THE OXFORD HANDBOOK OF
ENGLISH PROSE, 1640-1714

THE OXFORD HANDBOOK OF

ENGLISH PROSE, 1640–1714

Edited by
NICHOLAS McDOWELL
and
HENRY POWER

Great Clarendon Street, Oxford, OX2 6DP,
United Kingdom

Oxford University Press is a department of the University of Oxford.
It furthers the University's objective of excellence in research, scholarship,
and education by publishing worldwide. Oxford is a registered trade mark of
Oxford University Press in the UK and in certain other countries

© Oxford University Press 2024

The moral rights of the authors have been asserted

All rights reserved. No part of this publication may be reproduced, stored in
a retrieval system, or transmitted, in any form or by any means, without the
prior permission in writing of Oxford University Press, or as expressly permitted
by law, by licence or under terms agreed with the appropriate reprographics
rights organization. Enquiries concerning reproduction outside the scope of the
above should be sent to the Rights Department, Oxford University Press, at the
address above

You must not circulate this work in any other form
and you must impose this same condition on any acquirer

Published in the United States of America by Oxford University Press
198 Madison Avenue, New York, NY 10016, United States of America

British Library Cataloguing in Publication Data

Data available

Library of Congress Control Number: 2024946397

ISBN 978–0–19–874684–3

DOI: 10.1093/oxfordhb/9780198746843.001.0001

Printed and bound by
CPI Group (UK) Ltd, Croydon, CR0 4YY

Mr. Savill was asked by my Lord of Essex, his opinion touching Poets; who answered my Lord. *He thought them the best writers, next to those that write prose.*

Francis Bacon, *Apophthegms*

Acknowledgements

The editors are indebted above all to the patience and support of the contributors during the lengthy process of putting together this large book. The global events of 2020–21 can only partly be blamed for the time it has taken, and all the contributors have shown kindness and understanding in their tolerance of various delays: we hope they are glad to have stayed on board. At Oxford University Press, we would like to thank Jacqueline Norton for commissioning the volume and Aimee Wright for overseeing the production process. Thanks also to the University of Exeter for providing financial support for indexing (and to William Gallois for his help in arranging this).

Finally, we would like to acknowledge the congenial environment for editorial meetings provided by various establishments in and around mid- and east-Devon, including the Lamb Inn, Sandford; the Bridge Inn, Topsham; the Beer Engine, Newton St Cyres; the Agricultural Inn, Bramford Speke; and the Hour Glass Inn, Exeter.

Exeter, July 2024

Contents

List of Figures   xiii
List of Abbreviations   xv
Note on Texts   xvii
List of Contributors   xix

Introduction: An Age of Prose?   1
NICHOLAS MCDOWELL AND HENRY POWER

PART I: CONTEXTS

1. Circulation   15
   THOMAS KEYMER

2. Reception   40
   CYNTHIA WALL

3. Classical Inheritance   62
   FREYJA COX JENSEN

4. Continental Influences   81
   ALEXIS TADIÉ

PART II: CATEGORIES

5. Amatory Fiction   103
   MELISSA E. SANCHEZ

6. Antiquarian Writing   119
   THOMAS ROEBUCK

7. Biography and Autobiography   136
   JULIE A. ECKERLE

8. Bites and Shams JOHN MCTAGUE	152
9. Brief Lives and Characters KATE BENNETT	168
10. Circulation Narratives and Spy Literature ANDREA HASLANGER	184
11. Criminal Literature PAT ROGERS	200
12. Diaries ADAM SMYTH	216
13. Dissenting Writing NICHOLAS SEAGER	230
14. Encounters with the East MATTHEW DIMMOCK	250
15. Essays KATHRYN MURPHY	266
16. Fables and Fairy Tales JAYNE ELIZABETH LEWIS	283
17. Handbooks PADDY BULLARD	300
18. Heresiography and Religious Controversy NICHOLAS MCDOWELL	316
19. Histories NIALL ALLSOPP	332
20. Keys NICHOLAS MCDOWELL	350
21. Learned Wit and Mock-Scholarship HENRY POWER	366
22. Letters DIANA G. BARNES	379

23. Literary History NICK HARDY	400
24. Mock-Scientific Literature GREGORY LYNALL	417
25. New World Writing and Captivity Narratives CATHERINE ARMSTRONG	433
26. Periodical Literature BRIAN COWAN	450
27. Political Debate MARK KNIGHTS	468
28. Political Speculations NIGEL SMITH	486
29. Pornography HAL GLADFELDER	504
30. Radical and Deist Writing NICHOLAS MCDOWELL AND GIOVANNI TARANTINO	520
31. Recipe Books HENRY POWER	537
32. Religious Autobiography BROOKE CONTI	550
33. Scientific Transactions FELICITY HENDERSON	565
34. Secret Histories REBECCA BULLARD	584
35. Sermons WARREN JOHNSTON	600
36. True Accounts SOPHIE GEE	618
Index	637

Figures

1.1	Annual Book Production 1640–1700 (four-year intervals)	24
27.1	The fluctuations in press output, using data from ESTC	473
27.2	*Faction Display'd* (1709). © Trustees of the British Museum	476
33.1	Engraving of a flea in Robert Hooke, *Micrographia* (1665). Wellcome Collection. Attribution 4.0 International (CC BY 4.0). Source: Wellcome Collection.	581

Abbreviations

The following abbreviations have been used throughout.

EEBO   *Early English Books Online*
ODNB   *Oxford Dictionary of National Biography*
OED   *Oxford English Dictionary*

Note on Texts

In all quotations, punctuation, spelling, and italicization remain as in the original unless otherwise noted, apart from the modernization of the long s, i/j, and u/v. Unless otherwise stated, the place of publication for pre-1900 texts is London.

Contributors

Niall Allsopp is Senior Lecturer in English at the University of Exeter. His first monograph, *Poetry and Sovereignty in the English Revolution*, was published by OUP in 2020. It concerned political ideas and the reception of Thomas Hobbes by 1650s writers including Andrew Marvell, Margaret Cavendish, William Davenant, Abraham Cowley, and John Dryden. His recent publications on literature of the English Civil Wars include journal articles on marriage poetry and on the regional book trade. He is currently researching a project on occasional writing and political participation.

Catherine Armstrong is Reader in Modern History at Loughborough University and has been the Director of People & Culture for the School of Social Sciences and Humanities there since 2021. She is an Americanist who has published widely on both the colonial period and the nineteenth century. She has worked on the ways that notions of place, travel, and identity intersect for the first English migrants to North America, and for enslaved people in the southern States. She also sits on the board of the British Association of American Studies as co-treasurer. Her books include *Writing North America in the Seventeenth Century* (2007) and *Landscape and Identity in North America's Southern Colonies from 1660 to 1745* (2013), and currently she is researching her fourth monograph, under contract with Cambridge UP, entitled *Forgetting and Remembering Slavery: Cultural Legacies in the American South 1870–1939*.

Diana G. Barnes is Senior Lecturer in English Literary Studies at the University of New England, with particular interests in the gendering of intellectual history and the republic of letters. She has published widely on correspondence including that of Brilliana Harley, Lady Mary Wortley Montagu, Margaret Cavendish, letters embedded in Shakespeare's *Merry Wives of Windsor*, and a book on print letters, *Epistolary Community in Print, 1580–1664* (2013). Recently she has become interested in how early modern literature shaped the Australian settler-colonial mindset. Current research projects include an Australian Research Council funded study of early modern women's engagement with stoic discourse, a forthcoming edited collection on emotions and letters, and a contracted book on early modern bubbles.

Kate Bennett has research interests in early modern biography, early modern collecting, Alexander Pope, the work of John Aubrey, and the history of the anecdote. She held a junior research fellowship and a British Academy postdoctoral fellowship at Christ Church, Oxford, after which she was a Fellow in English at Pembroke College, Cambridge. After a break she returned to Oxford and for nine years taught English at

Magdalen College. She has been a member of the Centre for the Study of the Renaissance at Warwick University and a research fellow of New College, and she is a fellow of the Society of Antiquaries. In 2015 her two-volume edition of John Aubrey's *Brief Lives* was published by OUP, which was awarded the British Academy's Rose Mary Crawshay Prize, and was a *Times Literary Supplement* book of the year. She is currently writing a biography of John Aubrey.

Paddy Bullard is Head of the Department of English Literature at the University of Reading. He is the author of *Edmund Burke and the Art of Rhetoric* (2011) and of *Satire and Useful Knowledge in the Long Eighteenth Century: The Enlightenment Mock Arts* (2025). He is co-editor of *Jonathan Swift and the Eighteenth-Century Book* (2013), and editor of *The Oxford Handbook of Eighteenth-Century Satire* (2019) and *A History of Georgic Writing* (2022). He is principal investigator on the NERC-funded research project, 'Future Treescapes in Areas of Outstanding Natural Beauty: The Chilterns' (2023–24).

Rebecca Bullard is Senior Tutor at Trinity College, Oxford. She was previously an Associate Professor of English Literature at the University of Reading. She is the author of *The Politics of Disclosure: Secret History Narratives, 1674–1725* (2009), and co-editor of *The Plays and Poems of Nicholas Rowe, Volume I: The Early Plays* (2016) and *The Secret History in Literature, 1660–1820* (2017).

Brooke Conti teaches at Cleveland State University in Ohio. Her research focuses on the intersection of literature, religion, and politics in seventeenth-century England. She is the author of *Confessions of Faith in Early Modern England* (2014), as well as articles on Milton, Donne, Shakespeare, and Thomas Browne. She is co-editor, with Reid Barbour, of the new OUP edition of Browne's *Religio Medici* (2023) and is currently completing a second book manuscript, tentatively entitled 'Religious Nostalgia from Shakespeare to Milton'.

Brian Cowan is Professor of History at McGill University in Montréal, Canada. He is the author of *The Social Life of Coffee: The Emergence of the British Coffeehouse* (2005) and a member of the Multigraph Collective, who authored *Interacting with Print: Elements of Reading in the Era of Print Saturation* (2018). With Scott Sowerby, he edited *The State Trials and the Politics of Justice in Later Stuart England* (2021) and was also the editor of *The State Trial of Doctor Henry Sacheverell* (2012). He is president of the international *Groupe d'Intérêt Scientifique* (GIS)—*Sociabilités*, which has sponsored the Digital Encyclopedia of British Sociability: *DIGIT.EN.S* (https://www.digitens.org/en). His trilogy of monographs on the history of sociability is forthcoming with McGill-Queen's UP, and he is currently editing a collection, *Emotions and the City: Urban Sociabilities in Eighteenth-Century Britain and France*, for Routledge.

Freyja Cox Jensen is Associate Professor of Early Modern History at the University of Exeter. She read Ancient and Modern History at Christ Church, Oxford, before going on to complete her MA and PhD there. After a year spent as a stipendiary lecturer at

Merton College, Oxford, she returned to Christ Church in 2010 to take up a junior research fellowship, before joining the University of Exeter in 2012. She works on the reception of the classics, the intersection of print and performance, and practice research methodologies. Publications include 'The Popularity of Ancient Historians, 1450–1600', in *The Historical Journal* (2018), and *Reading the Roman Republic in Early Modern England* (2012).

Matthew Dimmock is Professor of Early Modern Studies at the University of Sussex. His publications include *Writing Tudor Exploration* (2022), *Elizabethan Globalism* (2019), *Mythologies of the Prophet Muhammad in Early Modern English Culture* (2013), and *New Turkes: Dramatizing Islam and the Ottomans in Early Modern England* (2005). He has recently collaborated with Andrew Hadfield to produce the expanded second edition of *Amazons, Savages, and Machiavels: Travel and Colonial Writing in English, 1550–1630: An Anthology* (2022) and is also editor of *William Percy's* Mahomet and His Heaven: *A Critical Edition* (2006) and the Quarto and Folio versions of *2 Henry VI* for the Norton Shakespeare, third edition (2015). He is currently editing volume 5 of the Oxford Hakluyt project; *Dido, Queen of Carthage*, for the AHRC-funded Thomas Nashe project; *Soliman and Perseda*, for the *Collected Works of Thomas Kyd*; and (with Jyotsna Singh) *The Tempest*, for the New Cambridge Shakespeare series.

Julie A. Eckerle is Professor of English and Gender, Women, and Sexuality Studies at the University of Minnesota Morris. She has published *Romancing the Self: Early Modern Englishwomen's Life Writing* (2013); the first print edition of seventeenth-century Englishwoman Dorothy Calthorpe's manuscripts, *News from the Midell Regions and Calthorpe's Chapel* (2022); and two co-edited volumes, *Genre and Women's Life Writing in Early Modern England* (2007; with Michelle M. Dowd) and *Women's Life Writing and Early Modern Ireland* (2019; with Naomi McAreavey). Her current work focuses on Alice Thornton's familial letters, Dorothy Calthorpe's textual literacy and authorial practice, and women's writing in and about seventeenth-century Ireland. She is a former President of the Society for the Study of Early Modern Women and Gender.

Sophie Gee is in the English department at Princeton University. Her most recent book, *The Barbarous Feast: Writing and Eating in the Eighteenth-Century World*, is forthcoming with Princeton UP. She is also the author of a monograph about literature and refuse in the eighteenth century, titled *Making Waste* (2010), and a historical novel rewriting *The Rape of the Lock* as a comedy of manners. She has written for *The New York Times*, the *TLS*, the *Washington Post*, and the *Sydney Morning Herald*, among others. Her new work is on the value and importance of public humanities.

Hal Gladfelder is Emeritus Professor of English and Comparative Literature at the University of Manchester, with a focus on literature and culture of the eighteenth and nineteenth centuries. His books include *Criminality and Narrative in Eighteenth-Century England* (2001) and *Fanny Hill in Bombay: The Making and Unmaking of John Cleland* (2012), and a critical edition of John Gay's *The Beggar's Opera* and *Polly* (2013).

His recent and current work focuses on the history of pornography and on the figure of the castrato in eighteenth-century Europe.

Nick Hardy was Birmingham Fellow and Lecturer in English at the School of English, Drama and American and Canadian Studies, University of Birmingham, until 2019, when he left his academic post to work full time as a trade union official, first at the University and College Union, and since 2024 as a strategic researcher at the International Transport Workers' Federation (ITF). His academic work concentrates on the relationship between religio-political conflict and intellectual culture in seventeenth-century Europe. His first monograph, *Criticism and Confession: The Bible in the Seventeenth Century Republic of Letters*, was published by OUP in 2017. His other publications have covered a range of topics, including natural law and materialism in the reception of the Lucretius, and new evidence for the translation of the King James Version of the Bible.

Andrea Haslanger is Senior Lecturer in English Literature at the University of Sussex. Her research spans literature and philosophy, with a particular focus on ethics, personhood, and violence. She is currently writing a book about ideas of peace in the long eighteenth century, titled 'Impossible Peace: Imagining Life After War'. Work from this project is forthcoming in *The People: Belonging, Exclusion, and Democracy*, edited by Benjamin Kohlmann and Matthew Taunton (2024). She has published articles about antislavery poetry, automata and the history of artificial life, pornography and the novel, and cosmopolitanism, in journals including *ELH*, *European Romantic Review*, *Modern Philology*, and *The Eighteenth Century: Theory and Interpretation*.

Felicity Henderson is Senior Lecturer in Archives and Material Culture at the University of Exeter. Her early research focused on university satire and performance in the seventeenth century, and commonplace books compiled by scholars at Oxford and Cambridge. She co-edited with William Poole the works of Francis Lodwick, an early fellow of the Royal Society, published as *Francis Lodwick: Language, Theology and Utopia* (2011). Since then, she has published widely on early modern scientific writing, particularly on Robert Hooke and the early Royal Society. Her recent biography, *Robert Hooke's Experimental Philosophy* (2024), explores Hooke's life and work through the lens of his own writing on scientific method. She is also currently preparing a new edition of Hooke's diaries for OUP.

Warren Johnston is Professor of History in the Department of English and History at Algoma University in Sault Ste Marie, Ontario, Canada. He is the author of *Revelation Restored: The Apocalypse in Later Seventeenth-Century England* (2011) and *National Thanksgivings and Ideas of Britain, 1689–1816* (2020). He continues to write and teach on the history of political, religious, and social ideas in early modern Britain. His current projects are focused on the history of seventeenth- and eighteenth-century sermons, including an examination of fast sermons in the 'long eighteenth century', and a collaborative project (with Newton Key) analysing the sermons preached in response to the 1683 Rye House Plot to assassinate Charles II.

Thomas Keymer is Chancellor Henry N. R. Jackman University Professor of English at the University of Toronto, where at different times he has served as Chair of the Department of English and Director of the University's Collaborative Program in Book History & Print Culture. He previously taught at St Anne's College, Oxford, where he remains a Supernumerary Fellow. His books include *Jane Austen: Writing, Society, Politics* (2020), *Poetics of the Pillory: English Literature and Seditious Libel 1660–1820* (2019), and, as editor, *The Oxford History of the Novel in English, Volume One: Prose Fiction in English from the Origins of Print to 1750* (2017). He has edited works by Defoe, Richardson, Fielding, Johnson, Beckford, and Austen in the Oxford World's Classics series, and he currently serves as co-General Editor of *The Cambridge Edition of the Works and Correspondence of Samuel Richardson*.

Mark Knights is Professor of History at the University of Warwick. His research focuses on early modern political culture in Britain and on the history of corruption in Britain and its empire. He is the author of *Representation and Misrepresentation in Later Stuart Britain: Partisanship and Political Culture* (2005, paperback) and *The Devil in Disguise: Deception, Delusion and Fanaticism in the Early English Enlightenment* (2011), both of which discuss political debate and prose. His most recent publication is *Trust and Distrust: Corruption in Office in Britain and its Empire 1600–1850* (2021). He is currently working on a cultural biography of a seventeenth-century merchant philosopher; a book charting the history of corruption in Britain and its empire from the 1620s to the 2020s; and the *Oxford Handbook of the History of Corruption*.

Jayne Elizabeth Lewis is Professor of English at the University of California, Irvine, and the author of *The English Fable: Aesop and Literary Culture, 1660–1740* (1995), *Mary Queen of Scots: Romance and Nation* (2000), and *Air's Appearance: Literary Atmosphere in British Fiction, 1660–1794* (2012). Her critical articles have centred on eighteenth-century literature, culture, ecology, religion, and medicine but have ventured as well into reception history and the psychoaesthetics of mysticism in modernist women's writing. She has also edited or co-edited several anthologies and essay collections, including most recently *Religion in Enlightenment England* (2016). She is currently completing a project on Helen Keller's 'correspondence' with Emanuel Swedenborg.

Gregory Lynall is King Alfred Chair in English Literature and Head of English at the University of Liverpool. He is co-director of the Literature & Science Hub research centre at Liverpool, and a former chair of the British Society for Literature and Science. His publications include *Swift and Science: The Satire, Politics, and Theology of Natural Knowledge, 1690–1730* (2012) and *Imagining Solar Energy: The Power of the Sun in Literature, Science and Culture* (2020), which won the 2022 European Society for the Study of English book prize in the 'Literatures in the English Language' open category.

Nicholas McDowell is Professor of Early Modern Literature and Thought at the University of Exeter. He is the author of *The English Radical Imagination: Culture, Religion, and Revolution, 1630–1660* (2003) and *Poetry and Allegiance in the English Civil Wars: Marvell and the Cause of Wit* (2008), and the co-editor (with Nigel Smith) of *The

Oxford Handbook of Milton (2009) and (with N. H. Keeble) of *The Oxford Complete Works of John Milton. Volume 6: Vernacular Regicide and Republican Writings* (2013). The first volume of his two-part intellectual biography of Milton, *Poet of Revolution: The Making of John Milton*, appeared with Princeton UP in 2020 and won the James Holly Hanford Award of the Milton Society of America. Currently he is completing the second volume and editing (with William Poole) the new Longman Annotated English Poets edition of *Paradise Lost*.

John McTague is Associate Professor in Eighteenth-Century Studies at the University of Bristol, where he teaches and researches late-Stuart and Hanoverian literary, political, and news cultures, the history and practice of print, and the history of historiography. He is the author of *Things That Didn't Happen* (2019), a scholarly editor (of Nicholas Rowe's *Tamerlane* and John Dryden's correspondence), and has published essays on Jonathan Swift, Delarivier Manley, political poetic miscellanies, the warming pan scandal of 1688–89, and 'practical' satires of the eighteenth century. He is a founding co-director of Bristol Common Press, a working historical print shop.

Kathryn Murphy is a Fellow in English Literature at Oriel College, and associate professor in the Faculty of English, University of Oxford. Her academic work focuses on early modern prose, poetry, and philosophy, and on the literary essay of all periods. She also writes essays and criticism on painting, sculpture, and Czech literature. She has co-edited volumes on Thomas Browne and on *The Emergence of Impartiality* (2013), and is co-editor, with Thomas Karshan, of *On Essays: From Montaigne to the Present* (2018). Her book *Robert Burton: A Vital Melancholy*, a study of distraction, attention, and *The Anatomy of Melancholy*, is forthcoming from Reaktion in 2025, and she is currently writing *The Tottering Universal: Metaphysical Prose in the Seventeenth Century*.

Henry Power is Professor of English Literature at the University of Exeter. He is the author of *Epic into Novel: Henry Fielding, Scriblerian Satire, and the Consumption of Classical Literature* (2015), and has edited Joseph Addison's miscellaneous prose writings for OUP. His edition of Alexander Pope's *Major Works* for the Oxford 21st-Century Authors series is forthcoming in 2025, and he is now editing (with Ian Calvert) Pope's translations from Homer for the new *Oxford Edition of the Writings of Alexander Pope*. He has held visiting positions at All Souls College, Oxford and at the Beinecke Library in Yale.

Thomas Roebuck is Lecturer in English at the University of East Anglia and works on the history of early modern British scholarship in the long seventeenth century. While tracing the intersecting intellectual trajectories of seventeenth-century scholars has taken him into the history of biblical studies and of travel to the Levant, his particular focus is on the history of British antiquarianism, on which he has recently published accounts of Edmund Gibson's 1695 revision of William Camden's *Britannia* and of the political and intellectual context of Henry Savile's edition of medieval historians (published 1596). His longer-term projects include an intellectual biography of the antiquarian, traveller, and expert on the Greek church, Thomas Smith (1638–1710). In recent years he has worked closely with libraries and heritage organizations in East Anglia to facilitate access to and understanding of their collections of early modern scholarly books.

Pat Rogers is Distinguished Professor Emeritus at the University of South Florida. He has written on aspects of eighteenth-century history and culture in several journals, including *Anglia, Arion, Bodleian Library Record, Book Collector, British Journal of Aesthetics, Burlington Magazine, Eighteenth-Century Ireland, English Historical Review, Journal of American Studies, Journal of Historical Geography, Journal of Literature and Science, Journal of Transport History, Journal of Victorian Culture, Medical History, Musical Quarterly, Notes and Records of the Royal Society, Proverbium, Quarterly Journal of Speech, Revue de Littérature Comparée,* and *Studies in Bibliography,* along with various antiquarian journals. He contributes to online sites, in particular the *Grub Street Project* and the *Literary Encyclopedia* on topics including adventurers, the criminal underworld, scarlet women, and Tyburn narratives. Among current works are essays in *The Edinburgh History of the British and Irish Press* (2023) and Brill's *Companion to the Reception of Homer from Byzantium to the Enlightenment* (forthcoming).

Melissa E. Sanchez is Donald T. Regan Professor of English and Comparative Literature and a Core Faculty member of Gender, Sexuality, and Women's Studies at the University of Pennsylvania. Her research and teaching focus on feminism, queer theory, and sixteenth- and seventeenth-century literature, and she is Director of Penn's Center for Research in Feminist, Queer, and Transgender Studies. Her books include *Erotic Subjects: The Sexuality of Politics in Early Modern English Literature* (2011); *Shakespeare and Queer Theory* (2019), and *Queer Faith: Reading Promiscuity and Race in the Secular Love Tradition* (2019). With Ania Loomba, she co-edited *Rethinking Feminism in Early Modern Studies: Gender, Race, and Sexuality* (2016).

Nicholas Seager is Professor of English Literature and Head of the School of Humanities at Keele University. He has published on British literature of the long eighteenth century, including Bunyan, Defoe, Haywood, Swift, Richardson, Goldsmith, Sterne, Johnson, and Austen. He is the editor of *The Cambridge Edition of the Correspondence of Daniel Defoe* (2022), co-editor with Daniel Cook of *The Cambridge Companion to Gulliver's Travels* (2023), and co-editor with J. A. Downie of *The Oxford Handbook of Daniel Defoe* (2023). His edition of Defoe's *The Fortunate Mistress*, with Marc Mierowsky, is forthcoming from Oxford World's Classics in 2024.

Nigel Smith is William and Annie S. Paton Foundation Professor of Ancient and Modern Literature at Princeton University. His major works include *Andrew Marvell: The Chameleon* (2010), *Is Milton Better Than Shakespeare?* (2008), *Andrew Marvell's Poems* (Longman Annotated English Poets series, 2003), *Literature and Revolution in England, 1640–1660* (1994), and *Perfection Proclaimed: Language and Literature in English Radical Religion 1640–1660* (1989). He has also edited George Fox's *Journal* (1998) and the Ranter pamphlets (1983; rev. edn, 2014), and co-edited several volumes, including *Radicalism in British Literary Culture, 1650–1830* (2002), with Timothy Morton; *The Oxford Handbook of Milton* (2009), with Nicholas McDowell; *Mysticism and Reform, 1400–1750* (2015), with Sara S. Poor; and *Politics and Aesthetics in European Baroque and Classicist Tragedy* (2016), with Jan Bloemendal. *Polyglot Poetics: Transnational Early Modern Literature* is forthcoming with Princeton UP. He also writes, performs, and records songs with 'The Unheard Melodies Project' and 'Second Flea'.

Adam Smyth is Professor of English Literature and the History of the Book at Balliol College, Oxford. He is the author of, among other books, *Material Texts in Early Modern England* (2019) and *The Book-Makers: A History of the Book in 18 Remarkable Lives* (2024), and the editor of *The Oxford Handbook of the History of the Book in Early Modern England* (2023). He is the co-founder and co-editor of *Inscription: The Journal of Material Text—Theory, Practice, History*.

Alexis Tadié is Professor of English Literature at Sorbonne University. He specializes in eighteenth-century literature, as well as in postcolonial literatures. He also has an interest in sports. He has published monographs on Laurence Sterne, Francis Bacon, John Locke, and Salman Rushdie, as well as tennis. He has edited volumes on early modern intellectual history, including *Fiction and the Frontiers of Knowledge* (2011, with Richard Scholar), *Dispute et Création en Europe à l'époque de la première modernité* (2019, with Jeanne-Marie Hostiou), and *Les règles du jeu à l'époque de la première modernité* (2024, with Clara Manco and Line Cottegnies), as well as *Sporting Cultures 1650–1850* (2018, with Daniel O'Quinn).

Giovanni Tarantino, FRHistS, is Associate Professor of Early Modern History at the University of Florence and honorary research fellow at the School of Humanities of The University of Western Australia. His interests lie in the intersections of religion, radical thinking, and emotional and cultural entanglements. His publications include *Twelve Cities – One Sea: Early Modern Mediterranean Port Cities and their Inhabitants* (2023, co-editor with Paola von Wyss-Giacosa); *Through Your Eyes: Religious Alterity and the Early Modern Western Imagination* (2021, co-editor with Paola von Wyss-Giacosa); *Feeling Exclusion: Religious Conflict, Exile and Emotions in Early Modern Europe* (2019, co-editor with Charles Zika); *Republicanism, Sinophilia, and Historical Writing: Thomas Gordon (c.1691–1750) and his 'History of England'* (2013); *Lo scrittoio di Anthony Collins (1676–1729): I libri e i tempi di un libero pensatore* (2007); and *Martin Clifford (1624–1677): Deismo e tolleranza nell'Inghilterra della Restaurazione* (2000).

Cynthia Wall is William R. Kenan, Jr Professor of English at the University of Virginia. She is the author of *Grammars of Approach: Landscape, Narrative, and the Linguistic Picturesque* (2019), *The Prose of Things: Transformations of Description in the Eighteenth Century* (2006), and *The Literary and Cultural Spaces of Restoration London* (1998), as well as an editor of Bunyan, Defoe, and Pope, and assorted essay collections.

INTRODUCTION
An Age of Prose?

NICHOLAS MCDOWELL AND HENRY POWER

In 'The Study of Poetry', originally written in 1880 to introduce an anthology entitled *The English Poets*, Matthew Arnold offered an account of English prose in the period covered by this volume that has proved remarkably tenacious:

> When we find Chapman, the Elizabethan translator of Homer, expressing himself in this preface thus: 'Though truth in her very nakedness sits in so deep a pit, that from Gades to Aurora and Ganges few eyes can sound her, I hope yet those few here will so discover and confirm that, the date being out of her darkness in this morning of our poet, he shall now gird his temples with the sun'—we pronounce that such a prose is intolerable. When we find Milton writing: 'And long it was not after, when I was confirmed in this opinion, that he, who would not be frustrate of his hope to write well hereafter in laudable things, ought himself to be a true poem'—we pronounce that such a prose has its own grandeur, but that it is obsolete and inconvenient. But when we find Dryden telling us: 'What Virgil wrote in the vigour of his age, in plenty and at ease, I have undertaken to translate in my declining years; struggling with wants, oppressed with sickness, curbed in my genius, liable to be misconstrued in all I write'—then we exclaim that here at last we have the true English prose, a prose such as we would all gladly use if we only knew how. Yet Dryden was Milton's contemporary.[1]

Arnold's subsequent assertion that the age of Dryden and Pope—the latter half of the seventeenth century and the opening decades of the eighteenth century—is 'an age of prose and reason' cumulates in his oft-quoted dictum that even though 'they may write in verse, though they may in a certain sense be masters of the art of versification, Dryden and Pope are not classics of our poetry, they are classics of our prose'. For Arnold, in

---

[1] Matthew Arnold, *Selected Prose*, ed. P. J. Keating (1970; Harmondsworth: Penguin, 1987), 357.

other words, English prose rose to such a position of dominance in the period of literary history surveyed by this *Handbook* that it shaped how even the finest English poetry was written. Arnold is sketchy on how and why 'true English prose' emerged at this time, but his repetition of 'imperious need' indicates it has something to do in his mind with the emergence of empire as well as the reaction to the experience of the Civil Wars and republican governments of the mid-seventeenth century: 'after the Restoration the time had come when our nation felt the imperious need of a fit prose. So, too, the time had likewise come when our nation felt the imperious need of freeing itself from the absorbing preoccupation which religion in the Puritan age had exercised.'[2]

Sweeping generalizations these may be, but, for all the many and elaborate twists and turns of literary criticism and theory in the subsequent 150 years, the influential critic John Guillory can still be found returning to them as intuitively 'right' in a recent consideration of the 'origins of modern prose style': 'Arnold's judgment rightly intuits a change in the position of poetry in response to a new gravitational force exerted by prose ... Readers of English literature know that prose changed in the latter end of the early modern period, and that by the eighteenth century the difference between modern and premodern prose was more or less established; but how did this happen?'[3] The persistence of Arnold's linking of the dominance of prose in the Restoration and early eighteenth century with imperial English nationhood and the emergence of the 'modern' probably has something to do with its compatibility with Hegel's notion of the 'prose of the world' as a trope for modernity, which became important to the ideas of prominent twentieth-century critical theorists such as Merleau-Ponty and Foucault.[4] Yet Guillory still feels he needs to address the fundamental question of how the change in English prose discerned by Arnold (as apparently by all '[r]eaders of English literature') actually happened. It is not the purpose of a multi-authored survey volume like the present one to provide a definitive answer to such a question (even if there were such a thing); but we propose that any attempt to do so has been hampered by the lack of critical work which brings together accounts and discussions of the multiple forms that English prose took in the later seventeenth and early eighteenth centuries.

The last substantial collection of multi-authored essays devoted exclusively to the topic of seventeenth-century English prose was edited by Stanley Fish over half a century ago, guided by an emphasis on stylistic criticism of a handful of major authors that now seems narrow in the age of databases like *EEBO* and *Eighteenth-Century Collections Online*, which make accessible and vivid the sheer amount of writing produced in print

---

[2] Arnold, *Selected Prose*, 358–9.

[3] Guillory, 'Mercury's Words: The End of Rhetoric and the Beginning of Prose', *Representations*, 138 (2017), 59–86 (62–3).

[4] *Hegel's Aesthetics: Lectures on Fine Art*, trans. T. M. Knox, 2 vols. (Oxford: Clarendon Press, 1975), 1:150. Hegel's phrase 'prose of the world' reappears as a chapter title in Michel Foucault's *The Order of Things* (1966) and as the title of a posthumously published book by Maurice Merleau-Ponty in 1973. See further Michal Peled Ginsburg and Lorri G. Nandrea, 'The Prose of the World', in Franco Moretti (ed.), *The Novel*, 2 vols. (Princeton, NJ: Princeton University Press, 2006), 2: 244–57.

(alone) between 1500 and 1800.[5] *The Oxford Handbook of English Prose, 1500–1640* (2013), edited by Andrew Hadfield, to which the present volume is a companion and sequel, now offers more ample coverage of the pre-Civil War period; it was preceded by two significant collections of new essays on 'English Renaissance Prose' and 'Early Modern Prose' with stated historical boundaries of 1650 or 1660 but which in practice included a couple of essays on post-1660 material.[6] Nonetheless one of the barriers to a greater appreciation of the efflorescence of English prose from the mid-seventeenth to the early eighteenth centuries has been the traditional division of the period in literature courses and anthologies into 'Renaissance', 'Civil War' (or 'Revolution'), 'Restoration', and 'Eighteenth Century' or (sometimes) 'Augustan'. A guiding principle of this *Handbook* is that the periodization that has conventionally segmented English literary history must be surmounted to obtain a more panoramic view of what has justly been called 'the golden age of English non-fictional prose'.[7]

It is in the 1630–60 period that we can observe a process whereby prose moves from the margins of cultural life in Britain to its centre, through the proliferation of newsbooks and polemical pamphlets, and in so doing 'becomes a way of living in print': an account of the so-called 'prosification' of the thriving London book trade of the later seventeenth century needs to trace its roots back to the unprecedented political and cultural crisis of the 1640s and 1650s, which witnessed rapid expansion in both the production and consumption of printed prose.[8] Indeed, the rise of prose became part of the polemic of the 1640s, as did every aspect of British cultural life. Alexander Brome's commendatory poem for Richard Lovelace's collection *Lucasta* (1649) is representative

---

[5] Stanley Fish (ed.), *Seventeenth-Century Prose: Modern Essays in Criticism* (New York: Oxford University Press, 1971). In 1987 Roger Pooley observed that 'the most astonishing of all gaps in English prose study is the absence of a single volume, general history of seventeenth-century prose' ('Prospects for Research in Seventeenth-Century Prose', *Prose Studies*, 10 (1987), 9–17 (12); Pooley attempted to fill that gap himself with his brief but brisk and lucid monograph, *English Prose of the Seventeenth Century, 1590–1700* (Harlow: Longman, 1992).

[6] Andrew Hadfield (ed.), *The Oxford Handbook of English Prose, 1500–1640* (Oxford: Oxford University Press, 2013); Margaret W. Ferguson and Susannah Brietz Monta (eds.), *Teaching Early Modern Prose* (New York: Modern Language Association, 2010), includes essays on John Bunyan, Aphra Behn, and Mary Astell; Neil Rhodes (ed.), *English Renaissance Prose: History, Language and Politics* (Tempe, AZ.: University of Arizona Press, 1997), includes essays on the Earl of Clarendon and Bunyan.

[7] Thomas N. Corns, review of Pooley, *English Prose of the Seventeenth Century*, in *The Review of English Studies*, 46 (1995), 259–60 (260). Ferguson and Monta observe that 'the renewed study of early modern prose has challenged the usual periodizations that divided sixteenth- and seventeenth-century courses and pre-1660 materials from those produced after the Stuart Restoration' ('Introduction', in Ferguson and Monta (eds.), *Teaching Early Modern Prose*, 1–18 (1)).

[8] Walter R. Davis, 'Genre and Non-fictional Prose', *Prose Studies*, 11 (1988), 85–98 (92). For the 'downwards dissemination' of print, particularly prose, due to the outbreak of Civil War and its literary effects, see Nigel Smith, *Literature and Revolution in England, 1640–1660* (New Haven: Yale University Press, 1994), 24 and *passim*; see also James Holstun (ed.), *Pamphlet Wars: Prose in the English Revolution* (London: Frank Cass, 1992). This period saw the rapid proliferation of the polemical newsbook; see Joad Raymond, *The Invention of the Newspaper: English Newsbooks, 1641–1649* (Oxford: Oxford University Press, 1996). For further discussion of the issues involved in assessing the growth in printed material in the 1640s and 1650s, see Chapter 1 on 'Circulation' by Thomas Keymer.

of royalist propaganda in its identification of the art of poetry with the Cavaliers and the artlessness of prose with the Roundheads. Brome laments 'the thick darkness of these verseless times, / These antigenious dayes', for which he blames the brutal instrumentality of the Parliamentary/Puritan cause: 'Their Prose unhing'd the State.' This polemical dichotomy shaped literary-critical attitudes towards the seventeenth century (including those of Arnold) until at least the mid-twentieth century. It was evident, for example, in the critical tendency to address Milton's poetry and prose as quite separate undertakings, the former timeless and above history and the latter contingent and partisan.[9] While no attempt has yet been made to account for the rise of English prose along the lines of the ambitious account by Wlad Godzich and Jeffrey Kittay of the 'emergence of prose' in thirteenth-century France as a 'signifying practice' yoked to the emergent political state, the process of 'prosification' in England identified by Arnold needs to be better understood in relation to the repeated political ruptures and transformed public sphere of the mid- and later seventeenth century.[10] This is one of the key aims of *The Oxford Handbook of English Prose, 1640–1714*, and central to our argument for coverage that stretches from Parliament's taking up of arms against Charles I in England to the death of Queen Anne, the last Stuart monarch.

One of the main reasons why there have been no attempts in the last thirty years to offer a substantive guide to prose of the post-1640 period is the difficulty of approaching anything like adequate coverage. The problem is not one peculiar to writing in English: prose remains 'one of the last undefined, untheorized bodies of writing in the early modern European languages. It is also the largest'.[11] There is an immense quantity and variety of material which crosses many generic and disciplinary boundaries, and much of it does not fit modern notions of what 'literature' looks like. A rough estimate of material included in the Short-Title Catalogue indicates that over eighty per cent of works printed between 1500 and 1700 were works of prose (and this excludes Bibles and texts of religious instruction such as catechisms).[12] The size of this *Oxford Handbook* enables us to give a real sense of that quantity and diversity. But even so, any reader familiar with the period will doubtless bemoan our lack of attention to one category or another among the almost inexhaustible range of material that might be included, in

---

[9] Alexander Brome, 'To Colonel Lovelace, on his Poems' (1648–9?), in Richard Lovelace, *Poems of Richard Lovelace*, ed. C. H. Wilkinson (Oxford: Clarendon Press, 1930), lines 4–5, 24. On the hold of this 'Roundhead-prose' / 'Cavalier-poetry' dichotomy on English literary criticism, see Nicholas McDowell, 'Early Modern Stereotypes and the Rise of English: Jonson, Dryden, Arnold, Eliot', *Critical Quarterly*, 48 (2010), 25–37; on the division of poetry and prose in the history of Milton criticism, see, e. g., William Kolbrener, *Milton's Warring Angels: A History of Critical Engagements* (Cambridge: Cambridge University Press, 1997).

[10] Wlad Godzich and Jeffrey Kittay, *The Emergence of Prose: An Essay in Prosaics* (Minneapolis: University of Minnesota Press, 1987).

[11] Elizabeth Fowler and Roland Greene (eds.), *The Project of Prose in Early Modern Europe and the New World* (Cambridge: Cambridge University Press, 1996), 1.

[12] Ferguson and Monta, 'Introduction', in Ferguson and Monta (eds.), *Teaching Early Modern Prose*, 4.

manuscript as well as in print.[13] Beyond the sheer amount of prose, other difficulties present themselves in any attempt to organize and select areas of focus. What should be the criteria for selection?

Authorship is probably not the most suitable category of selection. The prose writers that we now regard as important were not necessarily recognized as such in their time. Indeed, criteria of literary quality and authorial importance will always, to some extent, be anachronistic projections onto a period in which prose acts as a container for a vast array of discourses. One of the consequences of the rise of interest in recent years in areas including women's writing and the 'history of the book' has been a more omnivorous approach to literary culture, both in print and manuscript, and a greater appreciation of the material diversity of textual culture. It was one of the peculiarities of 'New Historicism' and its associated theoretical approaches that, despite their ostensible claims to retrieve the marginal, to deny a privileged status to the 'literary', and to collapse the divisions between 'text' and 'context', their practitioners tended to continue to use prose as context for Shakespeare and others firmly in the canon. 'New Historicism' defined itself as a 'cultural poetics' but, as Gary Saul Morson put it in his provocative manifesto for a 'prosaics' that would focus on representation of 'the ordinary, messy, quotidian facts of daily life': 'Poetics recognizes in prose only those aspects it shares with poetry, and denies artistic significance to the rest.'[14]

It is only in the last twenty years that distinctions between 'high' and 'low' cultural productions and between 'literary' text and 'historical' context have truly become subject to interrogation as the methodological approaches of literature and history have increasingly overlapped. Writing that would once have been deemed 'un-', 'sub-' or 'non-' literary is now the site of concerted literary and cultural analysis, establishing whole new fields of prose writing by women and by those outside social and educational elites.[15] A comparative analysis of prose has also been hampered in the past by the way in which the various prose discourses—historical, political, philosophical, and scientific as well as literary—have been appropriated by different disciplines: thus the writings of Thomas Hobbes, for example, were the preserve of political theory and not 'literature'. The emphasis placed on a mode of rhetorical analysis which is essentially literary in its techniques in 'contextualist' history has played a major role in breaking down these

---

[13] Scholarly work on manuscript culture has tended thus far to concentrate on the circulation of verse; for an exemplary study, see Harold Love, *English Clandestine Satire, 1660-1702* (Oxford: Oxford University Press, 2004).

[14] Gary Saul Morson, 'Prosaics: An Approach to the Humanities', *The American Scholar*, 57 (1988), 515-28 (526). Morson is much influenced by Mikhail Bakhtin's theories of the novel: see further Gary Saul Morson, *Mikhail Bakhtin: Creation of a Prosaics* (Stanford: Stanford University Press, 1990).

[15] See e.g., Betty S. Travitsky, 'The Possibilities of Prose', in Helen Wilcox (ed.), *Women and Literature in Britain, 1500-1700* (Cambridge: Cambridge University Press, 1996), 234-66; Naomi Conn Liebler, 'Introduction: The Cultural Politics of Reading', in Liebler (ed.), *Early Modern Prose Fiction: The Cultural Politics of Reading* (New York: Routledge, 2007), 1-17.

disciplinary boundaries.[16] The incorporation of interdisciplinary approaches into the humanities makes this a fitting, and indeed overdue, moment to attempt a large-scale account of later seventeenth- and early eighteenth-century prose, which must necessarily range across disciplines to provide anything approaching a comprehensive survey.

Nor is style the most helpful way of classifying prose in this period. Early and mid-twentieth-century interest in later seventeenth-century prose by eminent critics such as Morris Croll, R. F. Jones, George Williamson, and Joan Webber was emphatically stylistic in its focus; their debates over whether prose should be classified as 'Ciceronian' or 'Senecan', 'plain' or 'metaphysical', 'Royalist' or 'Puritan', were based on comparatively small samples of evidence and now seem overly reductive, as do related arguments for a decisive and polemical change to an anti-rhetorical, 'scientific' prose style related to the establishment of the Royal Society at the Restoration.[17] Elizabeth Fowler and Roland Greene self-consciously situate their 1996 collection, *The Project of Prose*, against this older vein of criticism by asserting that 'such a use of "style" effectively turns "prose" into an adjective and attenuates many of the relevant aesthetic and cultural issues'. At the same time, it can be objected that sensitivity to 'style' is important if prose is to hold its own as a formal concept and to avoid being seen, as it usually has been, 'as invisible, as coterminous with its contents'.[18] Some of the chapters in this *Handbook* pay close attention to the style of individual prose works and of the various sorts of prose writing, without advancing all-encompassing theories of the

---

[16] See e.g., Quentin Skinner, *Reason and Rhetoric in the Philosophy of Hobbes* (Cambridge: Cambridge University Press, 1995); Quentin Skinner, *Visions of Politics. Volume 1: On Method* (Cambridge: Cambridge University Press, 2002).

[17] See *Style, Rhetoric, and Rhythm: Essays by Morris W. Croll*, ed. J. Max Patrick and Robert O. Evans (Princeton, NJ: Princeton University Press, 1966), which includes '"Attic Prose" in the Seventeenth Century' (1921); 'Attic Prose: Lipsius, Montaigne, Bacon' (1923), and 'The Baroque Style in Prose' (1929); George Williamson, 'Senecan Style in the Seventeenth Century', *Philological Quarterly*, 15 (1936), 321–51; George Williamson, *The Senecan Amble: Prose Form from Bacon to Collier* (Chicago: University of Chicago Press, 1951); Richard Foster Jones, 'Science and English Prose Style, 1650–75', in Fish (ed.), *Seventeenth-Century Prose*, 53–89; Richard Foster Jones, *The Seventeenth Century: Studies in the History of English Thought and Literature from Bacon to Pope* (Stanford: Stanford University Press, 1951); Joan Webber, *The Eloquent 'I': Style and Self in Seventeenth-Century Prose* (Madison, Wisconsin: University of Wisconsin Press, 1968); Brian Vickers, 'The Royal Society and English Prose Style: A Reassessment', in Brian Vickers and Nancy Streuver (eds.), *Rhetoric and the Pursuit of Truth in the Seventeenth and Eighteenth Centuries* (Los Angeles, CA: Clark Memorial Lectures, 1985), 3–76. In his extensive survey of 'Sixteenth- and Seventeenth-Century Prose', John Carey concluded by lamenting that there 'are too many generalizations already about prose-style in this period', but his account is essentially structured by the same polarities of 'ornate' and 'plain' styles (in Christopher Ricks (ed.), *The Penguin History of Literature. Volume 2: English Poetry and Prose 1540–1674* (1970; London: Penguin Books, 1993), 329–411 (411)).

[18] Fowler and Greene (eds.), *Project of Prose*, 2–3; for the persistence of an inadequate division of seventeenth-century prose into 'ornate' and 'plain' styles, see also Debra Shuger, 'Conceptions of Style', in Glyn P. Norton (ed.), *The Cambridge History of Literary Criticism. Volume 3: The Renaissance* (Cambridge: Cambridge University Press, 1999), 181–6. Guillory returns to these issues of style with a more sophisticated, post-theoretical lens in 'Mercury's Words'; for an interesting defence of a return to stylistic criticism, see Stephanie Shirlan, 'The Forbidden Pleasures of Style: Seventeenth-Century Prose in Twentieth-Century Criticism', *Prose Studies*, 34 (2012), 115–28.

dominance of any particular stylistic approach. The great majority of our contributors are literary scholars and naturally pay attention to the literary texture and rhetorical ornament of prose as well as its cultural contexts and historical narratives. A scholarly emphasis on the rhetorical culture shared by many early modern prose writers has the virtue of retaining some continuity with the twentieth-century interest in prose style while demonstrating how formal literary analysis can open up wider questions of cultural history.[19]

The one area of early modern prose which has attracted sophisticated critical attention is the 'pre-history' of the novel: works such as Michael McKeon's *Origins of the English Novel, 1600–1740* (1987) and J. Paul Hunter's *Before Novels* (1990) have long since related the rise of prose fiction to genres such as the newsbook and the spiritual autobiography.[20] The obvious problem of such an approach for a critical history of prose is that it is inevitably both retrospective and teleological in its focus, motivated by what certain forms of prose *became* rather than the nature and interest of those forms of prose in themselves. As David Novarr once observed: 'we have the novel in mind when we separate prose into fiction and non-fiction.'[21] While this *Handbook* devotes several chapters to categories featuring prose fiction, contributors were asked to consider the prose in its own terms rather than those of what would become the novel. This point is related to the decision to choose 1714 as the historical boundary of the volume, aside from the fact that 1714 marks the end of the Stuart dynasty and so may be regarded as the endpoint of a process that began with the outbreak of civil war in 1640. By stopping before the appearance of the well-known prose fictions which appeared in the decade following Queen Anne's death—although of course contributors occasionally look beyond 1714 at moments in their chapters—the volume signals its singularity and distinction from critical works which present themselves as pre-histories of the novel.[22]

The format of *The Oxford Handbook of English Prose, 1640–1714* is consequently designed according to categories of prose, which follow simply in alphabetical order. These categories have been organized practically and flexibly rather than programmatically: some by form (e.g. 'Sermons'), some by subject matter (e.g. 'Political Debate'), and others by mode of publication (e.g. 'Periodical Literature'). This approach gives the

---

[19] A point made by Neil Rhodes, 'Introduction: History, Language and the Politics of English Renaissance Prose', in Rhodes (ed.), *English Renaissance Prose*, 1–18 (15).

[20] Michael McKeon, *The Origins of the English Novel, 1600–1740* (Baltimore: Johns Hopkins University Press, 1987); J. Paul Hunter, *Before Novels: The Cultural Contexts of Eighteenth-Century English Fiction* (New York: Norton, 1990).

[21] *Seventeenth-Century Prose*, ed. David Novarr (New York: Alfred A. Knoff, 1967), 11.

[22] See recently e.g., Thomas Keymer (ed.), *The Oxford History of the Novel in English. Volume 1: Prose Fiction in English from the Origins of Print to 1750* (Oxford: Oxford University Press, 2017); J. A. Downie (ed.), *The Oxford Handbook of the Eighteenth-Century Novel* (Oxford: Oxford University Press, 2016). An interesting example of a critical work which stretches back to the 1640s, though concerned with considering representation and description in prose in the retrospective terms of the development of the novel, is Cynthia Wall, *The Prose of Things: Transformations of Description in the Eighteenth Century* (Chicago: University of Chicago Press, 2006).

interpretative advantage of allowing contributors to explore a handful of key texts from a number of angles: so, to offer a couple of examples, Aphra Behn's *Love-Letters* appears in 'Amatory Fiction', 'Letters', and 'Secret Histories'; Jonathan Swift's *A Tale of a Tub* in 'Learned Wit and Mock-Scholarship', 'Mock-Scientific Literature', and 'Heresiography and Religious Controversy'; and *The Spectator* is treated not only from the vantage-point of 'Periodical Literature' but also from that of 'Fables and Fairy-Tales' and 'Circulation Narratives and Spy Literature'. Those authors now regarded as the leading exponents of prose in the period are thus not neglected but rather discussed within contexts other than their own perceived importance to later versions of literary history and from multiple, and in some cases, unconventional, perspectives. For more focused work on those now regarded as major prose writers of the period but who are relatively lightly treated in this volume, such as John Milton, Andrew Marvell, Thomas Hobbes, John Bunyan, and Daniel Defoe, readers can consult Oxford Handbooks already dedicated to those authors.[23] The shift away from authorship as a structuring principle does not mean that elements of evaluative criticism have been discouraged; but the principal aim of the volume chapters is descriptive, with contributors having been asked to ensure they provide coverage, whether through narrative or other forms of organization, right across the period of the *Handbook*'s focus. However, there has been no prescribed method of approaching each category of prose: some contributors seek to provide a general overview of developments, while others concentrate upon several important or particularly revealing instances of the type of prose writing that they discuss.

Although there will inevitably be some overlap in the writers, texts, and contexts discussed, this volume has also sought to avoid duplicating the emphases of other Oxford Handbooks dedicated to the literature of a specific period within our coverage (the English Revolution; the Restoration), or to a certain literary genre (narrative fiction; satire) that remains only one aspect of the infinite variety of uses to which prose was put in these seventy-four years.[24] It should be noted that there are no chapters specifically dedicated to women's writing, on the basis that such exceptionalism is neither true to the period nor appropriate to this *Handbook*'s organizing principles. However, the recovery of writing by women, both in print and manuscript, has been central to the rise in interest in prose as a topic in recent years and these discoveries and developments

---

[23] See Nicholas McDowell and Nigel Smith (eds.), *The Oxford Handbook of Milton* (Oxford: Oxford University Press, 2009); A. P. Martinich and Kinch Hoekstra (eds.), *The Oxford Handbook of Hobbes* (Oxford: Oxford University Press, 2013); Michael Davies and W. R. Owens (eds.), *The Oxford Handbook of John Bunyan* (Oxford: Oxford University Press, 2018); Martin Dzelzainis and Edward Holberton (eds.), *The Oxford Handbook of Andrew Marvell* (Oxford: Oxford University Press, 2019); Nicholas Seager and J. A. Downie (eds.), *The Oxford Handbook of Daniel Defoe* (Oxford: Oxford University Press, 2023).

[24] See Laura Lunger Knoppers (ed.), *The Oxford Handbook of Literature and the English Revolution* (Oxford: Oxford University Press, 2012); Downie (ed.), *Oxford Handbook of the Eighteenth-Century Novel*; Paddy Bullard (ed.), *The Oxford Handbook of Eighteenth-Century Satire* (Oxford: Oxford University Press, 2019); Steven N. Zwicker and Matthew Augustine (eds.), *The Oxford Handbook of Restoration Literature* (Oxford: Oxford University Press, 2025)).

are incorporated by contributors throughout the volume.[25] One of the concerns that characterizes this *Handbook* is its interest in the extent to which English prose can be said to exist as, or to develop into, a distinctive literary form during the 1640–1714 period. To that end, four longer introductory chapters are included to offer overviews concerning the changing mechanics and contexts of publication in the period, including censorship ('Circulation'); ways and theories of reading and receiving the various forms of prose ('Reception'); the influence of the classical heritage, which remained throughout this period the basis of school and university education ('Classical Inheritance'), and the role of relations with continental Europe, whether in terms of translation or the involvement of writers in travel and migration ('Continental Influences').

It was English Romantic writers and critics, pre-eminently Coleridge and Hazlitt, who first defined early modern prose 'as a distinct entity and granted [it] a literary status comparable with the achievements of Renaissance poetry and drama'. But their narrative of the rise of English prose was also one of decline, as a 'distinctive national product' was 'superseded by the homogenous European taste developed by the Restoration and eighteenth century'—a narrative that bears some comparison with Arnold's claim that something indubitably changed in English prose in this period, but which lacks the positive nationalistic spin of 'imperious need' that Arnold is able to put on the ironing out of stylistic idiosyncrasy.[26] While the influence of European (and particularly French) literature on English prose from the mid-seventeenth century onwards is one of the stories told by several chapters in this *Handbook*, the volume counters the Romantic narrative of national and qualitative decline with one of ever-expanding and cosmopolitan diversity.

One important area that there has not been room to explore adequately, even in this relatively capacious forum, is the status of Latin, still a living language in this period, and its relationship with vernacular prose: recent work on neo-Latin writing has emphasized the bilingual context of poetic composition in England up to the early eighteenth century, and some of the same claims hold true for writing in prose, as the chapters on 'Classical Inheritance' and 'Literary History' suggest.[27] It was as a Latin prose stylist that Milton was initially known across Europe, for instance, and Hobbes produced a new version of *Leviathan* (1651) in Latin in 1668, which has only recently received serious scholarly attention.[28] Addison may be best known for providing a refined model of English prose in *The Spectator*, but it is clear from his surviving university exercises that

---

[25] For a recent volume which features essays dedicated to prose writing by women, see Elizabeth Scott-Baumann, Danielle Clarke, and Sarah C. E. Ross (eds.), *The Oxford Handbook of Early Modern Women's Writing in English, 1540–1700* (Oxford: Oxford University Press, 2022).

[26] Rhodes, 'Introduction', in Rhodes (ed.), *English Renaissance Prose*, 1, 3.

[27] Victoria Moul, *A Literary History of Latin and English Poetry: Bilingual Verse Culture in Early Modern England* (Cambridge: Cambridge University Press, 2022); Sarah Knight and Stefan Tilg (eds.), *The Oxford Handbook of Neo-Latin Studies* (Oxford: Oxford University Press, 2015).

[28] See Joad Raymond, 'John Milton, European: The Rhetoric of Milton's Defences', and Estelle Haan, '*Defensio Prima* and the Latin Poets', in McDowell and Smith (eds.), *Oxford Handbook of Milton*, 272–90, 291–304; the Latin text of *Leviathan* is given a full scholarly appreciation for the first time in Thomas Hobbes, *Leviathan*, ed. Noel Malcolm, 3 vols. (Oxford: Oxford University Press, 2012).

he was equally at home writing in Latin—and indeed regularly cannibalized his earlier Latin prose writings in producing his English works.[29] Perhaps most strikingly, although Richard Bentley's *Dissertation Upon the Epistles of Phalaris* (1697) was one of the first major works of classical scholarship to be written in English, Bentley more frequently published in Latin, which he was said to have spoken 'as readily as he wrote it'.[30] A related issue is the potentially misleading implication of the term 'English prose': while the chapters which follow are concerned only with prose written in the English language, the authors who wrote this prose were not only English but from Ireland, Scotland, Wales, France, and elsewhere in origin, and thus in some cases—such as the Huguenot exile and translator of Rabelais in the 1690s, Pierre Antoine Le Motteux, discussed in the chapters on 'Keys' and 'Periodical Literature'—were not writing in their first language.

We hope that its format enables the volume to capture the diversity of written material that characterizes the period from the outbreak of the Civil Wars in 1640 to the end of the Stuart monarchy in 1714, while also having the virtue of freeing the organization of this material from the concerns (and anxieties) of periodization, authorial standing, and received hierarchies of quality and importance. This approach ensures that conventional categories of prose writing are covered ('Biography and Autobiography'; 'Essays'; 'Histories'; 'Literary History'; 'Periodical Literature'; 'Political Debate'; 'Sermons') but also allows us to pursue less familiar but rich avenues which properly convey the assortment of prose in this period, and hopefully provide much interest and entertainment in the process ('Bites and Shams'; 'Keys'; 'Mock-Scientific Literature'; 'Pornography'; 'Recipe Books'; 'True Accounts', and even (self-referentially) 'Handbooks'). Arnold's definition of a 'fit prose' was a narrow one, focusing on the balanced, the polite, and (one might almost say) the Augustan; we have spread our net more widely. While the focus of most of the contributions is on prose in print, chapters such as 'Diaries' also give a sense of how much activity went on in manuscript, and of the relationship between scribal and printed forms of prose. The volume covers both classically derived prose and the world of cheap print, 'elite' and 'popular' forms—often in the same chapter, as is case with a text such as Charles Gildon's *The New Metamorphosis* (1708) in 'Circulation Narratives and Spy Literature'.[31]

If there is one work that might be thought of as embodying the dynamic, contradictory energies of English prose in this period, however, it is Swift's *A Tale of a Tub* and the companion satires that appeared with it in 1704, *The Battle of the Books* and *The*

---

[29] On Addison's repurposing of his undergraduate orations, see Paul Davis, 'Addison's Classical Criticism and the Origins of Eighteenth-Century Aesthetics', *English Literary History*, 90 (2023), 693–721. The vast majority of Addison's surviving Latin work is in verse, on which see Estelle Haan, *Vergilius Redivivus: Studies in Joseph Addison's Latin Poetry* (Philadelphia, PA: American Philosophical Society, 2005).

[30] Kristine Louise Haugen, *Richard Bentley: Poetry and Enlightenment* (Cambridge, MA: Harvard University Press, 2011), 99.

[31] For specific discussion of cheap print in the earlier part of the period covered by this volume, see Joad Raymond (ed.), *The Oxford History of Popular Print Culture. Volume 1: Cheap Print in Britain and Ireland to 1660* (Oxford: Oxford University Press, 2011).

Mechanical Operation of the Spirit. The *Tale* stress-tests the boundaries between fiction and non-fiction, deriving much of its material from traditions of heresiography and religious polemic but also parodying aspects of the claims to realism and systematization that would become recognizable as aspects of the novel; the *Tale* looks back to the tradition of learned wit and mock-scholarship nurtured by Renaissance humanism but in doing so it also anticipates the 'Scriblerian' satire against philistinism and ignorance of the first half of the eighteenth century; the *Tale* satirizes the material forms of authorship and publication and appeared anonymously, yet the identity of its author soon became well known and celebrated; and the *Tale* is an ostensibly ideologically conservative work which also takes risky and even radical liberties in its mockery of forms of political, religious, and textual authority.

In the *OED*, 'prose' is generally defined in opposition to, or as part of a binary opposition with, poetry—as in Milton's undertaking to perform 'Things unattempted yet in prose or rhyme' in the opening invocation of *Paradise Lost*, where 'rhyme' simply stands in for verse itself. The binary opposition can seem to be embedded even in the term's etymological origins. 'Prose' derives from *prorsus* in Latin, meaning straightforward and direct and suggesting 'an ongoing forward movement', as opposed to verse, in which a line is 'turned' (*versus*): it is apparently the line-break that distinguishes verse from the potentially 'unlimited extendability' of a sentence in prose.[32] Some authors were evidently self-conscious about why they chose to write in prose rather than in other forms: in 1642 Milton famously referred to having 'the use ... but of my left hand' when writing in the 'cool element of prose', implicitly demoting prose below poetry—while at the same time going on to devote most of his career between 1641 and 1667 to publishing in prose, both vernacular and Latin, much of it extremely hot-tempered.[33] But prose has always existed and developed beyond a restrictive dualism with poetry—'the invention of prose' in classical Greece as the medium of 'almost all serious philosophy, history, medicine, mathematics, theology' has been seen as 'fundamental to the very foundation of Western culture'—and this *Handbook* sets out to offer a view unparalleled in its multi-dimensionality of English prose in its golden age.[34]

---

[32] Michael Peled Ginsburg, 'Turning: from Verse to Prose', in *Connotations: A Journal for Critical Debate*, 23 (2013–14), 189–206 (189–90).

[33] John Milton, *The Reason of Church-Government Urged against Prelaty* (1642), in *Selected Prose*, ed. William Poole (London: Penguin Books, 2014), 27.

[34] Simon Goldhill, *The Invention of Prose* (Oxford: Oxford University Press, 2002), 1, 4.

PART I
CONTEXTS

CHAPTER 1

CIRCULATION

THOMAS KEYMER

Metaphors

The pioneering medical researches of William Harvey, first published in 1628 and extended in his *De circulatione sanguinis* (1649), gave rise over time to a host of figurative applications.[1] In the *Spectator* (1711–12, 1714), the best-known essay periodical of the reign of Queen Anne, Joseph Addison and Richard Steele wrote literally about advances in medicine 'since the Circulation of the Blood has been found out ... by our Modern Anatomists'. But they also applied this language to other subjects, including changing fashion and its energizing effects on commercial activity: 'how far the Vanity of Mankind has laid itself out in Dress, what a prodigious Number of People it maintains, and what a Circulation of Money it occasions.'[2] It was in the economic realm above all that circulation metaphors caught on. Trade was the lifeblood of the nation, and it animated the body politic in comparable ways. The analogy became explicit in Daniel Defoe's mercantilist treatise *The Compleat English Tradesman* (1725–7), which took it as axiomatic that 'Trade ought to pass through as many hands as it can, and that the circulation of Trade, like that of the Blood, is the life of the Commerce'. London was the beating heart of this economic system, the vital organ that 'consumes all, circulates all, exports all, and at last pays for all, and this is Trade; this greatness and wealth of the City is the Soul of the Commerce to all the Nation.'[3] Defoe even structured his exhaustive socioeconomic survey, *A Tour thro' the Whole Island of Great Britain* (1724–6), in line with this view, dividing the work into 'Circuits' undertaken by the traveller-narrator as he observes and documents the circulation of trade.

---

[1] *Exercitatio anatomica de circulatione sanguinis* (1649), translated in 1653 as *Two Anatomical Exercitations Concerning the Circulation of the Blood*.

[2] Donald F. Bond (ed.), *The Spectator*, 5 vols. (Oxford: Clarendon Press, 1965), 4: 441 (no. 543, 22 November 1712); 4: 193 (no. 478, 8 September 1712).

[3] Daniel Defoe, *The Compleat English Tradesman*, 2 vols. (1725–7), 2, pt 2: 38; 2, pt 2: 142.

But what about the book trade specifically? 'Circulation' is now our standard term for the spread of print, as also for the transmission of manuscript, in terms of both scale (publication statistics) and reach (social, geographical). The word brings with it a range of benign connotations: of cultural lifeblood and its pulsing flow; of an organically connected national readership. But this sense of 'circulation' was slow to take hold. The *Oxford English Dictionary* gives no illustrations before the nineteenth century, and though examples are there to be found throughout the eighteenth, only a few predate the rise in the 1740s of 'circulating libraries', as pioneers like Samuel Fancourt called these new institutions (which had major, though not universally applauded, consequences for access to print thereafter).[4] Between 1640 and 1714, metaphors for book production and transmission often suggested more sporadic, violent, even baleful kinds of movement. Among the sources collected in D. F. McKenzie's and Maureen Bell's invaluable *Chronology and Calendar of Documents Relating to the London Book Trade 1641–1700*, we find one witness lamenting in 1679 that 'The Town swarms with pamphlets. Two or three appear every day.' A second observes in 1698 that 'Pamphlets fly about as thick, as is usual at the beginning of a parliament' (this witness singles out 'a violent satire on the King ... a scurrilous invective against Sir Thomas Littleton ... To these there are Answers, Replies, etc.'); a third deplores letters and pamphlets 'industriously spread' in 1692 by disaffected booksellers, and urges that 'speedy care must be taken to prevent the spreading of this infection, which creeps secretly into the bowels of the nation'.[5] In these reports and others like them, print swarms, flies around, creeps, as though locust-like or parasitic; it multiplies and poisons. Roger L'Estrange, a virtuoso of paranoid reading who in his dual office as Licenser and Surveyor of the Press was at the sharp end of press control in the Restoration era, fulminates about 'Numberless Shoals' of book and pamphlets, and about 'the *Vagabond License* of the *Press*'.[6] Such images of the boundless, wayward, and lawless were the stuff of his professional nightmares.

The hostile opinions cited above refer especially to factional or sectarian writing at moments of political crisis, which typically produce statistical spikes in the output of books and pamphlets. Similar points arise, however, in broader satires about Restoration print. For John Dryden in *Mac Flecknoe* (written *c.*1676 and circulated at first in manuscript copies), seventeenth-century London was a world clogged by ephemeral, odoriferous wastepaper, varying in political hue, but sharing the same abject fate in kitchens or privies:

---

[4] See Samuel Fancourt, *The Narrative* (1747), 4–5; David Allan, *A Nation of Readers: The Lending Library in Georgian England* (London: British Library, 2008), 119–62.

[5] D. F. McKenzie and Maureen Bell, *A Chronology and Calendar of Documents Relating to the London Book Trade 1641–1700*, 3 vols. (Oxford: Oxford University Press, 2005), 2: 230 (6 September 1679); 3: 268 (29 November 1698); 3: 132 (12 October 1692).

[6] Peter Hinds, *'The Horrid Popish Plot': Roger L'Estrange and the Circulation of Political Discourse in Late-Seventeenth-Century London* (Oxford: Oxford University Press, 2010), 9.

> From dusty shops neglected authors come,
> Martyrs of pies, and relics of the bum.
> Much Heywood, Shirley, Ogilby there lay,
> But loads of Shadwell almost choked the way.

Dryden amplified the excremental sneer when, on authorizing a print edition of *Mac Flecknoe* in 1684, he adjusted the allusion to his Whig rival Thomas Shadwell to read 'loads of Sh—'.[7] This was an act of sharpening more than concealment, and it stands now as one among many instances of a joke about repurposed print that runs through the period's satire: disposable sermons lining hatboxes, fugitive histories wrapping bacon, temporary poems wiping arses. No author was exempt. In a succinct later instance of the wastepaper trope, 'I'm glad you'l write', Lady Mary Wortley Montagu assured her personal and political adversary Jonathan Swift: 'You'l furnish paper when I shite.'[8]

We may turn to Swift for a more exuberant, albeit complexly ironic, account of proliferating print and its cultural effects. Swift's early masterpiece *A Tale of a Tub* (written in the 1690s, published in 1704, and now best known in its elaborately revised text of 1710) is at one level an allegory of religious schism between Catholicism, Anglicanism, and Dissent. But the *Tale* is also a gleeful satire on market-led modern authorship, written in the voice of a hackney author—ignorant, exploitative, slapdash, preening—who exemplifies the vices of commercial print culture, yet also embodies energies and attitudes in which Swift himself is imaginatively immersed, without any clear effect of satirical detachment. A shameless cheerleader for cultural debasement, the hack is also rhetorically compelling, even somehow winning in his ebullient opportunism. Fuelling the opportunism is a view of books, not as repositories of enduring truth or transcendent beauty, but as commodities to be hustled and hawked. The pretence of timeless value must of course be maintained, and Swift's hack begins by declaring his work 'calculated to live at least as long as our Language' and noting the paratextual formulae routinely used to distinguish a book from the herd ('*To observe what Trash the Press swarms with*, &c.').[9] His real instinct, however, is to embrace the swarming, and throughout the *Tale* he revels in a world of gratuitous textuality and mercenary print that has become, his prose suggests, the new norm.

The texts and the print concerned are typically fugitive. 'What is then become of those immense Bales of Paper, which must needs have been employ'd in such Numbers of Books?', he asks his work's dedicatee, Prince Posterity—a figure so hostile to modern writings 'that of several Thousands produced yearly from this renowned City, before the next Revolution of the Sun, there is not one to be heard of'. Happily, more new books

---

[7] *The Poems of John Dryden. Volume 1: 1649–1681*, ed. Paul Hammond (Harlow: Longman, 1995), 1: 323 (lines 100–3); see also, on the 1684 association between Shadwell and shit, 1: 315 (n. to line 15).

[8] Lady Mary Wortley Montagu, *Essays and Poems and Simplicity, a Comedy*, ed. Robert Halsband and Isobel Grundy (Oxford: Clarendon Press, 1993), 276.

[9] Jonathan Swift, *A Tale of a Tub and Other Works*, ed. Marcus Walsh (Cambridge: Cambridge University Press, 2010), 5, 28.

can be quickly thrown together to take their place, thanks not least to the 'great *Helps* and *Liftings*' to be had from other books; he puffs several examples of his own, vacuous, vainglorious, and alarmingly defiant of inherited values: '*A Dissertation upon the principal Productions of* Grub-street ... *A general History of* Ears ... *A modest Defence of the Proceedings of the* Rabble *in all Ages*.'[10] Such books can be sold in a range of formats geared to a stratified market, from superfluous high-end anthologies ('a faithful and a painful Collection ... in Twelve Volumes in Folio, illustrated with Copper-Plates') to lowbrow catchpenny chapbooks ('*Six-peny-worth of Wit*, Westminster *Drolleries, Delightful Tales, Compleat Jesters,* and the like'). They can be shifted by a range of paratextual tricks, from strategic dedications ('Your Lordship's Name on the Front, in Capital Letters, will at any time get off one Edition') to vaunting advertisements ('Our Great *Dryden* ... often said to me in Confidence, that the World would have never suspected him to be so great a Poet, if he had not assured them so frequently in his Prefaces').[11] Even so, the sell must be a hard one, for if Grub Street has now usurped Parnassus, and hallowed literary traditions have given way to the improvisatory chaos and fetishized novelty of the modern marketplace, shelf-lives are inevitably short. For the time being, Swift's hack exults in the privilege of 'being the *Last Writer* ... the *freshest Modern*' in a world where unripeness is all. But this position is by its nature precarious and must be monetized at speed. As he observes with mingled relish and disquiet, 'I am living fast, to see the Time, when a *Book* that misses its Tide, shall be neglected, as the *Moon* by day, or like *Mackarel* a Week after the Season'.[12] Annotating this line, Marcus Walsh cites a 1690 French source that Swift probably knew ('Les livres, comme les fruits, ont leur saison'). Yet awareness of Swift's borrowing, with the accompanying substitution, only heightens our sense of the creative surplus he injects: not fruit now but fish, and not any fish but specifically mackerel, a species notorious for rapid, noisome putrefaction.

One approach to the *Tale* would be to say that the picture it offers of the literary marketplace and proliferating print—aesthetically barren, ethically debased, culturally corrosive—implies a positive alternative to be found in manuscript circulation. Much of the *Tale*, with its companion piece *The Battel of the Books*, was drafted during Swift's period of intermittent employment at Moor Park, Surrey, as secretary to Sir William Temple, a distinguished retired diplomat and man of letters. The *Battel* intervenes on Temple's behalf in the controversy provoked by his 'Essay upon the Ancient and Modern Learning', published in 1690, which looks nostalgically back to traditions predating, and uncontaminated by, professional authorship and commercial production, and ranks modern literature and scholarship below the achievements of a classical golden age. In

---

[10] Swift, *Tale*, 23, 21, 84, 4. London's Grub Street was proverbially the home of garret-dwelling authors for hire, an association dating from the second quarter of the seventeenth century (*OED* gives illustrations from 1630 and 1648). Ear-cropping in the pillory was a penalty traditionally inflicted on authors or printers convicted of seditious libel, but mutilation was rare in practice after 1640.

[11] Swift, *Tale*, 38, 40, 16, 85.

[12] Swift, *Tale*, 85, 134.

this context, the *Tale* might seem to embody the same Moor Park values: the values of a manuscript culture characterized by gentlemanly amateurism, coterie circulation, and leisurely connoisseurship within a learned elite. At a time when the so-called Quarrel of the Ancients and Moderns still reverberated in England (its epicentre was in France), the hack expresses modernity in its worst aspects. He is mercenary, unprincipled, and cynically prolific: 'Fourscore and eleven Pamphlets have I writ under three Reigns, and for the Service of six and thirty Factions.' When his commonplace book, his index-learning, and his other channels of plagiarized content at last run dry, he will cheerfully resort to 'a pernicious Kind of Writings, called *Second Parts*' or attempt 'an Experiment very frequent among Modern Authors; which is, to *write upon Nothing*'.[13] To stress only these negatives, however, would be to miss the celebratory brio of the voice Swift creates in the *Tale*, to say nothing of the remarkable print career on which he was then himself embarking, in the first place as a party writer of notoriously unstable allegiance. Like his friend and ally Alexander Pope, whose great mock-epic of dumbed-down print, *The Dunciad*, first appeared in 1728, Swift was at once a devastating satirist, and a brilliant exponent, of commercialized literary culture. When his hack exults 'that Fate has flung me into so blessed an Age for the mutual Felicity of *Booksellers* and *Authors*', irony is only part of the story.[14]

NUMBERS

Yet was this in reality such a blessed age? The underlying conditions of population size, purchasing power, and literacy rates are hard to establish with great confidence, but the general picture is of uneven growth at best. The civil wars are thought to have cost more British lives proportionately than the First World War total of 3 per cent, and from the 1650s to the 1680s large outflows of emigration to North America, notably of Dissenters and others fleeing religious persecution and political turmoil, further thinned the population by as much as 8 per cent. At the time of the 'Glorious Revolution' in 1689, the British Isles remained sparsely inhabited and overwhelmingly rural, with an estimated 4.93 million people living in England, and another 300,000, 1.2 million, and 2 million respectively in Wales, Scotland, and Ireland (France had a population approaching 22 million). Only then was a demographic corner turned, as economic growth following the financial revolution of the 1690s supported a rise in the English population to around 5.44 million in 1726, up perhaps 10 per cent from its 1680s low. Much of the growth was associated with internal migration to London, a city of half a million in 1689, overtaking Paris at around this time as the largest in Christendom. This phenomenon

---

[13] Swift, *Tale*, 44, 118, 135.
[14] Swift, *Tale*, 117.

mainly accounts for an approximate doubling of the proportion of urban dwellers in England, to 20 per cent, between 1600 and 1700.[15]

The late seventeenth-century vogue for political arithmetic (a form of demographic and economic analysis that was another of Swift's many bugbears) provides interesting, though inevitably uncertain, evidence about income levels. Among the best-known exercises in this vein is Gregory King's calculation that in 1688, 91,586 families (nobility, gentry, merchants, freeholders, 'persons in offices', lawyers, naval officers) enjoyed an annual income of £80 or more, with below them a middling-sort tier of 420,000 families worth £40 or more annually. Books were a prestigious commodity for the propertied elite and other well-off consumers, and booksellers became increasingly adept at stimulating demand. But as James Raven points out, disposable incomes were squeezed throughout the Restoration by new fiscal efficiencies, so that 'by the 1690s ... the state extracted an unprecedentedly large income per capita, with much of the change imposed after 1660 and in response to the demands of war'.[16] Wealthy individuals continued to exercise patronage in the old way, subscription publishing established a new and more distributed patronage model, and the boom in party writing under William III and Queen Anne (those 'six and thirty Factions') gave professional authors a fresh, if precarious, income stream. But it is far from clear that middling-sort book buyers felt significantly wealthier than earlier generations, and if the much-debated 'consumer revolution' was indeed under way, there were many other luxuries, from clocks to china, competing with books for discretionary spending.[17]

Literacy rates are notoriously a matter of speculation, and of course literacy must be seen not as an absolute value but as a range of continuum points, beyond which the illiterate could still access print indirectly, via oral transmission or performance.[18] Julian Hoppit suggests that by 1714 perhaps 45 per cent of men and 25 per cent of women could read (Londoners were more likely to enjoy functional literacy than their rural peers), and he points to various factors, from the ready availability of newspapers in coffeehouses to the distribution of religious books by paternalistic gentry, to argue that some form of access to print was now extensive: 'even the poorest households might own printed works.'[19] That said, the cost of anything more than a basic chapbook or broadside ballad would have been prohibitive for the literate poor, and at best an occasional

---

[15] Julian Hoppit, *A Land of Liberty? England 1689-1727* (Oxford: Oxford University Press, 2000), 52-5; see also 66-9.

[16] Hoppit, *Land of Liberty*, 69-73; James Raven, 'The Economic Context', in John Barnard and D. F. McKenzie (eds.), *The Cambridge History of the Book in Britain. Volume 4: 1557-1695* (Cambridge: Cambridge University Press, 2002), 568-82 (581).

[17] See Lorna Weatherill, *Consumer Behaviour and Material Culture in Britain 1660-1760* (2nd edn, London: Routledge, 1996), esp. 93-136.

[18] See Paula McDowell, *The Invention of the Oral: Print Commerce and Fugitive Voices in Eighteenth-Century Britain* (Chicago: University of Chicago Press, 2017), 1-60.

[19] Hoppit, *Land of Liberty*, 169. The 1710s estimate (45 per cent of men, 25 per cent of women) is from David Cressy, *Literacy and the Social Order: Reading and Writing in Tudor and Stuart England* (Cambridge: Cambridge University Press, 1980), 175-7; Cressy proposes 30 per cent of men and 10 per cent of women for the 1640s.

splash for skilled artisans, shopkeepers, or tenant farmers. Book prices become easy to ascertain by the second quarter of the eighteenth century, but there is little evidence of standardized price-setting (by format and paper size) before the 1680s, and even under Anne it was unusual for anything more substantial than a long pamphlet to be advertised by price (typically sixpence for 30–50 pages, or a shilling beyond that, stitched but unbound). The most consistent source of evidence is the *Term Catalogues* listing of books published seasonally from 1668 to 1711, from which we learn that *A Tale of a Tub* was priced in 1704 at four shillings.[20] A high-end production such as Jacob Tonson's handsome edition of Dryden's Virgil (1697) cost subscribers two guineas, or five in the fine-paper format; Dryden believed small-paper copies to be selling for around £1.[21] Even unassuming books involved significant outlay in a market that was always sensitive to price. When the Stamp Act of 1712 added a halfpenny to the cost of a published half-sheet, several periodicals abruptly closed, and Swift observed (in a letter poised midway between gloating and lament) that 'Grubstreet is dead and gone last Week; no more Ghosts or Murders now for Love or Money'.[22] For a measure of other commodity prices in relation to books, Raven tells us that (after several decades of negligible inflation) 'in 1760 two shillings could buy a stone of beef or a pair of shoes'.[23]

We have somewhat greater clarity about printing and publishing capacity in London, thanks to the work of McKenzie, Raven, and others in archives such as the registers of the Stationers' Company, the body charged since 1557 with regulation of the book trade. Also of help is the towering paranoia of the Restoration surveyor Roger L'Estrange, who fretted in 1662 that a '*Glut* of *Poysonous* Libels' then on the market included '*Two-Hundred-Thousand* Seditious Copies ... Printed, since the blessed Return of his Sacred Majesty' (to which 'may be added divers *Millions* of the *Old Stock*'). Six years later, L'Estrange undertook a manuscript 'Survey of the Printing Presses wth the Names & Nombers of Apprentices Officers and Workmen belonging to every perticular Presse Taken 29º Julij 1668'; he had personally raided most of them, earning the nickname 'Towzer' (also 'Crack-Fart') in the process.[24] Then there are the quantitative possibilities of the English Short Title Catalogue (ESTC), which documents all known surviving

---

[20] Using newspaper advertisements and records of the book collector Narcissus Luttrell (1657–1732), Joseph Hone provides an illuminating chronology of 1702 books and prices in *Literature and Party Politics at the Accession of Queen Anne* (Oxford: Oxford University Press, 2017), 174–84.

[21] J. A. Downie, 'Paying for Poetry at the Turn of the Eighteenth Century, with Particular Reference to Dryden, Pope, and Defoe', *Digital Defoe*, 6 (2014), 1–18; John Barnard, 'The Large- and Small-Paper Copies of Dryden's *The Works of Virgil* (1697): Jacob Tonson's Investment and Profits and the Example of *Paradise Lost* (1688)', *Papers of the Bibliographical Society of America*, 92 (1998), 259–71. A gold guinea traded at a premium against silver coinage until 1717, when its value was fixed at 21 shillings (£1 1s.); it was worth up to 30 shillings in the 1690s.

[22] Jonathan Swift, *Journal to Stella: Letters to Esther Johnson and Rebecca Dingley 1710–1713*, ed. Abigail Williams (Cambridge: Cambridge University Press, 2013), 442 (7 August 1712).

[23] James Raven, *Judging New Wealth: Popular Publishing and Responses to Commerce in England 1750–1800* (Oxford: Clarendon Press, 1992), 57. That was a lot of beef: 14 lbs or 6.35 kg.

[24] Roger L'Estrange, *Truth and Loyalty Vindicated* (1662), sig. A2v; National Archives, SP 29/243 (126), transcribed in Barnard and McKenzie (eds.), *Cambridge History of the Book. Volume 4*, 794–6.

books, serials, newspapers, and selected print ephemera issued in Britain, Ireland, or the colonies before 1801, including at the time of writing 134,648 entries from 1640 to 1714.

Underlying all this evidence for the later Stuart period is the development of innovative publishing practices and print products in response to escalating demand, or, as Raven puts it, 'a book trade only erratically regulated by the State ... now driven by conspicuously new commercial opportunity'.[25] Numerous expansionary trends that took hold in the eighteenth century are already observable by the 1680s: improved transportation networks (with roads not so much circulating as radiating from London), which facilitated large-scale distribution to provincial, archipelagic, and colonial markets; efficient funding of bookselling ventures through new financial instruments and publication schemes like serialization and advance subscription; the formation of powerful book-trade 'congers' or cartels to distribute risk, share rights and stocks, and boost profits; the emergence of specialist publishers like Richard 'Novel' Bentley (1645–97), best known for his multi-volume collections, or Jacob Tonson (1655–1736), who nurtured a lucrative market for vernacular classics (Shakespeare, Milton, Dryden, Congreve). Raven discounts the estimate of Richard Atkyns' *Origin and Growth of Printing* (1664) that there were already 'at least 600 Booksellers that keep Shops in or about London, and Two or Three Thousand free of the Company of Stationers' ('bookseller' could mean a financing publisher, a retailer of books, or someone combining these roles; a freeman of the Stationers' Company won this status on completing a lengthy apprenticeship, or sometimes by patrimony). Atkyns was right, however, that the trade was buoyant overall. Around 650 booksellers are named more than twice on title pages between 1660 and 1700, and of these between 150 and 250 were publishers in something approaching the modern sense. The number of printing houses and printing presses was on the rise, albeit along a very jagged line, with estimated figures of 23 printing houses (46–51 presses in operation) in 1637, 40 in 1649, 59 in 1661–3, 48 in 1665, 33 (82 presses) in 1668, 55 (145 presses) in 1686, 48 in 1695, and 70 (150+ presses) in 1705. Then there were the 'supernumerary' (i.e. illegal) operators, fourteen of whom were summoned by the Stationers' Company in 1673 'to giue an Account vppon what Tearmes they keep their seuerall printing-houses'; L'Estrange watched the process closely and called for rigorous suppression.[26]

Book historians tend to represent the second half of the seventeenth century as a period of rising output, and this is no doubt true in general, though again with significant peaks and troughs along the way. That said, the surviving evidence must be evaluated with care, and the statistical table of 'Annual book production 1475–1700' offered by John Barnard and Maureen Bell in *The Cambridge History of the Book in Britain* for 1557–1695 is too often cited without regard to caveats elsewhere in the volume. The table alone records 848 published titles in 1640, a figure that soars with the collapse

---

[25] James Raven, *The Business of Books: Booksellers and the English Book Trade 1450–1850* (New Haven: Yale University Press, 2007), 83.

[26] Raven, *Business of Books*, 84, 47, 86; see also, for the 1673 investigation, McKenzie and Bell, *Chronology and Calendar*, 2: 48 and 59–60.

of political authority as civil war takes hold (2,034 titles in 1641, 3,666 titles in 1642), and then remains firmly above a thousand until the relatively quiet publishing years of 1664–71 (when L'Estrange was in his pomp, and untold losses to personnel, stock, capacity, and demand were no doubt entailed by plague and fire). Numbers surge again during the Exclusion Crisis of 1679–81, another period of political turmoil when press control buckled: 1,174 titles in 1678, 1,730 in 1679, 2,145 in 1680, 1,978 in 1681. Thereafter the annual total remains high until 1685, when the censorship regime bounced back under James II, and Towzer was once more off his leash. It rises further either side of the Glorious Revolution (1,941 titles in 1688, 2,514 in 1689, 2,302 in 1690), and remains elevated until the end of the century, with peaks of 2,066 titles in 1695 and 2,640 in 1700 (the highest annual total since 1660, the Restoration year, with its glut of unctuous panegyrics). The accompanying graph (Figure 1.1), based on the Barnard-Bell numbers, shows an unmistakable, though spiky, uptrend between the plague–fire years of 1665–6 and the end of the century, with a statistically perfect run of higher lows and higher highs observable throughout this period. The decade totals (all of which would now be somewhat larger, given ongoing additions to ESTC) are as follows:

Decade	1641–50	1651–60	1661–70	1671–80	1681–90	1691–1700
Number of titles	18,247	13,991	9,624	12,695	18,530	17,520

In view of the measures that generated these numbers in 2002, the corresponding figures for 1701–10 would probably be in the region of 19,300 titles, and c.20,000 titles for 1711–20.[27] Of all these totals, London imprints account for the great majority (varying by decade between 78 per cent and 88 per cent) at a time when provincial printing had yet to develop much scale. Oxford, Cambridge, and York, with their university or ecclesiastical privileges, were the only major production centres in the English provinces. Edinburgh still accounted for a larger number of published titles per annum than Dublin, but the Irish book trade grew fast after the Restoration, as printers and stationers eroded the monopoly patent of the King's Printer and founded the Guild of St Luke (in 1670) to regulate the trade. The number of booksellers in Dublin is thought to have quadrupled between 1660 and 1700; the number of printers also greatly increased.[28]

There is, in short, clear overall growth in published titles across the extended period, and, if one smooths for the spikes of political turmoil and regulatory incapacity, a firm upward trajectory. An economist might call it an ascending channel. Yet it remains incautious to say, as one politically focused book historian says, that during the Popish Plot panic of 1678–80 'in two years there was almost a doubling of the amount of books

---

[27] For the early eighteenth century, see Michael F. Suarez, 'Towards a Bibliometric Analysis of the Surviving Record, 1701–1800', in Michael F. Suarez and Michael L. Turner (eds.), *The Cambridge History of the Book in Britain. Volume 5: 1695–1830* (Cambridge: Cambridge University Press, 2009), 39–65. For technical reasons, Suarez's statistics cannot be mapped directly on to those of Barnard and Bell.

[28] Raymond Gillespie, 'Print Culture, 1550–1700', in Raymond Gillespie and Andrew Hadfield (eds.), *The Irish Book in English 1550–1800* (Oxford: Oxford University Press, 2006), 17–33 (23–4).

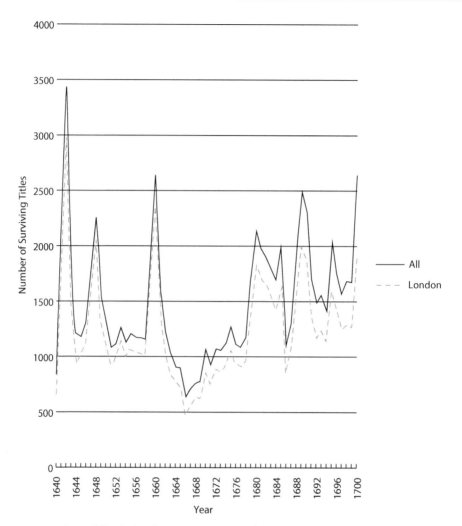

FIGURE 1.1 Annual Book Production 1640–1700 (four-year intervals). My thanks to Austin Long for creating this graph.

printed annually in London', or that in 1640–2 'the first civil wars produced more than a quadrupling of titles'.[29] Public crisis and book-trade overdrive are clearly inter-related, but there may also be an observer effect at work in the numbers, in which the very fact of crisis distorts survival rates. After all, much of what we know about output in the early 1640s, including many unique survivals, flows from the prodigious efforts at the time of George Thomason, a stationer who attempted a comprehensive collection of political and religious tracts as they came from the press. Thomason started with 22 titles in 1640, and in 1642 he purchased 1,966 titles, or 61 per cent of the London-published total;

---

[29] Hinds, *Horrid Popish Plot*, 9.

and he did it precisely because he saw the crisis as truly momentous, and important to document in full. What if he had started buying somewhat earlier in 1640, or had bought more voraciously at the outset of his project? Would we still think that publication rates were quadrupling, or would we recognize instead that moments of crisis spur acts of collection, and so inflate survival rates above levels seen during calmer periods (a point we might extend to the Exclusion Crisis material assembled by observers in and around 1680, notably Narcissus Luttrell and John, Lord Somers)? As D. F. McKenzie drily notes, 'metaphors of the trade exploding or bursting, or of books flooding or mushrooming, which lift the prose of so many historians of the period, do little to clarify its altered conditions or the exact nature of the evidence from which we infer their change'.[30] In some years, we may think we detect increased production when really the phenomenon we see is increased preservation; in all years, the products that happen to survive, and are duly recorded in ESTC, are only a proportion, unknown and variable from year to year, of actual production at the time. It is salutary to remember how many titles have been lost, or rather the impossibility of knowing how many—though, as McKenzie points out, common sense dictates that rates of loss will grow in severity the further back we go in time, so baking into our narratives of expansion a statistically exaggerating effect. Attrition rates are certainly enormous throughout the period covered by this volume, especially in low-prestige categories of output, and they should make us pause before treating any number as a guide to much more than survival now. McKenzie cites several Restoration and early eighteenth-century book-lists from which between 15 per cent and 60 per cent of items are lost. Barnard reports, from unusually specific archival evidence, that the Stationers printed 84,000 school primers in 1676/7; one known copy exists today.[31]

This leads on to a second major caveat, if we are concerned, at least, with the actual quantities of print being produced each year—those bales of paper so relished by Swift's hack—as opposed to the mere number of titles. On inspection, the latter figure turns out to tell us little about the former, for which the true measure would be the total number of signature sheets in any given title, adjusted for paper size and multiplied by the print-run of the title, added to the same calculation for every other title the same year. For a typical annual count of 1,200 titles, the bibliographical spadework involved in the first part of this task would be prohibitive, while the scarcity of print-run information (before large-scale archival sources kick in like the post-1710 ledgers of the printer William Bowyer) makes the second part pure guesswork. A run might be anywhere between 100 and 1,500 copies, or much more than that in a few categories of mass production such as almanacs, primers, and psalters. All these uncertainties notwithstanding, however, the likelihood remains that overall production volumes were expanding more rapidly than

---

[30] D. F. McKenzie, 'Printing and Publishing 1557–1700: Constraints on the London Book Trades', in Barnard and McKenzie (eds.), *Cambridge History of the Book. Volume 4*, 553–67 (560).

[31] McKenzie, 'Printing and Publishing', 558–9; John Barnard, 'The Survival and Loss Rates of Psalms, ABCs, Psalters and Primers from the Stationers' Stock, 1660–1700', *The Library*, 6th series, 21 (1999), 148–50.

the bare increase in titles suggests, so counterbalancing the upward distortions noted above in the trendline of title counts. For Raven, 'the gentle increase in the publication of new book and periodical titles in the decades following the Restoration hides an apparently enormous growth in the quantity of print, notably in religious and instructional small books'.[32] It might be added that the ephemeral tracts archived by Thomason in the 1640s were typically short pamphlets or single-sheet broadsides, inflating title counts with fugitive material that would mostly have been printed overnight in tiny runs. Yet each Thomason tract has the same impact on title counts as a massive publishing project of the kind familiar by the time Swift wrote the *Tale*: those painful collections 'in Twelve Volumes in Folio', a joke aimed especially at John Dunton, the prolific bookseller-author who is often held to embody the entrepreneurial energies of the post-Revolution trade.[33] In fact the typical Dunton production was on a smaller scale than this, but he and his contemporaries were certainly working their way through plenty of paper. Customs ledgers and port books from the late 1690s, in which print is a materially quantifiable commodity like any other, offer a nice glimpse of the tonnage involved: 175 hundredweight of books exported from England to Ireland (a figure that roughly doubled across the 1690s), 131 cwt to Holland, 119 cwt to Scotland, 108 cwt to Virginia.[34]

Manuscripts

There is a further crucial point if we are concerned with the circulation of texts, as opposed to print alone. None of the above numbers catches the hugely important phenomena of manuscript transmission and scribal publication—the distinction here being between the informal distribution practices of literary coteries and the commercial dissemination of handwritten copies produced in professional scriptoria. Groundbreaking monographs were devoted to these related vehicles in the 1990s (by Margaret Ezell in the first case, Harold Love in the second),[35] and subsequent studies have refined our sense of media succession in the age of print as a complex, extended, reciprocal process in which script was always of more than residual importance. Yet it is probably still true that we underestimate the ongoing vitality of manuscript media (with their attendant capacity to shape the message) throughout the period involved, and indeed beyond it. Major categories of prose flourished via manuscript transmission long before, even centuries

---

[32] Raven, *Business of Books*, 91.

[33] See J. Paul Hunter, *Before Novels: The Cultural Contexts of Eighteenth-Century English Fiction* (New York: Norton, 1990), 12–18, 99–106.

[34] Gillespie, 'Print Culture, 1550–1700', 24; see also Robert Welch, 'The Book in Ireland from the Tudor Re-Conquest to the Battle of the Boyne', in Barnard and McKenzie (eds.), *Cambridge History of the Book* 4, 701–18 (716). Printing began in Boston in 1639, but Virginia had no capacity until 1728.

[35] Margaret J. M. Ezell, *Social Authorship and the Advent of Print* (Baltimore: Johns Hopkins University Press, 1999); Harold Love, *Scribal Publication in Seventeenth-Century England* (Oxford: Clarendon Press, 1993).

before, they entered the realm of print—as sometimes occurred with the sanction of authors or executors, sometimes through the agency of unscrupulous publishers, sometimes as Victorian or later acts of scholarly retrieval.

There are cases, of course, in which manuscript meant pure secrecy, as with the diary of Samuel Pepys, which has been treated as a classic of Restoration prose since selections first appeared in the nineteenth century, but was originally protected by impenetrable cipher. Beyond this cipher, Pepys also used a hybridized argot or macaronic language of his own for moments of special discretion, as when in 1688 he buys and reads an imported pornographic book 'for information sake (but it did hazer my prick para stand all the while, and una vez to decharger)'.[36] Other manuscript diaries and journals, even when less confessional than this, were no doubt also intended for a readership of one. Personal letters, however, were increasingly valued as a literary form with its own special properties and rhetoric, and often circulated beyond their immediate addressees; sometimes they leaked further, a process resulting in sensational print volumes such as the 1697 *Familiar Letters: Written by the Right Honourable John Late Earl of Rochester, and Several Other Persons of Honour and Quality*. For Dorothy Osborne in her courtship letters of the 1650s to William Temple (Swift's later patron), the genre was a space of liberating stylistic informality, 'free and Easy as ones discourse, not studdyed, as an Oration, nor made up of hard words like a Charme'.[37] But alongside informality of style came intimacy of disclosure, a quality that enhanced public curiosity while reinforcing a determination within literary coteries to withhold epistolary material from print. As Thomas Sprat explained when excluding the poet Cowley's correspondence from his posthumous *Works*, 'In such Letters the Souls of Men should appear undress'd: And in that negligent habit, they may be fit to be seen by one or two in a Chamber, but not to go abroad into the Streets.'[38] Other forms of life-writing enjoyed wider manuscript readerships, including the spiritual autobiographies and conversion narratives that circulated within puritan sects and other religious communities as a means of sharing exemplary experience and bolstering group identity. They did so in ways that were often creatively informed by the materiality of script. As Kathleen Lynch puts it, 'we can best understand early modern self-representational experiments with form and method if we take into account the sensory engagements with paper, pen, and notebook'.[39]

---

[36] *The Diary of Samuel Pepys, Volume 9: 1668-9*, ed. Robert Latham and William Matthews (London: Bell & Hyman, 1971), 59 (9 February); the book was *L'Ecole des filles* (1655).

[37] Dorothy Osborne, *Letters to Sir William Temple*, ed. Kenneth Parker (London: Penguin, 1987), 131 (September 1653).

[38] Thomas Sprat, 'An Account of the Life and Writings of Mr. Abraham Cowley', in Cowley's *Works* (1668), sig. Adr.

[39] Kathleen Lynch, 'Inscribing the Early Modern Self: The Materiality of Autobiography', in Adam Smyth (ed.), *A History of English Autobiography* (Cambridge: Cambridge University Press, 2016), 59–69 (68); see also discussions of spiritual autography by Molly Murray and Tessa Whitehouse in the same volume. See further Chapter 7 on 'Biography and Autobiography' by Julie A. Eckerle and Chapter 12 on 'Diaries' by Adam Smyth.

Considerations of decorum or reputation, or simply the instincts of cultural conservatism, inclined many women writers to be averse to print; the aristocratic or professional defiance of a Cavendish or a Behn were not the norm. But the networks of creative sociability sustained by coterie circulation could also make manuscript a positive expressive choice, not only for poets such as Anne Killigrew, Katherine Philips, and perhaps the more reclusive Hester Pulter, but also for writers now best known for their religious, philosophical, or fictional prose. These include Elizabeth Singer Rowe, Catharine Trotter Cockburn, and Jane Barker, all of whom problematize our traditional binary between manuscript and print cultures by exploiting and sometimes intertwining the two, but who looked especially to script for a privileged means of inserting themselves in literary tradition while also engaging with the modern republic of letters. As Melanie Bigold writes, 'the circulation of their manuscript letters, treatises, devotions, poems, and essays reveals their concerted efforts to perpetuate classical constructs of civic friendship and, particularly, humanistic ideals of intellectual reciprocity'.[40] This practice was not inherently gendered, however; nor was it exclusively 'literary'. There were prudential reasons why some of the most important political treatises of the era, from Robert Filmer's divine-right *Patriarcha* (published 1680) to Algernon Sidney's republican *Discourses Concerning Government* (published 1698), circulated in manuscript until a generation after their authors' deaths—and even in manuscript the *Discourses* were a contributory factor in Sidney's execution for treason in 1683. The *Philosophical Transactions of the Royal Society*, inaugurated in print in 1665 to document and disseminate empirical science, did not prevent the ongoing use of manuscript exchange as a vital conduit of scientific communication.[41] Libertine wits of the Rochester and Buckingham circles found manuscript a congenial medium for obscene, blasphemous, or otherwise transgressive lampoons and libels, and their work found its way into handwritten miscellanies, some meticulously compiled, others messily extemporized, that circulated widely alongside print collections, with texts migrating between the two in both directions.

Manuscript also thrived as a commercial, albeit often underground, product. The regular and unofficial newsletter services of the Restoration were not displaced by the printed newspapers that began to proliferate in the 1690s, and could even trade on the perceived advantages of manuscript: confidentiality of access, authenticity of disclosure, a presumed immunity to censorship. Writing in 1688 about the thrice-weekly letter of John Dyer, a Tory newsmonger who may have employed as many as fifty scribes, L'Estrange estimated that 'there cannot upon a Fair Computation be so Few as Five Hundred Copies of it Spread over ye Kingdom'. Efforts to limit the reach of Dyer's news (fake news, it was often alleged) were strenuous but counterproductive,

---

[40] Melanie Bigold, *Women of Letters, Manuscript Circulation, and Print Afterlives in the Eighteenth Century: Elizabeth Rowe, Catharine Cockburn, and Elizabeth Carter* (Basingstoke: Palgrave Macmillan, 2013), 11.

[41] On distrust surrounding print among natural philosophers, see Adrian Johns, *The Nature of the Book: Print and Knowledge in the Making* (Chicago: University of Chicago Press, 1998), 444–542. See further Chapter 33 on 'Scientific Transactions' by Felicity Henderson.

and as Lord Treasurer Godolphin sighed after one of several indictments against Dyer, 'the consequence of it has been that his letters have been more sought after than they were before'.[42] Even more alarming was the varied and mainly manuscript category we now know (following Harold Love) as clandestine satire, which included not only inflammatory poems on affairs of state such as the 'Advice to a Painter' series by Andrew Marvell and others, but also prose characters, epigrams, lampoons, libels, polemics, prophecies, and more.[43] Remediation of this scribal material into print prompted special vigilance from the authorities, as when in 1671 the bookseller Thomas Palmer was fined and pilloried for his role in publishing a collection of 'Painter' poems: 'Not to be granted', L'Estrange briskly notes on Palmer's petition for clemency.[44] But manuscript transmission alone could be enough to make a satire viral, and within a few more years L'Estrange was pressing ministers to expose scribal works to the same legal regime as seditious print: 'The Question of Libells, extends it selfe (I conceive) to manuscripts, as well as Prints; as beeing the more mischievous of the Two: for they are com[m]only so bitter, and dangerous, that not one of forty of them ever comes to ye Presse, and yet by ye help of Transcripts, they are well nigh as Publique.'[45] Such was the association of manuscript with unconstrained utterance, and its perceived ability to fly beneath the radar of press control, that intriguing print-manuscript hybrids began to emerge. The printer Ichabod Dawks commissioned a special fount, Grover's Scriptorial, to lend an air of confidential authority to his thrice-weekly *Dawks's News-Letter* (1696–1716); the final sheet would also be left blank for last-minute manuscript addenda. Swift's literary career took off as the professional scriptoria entered decline, but some of his most politically audacious verse satires were published in incomplete printed texts filled out with manuscript insertions and annotations. These handwritten supplements are consistent enough across surviving copies to suggest, Stephen Karian reports, 'an effective and perhaps centralized mode of scribal publication'.[46]

LAWS

McKenzie's scrutiny of production (or survival) data also leads him to argue that the dampening effects of press regulation on book-trade activity have been overstated by

---

[42] BL, Add. MS 41805, fol. 93, quoted by Love, *Scribal Publication*, 12; Godolphin to the Duchess of Marlborough, 8 October 1702, quoted by Brian Cowan, entry for 'Dyer, John (1653/4–1713)', in *ODNB*.

[43] Harold Love, *English Clandestine Satire 1660–1702* (Oxford: Oxford University Press, 2004).

[44] McKenzie and Bell, *Chronology and Calendar*, 2: 6. For this episode and Elizabeth Calvert's 1670 indictment on a similar charge, see Martin Dzelzainis, 'Andrew Marvell and the Restoration Literary Underground: Printing the Painter Poems', *The Seventeenth Century*, 22 (2007), 395–410.

[45] 'Mr L'Estrange's Propositions concerning Libels, &c.', 11 November 1675, quoted by Love, *Scribal Publication*, 74; also summarized in McKenzie and Bell, *Chronology and Calendar*, 2: 94–5.

[46] Stephen Karian, *Jonathan Swift in Print and Manuscript* (Cambridge: Cambridge University Press, 2010), 8.

historians. When Parliament abolished Star Chamber in July 1641, it disabled the censorship regime that had operated under Charles I, and this measure is often cited as enabling the sudden efflorescence of a previously shackled press. But if the publishing boom of the following year is in large part a statistical artefact ('not an image of the actual historical situation but only a projection of what we happen to know of it'),[47] this assumption must be re-examined. In McKenzie's critique of the scholarly consensus (which persists), 'the impression that the trade was unusually productive in 1642 has time and again justified an undue emphasis on censorship as a constraint on printing before the abolition of the Court of Star Chamber ... and an equally misplaced celebration of the trade's new-found but short-lived freedom from licensing after that event'. Instead he proposes an alternative view, in which a ramshackle, underpowered, and wildly erratic press-control system, routinely flouted and sometimes defiantly faced down by printers and booksellers emboldened by commercial imperatives, was 'largely ineffective and of little significance to the trade as a whole'.[48]

The statutes alone look draconian. The 1643 Licensing Order (formally An Ordinance for the Regulation of Printing) required pre-publication approval and licensing of all titles as well as registration with the Stationers' Company, 'and the Printer thereof to put his name thereto'; extensive powers of search, seizure, and arrest were also mandated, 'and in case of opposition to break open doors and locks'. During the Long Parliament and under Cromwell, further legislation toughened provisions and penalties several times (1647, 1649, 1653, 1655) while transferring powers of investigation and enforcement from the Stationers to the state, and notably to the army (a process which, for the censorship scholar Cyndia Susan Clegg, 'reflects an extraordinary transformation in the conceptualization of press control').[49] All these measures were swept away at the Restoration, but after a period of reliance on royal proclamation, the emergency legislation that replaced them in 1662 (initially for two years, but with seamless renewal thereafter until 1679, and again from 1685 to 1695) was in some respects yet more stringent. The formal title of the 1662 Licensing Act ('An Act for Preventing the Frequent Abuses in Printing Seditious, Treasonable, and Unlicensed Books and Pamphlets; and for the Regulating of Printing and Printing Presses') places political repression ahead of commercial regulation, but the aim was to harmonize these two imperatives. Prohibition of all 'heretical seditious schismatical or offensive Bookes or Pamphlets' is emphasized in the preamble of the Act, to which end no book might be published without first obtaining a licence from the relevant authority (the Archbishop of Canterbury or the Bishop of London for divinity; the Lord Chancellor for law; the Secretary of State, which in practice would mean L'Estrange, for history, politics, and much else). The licenser

---

[47] D. F. McKenzie, *Making Meaning: 'Printers of the Mind' and Other Essays* (Amherst: University of Massachusetts Press, 2002), 115–16.

[48] McKenzie, 'Printing and Publishing', 560, 567.

[49] Cyndia Susan Clegg, *Press Censorship in Caroline England* (Cambridge: Cambridge University Press, 2008), 231; see also Jason McElligott, '"A Couple of Hundred Squabbling Small Tradesmen"? Censorship, the Stationers' Company, and the State in Early Modern England', *Media History*, 11 (2005), 87–104.

concerned would retain a manuscript to ensure consistency with the published version in all textual and paratextual matters. Printers were 'to set their Names thereto, and declare the Name of the Author if required'; they were to register the book with the Stationers' Company, and supply three printed copies for official deposit. Resuming various Star Chamber provisions from 1637, the Licensing Act also imposed strict reductions on the number of printers allowed to operate (twenty, with further limits for presses employed and apprentices trained), as well as on type-founders, booksellers, and importers. Extensive powers of search and arrest were instituted 'for the better discovering of printing in Corners without License', and heavy penalties 'by Fine Imprisonment or other Corporal Punishment' were specified for offenders. This is, like the prior legislation it built on and replaced, a forbidding document.

Yet what matters on the ground is not the letter of the law but the extent of compliance or enforcement. Before the Restoration, opposition to licensing (in sources ranging from Milton's *Areopagitica* (1644) to Leveller tracts by Lilburne and others) may have done little to dent the 1643 Order, but the fact that so much supplementary legislation was needed, including measures to militarize enforcement, makes clear that the press was still perceived by government as out of control. As indeed it was, and remained, in significant respects. McKenzie's analysis of print output in three specimen years reveals, in particular, that regulations to make print traceable were widely ignored. In 1644, 46 per cent of extant titles carry a printer's name and 32 per cent a bookseller's name; 22 per cent show no provenance at all, and only 20 per cent of books and pamphlets appear in the Stationers' Register. The corresponding figures for 1688 are 31 per cent (printer's name), 39 per cent (bookseller's name), 30 per cent (anonymous), 7 per cent (registered). From a total of 491 titles surveyed by McKenzie for the year 1668, the incidence of anonymous printing rises above 54 per cent (268 titles); fewer than 11 per cent (52 titles) bear any licensing imprimatur, and only 16 per cent (79 titles) are in the Stationers' Register. Across all three specimen years, author identification never reaches 50 per cent.[50] Most of the works concerned were no doubt unobjectionable in content, but they were all, one way or another, in breach of the law.

But what of more controversial works: the heretical, seditious, schismatic, or otherwise offensive? In his arduous dual office as Licenser and Surveyor, L'Estrange read extensively and vigilantly, and doubtless he personally kicked down a good few doors. But although he and others involved in policing the late-seventeenth-century book trade (notably Robert 'Hog' Stephens, a ferocious enforcer or 'Messenger of the Press') were energetic and ruthless, they were also notoriously susceptible to bribes, and in practice overwhelmed by the scale, complexity, and sheer labyrinthine obscurity of the world they were tasked to control. The resources at their disposal were basic and few, and in an age that long precedes the formation of hegemonic or monolithic states, to think of their dogged but endlessly frustrated efforts as acts of Orwellian or Foucauldian surveillance is to commit a rather obvious totalitarian fallacy. The absence of political hegemony

---

[50] McKenzie, *Making Meaning*, 131, 115, 118.

also produced a dangerous breakdown in licensing provisions between 1679 and 1685, when competing interests (the Whig metropolis, the Tory court) made renewal impossible, just as factional discourse was at its most violent. And although public opinion is sometimes treated as an invention of the eighteenth century, it was already a significant constraint on the punishment of offenders. No one responsible for press control would have wanted to repeat the disastrous Star Chamber misstep of 1637, when the pillorying and mutilation of William Prynne and two fellow puritan pamphleteers, intended as a ritual of humiliation, instead aroused widespread sympathy and anger (enough to have contributed, Lord Clarendon thought, to the outbreak of civil war).[51] Then there was the related problem of uncooperative juries, which became acute as London politics hardened and polarized between emergent categories of Whig and Tory during the Exclusion Crisis, but was evident during L'Estrange's first years in office. One can hear his frustration, not only with the rhetorical wiles of opposition satirists but also with the cat-herding process of jury management, when, having arrested the printer of *The Poor-Whores Petition to ... the Countess of Castlemayne* (1668), a politically charged work of proto-pornography, he despairs of securing a conviction: 'I can fasten nothing on *The Poor Whore's Petition* that a jury will take notice of.'[52]

The fact remains, however, that press control before the expiration of licensing in 1695 was always a formidable constraint, and sometimes simply a terror. L'Estrange may have been unable to cope with everything the press threw at him, but he coped with a great deal all the same. Randy Robertson estimates that, across the reign of Charles II, L'Estrange and his agents suppressed almost 3 per cent of total publications, and ruined numerous dissident book-trade professionals who died in prison or lost their livelihoods irreparably.[53] The system may have lapsed during the Exclusion Crisis, but throughout this period there were other mechanisms on which government could fall back, including proxy charges unaffected by the lapse such as unlicensed newsbook printing. Indeed, there are clear signs that the licensing lapse, far from disabling the authorities, only energized their work via other channels. The Whig pamphleteer Henry Care was prosecuted for seditious libel no fewer than five times between 1679 and 1685, and it was during one of Care's trials that Lord Chief Justice Scroggs articulated, with special determination, a new sense of priorities that was taking hold: 'It is hard to find the Author, it is not hard to find the Printer: but *one Author* found, is better than *twenty Printers* found.'[54] The pillories were busy during these years, as indeed was the execution block in the case of Algernon Sidney, who was arraigned for supposed complicity in a

---

[51] On this landmark case, see Kevin Sharpe, *The Personal Rule of Charles I* (New Haven: Yale University Press, 1996), 758–65.

[52] James Grantham Turner, *Libertines and Radicals in Early Modern London: Sexuality, Politics and Literary Culture 1630–1685* (Cambridge: Cambridge University Press, 2002), 190.

[53] Randy Robertson, *Censorship and Conflict in Seventeenth-Century England: The Subtle Art of Division* (University Park: Pennsylvania State University Press, 2009), 198; Robertson cites a 'Doleful Catalogue' of victims compiled in 1681 by the Baptist stationer Francis Smith.

[54] *The Triall of Henry Carr, Gent.* (1681), 7; see Lois G. Schwoerer, *The Ingenious Mr. Henry Care, Restoration Publicist* (Baltimore: Johns Hopkins University Press, 2001), 104–33.

treasonable plot, but whose Whig-republican *Discourses upon Government*, then still in manuscript, were also enlisted as evidence against him. With a beautifully sinister flourish of urban pastoral, the poet Oldham imagined a London that would soon run out of capacity to punish blasphemy and sedition, even 'Were every Street a Grove of Pillories'.[55] One victim was John Culliford, printer of, among other libels, an inflammatory sequel to Marvell entitled *The Second Part of The Growth of Popery and Arbitrary Government* (1682), whose ordeal in the pillory was widely illustrated.[56] Another was Jane Curtis, imprisoned and fined (though the pillorying may have been remitted) for publishing *A Satyr against In-justice: or, Sc[rog]gs upon Sc[rog]gs* (c.1679), a ballad probably composed by Stephen College, a Whig incendiary who was hanged for treason two years later. At that point, much was made at trial of College's alleged authorship of another broadside, *A Ra-Ree Show* (1681), which ridiculed the king as a tricksy puppeteer and urged onlookers to pull down the show.[57]

No printer was executed during the licensing lapse of 1679–85, but few can have felt entirely safe—and though censorship mechanisms were indeed as inconsistent and unpredictable as McKenzie suggests, that was their special terror. Every so often, as Voltaire might have said, the English would kill a printer to encourage the others—but no one would know quite when, or what for. In 1663, the printer John Twyn no doubt knew that he was taking a risk in handling a treatise, laced with topical import, on the godly duty to rebel against unjust rulers, which L'Estrange found in printed sheets when raiding Twyn's shop. But he cannot have expected to be hanged, drawn, and quartered for the offence (which he aggravated by refusing to identify the author) under medieval treason legislation; three of his associates were convicted of seditious libel and pilloried and fined. It is hard to believe that this gruesome episode was forgotten by book-trade professionals over the next few decades, even if other printers got away with much the same at other times—and in order to imprint the memory with proper firmness, Twyn's severed head was left to rot on a spike above Ludgate, in the heart of London's book-trade district. Nor could printers relax following regime change in 1689. William Anderton, an underground printer of Jacobite tracts, was hanged for treason in 1693 after being arrested by Stephens and fitted up (to make sure, since the printing evidence was circumstantial) with supplementary evidence of Stephens's invention.[58] To what extent these arbitrary flourishes of official violence affected production totals or inhibited circulation is impossible to say. But we may be sure that they brought home to printers,

---

[55] *The Poems of John Oldham*, ed. Harold F. Brooks with Raman Selden (Oxford: Clarendon Press, 1987), 177 ('The Thirteenth Satyr of Juvenal, Imitated' (1682), line 138).

[56] *The Second Part* is usually attributed to Robert Ferguson, though Culliford is named as author in one source (McKenzie and Bell, *Chronology and Calendar*, 2: 410).

[57] For Curtis, see Paula McDowell, *The Women of Grub Street: Press, Politics, and Gender in the London Literary Marketplace, 1678–1730* (Oxford: Clarendon Press, 1998), 71–2, 91; for College, Harold Weber, *Paper Bullets: Print and Kingship under Charles II* (Lexington: University Press of Kentucky, 1996), 172–208.

[58] Geoff Kemp, entry for 'Twyn, John (1619–1664)', in *ODNB*; Paul Hopkins, entry for 'Anderton, William (1663–1693)', in *ODNB*.

booksellers, and authors the need to be circumspect in all their procedures. In particular, the climate created by these episodes encouraged the development of protective strategies of disguise, from clandestine publishing techniques to literary indirection or, in Annabel Patterson's useful term, functional ambiguity.[59]

For complex reasons that had little to do with freedom of expression (at best an immature concept at the time), the Licensing Act lapsed again in 1695, and this time was never renewed, though numerous attempts were made to reintroduce it, or something like it, over the next few years. Other legislation stood in, to some extent, affecting different categories of output in different ways. The Blasphemy Act (1698) targeted unitarian, deist, and other heterodox publication, but beyond this specific goal, Mark Rose writes, 'probably was intended as a general warning to authors and booksellers not to take the end of licensing as a sign that anything might now be published'.[60] More severely, the Succession to the Crown Act (1707) made expression of Jacobitism in script or print a treasonable offence, and was used in 1719 to hang John Matthews, a nineteen-year-old journeyman involved in printing the incendiary pamphlet *Vox populi, vox dei*.[61] Further statutes enacted during the reign of Queen Anne, another era of ferocious partisan pamphleteering, made more indirect but no less significant contributions to press control. Among its other provisions, the groundbreaking Copyright Act of 1710 (formally the Act for the Encouragement of Learning) restored to the statute books the potentially intimidating requirement that proprietors register their ownership of new publications and deposit copies, now nine, with the Stationers' Company. This clause went beyond previous legislation in applying to all owners of literary property, not Company members only; as Jody Green writes, expanded registration 'remedied the greatest single problem that had faced would-be controllers of the English press for more than fifty years: the difficulty of finding and holding liable the authors of printed works, rather than their more easily located printers and distributors'.[62] Two years later, the Stamp Act was a wartime revenue-raising measure that imposed duties on several kinds of manufacture beyond newspapers and pamphlets, but from the government point of view its inhibition of cheap print was at least a welcome secondary effect, and probably a core motive. The odd historian still insists—with endearing faith in the transparency of eighteenth-century politics—that the Act aimed at no more than it said on the tin, which was to raise cash.[63] But in practice it put several troublesome periodicals

---

[59] Annabel Patterson, *Censorship and Interpretation: The Conditions of Writing and Reading in Early Modern England* (Madison: University of Wisconsin Press, 1984), 18 and *passim*.

[60] Mark Rose, 'Copyright, Authors, and Censorship', in Suarez and Turner (eds.), *Cambridge History of the Book. Volume 5*, 118–31 (127).

[61] For the appalling Matthews case (the last book-trade execution in England), see McDowell, *Women of Grub Street*, 74–82.

[62] Jody Greene, *The Trouble with Ownership: Literary Property and Authorial Liability in England 1660–1730* (Philadelphia: University of Pennsylvania Press, 2011), 5.

[63] See, for example, J. A. Downie's error-strewn review of Thomas Keymer, *Poetics of the Pillory: English Literature and Seditious Libel 1660–1820* (Oxford: Oxford University Press, 2019), in *The Review of English Studies*, 72 (2021), 188–90 (189).

out of business (the *Observator*, the *Medley*, and the *Protestant Post Boy* were among the casualties) and acted as a drag on others—though loopholes were then found, requiring further fiscal-cum-press-control legislation in 1725. Even the urbane *Spectator* got caught in the rain, and after doubling its price when the new duty came into force, it closed within the year, blaming the 1712 Act for reducing circulation 'to less than half the number that was usually Printed before this Tax was laid'.[64] The Stamp Act also dealt a further blow to book-trade anonymity: all pamphlets, on pain of a heavy fine, were to carry the name of the printer or publisher, and a copy was to be lodged with the Stamp Office within six days of publication.

These measures notwithstanding (with later statutes such as the Special Juries Act of 1730, which made it easier to secure book-trade convictions, and the Stage Licensing Act of 1737, which instituted pre-performance censorship of plays), there is a long-entrenched narrative, or set of related narratives, in which the 1695 lapse marks the end of state attempts to constrain free expression. Liberty of the press soon became a point of national self-perception and pride, for Tory authors as well as for Whigs. In the Elizabethan and Stuart volumes of his *History of England*, Hume emphasizes the brutalities once inflicted by despotic regimes on dissident writers: the severed hands, slit noses, branded faces, cropped ears. Now, by contrast, 'nothing is more apt to surprize a foreigner, than the extreme liberty, which we enjoy in this country, of communicating whatever we please to the public'.[65] Then there is the classic nineteenth-century statement of Thomas Babington Macaulay, for whom history unfolded as a story of enlightened progression towards liberal modernity, with the Glorious Revolution the defining event; here the end of licensing was among the Revolution's most momentous consequences, a watershed point in which 'English literature was emancipated, and emancipated for ever, from the control of the government'.[66] This emphasis reaches beyond the Whig historical tradition inaugurated by Macaulay. In Jürgen Habermas's classic twentieth-century account of the origins and development of the public sphere, a central component is the absence of licensing, or an 'elimination of the institution of censorship' that made possible the 'influx of rational-critical arguments into the press'. More recent scholarship has emphasized the rowdy, factious incivility of the spaces and organs on which Habermas bases his narrative, and his serene view of coffee-houses would certainly have startled officials who fretted at the time about what went on inside them. Overall, however, Habermas's account of the salutary consequences for print of

---

[64] *Spectator*, 4: 494 (no. 555, 6 December 1712). Soon after launch, Addison claimed a metropolitan circulation of 3,000 copies, with an estimated 'Twenty Readers to every Paper, which I look upon as a modest Computation' (1: 44; no. 10, 12 March 1711). Bond thinks circulation before the Stamp Act may have reached a high of 4,000 copies, and explains the readership estimate with reference to the coffee-house practice of reading aloud (1, p. lxxxiii).

[65] See David Hume, *The History of England from the Invasion of Julius Caesar to the Revolution in 1688*, intr. W. B. Todd, 6 vols. (Indianapolis: Liberty Fund, 1983), 5: 240 and *passim*; Hume, *Essays Moral, Political, and Literary*, ed. Eugene F. Miller (rev. edn, Indianapolis: Liberty Fund, 1985), 9 ('Of the Liberty of the Press', 1741).

[66] *The Works of Lord Macaulay, Complete*, ed. Lady Trevelyan, 8 vols. (1866), 4: 126.

public opinion and its institutions, and his emphasis on the 'unique liberties' of authors and the press in eighteenth-century Britain, retains much of its traction.[67]

As recently as 1979, J. A. Downie could open his otherwise still useful book about propaganda under Queen Anne with the observation that 'in 1695, with the expiry of the licensing act, state censorship of the press ceased'.[68] Yet ministers and their agents were less eager to attain enlightened modernity than that kind of claim would suggest. Clegg describes early modern censorship as drawing in improvisatory ways on a 'crazy quilt' of overlapping powers and prerogatives, and many of these mechanisms—the ancient doctrine of *scandalum magnatum*, for instance—still remained available for use, alongside the new legislation cited above.[69] Powers of proscription and general warrants could still be employed after 1695, as they vigorously were by Secretary of State Bolingbroke (architect of the Stamp Act) during his 1711 campaign against the Whig press. Journalists of varying political stripes, from John Dyer in 1694 to Nathaniel Mist in 1721, could be summoned to grovel for pardon at the bar of the House of Commons. Then there were the brazenly *ultra vires* routes, for it would be naïve to assume that the reigning ideology of rule of law—another much-touted component of national identity after 1689—was always a practical constraint on the great or those they employed. Authors, booksellers, and printers, as well as low-life targets like street-ballad hawkers, were routinely arrested and interrogated where no sound legal case existed, sometimes as a fishing expedition or on a slight hunch, sometimes just for the sake of intimidation. There could be outright violence. When in 1713 William Hurt, sentenced to two spells in the pillory as printer of the Whig *Flying Post*, was feted on the first occasion by a cheering crowd, a Tory mob turned up on the second, led, it was alleged, by men wearing Bolingbroke's livery; their attack left him close to death. When another key figure in Whig pamphleteering, John Tutchin, was acquitted of libelling the government after a botched trial, the Duke of Marlborough wrote privately that 'if I can't have justice done me, I must find some friend that will break his and the printer's bones'; the job was accomplished the following year, and Tutchin died from his injuries.[70]

Above all, there was the common law of seditious libel, which, with the related and sometimes pragmatically interchangeable charges of blasphemous and obscene libel, became ministers' primary mechanism for controlling the press after 1695. This was

---

[67] Jürgen Habermas, *The Structural Transformation of the Public Sphere* (Cambridge: Polity Press, 1989), 58, 59. For recent challenges to Habermas, see Brian Cowan, 'Making Publics and Making Novels', in J. A. Downie (ed.), *The Oxford Handbook of the Eighteenth-Century Novel* (Oxford: Oxford University Press, 2016), 55–70.

[68] J. A. Downie, *Robert Harley and the Press: Propaganda and Public Opinion in the Age of Swift and Defoe* (Cambridge: Cambridge University Press, 1979), 1. For a brilliant case study of one printer's tribulations in this environment, see Joseph Hone, *The Paper Chase: The Printer, the Spymaster, and the Hunt for the Rebel Pamphleteers* (London: Chatto & Windus, 2020), exploring the case of David Edwards, printer of the incendiary *Memorial of the Church of England* (1705).

[69] Cyndia Susan Clegg, *Press Censorship in Elizabethan England* (Cambridge: Cambridge University Press, 1997), 5.

[70] Lee Sonsteng Horsley, 'The Trial of John Tutchin, Author of the *Observator*', *Yearbook of English Studies*, 3 (1973), 124–40 (138), quoting Marlborough's letter to Harley of 1–11 October 1706.

retrospective as opposed to pre-emptive censorship, but it was censorship nonetheless, and throughout the reign of Queen Anne it proved a powerful and menacing tool. Sentences would vary in unpredictable ways (again, the effect was to intensify fears), but swingeing fines, a professionally ruinous prison term, and a disabling surety for good future conduct were the norm. Exposure in the pillory, for up to three spells, was added in the most egregious cases: a punishment of disgrace that could also be life-threatening at a time when supervising officials were often unwilling or simply unable to protect libellers from a mob of an opposing faction, or from the crowd in general. State-inflicted mutilation in the pillory was extremely rare after Prynne et al. under Charles I and the Quaker James Nayler under Cromwell, but the threat could never be quite discounted, and even after 1714, at least two forgers (Thomas Hayes in 1720, Japhet Crook in 1728) suffered ear-cropping and/or nose-slitting. Forgers, perjurers, and especially sexual offenders were the most likely categories of malefactor to be injured or pelted to death by the crowd, and eventually a long line of counterproductive episodes, from the Tory author John Shebbeare (1758) to the radical publisher Daniel Isaac Eaton (1812), led to the discontinuation of pillorying in book-trade cases. But the 'wooden ruff' held undoubted terrors in the early years of the century, and for every libeller who successfully converted his ordeal into a theatre of political defiance, another was taken down from the pillory traumatized or maimed. This sanction was used with special flair under Queen Anne by Secretary of State Harley, who (like Scroggs) preferred to look past printers and target authors—for whom, one satirist protested, 'large Fines, and Pil[lori]es, by thee | Were made the base Rewards of Poetry'.[71]

These were also the rewards of prose. The best-known case from Queen Anne's reign is that of Defoe, or, as Swift once sneered in *de haut en bas* style, 'the Fellow that was *Pillor'd*, I have forgot his Name'—a name, Claude Rawson observes, 'we know Swift did not forget, because in 1735, when reprinting his works, he added Defoe's name in a footnote without deleting the remark about having forgotten it'.[72] The libel at issue was *The Shortest Way with the Dissenters* (1702), a pamphlet of peculiarly unstable, perplexing irony that gave almost indiscriminate offence and was interpreted by ministers, possibly in good faith, as a threat to public order. *The Shortest Way* was, in the unusually emphatic language of the Old Bailey indictment drawn up against Defoe, 'a Seditious, pernicious and Diabolical Libel', its author 'a Seditious man and of a disordered mind', his intention that of 'perfidiously, mischievously and seditiously contriving, practicing and purposing to make and Cause discord between ... the Queen and her ... Subjects'.[73] Defoe was plainly terrified by the sentence that resulted, recoiling from a style of punishment he found intolerable 'as a Gentleman' (this, of course, was the point of Swift's

---

[71] *A Dialogue between Louis le Petite, and Harlequin le Grand* (1708?), p. viii; for Harley's activities and reputation as 'President of the Pillory', see Downie, *Robert Harley and the Press*, 80–100.

[72] Claude Rawson, *Satire and Sentiment 1660–1830* (New Haven: Yale University Press, 2000), 251; the remark comes in *A Letter Concerning the Sacramental Test* (1709).

[73] Paula R. Backscheider, *Daniel Defoe: His Life* (Baltimore: Johns Hopkins University Press, 1989), 103–4.

sneer) and pleading with Secretary of State Nottingham that 'Prisons, Pillorys and Such like ... are Worse to me Than Death'. Only weeks before the three consecutive spells in the pillory that awaited him in busy locations, he hoped to avoid the ordeal by pleading guilty in full to the florid indictment, 'Even to all the Adverbs, the Seditiously's, The Malitiously's'.[74] And though biographers still sometimes repeat the story of Defoe being pelted with flowers in the pillory by a sympathetic crowd, this anecdote is impossible to find in any source before the mid-nineteenth century, and was almost certainly a piece of Victorian myth-making. Defoe certainly did his best to stage-manage the episode, and emerged unscathed; he even had a poem distributed on the occasion (*A Hymn to the Pillory*) in which he likened his martyr status to that of Prynne. But the earliest documentary sources represent Defoe's gentle treatment by spectators not as an eruption of spontaneous sympathy but as a feat of hired protection and party muscle. A year after the anti-Stuart pamphleteer William Fuller lost an eye to crowd violence, his precautions were wise.

In a notable instance of the defter, slicker style of press control that would be perfected under Prime Minister Walpole in the 1730s, Defoe was then recruited to Harley's payroll. But he remained a loose cannon in later years, and in 1713 was forced to petition the Queen in abject style when imprisoned again for a series of pamphlets in which he impersonated a Jacobite voice with ironies that his enemies missed, or pretended to miss. Defoe reflected several times on the lessons of the *Shortest Way*, most interestingly, if also most indirectly, in *An Essay on the Regulation of the Press* (1704). There could be no more emphatic answer to the still persistent assumption that the end of licensing ushered in a golden age of expressive freedom. On the contrary, Defoe contends. Far from liberating authors, the absence of licensing left them newly imperilled, and their writing conditioned by an unrelenting state of anxiety or worse. Before 1695, he acknowledges, authors could never be sure exactly where they stood, but a licence constituted authorization. Uncertainties were far more debilitating, and dangerous, under the common law of seditious libel, which might be exerted in the most capricious or malevolent of ways, and after authors had committed themselves to print, and were thereby helplessly exposed. Under an unambiguous system of licensing, 'all Men will know when they Transgress, which at present, they do not; for as the Case now stands, 'tis in the Breast of the Courts of Justice to make any Book a Scandalous and Seditious Libel'. Good laws were like buoys marking hazardous rocks, 'and the Language of them is, *Come here at your peril*', whereas no such specificity applies with retrospective press control. Uniquely, 'the Crime of an Author is not known; and I think verily no Book can be wrote so warily, but that if the Author be brought on his Tryal, it shall be easy for a cunning Lawyer, ay for a Lawyer of no great Cunning, to put an *Innuendo* upon his Meaning, and make some Part of it Criminal'. Penalties were also impossible to predict, and Defoe cites the cases of Sidney and Anderton to deplore a censorship system that had come to operate by means of arbitrary victim selection and brutal exemplary

---

[74] *The Letters of Daniel Defoe*, ed. George Harris Healey (Oxford: Clarendon Press, 1955), 2, 8.

punishment. Merely on judicial whim, the same offence might generate anything from manageable financial loss to public execution: '*Fines, Whippings, Pillories, Imprisonment for Life, Halters and Axes.*'[75]

So yes, the press was indeed constrained after 1695, and with new intensity arising from the obscurities and ambiguities of the post-licensing regime. One might compare the situation with longstanding Marxist analyses of the 'Bloody Code' that, following the Glorious Revolution, emerged to protect property via a brutal combination of catch-all statutes, perfunctory trials, and exemplary hangings, compounded by erratic patterns of enforcement and ostentatious gestures of reprieve.[76] In the case of literature, however, the pain could also bring with it a measure of gain. Authors and publishers had no choice but to operate within the structures of intimidation and deterrence described by Defoe, but this was a discipline that could enable or energize as well as constrain, stimulating techniques of evasive irony and complicating indirection that we now think of as central achievements of the period's prose.[77]

---

[75] Daniel Defoe, *An Essay on the Regulation of the Press* (1704), 14, 15, 19.
[76] See the classic statement by E. P. Thompson, *Whigs and Hunters: The Origin of the Black Act* (2nd edn, London: Penguin, 1977).
[77] For this argument, see Keymer, *Poetics of the Pillory*, esp. 27–155.

CHAPTER 2

··

RECEPTION

··

CYNTHIA WALL

'*May I not write in such a stile as this? . . . why may it not be done?*' So asks the Narrator of John Bunyan's *The Pilgrim's Progress* (1678) in the prolegomena 'Apology'. Why not, indeed? Because, Bunyan's hypothetical critic accuses, '*it is feigned*'. The Puritan preacher answers stoutly: '*what of that, I tro / Some men by feigning words as dark as mine, / Make truth to spangle, and its rayes to shine.*'[1] He points out the many ways that fishermen and fowlers catch their prey—not only with '*Snares, Lines, Angles, Hooks and Nets*' and '*Lime-twigs, light, and bell*', but also with trout-tickling and bird-whistling. The seventeenth century as a whole erupted with a staggering array of new genres, as this *Handbook* explores: from amatory fiction to vade mecums, biographies and characters, captivity narratives and spiritual autobiographies, spy literature and secret histories, newspapers and essays, sermons and speeches, fables and recipes, and travel narratives and novels. This chapter begins its survey of the 'reception' of English prose from 1640 to 1714 with a look at its first consumers, the contemporary readers. Literacy rates rose significantly in the seventeenth century among women and the labouring classes; new kinds of readers prompted the new kinds of reading matters explored in this volume; the social layers of readers and the literary layers of genres inserted layers of perspective, of opinion, of simultaneously multiple points of view. The shifts from manuscript to print, the increasing practice of private reading, the reopening of public theatres, and the enclosing of private closets were all cause and consequence of new reading practices and prose styles. The swarm of new kinds of prose prompted debates about the quality of prose. The material for prose—the English language itself—came under fierce analysis. How does English compare to French or Italian or German or Latin or Greek? How does the English prose of *now* compare with the prose of *then*? How does the page instruct the reader how to read? What kind of prose is 'good' or 'elegant' or 'plain'? And says who? The critical reception of seventeenth-century prose continued to refine (and redefine) itself at accelerating speeds in the eighteenth and nineteenth centuries.

---

[1] John Bunyan, *The Pilgrim's Progress* (1678), ed. Cynthia Wall (New York: W. W. Norton, 2009), 6–7.

Consuming Prose: Readers and Reading Matters

'What woulde yee haue men doe? ... Sitte mooping always at their bookes, I like not that': so complains Atheos ('godless') in George Gifford's popular Puritan dialogue about his neighbour's religious zeal.[2] By the end of the sixteenth century, it seemed to some as if practically everyone could or should 'sitte mooping' at a book. According to *The Cambridge Economic History of Modern Britain*, in 1500 just over 10 per cent of men (basically, only aristocrats and gentry) and very few women could read; by 1600 about 25 per cent of men (including professional men) and 10 per cent of women were literate; by 1700 those rates had risen to 40 per cent and 25 per cent respectively.[3] Shopkeepers and apprentices, mistresses and maids, artisans and husbandmen, were swelling the ranks of the literate.[4]

Part of this was the work of the Reformation, which zealously promoted literacy. As Alec Ryrie notes, while private prayer and public worship were available to everyone, 'the illiterate were excluded from what was, to ministers at least, a central part of Protestant experience, and they "must needs fare the worse" '.[5] In *The Country Parson* (1652), George Herbert tells us that in the parson's house, all

> are either teachers or learners, or both, so that his family is a School of Religion, & they all account, that to teach the ignorant is the greatest almes. Even the walls are not idle, but somthing is written, or painted there, which may excite the reader to a thought of piety; ... especially the 101 *Psalm*, which is expressed in a fair table, as being the rule of a family. And when they go abroad, his wife among her neighbours is the beginning of good discourses, his children among children, his servants among other servants; so that as in the house of those that are skill'd in Musick, all are Musicians; so in the house of a Preacher, all are preachers.[6]

---

[2] George Gifford, *A Briefe Discourse of Certaine Points of Religion, Which is Among the Common Sort of Christians, Which May Bee Termed the Countrie Diuinitie* (1581), fol. 3r.

[3] David Mitch, 'Education and Skill of the British Labour Force', in Roderick Floud and Paul Johnson (eds.), *The Cambridge Economic History of Modern Britain, Vol. I: Industrialisation, 1700–1860* (Cambridge: Cambridge University Press, 2004), 332–56 (344).

[4] There has been a vast amount of writing on the subject of literacy and reading. See, for example, some classics: Thomas Laqueur, 'The Cultural Origins of Popular Literacy in England 1500–1850', *Oxford Review of Education*, 2 (1976), 255–75; Robert Darnton, 'First Steps Towards a History of Reading', *Australian Journal of French Studies*, 23 (1986), 5–30; David Cressy, 'Literacy in Context', in John Brewer and Roy Porter (eds.), *Consumption and the World of Goods* (London and New York: Routledge, 1993; repr. 1997), 305–19; Cecile M. Jagodzinski, *Privacy and Print: Reading and Writing in Seventeenth-Century England* (Charlottesville: University Press of Virginia, 1999).

[5] Alec Ryrie, *Being Protestant in Reformation Britain* (Oxford: Oxford University Press, 2013), 259, quoting Richard Rogers, *Seven Treatises, Containing Such Directions as Is Gathered Out of the Holie Scriptures, Leading and Guiding to True Happiness* (1603), 586.

[6] George Herbert, *A Priest to the Temple. Or the Country Parson His Character, and Rule of Holy Life* (1652; 2nd edn, 1671), 35.

Wife, children, even servants not only learn but *teach* their Bible, their psalms; reading is everywhere, even written on the walls. The gentlewoman Elizabeth Isham (1609-1654) recorded in her diary (c.1639) her 'pleasure at hearing one of her maids, who was literate, excitedly tell another, who was not, what she had just read in the Bible'.[7] People of all ranks read the Bible both privately and communally, repeating and memorizing it.[8] As Thomas Hobbes put it (disapprovingly):

> after the Bible was translated into *English*, every Man, nay every Boy and Wench, that could read *English*, thought they spoke with God Almighty, and understood what he said, when by a certain number of Chapters a day, they had read the Scriptures once or twice over, the Reverence and Obedience due to the Reformed Church here, and to the Bishops and Pastors therein, was cast off, and every Man became a Judge of Religion, and an Interpreter of the Scriptures to himself.[9]

The Quaker Margaret Fell quotes the Bible frequently if inaccurately in her pamphlet *Women's Speaking Justified* (1666)—inaccurately, because as Jane Donawerth argues, she had memorized several translations (including the King James and the Geneva) and created her own version, 'existing not on paper, but inside her'.[10] John Bunyan was the son of a tinker and would read aloud with his first wife the two books she brought as dowry: Arthur Dent's *The Plain Man's Pathway to Heaven* (1601) and Lewis Bayly's *The Practise of Piety* (1612). The Man the Dreamer sees in the opening of *The Pilgrim's Progress* is 'cloathed with Rags' but has 'a Book in his hand', because the pilgrim's mission is to '*read thy self*'.[11]

The literacy push was aided by an increasingly prosperous merchant class that afforded more leisure and more opportunities for education for many under their wing, particularly in London where the literacy of women in the late seventeenth century was, in David Cressy's word, 'precocious': 'Affected, perhaps, by the quickening commercial environment, the social demands of the city and the expanding availability of print, the women of Mrs Aphra Behn's London were as literate as men in the countryside.'[12] The Civil Wars destabilized a number of political and social as well as religious assumptions and traditions. The English publishing industry burgeoned with pamphlet wars and the new newspapers; every Man became a Judge of Politics and an Interpreter of the Pamphlets to himself. Works such as the *Philosophical Transactions* of the Royal Society popularized the new scientific discoveries and made natural philosophers of their

---

[7] Ryrie, *Being Protestant*, 260.

[8] W. R. Owens, 'Modes of Bible Reading in Early Modern England', in Shafquat Towheed and W. R. Owens (eds.), *The History of Reading, Volume 1: International Perspectives, c. 1500–1990* (London: Palgrave, 2011), 32–43 (35)35.

[9] Thomas Hobbes, *Behemoth, The History of the Causes of the Civil-Wars of England* (1682), 35.

[10] Jane Donawerth, 'Women's Reading Practices in Seventeenth-Century England: Margaret Fell's *Women's Speaking Justified*', *Sixteenth-Century Journal*, 37/4 (2006), 985–1005 (1005).

[11] Wall (ed.), *Pilgrim's Progress*, 11, 10.

[12] Cressy, 'Literacy in Context', 314.

readers. Samuel Pepys spotted Robert Hooke's *Micrographia* (1665) at his bookseller's and thought it 'so pretty that I presently bespoke it'; a few weeks later he 'sat up till 2 a-clock in my chamber, reading of Mr. Hookes Microscopicall Observacions' and found it 'the most ingenious book that ever I read in my life'.[13] The 'unruly energies of fiction production',[14] as Thomas Keymer notes, expanded the imaginative experience for the apprentice or servant; Lady Anne Clifford, Baroness de Clifford (1590–1676) would have her maid Moll Nevil read Sidney's *Arcadia* aloud.[15] Through access to the romance, the trickster tale, the picaresque adventure, 'the fixed destiny of walking contentedly in one's vocation was less unquestionable, more tenuous, especially given the social fluidity of positions of servitude'.[16] Lorna Weatherill has calculated that the number of books as a percentage of the total number of goods in London homes (based on inventories) rose from 18 per cent in 1675 to 34 per cent in 1715 and 56 per cent by 1725.[17] As J. Paul Hunter puts it, 'rural rebels, gentlefolk stymied by village life, urban émigrés, aspiring tradesmen, restless footmen, waiting maids hoping to better themselves', all became readers, 'raising their expectations of both art and life'.[18] Reading enabled private experience, private judgment, and private aspiration.

The ability to read and write was felt (and intended) to be empowering. Elizabeth Isham and Lady Anne Clifford delighted in the expansion of their maids' minds. The London schoolmaster David Brown argued in 1638 that through books and letters 'all high treasures of whatsoever nature or importance are both intended and prosecuted, ... friends that be a thousand miles distant are conferred with and (after a sort) visited; the excellent works of godly men, the grave sentences of wise men, and the profitable arts of learned men, who died a thousand years ago, are yet extant for our daily use and imitation'.[19] In 1645 the Puritan divine Samuel Torshell published his sermon *The Women's Glorie*, in which he declares that 'Women [are] capable of the highest improvements' in both piety and secular learning.[20] For Herbert's parson, teaching

---

[13] *The Diary of Samuel Pepys*, ed. Robert Latham and William Matthews, 11 vols. (Berkeley and Los Angeles: University of California Press, 2000), 6: 2, 18 (2 and 21 January 1665).

[14] Thomas Keymer, 'Introduction', in *The Oxford History of the Novel in English: Prose Fiction in English from the Origins of Print to 1750* (Oxford: Oxford University Press, 2017), p. xxii.

[15] Paul Salzman, 'Anne Clifford's Annotated Copy of Sidney's *Arcadia*', *Notes & Queries*, 56 (2009), 554–555 (555).

[16] Naomi Conn Liebler, 'Introduction', in *Early Modern Prose Fiction: The Cultural Politics of Reading* (New York and London: Routledge, 2007), 8.

[17] Lorna Weatherill, 'The Meaning of Consumer Behaviour in Late Seventeenth- and Early Eighteenth-Century England', in John Brewer and Roy Porter (eds.), *Consumption and the World of Goods* (London and New York: Routledge, 1993; repr. 1997), 206–27 (220): Table 10.4 'Changing ownership of goods in town and country'. The percentages of books owned in major towns held at 23 per cent between 1675 and 1715 and at 16–18 per cent in rural towns and villages.

[18] J. Paul Hunter, *Before Novels: The Cultural Contexts of Eighteenth-Century English Fiction* (New York: W. W. Norton, 1990), 85.

[19] David Brown, *The Introduction to the True Understanding of the Whole Arte of Expedition in Teaching to Write* (1638), sig. B4v.

[20] Quoted in Margaret J. M. Ezell, *The Oxford English Literary History. Volume 5: The Later Seventeenth Century, 1645–1714* (Oxford: Oxford University Press, 2017), 19.

psalms is 'the greatest almes'. John Evelyn admitted that '*Otium sine literis* [leisure without literature]' would be for him 'the greatest infelicity in the world'.[21] Donawerth argues that Fell's Bible was a 'political activist's Bible, one that refutes Catholic and Anglican practices' and that 'authoriz[ed] her to develop a class-based critique and to resist governmental authority when it contradicted that Word'. Evelyn advocated in 1684 for a public library in London so that the 'Noble-men' who were busy 'frequenting Taverns or Coffè-houses' would 'study & employ their time better, if they had books'. 'Indeed a greate reproch it is', he wrote, 'that so great a Citty as Lond: should have never a publique Library becoming it'.[22] Throughout the seventeenth century 'print-capitalism', as Benedict Anderson calls it, 'made it possible for rapidly growing numbers of people to think about themselves, and to relate themselves to others, in profoundly new ways'.[23]

And that is exactly what vexed others. Not all of the elite shared the joy of an Isham or Herbert. The nonconformist minister John Brinsley worried about women reading seditious pamphlets and 'turning from the way of the church of Christ in Old England, to the refined Error of separation'.[24] Puritan divine Richard Baxter repeatedly warned about the dangers of 'vain Romances, Play-books, and false Stories'.[25] Even Samuel Torshell feared for women's vulnerability to 'bad' books, warning: 'Away with your Tragedies, and Comedies, and Masques, and Pastoral, & whatsoever other names they have, that soften the spirit, and take away the savour of heavenly matters.' Evelyn, lover of literature in leisure and promoter of public libraries, worried that among his own class, 'not to *read men*, and converse with *living Libraries*, is to deprive our selves of the most useful and profitable of *Studies*: This is that deplorable defect which universally renders our *bookish* men so *pedantically morose* and impolish'd, and in a word, so very *ridiculous*.'[26] And in the early eighteenth century, Anthony Ashley Cooper, third earl of Shaftesbury, argued that he could not 'call a Man *well-read* who reads *many Authors*: since he must of necessity have more ill Models, than good; and be more stufft with Bombast, ill Fancy, and wry Thought; than fill'd with solid Sense, and just Imagination'.[27]

The numbers of new people reading, and thus the new commercial markets, produced a wealth of new kinds of reading material. Vernacular bibles, seditious pamphlets, tragedies, comedies, pastorals, romances, and feigned histories were just a few of the new kinds of reading material available to all these new readers—not to mention travel narratives (what Shaftesbury called tales of '*Barbarian* Customs, Savage

---

[21] Quoted in Jagodzinski, *Privacy and Print*, 3.

[22] Donawerth, 'Women's Reading Practices', 1005; *The Diary of John Evelyn*, ed. Guy de la Bédoyère (Bangor: Headstart History, 1994), 305 (13 February 1684).

[23] Benedict Anderson, *Imagined Communities: Reflections on the Origin and Spread of Nationalism* (rev. edn, London and New York: Verso, 1991), 36.

[24] John Brinsley, *A Looking Glasse for Good Women* (1645), quoted in Ezell, *Later Seventeenth Century*, 20.

[25] Richard Baxter, *A Christian Directory* (1673), 60, 292, 580.

[26] Torshell quoted in Ezell, *Later Seventeenth Century*, 20; Evelyn quoted in Jagodzinski, *Privacy and Print*, 3.

[27] Anthony Ashley Cooper, 3rd Earl of Shaftesbury, *Soliloquy: Or, Advice to an Author* (1710), 177–8.

Manners, *Indian* Wars, and Wonders of the *Terra Incognita*' that 'employ our leisure Hours'), popular accounts of scientific discoveries, domestic manuals, newspapers, essays, as well as 'books for young clerks, aspiring lawyers, and surgeons;... dictionaries and conduct books aimed at improving the reader's understanding of "hard words" they might encounter in this new reading matter'. The very proximity of new genre to new genre produced new genres. J. Paul Hunter argues that all the publications in the late seventeenth century that '*pretend[ed]* to tell actual tales', colourfully and wantonly blurring the distinctions between fact and fiction, created the generic space for the later novel: 'Without them there would have been no movement between species, no leap between kinds, no historical motion within accepted traditions'.[28] The multiplication of genres emblematizes a cultural interest in multiple points of view, in simultaneous layers of perspectives, that in turn become hallmarks of the genres themselves, in the writings about the past, the nation, the rest of the world; in the points of view of spies and convicts and travellers; in the double folds of irony and satire, fable and mock-genres; in the palimpsesting of history and fiction, evidence and speculation.

All these kinds of prose works, of course, are the subjects of the chapters in this volume; and all these new kinds of reading meant new ways of reading. The long-held assumption that the culture shifted from manuscript to print, from reading aloud to reading alone, has been steadily challenged in the work of, among others, Margaret Ezell (who has studied 'scribal authorship and the manuscript text in its social context'[29]); David Cressy (who demonstrates 'a layering, cross-referencing and impaction' instead of 'a great divide between oral and literate culture'[30]); Paula McDowell (who argues that the idea of an oral culture as something fundamentally different from print behaviour was actually the product of print behaviour[31]); and Abigail Williams (who traces the history of communal reading through the eighteenth century[32]). But there is no question that the experience of reading was fundamentally different from, say, going to a play or hearing a sermon: 'The ability to read granted independence from all those communal structures, as the interactions between reader, text, and author moved from the public forums of church and court to the privacy and solitude of the home and even to personalized private spaces within the home.'[33] The imagination could get to its restless inflaming work inside the private closet; we remember that in *Gulliver's Travels* (1726),

---

[28] Shaftesbury, *Soliloquy*, 178; Ezell, *Later Seventeenth Century*, 237; J. Paul Hunter, 'Protesting Fiction, Constructing History', in Donald R. Kelley and David Harris Sacks (eds.), *The Historical Imagination in Early Modern Britain: History, Rhetoric,, and Fiction, 1500-1800* ([Washington, D.C.]: Woodrow Wilson Center Press; Cambridge and New York: Cambridge University Press, 1997), 298–317 (312–13).

[29] Margaret J. M. Ezell, *Social Authorship and the Advent of Print* (Baltimore and London: The Johns Hopkins University Press, 1999), 38.

[30] Cressy, 'Literacy in Context', 311.

[31] Paula McDowell, *The Invention of the Oral: Print Commerce and Fugitive Voices in Eighteenth-Century Britain* (Chicago: The University of Chicago Press, 2017).

[32] Abigail Williams, *The Social Life of Books: Reading Together in the Eighteenth-Century Home* (New Haven and London: Yale University Press, 2017).

[33] Jagodzinski, *Privacy and Print*, 2.

'her Imperial Majesty's Apartment was on fire, by the Carelessness of a Maid of Honour, who fell asleep while she was reading a Romance'.[34] (And actually, on 3 November 1710, one Elizabeth Freke, daughter of a successful lawyer and landholder, recorded in her diary that her hair caught fire while she was 'sitting in my chamber all alone reading', although she doesn't say what exactly she was reading.[35]) As Hunter puts it, 'The difference now was that the dangers came to the solitary self; individuals would now be corrupted in their own private closets, the victims not of the example of others [as with the stage] and the temptation of communal experience but of their own willful choice, something they could not readily pass off as accident or public infection'. Stuart Sherman suggests that the *Spectator* 'offers to mirror its readers not in their social mode ... but in their private mode, at the level of consciousness that continues through each waking day whether they are engaged in talk or not'.[36] Even if communal reading (whether for pleasure *or* protection, as Williams argues) continued robustly into the eighteenth century and beyond, more kinds of people were reading more kinds of prose in the privacy of their own minds.[37]

'No' Tung Within Christendom May Compar' with Ours'

All these new readers reading all these new works prompted a closer look at quality as well as quantity. Was what England produced so prodigiously from its presses any good? Both the English language and the English 'style' became subjects of increasing and comparative interest in the seventeenth century and ever after. Opinion tended to be profoundly ambivalent. On the one hand, the language seemed unstable, unruly, unpolished, compared with French or Italian, Latin or Greek. And the style inherited from the Elizabethans now seemed overwrought, somehow over-elegant, for current needs and tastes. On the other hand, English is *English*, and our authors are better than their authors, damme![38]

In 1633 Charles Butler published *The English Grammar, or, The Institution of Letters, Syllables, and Woords in the English Tung*, in which he argues that (warning: Butler

---

[34] Jonathan Swift, *Gulliver's Travels*, ed. Paul Turner (Oxford: Oxford University Press, 1998), 43.

[35] *The Remembrances of Elizabeth Freke, 1671–1714*, ed. Raymond Anselment, Camden Fifth Series, Volume 18 (Cambridge: Cambridge University Press, 2001), 3; quoted inStephen Colclough, *Consuming Texts: Readers and Reading Communities, 1695–1870* (London: Palgrave Macmillan, 2007), 43.

[36] Hunter, 'Protesting Fiction', 307; Stuart Sherman, *Telling Time: Clocks, Diaries, and English Diurnal Form 1660–1785* (Chicago: University of Chicago Press, 1997), 115.

[37] 'Sometimes reading together was a preventative measure—particularly in the case of newly fashionable prose fiction, which was widely represented as dangerously titillating' (Williams, *Social Life of Books*, 3).

[38] 'Damn me!', used as a profane imprecation. The *OED* cites James Howell, *Epistolæ Ho-elianæ* (1645), v. xxxiv. 38: 'My Lord Powis ... said, "Dammy if ever he com to be King of England, I wil turn Rebell"'.

championed a phonetic alphabet, and among other things he chose to replace final silent e's with an apostrophe-like mark) '[t]he Excellenci of a Languag' (ingenuous Reader) doo'the [doth?] consist cheifly in three things, [1 Antiqiti', 2 Copious Eleganci', and 3 Generaliti']', and he declares that English is 'woorthily honoured' for all three.[39] Elegance appears in the 'pur' and fluent styl'' of all works of art and knowledge, in the 'strong Lin's of our deep' Divin's, the accurat' Speeches of our grav' Sages', and 'the eloquent Pleadings of our subtil Lawyers', such that 'no' Tung within Christendom may compar' with ours'. Butler's main criticism of his native language is the 'trubblous uncertainti'' of its orthography.[40] But Butler was in a minority. Critics of the current state of the English language compared it unfavourably to European languages, particularly the romance languages. Although Butler had asserted that the great beauty as well as antiquity of English derived from the Teutonic—'the Languag' spoken in Paradis''— most critics bemoaned the Germanic influence. 'Ours', said Dryden, is 'founded on the *Dutch*' and thus is 'full of Monosyllables, and those clogg'd with Consonants, and our Pronunciation is effeminate'. Not only is English 'abounding in Monosyllables', Joseph Addison amplified in 1711, but 'where the Words are not Monosyllables, we often make them so ... as in the Words, *drown'd, walk'd, arriv'd*, for *drowned, walked, arrived*, which has very much disfigured the Tongue, and turned a tenth part of our smoothest Words into so many Clusters of Consonants'. 'The *English Genius*', said Thomas Sprat, 'is not so airy, and discoursive, as that of some of our neighbors' due to 'its derivation from the rough *German*'. In general, argues Swift, 'our Language is less Refined than those of *Italy, Spain*, or *France*'.[41]

The sonic problem with the language was exacerbated by its unwieldy expansion. In *The History of the Royal Society* (1667), Sprat blamed the Civil Wars for drastically expanding the lexicon: 'for in such busie, and active times, there arise more new thoughts of men, which must be signifi'd, and varied by new expressions'; many 'fantastical terms' were introduced into the language 'by our *Religious Sects*', and 'many outlandish phrases' were, 'in that great hurry, brought in'.[42] Edmund Waller, in 'Of English Verse' (1686), lamented: 'who can hope his Lines should long / Last in a daily-changing Tongue? / ... We write in Sand, our Language grows, / And like our Tide ours overflows.'[43] Even Samuel Johnson in the Preface to his *Dictionary* (1755) was thinking with some wistfulness along the same lines: 'Language is only the instrument of science, and words are but the signs of ideas: I wish, however, that the instrument might be less

---

[39] Charles Butler, *The English Grammar, Or The Institution of Letters, Syllables, and Woords in the English Tung* (2nd edn, Oxford, 1634), 3.

[40] Butler, *English Grammar*, sigs. 3r–3v, 4v.

[41] John Dryden, *Troilus and Cressida: or, Truth found too late. A Tragedy* [1679] (1735), sig. A6v; Joseph Addison, *The Spectator*, ed. Donald F. Bond, 5 vols. (Oxford: Clarendon Press, 1965), 2: 33–4 (4 August 1711); Thomas Sprat, *The History of the Royal-Society of London, For the Improving of Natural Knowledge* (1667), 40, 42; Jonathan Swift, *A Proposal for Correcting, Improving, and Ascertaining the English Tongue* (2nd edn, 1712), 9.

[42] Sprat, *History of the Royal-Society of London*, 42.

[43] Edmund Waller, *Poems: &c. Written Upon Several Occasions, and to Several Persons* (1686), 237.

apt to decay, and that signs might be permanent, like the things which they denote.'[44]
The problems critics perceived in the English language infected the English style as well. Rather than sharing any of Butler's sense of a 'pur' and fluent styl', most seventeenth-century writers began to complain about an overly ornate, figuratively metastasized language. In 1605 Francis Bacon accused writers of

> hunt[ing] more after wordes, than matter, and more after the choiseness of the Phrase, and the round and cleane composition of the sentence, and the sweet falling of the clauses, and the varying and illustration of their workes with tropes and figures: then after the weight of the matter, worth of subiect, soundesse of argument, life of inuention, or depth of iudgement.[45]

This complaint continued throughout the seventeenth century. 'Impatience with metaphor' is how John Carey characterizes the 'fashionable opinions' of both Dryden and Hobbes. Dryden complained that 'we cannot read a verse of [John] *Cleveland*'s without making a face at it, as if every word were a Pill to swallow.'[46] The 'BRITISH MUSES' themselves—Shakespeare, Fletcher, Jonson, and Milton—created what Shaftesbury called 'this Dinn of Arms' with their penchant for 'wretched Pun and Quibble' or 'a false *Sublime*, with crouded *Simile*, and *mix'd Metaphor* (the Hobby-Horse and Rattle of the MUSES).'[47]

The English language and its writers did have their defenders, even among the ranks of critics and sometimes in their next breath. Sprat acknowledged that the language 'began to raise it self a little, and to sound tolerably well' from the time of Henry VIII to the beginning of the Civil Wars. Swift agreed. Dryden had his spokesman Neander defend Shakespeare as the English Homer and Jonson as its Virgil in *Of Dramatick Poesie, an Essay* (1668). The bards that Shaftesbury attacked for their wretched puns and crowded similes also 'provided us however with the richest Oar'. They threw off 'the horrid Discord of jingling Rhyme' and introduced blank verse, which John Dennis described as 'such Verse we make when we are writing Prose; we make such Verse in common Conversation.'[48] English, declared Thomas Rymer in 1674, is 'proper for great expressions' and so fittest for the genre of tragedy, while Spanish is too big, too much

---

[44] Samuel Johnson, *A Dictionary of the English Language*, 2 vols. (1755), 1, sigA2v.

[45] Francis Bacon, *The Two Bookes of Francis Bacon. Of the Proficience and Aduancement of Learning, Diuine and Humane. To the King* (1605), 18–19.

[46] John Carey, 'Sixteenth- and Seventeenth-Century Prose', in *English Poetry and Prose 1540–1674*, ed. Christopher Ricks, rev. edn (1986; Harmondsworth: Penguin, 1993), 329–412 (409) ; John Dryden, *Of Dramatick Poesie, an Essay* (1668), 23. Dryden does, however, forgive him for one 'highly Metaphorical' line because it is 'so soft and gentle, that it does not shock us as we read it': '*For Beauty like White-powder makes no noise, / And yet the silent Hypocrite destroyes*' ('To Prince Rupert', in *The works of Mr. John Cleveland containing his poems, orations, epistles, collected into one volume, with the life of the author* (1687), 272, ll. 39–40).

[47] Anthony Ashley Cooper, third Earl of Shaftesbury, *Soliloquy: Or, Advice to an Author* (1710), 64.

[48] Swift, *Proposal*, 17; Shaftesbury, *Soliloquy*, 64–5; John Dennis, *An Essay Upon the Genius and Writings of Shakespear* (1712), 3.

'the Kettle-drum to Musick'; the Italian 'termination in vowels is childish' and fit only for farce; German is 'rude and unpolisht'; and French 'too faint and languishing'. More generously than Rymer, Addison acknowledges the ways that any language can embody the best of its national characteristics, as in 'the light talkative Humour of the *French*', the 'Genius of the *Italians*, ... addicted to Musick and Ceremony', the 'Stateliness and Gravity of the *Spaniards*', and the 'blunt Honest Humour of the *Germans*'. And Addison, who so objected to the 'Clusters of Consonants', the monosyllables, and 'that *hissing* in our Language, which is taken so much notice of by Foreigners', concluded happily in that *Spectator* essay that in fact the language 'shows the Genius and natural Temper of the *English*, which is modest, thoughtful, and sincere'.[49]

Still, most agreed that English needed work. Since the Civil Wars, Swift argued, 'the Corruptions in our Language have ... at least equalled the Refinements of it'; a 'Licentiousness which entered with the *Restoration*' infected religion, morals, and language itself. One reason that Italian, Spanish, and French seemed superior was that those nations had long paid attention to their language and style. The *Académie française* was instituted by Cardinal Richelieu in 1635 to stabilize, 'smooth', and 'purif[y]' the French language. In England, on the other hand, 'Till the time of *King Henry the Eighth*, there was scarce any man regarded it, but *Chaucer*'. Dryden declared in 1679: 'It wou'd mortify an *English* Man to consider, that from the time of *Boccace* and of *Petrarch*, the *Italian* has varied very little: And that the *English* of *Chaucer* their Contemporary, is not to be understood without the help of an Old *Dictionary*.'[50] Sprat explicitly advocated for an academy along the lines of those in France and Italy in order to 'make a great Reformation in the manner of our Speaking, and Writing'. Some thirty years later Jonathan Swift was still calling for that sort of academy, or at any rate for *some* 'effectual Method for *Correcting, Enlarging*, and *Ascertaining* our Language' to catch up with the French who 'hath been polishing' theirs for 'these last Fifty Years'.[51]

'My Words Should Be Few and Savoury, Seasoned with Grace'

The generalization is that the later seventeenth century ushered in a new style of simplicity. Since R. F. Jones put science at the head of the School of Plain Language in 1930,

---

[49] Thomas Rymer, 'The Preface of the Translator', in R. Rapin, *Reflections on Aristotle's Treatise of Poesie. Containing The Necessary, Rational, and Universal Rules for Epick, Dramatick, and other sorts of Poetry* (1674), sigs. A4v–A5v (Rymer is talking about verse tragedy, but as part of the debate about the introduction of blank verse and its relation to prose); Addison, *Spectator*, 2: 35–6.

[50] Swift, *Proposal*, 17–18; Sprat, *History*, 39–40, 42; Dryden, *Troilus and Cressida*, sig. A6v. The play is dedicated to Robert, Earl of Sunderland, Principal Secretary of State. He adds that English 'abound[s] as much in Words, as *Amsterdam* does in Religions' (sig. A6v).

[51] Sprat, *History*, 41; Swift, *Proposal*, 6, 14.

there have been vociferous arguments about who influenced whom.[52] Following Bacon's complaint early in the century, Thomas Sprat describes the members of the Royal Society being 'most sollicitous' about 'the manner of their *Discourse*', famously arguing that '*eloquence* ought to be banish'd out of all *civil Societies*' because 'these specious *Tropes* and *Figures*' have brought 'mists and uncertainties ... on our Knowledg'; 'this vicious abundance of *Phrase*, this trick of *Metaphors*, this volubility of *Tongue*, which makes so great a noise in the World ... give[s] the mind a motion too changeable, and bewitching, to consist with *right practice*'. Dryden advised that 'wit is best convey'd to us in the most easie language, and is most to be admir'd when a great thought comes drest in words so commonly receiv'd that it is understood by the meanest apprehensions, as the best meat is the most easily digested'. Delarivier Manley proclaimed: 'There is something so eloquent and persuasive in Truth alone, without the Advantage of Oratory.'[53] Swift, who would read his own works to his servants to make sure his prose was clear at all levels, defined style as 'Proper Words in Proper Places'; as Ann Cline Kelly argues, he believed that 'stylistic decisions are existential decisions'.[54] M. A. Shaaber describes a period when '[t]erseness came to be preferred to copiousness ... [t]he effect sought was spontaneity, a direct and unvarnished reflection of the workings of the mind rather than the premeditated artifices of expression'.[55] In spite of what Sprat called the 'fantastical terms' introduced by the '*Religious Sects*', the Quakers George Fox and William Penn prided themselves upon their plain language. Fox wrote in his journal: 'I was to keep to "yea" and "nay" in all things; and that my words should be few and savoury, seasoned with grace.'[56] Penn described his own endeavours to '*express my self in* Plain *and* Proper *Terms, and not* Figurative, Allegorical *or* Doubtful *Phrases; that so I may leave* no room *for an Equivocal or Double Sence; but that the* Truth *of the Subject I treat upon, may appear* Easily *and* Evidently *to every common Understanding*'.[57] Bunyan introduced what C. S. Lewis describes as a biblically inflected prose of 'the fireside, the

---

[52] R. F. Jones argued in 1930 that the plain style promoted by the Royal Society influenced literary and sermonic prose ('Science and English Prose Style in the Third Quarter of the Seventeenth Century', *Publications of the Modern Languages Association*, 45 (1930), 977–1009). See Courtney Weiss Smith, *Empiricist Devotions: Science, Religion, and Poetry in Early Eighteenth-Century England* (Charlottesville and London: University of Virginia Press, 2016) for discussion of 'scientific, devotional, and poetic writing' (6). Weiss Smith traces the 'lines of influence [running] in both directions' (7).

[53] Sprat, *History*, 111–12; Dryden, *Dramatick Poesie*, 23; Delarivier Manley, *Memoirs of Europe, Towards the Close of the Eighth Century* (1710), quoted in J. B. Heidler, *The History from 1700 to 1800, of English Criticism of Prose Fiction* (Urbana: University of Illinois Press, 1928), 25.

[54] Jonathan Swift, *A Letter to a Young Gentleman, Lately entered into Holy Orders. By a Person of Quality* (1721), 6; Ann Cline Kelly, *Swift and the English Language* (Philadelphia: University of Pennsylvania Press, 1988), 4.

[55] M. A. Shaaber, *Seventeenth-Century Prose* (New York: Harper, 1957), 2. He acknowledges, of course, that 'all the world knows that casualness and spontaneity can be premeditated just as well as floridity, but they were the effects that the seventeenth century chose to premeditate' (2).

[56] Sprat, *History*, 42; George Fox, *The Journal*, ed. John L. Nickalls (Religious Society of Friends, 1975), 1–2.

[57] William Penn, *Primitive Christianity Revived in the Faith and Practice of the People called Quakers* (1696), sigs. B2v–B3r.

shop, and the land', and indeed, Swift declared he had been 'better entertained, and more informed by a Chapter in the *Pilgrim's Progress,* than by a long Discourse upon the *Will* and the *Intellect,* and *simple* or *complex Idea's'*. Certainly, the first half of the seventeenth century engaged in linguistic housecleaning on many fronts, scraping off Elizabethan ornament and rhythm and vocabulary in favour of an 'easie language ... drest in words so commonly receiv'd'.[58]

The historians of English prose agree in not oversimplifying. Paul Salzman notes that 'the ornate style survived into the 1660s, existing alongside the new plain romance style'. Although 'the influence that set up plain style as the prevailing model after the Restoration was that of the scientists', it has often been remarked that those seventeenth-century writers calling out loudly against metaphor in others—including Hobbes and Sprat—were quite happy to employ it themselves.[59] As Roger Pooley puts it, 'the attempts of early scientists to find a plain way of describing their experiments are fascinating, even at the crude level of catching them using metaphors when they had said they wouldn't'.[60] Or as Dryden said of Cleveland: 'he gives us many times a hard Nut to break our Teeth, without a Kernel for our pains.' N. H. Keeble reminds us that 'Quaker plainness' is not the same as Puritan plainness: 'For an early Quaker to write as "an Enlightened and Experienced Man" was to produce something far more rhapsodical, figurative, and allusive, something altogether more unbuttoned and unpredictable, than would satisfy the scrupulous desire for accurate exposition of a Baxter.' Let us simply say, with Peter Ure, that in the seventeenth century 'a demand for the plain and a taste for the subtle went together'.[61]

'Some Rules for Speaking and Action'

A combination of plain and subtle, of old and new, persisted on the page in both punctuation and syntax.[62] The usual story about punctuation is that its history reflects the shift from oral to print culture, from the rhetorical to the grammatical, from *telling* the reader how to read aloud to *showing* the reader how the sentence is

---

[58] C. S. Lewis, 'The Literary Impact of the Authorised Version', in *Selected Literary Essays,* ed. Walter Hooper (Cambridge: Cambridge University Press, 1969), 126–45 (140); Swift, *Letter to a Young Gentleman,* 24; Dryden, *Dramatick Poesie,* 23.

[59] Paul Salzman, *English Prose Fiction 1558–1700: A Critical History* (Oxford: Clarendon Press, 1985), 119; Shaaber, *Seventeenth-Century Prose,* 3.

[60] Roger Pooley, *English Prose of the Seventeenth Century, 1590–1700* (London and New York: Longman, 1992), 3.

[61] Dryden, *Of Dramatick Poesie,* 23; N. H. Keeble, 'The Politic and the Polite in Quaker Prose: the Case of William Penn', in Thomas N. Corns and David Loewenstein (eds.), *The Emergence of Quaker Writing: Dissenting Literature in Seventeenth-Century England* (Frank Cass, 1995), 112–25 (115) ; Peter Ure, 'Introduction', in Ure (ed.), *Seventeenth-Century Prose 1620–1700: The Pelican Book of English Prose. Volume 2* (Harmondsworth: Penguin, 1956), p. xvii.

[62] Portions of this section are derived from Cynthia Wall, *Grammars of Approach: Landscape, Narrative, and the Linguistic Picturesque* (Chicago: University of Chicago Press, 2019), chap. 3.

constructed.[63] And that is when the historian of punctuation gives the business any credibility at all; in 1728 Ephraim Chambers declared the rules for 'pointing' (as it was called) 'impertinent, dark, and deficient; and the practice, at present, perfectly capricious, authors varying not only from one another, but from themselves too'.[64] Later in the eighteenth century, Joseph Robertson would insist that punctuation is *not* 'an arbitrary invention, depending on fancy and caprice', but rather, 'founded on rational and determinate principles'.[65] The longer view sees indeed a sense of order from confusion sprung: the two strands of theory and practice—logical and elocutionary—were intertwined, both early on and into the nineteenth century. Order and confusion in different ways produced, if not gaudy tulips, a punctuation that sprang out more dramatically as both a busy little architect of the page and, aurally, D. F. McKenzie's 'handheld theatre of the book'.[66]

The author of *Some Rules for Speaking and Action; To be observed At the Bar, in the Pulpit, and the Senate, and by every one that Speaks in Public* (1716) puts the earlier elocutionary practice succinctly: 'A *Comma* stops the Voice while we may privately tell One, a *Semicolon* Two, a *Colon* Three, and a *Period* Four'.[67] Such practice emerged in the seventeenth century, in works such as Simon Daines's *Orthoepia Anglicana* (1640) and Christopher Cooper's *English Teacher* (1687). But as John Brightland instructed in 1711: 'The Use of these Points, Pauses, or Stops, is not only to give a proper Time for Breathing; but to avoid Obscurity, and Confusion of the Sence in the joining Words together in a Sentence.'[68] Says Thomas Dyche in 1716: 'THE *Stops* are used to shew what *Distance* of *Time* must be observ'd in *Reading*', but they are also 'absolutely necessary to *the better Understanding* of what we *write*, and *read*, that without a strict *Attention* to them, all *Writing* would be *confused*, and liable to many *Misconstructions*'. In 1775 William Cockin is still telling the counts of commas and colons, as well as 'the marks of interrogation (?) and admiration (!)' and the dash (albeit in a footnote).[69] (Elizabeth

---

[63] See Ellen Lupton, 'Telegrammar: From Writing to Speech', in *Period Styles: A History of Punctuation* (New York: Cooper Union, 1988), 7; Walter J. Ong, 'Historical Backgrounds of Elizabethan and Jacobean Punctuation', *Publications of the Modern Language Association*, 59 (1944), 349–360; Vivian Salmon, 'Early Seventeenth-Century Punctuation as a Guide to Sentence Structure', *The Review of English Studies*, 13 (1962), 347–408 (347–8).

[64] Ephraim Chambers, *Cyclopædia: Or, an Universal Dictionary of Arts and Sciences*, 2 vols. (1728), 2: 911.

[65] Joseph Robertson, *An Essay on Punctuation* (2nd edn, 1786), sig. A5v.

[66] D. F. McKenzie, 'Typography and Meaning: The Case of William Congreve', in Giles Barber and Bernhard Fabian (eds.), *The Book and the Book Trade in Eighteenth-Century Europe* (Hamburg: Hauswedell, 1981), 81–125 (83).

[67] *Some Rules for Speaking and Action; To be observed At the Bar, in the Pulpit, and the Senate, and by every one that Speaks in Public* (1716), 25. See also Isaac Watts, *The Art of Reading and Writing English; or, The Chief Principles and Rules of Pronouncing Our Mother-Tongue, Both in Prose and Verse* (2nd edn, 1722), 39–46.

[68] John Brightland, *A Grammar of the English Tongue* (1711), 149. This grammar was very popular and so presumably influential; it was in its eighth edition by 1759.

[69] Thomas Dyche, *A Guide to the English Tongue* (1716), 105; William Cockin, *The Art of Delivering Written Language; or, An Essay of Reading: In Which the Subject is Treated Philosophically as Well as with a View to Practice* (1775), 101 n.

Hamilton commented in the 1780s that the best prose style was 'always that which could be longest read without exhausting the breath'.[70])

Just as punctuation served both as stage direction for reading aloud and grammatical parser for reading alone in the late seventeenth and early eighteenth centuries, so the two basic English sentence styles of plain (the 'loose' or 'running' style) and fancy (periodic or Ciceronian) coexisted. Robertson defined the period sentence as 'a *circuit*, or a sentence, in which the meaning is suspended, till the whole is finished. It is called by Cicero, *verborum Ambitus* [circuit of words]'. In 1888 William Minto described the effect of the periodic structure as intending 'to keep the mind in a state of uniform or increasing tension until the *dénouement*'. When the subject matter is 'easy and familiar', says Minto, 'the reader, finding the sentence or clause come to an end as soon as his expectations are satisfied, receives an agreeable impression of neatness and finish'; when difficult or unfamiliar, 'or when the suspense is unduly prolonged, the periodic structure is intolerably tedious, or intolerably exasperating'. The periodic sentence was fashionable among the Elizabethans, but was considered by the seventeenth-century simplifiers (Bacon, Sprat, Dryden) both tedious and exasperating. As Shaaber argues, 'a casual, even jerky kind of sentence structure denied the writer's allegiance to Ciceronian periodicity; jingling and sweet-falling clauses gave way to aphorisms and witty conceits and images'.[71]

Where the period style, according to Richard Lanham, is basically hypotactic, the clauses ordered by 'balance, antithesis, parallelism, and careful patterns of repetition', the loose or running style is paratactic, a 'syntactic democracy'. He compares the two styles to period garden patterns:

> Styles in prose then are rather like styles in gardens. The periodic style is like the vast formal garden of a Baroque palace, all balanced squares and parallel paths. The land is rearranged in ways that the visual cortex can easily sort out. The running style, on the other hand, is like the informal garden which shapes nature without seeming to. Nature is not dominated and reformed but simply helped on the way it wanted to go anyway. We can wander—since there is no beginning, middle, and end—but again without fear of getting lost.

'Such a syntax', he continues of the running style, 'models the mind in the act of coping with the world. The coping is all small-scale, minute-to-minute tactics, not seasonal grand strategy'.[72]

The footprint scene from Daniel Defoe's *Robinson Crusoe* (1719) can model the confluence of all these points of punctuation and syntax—of speaking and action. Although Defoe's first novel lies just outside the purview of this *Handbook*, in it is embedded the

---

[70] Elizabeth Hamilton, *Memoirs of the Late Mrs Elizabeth Hamilton with a Selection from her Correspondence*, ed. Miss Benger (1819), 49–50.

[71] Robertson, *Essay on Punctuation*, 90; William Minto, *A Manual of English Prose, Literature, Biographical and Critical, Designed Mainly to Show Characteristics of Style* (3rd edn, Edinburgh and London, 1881), 5; Shaaber, *Seventeenth-Century Prose*, 2.

[72] Richard A. Lanham, *Analyzing Prose* (New York: Charles Scribner, 1983), 33, 54.

proses (if I may pluralize the term) of the seventeenth century: not only the styles of hypotaxis and parataxis, but also the genres of spiritual autobiography, travel narrative, fiction masquerading as history, and all marshalled by a punctuation that 'give[s] a proper Time for Breathing' and 'avoid[s] Obscurity, and Confusion of the Sence in the joining Words together in a Sentence', precisely by enacting the obscurity and confusion of Crusoe's mind in the act of coping with the world. Ian A. Gordon points to the 'effective paratactic series' in the footprint scene, where Crusoe sees the imprint of a single foot on the beach of his apparently not-so-deserted island: 'I stood like one thunderstruck, or as if I had seen an apparition: I listened, I looked around me, I could hear nothing, nor see anything. I went up to a rising ground to look further; I could see no other impression but that one.' The linking-words are absent, replaced by 'a firm pause or juncture'; the 'monosyllabic simplicity quickens to the magic of the discovery of the footprint'.[73] One clause follows breathlessly on another; the repetition of both action and syntax underscores the psychological astonishment.

Most nineteenth- and early twentieth-century critics find the power of Defoe's prose in its simplicity. In his *Cyclopædia of English Literature* (1844), Robert Chambers declares: 'His works of fiction still charm by their air of truth, and the simple natural beauty of their style.'[74] Anthony Burgess contrasts Defoe's style with the 'Latinate prose of those Elizabethans who fixed one eye on the Court and the Inns of Court'; Defoe consistently chooses the 'loose sentence' ('the culmination of decades of search for a perfect narrative manner') because it is more 'easily capable of giving the impression of immediacy'. They praised Defoe for the realism of his style, not its polish. According to William Minto, he was not 'a careful builder of sentences—studious of the arts of arrangement'; in the 'mechanical part of composition our author is singularly negligent' and 'his ungrammatical laxity would not be allowed in any modern writer'.[75]

But the 'mechanical part' of Defoe's prose has had its defenders. Samuel Taylor Coleridge argued that in fact 'De Foe was a first-rate master in periodic style'.[76] And W. R. Owens and P. N. Furbank demonstrate that 'Defoe, when he wanted, was very capable of constructing sentences and paragraphs on this plan' of the periodic, or '"teleological" or Ciceronian idea of a sentence'.[77] We can see the symbiotic powers of simplicity and periodicity if we look at the passage in full, with its complete original complement of punctuation:

---

[73] Ian A. Gordon, *The Movement of English Prose* (London: Longman, 1966), 30, 29, 8.

[74] Robert Chambers, *Cyclopædia of English Literature: A History, Critical and Biographical, of British Authors, From the Earliest to the Present Times* (1844), 3rd edn, rev. Robert Carruthers, 2 vols. (Edinburgh, 1876), 1: 566; Minto, *Manual of English Prose Literature*, 348.

[75] Quoted in Daniel Defoe, *A Journal of the Plague Year*, ed. Cynthia Wall (Harmondsworth: Penguin, 2003), 273.

[76] Coleridge was commenting on some 'exquisite paragraphs' in the *Farther Adventures of Robinson Crusoe* (1719); quoted in Pat Rogers, *Defoe: The Critical Heritage* (London: Routledge and Kegan Paul, 1972), 84.

[77] W. R. Owens and P. N. Furbank, 'Defoe and the "Improvisatory" Sentence', *English Studies*, 67 (1986), 157–66 (158).

> It happen'd one Day about Noon going towards my Boat, I was exceedingly surpriz'd with the Print of a Man's naked Foot on the Shore, which was very plain to be seen in the Sand: I stood like one Thunder-struck, or as if I had seen an Apparition; I listen'd, I look'd round me, I could hear nothing, nor see anything; I went up to a rising Ground to look farther; I went up the Shore and down the Shore, but it was all one, I could see no other Impression but that one, I went to it again to see if there were any more, and to observe if it might not be my Fancy; but there was no Room for that, for there was exactly the very Print of a Foot, Toes, Heel, and every Part of a Foot; how it came thither, I knew not, nor could in the least imagine. But after innumerable fluttering Thoughts, like a Man perfectly confus'd and out of my self, I came Home to my Fortification, not feeling, as we say, the Ground I went on, but terrify'd to the last Degree, looking behind me at every two or three Steps, mistaking every Bush and Tree, and fancying every Stump at a Distance to be a Man; nor is it possible to describe how many various Shapes affrighted Imagination represented Things to me in; how many wild Ideas were found every Moment in my Fancy, and what strange unaccountable Whimsies came into my Thoughts by the Way.
>   When I came to my Castle, for so I think I call'd it ever after this, I fled into it like one pursued; whether I went over by the Ladder as first contriv'd, or went in at the Hole in the Rock, which I call'd a Door, I cannot remember; no, nor could I remember the next Morning; for never frighted Hare fled to Cover, or Fox to Earth, with more Terror of Mind than I to this Retreat.[78]

Defoe's narrators' paragraphs are almost always single complex sentences connected by a series of semicolons and colons, which made Victorian editors apoplectic. If we compare the modernized passage quoted by Gordon with that of the first edition, we can see an actual weakening of energy and tension in the former. The modernized punctuation, which creates its pauses and junctures by imposing a colon and two full stops, makes two sentences with eight clauses. The gentler punctuation allows Crusoe to sit down (rhetorically) several times at the conveniently provided full stops; it is as if he really is privately and with deliberation telling the counts between clauses and periods. It creates a *calm* little paragraph of two sentences, relieving him of what presumably was considered repetitive pacings.

The whole typographical apparatus of the 1719 version, on the other hand, is far more mimetic of this mind-gob-smacking moment: beyond the fact that there are two additional clauses in this version, the capitalized and hyphenated 'Thunder-struck' bangs louder in the head; clause follows clause *follows clause* as Crusoe searches up, farther, up, down, listening and looking, hearing nothing and seeing nothing. And although this excerpted passage looks like one sentence with ten clauses (instead of two with eight), all hurrying faster with the one-count comma, when we insert it back into its original paragraphical context, we see that it is actually part of an even longer sentence that is the first of two in a paragraph that hinges between wandering around the

---

[78] Daniel Defoe, *The Life and Strange Surprizing Adventures of Robinson Crusoe, of York, Mariner* [...] *Written by Himself* (3rd edn, 1719), 181–2.

footprint and running from it. Such a syntax indeed displays a mind in the act of coping with the world, Crusoe's prose fleeing like one pursued. But one step back, and the passage as a whole—Defoe's prose—is conceptually periodic, in Lanham's terms: 'The mind shows itself after it has reasoned on the event; after it has sorted by concept and categorized by size; after it has imposed on the temporal flow the shapes through which that flow takes on a beginning, a middle, and an end. The periodic stylist works with balance, antithesis, parallelism, and careful patterns of repetition; all these dramatize a mind which has dominated experience and reworked it to its liking.'[79] Defoe was indeed a builder of sentences, studious of the arts of arrangement. The punctuation orchestrates both logistical and psychological drama; the plain prose moves within a Ciceronian circuit.

'He Is a Good English Writer'

Who was 'a good English writer', in the historian Henry Hallam's definitive pronouncement?[80] What defined English prose in and through the centuries? Part of the later reception of English prose was determined by late eighteenth-century linguistic engineering.[81] Elizabeth Closs Traugott has argued that the 'beginnings of the Modern English period are often associated with the publication in 1668 of John Dryden's essay, *Of Dramatic Poesy*, and Abraham Cowley's *Several Discourses by Way of Essays; in Verse and Prose*'. But she adds that two other phenomena had even greater consequences: 'the spread of English and the growth of concern with good and bad usage.'[82] The rise of prescriptive grammars in the eighteenth century was a product of a burgeoning interest in vernacular languages and prompted increasing attention to style. The seventeenth-century writers had seen themselves as dramatically improving English style, but the rise of what has been called prescriptivist grammar plunged the seventeenth-century writers back into the Miry Slough of Prose. Before 1700, thirty-four grammars were published in English about English; between 1700 and 1750 another thirty-four appeared; between 1750 and the end of the century: two hundred and five.[83] Grammatical and stylistic

---

[79] Lanham, *Analyzing Prose*, 54.

[80] Henry Hallam, *Introduction to the Literature of Europe in the Fifteenth, Sixteenth, and Seventeenth Centuries*, 4 vols. (1837–9), 4: 273.

[81] Laurel J. Brinton and Leslie K. Arnovick, *The English Language: A Linguistic History* (Oxford: Oxford University Press, 2006), 357. See also Ian Michael, *English Grammatical Categories and the Tradition to 1800* (Cambridge: Cambridge University Press, 1970).

[82] Elizabeth Closs Traugott, *The History of English Syntax: A Transformational Approach to the History of English Sentence Structure* (New York: Holt, Rinehart and Winston, 1972), 162.

[83] Michael, *English Grammatical Categories*, 588. Ingrid Tieken-Boon van Ostade argues that the increase in grammar production in the early eighteenth century 'seems due to the fact that it finally became clear, after the death of Queen Anne in 1714, that England would never have an Academy, despite recurrent pleas for one by men of letters such as Dryden in the early 1660s, Defoe in 1697, Addison in 1711 and Swift in 1712' ('Grammars, Grammarians and Grammar Writing: An Introduction', in van Ostade

changes were *designed*. Ben Jonson had simply called grammar 'the art of true, and well speaking a language'; in 1728, Ephraim Chambers reported that those who 'despise' grammar 'as only dealing in low, trivial Things, are exceedingly mistaken: It has, really, more Solidity than Shew'. Lindley Murray's 1795 *English Grammar* went into over three hundred editions during the nineteenth century. The art of speaking, reading, and writing acquired a moral and social authority. The English grammarians and stylists all came to agree with Kelly's characterization of Swift: that 'stylistic decisions are existential decisions'.[84]

English prose style thus became a matter for systematic investigation and pronouncement. Samuel Johnson anointed Sir William Temple (1628–99), for example, as 'the first writer who gave cadence to English prose. Before his time [writers] were careless of arrangement, and did not mind whether a sentence ended with an important word or an insignificant word, or with what part of speech it was concluded.'[85] Of Dryden's critical prefaces, he argues with measured ambivalence that

> They have not the formality of a settled style, in which the first half of the sentence betrays the other. The clauses are never balanced, nor the periods modelled: every word seems to drop by chance, though it falls into its proper place. Nothing is cold or languid; the whole is airy, animated, and vigorous; what is little, is gay; what is great is splendid ... Though all is easy, nothing is feeble; though all seems careless, there is nothing harsh; and though since his earlier works, more than a century has passed, they have nothing yet uncouth or obsolete ... His style could not easily be imitated, either seriously or ludicrously; for, being always equable and always varied, it has no prominent or discriminative characters.[86]

Of Addison, he assesses: 'His sentences have neither studied amplitude, nor affected brevity: his periods, though not diligently rounded, are voluble and easy'; and yet this very middleness, its neither-this-nor-that, becomes a very model of a modern *English* prose: 'Whoever wishes to attain an English style, familiar but not coarse, and elegant but not ostentatious, must give his days and nights to the volumes of Addison.'[87]

As the grammar industry grew, the 'reception' of seventeenth- and early eighteenth-century prose experienced an unhappy revolution. Carey McIntosh demonstrates that the number of examples of 'bad' English in prescriptive grammars after 1762 (by Bishop

---

(ed.), *Grammars, Grammarians and Grammar-Writing in Eighteenth-Century England* (Berlin and New York: Mouton de Gruyter, 2008), 1–16 (4).

[84] Jonson, *English Grammar* (1640), quoted in Tom Lundskær-Nielsen, *Prepositions in English Grammars until 1801—With a Survey of the Western European Background* (Odense: University Press of Southern Denmark, 2011), 114; Chambers, *Cyclopædia*, 1:177; Kelly, *Swift and the English Language*, 4.

[85] Quoted in James Boswell, *Life of Johnson*, ed. R. W. Chapman, intro. by Pat Rogers (Oxford: Oxford University Press, 1980), 921 (Thursday, 9 April 1778).

[86] Samuel Johnson, 'Dryden', in *Lives of the Poets*, ed. Roger Lonsdale, 4 vols. (Oxford: Oxford University Press, 2006), 2: 123.

[87] Johnson, 'Addison', in *Lives of the Poets*, 3: 38.

Lowth, George Campbell, Lord Kames, and Hugh Blair) 'are drawn from the writings of well-known authors of the first half of the eighteenth century, including Addison, Steel, Pope, Swift, and Bolingbroke'.[88] Blair, for example, fusses with the positions of Addison's adverbs:

> 'By greatness,' says Mr. Addison, in the Spectator, No. 412, 'I do not only mean the bulk of any single object, but the largeness of a whole view.' Here the place of the adverb *only*, renders it a limitation of the following word mean. 'I do not only mean.' The question may then be put, What does he more than mean? Had he placed it after *bulk*, still it would have been wrong. 'I do not mean the bulk *only* of any single object.' For we might then ask, What does he mean more than the bulk? Is it the colour? Or any other property? Its proper place, undoubtedly, is, after the word object.

Blair then proceeds to show how Shaftesbury, Swift, and Bolingbroke also transgress the rules of clearness and precision, unity, strength, and harmony. 'How often in the history of any of the Western languages', McIntosh remarks with some surprise, 'have school texts been filled with quotations from the major authors of fifty or seventy-five years earlier as examples of *bad* writing?'[89]

The nineteenth century revelled in producing full-scale taxonomies of English prose styles. While in some ways, at least in the eyes of nineteenth-century critics, seventeenth-century prose pulled itself out of the Slough the late eighteenth century had plopped it in, its literary reputation calcified in other ways. The Victorians were particularly fond of creating Eras (or perhaps it should be 'Æras') of Style. The Scottish biographer Robert Demaus (1829?–1874) 'conveniently' divides British literature into four periods: 'the *first* extending from Chaucer to Shakspere; the *second* from Shakspere to Pope; the *third* from Pope to Cowper; and the *fourth* from Cowper to the present day.' He gives rough chronological (monarchical) boundaries for the periods, and then their telling characteristics:

> The *first* period may be briefly characterized as one of rudeness, both in thought and expression, though by no means destitute of redeeming qualities; the *second* as one distinguished by grandeur of thought, not always, however, equally sustained, and dignity of expression, not, however, exempt from occasional rudeness; the *third* by grace and vivacity of thought without much depth, neatness and simplicity of expression without much dignity; and the *fourth* by a combination, with many peculiarities of its own, of the excellences of the two preceding periods.

It is the end of the second period and the beginning of the third that concern us here; he sees 'in the *second*, the influence of the revival of learning, and of the study of the

---

[88] Carey McIntosh, *The Evolution of English Prose 1700–1800: Style, Politeness, and Print Culture* (Cambridge: Cambridge University Press, 1998), 28.

[89] Hugh Blair, *Lectures on Rhetoric and Belles Lettres* (1783) (8th edn, New York: Jas. & John Harper, 1819), 103–4; McIntosh, *Evolution of English Prose*, 28.

great classical remains of antiquity' and in the third, 'polish and grace, neatness and liveliness'.[90]

The educationist Joseph Payne (1808–86) has rather larger but even more geologically proportioned categories in his *Studies in English Prose* (1868): 'FIFTH STAGE. / MODERN ENGLISH.—PERIOD OF RE-ESTABLISHMENT. (A.D. 1550–1867).' His concern in his introductory remarks to each period is linguistic, and his bird's-eye view discovers a stability in the language unperceived by Sprat, Waller, or Johnson:

> The English of the last three centuries is, by general consent, treated as Modern. This epithet is considered quite in harmony with the fact that the language in the course of that period has undergone great changes, and that the English of Tennyson and Carlyle is in many respects—not merely personal—very different from that of Lylie, Hooker, and Shakspeare. All its most important grammatical features were finally impressed upon it in the sixteenth century (the introduction of 'its' in the seventeenth century being nearly the only important exception); and although we have adopted many words which were formerly unknown, and invested many old ones with fresh meanings, yet the great bulk of the vocabulary remains the same. Neither the slight grammatical changes nor the accession of new words, nor the loss of old ones, has had the slightest tendency to disturb the essential character of the language.[91]

He rarely offers his own analysis of the prose of individual writers, relying instead on the earlier work of Johnson, Coleridge, Joseph Angus, Henry Hallam, and Edward Bulwer Lytton.

The historian Henry Hallam (1777–1859) became a leading figure for determining the nineteenth-century reception of seventeenth-century prose. His massive, four-volume *Introduction to the Literature of Europe in the Fifteenth, Sixteenth, and Seventeenth Centuries* (1837–9) overlooks almost no writer, no matter how minor (unless she was a woman); its judgments are extremely finely—and finally—drawn. Each writer is both grandly and minutely inspected and compared. Locke, for example, had not 'the luminous perspicacity of language we find in Descartes, and, when he does not soar too high, in Malebranche, but he had more judgment, more caution, more patience, more freedom from paradox, vanity and love of system, than either'. He paints the influential landscape of seventeenth-century English prose:

> The characteristics of English writers in the first division of the century were not maintained in the second, though the change, as was natural, did not come on by very rapid steps. The pedantry of unauthorized Latinisms, the affectation of singular and not generally intelligible words from other sources, the love of quaint

---

[90] Robert Demaus, *A Class-Book of English Prose, Comprehending Specimens of the Most Distinguished Prose Writers from Chaucer to the Present Time* (Edinburgh, 1859), 1–2.

[91] Joseph Payne, *Studies in English Prose: Consisting of Specimens of the Language in Its Earliest, Succeeding, and Latest Stages, with Notes Explanatory and Critical* (1868), p. xxxiv.

phrases, strange analogies, and ambitious efforts at antithesis, gave way by degrees; a greater ease of writing was what the public demanded, and what the writers after the Restoration sought to attain; they were more strictly idiomatic and English than their predecessors. But this ease sometimes became negligence and feebleness, and often turned to coarseness and vulgarity.

Hobbes, he says, is 'perhaps the first of whom we can say that he is a good English writer'.[92]

Sir Edward Bulwer Lytton (1803–73), a popular novelist, playwright, poet, and politician, was another authority figure in literary reception. He pulled Addison out of Blair's purgatory:

no praise of Addison's style can exaggerate its merits. Its art is perfectly marvelous. No change of time can render the workmanship obsolete. His style has that nameless urbanity in which we recognize the perfection of manner—courteous, but not courtierlike; so dignified, yet so kindly; so easy, yet so high-bred. Its form of English is fixed—a safe and eternal model, of which all imitation pleases—to which all approach is scholarship—like the Latin of the Augustan age.

He dials it back a bit when, after comparing Addison to the 'high-priest of eloquence', Jeremy Taylor, and 'the absolute command and the exquisite selection of words in Sir Thomas Browne', he concludes that Addison's 'jewels are admirably set, but they are not of the largest size, nor of the most precious water'.[93] The end of the nineteenth century brings us, among others, Matthew Arnold (1822–88), who follows the line from Wordsworth and Coleridge in *Lyrical Ballads* (1798, 1800) and, Addison-like, damns Pope, Swift, and early eighteenth-century poetry (and possibly early eighteenth-century prose) with faint praise. In 'The Study of Poetry' (1880), Arnold famously reclassified that poetry *as* prose: 'We are to regard Dryden as the puissant and glorious founder, Pope as the splendid high priest, of our age of prose and reason.' He carries on a rather facetious little discourse with us: 'Do you ask me whether Dryden's verse, take it almost where you will, is not good? ... Do you ask me whether Pope's verse, take it almost where you will, is not good?' The answer to both questions is: 'Admirable for the purposes of ... an age of prose and reason.' But neither poet has that 'high seriousness', that 'poetic largeness, freedom, insight, benignity'; alas, '[t]hough they may write in verse, ... Dryden and Pope are not classics of our poetry, they are classics of our prose'.[94] And so without sneering, Arnold teaches the rest to sneer.

---

[92] Hallam, *Introduction to the Literature of Europe*, 4: 273, 529, 530.

[93] Edward Bulwer Lytton, 'Style and Diction', in *Caxtoniana: A Series of Essays on Life, Literature, and Manners* (New York, 1864), 83–102 (83–4).

[94] Matthew Arnold, 'The Study of Poetry', in *Poetry and Criticism of Matthew Arnold*, ed. A. Dwight Culler (Boston: Houghton Mifflin, 1961), 306–27 (321–2). This essay was originally the general introduction to T.H. Ward's anthology, *The English Poets* (1880). See further the 'Introduction' by Nicholas McDowell and Henry Power.

'A Plain Earthenware Pot'

I have taken the topic of the 'reception' of English prose from 1640 to 1714 beyond what readers were consuming at the time and to write a kind of critical biography of that period's prose. Virginia Woolf said that all great novelists write 'a natural prose' that is based 'on the sentence that was current at the time'; criticism itself has a reception history that is based upon aesthetic (and political) assumptions current at the time.[95] Critical reception through time discovers the ways that authors and styles are not fixed in print but shapeshift within it. Swift's 'Proper Words in Proper Places' depends critically on the historical place of the words. The Royal Society Fellows, the Quakers, the playwrights of the late seventeenth century tossed out the 'wretched Pun and Quibble' and the 'false *Sublime*' of the late sixteenth and early seventeenth century in favour of words 'few and savoury, seasoned with grace'. The periodic sentence and the plain style jostled in place. Commas sparred with semicolons. The *belles lettres* of the late eighteenth century spurned the Addisonian adverbs. Addison himself is one of the bouncier ones bobbing up and down in the critical waters (his 'jewels' changing size with the temperature). Samuel Johnson booms out one set of magisterial pronouncements in one century; Thomas Babington Macaulay magisterially countermands in the next. The High Victorians relegated early eighteenth-century poetry to a kind of ultra-metrical prose, lacking high seriousness and poetic largeness; the Edwardians would rekindle the power. I choose to close with Virginia Woolf. After acknowledging that in *Robinson Crusoe* 'there are no sunsets and no sunrises', no poetic largeness per se, in fact 'nothing but a large earthenware pot', she demands in the end: 'And is there any reason, why the perspective that a plain earthenware pot exacts should not satisfy us as completely, once we grasp it, as man himself in all his sublimity standing against a background of broken mountains and tumbling oceans with stars flaming in the sky?'[96]

---

[95] Virginia Woolf, *A Room of One's Own* (London: Hogarth Press, 1929), 114–15.
[96] Virginia Woolf, 'Robinson Crusoe', in *The Common Reader, Second Series* (1932), ed. Andrew McNeillie (London: Hogarth Press, 1986), 51–9 (58).

CHAPTER 3

CLASSICAL INHERITANCE

FREYJA COX JENSEN

The classical inheritance was as much a part of English prose in the seventeenth and eighteenth centuries as it had been in the Renaissance years. Without the texts of ancient Greece and Rome, it is impossible to conceive of English literature as we know it, so greatly were the writers of the later Stuart period influenced by their ancient predecessors. Every part of the written tradition was informed by the classics, from the way in which language itself was constructed and manipulated, through the forms and genres in which works were attempted, to the ideas, morals, and ideological frameworks within which writers worked.

Whether ours is a period of change or continuity is a question that has occupied much space in the scholarship on the seventeenth and early eighteenth centuries. The turbulence of the civil war years, the ostensible 'new beginning' of the 'Restoration' of 1660, and the subsequent political struggles have all encouraged students of the period to look for novelty and innovation in the prose literature of the later Stuart era. On the other hand, the labels 'Augustan' or 'neoclassical' to describe the years from 1660 onwards have, despite cogent criticism, remained current in general usage, marking this as a period closely tied in the popular consciousness to the classical tradition. Various conceptions of 'neoclassical' or 'Augustan' literature—as being grounded upon a *Weltanschauung* denying the alterity of the past, which saw the classics as the embodiment of all human nature, eternally relevant; as meticulous imitation of classical paradigms at the expense of any real originality; or as a phase during which the elite was primarily interested in, and influenced by, classical texts, while the middling sort and its new interest in contemporary fiction gradually challenged this cultural hegemony—may all be seen, in part, to be reflected in the engagement of the period's prose writing with classical literature. Simultaneously, innovation and explicit rejections of earlier classicisms are also found in English prose from 1640 onwards.

Indeed, change and continuity are both apparent in our period. Classical models, *exempla*, and ideas were harnessed to numerous, sometimes conflicting agenda, as they had been throughout the Renaissance. The examples upon which writers drew were both Greek and Roman, republican and imperial. Individual English authors followed various literary precedents, depending upon their personal taste, political inclination, and artistic aims; and they naturally drew their inspiration from classical and non-classical sources. Attempts at finding a new, English prose style were founded upon classical bases, as well as upon the rejection of the classics: the works of Plato, Demosthenes, Seneca, Tacitus, and Plutarch influenced sustained attempts to develop an English *genus humile*, or 'plain style'—a move, in theory, at least, away from the oratorical style of the Ciceronians, towards prose that was more direct and exact in its representation of reality—yet Aristotle's *Rhetoric* remained a key text, dominating the understanding of rhetorical prose style throughout our period as it had done in the sixteenth century.

It is impossible to do more here than gesture towards both the formal and the wider cultural and artistic ways that English prose was shaped by the ancient world; more detailed analyses and observations may be found in a wide variety of scholarly publications produced in recent decades, since the resurgence of interest in classical reception, broadly conceived.[1] The following pages therefore present an overview of the more important means by which classical texts were assimilated into English cultural life and literature—grammar school and university education, and the reading of the classics in translation—and briefly sketch the genres of seventeenth-century prose writing owing most to the texts of the ancient world.

Education

No understanding of English prose in the early modern period can be achieved without an appreciation of the absolute centrality of classical literature to English learning, and thus to the intellectual development of nearly all male writers, and some women. The formal education provided by the grammar schools and universities was, in the seventeenth and early eighteenth centuries, still very much a classical one, based on the principles of Renaissance humanism. It was in this way that many readers and writers first encountered the classics; it was in the grammar schools that the precepts of classical rhetoric were first instilled in them, and it was here they received a thorough grounding in both the language and ideas of the major ancient authors.[2] This education was, of

---

[1] For example, on classical influences on various prose styles, see the numerous essays in Gordon Braden, Robert Cummings, and Stuart Gillespie (eds.), *The Oxford History of Literary Translation in England. Volume Two: 1550–1660* (Oxford: Oxford University Press, 2010), and Stuart Gillespie and David Hopkins (eds.), *The Oxford History of Literary Translation in England. Volume Three: 1660–1790* (Oxford: Oxford University Press, 2005).

[2] The most comprehensive and detailed studies of early modern school education are T. W. Baldwin, *William Shakespere's Small Latine & Lesse Greeke*, 2 vols. (Urbana, Ill.: University of Illinois Press, 1944) and Foster Watson, *The English Grammar Schools to 1660: Their Curriculum and Practice* (Cambridge: Cambridge University Press, 1908). More recent work detailing the curriculum and school practices includes Rosemary O'Day, *Education and Society 1500–1800* (New York: Longman, 1982), Helen M. Jewell, *Education in Early Modern England* (Basingstoke: Palgrave, 1998), and Peter Mack, *Elizabethan Rhetoric: Theory and Practice* (Cambridge: Cambridge University Press, 2002)

course, limited in its reach, available only to boys and young men, and then only to those whose financial circumstances allowed. It was not the only way that readers and writers encountered the classical tradition, but after the expansion of the schools and universities in the Elizabethan and early Stuart years, it is undeniable that by the mid-seventeenth century, more young men encountered the worlds of ancient Greece and Rome through formal education than at any time previously.

Continuity of practice was the defining feature of grammar school education throughout the seventeenth century, albeit not meeting with universal approbation. The curriculum was largely unchanged from that of one hundred years previously and was more or less consistent even though schools differed widely in their size and affluence. Boys worked their way through the same Latin exercises that had been set for several generations, assimilating the Latinate literary culture common across Europe. They read prose excerpts, in Latin and in English translation, from the best Roman authors—Caesar, Sallust, and Cicero—along with verse by Vergil, Horace, Ovid, and Terence, these authors serving as models of the ideal Latin style to which boys should aspire. By means of parallel translation, the composition of essays in accordance with the rules of classical rhetoric, and the emulation of the style of Cicero's epistles, students at the grammar schools were intended to become so fluent in Latin that reading and writing it came as easily, if not more so, than in their native tongue. This would, in turn, help them develop their English prose style, as they employed in the vernacular the rhetorical techniques modelled by the ancients.

Chief among the books used in schools, and exemplifying the educational ethos of the time, was Lily's Latin Grammar, which continued to enjoy the monopoly conveyed by its royal patent of 1547 until the end of the eighteenth century. Rules and rote learning were the methods used to effect the acquisition of rudimentary Latin, often enforced by strict classroom discipline. This was not yet the age of Greek, domestic printing and teaching resources not yet having attained their later strength. Nevertheless, the later seventeenth century did witness an increase in the teaching of Greek in the grammar schools, marking an improvement from the 'small Latin, and lesse Greek' of Shakespeare's schooldays; William Camden's Greek Grammar, first published in 1595 for use at Westminster School, was the most-used textbook, appearing with great regularity in twenty-four editions between 1640 and 1700.[3]

These standard texts were by no means universally regarded as useful pedagogical instruments or aids to better writing in English, however, and several educational theorists devoted many words to highlighting their substantial failings, and those of the system they embodied. John Milton condemned the formal methods of classical schooling both eloquently and passionately, lamenting the inefficiency of profitless parsing, boys spending 'seven or eight yeers meerly in scraping together so much miserable Latin, and Greek, as might be learnt otherwise easily and delightfully in one

---

[3] Ben Jonson, 'To the Memory of My Beloved, the Author, Mr William Shakespeare', in *Mr. William Shakespeares Comedies, Histories, & Tragedies* (1623), sig. A4r.

yeer'. '[F]orcing the empty wits of children to compose Theams, verses, and Orations' he saw as a 'preposterous exaction' of the 'poor striplings, like blood out of the nose, or the plucking of untimely fruit', and the most that could be hoped for the majority of schoolboys was that they floundered in the 'Grammatick flats & shallows where they stuck unreasonably to learn a few words with lamentable construction'.[4]

Protestations like these were of little avail, however, and Lily and Camden endured in use until long after the end of our period, a source of irritation to the more progressive pedagogues. The most constructive of these provided alternatives and supplements to the textbooks, and the later seventeenth century saw the beginning of a more child-friendly way of engaging with classical learning which, although not officially adopted, existed in tandem with more traditional methods, and which cannot but have facilitated the acquisition of Latin and Greek by larger numbers of boys, and a general advancement in the levels of education, erudition, and eloquence among the educated sorts. Edward Burles' *New English Grammar* (1652) sought to present the essence of Latin grammar plainly and clearly for teachers and boys in schools, and also for gentlemen whose Latin was somewhat rusty, 'for the recovery of what they have lost by discontinuance from their studies'.[5] A simpler way of learning Latin was of use far beyond the grammar schools, as Bathsua Makin observed in her essay on women's education (1673): 'there is very little advantage to the Child' in Lily's Grammar, because 'the whole Method swerves from the Rules of true Didactick ... All Rules ought to be plain, that they may be easily understood ... The Rules in *Lilly's Grammar* are not so.' Makin, along with Burles, advocated a move towards a simpler way of learning, based on teaching in English, or at least relating Latin more closely to English in order that children might better understand it; Lily's grammatical rules were ineffective 'because they are in Latin, a Tongue the Learner doth not understand; and which is worse, a great part of them is in verse, hardly intelligible to a Child if they are translated into Grammatical English'.[6]

Yet none of these authors disputed the importance of learning the classical languages in and of themselves as necessary prerequisites for the attainment of elegance when writing in English, and despite their attempts at reforming Latin education, Lily would remain the staple diet (and 'woful experience', as Makin put it[7]) of English schoolboys for decades to come. Moreover, a grammar school education taught boys more about the ancient world than just its accidence and syntax, and their deep familiarity with classical mores and habits of thought was facilitated by prose handbooks and dictionaries intended as aids to a fuller understanding of Greece and Rome, in order that the ancient examples, as well as the parts of grammar, were assimilated into young men's minds. Among the most popular was *Romanae historiae anthologia*, composed by Thomas

---

[4] John Milton, *Of Education* (1644), sig. A1v.
[5] Edward Burles, *Grammatica Burlesa, or, A New English Grammar Made Plain and Easie for Teacher & Scholar* (1652), title page.
[6] Bathsua Makin, *An Essay to Revive the Antient Education of Gentlewomen in Religion, Manners, Arts & Tongues with an Answer to the Objections Against this Way of Education* (London, 1673), sig. E3v.
[7] Makin, *An Essay*, sig. E3v.

Goodwin 'for the use of Abingdon Schoole'; he had previously been a master there.[8] First published in 1614, it appeared in twenty-two editions by the end of the century, suggesting a readership far greater than that for which it was initially intended; it sought to present 'An English exposition of the Romane antiquities, wherein many Romane and English offices are paralleld and divers obscure phrases explained'. Explaining such subjects as the topography of the city of Rome, the ordering of Roman society, religion, civil and legal procedures and processes, and the military arts, the book provided its readers with a complete guide to the context in which the ancient authors were writing. So useful was it throughout the seventeenth century that it was recommended as compulsory reading for first-year university students by the Cambridge tutor Richard Holdsworth, who stipulated that it be read 'before you come to other Latin authors, as being very useful in the understanding of them ... this being as it were a general comment to them all'.[9]

The classical culture prevailing in the grammar schools was even more strongly a feature of university education, because the range of authors and texts to which men were exposed was so much wider; a habit of mind that Mordecai Feingold has adjudged 'the inculcation of an almost intemperate love of the classics'.[10] It is hard to generalize about the precise nature of classical learning in the universities in the seventeenth and eighteenth centuries; Latin and Greek were largely unregulated by statute, and therefore throughout this period, as in earlier years, there appears to have been great diversity of practice.[11] Rhetoric was the central topic of study: at Cambridge, the core texts were Aristotle's *Rhetoric* and *Organon*; for the BA, Oxford required the reading of Vergil, Horace, and Cicero in addition to Aristotle, but otherwise, no stipulations were made. The available evidence—a patchwork of tutors' directives, library catalogues and inventories, notebooks, and commonplace books—indicates that the freedom from statutory expectations allowed colleges, tutors, and students to select any and all of the classical authors for study, though there was clear pedagogical opinion on which authors were superior, and the order in which they should be read. At Cambridge, Richard Holdsworth advocated the study of ancient history as of primary importance for young men: 'The necessity of this studie above the rest is the cause that it is to be continued through all the four yeares in the after noons, wheras other studies have each a parcel of your time alotted to them.'[12] This was not just for its grammatical or rhetorical quality, essential if men were to learn to write elegantly, but also for the moral

---

[8] Thomas Goodwin, *Romanae historiae anthologia: An English Exposition of the Romane Antiquities* (Oxford, 1614).

[9] Richard Holdsworth, 'Directions for a Student in the Universitie', transcribed in H. F. Fletcher, *The Intellectual Development of John Milton*, 2 vols. (Urbana, IL: University of Illinois Press, 1961), 2: 637. Although other authors have been proposed, the 'Directions' are commonly attributed to Richard Holdsworth, who is thought to have written them in the mid-1640s.

[10] Mordechai Feingold, 'The Humanities', in Nicholas Tyacke (ed.), *The History of the University of Oxford. Volume IV: Seventeenth-Century Oxford* (Oxford: Clarendon Press, 1997), 211–357 (229).

[11] Victor Morgan, *A History of the University of Cambridge, Volume II: 1546-1750* (Cambridge: Cambridge University Press, 2004), 438, 512; James McConica (ed.), *The History of the University of Oxford. Volume III: The Collegiate University* (Oxford: Clarendon Press, 1986), 152, 173–4.

[12] Transcribed in Fletcher, *Intellectual Development of John Milton*, 2: 637.

lessons it could teach. Seventeenth-century society continued to hold the humanist belief in the utility of the classical past, and its applicability to modern life; by reading the classics, young men might behold the patterns of human virtue and vice, and use them as a guide to living in the present, 'magistra vitae' and 'lux veritatis'.[13] This is presumably what Thomas Hobbes was thinking of when he attributed the Civil Wars of the mid-seventeenth century in part to an excessive zeal for the imitation of the classical past and its republican tendencies:

> Fourthly, There were an exceeding great number of Men of the greater sort, that had been so educated, as that in their youth having read the Books written by famous men of the Ancient Grecian and Roman Commonwealths, concerning their Policy and great Actions, in which Book the Popular Government was extol'd by that glorious Name of Liberty, and Monarchy disgraced by the Name of Tyranny: they became thereby in love with their form of Government: And out of these men were chosen the greatest part of the House of Commons: Or if they were not the greatest part, yet by advantage of their Eloquence were always able to sway the rest.[14]

It was the understanding that immersion in classical learning could lead to the wrong lessons being learned that prompted the composition of new advice literature on the reading of the ancient authors. Although the *ars historica* tradition was largely intellectually played out by the mid-seventeenth century, some renewed attempts were made to direct the young and the inexperienced toward the right messages in ancient prose writing. In 1685, Edmund Bohun translated into English Degory Wheare's inaugural lecture as Camden Professor of History at the University of Oxford, first delivered in 1623 and popular in print in Latin in the 1630s. Wheare's lecture had been printed in Latin several times in the Restoration period, by both Oxford and Cambridge printers, and now became available in the vernacular, editions appearing in 1685, 1694, 1698, and 1710. In the 1694 edition, Bohun added observations on the text and on history by Henry Dodwell, his 'Invitation to gentlemen to acquaint themselves with ancient history'; Dodwell had acceded to the Camden Chair in 1688 but was deprived in 1691 for refusing to take the Oath of Allegiance on religious grounds. The 'Invitation' demonstrates a clear appreciation of the continued relevance of the ancient world for the modern, approving Bohun's translation as 'an initiation of young Students in History' and seeking 'to recommend it to Gentlemen, who were not so well qualified either to read this Book, or the Histories concerned in it, in their Original Latin'.[15] Indeed, the practical application of classical learning to contemporary society is stated with no small degree of force:

> How much more beneficial would it be for the improvement of Husbandry if ... the Husbandmen understood Hesiod, Virgil, Cato, Varro, Columella, Palladius, Pliny,

---

[13] Cicero, *De Oratore*, 2.9.36: 'the guide of life, and the light of truth.'
[14] Thomas Hobbes, *Behemoth, or, An Epitome of the Civil Wars of the England* (1679), sig. A3r.
[15] Henry Dodwell, 'Invitation to Gentlemen to Acquaint Themselves with Ancient History', in Degory Wheare, *The Method and Order of Reading both Civil and Ecclesiastical Histories* (1694), sig A2v.

and the Geoponicks ... The like may be said concerning the other Discourses of the Antients, their Books of Architecture, of Mechanicks, of Hawking, Hunting, and Fishing, of cures of Beasts, nay even of Cookery. The usefulness of their Inventions in these concerns of Human Life are in a great measure lost for want of this conjunction of Knowledge and Practice.[16]

In the same way, when Roger L'Estrange produced a complete English text of Cicero's *De Officiis* in English in 1680, he did so for its great relevance to the world in which his readers lived:

as it was Composed in a Loose, and Troublesome Age, so was it accommodated also to the Circumstances of Those Times; for the assert-of [assertion of] the *Force*, and *Efficacy of Virtue* against the utmost *Rigour*, and *Iniquity* of *Fortune*. Upon which Consideration likewise, I have now turn'd it into English, with a regard to a Place, and Season, that extreamly needs it. I do not speak this, as if at any time it would have been Superfluous; but that Desperate Diseases *require the most* Powerful Remedies.[17]

As well as being a practical guide to good government for those in office, the work retained in the later seventeenth century the moral force that had made it so central a part of the earlier humanist canon:

It is a Lesson that serves us from the very *Cradle*, to the *Grave*. It teaches us what we Ow to *Mankind*; to our *Country*; to our *Parents*; to our *Friends*; to our *Selves*; what we are to do as *Children*; what, as *Men*; what, as *Citizens*: It *sets*, and it *keeps* us *Right* in all the Duties of *Prudence, Moderation, Resolution*, and *Justice*. It Forms our *Manners*; Purges our *Affections*; enlightens our *Understandings*; and leads us, through the *Knowledge*, and the *Love* of *Virtue*, to the *Practice*, and *Habit* of it.

L'Estrange's translation was intended to correct for the possible damage that might have been done to the text's appeal by its use in the formal education system; its importance was such that he sought to rehabilitate it among readers whose schoolroom encounters with the *de Officiis* might prejudice them against returning to it in later life, or paying its lessons the attention they deserved. His English prose version, L'Estrange argued, would be far more likely to have the desired effect of instilling moral lessons effectively, as well as improving the reader's relationship with the Latin original:

But tho', upon the whole matter, I do Highly approve of the *Usage* of *This Book* in *Schools*, I must confess yet, with Submission, that I am not at all satisfy'd in the *ordinary Way* of using it. For the cutting of it out into *Particles*, here and there a *Chop*,

---

[16] Dodwell, 'Invitation', in Wheare, *Method and Order*, sigs. A3r–v.
[17] Cicero, *Tullys Offices in Three Books Turned Out of Latin into English by Ro. L'Estrange* (1680), sigs. A4v–5r.

makes it a *Lesson*, to the Boys, rather of *Syntax*, then *Morality*; beside the *prejudice* that it suffers under the Trivial name of a *School-Book*; and the *disgust* which naturally continues with us, even when we are *Men*, for that which we were *whipt* for, when we were *Boyes*. Now the *Matter* of this Book being so *Excellent*; and truly the *Latin* of it hardly *Ciceronian*; it should be our bus'ness rather to inculcate the *Doctrine* then the *Stile*; and yet in *such manner* too, that the *One* may be *Attended*, without *Neglecting* the *Other*. And This may be effected to the Common Benefit of the *Schollar*, in *Both Kinds*; by, First, *Reading*, and *Expounding* These Offices, *Whole* to him, in *English*, before he be put to Hack, and Puzzle upon them by *Snaps* in the Original; the *One Facilitating*, and *Preparing* him for the *Other*. Let him be, *First*, and in his *Mother-Tongue*, instructed in the *Principles* of *Moral Duties*; and he shall then with the more *Ease, Profit*, and *Delight*, take the same Notions down in *Latin*, and Digest them. Whereas in beginning with the *Latin*, the *Pupil* has little more to do, then to bring together the *Nominative Case* and the *Verb*, without either *Understanding*, or *Heeding* the main *Scope*, and *Intent* of the *Book*.[18]

It is therefore clear that young men, and older ones, too, were intended to use classical learning for more than simply schoolwork. L'Estrange's condemnation of traditional educational methods notwithstanding, this was as true of the words they read as the sense those words conveyed. As early modern readers engaged with their texts, they also wrote, noting down salient words and phrases from their texts for use in oratory, prose composition, and polite conversation. The richness of classical allusions within seventeenth- and eighteenth-century prose owes everything to the commonplacing tradition: the collection of *copia* taken from the classical authors and the identification of *loci communes* or themes illustrated and exemplified by apophthegms and aphorisms. Bohun's translation of Degory Wheare's *Method* expresses concisely the importance of the practice of selecting these *exempla*: 'let [the reader] enquire into the Causes of every Action and Counsel; let him consider the circumstances of it, and weigh the success; and let him in each of these search out wherein any thing is well or prudently, ill or imprudently managed; and let him from thence draw up to himself a general Precept, Rule or Direction, and then prove or illustrate it with many Sentences or Examples.' Readers adhering strictly to the classic commonplacing method would record their selections simultaneously in two notebooks: the first was used for initial notes, the second being the true 'commonplace' book, in which extracts and phrases were organized according to a series of thematic headings, such as Honour, Duty, Love, the Good Leader, and so forth, each of these sections eventually acting as a store of examples where characters, situations, and deeds might be compared, cross-referenced, and studied for their virtues, vices, or vagaries. These examples were, as Wheare explains, of practical as well as academic value: 'there is a two-fold use of Examples: the first for our imitation of what is done by good men, and that we may learn to shun the ill actions of wicked men: The second is,

---

[18] *Tullys Offices*, sigs. A6v–7v.

that from particular Stories we may deduce and extract some Sentence, which may be generally usefull to us.'[19]

It is such systematic, highly organized note-taking which is responsible for the classical references used so widely and with apparent ease throughout the English writing of the seventeenth and eighteenth centuries—references so numerous and erudite that the modern eye may easily miss the more obscure. For the reader was not intended merely to make notes, but to learn these phrases and examples by heart. Just as Cicero advised the would-be orator to have to hand a store of examples on any number of given topics, so early modern readers memorized their classical phrases. Richard Holdsworth instructed his students: 'These Collections you shall render so ready and familiar to you by the frequent reading them over on evenings, or times set a part for that purpose, that they will offer themselves to your memory on any occasion.'[20] Through this practice, classical ideas, examples, and phrases entered everyday speech, writing, and thought in early modern England. The mature equivalent of the short moral sentences learned by schoolboys as examples of Latin grammar, the brief *sententiae* recorded by readers exemplified good rhetorical style and moral principles, and were used in scholarly disputations and tracts, in public speeches, in letters to friends and family, and in general conversation. Commonplacing and note-taking formed an ingrained part of literate culture in this period. The imitation of the great Latin and Greek authors, the recycling of their phrases in original prose compositions of many different kinds, and the appropriation of their wisdom was by no means seen as plagiarism. Rather, it was a means of paying homage to the rhetorical excellence of the ancient world, and of exhibiting one's learned credentials, used to the full by writers of all manner of texts.

Editions and Literary Translations

By 1640, most of the ancient authors had been translated into, and printed in, English. Until the second half of the seventeenth century, however, relatively few editions of classical texts were produced in England, readers relying for the most part on imported continental editions in the original classical languages, or on the one or two existing English translations. In the case of some texts, the only access readers had was through editions produced abroad, in Latin, Greek, or one of the European vernaculars. This was more common for Greek authors, or authors writing on Greek topics. These include relatively minor authors like Diogenes Laertius, whose biography of the Greek philosophers was printed in England for the first time in Greek in 1664, and did not appear in its own right in translation until 1688; but the story is the same for some of the more notable

---

[19] Dodwell, 'Invitation', in Wheare, *Method and Order*, sigs. Z3v, Z4r.
[20] Cicero, *De Inventione*, II.15.48; Holdsworth, 'Directions', in Fletcher, *Intellectual Development of John Milton*, 2: 651.

Greek and even Roman authors, too.[21] With the exception of *Platonis Menexenus* (1587), none of Plato's works was published in England until 1673, when a Latin translation, *De Rebus Divinis*, appeared, followed in 1675 by *Plato his Apology of Socrates, and Phaedo*.[22] Another such writer is Valerius Maximus. His *Facta et Dicta Memorabilia* (Memorable Deeds and Sayings) was a collection of the same kind of exemplary anecdotes as early modern readers were making, a manual for the orators of Valerius' own day. Judging by the evidence of library lists and notebooks, it was an extremely popular text, and was widely used in schools and universities. Yet it was only in 1675 that an English translation appeared, followed by a second edition and a Latin edition in 1678.[23] This example serves as a reminder of the continuing centrality of Latin texts, and of continental books, as part of the English book trade: the few English editions in no way reflect the extent to which this text was read and quoted in the later Stuart years.

But the period also saw the beginnings of a serious domestic Latin print trade, in terms of production rather than merely circulation, with English stationers printing their own editions of the classics in the ancient languages in increasing numbers.

The classics were also increasingly becoming available in other forms, broadening their reach beyond the members of the elite who had received an education in the exclusively male institutions of formal learning. A profit-driven print trade, an increasingly hungry and expanding market, and a healthy population of educated writers with an appetite for contributing to the sum of English learning created a flourishing tradition of literary translation, seeking to present in English as many of the ancient texts as possible. These translations, great in number and diverse in their nature and quality, occupied a central place in the literary landscape, shaping English writing throughout the period. They also represent sites where interlingual and intertextual encounters combined to produce an anglicized classical tradition: as the seventeenth century progressed, works of ancient history and literature became firmly embedded in the English literary context. Multiple translations of works were now, for the first time, on sale simultaneously, and they were increasingly available in a variety of formats and sizes, to suit the diverse tastes and budgets of an ever-growing readership, including women and those of the 'middling sort' who had not been classically educated.

Older translations, such as Thomas North's edition of Plutarch's *Lives*, first published in 1579, continued to be popular and influential.[24] Indeed, they remained the only English

---

[21] Diogenes Laertius, *Laertiou Diogenous Peri bion dogmaton kai apophthegmaton ton en philosophia eudokimesanton* (1664); Diogenes Laertius, *The Lives, Opinions, and Remarkable Sayings of the Most Famous Ancient Philosophers* (1688).

[22] Plato, *Platonis Menexenus* (Cambridge, 1587); Plato, *Platonis De rebys divinis* (Cambridge, 1673); Plato, *Plato his Apology of Socrates, and Phaedo* (1675).

[23] Valerius Maximus, *Q Valerius Maximus his Collections of the Memorable Acts and Sayings of Orators, Philosophers, Statesmen, and Other Illustrious Persons of the Ancient Romans* (1675); Valerius Maximus, *Romae antiquae* (1678); Valerius Maximus, *Valerii Maximi Dictorum factorumque memorabilium* (1678).

[24] The following editions were published: Plutarch, *The Lives of the Noble Grecians and Romans* (1657); Plutarch, *The Lives of the Noble Grecians and Romans* (Cambridge, 1676).

translations to be printed, when certain classical authors were out of vogue: Philemon Holland's Livy, which had first appeared in 1600, was printed throughout the seventeenth century, unrivalled by more modern versions, the taste for Livy having waned in favour of Tacitus. But these Elizabethan editions now competed for market share with modern renderings of many of the ancient authors, translations which reflected a new prose style and a changing political context, and publishers often forsook them in favour of more recent, fashionable, contemporary versions. These often made use of the better elements of earlier translators' work, but very much positioned themselves as part of a self-conscious programme of modernization, updating and improving upon what had gone before. Chief among the improvements to which translators laid claim were a more accurate text and a freer literary style. Thomas Lodge's collected works of Josephus, translated via the French and first published in 1602, enjoyed continued success until it was challenged in 1702 by Sir Roger L'Estrange's new translation, 'All Carefully Revis'd, and Compar'd with the Original Greek'.[25] This title-page advertisement of scholarly accuracy and fidelity to original sources reflects the same concerns over the quality of the Elizabethan translations exhibited by Dryden, writing in his preface to the new 1683 translation of Plutarch's *Lives*. North's 1579 translation was made via the French of Amyot, who had himself worked from a Latin translation: it was therefore 'only from the French, so it suffer'd this ... disadvantage, ... that it was but a Copy of a Copy, and that too but lamely taken from the Greek original'.[26] By contrast, the translation for which Dryden supplied the preface was made directly from the Greek by a team of well-qualified scholars; the work completely superseded North's translation and enjoyed great success for many decades to come.

The new translations were also important prose creations in their own right, reflecting the development of English literary style in the late Stuart age. Verse translations from Greek and Latin—including Pope's Homer, Dryden's Virgil, Horace, and Ovid, to name but a few—have received far greater critical attention than translations in prose, but both exhibit the same spirit of cultural appropriation and linguistic transformation, providing opportunities for translators to demonstrate their stylistic prowess and to contribute to the building of a peculiarly English model of neo-classicism that might challenge the dominance of France. Prominent men of letters, as well as less well-known scholars, turned these works into a new kind of English, appropriate for their time: Dryden translated the first part of Tacitus' *Annals*, published in 1698; Thomas Hobbes prepared a second edition of his 1629 translation of Thucydides, which was published in 1676.[27] The object, as with verse translations, was to convey the spirit of the

---

[25] Josephus, *The Works of Flavius Josephus: Translated into English by Sir Roger L'Estrange, Knight* (1702).

[26] Plutarch, *Plutarchs Lives, translated from the Greek by several hands ... The First Volume* (1683), sigs. B2v–3r.

[27] Tacitus, *The Annals and History of Cornelius Tacitus* (1698); Thucydides, *The History of the Grecian War in Eight Books ... Faithfully Translated from the Original by Thomas Hobbes of Malmsbury ... the Second Edition, Much Correction and Amended* (1676).

source text, rather than maintain slavish fidelity to the original grammatical construction, thereby offering an entirely modern work of English literature to readers, relevant to the concerns of the current age, which yet retained the authority and wisdom of the ancient world. Dryden's prefaces to a range of classical translations provide the most comprehensive statements of this philosophy:

> The common way which we have taken, is not a Literal Translation, but a kind of Paraphrase; or somewhat which is yet more loose, betwixt a Paraphrase and Imitation. It was not possible for us, or any Men, to have made it pleasant, any other way ... We have follow'd our Authors, at greater distance; tho' not Step by Step ... A Noble Authour would not be persu'd too close by a Translator. We lose his Spirit, when we think to take his Body. The grosser Part remains with us, but the Soul is flown away, in some Noble Expression or some delicate turn of Words, or Thought.[28]

Matthew Morgan, in his preface to the highly successful multi-volume edition of Plutarch's *Moralia* made 'by several hands' and first published in 1684, noted the dangers of being 'too faithful a translator'; the man who did this, 'by confining himself to the starch'd Method, he leaves the Sense as perplex'd as he found it ... He that goes this way to work, shall never make Plutarch intelligible'. This failure to write freely and elegantly in English, Morgan alleged, had been one of the chief detractions of the first English translation of the *Moralia*, that of Philemon Holland (1603): 'As for our Countryman, Dr. Holland, it must be allowed him, that he understood Greek, but whoever reads his Translation, and is impartial, must say, that he was by no means a Master of the English Tongue.'[29]

Indeed, translators in the later seventeenth century were scathing of the poor phrasing of their earlier colleagues, and frequently asserted the extent to which the language had improved since the Elizabethan age, as may be seen from Dryden's preface to the new translation of Plutarch's *Lives* (1683). This is not necessarily a reflection of the great advances in prose style that had taken place over the intervening century, and should perhaps be viewed as a wider literary trope as much as a genuine indication of progress; Dryden criticized North's 1579 translation of the text in much the same manner as he also criticized Shakespeare's verse, for example: 'the English language was then unpolish'd, and far from the perfection which it has since attain'd. So that the first Version is not only ungrammatical and ungraceful, but in many places almost unintelligible.'[30] Nevertheless, that later seventeenth-century translators sought to position themselves clearly in opposition to earlier styles of writing demonstrates, at the very

---

[28] Juvenal, *The satires of Decimus Junius Juvenalis translated into English Verse by Mr. Dryden and Several Other Eminent Hands* (1693), sig. n2v. Although this is a verse translation, Dryden's principle was the same for prose.

[29] Plutarch, *Plutarchs Morals translated from the Greek by Several Hands*, 2 vols. (1684), sigs. A3v–4r, A6r–v.

[30] Plutarch, *Plutarchs Lives ... First Volume*, sigs. B2v–3r.

least, a conscious desire to define their practice as new, particular, and deserving of literary acclaim. Modern prose translations not only provided the sense of the words but amplified the excellence of the text: 'the very Spirit of the Original, Transfus'd into the Traduction. And in one word; Plutarchs Worthies made yet more famous, by a Translation that gives a farther Lustre, even to Plutarch himself.'[31]

Significantly, the claims made by the late-Stuart translators in their prefaces seem generally more plausible than those of their sixteenth-century counterparts. Philemon Holland was perhaps only paying lip-service to the humanist ideal of improving the reach of classical learning when he avowed in 1600, in the preface to his magisterial and extremely expensive folio of Livy, that in translating it into English he was providing a service not just to the educated elite, but to 'the people in generall': 'A desire I had to performe in some sort, that which is profitable to the most, namely, an english Historie of that which of all others (if I have any iudgement) affourdeth most plenteous examples of devout zeale in their kind, of wisedome, pollicie, iustice, valour, and all vertues whatsoever.'[32] Even had that been his intention, the book was far beyond the reach of most purses. By the middle or end of the seventeenth century, on the other hand, it is far easier to believe such statements, with a century of development in the economy and the print trade enabling new consumers to partake of literary culture. The edition of Plutarch's *Lives* published by Jacob Tonson in 1683 was printed in octavo as a five-volume set. This was far more feasible a purchase for most members of the middling sort than the status-symbol folios of the Elizabethan period had been; the smaller size and concomitant price for each volume make it much more likely that Tonson believed his own words when he asserted in his preface to the reader that he produced the books 'for the service of my Country, and for a Common good.'[33] Similarly, William Leake, who published a pocket-sized translation of Cicero's *Cato*, informed his readers that he acted from similar motives: 'moved for the general good, to publish it thus abroad unto the world, beleeving that it will be a delight to the Aged, and a great benefit to the unlearned in the Latin Tongue, who may in their own Language read the sage wisdome of former times.'[34]

Translators, as well as the publishers who had the most to gain financially from selling their classical wares to an ever-wider market, believed (or at least, asserted) themselves to be writing for a readership far beyond the traditional, male, classically educated, scholarly elite, and for wider reasons than simply to educate future leaders and magistrates. Ferrand Spence, for example, prefacing his 1684 translation of Lucian, declared himself to be 'so public a spirited person, that I am willing to Communicate him to the Age.'[35] Not only were the Restoration translators more plausible in their avowal of public service as a spur to literary activity than earlier colleagues; prose literature was

---

[31] The publisher Jacob Tonson's epistle to the reader in *Plutarchs Lives ... First Volume*, sig. C6v.
[32] Livy, *The Romane Historie* (1600), sigs. A4r, A3v.
[33] *Plutarchs Lives ... First Volume*, sig. C6r.
[34] Cicero, *Cato Major, or, The Book of Old Age* (1648), sigs. A5v–6r.
[35] Lucian, *Lucians Works Translated from the Greek ... by Ferrand Spence* (1684), sig. †2v.

cited directly as a source of pleasure and entertainment by those who presented classical translations to the reader, as well as being educational. Dryden, while acknowledging the importance of history as a source of instruction to those who were engaged in public affairs, nevertheless stressed the enjoyment a well-crafted piece of historical prose could bring a reader, in his preface to Tonson's edition of Plutarch's *Lives*:

> I should take occasion to write somewhat concerning History it self: But I think to commend it is unnecessary: For the profit and pleasure of that study are both so very obvious, that a quick Reader will be before hand with me, and imagine faster than I can write. Besides that the post is taken up already, and few Authors have travell'd this way, but who have strewed it with Rhetorick, as they pass'd. For my own part, who must confess it to my shame, that I never read any thing but for pleasure, it has alwayes been the most delightful Entertainment of my life.[36]

Some translators even stated explicitly their sense that even those with the ability to read scholarly, classical texts might lack the time or inclination to do so, preferring something easier and lighter; thus they justified their production of abridged and excerpted translations as a 'short cut' to the assimilation of useful pleasant entertainment and historical knowledge, whatever the status of the reader. In his collaboration with John Chantry on a translation of Plutarch's *Lives* entitled *The Worthies of the World* (1665), David Lloyd addressed his dedicatee, the Duke of Monmouth, on the subject of his decision to translate and reduce the work in a manner that recognized not all audiences enjoyed their classical texts in learned form: 'It's in English, my Lord, because the unevennesse of his Greek should not exercise your patience; it's abridged, because the tediousnesse of the Story should not tire your Industry. It is fit that Learning in all the parts of it should put off it's harshnesse and impertinence, to endear its Notions to such its nobles Votaries as your Honour, in a way at once most pithy, and most polite.'[37] A similarly anti-intellectual aspiration was evinced by John Bulteel in his translation of the apophthegms of Plutarch, Diogenes Laertius, and others (1683). Dedicating the book to a female patron, Esther Woodward, he explained his rejection of the methods of earlier editors and translators, on the grounds that their work:

> smells too much of the Colledge. The mind loves to range freely here and there from Flower to Flower, like the Bees, without fixing too long upon any one, and so gather's that Honey which is distributed into little Cells, where every thing lyes in it's own place without disorder, and where every particular may be found out upon occasion. One would say, the mind were jealous of it's prerogative, and displeased when any one does undertake to cut out it's work, or prescribe any other Method besides it's own. Thence proceeds the disgust [that] is often taken in the Learning of

---

[36] *Plutarchs Lives ... First Volume*, 80.
[37] David Lloyd, 'The Epistle Dedicatory', in Plutarch, *The Worthies of the World, or, The Lives of the Most Heroick Greeks and Romans* (1665), sigs. A3v–4r.

the Sciences, where the Mind must be confined and obliged to certain rules for it's instruction.[38]

Like Lloyd, Bulteel abbreviated his source text when rendering it into English, as well as updating it and transposing it into the cultural and linguistic modes of his own time, defending his creative innovations as a profitable and reasonable response to the changing literary styles and reading habits:

> to make them the more quaint and concise, which is an essential property of an *Apophthegme*, I have pared away all the Superfluous Circumstances, because when we would see a thing perfectly well we must remove from about it every other Body that might hide or obscure it. Sometimes it was necessary to give things another Air and expression then the Author, to adapt it to the Language we speak, and the Age we live in ... If therefore an *Apophthegme* be met with here, which shall not be found in *Plutarch*, or that it speak otherwise then he relates it, let me not be rashly condemned, but first examine the reasons of it's variation upon the grounds above mentioned.[39]

Vernacular literary translations of the classics therefore took their place on the bookshelves of English private libraries alongside their Latin and Greek counterparts, freely available for all literate members of the household who cared to read them, including women: 'for you must know we Read Plutarch now 'tis Translated', wrote Elizabeth Rowe in the preface to her *Poems on Several Occasions* (1696), demonstrating her place within fashionable literate circles by means of reference to Tonson's best-selling edition of 1683.[40] The popularity of handbooks designed to facilitate a deeper understanding of the classics, such as Pierre Gautruche's *Poetical History*, translated from the French by Marius D'Assigny, further points to the appetite for classical learning among a new kind of reader: from its first appearance in 1671, ten editions were published before the end of the century.[41] Records of book ownership, such as book auction catalogues, confirm the success of these volumes: the classical authors were the books most commonly owned by men with private libraries, after the Bible and the prayer book.[42] These catalogues also remind us that readers continued to own editions in the classical languages, and older translations—it is never easy to determine which books in a library were actually read—acquired through inheritance or the second-hand book trade, or representing the acquisitions of a long lifetime. One such list dating from

---

[38] John Bulteel, *The Apophthegmes of the Ancients taken out of Plutarch, Diogenes Laertius, Elian, Atheneus, Stobeus, Macrobius and others: Collected into One Volume for the Benefit and Pleasure of the Ingenious* (1683), sigs. A6v–7r.

[39] Bulteel, *Apophthegmes*, sigs. A7r–8v.

[40] Elizabeth Rowe, *Poems on Several Occasions Written by Philomela* (1696), sig. A3v.

[41] Pierre Gautruche, *The Poetical Histories being a Compleat Collection of All the Stories Necessary for a Perfect Understanding of the Greek and Latine Poets and Other Ancient Authors* (1671).

[42] David Pearson, 'Patterns of Book Ownership in Late Seventeenth-Century England', *The Library*, 7th ser., 11 (2010), 139–67; David Pearson, *Book Ownership in Stuart England* (Oxford: Oxford University Press, 2021).

1688, prepared for the sale of books belonging to an anonymous 'learned, and eminent citizen of London, sometime-since deceased', includes editions of Hobbes' Thucydides (1676), Henry Holcroft's Procopius (1653), Diodorus Siculus translated by Henry Cogan (1653), and Robert Codrington's Quintus Curtius Rufus (1652), but also copies of the first edition of Hobbes' translation of Thucydides (in the 1634 imprint), and many of the great Elizabethan translations, in first editions and much later printings: the Appian of 1578, North's Plutarch, Lodge's Seneca, and Holland's Pliny and Ammianus Marcellinus, along with his translation of Plutarch's *Moralia*.[43] It was not uncommon for those of a more scholarly bent to own multiple editions of the same text; if the scraps of extant marginal evidence are representative of reading practices more widely, they apparently compared the editions in search of the perfect reading of the original text.

Literary Models

Classical texts exerted an undeniable influence on much English prose in the seventeenth and eighteenth centuries, inspiring writers and acting as models for a variety of different forms and genres. Some of the characteristics inherited from the classics are subtle, while others are plain to see; some authors directly avowed their adherence to the rules set out by their ancient predecessors, while others outwardly rejected certain classical authorities while following them implicitly. Recent publications provide detailed examples of all these, and the following paragraphs are simply a brief introduction to the more major literary debts owed by English prose to the Greeks and the Romans.[44]

Philosophical and discursive works of prose, composed as essays and dialogues, formed a more or less unbroken link to the classical tradition. Drawing upon, and adapting for their own purposes, the writings of the Greeks and the Romans, published writers and private gentlemen reflected upon the world, seeking wisdom that they might use in order to improve society, and live their lives more wholesomely and profitably. The essay form was believed to be essentially Senecan in origin; Platonic dialogues provided the pattern for philosophical enquiry; and classical authorities were essential to the successful discussion of almost every topic, while classical rhetoric provided the means by which to conduct it. Classical histories and historians acted as clear precedents for English writers to follow, and this they did throughout the seventeenth and eighteenth centuries. Greek and Roman models exerted a strong influence upon English historical writing, especially, though far from exclusively, the writings of Tacitus, the most

---

[43] Edward Millington, *A Catalogue of Books ... Contained in the Library of a Learned, and Eminent Citizen of London, Sometime-Since Deceased* (1688).

[44] For example, the essays in Patrick Cheney and Philip Hardie (eds.), *The Oxford History of Classical Reception in English Literature, Volume 2: 1558–1660* (Oxford: Oxford University Press, 2015); David Hopkins and Charles Martindale (eds.), *The Oxford History of Classical Reception in English Literature, Volume 3: 1660–1790* (Oxford: Oxford University Press, 2012).

popular of the ancient historians in the seventeenth century not only for his political acuity but for his eloquent phrasing and moralizing tone.[45] Although the late-Stuart historians largely abandoned the ancient tradition of invented speech-writing in favour of more objective evidence, the instructive nature of ancient history, with a focus on analysing causation and a multitude of oral examples illustrating a succinct narrative, was a classical trait that also marked the newly written English histories of Hobbes, Milton, Clarendon, and their colleagues. Similarly, the developing polemical genre of secret histories, inspired by Procopius and deployed most obviously in the war against 'popery and arbitrary government', invoked classical aims of analysing and exposing to the light the mysteries of state.[46] As Dryden explains in his 'Life of Plutarch':

> *Commentaries* or *Annals* are (as I may so call them) naked History: Or the plain relation of matter of fact, according to the succession of time, devested of all other Ornaments ... The method is the most natural that can be imagin'd ... The stile is easie, simple, unforc'd, and unadorn'd with the pomp of figures ... Of this kind the *Commentaries of Caesar* are certainly the most admirable; and after him the *Annals* of *Tacitus* may have place ... History properly so call'd may be describ'd by the addition of those parts, which are not requir'd to *Annals* ... dignity and gravity of stile is here necessary. That the guesses of secret causes, inducing to the actions, be drawn at least from the most probable circumstances, not perverted by the malignity of the Author to sinister interpretations, (of which *Tacitus* is accus'd;) but candidly laid down, and left to the Judgment of the Reader. That neither partiality or prejudice appear: But that truth may every where be Sacred ... Next to *Thucydides* in this kind, may be accounted *Polybius* amongst the *Grecians*; *Livy,* tho not free from superstition, nor *Tacitus* from ill nature, amongst the *Romans*.[47]

The writing of biography, too, witnessed significant developments over our period. In the ancient world, it had been conceived as a literary form in its own right, discrete from history, with its own particular value. This is how it began to be viewed in the later seventeenth century, following the tripartite distinction between different forms of history proposed by Francis Bacon in 1605:

> History which may be called just and parfite Historie, is of three kinds, according to the obiect which it propoundeth, or pretendeth to represent: for it either representeth a time, or a person, or an action. The first we call chronicles, the second lives, and

---

[45] On Tacitism and the development of Tacitean prose alongside other humanist models in early modern England by the beginning of our period, see Nicholas McDowell, 'Political Prose', in Andrew Hadfield (ed.), *The Oxford Handbook to English Prose 1500–1640* (Oxford: Oxford University Press, 2013), 360–79.

[46] See Rebecca Bullard and Rachel Carnell (eds.), *The Secret History in Literature, 1660–1820* (Cambridge, 2017), especially Rebecca Bullard's 'Introduction' and Martine W. Brownley, 'Secret History and Seventeenth-Century Historiography', 1–14, 33–45; see also Chapter 19 on 'Histories' by Niall Allsopp and Chapter 34 by Rebecca Bullard on 'Secret Histories'.

[47] *Plutarchs Lives... First Volume*, sig. G2r–4r.

the third narrations, or relations. Of these although the first bee the most compleate and absolute kinde of Historie, and hath most estimation and glory: yet the second excelleth it in profit and vse, and the third in veritie & sinceritie.[48]

Thomas Fuller, in his *History of the Worthies of England* (1662), followed Plutarch's insistence on the gathering of accurate facts when he prepared his work, accusing earlier 'biographists' of 'abominable untruths'.[49] The glimpses into the innermost workings of men's characters had long been responsible for the success of the classical collections of biographies, especially Suetonius' *Lives of the Twelve Caesars* or Plutarch's *Lives of the Noble Grecians and Romans*. Although there is perhaps little of this in Anthony Wood's antiquarian *Athenae Oxoniensis* (1691–2), much of Plutarch's concern with the interpretation of character as well as the accurate recording of facts can be found in John Aubrey's collective biographies, *Minutes of Lives* (later, of course, published as *Brief Lives*).[50] The same is true of the biographies of Izaak Walton, composed from 1640 onwards, including the lives of John Donne, Sir Henry Wootton, Richard Hooker, and George Herbert; while John Dryden's 'Life of Plutarch' employed the term 'biography' as it is used in modern English, meaning:

> the history of particular Mens lives ... confin'd in action, and treating of Wars and Counsels, and all other publick affairs of Nations, only as they relate to him, whose Life is written, or as his fortunes have a particular dependance on them, or connection to them: All things here are circumscrib'd, and driven to a point, so as to terminate in one.... Thus then the perfection of the Work, and the benefit arising from it are both more absolute in Biography than in History ... here you are led into the private lodgings of the hero; you see him in undress, and are made familiar with his most private actions and conversations.[51]

Numerous other kinds of writing engaged with the classical tradition to a greater or lesser extent (indeed, this extent continues to provoke debate among scholars). Some seventeenth-century writers traced modern imaginative literature or 'fiction' back to the prose romances of the ancient world.[52] The epistolary tradition was clearly rooted in the letters of Cicero, Pliny the Younger, and Seneca. The diarists owed more than a little to the commentaries of ancients such as Julius Caesar, as records of autobiographical and historical events composed using the writer's particular individual experience, giving

---

[48] Francis Bacon, *The Two Bookes of Francis Bacon. Of the Proficience and Aduancement of Learning, Diuine and Humane* (1605), sig. Cc3r.
[49] Thomas Fuller, *The History of the Worthies of England* (1662), sig. B4v.
[50] See Chapter 9 by Kate Bennett on 'Brief Lives and Characters'.
[51] *Plutarchs Lives ... First Volume*, sig. G4v; see also Chapter 7 by Julie A. Eckerle on 'Biography and Autobiography'.
[52] See, for example, Helen Moore, 'Prose Romance', in Cheney and Hardie (eds.), *Oxford History of Classical Reception in English Literature. Volume 2*, 291–310; Henry Power, 'The Classics and the English Novel', in Hopkins and Martindale (eds.), *Oxford History of Classical Reception in English Literature. Volume 3*, 547–68.

rise to the use of the word 'memoirs' in this sense from the late-1650s onwards[53]. Nor should we forget the many new works of English prose made by individuals for their private use, translations from any number of Greek or Latin texts that lived only within the pages of a manuscript notebook or in private, domestic readings and were never intended for any manner of publication. What is certain is that the classical inheritance continued to extend its influence across almost the whole corpus of English writing in the later Stuart period: an influence that would endure far longer than that dynasty or the one that followed.

[53] See *OED*, 'memoir, *n*.', 2.

CHAPTER 4

CONTINENTAL INFLUENCES

ALEXIS TADIÉ

SIR FOPLING (*to* EMILIA)   A thousand pardons, madam—some civilities due of course upon the meeting a long absent friend. The *éclat* of so much beauty, I confess, ought to have charmed me sooner.
EMILIA   The *brillant* of so much good language, sir, has much more power than the little beauty I can boast.
SIR FOPLING   I never saw anything prettier than this high work on your *point d'Espagne*.
EMILIA   'Tis not so rich as *point de Venice*.[1]

THIS brief exchange from *The Man of Mode* (1676) satirizes the introduction of foreign words in England and their affected use by fops in the period of the Restoration. Although the character of Sir Fopling Flutter appears ridiculous in part through his use of French words, Emilia's wit relies on an equal command of French expressions. Except for *point de Venice*, the *OED* cites Etherege's play as the first occurrence for all the French expressions used in this excerpt. Restoration comedy is perhaps the most visible, and indeed *brillant*, testimony of the import of French words in the English language in the period of the Restoration, when both the courtly circles that had been in exile in France during the Civil War and, later, the exile of Huguenots from France after the revocation of the Edict of Nantes in 1685, enhanced the contacts between the two languages. These contacts developed further through the exile of Jacobites at the Court of Saint-Germain. Aphra Behn, in her preface to her translation of Fontenelle, exclaims that 'it is Modish to Ape the *French* in every thing: Therefore, we not only naturalize their words, but words they steal from other Languages'.[2]

These linguistic borrowings have to be placed in the context of the importance of Latin for the evolution of the English language since the middle of the sixteenth century. Latin was crucial for the elaboration of a specialized language in disciplines ranging

---

[1] George Etherege, *The Man of Mode*, ed. Michael Neil (London: Methuen Drama, 2019), 3.2.153–60.
[2] Aphra Behn, 'The Translator's Preface', Bernard Le Bovier de Fontenelle, *A Discovery of New Worlds* (1688), sig. B2r.

from theology to botany or architecture. The second half of the seventeenth century saw a larger import of French words, although some did not survive later in the eighteenth century, after the French Revolution. In the second half of the seventeenth century French borrowings included military and diplomatic language, words belonging to the social register (such as *metier, faux pas, beau*), and vocabulary relating to arts and literature, dress, games, dancing, and food (e.g. *memoirs, ballet, nom-de-plume*, or *vinaigrette*).[3] The *OED* reports the expression *belles lettres* first came into use in the English language towards the end of the period covered by this handbook, in 1710, when Jonathan Swift introduced it in an essay for the *Tatler*. Borrowings from other European languages, such as Italian, did occasionally come by way of France, although words describing Italian products, social customs, and arts were particularly significant (in the arts, for instance, the vocabulary of architecture or of opera). The introduction of some Spanish words also testified to the links between England and Spain, while vocabulary relating to commerce, warfare, and art was occasionally borrowed from the Dutch. Such borrowings and exchanges prompted conflicting attitudes, the introduction of French words being seen in some circles as a corruption of the language—defenders of English praised its ancient, unaffected character and might even call for the rescue of 'our captivated Language from the Fetters of that Tongue'.[4] The opposition was of course as much social and political as it was linguistic because the French words which were criticized were likely to be those which were used by the courtly circles. It is worth noting that 'Words borrowed from French after 1500 make a very much smaller contribution than those borrowed before 1500 to the high-frequency vocabulary of modern English, or to its basic vocabulary (as reflected by basic meaning lists)'.[5]

This brief overview shows the importance of the French language as a main source for linguistic loans in the seventeenth century and is in many ways consonant with literary relations between England and the rest of Europe. Despite recurrent political tensions and indeed wars between France and England (such as the War of the Ligue of Augsburg of 1689-97 or the war of the Spanish succession of 1702-13) linguistic contacts between the two countries were crucial to literary and artistic evolutions, in England at any rate.[6] Books in French were accessible in the British Isles, in England as well as in Ireland—some were printed in London, in French. Translations from the French were ubiquitous, and a number of translations from other European languages came into English by way of French translations. All genres of literature were affected by the process. The theatre

---

[3] See Terttu Nevalainen, 'Early Modern English Lexis and Semantics', in Roger Lass, ed., *The Cambridge History of the English Language* (Cambridge: Cambridge University Press, 2000), 332–458 (368ff.); Richard Scholar, *Émigrés: French Words That Turned English* (Princeton: Princeton University Press, 2022).

[4] Quoted in R. F. Jones, *The Triumph of the English Language: A Survey of Opinions Concerning the Vernacular from the Introduction of Printing to the Restoration* (Oxford: Oxford University Press, 1953), 258.

[5] Philip Durkin, *Borrowed Words: A History of Loanwords in English* (Oxford: Oxford University Press, 2014), 348.

[6] This is also true of economic relations. The definitions of a national or of a foreigner could fluctuate according to circumstances. See Renaud Morieux, *The Channel: England, France, and the Construction of a Maritime Border in the Eighteenth Century* (Cambridge: Cambridge University Press, 2016), 328.

relied extensively on French plays, sometimes rewriting them under different titles, such as Wycherley's *The Plain Dealer* (1676), which is based on Molière's *Le Misanthrope*. With *Psyche* (1675), Shadwell translated and adapted the French *Psyché* by Molière, Corneille, and Quinault, and in so doing was not only bringing to England a French text but also a whole new conception of the theatrical performance—he also imported from France all the material possibilities of drama, complete with sets, machinery, dance, and singing. Access to French prose was made easy by numerous translations and collections, such as Richard Bentley's twelve-volume collection of novels, *Modern Novels*, published in 1692, each volume containing three to four novels. Some Spanish texts reached the English reading public by way of their French translations, such as the celebrated *Amadis de Gaula*, which was only translated directly into English in 1664. And the oriental tale came to inhabit the English literary tradition thanks to Galland's French translation of the *Arabian Nights*, early in the eighteenth century.

Numerous genres of European prose were available in English, ranging from fictions, including secret histories as well as more refined works such as *La Princesse de Clèves*, to history and travel literature, such as François Bernier's *Histoire de la dernière révolution des États du grand Moghol*, which was immediately translated into English, reprinted, and anthologized,[7] to philosophical treatises such as Fontenelle's *Entretiens sur la pluralité des mondes*, which was translated three times in the last quarter of the seventeenth century, or again to collections of moral philosophy such as La Rochefoucauld's *Maximes*, published in England towards the end of the century. It can therefore be argued that English prose in the period entertained close relationships with Continental prose, in particular in the French language, and it is one of the aims of this chapter to try and ascertain the extent to which English prose was indeed English in the period.

Divergences

The seventeenth century witnessed an increasing assertion of the Englishness of its literary and philosophical traditions. While at the beginning of the century Bacon thought that a Latin version of *The Advancement of Learning* (1605) was needed if his ideas were to circulate, the picture is different at the end of the seventeenth century when for instance John Locke's *Essay on Human Understanding* (1689) written in English travels to the Continent by means of the classic translation by Pierre Coste.[8] This phenomenon,

---

[7] Other French travel writers who were important sources for knowledge of the East include Jean-Baptiste Tavernier, whose *Six Voyages ... through Turky, into Persia and the East-Indies*, came out in an English translation in 1677 or Jean Chardin, whose *Travels ... into Persia and the East-Indies* were published in London in 1688.

[8] Locke of course knew French, went to France in 1670, and was acquainted with French philosophy. He started to translate Pierre Nicole's *Essais de morale* (first published 1671) in English. See *John Locke as Translator: Three of the Essais of Pierre Nicole in French and English*, ed. Jean S. Yolton (Oxford: Voltaire Foundation, 2000).

which also signals the wane of Latin as *lingua franca* and the continued development of vernacular traditions, is not limited to language use. Literary genres could indeed be enrolled to fashion a genealogy of national literature.

This is, for instance, the case for the essay. At the beginning of the century, Bacon writes in the dedication to his *Essayes* that 'The word is late, but the thing is auncient'. By emphasizing the recent borrowing of the word from Montaigne's French *Essais*, Bacon seems to imply the recent constitution of the category; but he is quick to place his enterprise in a long history which goes back for instance to Seneca's *Epistles to Lucilius*: essays are 'dispersed Meditacions, thoughe conveyed in the forme of Epistles'.[9] Such connections with the inheritance of Latin prose were perhaps necessary to emphasize continuity and, paradoxically perhaps, to distance his work from the French tradition of Montaigne. On the other hand, with Bacon's work, a distinctly English tradition was born. This is at any rate what William Hazlitt suggests when he takes stock of the genre, in order, perhaps, to find his own place in the genealogy.[10] The line includes writers such as Sir William Cornwallis, Ben Jonson, Abraham Cowley, or William Temple, before new forms developed in the eighteenth century in the periodical essays of Steele, Addison, or Johnson. This does not preclude the possibility for the 'English' essay to find inspiration across the Channel, in Montaigne in particular. Cornwallis, whose essays—first published in 1600–1—are contemporary with Bacon's, derives from Montaigne a tone, a style, and a manner that are characterized by a lack of flourish and a personal emphasis. Cowley's essays, written during the Restoration, are closer to Bacon in tone, but they lead to a last, personal essay. 'Of Myself' takes the form of a short autobiography, where the topics of the previous essays are applied to the life of the author, lessons drawn from the consideration of his own example, and we find the writer investigating something like his inner life.[11] The publication of a new translation of Montaigne by Charles Cotton, in 1685–6, which sparked a renewed interest in the genre of the essay and in the work of Montaigne in particular, further complicates the English character of the essay, in the seventeenth century at any rate.

Such ambivalence in the constitution of English generic traditions can be encountered in attitudes towards the prose romance. Like the essay, the romance claims connections with ancient texts, going back to Heliodorus's *Aethiopika*, but the English tradition finds in Sidney's 1590 *Arcadia* its most perfect incarnation, and critics have rightly identified this work as the acme of the genre in England. Recent revaluations of English romances have brought out important links between Sidney's work, for instance, and seventeenth-century romances, sometimes dismissed as imitations of a French genre,

---

[9] 'Dedicatory Epistles', in *The Oxford Francis Bacon. Vol. 15: The Essayes or Counsels, Civill and Morall*, ed. Michael Kiernan (Oxford: Oxford University Press, 1985), 317. See further Chapter 15 on 'Essays' by Kathryn Murphy.

[10] William Hazlitt, 'On the Periodical Essayists', in *Lectures on the English Comic Writers* (1819), 177–207.

[11] See Alan De Gooyer, 'Sensibility and Solitude in Cowley's Familiar Essay', *Restoration*, 25 (2001), 1–18 (18).

while the influence of Barclay's *Argenis* (published in Latin in 1621 and translated into English in 1625 and 1628) is generally recognized. Critics have underlined the resilience of romances in the seventeenth century and have called our attention to the important debates surrounding such texts. While Amelia Zurcher explains that romance is the dominant type of prose fiction in England in the seventeenth century, and that it should not only be read as political allegory, James Grantham Turner shows its complexities and transformations, contrasting old and new romance, insisting in particular on the fact that 'romance' and 'novel' were used in conflicting and fluctuating ways to define and categorize prose fiction.[12] Romance in the seventeenth century originally referred to chivalric romance, exemplified by *Amadis de Gaule*, but was on the wane during the period, while the 'new' genre centred on love between famous characters, and emphasized historical probability.

French romances circulated freely in England at the time; but certain writers recognized the importance of distinguishing a specific tradition in English. For instance, in the preface to his 1660 *Aretina; or, The Serious Romance*, entitled '*An Apologie for ROMANCES*', George Mackenzie rejects the attacks which the genre has endured; he defends its virtues, suggesting that romance is superior to history in that it teaches us not what was done but what should be done (something which Sidney had also underlined). He further praises the tradition to which such texts belong: '*who should blush to trace in these paths, which the famous* Sidney, Scuderie, Barkley, *and* Broghill *hath beaten for them, besides thousands of Ancients, and Moderns, Ecclesiasticks, and Laicks, Spaniards, French, and Italians, to remunerat whose endeavours, fame hath Wreathed Garlands.*'[13] He then alludes to Heliodorus as the great originator of the genre. Zurcher has suggested that such a striking enumeration which insists on British authors (Sidney, Barclay, Boyle) over and above French authors (Georges de Scudéry) 'confirms that in seventeenth-century Britain, English romance was not felt to be derivative of the French—if anything, the opposite was the case. And the fact that all of Mackenzie's examples are specifically prose romances suggests the importance of prose as a generic marker at mid-century'.[14] One would want to go further, though, and emphasize that at a time when French romances circulated widely, Mackenzie attempts to construct a different genealogy. In his apology, the author builds a narrative reminiscent of that ascribed to the essay, in which romance finds its roots in Antiquity, but enjoys a new life in the vernacular (*Aretina* is 'written originally in English'), away from the models which have come from abroad.

This is of course part of the rhetoric of prefaces; but such pronouncements show the ways in which authors tried to construct national histories for literary genres, in order to establish an alleged English specificity—even while, as is clearly the case with romance

---

[12] Amanda Zurcher, *Seventeenth-Century English Romance: Allegory, Ethics, and Politics* (New York; Basingstoke: Palgrave Macmillan, 2007); James Grantham Turner, 'Romance and the Novel in Restoration England', *Review of English Studies*, 63 (2012), 58–85.

[13] George Mackenzie, *Aretina; Or, The Serious Romance* (Edinburgh, 1660), 6.

[14] Zurcher, *Seventeenth-Century English Romance*, 65–6.

and to an extent with the essay, a number of French texts were available, and sometimes instrumental in shaping the genre. These two examples display the complexities of defining a tradition of English prose, and of articulating it to a significant body of work which may have come from the Continent. The invocation of the antiquity of the genre was perhaps seen as a further guarantee of the distinction of the contemporary, English practice. Such rhetorical strategies aimed at identifying a domain in which the genre could flourish. They remind us that the national tradition is also based on the construction of difference and on the rejection, or perhaps the rhetorical oblivion, of Continental practices.

Presences

These attempts cannot conceal the fact that, in seventeenth-century England, European texts were ubiquitous. This ubiquity took at least two forms: the circulation of books in other languages, and the publication of translations. In turn the circulation of foreign books relied mainly on the importation of books from the Continent—French books for instance came from France but also from Holland. Books in other languages were also published in London in the early modern era, sometimes to be exported to Europe—Italian, Dutch, and Spanish books were published in London from the sixteenth century, German and Portuguese books from the seventeenth century.[15] In London, a study of the book trade for the year 1709 showed that 26 per cent of publishers produced books in foreign languages. After English and Latin books, French books were by far the most numerous, representing, according to David Shaw, one out of every ninety publications up to 1800; they had been continuously published since the beginning of the sixteenth century.[16] Books in French were directed at a diverse market, made up of Huguenot *émigrés* and of natural philosophers for whom French might be the new *lingua franca*, not to mention the French market which saw the reintroduction of French clandestine literature by way of London. Such London publications included, alongside religious books or official documents aimed at the French-speaking community, grammar books to learn French, as well as books to teach English to the Huguenots. This phenomenon was amplified in the eighteenth century, with the publication in London of a number of French authors. The example of Voltaire, who had a great number of works published in London, is perhaps the most famous: his *Letters Concerning the English Nation* first

---

[15] See Barry Taylor (ed.), *Foreign-Language Printing in London, 1500–1900* (Boston Spa: The British Library, 2002), which contains chapters on French, Dutch, Italian, and Greek publishing in London. See for instance Stephen Parkin, 'Italian Printing in London 1553–1900', 133–74 (139): 'the few significant Italian language publications from the seventeenth century all seem to have been published at least partly with Italy in mind.'

[16] David J. Shaw, 'French-Language Publishing to 1900', in Taylor (ed.), *Foreign-Language Printing*, 101–22 (101).

came out in English in 1733 and were published the following year in French. While some English printers and booksellers specialized in the printing of French books, the circulation of French books in London in 1700 also relied on an important number of French booksellers, the result of emigration from France. David Shaw, following Katherine Swift, has given us a picture of the role of émigrés in the London book trade.[17] Some French book traders, in particular after the revocation of the edict of Nantes, found in London a place to pursue their activities. They were mainly based along the Strand for reasons linked to the presence of a French church which would have attracted potential buyers, because this was conveniently located near the Exchanges, and also because the area fell outside the control of the Stationer's Company. Their catalogues indicate that they published books in French and in translation, as well as Latin and English books. Among the books they published could be found grammars of the French language in English as well as translations from the French, suggesting, as pointed out by Shaw, that these booksellers retained some links with France. It also indicates that the circles of readers included their fellow émigrés, as well as a wider public who might have some interest in France or in the French language.

A similar picture, although on a smaller scale, obtains in Dublin. Máire Kennedy and Geraldine Sheridan explain that 'works in French were imported by Dublin booksellers in the last two decades of the seventeenth century, and there is also evidence that books from England, Holland and France passed through the other major Irish ports before 1700'.[18] While the London bookmarket was the main source of supply for such books, direct maritime routes between Holland and Ireland were important for access to these books. Hence, the picture is consonant with England, books in French dealing with subjects ranging from literature to the sciences being available on the Irish market. Of course, the market for such books, in 1700, was relatively narrow, confined mainly to groups of émigrés as well as to the upper classes. Some Huguenot writers published their works in French in Dublin, in particular religious books, but this wass still rare around 1700. This rapid sketch of the trade in foreign books in London and Ireland points to the circulation and availability of French texts on the book market, and indicates a measure of linguistic and literary contact between the two worlds. It also suggests, at the very least, the coexistence of different linguistic traditions within the same literary space.

Relations with Continental Europe are of course largely based on translations. Translations into English are the main vehicle of knowledge of European prose traditions for the English reading public. Following Mary Helen McMurran, '[w]e can say with some accuracy that during the Restoration and early decades of the eighteenth century in Britain, as much as 30 to 35 percent of the market of available novels

[17] David J. Shaw, 'French Emigrés in the London Book Trade to 1850' in Robin Myers, Michael Harris, and Giles Mandelbrote (eds.), *The London Book Trade: Topographies of Print in the Metropolis from the Sixteenth Century* (New Castle, De.: Oak Knoll Press and London: The British Library, 2003), 127–43.

[18] Máire Kennedy and Geraldine Sheridan, 'The Trade in French Books in Eighteenth-Century Ireland', in Graham Gargett and Geraldine Sheridan (eds.), *Ireland and the French Enlightenment, 1700–1800* (London: Palgrave Macmillan, 1999), 17396 (173).

were translations, mostly from French prose fiction ... It leveled off near the middle of the century, but translations from French still accounted for 15 to 20 percent of novels published in the second half of the century.'[19] Romance occupies pride of place in the prose works translated from French into English.[20] Although, as mentioned above, there was an effort to try and identify an English tradition of romance, the translations of French romances in the second half of the seventeenth century were particularly important—writers such as Mademoiselle de Scudéry were translated from 1652, while Madame de Lafayette's *Princesse de Clèves* was first translated in 1679 and was also the object of a rather free theatrical adaptation by Nathaniel Lee (first published in 1689 but performed a few years earlier).[21] The *Lettres portugaises*, published in 1669, were translated in 1678 under the title of *Five Love-Letters from a Nun to a Cavalier*, but were generally thought to be authentic letters written by a Portuguese nun to a French officer, and their success in English through the numerous editions of Sir Roger L'Estrange's translation proved of considerable importance for the development of prose fiction— such as Aphra Behn's *Love-Letters between a Nobleman and His Sister* (1684–7).[22]

Certain individual works influenced English prose, sometimes with a gap between the date of publication in the original language and their resonance in English. Such is the case for instance of Rabelais. Almost one hundred years after the publication of the original, the 1653 partial translation by Sir Thomas Urquhart renewed the interest in Rabelais, fostered again at the very end of the century when Peter Anthony Motteux revised Urquhart's translation of the first three books of *Gargantua and Pantagruel* (five books, 1532–64) and added his own version of the fourth and fifth books as well as a substantial commentary. Subsequent translations and revisions in the early eighteenth century proved important in developing that interest. Appreciation for Rabelais's prose combined with ambiguous attitudes towards his morality had been apparent since the sixteenth and early seventeenth centuries, when he was also read in French and quoted by the likes of Francis Bacon, Ben Jonson—who owned a copy—and John Donne, while Randle Cotgrave used frequent citations from *Gargantua and Pantagruel* in his great 1611 French–English dictionary.[23] Later engagement with Rabelais's prose and imaginary is clearly apparent in *Gulliver's Travels* (1726) and *Tristram Shandy* (1759–67).

---

[19] Mary Helen McMurran, *The Spread of Novels: Translation and Prose Fiction in the Eighteenth Century* (Princeton, NJ, and Oxford: Princeton University Press, 2010), 46.

[20] See further Stephen Ahern, 'Prose Fiction: Excluding Romance', and Jennifer Birkett, 'Prose Fiction: Courtly and Popular Romance', in Stuart Gillespie and David Hopkins (eds.), *The Oxford History of Literary Translation in English. Volume 3: 1660–1790* (Oxford: Oxford University Press, 2005), 328–38, 339–49.

[21] A number of French novels went through translations into English that were immediately adapted to the stage; see Ros Ballaster, 'Bring(ing) Forth Alive the Conceptions of the Brain: The Transmission of French to English Fiction between Stage and Page', in Jacqueline Glomski and Isabelle Moreau (eds.), *Seventeenth-Century Fiction: Text and Transmission* (Oxford: Oxford University Press, 2016), 183–97.

[22] See further Chapter 5 on 'Amatory Prose' by Melissa Sanchez.

[23] See Anne Lake Prescott, *Imagining Rabelais in Renaissance England* (New Haven: Yale University Press, 1998). On Motteux's Rabelais, see also Chapter 20 on 'Keys' by Nicholas McDowell.

The example of Rabelais shows further the complexities of the circulation of French texts, either in the original or in translation. Translations may come at a late stage and foster an interest in an author even as his or her fortunes may have waned in the country of origin. This is the case with Bocaccio, whose *Decameron* still enjoyed five English editions between 1620—perhaps translated by Florio—and 1684.[24] Similar gaps in time are apparent in translations of the Spanish picaresque, which appeared in the early seventeenth century, but then faded. In the later seventeenth century, the picaresque enjoyed a certain amount of popularity with the public thanks to translations of Cervantes's *Exemplary Novels* or of Quevedo. The first part of *Don Quixote* was translated in 1612 by Thomas Shelton and the edition was revised and reissued throughout the seventeenth century, serving as the reference-point, rather than John Philips's new translation of 1687, until at least Motteux's version of 1700–3. The curious case of the picaresque is that when English prose (and French prose a little earlier) develops an interest for the genre, it is no longer practised in Spain. This is even more striking in the eighteenth century when Fielding publishes *Joseph Andrews* (1742) 'in the manner of Cervantes'.

The clearest, and perhaps best studied, case of literature in translation shaping English prose in the late seventeenth century comes with the *Arabian Nights*, whose French translation by Antoine Galland, completed in 1717, changed the ways in which the East was perceived and represented in prose. It is in a translation from the French that the *Nights* became available to the reading public, in particular through chapbooks, although manuscripts had been circulating in learned circles. The English translation was published between 1705 and 1721. The *Nights* not only afforded an entry into another world but provided a number of eighteenth-century writers with narrative devices that they exploited, from Addison to Johnson and Beckford.[25] Other important texts of fiction translated into English at the time helped define certain types of prose, such as comedy: they include Charles Sorel's *Berger comique* (translated in 1653) and his *Histoire comique de Francion* (translated in 1655) as well as Scarron's *Roman comique*, a common reference for a number of satirical writers well into the eighteenth century (John Bulteel published a translation in 1665, and the *Works* came out in 1700), and Furetière's *Roman bourgeois*, translated as *Scarron's City Romance* in 1671. Imaginary voyages, already in vogue through Francis Godwin's *The Man in the Moone* (1638), were given new impetus through the translations of Cyrano de Bergerac, in particular his *Histoire comique des états et empires de la lune* translated for the first time in 1659 and a second time in 1687—it must be counted among the ancestors of *Gulliver's Travels*. But one of the most successful translations from the French in the seventeenth century was a work of pedagogy, Fénelon's *Les Aventures de Télémaque* (1699), the first translation of which came

---

[24] See Guyda Armstrong, 'From Boccaccio to the Incogniti: The Cultural Politics of the Italian Tale in English Translation in the Seventeenth Century', in Glomski and Moreau (eds.), *Seventeenth-Century Fiction*, 159–82.

[25] See Rosalind Ballaster, *Fabulous Orients: Fictions of the East in England, 1662–1785* (Oxford: Oxford University Press, 2005); and Claire Gallien, *L'Orient anglais: connaissances et fictions au XVIIIe siècle* (Oxford: The Voltaire Foundation, 2011).

out almost immediately in 1699–1700 and was the work of several hands, including the Huguenot refugee Abel Boyer; it was then retranslated by John Ozell in 1715. *Telemachus* proved of interest to young readers in England and in colonial America throughout the eighteenth century and was available in bilingual editions, pointing to its use as a textbook. Extremely popular genres in France, such as the fairy tale, found an echo in England through translations. Two names stand out: Madame d'Aulnoy, whose tales were translated several times in the early years of the eighteenth century (in particular in 1707 and in 1716); and Charles Perrault, whose *Histoires, ou contes du temps passé* (1697) came out in English in 1729.[26]

The works of both La Bruyère and La Rochefoucauld proved an important presence in seventeenth-century England. La Rochefoucauld was translated several times, including by Aphra Behn, who integrated an adaptation of his maxims in her *Miscellany* of 1685. She appropriated his persona, sometimes transforming it, and placed the maxims firmly in the courtly society of the Restoration, showing how a French text could also become relevant to the English philosophical and social contexts.[27] Behn was also one of the translators of the works of Fontenelle, the *History of the Oracles* (1688) and more famously *Discovery of New Worlds* (1688). Her interest in the latter text, as she states in 'The Translator's Preface', was fostered by the reputation of the author, the novelty of the subject in vernacular languages, and 'the Authors introducing a Woman as one of the speakers in these five Discourses ... for I thought an English Woman might adventure to translate any thing, a French Woman may be supposed to have spoken'.[28] Her preface further insists on the difficulties facing the translator, in particular because of the perceived differences in 'Genious and Humour' between the two nations. But she also mentions her corrections of mistakes in the original while insisting on the fact that she has endeavoured to remain faithful to the French text. This displays the importance of the process of translation; the changes to which she submits the text have been interpreted as a defence of religious toleration, thereby offering the translation as a contribution to philosophical debates in its own rights.[29]

This overview indicates the importance of the circulation of European, and mainly French, texts in seventeenth-century England. It shows how much of English prose in the late seventeenth century was in fact not originally written in English but came from diverse traditions. It displays the presence of literary and philosophical filiations and networks, which, in turn, because they are thus made available to the reading public as well as to writers, may serve as repositories of narrative devices, of stories to be retold, of future adaptations.

---

[26] See Chapter 16 on 'Fables and Fairy Tales' by Jayne Lewis.

[27] On Behn as translator, see Line Cottegnies, 'Aphra Behn's French Translations', in Janet Todd and Derek Hughes (eds.), *The Cambridge Companion to Aphra Behn* (Cambridge: Cambridge University Press, 2004), 221–34.

[28] Behn, 'The Translator's Preface', in *A Discovery of New Worlds. From the French. Made English By Mrs. A. Behn*, sig. A4r.

[29] Cottegnies, 'Aphra Behn's French Translations', 231.

NETWORKS

The publication of translations provides for English prose an overlapping web of texts and sources. The presence of Spanish picaresque forms, of French *nouvelles*, secret histories, not to mention libertine literature, as well as the resurgence of Italian novellas, goes some way towards providing a context for the emergence of fictional narratives in English, without constituting a single, identifiable 'influence': 'The English Restoration novel may thus be defined as a mode which draws on various sources; it is not just an imitation of any one, or even all, of the forms of French *nouvelle*.'[30] And indeed works such as Aphra Behn's *Oroonoko* (1688), William Congreve's *Incognita* (1692), or Delarivier Manley's *The Secret History of Queen Zarah and the Zarazians* (1705) all testify to the integration of various traditions into the crucible of English prose. The fact that a great number of writers were translators underlines the status of such texts in the early modern period. Interactions between the French and the English worlds of letters are thus crucial to an appreciation of the Englishness of English prose at the turn of the seventeenth century. In the seventeenth century, narratives of English traditions emerged in certain genres, such as the essay or the romance; later critics constructed similar histories, for the novel in particular. But the reality of literary exchanges is more nuanced. The importance of translations cannot be overstated: 'prose fiction was always already cross-national because of translation long before the rise of the novel.'[31] Translations were indeed a crucial element in the constitution of a multilingual European 'republic of letters', because translators were themselves part of the community of multilingual readers, and because 'the belief in linguistic intimacy between French and English, instilled along with the habits of translating, helped forge a closely knit milieu of bilinguals who could appreciate a variety of rendering styles'.[32] This meant in turn that the issue of a national tradition, or rather, of the national origin of given works, was not as pressing as we may now think.[33] In fact, it could be distinctly fuzzy, as when Brilhac's *Agnès de Castro, nouvelle portugaise*, translated by Aphra Behn in 1688, was put back into French for Madame d'Arconville's *Romans traduits de l'anglais* in 1761—where it was ascribed to Behn.

Thus, the emerging genre of the novel was also being shaped by French writers. Joan DeJean has reconsidered the novel at the turn of the century to emphasize its transnational character, bringing our attention to the careers of (French) women novelists who were part of the networks of writers whose texts were read in France and in Holland,

---

[30] Paul Salzman, *English Prose Fiction 1558–1700: A Critical History* (Oxford: Clarendon Press, 1985), 312.
[31] McMurran, *Spread of Novels*, 2.
[32] McMurran, *Spread of Novels*, 14.
[33] For McMurran, this is something that extends to the eighteenth-century novel: 'the novel's circulatory system looked much like that of premodern fiction: prose fictions were accepted, valorized, and transferred without the stamp of authorial or national identity' (*Spread of Novels*), 49.

as well as in England, both in French and in English. The example of the Huguenot writer Anne de La Roche-Guilhem, who, from 1687, spent the last twenty years of her life in London, is emblematic of such circulation. She wrote in French from London and derived an income from the publication of her novels, which were printed in Amsterdam and read throughout Europe, while some of her books were also published in London in English translation, sometimes more than once. The translations proved enduring and sometimes more successful than the French versions, implying at least different histories in different languages.[34] This suggests complex circulations, where the readership and indeed the fame of certain novels might be unpredictable and possibly need detours via the Continent to reach an audience closer to 'home'. Unlike Anne de La Roche-Guilhem, Mme d'Aulnoy was not a Huguenot, but she chose to live in London, where she wrote a number of her works. Her *Mémoires de la cour d'Espagne* (1690), *Mémoires des aventures singulières de la cour de France* (1692), and *Mémoires de la cour d'Angleterre* (1695) were all translated into English soon after publication in French and reprinted several times over. This further points to a history of the novel in English which takes in not only translations from the Continent but also writers whose presence in England was an important element in the success they may have enjoyed. Mme d'Aulnoy's reputation faded in France in the eighteenth century while she enjoyed relative acclaim in England, leading DeJean to ask paradoxically whether Mme d'Aulnoy does not, 'along with the other women writers who developed their talents in London, belong instead, to an extent worthy of some form of official recognition, to the English tradition of prose fiction?'[35]

As DeJean stresses, these findings resonate with certain aspects of one of the founding texts of criticism on prose writing, Pierre-Daniel Huet's 1670 *Traité de l'origine des romans*, originally published as the preface to Mme de Lafayette's *Zayde*, and translated into English in 1672.[36] Huet's treatise highlights the transnational character of the novel, whose origins are not to be ascribed to one specific nation, but go back to Antiquity and to the East—Egyptians, Arabs, Persians, Syrians—later to travel the globe, through conquests, assimilation, commerce, travels, historical circumstances. The story-tellers and troubadours from Provence are central to Huet's narrative of the spread of novels, through their travels and wanderings as well as through contact with a number of nations—according to Huet, for instance, the Italians would have developed their taste for novels when the Pope was in Avignon or when certain Normand nobles fought in Italy, and subsequently they would have been in contact with this tradition when they came to the university of Paris. In the history and the theory which were formulated

---

[34] Joan Dejean, 'Transnationalism and the Origins of the (French?) Novel', in Margaret Cohen and Carolyn Dever (eds.), *The Literary Channel: The Inter-National Invention of the Novel* (Princeton: Princeton University Press, 2002), 40–50. See also Alexandre Calame, *Anne de La Roche-Guilhen, romancière huguenote, 1644–1707* (Genève: Droz, 1972).

[35] DeJean, 'Transnationalism', 47.

[36] *Zayde, histoire espagnole, par M. de Segrais, avec un Traité de l'origine des romans, par M. Huet* (Paris, 1670–1).

in the late seventeenth century, as well as in the practice, the novel appears as a genre fostered by circulations and contacts with other languages and traditions.

The periodical press was a distinctive form of literary activity. French newspapers, alongside English ones, were published in London in the seventeenth century: 'There was clearly a market for news in French in the capital during these troubled times in the seventeenth century. A weekly newsbook *Le Mercure Anglois* appeared between June 1644 and December 1648 ... and a semi-weekly *Gazette de Londres* between November 1666 and December 1696.'[37] The *Mercure anglois* was itself replaced by the *Nouvelles ordinaires de Londres*, published by William Dugard in the middle of the seventeenth century. Later in the century, there was renewed activity on the part of French men of letters in London following the massive emigration of Huguenots, in particular from the 1680s until the end of the century (although the process started in the late 1660s). In parallel with such publications as the *Nouvelles de la république des lettres* or the *Bibliothèque universelle et historique*, published in the Netherlands, refugees in England took an active part in the development of the periodical press towards the end of the seventeenth century. As a consequence of the nature of the English social, economic, and intellectual life, the refugees tended to assimilate, sometimes becoming English, learning the language, and participating in the life of the country. The French Huguenot Jean (later John) de Fonvive set up the *Post Man* in 1695. Alongside his activities as playwright, librettist, polemicist, and translator, Peter Anthony Motteux, another Huguenot émigré, contributed to the fashioning of the new sociability through the first periodical in English. Originally boasting sixty-four pages, the *Gentleman's Journal, or, The Monthly Miscellany. By Way of Letter to a Gentleman in the Country. Consisting of News, History, Philosophy, Poetry, Musick, Translations, &c.* started its monthly publication in January 1692 and continued until October 1694. Although it claimed to distance itself from the *Mercure Galant*, it was explicitly modelled on the French publication, which reinforced Motteux's role as an intermediary between the French and English worlds of letters:

> The *French* have had a Letter of this nature, called, *Mercure Gallant*, every Month for many Years. Its Author, like most of the Panegyrists of the *French* Court, hath been accused of Profuseness in his Praises to an unsufferable Excess. I will strive to eschew his Fault, and avoiding trifling matters as much as possible, will altogether decline the Flatteries and Daubing that have prejudiced against him, all that love Candor and Impartiality as much as I do.

The first issue presented its readers with a variety of essays, ranging from accounts of opera and theatre, to disquisitions on natural philosophy, fables, translations of verse by Horace, songs, and enigmas. The opening letter of the first issue indicated clearly that the aim of the publication was to divert and benefit the public, while it celebrated

---

[37] Shaw, 'French-Language Publishing to 1900', 113. See further Chapter 26 by Brian Cowan on 'Periodical Literature'.

the achievements of the English armies. Given the central position of London, Motteux saw his periodical as a privileged position from which to convey news: 'I grant that from *London*, the Heart of the Nation, all things circulating to the other parts, such News of new Things as are sent me, may be conveyed everywhere, being inserted in my Letter.'[38] This required of course that news should be sent to the journal for the enterprise to succeed. Motteux intended not only to relay opinions but also to take an active part in the general conversation around the arts. The periodical, as conceived by Motteux, is a place where news may circulate, where the role of the publication is to convey news 'everywhere'.

The appropriation of forms and the circulation of words, languages, and literatures depended on such publications and on individuals like Motteux or Fonvive, who are both embodiments of the contacts between the English world of letters and the Continent, and the operators of such exchanges. While these writers are crucial to the circulation of news and texts and languages between France and England, after emigration they became full participants in the literary life of England, contributing to the development of English prose. These networks which link up France and England are of course connected to other, larger networks, through connections in the 'republic of letters', in particular between refugees in European countries. Pierre Des Maizeaux was active in circulating news from England to the Continent through his regular contributions to the *Nouvelles de la République des Lettres* between 1700 and 1710, reminding us that news could travel in different directions. He came to England in 1699, from Switzerland where he had fled with his family, via the Netherlands. He was an active member of Huguenot circles and was also close to the Royal Society, corresponding in particular with Hans Sloane.[39] He followed religious debates, belonging for instance to the deist Anthony Collins's circle.[40] Published in the section 'Extraits de diverses lettres', and representing about one-third of the pages devoted to newsletters, Des Maizeaux's contributions seem to have been the sole source of information on England available to the *Nouvelles de la République des Lettres*.[41]

While Des Maizeaux followed and discussed publications on religion, including the works on biblical prophecy of William Whiston as well as Latitudinarian and non-conformist books, the bulk of his letters concerned literary productions. In his despatches he did not hesitate to take sides, viewing events such as the controversy on the morality of the stage with a critical eye; he also surveyed the literary world with great attention, commenting for instance on the publication of Swift's *A Tale of a Tub* in 1704.

---

[38] *The Gentleman's Journal* (January 1692), 1.

[39] Elizabeth Grist, 'Pierre Des Maizeaux and the Royal Society', in Ann Thomson, Simon Burrows, and Edmond Dziembowski (eds.), *Cultural Transfers: France and Britain in the Long Eighteenth Century* (Oxford: Voltaire Foundation, 2010), 33–42.

[40] Ann Thomson, 'Des Maizeaux, Collins and the Translators: the Case of Collins' *Philosophical Inquiry Concerning Human Liberty*' in Thomson et al. (eds.), *Cultural Transfers*, 219–31. On Collins, see also Chapter 30 by Nicholas McDowell and Giovanni Tarantino on 'Radical and Deist Writing'.

[41] Joseph Almagor, *Pierre Des Maizeaux (1673–1745): Journalist and English Correspondent for Franco-Dutch Periodicals, 1700–1720* (Amsterdam: APA-Holland University Press, 1989), 47.

To these letters must be added news of publications on history and on science: 'The regular despatches from England gave the French readers a strong impression of a *dynamic* cultural activity in England. The newsletters must have left the readers with the notion that they were not far behind the literary and to some extent the scientific and political developments in England.'[42] He also became close to another French exile, Charles de Saint-Evremond, for a variety of reasons, including prestige, financial gain, and possible identification with his philosophical ideas. Saint-Evremond was not a Huguenot but, because he had antagonized Louis XIV's powerful minister, Colbert, had been in London and Holland since 1661, settling permanently in London in 1672. There, he became a prominent figure of literary circles, but, unlike the Huguenot writers, he is alleged never to have mastered fully the English language. Consequently, his reputation was based mainly on the circulation of his works in French and on his membership of various circles until his works began to be translated into English in the late 1680s and early 1690s. Des Maizeaux collected Saint-Evremond's works for a French edition published from London in 1705, and the English edition of 1714 included the life of the author written by Des Maizeaux.

While Saint-Evremond constitutes an interesting example of a French writer in exile, fully at home in the literary circles of the Restoration and conversant with English literary forms—he published for instance an essay on English comedy and composed a comedy, *Sir Politick Would-Be*, based on a character in Ben Jonson's *Volpone* (1606) and subtitled 'A la manière des Anglais'—the figure of Anthony (or Antoine) Hamilton throws further light on the literary and linguistic exchanges between France and England in the late seventeenth century. Hamilton was a Jacobite. He fought in Ireland, at the Battle of the Boyne, and was also at the siege of Limerick. He then sought refuge in France, where he joined James II at the court of Saint-Germain. His sister Elizabeth had married the Comte de Gramont. Hamilton wrote poetry and occasional pieces, in French, including parodies of oriental tales. He started writing the memoirs of Gramont in 1704, of which he completed the first two parts, the second in particular describing Gramont's life at the court of Charles II between 1662 and 1664 and based on Hamilton's own experiences as well as the recollections of his friend. First published in French in 1713, the *Mémoires de la vie du comte de Gramont*, which were subsequently translated by Abel Boyer and published in London in 1714, offered a controversial account of life at court, in particular of the amorous adventures of the future James II. His position as an English-speaking writer who published in French and became a literary figure in France constitutes a fascinating mirror image of the exiles who were part of the literary life of London at the time—although he moved in rather exclusive circles.

Such networks rested on individuals on both sides of the Channel, who circulated news and publications in different languages; Frenchmen writing in French about the English world of letters, Frenchmen writing in English and indeed becoming influential figures of London intellectual life, Frenchwomen publishing novels or tales written

---

[42] Almagor, *Pierre Des Maizeaux*, 70.

in French in London, Huguenot refugees publishing from London books in English as well as in French, or again Jacobites who found in French circles and letters a new home. Such complex activities emphasize the importance of cross-Channel exchanges, the interactions between languages, literary circles and traditions, and the extent to which political and social circumstances affected the developments of literary endeavours, the careers of writers, and indeed the language in which they wrote. They contribute to a reassessment of the divide between English and Continental prose, displaying a far messier picture than one might think originally. It is consonant with the findings of historians who have emphasized the importance of the much-understudied relationships across the Channel. Analysing the physical exchanges across the sea, as well as the historical construction of the Channel as an entity, Renaud Morieux has outlined 'the shared or intertwined history which connected southern Britain and northern France for long periods, in wartime as in peacetime'.[43] Such relations extend to the cultural sphere, even as the fascination of certain English circles for the French, and the unease it sometimes generated, might morph into outright rejection.[44] In assessing the nature of English prose it is therefore crucial to take into account its close connections, contacts, interchanges, and mixing with other parts of Europe, in particular with France. In the words of Ann Thomson and Simon Burrows, we need to consider 'how circumstances and channels of communication favoured the appropriation of certain aspects of the other's culture and how these aspects were adapted, contributing to the development of common learning and intellectual practice which was not confined to a particular national culture'. This situation has led some critics to examine the constitution of a 'Channel zone' of novelistic production at the turn of the seventeenth century, fostered by translations (real or spurious), imitations, adaptations, and rewritings of various kinds.[45]

Quarrels

This mostly irenic picture of contacts, exchanges, and circulations between the Continent and England, which fostered the development of English prose, suggests that, by the end of the seventeenth century, the English world of letters was suffused with French prose. This picture rests on networks of booksellers, translators, writers, and émigrés of one kind or the other. But such a situation proceeded in part from mass migrations following the revocation of the edict of Nantes. In England, the Huguenots gathered mainly in London, where three French churches were founded in the seventeenth century. It is estimated that between 50,000 and 70,000 people sought refuge

---

[43] Morieux, *The Channel*, 25.
[44] Se e.g. Gesa Stedman, *Cultural Exchange in Seventeenth-Century France and England* (Aldershot: Ashgate, 2013).
[45] Thomson and Burrows, 'Introduction', in Thomson and Burrow (eds.), *Cultural Transfers*, 4; see also the essays in Cohen and Dever (eds.), *The Literary Channel*.

in England, while about 10,000 fled to Ireland.[46] So the nature of the link between France and England rests on a degree of underlying violence which might occasionally surface—Motteux was for instance a public opponent of the policies of Louis XIV, and, in a pastiche of one of Boileau's odes, he attacked the poet and embraced the English language, abandoning publicly the language of a defeated France.[47]

These exchanges and contacts were sometimes built on quarrels—as indeed was much of literary life in the early modern period.[48] This may have affected translations as when Abel Boyer quarrelled with Ozell over who was responsible for the translation of Fénelon's *Télémaque* that appeared anonymously in 1699.[49] Like Motteux, Boyer was a Huguenot who integrated fully in the literary life of England. Born in France in 1667, he had moved to Holland in 1685, serving briefly in the Dutch army, before coming to England in 1689. His first publication was characteristic of publications by French Huguenots in England—*The Compleat French Master for Ladies and Gentlemen: Being a New Method, to Learn with Ease and Delight the French Tongue* (1694). It went through a number of editions (seventeen by the middle of the eighteenth century). Boyer translated both from and into French, notably publishing a French version of Addison's play *Cato* in 1713. A translator, a lexicographer, whose *Royal Dictionary* (1694) was a success both in England and in Europe, and a historian of the reigns of William III and of Queen Anne, he also wrote regularly for Abel Roper's *Post Boy*, a newspaper founded in 1695 that he subsequently took over. He then started in 1711 a new periodical, *The Political State of Great Britain*, in which he pursued a long-standing quarrel with Swift, whom he suspected of having barred him from becoming editor of the *London Gazette*.

The first, 1699 translation of Fénelon's *Télémaque* was begun by Isaac Littlebury, completed by Abel Boyer and Alexander Oldes, and reprinted several times in the early years of the eighteenth century. In the preface to a new 1719 edition, Boyer explained that various reprints introduced mistakes in the translation which were compounded by the fact that the original text they used had been defective. This had suggested to Boyer the necessity of a new translation, eventually carried out not by Boyer but by Ozell, and published in 1715. Boyer then proceeded to attack Ozell: 'in order to palliate his *Plagiarism*, he only corrected the *Printers Mistakes*, and made some Alterations in the Style; but it unluckily fell out, That *he alter'd every Thing for the Worse*.'[50] In reply to Ozell, who had claimed that he had corrected more than two hundred mistakes in the older translation, Boyer examined with scathing irony some of the alterations produced by Ozell in order to display the incompetence of the translator: 'I have hereto subjoyn'd

---

[46] Myriam Yardeni, *Le refuge protestant* (Paris: Presses Universitaires de France, 1985), 73.

[47] Motteux, *Ode de M. Boileau Despreaux sur la prise de Namur avec une parodie de la mesme Ode par le Sieur P. Motteux* ([1695]), 15.

[48] On quarrels in the early modern period see Jeanne-Marie Hostiou and Alexis Tadié (eds.), *Querelles et création en Europe à l'époque moderne* (Paris: Classiques Garnier, 2019).

[49] It was first published in 1699, and, as was frequently the case, not ascribed to any translator.

[50] *The Adventures of Telemachus ... Translated from the Last Paris Edition, Which is the Only Genuine, and Agreeable to the Author's Manuscript; and Dedicated to the King of France. Done into English by Mr. Is. Littlebury and Mr. A. Boyer* (1719), 1, 'Advertisement', p. x.

a *Sample* of his Alterations, which he is pleased to look upon as *Embellishments*, but which, if I am not mistaken, will, with all good Judges, rather pass for *Foils* to our Translation.'[51] This short quarrel throws light on the processes of translation, on debates over accuracy as well as over copyright and plagiarism, while suggesting that the circulation of texts between the French and English languages could be a complicated and antagonistic process. Similar arguments surfaced a little later in the more complex quarrel over the translation of Homer. Sometimes referred to as the 'seconde querelle d'Homère', it started in France with a fierce argument between two translators of Homer, Madame Dacier, who published her prose translation in 1711, and Antoine Houdar de la Motte, who used Dacier's translation to produce an edited version in alexandrine verse, although he did not know Greek. Ozell himself used Mme Dacier's translation for his own version of Homer in English verse published a year later, in which he claimed to have compared it with the Greek. In the preface he defended the superiority of the English language over the French to convey heroic subjects, upheld the use of blank verse, attacked previous translations of Homer (including Chapman's, for which he quotes the authority of Dryden), and generally argued for the improvements brought about by his own translation over Mme Dacier's. Acute arguments in France over the comparative merits of prose and verse to translate Homer thus found an echo in the English world of letters, where they later took on a life of their own. Debates surrounding Pope's translation of Homer renewed the controversy—hence Pope's scathing dismissal of Ozell when he reprinted in *The Dunciad* Ozell's own advertisement in praise of himself: 'As for my *Genius*, let Mr. *Cleland* shew better Verses in all *Pope*'s Works, than *Ozell*'s version of *Boileau*'s *Lutrin*... And Mr. *Toland* and Mr. *Gildon* publickly declar'd, *Ozell*'s Translation of *Homer to* be, as it was *prior*, so likewise *superior* to *Pope*'s.'[52]

This episode points to one of the defining quarrels of the age, that between the Ancients and the Moderns, Ozell having been identified as a 'Modern' by Pope. Although the quarrel has been studied in national contexts (largely as a French phenomenon) it is important to remember not only that it travelled across Europe, from Italy to Germany, via France and England, but also that it could be fought across the seas.[53] *A Tale of a Tub* and its companion piece *Battel of the Books* may thus be considered both in the context of a defence of Swift's former patron, Sir William Temple, who had been attacked by William Wotton, and within the European context of the quarrel between Ancients and Moderns, with arguments over the merits of Homer echoing the French dispute. The rhetoric of Swift's *Battel* drew on French texts in which the conceit of the war is used to address the parallel between both camps: Boileau's *Le lutrin* (1674), in which books become ammunition, and Gabriel Guéret's *La Guerre des auteurs anciens*

---

[51] *The Adventures of Telemachus*, p. xiii.
[52] Alexander Pope, *The Dunciad in Four Books*, ed. Valerie Rumbold (1999; London: Routledge, 2014), 135. On Ozell, see David Hopkins and Pat Rogers, 'The Translator's Trade', in *Oxford History of Literary Translation in English. Volume 3*, 81–95 (87–8).
[53] See Paddy Bullard and Alexis Tadié (eds.), *Ancients and Moderns in Europe: Comparative Perspectives* (Oxford: Voltaire Foundation, 2016).

et modernes (1671) and François de Callières's *Histoire poétique de la guerre nouvellement déclarée entre les anciens et les modernes* (1688), which both used the metaphor of war to intervene in the debate. The satire on mock-learning in the *Tale* is amplified in the *Battel* through physical encounters between books, with French authors of course involved in the fight—Descartes receives an arrow in the eye and dies, drawn 'into his own Vortex', while Perrault is thrown out of his saddle by Homer and hurled at Fontenelle, 'with the same Blow dashing out both their Brains'.[54] Swift's satire is at once an intervention in the local context of the dispute in England over the authenticity of the letters attributed to Phalaris, a reaction to the European context of the quarrel between Ancients and Moderns, and a satirical attack on the Moderns. It also shows that connections between the French and English worlds of letters could take on more antagonistic forms. The *querelle* found echoes in England, where arguments over the compared superiority of Ancients and Moderns could be equally defining for the age; it was also fought across the Channel, in Swift's *Battel*, as well as in the dispute over Homer: Mme Dacier attacked Pope's version of *Iliad* in the second edition of her translation (1719).

The *querelle* found its way into the periodical press, and further connected the French and the English worlds of letters. In the second and third issues of the *Gentleman's Journal* (February and March 1692), Motteux published a summary of the *querelle*, 'A Discourse Concerning the *Ancients* and the *Moderns*', which is one of the first accounts to be given in England of the general debate. The *Journal*'s contribution appeared between Temple's essay, published in 1690, and Wotton's reply of 1694.[55] It was clearly addressed to a more general reader than either of the two main contenders in the quarrel, and it can, at one level, be seen as an important element in the diffusion of the *querelle* from France to England and in the availability of its idiom. While it sided with the Moderns, and aimed at producing reasonable arguments in favour of their superiority, it never acknowledged that it was in fact a translation of Fontenelle's *Digression sur les anciens et les modernes* (1688), which thus found a discrete way into the English debate and perception of the controversy.[56]

Conclusion

The relationships between the English and Continental worlds of letters were thus in constant flux in the second half of the seventeenth century and well into the eighteenth

---

[54] *The Battel of the Books*, in *The Cambridge Edition of the Works of Jonathan Swift: A Tale of a Tub and Other Works*, ed. Marcus Walsh (Cambridge: Cambridge University Press, 2010), 157.

[55] See William Temple, 'Upon Ancient and Modern Learning', in *Miscellanea. The Second Part. In Four Essays* (1690), and William Wotton, *Reflections on Ancient and Modern Learning* (1694).

[56] The first translation to acknowledge authorship of the *Digression* was published with the fourth edition of John Glanvill's 1688 translation of *Conversations with a Lady, on the Plurality of Worlds*, in 1719. It was put into English by John Hughes.

century. There were occasional attempts at shaping certain English literary genres, but the contacts and circulations between England and especially France were particularly dynamic, in spite of political and military oppositions. Paradoxically, some of these antagonisms fostered the development of the English world of letters, with Huguenot writers finding a home in London and taking a defining part in the intellectual life of the country. In turn, through the networks of the Republic of Letters they contributed to the awareness of English prose on the Continent. Such circulations were compounded by the importance of translations in an age when texts might be translated several times over, while there was a certain amount of fuzziness over the origins of the translations—some were anonymous, others were 'by several hands'—leading in some cases to disputes over authorship. Texts could be translated in a succession of languages, in particular as European or oriental works made their way into English through French, while works written in English sometimes acknowledged the spirit—in the French idiom, 'à la manière de'—of other traditions. The development of the oriental tale or of the picaresque in the later eighteenth century constitute striking examples of such fertilization. This process was not confined to narrative genres but could also affect intellectual practice. For example, Marcus Walsh has traced the development of scholarly humanism in the later seventeenth century. In this narrative, the Low Countries are the pivot for the definition and practice of intellectual method, with simultaneous developments observable in France and England. Jean Le Clerc codified the modern standards of scholarly documentation, already exemplified in the Bible scholarship of Richard Simon and in the historical writing of Pierre Bayle: these Continental developments were reflected in the writings and the editorial practice of Richard Bentley and of a line of English literary editors that followed him, from Lewis Theobald to Edmond Malone.[57] Arguments developed in one intellectual environment could thus surface in another context, with different but recognizable effects.

The European world of letters was animated by controversies and disputes, some proving defining for the age: this is in particular the case for the quarrel between Ancients and Moderns, which articulated a number of more localized disputes, in different countries, literary genres, or indeed circles. Arguments over translations and the comparative merits of modern and ancient languages, not to mention other issues such as the morality of the theatre, could be heard in France and in England either as echoes or as disputes fought directly, sometimes with blurred chronological overlaps. All of this suggests, in the late seventeenth and early eighteenth centuries, the distinctly European character of English prose.[58]

---

[57] Marcus Walsh, 'Scholarly Documentation in the Enlightenment: Validation and Interpretation', in Bullard and Tadié (eds.), *Ancients and Moderns in Europe*, 97–112.

[58] On the transnational character of European prose in the seventeenth century, see recently Isabelle Moreau, 'Seventeenth-Century Fiction in the Making', in Glomski and Moreau (eds.), *Seventeenth-Century Fiction*, 1–18: 'Seventeenth-century prose fiction is a story of literary transmission and cultural exchange through complex processes of delocalization, translation, and derivation across national, linguistic, and generic boundaries' (16).

PART II
CATEGORIES

CHAPTER 5

AMATORY FICTION

MELISSA E. SANCHEZ

CONSIDERED by early critics to be tawdry and simplistic soft porn for women, amatory fiction was long seen as the embarrassing other to the novel's social and psychological realism.[1] In recent decades, however, feminist and historicist critics have demonstrated that amatory fiction in fact offers a complex analysis of gendered and political relations in the late seventeenth century.[2] Building on this work, I read seventeenth-century amatory fiction as a distinct and valuable archive for understanding the history of affect and sexuality, particularly as they are tied to methods of reading. In particular, this writing allows us to appreciate models of love and desire that do not assume the equation of true love with sexual innocence and bourgeois marriage that many critics have taken for granted. I focus on three prominent and popular mid- and late seventeenth-century prose works that depart strikingly from both the Renaissance romance's idealization of unrequited passion that preceded them and the eighteenth-century novel's idealization of middle-class respectability that followed them: George Thornley's translation of Longus's *Daphnis and Chloe* (1657), Roger L'Estrange's translation of *Lettres portugaises* (1678), and Aphra Behn's *Love-Letters Between a Nobleman and his Sister* (1684–1687). While Chloe in *Daphnis and Chloe* or Mariane of the *Five Love-Letters* might appear to be the opposite of the scheming, self-promoting Silvia in Behn's *Love-Letters Between a Nobleman and His Sister*, we might rather see the three as exploring the complexities

---

[1] For a description of amatory fiction's resemblance to both modern Harlequin romances and softcore pornography, see Toni Bowers, 'Sex, Lies, and Invisibility: Amatory Fiction from the Restoration to Mid-Century', in John Richetti et al. (eds.), *The Columbia History of the British Novel* (New York: Columbia University Press, 1994), 23–49. Ian Watt's *The Rise of the Novel* (London: Chatto and Windus, 1957) is the *locus classicus* for a genealogy that sees the novel proper as beginning with Defoe and therefore excluding the prose fiction of Behn, Manley, and Haywood. In a characterization that long held sway, John Richetti described amatory prose fiction as 'bad art' offering shallow pleasure (*Popular Fiction Before Richardson* (Oxford: Oxford University Press, 1969), 5).

[2] Important early feminist recoveries of the aesthetic and psychological sophistication of amatory prose fiction include Ros Ballaster, *Seductive Forms: Women's Amatory Fiction from 1684 to 1740* (Oxford: Clarendon Press, 1992), 31–66, and Bowers, 'Sex, Lies, and Invisibility'.

of eroticism as well as its interpretation. Refusing to idealize female sexual innocence and self-sacrifice, all three works accentuate the opacity of desire and motive. In these romances, characters, narrator, and reader alike are unable definitively to distinguish between innocence and knowledge and therefore to assign the guilt that sexual knowledge and the pursuit of self-interest are often understood to imply.

Erotic investment, as these texts show us, does not pit sincerity against inconstancy, desire against interest, passion against reason. It reveals these and other affects to exist in disturbing proximity for women as well as for men. As Lennard J. Davis and John Bray have argued, prose fiction reveals not the 'truth' of the self but its fictionality and instability. And insofar as fact and fiction are indiscrete categories, the 'questions of virtue'—hinging on benign motive, sincerity, and integrity—that Michael McKeon located as a central concern of the early novel are no more subject to final resolution than 'questions of truth'.[3] Because these works stress the difficulty of interpreting the 'truth' of desire, they also provide an important resource for thinking through recent debates that pit what has been called symptomatic or suspicious reading against the pleasure and receptiveness of surface reading or description. A paradigmatic statement of the ideological critique that takes a text's language as symptomatic in the psychoanalytic sense appears in Frederic Jameson's influential argument that by contrast to 'ordinary' reading, which assumes that 'the text means just what it says', '[i]nterpretation proper ... always presupposes, if not a conception of the unconscious itself, then at least some mechanism of mystification or repression in terms of which it would make sense to seek a latent meaning behind a manifest one'.[4] Characterizing this formulation as 'paranoid' reading, founded on the 'hermeneutics of suspicion' encouraged by Marx, Freud, and Nietzsche, Eve Kosofsky Sedgwick advocates in its place a 'reparative' mode of reading that accepts textual pleasure and acknowledges the limitations of criticism to unveil and master its objects.[5] In recent years a number of literary scholars have expanded on Sedgwick's provocation to propose that careful observation and description of a text's surface may offer a more nuanced and honest account of the work of the literary, with its conflicted investments and pleasures, than ideological critique.[6] Urging attentiveness to the words and formal features on a text's surface rather than the desire to plumb its ideological depths, surface or descriptive reading compels us to pay attention to the small details

---

[3] John Bray, *The Epistolary Novel: Representations of Consciousness* (London: Routledge, 2003), 1–28; Lennard J. Davis, *Factual Fictions: The Origins of the English Novel* (Philadelphia: University of Pennsylvania Press, 1996), 102–22; Michael McKeon, *The Origins of the English Novel, 1600–1740* (Baltimore: Johns Hopkins University Press, 1987).

[4] Frederic Jameson, *The Political Unconscious: Narrative as a Socially Symbolic Act* (Ithaca: Cornell University Press, 1981), 60.

[5] Eve Kosofsky Sedgwick, 'Paranoid Reading and Reparative Reading, or, You're So Paranoid, You Probably Think this Introduction Is about You', in *Novel Gazing* (Durham: Duke University Press, 1997).

[6] See Stephen Best and Sharon Marcus, 'Surface Reading: An Introduction', *Representations*, 108 (2009), 1–21; Heather K. Love, 'Close but Not Deep: Literary Ethics and the Descriptive Turn', *New Literary History* 41 (2010), 371–91; Mark Doty, *The Art of Description* (Minneapolis: Greywolf Press, 2010); Rita Felski, *The Limits of Critique* (Chicago: University of Chicago Press, 2015); and Sharon Marcus, Heather Love, and Stephen Best, 'Building a Better Description', *Representations*, 135 (2016), 1–21.

that disrupt any holistic, masterful account of literary truth. Amatory fiction puts its readers on notice that characters' (and narrators') words and actions cannot always be taken at face value, at the same time that it admits that the surface is all we have—we have no more access to interior 'truth' than character or narrator. Indeed, the psychological realism and complexity of amatory fiction lie in its attention to all that is uncertain, unavailable, and opaque to language and consciousness—these works struggle to describe what Doty calls 'the incompletely knowable'.[7] The self-conscious play with innocence and knowledge, truth, and fiction staged in amatory prose thereby might be understood as an early theory of reparative reading, but one that does not leave suspicion behind. For this fiction constantly gestures to subterranean motives and desires that neither we nor the fiction's characters can comprehend, teasing us with a depth that we cannot access.

Suspicious Minds; or, The Epistemology of Pastoral in *Daphnis and Chloe*

Longus's *Daphnis and Chloe* is the story of two young lovers who crave sex but don't know how to have it—want of skill, not conventional morality, is all that stands in their way. The most prominent characteristic of Longus's narrative is its consciousness of the artifice of pastoral itself, what Margaret Anne Doody describes as its conspicuous 'play with the never-ending reciprocities of Art and Nature' that 'at the outset warn the reader to be wary of complex artistries'.[8] The mimetic layers of *Daphnis and Chloe*, Froma I. Zeitlin argues, compel us to read through a double lens of 'naïve child' and 'sophisticated voyeur'.[9] Yet George Thornley prefaces his translation with an epistle to 'Young Beauties' that undermines Longus's central conceit, the comic and titillating naïveté of the title characters. For Thornley, childlike naïveté is a cover for sophisticated voyeurism, pastoral a covert form of pornography in that both turn on what McKeon has described as 'oscillation' between 'concealment and revelation' that registers 'the fundamental disparity between ... the will toward sexual activity and the unwillingness or inability to acknowledge it'.[10] Echoing a longstanding trope of advertising romances

---

[7] Doty, *Art of Description*, 137.

[8] Margaret Anne Doody, *The True Story of the Novel* (New Brunswick: Rutgers University Press, 1996), 45.

[9] Froma I. Zeitlin, 'The Poetics of *Erōs*: Nature, Art, and Imitation in Longus' *Daphnis and Chloe*', in Froma I. Zeitlin, John J. Winkler, and David M. Halperin (eds.), *Before Sexuality*, (Princeton: Princeton University Press, 1990), 417–64 (438).

[10] Michael McKeon, *The Secret History of Domesticity* (Baltimore: Johns Hopkins University Press, 2005), 544. As Ruth Perry and Ros Ballaster have argued, epistolary fiction offers a similar rhythm of arousal and delay (Perry, *Women, Letters, and the Novel* (New York: AMS, 1980), 158–9; Ballaster, *Seductive Forms*, 34–5).

as offering men the voyeuristic pleasures of reading works that aroused women readers, Thornley presents his translation of this Greek tale as 'A Most Sweet, and Pleasant Pastorall ROMANCE for Young Ladies'.[11] Thornley's prefatory epistle establishes a model of reading that equates his own disingenuous denials of lascivious intent with the romance's claims of the characters' innocence. Burlesquing what Doody describes as Longus's own 'play on the never-ending reciprocities of Art and Nature', Thornley opens this epistle by stating that '[t]his little, pleasant Laundschip of Love, by its own destiny and mine, belongs most properly to your fair eyes, and hands, and happier laps. And then, who would not lay his legge over a book; although that, sometimes, has been the complaint of a Schollar's solitude?' Having suggested the autoerotic uses of his book, Thornley immediately denies that he has any such thing in mind, instructing his readers to pause and contain themselves: 'But hold! there is nothing here to that purpose, but what Lycaenium taught her Schollar in the Wood.' Except for this one scene of erotic initiation, a trope that James Grantham Turner has seen as paradigmatic of early modern pornography, the tale offers no explicit descriptions of sex: 'in short', Thornley maintains, 'nothing to vex you, unless perchance, in your own conscience'.[12]

Thornley immediately follows this venerable romance disclaimer by alleging that those who miss the sexual content of *Daphnis and Chloe* only pretend to do so. The apparent naïveté of the title characters resembles that of a female readership whose innocence is a convenient pretence:

> Chloe knew well enough (though the Author makes her simple) what, and where, her Fancie was; and Daphnis too, needed not Lycaenium's Lanthorn to a plakit, or to follow Will with the wispe. But hark you Lady; and I will tell you a storie, one I had at a Tavern vesper ... A boy, and a Girle were got thither together: The boy opened his shop, and drew out all a young beginner had to show: the Girle askt him, what it was: The boy said, It was his purse: the Girle looked upon her selfe; And, if that be thy purse; Then (quoth she) my purse is cutt. And these are parallells to the simple rurals here ... But besides; it is so like your owne either simplicitie, or Art, you cannot but approve it here. You do not know what we meane, when we speak as plain as day. And now you have an Author too (which you never had before) to prove you do not counterfeit.[13]

The crude language of the epistle parallels the jokes told at a 'Tavern vesper' to 'the simple rurals' of the tale to follow. Thornley's epistle to female readers models not just

---

[11] Longus, *Daphnis and Chloe*, trans. George Thornley (1657), title page; all further references are to this edition. For the eroticization and trivialization of women's reading, see Heidi Brayman Hackel, '"Boasting of Silence": Women Readers in a Patriarchal State', in Kevin Sharpe and Stephen N. Zwicker (eds.), *Reading, Society, and Politics in Early Modern England* (Cambridge: Cambridge University Press, 2003), 101–21.

[12] 'To young Beauties', in *Daphnis and Chloe*, sigs. A3r–v; James Grantham Turner, *Schooling Sex: Libertine Literature and Erotic Education in Italy, France, and England, 1534–1685* (Oxford: Oxford University Press, 2003).

[13] *Daphnis and Chloe*, sigs. A3v–A4r.

what *Daphnis and Chloe* does, but also what those readers do with it, in a teasing alternation of art and nature, innocence and knowledge. Longus's 'simple ruralls' provide pleasure in that they allegorize women's 'own either simplicitie, or Art'. Like Chloe, who 'knew well enough' what she and Daphnis wanted, women cover their arousal with simplicity and thereby allow it to be spoken. Similarly, in his depiction of Daphnis and Chloe's pastoral innocence, Longus provides women an alibi to deny their own sexual pleasure. Chloe provides an exemplum of innocence that allows women to vow that they 'do not counterfeit' when they 'do not know what we meane, when we speak as plain as day'. They can always claim not to get the joke.

Read through the lens of Thornley's epistle, *Daphnis and Chloe* is less a straight story of innocence than a queer meditation on reading itself. As Simon Goldhill argues, the history of translation of, and commentary on, Longus testifies to 'the difficult question of *how far* to go in reading … If the fiction of innocence establishes the question of the whence of desire, the erotic narrative establishes a question of the reader's fiction of mastery, of control and self-control. Or: to read a *double entendre* with *sophrosune* [the virtue of self-control and temperance] is to miss the joke'.[14] Erotic fiction poses a unique and instructive challenge to a strong distinction between reparative and paranoid reading. For Thornley insists that Longus's professions of the lovers' innocence must be treated with suspicion. An early instance is Daphnis's mystified realization that although he has kissed 'young kids', 'a pretty whippet', and a calf, the kiss he shares with Chloe is 'a new thing'. The reader knows what Daphnis doesn't about the differences between kisses and is therefore encouraged to understand, before Daphnis does, that the freedom that he and Chloe share is not as innocent as the narrator suggests. When Chloe 'washed [Daphnis] stark naked with her own hands; and she her self, Daphnis then first of all, looking and gazing on her, washed her naked limbs before him' we understand that the pair get more pleasure from the experience than they let on, perhaps even to themselves.[15]

The old shepherd Philetis, who first informs Daphnis and Chloe that they are in love, is but one rightly suspicious reader of their innocence in the romance. Instructing that 'there is no med'cine for Love, neither meat, nor drink, nor any Charm, but only Kissing, and Embracing, and lying naked together', Philetis assumes greater knowledge than the pair is willing to admit, however, and his advice leads to another scene in which comic innocence becomes titillating foreplay. The pair take Philetis at his word and attempt the remedies of kissing and embracing 'with a bold, impatient fury' but 'durst not make the experiment' of lying naked together, 'for that was not onely an enterprise too bold for Maids, but too high for young Goatheards'. Despite their ostensible ignorance, Daphnis and Chloe distinguish between different forms of erotic contact. This unspoken sexual awareness appears in their 'sweet, erotic, amorous dreams; and what they did not in the day, that they acted in the night, and lay together stark naked,

---

[14] Simon Goldhill, *Foucault's Virginity: Ancient Erotic Fiction and the History of Sexuality* (Cambridge: Cambridge University Press, 1995), 30.

[15] *Daphnis and Chloe*, 20, 41–2.

kissing, clipping, twining limbs'. What they don't understand, the narrator explains, is penetration, so that when they eventually do attempt to act out their dreams, it is a disappointment: 'they lay a long while clinging together. But being ignorant of what after that was to be done, and thinking that this was the end of amorous fruition, most part of the day spent in vain, they parted, and drove their flocks home from the fields, with a kind of hate to the oppression of the night.' When, determined to find a remedy for their pain, they imitate the copulation of the sheep and goats they have been observing, they find no greater success: Daphnis 'lay down with her, and lay long; but knowing how to do nothing of that he was mad to do, lifted her up, and endeavour'd to imitate the Goats. But at the first finding a mere frustration there, he sate up, and lamented to himself, that he was more unskilfull than a very Tup in the practice of the mystery and the Art of Love'.[16]

Fortunately, Daphnis meets with another suspicious reader, a lusty neighbour woman, Lycaenium, who takes it upon herself to teach Daphnis about male and female genitalia. This is the scene singled out by Thornley as uniquely 'to that purpose' of arousal, but its blunt efficiency is far less titillating than the frustrations we have already witnessed: 'She, when she saw him itching to be at her, lifted him up from the reclination on his side, and slipping under, not without art, directed him to her Fancie, the place so long desired and sought.' The 'Fancie' that Thornley insists Chloe knows well in the epistle is here not just figurative desire but the literal vagina. John Winker has seen Lycaenium's warning that Chloe may 'squeak, and cry out, and bleed' when her hymen ruptures as a 'grim' reminder that *Daphnis and Chloe* depicts a patriarchal subtext of female pain and violation.[17] However, as Goldhill and Doody point out, Daphnis's literal response—he is terrified of blood and refuses to pass on his knowledge to the eager but bashful Chloe—may itself bespeak a patriarchal control of female pleasure and knowledge.[18] For Lycaenium's very determination to initiate Daphnis, just as 'another Youth taught me to play at this sport', attests that once 'well acquainted' with the physical act of sex women may experience not only pleasure but also mastery. In accentuating this pleasure as common to Lycaenium and Chloe through the euphemism 'Fancie', an anatomical meaning that appears to be unique to this translation, Thornley reinscribes the suspicion of innocence with which he prefaced the romance.[19]

Thornley's frank invitation to revel in double entendre in both his preface and his explicit translation might be instructively contrasted with J. M. Edmonds' bashfulness in the 1916 Loeb edition of Longus. Edmonds substitutes Latin for English in the passages describing the pair's attempt to emulate the goats' copulation, Lycaenium's initiation of Daphnis, Daphnis's fear of Chloe's blood, and the parasite Gnatho's attempts to seduce

---

[16] *Daphnis and Chloe*, 60, 62–3, 65, 74.

[17] *Daphnis and Chloe*, 133–5; John J. Winkler, *The Constraints of Desire: The Anthropology of Sex and Gender in Ancient Greece* (London: Routledge, 1990), 101–26.

[18] Goldhill, *Foucault's Virginity*, 35; Doody, *True Story*, 49.

[19] *Daphnis and Chloe*, 134–5. The *OED* records no such use, and Goldhill describes it as an 'unparalleled turn of phrase' (28).

Daphnis.[20] In Goldhill's analysis, Edmond's replacement of English with Latin is itself an interpretive act in that it 'recognizes the impossibility of an innocent reading' of these scenes and is therefore 'the reading that is most explicit about Longus's suggestiveness'.[21] Strikingly, however, there is no need to Latinize Thornley's translation of Longus's description of the actual wedding night: 'Daphnis now did the Trick that his Mistris Lycaenium had taught him in the thicket. And Chloe then first knew, that those things that were done in the Wood, were only the sweetest Sports of Shepherds.' Once Chloe has achieved the knowledge that rids her of what Doody aptly calls her 'technical, unwanted virginity', she ceases to be 'only' a shepherd, or (in the words of Thornley's prefatory epistle), a 'simple rural' and joins the readers in their superior, urbane knowledge. Thornley's final words, notably, are not a literal translation of Longus's *paidiōn paignia*, or 'children's play/children's games'.[22] Whereas Longus's phrase stresses sexual maturity, Thornley's calls attention to the epistemology of pastoral. Like the artifice of the pastoral wedding that concludes Longus's romance, pastoral codes permit not just the claim of innocence, but an eroticization of innocence requiring the complicity of the reader. In Thornley's hands, *Daphnis and Chloe* depicts not the journey from youth to maturity, innocence to knowledge, that Doody and Zeitlin have described.[23] Rather, by insisting that simplicity and sincerity may have been coy performances all along, Thornley highlights the pleasurable malleability of those very categories and thereby anticipates a central characteristic of the amatory prose of the decades to follow.

SURVIVING LOVE: *FIVE LOVE-LETTERS FROM A NUN TO A CAVALIER*

The tragic love depicted in the wildly popular *Les Lettres portugaises*, translated by L'Estrange as *Five Love-Letters from a Nun to a Cavalier*, would appear to be worlds away from the pastoral play of *Daphnis and Chloe*.[24] Drawing on Ovid's *Heroides* and the letters of Héloïse and Abelard, *Five Love-Letters* depicts love's bleak end rather than its hopeful onset. Yet, like Thornley's translation of Longus, *Five Love-Letters* plays with the relationships between convention and sincerity, innocence, and knowledge. As scholars have noted, *Five Love-Letters* was thematically and stylistically calculated to convey the devastation of unrequited love through the appearance of natural, spontaneous

---

[20] See J. M. Edmonds, *Longus's Daphnis and Chloe* (Cambridge: Harvard University Press, 1916), 149–51, 155–7, 207.
[21] Goldhill, *Foucault's Virginity*, 29.
[22] *Daphnis and Chloe*, 229. On the prevalence of games and sport in *Daphnis and Chloe*, see Doody, *True Story*, 50–1.
[23] Doody, *True Story*, 51–3; Zeitlin, 'Poetics of Erōs', 219.
[24] On the popularity of the *Five Love-Letters*, see Charles C. Mish (ed.), *Restoration Prose Fiction, 1666–1700* (Lincoln: University of Nebraska Press, 1970), 37.

prose.[25] Presented as the real letters of a real nun, the *Five Love Letters* are instrumental in forging an association between sincere, artless female passion and cynical, manipulative male interest.[26] And if the paradigmatic evidence of selfless, true, and virtuous love is unrequitedness, then Mariane is proven truthful and virtuous insofar as she is faithful to a lover who brings her pain rather than pleasure.

Accordingly, modern critics have understood the letters as themselves premised on fiction or delusion: Peggy Kamuf describes Mariane, their ostensible author, as 'more an hysterical voice than a character', writing letters 'punctuated only by the silence of her lover', and Ruth Perry and Warren Chernaik have concurred that Mariane's 'isolation' attests to the virtue of her passion, which, unlike the 'calculated rationality' of her libertine cavalier, seeks nothing in return.[27] To be sure, Mariane's letters begin by lamenting her unfaithful cavalier's 'absence'—a word that, along with 'gone', appears multiple times in the opening of the first letter—and she complains in the second, third, and fourth letters that he has not yet written. The fourth letter contrasts her continued epistolary activity with his lack of response, confessing that 'Tis not so much for your sake that I write, as my own; for my Business is only to divert, and entertain my self; Beside that the very Length of this Letter will make you afraid on't: And you'le never read it thorough neither'.[28] The potentially off-putting length of the letter, as Ruth Perry and Linda Kauffman have observed, turns it from an act of communication to a document of self-indulgence, from appeal to the other to consolation to the self.[29] It complicates, in other words, the virtue of Mariane's fidelity by suggesting that she derives gratification from her epistolary project. She writes not so much to please her lover as to 'divert' and 'entertain' herself.

Yet Mariane's isolation is not entire, nor is her devotion endless. For her first and last letters are themselves framed as responses to the cavalier's own letters, demonstrating that the *Five Love-Letters* are not to be read as mere apostrophe to an unresponsive

---

[25] Toni Bowers, *Force or Fraud: British Seduction Stories and the Problem of Resistance, 1660–1760* (Oxford: Oxford University Press, 2011), 68–70; Robert Adams Day, *Told in Letters: Epistolary Fiction before Richardson* (Ann Arbor: University of Michigan Press, 1966), 2–3.

[26] For this association of femininity, sincerity, and epistolarity, see Perry, *Women, Letters, and the Novel*, 114, 119, 128; Ballaster, *Seductive Forms*, 63–6; Warren Chernaik, 'Unguarded Hearts: Transgression and Epistolary Form in Aphra Behn's "Love-Letters" and the "Portuguese Letters"', *Journal of English and Germanic Philology*, 97 (1998), 13–33 (15, 19); Linda S. Kauffman, who traces the problems of the authenticity and authorship in the publication history of *Les Lettres portugaises* (*Discourses of Desire: Gender, Genre, and Epistolary Fiction* (Ithaca: Cornell University Press, 1998), 92–100); and John Richetti, *The English Novel in History, 1700–1800* (New York and London: Routledge, 1999), 20. See also Chapter 22 by Diana G. Barnes on 'Letters'.

[27] Peggy Kamuf, *Fictions of Female Desire: Disclosures of Heloise* (Lincoln: University of Nebraska Press, 1982), p. xviii, 45; Perry, *Women, Letters, and the Novel*, 110; Chernaik, 'Unguarded Hearts', 17. See also Kauffman, *Discourses of Desire*, who argues that Mariane's 'vocation' becomes 'iterative narrative' that sustains belief in a love that is definitively past (103).

[28] *Five Love-Letters from a Nun to a Cavalier Done out of French into English*, trans. Roger L'Estrange (1678), 81–2. All further references will be to this edition.

[29] Perry, *Women, Letters, and the Novel*, 102; Kauffman, *Discourses of Desire*, 107–10.

object but as dialogue, even negotiation, between two lovers whose interests diverge. Early in the first letter, Mariane complains that 'Your last Letter gave me such a Passion of the heart, as if it would have forc'd its way through my Breast, and follow'd you. It laid me three hours sensless'. At this point, her attachment is premised on hope: 'you may save your self the trouble too of desiring me to THINK of you. Why 'tis Impossible for me to forget you: and I must not forget the hope you gave me neither, or your Return, and of spending some part of your time here with us in *Portugal*.' Mariane's despair in the Fourth Letter notwithstanding, the Fifth Letter makes clear that the cavalier reads and responds to all four of her previous epistles. His cold politeness here extinguishes her optimism and, with it, her continued love. She runs out of patience, which (as their shared etymology suggests) is also to run out of passion:

> By the Impertinent Professions, and the most Ridiculous Civilities of your Last Letter, I find that all mine are Come to your hand; and that you have read them over too: but are as unconcern'd, as if you forsooth had no Interest at all in the Matter. Sot that I am, to lie thus at the Mercy of an Insensible, and Ungrateful Creature; and to be as much afflicted now at the Certainty of the Arrival of those Papers, as I was before, for fear of their Miscarriage! What have I to do with your telling me the *TRUTH OF THINGS*? Who desir'd to know it? Or the *SINCERITY* you talk of; a thing you never practis'd toward me, but to my Mischief. Why could you not let me alone in my Ignorance? Who bad you Write? Miserable Woman that I am! Me-thinks after so much pains taken already to delude me to my Ruin, you might have streyn'd one point more, in this Extremity, to deceive me to my Advantage, without pretending to excuse your self.[30]

Like 'THINK' in the First Letter, '*TRUTH OF THINGS*' and '*SINCERITY*' are typeset to stand out as direct quotations. Whereas the plea to 'THINK of you' in the First Letter is encouragement, it appears that the 'Impertinent Professions' and 'Ridiculous Civilities' mentioned in Mariane's Fifth Letter may be attempts to soften the blow of the 'TRUTH' with which she wants no traffic. The litany of rhetorical questions following the quotation of the cavalier's letter belies the Nun's performance (in the first four letters) of the self-sacrificing lover whose passion is proven sincere and selfless to the extent that it is *not* required: 'I'le rather endure any thing then forget you'; 'my Love does not depend upon your Manner of treating me'; 'I would rather chuse to Love you in any state of Misery, then agree to the bare Supposition that I had never Seen you'; and, most dramatically, 'should I survive this restlessness of thought, to lead a Life of more tranquility, and ease, such an Emptiness, and such an Insensibility could never consist.'[31] These earlier professions of fidelity, it turns out, engaged in a protracted delusion not about the cavalier, but about the selflessness of Mariane's own devotion. Now that she has received assurance that the cavalier will not return—a response all the more intolerable

---

[30] *Five Love-Letters*, 90–2.
[31] *Five Love-Letters*, 22, 29, 46, 63–4.

for its measured civility—Mariane faces the limits of a passion that she had heretofore represented to herself as boundless.

The 'different Ayre and stile' of the Fifth Letter indicates that her love is in fact both finite and relational. This final letter rejects the role of constant, self-abnegating beloved, insisting 'I am now at lenth perfectly convinc'd, that since I have irrecoverably lost your Love, I can no longer justify my own'. Writing, as Kauffman observes, proves to be a 'stategy of recuperation'. But this recuperation consists not in the saintly fiction of unrequitedness for which Kauffman and others would canonize Mariane, but rather in a new turn to a self-preserving rationality that aligns her with the cavalier, who was precisely the real addressee that critics intent on asserting Mariane's virtuous self-abnegation have denied exists.[32] It is his letters, Mariane notes, that have 'brought me to my self again': 'Your two last Letters I am resolv'd to keep, and to read them over oftener than ever I did any of the former, for fear of a Relapse'. In opposition to her embrace of irrational because self-destructive passion in the earlier letters, she here reluctantly admits that 'there's no resisting the force of Necessity and Reason'. She ends the letter with the possibility that 'I shall not write to you again for all This; for what Necessity is there that I must be telling of you at every turn how my Pulse beats?' The cessation of writing that she projects here is also the choice of 'Necessity and Reason' over the 'Extravagance of Choler, and Despair'—of self-protective calculation and restraint over self-sacrificing passion and fidelity.[33]

PASSION AND PRUDENCE: *LOVE-LETTERS FROM A NOBLEMAN TO HIS SISTER*

The gendered morality of the critical unwillingness to entertain the possibility that Mariane may indeed stop writing, signifying that she has chosen respect for herself over a romantic ideal of love that asks nothing in return, becomes particularly legible in responses to Silvia's increasing self-interest in Aphra Behn's *Love-Letters from a Nobleman to His Sister*. Behn's *Love-Letters* explores the complex negotiation of love and interest, devotion and self-preservation, that is the subtext of the *Five Love-Letters*. A fictionalized version of the scandalous elopement of the Whig Ford, Lord Grey of Werke, with his sister-in-law Lady Henrietta Berkeley, the first part of the *Love-Letters* advertises itself as a *roman à clef* that will provide the details not available in the transcripts that had been published shortly after Grey's trial for abduction in November of 1682 (and which would be published together with the seventh edition of Behn's fictional version in 1765); the second and third parts narrate

---

[32] *Five Love-Letters*, 83–4; Kauffman, *Discourses of Desire*, 116–17.
[33] *Five Love-Letters*, 114–15, 87, 117.

the secret, amorous history in tandem with the rebellion and fall of the Duke of Monmouth.[34] Yet the 'truth' that the *Love-Letters* reveals is inaccessibility of its characters' motives, even to themselves, along with the impossibility of the pure, selfless virtue that will characterize later fictional heroines in the eighteenth century. Even as Judith Kegan Gardiner designates Behn's *Love-Letters* the 'first English novel', she points out that it stands apart from the generic conventions it evokes, rejecting both the plot of 'love leading to marriage' and that of 'tragic adultery'.[35] Similarly, Ros Ballaster observes that 'the experience of conflicting interpretation, ambiguous reference, and slippage of meaning is one that is inscribed into [Behn's] novel itself and is, in fact, structural to its understanding of the necessarily "fallen" nature of political and sexual life'.[36] In this sense, *Love-Letters* picks up where the *Lettres portugaises* ends: with the aftermath of the decision to survive the end of love.

Philander and Silvia are typically read as the novel's villains, with Philander depicted as a vile aristocratic womanizer at best and a serial rapist at worst and Silvia as a 'sexual predator', 'unvarnished prostitute', a 'corrupt and tarnished' libertine mechanically pursuing 'empty conquests which give no pleasure'.[37] Their later lovers, Octavio and Calista, are usually treated as the virtuous brother–sister pair to offset Philander and Silvia's viciousness.[38] The critical outrage at Philander and especially Silvia has the effect not only of obscuring the ethical ambiguity of Octavio and Calista but also of supporting an ideal of female self-sacrifice that naturalizes the commodification and sexual violation of women. At the same time, the one mutually constant and passionate union that Behn depicts, that between Caesario (Monmouth) and Hermione (Lady Henrietta Wentworth), proves mutually self-destructive.[39] When Philander affirms that 'Self-Preservation' is 'the first principle to Nature', and when the narrator declares that Silvia was 'not of a Nature to dy for Love', they summarize the novel as a whole, which ultimately offers the same lesson that Mariane learns in the *Five Love-Letters*, when she confesses 'And yet I Live, (false as I am) and take as much pains to preserve my life, as to lose it.... If I had lov'd you so much as I have told you a thousand times I did, I had

---

[34] Examples of influential studies include Susan Staves, *Players' Scepters: Fictions of Authority in the Restoration* (Lincoln: University of Nebraska Press, 1979); Albert J. Rivero, '"Hieroglifick'd" History in Aphra Behn's *Love-Letters Between a Nobleman and His Sister*', *Studies in the Novel*, 30 (1998), 126–38; and Bowers, *Force or Fraud*.

[35] Judith Kegan Gardiner, 'The First English Novel: Aphra Behn's *Love Letters*, The Canon, and Women's Tastes', *Tulsa Studies in Women's Literature*, 8 (1989), 201–22 (201, 14).

[36] Ros Ballaster, '"The Story of the Heart": *Love-Letters Between a Noble-Man and His Sister*', in Derek Hughes and Janet Todd (eds.), *The Cambridge Companion to Aphra Behn* (Cambridge: Cambridge University Press, 2004), 138.

[37] For these phrases, see Richetti, *English Novel*, 23; Bowers, *Force or Fraud*, 132; Chernaik, 'Unguarded Hearts', 29, 33.

[38] See Bowers, *Force or Fraud*, 127–8; Ballaster, 'Story of the Heart', 143.

[39] Ballaster rightly remarks that Caesario loses authority and honour by falling prey to the same 'romantic illusion' that Silvia is educated to resist (*Seductive Fictions*, 109); Richetti contrasts the 'romanticized, tragic' portrait of Caesario/Monmouth's fall with the 'nasty refinements of Silvia's amoral individualism' (*English Novel*, 29).

been in my Grave long ere this'.[40] To chose self over other, life over death is ultimately a betrayal of an ideal of love as utterly selfless, persisting for its own sake and not altering in response to anything. But this is a necessary betrayal, one that is not cynical nor immoral but simply human.[41]

The manipulations and deceits that drive the plot of Behn's *Love-Letters* are almost never simple or straightforward substitutions of fiction for truth, performance for confession. The real motives and desires of the individual characters are consistently obscure, not only to those they dupe and betray but to themselves as well. Rather than offer the 'disclosure of inner truths', Behn's supplementation of first-person epistolary writing with third-person narration only accentuates the illusiveness of certain knowledge: 'private' thought is no more transparent than the 'public' rhetoric of letters.[42] To be sure, the extremity of the lovers' repeated—one might say repetitive—professions of conflicted passions is, as Bowers argues, at least in part rhetorical.[43] Yet the hackneyed conventions that Philander and Silvia enact in their letters are also expressed when they are all alone and have nobody to convince but themselves. Playing a role does not necessarily mean that one does not want to believe in it: as McKeon elegantly puts it, the characters of Behn's *Love-Letters* all embody a 'protoaesthetic willingness to suspend disbelief and enjoy the virtual pleasures of imagination'. Octavio's final letter to Silvia comes to a conclusion that might well apply to all of the characters in the novel, including himself: '*But oh! in vain I seek for Reasons from thee; perhaps thy own fantastic fickle Humour cannot inform thee why thou hast betray'd me.*'[44] Betrayal in Behn's *Love-Letters* is almost never only a matter of cold, premeditated choice. It is a result of characters driven by 'fantastic fickle Humour' that leads them not only to betray the trust of others but also as often as not to injure themselves.

Silvia's protracted affairs with Philander, Octavio, and Brilljard are the most striking instances of the opacity of motive that informs the *Love-Letters*. Her initial decision to run away with Philander and to marry his servant Brilljard in order to avoid being returned to her father attests to the sincerity of her love. However melodramatically she expresses it, she does in fact chose Philander over 'her Fame and Honour,... her friend, her Parents, and all her Beauties hopes for thee'. Silvia's real vulnerability appears in the novel's intermittent reports of the money that Philander sends her, as well as her later material dependence on Octavio, Brilljard, and, later, the Spanish nobleman Alonzo. Likewise, her affective response to Octavio is repeatedly described as not fully within her own control, however much she manipulates her responses to him in order to gain money, protection, or revenge. The narrator informs us that 'in spight of all her

---

[40] Aphra Behn, *Love-Letters Between a Noble-Man and His Sister*, 3 pts. (1684, 1685, 1687), 3: 452, 344; *Five Love-Letters*, 43.

[41] As McKeon argues, Behn writes at a time when the pursuit of self-interest is being reimagined as a natural dimension of human behaviour (*Secret History*, 536–7).

[42] McKeon, *Secret History*, 532; McKeon sees the third-person narrator as a figure for Silvia, and therefore a reliable witness of her character.

[43] Bowers, *Force or Fraud*, 119–23.

[44] McKeon, *Secret History*, 539; Behn, *Love-Letters*, 3: 310.

tenderness for *Philander*; [Silvia] found a soft emotion in her Soul, a kind of pleasure at his approach, which made her blush with some kind of anger at her own easiness' and that she 'had more Inclination than she yet had leisure to perceive' for Octavio.[45] In the third part, Silvia rapidly oscillates between Philander and Octavio because she 'could not indure to think of loosing either'; her deep attachment to Philander, as well as her vanity, lead her to act counter to her own self-interest, which would be to remain with the besotted and faithful Octavio, whom she has also come to prefer: 'now she fancies she found *Philander* duller in her Arms than *Octavio*.' Out of mere 'Pride', Silvia puts herself entirely in Philander's control, knowing that she is 'hasting to Ruin' but 'ashamed to own the Contrary' of the devotion she has just professed. Philander immediately confines her in a house in Cleves and forbids her contact with anyone but 'grave Ladies' and inhabitants of 'Monasteries'; Silvia 'regrets extreamly her conduct' as 'she every day saw what she had decay'd, her Jewels sold one by one, and at last her Necessaries' by Philander as, true to his name, he makes 'a hundred little Intrigues and Gallantries with all the pretty Women'.[46]

Silvia's odd obedience to Philander attests that truth and fiction, pragmatism and passion, are not opposites but intermingled. The impossibility of separating these motives appears more explicitly in the description of Silvia's conflicted reaction when Octavio takes holy orders:

> It was a great while before she could recover from the Indisposition which this fatal and unexpected Accident had reduced her: But as I have said, she was not of a Nature to dy for Love; and charming and brave as *Octavio* was, it was perhaps her Interest, and the loss of his considerable Fortune, that gave her the greatest Cause of Grief.... for she had this wretched Prudence, even in the highest Flights and Passions of her Love, to have a wise Regard to Interest; insomuch that it is most certain, she refused to give herself up intirely even to *Philander*; him, whom one would have thought nothing but perfect Love, soft irresistible Love could have compell'd her to have transgress'd withal, when so many Reasons contradicted her Passion: How much more then ought we to believe that Interest was the greatest Motive of all her after Passions?[47]

Puncturing the ideal that 'perfect Love, soft irresistible Love' cannot exist alongside 'Prudence' and 'Interest', Behn lets us know *now*, nearly 400 pages into the novel, that Silvia had 'refused to give herself up intirely even to *Philander*', although he aroused the 'highest Flights and Passions of her Love'. Attraction, desire, and passion are not without interest, and Silvia's 'Prudence'—her determination to shun a life of poverty—does not so much distinguish her from more seemingly sincere heroines like Chloe and Mariane as suggest the limits of a romance ideal of self-sacrifice. For had she 'give[n] herself up

---

[45] Behn, *Love-Letters*, 2: 297, 215; 3: 4.
[46] Behn, *Love-Letters*, 3: 235, 239, 291, 292–3.
[47] Behn, *Love-Letters*, 3: 344–5.

intirely' to Philander, had she not retained a 'wise Regard to Interest', Silvia would have been left to abject poverty, if not death. Being 'of a Nature to dy for Love' may be romantic, but it is hardly advisable. Nor does it make Silvia a 'sexual predator'. Critics are fond of quoting the novel's final description of Silvia's fate, in which having 'ruin'd the Fortune of that young Nobleman', Alonzo, she is expelled from Flanders by his uncle the Governor and 'forced to remove for new Prey, and daily makes considerable Conquests'. But this overlooks Alonzo's own predatory past (one that includes a seduction contest with Philander), which 'that young Nobleman' himself describes in gleeful detail. It also ignores Silvia's own genuine attraction to Alonzo, the 'thousand Agitations and Wishes' so intense that 'she durst no longer trust her self a Bed' with Alonzo in a comic, potentially homoerotic, scene in which, disguised as a man, she is lodged with Alonzo.[48]

Indeed, even the most seemingly virtuous characters, Octavio and Calista, act as much from a 'wise Regard to Interest' as from 'soft irresistible Love'. Octavio, upon learning that Philander intends to seduce his married teenaged sister Calista, is willing to allow that to happen if it will help his cause with Silvia. Octavio is initially distraught at the thought that an 'intrigue' with Philander 'might cost his Sister her Life, as well as her Fame'. But he recovers with disturbing speed when he remembers 'the more important Business of his Love'. His imagination of his sister's seduction verges on gleeful voyeurism: '*Well,* cry'd he;—*If thou beest lost* Calista, *thy ruin has laid a foundation for my happiness, and every Triumph* Philander *makes of thy Vertue, it the more secures my Empire over* Silvia ... *And thou* (continued he) *Oh perjur'd Lover and inconstant Friend, glut thy insatiate flame—rifle* Calista *of every Vertue Heaven and Nature gave her, so I may but revenge it on thy* Silvia!' Apostrophizing both Calista and Philander by turns, Octavio encourages a seduction that he knows can only harm his sister. At best, this harm will be emotional, through Philander's betrayal. At worst, it will be fatal, through the violence of her cuckolded husband, who, we later learn, '*had killed his first Wife; for which he was obliged to fly from the Court and Country of* Spain'.[49] Octavio's choice to put Calista at risk—and, not incidentally, to cheer on a betrayal that will cause Silvia pain—presents his passion *as* interest, the willingness to sacrifice not just everything but everyone to his desire. For even as he urges Philander to '*glut thy insatitate flame*', he understands his own union with Silvia as a reciprocal act of ruthless vengeance and conquest.

Calista's response to her own miserable marriage equally brings together passionate love with self-preservative prudence. Critics have made much of the ambiguity of rape and seduction in Philander's initial relations with Silvia and Calista, but—perhaps because the forced May-December marriage is a stock motif; perhaps because of an abiding assumption that sex within marriage cannot be rape—they have let pass without comment the scenes of unambiguous, and repeated, nonconsensual sexual contact

---

[48] Behn, *Love-Letters*, 3: 489, 353–62, 374–5.
[49] Behn, *Love-Letters*, 2: 167, 168–9; 3: 140.

to which Clarinau subjects Calista.[50] Philander learns from Clarinau's page that he had been married to Calista 'very much against her consent' just before he witnesses Clarinau 'fall upon her neck, her lovely Snowy neck, and loll, and kiss, and hang his tawny wither'd Arms on her fair Shoulders, and press his nauscious load upon *Calista's Body*'. Calista later tells Philander: 'but that he [Clarinau] had ever us'd to let her have four Nights in the Week her own, wherein he never distur'b her repose, she shou'd have been dead with his nasty entertainment'. Pregnant with Philander's child, she proposes that they flee together, for '*she vow'd if this unlucky Force of Flying had not happened to her, she had not been longer able to have indured his Tyranny and Slavery: But had resolved to break her Chain, and put herself upon any Fortune*' and she shoots Clarinau without hesitation when he attempts to stop their escape.[51]

Like Philander, Silvia, and Octavio, Calista is at least as motivated by the instinct of self-preservation as by the emotion of love. Calista's flight is itself a last resort, one undertaken because she cannot find a way to pass off Philander's child as Clarinau's. Having '*conceived the very first Night*' of her affair with Philander, Calista from that point cannot '*prevail for one Night with the old Count*', so that her '*Fears and Love increased with her growing Belly*' until, four months pregnant and unable to conceal her infidelity, she asks Philander to take her away. She escapes in order to liberate herself from her husband's '*Tyranny and Slavery*'; her love for Philander is secondary to self-protection. This mixture of interest and passion appears prominently in the narrative detail that Calista takes the time to '*put up all her Jewels, of which she had the richest of any Lady in all those Parts, for in that the old Count was over lavish*'. By contrast to Silvia, who initially fled her parents' home with nothing but the nightgown on her back, Calista does not impulsively '*put herself upon any Fortune*'.[52] She more prudently takes her fortune with her.

Calista's situation and actions illuminate Silvia's in many ways. The correspondence between the two women is made visible, as Gardiner notes, when they meet 'both conspicuously pregnant by Philander' and their jealous rivalry reveals that 'the stereotyping identifications between protagonist and virtuous woman fail'.[53] Both women are caught in a world that commodifies them. Calista has been forcibly—and profitably—married to 'an Old ill favour'd jealous Husband'. This unwanted but lucrative union may well have been arranged by Octavio, for when she is introduced into the narrative Calista has been 'lately' married and has 'no Parents but himself [Octavio] to right her wrongs'. Silvia's flight with Philander responded to her parents' determination to compel her to marry Forasco, and in their attempt to retrieve her they explicitly turn her into a commodity, offering a reward for her return. As she tells Octavio '*they put me into the weekly Gazette, describing me to the very Features of my Face, my Hair, my Breast, my Stature, Youth and*

---

[50] Bowers notes that Philander 'cynically takes advantage of Calista's mixed feelings' (*Force or Fraud*, 125); Richetti sees the exploitative sexuality of libertine seducers—but not husbands—as a mark of male dominance and class privilege (*English Novel*, 21).
[51] Behn, *Love-Letters*, 2: 149, 158, 358; 3: 142.
[52] Behn, *Love-Letters*, 3: 140–1, 143.
[53] Gardiner, 'First English Novel', 215.

Beauty, omitting nothing that might render me apparent to all that should see me, offering vast Sums to any that should give Intelligence of such a lost Maid of Quality.[54]

Given that all of the men in Behn's *Love-Letters* have shown themselves willing to treat women as commodities—even Octavio's largesse to Silvia upon her promise of celibacy is a bid to control her sexuality—the choices of wife, courtesan, or nun are all different forms of what McKeon aptly dubs 'sex work' insofar as they all provide sexual services, whether by regulating, satisfying, or denying the sexual urge.[55] And because sexuality can be directed toward self-interest, Behn's characters and narrators can never be sure which attachments and betrayals are driven by passion and which by interest. Ballaster notes that all we are left with at the end of the *Love-Letters* is a 'purely descriptive' account of Silvia's fate and laments the cynicism of a world in which 'Critical judgment is almost entirely abandoned' and 'even the narrator is unable to pass a moral judgment on her characters or her tale'. Silvia's refusal of the roles of 'distainful lady' or 'disdained whore' requires an identification with the male role—one that, it might be added, sees interest and pleasure as complements rather than opposites.[56] But I would argue that this refusal of a normative ideological judgement is amatory prose's unique contribution to the history of literature as well as the history of sexuality and affect. Rather than present an objective reality or morality, *Love-Letters*, like *Daphnis and Chloe* and the *Five Love-Letters*, offers descriptions of attachment and eroticism that always miss their mark, inducing equal parts suspicion and pleasure.

---

[54] Behn, *Love-Letters*, 2: 167; 3: 55. McKeon persuasively details the congruence between Octavio's language of aristocratic friendship and the self-interested exchange of women in marriage (*Secret History*, 514–15, 529). Ellen Pollack also discusses the congruence between patriarchy and fraternity in Behn's fiction; see 'Beyond Incest: Gender and the Politics of Transgression in Aphra Behn's *Love Letters between a Nobleman and His Sister*', in Heidi Hutner (ed.), *Re-reading Aphra Behn* (Charlottesville: University Press of Virginia, 1993), 15–66.

[55] McKeon, *Secret History*, 298; Ballaster, *Seductive Fictions*, 73. See also Susan Stave's insightful account of the correlation between duration of sexual possession and attributions of female morality, which hierarchize, wife, mistress, courtesan, and common prostitute ('Behn, Women, and Society', in Hughes and Todd (eds.), *Cambridge Companion*, 12–28 (25), and Catherine Gallagher's canny argument that, for Behn, the prostitute's self-alienation is also a form of self-possession ('Who Was that Masked Woman?: The Prostitute and the Playwright in the Comedies of Aphra Behn', *Women's Studies*, 15 (1987), 23–42).

[56] Ballaster, 'Love-Letters', 148, 149.

CHAPTER 6

ANTIQUARIAN WRITING

THOMAS ROEBUCK

THE last thirty years has seen a great outpouring of scholarship on seventeenth-century British antiquaries. Antiquaries' collaborative epistolary networks and the clubs and societies which shaped their work have been traced.[1] Their attempts to understand Britain's ancient monuments have been studied.[2] Their political commitments and their contributions to crucial debates about the status of the common law have been revealed.[3] The ways in which antiquaries shaped a sense of local and national identity have been explored.[4] In that context, too, Anglo-centric accounts of British antiquarianism have recently been powerfully challenged.[5] Scholars have studied antiquaries' methodologies, including the philological work embodied in their creation of dictionaries of medieval Latin or Anglo-Saxon grammars.[6] Their passion for

---

[1] Elizabeth Yale, *Sociable Knowledge: Natural History and the Nation in Early Modern Britain* (Philadelphia: University of Pennsylvania Press, 2016). On antiquarian clubs, see, for example, Diana Honeybone and Michael Honeybone (eds.), *The Correspondence of the Spalding Gentlemen's Society 1710–1761* (Woodbridge: Boydell Press, 2010).

[2] For instance, Angus Vine, *In Defiance of Time: Antiquarian Writing in Early Modern England* (Oxford: Oxford University Press, 2010), chap. 4.

[3] On antiquaries' royalist politics, for instance, see Jan Broadway, '"The honour of this Nation": William Dugdale and the *History of St Paul's* (1658)', in Jason McElligott and David L. Smith (eds.), *Royalists and Royalism During the Interregnum* (Manchester: Manchester University Press, 2010), 194–213. The classic account of the importance of antiquarianism for the development of the 'common law mind' remains J. G. A. Pocock, *The Ancient Constitution and the Feudal Law. A Reissue with a Retrospect* (Cambridge: Cambridge University Press, 1987).

[4] Jan Broadway, *'No Historie so Meete': Gentry Culture and the Development of History in Elizabethan and Early Stuart England* (Manchester: Manchester University Press, 2006).

[5] Kelsey Jackson Williams, *The First Scottish Enlightenment: Rebels, Priests, and History* (Oxford: Oxford University Press, 2020).

[6] On antiquaries and dictionary making, see John Considine, *Dictionaries in Early Modern Europe: Lexicography and the Making of Heritage* (Cambridge: Cambridge University Press, 2008), chaps. 5 and 6. For an introduction to the study of Anglo-Saxon in the seventeenth century, see John D. Niles, *The Idea of Anglo-Saxon England 1066–1901: Remembering, Forgetting, Deciphering, and Renewing the Past* (Chichester: Wiley Blackwell, 2015), chap. 4.

etymology has been uncovered, together with their desire to grasp the interrelationship between languages.[7] Attention has been paid to the interconnections between antiquarianism and natural history.[8] Antiquaries have also been studied as collectors of everything, from medieval manuscripts to art, statues, and coins.[9] We have seen accounts of antiquaries' books and reading habits.[10] The printing of antiquarian books has been examined.[11] Biographies of individual antiquaries have been written, as have synoptic treatments of the whole antiquarian tradition.[12]

In all this, however, with some notable exceptions, there has been relatively little attention paid to the ways in which antiquaries wrote—to antiquarian prose itself. This is understandable, for several reasons. For one thing, antiquarianism was a practice— a thing done—and that doing did not necessarily entail writing. Britain's antiquaries were usually (but not always) men who paid particular attention to the documents of the past.[13] Those 'documents' were usually written—medieval historians, Tower records, deeds of noble families. Such 'documents', however, did also encompass coins, inscriptions, urns, mosaics, prehistoric artefacts, bones, fossils, and much more. Perhaps a less anachronistic term than 'documents' would be 'monuments', which, especially in its Latin form, *monumenta*, encompassed everything from manuscripts to standing stones.[14] When antiquaries wrote about their discoveries, they did so in a huge variety of forms. 'Antiquarian writing' might most immediately call to mind the great county histories of the seventeenth century, which, in our period, encompassed classics

---

[7] See, for example, the introduction to Edward Lhuyd, *Archaeologia Britannica: Texts & Translations*, ed. and trans. Dewi W. Evans and Brynley F. Roberts (Aberystwyth: Centre for Advanced Welsh and Celtic Studies, National Library of Wales, 2009).

[8] Stanley Mendyk, *'Speculum Britanniae': Regional Study, Antiquarianism, and Science in Britain to 1700* (Toronto: University of Toronto Press, 1989).

[9] On antiquaries' collecting of medieval manuscripts, see Jennifer Summit, *Memory's Library: Medieval Books in Early Modern England* (Chicago: University of Chicago Press, 2008). For a different kind of antiquarian collecting, see Cinzia Maria Sicca, (ed.) *John Talman: An Early-Eighteenth-Century Connoisseur* (New Haven: Yale University Press, 2008).

[10] Sarah Griffin and David Shaw, 'William Somner and his Books: Provenance Evidence for the Networks of a Seventeenth-Century Antiquarian', in Claire Bartram (ed.), *Kentish Book Culture: Writers, Archives, Libraries and Sociability 1400–1660*, (Oxford: Peter Lang, 2020), 233–85. More generally see Nigel Ramsay, 'Libraries for Antiquaries and Heralds', in Giles Mandelbrote and K. A. Manley (eds.), *The Cambridge History of Libraries in Britain and Ireland: Volume 2: 1640-1850* (Cambridge: Cambridge University Press, 2006), 134–57.

[11] On the printing of Anglo-Saxon see Matthew Kilburn, 'The Learned Press: History, Languages, Literature, and Music', in Ian Gadd (ed.), *The History of Oxford University Press: Volume 1: Beginnings to 1780* (Oxford: Oxford University Press, 2013), 436–43.

[12] For a biography of an individual antiquary, see Theodor Harmsen, *Antiquarianism in the Augustan Age: Thomas Hearne, 1678–1735* (Oxford: Peter Lang, 2000). For a synoptic treatment of seventeenth-century antiquarianism, see Graham Parry, *The Trophies of Time: English Antiquarians of the Seventeenth Century* (Oxford: Oxford University Press, 1995).

[13] For antiquarian work supervised and directed by an aristocratic woman in this period see, *Anne Clifford's Great Books of Record*, ed. Jessica L. Malay (Manchester: Manchester University Press, 2015).

[14] For a detailed discussion of the usage of this term among scholars and antiquaries see Jan Marco Sawilla, *Antiquarianismus, Hagiographie und Historie im 17. Jahrhundert* (Tübingen: Max Niemeyer Verlag, 2009), 310–22.

of the genre such as William Dugdale's *Antiquities of Warwickshire* (1656) and Robert Plot's *The Natural History of Oxfordshire* (1677), but even these works, as we shall see, are structurally very different to one another. Seventeenth-century examples of this heterogeneous genre were ultimately attempts to deepen the chorographic accounts of each county offered by William Camden in his *Britannia* (1586–1607), a work which was revised and republished in the late seventeenth century as a *summa* of the progress made in this kind of county historiography during the seventeenth century.

But antiquarian writing was by no means limited to this kind of county history. Almost at the same time as Dugdale published his *Antiquities of Warwickshire*, he was also responsible for publishing one of the great compilations of medieval documents in his *Monasticon Anglicanum* (1655), the collection of monastic charters that he and the Yorkshire antiquary Roger Dodsworth (1585–1654) had amassed. Antiquaries produced other kinds of edition in this period, too, especially editions of medieval monastic historians, like those edited by William Fulman and Thomas Gale and published by Oxford University Press.[15] As well as directly producing editions of medieval documents, antiquaries also made catalogues of medieval manuscripts in this period, and increasingly brought them into print. Seventeenth-century catalogues of the celebrated library amassed by Robert Cotton (1570/1–1631) were written only in manuscript, but at the end of the century the nonjuror, Thomas Smith (1638–1710), who acted as librarian to the Cotton Library in the 1690s, brought an expanded version of those earlier catalogues into print.[16] But while many antiquaries were working towards publishing their findings, many others never intended to create systematic works for publication. Letters were not only a means for the major, publishing antiquaries to communicate with one another—for many seventeenth-century people with an interest in doing antiquarianism, letters were the primary form in which they wrote about what they did. Many such antiquaries never intended to produce finished, publishable works about their findings, and thus their work found ideal expression in the brief and disposable form of the letter.

The category of 'antiquarian prose' is, therefore, a bewilderingly broad one. Indeed, bewildering breadth is itself one of the most important characteristics of antiquarian prose. As Angus Vine has recently argued in a brilliant account of the subject, antiquarian works reflect a struggle to become at once both systematic and miscellaneous: 'systematic in the elaborate organizational principles that compilers often chose for them, but miscellaneous in their contents and methods of textual production.' Vine persuasively locates this tension between the 'accretive and accumulative' and the desire to be 'systematic' in the material culture within which antiquaries worked: mountains of miscellaneous notes had to be stitched together into some kind of coherent,

---

[15] *Rerum Anglicarum scriptores veteres*, ed. William Fulman and Thomas Gale, 3 vols. (Oxford, 1684–1691).

[16] Colin Tite, 'The Early Catalogues of the Cottonian Library', *British Library Journal*, 6/2 (1980), 144–57; Thomas Smith, *Catalogue of the Manuscripts in the Cottonian Library 1696 = Catalogus librorum manuscriptorum bibliothecae Cottonianae*, ed. and trans. Colin Tite (Cambridge: D.S. Brewer, 1984).

organized shape.[17] Vine's focus is largely on the late sixteenth century, but many of the same tensions he identifies are present within the antiquarianism of the seventeenth and early eighteenth centuries, too. Editions and catalogues of the mass of medieval documents were ways of bringing some kind of systematic order to those materials. Yet, as we shall see, medieval documents had a way of disrupting attempts to domesticate them to seventeenth-century prose. These tensions are given precise expression in the autobiographical account of the antiquary, Thomas Madox (1666–1727), of the process of researching and writing his massive history of the institution of the Exchequer in the eleventh and twelfth centuries. 'The first part of my business was', Madox writes, 'to make as full a collection from Records as I could, of Materials relating to the Subject.' This was not easy work: 'the labour of this cannot easily be estimated by any man who has not had some experience of it.' It is easy to see why many antiquaries never moved beyond this collecting phase. Madox, however, did. 'Those materials being ranged in a certain order in several books of *Collectanea*,' he explains, 'I reviewed them, and weighing what they imported, and how they might be applied, drew from thence a general scheme of the projected Design.' 'When I pitched upon Chapters or heads of Discourse,' he goes on, 'I took materials out of the stock provided, and digested them in proper places.' He would 'write down, in the draught of this Book', relevant 'Records or testimonies', before 'connecting and applying them afterwards, as the case would admit'.[18] Making collections, 'weighing what they imported', 'drawing from thence', 'digest[ing] them in proper places', 'connecting and applying': these are all the processes that the antiquary needed to go through in gathering and synthesizing the monuments of the past. It is easy to see how many antiquarian works ended up coming apart at the seams. The tensions within antiquarian prose are therefore the subject of the rest of this chapter.

That these tensions were felt to shape antiquarian prose writing is evident from some of the work which went into the revision of William Camden's *Britannia*, which was published in 1695.[19] The overall editor of the book was a young Oxford scholar of Old English, Edmund Gibson (1669–1748), and he was tasked with bringing together the scattered work of antiquaries from across Britain and Ireland into a coherent and publishable form. His letters to Arthur Charlett (1655–1722), the Master of University College, Oxford, vividly illuminate many of the challenges he faced in preparing this enormous antiquarian publication. One of these was getting the *style* of the book right. William Camden had written his original *Britannia* in Latin, and the book had been translated into English by the translator of classical texts, Philemon Holland, in an

---

[17] Angus Vine, *Miscellaneous Order: Manuscript Culture and the Early Modern Organization of Knowledge* (Oxford: Oxford University Press, 2019), 93–124 (124, 97).

[18] Thomas Madox, *The History and Antiquities of the Exchequer of the Kings of England* (London, 1711), p. iv.

[19] On the 1695 revision of the *Britannia* see Joseph M. Levine, *The Battle of the Books: History and Literature in the Augustan Age* (Ithaca and London: Cornell University Press, 1994), 327–36; Parry, *Trophies of Time*, chap. 12; and most recently, Thomas Roebuck, 'Edmund Gibson's 1695 *Britannia* and late-seventeenth-century British antiquarian scholarship', *Erudition and the Republic of Letters*, 5 (2020), 427–81.

edition published in 1610.[20] By the end of the seventeenth century, however, Holland's translation seemed crude; when the booksellers issued proposals for a new edition of the *Britannia*, they described the translation as 'very ill'.[21] In producing a new edition of the *Britannia*, specialists in the antiquities of each region were tasked with preparing translations of Camden's account of that region: the young Thomas Tanner (1674–1735) of Wiltshire, Edward Lhwyd of Wales, and so on. Each of these specialists then added a set of 'Additions' to their region, designed to bring the antiquarian scholarship on that area up to date. For some regions, multiple antiquaries contributed fragmentary sets of material: an inscription here, a hoard of coins there, and sometimes bits of modern economic history, too. When they did so, they wrote about it in different ways. This troubled Gibson. 'Now it was my design from the beginning', he explained to Charlett, 'to put all papers into form in their several Counties.' Unless he took a firm editorial hand, he risked 'an inequalitie of stile and composition, which would be the new consequence of several different pens', which 'must needs prove a great deformitie in the whole'.[22] This was a problem that Gibson would be far from entirely able to resolve.

Gibson's concern for the dangers of 'inequalitie of stile and composition' is a telling moment in the history of antiquarian prose. For one thing, despite antiquaries' reputation for sticking to the facts at the expense of eloquence, it demonstrates Gibson's concern for stylistic matters. As Joseph Levine has argued, even those who had a tendency to mock or condemn antiquarian learning in the seventeenth century were able to appreciate the need for antiquarian illumination of national history. Presenting the work with a polite and coherent smoothness was thus essential to making it palatable to readers for whom erudition was not automatically acceptable.[23] But, at a deeper level, Gibson's desire to avoid stylistic plurality reflects the nature of antiquarianism at the end of the seventeenth century. For all that William Camden drew on the work of many fellow antiquarian collaborators, his work was ultimately that of a single author.[24] Written in Latin, it had a fairly clear ambition to be received among the international world of European scholarship that had inspired the book in the first place. For all the perceived weaknesses (in the eyes of the late seventeenth-century antiquaries) of Philemon Holland's translation, it similarly had a singularity and unity to it as the work of an individual translator. The 1695 *Britannia* was, by contrast, many-headed: it represented diverse notions of what antiquarianism was and how it should be practised in the late seventeenth century, and diverse ways of writing about it. For some, antiquarianism was primarily focused on Roman antiquities and remains; for others, it focused on the

---

[20] Oliver D. Harris, 'William Camden, Philemon Holland, and the 1610 Translation of *Britannia*', *The Antiquaries Journal*, 95 (2015), 279–303.

[21] Bodleian Library, MS Wood 658, fol. 816r.

[22] Bodleian Library, MS Ballard 5, fol. 21r: letter of Edmund Gibson to Arthur Charlett, 1 Feb. 1693/4.

[23] Levine, *Battle of the Books*, 336–7: 'The popularity of the *Britannia* shows that the gap between learning and polite literature was not absolute; and indeed, it was generally believed that a little of antiquities, like a little philology, could well suit the man of affairs, as long as it was not overdone.'

[24] Angus Vine, 'Copiousness, Conjecture and Collaboration in William Camden's *Britannia*', *Renaissance Studies*, 28 (2014), 225–41.

middle ages; for others still, it could encompass modern economic history too. Some antiquaries prepared for Gibson coherently written and argued sustained treatments of particular counties, submitted to him as little booklets, which are made to seem monumental beside the contributions of other antiquaries, who sent letters, notes, drawings, off-cuts of printed broadsides, or even brass-rubbings.[25] By 1695, British antiquarianism had an almost uncontainable capaciousness to it, embodied materially in the profusion of documents which lie behind the 1695 *Britannia*. Gibson's task, therefore, was to try to contain these heterogeneous written and material forms, turning them into something capable of being printed.

For Gibson, 'inequalitie of stile and composition' was problematic. That was not so, however, for all antiquaries in the late seventeenth century, as Kate Bennett has argued in what is probably the most searching treatment of the form of seventeenth-century British antiquarian writing.[26] Her article's central concept emerges from Gibson's dismissal of John Aubrey's (1626–97) three-volume manuscript, *Monumenta Britannica*, as a 'mere rhapsody'. Aubrey's *Monumenta* not only contained his celebrated discussion of Stonehenge, but also ranged far more widely over British antiquities and architecture.[27] Gibson's dismissal of the work as a 'rhapsody' suggested, as Bennett explains, that he saw it as a loosely articulated series of miscellaneous materials, just the sort of thing that Gibson was attempting to avoid by trying to bring some stylistic unity to the *Britannia*. Turning Gibson's term of criticism on its head, Bennett argues that Aubrey deliberately embraced what she calls the 'rhapsodic book', one 'based in a new empirical evidence, impatient with rhetorical tradition, and incompatible with print culture; one which looked beyond the present to the needs of the future, and which infuriated traditionalists in its approach to authority'.[28] In its embrace of provisionality and its orientation towards the readers of the future, Aubrey's antiquarian writing, Bennett argues, stood as an implicit rebuke to the ideals of more conventional antiquarian scholars: rather Aubrey's inability to bring his antiquarian materials together into a form that editors (then or now) find readily publishable is not a failure, but intrinsic to his approach to prose writing.

Aubrey's embrace of the 'rhapsodic book' clearly went to extremes that dismayed his contemporaries, but we might suggest that tensions between the rhapsodic—provisional, fragmentary, future-oriented, reader-centric—and its opposite—unified, coherent, finished, and author-centric—were present within much antiquarian writing in late seventeenth-century Britain. As we have already seen, Gibson's approach to the heterogeneity of *Britannia* shows a desire to quell rhapsody. In other ways, though, even if he did not quite enthusiastically embrace rhapsody, he came closer towards it. For his whole conception of antiquarianism demonstrated the need to balance claims

---

[25] These materials are discussed in Roebuck, 'Edmund Gibson's 1695 *Britannia*'.

[26] Kate Bennett, 'John Aubrey and the Rhapsodic Book', *Renaissance Studies*, 28 (2014), 317–32.

[27] For a rich account of this work and its contribution to antiquarianism, see Kelsey Jackson Williams, *The Antiquary: John Aubrey's Historical Scholarship* (Oxford: Oxford University Press, 2016), chaps.1–3.

[28] Bennett, 'Rhapsodic Book', 318.

of provisionality and completeness. For him, Camden's *Britannia*, the masterpiece of British antiquarian prose, did not have an entirely monumental status. He articulates his vision of Camden, and with it his wider conception of antiquarian prose, in the 1695 *Britannia*'s 'Preface to the Reader'.[29] Here, he explains that Camden had won 'applause and commendation' from those who read his work, and had been 'stil'd the *Varro*, the *Strabo*, and the *Pausanias* of Britain'. He was, in other words, Britain's contribution to an antiquarian tradition which stretched back to the classical past. Even so, Camden was in need of '*Additions* and *Corrections*', which, 'in an Author of such an establish'd reputation', might risk looking 'too assuming, or be construïd a piece of envy and detraction'. However, supplementing and correcting Camden was not a mere exercise in chopping off the heads of tall poppies. It was inevitable that new antiquarian knowledge would have continued to emerge since Camden's time, and therefore supplementation and correction were no sign of weakness in the original author. But Gibson goes further. 'If Mr. *Camden* had liv'd to this day,' he argues, 'he had been still adding and altering.' Camden, in other words, was an author who had taken his place in a canonical, classical tradition, but who, on the other hand, simultaneously embodied the provisionality of antiquarian writing. To Gibson, British antiquarianism's greatest monument was a monument to a never-ending process of 'adding and altering'.

In seeing Camden in this way, Gibson was at odds with some of his contemporaries, who viewed his *Britannia* as a more stable classic. In the late seventeenth century, at the same time as canonical classics of the English literary tradition from the late sixteenth century and the early seventeenth century (like Shakespeare and Ben Jonson) were being established, so too were canonical classics of scholarship from exactly the same period.[30] Camden (and his *Britannia*, especially) was one of the foremost examples from early modern England of a scholar who deserved a place among the well-known names of the canon of Continental scholarship. This meant that, for some, Gibson's whole project of adding to the *Britannia*, and, perhaps even worse, translating it again into English, served to undermine the classic status of the work. For scholars engaged in antiquarian pursuits, such as the nonjuror Thomas Smith, Camden ought to be reprinted only in his original Latin. Moreover, for Smith, the most proper supplements to Camden were those compiled by either (ideally) Camden himself or (if necessary) those directly connected to him. In one of his letters to the young Thomas Hearne, who would become a leading antiquarian nonjuror of the early eighteenth century, Smith wrote that 'I have by mee' Camden's own copy of the 1607 *Britannia*, 'the last edition published in his lifetime' (deliberately discounting the English translation of the *Britannia* published in 1610 as not an *edition* of the book), in which various inscriptions have been 'added and inserted by himselfe in MS in their proper places, and more found out since his death.'[31]

---

[29] *Camden's Britannia, Newly Translated into English: With Large Additions and Improvements*, ed. Edmund Gibson (1695), sigs. A2r–v.

[30] See recently on this topic Emma Depledge and Peter Kirwan (eds.), *Canonising Shakespeare: Stationers and the Book Trade 1640–1740* (Cambridge: Cambridge University Press, 2017).

[31] Bodleian Library, MS Smith 127, p. 172. Camden's own copy of his *Britannia*, to which Smith is referring, is now Bodleian Library, MS Smith 1.

Supplementing Camden, therefore, was a privilege for Camden himself and those sufficiently intimately connected to Camden's legacy as to be able literally to have pasted manuscript additions into Camden's own copy of his book. It was not a matter to be opened to the multitude of Britain's antiquaries. Gibson's approach to the materiality of Camden's text was very different. Together with the booksellers who published the 1695 *Britannia*, he arranged for those responsible for each county to receive unbound leaves of the 1637 edition of the English translation of that county. Antiquaries could then write their own additions as marginalia in these unbound leaves. For Smith, authority lay in Camden's own personal copy of the book; for Gibson, Camden's book was literally and metaphorically unbound, ready for the supplements of antiquaries across Britain. In this context, Gibson's approach to the writing of antiquarianism seems comparatively anti-authoritarian, polyvocal, and even, to some extent, rhapsodic.

The tendency towards stylistic heterogeneity in seventeenth-century antiquarian prose was exacerbated by antiquaries' central subject: the medieval. It is true that, of course, since Britain had been a Roman province, there were some British antiquaries in this period who saw it as their specific remit to write almost exclusively about Roman Britain. One such was the schoolmaster, William Burton (1609–57), whose commentary on the Antonine Itinerary, one of the most important sources for understanding the geography of Roman Britain, was published in 1658, shortly after his death. This work is a word-by-word commentary, picking apart errors of copyists, analysing and emending grammatical solecisms, and locating Roman places in modern Britain with reference to archaeological finds. Burton was a classical antiquarian, proud of his ability to engage directly with the titanic figures of European scholarship despite being 'a poor Country Schoolmaster'.[32] Burton, however, was an extremely unusual figure in British antiquarianism. Most British antiquaries were medievalists, grappling with the languages and manuscripts of post-Roman Britain. Antiquaries were necessarily faced with the difficult question of how the archaic, unclassical, and often (in their terms) stylistically crude medieval tradition could be absorbed into contemporary prose.

Those who satirized antiquaries liked to suggest that their overfondness for antiquated things was not limited to the past's material remains but also extended to its language. The *New Dictionary of the Canting Crew* (1699), for instance, defined 'The Antiquary' as a 'curious Critick in old Coins, Stones and Inscriptions, in Worm-eaten records and ancient Manuscripts', who 'affects and blindly doats' on 'Relicks, Ruins, old Customs, Phrases and Fashions'.[33] Antiquated 'phrases' were part of the antiquary's misplaced enthusiasms, alongside coins, inscriptions, and manuscripts. Archaism was an acknowledged danger of antiquarian prose writing. This danger is perhaps voiced most clearly by the lawyer, James Harrington (1664–93), in the preface he wrote to the

---

[32] William Burton, *A Commentary on Antoninus His Itinerary or Journies of the Romane Empire, so for as It Concerneth Britain* (1658), 42.

[33] Quoted in Stuart Piggott, 'Antiquarian Studies', in L. S. Sutherland and L. G. Mitchell (eds.), *The History of the University of Oxford: Volume 5: The Eighteenth Century* (Oxford: Clarendon Press, 1986), 757–77 (757).

first volume of Anthony Wood's *Athenae Oxonienses* (1691), that enormous compilation of biographies of scholars who graduated from Oxford University from the time of Henry VII to Wood's present day. Harrington, in his preface to the work, is careful to defend the book's language, in particular. 'As to the Language,' he explains, 'the Reader may expect such Words as are suitable to the character of the Work, and of the Person.' Antiquaries, he explains, 'who always converse with old Authors', inevitably 'learn the dialect of their Acquaintance'. Indeed, for the antiquary, few words are 'recevi'd as English, but such as have been naturaliz'd by Spencer', suggesting (with gentle humour) that the famously archaic poet offered the accepted model for antiquaries' prose writing. But, Harrington goes on to say that antiquaries like Wood are right not to sugar-coat the writings of the past by updating their language. 'Originals are best express'd as found', he argues, 'without Alteration; and it is not only a misspent, but ridiculous labour, to change the old Expressions of a Deed; and to put a new Stamp upon a Medal.'[34] The difficult, archaic language of antiquated legal documents needs to be quoted without false embellishment. This process of absorbing old documents into antiquarian writing through quotation may roughen the smooth, elegant, polite verbal surface that Harrington's era admired, but it is inevitable in order to give a historically honest account of the past.

Some antiquaries did attempt to defend the gothic splendour of the Northern European writing of the early middle ages. Most notable here was the greatest Old English scholar of the age, the nonjuror George Hickes (1642–1715), who attempted to make a case for the rugged majesty of Icelandic sagas and other Northern European poetry.[35] But even those most sympathetic to Hickes and to the study of 'septentrional languages' were unpersuaded. Another Old English scholar, whom Hickes had mentored, the Bishop of Carlisle, William Nicolson (1655–1727), in his account of the Icelandic sagas, commented ironically that those who defended such poets assured us that 'the happiest flights we can meet with in the *Greek* and *Roman* poets, are dull Trash, if compar'd with the Seraphick Lines of a true *Cimbrian Scalder*.'[36] Perhaps more common, however, was a cautious acceptance that early medieval prose, especially Old English prose, had a certain roughness that was intrinsic to its nature. This raised fascinating questions about how such prose ought to be translated into Latin (and it was more common for almost this volume's entire period to see translations of Old English into Latin than into modern English). As translators of Old English, seventeenth-century scholars consciously sought to depart from perhaps their most prominent and significant sixteenth-century precedent. In 1568, the pioneering scholar of Old English and historian of Kent, William Lambarde (1536–1601), had published a collection of early medieval laws and treaties.[37] This book remained well known to seventeenth-century

---

[34] James Harrington, 'The Preface', in Anthony Wood, *Athenae Oxonienses*, 2 vols. (Oxford, 1691), 1: sig. a1v.
[35] On Hickes in general see *A Chorus of Grammars: The Correspondence of George Hickes and His Collaborators on the 'Thesaurus linguarum septentrionalium'*, ed. Richard L. Harris (Toronto: Pontifical Institute of Medieval Studies, 1992); for his work on Anglo-Saxon poetry, see 77–8.
[36] William Nicolson, *The English Historical Library* (1696), 131.
[37] William Lambarde (ed.), Ἀρχαιονομία, *sive de priscis anglorum legibus libri* (1568).

medievalists, and it was republished in Cambridge in 1644. To the leading scholars in that era, however, Lambarde's practice as a translator seemed to betray the true nature of Old English prose. Another pioneering Kentish Old English scholar, William Somner (bap. 1598, d. 1669), who in many ways consciously sought to model his career on that of Lambarde, voiced criticisms of his influential forebear in the preface to his great Old English dictionary, published in Oxford in 1659. Here, Somner explained that he had kept his translations literal, 'deliberately departing from that polite and elaborate style so greatly affected by William Lambarde in his own translation of the Anglo-Saxon laws'.[38] Not only, as he explained, were such paraphrastic translations unhelpful to the beginner in the language, the implication that Lambarde 'affected' such a 'polite and elaborate style' is that his Latin prose was not true to the rough-hewn nature of the original Old English.

This criticism was repeated and extended by the German scholar of Northern European languages and collector of Old English manuscripts, Franciscus Junius (1591–1677), who argued that Lambarde's translations were inferior to those of the middle ages because we ought 'rather to embrace translation of a rough and uncultivated age, than rashly adhere to those new translations which are more seemingly cultivated'.[39] These arguments were echoed by Edmund Gibson in the preface to his own edition of the Anglo-Saxon Chronicle and summarized by the antiquarian and cleric White Kennett (1660–1728) in his biography of Somner, who concluded that 'such an elegant and paraphrastic way of rendring old Records, was too much like paint on the face of a wrinkled matron, or a cap and feather upon gray hairs'.[40] There was a consensus among seventeenth-century antiquaries with a particular interest in Anglo-Saxon that the prose of that era ought to be rendered in a way which embraced its strange antiquity, rather than rendering it palatable to polite modern tastes.

Almost at the end of our period, Elizabeth Elstob (1683–1756) brought these debates about the proper translation of Anglo-Saxon texts into the vernacular. Elstob was by no means the first woman in England to take an interest in antiquarian texts, but she was the first to make substantive publications in the field.[41] Through her brother, William Elstob, she was introduced to the circle of the Oxford Saxonists, and her work was encouraged by George Hickes himself. She celebrated his mentorship in the preface to

[38] 'studiò politum illum & elaboratum fugiens stylum à *D. Gul. Lambardo* in suâ *Legum Saxonicarum* versione tantopere affectatum, ut parum aut nihil inde lector ad linguam originalem (*Saxonicam* scilicet quâ scribuntur:) intelligendam, commodetur' (William Somner, *Dictionarium Saxonico-Latino-Anglicum* (Oxford, 1659), sig. b1r).

[39] 'veterem potiùs horrentis incultíque saeculi versionem amplecti, quàm novitiis atque in speciem cultioribus temerè adhaerere' (Franciscus Junius, *Gothicum glossarium* (Amsterdam, 1684), sig. ***3v, published as an appendix to *Quatuor D.N. Jesu Christi Evangeliorum versiones perantiquae duae, Gothica scil. et Anglo-Saxonica* (Amsterdam, 1684)).

[40] *Chronicon Saxonicum*, ed. Edmund Gibson (Oxford, 1692), sig. b2v; White Kennett, 'The Life of Mr. Somner', published as a preface to his edition of William Somner, *A Treatise of the Roman Ports and Forts in Kent* (Oxford, 1693), 51–2.

[41] On Elstob see Jacqueline Way, '"Our Mother Tongue": The Politics of Elizabeth Elstob's Antiquarian Scholarship', *Huntington Library Quarterly*, 78 (2015), 417–40.

her 1709 edition of Aelfric's homily on the birthday of Pope Gregory the Great, who had been responsible for sending Augustine on a mission to Kent to convert the Anglo-Saxons. In that preface, too, she not only defended women's learning (and Old English learning in particular) but also theorized about how Old English prose ought to be translated into English. She explains that she has not done the translation 'with any great Elegance, according to the Genius of our present Idiom'. This methodological statement is far more than a conventional modesty topos. She goes on to explain that she kept her translation literal not only to help the reader decipher the unfamiliar language but also in order that the 'Saxon and the English might be discerned to be of the same Kindred and Affinity'. These aims, she concludes, 'would not be so well answer'd, by a Translation more polite and elaborate'.[42] Here she echoes in English the precise wording of Somner's criticisms of Lambarde's original translations of the Anglo-Saxon laws—that he had 'affected a polite and elaborate style'. In echoing Somner, she affirms her place as a modern successor to this tradition of antiquarian scholarship. But she departs from it, too, not only in that her translation is from Old English into the English vernacular, but also in that her translations aim to show 'Kindred and Affinity' between the ancient and the modern language, rather than to underline Old English's distance from the present. In the rest of the preface, Elstob is at pains to show that the modern Protestant church has many continuities with that of Anglo-Saxon England. Likewise, at the linguistic level, her prose shows that 'Kindred and Affinity' between the languages and eras, while stopping short of fully subsuming Old English prose into 'our present Idiom'.

British antiquaries of this period, then, had frequently to contend with a difficult question in their prose writing: how should they absorb or respond to the writing of the middle ages, when their own age valued very different kinds of prose style? We have found various kinds of responses to this problem, from humour, to defence of archaism, to subtle accommodation of the ancient to the modern (and vice versa). But perhaps one of the most wonderful examples of antiquarian integration of medieval into early modern prose is done in the simplest way: through quotation. This is found in the writing of William Dugdale, the revered herald, historian of Warwickshire, and leading expert on the Tower records in the seventeenth century.[43] Perhaps no antiquary did more in this period to bring the prose writing of medieval legal documents and charters to a seventeenth-century readership. But his use of medieval texts goes beyond mere source citation or cautious apologetics for archaism. Take, for example, the opening preface of his *Baronage of England* (1675), one of his final antiquarian works, which told the story of the lives, genealogies, and military exploits of England's medieval barons. He opens the work with a defence of history, which he initially gives over entirely to Cicero's *De Oratore*: 'There having been so much, and so well, in general, already spoken

---

[42] Elizabeth Elstob, *English-Saxon Homily on the Birth-Day of St Gregory* (1709), p. xi.
[43] On Dugdale's life see Jan Broadway, *William Dugdale; A Life of the Warwickshire Historian and Herald* (Gloucester: Xmera Press, 2011). For discussions of his life, scholarship, politics, and networks, see Christopher Dyer and Catherine Richardson (eds.), *William Dugdale, Historian, 1605–1686: His Life, His Writings and His County* (Woodbridge: Boydell Press, 2009).

in few words, by that great Orator Cicero, in commendation of History, That it is the Witness of times past, the Voice of Antiquity, the Light of Truth, and the Life of Memory; to offer more, were superfluous.' But Dugdale *does* decide it is necessary to supplement this piece of classical authority. He does so by quoting from the biography of Edward the Confessor written by the abbot, Aelred of Rievaulx (1110–67). 'Ailred, an old Monk of Rievaulx (who lived in the time of King Stephen, and Henry the Second)', Dugdale explains, gave a defence of historical biography in the preface to his *Vita S. Eduardi regis et confessoris* (1162–3). Aelred wrote (in Dugdale's translation) that 'by Recording the Lives and Actions of the Good, those who come after, have encouragement to imitate their Vertues; and, that nothing more inciteth the mind of Man, to an emulation of others, than to hear the report of their noble Atchievements'.[44] Dugdale here, without embarrassment or apology, places the medieval author alongside Cicero, effectively equating their authority and status. The quotation of Aelred mimics classical defences of historiography, suggesting direct continuities between the classical era and the high middle ages. Commonplaces from both eras flow directly into one another in Dugdale's prose. Dugdale does not simply tolerate or defend medieval 'monkish' prose: he simply treats it seamlessly with that of the Roman Latin classics. Here the antiquarian amassing of material does not suggest the pressures towards miscellaneity, but continuity and coherence.

We have seen that the larger antiquarian problem—the need to contain and discipline miscellaneous, contradictory, alien materials—shaped the prose in which antiquaries wrote. That antiquaries were concerned to bring some measure of formal and stylistic organization and even unity to the materials they studied does to some extent run counter to central concepts within the study of antiquarianism itself. Arnaldo Momigliano, in his founding article on the study of antiquarianism, made formal questions about the way in which antiquaries wrote central to the definition of antiquarianism. The question Momigliano asked in his celebrated article was: 'what is the difference between an antiquarian and a historian?' One crucial difference is in the form of their writing: 'historians write in a chronological order; antiquaries write in a systematic order.'[45] Beyond that, however, antiquaries were not concerned to burnish what they wrote with rhetorical elevation. Before the late eighteenth century, history, in Momigliano's argument, is a branch of rhetoric: it is an attempt to tell well-known stories of the past elegantly. Antiquarian research is, therefore, by contrast, unrhetorical: indeed, it is often written not only plainly but also in a crabbed, even pedantic style, as though specifically to display the fact that stylistic matters were unimportant. Although Momigliano describes antiquaries as writing in a 'systematic order', there is for Momigliano, as Vine has pointed out, something intrinsically *un*systematic to antiquarians.[46] This is the second point of Momigliano's distinction between historians and antiquaries: whereas the former

---

[44] William Dugdale, *The Baronage of England* (1675), sig. b1r.
[45] Arnaldo Momigliano, 'Ancient History and the Antiquarian', *Journal of the Warburg and Courtauld Institutes*, 13 (1950), 285–315 (286).
[46] Vine, *Miscellaneous Order*, 97.

produce 'facts which serve to illustrate or explain a certain situation', the latter collect all the items that are connected with a certain subject, whether they help to solve a problem or not. Historians seek to 'explain', antiquaries to 'collect'. Rhetorical and explanatory history is thus ranged against an unrhetorical and compilatory antiquarianism. By way of a conclusion to this chapter, I would like to revisit some of these questions and what they might tell us about British antiquarian prose in the seventeenth century.

There were certainly plenty of seventeenth-century antiquaries who argued that it was appropriate for antiquarianism to be written in a plain style. One of these was the natural philosopher and first keeper of the Ashmolean Museum, Robert Plot (*bap.* 1640, *d.* 1696). His *Natural History of Oxfordshire* was first published by the Oxford University Press in 1677.[47] Plot intended the work as a prolegomenon to a natural history of the whole of Britain, but in the end, only one more part, *The Natural History of Staffordshire* (1686), would be published. Plot's work emerges out of the tradition of county, chorographic antiquarianism, but he presents it, quite specifically, as a work of natural history. In the dedication of the work to Charles II, Plot states that the 'subject' of his work has 'alwaies deserved the notice, and the Enquirers into it, the favour of Princes'.[48] His *exempla* of princely patronage for his chosen subject are classical. 'Thus', he writes, 'had *Aristotle* in writing his Treatise of Animals the assistance of *Alexander*; and *Pliny* the Patronage of *Titus Vespasian* to his Natural History'. Whereas we saw Camden praised as the '*Varro*, the *Strabo*, and the *Pausanias* of Britain', Plot positions himself in a natural historical tradition which can be traced back to Pliny and even Aristotle. Nevertheless, it was commonly expected for the boundaries between antiquarianism and natural history to be porous in the seventeenth century, with the botanist, John Ray (1627–1705), providing lists of each region's plants to the new 1695 *Britannia*. Plot's book on Oxfordshire is organized according to natural historical categories—'Of the Heavens and Air', 'Of the Waters', 'Of the Earths' and so on. However, it is hard to keep antiquities out of these chapters, with a description of Oxford's location 'between the two Rivers of *Isis* and *Cherwell*' in the chapter 'Of the Waters' leading seamlessly into lists of Parliaments and Synods held in the city, drawing from 'an imperfect List in a MSS. in *Corpus Christi College* Library *Oxon.*'. Moreover, a whole tenth chapter was entirely devoted to 'Antiquities', including his famous account of the Rollright Stones (which he speculated might be a '*Danish* or *Norwegian monument*' to the 'election of their *Kings*') and an original (and correct) argument that the ancient British had coins before the Roman invasion.[49]

Plot opens his work with a defence of its plain style. His natural historical gleanings, Plot explains, 'I intend to deliver as succinctly as may be, in a plain, easie, unartificial

---

[47] Stanley Mendyk, 'Robert Plot: Britain's "Genial Father of County Histories"', *Notes and Records of the Royal Society of London*, 39 (1985), 129–58.

[48] Robert Plot, *The Natural History of Oxfordshire, Being an Essay toward the Natural History of England* (Oxford, 1677), sig. b1r.

[49] Plot, *Oxfordshire*, 308–58 ('Of Antiquities'), 337–43 (Rollright Stones), 308–13 (pre-Roman British coinage).

Stile, studiously avoiding all ornaments of Language'. Plot had already presented his work in Baconian terms, arguing that its remit—to cover both nature itself and nature 'as she is restrained, forced, fashioned, or determined, by Artificial Operations'—'may fall under the general notation of a *Natural History*' because 'things of Art (as the Lord *Bacon* well observeth)' are only different from 'those of Nature' in their efficient cause. It would be easy to attribute Plot's advocacy of the plain style for his natural historical antiquarianism to the Baconian influence of the Royal Society, to which he was elected soon after this book's publication.[50] There must be truth to this, but Plot was not new in advocating for a plain, unadorned style for antiquarian prose. In 1656, a few years before the founding of the Royal Society, William Dugdale had defended his own great work of county history, *The Antiquities of Warwickshire*, in not dissimilar terms. Although another classic of the same genre in which Plot wrote, this work also has many differences to his. Structurally, it is arranged not according to features of the natural world but according to the county's hundreds, its ancient administrative division that Dugdale dates to the Anglo-Saxon period. The hundreds themselves are ordered according to the county's rivers, a structuring device which echoes that of Camden's *Britannia*. Whereas Plot tends to focus on more ancient artefacts, Dugdale's work is stuffed with the evidences of medieval legal and administrative documents, which allow Dugdale to trace evolving place names, land ownership, and ecclesiastical administration. Despite this documentary focus, Dugdale does also provide a memorable description (and engraving) of a pre-historic axe, the kind of antiquity that would certainly have caught Plot's attention.[51] For all their formal differences, too, Dugdale also defends his work's lack of rhetorical adornment. 'In all which', he writes, near the end of his book's preface, 'and throughout the whole work, I have to my utmost, endeavoured the plainest style, as most meet (in my Judgment) for such a business.' Dugdale justifies this stylistic choice not in Baconian terms but with an appeal to classical authority. When he 'endeavoured the plainest style' he was, he explains, 'well remembring that of Cicero, how an Historian should be qualified'. He quotes Cicero's *De Oratore*, in which Catulus argues that the historian ought 'not of necessitie to be an Orator, *satis est non esse mendacem* [it is sufficient that he is not a liar]'. 'The truth is it', he goes on, 'which is principally to be aimed at', and he continues to quote Cicero: 'For who does not know the first law of History, never dare to speak falsehood? And then never dare not to speak the truth?'[52] Dugdale defends his work using the most well-known ancient statement on proper historical method, suggesting not only that he understood his work's plain style to be justified by classical rhetorical theory (rather than by anything more modern) but also that the boundaries (for Dugdale) between antiquities and history were blurred.

---

[50] Plot, *Oxfordshire*, 1–2. See further the chapter by Felicity Henderson on 'Scientific Transactions'.

[51] William Dugdale, *The Antiquities of Warwickshire* (1656), 778. For more on Dugdale's *Warwickshire*, see Graham Parry, 'The Antiquities of Warwickshire', in Dyer and Richardson (eds.), *William Dugdale*, 10–33.

[52] Dugdale, *Warwickshire*, sig. Bb4r. For the quotations, see Cicero, *De Oratore*, 2. 51, 62.

Dugdale was perfectly capable of *not* being plain when it was appropriate for him not to be. Indeed, the preface which we have just quoted begins with an almost bombastic quotation from Walter Raleigh's *History of the World*, which defends 'Historie' for having 'carried our knowledge over the vast and devouring space of many thousand years'.[53] Before he printed the *Antiquities of Warwickshire*, Dugdale circulated this preface (and the book's dedicatory epistles) to his fellow antiquary, William Somner (who had criticized Lambarde's 'polite and elaborate' translations of the Saxon laws), for his comments. The preface, Somner replied to Dugdale, is 'for the matter and contents, very pertinent, learned, and elaborate' and 'for the stile and language, such as the subject doth require, sober, serious and savoury, or (if you will rather) like the Author, grave'.[54] When 'grave' and 'elaborate' was required, Dugdale could produce it and Somner would approve of it, even if 'elaborate' was specifically a term of criticism when applied to Lambarde's translations of Anglo-Saxon prose. The detail of antiquities, on the other hand, required an appropriate plainness. We have seen, therefore, that there is much truth in Momigliano's distinction between history and antiquarianism in rhetorical terms. However, we have also seen that, for Dugdale, 'history' and 'antiquarianism', could not be firmly separated. If we return for a moment to Momigliano's own framework for thinking about antiquarianism, this is not surprising. For Momigliano, the firm distinction between history and antiquarianism only pertained to the writing of *classical* antiquities. 'The authority of the ancient historians was such the nobody was yet seriously thinking of replacing them', he writes. 'The situation was different', he goes on, when it came to medieval history. 'No cult of the Middle Ages had yet developed to compete with the idealization of Antiquity. No mediaeval chronicle', he argues, 'could claim such authority as to prevent the re-writing of mediaeval history'.[55] As we have seen, it is medieval history with which, ultimately, most British antiquaries were engaged. And as such, by the end of the seventeenth century, many would not have seen themselves purely to be writing 'antiquarianism' as opposed to 'history'.

One who certainly did not seem to draw such a firm distinction was the Cambridge scholar and physician, Robert Brady (c.1627–1700). Master of Gonville and Caius College, Cambridge, he was physician-in-ordinary to both Charles II and James II. Out of a mass of historical evidence from Tower records, in particular, he developed a historiographical theory which bolstered James II's absolutist ambitions. In 1684, Brady published his *Complete History of England*, the work in which his theory and practice as a historian were most fully developed. Whereas Whig-leaning historians were arguing that England's political liberties pre-dated the Norman conquest, for Brady, any such liberties flowed directly from the Anglo-Norman kings themselves, and were thus royal gifts. The Saxon period, to Brady, was one of servitude. These were arguments Brady continued to expound after the Glorious Revolution. His synthesis of deep research

---

[53] Dugdale, *Warwickshire*, sig. Bb1r.
[54] Letter of William Somner to Dugdale, 7 March 1655/56, printed in William Hamper, *The Life, Diary, and Correspondence of Sir William Dugdale, Knight* (1827), 304.
[55] Momigliano, 'Antiquarian', 292–3.

in historical sources, argument, and narrative have won him the respect of modern historians, although perhaps this synthesis was a little less original than is sometimes suggested.[56] For Levine, his *Complete History* was 'a new form of historical narrative that combined the annalistic form of the medieval chronicle with the antiquarian compilation of sources'.[57] Brady was certainly seen by contemporaries as both historian and antiquary. Thomas Smith, the Cotton Librarian and nonjuror whom we have already encountered, corresponded with Brady in the 1690s, in letters which make little effort to disguise their loyalty to James II. In one letter, Smith defends Brady from the accusations of the Whig historian, James Tyrrell (1642–1718), that Brady had failed to make reference to a crucial Tower record. According to Smith, Tyrrell was 'most disingenuously upbraiding you with your want of the knowledge of it, as if during those few years you had the custody of that inestimable treasure, you had been obliged to have read over every parchment there'. That inordinate task 'would take up the whole lifetime of an Antiquary or Historian', as though Brady might be well described as either and as though both would be interested in the Tower records.[58]

Many of the problems and tensions we have explored in this chapter—between a rhapsodic digressiveness and a striving after unity, between a prose of polyvocal embrace of medieval documents and a prose of polite, modern smoothness, between antiquities and history—come together in Brady's work. Brady gives voice to some of these tensions himself in his *Complete History*'s 'Letter to the Reader'. 'Through the whole Course of the History,' he writes, 'I have not Laboured after an Exact and Even Style.' He goes on to explain why 'an Exact and Even Style' has not proved attainable: 'nor can it be Expected where there is such Variety of Matter, and where Men are confined to, and limited by the Translation of other Mens Language.' 'There is nothing my own', he disclaims, 'but the Method and Version, and whether the last be Faithful and Just, as it ought to be, I Submit my self to the Censure of the Impartial Reader.' From a stylistic point of view, Brady, at least in his own estimation, did not even try to master the array of medieval documents with which his work bristled. There was simply too much 'Variety of Matter' and too much of 'other Mens Language'. But what he did have was 'Method', and in this he had a significantly easier job of mastering the diffuse energies of antiquarianism than did, say, Gibson, as he attempted to minimize 'inequalitie of stile and composition' in the revised *Britannia*. In other words, the rigorous argument Brady unfolded in his work was what allowed him to draw together the melee of Tower records available to him into a 'Complete History'. Nevertheless, the documents which crowd the margins, footnotes, and italicized quotations of his work show that 'an Exact and Even Style' was not obtainable. The simultaneous need to give antiquarianism a driving argument *and* to make sure that argument was bolstered by exact references emerged from the sharp divisions of seventeenth-century political culture, not least, in this case, those which precipitated the Glorious Revolution. Just as politics gave antiquarianism an argumentative focus,

---

[56] Pocock, *Ancient Constitution*, 182–228.
[57] Levine, *Battle of the Books*, 320.
[58] Bodleian Library, MS Smith 59, p. 9.

it also gave renewed energy to its polyvocality. However, to give antiquarianism such argumentative focus also seems contradictory to the nature of antiquarianism as a pursuit: to amass materials precisely *without* driving them towards such a conclusion. These are probably irresolvable tensions within the whole idea of 'antiquarian' writing, but perhaps they were never more acute or explored with greater self-consciousness than in the period of this volume.

CHAPTER 7

BIOGRAPHY AND AUTOBIOGRAPHY

JULIE A. ECKERLE

I<small>N</small> 1708, in epistolary comments about a proposed new edition of William Hamilton's *The Exemplary Life and Character of James Bonnell* (1703), Thomas Smyth, Bishop of Limerick, voiced concern about trends in biographical writing: 'It is a fault too Common among Such as apply themselves to the writing of Lives, that they are very Lavish & extravagant in the Commendation of those whos[e] character they pretend to publish: aiming rather to raise their vallue then give an impartial account of their merit, & studying more to shew their own Eloquence then to speak truth.' Smyth insists that he does not believe Hamilton, his likely addressee, to be guilty of such vanity and in fact professes his support of the printing of another edition of *The Exemplary Life*, since 'a faithfull Representation of those Christian Graces wch so Eminently appear'd in that Excellent person [i.e. Bonnell], must needs do the more good, the more publick it is made.'[1] Nonetheless, his comments provide a useful glimpse behind the scenes, as it were, of biographical writing in the early eighteenth century, near the end of a period of extraordinary development in the form.

Indeed, both biography and autobiography transformed dramatically in form, function, and scope over the course of the seventeenth and early eighteenth centuries, in no small part because of the tumultuous political and religious events that gave individual experience and testimony new value. For example, as Allan Pritchard explains in his useful survey of seventeenth-century biography, 'the two traditional categories of the lives of saints and lives of princes and other great public figures became in effect amalgamated or fused together' because 'religious and secular political issues were so closely linked' and '[t]he older type of the life of the prince was no longer possible after the beheading of the reigning king'. Furthermore, the traditional form in which the

---

[1] Thomas Smyth, letter (1708), National Library of Ireland, Dublin, MS 41,580/23. The hand is not clear enough to be *certain* of the addressee.

biographer 'attempts to assimilate his subjects with ideal models and to a large extent works deductively from those ideals' began to co-exist during this period with 'newer types of biography ... less concerned with similarities and more fully concerned with the differences between one individual and another'.[2] Exemplarity, long a driving motif of auto/biographical expression, remained key, but exactly how one established this aspect of his/her subject was less prescribed than had once been the case. At the same time, a fuller range of subjects became acceptable, in terms of both the individuals memorialized and the contexts in which they operated (religious, political, professional). Perhaps most significantly, as biographical and autobiographical prose developed over the period in question and began to incorporate themes beyond spiritual exemplarity, life-writers increasingly used the nascent genres to defend or justify their subjects' lives.

Given the political and cultural upheavals that characterized the period, this need to defend reputation, political allegiances, and behaviour—whether one's own, that of a close relative, or even of a political philosophy—is hardly surprising. But it does complicate both what we look for and what we find when we approach one of these texts. Does the narrative represent a life lived or, as Smyth implied in 1708, the biases, concerns, and reflections of the author? Although scholars and practitioners of the last century have made clear that no instance of auto/biographical expression is without a rhetorical agenda and at least some degree of fictionalization, intentional or otherwise, the degree to which these factors inform, shape, or distract from the 'facts' of a life was less theorized in the early modern period even as it clearly impacted how one reads a text and thus—to use Smyth's language—its ability to 'do ... good'. The shift from exemplarity as universal defining feature to a range of more explicitly selfish motives forced not only the genres of autobiography and biography but also their practitioners and readers to a new state of critical awareness.

Within this context, it is worth dwelling a bit longer on Hamilton's *Exemplary Life* of James Bonnell (1653–99), Accountant-General of Ireland. Although the text itself is in many ways typical and best read as the spiritual biography of an exemplarily pious man, the backstory of how it came to be written and published offers a valuable window into how late-seventeenth and early eighteenth-century individuals approached the biographical project at this key moment in the development of the form.[3] Among the familiar platitudes about the value of exemplary lives for the edification of readers, this story also demonstrates the investment of 'authorial' ego already observed by Smyth, the inter-personal conflicts over rhetorical purpose and biographical content, and some of the gendered realities that often informed life-writing projects at this time. Of course, being dead, James Bonnell had little to say about his posthumous *Life*. However, almost

---

[2] Allan Pritchard, *English Biography in the Seventeenth Century: A Critical Survey* (Toronto: University of Toronto Press, 2005), 12, 6. Although the term 'biography' began to be used in the seventeenth century, 'life' was far more common.

[3] For religious autobiography in the period covered by this volume, see Chapter 32 on 'Religious Autobiography' by Brooke Conti.

immediately after his death on 28 April 1699, his widow, Jane (c.1670–1745), reached out to their mutual friend, William King (1650–1729), then Bishop of Derry, with a fervent hope that he would write her husband's life and publish her husband's writings, especially his meditations and excerpts from his letters. King refused both tasks, initially in quite polite terms, but found himself refusing again and again, for many months and in many letters, until Jane finally gave up and asked Hamilton (d. 1729), Archdeacon of Armagh, to take on the project. Jane and King's voluminous correspondence in the interim records a passionate disagreement about the ethics of biographical writing (not to mention related debates about appropriate degrees of grief and the responsibilities of friendship). For Jane, as with many women of this period who wrote their husbands' or fathers' lives, such projects fulfilled the duty they felt to memorialize (and perhaps redeem, depending on the circumstances) their loved one's reputation and often provided a means of dealing with grief over the individual's passing.

Regarding the first motive—a spouse's duty to memorialize—Jane is quite explicit and insistent. Writing to her husband's kinsman Reverend John Strype (1643–1737), himself a writer of lives, in October 1699, she says, 'I think I ought to do all y^t is possable to perpetuat the memory of such a saint'.[4] Similarly, in a letter to King the following March, she expresses her confidence that he will do all in his power 'to preserve the memory of such a man who I may say deserved it from y^u if the sincer[e]st frendship may merit any thing'.[5] As that confidence wanes over the subsequent months, Jane's manipulative rhetoric intensifies. Thus she expresses disbelief in a January 1701 letter about King 'den[y]ing to doe Iustice to the memory of [his] frend' by not publishing Bonnell's writings, and she questions whether a man of King's position and temper could possibly write Bonnell's life appropriately anyway:

> I must acknowledge to be in a temper to writ such a Life woud need such recollection & sedeatness of temper as is not easily to be attained in the midst of such incombrance as y^u are engaged in, but the way to be in such a temper, would be to set about such a work, the dwelling much upon his life, & conversing with his heavenly remains, must put one in such a temper if they be not utterly lost to all sence of piety. My earnest desire was that y^u shoud set about it when the sence of the loss y^u had, was fresh in y^r memory, & had made some impression on y^u, then y^u woud have neither wanted temper nor words to have represented him in a true Light, but alas we are all apt to let such things wear too soon of [i.e. off], … may I never forget [my loss] I humbly beg[.][6]

---

[4] Strype published *Memorials of … Thomas Cranmer* in 1694, the first of what Diarmaid MacCulloch describes as 'Strype's Series of Studies of Worthies of the Mid-Tudor and Elizabethan Periods, Mostly Archbishops' (*All Things Made New: The Reformation and Its Legacy* (Oxford: Oxford University Press, 2016), 267); Jane Bonnell, letter to Rev. J. Strype (19 Oct. 1699), Trinity College, Dublin, MS 2929, fols. 249-60 (fol. 250). The manuscript contains transcribed copies of original letters in the Strype Correspondence at Cambridge.

[5] Jane Bonnell, letter to William King (16 March 1699/1700), Trinity College, Dublin, MS 1995-2008/673.

[6] Jane Bonnell, letter to William King (28 Jan. 1700/1701), Trinity College, Dublin, MS 1995-2008/752.

Not only does this passage reveal Jane's bold character (a consistent feature of her ample correspondence), but—more pertinently for the purposes of this chapter—it also demonstrates how quickly a textualized life becomes merged with the identities of its writers, readers, and, in Jane's case, commissioners. First, Jane insists, simply writing the life of a sedate and pious man will endow the author with said temper and piety (no matter, apparently, the state of mind and soul with which he begins the work). By a similar logic (the foundational logic of exemplarity), reading the life of a pious man will improve the piety of the life's readers. But Jane, too, will be elevated in piety and reputation as the ideal widow behind both text and man. Indeed, nearly two years after her husband's death, Jane's insistence that Christian duty requires Bonnell's friends and loved ones to share his piety with the world is so closely intertwined with her own sense of self—and the pious sense of self that such a project, if successful, would reinforce—that it is nearly impossible to distinguish the two. Quite simply, to publish her husband's life and writings is to be an exemplary widow.

Yet grief, the second impulse common to the writing and publishing of a deceased spouse's life, is also at work here. To explain why she has spoken of her husband at such length in her 1699 letter to Strype, Jane says simply, 'I coud spend my life time in speaking or writing of him'.[7] She uses slightly different terms when she writes to King just five days later: 'I think I am now very indifferant as to all things of this world, only an earnest desire to see that work set about [and] published.'[8] In both cases, Jane's comments suggest that getting her husband's life and work published not only makes her an exemplary widow but also enables and in part enacts her grieving. For King's part, he insists that his respect and love for his deceased friend have led him to a quite different conclusion about the projects Jane has proposed. In a December 1700 letter to her, King cites Bonnell's own opinion against printing another man's writings after his death, adding that he has no reason to believe Bonnell wanted his own work to be an exception. He reinforces this claim in a late April 1701 letter, explaining, 'I find a passage that Contains at full ... Bonnells opinion Concerning the Censure that may be past on him if any one shou'd see ye papers that he says he made his Confessors'.[9] Like his correspondent, King's rhetoric gradually grows more heated—'In short Madam I think you wrong in this whole matter and managem^t. towards his memory'—even as he insists that he is enacting respect for his dear friend by refusing a task that would not only defy Bonnell's 'Judgment and Desire' but also expose him to the 'injury' that King himself has witnessed 'Done great Men by posthumous works'.[10] King's sense of the moral responsibility of writing a man's life is so acute, in fact, that he provides some advice for Bonnell's ultimate biographer even though he wants nothing to do with the project himself: 'However [whoever] writes his life if they do him Justice must say amongst other

---

[7] Bonnell, letter to Rev. J. Strype, Trinity College, Dublin, MS 2929, fol. 253.
[8] Jane Bonnell, letter to William King (24 Oct. 1699), Trinity College, Dublin, MS 1995–2008/631.
[9] William King, letter to Jane Bonnell (27 April 1701), Trinity College, Dublin, MS 750/2/2/121.
[10] William King, letter to Jane Bonnell (22 July 1701), Trinity College, Dublin, MS 750/2/2/27; William King, letter to Jane Bonnell (4 Dec. 1700), Trinity College, Dublin, MS 750/2/2/29.

things that he was a[cc]urate in his method, curious in his thought, Choice in this [sic] words, delicate in the turnes of sentences and Just in his Expressions, print only what agrees with this and Youl do his memory Justice.'[11] Clearly, King and Jane share a deep respect for Bonnell even as their disagreement about his textual life reveals that the moral imperative of biographical writing is not a straightforward matter nor the project—once determined on—totally distinct from the motives and personalities behind it.

Ultimately, as the very title of Bonnell's *Life* makes clear, Hamilton chose to write according to the exemplarity tradition and thus composed his text with the goal of edifying readers via the model lived by James. This rationale appears most explicitly at the beginning of Part II:

> I shall now enter upon that part of this work, for the sake of which the rest was put together, and without which the world is not much concerned to know his story, and that is, particularly to describe his character and excellences: to recommend him as a pattern worthy our imitation, in all the duties of the Christian life; and to shew from him, how beautiful Christianity is, when reduced to practice; when it becomes a rule of life and manners; and not, as it is with most men, confined to the thoughts, and made an unactive notion of the mind.[12]

Hamilton here conveys the theory of the exemplary life, which enables the dead to speak, as it were, to readers. So says D. Cumyng when he writes to Jane in April 1705 in advance of a new edition.[13] He further distances *The Exemplary Life* from the troublesome trends noted by Smyth: 'I am well sattisfied that the Main design in the Publication of M. Bonnells life was not to Erect a monument for or to perfume the memory of the Dead (tho. Much of that be verie allowable where there was so verie Much Merit as in your Excellent Husband). But that the prime Intention of printing and Reprinting it was, and is, to doe good to the Living.'[14] Thus the story of 'How James Bonnell's *Life* Came to be Written' appears to have a happy ending. Even Jane's epistolary relationship with King survived their barbed debate, continuing for the rest of King's life.

However, thanks to their correspondence, we know that there is more to the story, including the likelihood that Bonnell's life as depicted on the page differed from how it was actually lived. Although there is no indication that Jane kept any scandalous details about her husband secret, she does explain in an early letter to King that she has taken the liberty of having 'a frend … coppy [Bonnell's letters to Jane] & leave out such parts as did not releat to religious matters'.[15] The edited copies are the ones she then shared with King and, later, Hamilton. This decision further reinforces the

---

[11] William King, letter to Jane Bonnell (27 April 1701), Trinity College, Dublin, MS 750/2/2/121.
[12] William Hamilton, *The Exemplary Life and Character of James Bonnell* (8th edn, London, 1829), 70.
[13] Jane's correspondent in this case was almost certainly the Presbyterian medical doctor Duncan Cumyng, who practiced in Dublin.
[14] D[uncan] Cumyng, letter to Jane Bonnell (18 April 1705), National Library of Ireland, Dublin, MS 41,580/23.
[15] Jane Bonnell, letter to William King (24 Oct. 1699), Trinity College, Dublin, MS 1995–2008/631.

ethical challenges of auto/biographical writing that, in this instance, the epistolary record allows us to see. What is suitable for inclusion in a life story? Whose approach to the moral justification of such a project is correct? How much of the author (or of a behind-the-scenes director or editor like Jane) appears in the biography ultimately written? And—perhaps most importantly—when is 'the world ... concerned to know [an individual's] story'?

*

Many readers and writers found auto/biographical stories worth their time in the period 1640–1714. Yet it is important to acknowledge that what the terms 'autobiography' and 'biography' mean to us in the twenty-first century is quite different from what they meant to individuals in the seventeenth and early eighteenth centuries. Indeed, a recent work like Adam Smyth's *A History of English Autobiography* demonstrates quite convincingly that there is 'a crucial pre- or counter-history to the better-known story of autobiography's nineteenth-century origins', according to which Jean-Jacques Rousseau's 1782 *Confessions* marks autobiography's 'real beginning'.[16] According to our revised understanding, however, autobiographical forms existed well before Rousseau and in fact adapted as necessary to social, political, and spiritual needs. The mid-seventeenth-century regicide may have been the most shocking and influential of the period's events, but many other developments—such as 'the spread of Protestant doctrines about introspection and unmediated relationships with the divine' and 'the development of experimental science'—also 'helped to produce a cultural environment that privileged both self-reflection and an ideologically nuanced approach to individuality'.[17] The auto/biographical forms that developed along with and in response to these shifts were characterized by fluidity, multiplicity, hybridity, and experimentation. Indeed, Smyth argues that not only has 'a sense of generic unfixity and experimentation ... always been ... a central trait of autobiography' but it is also, in fact, 'a *condition* of autobiographical writing'.[18]

Scholars were slow to acknowledge both this aspect of auto/biographical expression and the genres' earliest incarnations in large part because they did not conform to the strict definitions fixed post-Rousseau. In modernity, autobiography has generally been thought to depend on the construction of a cohesive self (especially a *male* self) over time, as well as 'an authoritative perspective that consistently controls the presentation of this self', typically composing from a mature age late in life, whereas biography

---

[16] Adam Smyth, 'Introduction', in Smyth (ed.), *A History of English Autobiography* (Cambridge: Cambridge University Press, 2016), 1–10 (2). The dates most often noted for the first recorded usage of the term 'autobiography' are 1797 and 1809; see, respectively, David Booy, 'Introduction', in Booy (ed.), *Personal Disclosures: An Anthology of Self-writings from the Seventeenth Century* (Aldershot: Ashgate, 2002), 1–19 (3); Felicity A. Nussbaum, *The Autobiographical Subject: Gender and Ideology in Eighteenth-Century England* (Baltimore: Johns Hopkins University Press, 1989), 1.

[17] Michelle M. Dowd and Julie A. Eckerle, 'Introduction', in Dowd and Eckerle (eds.), *Genre and Women's Life Writing in Early Modern England* (Aldershot: Ashgate, 2007), 1–13 (1).

[18] Smyth, 'Introduction', in Smyth (ed.), *History of English Autobiography*, 6–7 (emphasis added).

similarly traces the cohesive life narrative of an important public individual.[19] Not only do these definitions fail to account in any way, shape, or form for the auto/biographical expression of *women*—as the last few decades of feminist scholarship have amply demonstrated—but they also fail to account for much of the life-writing that was written before the modern period by writers of either gender.[20] The early modern use of different terms, such as 'history' as a synonym for 'life' and 'memoir' for both biographical and autobiographical accounts, further complicates matters.

Given our current understanding of these pre-modern forms, it may well be more useful to approach auto/biographical writing as a *practice* rather than a genre. Certainly, this is Michael Mascuch's method in *Origins of the Individualist Self*, in which he approaches autobiography as 'cultural practice': 'autobiography is a performance, a public display of self-identity, even when composed secretly for an audience of one.'[21] Regardless of whether one thinks of a 'practice' or 'genre', however, it is essential to develop a broader terminology and at the very least to acknowledge the lack of stability of both the terms and assumed forms of 'biography' and 'autobiography'. In this unblinkered condition, we can see auto/biographical expression *everywhere* in the pre-modern period, including in many of the forms of prose writing surveyed in the chapters of this volume: recipe books, inscriptions designating book ownership, letters, diaries, mothers' and fathers' legacies, monument inscriptions, almanacs, commonplace books, marginalia, the *responsa scholarum* composed by new university students, fictional forms like poetry and romances, occasional meditations, prefaces, and more.[22] One way of dealing with this often overwhelming mass of auto/biographical material has been to use the term 'life-writing', defined by Marlene Kadar as 'a less exclusive genre of personal kinds of writing'.[23] However, for the purposes of this chapter, that would be

---

[19] Dowd and Eckerle, 'Introduction', 3. The most typical incarnation of this definition is Phillippe LeJeune's: 'a retrospective prose narrative produced by a real person concerning his own existence, focusing on his individual life, in particular the story of his personality' (quoted in Smyth, 'Introduction', 2). Even in the late twentieth century, Michael Mascuch defined autobiography as 'the unified, retrospective first-person narrative [that] uniquely totalizes its subject as both author and hero' (*Origins of the Individualist Self: Autobiography and Self-Identity in England, 1592–1791* (Stanford, Calif.: Stanford University Press, 1996), 23).

[20] See especially Shari Benstock, *The Private Self: Theory and Practice of Women's Autobiographical Writings* (Chapel Hill: University of North Carolina Press, 1988); Sheila Ottway, 'Autobiography', in Anita Pacheco (ed.), *A Companion to Early Modern Women's Writing* (Oxford: Blackwell, 2002), 231–47, and Sidonie Smith and Julia Watson, *Women, Autobiography, Theory: A Reader* (Madison, Wisc.: University of Wisconsin Press, 1998).

[21] Mascuch, *Origins of the Individualist Self*, 8–9.

[22] On *responsa scholarum*, see Molly Murray, 'The Radicalism of Early Modern Spiritual Autobiography', in Smyth (ed.), *History of English Autobiography*, 41–55. See further this volume's chapters by Kate Bennett ('Brief Lives and Characters'); Adam Smyth ('Diaries'); Nicholas Seager ('Dissenting Writing'); Niall Allsopp ('Histories'); Diana G. Barnes ('Letters'); Catherine Armstrong ('New World Writing and Captivity Narratives'), and Brooke Conti ('Religious Autobiography').

[23] Marlene Kadar, 'Coming to Terms: Life Writing—From Genre to Critical Practice', in Marlene Kadar (ed.), *Essays on Life Writing: From Genre to Critical Practice* (Toronto: University of Toronto Press, 1992), 3–15 (4). Similarly, in his 'Introduction' to *Personal Disclosures*, Booy prefers phrases like 'self-writing', 'writings about life-experience', and 'autobiographical expression', because they 'at least

to cast far too wide a net. Instead, I focus on rather traditionally conceived autobiography and biography while recognizing that stand-alone incarnations of these generic forms came to be in a milieu in which deeply reflective and engaged human beings—both male and female and of the full range of religious and political persuasions—used and manipulated a variety of forms and models for a variety of personal and political purposes.

Female-authored biography, only a short step from the 'female-commissioned' life considered in my introduction, is best represented by two women on opposite sides of the civil war crisis: Royalist Margaret Cavendish (1623–73) and Parliamentarian Lucy Hutchinson (1619/20–81). Their politically driven apologia for their husbands are characterized by many of the aspects of auto/biographical expression I have identified, such as incorporating multiple genres, idealizing their subjects, and—at least in Cavendish's case—defying the more modern expectations of narrative cohesion. Most significantly, they demonstrate how, in seventeenth-century lives, exemplarity gives way to more urgent motives and themes, most often the defence of a reputation.

In *The Life of John Hutchinson*, first printed in 1806 but written from 1664 to 1671, Hutchinson's primary task is undoubtedly political, as her Puritan husband, John (1615–64), was a signatory of Charles I's death warrant and had died in prison in September 1664.[24] Therefore, although in her preface she describes the writing of his *Life* in the fashion of Jane Bonnell as 'consolatory' and claims it will serve as both a 'monument' to her husband and 'the preservation of his memory' for their children, what is really at stake is John's reputation.[25] How she goes about this, however, is less predictable, for she builds *The Life* around the theme of her husband's divinely ordained life, even though—at the time of her writing—God's chosen side seems rather clearly to have been the Royalists. Indeed, according to the traditional Royalist interpretation of events, '[t]he Civil War and Interregnum were seen as divine judgment upon the merely conditional and partial obedience which subjects had granted to their sovereign'.[26] Yet Hutchinson's text counters and challenges this narrative. It refuses to assign a moral victory to the other side or to apologize for her husband's Parliamentarianism but instead—in the immediate aftermath of the monarchy's restoration—makes a hero of a man whose signature on a king's death warrant had helped to destroy said monarchy in the first place. Hutchinson co-opts the Royalist tale of moral righteousness to create the kind of hero praised and admired in Royalist narratives: her husband was an exemplary Christian

---

encompass the heterogeneity of seventeenth-century texts in which some form of self-revelation occurs' (3).

[24] Although editors since the first published edition have identified the text as *Memoirs of the Life of Colonel Hutchinson*, I use the abbreviated version of Hutchinson's own heading, 'The Life of John Hutchinson of Owthorpe in the County of Nottingham, Esquire'.

[25] Lucy Hutchinson, *Memoirs of the Life of Colonel Hutchinson with a Fragment of Autobiography*, ed. N. H. Keeble (London: J. M. Dent, 1995), 16–17. Cited hereafter as Hutchinson, *Life*.

[26] N. H. Keeble, 'Obedient Subjects? The Loyal Self in Some Later Seventeenth-Century Royalist Women's Memoirs', in Gerald Maclean (ed.), *Culture and Society in the Stuart Restoration: Literature, Drama, History* (Cambridge: Cambridge University Press, 1995), 201–18 (202).

man whose very 'soul conversed with God' and whose heart '*in all times* ... was sincere and steadfast to the Lord' (emphasis added).[27]

Needless to say, this particular construction of Colonel John Hutchinson requires strategic manoeuvres, perhaps the most telling of which is Hutchinson's insertion of herself into John's biography as a key agent in saving him from execution. Although her husband, being the loyal and steadfast man he was, appeared bent on 'being a public sacrifice', Hutchinson explains that *she* chose the disloyal route. Characteristically using the third-person voice to narrate her actions as John's wife, she explains that 'herein only in her whole life, [she] resolved to disobey him' by writing 'a letter in his name to the Speaker' of the Commons asking for mercy; significantly, she does not explain what the letter said.[28] In this way, she effectively preserves John's reputation as a republican even though, as Derek Hirst points out, we now know that the letter actually contained both confession and regret, elements that could prove shameful to the 'noble commonwealthsman' she has been at such pains to construct. Seemingly taking the fall as disobedient wife, Hutchinson thus preserves both her husband's reputation and his integrity, the latter being a key aspect of the virtuous man she has created on the page and for posterity. Yet the real man, Hirst reminds us, exhibited increasingly Royalist behaviours that Hutchinson consistently misrepresents in her text, thus leading to Hirst's convincing conclusion that '[t]he steadily virtuous Colonel she presented was not the Colonel she lived with' but instead a man more in line with her *own* republican values and with the kind of man she *wished* her husband to be.[29] According to this reading, then, claiming authorship of the confessional letter preserves the fiction of his loyalty to the republican cause and in the process points quite compellingly to Hutchinson's self-serving motives. John's reputation as a devoted Parliamentarian remains intact.

Margaret Cavendish had her own agenda, of course, for writing *The Life of William Cavendish Duke of Newcastle* (1667), an active Royalist (1593–1676) who spent a number of years in exile, often with the court, and who—unlike John Hutchinson—was alive when his wife wrote and published his biography. Cavendish is notorious for writing and living according to her own terms, and her approach to life-writing is no different. For example, in the conclusion to her autobiography, *A True Relation of My Birth, Breeding, and Life* (1656), she confidently refutes her text's need to appeal to readers: 'Readers will scornfully say, why hath this Ladie writ her own Life? Since none cares to know ... how she lived, ... I answer that it is true, that 'tis to no purpose, to the Readers, but it is to the Authoress, because I write it for my own sake, not theirs.'[30] Cavendish thus blatantly disregards and deconstructs the primary point of 'life' writing from the point of view

---

[27] Hutchinson, *Life*, 17, 22.

[28] Hutchinson, *Life*, 280–1. Whether Hutchinson actually composed the letter or simply wrote down what her husband dictated is a source of much speculation.

[29] Derek Hirst, 'Remembering a Hero: Lucy Hutchinson's *Memoirs* of Her Husband', *English Historical Review*, 119 (2004), 682–91 (683–4, 689).

[30] Margaret Cavendish, *A True Relation of My Birth, Breeding, and Life*, in Sylvia Bowerbank and Sara Mendelson (eds.), *Paper Bodies: A Margaret Cavendish Reader* (Peterborough, Ontario: Broadview, 2000), 63.

of practitioners like Hamilton and acknowledges the selfishness at the heart of all auto/biographical expression. Whether her own life or her husband's, she is a part of the narrative, and she writes for *her* sake.

Even so, she insists in her preface to William's *Life* on its 'historical trut[h]' (lvii), a claim that is only reinforced by the fact that she calls it a 'history', specifically 'a particular history', or 'the history of the life and actions of some particular person' (lv).[31] Such claims to her story's historical veracity increase the likelihood that her text will achieve what James Fitzmaurice calls '[h]er primary goal' for writing it in the first place: 'to defend her husband's reputation against charges that he should not have left England after the defeat of his army at the Battle of Marston Moor.'[32] Cavendish's post-Restoration biography thus intervenes in the historical record in such a way that may well have helped 'to promote her husband's claim to greater favor from the king', as money and land were doled out to Charles II's loyal supporters. But Cavendish's narrative intervenes in the familial record as well, and it is here that her authorial investment in the writing of her husband's life becomes clear. Cavendish 'revisits the major events and losses of *her* life, through a detailing of *William* Cavendish's life, career, and losses': she does so, Elspeth Graham argues, 'to inscribe her [self] even more firmly into the activities and buildings that embody [her husband's] being'.[33] This motive makes sense in light of Cavendish's famous concern that, as William's *second* wife, she might be forgotten by history, the very concern that she claims informed her decision to write *A True Relation*: 'lest after-Ages should mistake, in not knowing I was ... second Wife to the Lord Marquis of *Newcastle*, for my Lord having had two Wives, I might easily have been mistaken, especially if I should dye, and my Lord Marry again.'[34] Fitzmaurice suggests, however, that Cavendish intends, via *The Life*, 'to establish herself as a serious historian', albeit 'a historian of "some particular person"', which is, in our own parlance, 'a biographer or practitioner of life writing'.[35] Quite possibly both motives are true, as Cavendish and Hutchinson's texts demonstrate nothing so much as the genre's ability to absorb and balance personal, political, and even spiritual goals that may or may not coincide with what a life's subject may have wanted. Indeed, giving further credence to the concern expressed by Thomas Smyth a few decades later, Cavendish and Hutchinson also write their selves, their desires, and their voices into the textual after-lives of their husbands.[36]

---

[31] Margaret Cavendish, 'The Preface', in C. H. Firth (ed.), *The Life of William Cavendish Duke of Newcastle*, (London: John C. Nimmo, 1886), pp. liii-lxiv (lvii-lv).

[32] James Fitzmaurice, 'Margaret Cavendish's *Life of William*, Plutarch, and Mixed Genre', in Line Cottegnies and Nancy Weitz (eds.), *Authorial Conquests: Essays on Genre in the Writings of Margaret Cavendish* (Madison, Wisc.: Fairleigh Dickinson University Press, 2003), 80-102 (82).

[33] Elspeth Graham, 'Intersubjectivity, Intertextuality, and Form in the Self-Writings of Margaret Cavendish', in Dowd and Eckerle (eds.), *Genre and Women's Life Writing*, 131-50 (147).

[34] Cavendish, *A True Relation*, in Bowerbank and Mendelson (eds.), *Paper Bodies*, 63.

[35] Fitzmaurice, 'Margaret Cavendish's *Life of William*', 84.

[36] Scholars of both women have gone so far as to claim that their lives of their husbands can also be read as autobiography. Graham, for example, argues that Cavendish's *Life* is 'a further version of her own story' ('Intersubjectivity, Intertextuality, and Form', 131), whereas Susan Cook claims that Hutchinson's

This is not to say, however, that they do *no* work on behalf of their husbands. On the contrary, as already noted, they work hard to redeem their spouses where necessary and to solidify for them the best reputations possible. They do the work, in other words, of textual stewardship, much as their little-known contemporary Dorothy Calthorpe (1648–93) does for her father and grandfather in a biographical romance that she wrote between 1672 and 1684 and that has survived in its original manuscript form.[37] On the surface, Calthorpe's narrative is quite different from Hutchinson and Cavendish's. Titled 'A Short History of the Life and Death of Sr Ceasor Dappefer', the narrative is better approached as a romance, specifically a *roman à clef*, rather than a biography. Yet, like Cavendish, Calthorpe insists on the veracity of her 'history', claiming only to have changed her characters' names 'to deuert my selfe and make my story pleasenter'. Furthermore, she explains at the end of the narrative:

> the designe of this Littell Mem-oise [i.e. memoir] was only to giue a true relation of my owne famely ... to tell the truth of all the accidents that happned from my grandfather to my fathers death haueing no reason to un-reauell any furder because he prouided for us all out of his own industerry without being be-holding to his famely therefore I begine with the father and end with the Son[.][38]

Calthorpe's romance-like narrative traces her patriarchs' history in precisely this way, just as her characters precisely align with their historical counterparts, starting with the character Sir Ceasor Dappefer representing Calthorpe's paternal grandfather, Sir Henry Calthorpe (1586–1637). More significantly, as this passage foreshadows with its reference to her father having sufficiently provided for his family, the story reveals both Henry and his son James (Calthorpe's father and 'Jewlious' in the romance) to be exemplary Christian men in the tradition of the earliest Calthorpe ancestors, men who were literally 'dapifers', or stewards.

Although I do not argue here that Calthorpe's 'Short History' is actually a seventeenth-century 'life', it does share many of the genre's goals and traits. More to the point, Calthorpe's construction of her male forebears as ideal stewards resonates with and underscores the work with which women often engaged in biographical projects. Not only were Calthorpe's father and grandfather responsible stewards of the family's money and property, her text suggests, but she, too, enacts responsible stewardship by recording

---

Life is 'her own story as much as ... that of her husband' ('"The Story I Most Particularly Intend": The Narrative Style of Lucy Hutchinson', *Critical Survey*, 3 (1993), 271–7 (272).

[37] The manuscript (which I call *Calthorpe's Chapel* for the red-inked chapel that appears on the volume's first page) was sold at a Sotheby's auction in 2006 and now resides at Yale's Beinecke Rare Book and Manuscript Library (MS Osborn b421 vo. 1). For more on Calthorpe and her manuscripts, see my introduction in Dorothy Calthorpe, *News from the Midell Regions and Calthorpe's Chapel*, ed. Julie A. Eckerle (New York and Toronto: Iter Press, 2022), 1–76.

[38] Dorothy Calthorpe, *A Short History of the Life and death of Sir Ceasor Dappefer*, in Eckerle (ed.), *News from the Midell Regions*, 131–2. I have silently amended Calthorpe's idiosyncratic use of the uppercase 'L' where appropriate.

their story and characters for posterity (not to mention via her own not-insignificant philanthropic bequests delineated in her will).[39] 'A Short History' demonstrates how approaching biographical writing as a form of stewardship can instruct our reading of many of the period's lives by writers of both genders but especially women.[40]

That said, the many biographies of women written at this time tend to have less defensive work to do than the kinds of texts I have been describing. Rather, male-authored biographies of women are almost exclusively spiritual lives, whether they appear first in the form of a funeral sermon or whether they are produced—as we have already seen—from the pen of a grieving spouse. For example, the Dutch physician Arnold Boate (1606–53) published the life of his Irish wife, Margaret, *The Character of a Trulie Vertuous and Pious Woman* (1651), just months after her death. In quite familiar tones, he explains that he wrote the text 'to serve me instead of a pourtrait', to provide her 'a farre statelier monument', and—inevitably—to provide 'principallie for the advantage and edification of others'.[41] There seems little to redeem or justify in the lives of women thus eulogized as exemplary Christian wives, though Boate does expend a few words explaining (and, indeed, justifying) his wife's love of the controversial romance genre. It is, without a doubt, early modern *men* whose lives most warranted secular biographies (or autobiographies), especially when their lives were thought to model an aspect of exemplary living, to offer a touchstone in a moment of cultural change or crisis, or to represent in a single individual the beliefs of a group.

One of the more intriguing examples of the last category is the *Memoirs* (1698–9) of the republican soldier and statesman Edmund Ludlow (c.1617–92). Like another influential autobiography from this period, *The Life of Edward Earl of Clarendon* (1759), Ludlow's text can be read as self-vindication. It is, likewise, the life of a controversial figure, in this case a man who actively fought against the king's party, who was one of the judges who sealed Charles I's fate, and who later turned against Oliver Cromwell when he became Protector in 1653. Like Edward Hyde, Earl of Clarendon (1609–74), Ludlow wrote his story from post-Restoration exile, in this case in Switzerland. And like Clarendon's *Life*, Ludlow's manuscript did not see print until after his death but was ultimately issued in three volumes, subsequently providing a primary source of civil war 'history' for those who came after. Yet Ludlow's *Memoirs* also represents the particular perspective of late seventeenth-century republicans; indeed, in its published form, the *Memoirs* seems to represent this group far better than it represents Ludlow himself. This is because, as became fully accepted by scholars and historians only in the 1970s, the

---

[39] Most notable was her founding of an almshouse in Ampton, Co. Suffolk; see the introduction to my edition of Calthorpe's writing for more information.

[40] See also Julie A. Eckerle, 'Women's Life Writing and the Labour of Textual Stewardship', in Elizabeth Scott-Baumann, Danielle Clarke, and Sarah C. E. Ross (eds.), *The Oxford Handbook of Early Modern Women's Writing in English, 1540–1700* (Oxford: Oxford University Press, 2022), 231–44; and Julie A. Eckerle, 'Life-Writing Dapifers: Early Modern Women as Textual Stewards,' in Katherine Scheil and Linda Shenk (eds.), *Early Modern Improvisations: Essays in History and Literature in Honor of John Watkins* (Routledge: New York, 2024), 161–71.

[41] Arnold Boate, *The Character of a Trulie Vertuous and Pious Woman* (Paris, 1651), sig. A3r.

Memoirs as it was ultimately published had been significantly, silently revised by the republican John Toland (1670-1722). Thus, the authorial voice of Ludlow's autobiographical manuscript, 'A Voyce from the Watch Tower', appears on the page of the published *Memoirs* quite differently. As Blair Worden's detailed analysis of both texts compellingly demonstrates, in the print version, 'Ludlow's views and character were brought into line with a late seventeenth-century political programme. Ludlow the Puritan became Ludlow the radical Whig or "real whig". Ludlow the builder of a godly commonwealth became a spokesman for the country against the court'.[42] Furthermore, the revised text largely removes the religious tone and content that are essential to *A Voyce* and to Ludlow's intent in writing it. Indeed, in written directions for the possible publication of *A Voyce* after his death, Ludlow insisted that only his wife or close relatives should handle the project if deemed worthy and that, 'if revised for publication, [it] should be "made to speake noe other than my principle ... in relation to" religion'. Yet, as Worden states the case quite starkly, '[t]he text of 1698 broke this rule at every turn', seemingly to serve the political goals of the text's editor/reviser and of its printer, John Darby, all of whose publications at this time 'that were intended to revive the political enthusiasms of mid seventeenth-century England ... removed or subordinated the religious ones'.[43]

Therefore, even though Ludlow appears in both *A Voyce* and the *Memoirs* as loyalty personified, a man who puts England's welfare before all else much in the manner of Hutchinson's John, the end to which this loyalty works varies according to the text in which it appears. Whereas *A Voyce* emerges from an individual's experience of exile and disappointment, the *Memoirs* emerges from the radical Whig milieu surrounding Darby and his writers, a group eager to use disappointment in William after 1688 as a rallying cry. Ludlow—both the man remembered and admired for his heroic exploits (even in 1689, when he had returned to England to support the Williamite cause and found himself sent back to Switzerland instead) and the character in the *Memoirs*—simply became their vehicle. Once again, then, we have the historical subject of a text transformed into a somewhat fictional character according to the desires and goals of an author, although in Ludlow's case, it is an autobiographical text that is so transformed rather than a biographical one. Autobiography and biography become auto/biography not just in academic shorthand but in reality as well, and generic distinctions once again seem increasingly unhelpful.

The case of Clarendon's *Life* returns us to the more typical autobiography motivated above all else by self-defence, as his hybrid text comprises a self-serving combination of political analysis, history, and autobiography. Perhaps better known for his *History of the Rebellion and Civil Wars in England* (1702-3), which Pritchard describes as 'a work of collective biography as well as a history', Clarendon tells essentially the same history in his *Life*, albeit this time with a focus on himself in the midst of said rebellion, thus forgoing battlefield scenes for diplomatic negotiations in the various locations of the

---

[42] Blair Worden, 'Whig History and Puritan Politics: The *Memoirs* of Edmund Ludlow Revisited', *Historical Research*, 75 (2002), 209-37 (210).

[43] Worden, 'Whig History and Puritan Politics', 213, 221.

exiled court.[44] The fact that Clarendon wrote his *Life* from his own post-Restoration exile tells us a great deal about his motives. Dismissed from office and then impeached for high treason in 1667, Clarendon fled to France, where he continued to defend himself against the various charges against him and did a great deal of writing. Clarendon used personal story combined with political history to tell a tale in which he emerges as the most loyal of royal servants, a man who frequently denied or at least resisted various titles and positions precisely because he did not want to expose himself to jealousy and slander. The first volume of his *Life* lays the groundwork for this defence, long before the chronological moment demands it, by including numerous instances of such humility and loyalty. Thus we learn of Hyde's decision to give up a law career in order to commit to public service, 'which he saw so much concerned the peace and very being of the kingdom'; rejection of the positions of solicitor-general in 1641 and secretary of state (twice) in 1643; and absolute horror at the discovery of his daughter Anne's secret marriage to the Duke of York in 1660.[45] This last incident is a particularly important episode in Clarendon's *Life*, since it reveals so many key aspects of the character he wishes to record for posterity, including his willingness to put country before family and king before daughter. Essential elements of this narrative include his surprise—'nobody was so surprised and confounded as the chancellor himself'; his horror that he will be seen as having schemed for the crown, 'which as himself his soul abhorred'; his desperation to think of his family's inevitable banishment, which would separate him from the work and country he loves; his preference that Anne 'should be the duke's whore than his wife'; his absolute opposition to the marriage, even when supported by Charles II; and his desire that the king punish his daughter instead by beheading her.[46] All of these responses inform the way in which Clarendon will handle the crises that lay ahead in the chronological narrative but that he, as retrospective author, has already lived through. And all construct a very particular character, 'the indomitably humble Chancellor', a man who is simply incapable of ambition, much less treason.[47]

The defensive tone throughout *The Life* but particularly in the section *The Continuation of the Life* makes this point explicit, whether the autobiography was originally intended for private use (as 'The Preface to the First Edition' claims) or a more public audience. Readers are informed that incidents have been chosen that will be 'sufficient manifestation of the integrity of the chancellor, and how far he was from being that corrupt person, which his most corrupt enemies would have him thought to be'. A similarly confident disclaimer also precedes the lengthy discussion of the period and negotiations leading up to Charles II's marriage to Catherine of Braganza, another event for which Clarendon was blamed: 'I shall here ... make it appear to all the world, how

---

[44] Pritchard, *English Biography*, 13. See further Niall Allsopp's Chapter 19 on 'Histories'.
[45] Edward Hyde, *The Life of Edward Earl of Clarendon*, 2 vols. (Oxford: Clarendon Press, 1827), 1: 87, 100, 168, 204.
[46] Hyde, *Life of Edward Earl of Clarendon*, 1: 372, 273, 378–9.
[47] Carolyn D. Williams, '*Pamela* and the Case of the Slandered Duchess', *Studies in English Literature*, 29 (1989), 515–33 (517).

far the chancellor was from being the author of that counsel, ... and that he did nothing before, in, or after that treaty, but what was necessary for a man in his condition, and what very well became a person of that trust and confidence he was in with his master.' Indeed, just as the king of Clarendon's *Life* seems not at all bothered by his brother's unorthodox choice of bride in the Anne Hyde incident, here the king not only values Clarendon's input throughout the negotiations but also says of his Lord Chancellor 'that few men were so scrupulous'.[48]

Despite the claim in 'The Preface' that Clarendon wrote his *Life* 'only for the information of his children', then, it is far more likely that he hoped to use the text along with much of his other writing from exile in order to help clear his name.[49] Manuscript narratives are commonly marked by an insistence on personal use and private intent, but the reality is often quite different. Especially for a public figure like Clarendon, broad manuscript circulation was likely. Not only did he seize the leisure of exile to record the history of his country, his king, and himself, but he also specifically chose a genre that was particularly suited to the work of self-defence, or—we might say—the stewardship of his own reputation. In similar, albeit less-known terms, the Royalist Lady Anne Halkett (1621/22–99) wrote an autobiographical narrative in which she explains how she became romantically involved with a married man while helping the Duke of York escape England; Anne Wentworth (c.1630–fl. 1677) used the autobiographical mode to justify her decision to leave her husband; and Alice Thornton (1626/27–1706/7) in multiple autobiographical accounts responded to the scandal that arose when she arranged for her daughter's marriage at the age of fourteen.[50]

In short, as this brief survey demonstrates, seventeenth- and early eighteenth-century auto/biography was often political and often spiritual but nearly always motivated by agendas of personal, familial, or public vindication. These texts co-existed alongside many other sub-genres, including prison narratives, profession-based memoirs, and family histories. In Pritchard's discussion of the category of family history, he argues that it is 'one of the most ... neglected types of biographical writing in England during this period'. Certainly, its study is hindered not only by its archival and manuscript nature, as Pritchard notes, but also—once again—by generic hybridity. Is a history of a family a history, a biography, or simply a narrative approach to genealogy? Do the biographical sketches contained therein rank as biography proper or brief lives? And are such texts

---

[48] Hyde, *Life of Edward Earl of Clarendon*, 1: 521, 488, 523.
[49] Hyde, *Life of Edward Earl of Clarendon*, 1, p. i.
[50] Many different titles have been applied to Halkett's *Autobiography*; see *Lady Anne Halkett: Selected Self-Writings*, ed. Suzanne Trill (Aldershot: Ashgate, 2007), pp. xxxvi–xxxvii. Wentworth discusses her controversial decision in both *A True Account* (1676) and *The Vindication of Anne Wentworth* (1677), which can be found in *The Early Modern Englishwoman: A Facsimile Library of Essential Works*, ser. 2, *Printed Writings, 1641–1700: Pt. 1, vol. 2, Life Writings*, II, ed. Elizabeth Skerpan-Wheeler (Aldershot: Ashgate, 2001). Thornton produced multiple versions of her manuscript life; see Raymond A. Anselment, 'Seventeenth-Century Manuscript Sources of Alice Thornton's Life', *Studies in English Literature*, 45 (2005), 135–55. A digital edition of Thornton's four books edited by Cordelia Beattie, Suzanne Trill, Joanne Edge, and Sharon Howard is newly available at https://thornton.kdl.kcl.ac.uk/.

driven by the spiritual exemplarity of religious lives, the justification of political lives, or more private agendas rooted in each individual family's background? Perhaps not surprisingly, this last question can be answered with a simple 'all of the above'. 'Like the religious biographers,' Pritchard writes, 'the family historians often display an exemplary aim, an intention of showing descendants what to emulate or shun by the examples of their forebears.' Yet 'the emphasis is not on piety or learning, ... but on family status and alliances, management of estates, and public and military service'.[51] Thus, while typical examples of this sub-genre include massive accounts like Sir Hugh Cholmley's *The Memoirs of Hugh Cholmley* (1650s; first printed, 1787), which includes lives of various Cholmleys, and Gervace Holles's *Memorials of the Holles Family, 1493–1656* (c.1658; first printed, 1937), Calthorpe's *Short History* also participates in this work, creating as it does a multi-generation history of the Calthorpe family in which the exemplary virtue of Christian stewardship defines the family and its legacy.

The lesson of generic hybridity across gendered, political, and religious lines in the auto/biographical prose of 1640–1714 is that rhetorical analysis is a far more valuable approach to this material than categorization or definition. This approach demonstrates—perhaps paradoxically for texts focused so intently on particular *persons*—that they are not necessarily linked to authorial attributes like gender and political allegiance. Indeed, such details often pale in the face of the numerous *shared* characteristics of biographical and autobiographical prose in the period. Therefore, although the unique circumstances of a given author at a particular historical moment certainly shape the text that is written, key shared features nonetheless remain. Careful consideration of the rhetorical work performed in and by these texts thus has as much to tell us about textual and literacy practices as it does about the pressures and anxieties that informed human experience in civil war and post-civil war England.

---

[51] Pritchard, *English Biography*, 199, 201.

CHAPTER 8

BITES AND SHAMS

JOHN MCTAGUE

Prose lends itself to shamming, hoaxing, and other forms of sociable deceit more readily than verse or drama. That may be because the translucent deadpan upon which shamming relies is more readily achievable in a medium associated with apparently 'straight-forward' kinds of writing like scientific report, travel writing, political theory or debate, and literary criticism. The generic commodiousness of prose is also well suited to the ways in which shams and bites rely on a generic, tonal, or contextual metamorphosis. Kate Loveman has demonstrated the ways in which various kinds of deceptive or mock-deceptive social and literary practices contribute to the development and reception of eighteenth-century novels. We are familiar now with the idea of a 'sham' as something connected with deception and fakery. Loveman points out that the origins of the word 'sham' in the late seventeenth century are connected to the embarrassment of being caught out, the etymological link with 'shame' keeping alive a sense of 'the social stigma of deception', even while the popularization and social refinement of the practise in this period mollified the seriousness of such ignominy.[1] 'Bites' were jokes in which one took in one's audience with a plausible lie, before revealing that you had caught them out by declaring 'a bite!'; as with many shams, the 'exposure' of a bite is an inherent feature.[2] The fact that 'bite' is an angling metaphor helps us see it as sublimated conflict, a 'civilized' or leisured kind of pursuit. We remain occasionally liable to fall for things 'hook, line, and sinker'. Depending on for how long one has been 'played', a bite may well produce the mortification attendant on discovering oneself to have been out of one's element, but the labelling of the trick *qua* trick through the cry of 'a bite' is akin to a sports fisherman releasing his catch back into the river.[3]

---

[1] Kate Loveman, *Reading Fictions, 1660–1740: Deception in English Literary and Political Culture* (Aldershot: Ashgate, 2008), 12.
[2] See Loveman, *Reading Fictions*, 154–5.
[3] *OED*, 'play, v.', 4.b., illustrated with the following quotation from Defoe's *Moll Flanders* (1722): 'Yet I had hook'd him so fast, and play'd him so long that I was satisfied he would have had me in my worst Circumstances.' On the importance of mortification in the operation of some related 'practical satires',

This emphasis on 'biting', catching, and pursuit may give the impression that shamming is a competitive endeavour. There may at certain times be winners and losers, but bites and shams are not only, and perhaps not even primarily, concerned with catching people out. Loveman has shown that these sociable activities are driven by 'feigned credulity', a suspension of disbelief that extends or re-appropriates an agreeable deception.[4] The fun, such as it is, does not stop when a hoax is perceived as a hoax. One helpful analogue might be the surprise party, the real pleasure of which, for the guest of honour and others, is not the moment of revelation, but the realization—and often the subsequent narration—of the emotional, financial, and logistical investment in the party, and the (benevolent) subterfuge involved. What the revelation reveals, indeed, is an alternate history: the guest of honour has been experiencing a history in which there was no party, but really there was a party all along. Those things, not the revelation itself, are the party's substance. The surprise, a shifting of the ground, is only the beginning.

Surprise, You're Dead

In this period the character and reach of shams were transformed by changes in communications technology. The same is true of other cultural forms, but the changes in the printing industry and the machinery for the distribution of information made differently available to the shammer and their audience certain shared discourses or languages. No longer confined to making a companion look foolish in a tavern, coffee shop, or at court, the shammer could now hide behind and manipulate the characteristics of 'straight' publications with which a wider public were familiar. There were more places to hide, and, paradoxically enough, those hiding places were more public. When Jonathan Swift predicted and then 'reported' the death of the astrologer John Partridge in the spring of 1708, and maintained that pretence for the next couple of years, he concealed himself behind a kind of obtrusive camouflage that has become less noticeable over time, because the life and works of his target have also faded from memory.[5] In this series of pamphlets known as the 'Bickerstaff Papers', the target is less the practice of astrology than its underhanded use for propagandic scaremongering. More people knew about John Partridge than had heard of Jonathan Swift in the spring

---

see John McTague, 'Satire as Event', in Paddy Bullard (ed.), *The Oxford Handbook of Eighteenth-Century Satire* (Oxford: Oxford University Press, 2017), 509–24.

[4] See Loveman, *Reading Fictions*, 66–9.

[5] On the hoax's effect on Partridge (and its 'real life' limits), see John McTague, 'A Letter from John Partridge To Isaac Manley, 24 April 1708: Provenance and Authenticity', *Notes and Queries*, 59 (2012), 197–202. For more detail on the timing and effect of the individual pamphlets contributing to this sham, see Jonathan Swift, *Parodies, Hoaxes, Mock Treatises*, ed. Valerie Rumbold (Cambridge: Cambridge University Press, 2013), particularly the headnotes and textual accounts of *Predictions for the Year 1708* (1708), *The Accomplishment of the First of Mr. Bickerstaff's Predictions* (1708), and *A Vindication of Isaac Bickerstaff Esq.* (1709), and also Appendices D and E. Cited hereafter as Swift, *Parodies*.

of 1708. The latter was at an early stage of his career, but Partridge was the country's foremost almanac maker, and had developed a persona as a 'no-popery' Whig, a persona grounded in his involvement in the birth of radical Whiggism in the reigns of Charles II and James II. Much more than a distaste for astrology, it is Partridge's public identity that both provokes Swift and provides him with the materials for his parody.

In the 1680s, Partridge was a member of the radical Whig Green Ribbon club, which organized oppositional propaganda, including the infamous Pope Burnings and the mass petition of 1680 presented to Charles II, which he also signed.[6] In 1683, bathetically enough, he was also almost involved in the Rye House Plot to assassinate Charles II and his brother James in Hertfordshire. '*Partridge* offered to joyn in it,' says an informant, 'if it were to be done in Town, but was not able to Ride and therefore would not joyn in the Attempt out of *London*.'[7] The same account accuses him of casting illegal nativities for the royal family, allegations repeated in print throughout his career, and Partridge himself frequently insisted on his radical past as a source of authority and identity.[8] Swift will have held in disdain the grandstanding of this tradesman turned rebel and demagogue. He was not the first to notice this aspect of Partridge's personality, however, and his hoax draws on what we might think of as an 'anti-Partridge' tradition.

At the end of 1687, as the opposition to England's Catholic monarch James II reached fever pitch, Partridge published a pamphlet entitled *Mene Tekel*, named for the phrase written on a wall by a disembodied hand during Belshazzar's feast, in the fifth chapter of the Book of Daniel ('MENE, MENE, TEKEL, UPHARSIN'). Daniel interprets the phrase as a divine prophesy of the downfall of Belshazzar, the last king of the Babylonians, and the takeover of his kingdom by the Medes and Persians. The pamphlet's title rather bluntly positions Partridge as a clairvoyant uniquely able to interpret the meaning of things everyone can see, but not understand—in the Bible, Belshazzar summons Daniel after his advisers have all failed to interpret the phrase. In the analogy implied by the title, James II is Belshazzar. *Mene Tekel* was filled with vague forebodings, warning of 'some villainous contrivance' by 'the papists', for instance.[9] One particular prognostication made the pamphlet, and Partridge, notorious. Having predicted 'some great *Irruption* in the *State*, or alteration in the *Government* by the death of the then *King, Prince*, &c.,' he goes on to identify his target: 'Now suppose the question was Asked,

---

[6] Melinda Zook, *Radical Whigs and Conspiratorial Politics in Late Stuart England* (University Park: Pennsylvania State University Press, 1999), 7–13. Partridge is listed as a member of the club in Pepys Library, Magdalene College, Cambridge, MS 2875. For Partridge's propagandic efforts whilst in exile in Holland, see John McTague, '"There is No Such Man as Isaack Bickerstaff": Partridge, Pittis, and Jonathan Swift', *Eighteenth-Century Life*, 35 (2011), 83–101.

[7] Thomas Sprat, *Copies of the Informations and Original Papers Relating to the Proof of the Horrid Conspiracy Against the Late King* (1685), 62.

[8] See Swift, *Parodies*, 36–40; George Parker, *An Ephemeris of the Coelestial Motions* (1699), sigs. A4v, A7; and Ned Ward, *The World Bewitch'd* (1699), 11–12. Partridge glories in his political past in the dedication to fellow radical Joseph Tiley in *Defectio Geniturarum* (1697), sigs. A2–A2v.

[9] Partridge, *Mene Tekel being an Astrological Judgment on the Great and Wonderful Year 1688* (1688), sig. A3v.

Whether a man of 55 years of age, under such a Crowd of directions, could live or not? why really I must needs say, if it was my own Brother's Case, I should not think it was possible to Escape with his life.'[10] James II, of course, was 55 in 1688. The invasion of William of Orange in November 1688, and the subsequent revolution, granted, did not lead to James II's death, though he did flee to France with (some of) his family. Unruffled by such a technicality, in 1689 Partridge issued *Mene Mene Tekel Upharsin*, celebrating the success of his prediction, with the following audacious qualification:

> I find some peevish People are apt to exclaim against *Astrology*, because the late *King* did not dye in *October* or *November* 1688, pretending that I had said in Print he would then die, but I would very fain have them show it to me where I have so said ... For the effect is so like *Death* that it doth as well for the Deliverance of the *Nation*, and I hope they cannot say but it happened at the same time I had predicted it too. It is indeed a *Civil Death*, and to him I think worse than *Death*.[11]

This retrospective adjustment of a prediction informs the execution of Swift's parody.[12] N. F. Lowe has shown that Swift read about this episode in his copy of the French philosopher Pierre Bayle's 1705 critique of the affair.[13] Reading *Mene Tekel* as bald Williamite propaganda, Bayle declares, 'certain people believed that [Partridge] hazarded hopes and wishes more often than judgements, ... to give courage to his party, and to give cause for alarm amongst the papists' (the French makes Partridge's scaremongering sound more like projectile warfare: 'pour jeter l'allarme parmi les Papistes'). Partridge, writes Bayle, was encouraged to predict James's death by the 'principal plotters' of the revolution, who 'ordered him to insist on the certain death of the king'. Their motivation was the 'great difficulty' (or 'grand embaras') that would be caused by James remaining in the country following William's invasion; Partridge's prediction was intended to make James 'fear the same fate as his father', Charles I (i.e. beheading). 'These threats were rumoured abroad,' he continues, 'so that ... he would be thrown into such a consternation that he would take flight, and they could then pretend that he had abdicated and thus the throne was vacant.'[14]

Mene Tekel, for Bayle, was emblematic of the propagandic (or even casuistic) means by which the Williamite administration avoided the 'grand embaras' of the English throne being won by force. Bayle was not the only source of this information about and criticism of Partridge, which is pre-empted by English writers.[15] In 1687 the rival

---

[10] Partridge, *Mene Tekel*, sig. A5v.
[11] Partridge, *Mene Mene, Tekel Upharsin* (1689), sigs. A3–A3v.
[12] On Swift's *A Vindication of Isaac Bickerstaff*'s capitalization on the idea of a 'civil death', see McTague, 'Satire as Event'.
[13] N. F. Lowe, 'Why Swift Killed Partridge', *Swift Studies*, 6 (1991) 70–82.
[14] Pierre Bayle, *Continuation des Pensées Diverses [. . .], à l'occasion de la Comete* (Rotterdam, 1705), 200, quoted and translated in Lowe, 'Why Swift Killed Partridge', 73–4.
[15] Swift arrived in England in January 1689, so may have encountered *Mene Tekel* or its follow-up first hand. See also his connection with Partridge's birthplace East Sheen and his friend Isaac Manley (McTague, 'A Letter from John Partridge', 198).

astrologer John Gadbury cast him as a '*Libeller*' who '*Forged*' his prognostications 'on purpose to Create *Disturbances*' (which latter phrase we might translate as 'pour jeter l'allarme').[16] In 1699, the Tory writer Ned Ward insisted: '[Partridge] never could Foretell any thing by the Heavens, but what was communicated to him upon Earth by wiser Noddles than his own, or else the Prophecies in his *Mene-Tekel* would have prov'd as false as his Calculation of the late King's Nativity, who was to dye, according to his Judgement, many Years ago; but is still living in spight of his croud of Directions.'[17] 'Croud of Directions' is a direct quotation: ten years after its publication, *Mene Tekel* was notorious enough for such a reference to have been understood.[18] Swift's obtrusive camouflage depends on that kind of understanding. Swift does not produce a mock-up of a Partridge text or adopt his voice; nor does he publish in Partridge's name. Rather, his persona Bickerstaff makes a series of moves which are unmistakably 'Partridgean', in a kind of burlesque performance. Bickerstaff's urbane politeness distinguishes his voice from Partridge's, also serving as a kind of screen for the mean-spiritedness of his attack. This screen was more translucent in 1708. By turning Partridge's manner of proceeding against him, Swift made plain the motivation for his sham.

The hoax on Partridge is a self-fulfilling prophecy that establishes its own context. As with *Mene Tekel*, the assassination heralded by Bickerstaff's *Predictions for the Year 1708* is not set in motion by the influence of the stars, but the sway of public opinion (or the representation thereof). Like Partridge, Swift 'hazarded hopes and wishes more often than judgements'. He declares one of his 'hopes'—that Partridge would 'infallibly dye upon the 29th of *March* next'—to be an astrological judgement.[19] Bayle's reading of *Mene Tekel* is effectively re-enacted in *The Accomplishment of the First of Mr. Bickerstaff's Predictions*, published just after the day Bickerstaff appointed for Partridge's death. Here, an incredulous reader of Bickerstaff's prediction is gradually converted to credulity by the incontrovertible evidence of Partridge upon his deathbed. This reader reports, 'I saw him accidentally once or twice about 10 Days before he died, and observed he began very much to Droop and Languish'.[20] The witness then asks Partridge 'whether the Predictions Mr. *Bickerstaff* had publish'd relating to his Death had not too much affected and work'd on his Imagination'. Partridge's reply cuts right to the heart of the hoax:

> He confess'd he had often had it in his Head, but never with much Apprehension till about a Fortnight before; since which Time it had the perpetual Possession of his Mind and Thoughts, and he did verily believe was the true Natural Cause of his present Distemper: For, said he, I am thoroughly perswaded, and I think I have very

---

[16] John Gadbury, *A Reply to That Pernicious and scandalous Libel lately Printed in Holland* (1687), sigs. B1–B2v.
[17] Ward, *The World Bewitch'd: a Dialogue Between Two Astrologers and the Author* (1699), 5.
[18] Partridge, *Mene Tekel*, 10.
[19] Swift, *Parodies*, 49.
[20] Swift, *Parodies*, 61–2.

good Reasons, that Mr. *Bickerstaff* spoke altogether by Guess, and knew no more what will happen this Year than I did my self.[21]

Thus, Swift's 'Partridge' accuses Bickerstaff of guesswork and admits the charade of his own astrology at the same time as admitting the efficacy of Bickerstaff's words as words, the 'true Natural Cause' of his illness. While declaring astrology to be false, the 'fact' of his impending death confesses the power of public utterance. Partridge's 'apprehension', like 'l'allarme' which he had tried to spread amongst 'les Papistes' in 1688, is a result of the representative force of Bickerstaff's conjectures. These conjectures derive their force from readers' willingness to go along with the sham. Swift reflects here upon the desire of Partridge's Williamite advisers that James II would 'fear the same fate as his father, and that this fear would make him run away'.[22] Not taking the risk of Partridge removing himself, Swift represents his *Predictions* as a success in *The Accomplishment* and subsequent pamphlets (including *A Vindication of Isaac Bickerstaff* (1709), which ingeniously answers Partridge's protestation that he was yet living). The speaker of the *Accomplishment* declares, 'whether [Bickerstaff] has not been the Cause of this Poor Man's Death, as well as the Predictor, may be very reasonably disputed'.[23] The hoax explains its working even as it unfolds; its unfolding, in effect, is the explanation. Swift's burlesque of Partridge reveals to the participating reader the failings (or rather the lamentable success) of propaganda. When either Swift himself, his readers, or his collaborators go along with Bickerstaff's prediction, speaking of Partridge as dead when they know he is alive—and sometimes imagining doing so to his face—they treat him as he was known to have treated James II in 1688.[24] They are not just suspending disbelief, but performing a kind of wilful ignorance that apes the 'Popish' passive obedience Partridge had spent his career raging against. When Daniel Defoe impersonated an intolerant 'High Church' Anglican in 1702's *The Shortest-Way with the Dissenters*, he encountered a readership far less cooperative.

A Frustrated Ventriloquist

Loveman suggests that shamming and sociable deceit were practices or discourses that helped to take the practically violent edge off political and religious dispute.[25] Swift's 'assassination' of Partridge shows that imitative satire can sometimes be a kind of sublimation of older forms of violent extra-legal redress. In the case of *The Shortest-Way*

---

[21] Swift, *Parodies*, 62.
[22] Lowe, 'Why Swift Killed Partridge', 74.
[23] *Parodies*, 64.
[24] Swift does this himself in *A Vindication of Isaac Bickerstaff*, through an imagined reader in the *Accomplishment*, and with undetermined collaborators in *'Squire Bickerstaff Detected* (1708). On the authorship of *'Squire Bickerstaff Detected*, see Swift, *Parodies*, appendix D.
[25] Loveman, *Reading Fictions*, 106.

with the Dissenters, however, this mooted prophylactic effect of shamming fails. In this anonymous pamphlet, Defoe appropriated the voice of his enemies—'High Church' Anglicans opposed to the toleration of dissenting (or non-Anglican) Protestants— in order to expose the persecutory impulse behind their violent rhetoric. His speaker, declaring that 'the time of mercy is past', insists that the best way of dealing with dissenting Protestants would be to hang their preachers and banish those found attending services. This is presented as an act of exemplary or preventative justice, even charity: 'I am not supposing that all the Dissenters in England should be hanged or banished, but as in cases of rebellions and insurrections, if a few of the ringleaders suffer, the multitude are dismissed, so a few obstinate people being made examples there's no doubt but the severity of the law would find a stop in the compliance of the multitude.'[26] Violence is repackaged as restraint: the least that can be done. This is a proposal that 'saves' the nation the logistical but not the moral cost of murdering *all* of the dissenters. Defoe's purpose is to show what will happen if High Churchmen's prejudices are left unchecked. That project backfired because the pamphlet's anonymity failed. Broadly speaking, this meant that the sedition of Defoe's speaker was made his responsibility by a court that could not be swayed by his protestation that he was 'making other peoples' thoughts speak in his words'.[27] Defoe's disguise held from the pamphlet's publication on 1 December 1702 until John Tutchin identified him in his newspaper *The Observator* for 31 December–2 January.[28] A warrant for his arrest was issued on 3 January 1703, and a reward offered for his capture, which he evaded until 21 May. In the meantime he had been indicted for seditious libel.[29] At his trial on 7 July he was found guilty, given an unusually heavy fine, and ordered to stand in the pillory, which he did on 29, 30, and 31 July.

To stand in the pillory in the neighbourhood where one lives and works is a compromising situation, but in a sense the position Defoe wrote from was already compromised. He was opposed in principle to occasional conformity, a practice that gave his fellow dissenters access to public office by taking communion once a year in the Anglican Church, thereby circumventing the rigours of the Test Act, which excluded all but Anglican men from such roles. For Defoe, this privileged worldly aspiration over

---

[26] Daniel Defoe, *The True Born Englishman and Other Writings*, eds. P. N. Furbank and W. R. Owens (Harmondsworth: Penguin, 1997), 141.

[27] *A Brief Explanation of a Late Pamphlet, Entitled, The Shortest Way with the Dissenters* (1703), in Furbank and Owens (eds.), *The True Born Englishman*, 147. In cases of seditious libel at this time, the criminality of a tract was determined by the court; the jury simply decided whether the defendant was responsible for its dissemination. For the literary consequences of seditious libel, see Thomas Keymer, *Poetics of the Pillory: English Literature and Seditious Libel, 1660–1820* (Oxford: Oxford University Press, 2019).

[28] For a narrative of Defoe's arrest see Paula R. Backscheider, 'No Defense: Defoe in 1703' *Publications of the Modern Language Association*, 103 (1988), 274–84; see also Keymer, *Poetics of the Pillory*, 121–47.

[29] For the indictment see Backscheider, 'No Defense', 277. The arrest warrant accuses Defoe of the more capacious and serious offence of high crimes and misdemeanours, perhaps because of suspicions of the possibly treasonous dissemination of the pamphlet in the Netherlands by John Toland (see J. D. Alsop, 'Defoe, Toland, and *The Shortest Way with the Dissenters*', *Review of English Studies*, 43 (1992), 245–7).

the religious integrity of the dissenting community.[30] However, he was also faced with a High Church campaign to abolish occasional conformity that was riven with violently persecutory rhetoric, and bound up with party and dynastic politics.[31] It was a campaign which seemed to be seizing on the issue of occasional conformity as a means of bringing about the political disenfranchisement of dissenting Protestants, if not their outright persecution. In *The Shortest-Way*, Defoe sought to expose the ways in which opposition to occasional conformity was being used by High Church polemicists as a kind of dog-whistle, appealing to those opposed to protestant dissent in general, while affecting a sort of 'legitimate' concern about one particular practice.[32] The culture of printed prose polemic in which Defoe was operating thrived on anonymity, pseudonymity, and the various kinds of personation enabled by the printed page; the party conflict that encouraged such practices and made them effective also made them dangerous. Conscious of his compromised position as a writer who had previously argued *against* occasional conformity, Defoe sought to separate man from persona by fashioning a golem from High Church opinion, extrapolating a character and a voice from the language of intolerant contemporaries. Following his identification as the author, the complexity of his position was converted into evidence of treachery, a compromised integrity. Those qualities are made legible—or rather created—by the violent reattachment of fictional persona with flesh-and-blood author.

The conclusion of this affair in the pillory is hard to ignore, and so most readers of this pamphlet have sought to identify what went wrong. Modern critics have argued that Defoe did not signal his irony well enough, or that he was too clever for some parts of his readership, and not clever enough for others. As Ashley Marshall has argued, most of these responses take as read that Defoe's pamphlet was ironic (a position unhelpfully encouraged by Defoe following his arrest). Dismissing the dominant '"failed hoax" reading', Marshall argues that *The Shortest-Way* was not an irony but a 'monitory satire', designed to warn readers by way of demonstrative impersonation. For Marshall, it was 'the unforeseen exposure of the author's identity' that landed him in the pillory.[33]

---

[30] On the occasional conformity debate and Defoe's participation therein, see D. N. Deluna, 'Ironic Monologue and "Scandalous 'Ambo-Dexter' Conformity" in Defoe's "The Shortest Way with the Dissenters"', *Huntington Library Quarterly*, 57 (1994), 319–35.

[31] Drawing attention to the particular passages censured by Parliament, Joseph Hone has persuasively argued that Defoe's pamphlet was controversial less because of his speaker's views on occasional conformity, and more because it was read as 'a Jacobite libel—and one that implicated the queen and government to boot' (*Literature and Party Politics at the Accession of Queen Anne* (Oxford: Oxford University Press, 2017), 161–2).

[32] For Hone, Defoe was 'bringing the underlying Jacobitism of High Church propaganda to the surface' (*Literature and Party Politics*, 166).

[33] Ashley Marshall, 'The Generic Context of Defoe's *The Shortest-Way with the Dissenters* and the Problem of Irony', *Review of English Studies*, 61 (2009), 234–58 (235–6)6. Loveman entertains the possibility that *The Shortest-Way* was 'a deception which Defoe did not want to be penetrated', before suggesting that it was 'an open-ended stratagem': both a deception never meant to be discovered *and* a hoax which would be (*Reading Fictions*, 137). Such a strategy, deliberately taken from the outset, would be remarkably risky for Defoe.

Characterizing the pamphlet as a 'clandestine polemic designed to alarm moderates away from Tory policy', Joseph Hone sees it as a 'cloak and dagger operation' intended to 'elicit attack from all quarters'; again, Defoe looks to have succeeded in these aims until it became clear the pamphlet was his. In these readings, *The Shortest-Way* was conceived as a kind of inoculation, an irritant introduced into a system, triggering a managed response that secures it against future infection.[34] Defoe's exposure meant that the ensuing immune response rejected him along with the pamphlet.

Rather than creating an 'ironic' text in which the intending author and speaker jostle for position, then, Defoe sought to hive his High Church speaker off into their own hermetically sealed pamphlet, hoping to provoke response. There are signs of such a plan, and its failure, in the earliest responses, one of which may have been by Defoe himself. This pamphlet, of which there are two printings, is *Reflections upon a Late Scandalous and Malicious Pamphlet Entitul'd The Shortest Way with the Dissenters* (1703).[35] It reprints the original text, then comments on it in an attached essay. *Reflections* and Tutchin's *Observator* for 23–6 December are the only written responses to *The Shortest-Way* that we can confidently say precede the revelation of Defoe's authorship. Frank Bastian identified *Reflections* as Defoe's in 1981.[36] The rationale for Bastian's attributions to Defoe has been discredited in general, though some contemporary readers thought that *Reflections* was either Defoe's or the work of 'some of his Accomplices'.[37] Determining its authorship matters less than the fact that this early and supportive response seeks to maintain the separation of author and persona (and so it corroborates Marshall's account):

> there are various Conjectures, as to the Author and his Party: Some think him a Papist, some a Nonjurant [i.e. High Church] Parson, and others think him a Dissenter. I don't much concern my self which of the three he belongs to, or what his Design may be, or if he act in Disguise[.] But since he speaks the Language of the

---

[34] In 1703's *Brief Explanation* Defoe explains the effect of the pamphlet in similar terms: 'when the persecution and destruction of the dissenters, the very thing they drive at, is put into plain English, the whole nation will start at the notion, and condemn the author to be hanged for his impudence' (Furbank and Owens (eds.), *The True Born Englishman*, 147). Similarly, the author of *The Fox with his Fire-brand Unkennell'd and Insnar'd* (1703) accuses Defoe of dressing up the church and state in lion and bear skins, as Romans did primitive Christians 'the better to bring their Dogs to worry them' (3).

[35] The other has a pluralized title, *Reflections on some Late Scandalous Pamphlets*, and the contents are differently ordered. The new title page also cites two 1702 pamphlets Defoe insisted he was using as source material: Henry Sacheverell's *The Character of a Low Churchman* (1702) and Charles Leslie's *The New Association* (1703). It is likely this version was published after Defoe's arrest. It resembles his attempts to defend *The Shortest-Way* by declaring it to be an assemblage of High Church works, as when a 1703 edition of the pamphlet declares it to be 'Taken from Dr. Sach-----ll's Sermon, and Others' on the title page. That the modification of the title page of *Reflections* follows that of *The Shortest-Way* further suggests of Defoe's involvement in, if not authorship of, *Reflections*.

[36] Frank Bastian, *Defoe's Early Life* (Totowa, N.J.: Barnes & Noble, 1981), 281.

[37] *The Fox with his Fire-brand*, 10. On Bastian's methods, see Pat Rogers's review in *The Scriblerian*, 15 (1983), 126–7, and Robert James Merrett, 'A Review Essay: Fact and Myth in Defoe's Fiction', *Modern Language Studies*, 17 (1987), 75–81.

two former, I attack him as such, for let him be serious or otherwise, it's plain that he argues their Cause, and insists upon the same Topics that are to be found in their Pamphlets and Sermons.[38]

Care is taken not to conflate the 'monster [that] makes the world afraid' with its creator.[39] Bastian uses his attribution of this pamphlet to Defoe to read *The Shortest-Way* as 'a brilliant piece of impersonation, intended as a target': that is, to attract the kind of attention paid to it by *Reflections*. Nor is *Reflections* the only early response to disregard authorship and to use *The Shortest-Way* in order to discredit High Churchmen. Tutchin's first take on the piece reads very much like the passage just quoted, and may well be a response thereto: 'Whatever the author be, 'tis no great matter, but the book is a System of the *High-Flyers Divinity* and *Politicks*, and I am glad those People have at length given the World a Sample of their Morals and good Nature: ... herein those People are drawn to the Life, and those who know their Marks and Character, will the better know how to avoid them.'[40] If the present account of the purpose of *The Shortest-Way* is correct, here is confirmation of its initial success; that the success was short-lived is confirmed in the same newspaper a week later. Having learned that Defoe was the author, Tutchin shifts his focus from the content of the pamphlet to what it says about Defoe's character. '[P]erhaps,' he fulminates, 'there was never a greater piece of Villainy impos'd upon Mankind.' The pamphlet is 'Unchristian and Irreligious', 'a Cheat that even a Heathen would have blush'd to expose to the World.'[41]

What was an instructive warning is now thought of in ethical terms as a kind of treachery. Others recognized that the attribution was Defoe's undoing. Indeed, the author of *The Fox with his Fire-brand Unkennell'd and Insnared* (1703) reads the publication of *Reflections* as part of a (failed) conspiracy specifically designed to protect against the discovery of Defoe's authorship: 'And [lest] this *Short Way with Dissenters* shou'd lose its efficacy, by being damn'd in the Discovery, they have fetch'd a wider Compass with their *Short Way*, and printed it over again at length, with a sham Answer at the Tail of it, that, like a Comet, it might be the more regarded, and blaze the more.'[42] *The Shortest-Way* and Defoe were, precisely, 'damn'd in the discovery'. The attribution enables not just his prosecution but a series of *ad hominem* attacks disguised as interpretations. Unable to distance himself effectively from the pamphlet, he was obliged to look to irony, a form of internal distancing and division, for his defence. Tutchin's abrupt about-turn demonstrates that the 'irony' of *The Shortest-Way* is not a characteristic of the pamphlet itself, but situational, produced by being 'damned in the discovery'.[43] In reading *The*

---

[38] *Reflections upon a Late Scandalous and Malicious Pamphlet Entitul'd The Shortest Way with the Dissenters*, p. iii.
[39] Daniel Defoe, *A Hymn to the Pillory* (1703), 6.
[40] *The Observator* (23–6 December 1702).
[41] *The Observator* (31 December 1702–2 January 1703).
[42] *The Fox with his Fire-brand*, 10.
[43] As Hone puts it, those features of the text identified by previous critics as ironic 'tells' 'are only visible and ironic when one knows what one is looking for, which readers in 1702 did not' (*Literature and Party Politics*, 163).

Shortest-Way in the knowledge that Defoe is the author, and that his authorship landed him in the pillory, we read with the historical equivalent of dramatic irony. Dramatic irony is a kind of privileged knowledge unevenly distributed across the theatrical space; the characters know less than the audience, and their actions remain cruelly *and significantly* uninformed by that knowledge. When Defoe wrote *The Shortest-Way*, he did not know that he was becoming the protagonist in a dramatically ironic plot. This is not to say that Defoe could not possibly have predicted discovery or even prosecution, but that is not the same as openly courting it (as ironic hoaxers, in fact, normally do).[44] *The Fox* reads the 'failure' of *The Shortest-Way* not as a failure in the conception or writing of a pamphlet but as the foiling of a hoax-in-process. The opening pages lambast Defoe for calculatedly misusing the term 'Irony' in his *Brief Explanation*; according to this pamphleteer, by 'Irony', Defoe really just means 'deceptive impersonation'. The speaker then makes an instructive comparison: 'If this were *Irony* too, so was *Guy Fawx*'s dark Lanthorn, when it came to blow up the Government!'[45] This 'dark Lanthorn', used to light Fawkes's way beneath the Houses of Parliament, was also a device capable of concealing its light and his presence. That is, the pamphlet reads Defoe's disguising 'Irony' (i.e. imitation) as both the delivery mechanism for the pamphlet's 'explosive' contents, and the covert means of lighting the touch paper. Drawing a parallel with the thwarted gunpowder plot allows the pamphlet to ridicule Defoe's failure without foregoing the grounds for attacking him. Both Fawkes and Defoe were 'damn'd in the Discovery', and the discovery of both, which foiled at the same time as revealing their designs, was an opportunity to burn them in effigy.

Swallowing Keys

In 1704, Defoe complained of readers who ignored 'the good or ill in the book', basing their impressions instead on partisan reports of 'the Character of the Author'.[46] Such a distaste for naïve or malevolent biographical reading also motivates the two shams perpetrated by Alexander Pope, in 1713 and 1715: his imitation of the Whig poet and critic Thomas Tickell in *The Guardian*, and *A Key to the Lock*, a pamphlet purportedly written by one 'Esdras Barnivelt', apothecary, offering a wrongheaded political-biographical reading of Pope's mock-epic *The Rape of the Lock* (1714), where the lock of hair represents a peace treaty, the protagonist Belinda is Queen Anne, Sir Plume is Eugene of Savoy, and so on. Both shams are impersonations that involve a disguised Pope writing to and about himself.

The publication of Pope's pastorals in a 1709 miscellany published by Jacob Tonson was his public debut. The same volume carried the pastorals of Ambrose Philips. The

---

[44] On courting discovery, see McTague, 'Satire as Event', 513 and n. 25.
[45] *The Fox with his Fire-brand*, 4.
[46] Daniel Defoe, *An Essay on the Regulation of the Press* (1704), 7.

two poets had very different ideas of what pastoral poems should do. Philips's looked back to an earlier English tradition (particularly that associated with Edmund Spenser), engaged with modern politics, and insisted on an English rather than a classical mythology. Contemporaries connected the manner of Philips's pastorals with the perceived 'rusticity' of Theocritus, a connection that may have more to do with their juxtaposition with Pope's pastorals than any strenuous effort on his part.[47] While necessarily looking back to Theocritus, Pope's pastorals were dominantly Virgilian, classicized, and they remained aloof from contemporary concerns. Philips received the lion's share of commendation in print, though Pope's poems had been approved of less publicly.[48] Much of Philips's praise came from the literary circle he belonged to at Button's Coffee House, presided over by Joseph Addison (Pope had attended sporadically; by 1713 his sympathies were drifting elsewhere). Richard Steele's early praise of Philips in the *Tatler* did not even mention that Pope's poems appeared in the same volume.[49] Pope endured several more indirect snubs before he was provoked by a series of essays in Steele's newspaper *The Guardian* by another member of the Button's circle, Thomas Tickell (though Pope assumed they were by Steele). These essays offered a history of the pastoral which championed precisely those things that Philips's poems prioritized, lauding him as the poetic heir of Theocritus and Spenser. The illustrations are overwhelmingly taken from Philips.[50] Pope's response was to pen a continuation of the series later in 1713, *Guardian* 40, purportedly in Tickell's voice, appearing to compare Pope's pastorals unfavourably with Philips's, but parodically exposing the sycophancy and superficiality of Tickell's reading.

As Pope illustrates here the extent and effect of Tickell's author-worship, so in *A Key to the Lock* (1715) he responds to increasingly prejudicial public attacks on his personal and political character.[51] His persona Barnivelt declares, in an inversion of Defoe's complaint: 'It is a common and just Observation, that when the Meaning of any thing is dubious, one can no way better judge of the true Intent of it, than by considering who is the Author, what is his Character in general, and his Disposition in particular.' Barnivelt knows very little about Pope's character except that he is a Catholic, which is more than enough for him. The apothecary is an obstinate and invasive reader, a meddlesome physician: addressing Pope, he says, 'I must take leave to make you my Patient, whether you

---

[47] For the political-cultural context of this affair, see Abigail Williams, 'The Diverting Muse: Miscellanies and Miscellany Culture in Queen Anne's Reign', in Cedric D. Reverand II (ed.), *Queen Anne and The Arts* (Lewisburg: Bucknell University Press, 2015), 119–34, esp. 127–34.

[48] Edward Heuston, '*Windsor Forest* and *Guardian* 40', *Review of English Studies*, 29 (1978), 160–68 (161).

[49] *Tatler*, no. 10 (3 May 1709); Pat Rogers, *A Political Biography of Alexander Pope* (London: Pickering & Chatto, 2015), 65.

[50] Tickell's essays appear in *The Guardian*, nos. 22, 23, 28, 30, and 32, between 6 and 17 April 1713. The only time Pope appears, Tickell pointedly quotes not from his pastorals but his loose translation of Chaucer, 'January and May'.

[51] For details of such accusations see J. P. Guerinot, *Pamphlet Attacks on Alexander Pope, 1711-1744* (London: Methuen, 1969).

will or no.'[52] As well as being a form of forced entry, the 'key' Barnivelt provides for Pope's work, like many early modern medical treatments, manufactures more 'symptoms' than it alleviates. Possessing a key, Pope shows us, may enable you to open a door, but it does not necessarily equip you to deal with whatever lies beyond.[53]

Both *A Key to the Lock* and *Guardian* 40 parody modes of reading which extrapolate a total interpretation from a literally and metaphorically partial view. Barnivelt's interpretative framework takes no prisoners. As is well known, *The Rape of the Lock* has its origins in and partly represents a dispute between two noble Catholic families, a circumstance explained in the prefatory material to the poem from its first publication. Barnivelt gets around this apparent obstacle to his reidentification of Pope's characters by converting it into a conspiracy: 'What confirms me in this Opinion, is an accidental Discovery I made of a very artful Piece of Management among his Popish Friends and Abettors, to hide this whole Design upon the Government, by taking all the Characters upon themselves.' Any square pegs which happen not to fit into Barnivelt's round holes are likewise dismissed as deliberate obfuscations, as in his insistence that Sir Plume is the avatar of Prince Eugene of Savoy: 'His Earnest Eye, or the Vivacity of his Look, is so particularly remarkable in him that this Character could be mistaken for no other, had not this Author purposely obscur'd it by the fictitious Circumstance of a *round, unthinking Face*.'[54] Barnivelt's singlemindedness is echoed in the absurd pedantry of *Guardian* 40's championing of Philips's 'rusticity'. Here the speaker takes Virgil himself to task, making some editorial suggestions: 'might he not have said *Quoi* instead of *Cui*; *Quoijum* for *Cujum*; *volt* for *vult*, &c. as well as our Modern [Philips] hath *Welladay* for *Alas*, *Whilom* for *of old*, *make mock* for *deride*, and *witless Younglings* for *simple lambs*, &c. by which Means he had attained as much of the Air of *Theocritus*, as *Philips* hath of *Spencer*.'[55]

Such an 'Air'—he might as well have said 'whiff'—of Spenser, Pope implies, is the closest that Philips will ever get: affected archaisms are a 'key' to pastoral simplicity that get you no more than a foot in the door. Discussing *A Key*, Tim Morris observes that 'the contemporary hermeneutic condition, Pope recognizes, is one where meaning exists before interpretation, thus rendering interpretation teleological': Barnivelt's reading, resting on the erroneous identification of the lock with the Barrier Treaty, is 'reverse engineered'.[56] Such a presumptuous teleology is precisely the focus of Pope's parody of Tickell's essays. He signals Tickell's obsession with Philips in the epigram from Virgil,

---

[52] *A Key to the Lock* (1715), in *Selected Prose of Alexander Pope*, ed. Paul Hammond (Cambridge: Cambridge University Press, 1987), 77.

[53] See further Chapter 20 by Nicholas McDowell on Pope's *A Key to the Lock* and the literary category of 'Keys'.

[54] Hammond (ed.), *Selected Prose*, 77, 80.

[55] 'Contributions to *The Guardian* (1713)', in Hammond (ed.), *Selected Prose*, 41.

[56] Tim Morris, 'Lock and Key: Hermeneutics, Symbols, and Signifying in Pope's *The Rape of the Lock*', *English*, 64 (2015), 183–203 (199, 202); see also Freya Johnston, 'Alexander Pope: Unlocking the Key' *Review of English Studies*, 67 (2016), 897–913 (911).

which, translated, reads 'Corydon and Thyrsis had driven their flocks together. From that day Corydon is the one and only Corydon for us'.[57] The epigram narrates the publication of both poets' pastorals by Tonson (the driving together of the flocks of Corydon-Philips and Thyrsis-Pope) and their reception, which consisted of repeated citation of Philips to the exclusion of Pope. Picking up where Tickell left off, Pope also offers numerous illustrations from his rival's poems. Using the satirical commonplacing technique that he would later perfect in *Peri Bathous* (1727) and *The Dunciad Variorum* (1729), Pope places the worst passages from Philips next to his own work, declaring that 'it will be obvious how much *Philips* hath the Advantage'; the juxtaposition of quotations answers the question 'how much' with 'not at all'. Nevertheless, the speaker keeps insisting on Philips's primacy, thereby allowing Pope not just to ridicule that poet's work, but simultaneously to demonstrate the superficiality of Tickell's 'criteria' for pastorals. There are moments when Pope cannot resist some self-praise, refracted through layers of irony, as the speaker declares that he 'deviates into downright poetry', or that 'it must be confessed [he] hath a knack of Versifying'.[58] With wonderful deadpan, the speaker provides descriptions in which 'no Man can compare with' Philips: incomparability, of course, cuts both ways. Here is an incomparable instance of 'beautiful rusticity', and Pope's commentary thereon:

> *O woful Day! O Day of Woe, quoth he,*
> *And woful I, who live the day to see!*

That Simplicity of Diction, the Melancholy Flowing of the Numbers, the Solemnity of the Sound, and the easie Turn of the Words, in this *Dirge* (to make use of our Author's Expression) are extreamly Elegant.[59]

For Pope's parodic purposes, 'Simplicity', 'Melancholy', and 'easie' are all qualitative descriptors perfect in their ambivalence. More faux-rhetorical questions follow: 'How he still Charms the Ear with these artful repetitions of the Epithets; and how significant is the last Verse! I defy the most common Reader to repeat them, without feeling some Motions of Compassion.' Just as the participants in Swift's hoax continue to insist that Partridge is dead in full knowledge of his continued existence, so Pope's tasteless speaker relentlessly insists on Philips's primacy in spite of clear evidence—evidence that he has unwittingly provided—to the contrary.[60] Pope's achievement in *Guardian* 40 is to imitate a prejudicial and inflexible form of reading while shedding light on its insufficiency

---

[57] Virgil, *Eclogues. Georgics. Aeneid: Books 1-6*, trans. H. Rushton Fairclough, rev. G. P. Goold (Cambridge, MA: Harvard University Press, 1916), 66–7; 72–3 (lines 2 and 70 of *Eclogue* VII).

[58] Hammond (ed.), *Selected Prose*, 42. Citing criticism written by fools as a form of self-praise is another dominant technique of *The Dunciad Variorum*.

[59] Hammond (ed.), *Selected Prose*, 43.

[60] Hammond (ed.), *Selected Prose*, 44; see in particular *'Squire Bickerstaff Detected*, in Appendix D of Rumbold (ed.), *Parodies*.

by leaving ajar doors that open out onto his own pastorals. In other words, Pope finds a way to promote himself within an excoriating parody of sycophantic puffery.

These shams were not primarily intended to 'fool' people. Indeed, one of the things Pope ridicules through Barnivelt is the idea that the populace were routinely 'seduced' by political deceptions, as the apothecary reads *The Rape of the Lock* as a propagandic Trojan horse: 'Many of these sort of Books have been bought by honest and well-meaning People purely for their diversion, who have in the end found themselves insensibly led into the Violence of Party Spirit.'[61] However, some have supposed that Pope's *Guardian* 40 did lead readers insensibly into error.[62] In 1782, Joseph Warton reported that the 'secret grounds of Philips's malignity to Pope, are said to be the ridicule and laughter he met with … for mistaking the incomparable ironical paper in the Guardian, N°. 40 … for a serious criticism on pastoral poetry'.[63] The anecdote is implausible: Philips had reasons to be aggrieved, certainly, but he surely saw the paper for what it was. *Guardian* 40 is just too funny, and too blatantly a parody of Tickell's idolization of him, to be mistaken for anything else. A truly inattentive reader might mistake this for a paper written by one of Pope's well-wishers, but it is difficult to imagine anyone—especially someone so closely concerned—reading this essay 'straight'. Similarly, Maynard Mack is positive that Richard Steele 'printed the piece without catching its satirical tone'.[64] In 1925, Bonamy Dobrée contended that Steele accepted the paper with a 'twinkle in his eye', knew it was Pope's, and only pretended to the injured Philips that he had been duped.[65] For Mack, such a reading is improbable because it 'requires us to suppose [Steele] knowingly involved in depreciating two staunch Whigs'.[66] However, the alternative requires us to suppose Steele a very inexpert reader.

The source of much of this uncertainty appears to be Pope's literary executor William Warburton, who wrote in his 1770 edition of Pope's works: 'These papers were sent by an unknown hand to Steele, and the irony escaping him, he communicated them to Mr. Pope, declaring he would never publish any paper, where one of the Club was complimented at the expence of another. Pope told him he was too delicate, and insisted that the papers should be published in the *Guardian*. They were so. And the pleasantry escaped all but Addison.'[67] Warburton is writing twenty-six years after Pope's death and

---

[61] Hammond (ed.), *Selected Prose*, 77. Howard Erskine-Hill has argued that *A Key* is essentially a double-bluff: that there *were* Jacobite meanings encoded in the poem, and that Pope pre-empted their discovery by making all political interpretation seem absurd (*The Poetry of Opposition and Revolution: Dryden to Wordsworth* (Oxford: Oxford University Press, 1996) 85–8). However, that is not quite the same as the pamphlet being read 'straight'.

[62] On the dangers and the appeal of assuming that contemporaries were taken in by hoaxes, see McTague, 'Satire as Event', and the caveats in Loveman, *Reading Fictions*, 13–15.

[63] Joseph Warton, *An Essay on the Genius and Writings of Pope*, 2 vols. (1782), 2: 240.

[64] Maynard Mack, *Alexander Pope: A Life* (New Haven: Yale University Press, 1985), 216.

[65] Bonamy Dobrée, *Essays in Biography* (London: Oxford University Press, 1925), 268–70.

[66] Mack, *Alexander Pope*, 855. Steve Van-Hagen follows Mack in saying that Steele was 'tricked' ('Literary Technique, the Aestheticization of Labouring Experience, and Generic Experimentation in Stephen Duck's *The Thresher's Labour*', *Criticism*, 47 (2005), 421–50 (425)).

[67] *The Works of Alexander Pope Esq.* ed. William Warburton, 9 vols. (1770), 9: 89. The 'Club' is that which met at Button's Coffee House.

fifty-seven after the publication of *Guardian* 40.[68] Even if the details of this anecdote are accurate, however, it does not necessarily add up to proof that Steele was hoodwinked. Like Mack, Warburton is assuming that Steele cannot have published the paper in the full understanding of its ironies. That he contacts Pope to ask permission to publish might seem to corroborate this, but only if we ignore the context. Pope wrote the essay, we should recall, because Steele had published not one but six papers where 'one of the Club' (Philips) had been complimented at the expense—or at least to the exclusion—of another (Pope).[69] For Steele to say this seriously to Pope would require considerable front. More likely: Steele is speaking with a twinkle in his eye, feigning credulity (and innocence) while surreptitiously communicating to Pope his cognizance of the paper's authorship and intended targets. Pope's reply, that Steele is 'too delicate', now reads as a riposte fizzing with a reciprocal irony, for Steele had been anything but delicate in this affair. In so replying, Pope demonstrates his knowledge that Steele is pretending not to know what Steele does, in fact, know: that Pope wrote *Guardian* 40, and that the editor of that newspaper was one of its secondary targets.

In the eighteenth-century accounts of this incident there is variance in the assignment of roles but not the basic shape of the narrative. We hear that Tickell was duped (Warton), that Steele (and everyone except Addison) was tricked (Warburton, repeated by Johnson in his 'Life of Pope'), and elsewhere that Addison fell for the impersonation, with Steele nowhere to be seen.[70] All of these writers are working with a simplistic but appealing conception of shamming as a competitive endeavour involving perpetrators and victims, disagreeing only as to personnel. However, supposing that Steele was tricked adds nothing to our understanding of Pope's sham, which depends on the perception of irony for its effect. The Bickerstaff papers, *A Key to the Lock*, and *Guardian* 40 remain intelligible and entertaining. These qualities are not affected materially by their having pulled the wool over 'real' readers' eyes, or having failed to do so. With the complex exception of Defoe's frustrated impersonation, the texts discussed here deliberately signpost their shamming, and readers were then and are now more than capable of following those directions. A surprise party does not end with but is sustained by the narration of the surprise and its effects. The surprise need not even be genuinely surprising, so long as the guest of honour is able to feign credulity appropriately. The same is true of these eighteenth-century bites and shams.

---

[68] The note did not feature in any of his previous editions of the *Works* (1751; 1753; 1766).
[69] i.e. Tickell's five *Guardian* papers and *Tatler*, no. 10.
[70] Joseph Spence, *Observations, Anecdotes and Characters of Books and Men*, ed. James M. Osborn, 2 vols. (Oxford: Clarendon Press, 1966), 1: 171.

CHAPTER 9

BRIEF LIVES AND CHARACTERS

KATE BENNETT

'THE seventeenth century is rich in short studies or characters of its great men' in 'public life', stated David Nichol Smith in his 1918 Clarendon edition of *Characters from the Histories & Memoirs of the Seventeenth Century*.[1] Nichol Smith borrows his terminology and the majority of his material from Edward Hyde, Earl of Clarendon, whose autobiography and *True Historical Narration of the Rebellion and Civil Wars in England* (1702–4) include a series of confident, elegant, pen-portraits which lament, censure, and praise the key players in seventeenth-century England. Short studies of 'great men' would certainly be one way of describing the biographical collection of the Royalist clergyman David Lloyd, *The States-Men and Favourites of England Since the Reformation* (1665), dedicated to 'the Hope of England, its Young Gentry'.[2] Lloyd presents those young gentry with airbrushed portraits of their forebears, to encourage them to carry on the good work now they are back in power. Yet if we look beyond Lloyd and Clarendon, there are sharp pens ready to puncture such complacency. In John Gay's 1729 satire *The Beggar's Opera*, Mrs Peachum, who with her husband runs a criminal syndicate, assures a promising pickpocket that he will be a 'great Man in History' provided he can escape the gallows.[3] In his biographical collection, *Brief Lives* (compiled c.1680–1), John Aubrey depicts 'great men', not in 'public life', but in vulnerable situations: in hiding, in defeat, in childhood, in prison, unhappily married, unwell, alcoholic, in old age, or suffering a posthumous neglect. In addition he includes many studies of women and the humbly born, alongside details of people like John Gregory, a celebrity barber known for his excellent wigs.[4]

---

[1] David Nichol Smith (ed.), *Characters from the Histories & Memoirs of the Seventeenth Century* (Oxford: Clarendon Press, 1918), p. ix.
[2] Lloyd, *The States-Men and Favourites of England Since the Reformation* (1665), sig. A2.
[3] John Gay, *Dramatic Works*, ed. John Fuller, 2 vols. (Oxford: Clarendon Press, 1983), 2: 10.
[4] John Aubrey, *Brief Lives with an Apparatus for the Lives of our English Mathematical Writers*, ed. Kate Bennett, 2 vols. (Oxford: Oxford University Press, 2015), 1: 580. All citations are to this edition.

Aubrey also makes space for carefully garnered comic anecdotes. In his life of William Butler, famous Cambridge physician, a great man and a 'man of great Moodes', memorialized in numerous 'merry stories', we hear that Butler would be fetched home from the tavern by his maid. Nell would appear at nine o'clock with a lantern and scold, 'come you home you drunken Beast'. Nell would go on calling Butler a drunken beast until she stumbled in the darkness, whereupon he would call her 'drunken beast' back; and so 'they did drunken-beast one another' the whole way home.[5] In Aubrey's hands, the brief life, like the public house, is accommodating. It finds room for anecdotal 'particulars which are gratefull [pleasant] … to talk over among Friends' but which are 'not so proper perhaps to appear in a publick Writing'. These are the faintly apologetic words of Abraham Hill, Fellow of the Royal Society, in a biographical preface to the complete works of Dr Isaac Barrow, Master of Trinity College, Cambridge. Although this was a serious publication, an edition of sermons and mathematical works, Hill tells us that Barrow could not resist fruit, that he smoked, and that he was sensitive to cold.[6] Another of Barrow's biographers, Walter Pope, tells the story of his being attacked by a great mastiff in the middle of the night while on the way to the privy in a friend's garden. Barrow, who had fought schoolboys as a child and pirates as a young man, seized the dog by the throat, and then lay on top of it and called for help. He did not harm it, however, reflecting that it was only doing its duty as a guard dog.[7]

Pope describes these stories as digressions, 'sometimes going out of the way for a season, to make the Narration more delightful', and maintained that in the case of a 'great man' such as Barrow, 'less considerable' circumstances like these were 'worthy to be transmitted to Posterity'.[8] This sounds reasonable enough: the Greek biographer Plutarch had done the same. In an account of the 'various' style of biography in his 'Life of Plutarch', Dryden ascribes to '*Biographia*, or the Histories of particular Lives' a special quality of intimacy, defined by their characteristic 'descent into minute circumstances, and trivial passages of life' in which 'the Pageantry of Life is taken away' through the recounting of personal anecdotes.[9] However, this is not merely an adherence to convention. Barrow, like Butler, was defiantly eccentric, a figure cherished in Cambridge, but out of place elsewhere. Pope claims that when Barrow gave a sermon in London, his slovenly dress and uncombed hair prompted a stampede amongst the congregation, some climbing over the pews in a rush to get out of the church.[10] While Clarendon's 'characters' present an account of those in power and exercising that power, the brief life seeks out oddity and quirky detail. Aubrey's *Lives* are often defences of the

---

[5] Aubrey, *Brief Lives*, 1: 80.

[6] Abraham Hill, *Some Account of the Life of Dr. Isaac Barrow* (1683), sigs. a2v, c2-2v. This is the biographical preface to *The Works of Isaac Barrow*, ed. John Tillotson, 4 vols. (1683–7).

[7] Walter Pope, *The Life of the Right Reverend Father in God Seth, Lord Bishop of Salisbury* (1697), 128, 137.

[8] Ibid. pp. 137, 228..

[9] John Dryden, 'The Life of Plutarch', prefixed to *Plutarch's Lives, Translated from the Greek by Several Hands*, 5 vols. (1688), 1: 60.

[10] Pope, *Life of Seth [Ward] . . Bishop of Salisbury*, 139.

unconventional; he had a particular interest in the self-made and those, especially those clergymen, who gave more time to their private intellectual studies than to their day job.[11] He metes out cheerful and indulgent treatment to turncoats, cowards, crackpots with half-baked ideas, and people who, rather than maintaining chastity (women) or honour (men), chose instead to take lovers, write poetry, study interesting subjects, or simply 'to sleepe in a whole skin'.[12] Aubrey makes the marginal central, he connects the provinces to the metropolis, and his lives are digressive in more ways than one. On the page, his chaotic, vital, and inchoate lives make use of non-linear forms: the marginal note, the footnote, the interlined qualification, scribbled suggestions, gaps between words, or entire blank pages.[13]

The character-writer John Earle begins his collection with a character of the 'Child', who is:

> a Man in a small Letter, yet the best Copie of *Adam* before he tasted of *Eve*, or the Apple; and hee is happy whose small practice in the World can only write this Character. Hee is natures fresh picture newly drawne in Oyle, which time, and much handling, dimmes and defaces. His Soule is yet a white paper unscribled with observations of the world, wherewith at length it becomes a blurr'd note booke.[14]

Like Earle's picture of sullied innocence, the much-handled brief life is an emblem of the compromises, eccentricity, and self-assertion of middle age and of the 'blurr'd' knowledge of a world which had lived through civil war. Earle acknowledges the radical incompatibility between the complexities of experience and observation, and an adherence to 'happy' biographical form. The brief life rejects form to explore elements which fall outside such boundaries as the narrative of its subject's career, the exemplary tale, or the purely satirical character. It actively cultivates the marginal.

As a result of the seventeenth century's wars, and their aftermath, a good number of people found themselves living in the margins. In his life of Francis Mansell, his predecessor as Principal of Jesus College, Oxford, Leoline Jenkins describes how, in the last stages of the Civil War, Royalists retreated to Glamorgan which, as it 'happened to be one of the last that became subject to the Rebells, so it was the Refuge of many Persons of Quality that came for shelter to their Persons and Consciences there, when the Parliament-Armes had driven them out of their own homes'. But the 'Rebell-Soldiery' soon came, and they found Mansell 'using the Liturgy in Publick twice a day'. Jenkins says that they burned his common-prayer books, 'layd hands on his person and one

---

[11] Kate Bennett, 'John Aubrey and the "Lives of our English Mathematical Writers"', in Eleanor Robson and Jacqueline Stedall (eds.), *The Oxford Handbook of the History of Mathematics* (Oxford: Oxford University Press, 2009), 329–52.

[12] Aubrey reports that Sir Jonas Moore gave this reason for holding back from the competition to survey Ireland (Aubrey, *Brief Lives*, 1: 46).

[13] Kate Bennett, 'The Making of *Brief Lives*', in Aubrey, *Brief Lives*, 1: cvii–xxx.

[14] John Earle, *Micro-cosmographie, Or, A Peece of the World Discovered: In Essayes and Characters* (1628), no. 1, 'A Child'.

Clements a Farrier (by Trade) but a Preacher by Profession, ript and Toare his Canonicall Cassock about him that it dangled from his Girtle downewards, in so many small shreads or thongs as made them greate Sporte', an indignity which Mansell received with exemplary Christian patience.[15] Even Clarendon, a central figure both politically and historiographically, wrote his autobiography and his *History of the Rebellion* while in exile in France. For Royalist writers, telling the story of their times in terms of loyalty or its opposite, life-writing meant settling scores. In his account of the Long Parliament, Clarendon presents loyalty in general terms, maintaining that most MPs were 'persons of wisdom and gravity' who had 'all imaginable duty for the King', if not his court, and 'had no mind to break the peace of the kingdom'. He then turns to the biographical character to associate revolution with distinctive, aberrant, and overreaching personal qualities: these men have extraordinary 'fierceness and barbarity', predisposing them to rebellion. He begins with John Pym as a relatively harmless character, before turning to John Hampden as 'a man of much greater cunning, and it may be of the most discerning spirit and of the greatest address and insinuation to bring any thing to pass which he desired of any man of that time'. Of Sir Henry Vane the younger, Clarendon has it that he 'was a man of great natural parts and of very profound dissimulation, of a quick conception and very ready, sharp, and weighty expression'. Paul Seaward perceptively comments that 'with its lists of the dead and its sketches of their characters', Clarendon's *History* is a 'royalist war memorial'.[16]

Memorial is a central purpose both of the brief life and the biographical character. The historian Anthony Wood devoted a lifetime to celebrating the achievements of the city and university of Oxford, and in expressing his anger and indignation at the effects of the Civil War and its aftermath on his beloved city. Oxford had supported the king in the Civil War and had been the centre for the exiled court. In 1647, those college fellows who would not take an oath of loyalty to the victorious parliament were expelled, their places taken by scholars from the puritan university of Cambridge. There were many ways in which college men experienced rupture of their cherished traditions in the period, and Wood's work on the city, university, and writers of Oxford was one long song of love and hatred. As Wood vowed in a private letter, he was determined 'to spend my self and be spent to rake' Oxford 'out of dirt and ashes'.[17] One result of his devoted raking was the 1691 *Athenæ Oxonienses,* an immense, formidably researched, and waspishly censorious biographical catalogue of Oxford-educated writers. It caused outrage on publication, as Wood refused to observe conventions regarding what was fit for, in Abraham Hill's phrase, 'a publick Writing'. He was preoccupied with exposing venality, self-interest, and corruption; and the first thing he declares in his preface is that he is himself pure in heart. 'It is well known', he claims, 'that the Author of this Work hath through the whole course of his life, declin'd the pursuit of any private interest or advantage, and

---

[15] Leoline Jenkins, *The Life of Francis Mansell, D. D.* (London: 1854), 11–12, 17–19.
[16] Edward Hyde, Earl of Clarendon, *The History of the Rebellion*, ed. Paul Seaward (Oxford: Oxford University Press, 2009), p. xxv, 59, 61.
[17] Quoted in Aubrey, *Brief Lives*, 1: lxiii.

hath only, according to his abilities, endeavour'd to promote the honour and glory' both of the nation and of the university. And then he defines the work as a 'Register' of the university's 'Heroes'. But of course, many were not heroes, and, Wood asserts, 'it is no excellence in an Historian to throw a veil on Deformities'.[18]

Unveiling deformity of this kind was the natural province of ephemeral libels. It was a highly risky principle in a printed work intended for posterity. Wood was successfully prosecuted on publication for including a detail with which Aubrey had supplied him. This was the allegation that Clarendon had taken bribes as Lord Chancellor. Wood was fined, expelled from the university, and the offending passages of his book were burned.[19] This was for a special offence of *scandalum magnatum*, libelling a person of high birth, but Wood offended more modest people, too. He could be very sharp-tongued. He describes how the academic Edmund Gayton was ejected from the university in 1647, and 'lived afterwards in London in a sharking condition' (presumably sponging on others or cheating at cards) and writing 'trite things meerly to get bread to sustain him and his wife ... He hath written some good, others most vain and trashy things'. Wood lists all of these in his bibliography, 'according to method', although he maintained they were 'fit to be buried in oblivion'. So he included Gayton's *Wit Revived*, 'published under the name of Asdryasdust Tossoffacan', a ballad 'on the Gyants in the Physick Garden in Oxford', these giants being topiary trees, and a song about a banquet in St John's College, Oxford. This recounts how Charles I was served a procession of marzipan and jelly academics, bowing to him in hood and gown and holding little maces. The queen's dwarf, we are told, ate the verger in one mouthful.[20] Despite Wood's depreciatory comments, he avidly obtained copies of all these texts, and it is due to his efforts that they survive among his vast collection of printed books and ephemera, source and companion volume to his biographical collections.[21] Wood's 'method' was consistency of editorial approach combined with scrupulous archival and bibliographical comprehensiveness. For the first time in English biography Wood insisted on precise evidence for such matters as date and place of birth, checking wills, inscriptions, archives, glass windows, and personal testimony. This assiduousness was not appreciated. One infuriated Oxford fellow said to another that he 'was amazed at the Indiscretion and Injudiciousness' that Wood had showed in including such detail, 'heaping up things, that are meerly trivial & impertinent'.[22]

Wood's most active and proactive collaborator in the 'heaping up' was Aubrey, who for twenty-eight years loyally supplied him with a mass of letters, publications, ephemeral printed texts, and manuscript biographies of unique interest and value.[23] His *Brief*

---

[18] Anthony Wood, *Athenæ Oxonienses*, 2 vols. (1691–2), 1, sigs. a–av.
[19] Wood, *Athenæ Oxonienses*, 2: 221; Andrew Clark (ed.), *The Life and Times of Anthony Wood*, 5 vols. (Oxford, 1891–5), 4: 1–50.
[20] Wood, *Athenæ Oxonienses*, 2: 271.
[21] See Bodleian Library, Oxford, MS Wood 416, fols. 4, 92; MS Wood 423 fol. 38.
[22] Quoted in Kate Bennett, 'John Aubrey and the Rhapsodic Book', *Renaissance Studies*, 28 (2014), 317–32 (318).
[23] Aubrey, *Brief Lives*, 1: xcvi–cvi.

Lives was based on the same degree of research. In the preface he asserts that the work contained 'the Trueth'. This, he explained, was 'exposed so bare, that the very pudenda are not hid', and contained content so inflammatory that it required to be kept out of the public view for decades to prevent its being destroyed.[24] While Clarendon said of the brilliant lawyer and scholar John Selden that 'if he had some infirmities with other men, they were weighed down with wonderful and prodigious abilities and excellencies in the other scale', Aubrey, who also admired him, recorded the view of his saddle-maker, that 'Mr Selden had got more by his Prick, then ever he had done by his practise', referring to his advantageous relationship with the countess of Kent.[25] Archival scrupulousness, the views of saddle-makers, and political score-settling were all principal features of the brief life. Edifying whitewash was not; and many brief lives and characters, therefore, remained in manuscript, written for posterity and intended to be published, if at all, after their authors' deaths.

Clarendon said of Selden that he 'was a person whom no character could flatter, or transmit in any expressions equal to his merit and virtue'.[26] He was using the term character to mean a short biographical sketch, focused on a confident, evaluative, account of personality. This sense emerges gradually in our period, as 'character' becomes an increasingly rich and complex term.[27] However, in the earlier seventeenth century, the prose 'character' mainly referred to the 'Theophrastan character', a pen-portrait of a contemporary moral or social type: an 'idle gallant', for example, or a 'player'. Our professed distrust of stereotypes is alien to the seventeenth century, which valued them as an essential moral exercise. The character operates through the permanence of moral typology on the one hand, and contemporary modes on the other, shaped and articulated by social observation, ironical detachment, and wit. In the 1620s, John Earle's 'Gallant' talks only of jests in plays and loves to 'heare his Spurs gingle' when he walks. By the Restoration, Samuel Butler's 'Modish Man' understands 'exactly to a day what times of the year the several and respective sorts of colour'd ribbands come to be in season, and when they go out again', and 'sees no plays but only such as he finds most approv'd by men of his own rank and quality'. These he attends assiduously, climbing on his bench between the acts and keeping time to the incidental music 'with his comb and motion of his person'.[28]

---

[24] Aubrey, *Brief Lives*, 1: 38.
[25] Clarendon, *History*, 436; Aubrey, *Brief Lives*, 1: 406.
[26] Aubrey, *Brief Lives*, 1: 406.
[27] Recent works which discuss the Theophrastan character include Deidre Shauna Lynch, *The Economy of Character: Novels, Market Culture, and the Business of Inner Meaning* (Chicago: Chicago University Press, 1998); Jessica Martin, *Walton's Lives: Conformist Commemorations and the Rise of Biography* (Oxford: Oxford University Press, 2010); John Frow, *Character and Person* (Oxford: Oxford University Press, 2014); Andrea Walkden, *Private Lives Made Public: The Invention of Biography in Early Modern England* (Pittsburgh, PA: Duquesne University Press, 2016).
[28] Earle, *Micro-cosmographie*, no. 30, 'An Idle Gallant'; Samuel Butler, *Characters and Passages from Note-Books*, ed. A. R. Waller (Cambridge: Cambridge University Press, 1908), 240.

Although it is often treated essentially as a hominid early form which evolved into the fully erect representations of the novel, the character is essentially a classificatory system. Like the brief life, it has a flexible and lasting cultural role. Collections of characters and brief lives offer museums of humankind and a variety of systems with which to approach them. But the character itself adapts according to the various kinds of collection early modern people chose to amass and define. It develops over the long seventeenth century from a largely ethical, typological function to one which, while continuing to entertain, edify, and comfort itself by identifying bad men, time-wasters, and fools, responds to other needs. The character comes in handy when articulating choices, affirming preferences, fighting battles, and maintaining boundaries. Heiresses use them to discriminate between suitors; professionals use them to disparage pretenders to competence in law or medicine; politicians use them to describe their constituencies and the power-play within them; religious writers explain the godly life through them; members of niche groups qualify each others' weaknesses and personalities; historians use them to take stock of their times, and satirists, to laugh at them.

The genre ultimately derived from the Greek writer Theophrastus, whose 'ethical characters' were first published in a Latin translation by Isaac Casaubon in 1592.[29] The first English character-writer, Bishop Joseph Hall, brought out his *Characters of Vertues and Vices* in 1608. Authorized by Biblical allusion and explicitly exemplary, these exhorted the reader to follow virtue (the Penitent, the Faithfull Man, the Patient Man) and to shun vice (the Superstitious, the Envious, the Flatterer). John Bunyan used a version of Hall's exemplary character in his allegorical prose fiction, *The Pilgrim's Progress* (1678), in the dialogue in which Faith and Christian learn about Talkative.[30] A character collection was published in 1614 under the name of Sir Thomas Overbury, a courtier who had died in prison a couple of years earlier.[31] The true authors of the 'Overbury' characters are not known; they must have been commissioned or written by Lawrence Lisle, the publisher of the collection. They are to some degree arranged in moralizing pairs: a 'good Woman', a selfless helpmeet, is followed immediately by her antetype, a 'very very Woman', who just wants to have fun. Although they mainly offer versions of social types, there are some characters of places, 'A Taverne', 'A Bowle-Alley', and 'Paules Walke' in St Paul's Cathedral, which at this date was a thronged public forum where news and gossip might be exchanged. The Overbury characters were allegedly '*written by himselfe and other Learned Gentlemen his Friends*', invoking an association between the character and an informal, coterie setting in which these were concocted just for entertainment, or, as Edward Blount was to put it, 'written especially' for the

---

[29] See Richard A. McCabe, *Joseph Hall: A Study in Satire and Meditation* (Oxford: Clarendon Press, 1982), chap. 3.

[30] John Bunyan, *The Pilgrim's Progress*, ed. N. H. Keeble (Oxford: Oxford University Press, 1984), 64–5.

[31] *A Wife now The Widdow of Sir Thomas Overburye [...] Whereunto are added many witty Characters and conceited Newes, written by himselfe and other Learned Gentlemen his Friends* (London, 1614). See Bruce McIver, '"A Wife Now the Widdow": Lawrence Lisle and the Popularity of the Overburian Characters', *South Atlantic Review*, 59/1 (1994), 27–44.

author's 'private recreation, to passe away the time in the Country & by the forcible request of Friends drawne'.³²

Blount was describing the characters of John Earle, copies of which had circulated in manuscript, and which Blount published anonymously in 1628 as *Micro-cosmographie, Or, A Peece of the World Discovered: In Essayes and Characters*. Like the 'Overbury' characters, the Earle collection burgeoned in later editions: the original fifty-four characters grew to seventy-eight, which were still being printed regularly into the nineteenth century. Some of the character types were repeated over and over by successive writers. Earle revisits Overbury's 'Bowle-alley', 'Taverne', and 'Paules-Walke', while the Restoration character-writer Samuel Butler offers new versions of Earle's characters of antiquary, herald, drunkard, 'Sharke', and so on, while adding scores more.³³ The character burgeoned during the long seventeenth century. Editions of Theophrastus continued to be published, and the early English versions, particularly Earle's, remained very popular and went through many editions. Robert Hooke picked up a copy of the 1615 edition of Overbury for sixpence in 1675.³⁴ Butler's Restoration collection, which he left in manuscript, offers us over two hundred characters, including a republican, a modern critic, a politician, a tedious man, a small poet, a banker, a highwayman, a sot, a pimp, and a tennis player. Butler is an exceptionally sharp social critic, acutely aware of intellectual trends: the *Characters* begin with his longest, an essay on 'A Modern Politician', a critique of the political thought of Thomas Hobbes. He is wryly fascinated by scientific culture. The *Characters*, which include 'a Virtuoso' and 'A Mathematician', are preoccupied by museum exhibits—his 'Fool' is 'the skin of a man stuff'd with straw, like an alligator'; by alchemy—the 'Ignorant Man' is like lead in the alchemical 'test of metals'; by medicine—the Fencer is a 'duel-Doctor' whose prescriptions 'destroy as many as they preserve'; and by mechanics: the 'Affected' man is 'a Piece of Clockwork, that moves only as it is wound up and set, and not like a voluntary Agent. He is a mathematical Body, nothing but *punctum, linea & superficies* [point, line, and surface], and perfectly abstract from Matter'.³⁵

It is a genre which relies on amplification. In one of Margaret Cavendish's 'sociable letters', she describes a lavish and bizarre feast of literature, course upon course of 'Poetical Meats', in which 'characters' form the 'olio' of the banquet.³⁶ The olio is a mixed stew, a compound of many delicious ingredients, such as Butler's 'Huffing Courtier', a ridiculous creature who 'carries his elbows backward, as if he were pinioned like a trust-up Fowl, and moves as stiff as if he were upon the Spit'. The formula is simple, relying not only on a medley of people depicted but on a rich mixture of similes and statements. In his character of 'A Lover', Butler could be describing a mediocre character-writer when

---

[32] Blount, foreword in Earle, *Micro-cosmographie*, sig. A2v.
[33] Butler, *Characters*, 42, 76, 111, 258.
[34] *Diary of Robert Hooke*, ed. H. W. Robinson and Walter Adams (London: Taylor & Francis, 1935), 168.
[35] Butler, *Characters*, 184, 221, 223, 229.
[36] Margaret Cavendish, *CCXI Sociable Letters* (1664), 420.

he says that 'all Lovers are Poets for the Time being, and make their Ladies a Kind of mosaic Work of several coloured Stones joined together by a strong Fancy'.[37] The character serves to entertain friends; and in the hands of some writers the brief life, too, is a feast of friendship and community. Characters map a peopled territory, a 'Micro-cosmographie or Peece of the World', composed of ties of friendship and interest, against which dysfunction can be measured and laughed at. Aubrey's *Lives* have many digressions and marginalia in which other lives flourish; the brief life deals, not merely in individuals so much as in circles of influence.

The character is embedded in place. The playwright William Congreve wrote in 1695 to the literary critic John Dennis from the fashionable spa of Tunbridge Wells. Displaying a mastery of epistolary etiquette, he protested that he was unable to fulfil his wish of 'making Observations' of the spa because Dennis's letters from London were simply too excellent and he could not compete. Then, deploying a late form of the character of place which was demonstrated in Overbury and Earle's tavern and bowling alley, he characterizes the spa as the 'anti-Hypocrene' source of 'quantities of excrable' satires and lampoons, and full of provincial bores stuffing themselves with food. There must have been something in the water which made them all so dull, and he proposed a scientific experiment to find it out. He then suggests that a play might be written about them, full of 'Entertaining and Ridiculous Humours', characters in the sense developed by Ben Jonson. But he will not compose prose characters, for 'were the Company better, or worse, I would have you expect no Characters from me; for I profess my self an Enemy to Detraction; and who is there, that can justly merit Commendation?'[38] The term might be used, as Congreve does here, to denote a witty satirical portrait which might entertain a conversational partner or the recipient of a letter, but which was also sufficiently polished to merit further transmission once it had been extracted from the immediate context. As a form, Congreve suggests, the character is more polite, more positive and civilized, than the satires and lampoons written by the bores merely for 'detraction' and to mediate ephemeral chit-chat.

This sense of the character as polite satire is demonstrated in the letters written by the Bedfordshire gentlewoman, Dorothy Osborne, to her lover, and eventual husband, Sir William Temple, with whom she was carrying on a clandestine courtship, opposed by both families. Osborne's father and brothers were subjecting her to close surveillance while putting pressure on her to accept a number of rival suitors. Osborne succeeded in dismissing these men one by one, while keeping up her morale and developing her relationship with Temple in a manner consistent with the couple's sense of discretion and appropriate conduct, a decorum which embraced the form of the letter itself. Letters, she thought, should be like conversations: 'free and Easy as ones discourse', not 'studdyed' like formal academic 'orations'. For Osborne, there was a proper way to discourse confidentially, to conduct amours, and to discuss the characteristics of men with

---

[37] Butler, *Characters*, 37, 170.
[38] *The Works of William Congreve*, ed. D. F McKenzie, 3 vols. (Oxford: Oxford University Press, 2011), 3: 139–40.

the intention of selecting one of them for a husband or entrusting them with business matters. Indeed, this mode of discourse constituted a form of due diligence to be conducted with skill, positioning the speaker as neither a foolish, loose-tongued gossip, nor a gullible social ignoramus, while at all costs avoiding being a bore. In her letters Osborne briefly characterizes each of her unwelcome 'Servants'. The grave and scholarly Sir Justinian Isham, for example, made her 'sport' by writing her a love-letter which 'was the most sublime nonsense that in my life I ever read, and yet I beleeve hee decended as low as hee could to come neer my weak understanding'.[39]

Osborne tells Temple of conversations with her brother in which she has had recourse to anecdotes of her neighbours and her acquaintance as examples of successful or unfortunate marital choices, in a way which suggests how the readership of the romance and the emergent novel might develop out of a seventeenth-century sense of the profitable use of gossip. In her situation, Osborne's reputation was clearly of particular importance. Within a context of confidential talk and private correspondence, Osborne displays herself in the act, both of reflection and of prudent negotiation. And in part to maintain a character of prudence before her brothers and of fidelity before her lover, and in part to entertain, Osborne presents further examples of her observations, in a manner clearly informed by the Theophrastan character. Her compendious satire is a perfect example of what Margaret Cavendish meant when she called the character the 'olio', or satirical stew, for Osborne is attentive to the character's vulgarly crowding and exterior quality, heaping up 'a great many ingredients' before concluding with a contrasting vision of private and loyal married love:

> There are a great many ingredients must goe to the makeing mee happy in a husband, first, as my Cousin [Elizabeth] Fr[anklin]: says, our humours must agree, and to doe that hee must have that kinde of breeding that I have had and used that kinde of company, that is hee must not bee soe much a Country Gentleman as to understand Nothing but hawks and dogs and bee fonder of Either than of his wife, nor of the next sort of them whose aime reaches noe further then to bee Justice of peace and once in his life high Sheriff, who read noe book but Statut[e]s and study's nothing but how to make a speech interlarded with Latin that may amaze his disagreeing poore Neighbours and fright them rather then perswade them into quietnesse; hee must not bee a thing that began the world in a free scoole, was sent from thence to the University, and is at his farthest when hee reaches the Inns of Court, has noe acquaintance but those of his forme in these places, speaks the french hee has pickt out of Old Laws, and admires nothing but the Storry's hee has heard of the Revells that were kept there before his time; hee must not bee a Towne Gallant neither that lives in a Tavern and an Ordinary, that cannot imagin how an hower should bee spent without company unlesse it bee in sleeping, that makes court to all the Women hee sees, thinks they beleeve him and Laughs and is Laughed at Equaly; Nor a Traveld Mounsieur whose head is all feather inside and outside that can talk of nothing but

---

[39] *The Letters of Dorothy Osborne to William Temple*, ed. G. C. Moore Smith (Oxford: Clarendon Press, 1928), 90.

dances and Duells, and has Courage Enough to were slashes when every body else dy's with cold to see him; he must not bee a foole of noe sort, nor peevish nor ill Natur'd nor proude nor Coveteous and to all this must be added that he must Love mee and I him as much as wee are capable of Loveing.[40]

Dorothy's letter was accompanied by a volume of Madeleine de Scudéry's immense novel, *Le Grand Cyrus* (10 vols., 1649–53), which she wanted Temple to read. This gift formed a part of her courtship, for she says in her next letter that she identifies with the outlook of the fictional character Doralize, in particular in her romantic preferences: 'I am of her opinion in most things … in her Character of L'honnest homme that she is in search of.'[41] A 'Character' in Osborne's sense is a person whom you have not yet met but whose nature you will be able to penetrate, and whose actions you will be able to predict, because you already have the key to their personality. She offers the possibility that these men may be identified with real people, but she is careful not to be too precise as to who they may be. She also avoids the indecorum of telling her future husband how to behave. The character is a form which may allow the female user to demonstrate her values, taste, wit, social knowledge, and wisdom without the risk of censure, since no one individual is usually identified.

Sometimes, of course, they were identified. Butler offers a character of 'A Duke of Bucks', a debauchee who sleeps all day and chases pleasure all night. Employing the genre of the character, rather than just adding to the mountain of satires on Buckingham, makes its own point; this was a one-off, pure monster, rather than a portrait of a class of man who needed collectively to have the monstrosity of their failings pointed out.[42] In the coffee house one January evening in 1675, 'Mr. Aubery told' Robert Hooke 'of Mr. Henshaws character from Lord Brouncker.'[43] Hooke, Aubrey, and Thomas Henshaw were close friends and fellows of the Royal Society: William Brouncker, 2nd Viscount Brouncker, was its unpopular president. We cannot be sure what this 'character' was. It may have been simply what Brouncker thought of Henshaw. Or it may have been a character assassination relayed through confidential talk: just the kind of gossip which *Brief Lives* is famous for recording. The ambiguity of this example demonstrates that the spoken character, by this period, might be both particular to an authorial point of origin (here, Brouncker), and also a synonym for a reputation, which is owned—precariously—by its subject (here, Henshaw). Brouncker may have skilfully translated a quality agreed to be possessed by Henshaw, and Aubrey may have found a means to translate that quality into a form of anecdotal performance.

Hooke, meanwhile, was creating his own characters. In his *Micrographia* (1665), the curator of experiments to the Royal Society presented the learned world with an insight into the appearance and intimate habits of a familiar nuisance. Hooke was not the first to

---

[40] *Letters of Dorothy Osborne*, 105.
[41] *Letters of Dorothy Osborne*, 109.
[42] Butler, *Characters*, 33.
[43] *Diary of Robert Hooke*, 212.

examine a head louse under a microscope, yet in its precise observation and rich empirical detail his work was vastly more ambitious than anything that had come before it. His images remained the most accurate available for centuries. The engraving of the louse is the largest in *Micrographia*: nearly two feet long, the unfolded image is twice the size of the volume which contains it. Hooke's louse is a character in all senses. It is grandiose. It holds on to a single, vast human hair with its little hooked claws, and keeps its head high. It is a masterly portrait: Hooke even included the louse's shadow. The poet Andrew Marvell immediately saw its potential, appropriating it for his own verse satire aimed at Clarendon and his cronies: *The Last Instructions to a Painter* (1667) contains a portrait of the Royalist courtier Thomas, Lord Clifford of Chudleigh, who had done very nicely out of the Anglo-Dutch War, as the 'Comptroller' at whom 'all men laugh / To see a tall louse brandish his white staff'.[44] In the satirist's eyes, the respiratory orifices along the thorax appear like the folds of a robe of state; the reproductive organs like neat court shoes; the hair which it clutches like a ceremonial staff of office. The louse stimulates both curiosity for knowledge and satirical laughter, for Hooke himself began his account with a character of the parasite and goes on to a precise consideration of its anatomy:

> This is a Creature so officious, that 'twill be known to every one at one time or another, so busie, and so impudent, that it will be intruding it self in every ones company, and so proud and aspiring withall, that it fears not to trample on the best, and affects nothing so much as a Crown; feeds and lives very high, and that makes it so saucy, as to pull any one by the ears that comes in its way, and will never be quiet till it has drawn blood: it is troubled at nothing so much as at a man that scratches his head, as knowing that man is plotting and contriving some mischief against it, and that makes it oftentime skulk into some meaner and lower place, and run behind a mans back, though it go very much against the hair.[45]

In his ode to the Royal Society, published two years later in 1667, Abraham Cowley praises the Society for forcing its way into Nature's secrets, teaching 'the curious Sight to press / Into the privatest recess / Of her imperceptible Littleness'.[46] However, in Hooke's character, it is the saucy louse, and not the observant natural philosopher, who intrudes into private places. Cowley imagines a feminine abstraction, the 'privatest recess', but Hooke employs a very different analogy, characterizing the louse as a frequenter of a place thronged with great men, like the chambers of Whitehall. As in Dorothy Osborne's list of unacceptable suitors, characters belong in crowds. *Micrographia* has in its prefatory matter a carefully articulated and sustained argument for the nonpartisan nature of

---

[44] *Poems of Andrew Marvell*, ed. Nigel Smith (Harlow: Longman, 2003), 367, lines 17–18.

[45] Robert Hooke, *Micrographia* (1665), 211; the engraving is facing, 212. This might remind us that Theophrastus was not only the first character-writer, but also the first botanist. Hooke himself possessed copies of both the 'Overbury' characters and a 1534 selection from Theophrastus's *History of Plants*; see *Bibliotheca Hookeiana* (1703), 3.

[46] Abraham Cowley, 'To the Royal Society', in Thomas Sprat, *History of the Royal-Society of London* (1667), sig. B3.

scientific enquiry, and if we take Hooke's hint to read the science as a counterpoint to the satire, the royal crown to which the louse aspires proves merely to be the scalp that every one of us has. But nothing was nonpartisan in the 1660s. Hooke's louse is a republican, or at least an aspiring upstart; and Hooke jokes that he obtains his 'information' on him from a Royalist newspaper, 'my faithful *Mercury,* my *Microscope*'. Butler, in his character of 'A Liar', explains that the liar's 'discourse is a kind of microscope, that represents things much bigger than they are, but not so true to the object'; a respectful qualification, and an unusual one: the microscope and the scientific publication remained a satirist's staple for decades.[47]

In the Preface to *Micrographia,* Hooke insists that 'there should be a scrupulous choice, and a strict examination, of the reality, constancy, and certainty of the Particulars that we admit'. He characterizes *Micrographia* as 'Pictures and Observations'.[48] In its respect for the value of observation, pursuing the smallest and humblest of details in the search for the truth, Hooke's natural philosophy has an affinity with the brief life. In *Brief Lives*, Aubrey, one of Hooke's closest friends, and his biographer, also used his eyes. He noted that Hooke's 'head is lardge: his eie full and popping, and not quick. a grey eie'. The physician William Harvey told him that Sir Francis Bacon's were 'delicate, lively, hazel' eyes, 'like the Eie of a Viper'. Meanwhile Aubrey was himself observing that Harvey was exceptionally short and his dark complexion was the colour of 'wainscott'. He measured Thomas Hobbes's head and noted that it had a 'mallet' form, and that the Royalist journalist Sir John Berkenhead had 'great goggli eyes'.[49] When Hooke shone a 'very bright light' on the louse he saw 'its two black shining goggle eyes', but could find no eye-lids, discovering instead, two protective horns.[50] The brief life is a biographical microscope, which turns a sharp eye on processes and surfaces, bristles and mandibles, rather than offering the eulogy and moral exemplarity which had long been the province of life-writing. As Aubrey said, 'the very pudenda are not hid'.

This is a radical rejection of a deep strain. David Lloyd's exemplary lives are all presented as 'Observations', and he gave a long quotation from Bacon's *Advancement of Learning* (1605) as a preface, but this was merely old wine in new bottles and a gesture, perhaps, to the intellectual interests of his patron, Isaac Barrow.

In this period the exemplary, the rhetorical, and the minutely observed were not easily separated, even in scientific writing. Henry Power, who published a series of 'Microscopical Observations' the year before *Micrographia,* began his account of the house spider: 'now let us see what we can discover in *Ovid's Lydian*-Spinstresse, that proud Madam which *Pallas*, for her Rivalship, transformed into the Spider; which hath not only the Character of *Aristotle,* but of *Solomon* himself, for a wise and prudent

---

[47] Butler, *Characters,* 237. See further Chapter 24 by Gregory Lynall on 'Mock-Scientific Literature' and Chapter 33 by Felicity Henderson on 'Scientific Transactions'.

[48] Hooke, *Micrographia,* sigs. a2v, g1v.

[49] Aubrey, *Brief Lives*, 1: 98, 200, 210, 268, 2: 820.

[50] Hooke, *Micrographia,* 211–12. A parallel between Aubrey and Hooke as microscopic writers is also made in Walkden, *Private Lives Made Public,* chap. 4.

Animal.' Power sees no incongruity in alluding to Ovid's *Metamorphoses* and offering the spider as a moral emblem ('character') in the same breath as reporting that 'in the *Microscope*' its 'body and limbs is all stuck over with small silver hairs, which the very ayr will waft to and fro'.[51] For Aubrey, this was precisely the problem. 'Pox take your Orators and poets', he said in 1679, 'they spoile lives and histories'. He was talking about Dryden's interventions in a collaborative life of Hobbes, merely intended to make a 'better picture' of Hobbes at the expense of the more prosaic facts.[52] Clarendon, however, exemplifies another and far more sinister form of bias. His character of John Pym is inserted in the *History* at the point of Pym's death from the 'torment and agony' of a disease that was defined in the postmortem examination as a 'large abcesse or imposthume', possibly bowel cancer. Clarendon, however, drawing on Royalist gossip and satire, and ignoring the fact that Pym's corpse was publicly shown in Westminster Abbey, says Pym died of the 'lothsome' disease 'morbus pediculosus'.[53] This was phthiriasis, a hideous, legendary sickness, in which a mass of tumours was believed to arise spontaneously within the sufferer's skin, and then to burst, releasing a swarm of lice, the transubstantiated matter of the afflicted. In the writings of ancient and partisan authorities such as Josephus and Plutarch, phthiriasis appears as a terrible divine punishment reserved for tyrants and enemies of religion, such as Herod the Great and Sulla.[54]

Aubrey, by contrast, did not merely record gossip, nor was he partisan. For example, he took the trouble to visit Milton's apothecary to get the best authority for the date and cause of the republican poet's death, and also made enquiries as to the gradual onset of his blindness, similarly a subject of Royalist gossip. What he wanted to put in the place of moralizing, oratory, and manipulation of the facts was 'minutenesse', microscopic detail, in order to 'make a better picture'.[55] But even he still found a role, not only for anecdotes but also for the character. Describing the Elizabethan solicitor-general Sir Justice Popham, 'a huge, heavie, ugly man', who, the story goes, resolved to leave off his misspent youth of purse-taking and profligate company and 'stick to the studie of the law', Aubrey added in the margin of his *Brief Lives* a reference to the (presumably emblematic) 'picture of a Common Lawer. he must have An Iron head a brazen face and a Leaden breech'.[56] And struggling to construct a life of the Restoration actor John Lacy out of very sparse details, Aubrey makes a note to consult 'Dr Earles character of a Player'.[57] It is impossible to be sure what part of Earle's

---

[51] Henry Power, *Experimental Philosophy* (1664), 11–12.
[52] Aubrey, *Brief Lives*, 1: xc–xci.
[53] Clarendon, *History*, 202.
[54] Jan Bondeson, 'Phthiriasis: The Riddle of the Lousy Disease', *Journal of the Royal Society of Medicine*, 91 (1998), 328–34. Bondeson discusses the case of Pym (330–1), arguing that although it was certainly a matter of legend, the disease was also in some cases a genuine one, caused by a subspecies of the louse which infects birds in this way but which has not been observed to infect humans since the 1870s.
[55] Aubrey, *Brief Lives*, 1: 665; 2: 1627–8.
[56] Aubrey, *Brief Lives*, 1: 284–5.
[57] Aubrey, *Brief Lives*, 1: 559; Earle, *Micro-cosmographie*, no. 38.

character might have been thought suitable to add to the brief life. But Aubrey did not make a firm distinction between the brief life and the character: he felt that the character encapsulated as a general rule what his *Lives* demonstrated as particular and telling instances. Although the brief life was not didactic, it had strong empirical principles. It garnered the fruits of experience. In his brief life of Shakespeare, Aubrey states that Shakespeare and Ben Jonson did 'gather Humours of men dayly wherever they came'.[58]

In an unpublished treatise, 'An Idea of Education of Young Gentlemen' (c.1684–90), Aubrey laid out a plan for an entirely modern school, with a new and progressive curriculum, intended to produce a governing class who were prepared for the life of action, negotiation, and statesmanship which lay ahead of them. Aubrey spent decades on this work, and it includes much of his own experience as well as that of his acquaintances. There is a chapter on how children were to have 'their understandings opened with the Ethicks'. He proposed that each child keep a notebook in which they would record their personal 'Observations' of their fellow men, 'Mores Hominum'. Aubrey anticipates the objection that this would be rather pointless, 'it may be sayd, that that is as old as Horace etc:' who had employed the phrase in his *Ars Poetica*; 'but the application of it to Youths' is 'usefull. Wherefore I would have 'em to read Mankind dayly, as well as bookes: and to insert their Observations in … pocket Note-bookes' as Jonson and Shakespeare had done. Jonson's plays, Aubrey explains, are 'not only Dramatique Poetrie: but there are admirable Essaies, and Characters, and Mores Hominum excellently described'. This is an allusion, perhaps an unconscious one, to the title of Earle's character collection, *Micro-cosmographie, Or, A Peece of the World Discovered: In Essayes and Characters*. Aubrey describes these pocket notebooks as 'a Nest-egge', repositories or 'Stores from observation and Experience: a way as farre beyond the common way of Precept, as the Knowledge of a Traveller exceeds that which is gotten by a Mappe'. Jonson 'dayly read Men, and made his Observations as he walkt-along the streetes', and his eminence as a playwright was based on his assiduity as a *flâneur*.[59]

Aubrey, who admired above all people creative thinkers, those who observed their fellow men rather than relying exclusively on the learning of the library, is appropriating Jonson for his own purposes. He felt his century needed to understand itself better, so that it could prepare itself for beneficial change; and that collections like his might prove an invaluable resource for posterity. As we saw with Dorothy Osborne, characters, like personal testimonials, might support prudent calculations and predictions, such as whom to trust with your money or your hand in marriage; and they certainly might be employed to justify a choice of that kind. They were a nest egg and a collection: the more, the better; and, like money, they accrued value and were there when you needed them. Aubrey's financial prodigality, if that is what it was, has always been associated with the writing of *Brief Lives*, as an assumed cause and effect. Yet he believed his unpublished

---

[58] Aubrey, *Brief Lives*, 1: 365.
[59] Bodleian Library, Oxford, MS Aubrey 10, fols. 46, 94, 95, 106.

collections to constitute, rather, a laying up of stores. Collecting people is accounting for the productive use of one's time.

The character was a conservative form: while it mocked bores, it also pleased them. Its function as easy-reading moral criticism had a particular appeal to those popular writers who were lampooned as Dunces by Pope. Nahum Tate, who most famously adapted *King Lear* to give it a happy ending in 1681, published a version of Joseph Hall's *Characters* in 1691, in ponderous rhyming couplets: 'The Hypocrite to sadness can convert / His looks, while Mirth is Rev'lling in his Heart, / Then Jugler-like with Pleasure does retreat, / To think how smoothly he has pass'd the Cheat.' Eustace Budgell published a translation of Theophrastus in 1714. In an obsequious dedicatory epistle to Charles Montagu, Lord Halifax, Budgell said that it was one of 'those Works which tend directly to *Use*, and improve the Judgement by giving us an Insight into *Men* and *Manners*', a statement which by this period was tediously conventional.[60] Insightful observation led on one hand to political stock-taking, moral satire, and disenchantment. But, on the other hand, it was a serious and conscientious obligation. It led to the discovery of scientific and social rules, and to new verbal and visual forms to record them. In the Restoration, these two principles, satire and science, linked by a new valorization of observation, prudence, and experiment, shaped a new direction for the two forms of character and brief life.

---

[60] Nahum Tate, *Characters of Virtue and Vice ... Attempted in Verse from a Treatise of the Reverend Joseph Hall* (1691), 17; Eustace Budgell, *The Moral Characters of Theophrastus. Translated from the Greek* (1714), sig. A3v.

CHAPTER 10

CIRCULATION NARRATIVES AND SPY LITERATURE

ANDREA HASLANGER

More than half a century before the ascendancy of tales told by things (a sofa, a coach, a pair of slippers) or by animals (a hare, a bird, a squirrel), a more ragtag and diffuse set of texts concerning circulation emerged in England. These narratives are related by observers whose powers of observation are unsuspected and who are, to a greater or lesser degree, anonymous: spies, speaking coins, editorial personae, and in one notable case, a man metamorphosed into a lapdog. In letters or in episodic prose, these tales describe the narrator's travels, whether local, national, or international, and the people he or she meets along the way. They peek into aristocratic homes, confessionals, royal palaces, pubs, markets, gambling houses, and thieves' dens, relating episodes at turns scandalous and utterly quotidian. Though attention is given to the narrator's own condition and concerns—the spy's garb, the coin's previous existence as a bracelet, the dog's sore paws—the primary focus is on scenes and characters he or she meets, which offer studies of individual as well as national character and reflections on the history of England since the Civil Wars. These narratives use the fiction of an invisible or unnoticed observer to generate an outsider's perspective that is able to see what others cannot, not only in the sense of witnessing private scenes up close, but also in the sense of detecting broader patterns and phenomena from afar and in aggregate. They participate in the making of English national identity and the representation of the urban public as a collective, negotiating questions of virtue and value and standards of behaviour in the process.

Spy and circulation narrators act as repositories of information, whose memories and minds, undiminished by the passage of time, record their every observation. The mental continuity of these narrators is notable not only because it persists in spite of changes in state (like a coin's reminting, or animal metamorphosis), but also because what it records is less concerned with the self than with the representation of other persons, positions, views, and attitudes. Here, mindedness is associated not with inwardness or inner workings but with outwardness and display, and with a capacity to show others what they otherwise do not or cannot see. Spy and circulation narrators, this chapter argues, work to shape public opinion by embodying or even objectifying particular attitudes about popular topics like sexual morality, trade, statecraft, and national character. They offer first-person narratives that are neither strictly personal nor individual, but that use the first person to authenticate the attitudes they give voice to. While they share certain features in common with the it-narrative and the novel, they are distinct from both. Unlike the it-narrative, which comes into relief at mid-century, these texts are not defined by their nonhuman narrators per se, but instead by their multifarious strategies for exposing the unseen and generating new ways of looking at types and groups of people.[1] Unlike the novel, which appears by the second decade of the century, and which also employs letters and other fictions of access to depict private places and lives, the texts under discussion here do not offer sustained treatment of characters' experiences, thoughts, or feelings.[2]

The analysis that follows begins with a brief survey of circulation narratives and spy literature. From there it moves to detailed readings of Charles Gildon's *The New Metamorphosis* (1708) and *The Golden Spy* (1709) alongside selected issues of the *Tatler* and the *Spectator*. Its objective in focusing on these texts in particular is not only to demonstrate how metamorphosis is used to generate continuity of character across different physical forms, but also to evaluate how this bears on the more familiar connection between currency and national identity in tales about coinage. Throughout, the argument is sensitive to how the device of the spy or the circulation narrator performs a taxonomic function, categorizing certain persons and behaviours and encouraging particular beliefs. Overall, the chapter has three main aims: first, to demonstrate just how variable, multifarious, and resistant to categorization circulation narratives and spy literature from the period can be; second, to offer close analysis of the role of metamorphosis, animation, and mindedness in these texts, with reference to the it-narrative and the novel, as well as to figure, personification, and materialism; and third, to suggest that these texts can be seen to generate a model of character concerned not with inwardness but instead with making visible or recognizable shared views or attitudes.

Circulation narratives and spy literature are distinct categories that nevertheless overlap substantially between 1688 and 1714. These two categories are best seen not as exhaustive or mutually exclusive, but instead as a way of bringing into relief certain

---

[1] The appearance of the it-narrative is often dated to Francis Coventry's *The History of Pompey the Little, or the Life and Adventures of a Lapdog* (1751) or Charles Johnstone's *Chrysal, or the Adventures of a Guinea* (1760). For a compendious collection of it-narratives as well as a discussion of the category itself, see Mark Blackwell et al. (eds.), *British It-Narratives, 1750–1830*, 4 vols. (London: Pickering and Chatto, 2012). See also Mark Blackwell (ed.), *The Secret Life of Things: Animals, Objects, and It-Narratives in Eighteenth-Century England* (Lewisburg: Bucknell University Press, 2007).

[2] Even so, some of the narrative strategies of these pre-novelistic texts arguably anticipate and influence later novelistic modes. Charles Gildon's *The Post Boy Robb'd of His Mail* (1692–3) uses the letter to peek into private lives, purporting to publish a bag of stolen letters. There are also more general parallels between the spy or circulation narrator and the omniscient narrator, who is a kind of spy, able to access characters' minds without being detected by them.

characteristics for further consideration. The definition of each category offered here, therefore, is intended to keep in view the multiple affiliations many of these texts have, and to examine, at least briefly, certain preoccupations shared by circulation and spy narratives from the period. The term 'circulation narrative' is a relatively recent invention, approximately two and a half decades old, and describes a prose work told by a nonhuman narrator that moves from one owner to the next.[3] The term 'circulation narrative' is often used interchangeably with 'it-narrative' when discussing texts from mid-century on, but for reasons both chronological and formal, this chapter makes the claim that circulation narratives should be understood as distinct from it-narratives.[4] The circulation narratives written before 1714 include Joseph Addison's *Tatler* no. 249 (1710) on the adventures of a shilling as well as two texts by Charles Gildon, *The New Metamorphosis* (1708) and *The Golden Spy* (1709), which are narrated by a man turned into a dog and an international collection of speaking coins. Each of these works concerns a series of connected episodes that occur as the narrator moves from place to place. They are life stories, organized chronologically and spanning many years, but, unlike more familiar varieties of autobiography, they are not told by a human narrator and are not bounded by the parameters of an ordinary human life. Circulation narrators change shape, lose and regain the power of speech, observe countless human beings, and, in the case of the tales told by coins, live for centuries without forgetting anything. They possess knowledge that surpasses the boundaries of a single body or a single age: what they have to say differs from case to case, but there is a general focus on human foibles and desires running throughout. In discussing these texts, scholars often focus on the representation of precious metals and money, and therefore treat *Tatler* no. 249 alongside *The Golden Spy* without giving much attention to *The New Metamorphosis*, but all three are important examples of the varieties and uses of circulation in the first decade of the eighteenth century.

Like circulation narratives, spy literature also involves a roving narrator: it comprises letters or dispatches from a disguised foreigner or an invisible persona who comments on politics, cultural customs, and behaviours at home or abroad. Like the circulation narrator, the spy is able to see how people behave when they think no one is watching,

---

[3] See Liz Bellamy's chapter on 'The Novel of Circulation', in *Commerce, Morality and the Eighteenth-Century Novel* (Cambridge: Cambridge University Press, 1998), 119–28.

[4] There is not critical consensus on this point. To some scholars, Gildon's *Golden Spy* and the adventures of a shilling detailed in *Tatler* no. 249 are founding it-narratives that prefigure later tales told by coins and banknotes. To others, the comparative scarcity of such texts, and the long gap between their appearance and the publication of later it-narratives at mid-century, makes such a claim untenable. For different readings of Gildon in relation to this question see Liz Bellamy's introduction to *British It-Narratives*, 1, pp. ix–xxviii; Courtney Weiss Smith, *Empiricist Devotions: Science, Religion, and Poetry in Early Eighteenth-Century England* (Charlottesville: University of Virginia Press, 2016); Jonathan Lamb, 'Modern Metamorphoses and Disgraceful Tales', *Critical Inquiry*, 28 (2001), 133–66; Scott Nowka, 'Talking Coins and Thinking Smoke-Jacks: Satirizing Materialism in Gildon and Sterne', *Eighteenth-Century Fiction*, 22 (2009–10), 195–222; and Christopher Flint, 'Speaking Objects: The Circulation of Stories in Eighteenth-Century Prose Fiction', *Publications of the Modern Language Association*, 113 (1998), 212–26.

and to travel widely in pursuit of intelligence. The most influential spy narrative from the period is the tremendously popular *Letters Writ by a Turkish Spy* (1687, 1691–4), which reports on seventeenth-century France and was translated into English from French in several instalments.[5] It inspired a number of imitations and adaptations, ranging from epistolary fictions like Charles Gildon's *The Post-Boy Robb'd of His Mail* (1692–3), to urban reportage like Ned Ward's *London Spy* (1698–1700) and Addison and Steele's *Tatler* (1709–11) and *Spectator* (1711–14), to further fictions of Eastern correspondents like Daniel Defoe's *Letters Writ by a Turkish Spy in Paris* (1718) and Montesquieu's *Persian Letters* (1721). The content of these texts includes reflections on England as well as other European nations from the perspective of an observer who is separated either by invisibility or by cultural difference from the scenes he observes. The Turkish spy's remarks about Europe are a device of defamiliarization, what Ros Ballaster calls a '"reverse" gaze [through which] the eastern spy/traveller puts the West on display to his correspondents "back home"'.[6] The desire to put the West in general and England in particular on display also animates the personae of Ward's London Spy and Addison and Steele's Mr. Spectator. While there are important distinctions between the fictionalized Turkish or Eastern spy and the periodical personae of Ward, Addison, and Steele, all use a technique of abstraction to generate their commentary. They relate their observations from a position of comparative invisibility, which does not offer and is in fact at odds with a detailed rendering of the spy's personality or self. Clearly, this technique of abstraction interacts differently with national identity in each case, but overall it facilitates the presentation of judgements about national character, class, religion, and other matters in the guise of factual report.

The fictional spy is, by definition, a figure who cannot be known but who disseminates information about others. For the spy, as for the omniscient narrator, the position of knowing others while remaining relatively unknown is made possible by a kind of invisibility, an assumed identity, or a difference in kind—this difference in kind can be, for instance, that between the coin narrator and the humans it observes. In cases where the spy is not human, and is an animal or a thing, the spy's ability to communicate, even its sentience, can require explanation. The texts under discussion here account for their nonhuman narrators' capacities by describing them as the product of metamorphosis or, less frequently, dream vision. Both metamorphosis and dream vision involve transformation, whether from one outward form to another (a man turning into a lapdog) or from silence to speech (a coin rising up from the table and starting to speak). What is more, transformation connects previous and present states: as the man becomes a dog, or the silent coin suddenly speaks, the memory of what came before is preserved. Because of this continuity, metamorphosis can use its movement across forms and across different degrees of animation to reflect on the social distribution of power within and across species. Unlike the it-narrators who are born as, say, sedans or as coats

---

[5] Ros Ballaster details the complicated publication history of this text in *Fabulous Orients: Fictions of the East in England, 1662–1785* (Oxford: Oxford University Press, 2005), 145–6.

[6] Ballaster, *Fabulous Orients*, 149.

and who spend their entire lives as such, until they are discarded or salvaged or used up, the spy and circulation narrators of the two prose texts that are the focus of this chapter, *The New Metamorphosis* and *The Golden Spy*, transform over the course of their tales. Metamorphosis makes them, and though it is not the only explanation offered for their unusual abilities, it is by far the most important one.[7] Their movement from one state to another is inseparable from their capacity as observers and spies and their ability to comment on the behaviour of the humans they witness.

The sort of metamorphosis at issue in Gildon's *The New Metamorphosis* is at once more sustained and less serious than one might expect: more sustained because a single transformation lasts for hundreds of pages and less serious because it is frequently used as a device to deliver moralizing parables or *roman à clef* tales. Metamorphosis, in other words, not only situates Gildon's texts within a recognizable tradition, but solves a narrative problem of how to secure access to private scenes and hidden thoughts. *The New Metamorphosis* rewrites Apuleius's *The Golden Ass*, repurposing metamorphosis as a stronger spyglass for scandal. Its major revision to Apuleius's text is to replace the ass, which 'could scarce come into any Place where there cou'd be any Secret Transacted' with a lapdog, an animal that 'is admitted to the Clossets [sic], Cabinets, and Bedchambers of the Fair' and is therefore a far superior 'Machine for the Discovery of Secret Vices'.[8] Gildon cannily adapts an ancient tale of intrigue into a modern one, bolstering his semi-pornographic, anti-Catholic romp through the bedrooms of Italy with this reference to an ongoing tradition of metamorphosis and textual revision.

Notably, the metamorphosis of the title occurs nearly halfway through the text, towards the end of the first volume. This does not mean that readers have to wait patiently—or skip ahead—to find scandalous scenes. The narrator, Don Fantasio, is able to act as a spy in his human as well as his canine guises, thanks to the access he is granted first as a man who looks young enough to be a child and later as a luxurious pet. While still a human, he is taken on as an attendant of the beautiful Theresa, who undresses and bathes in front of him, 'For under the Notion of a Child, she believ'd all her Permissions inoffensive'. After Don Fantasio tells her a love story to entertain her while she is bathing, he falls into the water and she exclaims: 'Oh! My dear little Miniature of Man, that thou wert as capable of easing my Pains as thy Tongue has been of raising them!'[9] Things unfold rather predictably from here, and Don Fantasio continues his assignations with

---

[7] Because metamorphosis is so rarely a feature of it-narratives, it has not received much discussion in the scholarship, with the exception of Lamb's 'Modern Metamorphoses and Disgraceful Tales'. The explanations of why things talk offered in later it-narratives, when there are explanations offered at all, very rarely mention metamorphosis. Instead, they discuss materialism, philosophy of mind, and transmigration, among other phenomena. For discussions of the materialism of later it-narratives, see Jonathan Lamb, *The Things Things Say* (Princeton, NJ: Princeton University Press, 2011), as well as the essays collected in Blackwell (ed.), *The Secret Life of Things*. For a reading of *The Golden Spy* that makes a case for its satirical engagement with materialism, see Nowka, 'Talking Coins and Thinking Smoke-Jacks'.

[8] Charles Gildon, *The New Metamorphosis: or, The Pleasant Transformation: Being the Golden Ass of Lucius Apuleius of Medaura*, 2 vols. (2nd edn, London: 1709), 1, np.

[9] Gildon, *New Metamorphosis*, 1: 22, 45.

Theresa as a kind of living Signior Dildo, witnessing her encounters with other lovers as well. This comparatively happy period ends when the Cardinal, whose palace Theresa resides in, makes advances on Don Fantasio. Don Fantasio flees the palace, dressed in Theresa's clothes; his subsequent adventures keep him concealed, first in women's clothes and then in a trunk, in which he is carried to Invidiosa, an old woman who saves him from the Cardinal's search party by transforming him.

Gildon, like Apuleius before him, explains the phenomenon of the nonhuman narrator, who is a human at the story's beginning and who turns back into a human to write the manuscript, through metamorphosis. Apuleius, in his preface, says that the reader might enjoy the novel '[i]f you are not put off by the Egyptian story-telling convention which allows humans to be changed into animals and, after various adventures, restored to their proper shapes'.[10] In both Apuleius and Gildon's versions of the tale, the stagecraft of metamorphosis relies on a fateful pot of ointment borrowed from an old woman with magical powers. Lucius's potion in Apuleius comes from his lover's mistress, who transforms herself into animal shapes to seduce much younger men; Don Fantasio's comes from Invidiosa, a woman trained in the 'Art of Magic' who herself transforms from 'an old, wither'd, Paralitic Hag' into a beautiful young woman when she forces Don Fantasio to sleep with her.[11] Lucius is transformed out of curiosity; Don Fantasio out of necessity, to escape imminent capture and punishment. In each case, metamorphosis lasts longer and creates more hardships than expected: the miraculous antidote requires the intervention of the goddess Isis in *The Golden Ass* and a trip all the way across Europe to visit an English physician in *The New Metamorphosis*.

In both Apuleius and Gildon's versions of the tale, metamorphosis encompasses changes in outward appearance rather than memory or mind. Apuleius makes it clear that even while Lucius is an animal, he retains his human mind: Lucius says at one point, in answer to an imagined reader's objection: 'I was an ass, I agree; but I still kept my human intelligence.' The same is true in *The New Metamorphosis*, where Don Fantasio remembers all 'the Discoveries [he] has made' as a dog after his 'Restoration' to the 'State of Humanity'.[12] Metamorphosis's conservation of mind makes it possible for the metamorphosed narrator to remember and ultimately relate what has happened: it allows the narrator to remain known to himself while becoming unknown to others, even his intimates. But what the narrator relates is invariably in service of exposing the follies of mankind: metamorphosis is not an instrument of individual self-knowledge in these texts so much as a technique of making visible a broader pattern of 'secret vices'. More to the point, metamorphosis facilitates the pursuit of ever better and more scintillating scenes of witness.

In *The New Metamorphosis*, Gildon's use of metamorphosis is localized and does not signal a wholesale materialism that entertains the possibility that apparently inanimate things may think, feel, even speak. Unlike its source text, *The Golden Ass*, *The New*

---

[10] Lucius Apuleius, *The Golden Ass*, trans. Robert Graves (London: Penguin, 1960), 25.
[11] Gildon, *New Metamorphosis*, 1: 238–9.
[12] Apuleius, *Golden Ass*, 225; Gildon, *New Metamorphosis*, 1: 324.

Metamorphosis does not imply that metamorphosis might be at work elsewhere in the world of the story and therefore a chair or a horse or a locket might be a human in another guise. The protagonist Lucius expresses the point memorably in *The Golden Ass*: 'I wondered whether the stones I kicked against were really, perhaps, petrified men, and whether the birds I heard singing were people in feathered disguise ... and I began to entertain doubts about the trees around the house, and even about the faucets through which the fountains played.'[13] This idea of the apparently inanimate being animated, of every thing being a person in disguise, unsettles what are otherwise clear divisions between different categories of being and suggests a way of looking at the world which acknowledges that one's perceptions may be mistaken and that any sort of thing might be minded. *The New Metamorphosis* entertains no such uncertainties or doubts beyond its central transformation of Don Fantasio: it reserves the infinite permutations of possibility not for the idea that a cabinet or a flower or a shoe might be a human in disguise, but for an endlessly renewable display of human vice in every room and every mind. The question raised by metamorphosis, then, is not whether things might be persons, but whether humans might be monsters.[14]

For these reasons, we might ask how seriously to take the metamorphosis in *The New Metamorphosis*. It is hardly the case that Gildon's text is interested in what it is like to be a dog; its focus, instead, is on what a dog can see. As a lapdog, Don Fantasio witnesses countless scenes of seduction, coercion, manipulation, and deceit between priests, friars, and nuns, who use sex as a tool of power and punishment.[15] His metamorphosis only intensifies the text's anti-Catholic, semi-pornographic agenda. Inasmuch as metamorphosis is so clearly used as a narrative 'machine', Don Fantasio's experience as a dog appears to be yet another excuse for looking into confessionals and friars' cells to detail 'the Vices of *Italy*'. But there is more at issue here than finding new ways to tell old stories. Don Fantasio's transformation from human to dog also allows him to escape the sexual violence that he sees other humans subjected to and that he himself experiences.[16] To be a human in *The New Metamorphosis* is to be subjected to the will of those more powerful than you and to be used privately in ways that are denied publicly. Don Fantasio's travels expose him to the unpleasant recognition that whatever codes of morality, benevolence, or justice might appear to govern mankind are

---

[13] Apuleius, *Golden Ass*, 47–8.

[14] On this point, see Lamb's remark that things' bleak disclosures about humans threaten 'human sympathy' ('Modern Metamorphoses and Disgraceful Tales', 154). In *The New Metamorphosis*, Don Fantasio does mention in passing that Invidiosa has transformed other humans, but this is not a central part of the plot.

[15] There is little to stitch these scenes together, and when the nuns' education is offered up as a partial explanation for these 'various Scenes of *Lewdness*', the mention of *The School of Venus* (1680) drives home the point that the author of *The New Metamorphosis* is conversant with contemporary pornography (Gildon, *New Metamorphosis*, 2: 331, 333).

[16] Gildon, *New Metamorphosis*, 2: 324. In this regard, it echoes the tales of Ovid's in which metamorphosis succeeds rape. The fundamental way in which being a dog is better than being a human in *The New Metamorphosis* is that it protects Don Fantasio from being raped by a man, which is depicted as the ultimate humiliation and a specifically Catholic threat.

in fact superseded by individuals' violent pursuit of their own wills and their use of others as playthings. The gravity of this message is tempered somewhat by the text's satirical aims: it may be more accurate to limit the damning verdict on mankind to the European locales in which its stories take place, or rather to the strict moral codes of conduct that these locales are bound by.

The New Metamorphosis pioneers a technique that also appears in The Golden Spy and in Tatler no. 249, whereby a sentient nonhuman observer is able to see aspects of human life and behaviour that humans themselves cannot.[17] Metamorphosis exposes morals as they relate to economy and exchange in The Golden Spy, which has been of interest for just this reason. The golden spies of Gildon's title are a collection of international coins that come to life at night and entertain their human owner with tales of their adventures. A louis d'or, a guinea, and 'some *Dutch, Spanish,* and odd *Italian* pieces of Gold' enrapture the human narrator, who converses with them in the privacy of his lodgings.[18] The coins' 'Intelligence'—the information they have gathered and their capacity to do so in the first place—is explained in two ways by the text. Initially, it is associated with materialism, or the '*Sensibility of Things* which we generally not only esteem mute but inanimate'; subsequently and repeatedly, it is attributed to metamorphosis, and specifically to the fact that some of the coins contain the gold Jupiter turned into when he rained down on Danaë, impregnating her with Perseus. The important point here is that metamorphosis provides the predominant explanation for the coins' exceptional capacities and is associated not only with changing physical shape, but with exerting control over particular humans. Even a grain of this divine gold is irresistible: it allows its possessors to pursue their desires and to enforce their will on others, as Jove does in his many guises.[19] This does not make the coin the master of its owner so much as making it an extension of its owner's capacities. The louis d'or (or 'd'ore', as Gildon puns), the first coin to speak, explains that he has 'had multitudes of Masters, and Shapes full as various' since descending 'from Heav'n in that *show'r* with *Jove*'. He has been an ornament on generals' swords, a ring on ladies' fingers, a coin held by politicians, clergymen, gamesters, pimps, and bawds; he has travelled throughout England and has 'been of all Parties and Factions' and 'every station of Life, from the *Prince* to the *Peasant*'.[20] Like Ned Ward's London Spy or the later Mr. Spectator, the louis d'or claims to have access to everyone; in contrast to these other spies, the coin's access depends on its metamorphic properties and its presumed insensibility.

The metamorphosis of The Golden Spy concerns the powers of gold, both in the sense of gold's capacities of perception and in the sense of its ability to enchant the humans

---

[17] The influence moves in both directions: the Tatler is also cited as a source for Gildon. The 'Epistle Nuncupatory' associates the coins' spying prowess with techniques used in the Tatler, which has 'lately ... crept like the Fops of the Times into the Closet of the *Great* and the *Fair*' (Charles Gildon, The Golden Spy (1709), np).

[18] Gildon, Golden Spy, 304.

[19] Gildon, Golden Spy, 2, 8–9.

[20] Gildon, Golden Spy, 9, 12, 14.

who desire or possess it. The coin narrators of *The Golden Spy* speak like humans but are not humans: their clear, articulate English allows them to communicate their wisdom to the human narrator, who converses with them over the course of six nights, during which they tell him stories of love, intrigue, and deceit and discuss the political character of their home nations. Notably, the circulation narrative actually impedes continued circulation: the human narrator does not dream of spending his coins, for he cannot be certain that other coins would speak, and even if they did, they would say different things.[21] But while the narrator's wishes inhibit the coins' circulation, they do not inhibit the circulation narrative: the coins are able to offer up-to-date observations, having been taken out of circulation only very recently. In addition, the narrative itself circulates in the hopes of enriching its author and publisher. Therefore, to say that the coins' narrative survival is at odds with the realization of their financial potential may be to take an overly limited view, given that the author is attempting to turn their chatter back into coinage.

When money talks in Gildon's text, what it says concerns its use, its endurance, and its observations about its power to motivate moral and immoral behaviour. Readers might wonder whether money theorizes its value, and to what extent its remarks concern contemporary changes in the English and European economy. Certainly, the choice of a coin narrator is topical, not only because of recent debates about recoinage, which culminated in the melting down of clipped coins to produce standardized coins with ridged edges, but also because of ongoing concerns about international trade and 'about how money was supposed to work, how the economy ought to be ordered'.[22] But even though Gildon's speaking coins appear at a historical moment that makes it tempting to suggest that they might encapsulate an ongoing shift in how money and value is conceived, they do not neatly map onto the development of a specifically modern way of thinking about money and value. They do not theorize monetary value as a human construction, nor do they offer readers much guidance about what to do with their money, whether to spend or to save, beyond remarking that gold thrives when it enjoys 'absolute Freedom of circulating with the Sun about the World'. Even if the subtext of encouraging spending is clear enough, there is little direct suggestion that gold's circulation might enrich the nation or the globe, and it is notable that the text describes economic mobility gotten from gambling as a kind of metamorphosis, associating it with fantastic transformation rather than industrious self-improvement. The louis d'or says early on: 'The Metamorphoses of this Mystery [gaming] are greater than those of *Ovid*; for here Footmen, Porters, Butchers, Tapsters, Bowl-Rubbers are transform'd into Gentlemen,

---

[21] Not all coins speak, as the louis d'or explains: some coins, he notes, 'have had the Power of Speech, but by prostituting that Faculty, have for a time quite lost it; but ... the rest neither ever had or ever would enjoy that Prerogative' (Gildon, *Golden Spy*, 6).

[22] Smith, *Empiricist Devotions*, 109. For discussions of concepts of currency and value in relation to coinage, see also Brad Pasanek, *Metaphors of Mind: An Eighteenth-Century Dictionary* (Baltimore: Johns Hopkins University Press, 2015), 51–9; and Sean Silver, *The Mind is a Collection: Case Studies in Eighteenth-Century Thought* (Philadelphia, PA: University of Pennsylvania Press, 2015), 130–3, 229.

and Companions for Ministers of State, and Princes themselves; and on the other hand, Lords, Knights, and Squires into Scoundrels, excluded from the Conversation of the Chambermaid.'[23] The rising and falling fortunes of the high and the low are at once represented as out of their control and as a species of magic. The metamorphic power that allows money to speak allegorizes money's power to transform one's fortune or state. But it also uses a form that is fundamentally associated with fanciful tales to do so: money's magic might be something of a fiction, and money might require fictions to represent its power.

Inasmuch as *The Golden Spy* can be read as a text that reflects on contemporary conditions, including those of a changing economy in the decade and a half after the foundation of the Bank of England and the recoinage debate, its remarks on these issues cannot be disaggregated from its moral tales, which discuss the gold's existence before becoming money. When the coins describe their history before being minted, they tell centuries-old stories akin to those that populate *The New Metamorphosis*, replete with scenes of manipulation, coercion, mistaken identity, and rape. These tales stretch back at least to the fourteenth century. In one such tale, a mercenary gallant who had hoped for a loan from his lover steals her necklace instead, ingesting it pearl by pearl but leaving the locket, which is too large to swallow and in which the trusty narrator is lodged, watching the whole thing. In another, a woman is bewitched by a lover, who has given her his miniature 'tinctur'd' with divine gold; she pits a second suitor against him, causing the second suitor to fall to his death. Tales like these are evidence of gold's immortality and its accordingly long spying career; they also illustrate how money and sex are timeless prime movers. The human narrator makes just this point when he introduces the final night of conversation with his golden spies, remarking that the depravities of the present age are no better or worse than those of the past: 'Men were always the same in their Desires, in their Sins, in their Follies, and not very different in their Knowledge; if one Age lost it, the succeeding ones revived it.'[24] Doubtless, such remarks suggest a universal economy in which acts and goods are exchanged, and appear to erode the historical specificity of the guinea's discussion of the present. But this pabulum about the universality of human vice and the cycles of history belies the text's rather more interesting relation to its contemporary moment and to the process of generating historical consciousness, which it does in part through the coin's sheer longevity.

The history offered up in *The Golden Spy* appears to be national—a nation's coin consolidates what the nation stands for—but defines the nation in relation to its neighbours and its empire in ways worth highlighting here. Coins are presented as portable tokens of national character: each is stamped with the profile of a sovereign, whose face the human narrator sees when he holds the coin up for closer examination. When the coin speaks, it does not speak as the sovereign per se, but as representative

---

[23] Gildon, *Golden Spy*, 7, 10.
[24] Gildon, *Golden Spy*, 20, 276.

of its nation.[25] The international chorus in *The Golden Spy* allows English identity to be defined in contrast to European identity and facilitates the text's serious as well as satirical aims. Foreign coins present caricatured accounts of other nations, suggesting for example that Italian politicians and even the Pope are in the thrall of women who control their every move. Predictably, the foibles of the French attract the strongest criticism. In the most extended political discussion in the text, on the sixth and final night, the louis d'or discusses gold's pre-eminence as a French state actor, particularly during the War of the Spanish Succession: Louis XIV goes to war carrying gold (that is, money), whereas England goes to war carrying iron (that is, weapons). In France, coins are the 'true Troops of the Household' and 'No Fort, no Ramparts, no Bulwarks or Walls, but fall down like those of *Jericho*' at their approach. The magic of gold once again is its power to buy anyone or anything, including enemies, foreign territories, and peace. France's victories are cheapened by its reliance on what is seen as a dishonourable and decadent strategy, but the discussion breaks off without offering much resolution to the question of how England should approach war and peace. The human narrator's intervention acknowledges the power of gold but stops short of prescribing its uses: 'In effect, Gentlemen, said I … you are the Darlings of the Age, your Empire is over all, and you are the Arbitrators of *War* [and] *Peace*; but to the Shame of those who advanced you to that Power be it spoken.'[26]

The connection between gold's notional empire and the empire that secured its extraction shadows English patriotism throughout *The Golden Spy*. Certain aspects of the guinea's history, which would have been familiar to contemporary readers, go unmentioned. Guineas are coins minted from 'Guinea' gold from the West coast of Africa, introduced by Charles II in 1663 and named to honour the Company of Royal Adventurers Trading to Africa (later called the Royal African Company), which held a monopoly on English trade with West Africa. The imported gold in the guinea, stamped with the sovereign's face, indicates that England's national identity is not simply defined in opposition to the Continent in the ways discussed above, but manufactured from resources that, by the early 1670s, are extracted from a region where the English are trading in enslaved persons. The geopolitics of currency, like those of the coin itself, encompass the conditions of its production (the metal it is made from, the human labour that extracts that metal, the trade through which the metal is obtained) and those of its circulation (what it is used to buy, how it is valued, whether it is kept or spent, and so on). To see a coin as born when it is minted, rather than born when it is extracted, is to start its autobiography a bit late. Likewise, to consider national identity as separable from international relations of empire and trade is similarly selective. The representation of English liberty figured forth in the guinea depends on the enrichment England obtains from African commodities, including persons treated as property. Therefore, the irony

---

[25] Other contemporary texts that express an interest in numismatics and national history and character include John Evelyn, *Numismata* (1697), and Joseph Addison, *Dialogues Upon the Usefulness of Ancient Medals* (1721).

[26] Gildon, *Golden Spy*, 288, 204.

in the guinea's remark, intervening in a debate about which nation is best, hardly needs highlighting: '[W]hat Nation can compare with the *English*, who are not content to be rich and free themselves when almost all the World is in slavery, but extend their Power to the Relief of the distress'd on the Continent.'[27]

The guinea's general lesson for readers is a familiar, patriotic one that subordinates all English statecraft to the maintenance and spread of liberty. The idea that coins can act as narrators of history and proponents of patriotism appears in an even more distilled manner in *Tatler*, no. 249. The shilling that comes alive and speaks with 'a soft Silver Sound' relates that it was born in a mine in Peru and 'naturalized' in England when stamped with the 'Face of Queen *Elizabeth*', effectively becoming English when made into English currency. The shilling passes from the hands of the apothecary to the herb-woman to the butcher to the brewer and on and on; it is able to 'fetch in a Shoulder of Mutton, sometimes a Play-Book', satisfying the needs and desires of those who spend it. The shilling is happy when on the move ('we Shillings love nothing so much as travelling') and is miserable when it moulders in a miser's chest or in an old woman's 'greasy Purse'.[28] It feels shame as it remembers having been used to recruit soldiers to fight against the king in the Civil Wars, for it is a good patriot. At the conclusion of the number, it is clipped and then remade, shiny and new, as a shilling stamped with William III's profile, given in charity to a blind man.

The shilling has a far clearer agenda than Gildon's golden spies: it encourages a positive attitude to spending and suggests that the proper use of money brings happiness, satisfaction, and greater good. The shilling's liveliness—its animation—is an effect of personification, which, as Liz Bellamy observes, is 'implicit in the physical characteristics of currency'.[29] The coin's face invites the fiction of that face's speech. But the speech, as is clear from the brief summary above, is intended to shape its readers' opinions: what are represented as the coin's natural sentiments are in fact the views of a particular group of people. In the broader context of the *Tatler* and the *Spectator*, such a strategy appears frequently: figures, including personification and allegory, are often used as explanatory devices for economic or commercial phenomena. *Spectator*, no. 3, describes the figure of Lady Credit coming to life in a dream, where she is surrounded by symbols of statecraft and empire and flanked by bags of money. Her physical appearance changes in response to the nation's fortunes; she can go from healthy to skeletal in a moment, and she can recover equally quickly. When she falls ill, the heaps of money around her turn into bags of air, and the piles of gold into piles of paper. Lady Credit offers a vision of the body politic whose swings from health to sickness and back again are caused by a further cast of allegorical characters, including tyranny, anarchy, bigotry, liberty, moderation, and the 'Genius of *Great Britain*'.[30] A reader would be hard pressed to mistake good and bad

---

[27] Gildon, *Golden Spy*, 40. I am not suggesting that Gildon intends this to be ironic, only that it reads as such.
[28] *The Tatler*, ed. Donald F. Bond, 3 vols. (Oxford: Clarendon Press, 1967), 3: 269–71.
[29] Blackwell et al. (eds.), *British It-Narratives, 1750–1830*, 1, p. liii.
[30] Donald F. Bond (ed.), *The Spectator*, 5 vols. (Oxford: Clarendon Press, 1987), 1: 17.

here, but the fact that metamorphosis is used to explain these sudden shifts from coin to air and back again means that human agents are absent from the explanation of economic stability and growth.

Lest this appear to be a primal scene of commodities snatching agency away from humans, it is not. Instead, the use of animation and figure is directed toward generating a particular attitude toward commerce, trade, and exchange, whereby the narrator's responses act as a guide for those of the reader. If the shilling's happiness and shame are meant to elicit the same emotions in the human reader, so too are Mr. Spectator's worry at seeing an emaciated Lady Credit, or his 'Pleasure' at witnessing 'the prosperous and happy Multitude' at the Royal Exchange intended to model appropriate responses.[31] We see just such a set-up when Mr. Spectator positions himself in *Spectator*, no. 69, as a passive witness, unrecognized, 'justled', 'lost' in a crowd. As he watches transactions occur around him, he reflects on how commerce is part of the plan of 'Nature' to distribute goods around the globe and make different regions mutually dependent in pursuit of a 'common Interest'. Such an argument benefits Britons in particular, who can 'refresh' their eyes with vistas of 'green Fields' and their 'Palates ... with Fruits that rise between the Tropicks'.[32] On this account, the fruits which appear to rise of their own accord do Nature's bidding, as do the merchants who trade them. One way of reading *Spectator*, no. 69, then, is as an account of Nature as animating force, and as an attempt to produce a theorization of trade and the place of human agency within it that is compatible with determinism or divine design or both.[33] But Mr. Spectator himself, even as he is spokesman of Nature's wisdom, takes liberties with his own role and his place in the natural order. As a spy, he enjoys apparently plastic national identity, assuming and shedding citizenship easily: 'I am a *Dane, Swede,* or *French-Man* at different times, or rather fancy myself like the old Philosopher [who claimed to be] a Citizen of the World.'[34] Mr. Spectator's aphoristic cosmopolitanism imagines the possibility of dipping into different national identities simply by moving through crowds. Superficial as this might be, it aspires to provide a complete view by assembling what it imagines to be outsiders' perspectives. In doing so, it clearly borrows from the tradition of the Turkish spy.

Perhaps the most radical transformation depicted in *Spectator*, no. 69, however, is the final one. Mr. Spectator imagines that a statue of a past king at the Royal Exchange comes to life and observes the changes England has undergone since his reign:

> When I have been upon the '*Change,* I have often fancied one of our old Kings standing in Person, where he is represented in Effigy, and looking down upon the wealthy Concourse of People with which that Place is every Day filled. In this Case, how would he be surprised to hear all the Languages of *Europe* spoken in this little Spot of his former Dominions, and to see so many private Men, who in his Time

---

[31] *Spectator*, 1: 294.
[32] *Spectator*, 1: 294–6.
[33] See Weiss Smith, *Empiricist Devotions*, 129.
[34] *Spectator*, 1: 294.

would have been the Vassals of some powerful Baron, Negotiating like Princes for greater Sums of Mony than were formerly to be met with in the Royal Treasury![35]

The sovereign comes to life to witness historical change and to authenticate a particular interpretation of this change. He looks out at his subjects, collected here as a commercial people, and feels surprise at their and the nation's enrichment. His response acts as a judgement of sorts: it indicates just how well the nation is doing, just how much it has improved. Of course, Mr. Spectator is less interested in what the late king would actually say, were he to be resurrected, than in what he can be made to think and say. The king is yet another persona for Mr. Spectator, but a very potent one, who can be mobilized as a symbol of national identity, uniquely qualified to comment on the nation's path. And yet, the king is a mouthpiece. Like the coin stamped with the sovereign's face, the effigy of the king invites personification, animation, ventriloquy.

To have a past century's king witness the present and marvel at it is clearly a contrivance. But we might understand the contrivance in at least two ways. The first is as a technique or tool for advancing economic ideology, and the second is as a mode of representing a nation to itself, and therefore as a technique of narrative more generally. In *Spectator*, no. 69, these two phenomena are inseparable: one cannot prise them apart because the nation is presented to itself in economic terms, as a trading public that has a 'kind of additional Empire' at home. But there is a broader application of the second, inasmuch as the personified king, like the speaking coins and other animated figures this chapter has considered, acts as a character through whom a representation of national character or history is formed. We might think of the king as a way of marking out, giving shape to, even personifying a historical point of view that England has benefited from the recent growth in trade. To call such a view 'historical' draws attention to the fact that history is undertaken from a particular perspective, here literally figured as a point of view. The personification of the king's image, like the speaking shilling and Gildon's collection of coins, all offer up points of view. These points of view are associated with physical objects that a reader can imagine or has seen: these objects are material, they exist, they have faces.[36] But more than that, they have opinions: the stories that they tell, as discussed above, contain judgements, claims, and generalizations about groups and classes of people. These opinions are represented as their own, and as a kind of objective report. But they are not their own, or not exactly. Circulation and spy narrators act as vehicles for, and storehouses of, particular attitudes concerning public opinion, national identity, and related concerns. They might also be described as personifications

---

[35] *Spectator*, 1: 296. Addison's 'effigy' likely refers to a statue: a statue of Charles II stood in the middle of the Exchange after it was rebuilt following the great fire. The statue of Charles II is also mentioned in the portion of *The London Spy* that describes the spy's visit to the Exchange, where he finds himself amidst 'the people of sundry nations' (Ned Ward, *The London Spy*, ed. Paul Hyland (East Lansing: Colleagues Press, 1993), 62).

[36] For a reading of material history and its generation of 'speaking subjects', see Sean Silver, 'John Evelyn and Numismata: Material History and Autobiography', *Word and Image*, 31 (2015), 331–42.

of such attitudes, for they house them within forms that, to greater or lesser degrees, are anthropomorphized but remain at or beyond the borders of the human.

In this light, the texts considered here invite further consideration in relation to several broader issues: the development of character in early prose fiction; the use and theorization of figure, particularly personification, across the century; and the mediation of opinion through print and the public sphere. Circulation and spy narrators have remarkable powers of observation, capacious minds, and extensive memories—or so we are led to believe—but they do not use these powers in service of the searching psychological examination of themselves or even, really, of others. These texts are not focused on individuals and never stay in one place for long; their incessant movement maximizes the number of scenes they can observe and expose.[37] For these reasons, they differ from the sorts of human protagonists later novels represent, though some of the narrative techniques of circulation and spy narratives appear in novels, notably the letter, torn open by someone curious to understand its contents and its author. The letter is offered up as a familiar object, but it is also offered up as an objectification of an inner state.[38] The circulation or spy narrator is less an objectification of an inner state than an objectification of an attitude that is neither private nor individual, but collective and meant to be adopted collectively.

As an objectification it holds particular interest for critics compelled by the relations between persons and things. Persons and things have been the subject of much critical reflection in recent decades, as evidenced by the appearance of thing-theory, the renewed interest in personification, and the discussion of those excluded from legal personhood.[39] There are at least two different critical impulses that animate this turn to persons and things: the first is a desire to think through materiality and objecthood as thoroughly as possible; the second is a recognition of the power that the categories of person and thing hold in law and in life. Scholarship on it-narratives considers both of these concerns and combines attention to twentieth- and twenty-first century arguments with readings of seventeenth- and eighteenth-century philosophy and law. It often focuses in particular on the commodity in relation to fashion and the

---

[37] As Bellamy notes, this exposure takes the form of the devil flying around and lifting the roofs off houses in Alain René Le Sage's *Le Diable Boiteux*, translated into English in 1708 as *The Devil Upon Two Sticks*. Bellamy suggests that *The Golden Spy* is 'roughly based on' the translation (*Commerce, Morality and the Eighteenth-Century Novel*, 119).

[38] On the topic of fictional characters being made physically legible, see Deidre Lynch, *The Economy of Character: Novels, Market Culture, and the Business of Inner Meaning* (Chicago: University of Chicago Press, 1998), esp. 99.

[39] There are too many titles to give a comprehensive list here, but see for example Arjun Appadurai (ed.), *The Social Life of Things: Commodities in Cultural Perspective* (Cambridge: Cambridge University Press, 1986); Bill Brown (ed.), *Things* (Chicago: University of Chicago Press, 2004); Lynn Festa, *Sentimental Figures of Empire in Eighteenth-Century Britain and France* (Baltimore: Johns Hopkins University Press, 2006); Saidiya V. Hartman, *Scenes of Subjection: Terror, Slavery, and Self-Making in Nineteenth-Century America* (Oxford: Oxford University Press, 1997); and Monique Allewaert, *Ariel's Ecology: Plantations, Personhood, and Colonialism in the American Tropics* (Minneapolis: University of Minnesota Press, 2013).

appetite for luxury; elsewhere, it considers the nexus of person and thing in relation to the commodity fetish (the commodity draws life force from the worker) and chattel slavery (the law treats the enslaved person as property).[40] These readings of it-narratives are compelling not only because they think about the category of fiction capaciously, demonstrating how rhetorical figures are involved in the making and unmaking of legal persons, but also because they have ethical urgency.

The framework of persons and things, which it-narratives fit into, and through which they can be read, does not clearly apply to the texts under discussion here. These circulation and spy narrators are nonhuman as well as invisible and often international, but the category distinctions most often at issue in these texts are not those between thing and person (or animal and person, for that matter). Instead, they are social and cultural: distinctions between the French and the English, between Catholics and Protestants, between the wealthy and the poor, the entitled and the unassuming. The sorting activity that Don Fantasio and Mr. Spectator and other narrators assist with concerns being able to distinguish, and therefore to negotiate, between desirable and undesirable behaviours and identities. This is often done crudely rather than precisely, and it can be in service of satire and scandal as well as the cultivation of social and moral judgement. Either way, the practice is highly ideological. Viewed more broadly, it might be contextualized alongside other contemporary accounts of judgement and social distinction, notably the impartial spectator central to Adam Smith's theory of sympathy. The circulation or spy narrator, like the impartial spectator, purports to offer a view from the outside, an objective account. Both externalize something that is subsequently meant to be internalized, and both are engaged in the construction of a specifically English (later British) set of values. Each contributes to the history of narrative form's involvement with social distinction and the making of received opinion.

---

[40] See Festa, *Sentimental Figures of Empire*, especially chaps. 3 and 4.

CHAPTER 11

CRIMINAL LITERATURE

PAT ROGERS

Crime is always with us, and the literature of the subject goes back a long way. These days we tend to reject a sharply etiological or teleological narrative in discussing genres, and prefer to view forms such as the novel as exhibiting discontinuity rather than steady development. We are receptive to what Gaston Bachelard called 'epistemological breaks', and look with suspicion on linear accounts of historical evolution.[1] Nevertheless, it remains true that books about crime in the long seventeenth century changed more or less *pari passu* as the nature of crime evolved. New categories of crime came into being in the English legal code, both by statute and common law. New offences were committed in new social circumstances and new spaces (largely urban), and often by new sorts of offender. The mechanisms of justice were reformed in some areas; different bodies became responsible for administering certain branches of the legal system. While policing showed itself stubbornly resistant to innovation for a long time, the role that judges, lawyers, and juries played in the drama of the courtroom was considerably modified over the period. All these developments in real life were reflected in the stories of those who found themselves on the wrong side of the law.

In the period covered by this volume, the map of literature underwent its own profound change, or series of changes. Some of these have to do with the gradual displacement of epic from a central position within the kinds, a process delayed but not finally impeded by the work of Milton. Naturally the effect of this was felt most strongly in poetry; but it also altered the opportunities for writers in prose. The most obvious consequence was to scale down the expectations of readers, in terms both of aspects such as plot (with fewer grand national themes, and fewer characters such as emperors and queens) and style (with fewer heroic properties in the language used). As a consequence, genres dealing with everyday people and distinctly sub-heroic actions achieved more prominence. One beneficiary was the literature of crime, where authors could exploit

---

[1] Gaston Baudrillard, *The Formation of the Scientific Mind: A Contribution to a Psychoanalysis of Objective Knowledge*, trans. Mary McAllester Jones (Manchester: Clinamen, 2002), 24.

this more open and potentially 'democratic' situation. Books in this field commonly dealt with low life, and with rare exceptions—such as mock-heroic treatments of a figure such as the thief-catcher Jonathan Wild—the verbal texture was correspondingly lacking in any form of grandeur or magniloquence.

As other chapters in this volume demonstrate, prose was gaining ground against poetry as the most natural medium of expression. Some poets were able to make effective use of criminal issues, most obviously in satiric contexts. A good example is Robert Gould's 'Satyr Upon the Play-House' (1688), which directs its main assault on the London theatrical world around Covent Garden, with the help of much scabrous misogyny. This also brings out some insalubrious connections with prostitutes, thieves, and superannuated members of the army and navy with no obvious means of a legal livelihood. For the most part, however, it was prose that would emerge as the most effective vehicle of social commentary.

One more consideration needs to be mentioned. Overwhelmingly the literature on crime is dominated by moral diatribes by theologians and social observers on the one hand, and by hostile portrayal in plays, pamphlets, and chapbooks. Little that resembles modern criminological analysis went on until the third quarter of the eighteenth century. This is when writers such as the Fielding brothers (Henry and John, both London magistrates) in England and the great penologist Cesare Beccaria in Italy began to survey the cause and patterns of illegal behaviour, with the aim of giving a more rational basis for the scale of punishments. Meanwhile, a stray journalist might quote scary figures about the number of murders or gin-drinkers. But it was only when Sir Frederick Eden produced his *State of the Poor* in 1797 that reliable data about the income and lifestyles of the lower classes could be brought to bear on issues affecting the prevalence of various crimes. Statistics, the bedrock of criminology today, made little headway in our period, despite the beginnings of political arithmetic at the end of the seventeenth century in the hands of John Graunt, William Petty, and Gregory King.

The Legal Background

The years 1640–1714 saw a large number of developments in the law and its implementation, though perhaps fewer radical changes than had occurred under the Tudors. Some of these changes left a marked impact on the literature of crime, others less so. There were few new categories of crime but some offences became more prominent, although violations of property began to show up more prominently than before in relation to assaults upon the person. There are of course variations between different parts of the country, with the growing dominance of London skewing the picture. At the start of the period the capital had a population of around 250,000; by the end this had grown to something like 650,000, and it continued to advance rapidly with suburbs spreading in almost every direction. The city could not handle the increase in crime, with its archaic system of law enforcement based around an untrained corps of magistrates supported by parish officers who were often unwilling or incompetent. This way of doing things held up reasonably well in rural areas, where Justices of the Peace retained some degree of natural authority and could compensate to some degree for the inadequacy or corruption of inferior parochial officers. But it was patently unfitted to patterns of wrongdoing that evolved in the close spaces of modern urban life, where the absence of effective policing made the world safe for many would-be offenders. Maintaining the large number of prisons, from the principal gaols like Newgate downwards, involved a large outlay of time and money, and the municipal authorities naturally farmed out their running to private contractors. Most provincial towns could get away with a single gaol with one or two tiny roundhouses. Not surprisingly London is the setting for a disproportionate number of criminal narratives.

Court procedures underwent some modification over time. One survival was the old method of trial by 'altercation', in which cases of felony were largely conducted by the judge without any intervention by counsel on either side. It was not until just after the close of this period, in the second quarter of the eighteenth century, that the 'adversarial' system emerged, with defence counsel allowed to speak on behalf of their clients and to cross-question witnesses.[2] Similarly it was not until 1730 that legislation was passed making English rather than Latin the language of record for courts and statutes, which may have meant that more members of the general public were able to understand the points at issue in some criminal literature. Again, London was unique in the existence of the Old Bailey Sessional Papers, which began to be issued regularly in the 1670s, providing a major source for writers from that day right down to the present. Equally useful for many seventeenth-century cases are the various incarnations of the *Newgate Calendar*, which were immensely popular in later decades, having their origin in compilations from the first quarter of the eighteenth century.

One firmly established aspect of the courts lay in the jury system, which came into being as a result of the abolition of trial by ordeal in 1215, and remained a bulwark of the law throughout Tudor and Stuart England. The distinguished historian of crime J. M. Beattie has argued that 'the late seventeenth century was the heroic age of the English jury, for in the political and constitutional struggle of the reigns of Charles II and James II, trial by jury emerged as the principal defence of English liberties'.[3] This is undoubtedly true, but it should be added that the juries and grand juries who heard such cases were again based in London, where members of the panel tended to be men of greater substance (often in trade), education, and independence than their provincial equivalents. Other set-pieces in the capital were the great show trials that often greeted unpopular political figures on their demise, later recorded in elaborate detail in volumes of *State Trials*. At the very top of the social hierarchy, the unfortunate individual might

---

[2] See e.g., John H. Langbein, *The Origins of the Adversary Criminal Trial* (Oxford: Oxford University Press, 2003).

[3] J. M. Beattie, 'London Juries in the 1690s', in J. S. Cockburn and Thomas A. Green (eds.), *Twelve Good Men and True: The Criminal Jury Trial in England, 1200–1800* (Princeton, NJ: Princeton University Press, 1988), 214–53 (214).

face impeachment by parliament, with his life at stake, a fate hardly less grisly than that suffered by Charles I himself leading up to his execution in 1649 (the event rings of course through English literature for generations to come). Neatly for our purposes, the impeachment of the Earl of Strafford in 1640 was followed by his attainder and beheading in the following year. At the other end of the period, the Earl of Oxford fell from power just as Queen Anne died in 1714; a year later he was sent to the Tower while parliament began to exact its familiar revenge on an outgoing minister. The impeachment failed, and no prime minister since has undergone the same experience—not even Robert Walpole, who had collected an immense range of enemies before he was deposed in 1742. One crime had effectively disappeared for ever: that of being at the head of a government.

Nor has anything occurred in the intervening centuries that resembles the Bloody Assizes held in 1685 at Winchester and West Country towns following the Monmouth rebellion. Over 1,400 rebels were imprisoned and then taken to court. The fearsome Lord Chief Justice, George Jeffreys, presided over the hearings, and the outcome saw almost 400 people sentenced to be hanged, or less mercifully hanged, drawn, and quartered. Hundreds more were transported to the West Indies. Neither her sex nor her genteel status could save Dame Alice Lisle from a sentence to be burned at the stake for harbouring fugitives after the Battle of Sedgemoor, though this was later reduced to beheading by James II in acknowledgement of her social rank. The episode aroused huge passions and a spate of pamphlets followed. Jeffreys, already reviled in some quarters for the way he had handled the trials of Titus Oates and Algernon Sidney, found himself the subject of scurrilous ballads and lampoons, which were renewed after he was captured attempting to flee the country in 1688. Such egregious individuals naturally received more than their share of attention in the prints, but the savage treatment they received was not all that unlike the general tone of contempt meted out to criminals of all descriptions in biographies and chapbooks.

One notable disparity visible across the period concerns the declining role of the upper classes in recognized breaches of the order. As J. A. Sharpe has observed: 'By 1550 the gentry were less likely to be involved in organised crime', though they were 'still capable of acts of savage violence'. A century later the trend had had become more marked, as 'habits of restraint spread among the landed orders'.[4] An occasional grandee might run into trouble, such as the Irish bishop John Atherton, hanged for buggery in 1640. This episode prompted a number of works including the customary penitential outpouring, and was sufficiently alive to provide copy for the unscrupulous bookseller Edmund Curll in *The Case of John Atherton, Bishop of Waterford in Ireland; who was Convicted of the Sin of Uncleanness with a Cow, and other Creatures* (1710).[5] Sometimes, too, highwaymen are given implausibly lofty social backgrounds in popular narratives; in reality, this was a career path generally embarked on by desperate and impoverished

---

[4] J.A. Sharpe, *Crime in Early Modern England, 1550–1750* (Harlow: Longman, 1984), 96.
[5] The case also more recently inspired a fascinating work of historical reconstruction in Peter Marshall, *Mother Leakey and the Bishop: A Ghost Story* (Oxford: Oxford University Press, 2008).

individuals who had no legitimate way of making ends meet. Among the few exceptions might be the supposed French-born 'gentleman' Claude Duval, hanged in 1670 and the subject of a good deal of myth-making, even though the deathbed memoirs make it clear his origins were humble. He later entered the ballad repertory, when his 'frolicsome intrigues' were set out. The original *Memoires of Monsieur Du Vall: Containing the History of His Life and Death* (1670) state that numerous women were present when he was dispatched at Tyburn, and then followed his corpse to a tavern where he lay in state prior to burial at St Paul's, Covent Garden (aptly known today as the actors' church). Very little of this has any basis in reality. But, of course, writers could add a titillating whiff of scandal by bending the truth; and this is one reason why we should not read works in this category as dependable accounts of the history of crime.

For the most part the criminal classes were just that, a subset of the population identifiable by poverty, humble origins, little education, and the lack of any resources to challenge the power of the law when they came before the courts. Their lives were marked by insecurity, as they often moved restlessly in terms of geography and occupation, with diminishing family ties. It was quite usual for men discharged from the army or navy to enter this segment of the population. As has always been the case, they were predominantly male, and disproportionately young. Sometimes they entered into a form of collective action which might be seen as approaching gang life, but there was little organized crime outside the capital for most of the period. Such a life history made for lively tales full of picaresque incident and for moralizing fables recounting the fall of idle apprentices—both modes of writing which seemed to attract a wide readership. The story of the wicked young servant George Barnwell had appeared in a ballad long before it was translated by George Lillo into a hit drama, *The London Merchant* (1737), or before it became a favourite subject for chapbooks.

As for punishment in early modern Britain, the notion of the Tudors as particularly bloodthirsty, spurred by episodes such as that of the Marian martyrs, needs some refinement. Only about a dozen capital crimes stood on the statute book in the sixteenth century, including treason, coining, murder, and rape—with, significantly, piracy and highway robbery already included. Buggery was added to the list, and this would remain a hanging offence until 1861. All these form staple elements in the literature of roguery, though opportunities to document real-life high treason were not as frequent as some authors may have wished. The tally for this ultimate breach of tolerable behaviour gradually mounted to about fifty in the 1690s. Again, a marked shift appeared as the period came to an end: the notorious Black Act of 1723 almost doubled the total number of capital offences, and within less than a century the score went above 200. While many of these offences were rarely prosecuted, and many sentences commuted, the laws remained on the books *in terrorem*. These developments gave rise to an expansion of the already lucrative trade in narratives of courtroom drama, as well as dying words and confessions of those carried to their death on the scaffold. Tyburn Tree had been erected in 1571 and an elaborately choreographed procession to the site from Newgate prison developed. After the Restoration, among those hung up in chains at Tyburn were four regicides specially disinterred so they could be subjected to posthumous humiliation: one of these was Oliver Cromwell, whose severed head was later stuck on a pole outside Westminster Hall. Fictional chroniclers of ghastly and Gothic scenes did not have to make them all up themselves.

A mode of punishment with a strong symbolic charge was the pillory. We should be clear that people were not dispatched to this ignominy on capricious grounds. Beattie has pointed to a selection process, by which judges reserved the sentence for 'acts that aroused deep public anger and hostility, either because of the vulnerability of the victim (a child, for example) or because the offense was both damaging and difficult to prevent'. He goes on to explain that the aim of punishment by public exposure was to forewarn potential victims by marking out the offender to the public as someone not to be trusted.[6] Men and women alike were sent to the pillory for a variety of cheats, such as pretending to tell fortunes, cheating at cards, and making false accusations. But the most significant victims were those convicted of sedition, such as Daniel Defoe in 1703. Legend has it that the author was garlanded with flowers when he stepped off the rostrum at Charing Cross and heard his health drunk by spectators. But Thomas Keymer has recently shown that this, too, was probably a myth.[7]

Trials for sedition actually increased around the turn of the century, after the lapse of the Licensing Act in 1695. Keymer's important book demonstrates that authors and publishers were more likely to fall foul of the law in this phase than they had been when official censorship was in place. We do not ordinarily think of state trials as the subject matter of criminal literature, regarding 'private' offences such as theft and murder as supplying more human interest. What we now understand better is that the logic behind prosecutions for libel, blasphemy, or obscenity (all of which might come under the rubric of sedition) contributed to a wider discourse concerning the nature of criminality. It follows that we ought to take cognizance of such proceedings after the discovery of the Popish Plot, when men of considerable substance were taken to court. These narratives have been excluded from the canon up till now. Yet, even if they lack the thick description of more artistic writing, transcripts of judicial hearings in these 'political' cases surely belong in the literary record, along with tales describing the raffish activities of the picaroon, the tricks of the swindler, the exploits of the pickpocket, or the wiles of the prostitute.

One issue that has received increasing attention of late is the part played by women in criminal activity. The exact incidence of females in various categories varies by date, by geographical location, by age, and by the specific offence. But as a very rough estimate we could say that overall not much more than 10 per cent of indictments concerned women. The conviction rate was probably about the same as for men, but sentences

---

[6] J. M. Beattie, *Crime and the Courts in England 1660–1800* (Princeton, NJ: Princeton University Press, 1986), 464–8 (464). See also J. M. Beattie, *Policing and Punishment in London 1660–1750: Urban Crime and the Limits of Terror* (Oxford: Oxford University Press, 2001).

[7] Thomas Keymer, *Poetics of the Pillory: English Literature and Seditious Libel, 1660–1820* (Oxford: Oxford University Press, 2019), 132–48; for the spike in actual and threatened prosecutions for libel, see 89–100.

tended to be a little more gentle, and these were commuted more often. In addition, pregnant women could plead their belly to delay their punishment, which is what Defoe has the heroine's mother do in *Moll Flanders*, a novel that was set notionally during the latter part of the seventeenth century but published in 1722. With some offences women form a majority of those prosecuted, such as for obvious reasons prostitution and infanticide, but they also appear very frequently in cases involving the theft of household goods and clothing: they proved to be some of the deftest pickpockets in life as in literature. We might think of Moll once again, together with a possible real-life model 'Jenny Diver', alias Mary Young. A few women gained notoriety for particularly heinous murders, including the arsenic poisoner Elizabeth Mason in 1712. It should be added that since the most common occupation by far was that of household servant, women appear as witnesses regularly in cases of domestic robbery (and they also give crucial testimony in the rare consistory court hearings for divorce). They were sometimes used as informants, a notoriously unpopular group within the criminal subculture.[8]

A more atypical breach of the law concerned the crime of witchcraft. Sharpe tells us 'around 90 per cent of persons indicted for witchcraft at the Home Circuit assizes between the passing of the Elizabethan statute in 1563 and the abolition of laws against witchcraft in 1736 were women'.[9] This seems to be a representative figure though possibly a little high. Periodically there was a spike in prosecutions, commonly the work of fierce activists such as the witch-hunter Matthew Hopkins in East Anglia at the time of the Civil War. The last executions of witches took place in Exeter—three women from North Devon in 1682 and finally Alice Molland in 1685. But later still, one of the last persons to be indicted in England was Jane Wenham, tried and convicted at Hertford in 1712, but whose sentence was set aside by the judge. She became the subject of a pamphlet war, instigated in part by the ever-alert Edmund Curll—something that attests to the popular appeal of works on the subject. Four years later came the very last known conviction, involving a woman and her daughter aged nine. Witchcraft did not cease to be a subject of discussion, and the events at Salem in 1692 were familiar to a British audience, with *A True Account of the Tryals, Examinations, Confessions, Condemnations, and Executions of divers Witches, At Salem, in New England* soon rushed into print. But this was one species of criminal writing which lost some of its urgency as our period drew to a close.

The rapid survey attempted here can do no more than sketch in the background with the broadest of brushes. Inevitably many aspects of the world of crime have been omitted. What should emerge overall is a society poised between the older inherited

---

[8] Useful discussion of issues related to this topic will be found in the essays collected in Jenny Kermode and Garthine Walker (eds.), *Women, Crime and the Courts in Early Modern England* (Chapel Hill: University of North Carolina Press, 1994), and Anne Laurence, *Women in England 1500–1760: A Social History* (New York: St Martin's, 1994), 245–71. For an argument that 'the legal situation of the majority underwent serious erosion in early modern England', see 'The Law and its Administration', in Sara Mendelson and Patricia Crawford, *Women in Early Modern England 1550–1720* (Oxford: Clarendon Press, 1998), 34–48.

[9] Jim Sharpe, 'Women, Witchcraft and the Legal Process', in Kermode and Walker (eds.), *Women, Crime and the Courts*, 106–24 (106).

attitudes and practices (visible, for instance, in the altercation model of court proceedings) and the newer forms of penal treatment that began to appear with the Hanoverian accession in 1714. Sometimes the change would be in the direction not of liberalization but of greater severity, as was revealed by the ferocious Black Act of 1723 already mentioned.[10] Only at the end of our period did the growth of a new financial regime initiate a crucial development, as institutions like the Bank of England and the great trading companies came to the fore in the 1690s, bringing with them new financial instruments supplying credit for the rapidly expanding markets. One consequence was a fresh emphasis on white collar crime, with fraud, forgery, and embezzlement appearing more frequently in the list of prosecutions. Counterfeiting coin had been high treason since the medieval period, but William III enlarged the scope of the offence. The provisions extended beyond our period: women could be burned at the stake for coining until 1790, and either sex could notionally be hanged until 1965. In many ways this world seems remote in its cruelty and its blunt approach to punishment. It may or not be surprising then that some of the literature of crime strikes us as almost nonchalant and even coolly indifferent in tone, even where the offence is brutal and the penalty harsh. Unavoidably, people wrote about crime with a different set of expectations from our own.

Rogue's Tales

Writers in this period inherited a number of forms that had proved popular in Elizabethan and Jacobean literature, which could be adopted to fit new purposes.[11] These included stories of rogues, cutpurses, and cony catchers such as the semi-legendary Moll Cutpurse, alias Mary Firth, whose deeds as violent gang boss, thief, prostitute, transvestite, and lesbian threatened just about every conventional standpoint of the time. She had been portrayed by Dekker and Middleton in a play, *The Roaring Girle*, as early as 1611, but retained enough copy value to be used in later generations. In 1662 two versions of her life appeared. Once was entitled *The Life and Death of Mrs. Mary Frith commonly called Mal* (sic) *Cutpurse Exactly Collected and now Published for the Delight and Recreation of all Merry Disposed Persons*, an extensive treatment which soon morphs into a first-person recital and ends with the subject's will, as 'serious' biographies commonly did. A much shorter chapbook version has a longer title: *The Womans Champion; or, The Strange Wonder being a True Relation of the Mad Pranks, Merry Conceits, Politick Figaries, and Most Unheard of Stratagems of Mrs. Mary Frith Commonly Called Mall Cutpurse living near Fleet-Conduit; even from her Cradle to her Winding-sheet. Containing Several Remarkable Passages Touching the*

---

[10] See the masterly survey by E. P. Thompson, *Whigs and Hunters: The Origins of the Black Act* (Harmondsworth: Penguin, 1977).

[11] For the pre-1640 context, see Craig Dionne and Steve Mentz (eds.), *Rogues and Early Modern Culture* (Ann Arbor: University of Michigan Press, 2004).

Constable, Counters; and Prisoners, and her Last Will and Testament to Squire Dun, as a Legacy for his Latter Days. With her Divining Prophesie, concerning Wicked Plots, and Hellbred Conspiracies. Extracted from the Original; Published According to Order. Both texts naturally draw on their predecessors, and the short version displays if not exactly criminal behaviour on the part of the publisher (there was as yet no broad legal framework of copyright), then certainly a form of shameless exploitation appropriate to Mary Frith's story. The tale, told at breakneck speed, is bookended by a crude woodcut at the start and a verse epitaph with an acrostic at the end. A century later, these same features would reappear in chapbook versions of Defoe's novels *Moll Flanders* (1722) and *Roxana* (1724).

A little less exotic are the pamphlets devoted to the life of the adventuress Mary Carleton, who was executed at Newgate in 1672. Her capital offence was to return from a sentence of transportation in Jamaica, imposed for theft, after which she returned to her former scams in the guise of a rich heiress. Her supposed autobiography, *The Counterfeit Lady Unveiled* (1673), was actually written by Francis Kirkman, and it was used in an abridged form by 'Capt. Alexander Smith' in late editions of his compendious assortment of criminal lives. There were, however, many other treatments of Carleton's life, including a facetious elegy and even a play in five acts loosely based on her career, *The Witty Combat: or The Female Victor* (1663).

As many of the titles suggest, the appeal of such works is overwhelmingly that of simple entertainment. The 'hellbred conspiracies' about which Moll Cutpurse warned seem no more than afterthought. While this insouciant treatment of criminal behaviour survived throughout the period, with solemn moralizing tracts occupying a different area of discourse, more effort is sometimes made towards the later part of the century to incorporate a sense of outrage along with the tolerant comedy that had prevailed. Wrongdoers usually take a minor role among the anecdotes retailed in jestbooks (a category so named only in the nineteenth century), which had emerged in the Renaissance, slightly later in England than in other European countries. Nevertheless, the tone of collections of 'merry' diversions does not differ greatly from that found in the average rogue's tale. We might not instantly realize from the formulaic opening words of the title of one book exactly what we are dealing with: *A Pill to Purge Melancholy* (1652). But if we go on a little further, the subject matter becomes clear: *or Merry Newes from Newgate: Wherein is Set Forth, the Pleasant Jests, Witty Conceits, and Excellent Couzenages, of Captain James Hind, and his Associates*. On this showing Hind is no more than a conman and scumbag, whose mission in life is to deprive generally innocent people of their entire savings. In his exploits he shows some resourcefulness and cunning, but no extreme physical bravery. The author stresses the element of 'waggery' in which Hind delighted, for example when he borrows a prostitute's clothes and tricks an 'old rusty *Lawyer*' he accosts in the Temple into paying him ten shillings in expectation of sex. As with most of these stories, scorn is reserved for dupes, cullies, and foolish constables in the mould of Dogberry. In spite of what the title may suggest, there is no sign in the brief narrative that Hind has received, or will get, his comeuppance at the hands of the law. Other versions of his career, such as *The English Gusman* (1652), adopted a more picaresque approach. As we shall see presently, his true-life story took a harsher course than these narratives would have us believe.

Picaresque

Perhaps the most important literary innovation that made itself felt in the period came with the appearance of picaresque fiction. The genre was already well established on the Continent, following on from its earliest incarnation in *Lazarillo de Tormes* (1554) with its development in *Guzmán de Alfarache* (1599: 1604) by Matteo Alemán and *El Buscón* (1626) by Francisco de Quevedo, all soon translated into English. However, although there are a few traces visible in Thomas Nashe's *The Unfortunate Traveller* (1594), picaresque did not really get going in Britain until well into the seventeenth century. The most important document is the first part of *The English Rogue Described in the Life of Meriton Latroon, a Witty Extravagant being a Compleat History of the most Eminent Cheats of both Sexes*, produced by Richard Head in 1665. Soon afterwards Francis Kirkman added three sequels, with some input possibly from Head: these are less fresh and lively. Head himself went on to write a number of other books which did not enjoy the huge success that the *Rogue* had earned: the most interesting in the present context is *The Canting Academy, or, The Devils Cabinet Opened wherein is Shewn the Mysterious and Villanous Practices of that Wicked Crew, Commonly Known by the Names of Hectors, Trapanners, Gilts, &c.: to which is Added a Compleat Canting-Dictionary, both of Old Words, and Such as Are Now Most in Use* (1673), which has retained currency as it preserves the history of thieves' argot.

To a degree Head may have invented, or at least adapted, the idiolect of the criminal subculture of his time. In any case *The English Rogue* provided a template for a great deal of literature in the same vein, an influence that extends to the early novels of Tobias Smollett. Comparatively formal in style, the book nonetheless creates a vivid first-person identity in the shape of an Irish adventurer cast adrift in a rough and hostile world where he needs to live by his wits to survive. A section from the opening chapter exemplifies Head's verbal exuberance and fondness for puns, along with some Sternian musings on the genetic pathways through which parents do and do not pass on their attributes to children:

> By this time my mother drew near her time, having conceiv'd me in *England*, but not *conceiving* she thus should *drop* me in an *Irish Bog*. There is no fear that *England* and *Ireland* will after my decease, contend about my Nativity, as several Countreys did about *Homer*; either striving to have the honour of first giving him breath. Neither shall I much thank my Native Country, for bestowing on me such principles as I and most of my Country-men drew from that very air; the place I think made me appear a Bastard in disposition to my Father. It is strange the Clymate should have more prevalency over the Nature of the Native, than the disposition of the Parent.

The son is very different from his parents. It will be noted that the canard about Irish 'blarney' was already current:

> For though Father and Mother could neither flatter, deceive, revenge, equivocate, &c. yet the Son (as the consequence hath since made it appear) can (according to the common custom of his Country-men) dissemble and sooth up his adversary with expressions extracted from Celestial Manna, taking his advantage thereby to ruine him: For to speak the truth, I could never yet love any but for some by-respect, neither could I ever be perswaded into a pacification with that man who had any way injured me, never resting satisfied till I had accomplisht a plenary revenge, which I commonly effected under the pretence of great love and kindness. Cheat all I dealt withal, though the matter were ever so inconsiderable. Lie so naturally, that a Miracle may be as soon wrought, as a Truth proceed from my mouth. And then for Equivocation, or Mental Reservations, they were ever in me innate Properties. It was always my Resolution, rather to dye by the hand of a common Executioner, then want my revenge, though ever so slightly grounded.[12]

This anticipates the bold revelations of literary crooks like Fielding's Jonathan Wild and Thomas Mann's Felix Krull. But we can also detect in this passage faint traces of an interior monologue, previously little seen in Western literature, which opens the way towards the autobiographic modes of later writing, such as the *Bildungsroman*, the self-directed irony of Shandean novels such as Jean Paul's *Titan* (1800–3), or the sinuous involutions of Vladimir Nabokov's memoir, *Speak, Memory* (1951).

Among Head's imitators was the author of *The Life & Death of Captain William Bedloe, one of the Chief Discoverers of the Horrid Popish Plot wherein all his more Eminent Cheats, and whatever is Remarkable of him, both Good and Bad, is Impartially Discover'd* (1681). The style is a little more colloquial, with more emphasis on concrete details than is the case with *The English Rogue*. Bedloe was a real individual who had acted as an informer against Catholics in the wake of Titus Oates, supplying undependable evidence to Judge Jeffreys among others. However, the author of the biography devotes more than half of his space to the various frauds that his hero committed, and shows most relish for episodes such as one where Bedloe adopts a disguise to enter a convent in Flanders and impregnates several of the nuns. Impostures for the purposes of gaining money and sexual titillation trump political intrigue whenever these authors seek to make crime a suitable subject for extensive narrative. Men or women behaving badly in pursuit of power or influence in matters of state do not figure as centrally, at least until a time just after the turn of the century when the vein of 'secret history' was imported from France to reveal in a coded form the misdoings of members of Queen Anne's court.[13]

Picaresque as narrowly defined involves the adventures of an individual, usually young and male, often an orphan, as he fights his way from poverty in his travels through

---

[12] Richard Head and Francis Kirkman, *The English Rogue, Continued in the Life of Meriton Latroon, and Other Extravagants, Comprehending the Most Eminent Cheats of Both Sexes* (1680), 7–8.

[13] See Chapter 34 by Rebecca Bullard on 'Secret Histories'.

the world. Mostly he operates on the fringe of delinquency, rarely committing the more heinous types of crime. His attitude to life, mirrored in the general tone of the story, tends to be harshly realistic and cynical. The strict form was observed less scrupulously in Britain than in Spain or France, and nothing emerged in the short term which rivalled Alain Le Sage's *L'Histoire de Gil Blas de Santillane*, which began to appear in 1715 just as our period closes. The book would be translated by Smollett (1749), and often published in abridged editions for generations to come. Nevertheless writers in the English language would prove adept in adapting and extending pure picaresque, for example in Smollett's own *Humphry Clinker* (1771), which merges the genre with travel narrative, epistolary fiction, and the novel of satire on class distinctions. Equally Fielding takes the picaresque into new areas by adding a strong Cervantic element to *Tom Jones* (1749). Defoe gave both of his female adventurers, Moll Flanders and Roxana, some of the survival skills of the pícaro. Women writers employed the form less often, but it would leave its traces in works such as Charlotte Lennox's *Harriet Stuart* (1750). This enduring afterlife is worth emphasizing, because no other brand of seventeenth-century fiction lasts as long within the mainstream: the line extends forward to Dickens, Thackeray, and Mark Twain, arguably as far as Thomas Mann, Saul Bellow, Günter Grass, John Barth, and John Kennedy Toole—some might add Angela Carter. Most of these writers were fully conscious of a debt to their predecessors from the 1600s.

Pirates and Highwaymen

Two modes of writing gained increasing prominence in the period. They tell the stories of wrongdoers on land and on sea whose exploits had given them a certain cachet. They are found in both fictional and nonfictional contexts, as well as in a blend of the two—often the subjects of the narrative existed in real life, but their experiences are altered to suit the needs of the form—so that they are presented as more glamorous or more successful than was actually the case. Depending on the approach of the writer, their faults could be glossed over by comic means (something we have already seen in the case of Captain Hind's adventures) or else sententiously emphasized, as with the penitential accounts of street-robbers dispatched at Tyburn.

There had of course always been highway robbery and piracy on the high seas. However, both crimes seem to have promoted greater anxiety after the Restoration, leading to a kind of moral panic that could be partly assuaged by tales of the ultimate capture and punishment of the wrongdoer, as happens in most of the tales told in the period. The more banal and domestic world is that of highwaymen, commonly lumped together in the literature with footpads and housebreakers who worked chiefly in the city. It may be objectively true that there were more crimes on the highway in 1714 than in 1640, although indictments fluctuated over time and place, and the exact figures are often lacking. We know that in some areas of the home counties rural property crimes fell after the social turmoil of the Civil War and Protectorate, spiking again around the

1670s and the 1690s—though the number of indictments was always much lower than in the second half of the eighteenth century. How much this has to do with prosecutorial zeal is not clear. What can be said is that the ownership of movable property increased in this phase of history for all segments of society except the very poorest. Despite efforts by the authorities to improve the state of roads under the Tudors and periodic legislation, most highways remained in a wretched condition at the outset of the Civil War, but gradually things got better so that travel times by the end of the century were distinctly shorter than a hundred years earlier. The technology of building coaches made some advance and, in addition to a growing number of private vehicles, regular stagecoaches became frequent on all the main roads out of London by the 1660s. Mounted carriers had carried mail along the same routes from the time of Charles I.

Integral to these developments was the appearance of coaching inns, often quite modest at first, which proved useful to the commission of crime as well as to travellers. It is not surprising that these inns regularly appear in fictional and nonfictional lives of highwaymen. To take a single example, in the second part of *The Scotch Rogue: or, The Life and Actions of Donald Macdonald a High-land Scot* (1706), the narrator describes 'his Introduction into the Society of High-Way-Men, the Robberies he committed amongst them; and how he was made Captain of the Gang'. He signs up to join the gang in an inn, meets his comrades there, encounters victims there, and is arrested there by officers. Macdonald writes in the first person, as is common, and operates in Scotland, which is unusual, because the greater proportion of highway stories take place around London, where the highest concentration of wealth was found. Indeed, the perpetrators frequently have their base in the capital and meet their end in the city.

All these factors would help to explain a surge in accounts of highway robberies late on in the period. There is only a scattering of such items in most years up to the 1680s: among the more notable is the life of Claude Duval in 1670, already mentioned. In the last decade of the century, some members of the fraternity such as James Whitney and William Davis, the 'Golden Farmer', achieved widespread notoriety after their trial and execution—generally a robber had to be caught to be properly recognized, as only then did any halfway reliable information come to light. Again, we find that in 1714 some developments were only just on the point of emerging. Not wholly by coincidence, it was around the second decade of the new century that the project to improve roads gained a sudden momentum, just as collective lives of highwaymen began to appear with increasing frequency. The most notable of these was the work of 'Capt. Alexander Smith', first issued in 1714 as *The History of the Lives of the most Noted Highway-men, Foot-pads, House-breakers, Shop-lifts, and Cheats, of Both Sexes, in and about London, and Other Places of Great-Britain, for above Fifty Years Last Past*, which was reissued a number of times in the immediately following years, with an expanded version in three volumes in 1719. Rather more than half the subjects in the original collection were highway robbers, and almost as many housebreakers. Five individuals are described as 'Murderer and Highway-man', although Smith's tone does not pick these out as especially heinous criminals in the context of those covered. Among this latter group was James Hind, a far less cosy character than he had seemed in the 1652 chapbook, as we are now told of his long stay in Newgate, his conviction for murder, and his ultimate fate: to be hanged, drawn, and quartered at Worcester gaol aged 34. In the expanded version we meet old friends such as Moll Cutpurse: it was indeed through the agency of Alexander Smith that the fame of many malefactors was passed down to posterity. This point has a wider significance related to the history of genres: collective and collaborative works started to play a more important part in the dissemination of literature in this period, with consequences for works on science and technology, lexicography, and biography.[14]

Another conspicuous case in Smith's gallery of rogues is that of Jack Hall, a housebreaker and 'most notorious Malefactor' who 'deservedly suffer'd death at *Tyburn*' in 1707. Hall had been the subject of a supposedly penitential account of his own life in 1708, published as *Memoirs of the Right Villanous John Hall, the Late Famous and Notorious Robber, Penn'd from his own Mouth some Time before his Death*, which came complete with the customary elegy, epitaph, and pious reflections (it was reprinted, aptly once more, in 1714). This item is still consulted because it contains a short lexicon of thieves' cant. But Hall was no more than a run-of-the-mill burglar, connected with a gang active at the start of the century, some of whom may have pioneered the kind of thief-taking activity which Jonathan Wild soon after took to new lengths. As is widely known, the exploits of Wild and the gaolbreaker Jack Sheppard prompted a spate of criminal lives in the mid-1720s that told the story of these men and their colleagues, with a literary afterlife in John Gay's *Beggar's Opera* (1728) and Fielding's *Jonathan Wild* (1743). The readership in 1714 may have been poised for such mordant satires, aligning crime with the evil practices of government and high society: but the time had not quite come.

Lincoln B. Faller has written of 'the oddity of the highwayman as hero and social critic', and there is certainly some moral ambiguity about the way some gentlemen of the road were presented, though in most cases they were shown as dissolute and socially destructive.[15] But at least their activities were confined to a small area, the majority did not commit acts of violence, and they did not seriously challenge the authority of the state. What is more surprising is the glamorization of pirates, who disrupted trade in a more fundamental way, who made it their professed business to extirpate all forces of authority whom they encountered (which could mean sinking a ship and sending all its crew to the bottom of the ocean), and who did not have any recognizable place in civilized society. Accounts of their exploits, albeit these come with dubious authority, paint an unattractive picture of men (usually) living in a coarse and brutal fashion, with little respect for human life. This impression would be strengthened by the widespread currency of two collections, in particular: those of Alexandre Olivier Exquemelin and

---

[14] See e.g., Chapter 33 on 'Scientific Transactions' by Felicity Henderson.

[15] Lincoln B. Faller, *Turned to Account: The Forms and Functions of Criminal Biography in Late Seventeenth- and Early Eighteenth-Century England* (Cambridge: Cambridge University Press, 1987), 174–93. In a later book the same author writes that 'the two earliest forms of criminal biography owed their wide popularity as well as most of their distinctive features to a powerful array of social, political, religious, and moral concerns specific to the late seventeenth and early eighteenth centuries'. This appears to refer to lives of highwaymen and murderers (Lincoln B. Faller, *Crime and Defoe: A New Kind of Writing* (Cambridge: Cambridge University Press, 1993), p. xiii).

'Capt. Charles Johnson'. The first was published in Dutch as *De Americaensche Zee-roovers* in 1678, and translated into English, probably out of Spanish, as *The Bucaniers of America* in 1684. The work captured the imagination of the age as few others managed to do. The text was rendered into several languages, imitated, fictionalized, and, of course, pirated. Remarkably the English translator sees the production as the 'glorious Actions' of the Nation, which refers principally to the 'hero' Henry Morgan, the privateer and more bluntly pirate who ravaged the Spanish in the Caribbean in the 1670s and 1680s. Morgan was able to use reasons of state to justify some actions that barely qualified as acceptable even in his day, as with the sack of Panama in 1671 that involved torture and perhaps rape.

Exquemelin stood alone until just after the end of the period. A spate of new piratical enterprises followed the appearance of his book, and many of these were brought together by 'Capt. Charles Johnson' in his collection *A General History of the Robberies and Murders of the Most Notorious Pyrates* (1724), sometimes attributed to Defoe but without any solid basis. Johnson concentrates almost exclusively on English examples, among them figures still alive in the imagination of filmmakers and other exponents of popular culture: they include the female pirates Mary Read and Ann Bonny, whose names are highlighted on the title page. Along with them come Edward Teach ('Blackbeard'), Stede Bonnet, the former merchant seaman Bartholomew Roberts, and Henry Avery, 'the king of pirates'. Avery even became the subject of tragicomedy in *The Succesful Pyrate* in 1712, and figures in Defoe's journalism and fiction. All these individuals were active in what is called, somewhat inaptly, the golden age of piracy. That is, they operated mainly in the Caribbean and North Atlantic waters approximately between the years 1685 and 1720. At least one, Roberts, had served on the crew of a slave ship, but this was not of any interest to those who wrote about these figures and embellished their careers in fiction. There was after all nothing in the passive sufferings of the human commodities transported across the Atlantic that appealed to those looking for exciting adventures or daring exploits. The slaves were cargo, rather than human beings with their own agency.

David Cordingly has written: 'The accounts of pirate life given by Exquemelin and Captain Johnson suggest an anarchic round of drinking and gambling and womanizing, interspersed with fierce raids on helpless victims.' He concedes that a lot of this really did go on, but adds that pirate life at sea was well organized, 'and similar in many respects to life on a merchant ship'.[16] Whatever the truth of their representations, such narratives struck an obvious chord among contemporary readers, and they left their mark on English fiction of the eighteenth and nineteenth centuries. The tales have an exotic flavour; they describe bursts of intense action, punctuated by short lulls in which the manners and mores of this outré group could be held up for inspection; and they have an obvious teleological curve, which leads us inexorably to Execution Dock as the final bourne of any piratical career. Johnson's collection ends with 'An abstract of the civil

---

[16] David Cordingly, *Under the Black Flag: The Romance and the Reality of Life among the Pirates* (New York: Random House, 1995), 90.

laws and statute law now in force, in relation to piracy'. Writers and compilers needed to reassert conventional morality, as expressed by the law, as the stories came to an end, even if their appeal had lain in the brash overthrow of normal restraints on behaviour.

Conclusion

Change is apparent throughout the period, whether in the fashionability of literary genres, in the legal framework, or in public attitudes to crime. A new window on the subject was opened late in the period by journalism: the periodical press had existed during the Civil War, but it had been suppressed under Charles II, and it is not until the reign of Anne that we first encounter daily, weekly, biweekly, Sunday, and evening newspapers, together with a range of other serial organs. Crime was naturally a main focus of these journals, and trials were given extensive coverage almost overnight—a major departure. Thus, by 1722 it was possible for metropolitan readers to have several day-to-day accounts of a sensational case of attempted murder in Suffolk, which could not have happened even twenty-five years earlier. Provincial papers soon got in on the act. Another significant innovation came with the appearance of the Old Bailey Session Papers, mentioned earlier. Dying speeches at the place of execution became a staple industry in the hands of a man like John Applebee, who from 1715 ran a weekly newspaper carrying trial reports which were then expanded into short pamphlets, *Applebee's Original Weekly Journal*. Applebee's business depended on his close contacts with the ordinary or chaplain of Newgate prison, successively Thomas Purney and James Guthrie, whose high-minded account of 'the behaviour, confession, and dying words of the malefactors who were executed at Tyburn' accompanied the grisly ceremony on each hanging day.[17]

By the end of our period, then, the public had a diverse array of sources of information, far larger than their grandparents had enjoyed seventy years earlier. The variety of literary forms expanded to meet the needs of a new class of readership, occasioned in part by a slow rise in the number of literate men and women. More detail and specificity could now be supplied, so that the timeless and almost legendary quality of narrative forms such as the street ballad came to seem a little old-fashioned. The literature of crime would start to embrace some features of modernity, only present in a fitful and fragmentary way up till then.

---

[17] On Applebee, see e.g., Andrea McKenzie, 'The Real Macheath: Social Satire, Appropriation, and Eighteenth-Century Criminal Biography', *Huntington Library Quarterly*, 69 (2006), 581–605.

CHAPTER 12

DIARIES

ADAM SMYTH

In one of the richest recent meditations on the diary as genre, practice, and theoretical problem, Philippe Lejeune acknowledges the difficulty of offering a single, stable definition of the textual form we associate, perhaps too easily, with Samuel Pepys, John Evelyn, Elizabeth Mordaunt, Elias Ashmole, Samuel Jeake, Elizabeth Freke, Ralph Josselin, Roger Lowe, Anne Clifford, Nehemiah Wallington, and many others. The closest Lejeune comes to a definition is 'a series of dated traces [*série de traces datées*]', but he prefers instead to itemize the diary's potential formal traits, approaching genre through the accumulation of tendencies: 'Discontinuous. Full of gaps. Allusive ... Redundant ... repetitive ... Non-narrative.' We might add others. The diary is often (but not always) written close to the events described, in contrast to the retrospective gaze of the autobiographer, and certainly diaries generally create the *effect* of an immediacy of composition. The diary is written, inevitably, with other readers in mind (at the very least, God and the writer's future self), sometimes including family or community members, but is not generally composed with the prospect of wide, printed circulation, and generally works with the expectation or rhetoric (if not the fact) of private composition and consumption.[1]

Each of these traits could be subject to debate, so if it is hard to say what a diary is, can we say what it is like? The diary, Lejeune suggests, is 'a piece of lacework, a sport'; it is a kind of rhythm, both in its 'internal morphology' of themes and form, and in the external process of its composition. The diary is like 'musical improvisation', requiring 'both mastery of a technique and immediate acceptance of the unknown'. The diary is 'antifiction' (Lejeune's neologism), written with no knowledge of where and when it will end: 'a daunting face-off with time', 'a dream of defeating death'. The diary is 'made up of more empty space than filled'. It is a sculpture, given 'form by removing nine-tenths of its material', and 'a silhouette in a sketchbook with three pencil strokes'.[2]

---

[1] Philippe Lejeune, *On Diary*, ed. Jeremy D. Popkin and Julie Rak, trans. Katherine Durnin (Honolulu: The University of Hawai'i Press, 2009), 179, 170.

[2] Lejeune, *On Diary*, 181, 182, 202, 209, 202, 181, 176.

Why is the diary hard to pin-down? In the seventeenth century, this sense of evasiveness plays out on the level of terminology, as the noun 'diary' (the *OED*'s first usage date of 1581 in fact overlooks several earlier texts)[3] jostles with an array of other descriptors, including memorial, journal, daybook, diurnal, diet-book, calendar, and ephemeris. This fluidity of terminology tells us something important about the way that the diary was protean, and was often entangled with other genres of writing: the line between diary and commonplace book, miscellany, or recipe collection, for example, is not always easy to draw, and in fact that generic crossing-over was a particular feature of life-writing at this time (so we need to notice it, and not approach it as a problem). Readers who study the diary need to attend to these rhetorical and even literary qualities—the diary's overlappings with other forms; its own conventions; its mechanisms of persuasion—rather than using the diary as a neutral historical document, as a window on to a moment. This chapter will keep this generic messiness in mind by working with an expansive sense of form, both in terms of genre and materiality.[4]

The rise in forms of self-representation more generally, and in the diary in particular, can be attributed to a range of factors: Protestantism's emphasis on the individual, in terms of his or her relationship with God, and the injunction to turn within and search for signs of redemption; the 'heightened sense of history and self-consciousness' that the extraordinary events of the Civil War induced;[5] the boom in print culture and the rise of literacy rates, particularly in the later seventeenth century, which meant individuals had before them, suddenly, many more models for imagining experience, life, and self;[6] the growth in the 1620s of corantos—weekly pamphlets of foreign news, precursors to newspapers, printed abroad—and then in mid-century of titles such as *Mercurius Aulicus* and *Mercurius Britanicus*, texts which disseminated in print frequent, regular, chronological accounts of the present;[7] the growth of experimental science and an attention to the particular, material conditions of experience;[8] the spread of systems

---

[3] For example, William Patten, *The Expedicion into Scotlande* (1548) is 'set out by way of diarie, by W. Patten Londoner' (title page).

[4] For discussions of forms of autobiography more generally, see Ronald Bedford, et al. (eds.), *Early Modern Autobiography: Theories, Genres, Practices* (Ann Arbor: University of Michigan Press, 2006); Michelle M. Dowd and Julie A. Eckerle (eds.), *Genre and Women's Life Writing in Early Modern England* (Ashgate: Aldershot, 2007); Felicity A. Nussbaum, *The Autobiographical Subject: Gender and Ideology in Eighteenth-Century England* (Johns Hopkins: Baltimore and London, 1989); James Olney (ed.), *Autobiography: Essays Theoretical and Critical* (Princeton, NJ: Princeton University Press, 1980); Adam Smyth, *Autobiography in Early Modern England* (Cambridge: Cambridge University Press, 2010); and Adam Smyth (ed.), *A History of English Autobiography* (Cambridge: Cambridge University Press, 2016). See also Chapter 7 by Julie A. Eckerle, 'Biography and Autobiography'.

[5] Sharon Cadman Seelig, *Autobiography and Gender in Early Modern Literature: Reading Women's Lives, 1600–1680* (Cambridge University Press: Cambridge, 2006), 4. See also Chapter 32 by Brooke Conti on 'Religious Autobiography'.

[6] See Chapter 1 by Thomas Keymer on 'Circulation'.

[7] See Chapter 26 by Brian Cowan on 'Periodical Literature'.

[8] See Chapter 33 by Felicity Henderson on 'Scientific Transactions'.

of financial accounting which encouraged a broader interest in recording transactions, and in 'setting things to rights', to use Pepys's exacting phrase.[9]

For Lejeune, and for many other critics, the diary is a form associated with a modernity that begins in the late eighteenth century, but this version of literary history effaces the diary's lively earlier presence. Oxford diarist, antiquarian, historian, and man of controversy Anthony Wood (1632–95)—or, as he tried to style himself in his later writing, Anthony à Wood—presents, contextualized in relation to other writers, an excellent test case for a study of the form. This is partly because of the web of life-writing texts Wood left behind (including a diary, a long run of annotated almanacs, and an autobiography), but also because Wood thought carefully (and occasionally deeply) about the relationship between writing, memory, and life.[10] Wood was certainly not by instinct a theoretician—he would have recoiled from the term—but the intense hostility his writings induced, particularly his mountainous catalogue of bookish Oxford lives, *Athenae Oxonienses* (1691–2), caused Wood to reflect on the kind of work he was doing and to offer a series of justifications of the ways lives might be recorded and be made to endure.[11]

Central to so much seventeenth- and eighteenth-century diary-writing was the process of transferring text between different book forms: the movement and revision of notes about a life, from an initial and usually brief register, most commonly in the blank pages or spaces of a printed almanac, towards a fuller, more sustained narrative. Many life-writing texts from the period, including texts we could recognize as diaries, were produced in this way: the tireless and prolific Warwickshire antiquarian Sir William Dugdale, for example, kept annotated almanacs for most of his life: fifty heavily annotated volumes survive from 1626, when Dugdale was twenty-one, until his death in 1686, and there may have been more.[12] This mass of information subsequently fed into Dugdale's many writing projects, including *Monasticon Anglicanum* (1655), *The Antiquities of Warwickshire* (1656), *A Short View of the Late Troubles in England* (1681), and also his own brief autobiography, later enlarged by Anthony Wood.[13] Such a working method unravels the assumption that diaries are spontaneous, artless transcriptions of lived reality, suggesting instead the work of careful stages of revision: which is not to suggest they were false or disingenuous, but rather that they were more complicated and more literary in nature than critics often assume.[14] Critics seeking to raid diaries

---

[9] *The Diary of Samuel Pepys*, ed. Robert Latham and William Matthews, 11 vols. (1970; Berkeley and Los Angeles: University of California Press, 2000–1), 7: 170 (18 June 1666).

[10] N. K. Kiessling, 'The Autobiographies of Anthony Wood', *The Bodleian Library Record*, 19 (2006), 185–215.

[11] On Wood, see also Chapter 9 by Kate Bennett on 'Brief Lives and Characters'.

[12] The originals are kept at the Dugdale home at Merevale; microfilm copies are available at Warwick Record Office, MI 318.

[13] William Hamper, *The Life, Diary and Correspondence of Sir William Dugdale* (London, 1827). On antiquarian writing in this period, see also Chapter 6 by Thomas Roebuck.

[14] For a (mis)reading of diaries in terms of their 'guileless disclosure', see Roger Cardinal, 'Unlocking the Diary', *Comparative Criticism*, 12 (1990), 71–87 (78).

for nuggets of artless historical fact often neglect the complex compositional scaffolding within which diaries come into being.

In the production of his diaries, Wood adheres to this writing-through-revision paradigm: making notes first in what scholars call his 'almanac diaries' from 1657 to the year of his death in 1695; then returning to revise this material into a first-person narrative in manuscript quarto of sixty-three pages, covering 1632–60, a text Wood titled 'The Diarie of the Life of Anthony à Wood Historiographer and Antiquarie of the most famous Universitie of Oxford' (British Library MS Harley 5409); and then in turn revising this account to produce 'Secretum Antonii' (Bodleian MS Tanner 102), sixty-nine pages of manuscript folio of Wood's life, now conveying in a detached third person a more sober account of a life, largely stripped of what Wood called 'exploits' or 'frolicks', and covering 1632–72.

Wood's most sustained form of annotation was the insertion of handwritten notes of his activities on pages bound opposite the almanac's printed monthly calendar.[15] In part because of the fullness of Wood's 'Diarie' and 'Secretum Antonii', the annotated almanacs have received little analysis, but these staccato records are, as so often in the diary culture of the time, a crucial first stage in the construction of Wood's daily self. The notes are overwhelmingly financial in nature, in the sense that the majority of actions noted have a monetary value attached: this was the dominant variable for inclusion, and, since Wood's later, fuller diary and autobiography grew out of the almanac annotations, financial expense might be said to be one structuring paradigm for Wood's sense of self. Even activities that we would not classify as primarily financial (such as a visit to a church to examine the monuments) were logged and had a rationale as expenses ('the 3 day: giuen to the porter of Mag: Coll: to see the chappell—6d – 0').[16]

The principal topics of annotation, and thus the main coordinates of Wood's diary-self, are as follows:

1. a bibliographical economy: the purchase, binding, borrowing, and lending of books ('to Beckford for binding of Camden's remains—6d – 0')
2. reading notes ('I began ˄^{to} Read Lelands Collections: Bib: Bod')
3. theatre visits ('in ye morn: a comedy called a mad world my masters—0 – 6d – 0 in ye afternoon, a comedy called ye milkmaids—0 – 6d')
4. reforms to his home ('This month of feb: 1659. I set up my chimney wch cost me about 20^s. as also ye Window in my study')
5. money lent to individuals
6. social life, usually centred on a tavern ('spent at ye merem: Tau: wth Jo: Drope –1s—1d—0')
7. music, participation in ensembles ('the 13 and 20 I plaid at the musick Schole')

---

[15] For a comparable set of annotated almanacs, acquired by the Bodleian Library in 2011 and at the time of writing awaiting a first sustained analysis, see the twenty almanacs of Frances Wolfreston (BL, MS Don. E. 246). For the form in general, see Smyth, *Autobiography in Early Modern England*, chap. 1.

[16] MS Wood's Diaries 1, fol. 23.

8. visits to churches and colleges
9. expenses at barber, cobbler, tailor, often bundled under the catch-all category 'spent'
10. health of self, especially notes of 'vomits' or purges
11. deaths of friends, acquaintances, figures of renown, often struck through indicating transfer to another text ('old Mr Sterne chaplain of New Coll: died & was buried in ye cloister of ye same Coll').[17]

Wood maintains these central topics and this mode of diary-as-annotation across his five decades of almanac use. His records have certain striking material features, too: some contain gaps for names and dates to be added subsequently; there are glued-in smaller sheets with handwritten lists such as 'Fellowes of Lycn y^t left their fellowship for non-conformity';[18] and parts of, and sometimes whole, pages have been torn out, leaving fragments or stubs. Such moments, when the note-taking strains against the coherence of the book, are representative of an important tension in diary-writing: that is, between writing that is contained within a single bound book and writing that occurs across loose sheets and manifold sites; between a written selfhood that is bounded, possessed of some sense of material and conceptual unity (it is a thing which can be located between two covers), and a sprawling written selfhood that is less bibliographically policed. Lejeune organizes this tension into an opposition between continuous and discontinuous writing, between the bound book and the loose sheet, but in fact almanacs are powerful and therefore frequent sites for diary-writing in part because they constitute that apparently impossible bibliographical object, the never-ending notebook—the book that becomes, upon completion, part of a longer run of books.[19] Wood opens each year's diary notes with a record of his purchase of the almanac he is at that moment annotating ('ye 2^d for this Almanack—0 – 3d'):[20] a record that, repeated across all almanacs, draws the single book into a relationship with others, and a moment of *mise en abyme* in which the materiality of writing becomes the subject of record, rather as Pepys collapses the gap between writing and experience in his note: 'I staid up till the bell-man came by with his bell just under my window as I was writing of this very line, and cried, "Past one of the clock, and a cold, frosty, windy morning"'.[21]

We can see the process of revising the self by tracking across almanac, 'Diarie', and 'Secretum Antonii', noting the different written versions of Wood's life and subjectivity he constructs for a single day. On 27 March 1657, Wood attended the funeral of Jane Wickham; because there was a small cost incurred (one shilling for the hire of a horse), Wood notes the following in his almanac: 'the 27 I gaue 1^s for the hiring of a

---

[17] MS Wood's Diaries 1, fols. 25v, 28; 5, fol. 22v; 4, fol. 10; 5, fol. 8; 1, fol. 28; 6, fol. 18v.
[18] MS Wood's Diaries 6, fol. 22.
[19] Lejeune doesn't discuss almanacs but 'procedures that restore continuity: numbering, which turns each notebook into the page of a larger notebook' (Lejeune, *On Diary*, 176).
[20] MS Wood's Diaries 4, fol. 7.
[21] Pepys, *Diary*, 4: 47.

horse to goe to m^rs Wickhams Buriall att Casington: she died the 25 day of march.'[22] Wood's money-driven record orientates the event in a counter-intuitive direction: the fact of Jane Wickham's burial (which seems to us significant) is tagged on to a shilling for a horse (which seems not). The annotation is struck through, indicating a process of textual transfer, and in the 'Diarie', Wood writes up this day like this:

> 27 Mar. Fri. I rode to Garsington with the Corps of Jane Wickham the widdow, and sometimes the second wife of William Wickham of the same place Gent. to see and attend her burial in the Chancel of the church there neare the Remaines of the said William Wickham. This woman who was sister to Henry Brome of Clifton neare Banbury in Oxfordshire (of the familie of the Bromes of Halton) and died in Oxon, 25 March. I did not survey then the monuments of the church, because of the company there[.]

In 'Secretum Antonii', Wood presents the following:

> 27 Mar. Fri. At the funeral of Jane Wickham the widdow, and sometimes the second wife of William Wickham of Garsingdon neare Oxôn Gentleman. Shee was buried in the Chancel of the church there by the Remaines of the said William Wickham. This woman was sister to Henry Brome of Clifton neare Banbury in Oxfordshire (of the same Familie with the Bromes of Halton) and died in Oxon, 25 March. AW did not then survey the monuments in Garsingdon church, because of the company there, but rode immediatly home to Oxôn –[.][23]

As with this example, the most common revision is the shift from first to third person, with a consequent effect of detachment and objectivity; from brevity to fullness; from something like immediacy to reflection and evaluation. The point, here, is not that Wood is a diary outlier, disingenuously or even deceitfully fashioning a false self; rather, Wood illustrates, in an unusually overt way, the process of writing and revision that lies behind many diaries and forms of life-writing from this period. What was, in the 'Diarie', 'I remember one Franc. Croft whom I found to be one of the chaplaynes of Merton College' becomes in the autobiography: 'Mr Francis Croft, whome AW found to be one of the chaplaynes of Merton College'; 'My Brother Edward died to the great Reluctancy of Friends and Relations' becomes 'Edward Wood died to the great Reluctancy of his Friends and Relations'; and 'My mother, my two brothers Robert and Christopher & my self gave 5^li to Merton college, towards the casting of their five Bells into eight' becomes 'AW, his mother, and his two Brothers Robert and Christopher Wood gave 5^li to Merton college, towards the casting of their five Bells into eight'. This is partly about shifting conceptions of substantiation—where the collectively circulating 'This is mention'd' appears a more robust truth than 'This

---

[22] MS Wood's Diaries 1, fol. 16.
[23] *The Life of Anthony Wood in His Own Words*, ed. N. K. Kiessling (Oxford: Bodleian Library, 2009), 51.

I mention'—but it is also about Wood's attempt to create a more sober, detached sense of a life. Some of these revisions are more spectacular. Thus, in the earlier 'Diarie', Wood describes a semi-drunken cavort with companions to Farringdon Fair 'to disguise our selves in poore habits, and like contry fidlers scrape for our livings', along with reports of dining, dancing, and music at 'the In standing on the road going to Farringdon'. This sits oddly with the version of Wood familiar to posterity, and indeed at the time of writing Wood craved its suppression: 'Most of my Companions would afterwards glory in this, but I was ashamed and could never endure to heare of it.' When the same event is written up in 'Secretum Antonii', Wood attempts to enact this desire for an edited life, even if his commitment to the historical record requires him to log some kind of notice: 'Latter end of 1654. AW having by this time obtain'd proficiency in musick, he and his companions were not without silly Frolicks—not now to be maintaind—'.[24] This is a Wood more like, or less unlike, the version fashioned in *Athenae Oxonienses*, where Wood describes himself as 'an Admirer of a solitary and retired life', a stranger to 'Coffee-houses, Assignations, Clubbs, &c. [and] ... [only] a degree different from an Ascetick': not a million miles from Anthony Powell's unappealing but plausible description of Wood as 'one of those uninviting pedants ... a lonely unpopular recluse'.[25]

This sense of Wood's written life as repeated, amplified, or dispersed across three texts, and of the need for modern scholars to read the diary in relation to these other representations, characteristic of writing from this period, creates a problem for later editors. Editors often respond to this textual network by extracting a certain kind of information to build a single new text out of the variety: from the parliamentary diaries and annotated books belonging to historian and MP Narcissus Luttrell (1657–1732), for example, Thomas Macaulay produced *A Brief Historical Relation of State Affairs from September 1678 to April 1714* (1857); and, much more recently, by patching together John Aubrey's words scattered across his various genres of writing, biographer Ruth Scurr constructed the diary that Aubrey never wrote.[26] The nature of the new text produced will alter according to the historical moment in which the editor works, and the use they wish to make of the past: Macaulay wanted a chronicle of public state affairs; Scurr sought a lively, somewhat Pepysian character. The problem with such responses is that they bring the original sprawl of texts into a false coherence: the constructed text, and the subjectivity it conveys, are anachronistically tidy and centripetal, and we need to learn to read the diary on its original, networked terms. Wood's final 'not without silly Frolicks—*not now to be maintaind—*' might refer to the drunken lifestyle, or the written record of the drunken lifestyle, and in muddling the difference between life and text,

---

[24] Kiessling (ed.), *Life*, 44, 192–3.
[25] Wood, *Athenae Oxonienses*, 2 vols. (Oxford, 1691–2) 1, 'To the Reader', n.p.; Anthony Powell, *John Aubrey and his Friends* (London: Hogarth Press, 1948), 127, quoted in T. A. Birrell, 'Anthony Wood, John Bagford and Thomas Hearne as Bibliographers', in Robin Myers and Michael Harris (eds.), *Pioneers in Bibliography* (Winchester: St Paul's Bibliographies, 1988), 25–39 (25–6)).
[26] Ruth Scurr, *John Aubrey: My Own Life* (London: Chatto & Windus, 2015).

between an embarrassing past and an editor's erasure, Wood is expressing something fundamental about a seventeenth-century sense of self: that is, the degree to which life is conceived as, and described in terms of, a text.

Wood's commitment to closing the gap between life and writing is most apparent in his investment in what we would now call bio-bibliography: the narration of a life through the recounting of written, usually printed, works.[27] Although the *OED* offers 1808 at the first date for this term, Wood did much to establish this form: it dominates *Athenae Oxonienses*, where the 1,500 Oxford lives from between 1500 and 1690 are organized around book titles, and publication and format ('qu[arto]') details, along with Wood's brand of gossipy, first-person literary history. Here is an example of one of the many minor divines about whom, without Wood, we would know little:

> JASPER FISHER, a Gentlemans Son, was born in *Bedfordshire*, entred a Com. of *S.M. Magd.* hall in Mich. Term 1607, took the degrees in Arts, became afterwards Divinity or Philosophy reader of *Magd.* Coll. Rector of *Wilden* in his own Country, about 1631, and at length D. of D. He hath written and published
>
> > *Fuimus Troes Æneid.* 2. The True Trojanes, being a story of the Britains valour at the Romans first invasion. *Lond.* 1633. qu. Before which time, it had been once, or more, publickly represented by the Gentlemen-Students of *Magd.* coll. in *Oxon*
> >
> > Several Sermons, as (1) *Serm*. On Malac. 2.7. Printed 1636. in oct. &c. This person who was always esteemed an ingenious man while he lived in *Magd.* coll. as those that knew him, have divers time informed me, lived several years after this, (1633) but when he died, or what other things he hath published, I cannot learn.[28]

It may be that Wood's memory operated not according to the paradigm of Giulio Camillo's mind's-eye theatre famously described by Frances Yates, but rather through the form of the bibliography: that is, the story of a life draped over the skeleton of a list of (printed) works.[29] Certainly, when Wood describes the hanging of Anne Green, 'a servant Maid', on 14 December 1650, for the 'murdering her Bastard child', Wood's account slides inexorably towards an account of the printing of a ballad of the event:

> After she had suffer'd the Law, she was cut downe, and carried away in order to be anatomiz'd by some yong Physitians, but they finding life in her, would not venter upon her, only so farr, as to recover her to life. Which being look'd upon as a great wonder, there was a Relation of her Recovery printed, and at the end several Copies of Verses made by the yong poets of the Universitie were added.[30]

---

[27] For the development of bio-bibliography in the late seventeenth century in the works of Thomas Fuller, Edward Phillips, William Winstanley, Gerald Langbaine, and others, see Adam G. Hooks, *Selling Shakespeare: Biography, Bibliography and the Book Trade* (Cambridge: Cambridge University Press, 2016).

[28] *Athenae Oxonienses*, 1: 528.

[29] Frances A. Yates, *The Art of Memory* (Chicago: University of Chicago Press, 1966), 129–59.

[30] Kiessling (ed.), *Life*, 34.

What started as an account of Anne Green's death-then-life becomes a description of a pamphlet, described to the cadence of the title page (Wood has in mind Richard Watkins' *News from the Dead ... Whereunto Are Added Certain Poems, Casually Written Upon That Subject* (1651)), and the effect is of a writer who finds it hard to keep life, and the written record, distinct.

This is in part because print is at this moment fast becoming the medium of permanent historical record: books are, in Wood's words, things 'left to Posterity'.[31] Wood's lament for the 'obliteration' of devotional paintings 'in various and antique shapes' on the back of the stalls in Merton College Choir—'daubed over with paint by the command of the [Parliamentary usurpers]'—is to some degree mitigated by his note, in 'Secretum Antonii', that 'AW had before this time transcrib'd them, which were afterwards printed—See *Hist. et Antiq. Univ. Oxon* lib. 2 p. 91'.[32] Conversely, events that were not recorded were for Wood not quite real, or quickly ceased to be real: thus Wood's cautionary tale of Rector Hodges of Wytham, Berkshire, 'a very good scholar and fit in many respects to oblige posterity by his Pen', who, by merely 'delighting himself in Mirth ... could never be brought to set pen to paper for that purpose'.[33] This sense of identity-through-publication applies to Wood's own sense of self, manifest in his notes in his almanac diaries, and in his 'Diarie' and 'Secretum Antonii'. Wood is fascinated and, one senses, feels uniquely substantiated when his life is recorded in manuscript ('18 Oct. [1647] St Lukes day and Munday he was entred into the Buttery-Books of Merton college') or, especially, in print. Wood digs out these moments of textualized, printed selfhood, and presents them like a child who has found a coin in the road: 'Received from Dr Savage Master of Balliol col*lege* his book lately printed, entitled *Balliofergus* &c. in requital for what AW had done in order to its composition—In the said book p. 28 he calls AW *his friend*.'[34]

This sense of life- and diary-writing organized around an attention to listing works— a record of life filtered through something like bibliography, *avant la lettre*—is evident in other diaries, including the 145 octavo notebooks kept by Thomas Hearne between 1705 and 1735. What Hearne called his 'Remarks and collections' was a blend of gossip, politics, intellectual history, publishing news, and his particular brand of voyeuristic social history:

> July 30 [1723]. Some Years agoe came out at Oxford a Poem, called *Merton Walks*, the Walks in the Garden of that Place being every Sunday Night, in the pleasant time of the Year, thronged with young Gentlemen and young Gentlewomen, which growing scandalous, the Garden Gate was at last shut up quite, and thereupon the young Gentlemen and others betook themselves to Magdalen College Walk, which is now every Sunday Night in Summer time strangely filled, just like a Fair, which hath

---

[31] *Athenae Oxonienses*, 1: 6, s.v. 'William Galeon'.
[32] Kiessling, *Life*, 70.
[33] Kiessling, *Life*, 32.
[34] Kiessling, *Life*, 24, 111.

occasioned a printed Letter, giving an Account of an Accident that happened there between a young Gentleman and a young Woman.[35]

That these figures worked in university and library contexts—Hearne was Assistant and Second Keeper at the Bodleian and, through his cataloguing work, one of the 'pioneers of bibliographical method'—perhaps makes such a self-writing mode unsurprising.[36]

But, more broadly, the debts of Wood and Hearne to bibliography as a paradigm for ordering experience illustrates one crucial feature of diary-writing in this period: that is, the manner in which diaries began not with a writer seeking to construct a record of their life *in toto* but with some other, more focused agenda, out of which a broader life-record subsequently emerged, while often retaining the originating structure. Samuel Jeake's Rye diary has as its foundation an astrological record of the late seventeenth century;[37] Celia Fiennes' journals describe her journeys on horseback around Britain between 1684 and about 1712;[38] financial account books, like Lady Anne Clifford's, often tip over into narrative self-representation;[39] the 'Baptisms Marriages Burials 1665–1671' noted by Reverend John Wade of Hammersmith are surrounded by Wade's extended private shorthand diary;[40] the journals or memoranda of John Locke and Robert Hooke have as their originating or dominant focus a record of the weather.[41] Hooke's first entry from Sunday 10 March 1672 records his entangling of self and weather: '*Sun* 10 [mercury] fell from 170 to 185. most part of ye Day cleer but cold & somewhat windy at the South–[I was this morning better with my cold then I had been 3 months before] [moon] apogeum—It grew cloudy about 4. [mercury] falling still—.'[42]

The role of religion as a catalyst and ordering structure for diary-writing has long been seen as central by critics, particularly Protestantism's stress on the single believer and

---

[35] *The Remains of Thomas Hearne: Reliquiæ Hearnianæ*, ed. John Buchanan-Brown (Carbondale: Southern Illinois University Press, 1966), 259. Hearne is referencing John Dry, *Merton Walks, or, The Oxford Beauties, a Poem* (Oxford, 1717).

[36] Birrell, 'Wood, Bagford and Hearne as Bibliographers', 37.

[37] *An Astrological Diary of the Seventeenth Century: Samuel Jeake of Rye 1652–1699*, ed. Michael Hunter and Annabel Gregory (Oxford: Oxford University Press, 1988).

[38] *The Illustrated Journeys of Celia Fiennes 1685-c.1712*, ed. Christopher Morris (Stroud: Alan Sutton, 1995).

[39] Cumbria Record Office, Kendal, WD/Hoth/A988/17. For Clifford's financial record-keeping and its relation to her other life-writing forms, see Smyth, *Autobiography in Early Modern England*, 72–93.

[40] Hammersmith and Fulham Archives, DD 71/1-2. There is a transcript, which includes a translation of the shorthand, by Albert Foyer: 'Private Diary and Accounts of the Rev. John Wade, Minister of Hammersmith in the 17th Century' (unpublished transcript, Hammersmith 1956), DD 818/10.

[41] Locke's 'Weather Diary, Oxford and London June 1666-June 1683; Otes Dec 1691-May 1703' is Bodleian Library, MS Locke d. 9, 531–471 *rev.*; Hooke's journal or memorandum book covering 1672 to 1683 is Guildhall Library, MS 1758.

[42] Guildhall Library, MS 1758, fol. 2r. For a transcript and discussion, see Felicity Henderson, 'Unpublished Material from the Memorandum Book of Robert Hooke, Guildhall Library MS 1758', *Notes & Records of the Royal Society*, 61 (2007), 129–75 (135).

the search within for signs of grace. According to Wood's friend and fellow antiquary Thomas Tanner, Wood in his final days in November 1695 'seems to be very sensible that his time is short, tho' truly he spends his spirits more in setting his Papers in Order, than in providing for another World'.[43] Yet, for many diarists, there was an intimate relationship between spiritual faith and first-person life-writing. While there is certainly a strong tradition of Catholic writers producing life-writing, as Nicky Hallett has recently demonstrated, critics have long argued that Puritanism encouraged an attention to the particular, no matter how apparently negligible: God's interventions, and one's predestined spiritual condition, might be discerned in the smallest action.[44] Along with this tendency towards observation and self-surveillance, Puritanism placed great weight on the need to remember perceived signs of God's benevolence and, simultaneously, created an anxiety about the individual's tendency towards forgetfulness. The spiritual diary, the log of actions in which God's purpose might be discerned, is the product of these pressures, a detailed record of the minutiae of the day as a mechanism through which the writer's spiritual condition might be understood, and due thanks to God expressed. The form is sprawlingly enacted in the diaries of Nehemiah Wallington, 'that lonely, God-struck artisan', who trawled over and over apparently inconsequential events of the 1630s, 1640s, and 1650s to discern his Lord's hand, and in the diaries of the vicar of Earls Colne, Ralph Josselin.[45]

Spiritual guides published in the seventeenth century helped catalyse these forms of spiritual diary-keeping. In *A Fountaine of Teares* (1646), John Featley stressed that, in order to 'see my God with joy', the Christian's sins 'must be seene by mee, and be bewayled by mee', and to this end, 'I will therefore sitt downe, and consider with my selfe, and examine my selfe how I have spent the day; before I betake my selfe to the rest of the night'. Featley provides a list of thirty-eight questions—from 'At what time, in the morning, did I arise from my bed?', and 'What first did I?', to 'What sighes, and groanes have I sent to heaven for pardon for it?'—which, once answered, will yield 'mine account', a textual record of little actions that, accumulatively, constitutes a written self.[46] In *The Journal or Diary of a Thankful Christian* (1656), John Beadle described a similar dynamic when he imagined a broader, proto-secular diary growing out of the process of spiritual self-accounting he urged on Christians: while the diary would begin as a record of 'all Gods gracious dealings with us', it might soon expand to include 'the severall occurrences of the Times we meet with, as they have reference to the Countrey and Nation we live in. It is good to keep an History, a Register, a Diary, an Annales, not

---

[43] Kiessling, *Life*, 163.

[44] Nicky Hallett, *Lives of Spirit: English Carmelite Self-Writing of the Early Modern Period* (Aldershot: Ashgate, 2013). See further Chapter 32 on 'Religious Biography' by Brooke Conti.

[45] Paul S. Seaver, *Wallington's World: A Puritan Artisan in Seventeenth-Century London* (Stanford: Stanford University Press, 1985), 39; *The Diary of Ralph Josselin, 1616-83*, ed. Alan Macfarlane (Oxford: Oxford University Press, 1991).

[46] John Featley, A *Fountaine of Teares* (Amsterdam, 1646), 89–91.

onely of the places in which we have lived, but of the mercies that have been bestowed on us, continued to all our dayes'.[47]

The spiritual diary of Elizabeth, Viscount Mordaunt, covering the years 1656–78, is illustrative of the kind of first-person life-writing encouraged by the guides of Featley, Beadle, and others. Mordaunt's diary consists principally of prayers composed in response to, or occasionally in anticipation of, particular occasions ('April, the 22nd, 1649. After the berthe of my son John'; 'A Prayr of thanks geuing For my deare Hosband's recouer from His greate and dangerus illnes July ye 16th 1662'), in addition to resolutions for future virtuous actions ('What I promos to pay to ye poure euery yere, so long as God shall enabell me').[48] Self-representation is refracted here through prayer, and the temporality of Mordaunt's life-records-as-prayers is complicated: the records look both back and forwards, responding to events and aspiring to better ways to live. In this respect they enact a tension that is always at work in diaries: the notion that the diary records life as it has been lived, alongside the conception of the diary as a mechanism for better living. Self-reflection is both a meditation on what has been and a desire to live differently in the future: a paradox exploited by John Dunton, the consistently eccentric bookseller and (he claimed) author of over 600 titles, who in 1705 published a blend of spiritual autobiography and travel narrative, peppered with transcripts of letters to and from his wife, entitled: *The Life and Errors of John Dunton: Late Citizen of London; Written by Himself in Solitude. with an Idea of a New Life; Wherein is Shewn How He'd Think, Speak, and Act, Might He Live Over His Days Again.*

Mordaunt's text is also expressive of the tendency of spiritual accounting to overlap with systems of financial accounting: a tendency that can be traced back to St Paul, in Romans 14:12 ('every one of us shall give account of himself to God'), and Matthew 25:19 (the 'lord of those servants cometh, and reckoneth with them'), but which was given life through the intertwining of religious and financial discourses in guides to spiritual wellbeing such as Isaac Ambrose's popular *Media: The Middle Things* (1649). For almost two months in 1657, Mordaunt borrowed from financial record-keeping to write her diary, dividing her pages in two, and distributing records between these columns, headed, like columns in a double entry book-keeping account, 'To returne thanks for' and 'To ask perden for'.[49] Under 'To returne thanks for', Mordaunt includes entries such as 'For my helthe and safety, and that of my Husbands'; and 'for all mercys granted this day to me'. Under 'To ask perden for', Mordaunt notes 'Ofended by disputing with my Husband, and therby geuing him a trubel, hauing bin weded to my owne opinion, and not yielding'; 'Hauing bin angery to day in my house with Lady P— and for hauing bin dull at prayrs'. Mordaunt calls the text her 'account' ('Lord my ofences ar many and my account but

---

[47] John Beadle, *The Journal or Diary of a Thankful Christian* (1656), 10–11. Featley and Beadle are discussed in Sara Heller Mendelson, 'Stuart Women's Diaries and Occasional Memoirs', in Mary Prior (ed.), *Women in English Society, 1500–1800* (London and New York: Methuen, 1985), 181–210 (186).

[48] *The Private Diarie of Elizabeth, Viscountess Mordaunt*, ed. Robert Jocelyn (Duncairn: privately printed, 1856), 28, 41. The current location of the original manuscript is unknown.

[49] This section is reproduced as an appendix to the *Private Diarie*, 225–39.

seldum mayde'), a word that suggests numbering, narrative, and more broadly a sense of accountability. And while Mordaunt abandoned this format, the structure she employed was clearly borrowed from financial accounting's columns of credit and debit.[50]

This collision between prayer, finance, spiritual self-accounting, and diary is more generally expressive of the way in which the diary migrated into, or informed, other genres of writing. By way of conclusion, I will briefly mention two such blurrings with what we might call canonical literary texts, in the form of an example of early literary journalism, and the genre-bending fictions of Daniel Defoe. The Whiggish literary journal *The Tatler* (1709–11) is organized around dispatches from London's four most popular coffee-houses (White's, Will's, the Grecian, and St James's), dispatches that convey the latest scandal, rumour, and news ('Letters inform us that …'). *The Tatler* is a text that produces, even from the reading distance of more than three centuries, a powerful sense of the now-ness of London: gossipy, urgent, excited, fizzing with life. This is prose that seems whispered in the reader's ear, or scribbled in a notebook with the ink still wet. In addition to these coffee-house reports, Richard Steele (and later both Jonathan Swift and Joseph Addison) wrote in the first person as 'Isaac Bickerstaff' and supplied regular 'lucubrations' (that is, nocturnal writings).[51] Composed 'From my own Apartment', and dated to the day, these biting but sociable digressions include entries such as '*June* 14. I am just come hither at Ten at Night, and have ever since Six been in the most celebrated, tho' most nauseous, Company in Town'; '*November* 7. I was very much surpris'd this Evening with a Visit from one of the Top Toasts of the Town, who came privately in a Chair, and bolted into my Room, while I was reading a Chapter of *Agrippa* upon the Occult Sciences'; '*April* 12. I had Yesterday Morning a Visit from this learned Idiot'; and

> *From my own Apartment, June 27.*
> Being of a very spare and hective Constitution, I am forced to make frequent Journies of a Mile or two for fresh Air; and indeed by this last, which was no further than the Village of *Chelsea*, I am farther convinced of the Necessity of travelling to know the World. For as it is usual with young Voyagers, as soon as they land upon a Shore, to begin their Accounts of the Nature of the People, their Soil, their Government, their Inclinations, and their Passions, so really I fancied I could give you an immediate Description of this Village, from the five Fields where the Robbers lie in wait, to the Coffee-house where the *Literati* sit in Council.[52]

---

[50] For key work on spiritual diaries, see Effie Botonaki, *Seventeenth-Century English Women's Autobiographical Writings: Disclosing Enclosures* (Edwin Mellen Press: Lampeter, 2004); Cynthia Garrett, 'The Rhetoric of Supplication: Prayer Theory in Seventeenth-Century England', *Renaissance Quarterly*, 46 (1993), 328–57; Retha M. Warnicke, 'Lady Mildmay's Journal: A Study in Autobiography and Meditation in Reformation England', *Sixteenth-Century Journal*, 20 (1989), 55–68; Maria Magro, 'Spiritual Autobiography and Radical Sectarian Women's Discourse: Anna Trapnel and the Bad Girls of the English Revolution', *Journal of Medieval and Early Modern Studies*, 34 (2004), 405–37.

[51] See further Chapter 8 by John McTague on 'Bites and Shams'.

[52] Donald F. Bond (ed.), *The Tatler*, 3 vols. (Oxford: Oxford University Press, 1967), 1: 219 (No. 29, 16 June 1709); 2: 68 (No. 91, 8 November 1709); 2: 385 (No. 158, 13 April 1710); 1: 251 (No. 34, 28 June 1709).

The serial updates of 'Bickerstaff' from the front line of his apartment grow out of a tradition of diary-writing, and these first-person, punctual reports of the recent past possess that sense of present-tense animation that can characterize that form. These *Tatler* entries are not diaries in a literal sense, but they are shaped by, and in part aspire to resemble, that genre. As Stuart Sherman has put it, they might be read as 'instalments in the cumulative self-portrait of a fictional narrator'.[53]

Daniel Defoe's *A Journal of the Plague Year* (1722) is a first-person, chronological, retrospective, semi-fictionalized account of one man's experience of the plague of 1665. The book was written as the 1722 plague in Marseille threatened to spread to London, and is in part an alarmed warning of what might happen next; but Defoe's overt subject is the London plague of fifty-seven years before, when Defoe was five years old. Generically, *A Journal* is complicated, or evasive, or playful, or some combination of all three: Defoe combines features of the diary and autobiography with statistical material drawn from weekly bills of mortality such as *London's Dreadful Visitation* (1665), alongside an inclusive desire to note down the most urgent features of 1665 that looks, now, like early journalism. The text flickers between historical fiction, memoir, audit, practical handbook ('I mention this Story also as the best Method I can advise any Person to take in such a Case'), and diary, and Defoe is acutely aware of these complexities.[54] (The book is published under the initials 'H. F.', and the account may have a relation with the journals of Defoe's uncle, Henry Foe.) The presence of the diary as a generic influence is particularly strong: thus the precise renderings of place and time; the many moments of enquiry into the purposes of a seemingly inscrutable God; and the narrator's tendency towards introspection ('I now began to consider seriously with my Self, concerning my own Case').[55] Such experiments in the production of what we might call the truth-effect were central to Defoe's literary ingenuity, as seen in *The Life and Strange Surprizing Adventures of Robinson Crusoe* (1719), *Memoirs of a Cavalier* (1720), and *The Fortunes and Misfortunes of the Famous Moll Flanders* (1722), all of which have baffled and provoked critics seeking a literary history organized around tidy generic classifications. In part this reflects Defoe's ongoing literary experiments with fact and fiction, but it also says something important about the diary as a form: its capacity to travel into other kinds of writing; its appeal to literary authors; and the urgent power it possesses for generating a sense of the real, the lived, the present—that great haunting aesthetic that Philip Lejeune identifies as the capacity to produce in readers 'the feeling of *touching time*'.[56]

---

[53] Stuart Sherman, 'Diary and Autobiography', in *The Cambridge History of English Literature*, ed. John Richetti (Cambridge: Cambridge University Press, 2005), 653–72 (653). Sherman notes the migration of the diary into parts of *The Tatler*.

[54] Daniel Defoe, *A Journal of the Plague Year*, ed. Paula R. Backscheider (New York and London: W.W. Norton, 1991), 13.

[55] Defoe, *Journal*, 11.

[56] Lejeune, *On Diary*, 209.

CHAPTER 13

DISSENTING WRITING

NICHOLAS SEAGER

The extent and variety of dissenting writing in late Stuart Britain attests to the vital role prose played in sustaining the culture of nonconformity during its persecution. Dissenters contributed pamphlets to political and religious controversies, debating questions of doctrine and ecclesiology, defending their abstention from the national church, and promoting their civil rights. They employed private manuscript forms including diaries, commonplace books, and correspondence to explore their personal faiths and identities and to strengthen familial, social, professional, and congregational ties. They published sermons, religious treatises, and biblical commentaries with hortatory and pastoral purposes. Dissenters wrote biographies and histories, and many chronicled their congregations' activities in manuscript Church Books. Because of Puritanism's focus on individual grace, dissenters excelled in autobiographical genres: pre-eminent examples include the Baptist John Bunyan's *Grace Abounding to the Chief of Sinners* (1666), the Quaker George Fox's *Journal* (1694), and the 'Presbyterian' Richard Baxter's *Reliquiae Baxterianae* (1696).[1] Dissenting prose extends to newspapers, travel writing, children's books, and fiction, where its greatest achievement in this period is Bunyan's *The Pilgrim's Progress* (1678–84). Dissenters produced cheap popular print as well as expensive multivolume works. Authors range from erudite ministers such as the Independent John Owen to people traditionally denied a voice, including working-class authors like Bunyan and women such as Agnes Beaumont and Anne Wentworth. Though richly heterogeneous, dissenting prose has several shared modes: patience and defiance; encouragement and exhortation.

This chapter is divided into four sections. The first addresses the legal and material conditions of dissenting authorship, particularly censorship and distribution. In adversarial circumstances, nonconformists emphasized the religious and political

---

For feedback on drafts, I thank Rachel Adcock, Ann Hughes, and Nicholas McDowell.

[1] Baxter never designated himself a Presbyterian but acknowledged that the term was applied to nonconformists like himself who favoured 'moderate Episcopacy' (*Reliquiae Baxterianae* (1696), pt. 2, 278).

efficacy of writing, and communication became a duty. The second section evaluates dissenters' responses to historical affairs, from proscription following the Restoration to a limited state of toleration after 1689. Reacting to their experiences, dissenters mounted powerful arguments for freedom of conscience, religious pluralism, and individual rights which helped shape modern conceptions of selfhood and liberalism. The third section examines literary features of dissenters' writing: their defences of 'graceful' prose style against the rational and moral norms promoted by conformists, and their experiments with genre that occasioned new modes of self-expression. The final section explores two prominent tropes of dissenting experience: pilgrimage and imprisonment. Nonconformists conceived of themselves as spiritual wayfarers journeying from this world to the next. They often found their progress arrested by incarceration; but many used that experience productively in order to affirm their faith and compose works that contributed to the flourishing literary culture of dissent.

CONDITIONS OF AUTHORSHIP

Writing as a dissenter was potentially hazardous but essential for the survival of nonconformity, embodying as well as articulating defiance in the face of persecution. It was facilitated by a burgeoning print culture which dissenters embraced. For the Independent Christopher Ness, 'The Art of Printing was bestow'd as a special Gift by a gracious God ... *Printing* is like a *Wing*, on which *knowledge flies* throughout all the *Habitable World*, and is at this day a *famous Instrument* of Gods holy Spirit, to publish his Sacred and *Infallible Truth*'. However, Ness continues, 'Satan do use it also to spread his *damnable Errors*', which necessitated controversy, not quiescence.[2] The godly felt called upon to write by the highest authority. 'Being Silenced, Writing is the far greatest part of my remaining Service to God for his Church, and without the Press my Writings would be in vain', wrote Baxter, one of many ministers banned from preaching who took to the pen.[3] Baxter did so because 'the Press hath a louder voice than mine' and '*Books* may be at hand' when pastors 'are persecuted and forbid to preach'.[4] Authorship, then, took on some of the authority and urgency of preaching when that activity was circumscribed by law.

Writing was a potent means of self-vindication for those traditionally denied a voice. For example, defending herself in print when excluded by her Baptist congregation, Anne Wentworth insisted that God instructed her to 'discover my Husbands cruelty', so she was 'commanded to write' despite incurring hostility. In Wentworth, the religious impulse to write despite prohibition, experienced by many

---

[2] Christopher Ness, *A Distinct Discourse and Discovery of the Person and Period of Antichrist* (1679), 94–5, 96.
[3] *Reliquiae Baxterianae*, pt. 3, 86.
[4] Richard Baxter, *True Christianity* (1655), sig. A4v; *A Christian Directory* (1673), 60.

dissenters, has a proto-feminist potential: 'Men will not suffer me to glorify God, though I am commanded of God so to do: but they persecute me for it.'[5] She asserts the greater authority of spiritual inspiration over wifely submission. However, doing God's work could be onerous as well as liberating, as the Quaker Thomas Ellwood acknowledged: 'Fain would I have been excused from this Service, which I judged too heavy for me: Wherefore I besought the Lord to take this Weight from off me ... But the Lord would not be entreated: but continued the Burden upon me, with greater weight; requiring *Obedience* from me, and promising to assist me therein. Whereupon I arose from my Bed, and in the Fear and Dread of the Lord, committed to Writing what He, in the Motion of his *Divine Spirit*, dictated to me to write.'[6] Hardship was inevitable, but duty demanded perseverance that would be aided by inspiration.

Conformists saw dissenting writing as incendiary, not inspired. Censorship was accordingly strict. The 1662 Licensing Act forbade the printing of anything 'contrary to ... the doctrine or discipline of the Church of England', and Roger L'Estrange, surveyor of the press, was resolved to suppress sectarian writing. Aligning the democratization of print with factiousness, L'Estrange complained that 'there have been *Printed*, and *Reprinted* since [the] *Restauration*, not so few as a *Hundred Schismatical Pamphlets*, against *Bishops*, *Ceremonies*, and *Common-Prayer*', three aspects of the Restored Church to which nonconformists objected. L'Estrange computed that 'since *the late Act for Uniformity* [1662] there have been Printed near *Thirty Thousand Copies of Farewel-Sermons* ... in Defiance of the *Law*'.[7] The spate of sermons delivered and then published upon the 'great ejection' of nonconforming ministers posed a challenge to the restoration of episcopal and monarchical authority, helping to consolidate the nonconformist movement.[8] Dissenting writing was often illegally published without a licence, utilizing anonymity and false imprints. Disguised styles were employed in licensed works: ambiguity and obliquity were invaluable tactics to circumvent censorship. Manuscript circulation persisted alongside the illicit printing and covert distribution networks that disseminated nonconformity through print.

The authorities could refuse licences, were permitted to expurgate texts, and could search premises suspected of printing seditious material as well as seize private papers and intercept letters. Though the Licensing Act lapsed in 1679 and pre-publication censorship was thereafter patchy until terminating in 1695, laws of seditious libel and blasphemy meant that printers and authors could still be imprisoned, fined, and pilloried, as happened to the Presbyterian Daniel Defoe for *The Shortest-Way with the Dissenters*

---

[5] Anne Wentworth, *Englands Spiritual Pill* (1679), 5; *A Vindication of Anne Wentworth* (1677), 7; *A True Account of Anne Wentworth* (1676), 9.

[6] *The History of the Life of Thomas Ellwood* (1714), 77–8. Ellwood recollects writing *An Alarm to the Priests* (1660).

[7] Roger L'Estrange, *Considerations and Proposals in Order to the Regulation of the Press* (1663), sig. A3v.

[8] See David J. Appleby, *Black Bartholomew's Day: Preaching, Polemic and Restoration Nonconformity* (Manchester: Manchester University Press, 2013).

(1702).[9] Amid the High Church resurgence following Queen Anne's succession, Defoe impersonated a genocidal Anglican cleric to insist that the Church's 'implacable Enemies' must be '*rooted out from the Face of this Land for ever*'.[10] Defoe angered not only Anglicans duped into agreement with a dissenter's pastiche of their views but also his coreligionists who feared repercussions would follow provocation. The government deemed the work seditious and ordered it be burned.

Such adverse publishing conditions indicate the determination of dissenting authors, printers, and booksellers to get works out. Echoing L'Estrange's view of a baleful proliferation of dissenting works, the nonjuror Charles Leslie complained as late as 1704 that 'it wou'd be the work of a *Society* of *Writers*, such as they have, to Answer every one of that *Multitude* of *Pamphlets*, which, now more than ever, come out Thick and Threefold upon us every Day, to *Propagate* their Abhorr'd *Principles* of *Schism* and *Rebellion*'.[11] Though Leslie exaggerates both the coherence and radicalism of nonconformity, the dissenters did enjoy a cultural presence and literary productivity that belied their modest numbers.[12] Their works extend the move away from writing belonging exclusively to an elite, which gained impetus during the 1640s and 1650s and could not be reversed after 1660. Their books comprise a vibrant literary tradition rather than one in decline or narrowly defensive.[13] Writing is crucial for an imperilled group that fears for its own extinction.

Persecution and Toleration

Dissent was borne of and shaped by historical circumstances, though many dissenters held beliefs that turned them away from politics as a merely worldly concern. The Presbyterian John Howe thought that Christians should mind 'the various alternations of Political Affairs' with 'unconcernedness' and instead cultivate inner quietude.[14] Historical experience made such stoicism, or even passive resistance, difficult in practice.[15] In the Declaration of Breda, before the Restoration, Charles II professed care for 'tender consciences', pledging that 'no man shall be disquieted or called in question

---

[9] See Chapter 8 by John McTague on 'Bites and Shams' and Chapter 11 on 'Criminal Literature' by Pat Rogers.

[10] [Daniel Defoe], *The Shortest-Way with the Dissenters* (1702), 15, 29.

[11] Charles Leslie, *The Wolf Stript of his Shepherd's Clothing* (1704), 3.

[12] Dissenters comprised about 4 per cent of the population in the 1660s and about 6 per cent by the 1710s: Michael Watts, *The Dissenters: From the Reformation to the French Revolution* (Oxford: Clarendon Press, 1978), 269–70.

[13] On the rich tradition of dissenting literature, see N. H. Keeble, *The Literary Culture of Nonconformity in Later Seventeenth-Century England* (Leicester: Leicester University Press, 1987).

[14] John Howe, *The Vanity of this Mortal Life* (1672), 109.

[15] On nonconformist radicalism, see Richard L. Greaves, *Deliver Us from Evil: The Radical Underground in Britain, 1660–1663* (Oxford: Oxford University Press, 1986) and *Enemies Under His Feet: Radicals and Nonconformists in Britain, 1664–1677* (Stanford, CA: Stanford University Press, 1990).

for differences of opinion in matters of religion which do not disturb the peace of the kingdom'. However, Charles proved unable to prevent the reestablishment of strict church polity and the penal legislation against dissent that passed from 1661 to 1665: the 'Clarendon Code', including the Corporation Act that required municipal office holders to take Anglican communion and the Conventicle Act that forbade unofficial religious gatherings. Nonconformists' worship was punished by fines and imprisonment, their civic participation was restricted, and they were victims of casual as well as official opprobrium and violence. Persecution varied by geography, chronology, and denomination, but nonconformists were lumped together and their worship proscribed.

The several sects that were thus legally united had conflicting agendas. Presbyterians were reluctant nonconformists who supported an inclusive national church; their failure to attain comprehension enlarged and moderated the dissenting movement. Independents (or Congregationalists) were not far removed in doctrine from Presbyterians but believed in the autonomy of each church without direction from a higher human authority. Baptists were more radical separatists who also favoured a congregational basis of church membership. Congregationalists and Baptists generally hoped for toleration, not comprehension.[16] Quakers' beliefs about the individual's inward, direct experience of God put them beyond the pale as much for other nonconformists as for Anglicans; for them persecution was continued, not initiated, in the 1660s.[17] The main barriers to conformity for those dissenters who desired it were the requirement for episcopal (re)ordination of ministers, the obligation to accept the Book of Common Prayer and renounce the Solemn League and Covenant, and adherence to the Anglican liturgy. For dissenters, the Restoration was a betrayal of promises, as lawful worship was defined even more narrowly than by Laud before the Civil Wars. As one said, 'Present Conformity is foreign and quite of another nature from conformity heretofore; Conscience being now much more forced and violated by them in the Chair'.[18]

Many dissenters set about challenging the magistracy's right to legislate in matters of worship; and those who accepted the magistracy's authority in this area demanded different legislation. The Quaker Edmund Burrough argued, 'If any man shall assume to *prescribe God a way* how he must be *Worshipped*, and shall *limit his Spirit* from this, or to the other *way of Religion*, and think *to be Lord in mens Consciences* in *religious Matters*, such are but *Usurpers*'.[19] Dissenters developed potent arguments for religious freedom and individual rights, denying the government's authority 'to command any

---

[16] On Baptist writing, see A. C. Underwood, *A History of the English Baptists* (London: Baptist Union, 1947); Rachel Adcock, *Baptist Women's Writing in Revolutionary Culture, 1640–1680* (Aldershot: Ashgate, 2016).

[17] On Quaker writing, see Thomas N. Corns and David Loewenstein (eds.), *The Emergence of Quaker Writing: Dissenting Literature in Seventeenth-Century England* (London: Cass, 1996); Kate Peters, *Print Culture and the Early Quakers* (Cambridge: Cambridge University Press, 2005); Catie Gill, *Women in the Seventeenth-Century Quaker Community* (Aldershot: Ashgate, 2005).

[18] A. B., *A Letter from a Minister to a Person of Quality, shewing some Reason for his Non-conformity* (1679), 2.

[19] Edmund Burrough, *A Visitation of Love unto the King* (1660), 14.

Person to do what God forbids, or to forbid what God commands, in matters Civil, Spiritual, or Ecclesiastical'.[20] They deemed the imposition of uniformity presumptuous. The Presbyterian Thomas Manton bewailed 'that the Traditions of Men should be made equal in dignity and authority with the express Revelation of God'.[21] God created diversity, not uniformity, and gave humans the faculty of conscience, which must be exercised. Uniformity was moreover unfeasible. Ralph Wallis wrote that, 'If there was an Act of Parliament, that all men should have faces one like another, and propose one man for a Pattern, it would be as easily brought to pass, as to compel all men to be of one Judgment; for he that hath a hand in forming the face, hath a hand in forming the Judgment'.[22]

Pluralism and individualism were invoked to counter arguments for uniformity. The Quaker Francis Howgill complained that conformists 'would have all Shoos made by their Last, though they will not fit every mans feet. Faith is the gift of God, there are divers degrees and measures according to the mind and good pleasure of the giver'.[23] Whereas conformists held to the view that religious uniformity was vital to national unity, for dissenters diversity of opinion was a sign of intellectual and religious vitality. According to the Independent Charles Wolsley, 'As Knowledge encreaseth, it expatiates it self into variety of Thoughts and Principles; and as it enlargeth all other Sciences, so [it does] Religion'.[24] Coercion is a violation of God's will because it disregards the diversity in the creation and stifles the individual's responsibility to God for their own spiritual wellbeing. 'Without all Exception', proclaimed Burrough, 'every man [should] be permitted in the free exercise of Conscience, without any kind of Force put upon him ... to follow that Religion, and to live in such Faith, and perform such Worship to God, as he does trust his own Soul withal, and give account thereof before God in the day of dreadful judgment.'[25] John Corbet countered arguments that religious uniformity buttressed political order by suggesting *au contraire* that blind acceptance of prescribed faith could produce civil unrest: 'A people nuzzled in ignorance and superstition [those who accept uniformity] are more easily seduced from their obedience to Magistrates, and carried headlong by those that have dominion over their Consciences. But Understanding and Knowledge [characteristics of dissenters] makes men considerate, and more easily manageable by a just and prudent Government.'[26] Even more pragmatically, the godly contended that toleration was in the national interest, as unity was good for trade.[27]

On the whole, persecution bolstered rather than weakened dissenters' convictions. As the Quaker William Penn put it, 'If we had wanted a *Proof* of the Truth of our *Inward Belief* and *Judgment*, the very Practice of them that *opposed* it, would have abundantly confirm'd

---

[20] *The Saints Freedom from Tyranny Vindicated* (1667), 40.
[21] Thomas Manton, *XVIII Sermons on the Second Chapter of the 2d Epistle to the Thessalonians* (1679), 344.
[22] Ralph Wallis, *More News from Rome* (1666), 9.
[23] Francis Howgill, *The True Rule, Judge, and Guide of the True Church of God Discovered* (1665), 9.
[24] Charles Wolsley, *Liberty of Conscience, The Magistrates Interest* (1668), 8.
[25] Burrough in William Caton, *The Testimony of a Cloud of Witnesses* (1662), sig. B1v.
[26] John Corbet, *A Discourse of the Religion of England* (1667), 20.
[27] See e.g., Slingsby Bethel, *The Present Interest of England Stated* (1671), 13.

us'.[28] For Bunyan, 'Persecution of the godly was, of God, never intended for their destruction, but for their *Glory*, and to make them shine the more when they are beyond this valley of the shadow of death'.[29] John Owen pointed out that historically persecution was used 'to drive Truth, and the purity of the Gospel, out of the World, and to force all men to center in a Profession and Worship, framed to the Interest of some few men, who made no small advantage of it'.[30] The Bible provided prototypes of God's people being oppressed: '*Many and great in all Ages unto this day have been the* Afflictions, Tryals, *and* Oppressions *of the* Righteous, *as have been foretold by the holy Prophets, Christ and his Apostles since the world began*', wrote the Quaker John Crooke.[31] As well as scripture, emergent conceptions of English national identity, increasingly framed in terms of constitutional liberty, provided a basis for protest. Of the Second Conventicle Act (1670), Howe complained:

> Our *Magna Charta* was torn in Pieces; the worst and most infamous of Mankind, at our own Expence, hired to accuse us; multitudes of Perjuries committed; Conviction made without a Jury, and without any Hearing of the Persons accused; Penalties inflicted; Goods rifled; Estates seiz'd and imbezel'd; Houses broken up; Families disturb'd, often at most unseasonable Hours of the Night, without any Cause, or Shadow of a Cause, if only a malicious Villain could pretend to suspect a Meeting there.[32]

Dissenters provided numerous countercultural narratives that made their suffering their glory, but they also appropriated mainstream understandings of the liberties of person and property, what Penn styled the 'undoubted Birthright of English Freedoms'.[33]

In the 1670s and 1680s, dissent was a pawn in the Crown's tussles with Parliament.[34] Charles II's 1672 Declaration of Indulgence, suspending the penal laws, promised alleviation from persecution but on questionable terms. 'Some think by accepting of y^m wee give ye King a power above the lawes', wrote Philip Henry; 'others think twill end in ... a Massacre, it being now known where such people [dissenters] may bee met with, as if they all had but one neck'.[35] A decade of persecution explains Henry's far-fetched fear that indulgence was a ruse to enable extermination, but he more accurately feared that Charles was exercising the royal prerogative to promote Catholics' rights. The Presbyterian MP William Love advocated resisting indulgence on terms that endorsed

---

[28] William Penn, *No Cross, No Crown* (1682), 155.

[29] John Bunyan, *Seasonable Counsel* (1684), 211.

[30] John Owen, *A Peace-Offering in an Apology and Humble Plea for Indulgence and Liberty of Conscience* (1667), 27–8.

[31] John Crooke, *The Cry of the Innocent for Justice* (1662), 3.

[32] John Howe, *The Case of the Protestant Dissenters, Presented and Argued* (1689), 2.

[33] William Penn, *The Great Case of Liberty of Conscience Once More Briefly Debated and Defended* (1670), 4.

[34] See e.g., Douglas R. Lacey, *Dissent and Parliamentary Politics in England, 1661–1689* (New Brunswick: Rutgers University Press, 1969); Jacqueline Rose, *Godly Kingship in Restoration England: The Politics of the Royal Supremacy, 1660–1688* (Cambridge: Cambridge University Press, 2011), 163–202.

[35] *Diaries and Letters of Philip Henry*, ed. Matthew Henry Lee (1882), 253.

the king's 'dispensing power': 'I had much rather see the Dissenters suffer by the Rigour of the Law, tho' I suffer with them, than see all the Laws in *England* Trampled under Foot of the Prerogative ... and, I hope, the *Dissenters* understand [the] Liberty of *English Men*, better than to accept of it in an Illegal manner.'[36]

The Indulgence exposed divisions within as well as between Presbyterianism and Congregationalism. Many thought that dissenters had more to gain than to lose: 'Supposing we refuse Licenses [to preach]', one asked, 'will that secure our Civil Rights? Nothing less! The Law hath taken them all from us. Fines, Imprisonments, Seizures, Banishment, Outlawry, yea Death it self is our hire by Law. Indulgence defendeth us from these Laws, and thereby continueth our National Priviledges, so far is it from taking them away.'[37] This passage combines civic and theological understandings of 'the Law', indicating dissenters' propensity to view temporal experience in spiritual terms. The Indulgence further consolidated the nonconformist movement, suggesting that toleration without, rather than comprehension within, the Church was its best hope. However, a year later, in 1673, the Indulgence was withdrawn and the Test Act passed. This Act required holders of public office to take Anglican communion; parliament was targeting Catholics but the Act further disenfranchised dissenters as well. Increasingly a coherent political interest, the dissenters allied with the Whigs in support of the unsuccessful effort, from 1679 to 1681, to have the Catholic James, Duke of York excluded from the royal succession, a move that led to renewed persecution of dissent until James, now king, issued two new Declarations of Indulgence in 1687 and 1688. James had hoped to unite dissenters and Catholics, but he succeeded only in uniting dissenters with the Anglicans who had formerly supported his right to the throne. Thus he secured his own downfall. The dissenters' reward for supporting the Glorious Revolution was the 1689 Toleration Act. 'It comes to us as the Fruit of the Prayers and Tears, the Sufferings and Hardships, the Conflicts and Vows of our Fathers before us', said Edmund Calamy III.[38] Dissenters insisted that toleration was achieved through their steadfastness, not merely bestowed by lenient lawmakers.

Though the Toleration Act left penal legislation intact and put paid to the hopes for comprehension, it secured freedom of worship for all Protestants.[39] It therefore jettisoned the idea of national religious unity in favour of state-guaranteed pluralism, albeit with severe limitations (Catholics and non-trinitarians were excluded). Historians still debate just how revolutionary the Toleration Act was.[40] Something of that debate is anticipated in Defoe's objections to the High Church party's efforts to downplay the Act's

---

[36] In *Defoe's Review* (1704–13), ed. John McVeagh, 9 vols. (London: Pickering and Chatto, 2004–11), 2: 263.

[37] *Vindiciæ Liberatatis Evangelii: or, A Justification of our Present Indulgence, and the Acceptance of Licences* (1672), 25.

[38] Edmund Calamy, *A Continuation of the Account of the Ministers ... Ejected and Silenced after the Restoration*, 2 vols. (1727), 2, p. xxxviii.

[39] The Revolution settlement also established the Presbyterian Church of Scotland, making Episcopalians 'dissenters' there, a reversal of the situation in England.

[40] Ole Peter Grell et al. (eds.), *From Persecution to Toleration: The Glorious Revolution and Religion in England* (Oxford: Oxford University Press, 1991).

significance; they 'reduc[e] the Toleration to such a Pitch, that they would no more have it allow'd to be a Toleration, but an Exemption from the Penalty of certain Laws', Defoe complained.[41] Toleration certainly imbued early eighteenth-century dissenters with greater confidence, and they even turned the accusation of schism back on unbending Anglicans. The Presbyterian George Trosse said that 'the *Imposers* of any disputable Doctrines, or Rites and Ceremonies, as *necessary Conditions of Communion … These, These* are the great Dividers of the Church, and disturbers of her Peace'.[42] James Owen stated that 'the *Schism* lies at the Door of those who contriv'd the *Act of Uniformity*.'[43]

Upon her coronation, Queen Anne promised to uphold the toleration but also specified that the national interest and that of the Church were one and the same, contributing to a climate of renewed anxiety, enflamed by attacks from Anglicans and dissenters alike on occasional conformity—the practice of nonconformists taking Anglican communion in order to qualify for civil office. Defoe in particular felt that if people could conform occasionally for the sake of gaining places, they should conform permanently for the sake of unity: 'If a Man dissent from the Church, let him do so, and his Principle being well-grounded for such Dissent, let him hold it; if not well-grounded, let him leave it.'[44] For Defoe and others, dissent seemed to have slipped from being a principled religious collective to a dependent arm of a political party, the Whigs. In a series of publications during Anne's reign, Defoe endeavoured 'to Represent to the Dissenters the ground they have lost and the Injury they have done Themselves by joyning into Parties and Meddling with Politicks'.[45] Hopes for the repeal of the Test Act and Corporation Act under William III seemed distant when further anti-dissent legislation passed in the last years of Anne's reign, including the 1711 Act against occasional conformists taking offices and the 1714 Schism Act, which outlawed dissenting schools (it was never enforced). The Whig ascendency following the Hanoverian succession in 1714 ushered in a new age of dissent, securing the freedoms attained in 1689.

Style, Spirituality, and Self-Fashioning

We have seen that dissenting writing was viewed by the mainstream with mistrust. Conformists associated it with democratic proliferation, an eructation of erroneous, seditious, and self-regarding views. Pre-Civil War arguments about Puritans' preference

---

[41] Daniel Defoe, *An Essay on the History of the Parties, and Persecution in Britain* (1712), 20.
[42] George Trosse, *A Discourse of Schism* (1701), 12–13. On the accusation of schism against dissenters, see Chapter 18 on 'Heresiography and Religious Controversy' by Nicholas McDowell.
[43] John Owen, *Moderation still a Virtue* (1703), 17.
[44] Daniel Defoe, *The Opinion of a Known Dissenter on the Bill for Preventing Occasional Conformity* (1702), 1.
[45] *Letters of Daniel Defoe*, ed. G.H. Healey (Oxford: Clarendon Press, 1955), 374.

for a 'plain style' in prose and preaching versus Anglican ornateness were reversed in the Restoration, as Anglicans set themselves up as the guardians of lucidity against the verbal excesses of nonconformity.[46] This disagreement about style concerned what constitutes 'sense' and 'senselessness', the authentic and the affected. For conformists, plainness in religious discourse meant a clear exposition of moral duties, but for dissenters it meant a sincere articulation of the experience of grace, which was often ineffable in prosaic terms. Conformist writing sought the moral concurrence of its readers but nonconformist writing often aimed to move them emotionally. Its affective intensity embarrassed the increasingly rational Anglican Church. An older critical understanding of dissenting literature as pathologically introspective and individualistic, focused on the tortuous anxieties attendant on Calvinist predestination, has been tempered by recent scholarly attention to 'godly' or 'graceful' reading, which emphasizes the role of writing and reading in producing supportive communities of believers and engendering salvific hope.[47] Back in the late seventeenth century, whether pigeonholed as gloomy or 'enthusiastic', dissenting writing was consistently denounced by conformists.

Anglican attacks on nonconformist writing levelled charges of affectation and obscurity, alleging that dissenters simultaneously made truth opaque and error plausible. Anthony à Wood claimed that, in his *Discourse of Communion with God* (1657), John Owen 'doth strangely affect in ambiguous and uncouth words, canting, mystical and unintelligible phrases to obscure sometimes the plainest and most obvious truths: And at other times he endeavours by such a mist and cloud of senseless terms to draw a kind of vail over the most erroneous doctrines'.[48] The charge of uncouthness indicates a snobbish social attitude that accompanies the distaste for theological obscurity. Samuel Parker labelled dissenters 'the rudest and most barbarous People in the World', accusing them of 'hiding themselves in a maze of Words ... rowling up and down in canting and ambiguous Expressions' and 'affected Phrases'.[49] L'Estrange astutely recognized that a shared, codified language forged a collective identity, complaining of '*a Privy* Cypher *of* Intelligence *betwixt Themselves, and the* Cant, *or* Jargon *of the* Party'. He recognized that language did not just reflect differences of outlook but constituted and consolidated them, especially in conditions of censorship: '*They fly from us in their* Speech, *their* Manners, *their* Meaning, *as well as in their* Profession ... *and they make it a point of* Honour *to maintain the Freedome of their* Own Tongue, *in token, that they are not yet a* Conquer'd Nation.'[50] The Episcopalian Robert South pointed to 'a Set of fantastical

---

[46] Roger Pooley, 'Language and Loyalty: Plain Style at the Restoration', *Literature and History*, 6 (1980), 2-18 (4).

[47] Compare John Stachniewski, *The Persecutory Imagination: English Puritanism and the Literature of Religious Despair* (Oxford: Clarendon Press, 1991) with Michael Davies, *Graceful Reading: Theology and Narrative in the Works of John Bunyan* (Oxford: Oxford University Press, 2002) and Andrews Cambers, *Godly Reading: Print, Manuscript and Puritanism in England, 1580–1720* (Cambridge: Cambridge University Press, 2011).

[48] Anthony à Wood, *Athenae Oxonienses*, 2 vols. (1691-2), ed. Philip Bliss, 3rd edn, 4 vols. (1813-20), 4: 105.

[49] Samuel Parker, *A Discourse of Ecclesiastical Politie* (1670), pp. xiii, xvii–xviii.

[50] Roger L'Estrange, *The Casuist Uncas'd* (2nd edn, 1680), sig. A2r.

new-coin'd Phrases, such as *Laying hold on Christ, getting into Christ*, and *rolling themselves upon Christ*, and the like; by which if they mean any Thing else but obeying the precepts of Christ, and a rational Hope of Salvation thereupon, (which, it is certain, that generally they do not mean) it is all but a *Jargon* of empty, senseless Metaphors.'[51] As South acknowledges, dissenters did *not* mean obedience to precepts: for them, salvation was by the free gift of grace, not compliance with edicts. 'Herein lies the most material difference between the sober Christians of the Church of *England*, and our modern Sectaries,' Parker explained, 'That we express the Precepts and Duties of the Gospel in plain and intelligible Terms, whilst they trifle them away by childish Metaphors and Allegories, and will not talk of Religions but in barbarous and uncouth Similitudes.'[52] To Anglicans in the prevailing rationalist and latitudinarian mould, duties were concomitantly logical and ethical. By contrast, the language of grace defied standards of rational verifiability.

If the analogical mode of nonconformist writing—its metaphors, allegories, similitudes, and biblical allusions—seemed childish, vulgar, or zany to many Anglicans, for dissenters it was appropriate to the state of grace and suited to defiance of persecution. Facing down her detractors (Baptists rather than Anglicans), Anne Wentworth had recourse to a rich vein of metaphors that proliferate in her prose, replicating the smothering of anger and vanity by revelatory truth that she describes:

> [God] will raise truth up more bright to break their Head [Psalm 68:21], they have kicked against the Pricks, and burthened themselves with a burthensome Stone [Zechariah 12:3], they would not bare truth at first, but tread so hard upon it, and truth as a bed of Cammamile grows so strong to overcome them all at last, for what is so strong as truth, dying men are not, for they are rotten reeds, and shall wither as the grass, and be soon cut of, but truth liveth and abideth for ever [Isaiah 40:6–8]; now they have tryed all their strength and done all they can, they are lighter than Vanity [Psalm 62:9], and will appear as they are, but dying, angry Men.[53]

The passage communicates a frantic mental state. Its alliteration, rhyme, and consonance ('bright to break'; 'kicked against the Pricks'; 'rotten reeds'; 'tread so hard') give it an idiosyncratic verve and gusto. The possible pun on bearing or baring truth would point both to her detractors' discomfort with exposure and her own capacity, unlike them, to withstand hardship. The biblical allusions are associative, suggestive, and accretive, which is typical of dissenters' abilities to draw on scripture for a rich fund of analogues.

In *Grace Abounding*, Bunyan reached for an emblematic style that he presents simultaneously as 'plain and simple' and as a religious test for the reader: 'I have sent you here enclosed a drop of that honey, that I have taken out of the Carcase of a Lyon (Judg. 14:5–8). I have eaten thereof my self also, and am much refreshed thereby ... The Philistians

---

[51] Robert South, *Twelve Sermons*, 6th edn, 5 vols. (1727), 3: 165. The first volume originally appeared in 1692.
[52] Parker, *Discourse of Ecclesiastical Politie*, 75.
[53] Wentworth, *True Account*, 4. Biblical references added.

understand me not.'⁵⁴ The style promoted here is sufficiently lucid to be accessible by the meanest reader, but the 'Language of *Canaan*' (which leads Faithful and Christian to be labelled 'Bedlams and Mad' at Vanity Fair) sorts the righteous from the ungodly.⁵⁵ Decorous language, for its own sake, would be unsuitable:

> I could also have stept into a stile much higher than this in which I have here discoursed, and could have adorned all things more than here I have seemed to do: but I dare not: *God* did not play in convincing of me; the *Devil* did not play in tempting of me; neither did I play when I sunk as into a bottomless pit, when *the pangs of hell caught hold upon me*: wherefore I may not play in my relating of them, but be plain and simple, and lay down the thing as it was: He that liketh it, let him receive it; and he that does not, let him produce a better.⁵⁶

The equation of a 'higher' style with irresponsible playing and the desire for plainness suggest an attempt to attenuate the dangers of misprision inherent to writing. The emblematic mode that would render experience as metaphor, this world as a shadow of that to come, co-exists with the psychological extremis ('pangs of hell') and empiricism ('the thing as it was') that increasingly came to characterize literary realism as practised in the novels of later nonconformists like Defoe and Samuel Richardson.

Dissenters' views of language were conflicted. On the one hand, style might be a reliable gauge of sincerity, but on the other it could be mere outward profession of faith, quite distinct from true gracefulness, as with Talkative in *The Pilgrim's Progress*. The Quaker George Keith was among those dissenters alert to the inadequacy of words to articulate the experience of grace or indeed to help believers attain that condition: 'How insufficient words, (even the best of words, Scripture words, though there were as many books of Scripture as the whole world could contain) are to reveal or to give the knowledge of God unto man, many, yea the most of things natural, and created cannot be understood of or by words, words being but figures, emblems, signs and representations of things, come always short of the things themselves.'⁵⁷ This insufficiency was acutely felt by Quakers, given their emphasis on the inner light rather than textual authority.

This difficulty in interpreting words was troubling because a major preoccupation of nonconformist writing was to ascertain one's spiritual condition. The Quaker John Swintoun stated the matter with urgency: 'The sum, the main end of all to be minded, is, What spirit thou art born off, led by, possessed with, joyned to: for who are born of the Spirit, are led by the Spirit; and who are joyned to the Lord, are one Spirit. So all know what spirit you are of; for this is the tryal of this day, to try what spirit any are of: and this shall abundantly be manifested before this day be over ... and it is he or they,

---

[54] John Bunyan, *Grace Abounding to the Chief of Sinners*, ed. John Stachniewski (Oxford: Oxford University Press, 1998), 3. All references are to this edition.

[55] John Bunyan, *The Pilgrim's Progress*, ed. James Blanton Wharey and Roger Sharrock (Oxford: Oxford University Press, 1960), 90–1. All references are to this edition.

[56] Bunyan, *Grace Abounding*, 5.

[57] George Keith, *Immediate Revelation* (1668), 38.

who endures to the end, receive the Crown.'[58] The repetition conveys the anxiety that lay behind the most pressing question to which diarists and spiritual autobiographers sought answers: whether they would receive spiritual regeneration, which John Owen defined as 'the infusion of a *new real Spiritual* Principle into the Soul and its Faculties, of Spiritual Life, Light, Holiness, and Righteousness, disposed unto, and suited for the Destruction or Expulsion of a contrary inbred habitual Principle of sin and enmity against God, enabling unto all Acts of Holy Obedience'.[59] For those writing in the Calvinist tradition, grace is freely given by God, but the believer is obliged to enhance her or his preparedness to receive it. What Elianor Stockton called 'the worke of self examination' became a crucial component of this process.[60] Spiritual (auto)biographies or conversion narratives proliferated because recounting one's religious experience would help to situate the self in God's larger plan.

The Presbyterian James Janeway's description of his brother John's spiritual diary gives a thorough 'account' of the many motivations for his diurnal writing, employing the metaphor of commercial book-keeping common among dissenters:

> He kept a *Diary*, in which he did write down every evening what the frame of his spirit had been all the day long, especially in every duty. He took notice what incomes and profit he received; in his spiritual traffique; what returns from that far-country; what answers of prayer, what deadness and flatness, and what observable providences did present themselves, and the substance of what he had been doing; and any wandrings of thoughts, inordinancy in any passion; which, though the world could not discern he could. It cannot be conceived which do not practise the same, to what a good account did this return! This, made him to retain a grateful remembrance of mercy, and to live in a constant admiring and adoring of divine goodness; this, brought him to a very intimate acquaintance with his own heart; this, kept his spirit low and fitted him for freer communications from God; this, made him more lively and active; this, helped him to walk humbly with God, this made him speak more affectionately and experimentally to others of the things of God: and, in a word, this left a sweet calm upon his spirits, because he every night made even his accounts; and if his sheets should prove his winding-sheet, it had all been one: for, he could say his work was done; so that death could not surprise him.[61]

Self-knowledge and composure befitting spiritual receptivity, alertness to God's providential communications and to one's own failings, the understanding of grace that enables evangelism: these are the benefits of diary-keeping that Janeway recalls.[62]

---

[58] John Swintoun, *Some Late Epistles to the Body* ([Scotland?], 1663), 3.
[59] John Owen, Πνευματολογια: *or, A Discourse Concerning the Holy Spirit* (1674), 182.
[60] 'Occasional Reflections of Mrs Stockton', Dr Williams's Library, MS 24.8, fol. 12r.
[61] *Invisibles, Realities, Demonstrated in the Holy Life and Triumphant Death of Mr. John Janeway* (1673), 58–9. See also, e.g., the Independent Bartholomew Ashwood's *The Heavenly Trade, or, The Best Merchandizing* (1678) and the Presbyterian George Swinnock's *The Christian Man's Calling: or, A Treatise of Making Religion Ones Business*, 3 vols. (1662–5).
[62] See further Chapter 12 on 'Diaries' by Adam Smyth.

Uncertainty and anguish were invariable companions of dissenting faith: the ideal of the sanctified life and onus to interrogate oneself placed incredible strain, and nonconformist works comprise a rich record of emotional and bodily suffering. Wentworth, probably a victim of marital violence and ostracized by her community, saw her suffering metamorphosed into glory: God is pleased 'to turn all the fierce wrath of man, which has been against me, into his own praise: And to change all the evil mine Enemies have thought and done against me, into a sweet designe for good; making all my *unspeakable sufferings* from man, my *wonderful supports* and *deliverances from God*, a *figure* of his *intended dispensations* towards his *Enemies*, and *people* in this Nation'.[63] Affliction was paradoxically evidence of divine solicitude, extending here from the individual to the country at large.[64] The Independent Thomas Goodwin turned to a numismatic figure to advise readers: 'That your graces are so highly valued by God, is the reason, why he tryes them; he would not be at the pains and cost of it, else. And *they being tryed*, and holding to be right, and true gold indeed, they have thereupon his *approbation* upon that tryal; and he sets his *Royal Tower Stamp*, and mark upon them.'[65]

Afflictions were instructive trials, conferring greater self-understanding, and it seems that recording experiences in writing or orally helped elicit these insights. The Independent Mary Franklin wrote: 'I looked upon it as an honour that the Lord should count me worthy to suffer anything for his sake ... and that I should have the honour to be one of those that should help to fill up the measure of Christ's sufferings [Colossians 1:24].'[66] 'He that will live Godly in Christ Jesus', wrote the Quaker Sarah Chevers, 'must suffer Persecution; it is an evident token [of grace].'[67] And in similar vein Thomas Manton counselled that 'God's tempting is not to inform himself, but to discover his Creatures to themselves and others ... that what is known to him, and yet unknown to our selves, that that which lodgeth and lyeth hid in our Heart, may be discovered to us'.[68] 'In *tryals* we discern the *sincerity* of grace, and the *weakness* and *liveliness* of it; and so are less strangers to our own hearts,' Manton insisted.[69] The lions before Palace Beautiful in *The Pilgrim's Progress* alarm Christian until Watchful hollers reassurance: 'Fear not the Lions, for they are Chained; and are placed there for a trial of faith where it is; and for discovery of those that have none: keep in the midst of the Path, and no hurt shall come unto thee.'[70] Personal affliction and political persecution

---

[63] *Vindication*, 1–2. See further Katharine Gillespie, *Domesticity and Dissent in the Seventeenth Century: English Women's Writing and the Public Sphere* (Cambridge: Cambridge University Press, 2004), 202–3.

[64] Compare *The Narrative of the Persecutions of Agnes Beaumont* (1674).

[65] *Patience and its Perfect Work, Under Sudden and Sore Tryals* (1666), 14.

[66] 'The Experience of Mary Franklin', *Transactions of the Congregational Historical Society*, 2 (1905–6), 387–401 (397).

[67] *This is a Short Relation of some of the Cruel Sufferings (for Truth's Sake) of Katherine Evans and Sarah Cheevers* (1662), 87.

[68] Thomas Manton, *A Practical Exposition of the Lord's-Prayer* (1684), 413.

[69] Thomas Manton, *A Practical Commentary ... on the Epistle of James* (1653), 20.

[70] Bunyan, *Pilgrim's Progress*, 45–6.

are turned to the beneficial end of self-understanding and assurance of God's watchfulness, which will ideally produce the tranquillity conducive to grace. Accordingly, Howe insisted, 'this present state is only intended for trial to the spirits of men, in order to their attainment of a better state in a better world'.[71] Such arguments informed academic theodicy as well as ordinary people's life-writing. But Howe had no truck with Anglican arguments that penal laws were for the dissenters' own good, sarcastically answering Bishop Thomas Barlow's claim that persecution was a form of charity designed to save dissenting souls: 'We must, it seems, understand all this Rigour your Lordship shews, to proceed from Love, and that you are for destroying the Dissenters, only to mend their Understandings'.[72]

Writing was vital for self-fashioning and self-enquiry, but dissenters also advocated (in the words of the Presbyterian Thomas Gouge) 'communicating your experiences, your comforts and supports one to another, exhorting one another, and provoking one another to love and to good works'.[73] Unlike impersonal episcopal gatherings, dissenting congregations, in Stephen Lobb's words, help 'each other towards heaven, by provoking each other to Love and to Good works'.[74] Dissenters saw writing as a means to enjoin and encourage others through exemplary narratives. For sure, the primary purpose of narrating a life was to ascertain one's own spiritual wellbeing, but the educational function is crucial too. In writing, said Oliver Heywood, 'tis my desire to search & see what obedience & grounds of hope I haue to beleeve & be persuaded that my soul is built upon the rock of ages, that I am within the bond of the covenant, and sealed up to the day of redemption, w[hi]ch I doe to this end that I may give diligence to make my calling, and election sure, not in itselfe, but to my selfe'.[75] He acknowledges that his explorations cannot affect the eschatological outcome, but it is his duty to seek confirmation of election; and it may also provide solace for others, for although every believer's experience is unique there are shared patterns. Ordinary lives could be every bit as instructive as eventful ones: Matthew Henry said that the life of his father Philip '*is more adapted to general use*' because conducted in a '*low and narrow Sphere*' and especially because it '*consist*[s] *not in the* Extasies *and* Raptures *of Zeal and Devotion, which are looked upon rather as* admirable *than* imitable: *But in the long series of an even, regular, prudent, and well order'd Conversation, which he had in the World, and in the ordinary business of it*'.[76] Baxter described the didactic value of memorializing lives: 'The true History of exemplary Lives, is a pleasant and profitable recreation to young persons; and may secretly work them to a liking of Godliness and value of good men, which is the beginning of saving Grace'.[77]

---

[71] John Howe, *The Blessednesse of the Righteous Opened* (1673), 4.
[72] Edmund Calamy III, *Memoirs of the Life of the Late Revd. Mr. John Howe* (1724), 111.
[73] Thomas Gouge, *The Young Man's Guide* (1670), in *Works* (1815), 358.
[74] Stephen Lobb, *The True Dissenter* (1685), 85–6.
[75] Oliver Heywood, *His Autobiography, Diaries, Anecdote, and Event Book*, 4 vols. (1881–5), 1: 134.
[76] *An Account of the Life and Death of Mr. Philip Henry* (1698), sig. A5v.
[77] Richard Baxter, 'To the Reader', in Samuel Clarke, *Lives of Sundry Eminent Persons* (1683), sig. A3v.

Pastoral writing and practical divinity, modes that sought to comfort and direct other Christians, were as important as self-scrutinizing genres. Unsurprisingly, the ministerial office occasioned additional doubts, one of the important differences between clerical and lay strands in dissenting writing. Heywood was one of those who fretted over the duty of counselling others: 'I find christians of different tempers, some apt to run into one extreme others into another. I find it very hard to suit every condition, so as to giue every one their grain of allowance and yet indulge them in no sin, to curb their frowardnes so as not to nip the buddings of grace, and prevent the sproutings of what is good in their harts and liues.'[78] In this passage, the pastor is a gardener who tends plants with care. Richard Alleine defined ministers as 'good Stewards' but kept the emphasis on believers' need to 'apply the Word of God aright'; he particularly worried that the 'distressed' grasped at every 'affrighting word in a whole Sermon'.[79] Pastoral writing was thus a fine balance between providing reassurance and ensuring vigilance; two tropes that helped writers to strike this balance were imprisonment and pilgrimage.

Prisoners and Pilgrims

As well as focusing on the present as a means of understanding the future, dissenters in this period looked for instruction to the recent past. Commemoration was vital to dissenting identity. In addition to histories and biographies, gravestone epitaphs memorialized worthy lives. The Baptist Vavasor Powell's epitaph at Bunhill Fields Burial Ground called him 'a successful Teacher of the past, A sincere Witness of the present, and an useful Example to the future Age', and recounted his hardships: 'Being called to several Prisons, he was there tried, and would not accept Deliverance, expecting a better Resurrection.'[80] Incarceration is here a figure of temporal existence. Powell was one of many dissenters who died in prison. The Baptist Francis Smith's epitaph enumerates life's challenges similarly to Janeway's diary:

> Here lyeth the Body of FRANCIS SMITH, Bookseller, who in his Youth was settled in a separate Congregation, where he sustained, between the Years of 1659 & 1688, great Persecution by Imprisonments, Exile, and large Fines laid on Ministers and meeting houses, and for printing and promoting Petitions for calling of a Parliament, and several Things against Popery, and after near 40 Imprisonments, he was fined 500 l. for printing and selling the speech of a noble Peer, and three times Suffered Corporeal Punishment. For the said Fine, he was 5 Years Prisoner in the *Kings Bench*: His hard Duress there, utterly impaired his Health. He dyed House-Keeper in the Custom-House, December the 22nd 1691.[81]

---

[78] *Autobiography*, 1: 206.
[79] Richard Alleine, *Godly-Fear: or, The Nature and Necessity of Fear, and its Usefulness* (1674), 220.
[80] *History of the Bunhill Fields Burial Ground* (1902), 56–7.
[81] The controversial 'speech' was Anthony Shaftesbury's *Speech of a Noble Peer of the Realm* (1681).

Indignation at Smith's suffering combines with respect for his patience under such conditions and gratitude for its eventual alleviation after toleration.

Prison experiences of dissenters across the period vary from relatively comfortable confinements with access to friends, books, and writing materials to instances of overcrowding, abuse, and death from malnutrition, disease, or violence. Prison writing—a composition during or about confinement—forms an important subset of dissenting writing. Sharon Achinstein argues that 'for the prisoner who saw himself in a story larger than his personal experience, prison was ... a pulpit, a privileged space for expressing disobedience'.[82] George Fox, for instance, made the Pauline connection between incarceration and inspiration; he was motivated by the need to reassure those at large: 'During the time of my imprisonment in Worcester ... I writ several books for the press ... many papers and epistles to friends, to encourage and strengthen them in their services for God.'[83] Imprisoned for illegally preaching, the Quaker Leonard Coale reassured his congregation that through print he could nonetheless make 'a Visitation unto you all, that you may consider what you are doing'.[84] The monitory, hortatory, and comforting aims of such writing are given additional force by the adverse conditions in which they were composed: incarceration enhanced a dissenting writer's authority.

The body's confinement offset or even facilitated the spirit's freedom. According to George Hughes, 'Free communion with God in prison is worth a thousand liberties, gained with loss of liberty of spirit. The Lord keeps us his free men'.[85] From Dorchester jail, the Presbyterian Isaac Clifford echoed the sentiment that confinement solidified faith:

> The fear of a prison is more than the harm. We have great cause to praise God, who hath made a prison very comfortable. I was never better in health or more cheerful in spirit than since my imprisonment, glory be to God. The best liberty which none can take away we have here, and enjoy much peace and quietness and precious opportunities, which many who are abroad much want. We have this advantage by a prison, we are free from the fears and snares, [that] much disturb and endanger others.[86]

Reassurance from those in peril was intended to strengthen the resolve of those who feared it. Matthew Newcomen told his Essex congregation to read about the Marian martyrs in Foxe's *Actes and Monuments* (1563): 'The reading how chearfully they went to Prison, and to the stake will embolden you against the feares of sufferings, and death.'[87]

---

[82] Sharon Achinstein, *Literature and Dissent in Milton's England* (Cambridge: Cambridge University Press, 2003), 73.

[83] Fox, *Journal* (1694), 196.

[84] Leonard Coale, *To the Bishops and their Ministers* (1671), 3.

[85] Edmund Calamy III, *An Abridgement of Mr. Baxter's History of his Life and Times*, 2 vols. (1713), 2: 232.

[86] *Letters of John Pinney, 1679–1699*, ed. Geoffrey F. Nuttall (London and New York: Oxford University Press, 1939), 1–2.

[87] Matthew Newcomen, *The Second and Last Collection of the late London Ministers Farewell Sermons* (1663), 165.

The theology of beneficial affliction that, as we have seen, developed more generally in Restoration dissenting writing deeply informs ideas of incarceration.

'I never had in all my life so great an inlet into the Word of God' as in prison, Bunyan wrote: 'them Scriptures that I saw nothing in before, are made in this place and state to shine upon me.' Prison made Bunyan aware of what it meant to have God 'stand by me at all turns.'[88] *The Pilgrim's Progress* is among the greatest works of prison writing, its first part composed during the years Bunyan spent in jail for unlicensed preaching. The allegory begins with a dreamer's vision, facilitated by confinement: 'As I walk'd through the wilderness of this world, I lighted on a certain place, where was a *Denn [The Gaol]; And I laid me down in that place to sleep: And as I slept I dreamed a Dream.'[89] Life is a pilgrimage, a journey through wilderness, and prison is a resting place where creativity may take hold. The subject of the dreamer's vision, the man who becomes Christian, informs Evangelist: 'If I be not fit to go to Prison, I am not fit (I am sure) to go to Judgement, and from thence to Execution.'[90] Worldly trials and tribulations, then, pale in comparison to eschatological judgement, though the confinements Christian and Hopeful undergo register as traumatic physical and psychical experiences, not mere metaphors, such as that by Giant Despair in Doubting Castle: 'The *Giant* therefore drove them before him, and put them into his Castle, into a very dark Dungeon, nasty and stinking to the spirit of these two men: Here then they lay, from *Wednesday* morning till *Saturday* night, without one bit of bread or drop of drink, or any light, or any to ask how they did. They were therefore here in evil case, and were far from friends and acquaintance.'[91] Release comes not through legal intervention but through religious faith, as Christian, after a period of prayer, recollects the key called 'Promise' which signifies that a propensity to sin or to doubt does not amount to an unregenerate state.

Much of the power of *The Pilgrim's Progress* resides in its combination of realistic particularity with representative typicality, mimesis with allegory. The imprisonment playing out in real time, '*Wednesday* morning till *Saturday* night', is a nice instance of this. Folkloric and romance features (like giants) combine with quotidian detail and biblical allusion. Christian's key would have resonated as more than a symbol with those of his readers who had seen the inside of a cell, but it also recalls the 'keys of the kingdom of heaven' in Matthew 16:19 and Peter's miraculous prison escape in Acts 12:10. The popularity of *The Pilgrim's Progress*, then, can be considered in terms of its appeal to different kinds of audience: it found readers among ministers and laity, adults and children, Anglicans and nonconformists.[92] Dissenting writing, to a greater extent than Anglican work, frequently concerns itself with different kinds of reader, in terms of both educational level and spiritual feeling. *The Pilgrim's Progress* is a prime instance of this,

---

[88] Bunyan, *Grace Abounding*, 87, 88.
[89] Bunyan, *Pilgrim's Progress*, 8. Square brackets indicate Bunyan's marginalia.
[90] Bunyan, *Pilgrim's Progress*, 10.
[91] Bunyan, *Pilgrim's Progress*, 114.
[92] See further the essays in part IV of Michael Davies and W. R. Owens (eds.), *The Oxford Handbook of John Bunyan* (Oxford: Oxford University Press, 2018).

as it makes abstruse doctrine clear and engaging. For example, the Calvinist doctrine of justification by faith is elaborated in the pilgrims' conversations with the Arminian character Ignorance, who erroneously believes that, 'I shall be justified before God from the curse, through his gracious acceptance of my obedience to his Law', a view which Christian derides as the 'pitiful old self-holiness'.[93] By contrast, Hopeful and Christian adhere to a conception of original sin as something that cannot be expunged through human effort ('the sin that cleaves to my best performance') and of Christ's righteousness imputed to the saintly through the propitiatory atonement ('without the righteousness of this Christ, all the World could not save me'; 'He is Mediator between God and us').[94] Ignorance dismisses the pilgrims' theology as 'the fruit of distracted brains', but it is he who is cast into Hell at the very gates of Heaven.[95] The ideas discussed in dialogues with Ignorance reinforce earlier parts of the allegory, such as Christian's fear of Mount Sinai, emblem of the Mosaic Law that cannot bring about salvation, as a hill flashing fire that might fall on his head, and the carnal temptations of Adam the First.[96] Allegory allows Bunyan to combine narrative entertainment with doctrinal exposition in order to juxtapose multiple positions, reflecting the variegated religious world in which he lived, but of course to steer readers away from doctrinal errors. In *The Pilgrim's Progress* Bunyan employs character, setting, and situation as emblems to capture a distinctly dissenting mindset; and he provides readers with instructional accounts of the hallmarks of dissenting experience such as religious doubt, Christian fellowship, and persecutory imprisonment.

Conclusion

In 1662, nonconformity was a rather artificial category which brought together disparate groups. By 1714, manifold internal differences remained, but a more cohesive understanding of dissent had developed. Its culture of writing helped to consolidate and perpetuate nonconformity to the extent that more and more works appeared that represent *writing by dissenters* rather than *dissenting writing*: that is, works that can be classified on bases other than the religious persuasions of their authors. So, in her travel writings, compiled in manuscript around 1702, Celia Fiennes has much to say from a dissenter's perspective about varieties of religious worship, and the diaristic form she adopts owes something to dissenting modes of self-fashioning; but Fiennes's texts are not first and foremost 'dissenting writing'.[97] The poet and librettist John Hughes's preface to his edition of Spenser makes influential arguments about allegory arguably informed by

---

[93] Bunyan, *Pilgrim's Progress*, 147, 151.
[94] Bunyan, *Pilgrim's Progress*, 140–3.
[95] Bunyan, *Pilgrim's Progress*, 148, 163.
[96] Bunyan, *Pilgrim's Progress*, 20, 69.
[97] *The Journeys of Celia Fiennes*, ed. Christopher Morris (London: Cresset Press, 1947).

his nonconformist background, but again his essay need not be hived off from literary criticism more broadly and labelled 'dissenting prose'.[98] The greatest literary work of eighteenth-century dissenting prose is Defoe's *Robinson Crusoe* (1719). Its protagonist conceives of his adventures as pilgrimage and his confinement as imprisonment; his twenty-eight-year sojourn on a desert island that invigorates his religious belief even coincides with the period of dissenting persecution in Restoration England (Crusoe is born in 1632, stranded when he is twenty-seven, and rescued twenty-eight years later, making island captivity a figure for the persecution of nonconformity). Defoe's novel emerges from dissenting literary culture, but its reach extends much further: it has a plausible claim to being the first novel in English and has attained a global, mythic status. This chapter has focused on writing by dissenters about dissenting experience in the period 1660 to 1714; to some extent, the triumph of the tradition is not just the perennial endurance of its literary greats but also the increasing obsolescence of 'dissenting writing' as a cogent, stand-alone category in the eighteenth century.[99]

[98] *The Works of Mr. Edmund Spenser*, ed. John Hughes, 6 vols. (1715).

[99] Since this essay was written, two valuable sources for the study of dissenting writing in the period have been published: John Coffey (ed.), *The Oxford History of Protestant Dissenting Traditions, Volume I: The Post-Reformation Era, 1559–1689* (Oxford: Oxford University Press, 2020); and Andrew C. Thompson (ed.), *The Oxford History of Protestant Dissenting Traditions, Volume II: The Long Eighteenth Century c. 1689–c. 1828* (Oxford: Oxford University Press, 2018).

CHAPTER 14

ENCOUNTERS WITH THE EAST

MATTHEW DIMMOCK

WRITING in 1681 on behalf of the Royal Society, Robert Hooke publicly endorsed the prose 'History' as the primary medium for accounts of the wider world. Every effort needed to be made, Hooke wrote, to rescue existing knowledge from obscurity, to translate available material into English or Latin, and to procure new accounts from English merchants, seamen, and travellers. Instructions were to be circulated concerning what was 'pertinent and considerable', public enthusiasm was to be generated, and 'fit Persons' were to be identified that might facilitate the process, 'fitted to engage, and careful to collect' the necessary raw materials which would then be 'Compose[d] into Histories'.[1]

Although he mentions the need for 'a good History of most our West-Indian Plantations', Hooke's interests (connected to the East India Company that he hoped would be a partner in this enterprise) lay to the east. He personally ushered through the press Robert Knox's *An Historical Relation of Ceylon* (1681), encouraged the writing of Samuel Baron's *Description of the Kingdom of Tonqueen* (written in 1686, first published in 1732), and organized the printing and distribution of Simon de la Loubère's *A New Historical Relation of the Kingdom of Siam, wherein a full account is given of the Chinese way of Arithmetick and Mathematick* (1693).[2] These were 'hybrid products of encounter' that brought new 'easts' to English readers in new ways, offering detailed, intimate,

---

[1] Robert Hooke, 'Preface' to Robert Knox, *An Historical Relation of the Island Ceylon, in the East Indies* (1681), sig. A2v.

[2] Knox, *An Historical Relation*, sig. a3r; Samuel Baron, 'A Description of the Kingdom of Tonqueen', in Awnsham Churchill and John Churchill (eds.), *A Collection of Voyages and Travels*, 6 vols. (1705–32), 6: 1–40; Simon de la Loubère, *A New Historical Relation of the Kingdom of Siam, wherein a Full Account is Given of the Chinese Way of Arithmetick and Mathematick* (1693). For more on Hooke's connection to each of these texts see Lisa Jardine, *The Curious Life of Robert Hooke: The Man Who Measured London* (London: HarperCollins, 2003), 272–87.

and sometimes clandestine entry into hitherto unknown territories and cultures.[3] In these terms they are characteristic of the innovations in late seventeenth- and early eighteenth-century prose that persistently looked eastward for sources, content, settings, and inspiration.

'How much of the present Knowledge of the Parts of the World is owing to late Discoveries', Hooke notes, 'may be judged by comparing the Modern with the Ancients' Accounts thereof'. His point was that through determination, perspicacity, and institutional willingness the contemporary world had become finite: knowable, containable, and, in the right circumstances, eminently communicable to an English reader. But Hooke's opening observation also entails the acknowledgement that 'Histories' had generically always been the repository for such knowledge, despite the fact that few early examples had 'scaped the Injury of Time' and others remained 'for the most part Imprison'd in the Cells of some Library or Study, accessible to a small number of Mankind' and subject to loss or decay.[4] The potential appeal of such writing was as broad as its definition: for Hooke a 'History' comprised a carefully shaped narrative of 'Discoveries and Observations' that needed to be, like Robert Knox himself, 'no ways prejudiced or byassed by the vain-glory of telling Strange Things' that might 'swarve from the truth of Matter of Fact'.[5] Ideally it would also be written by 'Ingenuous' and 'knowing' intermediaries: men whose identities were formed in the interstices generated by the newly global reach of English mercantilism such as Knox, a captive in Ceylon for near-twenty years, or Baron, the offspring of Dutch and Vietnamese parents who became a 'naturalised Englishman'.[6] An attention to such 'authentic' lives, and their narrative equivalents, were also a key feature of late seventeenth- and early eighteenth-century prose writing of, and about, the east.

Hooke's assertion that history was, and since the establishment of writing had always been, the universal mode through which literate cultures recorded and encountered the wider world is a skewed reflection of his own intellectual traditions, but it was the dominant view of his contemporaries.[7] The literary legacy of a pre-Columbian past in which the world lay to the east and southeast, and England sat on a distant northern edge of the dominant global powers, remained potent throughout this period. Some of the most well-known medieval accounts of eastern travel continued to be reprinted (even if their veracity was increasingly questioned), such as the perennially popular *Travels* of the fictional Englishman Sir John Mandeville, originally circulated in the late fourteenth century, with English editions appearing throughout the early modern period, including the edition published by Chiswell, Walford, Wotton, and Conyers in 1696.[8] Presenting

---

[3] Anna Winterbottom, *Hybrid Knowledge in the Early East India Company World* (Basingstoke: Palgrave Macmillan, 2016), 40.

[4] Hooke, 'Preface', sig. a2r.

[5] Hooke, 'Preface', sig. a3v.

[6] Hooke, 'Preface', sig. a3r. The extraordinary life, career, and output of Samuel Baron are all considered at length in Winterbottom, *Hybrid Knowledge*, 26–53.

[7] See further Chapter 19 on 'Histories' by Niall Allsopp.

[8] John Mandeville, *The Voyages & Travels of Sir John Mandeville . . . with Woodcuts* (1696). Further editions of the text appeared in 1722 and 1750.

a Eurasian world in the aftermath of sustained Mongol advances, Mandeville's text was part-pilgrimage, part-romance inflected *itinerario*, and part-religious delineation of those states beyond Christendom's south-eastern fringes.[9]

Although influential and widely read, imitated, and parodied, the *Travels* was not typical either of prose writing from these earlier periods or of the *Chansons* tradition in which Muslim/Christian engagements were presented in epic verse. Most accounts of the 'oriental regions' that correspond to Hooke's requirements of history were of the Latin chronicle or *annale* type, such as Ranulf Higden's fourteenth century *Polychronicon*, supplemented by a plethora of prose polemics, perhaps most influentially Riccoldo da Montecroce's *Contra Legem Sarracenorum* (1300), and Robert of Ketton's Latin translation of the Qur'ān itself, *Lex Mahumet pseudoprophete* (1143), the pre-eminent version circulating in Christendom for over five centuries.[10] All these writings sought to define 'eastern' cultures by their presumed adherence to 'Maumet' or 'Mahomet', a false pseudo-prophet who had cynically fabricated a new religion—Mahometanism—out of elements of Christianity, Judaism, and his own self-interested and Epicurean invention.[11] From a late medieval and early modern Christian perspective this non-religion dominated Asia, Africa, and the Mediterranean, and it was the filter through which these 'old worlds' were understood. For a substantial part of that history 'Mahometanism' was also represented as an existential threat, particularly following the Ottoman conquest of Constantinople in 1453.

For the later seventeenth century this was a complex inheritance that was variously engaged, reproduced, endorsed, reinvented, and overturned, repeatedly and invariably in prose. One finds little more than a crystallization of earlier polemical traditions in one of the more surprising innovations of the mid-century: the appearance of the first English translation of the Qur'ān, *The Alcoran of Mahomet* of early 1649. Based on a French version of two years earlier by the French diplomat André du Ryer, rather than done directly from Arabic, and derided by subsequent English translators, this *Alcoran* was nevertheless 'one of the more popular books of seventeenth century England'.[12] The

---

[9] These contexts for Mandeville and his sources are discussed in William of Tripoli, *Notitia de Machometo: De statu Sarracenorum*, ed. Peter Engels (Würzburg: Corpus Islamo-Christianum, 1992), 52–74, and John Tolan, *Saracens: Islam in the Medieval European Imagination* (New York: Columbia University Press, 2002), 203–9. See also Matthew Dimmock, 'Mandeville on Muhammad: Texts, Contexts and Influence', in Ladan Niayesh (ed.), *A Knight's Legacy: Mandeville and Mandevillian Lore in Early Modern England* (Manchester: Manchester University Press, 2011), 92–107.

[10] See the relevant sections in Tolan, *Saracens*, and in Norman Daniel, *Islam and the West: The Making of an Image* (1960; 2nd edn, Oxford: Oneworld Publications, 1993).

[11] This misrepresentation is considered at length in Matthew Dimmock, *Mythologies of the Prophet Muhammad in Early Modern Culture* (Cambridge: Cambridge University Press, 2013).

[12] Ziad Elmarsafy, *The Enlightenment Qur'an: The Politics of Translation and the Construction of Islam* (London: Oneworld, 2009), 9. In the preface to his own translation—the dominant translation for at least two centuries—George Sale would write that the anonymous 1649 translator was 'utterly unacquainted with the Arabic, and no great master of the French' and had 'added a number of fresh mistakes of his own to those of Du Ryer, not to mention the meanness of his language, which would make a better book ridiculous' (George Sale, *THE KORAN, commonly called the Alcoran of Mahomet* (1734), p. vi.

poetic nature of the original Arabic is lost, replaced by an over-close adherence to Du Ryer's original, a reflection perhaps of an abiding presumption that the Qur'ān was 'ridiculous'.[13] Thomas Carlyle would typify this view in his lament that it was 'as toilsome a reading as I ever undertook'. Like many earlier Christian readers, working with Latin or later English translations in prose, he found it a 'wearisome confused jumble, crude, incondite; endless iterations, long-windedness, entanglement', little more than 'endless stupidity'.[14]

The 1649 *Alcoran of Mahomet* appeared soon after the regicide and after a struggle with the Parliamentary authorities, who allowed its printing only after sober consultation and the addition of a 'Caveat' by the cleric and polemicist Alexander Ross.[15] Towards the beginning of his text Ross pointedly notes that: 'I know the publishing of the *Alcoran* may be to some dangerous and scandalous; dangerous to the Reader, scandalous to the higher Powers, who notwithstanding have cleared themselves by disliking the publishing, and questioning the publishers thereof: but for the danger, I will deliver in these ensuing Propositions my opinion, yet with submission to wiser judgments.'[16] Intriguingly then, the responsibility for the text thus falls upon on the reader, for whom it may be 'dangerous', particularly since the anonymous translator and the authorities had sought in different ways to absolve themselves of responsibility for its publication. Although initially he apparently offers the volume to all who care to pry into the 'Turkish vanities' contained within, later in his 'Caveat' Ross anxiously refines this point about reading: 'But before I end,' he writes, 'give me leave to clear my self again in this point, that it is *not* my meaning all should have the liberty to read the *Alcoran* promiscuously.'[17] There follows an anecdotal litany of justificatory examples: 'that Sword which may without danger be handled by a sober Man, cannot without danger be touched by a mad Man.' 'If all Men were like Bees, to suck Hony even out of Henbane,' Ross reflects, 'there might be no danger in reading the *Alcoran*, but most Men are like Spiders, suck securely Poyson even out of the sweetest Roses.'[18] As a result—and this is Ross's most direct assertion of how the Alcoran should be read and by whom: 'they only may surely and without danger read the *Alcoran*, who are intelligent, judicious, learned, and thoroughly grounded in Piety, and principles of Christianity.' In contrast, 'weak, ignorant, inconstant, and disaffected minds to the Truth, must not venture to meddle with this unhallowed piece, lest they be polluted with the touch thereof... and if we will not venture to go into an infected House without preservatives, much less should any dare to

---

[13] Samuel Purchas, *Purchas his Pilgrimage, or, Relations of the World and the Religions Observed in All Ages and Places Discovered* (1613), 211.
[14] Thomas Carlyle, *On Heroes, Hero-Worship and the Heroic in History* (London: Chapman and Hall, 1907), 64–5.
[15] See Matthew Birchwood, *Staging Islam in England: Drama and Culture, 1640–1685* (Cambridge: D. S. Brewer, 2007), 64–5.
[16] Alexander Ross, 'A Needful Caveat', *The Alcoran of Mahomet* (1649), sig. Ee1r.
[17] Ross, 'A Needful Caveat', sig. Ee6r (my emphasis).
[18] Ross, 'A Needful Caveat', sig. Ff3v.

read the *Alcoran*, that is not sufficiently armed with Grace, Strength, and Knowledge.'[19] This was a Royalist cleric writing in support of orthodoxy: any justification he offered for the publication of the Alcoran needed to be strongly tempered with moral guidance and Christian authority.

The element of Ross's equivocal justification for a reading of the Alcoran—now on the open market, free to be purchased by all—that most interests me is his insistence that he does not believe all should have the 'liberty' to read it 'promiscuously'. Rather than 'casually', a meaning this word gained only in the eighteenth century, Ross means his readers should not read it 'without distinction, discrimination, or order'; presumably without seeking suitable guidance.[20] There is, however, a more direct context for this word. Ross uses it intending to respond to, if not deliberately to echo, John Milton, who in *Areopagitica* (1644) had argued vehemently for intellectual liberty and unlicensed printing, subjects of direct relevance to the 1649 *Alcoran*. In *Areopagitica* Milton had written: 'Since therefore the knowledge and survay of vice is in this world so necessary to the constituting of human vertue, and the scanning of error to the confirmation of truth, how can we more safely, and with lesse danger scout into the regions of sin and falsity then by reading all manner of tractats, and hearing all manner of reason? And this is the benefit which may be had of books promiscuously read.'[21] Milton is clearly in favour of 'promiscuous' reading (by which he means random or undiscriminating; perhaps even unrestricted), since God has given man a questioning mind and he can only truly comprehend through exposure to error—thus all books should be published as means to better understand truth.

So in the context of the 1649 Alcoran, this reference is a curious one: Ross appears to deny Milton's affirmation of the benefits of promiscuous reading—he does not believe all should have the 'liberty' to read this particular book 'promiscuously'—and yet he seems to make Milton's argument repeatedly in his 'Caveat': that a reading of the Alcoran is (in suitably Christian hands) an affirmation of true faith. This is of course the dilemma that Ross faces from the off: he is required to justify the translation and publication of the Qur'an whilst necessarily condemning its content. So at the very opening of his essay, he supposes the 'great *Arabian* Impostor' has 'at last after a thousand years' come via France to arrive 'in *England*; his *Alcoran*, or gallimaufry of Errors ... hath learned to speak *English*' and been invited in by the translator:

> no otherwise than some Monster brought out of *Africa,* for people to gaze, not to dote upon; and as the sight of a Monster or mishapen creature should induce the beholder to praise God, who hath not made him such; so should the reading of this *Alcoran* excite us both to bless God's goodness towards us in this Land, who enjoy the glorious light of the Gospel, and behold the truth in the beauty of holiness; as also to

---

[19] Ross, 'A Needful Caveat', sig. Ee6v.
[20] *OED*, s.v. 'promiscuous, adj.', 1.a.
[21] Milton, *Areopagitica; A Speech of Mr. John Milton for the Liberty of Vnlicens'd Printing, to the Parliament of England* (1644), 13.

admire God's Judgments, who suffers so many Countreys to be blinded and inslaved with this mishapen issue of *Mahomet*'s brain.[22]

Elsewhere in this passage, and throughout his 'Caveat', Ross draws upon the key elements of a medieval biography of 'Mahomet' and repeatedly affirms this figure's authorship of the text, thus refuting divine revelation. It is the monstrosity of the Alcoran that offers him the chance to justify its appearance in England in 1649—the book is a monster born of a monstrous birth from a monster and people should appraise it as a prodigy that reminds them of the grace of God and of the perfection of their own faith. This is a similar rhetorical device to the one Luther employed to justify the printing of the Qur'ān in Latin in the previous century, yet Ross goes further. He enumerates a lengthy list of those heresies, ranging from the 'damnable errors' one might find recorded in Scripture, to 'the modern Histories of the East and West *Indies*' and 'the damnable Heresies of the modern *Familists*, who deny Christ's Divinity, making as many Christs as there be illuminated in their Congregations'. He asks, 'are not also the Heresies of the *Socinians, Anti-trinitarians, Adamites, Servetians, Antisabbatarians*, and many others exposed to the view of all that will read them?'[23] If all these heresies are readily available to English readers then, Ross asks, what justification can there be for prohibiting the Alcoran? The intention here is to castigate the current religious settlement and the proliferation of sectarianism in England, but in doing so he also lambasts the freedom with which the previously unknown religions of east and west were being delineated in English prose, in precisely those histories Hooke would champion later in the century.[24] Lamenting this decent into relativism, Ross draws attention to the fragile religious tolerance that existed in the mid-seventeenth century and dramatically alleges that in all this chaos the arrival in England of Mahomet (and thus Islam) was somehow inevitable.

The 1649 *Alcoran of Mahomet* was something of a curiosity. It may have been one of the more popular books of the period (and a second edition appeared in the similarly momentous year of 1688), but it was never intended for serious study.[25] It was indirectly the product of a sophisticated French orientalist culture, clearly indebted to the Alcoranic translations of the past and their polemical apparatus, but was also tied absolutely to the circumstances of its production as a rather ephemeral, inexpensive piece of political pamphleteering.[26] Just as readers were clamouring to access the words of the 'Arabian

---

[22] Ross, 'A Needful Caveat', sig. Ee1r.
[23] Ross, 'A Needful Caveat', Ee1v.
[24] Compare the discussion of 'Heresiography and Religious Controversy' in Chapter 18 by Nicholas McDowell.
[25] There is abundant evidence that the *Alcoran* was highly sought after upon its initial publication, and large numbers of copies remain extant in libraries across the UK and the US, testifying to its reach. The impact of the text (and the identity of its translator) is explored in detail, and with differing conclusions, in Noel Malcolm, 'The 1649 English Translation of The Koran: Its Origins and Significance', *Journal of the Warburg and Courtauld Institutes*, 75 (2012), 261–95, and Mordechai Feingold, '"The Turkish Alcoran": New Light on the 1649 English Translation of the Koran', *Huntington Library Quarterly*, 75 (2012), 475–501.
[26] Dimmock, *Mythologies of the Prophet Muhammad*, 164.

Imposter' in rather undistinguished English prose, the most prominent of English Arabists, Edward Pococke, was creating a legacy that would have profound implications for later prose engagements with Islam and Islamic cultures. Pococke's audience was constituted primarily of fellow scholars across Europe and accordingly he wrote in Latin and in Arabic rather than English—producing, most notably, his *Specimen historiae Arabum* (1650) and the accompanying *Notae* 'which feature a new methodology for the study of Islam that relies exclusively on Arabic sources'.[27] The early seventeenth century had seen an emerging interest in the incorporation of non-Christian sources into narratives of travel, cosmography, and histories of religion. Pococke's commitment to translating Arab/Islamic histories from original, authenticated sources as the first Laudian Professor of Arabic and Regius Professor of Hebrew at the University of Oxford (a position established in 1636) marked a major development in such work. The shifts in perspective that this work entailed and promoted were already well underway elsewhere in Europe—as for example in Johann Heinrich Hottinger's *Historia orientalis* (1652), the first attempt to offer an account of Muhammad based on Arabic, Hebrew, and Syriac manuscripts—and would be exemplified later in the century by the posthumous publication of Barthélemy d'Herbelot's *Bibliothèque Orientale* (1697), which can be regarded 'as the first encyclopedia of Islam'.[28]

Pococke's work impacted all subsequent English writing on Arabic and Arabic cultures, not least in a gathering determination to excavate knowledge and to challenge established Christian mythologies about such peoples and their religious beliefs. This is abundantly evident in a series of later works that focused on the figure of the Prophet Muhammad in the final decades of the seventeenth century, although with profoundly different agendas, to shift the parameters of English understanding: works such as Lancelot Addison's *The First State of Mahumedism* (1678), Humphrey Prideaux's *The True Nature of Imposture fully dsplayed in the life of Mahomet* (1697), and an incendiary text circulated only in manuscript, Henry Stubbe's 'The Originall & Progress of Mahometanism' (c.1671). Each writer sought authenticity; to free 'Mahomet' and his doctrine from 'many ridiculous but usual stories concerning them both; which the present Mahumedans laugh at'.[29] Each sought to inform and to intervene: Addison to press a Royalist, orthodox Anglican position, Prideaux to attack antitrinitarianism, which had found a means to cement and articulate a political and religious manifesto through Islam. This made such radical English Protestants easy to attack, but for the radicals a 'sympathetic identification with Islam' was a means to achieve 'historical,

---

[27] Nabil Matar, 'Edward Pococke', in David Thomas and John Chesworth (eds.), *Christian-Muslim Relations: A Bibliographical History* (Leiden: Brill, 2016), 445–508 (450).

[28] Guy G. Stroumsa, *A New Science: The Discovery of Religion in the Age of Reason* (Cambridge, MA: Harvard University Press, 2010), 131; Maxime Rodinson, *Europe and the Mystique of Islam* (London: I. B. Tauris & Co, 1988), 44.

[29] Lancelot Addison, *The First State of Mahumedism being an Exact Account of Mahumed, the Author of the Turkish Religion* (1678), sig. A2v.

philosophical, and ideological coherence'.[30] Stubbe, although the least read in this period, was certainly the most original, and his work usefully demonstrates this point. He found in 'Mahometanism' a truer Noahic form of Christianity, uncorrupted by Pauline innovation and subsequent events, as the present Christian churches had been. He also attempted to forge a new, experimental prose that might do justice to his subject; writing that gains lyricism and expression in its emulation of the cadences of the Arabic sources Stubbe was consulting (including the Qur'ān and the Hadith).[31] His opening is particularly striking; a description of the Prophet Muhammad that describes him as a 'great soul' in whom 'the Awfullness of Maiesty seem'd to bee temper'd with admiral sweetness which at once imprinted in the beholders Respect Reverence & Love'. Moreover, Stubbe writes, the 'Arabians compare him to the purest streams of some River gently gliding along which arrests and delights the Eyes of every approaching Passenger'.[32] In content and in form this was something quite new.

Stubbe's writing and ideas were directly indebted to Pococke, whom he quotes approvingly, and they would resurface in the work of early eighteenth-century radicals like John Toland.[33] Many other writers looked to augment Pococke's attention to original sources whilst continuing, like Stubbe, to look east. The book which would have greatest influence was a very different prose work: Paul Rycaut's *The Present State of the Ottoman Empire* (1666). It followed the earlier example of Richard Knolles' imperious *The Generall Historie of the Turkes* (1603), with which it was published in an edition of 1700, but Rycaut conspicuously departed from precedent by arguing for the importance of continuing peace and cordial commercial relations with the Ottomans, and explicitly drawing on his first-hand experience of Ottoman courtly life and records (as secretary to Sir Heneage Finch, earl of Winchelsea, Charles II's ambassador in Istanbul).[34] He offered the reader an opportunity to 'penetrate further into the mysteries of this polity', to step beyond the caricatures of barbarity, and (as Stubbe was simultaneously doing) drew upon the Qur'ān and the Hadith.[35] Perhaps more importantly, he also provided his readers with a 'rich collection of anecdotes about people at the Turkish court', which no

---

[30] Humberto Garcia, 'A Hungarian Revolution in Restoration England: Henry Stubbe, Radical Islam, and the Rye House Plot', *The Eighteenth Century*, 51 (2010), 1–26 (1); see also Justin Champion, *The Pillars of Priestcraft Shaken: The Church of England and its Enemies, 1660–1730* (Cambridge: Cambridge University Press, 1992), 101–27; and James R. Jacob, *Henry Stubbe, Radical Protestantism and the Early Enlightenment* (Cambridge: Cambridge University Press, 1983).

[31] Stubbe's sources are outlined in detail in the opening sections of Nabil Matar (ed.), *Henry Stubbe and the Beginnings of Islam: The Originall & Progress of Mahometanism* (New York: Columbia University Press, 2013).

[32] Quoted in Dimmock, *Mythologies of the Prophet Muhammad*, 196. The full text is also reproduced in Matar (ed.), *Henry Stubbe and the Beginnings of Islam*.

[33] See Champion, *The Pillars of Priestcraft Shaken*, 125–54, and Dimmock, *Mythologies of the Prophet Muhammad*, 196–8. On Toland, see also Chapter 30 on 'Radical and Deist Writing' by Nicholas McDowell and Giovanni Tarantino.

[34] As Rycaut relates in the final concluding section of his *The Present State of the Ottoman Empire* (2nd edn, 1667), 49–50.

[35] Rycaut, 'The Epistle to the Reader', in *The Present State* [n.p.].

doubt contributed to its considerable popularity.[36] Rycaut's book rapidly became canonical: it was certainly read by John Locke, Samuel Pepys, Montesquieu, Leibniz, Racine, and Sir William Temple, and later readers include Thomas Jefferson and Lord Byron.[37] James Sutherland suggests that it was 'probably in every gentleman's library' in this period.[38] Rycaut offered novel, privileged access to the east, crafting for his readers the vicarious thrill of penetrating the very essence of the Ottoman imperium in a clear prose style apparently unclouded by prejudice.

The influence of Edward Pococke's scholarship also worked in other ways: later in life he collaborated with his son, Edward Pococke Jr, to publish Ibn Ṭufayl's twelfth century *Risālat Ḥayy b. Yaqẓān fi asrār al-ḥikma l-mashriqiyya*, in Arabic with facing Latin translation, as *Philosophus autodidactus. Sive epistola Abi Jafar ebn Tophail de Hai ebn Yokdhan* (1671). This tale related the solitary life of Ḥayy ibn Yaqẓān who grew up on an island without human interaction and who gradually found his way to a profound connection with God. Later he would meet other men who attempted to bring his spiritual insights to a wider constituency but, due to the corruption of the world, the enterprise failed. The Pocockes' literal translation was to have considerable influence, in and beyond England. Critics have long postulated a second- or third-hand impression on Daniel Defoe's early novel *Robinson Crusoe* (1719), and have found its echoes in the work of many other European novelists, as well as in the thought of John Locke.[39] More immediately it prompted a rush of vernacular translations, first in Dutch, and then in English versions undertaken by the Quaker George Keith in 1674 (as *An account of the Oriental philosophy, Shewing the wisdom of some renowned men of the East*), the High Anglican George Ashwell in 1686 (as *The History of Hai eb'n Yockdan, an Indian Prince, or, The Self-Taught Philosopher*), and then a new translation from the Arabic by British orientalist scholar Simon Ockley in 1708 (as *The Improvement of Human Reason, Exhibited in the Life of Hai Ebn Yokdhan. Written in Arabic Above 500 Years Ago, by Abu Jaafar ebn Tophail*).[40]

The titles of the Keith, Ashwell, and Ockley translations give a useful sense of their orientation: Keith's an attempt to enlist Ṭufayl's text to the Quaker cause; Ashwell's motivated in part as a response to Keith, but also to court a more general reader; and Ockley's a more scholarly enterprise to correct earlier wrongs. All, as Nabil Matar has noted, partake in a kind of de-Islamicisation of their source that is typical of English

---

[36] Phyllis Lachs, quoted by John Anthony Butler in the 'Introduction' to his edition of *Sir Paul Rycaut: The Present State of the Ottoman Empire, Sixth Edition* (Tempe: Arizona Center for Medieval and Renaissance Studies, 2017), 1–114 (38).

[37] Butler, 'Introduction', *Sir Paul Rycaut*, 38.

[38] James Sutherland, *English Literature of the Late Seventeenth Century* (Oxford: Clarendon Press, 1969), 290.

[39] See Srinivas Aravamudan, *Enlightenment Orientalism: Resisting the Rise of the Novel* (Chicago: University of Chicago Press, 2012), 15–17.

[40] The translations and editions of Ṭufayl's text are comprehensively detailed in L. I. Conrad, 'Research Resources on Ibn Ṭufayl and Ḥayy ibn Yaqẓān', in L. I. Conrad (ed.), *The World of Ibn Ṭufayl: Interdisciplinary Perspectives on Ḥayy ibn Yaqẓān* (Leiden: E. J. Brill, 1996), 267–94.

approaches to such material in this period: but all do acknowledge their text's Islamic origin and the intrinsic value it has for the 'Western reader'.[41] And indeed it is the anticipated experience of the reader that is of paramount concern for each of the different versions of *Ḥayy ibn Yaqẓān* circulating in England by the early eighteenth century. The reader was to be challenged by something new yet edifying; by something strange—but at least for Ashwell, who states it explicitly in his opening, the reader was also expected to find pleasure in this encounter.[42]

This too is a departure from the tone of most earlier prose writing on these topics, the primary concern of which was polemical, evangelical, or historical (or a combination of all three), and for the most part seems loftily unconcerned with the predilections of its readers. Returning to Robert Hooke's preface to Knox's *Historical Relation of the Island Ceylon* with which I opened this chapter, we find precisely the same preoccupation with the 'penetration' of an eastern culture; with the authenticity of what is related; and with a clear consciousness of the pleasures attendant on the experience of reading such material. Although Hooke's stated purpose in endorsing and supporting Knox's publication was the extension of a natural knowledge of the world it offered, he recognized the necessity of courting and cultivating a variety of readers. It seems that an affirmation of the author's probity and of the truthfulness of his account was no longer enough.

For Hooke, the book was not solely intended for those interested in geography; rather 'most readers, though of differing Gusts' might 'find something pleasant to their Pallat'. He goes on: 'the Statesman, Divine, Physician, Lawyer, Merchant, Mechanick, Husbandman, may select something for their Entertainment.'[43] Later, reminding the reader of Knox's extraordinary nineteen years in captivity (and thereby connecting the text to the well-established and more sensationalist prose genre of the captivity narrative), Hooke indulges in a rather uncharacteristic rhetorical flourish, exhorting his readers to: 'Read therefore the book it self, and you will find your self taken Captive indeed, but used more kindly by the Author, than he himself was by the Natives.'[44] This implies again the centrality of the imagination to reading this kind of 'historical' prose, and a willed identification with the central protagonist, whether traveller, captive, diplomat, or even 'oriental' that we tend to assume is the province of fiction. All this talk of authenticity, truth, penetration, and identification also suggests elements of an 'orientalist' dynamic, in Said's terms, well before the specific geo-political circumstances in which 'high' Orientalism could come about.[45] But fiction is an important context: Hooke was well aware that he was pitching to a market 'so taken up of late with *Novels* and

---

[41] Nabil Matar, *Islam in Britain, 1558–1685* (Cambridge: Cambridge University Press, 1998), 101–2.
[42] George Ashwell, *The History of Hai eb'n Yockdan, an Indian Prince, or, The Self-Taught Philosopher* (1686), 'The Preface', sig. B5v.
[43] Hooke, 'Preface', sig. A3v.
[44] Hooke, 'Preface', sig. A4r. See further Chapter 25 on 'New World Writing and Captivity Narratives' by Catherine Armstrong.
[45] See Edward Said, *Orientalism* (New York: Pantheon, 1978). The challenges of its early modern application are cogently articulated in Gerald MacLean, *Looking East: English Writing and the Ottoman Empire before 1800* (Basingstoke: Palgrave Macmillan, 2007), especially 17–20.

Romances', and he signals the increasingly porous boundaries between prose fiction and the historical, geographical, philosophical worlds of non-fiction (even as he rejects that porosity).[46] It was happening all around him: as well as a potential debt to *Ḥayy ibn Yaqẓān*, Defoe's *Robinson Crusoe* also owes something of its genesis to Knox's captivity and his *Historical relation*.[47]

As earlier examples have demonstrated, information, goods, and narratives were carried together from east to west and found receptive English audiences. There was of course movement in the other direction too, but even in the late seventeenth and early eighteenth centuries England remained on the periphery of global empires and the trade routes that bound them, and was therefore a net importer of such narratives; a means of writing and translating the English into the world.[48] Recent scholarship has turned away from the insistence of an earlier tradition that tales from, and of, the orient were merely exotica, their influence limited and popularity short-lived. That tradition is summed up by Martha Pike Conant, who argued that 'the oriental tale was alien; and incident, atmosphere, fancies, understood and liked by Eastern listeners, seemed too grotesque and incredible to make more than a limited appeal to untravelled English readers. They welcomed, rather, with characteristic heartiness the homely, realistic background of Defoe's stories'.[49] Srinivas Aravamudan, Ros Ballaster, Peter Caracciolo, Robert Irwin, and others have since demonstrated the fallacy of this position, and the opposition set up here between Defoe's English homeliness and the outlandish oriental narrative is (as I have already suggested) simply unsustainable.[50] As a result of precedent and geo-political circumstance, by the later seventeenth-century English writers and readers instinctively looked to the east for stories, for settings and for alternative ways of articulating the self and society. The results were

---

[46] From the opening line of the 'Preface' to Daniel Defoe, *The Fortunes and Misfortunes of the Famous Moll Flanders, &c* (1722), sig. A1r.

[47] As Anna Winterbottom notes, Knox's book was used by John Locke in his *Second Treatise of Government* (c.1689) and may have provided some inspiration for Defoe's *Robinson Crusoe* (1719) and *Captain Singleton* (1720): see Winterbottom, *Hybrid Knowledge*, 142–3. It is certainly clear from the later of these two novels that Defoe knew Knox's book, even if the two do not seem to have met. The connection between *Robinson Crusoe* and Knox's own life story has been fully elaborated in Katherine Frank, *Crusoe: Daniel Defoe, Robert Knox, and the Creation of a Myth* (New York: Pegasus Books, 2012).

[48] See for instance Nabil Matar's two important volumes on this topic: *In the Lands of the Christians* (London: Routledge, 2003) and *Europe through Arab Eyes, 1578–1727* (New York: Columbia University Press, 2009).

[49] Martha Pike Conant, *The Oriental Tale in England in the Eighteenth Century* (New York: Columbia University Press, 1908), 236–7; also quoted in Robert Irwin, 'The *Arabian Nights* and the Origins of the Western Novel', in Philip F. Kennedy and Marina Warner (eds.), *Scheherazade's Children: Global Encounters with the* Arabian Nights (New York: New York University Press, 2013), 143–53 (145).

[50] Aravamudan, *Enlightenment Orientalism*; Ros Ballaster, *Fabulous Orients: Fictions of the East in England 1662–1785* (Oxford: Oxford University Press, 2005); Peter Caracciolo, 'The House of Fiction and le jardin anglo-chinois', *Middle Eastern Literatures*, 7 (2004), 199–211, and his 'Introduction: Such a Store House of Ingenious Fiction and Splendid Imagery', in Caracciolo (ed.), *The Arabian Nights in English Literature: Studies in the Reception of* The Thousand and One Nights *into British Culture* (Basingstoke: Macmillan, 1988), 1–80; and Irwin, '*Arabian Nights* and the Origins of the Western Novel'.

spectacular, profoundly enriching English prose in ways that reverberated through subsequent centuries.

Sometimes these narratives came directly from source, but more often at this point they came through the more advanced and better connected French orientalist milieu. New forms of prose writing were generated in these encounters, most inventively and influentially in the burgeoning sphere of print fiction. Here allegory and allusion allowed English writers to test the conventions of eastern despotism and depravity (and to titillate at the same time) while simultaneously measuring their own monarchical system—and individual monarchs—in equivalent terms. Fiction also offered a conceptual space in which versions of the east might be inhabited and a means of assimilating other narrative structures, such as the elaborately framed story sequence, popularly known as the 'oriental tale', in the process forging what Ballaster has suggested are 'new models of subjectivity'.[51]

The genre of the 'secret history' or the 'scandal novel' is an early example of a fictional engagement that looks east in order to look inwards, in this case tailored for the particular circumstances of the Restoration court.[52] The first, *Hattige: or the Amours of the king of Tameran, A Novel* (1680) was a translation of Sébastien Brémond's *Hattigé* and is a bawdy satire of disguise, cross-dressing, and infidelity centred upon the titular Hattige, a version of the infamous Barbara Palmer, countess of Castlemaine, the most prominent of Charles II's mistresses in the first half of his reign. This was followed by the anonymous *The Amours of the Sultana of Barbary* (1689), an extraordinarily detailed mapping of Charles II's court onto the Ottoman reign of Achmed I (1603–17), focusing on the intrigues and career of Indamora (who becomes at Achmed's gift the Sultana of the title). Indamora is the surrogate of Louise de Kéroualle, later Duchess of Portsmouth, and a controversial French mistress of the English king. An even more complicated, multi-generational transposition of Ottoman onto English court comes in Peter Belon's two-part *The Court Secret* (1689) in which Charles I is figured as Ottoman Sultan Selim I (1512–20), his sons Charles and James erroneously identified with Selim II (1566–74) and Murad III (1574–95), and the French king Louis XIV as Persian monarch 'Abbas I (1588–1629).[53]

Ballaster notes that in such books, Charles II, as 'elsewhere in oriental scandal fiction, is treated lightly', and is not the raging lascivious tyrant one might expect. As a result she finds that 'the presentation of a gentle easygoing king sits uneasily with the oriental analogue'.[54] This perhaps downplays the range and flexibility of the Ottoman role in English culture: over a century of imaginative engagement had generated numerous different positions the despot might occupy. Rycaut describes 'a free and open trade and amicable correspondence and friendship with this people' that had been 'maintained for

---

[51] Ballaster, *Fabulous Orients*, 6.
[52] See further Chapter 34 on 'Secret Histories' by Rebecca Bullard.
[53] Erroneously because Selim II and Murad III were the sons of Suleiman I ('the Magnificent', who ruled 1520–66), who was himself son of Selim I.
[54] Ballaster, *Fabulous Orients*, 174.

the space of above eighty years', a rich history that should not be underestimated when considering fictional engagements.[55] The novel form also allowed greater nuance, intimacy, and depth than the popular stage, where stock types dominated; and each of these 'secret histories' are claimed, ostensibly at least, to be true, authentic portrayals and are based on the presumption of a reader's sophisticated familiarity with Ottoman court culture and insatiable desire for more.[56] Two defining elements of these satires come to the fore: the elision of an English monarchical system with Ottoman despotism; and, closely connected, the pivotal political role played by women, in each case extending their influence beyond the harem (a space of endless fascination for English writers and readers) and encompassing both ruler and structures of governance. As the reader moves through these works they actively collapse into one another eastern and western, Islamic and Christian, in a thrilling indictment of both.

Another innovative, influential, and popular volume of the period that similarly offers an apparently authentic and privileged intimacy in relation to eastern and western matters is *Letters Writ by a Turkish Spy* (published in English in eight volumes between 1691 and 1694, and repeatedly thereafter), initially based on a number of short volumes in French by Genoese author Giovanni Paolo Marana that had been published in Paris and Amsterdam between 1684 and 1686. Daniel Defoe would extend the account in his *Continuation of Turkish Letters Writ by a Turkish Spy in Paris* (1718) and Marana's text also provided inspiration for Montesquieu's celebrated *Lettres Persanes* (1721), alongside being a less explicit influence on Fielding, Smollett, and a host of later English writers. Across the six hundred letters written by Mahmut (the Turkish spy) to a variety of correspondents, the reader is offered apparently unmediated access to the clandestine observations of a strange observer on the momentous European politics of the time, and thus intimate access to Mahmut himself. Marana's initial preface spins an elaborate frame in which the original letters were found abandoned and then translated from their original Arabic into Italian, and from Italian into French, and then from French into English: a suitably labyrinthine trail. He thereby reassures his reader that they hold in their hands 'a *real History*' rather than a '*Romance*' that faithfully reproduces Mahmut's prose style, for he is commended for explaining himself 'neatly' and speaking of things 'with great Frankness'; his 'Style shews a great Liberty of Spirit, and never Passion.'[57]

In terms that are similar to those used by Robert Hooke, Marana exhorts his 'Gentle Reader' to peruse 'without fear of tiring thy self, or being deceived', and then makes an argument reminiscent of Rycaut's earlier sympathies:

> though these Letters be neither *Greek* nor *Latin*, nor written by a *Christian*, they contain nothing of Barbarous; and though the Ignorant be in great Numbers amongst

---

[55] Rycaut, *Present State*, 49.

[56] The 'oriental' drama of the majority of this period is considered in Birchwood, *Staging Islam in England*, passim.

[57] Giovanni Paolo Marana, *Letters Writ by a Turkish Spy, Who Lived Five and Forty Years, Undiscovered, at Paris* (1687), sig. A5r.

the *Turks*, there are yet Men of great Understanding, that write the *Annals* of the *Ottoman* Empire, though they are not easy to come by; for, their Books not being printed, they scarce ever reach us. We may notwithstanding believe, That amongst this Nation, that we term Barbarous, there are great and wise Captains, good Men, and learned Authors...[58]

English readers and audiences of all types had long been interested in the reputation of their country and their faith in the Ottoman court, a perspective supplied by the reproduction of Anglo-Ottoman courtly correspondence by Richard Hakluyt and Samuel Purchas in the late sixteenth and early seventeenth centuries.[59] Maroma skilfully exploits the truth-claims embedded in such letters and his readers' hunger for intrigue, but his prefatory assertions also accord with contemporary re-evaluations of Islam and the Ottomans by Pococke, Stubbe, Ockley, and Rycaut. Articulating this kind of national self-examination through a non-Christian had been a satirical device of long-standing, as in Mandeville's use of the Soldan of Egypt in his *Travels* to lambast immoral Christian conduct.[60] However, it was Maroma's decision to centre the *Letters Writ by a Turkish Spy* on an engaging and curious but relatively minor figure, perpetually paranoid of discovery, and to comprehensively articulate the events of the day through his plausibly alien (but not too alien) perspective, that brought a new form and a new kind of intimacy to English prose.

The popularity of the voice of the Turkish spy in English culture at the very end of the seventeenth century generated a series of more directly ventriloquized interventions, such as the anonymous *A Letter from an Arabian Physician* (1706?) and the pseudonymous Abdulla Mahumed Omar's *Mahomet No Imposter* (1720). Alongside the various English translations of *Ḥayy ibn Yaqẓān*, this popularity also contributed to an even greater demand for authentic eastern voices, one met by translators such as Antoine Galland and his *The Remarkable Sayings, Apothegms and Maxims of the Eastern Nations* (originally *Les paroles remarquables*), published in English in 1695, Gilbert Gaulmin's *The Fables of Pilpay* (originally *Les Fables de Pilpay*), translated by Joseph Harris and published in 1699, and François Pétis de la Croix's *Turkish Tales* (originally *Contes Turcs*), which appeared in English in 1708.[61] All would be eclipsed by the extraordinary popularity of Galland's confected version of the *Arabian Nights' Entertainments* from a number of different sources, which seems to have appeared in English translation as early as 1705, although no early translation remains extant.[62] It would be extensively

---

[58] Marana, *Letters Writ by a Turkish Spy*, sig. A6r.
[59] Numerous letters from various Ottoman Sultans and other non-Christian potentates are reproduced in Hakluyt's *The Principall Nauigations, Voyages and Discoueries of the English Nation* (1589) and in the expanded, multi-volume edition of 1598–1600, as well as in Purchas' continuation of that text, *Hakluytus Posthumus, or, Purchas his Pilgrimes* (1625).
[60] As in the early English printed edition, *Here Begynneth the Boke of Iohn Mandeville* (1496), sig. C2r.
[61] These translations are discussed in further detail in Ballaster, *Fabulous Orients*, 114–30 and 343–58.
[62] The extent of Galland's invention of the *Arabian Nights* has been extensively discussed, and will not concern me here. On this topic see Caracciolo (ed.), *The Arabian Nights in English Literature* and Robert Irwin, *The Arabian Nights: A Companion* (London: Allen Lane, 1994).

imitated, parodied, referenced, and retranslated by Galland's contemporaries and throughout the eighteenth and nineteenth centuries, triggering an English craze for all things 'Arabian' that extended from the literary into fine art, fashion, theatre, architecture, home furnishings, and beyond. Its stories spread 'irrepressibly' and it 'was read in public and in private, in bedrooms and in coffeehouses; it was passed on in different print versions, and its characteristic features entered European culture and operated profound cultural transformations'.[63]

The famous framing narrative—in which the king Schahriar, wounded by his wife's infidelity, is prevented from slaughtering each wife the morning after their marriage by his latest bride, the plucky Scheherazade, who spins tales to him and her sister Dinarzade through each night in the royal bedchamber—is, Galland insists in the opening lines, taken from the 'Chronicles of the *Sassanians*, the Ancient Kings of *Persia*'. As in every other prose text I have discussed, Galland goes to considerable lengths to establish the authenticity of his source: he 'was forced to send for it from *Syria*' and the English preface remarkably asserts an almost ethnographic veracity for the work: the reader will find all 'the Eastern Nations, Persians, Tartars, and Indians, are here distinguish'd, and appear such as they are, from the Sovereign to the meanest Subject'.[64] Yet the same tension identified in Robert Hooke's introduction of Knox's *Historical Relation* between absolute probity and a need to provide entertainment can also be found here. Galland acknowledges (in apparent contradiction of the English preface) that the text is both 'fabulous' and 'diverting'.[65] Particular emphasis is placed on the structure of the tales: what could be more 'ingenious, than to compose such a prodigious Quantity of pleasant Stories, whose Variety is surprizing, and whose connexion is so wonderful?' Indeed, in a striking validation of the orient as a primary source of narrative invention, the preface insists that the *Arabian Nights' Entertainments* shows 'how much the *Arabians* surpass other Nations in composures of this sort'.[66]

From its opening intimacies, Galland's version of the *Arabian Nights' Entertainments* offers all the elements of the earlier secret histories and the epistolary spy fiction combined: courtly scandal, sexual indiscretion, powerful female voices, and tyranny, but it extends the palette way beyond the confines of earlier pseudo-oriental tales, rendering them largely irrelevant, to draw on 'strange' alternative mythologies that had only hitherto been glimpsed by English readers. In that sense it similarly reflects the earlier prominence of texts like the *Alcoran of Mahomet* and the English translations of *Ḥayy ibn Yaqẓān*. The *Arabian Nights* was a text explicitly created for an early eighteenth-century readership, and its prose is crafted accordingly, but, in its unpredictable bucking of western narrative convention and its polyphonic clamour, it

---

[63] Philip F. Kennedy and Marina Warner, 'Introduction', in Kennedy and Warner (eds.), *Scheherazade's Children*, 1–24 (3).

[64] *Arabian Nights Entertainments: Consisting of One Thousand and One Stories Told by the Sultaness of the Indies* (5th edn, 1718), sigs. A2v, A3v.

[65] *Arabian Nights Entertainments*, sig. A2v.

[66] *Arabian Nights Entertainments*, sig. A3r.

nevertheless fundamentally challenged English (and wider European) notions of what prose could do.

Robert Hooke's distrust of 'the vain-glory of telling Strange Things' would certainly have rendered the form and content of the *Arabian Nights* suspicious had he been able to read it (he died two years before it was first published in English). But in all its uncategorizable glory, it—along with the various types of oriental engagement that preceded it—did offer a means for the English to inhabit, and to be inhabited by, eastern cultures. Hooke's intention was always that the national interest was best served by encouraging the writing of prose histories that rendered the wider world knowable. The different ways in which English readers were able to engage the east in prose, through scholarship and translation across the seventeenth and early eighteenth centuries, certainly enabled that desire, breaking down preconceptions in the process. But it was the imaginative engagement that this work engendered that would transform English conceptions of the self and its articulation in ways that Hooke could not have imagined.

CHAPTER 15

ESSAYS

KATHRYN MURPHY

In the period 1640–1714, over 1,500 separate works were printed in Britain with either 'essay' or 'essays' in the title. They address a bewildering variety of subjects, at lengths ranging from a single sheet to hundreds of pages, encompassing both facetious accounts of 'the art of pleasing women', and the scholarly monuments of John Wilkins's *Essay towards a Real Character, or Philosophical Language* (1668) or John Locke's *Essay Concerning Human Understanding* (1690). Essays were written in both prose and verse. Their subjects included gunnery; dancing; tea; the waters of Tunbridge; the being and attributes of God; whoring; the immortality, transmigration, rationality, and sleep of the soul; the Isle of Man; the migration of birds; the loyalty of Presbyterians; 'the original of fountains'; penmanship; trade in Ireland; marine architecture; the true happiness of man; drinking; the mind of Moses; grace; grief; lying; the Lord's prayer; taxes; the arts of love, cocking, oratory, self-government, war, navigation, grammar, astrology, feeling the pulse; cloths; covetousness; and nothing.

The miscellaneity of essay-writing has been a feature of the genre from its origins in the *Essais* of Michel de Montaigne, first published in French in 1580, which by the third edition of 1595 included 107 chapters on topics varying from thumbs to the concept of experience. Warren Boutcher encourages us to see the essay before 1800 not as a distinct genre, but as one name of many given to works in a broadly miscellaneous tradition, part of an erudite and humanist culture, and related to the habit of dispersed antiquarian and philological commentary.[1] This accords with such titles as Mark Hildesley's *Religio jurisprudentis, or, The Lawyer's Advice to His Son in Counsels, Essays, and Other Miscellanies* (1685), John Norris's *A Collection of Miscellanies Consisting of Poems, Essays, Discourses, and Letters* (1687), and William Temple's *Miscellanea* (1680) or the opening statement in the 'Vindication of Montaigne's Essays', appended to Charles Cotton's translation: 'The Essays of *Michael de Montaigne* are justly rank'd amongst Miscellaneous

---

[1] Warren Boutcher, 'The Montaignean Essay and Authored Miscellanies from Antiquity to the Nineteenth Century', in Thomas Karshan and Kathryn Murphy (eds.), *On Essays: Montaigne to the Present* (Oxford: Oxford University Press, 2020), 55–77.

Books.'[2] To acknowledge that the essay participates in a longer tradition of miscellanies does not, however, account for the popularity of the word 'essay' in titles of this period, nor for its centrality to developments in the culture of knowledge, nor why Locke's *Essay* could be called such, not as an aberration, but as an exemplification of that culture; nor for the fact that essaying, as a way of writing and of taking up an attitude, might in fact be characteristic of the age.

Though there are typical topics for essays—experience, drunkenness, solitude, liberty, books, idleness among them—the characteristic feature is rather that an essay is about something, than what it is about. This is clear in one of the earliest definitions of the genre, designed for schoolboys, in Ralph Johnson's *The Scholars Guide* (1665): '[a]n Essay is a short discourse about any vertue, vice, or other common-place.'[3] John Kersey's *New English Dictionary* (1702), the first English lexicon to define 'essay' as a work of literature, offers the definition a 'tryal, or a short Discourse upon any subject.'[4] However, this 'uponness' or 'aboutness' does not distinguish the essay from a number of other possible names for non-fiction prose: treatise, discourse, lecture, sermon, account, inquiry, letter, etc. Defining what is specifically essayistic has thus been a critical preoccupation. Ted-Larry Pebworth has argued that what distinguishes the essay is its intention 'to give the impression of a mind thinking on a subject with no predetermined goal or formulaic conclusion toward which it need aim ... a record of a mind apparently roaming freely', and that this lack of teleology separates it from other forms of discourse on particular subjects.[5] While this sorts well with essays in the Montaignean vein in the early to mid-seventeenth century, it is difficult to square with the works of the later seventeenth century, many of which have definite designs on persuasion. Indeed, the frequent locution 'an essay towards ...', first appearing in Seth Ward's *A Philosophicall Essay towards the Eviction of the Being and Attributes of God* (Oxford, 1652), outright conflicts with the idea of purposelessness, even as it implies that any hazarded purpose may yet be incomplete.

Part of the problem is that criticism has been preoccupied with more or less canonical works which are recognizably 'literary', and with telling the prehistory of what has been called 'the golden age of essay writing, from 1710 to 1775'.[6] In such an account our period sees a shift from the retired reflections of Abraham Cowley and William Temple, written in the 1650s, to the flourishing of the periodical essay in *The Tatler* and *The Spectator*, founded by Joseph Addison and Richard Steele and published in 1709–11 and 1711–12, respectively. It includes writers like Owen Felltham, James Howell, and Thomas Browne,

---

[2] 'A Vindication of Montaigne's Essays', *Essays of Michael Seigneur de Montaigne*, trans. Charles Cotton (4th edn, 1711), 1.

[3] Ralph Johnson, *The Scholars Guide* (1665), 12–13.

[4] John Kersey, *A New English Dictionary* (1702), s.v. 'essay'.

[5] Ted-Larry Pebworth, 'Not Being, but Passing: Defining the Early English Essay', *Studies in the Literary Imagination*, 10 (1977), 17–27 (18, 21).

[6] Paul J. Korshin, 'Johnson, the Essay, and *The Rambler*', in Greg Clingham (ed.), *The Cambridge Companion to Samuel Johnson*, (Cambridge: Cambridge University Press, 1997), 51–65 (65); see also Denise Gigante (ed.), *The Great Age of the English Essay: An Anthology* (New Haven: Yale University Press, 2008).

who participate in 'the spirit of the essay' without using the word.[7] It takes in Charles Cotton's retranslation of Montaigne in 1685, intended to replace Florio's supposedly unfaithful and error-ridden version of 1603, and the increasing association of the essay with literary and cultural criticism, most notably in Dryden's *Of Dramatick Poesie, an Essay* (1668), the third Earl of Shaftesbury's *Characteristicks* (1711), Pope's *An Essay on Criticism* (1711), and Addison's essays on the imagination and on Milton in the *Spectator*.

This perspective, however, takes for granted the later, literary sense of the term 'essay' and smooths out the heterogeneity of the essays of the period, ignoring the majority of what the period called essayistic and bemoaning the fact that 'the writers of the late Renaissance occasionally applied the word to works which were not true essays'.[8] This is itself in part the result of the critical interventions of the essayists of the period, such as Addison, who establish a separate and narrower sphere of the 'literary', distinguishing works of the imagination from proposals for improvement in innumerable fields, and considerations on miscellaneous topics.[9] To account for the shift from the leisured reflections of Cowley and Temple to the periodical publications of the early eighteenth century without reference to the larger body of essayistic writing, however, misses how the emergence of the essay as the period's dominant mode of discursive and argumentative writing tells a wider story about shifts in cultural and intellectual priorities, and about the capacities of the essay as form. In this chapter, then, I take a different tack, asking what work the term 'essay' does for such disparate projects, and why its implications of provisionality and experiment were compatible with the aims of so many different styles of the period's writing.

A FROTHY DISTEMPER?

Shaftesbury's 'Soliloquy; or, Advice to an Author' aims to rid the world of a 'frothy Distemper' to which 'Writers of MEMOIRS and ESSAYS', who 'entertain the World so lavishly with what relates to *themselves*', are subject:

> Who indeed can endure to hear *an Empirick* talk of his own Constitution, how he governs and manages it, what Diet agrees best with it, and what his Practice is with himself? The Proverb, no doubt, is very just, *Physician cure thy-self*. Yet methinks one shou'd have but an ill time, to be present at these bodily Operations. Nor is the Reader in truth any better entertain'd, when he is oblig'd to assist at the experimental Discussions of his practising Author, who all the while is in reality doing no better, than taking his Physick in publick.[10]

---

[7] Hugh Walker, *The English Essay and Essayists* (London: J. M. Dent, 1915), 84, on Howell.
[8] Pebworth, 'Not Being but Passing', 17.
[9] See Karen Collis, 'Shaftesbury and Literary Criticism', *Review of English Studies*, 67 (2016), 294–315.
[10] Anthony Ashley Cooper, Third Earl of Shaftesbury, *Characteristicks of Men, Manners, Opinions, Times*, ed. Philip Ayres, 2 vols. (Oxford: Clarendon Press, 1999) 1: 90.

Shaftesbury wrinkles his nose at the indecorous self-exposure of essayists. Among the ironies of his complaint is that Shaftesbury's own 'Sensus communis: an Essay on the Freedom of Wit and Humour' was collected alongside 'Soliloquy' in the *Characteristicks*. More puzzling, however, is the question of which essayists might be bearing the brunt of his disdain.

Certainly, Montaigne himself accords with the description. In chapters such as 'Of Experience' and 'Of the Resemblance of Children to Their Fathers', Montaigne does indeed take his physic in public, detailing his personal regimen, his experiences of sex and impotence, and struggles with urinary stones. It was not only Shaftesbury who found such features distasteful. Montaigne's reputation in the later seventeenth century was for 'Bawdery', particularly in the Florio translation of 1603, and remedying such defects was part of the prompt for Charles Cotton's 'pared-down, antiseptic' version of 1685.[11] But the confessionalism in Montaigne's English followers is more decorous, an account of idiosyncrasies of mind rather than body. Moreover, such imitators tend to be reluctant to acknowledge the influence. Thomas Browne, who did not call his works 'essays', objected when Thomas Keck, in annotations on *Religio Medici*, identified several parallel passages in Montaigne, and claimed in a manuscript note that 'when I penned that peece I had never read 3 leaves of that Author (& scarce any more ever since)'.[12] Nonetheless, *Religio Medici*, in its playful self-scrutiny and confessional tone, does invite the comparison, and, since Browne was himself a physician, seems a possible target of Shaftesbury's complaint. But Browne did not seek to take his own medicine in public: putting his name in 1643 to an authorized edition, he insisted that it had been written 'for my private exercise and satisfaction' during 'leisurable hours'; the 'intention was not publike', and it was 'directed to my selfe'.[13]

William Temple's early essays, preserved in a manuscript headed 'ESSAYS by Sr W.T. | Written in his Youth at Br[ussels] | in 1652', explicitly court an association with Montaigne, including an anecdote of seeking a copy of the *Essais* in Paris. Temple's essays move between commonplaces on a variety of Montaignean topics (the inconstancy and variety of judgement, reverie and idle fancy, fortune, envy, honour) and first-person meditation on his own characteristics, which at times show direct parallels with passages in Montaigne and indeed Browne, especially on the topics of idiosyncrasy and human variety:

> Tis folly to judge of others by our selves, there is as greate variety of humours as there is of faces, as much diversity in the temper of our minds as in the cons[t]itution

---

[11] See William M. Hamlin, *Montaigne's English Journey: Reading the Essays in Shakespeare's Day* (Oxford: Oxford University Press, 2013), 50, 65, quoting the manuscript comment of one Abiel Borfet in his copy of Florio's Montaigne c.1680. See also Philip Ford, 'Charles Cotton's Montaigne', *Montaigne Studies*, 24 (2012), 105–20, and Nicolas H. Nelson, 'Montaigne with a Restoration Voice', *Language and Style*, 24 (1994), 131–44.

[12] British Library, MS Sloane 1896, fol. 20.

[13] Thomas Browne, *Religio Medici and Other Works*, ed. L. C. Martin (Oxford: Clarendon Press, 1964), 1–2.

of our bodyes ... nay more then this, besides the difference of kinds and degrees, time and occasions make a difference in the same mind. I may bee sometimes of one opinion sometimes of another, surfet at the sight of that to morrow wch to day I long for.[14]

Nonetheless, as his sister Lady Martha Giffard reported, though the essays were 'still in his Famely ... he would never suffer them to goe further'. His much-admired later essays, published under the collected title of *Miscellanea* from 1680, divest themselves of both the Montaignean influence and the confessional tone. They turn to matters of public import or antiquarian interest: 'An Essay upon the Advancement of Trade in *IRELAND*'; 'Upon the Conjuncture of Affairs in *Octob.* 1673'; 'An Essay upon the Cure of the GOUT by *Moxa*'. That this was deliberate self-restraint is made clear by Lady Giffard, who contrasted the early essays, which display 'such a spirit & range of fancy & imagination [as] has seldome bin seen', with what 'he has writt since with more Judgement & thought'; public decorum required the subordination of wit and fancy to judgement and reason, though it 'cost him afterwards so much pains to suppress [fancy and imagination] in all he writt & made publick'.[15]

Despite Shaftesbury's censure, then, consigning Montaignean or Brownean confession to youth and privacy is a pattern, and part of a process of redeeming the name of the essay for a decorous exposure of the private person in public. Sir George Mackenzie's *Religio Stoici* (1663) was republished in his posthumous *Essays upon Several Moral Subjects* (1713), retitled *The Religious Stoic* and thus divested of its Brownean tincture, and marked as juvenile work: 'His *Virtuoso* or *Stoic* shews us what solid Fruits his green and tender Years were able to produce: For he was not Five and Twenty Years old when he writ it.'[16] Though Abraham Cowley closes his *Severall Discourses by Way of Essays, in Verse and Prose* with an essay entitled 'Of My self', it is not confessional; he confines his attention to tracing his disposition towards privacy, retreat, and resistance to exposure in the public world.[17] The title of John Hall's *Horae Vacivae, Or, Essays* (1646) equates essays with idle hours; Francis Boyle, Viscount Shannon's 1690 *Moral Essays* call them the 'small Issue and Recreation of my own private Thoughts and Meditations, during my two Years Retirement in the Country'.[18] Joseph Glanvill published a series of revisions of an argument against dogmatism, which began with a close imitation of Browne's style, in *The Vanity of Dogmatizing... Manifested in a Discourse of the Shortness and Uncertainty of our Knowledge* (1661). He shed the Brownean tone in *Scepsis Scientifica: or, Confest Ignorance, the Way to Science; in an Essay of The Vanity of Dogmatizing* (1665), dedicated

---

[14] *The Early Essays and Romances of Sir William Temple Bt.*, ed. G. C. Moore Smith (Oxford: Oxford University Press, 1930), 161–2. Cf. e.g., the opening of Montaigne's 'Of repentance', or *Religio Medici*, 1.6, 1.15, 2.2.

[15] Giffard, 'Life of Sr William Temple', in Temple, *Early Essays*, 6.

[16] Mackenzie, *Essays upon Several Moral Subjects* (1713), p. ix.

[17] Abraham Cowley, 'Of My self', in *The Works of Mr. Abraham Cowley* (1668), 143–8.

[18] See [Francis Boyle], 'The Preface to the Reader', *Moral Essays and Discourses, Upon Several Subjects* (1690), sig. A2.

to the Royal Society, and published a final, plainer version of the argument in his *Essays on Several Important Subjects in Philosophy and Religion* (1675), under the title 'Against Confidence in Philosophy'. Again, the 'Preface' to Glanvill's *Essays* establishes a deliberate distance between what was 'written when I was very young', and what came forth when 'more maturity of judgment is expected'.[19] The arc of Glanvill's shifts in style encapsulates a move in the essay from the metaphysical prose of the earlier seventeenth century to the plainer style of the Restoration and after; and an equivocation between 'essay' as the marker of the idlings of private hours, and an individual's considerations of public benefit.

What is, in these writers, a biographical putting away of the childish things of confession, or a consigning of the imitation of Montaigne or Browne to retirement and the irresponsibility of leisure, amounts to a trend in the period's essay-writing, which, as we will see, increasingly divests itself of idiosyncrasy, while remaining interested in the particular. It also suggests that Shaftesbury's objection to the frothy distemper of the essayist and memoirist, in the early eighteenth century, tilted at something of an antique straw man.

Experimental Discussions

The terms of Shaftesbury's complaint nonetheless suggest something important about the period's essays. His use of the '*Empirick*' as analogy for the essayist, and his insistence on practice, bodily operations, and especially 'experimental Discussions', associate the essay with the rise of empirical and experimental philosophy, canonized by the foundation of the Royal Society in 1660, and with the increasing valorization of experience as the ground for knowledge.[20] It recognizes the range of meanings of the word 'essay': a trial, an attempt, a taster, an experiment, an experience. Shaftesbury's harping on 'practice' meets both the sense of the essay as a tentative sketch or draft, and its preference for learning from lived experience, rather than theory or dogma. As well as a calque for 'essays', 'experimental discussions' is a tautology, since 'discussion' etymologically means a trial, test, examination, investigation.[21] Behind Shaftesbury's distaste for the confessional essayist lies a wider dismay at the replacement of philological and erudite learning with practical experiments.

---

[19] Joseph Glanvill, 'Preface', in *Essays on Several Important Subject in Philosophy and Religion* (1676), a2v.

[20] See further Kathryn Murphy, 'Of Sticks and Stones: The Essay and Experience in the Seventeenth Century', in Karshan and Murphy (eds.), *On Essays*, 78–96.

[21] 'Discussion' comes ultimately from Latin *discutio*, meaning to shatter, scatter, or dash to pieces, or, in medical contexts, to disperse; in post-classical Latin it comes to mean 'examine', 'investigate', 'try'. See *OED*, s.v. 'discuss, v.', and for the sense of 'trial', 'examination', just obsolete in Shaftesbury's time, see *OED*, s.v. 'discuss, n.'.

This is no accident. The most sustained examination of the potential of the essay as a genre in the period comes not from a critic or philologist but from the experimentalist, and founder member of the Royal Society, Robert Boyle. In the 'Proemial Essay [...] with some considerations touching Experimental *Essays* in General', prefacing his *Certain Physiological Essays* (1661), Boyle sets out to explain to an imagined addressee, Pyrophilus, 'why I have cast [these experiments] into Essayes, rather than into any other form'. His reasons are revealing about the associations of the essay in the period more generally. In natural philosophy, writers have felt compelled to write 'compleat Systems', and have thereby been repetitious, purveyed unexamined truths, given the impression that knowledge is already complete, smothered their originality in 'a Rhapsody of trite and vulgar Notions', and suppressed useful nuggets which couldn't be made to fit.[22] '[T]hat form of Writing which (in imitation of the French) we call Essaies' offers the opposite: 'the Reader needs not be clogg'd with tedious Repetitions of what others have said already', while 'the Writer, having for the most part the Liberty to leave off when he pleases, is not oblig'd to take upon him to teach others what himself does not understand, nor to write of any thing but of what he thinks he can write well.'[23] This ability to stop *ad libitum* chimes unexpectedly with Pebworth's criterion for the 'true essay', where essayistic writing exhibits the mind in the aimless act of thinking. For Boyle, however, this serves the advancement of learning. The essay can busy itself with trivialities, Boyle argues, without pre-emptively feeling an obligation to build a superstructure of theory on them. Enriched with 'real Experiment or Observation', it offers the reader independence: 'let [the writer's] Opinions be never so false, his Experiments being true, I am not oblig'd to believe the former, and am left at liberty to benefit by the later.'[24] It is, for Boyle, not only the right genre in which to transmit observation and experiment but also a way of prompting reflection and further thought on the part of the reader, an epistemological tool.

Shaftesbury's association of the essayist with the empiric's experiments, then, is well grounded, as the various qualifiers which essays could attract attest: chymical, hydrological, physico-medical, physiological, anatomical, practical.[25] But the sense of experiment ramifies beyond what we would now recognize as scientific pursuits into a more generally tentative and testing mode. When Addison wrote that '[a]n Essay Writer must practise in the Chymical Method, and give the Virtue of a full Draught in a few Drops', his metaphor touched not only on the sense that essays, being typically 'loose Tracts and single Pieces' rather than 'a bulky Volume', must offer the quintessence of their subject; he also implied a metaphorical context of the alchemist's trial and assay. He shared Boyle's sense of the essay as a space of liberty in *Spectator*, no. 249: 'When I make Choice

---

[22] Francis Boyle, 'Proemial Essay', in *Certain Physiological Essays* (1661), 3–5.
[23] Boyle, 'Proemial Essay', 9.
[24] Boyle, 'Proemial Essay', 10.
[25] See e.g., John Colbatch, *A Physico-Medical Essay Concerning Alkaly and Acid* (1699); Robert Eliot, *An Anatomical Essay* (Edinburgh, 1702); William Oliver, *A Practical Essay on Fevers* (1704); William Simpson, *Hydrological Essayes, or, a Vindication of Hydrologia Chymica* (1670).

of a Subject that has not been treated on by others, I throw together my Reflections on it without any Order or Method, so that they may appear rather in the Looseness and Freedom of an Essay, than in the Regularity of a Set Discourse.' *Spectator*, no. 124, underlined the essay's tentative and speculative nature by referring to its 'broken Hints and irregular Sketches'.[26] The typical locutions of many titles underline this preoccupation with the ad hoc and tentative: 'by way of essay', 'an essay at', 'an essay towards'. 'Essay' could be equated with 'proposal', as in the anonymous *An Essay to a Further Discovery of Terra Firma; or, A Proposal to a More Firm Ascertaining of Title in Lands* (1663), or could be a way of tiptoeing towards a contentious subject, like Edward Stephens's *An Essay Towards a Proposal for Catholick Communion* (1705).

In these titles, it is not clear whether 'essay' names the form of the written text, or just strikes the note of tentativeness. In some natural philosophical titles, 'essay' hovers between the book and the experiment it describes, as in Jean Béguin's *Tyrocinium chymicum, or, Chymical Essays Acquired from the Fountain of Nature and Manual Experience* (1669), or Boyle's own *Essays of the Strange Subtilty, Determinate Nature, Great Efficacy of Effluviums* (1673). This ambiguity is more general. 'Essay' was not simply a form in fashion but a word in vogue, often signalling a stance towards a topic rather than a form of writing. John Locke captured this double sense in the preface to later editions of his *Essay Concerning Human Understanding*: 'If any, careful that none of their good thoughts should be lost, have publish'd their censures of my *Essay*, with this honour done to it, that they will not suffer it to be an *Essay*, I leave it to the publick to value the obligation they have to their critical Pens.'[27] 'My *Essay*' refers to his book; 'an *Essay*', however, is an attempt and experiment, with the implication that such writing is to be deemed heuristic and probative rather than final.

This sense of attempt well suited the emerging cultures of national improvement, with which Baconian advancement of learning was so often associated. The intelligencer Samuel Hartlib published *An essay for Advancement of Husbandry-Learning, or, Propositions for the Erecting Colledge of Husbandry*, written by Cressy Dimmock, in 1651, and essays as suggestions for the bettering of English trade, economy, or various arts and crafts useful to the nation abound in later publications. Cowley's *Essayes* might be thought to land squarely on the side of the 'literary', with their Montaignean titles ('Of Liberty', 'Of Solitude', 'Of My self'). But the essay 'Of Agriculture', though beginning with discussion of Virgil, proposes a college of agriculture, and suggests that the teachers 'should be men not chosen for the Ostentation of Critical Literature, but for solid and experimental Knowledge of the things they teach such Men; so industrious and publick-spirited as I conceive Mr. *Hartlib* to be'.[28]

---

[26] *Spectator*, no. 124 (Monday, 23 July 1711) and no. 249 (Saturday, 15 December 1711), in Donald F. Bond (ed.), *The Spectator*, 5 vols. (Oxford: Oxford University Press, 1965), 1: 505–6 and 2: 465.

[27] John Locke, *An Essay Concerning Human Understanding*, ed. Peter H. Nidditch (Oxford: Oxford University Press, 1975), 12.

[28] Cowley, *Works*, 102. Cowley also wrote a proposal for a college of improvement in his *A Proposition for the Advancement of Learning* (1661).

Daniel Defoe's anonymous publication of 1697, *An Essay upon Projects*, likewise contained, in 'Of Academies', schemes for arbiters of English, military colleges, and the education of women. The book, which was Defoe's first, consists of twelve chapters which propose enhancements to the economy, trade, and productivity of England. It also addresses projecting itself. His preface refers to the '*Projecting Humour of the Nation*', and the introduction claims that the period is '*The Projecting Age*'.[29] 'The History of Projects' dates that epoch's inauguration: 'about the Year 1680. began the Art and Mystery of Projecting to creep into the World.'[30] Projecting is at once what is now called inventing—the ingenious devising of 'Engines, and Mechanical Motions'—and the proposing of schemes aimed at once at '*Publick Good,* and *Private Advantage*'.[31] Defoe's chapters thus propose, among other things, methods for the improvement of banks, credit, highways, 'assurances', 'friendly-societies', wagering, and the care of the mentally ill.

The sense in which these are 'essays' is bound more to their projecting than to their style. In the introduction, the word 'Essay' appears twice in its sense as proposal or attempt: Defoe's description of the '*Projecting Age*' is offered, he says, 'but as an Essay at the Original of this prevaling [sic] Humour of the People', while if, in the book, he has 'given an Essay towards any thing New, or made Discovery to advantage of any Contrivance now on foot, all Men are at the liberty to make use of the Improvement'. Like Boyle, Defoe hands to the reader the duty of carrying out what is proposed by the essay's projecting mood.[32] 'Essay' for Defoe is thus equivalent to projecting itself. It participates in the same spirit as his proposals for the management of chance in schemes of insurance and friendly societies, and in the economies of risk and venture, hazard, probability, speculation, and credit, attendant on the emergence of the new capitalist economy. In his conclusion, however, Defoe returns to 'essay' as a kind of writing. In terms of freedom similar to those of Boyle and Addison, he tells his reader 'I have endeavour'd to keep to my Title, and offer'd but at an *Essay*; which any one is at liberty to go on with as they please'. Again, the liberty of the writer's hypothetical projection is passed on to the reader. Defoe turns in the final sentences, however, to style, stating that he has been 'careful' to make his book rather 'speak *English* suitable to the manner of the Story, than to dress it up with Exactness of Stile; chusing rather to have it Free and Familiar, according to the Nature of *Essays*, than to strain at a Perfection of Language, which I rather wish for, than pretend to be Master of'.[33] The free and familiar essay, ad hoc, tentative, and directed to the future and to the reader at liberty, is thus for Defoe a style in sympathy with the projecting endeavours of the age.

---

[29] Defoe, *An Essay upon Projects* (1697), p. ii, 1.
[30] Defoe, *An Essay upon Projects*, 25.
[31] Defoe, *An Essay upon Projects*, 28.
[32] Defoe, *An Essay upon Projects*, 9, 10.
[33] Defoe, *An Essay upon Projects*, 335–6.

The Deinstitutionalization of Philosophy

Proposals for new educational institutions, such as those of Cowley and Defoe, corresponded to a wider dissatisfaction with the present state of learning and the institutions which offered it; or, in many metaphors, confined or entrapped it.[34] 'It was said of *Socrates*', Addison wrote in *Spectator*, no. 10, 'that he brought Philosophy down from Heaven, to inhabit among Men; and I shall be ambitious to have it said of me, that I have brought Philosophy out of Closets and Libraries, Schools and Colleges, to dwell in Clubs and Assemblies, at Tea-tables, and in Coffee houses.'[35] Shaftesbury, too, claimed that '[Philosophy] is no longer *active* in the World; nor can hardly, with any advantage, be brought upon the publick *Stage*. We have immur'd her (poor Lady!) in Colleges and Cells[.]'[36] Addison and Shaftesbury agree that philosophy must be liberated and restored to the sociable world. David Hume, in his 'Of Essay-Writing', wrote that 'the Separation of the Learned from the conversible World seems to have been the great Defect of the last Age'. Hume saw his own role as mediation: to act as an 'Ambassador from the Dominions of Learning to those of Conversation'.[37] The establishment of diplomatic relations was the work of the essayists of the earlier period.

Philosophy could be liberated from colleges and cells to take up a place either in the private zones invoked by Cowley's 'Of Liberty', 'Of Solitude', and 'Of Gardens', Temple's 'Of the Gardens of Epicurus', or Mackenzie's 'Moral Essay, preferring Solitude to Publick Employment'; or in the sociable world endorsed by periodical essayists. The former fantasize a space in which freedom of thought is licensed, whether garden, country house, library, or study. The latter emphasize the public space of the coffee-house and places of urban gathering and free exchange, the streets, markets, and bourse. The *Tatler*, in its opening number, made clear that certain kinds of knowledge and news were specific to particular venues: 'All accounts of gallantry, pleasure, and entertainment, shall be under the article of White's Chocolate-house; poetry, under that of Will's Coffee-house; learning, under the title of Grecian; foreign and domestic news, you will have from St. James's Coffee-house; and what else I have to offer on any other subject shall be dated from my own apartment.'[38] That the *Tatler*, by the end, was almost exclusively 'dated from my own apartment' does not signal a retreat, but rather the increasing influence of

---

[34] *Spectator*, no. 305 (19 February 1712), satirizes such schemes in a proposal for an academy for politicians. See Bond (ed.), *Spectator*, 3: 95–100.

[35] *Spectator*, no. 10 (12 March 1711), in Bond (ed.), *Spectator*, 1: 44.

[36] Shaftesbury, *Characteristicks*, 2: 4–5.

[37] David Hume, *Essays Moral, Political, and Literary*, ed. Eugene F. Miller (Indianapolis: Liberty Press, 1987), 534, 535. See further Fred Parker, 'The Sociable Philosopher: David Hume and the Philosophical Essay', in Karshan and Murphy (eds.), *On Essays*, 114–31.

[38] Richard Steele, *The Tatler*, no. 1 (April 12 1709).

Addison, and the priority given to miscellaneous essays rather than news as the periodical progressed.[39]

The question was also one of style. Terms of art erected barriers around what Shaftesbury calls 'the graver Subjects', a verbal barrier to the uninitiated.[40] Defoe's commendation of the 'Free and Familiar' style of the essay was also a matter of avoiding institutional shibboleths. In 'On Academies', he recommended the foundation of a society 'to encourage Polite Learning, to polish and refine the *English* tongue', and asserted that '[t]here should be room in this Society for neither *Clergyman*, *Physician*, or *Lawyer*'—the professions emerging from the three higher university faculties of theology, medicine, and law—because 'their several Professions do naturally and severally prescribe Habits of Speech to them peculiar to their Practice, and prejudicial to the Study I speak of'. The essayistic spirit of projecting was to avoid the demarcation disputes and *déformations professionnelles* attendant on specialism.[41]

The essayist thus took up position as Hume's 'Ambassador', a mediator of privileged information. This accounts for the range of titles which taught mechanical and other arts, attempting to codify skilled or artisan knowledge in literary form, such as William Walgrave's *Essay to Gunnery* (1681); William Machrie's *Essay upon the ... Art of Cocking* (Edinburgh, 1705); William Sutherland's *The ship-Builders Assistant: or, Some Essays Towards Compleating the Art of Marine Architecture* (1711), and E. Pemberton's *An Essay for the Further Improvement of Dancing* (1711). The apparent triviality of some of these 'arts', or the evident futility of attempting to teach bodily movements through the medium of print, also gave rise to a subgenre of what Paddy Bullard has called 'Scriblerian mock-arts'. Bullard identifies as the earliest example the squib 'Critical Essay upon the Art of *Canting*, Philosophically, Physically, and Musically, considered' named among the 'Treatises wrote by the same author' on the reverse of the title page of Swift's *Tale of a Tub* (1704).[42]

The periodical press popularized philosophy and other forms of knowledge. The periodical's miscellaneity allowed shifts from the philosophical to the fashionable in the course of a week, but with equally clear direction as to good taste in each. In the first number of the *Tatler*, Steele set as his task to instruct 'Politick Persons, who are so publick-spirited as to neglect their own Affairs ... *what to think*'. The *Spectator* veered between Milton and the imagination, and petticoats and party-patches. John Dunton's *Athenian Mercury*, which ran from 1691–7, invited questions from its readers which would be answered by the anonymized 'Athenians': Dunton, Samuel Wesley,

---

[39] For a similar passage, see *Spectator*, no. 1 (1 March 1711), in Bond (ed.), *Spectator*, 1: 3–4. On the retreat from, and critique of, news in *The Tatler* and *The Spectator*, see Brian Cowan, 'Mr Spectator and the Coffeehouse Public Sphere', *Eighteenth-Century Studies*, 37 (2004), 345–66; see also Chapter 26 on 'Periodical Literature' by Brian Cowan.

[40] Shaftesbury, *Characteristicks*, 2: 6.

[41] Defoe, *Essay upon Projects*, 234, 235.

[42] See Paddy Bullard, 'The Scriblerian Mock-Arts: Pseudo-Technical Satire in Swift and his Contemporaries', *Studies in Philology*, 110 (2013), 611–36 (617) . See also Chapter 17 by Paddy Bullard on 'Handbooks' and Chapter 24 by Gregory Lynall on 'Mock-Scientific Literature'.

and Richard Sault. The purpose was to 'use the anonymity of print to create a dialogue between readers and a group of "experts" who could answer their candid questions'.[43] Though some questions turned on matters of conduct, many others were philosophical, in a broad sense: 'Whether There be a Species in Nature of Which One Creature Does Only Exist?'; 'Who Was the First Philosopher?'; 'Whether Bees Make That Humming Sort of a Noise with Their Mouths or with Their Wings?'[44] While the appeal evidently rested on the pleasing miscellaneity of the contributions, the purpose was also the mediation of learning to those who lacked it.

This might seem to trespass on the dogmatic or didactic mode that Boyle insisted was antithetical to the form. But even in the model of the question and answer, or in the *Tatler*'s teaching of what to think, the essay treats the transmission of knowledge very differently to the genres of academic proof and debate taught in the universities. Scholastic disputation and dialectic relied on agonistic models of argumentation, in which truth emerged from the combat of arguments *pro* and *contra*. Philosophy was adversarial. The pursuit of truth was a binary competition, with little room for doubt, indecision, or compromise.[45] Though this picture ignores the subtlety of medieval and early modern training in logic and philosophy, it is a common caricature in Montaigne, who uses attacks on Aristotle, logic, and metaphysics as part of his assertion of doubt, variety, and uncertainty as the human condition.[46] Essayistic tentativeness and the hazard of projection, with its invitation to the reader to revise the ideas proposed, counter the enclosure of knowledge within the immurement of scholastic and institutional strife. Locke's 'Epistle to the Reader' in his *Essay* situates the work's origins in an occasion on which 'five or six Friends [met] at my Chamber' in order to 'discours[e] on a Subject'.[47] Even *The Athenian Mercury*, in inviting the reader's questions, admits a collaborative model of the production of knowledge. The essay was thus a component of what has been called 'the revolution of mediation' in the period and of the establishment of Hume's 'conversible World'.[48]

---

[43] Robert DeMaria, Jr., 'The Eighteenth-Century Periodical Essay', in John Richetti (ed.), *The Cambridge History of English Literature, 1660–1780* (Cambridge: Cambridge University Press, 2005), 527–48 (529).

[44] From the contents page to the fourth collected volume, printed as the frontispiece to Gilbert D. McEwen, *The Oracle of the Coffee House: John Dunton's Athenian Mercury* (San Marino, CA: Huntington Library, 1972). On the essayism of the *Philosophical Transactions* of the Royal Society, see Scott Black, *Of Essays and Reading in Early Modern Britain* (Basingstoke: Palgrave, 2006), 72–3; see also Chapter 33 by Felicity Henderson on 'Scientific Transactions'.

[45] See Anita Traninger, 'Taking Sides and the Prehistory of Impartiality', in Kathryn Murphy and Anita Traninger (eds.), *The Emergence of Impartiality* (Leiden: Brill, 2013), 33–6(33–6).

[46] See Ian Maclean, 'Montaigne and the Truth of the Schools', in Ullrich Langer (ed.), *The Cambridge Companion to Montaigne* (Cambridge: Cambridge University Press, 2006), 142–62.

[47] Locke, *Essay*, 7.

[48] See Bullard, 'Scriblerian Mock-Arts', 615–16, and Clifford Siskin and William Warner, *This Is Enlightenment* (Chicago: University of Chicago Press, 2010), on 'the revolution of mediation'. On the increasing value accorded decorum in philosophical and scholarly endeavour, see Steven Shapin, *A Social History of Truth: Civility and Science in Seventeenth-Century England* (Chicago: University of Chicago, 1994), 240, 309.

The Conversible World

As Addison's mention of Socrates suggests, a model of heuristic questioning and dialogue was an alternative ideal to the supposed dogma and antagonism of academic genres. For Shaftesbury, Socrates was '*a perfect Character*' who practised 'a certain exquisite and refin'd Raillery which belong'd to his Manner, and by virtue of which he cou'd treat the highest Subjects, and those of the commonest Capacity both together, and render 'em explanatory of each other'.[49] The Socratic model was ironic, and itself attracted ironic treatment. *Tatler*, no. 66, pastiched Plato's *Symposium*: 'The Subject of the Discourse this Evening was Eloquence and graceful Action. *Lysander*, who is something particular in his Way of Thinking and Speaking, told us, A Man could not be Eloquent without Action.'[50] But facetiousness rather affirmed than undermined sympotic freedom, as Shaftesbury argued: 'A Freedom of Raillery, a Liberty in decent Language to question every thing, and an Allowance of unravelling or refuting any Argument without offence to the Arguer, are the only Terms which can render such speculative Conversations any way agreeable.'[51] The Socratic method avoids dogma and performs philosophy as a social activity, in which the method of question and answer invites both parties to the conversation to relish the pleasures of thought, and to revise their positions collaboratively. The essay's characteristic combination of serious and comic, and its aim to lure philosophy from the lecture-hall to the coffee-table, thus find a forebear in Platonic dialogue.

Nonetheless, as we have seen, Shaftesbury did not have a high opinion of essayists. Indeed he sets the essay in counter to the heuristic, civic, and sociable value of the dialogue, wondering repeatedly '[w]hy we Moderns, who abound so much in *Treatises* and *Essays*, are so sparing in the way of Dialogue; which heretofore was found the politest and best way of managing even the graver Subjects'.[52] For Shaftesbury, the dialogue, in which '*the Author* is annihilated', countered the wayward idiosyncrasy of the essay's confessionalism and preoccupation with the first person. But other writers equated the possibilities of the dialogue precisely with the essay. In Jeremy Collier's *Essays upon Several Moral Subjects* (1698), conversation initiates interlocutors and readers both into an enlightened breadth of view. He deploys two characters: Philotimus, whose name means 'lover of glory', puts forward fashionable ideas which he is then forced to defend and ultimately relinquish in the face of the more considered and learned positions of Philalethes, or 'lover of truth'. The dialogic essay exposes contemporary excesses to the counterpoise of conversation, and tests ideas as natural philosophical experiments test the properties of matter. Samuel Parker's 'The Foundations of Dr. *Burnet*'s Theory of the Earth, Consider'd in a Conference between *Philalethes* and *Burnetianus*', for example,

---

[49] Shaftesbury, *Characteristicks*, 1: 105.
[50] *Tatler*, no. 66 (10 September 1709), 453.
[51] Shaftesbury, *Characteristicks*, 2: 42.
[52] Shaftesbury, *Characteristicks*, 2: 6; see also 1: 107–9.

uses the dialogue as an opportunity to present objections to Burnet, while admitting the possibility of reciprocal refinement: Philalethes requests of Burnetianus 'leave to communicate a thought or two of my own, and be free to find what flaws you can'.[53]

Shaftesbury's recommendation of dialogue as a counter to the waywardness of soliloquy is literalized in the ways in which Collier's and Parker's dialogic essays are staged as the interruption of perplexed or wrong-headed solitude. Parker uses the trope to bizarre effect in 'Of the Weather'. He begins with a moonlit walk, in which the first-person persona revolves knotty issues raised at dinner. His meditations are interrupted by 'a person of a sage and serious Countennace [sic], wrapp'd in a Morning-Gown, with a large Ruff round his Neck, a Broad-brim'd, high-crown'd Hat upon his head, under his right arm a Terrestrial Globe, and under his Left a load of Books'. This 'person' is the ghost of Francis Bacon: it is a visitation by the patriarch of English essay-writing. His appearance is prompted by 'what I overheard of your Soliloquy' on the 'unaccountableness of the Weather', something Bacon, both through his lifetime's study and the extra knowledge gained by his 'retreat from this neather world', is well equipped to address. Despite the epistemological advantage granted by the afterlife, Bacon adheres to the principles of the essayistic dialogue, engages to show the reasonableness of his 'Assertions', and grants the persona to 'the liberty of interposing, when any Scruples arise'.[54]

The purging of idiosyncrasy is explicit in Collier's 'Of General Kindness'. The dialogue begins with Philotimus alone, pondering, like Hamlet, what a piece of work is man:

> *Philot.* What false, humoursome, insipid Creatures are Men! Sure these are none of the best Things God ever made! Upon the Whole, I think one might as good disband, and turn Hermit, as be troubled with them any longer. [...]
> *Philal.* What Mr. *Hob*'s Ghost! No less than a Satyr upon your whole Kind? I'm not sorry I have interrupted your Soliloquies, except they had been better natured.[55]

Again, a soliloquy is interrupted. Philalethes's intervention identifies Philotimus with fashionable opinion, Hobbesian philosophy, and the satirical vein of court libertines, with the ghost of Hamlet's adolescent misanthropy in the background. The question of whether Hobbesian self-love is a basis for hating or loving your fellow men absorbs much of the following conversation. Philalethes administers the corrective of conversation to Philotimus's cynical soliloquy. He begins, like Socrates, from things which seem self-evident:

> *Philal.* Are not you a man, *Philotimus*?
> *Philot.* What then?
> *Philal.* Then, by your own Confession, 'tis forty to one but that some Part of the disagreeable Character belongs to your self.[56]

---

[53] Parker, *Six Philosophical Essays* (1700), 2.
[54] Parker, *Six Philosophical Essays*, 36–8.
[55] Jeremy Collier, *Essays upon Several Moral Subjects. Part I* (3rd edn, 1698), 147–8.
[56] Collier, *Essays*, 148.

Since Philotimus possesses common human nature—a vivid strain in Montaigne's essays—misanthropy is a form not of self-love but of self-hatred. Like Socrates, Philalethes leads Philotimus towards self-contradiction, here with the additional poignancy that self-contradiction is achieved by recognizing what is most general and least individual about the self. Philotimus must shift from solitary idiosyncrasy to what he shares with all other men, on the basis of which self-love turns out to be an expression of universal benevolence. 'General Kindness', says Philalethes in the capstone of his argument, 'springs from a generous Root':[57] not only from a benevolent motive but also from the etymological root of 'generous' in genus, belonging to the general kind. The essay's title gains a significant double sense. The dialogic movement of Philalethes's argument rebukes the association of the essay with Montaignean idiosyncrasy; and in this, it enacts one of the major shifts in essayistic writing in the period.

Against Idiosyncrasy

The advocacy of the dialogue in Shaftesbury, Collier, and Parker, the move away from the Montaignean confessional style of the earlier period, the issuing of periodicals anonymously or as if from a 'Committee', as in the early numbers of the *Spectator*, and the communal reading of them in coffee-shops: all these suggest a move away from the individual voice.[58] It is an ideal suggested in the title of Shaftesbury's 'Sensus Communis'. Common sense is not just a sturdy objection to the metaphysical, improbable, or extreme: it is a sense of community, the sense made by communities, and an encouragement to stress what is common rather than idiosyncratic in human nature.[59] One model of 'polite conversation', exemplified by Shaftesbury and the dialogic essayists, is as a middle ground on which participation is only permitted after personal idiosyncrasy had been set aside.[60]

To argue that the essay moves towards such 'common sense' seems contradictory, not only because it denies the personal voice and intimacy deemed characteristic of the essay form, even by Shaftesbury, but because it seems at odds with a significant development in the periodicals of the period: the emergence of pseudonymous personae. A persona, after all, appears to insist on establishing the essayistic voice as issuing from someone, from somewhere. That things are more complicated is suggested by Shaftesbury's objection to 'AN AUTHOR who writes in his own Person', because he 'is no certain Man; nor

---

[57] Collier, *Essays*, 175.
[58] For the fictional 'Club' or 'Society' responsible for the *Spectator*, see nos. 1 and 2 (Bond (ed.), *Spectator*, 1: 6–7); and for the borrowing of the 'club motif' from Defoe's *Review*, see Cowan, 'Mr Spectator', 350.
[59] See Shaftesbury's philological footnote on 'sensus communis', *Characteristicks*, 1: 58–9.
[60] On this model and counters to it later in the eighteenth century, see Jon Mee, *Conversable Worlds: Literature, Contention, and Community, 1762–1830* (Oxford: Oxford University Press, 2011), esp. 1–80.

has any certain or genuine Character: but sutes himself … to the Fancy of his Reader'. Attention is thus drawn 'from the Subject, towards *Himself*'.[61] For Shaftesbury, the individual lacks 'genuine Character'. The antidote, however, is not a magisterial view from nowhere, but a persona which, paradoxically, permits a freeing certainty, a character without idiosyncrasy—a man without qualities. For Shaftesbury, the 'good Poet and Painter … hate *Minuteness*, and are afraid of *Singularity* … 'Tis from the *many* Objects of Nature, and not from *a particular-one*, that those Genius's form the Idea of their Work'.[62] Writers on serious subjects, he suggests, should practise the same abstraction. This is the opposite of Montaigne's self-imposed task—to portray in all its changeability one particular human being. For Shaftesbury, to write with common sense means sifting idiosyncrasy from yourself, and promoting what belongs to kind or genus.

This is how Addison inaugurates the *Spectator*. The persona of Mr Spectator is established not as an assertion of personality but as an avoidance of it. 'I live in the World', he writes, 'rather as a Spectator of Mankind, than as one of the Species; by which means I have made my self a Speculative Statesman, Soldier, Merchant, and Artizan, without ever medling with any Practical Part in Life.… I have acted in all the parts of my Life as a Looker-on, which is the Character I intend to preserve in this Paper'. To be 'one of the Species' is to be an individual. A mere spectator, however, is free to identify with any man, without being a particular one. The essayistic persona of the 'Looker-on' thus resists the commitments of idiosyncrasy. Masked and yet public, singular but not individual, it preserves the liberty of privacy, while coming forth in public. Mr Spectator's presence everywhere, and participation nowhere, allows a paradoxically disinterested interest. The antagonisms of the Civil Wars and Protectorate, and the rise of political party, made of the essay's conversational model of addressing topics and resolving conflict a way of promoting a different kind of discourse, associated with the emergence of impartiality. Mr Spectator affirmed that he had 'never espoused any Party with Violence'.[63] The emphasis is on resistance not to party but to vehemence in espousing one: no-one would have doubted where the *Spectator*'s political sympathies lay (with the Whigs).[64] William Penn could write a *Protestants Remonstrance Against Pope and Presbyter in an Impartial Essay Upon the Times or Plea for Moderation* (1681), which names its own party in the title while attempting to find a middle ground. Claims of impartiality could be, in themselves, party claims. Defoe's *Review* (1704–13) initially bore the title 'A Weekly Review of the Affairs of France: Purg'd from the Errors and Partiality of Newswriters and Petty-Statesmen, of all Sides'. But it was itself, of course, a 'propaganda machine' for the government.

---

[61] Shaftesbury, *Characteristicks*, 1: 107.
[62] Shaftesbury, *Characteristicks*, 1: 78.
[63] Bond (ed.), *Spectator*, 1: 4–5. See Kathryn Murphy and Anita Traninger, 'Introduction', in Murphy and Traninger (eds.) *Emergence of Impartiality*, 1–31; on the *Spectator*, and on Addison's abandonment of impartiality in *The Freeholder* (1716), see 12.
[64] On the apparent impartiality and politeness of *The Spectator* as political stratagem, see Cowan, 'Mr Spectator', 348, 351, 359.

And yet, as Robert DeMaria has argued, 'the periodical essay par excellence is not bound as much by partisan politics as by a less tendentious involvement with the public sphere of private individuals'.[65] The persona-driven periodical thus serves the same aim, paradoxically, as the essays of retreat and retirement. George Mackenzie's 'Moral Essay' (1665), written shortly before he accepted a position as advocate for Dundee, argued that 'solitary Persons' were happier than 'great Men', since 'when any disinterested Subject is fallen upon with them, it is spoke to with so much Constraint, and the Speakers are so hemm'd in by Discretion and Respect, that the Discourse is manag'd with much Disadvantage'. In privacy, however, 'the most hidebound Orator can pour his Conceptions into his Neighbours Bosom, in their natural Set and Fashion, and with as little Alteration as a Discourse receives by being cast off the Press upon Paper'.[66] Printing here models an intimate form of publicity. The shift from retirement to the press mimics the larger change from patronage to the purchasing decisions of readers as the main conditions of earning financial reward through writing. The solitary manuscript essayist retreats from the world in order to cease wearing a constricting mask. The professional print essayist dons a mask which liberates him. In both circumstances, the effect is a paradoxically public privacy, a zone of simultaneous freedom and common sense.

To call your work an essay in this period was thus as much to characterize the spirit and intention of its writing, as to name its form: to suggest an investment in the experimental and projecting spirit; to resist the antagonism of academic disputation, the premature conclusions of system, and (at least apparently) the various forms of partisanship which characterized the period; and above all to claim a liberty of form and thought both for the writer and their reader. It is Shaftesbury, again, who despite himself supplies the most revealingly essayistic account of the relation of the essay to this controversial age. The philosophy he recommends rests on 'a certain way of Questioning and Doubting, which no-way sutes the Genius of our Age. Men love to take Party instantly. They can't bear being kept in suspence. The Examination torments 'em'.[67] For all his distaste for essayists, Shaftesbury's terms are Montaignean. Montaigne's personal emblem was a pair of scales, and he took as a motto the Pyrrhonian keyword '*epechō*': I suspend judgement, I remain in suspense. 'Examination' recalls its etymological sense in Latin *exāmen*, 'an apparatus for weighing, scales or tongue of a balance, process of weighing'.[68] 'Essay' itself derives from the related word '*exagium*', or process of weighing. The essay—prose in suspense, dialogic, a postponement of decision—is thus both the apt genre for impartiality, and, despite its prior association with confession and idiosyncrasy, for the emergence of the conversible world.

---

[65] DeMaria, 'Eighteenth-century periodical essay', 531, 528.
[66] Mackenzie, *Essays*, 132–3.
[67] Shaftesbury, *Characteristicks*, 2: 7.
[68] See *OED*, s.v. 'examen'. On Montaigne's motto see Richard Scholar, 'Reasons for Holding Back in Two Essays by Montaigne', in Murphy and Traninger (eds), *The Emergence of Impartiality*, 65–86.

CHAPTER 16

FABLES AND FAIRY TALES

JAYNE ELIZABETH LEWIS

> What can be said more to the Honour of This *Symbolical* Way of Morallizing upon *Tales* and *Fables,* then that the Wisdom of the Ancients has been still Wrapt up in *Veils* and *Figures;* and their Precepts, Councels, and salutary Monitions for the Ordering of our Lives and Manners, Handed down to us from all Antiquity under *Innuendo*'s and *Allusions*? For what are the *Aegyptian Hierogliphicks,* and the whole History of the *Pagan Gods;* The Hints, and Fictions of the Wise Men of Old, but in Effect, a kind of *Philosophical Mythology:* Which is, in truth, no other, then a more Agreeable Vehicle found out for Conveying to us the Truth and Reason of Things, through the *Medium* of *Images* and *Shadows.*
>
> Roger L'Estrange, *Fables of Aesop* (1692)

EVERY story has a moral, and that of English prose would seem to be no exception. Its didactic turn toward 'Precepts, Councels, and salutary Monitions for the Ordering of our Lives and Manners' after the Whig coup of 1688 is a truth all but universally acknowledged.[1] Wlad Godzich and Jeffrey Kittay depict modern prose as a 'signifying practice' whose defining 'subterfuge' is 'not to be recognized for what it is but for the way things are'.[2] Both from this perspective and in the historical context of post-1688 literature's mounting mandate to involve itself with the lives of ordinary readers, the ancient fable was easily adapted to respond to new pressures on English prose. Revitalized by an emergent culture of popular print, the fable's time-tested ability to deliver 'the Truth and Reason of Things' by way of 'Agreeable Vehicle' bred confident new experiments on the order of Roger L'Estrange's massive *Fables of Aesop and Other Eminent Mythologists* (1692). Indeed, on the brink of the 1695 lapse of the Licensing Act

---

[1] Roger L'Estrange, 'Preface', *Fables of Aesop and Other Eminent Mythologists with Morals and Reflexions* (1692), sig. A3v.
[2] Jeffrey Kittay and Wlad Godzich, *The Emergence of Prose: An Essay in Poetics* (Minneapolis: University of Minnesota Press, 1987), 3, 175.

that would expand the English reading public, L'Estrange justified the humble fable's otherwise improbable rise as an 'eminent' prose subgenre on the basis of its relationship not to fiction but to reality.

Recent students of the fables that proliferated in an increasingly literate society have emphasized the figural and political dimensions of their story portions, or the implications for modernizing conceptions of personhood and power encoded in the speaking animal pretence.[3] Far less attention has gone to the moral portion that turned every fable from a patent fiction into a method of practical instruction, still less to the 'signifying practice[s]' that mediated fables themselves. Likewise, students of the fairy '*Tales*' whose way into popular print culture was cleared by the wave of prose fables that crested in the 1690s lament their supposed flattening into a precept delivery system over the course of the eighteenth century.[4] That by the middle of the eighteenth century '*Tales* and *Fables*' alike had become models for children's literature at its most pedestrian and irritatingly pedagogical has seemed like a demotion after their sophisticated fashioning for adult readers in L'Estrange's day. Yet even the first literary fairy tales in English were overtly moralized, and the moral symbologies that oriented them to 'the Truth and Reason of Things' complemented those of fables. In both instances, prose proved uniquely hospitable to 'a kind of *Philosophical Mythology*', one equally reflexive and referential, open-ended and formally coherent.

Such dualities could co-exist because the morals that defined these kinds of philosophical mythology were seldom only prescriptions for conduct or lessons in life. An ideation given objective form, 'the Moral' was always first a dynamic 'Impression'

---

[3] On the eighteenth-century fable's role in 'restor[ing] the animal as a distinctive mode of being and relation', see Heather Keenleyside, *Animals and Other People: Literary Forms and Living Beings in the Long Eighteenth Century* (Philadelphia; University of Pennsylvania Press, 2016), 16–17, and the complementary view developed by Frank Palmeri, *Humans and Other Animals in Eighteenth-Century British Culture: Representation, Hybridity, Ethics* (Aldershot: Ashgate, 2006). Seventeenth-century fables are analysed as political writing by Terence Allott, '"Brutes Turn'd Politicians": The Seventeenth-Century Fable', *New Comparisons*, 7 (1989), 20–32; Stephen H. Daniel in 'Political and Philosophical Uses of Fables in Eighteenth-Century England', *The Eighteenth Century*, 23 (1982), 165–71; Mark Loveridge, *A History of Augustan Fable* (Cambridge: Cambridge University Press, 1998), 102–42; and Annabel Patterson, *Fables of Power: Aesopian Writing and Political History* (Durham: Duke University Press, 1991). On fables as figuration, see Jayne Elizabeth Lewis, *The English Fable: Aesop and Literary Culture, 1651–1740* (Cambridge: Cambridge University Press, 1995), and Anja Müller, 'Picture AEsops: Re-vision of AEsop's Fables from L'Estrange to Richardson', in *1650–1850: Ideas, Aesthetics, and Inquiries into the Early Modern Era*, 10 (2004), 33–62.

[4] The fairy tale's conversion into moral pedagogy is taken up by David Blamires, 'From Madame d'Aulnoy to Mother Bunch: Popularity and the Fairy Tale', in *Popular Children's Literature in Britain*, ed. Julia Briggs, Dennis Butts, and M. O. Grenby (Farnham: Ashgate, 2007), 69–86; Christine A. Jones, 'Madame D'Aulnoy Charms the British', *Romantic Review*, 99 (2009), 239–56. This trend is critiqued in Jack Zipes, *Fairy Tales and the Art of Subversion: The Classical Genre for Children and the Process of Civilization* (New York and London: Routledge, 2006); see also Lewis C. Seifert, *Fairy Tales, Sexuality, and Gender in France, 1690–1719* (Cambridge: Cambridge University Press, 1996). Aileen Douglas provides a comprehensive and insightful account of the moral trend in later eighteenth-century fairy tales as developed by women in 'Women, Enlightenment, and the Literary Fairy Tale', *Journal for Eighteenth-Century Studies*, 38 (2015), 181–94.

grounded in literary experience. Charged with 'conveying to us the Truth and Reason of Things', moralized '*Tales* and *Fables*' thus made visible the notional '*Medium*' within which all 'Things' come to mean. As Robert Samber's dedicatory preface to his 1729 translation of Charles Perrault's fairy tales ('with Morals') would put it, nothing can surpass the 'Excellency of Instruction by Fable ... there being nothing in the Productions of the Mind as delightful and diverting and at the same time so instructive'.[5] After John Locke, 'the Mind' was famously conceived—and spatially expressed—on the model of the printed page.[6] But Jonas Barish suggests that the temporal 'processes of live thought' themselves were dynamically structured on the model of the modern sentence as, defying predetermined schemes, it makes its way from clause to clause, building experience and thence meaning both in and between lexical incidents.[7] In turn, it was through their playful yet purposive engagement with a conception of '*Medium*' exemplified in the dynamics of modern prose that '*Tales*', like '*Fables*', moved in two different directions. One was toward what we might call moral realism. The second was toward what we might call moral irony. Fabulous vacillation between these possibilities illuminates more than one 'Truth' about English prose in transition.

MORAL REALISM: AESOP IN PROSE

Changes in English prose in the second half of the seventeenth century have long been linked to English philosophy's empirical pivot. Anti-Ciceronian matching of words to things, of propulsive, associative syntax to open-ended inquiry, and of mobile, fungible linguistic units to consensually verifiable referents in the world beyond the book often ends in a show of spurning fantastic figures, 'Hints, and Fictions'. An amplified call for 'sensible words', in Murray Cohen's now classic formulation, complemented both the concrete example's growing reputation as the best precept and the rise of probabilist reckoning.[8] Thomas Sprat's push for 'larger, fairer, and more moving Images'

---

[5] Robert Samber, 'To the Right Honourable, the Countess of Granville', in Charles Perrault, *Histories or Tales of Past Times*, trans. Samber (1729), sigs. A3r-v. This volume, marking Perrault's arrival in English literature, includes such eventually canonical tales as 'Cinderella', 'The Blue Beard', and 'The Sleeping Beauty in the Wood', all equipped with morals.

[6] Brad Pasanek, *Metaphors of Mind: An Eighteenth-Century Dictionary* (Baltimore: The Johns Hopkins University Press, 2015).

[7] Jonas A. Barish, 'Prose as Prose', in *Seventeenth-Century Prose: Modern Essays in Criticism*, ed. Stanley Fish (New York: Oxford University Press, 1971), 309–35 (311).

[8] Murray Cohen, *Sensible Words: Linguistic Practice in England, 1660–1720* (Baltimore: The Johns Hopkins University Pres, 1977). See also John Wallace '"Examples are Best Precepts": Readers and Meaning in Seventeenth-Century Poetry', *Critical Inquiry*, 1 (1975), 273–90; Richard Kroll, *The Material Word: Literature Culture in the Restoration and Early Eighteenth Century* (Baltimore: The Johns Hopkins University Press, 1991); Douglas Lane Patey, *Probability and Literary Form: Philosophic Theory and Literary Practice in the Augustan Age* (Cambridge; Cambridge University Press, 1989); and Courtney Weiss Smith, *Empiricist Devotions: Science, Religion, and Poetry in Early Eighteenth-Century England* (Charlottesville; University of Virginia Press, 2016).

that might 'represent *Truth*, cloth'd with Bodies, and ... bring Knowledge back again to our very Senses, whence it was first derived' reinforced Locke's contention that "'tis the Knowledge of Things that is only to be priz'd" while affirming his 'Preference to one man's Knowledge over another's, that it is of Things as they really are and not of Dreams and Fancies'.[9]

How then to explain the sudden proliferation of fables and fairy tales, quasi-pictorial fictions, literary 'Dreams and Fancies'? Sprat's equation of empirical 'knowledge' with 'Images' and clothing offers one clue as to why L'Estrange strove to make 'acceptable in prose' the fantastic contents of his *Fables of Aesop and Other Eminent Mythologists* in 1692.[10] L'Estrange challenged verse's predominance in earlier fable collections like the two John Ogilby had published in 1651 and 1668 and Francis Barlow's sumptuous 'Catholic' Aesop, whose 1687 edition carried couplets courtesy of Aphra Behn.[11] Such productions often married 'Dreams and Fancies' to 'Things as they really are'. But the signifying practice that conditioned them—verse—was obviously contrived. By contrast, L'Estrange's improvisational sentences belonged to what Cynthia Wall calls 'the prose of things'.[12] On every crowded page, a rambling apologue precipitated an even more loosely-jointed 'Moral' that in turn prompted a shapeless, if substantive, paragraph of 'Reflexion'. The pages of L'Estrange's *Fables* thus appear crowded, bulky, and formally unconstrained—visibly integrating verbal forms with the sensible world that fables seemed to reference by way of both their garrulous, sceptical animal interlocutors and their pretence of application to the 'Truth' beyond their pages. In turn, story's spontaneous coupling with moral sparked a 'Reflexion' that reintegrated that truth with the movements of the mind. It was prosaic enterprises like L'Estrange's that most handily transported fables and their morals from mid-seventeenth-century Puritan textbooks to early eighteenth-century periodicals like the *Tatler* and the *Spectator* devoted to the practical culture of the popular mind.

In a 1711 essay assessing the fabular 'Way of Writing' that had become vital to his own undertaking, Addison's Mr Spectator thus deemed 'Fables' more than 'the first Pieces of Wit that made their Appearance in the World'.[13] As rudimentary symbolic forms, they were equally suited to the practical demands of a new 'World', even as their appearance in 'Pieces' presupposed the literary medium as bridge to the old one. In the Aesopian collections of the period, fables' ability to make that medium visible as an empirical determinant of identity, meaning, and value underwrote their conventional identity as

---

[9] Thomas Sprat, *History of the Royal Society of London* (1667), 112; John Locke, *An Essay concerning Human Understanding*, ed. Peter Nidditch (Oxford: Clarendon, 1975), 4.4.1.

[10] The phrase 'acceptable in prose' is from the 'Preface' to *Aesop Naturaliz'd* (4th edn, 1727), sig. A2.

[11] See Line Cottegnies, 'Aphra Behn's French Translation', in *The Cambridge Companion to Aphra Behn*, ed. Derek Hughes (Cambridge: Cambridge University Press, 2004), 20–32.

[12] Cynthia Wall, *The Prose of Things: Transformations of Description in the Eighteenth Century* (Chicago: University of Chicago Press, 2014).

[13] Joseph Addison, *Spectator*, no. 183 (29 September 1711), in Donald F. Bond (ed.), *The Spectator*, 5 vols. (Oxford: Oxford University Press, 1987), 2: 247.

'Precepts' that are 'gilded with Delight'.[14] Fables' reflexivity became a feature of their oblique realism. A cock digging a 'Diamond'—or in some versions a 'precious Stone', in others a 'Jewel'—out of a dunghill fails to recognize its value at the outset of virtually every prose fable collection of the period.[15] The verbal ingredients of the story varied from volume to volume, as did assessments of the bird's virtue and intelligence. Ever the same, however, was the gem's equation with the 'Moral' of the story. Fables' readers learned on the job both how to attribute depth to the reading matter before them and how to extract portable value from it. The fable's reflexivity went hand in hand with the self-explicating forward momentum of its moral reasoning, binding it to Barish's 'processes of live thought'.

The cock and diamond typically introduced prose collections of the fables of Aesop, whose numbers skyrocketed after 1688; a second wave followed the 1695 lapse of the Licensing Act. But our hermeneutic rooster is largely absent from the rhymed collections with which those in prose competed in a burgeoning literary marketplace whose freedoms were often understood to extend those of the mind under the political and cultural ideals of the Whig ascendancy. If Restoration poets had been likeliest to craft verse Aesops for elite consumption, Williamite projects of social and moral reform spawned a new breed of fabulist eager to renew the pedagogical ambitions and transparently rhetorical vows of his republican-era counterparts. L'Estrange was quick to augment and reissue his copious 1692 *Fables of Aesop and Other Eminent Mythologists*, even changing its title to the more prosaic *Fables and Storyes Moralized* (1699). Both volumes competed with popular reprints of *Aesop's Fables, With their Morals in Verse. And in Prose* (1650). The Anglican cleric Philip Ayres's *Centuries of Aesopian Fables in English Prose* (1689) congratulated itself on a 'plain Style' that managed to complement the notion that 'the representing of ... pleasant Ideas to the Reader's Fancy ... is like the placing of Pictures before their Eyes'.[16] Translations of the Dutch prose fabulists Johan de Wit and Pieter de la Court circulated alongside Locke's own 1703 *Aesop's Fables* 'in English and Latin, interlineary, for those who not having a Master, would learn either of these Tongues'.

Locke's long title touts the fable's oft celebrated autodidactic potential. This potential was often tied to the physical properties of the modern book, including the lineation that can be adjusted without loss of meaning only in prose. Inflected by primers like Johan Comenius's *Orbis sensualim pictus* (1675), modern English prose fables claimed both to shape their readers' minds and to change them simply by italicizing verbal equivalents, placing transliterated sentences side by side for comparison, or keying phrases to illustrations. Pitched at the point of interpretation rather than at that of representation, even the speaking animal fable's realism was confirmed by its openness to

---

[14] Isaac Littlebury, 'Preface', in François Fénelon, *The Adventures of Telemachus*, trans. Littlebury (1699–1700; 3rd edn, 1701), sig. A1v. All references are to the 1701 third edition.

[15] L'Estrange, *Fables*, 1; Philip Ayres, *Mythologia Ethica; or Three Centuries of Aesopian Fables in English Prose* (1689), 2; John Locke, *AEsop's Fables in English and Latin, Interlineary* (1703), 1.

[16] Ayres, 'Epistle Dedicatory', *Mythologia Ethica*, sig. A3.

the building of meaning as a step-by-step process that unfolds through the manipulation of objects at a low angle to the plane of ordinary life in time. Meanwhile, fables' familiar style and homely cast of characters, beginning with the illiterate, 'Blobber-lipp'd', black slave, Aesop himself, made prose fables a viable literary replacement for the bodies of living schoolmasters.[17] Here independent minds could act upon themselves as they interacted with the bookish bodies of fables. 'In short', Addison's ever-apt Mr Spectator was to summarize, 'by this Method a Man is so far o'er-reached as to think he is directing himself, whilst he is following the Dictates of another'.[18]

Aesopian 'Method' appealed to the literate, liberal 'Man' because, transparently underhanded, it preserved a delicate balance of authority between fable and reader. This appeal was amplified when, under the patent guise of dispensing—or of not dispensing—'Advice', fables initiated (prosaic) processes of 'following' and 'consequenc[e]' that that same man could track for himself. Similar opportunities were soon available to 'the *British Ladies*'. The first literary fairy tales arrived in England via translations of the *Contes de fées* of the disreputable French countess Marie-Catherine d'Aulnoy (1650/1–1705). Throughout the eighteenth century, fairy tales would be imported from the French of such elite *conteuses* and *conteurs* as the aristocrats Marie Jeanne L'héritier, Henriette Julie de Murat, and Jean, Chevalier de Mailly; the Bourbon finance minister, Charles Perrault, and the royal tutor, François Fénelon.[19] Until well after the death of Queen Anne, however, it was d'Aulnoy's fairy tales that epitomized an emergent subgenre. 'Happily interwoven with [her] Novels', so as to 'shew her Judgment more refined and stronger', d'Aulnoy's *Tales of the Fairies* exploited the textual medium's potential to integrate matter, form, and the movements of the mind so as to institute new forms of literary authority and authorial identity.[20] The intricate, internally reflexive morals attached to d'Aulnoy's prose stories seldom admitted of a single meaning. Instead, in the manner of L'Estrange's 'Reflexions', they bent back toward the prose narratives that they accompanied.

The first of three early eighteenth-century translations of d'Aulnoy's *Tales of the Fairies* appeared posthumously at the hands of a consortium of publishers in 1707, bundled with the 'Memoirs of her Life', her letters, and her Spanish 'Novels and Histories'. This paratextual material integrated both these eighteen fairy tales' semi-mythic setting 'on a Time' and their ties to the oral culture of aristocratic French salon culture with the progressive present time of their reading in English. Although modern scholars have seen what Addison called the 'Fairie way of Writing' as the source of an escapist 'pastoral of

---

[17] L'Estrange, 'Life of Aesop', in *Fables*, 1. Aesop was allegedly hunchbacked, black, and afflicted with a speech impediment; see Patterson, *Fables of Power*, 13–44; and Lewis, *English Fable*, 71–98.

[18] Addison, *Spectator*, no. 183 (29 September 1711), in Bond (ed.), *Spectator*, 2: 248.

[19] A helpful survey of eighteenth-century English translations of French fairy tales is Nancy B. Palmer and Melvin D. Palmer, 'The French "Conte de Fée" in England', in *Studies in Short Fiction*, 11 (1974), 35–44. For a detailed reading of the fairy tale as women's writing, see Elizabeth Harries, *Twice upon a Time: Women Writers and the History of the Fairy Tale* (Princeton, NJ: Princeton University Press, 2001).

[20] Preface to Marie-Catherine d'Aulnoy [d'Anois], *A Collection of Novels and Tales of the Fairies*, 3 vols. (1728), 1, p. viii.

reading' or as a disingenuously 'distressed genre', d'Aulnoy's tales were often detached from the past.[21] 'The Empire of the Fairies, had not flourish'd many Centuries', begins a later translation of the popular tale of Graciosa and Percinet, 'but there reigned in the Eastern Countries, a King and Queen, with so much Clemency and Justice, that they had gain'd the Hearts of all their Subjects.'[22]

D'Aulnoy's interest in right rule recognized through its affective influence on its subjects marks yet another aspect of what would count as realism for liberalizing English political imaginations. Other adaptations to 'the Truth and Reason of Things' were more subtle and systemic: from the start, d'Aulnoy's fine-spun stories of lovesick princes transformed into charismatic bluebirds and princesses who spout mouthfuls of diamonds mixed unexpectedly with the volatile matter of vernacular English. Before 1714, two early translations of the first literary fairy tale in English, d'Aulnoy's *L'ile de la Félicité* ('The Isle of Happiness') were embedded in English renderings of her long prose romance, *Histoire d'Hippolyte* (1690). Both versions adopted colloquial vocabularies and syntaxes loosened from d'Aulnoy's elegant salon French into a less varnished frame of reference realized in contemporary English. Indeed, it has been observed that because d'Aulnoy's first, anonymous translator lent the story 'a markedly English flavor, it was [long] regarded as a native English work'.[23] Responsiveness to linguistic environment translates into characterological realism, such that even crones act against archetype, declining drink on the practical grounds that, were they to indulge, 'we should bounce about like mad in our Cups'.[24]

Cross-bred with an explicitly British 'History' and the linguistic and mental ventures often thought able to realize it, d'Aulnoy's tales competed with the first English translations of *L'aventures de Télémaque* (1699), the French cleric François Fénelon's 800-page prose extension of Homer's *Odyssey* for the pedagogical benefit of Fénelon's pupil, Louis XIV's grandson. Balancing his young reader's tenderness against the probability of his ascent to political authority in the future, Fénelon's moralized tale strategically replaced Homer's epic protagonist with his son Telemachus and doubled down on Homer's already episodic structure, repeating it with several telling differences that shifted the narrative centre from Telemachus to the didactic prose framework that makes him visible to the mind's eye. If Telemachus as character is less significant than Telemachus as didactic function, and if neither is as significant as the moralized story form itself, most significant of all is the newly prominent figure of Mentor, whose name and style of speech make him a walking model of emergent English prose values: 'His Discourse seem'd short, and they wish'd he had spoken longer. All he had said, remain'd

---

[21] Kevin Pask, *The Fairy Way of Writing: From Shakespeare to Tolkien* (Baltimore: The Johns Hopkins University Press, 2013), 69; Susan Stewart, *Crimes of Writing: Problems in the Containment of Representation* (New York: Oxford University Press, 1991), 66.
[22] d'Aulnoy, *The History of the Tales of the Fairies*, 3 vols. (1734), 1: 7.
[23] Palmer and Palmer, 'The French "Conte de Fée" in England', 35.
[24] d'Aulnoy, *The History of Hippolyte, Count of Douglas* ([1690] 1691), 8. See also Paula R. Backsheider, *Elizabeth Singer Rowe and the Development of the English Novel* (Baltimore: The Johns Hopkins University Press, 2013), 90–1.

as it were Engraved in their Hearts; his Speech made him believ'd; every one was greedily attentive both with their Ears and Eyes, to catch the least Syllable that came out of his Mouth.'[25] When Mentor is revealed to be Minerva in disguise, the prose style that he embodies takes on the charismatic, mysterious, even supernatural authority once reserved for philosophers, mystics, and kings.

Minerva metonymically represents a covert matrix of female tutors whose instruction subtly organizes the narrative as a whole. This matrix includes the seductive nymph Calypso, who early on dispatches Homer's plot in a two-page summary that transforms his majestic epic in verse into a didactic prose history tailored to the modern reader.[26] This transformation clears the way for a protracted series of invented episodes. Each is fixed within a moralized frame whose irenic stance against luxury, absolute monarchy, and war in favour of trade and limited monarchy got the book censored in France.[27] No such fate met its Whiggish English translation, the first instalment of which appeared in 1699 at the hands of Isaac Littlebury, translating for Awnsham and John Churchill, who were also the publishers of Locke's *Thoughts Concerning Education* (1693). The popularity of *The Adventures of Telemachus*, especially as a moral guide for young boys, was evident in its eight English editions by 1713.[28] An opera based on the Calypso episode was staged in London as early as 1712, attesting to the work's intermedial potential. While Hanoverian adaptations would turn *Telemachus* into a scene of speculation and debate about the nation's political future, the text's initial and persistent meaning for English readers was reflexively pedagogical.[29] A 1712 rendering in a mere ninety-nine pages of verse justified its own existence on the grounds that 'the Stile is so poetical', and 'the materials so well furnish'd out, that nothing but an easy Talent at Versification seems wanting to make the whole a very entertaining Poem'. But if *Telemachus* was to break the literal suspense entailed in entertainment and move forward into the world, prose was in order.[30] So twelve *Telemachi* in prose dutifully materialized before the end of the eighteenth century.

Littlebury's preface to the first English edition of what was now *The Adventures of Telemachus* proposed that Fénelon 'involve[d] his Instructions in Fable' because 'he lives under a Monarchy that will not suffer open and undisguised Truth'. The trope of constrained speech linked the Telemachus franchise to the Aesopian corpus, where

---

[25] Fénelon, *Adventures of Telemachus*, trans. Littlebury, 356.

[26] Adeline Johns-Putra, 'Gendering Telemachus: Anna Seward and the Epic Rewriting of Fénelon's *Télémaque*', in *Approaches to the Anglo and American Female Epic, 1621–1982*, ed. Bernard Schweitzer (Burlington, VT: Ashgate, 2006), 87–97.

[27] On *Télémaque* as an allegory of political economy, see Paul Schuurman, 'Fénelon on Luxury, War, and Trade in the Telemachus', *History of European Ideas*, 38 (2012), 179–99.

[28] *Telemachus*'s history within the growing body of eighteenth-century children's literature is taken up by Ruth B. Bottigheimer in 'Fairy Tale, Telemachus, and *Young Misses Magazine*', *Children's Literature Association Quarterly*, 28 (2003), 171–5.

[29] See e.g., Doohwan Ahn, 'From Idomenius to Protesilaus: Fénelon in Early Hanoverian Britain', in *Fénelon in the Enlightenment: Traditions, Adaptations, and Variations*, ed. Christoph Schmitt-Maaβ, Stefanie Stockhorst, and Doohwan Ahn (Amsterdam: Rodopi, 2014), 99–128.

[30] Preface, *The Adventures of Telemachus in Verse* (1712), sig. A3v.

the slave Aesop's oft-reprised biography treats his cryptic utterances as evidence of an oppressive sociopolitical environment that repudiates truth spoken to power.[31] Just as the *Life of Aesop* actually demystifies his fables themselves, however, Littlebury's claim regarding 'Truth' disguised reframes what follows as truth *un*disguised, at least for English readers. In their carefully posited vulnerability to literary impression, those readers' resemblance to the naïve Telemachus joined forces with their distance from him, bringing them into the ethical and political reasoning that unfolds sequentially over the book's many pages. Its first English preface thus naturally praised 'that Virtue, Wisdom, and ardent Desire to procure the Good of Mankind, which are enterwoven [sic] in the following Story'.[32] As it prolonged the moral life of prose in an unstable social and political context, such interweaving of intention and 'Story' made Fénelon's didactic fantasy a natural tributary to the English novel, and even a trainer of the mentality that sustained it. (Tobias Smollett's highly regarded translation of *Telemachus* would appear posthumously in 1776.) Telemachan dispositions of mind came with a political spin: an array of Mediterranean political cultures unimagined in Homer imposed on Fénelon's narrative a spatial configuration that in itself pointed up precepts of right governance by way of examples both positive and negative: ''tis the Law and not the Man that ought to reign' is the recurrent lesson.[33] Such morals, matched to the reader's supposedly free movement through the pages of *Telemachus*, flattered Williamite ideology and Whig sensibilities. But then again Fénelon himself had freed the Homeric text for future generations.

As moralized imports that could be assimilated into a native economy and metabolized through the mentalities they scripted, English adaptations of 'eminent' non-native 'Mythologists' from Aesop to d'Aulnoy and Fénelon invite comparison with contemporary translations of François Pétis de la Croix's *Contes turcs* (1707) and *Mille et un jours* (1710–12), not to mention *The Arabian Nights' Entertainments*, Grub Street's best-selling 1706 translation of the first part of the French orientalist and archaeologist Antoine Galland's *Mille et une nuits* (1704–17). Ros Ballaster stresses complicity between the appropriation of these exotic literary forms and the advance of empire.[34] But even orientalist fantasy bound reason and imagination within prosaic habits of mind. Rival translations by Abel Boyer and William King of what were now packaged as 'Turkish Tales' and 'Persian Tales' were often broken down into individual tales that could be recycled as didactic fables in the pages of popular periodicals, the most notable being Eustace Budgell's conversion of the story of Fadlallah and Zemroude for *The Spectator* into 'a Story in some Measure applicable to [a] Piece of Philosophy' from Locke.[35]

---

[31] Fénelon, *Adventures of Telemachus*, trans. Littlebury, sig. A3v; Patterson, *Fables of Power*, 13–14.
[32] Fénelon, *Adventures of Telemachus*, trans. Littlebury, sig. A3v.
[33] Fénelon, *Adventures of Telemachus*, trans. Littlebury, 164.
[34] See e.g., Ros Ballaster, *Fabulous Orients: Fictions of the East in England, 1662–1785* (Oxford: Oxford University Press, 2005), 1–17; see also Chapter 14 on 'Encounters with the East' by Matthew Dimmock.
[35] *Spectator*, no. 578 (9 August 1714), in Bond (ed.), *Spectator*, 4: 575. See Mark Blackwell, 'The People Things Make: Locke's *Essay concerning Human Understanding* and the Properties of the Self', *Studies in Eighteenth-Century Culture*, 35 (2006), 77–94.

Meanwhile, the English *Arabian Nights* has since been singled out for 'flat dependent clause[s]' and 'prosaic ending[s]' that contrast with the 'fairy-tale magic effect' of Galland's French.[36] As Ballaster has shown, for all their investment in the narrative pleasures of indeterminacy and sensuous immediacy, the English translations of these works sustained reputations as historical and anthropological documents whose moral points depended on their grounding in the manners and mores of Middle Eastern society—a double-barrelled moral realism less at odds with an overtly fabulous, narratively self-reflexive texture than dynamically 'enterwoven' with it.[37] In this interweaving, and the open-endedness it guaranteed, irony found a foothold of its own.

Moral Irony

Introducing Viktor Shlovsky's classic 1929 *Theory of Prose*, Gerald R. Bruns ventures that 'modernity begins with the recognition that the object before me is not a sign but a random particle'; hence it 'begins to discover that the book of the world is written in prose'. For Bruns, this means that 'the prose world is a place of violent interruption; it is the nonlinear region of pure historicality that can only be described by means of... the slow breaking down of entities piece by piece' to yield 'an unpredictable and dangerous world in which everyone is someone's victim'. Mastery of a contingent, aleatory atomistic world arises through ascertainment of its inherent 'syntax' even as each of that syntax's constitutive particles can be understood as 'nothing in itself but only a combinatory potential'.[38] The modern fabulist articulated this prosaic worldview both structurally and thematically. His fables, so often gathered into a collection, could break free of their bindings and turn up in other literary venues, as had Pétis de la Croix's story of Fadlallah and Zemroude. In the plots that animate these discrete, infinitely recombinant literary 'Pieces'—especially those, in Addison's phrase, 'raised upon Vegetables and Brutes'—animal protagonists jockey for power, quarrel, manipulate, and intimidate one another.[39] The Hobbesian morals that arise from their contests for domination ironically confirm the stable rule of the world's instability and reversibility, power's arbitrariness and its assertion via the control of representation: 'Innocence is no Protection against the Arbitrary Cruelty of a Tyrannical Power'; 'Honours change Manners'; 'Fraud should be repaid with fraud; and he who studies to cheat others, must not wonder when paid in his own Coin.'[40]

---

[36] C. Knipp, 'The "Arabian Nights" in England: Galland's Translation and Its Successors', *Journal of Arabic Literature*, 5 (1974), 44–54 (52).

[37] Ballaster, *Fabulous Orients*, 74.

[38] Gerald R. Bruns, 'Introduction', in Viktor Shklovsky, *Theory of Prose*, trans. Benjamin Sher (Elmwood Park, IL: Dalkay, 1990), pp. ix–x.

[39] *Spectator*, no. 143 (14 August 1711), in Bond (ed.), *Spectator*, 2: 248.

[40] L'Estrange, *Fables*, 3, 241; Ayres, *Centuries*, 3.

At the same time, the morals of the fables bid for dominance in their own right, only to ironize that dominance through the very necessity of formal assertion. Moral authority was further compromised by the variability that could be tracked from telling to telling—a legacy of the 1640s and 1650s, when the same fables anchored Civil War propaganda on both sides.[41] L'Estrange's landmark *Fables of AEsop* revelled in the resulting multivalence, dishing out as many as half a dozen sometimes contradictory morals and reflections for every fable. If his fables' homely, colloquial diction and syntax won readerly trust in their logic, L'Estrange's morals exposed those qualities as pretence. They did so by laying out the many meanings that arose from any given story—rendering any single meaning an obvious imposition—and through figurative language so ubiquitous that the morals begin to read like stories too. Consider the lead fable in L'Estrange's 1692 collection. Here, a wolf 'lapping at the Head of a Fountain ... spy'd a *Lamb*, paddling at the same time, a good way off down the Stream', and tears him to pieces for 'dar[ing to] lye muddling the Water that I'm a drinking'. Many morals come to mind. The first—playfully reflexive in L'Estrange's highly figurative (if also markedly colloquial) formulation—is that ''tis an Easie Matter to find a Staff to Beat a Dog'. A second moral—'Innocence is no Protection against the Arbitrary Cruelty of a Tyrannical Power'—yields the further 'Reflexion' that 'PRIDE and Cruelty never want a Pretence to do Mischief'; followed by the still further 'Reflexion' that 'the Plea of *Not Guilty* goes for Nothing against Power: For Accusing is Proving, where Malice and Force are Joyn'd in the Prosecution'.[42] The play of morals and reflection is stabilized not through the referential pretext but rather through the negative act of exposing that pretext as pretence; and through the positive inferential process of successively 'Joyn'd' meanings whose terminus, like the play of mind it initiates, is always receding beyond the horizon of the page.

L'Estrange's irony was supported by the same empirical elements that sustained his realism: a typographical medium able to display multiple realities simultaneously in space and a Lockean process of thought keyed to the reader's temporal movement from the sensuous impact of the fable through to moral impression and thence to reflection. Such ploys undermined prose's pretence of transparency without actually compromising its authority as a medium of 'Truth and Reason'. As Roland Greene and Elizabeth Fowler propose: 'unlike poetry, which is often said to be ... autonomous and invisible ... prose is often seen as invisible, coterminous with its contents.'[43] As a fable's moral brings its 'madness' to the centre of attention, prose too becomes visible as convention. While such exposure compromised a fable's signal pretence of transparency, it introduced the second-order transparency of self-reflection. This transparency stemmed from the playful fusion of any member of a fable's cast of characters with that

---

[41] Patterson, *Fables of Power*, 82–7.
[42] L'Estrange, *Fables*, 2–3.
[43] Roland Greene and Elizabeth Fowler, 'Introduction', in Greene and Fowler (eds.), *The Project of Prose in Early Modern Europe and the New World* (Cambridge: Cambridge University Press, 1996), 4.

character's representational function. As Charles Montagu and Matthew Prior observed in 1687, a fable's 'Characters [are] the same throughout, not broken or chang'd, and always conformable to the Nature of the Creatures they introduce'.[44] Yet such 'Characters' open the authority of the morals applied to them to investigation, critique, and re-adjustment. For instance, James Gordon's 1701 *Remarks on Roger L'Estrange's Edition of Aesop's Fables* were not designed to refute the hard-scrabble moral universe in which L'Estrange's plots unfolded; indeed, when Gordon read that 'AEsop's Cock, in preferring a Barley-Grain to a Diamond, is an Emblem of such Fools as Midas', he ruled it a 'better Demonstration, than that of a circle in a Triangle'. Nonetheless, Gordon treated L'Estrange's characters, like his morals and reflections, as prompts to his own 'Historical Illustrations'. These in turn generated new 'Supposition[s]'.[45] So were modern fable readers made into fabulists in their own right.

The Phrygian slave Aesop himself was fast becoming interchangeable with any number of other fabulists. The Anglican cleric Philip Ayres's *Mythologia Ethica* figured fabulous authorship not only in Aesop but in the Roman slave Phaedrus, and even in Chiron the Centaur, since after all 'every one of us partake of two different Natures or Qualities; the one of a Man, and the other of a Beast'.[46] Likewise, their obvious mediation through chains of non-English authors seems to sit awkwardly with fables' didactically usable claims to sensuous immediacy by way of animal actors, supplementary illustrations, and words brought as close as possible to the status of things. Joseph Harris's 1699 translation of the fables of the Brahmin Pilpay (sometimes known as Bidpai) dutifully found them to 'contain[n] many useful Rules for the Conduct of Humane Life', but most of his energy was devoted to the book's migrations from 'Indolstan', where 'the Author of this Treatise' had 'compos'd this little Work', to Persia, then into 'the Ancient *Persian* Tongue', followed by Arabic and at last French. 'This last Translation surpass'd all the Rest', Wright notes, and 'from thence it was that we translated ours'.[47]

Fables always lived at points of transition between languages. Just as Aesop was fabled to have turned from a slave into a free and speaking subject, so were modern fables useful for teaching the young how to read Latin, French, and even English itself. This charge had gained new momentum with literacy's expansion in the seventeenth century. But the pragmatism that it embodies opened the way to irony as well as to instrumentality. L'Estrange admitted as much when he foregrounded the pedagogical uses of his *Fables of Aesop*—a strategy that, as Line Cottegnies suggests, helped someone whose politics had become unpopular to prevail in a 'competitive literary

---

[44] Charles Montagu and Matthew Prior, *The Hind and the Panther Transvers'd to the Story of the Country Mouse and the City Mouse* (1687), in *Literary Works of Matthew Prior*, ed. H. Bunker Wright and Monroe K. Spears, 2 vols. (Oxford: Oxford University Press, 1959), 2: 35.

[45] Gordon, *Remarks on Roger L'Estrange's Edition of Aesop's Fables* (1701), 1.

[46] Ayres, Preface to *Mythologia Ethica*, sig. A1v.

[47] Joseph Harris, 'Advertisement', in *The Fables of Pilpay, a Famous Indian Phylosopher* (1699), sigs. A4v–A5.

market'.[48] 'This *Rhapsody* of *Fables* is a Book Universally Read, and Taught in All our Schools', L'Estrange declared,

> but almost at such a rate as we Teach *Pyes* and *Parrots,* that Pronounce the Words without so much as Guessing at the Meaning of them: Or to take it Another way, the Boys Break their Teeth upon the Shells, without ever coming near the Kernel. They Learn the *Fables* by *Lessons,* and the Moral is the least part of our Care in a Childs Institution: so that take Both together, and the One is stark Nonsense, without the Application of the Other.

L'Estrange's figures of speech ironize the complaint they level. Prose promises some deliverance from the resulting hall of mirrors, but at a cost:

> To supply this Defect now, we have several English *Paraphrases* and *Essays* upon *Aesop,* and Divers of his Followers, both in *Prose* and *Verse*: the Latter have perchance Ventur'd a little too far from the Precise Scope of the Author, upon the Privilèdge of a Poetical License: And for the Other of Ancient Date, the *Morals* are so *Insipid* and *Flat,* and the *Style* and *Diction* of the *Fables,* so *Course* and *Uncouth,* that they are rather *Dangerous,* than Profitable, as to the purpose they were Principally Intended for; and likely to do Forty times more Mischief by the One then Good by the Other. An *Emblem* without a *Key* to't, is no more then a *Tale of a Tub*; and that Tale sillily told too.[49]

L'Estrange both exercised 'the Privilèdge of a Poetical License' and blew the whistle on fables' potentially endless play of meaning. But it was the tension between a profitless '*Tale* of a *Tub*' and the profit margin that widened whenever a moral hit home that brought his own fables to life, pushing the form in opposite directions over the next decades. Nobody can accuse Locke's own interlineary Aesop of being 'sillily told'. Rather, the collection realized the didactic model that Locke had recently put forward in his *Thoughts concerning Education,* which prosaically recommended that a boy could be taught Latin:

> by taking some easie and pleasant Book, such as *Aesop's Fables,* and writing the *English* Translation (made as literal as it can be) in one Line, and the *Latin* Words which answer each of them, just over it in another. These let him read every Day over and over again, till he perfectly understands the *Latin* … and then go on to another Fable till he be also perfect in that … And when he comes to write, let these be set him for Copies, which with the exercise of his Hand, will also advance him in *Latin*.[50]

---

[48] Line Cottegnies, '"The Art of Schooling Mankind": The Uses of Roger' L'Estrange's *Aesop's Fables* (1692)', in Anne Dunan-Page and Beth Lynch (eds.), *Roger L'Estrange and the Making of Restoration Culture* (Aldershot: Ashgate, 2008), 131–48 (133).

[49] L'Estrange, Preface to *Fables,* sig. A4r.

[50] John Locke, *Some Thoughts concerning Education* [1693], in *Educational Writings of John Locke,* ed. James Axtell (London: Cambridge, 1968), 259.

Yet if mechanical repetition supports the progressive activity of linear transcription, it also potentially reduces it to absurdity: 'When by these gentle ways he begins to be able to *read*, some easy pleasant Book suited to his Capacity, should be put into his Hands, wherein the entertainment, that he finds, might draw him on, and reward his Pains in Reading, and yet not such as should fill his Head with perfectly useless trumpery, or lay the principles of Vice and Folly.' Locke's 'gentle ways' reconcile repetition and its attendant ironies with novel occurrence in the experience of 'draw[ing] out'. Yet these 'ways' persist in generative tension both with the lure of 'useless trumpery' and with the logic of unintended consequences built into prosaic movement forward toward the 'useful Reflections' that can be afforded to the 'grown Man'.[51]

If fables ironize Locke's prosaic realism, they exert the opposite influence on Jonathan Swift's *Tale of a Tub* (1704). Like L'Estrange's '*Emblem* without a *Key* to't', the satire's title parrots a popular term of contempt; the text that follows enacts a dysphoria of ungrounded signage that empties allegory of its pretence to stable meaning and real content. In subjoining *The Battel of the Books* to his *Tale*, however, Swift shifted the ironies into the 'Publick Libraries', where they are stabilized and objectified within the fabular tradition.[52] Interminable conflict between 'Antient' and 'Modern' signifying practices, waged between rival books, is 'aesopically' enacted in a quarrel between a bee and a spider. The impasse between the two is resolved when Aesop bursts through the bindings of a book that had 'chained him fast among a Shelf of Moderns' and defects to the ancient side, there to moralize on the 'two Cases so parallel and adapt to each other'—'That in the Window, and this upon the Shelves'.[53] While the 'Battel' itself stops *in medias res*, Aesopian narration nonetheless supplies a stable lexical praxis that guarantees the text's legibility to ancient and modern readers alike.

And what of the ironies that attended 'the Fairy Way of Writing'? In Addison's oft-cited assessment, this was 'a Kind of Writing, wherein the Poet quite loses sight of Nature and entertains his Reader's Imagination with the Characters and Actions of such Persons as have in them no Existence, but what he bestows on them'.[54] But Addison's verdict had little to do with the fairy tales that his English contemporaries were actually reading. Those same tales also defy the Oxford antiquarian John Aubrey's observation that 'till a little before the Civil-warres, the ordinary sort of people were not taught to reade: now-a-days Books are common, and most of the poor people understand letters; and the many good Bookes, and variety of Turnes of Affairs, have put all the old Fables out of dores and the divine art of Printing and Gunpowder have frighted away Robin-good-fellow and the Fayries'.[55] In reality, the first fairy tales in English were not only imports

---

[51] Locke, *Some Thoughts concerning Education*, 274.

[52] *The Cambridge Edition of the Works of Jonathan Swift: A Tale of a Tub and Other Works*, ed. Marcus Walsh (Cambridge: Cambridge University Press, 2010), 146. On L'Estrange and the political key to his *Fables*, see also Chapter 20 on 'Keys' by Nicholas McDowell.

[53] Swift, *Tale of a Tub*, ed. Marcus Walsh, 151.

[54] *Spectator*, no. 419 (1 July 1712), in Bond (ed.), *Spectator*, 3:570.

[55] John Aubrey, *Remaines of Gentilisme and Judaisme* (1686–7), in *Three Prose Works*, ed. John Buchanan-Brown (Fontwell, Sussex: Centaur, 1972), 132.

from the French but, as such, a product of expanding literacy. Apart from a 1682 broadside version of the indigenous legend of Tom Thumb (the subject of a facetious scholarly examination by the physician William Wagstaffe in 1711), the first fairy tales came from other books. The transfer was facilitated by the prose form. D'Aulnoy's *Les contes de fées* (1697–8) and *Contes nouveaux, ou les fées à la mode* (1699) were both framed by longer narratives; they also present even the conceit of their origins in French salon culture as an aspect of their core preoccupation with women's writing and women's reading—a preoccupation that made the tales a major influence on such later female novelists as Elizabeth Sheridan, Sarah Fielding, and even Ann Radcliffe.

As Aileen Douglas explains, however, d'Aulnoy's fairy tales are centred not just on women's writing but on 'female moral autonomy and active female reason'.[56] Their didactic ambitions can be realized only in this context, as d'Aulnoy acknowledges in the preface to her 1707 *Tales of the Fairies*: 'I hope to continue the Design I have begun in justification of women ... and I shall shew by this recital of their Adventures ... that outward Appearances are frequently deceitful, and that there is more misfortune than Irregularities in the Conduct of Women'.[57] This moral might conceivably yield prose narrative in the manner of d'Aulnoy's contemporary Charles Perrault, whose fairy tales 'with Morals' were later recommended on the grounds that, 'childish in its Appearance' though a fairy tale 'may sometimes be, it carries notwithstanding in the Bottom, a most solid sense, and wraps up and enfolds the most material and important Truths'.[58] And it is true that the morals that framed d'Aulnoy's fairy tales also linked them to 'material and important Truths'. But these entwine with her prose style in subtle ways that have plunged the many critics who agree that they must be prescriptive into fierce dispute as to what they actually prescribe.[59] The English dedication to the 1716 *History of the Tales of the Fairies* is inconclusive on this point, detecting in the tales a '*Check* to the *Levity* of those Ladies who spend so much Time in Discourse inconsistent with their Duties and Characters'. Female readers are thus enjoined to 'prove in *reality* what they appear to be, *Bright and Conspicuous*, and make use of those Spare Hours, devoted to innocent Diversion, in something Instructive to the rest of the World, that Mankind may treat them with more Respect, by a civiliz'd *Conversation*, and the Ladies become more Illustrious'.[60]

Against this background, it is striking that d'Aulnoy's tales should have been promoted on the title page for their capacity for 'shewing': the tale of Garciosa and Percinet 'shewing the Cruelty of a proud Mother-in-Law to an innocent, dutiful Virgin'; that of 'Prince Avenant, and the Beauty with the Locks of Gold; shewing what Difficulties and

---

[56] Douglas, 'Women, Enlightenment, and the Literary Fairy Tale in English', 181.

[57] Marie-Catherine d'Aulnoy, *The Countess D'Anois's Memoirs*, in *Diverting Works of the Countess D'Anois* (1707), 135.

[58] Samber, 'To the Right Honourable, the Countess of Granville', in *Histories or Tales of Past Times*, sig. A4v.

[59] For example, did fairy tales proscribe female agency or subtly enable it? Douglas glosses debates on this issue ('Women, Enlightenment, and the Literary Fairy tale in English', 182).

[60] B. H., 'To the British Ladies', in *History of the Tales of the Fairies* (1716), sig. A2.

Dangers Love will surmount'; the story of 'the king of the Peacocks, and the princess Rosetta; shewing the Vanity of Covetousness, Pride and Envy'. Only the last of these 'shewings' comes close to limiting the meaning of the tale in question, or of moulding it into a moral precept. In keeping with L'Estrange's '*Symbolical* Way of Morallizing', 'shewing' was best understood simply as 'shewing'—as making the process of reflexive ideation the *foundation* of moral reason, not just a means to that end. D'Aulnoy's fables are thus grounded in process of thought, their realism reconciled with characters that 'have in them no Existence'.

English prose style foregrounds the subtleties of this process, making those subtleties part of the lexical event of the fairy tales themselves. Throughout d'Aulnoy's fiction, 'thus' and 'therefore' connect embodied ideas even as the fairy tales are anchored in language worlds made up of rumour and reputation. This fabulous foundation supports a form of realism that redefines the prosaic as a formal (and often witty) series of prescriptions for making meaning. For example, of the spoiled and temperamental princess at the centre of the eponymous *The Fair One with Golden Locks*, we are told that, 'because she was so extremely Amiable, she was called *The Fair One with Locks of Gold*: For her Hair was finer than Gold'. In the same tale, a 'young Stripling at the Court ... because of his comely Grace and Wit, [is] call'd Avenant, or the Handsom'. As the English translation emphasizes, D'Aulnoy's irony goes hand in hand with her interest in literary transference. Avenant thus travels with a 'table-Book in his Pocket, and when any curious Thought came into his Head, fit to be made use of in his Speech, [he] wrote it down in his Book, that he might forget nothing'.[61]

Because grounded in symbolic experience, d'Aulnoy's fairy tales redistribute power both thematically and syntactically.[62] Like Aesop's, her animals possess not only language but the capacity to reflect upon their own sensations. Irenic, egalitarian, and sympathetic, the ethical result contravenes the court aesthetic in which it is expressed. When Avenant compassionately tosses a beached carp back into a stream, the fish 'began to feel the coolness of the Water'; an owl ensnared 'cr[ies] out like an Owl in Despair'. D'Aulnoy's morals are thought experiments whose playful indeterminacy compensates for their realist content: 'men are only made to torment one another, or else to persecute poor Creatures that do 'em neither Wrong nor Damage.' Her rendering of objects as dynamic ideations thus naturally recognizes in those objects the potential for transformation: poor women turn into chickens, besotted princes into bluebirds.[63]

These tales thus present as the 'kind of Philosophical Mythology' that L'Estrange had in mind. But 'Philosophical' did not in this case necessarily mean Lockean. D'Aulnoy

---

[61] D'Aulnoy, *The Fair One with Golden Locks*, in *Diverting Works*, 393–5.

[62] On eighteenth-century children's literature's suspense between 'the claims of judgment and those of imagination', see Geoffrey Summerfield, *Fantasy and Reason: Children's Literature in the Eighteenth Century* (London: Methuen, 1984), 20.

[63] D'Aulnoy, *The Fair One with Golden Locks*, in *Diverting Works*, 395–6. On the occult aspect of these transformations, see D. J. Adams, 'The "Contes de fees" of Madame D'Aulnoy: Reputation and Revaluation', *Bulletin of the John Rylands University Library*, 76 (1994), 5–22.

was acquainted with the neo-Epicurean Pierre Gassendi's *Animadversions* (1658), which are grounded in the same premise that undergirds Locke's empiricism: 'nothing is in the intellect that has not been in the senses.' But for Gassendi, the content of the senses includes the material impressions of the imagination—'*phantasia*'—whose sensory foundation, though it arises from within the body, is no less real than those which originate outside it. Gassendi's empiricist *phantasia* not only shapes d'Aulnoy's prose style but is the same in both human beings and animals, a paradigm for the sympathy that passes between Avenant, the fish, and the owl. Why was such a paradigm better communicated in prose than in verse? Perhaps because of prose's historical claims to transparency, its protean identity as neither a genre nor a medium.[64] Fables and tales ironized the realist pretences that arise from that very ambiguity, checking prose's claims to tell the truth even as they exploited it. So did they realize a uniquely modern moral.

---

[64] Greene and Fowler, 'Introduction', in Greene and Fowler (eds.), *Project of Prose*, 5.

CHAPTER 17

HANDBOOKS

PADDY BULLARD

THE second half of the seventeenth century saw a notable increase in the numbers of printed books that conveyed instruction on practical matters—volumes of 'how-to' advice, manuals, guides to conduct, and all sorts of *vade mecum*. The rate at which their ranks expanded indicates their importance to the history of the period's prose, but they remain (as they have always been) hard to evaluate and to categorize. Because they are practical books, it is convenient to describe them in terms of function. Their growing numbers reflect the practical needs of a new and expanding readership among women, skilled workers, and the urban middle class.[1] Rates of apprenticeship were declining and the guild control of trades was loosening throughout the period, while towns and cities swelled with an influx of young workers from the countryside, cut off from the personal instruction they might have received in more stable communities.[2] As J. Paul Hunter speculates, print culture seems to have taken over 'functions that the oral culture could no longer handle, becoming a vehicle of social change as well as a measure of it'.[3]

A step up the social scale, newly polite or ennobled people needed to learn how to present themselves: hence, as Lynette Hunter has explained, the growing demand for books on 'sugarwork, that sure indication of wealth, on the ordering of feasts, on the "dressing" (breaking in) of horses and on the construction of knot gardens'.[4] These new readerships brought a general increase in capacity for the trade. The well-established

---

[1] For a general account of this trend, see introduction to Natasha Glaisyer and Sara Pennell (eds.), *Didactic Literature in England, 1500–1800: Expertise Constructed* (Aldershot: Ashgate, 2003), 1–15; the standard bibliographical survey is Jochen Hoock and Pierre Jeannin, *Ars Mercatoria: Eine analytische Bibliograpie*, Band 2: 1600–1700 (Paderborn: Schöningh, 1993).

[2] Joan Lane, *Apprenticeship in England, 1600–1914* (London: UCL Press, 1996), 211–17; James R. Farr, *Artisans in Europe, 1300–1914* (Cambridge: Cambridge University Press, 2000), 10–44.

[3] J. Paul Hunter, *Before Novels: The Cultural Contexts of Eighteenth-Century English Fiction* (New York: W.W. Norton, 1990), 253.

[4] Lynette Hunter, 'Books for Daily Life: Household, Husbandry, Behaviour', in John Barnard and D. F. McKenzie (eds.), *The Cambridge History of the Book in Britain. Volume IV, 1557–1695* (Cambridge: Cambridge University Press, 2002), 514–32 (516).

market for advice books aimed at genteel, professional, and mercantile men seems to have expanded at the same time, helped by the fashionable (if intermittent) involvement in the mechanical arts of natural philosophers and virtuosi.[5] Their interest contributed to the increasing specialization of volumes of practical instruction—general guides to husbandry, for example, being joined by more focused studies of sylviculture or botany—and so to the proliferation of titles. The biographer John Aubrey recalled how 'Till about the year 1649 'twas held a strange presumption for a man to attempt an innovation in learning; and not to be good manners to be more knowing than his neighbours and forefathers. Even to attempt an improvement in husbandry, though it succeeded with profit, was look't upon with an ill eie'.[6] As we shall see, the year of the execution of Charles I marks a watershed in the history of the literature of improvement as well: a renewed spirit of practical endeavour, ever eager to challenge the jealousy of neighbours and forefathers, demanded books that showed all kinds of readers how to make and do.

These broadly socio-economic explanations for the rising profile of instructional literature provide a necessary basis for surveys of the books themselves. They also leave many questions unanswered. Above all, they assume a workable alignment between the needs of readers, the usefulness of the texts, and the intentions of authors and booksellers.[7] For many (and perhaps a majority) of texts all three of these factors are in fact complicated. In terms of motives for reading, instructional literature is often appreciated as pastoral—that is, as Arcadian fantasy with a political shadow. To use a well-known twentieth-century example, Elizabeth David's first three cookery books up to *Italian Food* (1954) appeared during the years of post-war rationing. Lack of ingredients rendered them almost useless to her readers in the kitchen: what they offered were evocations of plenty.[8] Looking back to the seventeenth century, Izaak Walton's *Compleat Angler* (1654) made comparably nostalgic appeals to readers at a time of civil war, with descriptions of the cooking and eating of the catch playing an important part in the book's effect. Walton also writes with an irony like David's about the practicability of his advice. In terms of usefulness, it is common for how-to books to offer instruction in processes that are circumstantially difficult, or even logically unspecifiable. No novice can learn how to fish or to swim or to dance by reading a book on the subject, and yet such books continue to be written and read as though she can.[9] Elizabeth Eisenstein

---

[5] Adrian Johns, *The Nature of the Book: Print and Knowledge in the Making* (Chicago: University of Chicago Press, 1998), 446–75; Walter E. Houghton, Jr, 'The History of Trades: Its Relation to Seventeenth-Century Thought: As Seen in Bacon, Petty, Evelyn, and Boyle', *Journal of the History of Ideas*, 2 (1941), 33–60.

[6] John Aubrey, *Natural History of Wiltshire*, ed. John Britton (1847; repr. Newton Abbot: David & Charles, 1969), 5.

[7] See further Chapter 31 on 'Recipe Books' by Henry Power.

[8] Charles Rosen, 'The Cookbook as Romantic Pastoral', in *Romantic Poets, Critics, and Other Madmen* (Cambridge, MA: Harvard University Press, 1998), 76–82.

[9] Michael Polanyi, *Personal Knowledge: Towards a Post-Critical Philosophy* (Chicago: University of Chicago Press, 1958), 62–3.

worried about the oddness of that fact and observed that something more oblique than simple utility was usually in play with instructional books.[10]

When one thinks about this characteristic obliqueness in terms of authors' intentions, it is notable that the common choice of the word 'didactic' as a gather-all label for the period's practical and instructional literature begs many more questions than it answers.[11] For example, why is it that instructional books calling themselves *Manuals* so frequently compile information on topics with which the reader is assumed to be familiar? William Badcock's *Touchstone for Gold and Silver Wares* (1677) is actually a survey of the trade's statutory regulation, for example, while Edward Welchman's *The Husband-man's Manual* (1706) turns out to be a devotional guide. Why does the informative purpose of texts like these lie at such an angle to the information they convey? In the case of Walton's *Compleat Angler*, sporting instruction provides thin cover for a range of undeclared agendas—antiquarian, convivial, confessional, and political. To read such books only in terms of didactic function is to ignore more than half of what they do as texts. There is the danger of anachronism here as well, since early modern writers generally reserved the term 'didactic' for the class of discursive poetry that descended from Lucretius and Virgil's *Georgics*: it is not a label that they would have applied, for example, to John Brown's *Capenters Rule* (1656) or to Hannah Woolley's *Cook's Guide* (1664).

This chapter is a survey of books of practical instruction printed in Britain during the second half of the seventeenth century. Its purpose is to offer an alternative perspective on these publications, one that does not define them only in terms of instrumental function and socio-economic context (although those terms remain important). Instead, it tries to think about them in terms of genre—that is, as written works that can be gathered together by family resemblance or shared genealogy, despite apparent functional differences. It takes as its starting point one of the most common words used in the titles of practical instruction books: *manual*. A focus on books that call themselves 'manuals' has several advantages. They form a very diverse class of publication, ranging from austere ethical treatises to the most everyday tradesman's guides and 'ready reckoning' tables. Within this diversity, a very high proportion of them display family resemblances to pre-modern texts with which they share their 'manual' title (which aligns in turn with the ancient Greek *enchiridion* and the Anglo-Saxon *handbook*). The class has historical depth.

Another advantage is that books bearing the title *Manual* tend to be more than usually self-conscious about their genre and format. This is due to the affordance that the word 'manual' gives to books for different kinds of figurative self-identification. Manuals describe themselves as books that are only as big as a hand, that are to be held in hand or kept handy, that describe processes carried out by hands or by hand-held tools, that are structured around digital (and hence manual) indexing. When considering

---

[10] Elizabeth L. Eisenstein, *The Printing Press as an Agent of Change* (Cambridge: Cambridge University Press, 1979), 239–44.

[11] The literature of practical instruction is labelled 'didactic' by, among many others, Hunter, *Before Novels*, and by Glaisyer, Pennell, and their contributors in *Didactic Literature*.

the spectrum of 'manual' texts that self-identify in this way—a spectrum that ranges from sublime treatises of philosophical contemplation at one extreme to the most stolid account of mechanical process at the other—one is struck by how often books from one end of the spectrum display a sense of ideas or of modes at the other end. The regimen of the Stoic reveals an unexpected concern for the skills of the carpenter, while the guide to fishing turns out to have much to say about meditation and prayer. Taken together, these characteristics indicate coherence within the diversity of the group. They also encourage us to bring other books into the selection that do not call themselves 'manuals' but that bare an adequate resemblance to texts that do.

The Range of *Manuals*

As far as classical influences are concerned, the early modern *Manual* genre was shaped most profoundly by a compilation of moral maxims, the *Enchiridion* of the Stoic philosopher Epictetus. The *Enchiridion* offered snapshots of Epictetus's thought assembled by his pupil, Arian of Nicomedia, who also transcribed the more subtle *Discourses* directly from his master's lectures.[12] Nevertheless, the former was by far the more popular of the two works during the early modern period, due in large part to a distinctive English translation published by John Healey in 1610 as *Epictetus his Manual*. The book offers a regimen for self-mastery that involves the internalizing of its literary form in the reader's conscience. 'At all occasions, be ready to turn to thine own thoughts, and therin search the proper instructions which thou hast concerning the uses of whatsoever befalleth thee', Epictetus advises: 'If thou meetest with paines, make thy buckler of pacience, which also is the surest shield for the repulse of repoache …'[13] Having instrumentalized the mind (internally) by making it like a book of instructions, the *Enchiridion* turns, with a sharp inversion of figurative logic, to weaponizing it (externally) as a shield and buckler. Healey develops the idea of the text-as-tool further in his dedication of the book to John Florio. He reminds Florio that the manual of Epictetus 'hath beene held by some the hand to Phylosophy, the instrument of instruments … It filles not the hand with leaues, but files ye head with lessons: nor would bee held in hand, but had by hart to boote'.[14] The 'instrument of instruments' is the hand, according to Aristotelian commonplace, so Healey is pushing well beyond the conventional identification of manuals as books for holding. He suggests instead that Epictetus's manual is, like the hand itself, a meta-instrument: it is capable of doing, of making, of manipulating other conceptual tools.

There is evidence that the self-regulatory processes described and enacted in Epictetus's *Enchiridion* had some local impact on seventeenth-century philosophical

---

[12] A. A. Long, *Epictetus: A Stoic and Socratic Guide to Life* (Oxford: Oxford University Press, 2002), 9.
[13] *Epictetus his Manuall. And Cebes his table*, trans. John Healey (1610), 17–18.
[14] *Epictetus his Manuall*, sigs. A3r–A4v.

practice as Healey hoped. When Henry More called his 1668 treatise *Enchiridion ethicum* (later translated into English as *An Account of Virtue*, 1690), he inherited with the title a technical sense of what ethical philosophy should do. As a writer of philosophy it would be wrong, for example, to offer precepts attainable only with the perfection of nature ('which is virtue', according to More). His ethics is conducive rather to the perfection of human life, which is felicity: 'so you are not to expect Precepts how to *dispute*, but how to live, and how to be *happy*.'[15] Nobody took More's insistence that ethical theory should be 'consentaneous' with liveable ends more seriously than Anthony Ashley Cooper, third Earl of Shaftesbury. During a series of 'retreats' from public life to Rotterdam in 1698 and 1703, he wrote a manuscript *Askêmata*, or philosophical regimen. Associated with this manuscript is a seven-sheet vellum 'pocket encheiridion', as Shaftesbury called it, known as the *Parchment*, which seems to have served as a portable index to themes explored more fully in the *Askêmata*.[16] Shaftesbury copied out sentences from Epictetus's *Enchiridion* and similar texts into the *Parchment* in two tiny columns, with his own precepts and reflections in a column of footnotes below. On the final page of the *Parchment* Shaftesbury drew an open hand, with a set of curious pictograms (also found in the *Askêmata*) radiating out from it. Commentators usually interpret the drawing as a Stoic flinging-away of certain oppressive worldly concerns, represented by the emblem.[17] But it is worth remembering that Shaftesbury drew the hand in what he described as a 'manual'. Given that the emblems align serially with the hand's five fingers, it seems more likely that it represents a manual (or rather digital) process for indexing ideas—a method for ordering them, rather than a release from them.

Shaftesbury's Stoic regimen owes its intensity to a Christian tradition of manual-based devotional practice, associated particularly with St. Augustine's *Enchiridion ad Laurentium*. Healey had stressed the link between sacred and secular meditation, describing his translation of Epictetus as 'the hand-maide of a greater body of *Saint Augustines*'.[18] In fact the debts went both ways: the *Enchiridion ad Laurentium* dwells much upon Stoic themes, particularly with its repeated prayers for *apatheia*, for 'a refuge for my soule from the parching heate of worldlie cogitations'.[19] A modern devotional manual that described a more robust and outward-facing form of devotion was Erasmus's *Enchiridion militis Christiani* (1501). Erasmus figured his manual as a small dagger, 'which you should never lay out of your hands, no not at Tale, nor in your Chamber, that if ever you be forced to engage in the Affairs of this World, and will not

---

[15] Henry More, *An Account of Virtue, or, Dr. Henry More's Abridgment of Morals* (1690), 1, 27; cf. *All the Works of Epictetus*, tr. Elizabeth Carter (1758), 54 (*Discourses*, I. xv): 'For the Subject-matter of a Carpenter is Wood; of a Statuary, Brass; and so, of the Art of Living, the Subject-matter is each Person's own Life.'

[16] Anthony Ashley Cooper, Third Earl of Shaftesbury, *Standard Edition: Complete Works, Correspondence and Posthumous Writings*, ed. Wolfram Benda et al., 21 vols. (Stuttgart: Frommann-Holzboog, 1991–), Band II, 6, *Askêmata*; 'Parchment', 473–508.

[17] Shaftesbury, *Askêmata*, 508.

[18] *Epictetus his Manuall*, sig. A3r.

[19] *Augustines Manuel*, trans. Thomas Rogers (1581), 9; cf. 74, 76.

carry about you that compleat Armour [i.e. Bible], you may nevertheless be sure not to let that lyer in wait [i.e. the devil] at any time set upon altogether unarmed...'[20] The development of the 'armour' image must owe something to Epictetus's buckler. The distinctive thing about Erasmus's figuration of his manual, however, is that he makes no claim for its sufficiency as an instrument of spiritual defence. It does not contain all the information that one needs in order to use it effectively: 'it is very small', he counsels, 'yet if you know how to use it skilfully, together with the shield of Faith, you easily sustain the most violent Assaults of the Enemy.'[21] The implication is that these skills are not to be specified within the book: they must be acquired by experience, devotional practice, and reference to the Bible. And yet this is precisely the sort of practical guidance one might reasonably expect to find in a 'how-to' handbook. This division between instrumentation and instruction in the account that such books give of their functions becomes an increasingly prominent feature of the seventeenth-century manual.

The most important seventeenth-century English text in this tradition is *A Manual of the Private Devotions of Lancelot Andrewes*, first published as a complete translation in 1648. The original Greek text was published later as *Preces privatae*, edited by John Lamphire in 1675. Several different autographs and copies of the manuscript circulated after Andrewes's death, and its seventeenth-century editors made much of those material witnesses. 'Had you seen the *Original Manuscript*,' wrote Richard Drake of the copy he translated, now at Pembroke College, Cambridge, 'happie in the glorious deformitie thereof, being slubber'd with His pious hands, and water'd with His penitential tears, you would have been forced to confess *That Book* belonged to no other then pure and Primitive Devotion.'[22] Another manuscript copy of the *Preces*, now in the Bodleian Library, Oxford, had been given by Andrewes to William Laud. Laud's own *Officium quotidianum, or, A Manual of Private Devotions* appeared in a strikingly austere edition of 1649, marketed as a Royalist talisman in the year of King Charles's execution, and four years after his own. A third important text in what would become a significant high-Anglican sub-genre is Jeremy Taylor's *Golden Grove, or, A Manuall of Daily Prayers* (1654). Taylor gives interesting indications of how these books were intended to be used: 'Reade not much [of them] at a time', he advises, 'but meditate as much as your time and capacity and disposition will give you leave ever remembring, that little reading, and much thinking; little speaking, and much hearing; frequent and short prayers, and great devotion, is the best way to be wise, to be holy, to be devout.'[23] The strange idea emerges of the manual being used as a therapeutic clog to discourse, a voluntary impediment (as it had been sometimes for the Stoics) to the unpredictable flow of one's thoughts. In the case of the supremely eloquent sermonizer Andrewes this conception took on a special force. As Richard Drake explained, by using his manual for private devotions Andrewes made sure that he never 'appear[ed] before *His God* emptie,

---

[20] Erasmus, *A Manual for a Christian Soldier* (1687), 30–1.
[21] Erasmus, *Manual*, 31.
[22] Lancelot Andrewes, *Manual of the Private Devotions*, tr. Richard Drake (1648), sigs. A8v–A9r.
[23] Jeremy Taylor, *The Golden Grove, or, A Manuall of Daily Prayers* (1654), 58.

or with that which cost Him nothing'—as the spontaneous prayers of the Puritans cost them nothing, so the implication goes. Instead Andrewes used his manual as a goad to humility. In his *Holy Living* (1650) Jeremy Taylor tried to explain the process of using a manual to externalize, and thus depersonalize, one's thoughts. One can do so either by writing them down—and later reading them as though they were another's—or simply by reading someone else's formulations of ideas that one has oneself: 'I can better be comforted by my own considerations, if another hand applyes them, then if I do it my self', reasoned Taylor, 'because the word of God does not work as a natural agent, but as a Divine instrument'.[24] This is writing instrumentalized in a new way: not as a tool for creating one's own outward-facing discourse, but as a means of ventriloquizing oneself, thus turning inwards, and looking there for signs of grace.

The printed texts of the private manuals made by Andrewes and Laud were souvenirs of relic-like manuscripts, and they presented themselves in turn as objects to be solemnized by use. Moving another step along the spectrum of manuals, from divinely meditative towards the stolidly mechanical, it is curious to see how a third class of handbook occupying the middle of the range, the statesman's *vade mecum*, never really took off for seventeenth-century booksellers. This non-appearance is not especially surprising. The example of Bacon and later Sir William Temple made the essay a far more eligible medium for prudential maxims, and the intensity of the devotional manuals was in any case hard for statesmen to match. But some attempts were made. The *Precepts* attributed in 1636 to William Cecil, Lord Burghley, is a case in point. Printed originally 1611 as a broadside of 'ten precepts' and later padded thinly with similar texts associated with Francis, Earl of Bedford, and with St. Augustine, the *Precepts* are curt, cautious, and rather banal, only occasionally raising themselves to an irritable liveliness: 'Suffer not your Sonnes to passe the *Alpes*', we are advised, 'for they shall exchange for theyr forraine trauell ... but others vices for thyr owne vertues'.[25] Readers disappointed by the *Precepts* could turn to another manual apparently written by Cecil's most dynamic associate, *Arcana aulica, or, Walsingham's Manual of Prudential Maxims* (1652). The hook is an apparent link with Sir Francis, but the Walsingham in question turns out to be a minor Royalist called Edward, and the text itself an unattributed translation of Eustache du Refuge's *Traité de la Cour*. An anonymous manuscript fragment of the *Traité* had come into Edward's possession in Paris, and he failed to identify it, though John Reynolds had translated the complete text as early as 1622. Turning to statesman/jurists, there were reports that Sir Edward Coke had kept a curious handbook: towards the end of his life Coke found 'leisure to peruse what formerly he had written, even thirty books with his own hand', reported Thomas Fuller, 'most pleasing himself with a Manual, which he called his *Vade mecum*, from whence at one view he took a prospect of his life pass'd, having noted therein most remarkables'.[26] The manuscript was among

---

[24] Jeremy Taylor, *The Rule and Exercise of Holy Living* (1650), 264–5.
[25] Burghley, William Cecil, Baron, *Precepts, or, Directions for the Well Ordering and Carriage of a Mans Life, through the Whole Course thereof* (1636).
[26] Thomas Fuller, *History of the Worthies of England* (1662), 251.

papers seized from Coke by King Charles in 1634. It resurfaced among the Harley MSS in the British Library during the nineteenth century, but turned out to be little more than an abbreviated list of family appointments, births, deaths, and marriages.[27]

The appearance (and, in the case of Burghley's *Precepts,* calls for new editions) of these statesman's manuals indicate an appetite among readers for books of worldly maxims by authors with experience of public life. This appetite would be satisfied later in the century by translations of Baltazar Gracian's *Art of Prudence* (1647, trans. as *The Courtier's Manual Oracle,* 1685). But it is also evident from the success of a similar work by a non-statesman, the emblematist Francis Quarles's *Enchiridion* (1640), which appeared in twenty-five editions/impressions to 1700. Quarles's collection of three hundred maxims are highly conventionalized, giving the impression, when read sequentially, of having been composed as rhetorical exercises. Their most common scheme is that of a general assertion, followed by an antithesis, followed by a chiastic conceit (often the figure anadiplosis): for example, 'Give not thy tongue too great a liberty, lest it take thee prisner', Quarles advises in 'Cento II, Chapter 35': 'A word unspoken is like the Sword in thy Scabberd, thine; If vented, thy Sword is in anothers hand: If those desire to be held wise, be so wise as to hold thy tongue.'[28] Typically of seventeenth-century manuals, and consistently with this sort of rhetorical patterning, there is evidence of formal self-consciousness scattered throughout the copy. 'Cento II, Chapter 58' is even concerned with the keeping of a manuscript notebook-manual. It uses the practice as an analogy for the evaluation of priests: 'The Clergy is a Coppy Booke', Quarles suggests; 'Their Life is the Paper, whereof some is Purer, some Courser: Their Doctrine is the Copies; some written in a Plaine Hand, others in a Flowrishing Hand... Among them all, chuse one that shall be most Legible, and Usefull, and fullest of Instructions. But if the Paper chance to have a Blot, Remember, the Blot is no part of the Coppy.'[29] The analogy has great dynamism. It adverts at once to a scene of authorial composition and to that of the reader taking notes for a manual of their own. There is a corresponding doubleness to the knowledge it evokes. On one hand it concerns the parishioner's ethical assessment of a priest (that is, knowledge of the different characters or 'wits' of men), on the other it concerns the priest's knowledge of church doctrine, his capacity to pass on appropriate 'Instructions'. Somehow these two kinds of knowledge are bound together by the analogy, made personal—but not, as one might expect, public—as they are assembled in that particularly intimate possession, the copy book.

Handbooks for professionals occupy the next station along the spectrum of manuals, from the sublime to the mechanical. Medical manuals are a particularly interesting case in point, because of the distinctive conjuncture that several of them make between ancient learning, instrumental skill, and other less official forms of knowledge. Certainly, the manual was not a genre associated with medically minded natural philosophers.

---

[27] 'Sir Edward Coke's "Vade Mecum"', *Collectanea Topographica et Genealogica,* 8 vols. (1840), 6: 108–22.
[28] Francis Quarles, *Enchiridion Containing Institutions* (1640), 32.
[29] Quarles, *Enchiridion,* 58.

Alexander Read's *Manual of the Anatomy of Man* (1634), based on his earlier synopsis of Helkiah Crooke's *Sōmatographia anthrōpinē, or, A Description of the Body of Man* (1611), is typical of this group of texts, in so far as it presents itself as supplementary to an imagined course of practical investigation in the dissection theatre. Anatomy is 'an artificiall separation of the parts of the body of section, practised to attaine to the knowledge of the frame of it', which means that Read's *Manual* is really only a description of the descriptions one can achieve by its means.[30] Read's stubborn modesty of method is shared with another often-reprinted mid-century manual, Thomas Brugis's *Vade Mecum, or, A Companion for a Chirurgion* (1652). Brugis was, like his master the Parisian anatomist Jean Riolan the younger, and as Alexander Read was widely assumed to be, a Galenist, and opponent of William Hervey's new doctrines concerning the circulation of blood.[31] Following Brugis, an English translation by Nicholas Culpepper and 'W.R.' of Riolan's *Manuel anatomique* (Paris, 1653) appeared in 1657, in which the genre of the medical manual is itself traced back to Galen's *Synopsis de pulsibus*.[32] Scientifically cautious and resolutely anti-theoretical, Brugis's manual emphasizes the traditions of practice inherited by 'the Physitian, who is *Manus Dei,* and to whom he hath given knowledge, that he might bee glorified in his wondrous works ... let him [the physician] consider with what care, diligence, and respect, he ought to behave himselfe towards this noble peece of workmanship [human body]'.[33] Brugis attributed his firmly practical method to the example of John Woodall in *The Surgions Mate, or, A Treatise ... of the Surgions Chest* (1617), with whom he shares a particular interest in scalpel technology.[34] But he also shares a milieu with Elizabeth Grey, Countess of Kent's enduringly popular *Choice Manual of Rare and Select Secrets in Physick and Chyrurgery* (1653), and with John Sadler's hermetic receipt book, *Enchiridion medicum: An Enchiridion of the Art of Physic* (1657), translated from Latin by Robert Turner, another outspoken defender and popularizer of Paracelsus, and opponent of Hervey. It is striking that these titles all appear within a few years of one another during the mid-1650s.

The expanding market for medical manuals during the 1650s is an indication of the general increase in books published for a new readership that included women and younger members of the urban petit-bourgeoisie. The flourishing of titles aimed at junior legal functionaries and clerks, including Walter Yonge's *Vade Mecum of Statutes* (1643) and *The Young Clerk's Companion, or, A Manual for his Daily Practice* (1664), is another significant instance of this trend. The trade's cultivation of a newly powerful female readership for practical guides had deeper roots. For example, Sir Hugh Plat's *Jewell House of Art and Nature* (1594) and supplementary *Delightes for Ladies* (1600)

---

[30] Alexander Read, *The Manual of the Anatomy of the Body of Man* (1634), 1.
[31] For context see Roger French, *William Harvey's Natural Philosophy* (Cambridge: Cambridge University Press, 1994), 140–9.
[32] Jean Riolan, *A Sure Guide, or, The Best and Nearest way to Physick and Chyrurgery*, tr. Nicholas Culpepper and W. R. (1657), 3.
[33] Thomas Brugis, *Vade Mecum, or, A Companion for a Chirurgion* (1652), sigs. A5v–A6r.
[34] Brugis, *Vade Mecum*, 138–40.

had thrived under the patronage of women readers, as had the continuously popular rural guides written by Gervase Markham, who made much of his indebtedness to aristocratic women for information.[35] Hannah Woolley, whose successful books for this readership ranged across topics such as conduct, cosmetics, and cookery, wrote of the social upheavals that made her information particularly valuable during the second half of the century: 'I find so many Gentlewomen forced to serve,' she wrote in her compendious *Queen-Like Closet*, 'whose Parents and Friends have been impoverished by the late Calamities, *viz*. the Late Wars, Plague, and Fire, and to see what mean Places they are forced to be in, because they want Accomplishments for better.'[36] The knowledge in which Woolley dealt sold itself as a life raft, giving her uprooted readers at least a degree of buoyancy among the rapid currents of late-Stuart society.

Finally, at the far end of the generic spectrum from Bishop Andrewes or Epictetus, an increasingly specialized body of manuals concerned itself with mechanical processes, or tabulated information (often arithmetical) for working people. It is with these titles that the social instability registered by Woolley can be seen to affect generic codes governing the literary forms that manuals took. It is true that guilds or more informal structures of authority within the trades continued to restrict the publication of mechanical knowledge from which manual workers made a living. In his *Touchstone for Gold and Silver Wares* Thomas Badcock side-stepped the issue by focusing on the legal regulatory frameworks that governed work on precious metals: 'What I have here discovered', he protested, 'is not the Honest Mystery or Craft in Working and Fashioning the Wares, (which in all Trades is to be conceal'd) but the Publique Rules of our Laws ... to prevent Deceit in the Exercise of that Mystery ...'[37] Famously, John Evelyn was obliged to abandon his work on the Royal Society's Baconian project for the compilation of a public register of mechanical knowledge, because he found tradesmen so resentful of his attempts to codify their expertise.[38] As the Royal Society's attention turned in the last decades of the seventeenth century from fructiferous to luciferous knowledge (that is, from productive processes to experimental science), one of its very few fellows from the artisan classes, the instrument maker, author, and printer Joseph Moxon, quietly succeeded where Evelyn and several others had failed. His *Mechanick Exercises* adopted a revolutionary periodical format to deliver manuals for a whole ecology of artisanal trades, culminating with an account of what Moxon took to be the supreme mechanical technology of his day (and that which included all the others), hand-press printing. Moxon, a liveryman of the Weavers Company from 1664, was free to reveal the mysteries of the print shop because he had no affiliation with the Stationers

---

[35] Hunter, 'Books for Daily Life', 517–19.
[36] Hannah Woolley, *The Queen-like Closet, or, Rich Cabinet Stored with all Manner of Rare Receipts* (1670), 379.
[37] [William Badcock], *A Touch-Stone for Gold and Silver Wares, or, A Manual for Goldsmiths* (1677), A7r.
[38] Evelyn to Boyle, 9 May 1657, *The Correspondence of Robert Boyle*, ed. Michael Hunter et al., 6 vols. (London: Routledge, 2001), 1: 212–13.

Company—they would never have permitted a member to divulge their industrial secrets.[39]

With Moxon we arrive at the mechanical end of the spectrum of seventeenth-century manuals. Moxon had been responsible, as printer and as author, for a variety of manuals, and the *Mechanick Exercises* shares the genre's self-defining relationship with the 'instrument of instruments', the hand. But he was careful to limit the terms of that association. He had originally intended to title his text *The Doctrine of Handycrafts*, until reflecting that the manual processes themselves, with all the haptic skills and tacit knowledge they entail, were really something quite distinct from what a manual can teach: 'I shall not undertake that with the bare reading of these *Exercises* any shall be able to perform these Handy-works', Moxon stipulated, 'but I may safely tell you that these are the Rules that every one that will endeavour to perform them must follow; and that by the true observing them, he may, according to his stock of Ingenuity and Zeal in diligence, sooner or later inure his hand to the *Cunning* or *Craft* of working like a *Handy-craft*.'[40] In other words, Moxon's *Mechanical Exercises* lays out principles for the regulation of manual processes, not functional descriptions of the processes themselves. The distinction is analogous to the one made by the writers of religious manuals, which they presented as instruments that help facilitate devotional practices, usually by depersonalizing acts of prayer, rather than as guides to those processes as such.

The *Mechanick Exercises* also marks some of the limits of the manual, considered generically. Manuals from across the spectrum identify themselves in terms of smallness. To add another example to those discussed already, John Evelyn writes in *Kalendarium hortense, or, The Gard'ners Almanac* (1666) of how the imperfection of a previous '*Impression*' of the text led him 'to publish this *second Edition* in a smaller *Volume*, that as an *Enchiridion* it may be the more ready and useful'.[41] By issuing the *Mechanick Exercises* in twelve-sheet quarto instalments Moxon retained the portability of the manual, even as the regular periodical issues built up into a larger book that looked—in terms of bulk, of comprehensiveness, of systematic arrangement—more like an encyclopaedia. Another common feature of the manuals discussed above is their epitomizing function. One typical manual-writer boasts of designing his book so that it 'may more easily be read and remembered by such as have neither time to read large Books, nor Money to buy them', and there is usually an implicit claim that the tiny volume contains the essence of several big ones.[42] Another, Nicholas Stone, resorts once more to hand imagery in the 'Proem' of his *Enchiridion of Fortification* (1645) when explaining how for his manual he has 'pickt out the most select, and choice flowers (of those many which have been gathered out of that great nursery of *Martiall discipline*, by *Samuel Maralois*, & others

---

[39] Lisa Maruca, *The Work of Print: Authorship and the English Text Trades, 1660–1760* (Seattle: University of Washington Press, 2007), 34.

[40] Joseph Moxon, *Mechanick Exercises, or, The Doctrine of Handy-works* (1677), sig. A4r.

[41] John Evelyn, *Kalendarium hortense, or, The Gard'ners Almanac* (1666), 8–9.

[42] John Rawlett, *The Christian Monitory, Containing an Earnest Exhortation to an Holy Life* (1686), 3–4.

of great skill therein, and profound *Mathematicians*, directed to the most necessary by mine own experience) as it were into one handful…'[43] Moxon, by contrast, barely refers to the authority of earlier authors, following instead the Royal Society maxim of *nullius in verba*, and defining the master of a trade as he 'who by his own Judgement, from solid reasoning with himself, can either perform, or direct others to perform from the beginning to the end, all the Handy-works and Physical Operations' of the craft.[44] Of course, manuals continued to be published in increasing numbers through the eighteenth century. But Moxon's *Mechanick Exercises* perhaps marks the point at which the manual genre loses a sense of its purpose—the fixing and indexing of knowledge for purposes of portability—as a literary system.

The Compleat Angler as Handbook

The foregoing survey of manuals has brought to light some trends across the spectrum of books that offered practical instruction to seventeenth-century readers. They are a distinctive class of books in terms of format. Often they are tiny, duodecimo or smaller, with several titles selected here surviving in copies with pages of barely 2 by 4 inches, those by Andrewes and Quarles being representative in this respect. Their singular appearance prompts self-consciousness about form in the text itself, often expressed in terms of intended portability, hand-like smallness, finger-like articulation (for purposes of indexing), or hand-tool-like instrumentality. Their smallness also leads to reflections about what they leave out, particularly when they omit instructions regarding skills or arts with which they are ostensibly concerned. Often they present themselves as adscititious to the personal processes one might have expected them to specify as guides. Those processes themselves share certain characteristics: they tend to involve self-reflection, privacy (rather than communal reference), and a powerful focus of engagement, whether it be the regular prayerfulness of the *devot* or the commitment to manual practice of the tradesman.

There remains a question, however, whether this distinctive range of features translates itself beyond the relatively narrow spectrum of books that call themselves manuals or enchiridions (intensely pious or stolidly practical), to the more general class of seventeenth-century literature that offer hand-held practical instruction. From this wider category of seventeenth-century manual, one title has remained consistently popular among general readers: Izaak Walton's *The Compleat Angler, or The Contemplative Man's Recreation* (1653). It seems right to categorize *The Compleat Angler* as a manual, although it is seldom read primarily for practical instruction.

---

[43] Nicholas Stone, *Enchiridion of Fortification, or, A Handfull of Knowledge in Martiall Affaires* (1645), 4–5.

[44] Joseph Moxon, *Mechanick Exercises, or, The Doctrine of Handy-works. Applied to the Art of Printing. The Second Volumne* [sic] (1683), 6.

Other qualities have kept it in print for three-and-a-half centuries: the attractiveness of its blend of tavern mirth and pious elegy is one; the eccentricity of its assemblages of popular songs, receipts, learned anecdote, and personal memorial is another. The enduring popularity of fishing as a pastime for the bookish classes must have played a part. Whatever its literary qualities, however, the avowed intention of *The Compleat Angler* is practical: 'for I know [the art of fishing] is worthy the *knowledge* and *practise* of a wise man.'[45] So to what extent are the features identified across the spectrum of seventeenth-century books that describe themselves as manuals relevant to Walton's odd and playful handbook?

In the first place, *The Compleat Angler* shares with several of the manuals mentioned above (devotional and mechanical) a consciousness that the processes to which it is a guide are, in practical terms, all but unspecifiable by means of written discourse. Given the prominence of Walton's discussion of this problem, it seems likely that his book's title, with its insistence on completeness, is ironic, or at least intended to cause reflection. The book cannot give an adequate description of the subtle skills that distinguish the best anglers. One is invited to consider, perhaps, how the art of fishing can be perfected only in the person of the 'the angler', not in a technical discourse. In his preface Walton frames this problem—'how to make a man that was none, to be an Angler by a book'—in ethical terms, always stressing the personal nature of the knowledge involved. He tells the story of the celebrated fencer George Hale, who was laughed at when he published *The Priuate Schoole of Defence* (1614): 'Not but that something usefull might be observed out of that Book', Walton hastens to say; 'but that Art was not to be taught by words; nor is the Art of Angling.'[46] In fact Hale's manual is much more reflective about this question than Walton's remarks suggest. The *Private School of Defence* calls itself 'an Art Geometricall', laying out processes that are describable in rational terms, but profoundly subject to uncertainties of circumstance (in a similar move Walton compares fishing to mathematics). Hale also likens fencing to the art of logic: 'since as in [disputation], many subtilties and nimble inuentions oppresse and wrest the best expositions: so in those of exercise of the body, the inequalitie of place, as the slipping of ground, dazeling of sight, many times disorder the best and surest way of *Defence* and *Knowledge*.' The point is that the practical part of sword fighting is really an art of discretion—of improving the contingent circumstances in which the 'Geometricall' use of the sword takes place—rather than an art focused on the instrumental end of overpowering an enemy with a sword. It is a discourse on probability before the scientific discourse of probability had fully developed.[47] And, as Walton also shows, written discourse is good for describing that sort of ethical condition. It allows the author to insert something analogous to the artist's cunning into otherwise prescriptive narratives.

---

[45] Izaak Walton, *The Compleat Angler, 1653–1676*, ed. Jonquil Bevan (Oxford: Oxford University Press, 1983), 178.

[46] Walton, *Angler*, 170.

[47] See Ian Hacking, *The Emergence of Probability: A Philosophical Study of Early Ideas about Probability, Induction, and Statistical Inference* (Cambridge: Cambridge University Press, 1975), 57–62.

In the *Compleat Angler* Walton talks about this shift from external ends in terms of his art's status as a pastime—that is, as a 'recreation' defined more by internal dynamics (contemplation, fellowship, emulation). Many of the manuals considered in this chapter have presented themselves as tools for facilitating daily regularities, rather than as books for holiday time. To add another example, William Brough, in *Sacred Principles, Services, and Soliloquies* (1649), insists that his manual is '... calculated chiefly for the Meridian of their minds who fall to their Prayers not by *fits*, but *Courses*; and read Books, not to *passe* the time *away*, but well. Taking them in hand, not as *Recreations* of their thoughts, but *Businesse* of the mind'.[48] Always remembering that the opposition of business to recreational time is one that binds both terms together in mutual definition, it is striking how insistently Walton, in the *Compleat Angler*, presses his claims in the opposite direction: 'And I wish the *Reader* also to take notice, that in writing of it I have made my self a *recreation* of a *recreation*; and that it might prove so to him, and not read *dull* and *tediously*, I have in several places mixt (not any scurrility, but) some innocent, harmless mirth...'[49] We understand that by '*recreation* of a *recreation*' Walton means above all that he has pleasantly passed his time writing about a pleasant pastime. But the curious doubling of the word 'recreation' signals further meanings. 'Recreation' also implies re-making or reduplication, and as such refers to Walton's representation of the art of angling in text (that is, he has 'recreated' fishing in his book). The effect of this verbal ambiguity is to offer the first of several glimpses, behind the pleasant and ephemeral recreation that fishermen enjoy as individuals, of something more substantial: of knowledge and skill passed (or re-created) from person to person, of still deeper social and cultural alignments (in Walton's case, loyalty to the Laudian group within the sequestered clergy of the Church of England) that those exchanges articulate.[50]

When one looks closer for those things about which *Compleat Angler* remains silent, it is apparent that they fall into one of two categories: they are things either too ordinary or too sublime to mention. Breaking off a discussion about the use of dead bait when fishing for the tyrant of the river, the pike, Walton brushes aside 'that [which] you may be taught by one day's going a-fishing with me, or any other body that fishes for him'.[51] The use of drag-hooks in night-time eel fishing is likewise 'too common to be spoken of, and an hours fishing with any Angler will teach you better ... than a weeks discourse'. Concluding his chapter on fish ponds Walton gestures to observations on the subject made by earlier writers, but advises us that their instructions are redundant, 'as if a man should tell a good Arithmetician, that twice two, is four'.[52] On the other hand, Walton depicts his experienced angler 'Piscator' catching many fish with the same rod and line

---

[48] William Brough, *Sacred Principles, Services, and Soliloquies, or, A Manual of Devotions* (1649), sig. A2v.
[49] Walton, *Angler*, 169.
[50] B. D. Greenslade, 'The Compleat Angler and the Sequestered Clergy', *The Review of English Studies*, 5 (1954), 361–6.
[51] Walton, *Angler*, 289.
[52] Walton, *Angler*, 359.

that proves useless in the hand of his pupil. The difference is explained in terms of an indescribable subtlety of gesture: 'you have my *Fiddle*,' crows Piscator, 'that is, my very Rod and Tacklings with which you see I catch Fish; yet you have not my *Fiddle-stick,* that is, you have not skill to know how to carry your hand and line.'[53] Rather than make himself anxious about the elusiveness of such skills, Walton makes merry with it. At one point he gives the receipt for a particularly effective fish-bait in Latin, 'lest it should be made common.'[54] There is a similar playfulness in his association of certain fish-attracting preparations with alchemical processes: 'there is a mysterious Knack' to making them, he advises, which 'is not attainable by common capacities, or else lies locked up in the brain or breast of some chymical man.'[55] The manual instructions of *The Compleat Angler*, in their self-conscious incompleteness, lie in the middle between practices that are too ordinary to mention, or too esoteric to be shared.

However, the exclusions marking most clearly the outlines of this 'art' are ethical ones. Walton does not support his frequent assertions 'that *Angling* is an *Art*' (rather than a common knack) with any very substantive argument, but he does bolster them invariably with allusions to the virtues of proficient anglers. More than once Piscator argues that fishing 'is an Art, and an Art worth the knowledge and practice of a wise man.'[56] In a similar locution he tells his pupil to doubt not 'but that *Angling* is an Art, and an Art worth your learning: the Question is rather, whether you be capable of learning it? For *Angling* is somewhat like *Poetry*, men are to be born so ... [and] having once got and practis'd it, then doubt not but *Angling* will prove to be so pleasant, that it will prove to be like Vertue, *a reward in itself*.'[57] In another passage where he suggests that angling represents a distinctive blend of the contemplative and active, it is action that bears the most important part: 'for they say also, *That action is Doctrinal, and teaches both art and virtue, and is a maintainer of humane society*.'[58] If angling is an art made up of practical banalities—if it is an easy one in technical terms—then it is surprisingly exclusive in ethical terms. In the process of acquiring the art an artist will take on a remarkable complex of moral and personal qualities. Once again, *The Compleat Angler* is consistent in refusing even to try to denote how this process should take place, except by observation and practice. Like many seventeenth-century manuals, its silence on this matter itself communicates a profound trust in human experience and process, and in the tacit component of the art to which it is nothing more (so it claims) than an inessential support.

At which point on the spectrum of seventeenth-century manuals, from contemplative to mechanical, does *The Compleat Angler* finally sit? On one hand, Walton's memorializations of Carolinian churchmen, and his continued loyalty to the Laudian sequested clergy that produced manuals of devotion like those of Andrewes and Taylor,

---

[53] Walton, *Angler*, 252.
[54] Walton, *Angler*, 279.
[55] Walton, *Angler*, 344.
[56] Walton, *Angler*, 139.
[57] Walton, *Angler*, 190.
[58] Walton, *Angler*, 193.

encourage us to place his book at the sublime end of the range. The intelligence with which Walton writes about what his book leaves out recalls their piously practical exclusions as well, despite the obvious dissimilarities of tone. Seventeenth-century prayer manuals are material accoutrements to intensely personal and regularized processes of devotion, but only rarely do the authors stand back from those processes to reflect upon them directly. In a different context, Walton also declines to write about his art as a physical practice, choosing to fill his pages with learned anecdote and informal natural history, rather than with descriptions of haptic gestures. On the other hand, Walton's faith in the sufficiency of observation, reason, and experience as guides to those who would acquire the angler's art does anticipate the direction in which Moxon would take the mechanical manual. Like Moxon, Walton doubts the mysteriousness of the mysteries upon which he is commenting, while at the same time insisting on the value of the practitioner's personal knowledge, and particularly on the social and moral relations that they represent. As such, *The Compleat Angler* faces both ways along the spectrum of seventeenth-century manuals.

CHAPTER 18

HERESIOGRAPHY AND RELIGIOUS CONTROVERSY

NICHOLAS MCDOWELL

JONATHAN Swift's *A Tale of a Tub* and the *Mechanical Operation of the Spirit*, published with the *Tale* in 1704, were mostly written in the 1690s and, for all the complexities of Swift's allegiances at this time, it seems clear that he set out, at least, to write against the impact of the 1689 Toleration Act and to contribute to 'the project of contemporary High Church and Tory polemic to collocate modern Dissent with antinomian fanaticism'.[1] The *Tale* has been found to echo the new wave of anti-Quaker propaganda that appeared in the aftermath of the Act.[2] Ian Higgins, arguing that Swift's position in the *Tale* is that of a High Church cleric with Jacobite leanings, has shown that 'Swift's satire of hubris and self-sufficiency in learning and religion, connection of modern Dissent with Gnosticism, and specific animus against Quakers and the doctrine of the Inner Light' has particular analogues in the pamphlets of the prolific Jacobite polemicist Charles Leslie (1650–1722).[3] Earlier critics have looked to the great Restoration verse satire on Civil War Puritanism and sectarianism, Samuel Butler's *Hudibras* (3 parts, 1662–78), which is in turn indebted to royalist polemic of the 1640s, and before that to an Anglican tradition of anti-Puritan invective that stretches back to the late Elizabethan period.[4]

---

[1] Ian Higgins, *Swift's Politics* (Cambridge: Cambridge University Press, 1994), 97, 103; see also the chapter on the *Tale* in Clement Hawes, *Mania and Literary Style: The Rhetoric of Enthusiasm from the Ranters to Christopher Smart* (Cambridge: Cambridge University Press, 1996), 101–28.

[2] Hugh Ormsby-Lennon, 'Swift and the Quakers (I)', *Swift Studies*, 4 (1989), 34–62; 'Swift and the Quakers (II)', *Swift Studies*, 5 (1990), 53–89.

[3] Higgins, *Swift's Politics*, 105–9 (105).

[4] Philip Harth, *Swift and Anglican Rationalism: The Religious Background of* A Tale of a Tub (Chicago: University of Chicago Press, 1961); Thomas L. Canavan, 'Robert Burton, Jonathan Swift, and the Tradition of Anti-Puritan Invective', *Journal of the History of Ideas*, 34 (1973), 227–42; J. R. Crider, 'Dissenting Sex: Swift's "History of Fanaticism"', *Studies in English Literature*, 18 (1978), 491–508; *The Cambridge Edition of the Works of Jonathan Swift: A Tale of a Tub and Other Works*, ed. Marcus Walsh (Cambridge: Cambridge University Press, 2010), pp. liv–lxvi. All references to Swift's writings are to Walsh's edition unless otherwise indicated.

Indeed it is part of Swift's polemical strategy to suggest that groups like the Quakers are simply another manifestation of sectarian heresy that reappears throughout the history of Christianity: the first epigraph on the title-page of *A Tale* is from the great catalogue of heresies, *Adversus haereses*, compiled by the second-century Church Father Irenaeus. Swift made an abstract of Irenaeus in 1697, when he was probably writing *A Tale*.[5] Irenaeus's method, as Ronald Paulson observed, is to 'employ the jargon which was common among the heretics themselves' rather than to controvert their theology, expecting the reader to acknowledge the perversity of such behaviour and belief.[6] Swift draws attention to this strategy on the title-page of the 1710 edition of the *Tale* by reproducing from Irenaeus some meaningless lines—in his notes Swift describes them as 'gibberish'—supposedly derived from Hebrew and used as a chant in the initiation ceremony of a Gnostic sect.[7]

Such demonstrations of how the *Tale* and the *Discourse* are indebted to a long literary tradition of anti-sectarian polemic and heresiography do not explain why, when they were first published (anonymously), they were linked by some readers with deism and widely regarded as subversive of religious orthodoxy: such was the negative response that Swift had to attach an (anonymous) 'Apology' to the 1710 edition.[8] We have no real grounds, though, for thinking Swift to be consciously disingenuous when he assures us in the 'Apology' that his intention was 'to see the follies of fanaticism and superstition exposed, though in the most ridiculous manner'. The *Tale*, he maintains, 'celebrates the Church of England as the most perfect of all others in discipline and doctrine', attacking 'nothing but what [its clergy] preach against'.[9] What provoked contemporaries and fascinates modern critics, and what distinguishes Swift's satires on enthusiasm from the tradition of anti-heretical writing from Irenaeus to Samuel Butler to Charles Leslie, is the creation of authorial and narrative voices that are themselves the object of satire. In the *Discourse* and the sections of the *Tale* concerned with sectarian behaviour the narrator is both heretic and sympathetic heresiographer, enthusiast and admiring historian of enthusiasm, 'describing, with reverence, the customs of his friends'.[10]

The religious and political conflicts of the English Civil Wars remained 'live issues' for Swift and his contemporaries, and they returned obsessively to the events, arguments, and also texts of the 1640s and 1650s to fight their ideological battles.[11] The distinctiveness

---

[5] *A Tale of a Tub*, ed. A. C. Guthkelch and D. Nicol Smith, rev. edn (Oxford: Oxford University Press, 1973), p. lvi.

[6] Ronald Paulson, *Theme and Structure in Swift's 'Tale of a Tub'* (New Haven: Yale University Press, 1960), 77; on Irenaeus, see also 76–9, 97–105, 122–3, 146–9, 236–8.

[7] *Tale of a Tub*, 20.

[8] Frank T. Boyle, '"Profane and Debauched Deist": Swift in the Contemporary Response to A *Tale of a Tub*', *Eighteenth-Century Ireland*, 3 (1988), 25–38. On deism in this period, see further Chapter 30 on 'Radical and Deist Writing' by Nicholas McDowell and Giovanni Tarantino.

[9] The point is made by Marcus Walsh, 'Text, "Text", and Swift's "A Tale of a Tub"', *Modern Language Review*, 85 (1990), 290–303 (301–2).

[10] Paulson, *Theme and Structure in Swift's 'Tale of a Tub'*, 78

[11] See e.g., Ashley Marshall, *Swift and History: Politics and the English Past* (Cambridge: Cambridge University Press, 2015).

of Swift's narrative mode in the satires on enthusiasm comes into sharper focus if we compare them with superficially similar examples of polemical prose narrative of the 1640s, when anti-sectarian and heresiographical writing became one of the most common literary modes of a newly unregulated polemical print culture. Editors tell us that 'a tale of a tub' refers to 'an old expression meaning a cock-and-bull story and also the icon, to which [the tale-teller] himself refers, of the mariners throwing out an empty barrel to distract an inquisitive and threatening "whale"'. The tale-teller, after all, refers to this custom in his 'Preface', advising that the whale which his tub is supposed to distract is '*Hobs's Leviathan*, which tosses and plays with all other Schemes of Religion and Government'.[12] But *A Tale of a Tub* is hardly limited in its targets to Hobbesian free-thinking: it is also a tale of tub preachers, as in the title of the anti-sectarian pamphlet published in 1642 by the prolific Royalist satirist John Taylor (1578–1653): *A Tale in a Tub, or, A Tub Lecture. As It Was Delivered by Mi-Heele Mend-Soale, an Inspired Brownist, & a Most Upright Translator. in a Meeting House Neere Bedlam, the One and Twentieth of December, Last 1641.* The woodcut on the title-page of Taylor's pamphlet is dominated by the tub from which 'Mi-heele Mend-soale' preaches (the woodcut had previously been used in Taylor's *A Swarme of Sectaries and Schismatiques* (1641)). The replacement of the pulpit by a tub becomes emblematic for Taylor of the breakdown of religious and social decorum in Civil War England—in the proper and natural order the cobbler should concern himself with mending soles, not souls. Social disruption is automatically accompanied by sexual excess: in Taylor's *Love One Another: A Tub Lecture, Preached by John Alexander, a Joyner* (1642), the tub preacher explains to his listeners that the Christian injunction to 'love one another' is in fact a justification of wife swapping. Taylor's technique in *A Tale in a Tub* and *Love One Another: A Tub Lecture* is to ventriloquize, without any kind of framing device, the voice of the tub preacher explicating, or 'translating', a line of pseudo-Scripture. In another pamphlet Taylor explains why he employs such satirical techniques: 'I hold it altogether unnecessary to write or speak of you but in the way of mirth ... a Tub is more necessary for a cobbler than a Pulpit, thus farre I hold with your Apologie; but, not withstanding, if I prove you not all *Madmen* and *Fooles*, to maintain the Proverbe, I will give you leave to ride me.'[13] Sectarian fools are recognized, Taylor insists (as did Irenaeus), by their folly.

Although none of Taylor's pamphlets are included in Swift's lists of his books, it has been suggested that Swift's central satiric parable in the *Tale* of the three brothers Peter, Martin, and Jack may have been influenced by Taylor's 1641 pamphlet *A Dialogue Betwixt Three Travellers*.[14] Taylor's overtly comic treatment of mechanic and women preachers in fictional prose narratives, which are presented as accounts of real sectarian

---

[12] Jonathan Swift, *Major Works*, ed. Angus Ross and David Woolley (Oxford: Oxford University Press, 2003), 617 n. 62; *Tale of a Tub*, 25.

[13] John Taylor, *An Honest Answer to the Late Published Apologie for Private Preaching. Wherein is Justly Refuted their Mad Forms of Doctrine. As Preaching in a Tub* (1642), sig. A2r.

[14] Higgins, *Swift's Politics*, 135. On the central narrative in the *Tale*, see further Chapter 21 on 'Learned Wit and Mock-Scholarship' by Henry Power.

excesses, certainly seems to offer a closer literary model for Swift's prose satires than the mock-heroic couplets of Butler's *Hudibras*. Yet where Taylor simply impersonates sectarian enthusiasts to parody their behaviour and reduce to absurdity their ideas, Swift creates a narrator who records and comments on sectarian activity, and so is separated from it, but who is at the same time encompassed by the satire because he takes that activity so seriously and is in fact himself *part of it*.

A voluminous collection of supposedly 'real' anti-sectarian narratives from the 1640s that Swift did own was the most notorious of all the Civil War heresiographies: *Gangraena: or a Catalogue and Discovery of many of the Errours, Heresies, Blasphemies and pernicious Practices of the Sectaries of this time*, was published in three parts in 1646 and compiled by the Presbyterian divine Thomas Edwards (c.1599–1648), still best known as the 'shallow Edwards' condemned by Milton in his sonnet 'On the New Forcers of Conscience Under the Long Parliament' (1646). In Swift's library catalogue of 1715, written in his own hand, is the listing 'Edward's Gangraena, compleat'—in other words, all three parts.[15] Despite the publication of the three separate parts in 1646 and the reprinting of the first part three times in two months, there were no reissues of any part of *Gangraena* after 1646 and the text was not published in composite form until a 1977 facsimile edition. Swift may thus have gone to the trouble of locating the three different parts of a text that was some fifty years old when he was composing the *Tale*—the very fact Swift describes his copy as 'compleat' indicates awareness of its multi-part form.

Gangraena is the most ambitious of the many attempts in seventeenth-century England to compile a catalogue of current heresies on the model of Irenaeus, to whom Edwards himself refers with admiration.[16] Edwards sought to catalogue the heretical beliefs supposedly at large in England to persuade Parliament to impose censorship on heretical books and establish a compulsory Presbyterian church discipline, replacing the disintegrated episcopal structure of the Church of England. Edwards's message was an urgent one. As he declares at the beginning of the book:

> For now things are grown to a strange passe, (though nothing is now strange) and every day they grow worse and worse, and you can hardly conceive and imagine them so bad as they are, no kinde of blasphemy, heresie, disorder, confusion, but either is found among us, or a coming in upon us, for we instead of a Reformation, are grown from one extreme to another, fallen from *Scylla* to *Charibdis*, from Popish Innovations, Superstitions, and Prelaticall Tyranny, to damnable Heresies, horrid Blasphemies, Libertinisme and fearfull Anarchy.[17]

---

[15] William LeFanu, *A Catalogue of Books Belonging to Dr Jonathan Swift of St Patrick's, Dublin Aug. 19. 1715: A Facsimile of Swift's Autograph with an Introduction and Alphabetic Catalogue* (Cambridge: Cambridge Bibliographical Society, 1988), 17.

[16] See Ann Hughes, *Gangraena and the Struggle for the English Revolution* (Oxford: Oxford University Press, 2004), 66–75; Thomas Edwards, *Gangraena*, 3 parts (1646; repr. Exeter: Rota Press, 1977), 1: 142, 2: 97. All references to *Gangraena* are to this facsimile reprint.

[17] *Gangraena*, 1, sig. A3.

Edwards is particularly close to Irenaeus in his preference for simply reporting what the heretics of Civil War England have done and said rather than arguing with them on theological or doctrinal grounds. He says that he will recount the blasphemous ideas and actions of the heretics 'in their own words and phrases syllabically, as neer as possible can be, or I can remember them' and insists that 'the naming of them will be sufficient confutation'.[18]

When it appeared, *Gangraena* was a 'publishing sensation': it has been called 'the most famous printed book in an era [the Civil Wars] in which printed texts played a crucial role' (although the *Eikon Basilike* (1649), the supposed record of Charles I's thoughts in his captivity, was soon to take on that mantle).[19] It can seem like a fool's errand to look and argue for specific 'sources' for the *Tale* given the chaotic multiplicity of discourses swarming around behind the work: as Claude Rawson has observed, the *Tale* assimilates 'an immense body of reading, beyond specific sources, and different from the sum of its parts'.[20] But anti-sectarian polemic is unquestionably one of the discourses that are refracted through the parodic lens of the *Tale*, and a comparison of Swift's satires with the best-known English heresiography of the seventeenth century offers another perspective on their provocative and perplexing prose form; and also another way of thinking about Swift's crucial inclusion of his narrators in the sectarian madness that they claim to record with quasi-scientific objectivity.

Gangraena emerged from the growing anxiety amongst Presbyterians that the reformation of the church on Presbyterian lines was being subverted by the rise of the Independents, generally more tolerant of sectarianism. Hence the Independents are blamed throughout *Gangraena* for the proliferation of popular heresy in an effort to discredit Independent influence within Parliament and the army: *Gangraena* is more immediately a massive attack on Independency than Anabaptism or antinomianism. Indeed, Hughes has shown *Gangraena* to have been of central importance in constructing the very binary divisions of Presbyterian and Independent that it purports to describe—a striking example of how a text can shape historical reality.[21] The important point here, though, is that *Gangraena* is not 'Anglican' anti-Puritan satire, which is the tradition the *Tale* is usually placed in, but Puritan anti-sectarian polemic. Throughout his life, Swift conflated Presbyterianism with sectarian dissent: in his genealogy of heresy in the *Tale*'s narrative of Peter, Martin, and Jack, the origins of the Æolist sect, whose scatological devotional practices are uproariously described in Section XVII and who, Swift tells us in a gloss, represent 'All pretenders to inspiration whatsoever', are traced back to Jack (Calvin). Section XI of *A Tale* includes an extended parody of the Calvinist doctrine of double predestination that Edwards repeatedly asserts is orthodox Christian doctrine. Just as Edwards argues that all the sects in revolutionary England develop from the same root, Independency, so Swift presents all sectarian dissent as springing from the same

---

[18] *Gangraena*, 1: 4–5.
[19] P. R. S. Baker, entry for Thomas Edwards in the *ODNB*; Hughes, *Gangraena and the Struggle*, 2.
[20] Claude Rawson, 'Behind the Tub', *Times Literary Supplement*, 5293 (September 10 2004), 3–4 (3).
[21] See the full discussion in Hughes, *Gangraena and the Struggle*, chap. 5.

root of Calvinist belief. Towards the end of his career, in *The Presbyterians Plea of Merit; In Order to Take Off the Test, (in Ireland,) Impartially Examined* (1733), Swift responded to Presbyterian claims that their loyalty to the English monarchy was exemplified historically by their opposition to the execution of Charles I by insisting that '[n]o other [motive] can possibly be assigned, than perfect Spite, Rage, and Envy, to find themselves wormed out of all Power, by a new infant Spawn of *Independants*, sprung from their own Bowels'. The Presbyterians were the 'Parent Sect' of the Independents, and 'after the Restoration', the Independents, regicidal and tolerationist, 'mingled with the Mass of *Presbyterians*; lying ever since undistinguished in the Herd of Dissenters'.[22] So, when he read Edwards's rhetoric about the 'godly orthodox Presbyterians', Swift would immediately have been distanced from the text by his own conviction that the Presbyterians were themselves the most dangerous of heretics. For Swift, the fervent Presbyterian Edwards was himself an original species of sectarian enthusiast. One of the explanations often advanced for Swift's taking to religious satire in the *Tale* is, after all, his experience in 1695–6 of being an Anglican clergyman in the Presbyterian stronghold of Kilroot, near Belfast.

Other Restoration Anglican and Tory polemicists had seen in *Gangraena* the opportunity to damn the Presbyterians with their own words. In William Dugdale's 1681 polemic against dissent, designed to intervene in the Exclusion crisis, orthodox Presbyterians and radical sectarians are lumped together as a threat to religious order and morality and *Gangraena* cited extensively to demonstrate the dangers of toleration. Dugdale refers to Edwards as 'one of their own Ministers of the Gospel (as he stiles himself)' who 'instances no less than one hundred seventy-six Heretical and Blasphemous Tenets, broached by the Sectaries (the Offspring of the *Presbyterian*)'.[23] Edwards's quest for comprehensiveness across his three volumes (of which more below) is here turned against him. Dugdale may have got the idea from Roger L'Estrange's *The Dissenters Sayings* (1681), in which L'Estrange (1616–1704), who had assiduously sought to suppress dissenting literature in his role as Licenser of the Press from 1663 to 1679, extracts arguments against toleration from Presbyterian tracts and polemics so that the dissenters 'themselves shall be allow'd to be their own Advocates' and the 'Reader may himself to be gotten into the Phanaticks fansie Trying-Room; where he sees all their Dresses, & Disguises; their Shifts of Masques & Habits'. *Gangraena* is a key source for L'Estrange in his section on 'The Fruits of Toleration' and is quoted extensively and at length: in *The Dissenters Sayings. The Second Part*, also published in 1681, he includes one-line summaries of several of the most sensational narratives of sectarian behaviour in *Gangraena*.[24] Swift was perhaps encouraged to get hold of *Gangraena* by reading L'Estrange. Swift specifically names L'Estrange in the 1710 'Apology' prefixed to the *Tale* as one of the writers he 'personates' and he owned and annotated a copy of *The Dissenters*

---

[22] [Swift], *The Presbyterians Plea of Merit; In Order to Take Off the Test, (in Ireland,) Impartially Examined* (1733), 8–9.
[23] William Dugdale, *A Short View of the Late Troubles in England* (Oxford, 1681), 573.
[24] Roger L'Estrange, *The Dissenters Sayings. Two Parts in One* (1685 [1705]), 65, 93.

Sayings. Two Parts in One, which combined L'Estrange's two 1681 pamphlets with some other anti-sectarian and anti-Dissenter material, although this was not published until 1705.[25] In the same year that the *Tale* was published, Mary Astell cited *Gangraena* extensively in a polemic against the toleration of occasional conformity, *Moderation Truly Stated* (1704); responding in *A Fair Way with the Dissenters* (1704) to a Presbyterian critic of her views, Astell declared that 'those Expressions about Schism, which our Author is so offended at, are the very words of Mr Edwards the Presbyterian'.[26] Such recourse to the major heresiography of the Civil Wars to fight the polemical battles of 1681 and beyond exemplifies how controversialists of the late Restoration felt themselves still to be embroiled in the religious conflicts of the 1640s and 1650s.

Gangraena was seen, then, by other late seventeenth- and early eighteenth-century critics of dissent and toleration as a particularly useful resource because, according to the polemical logic by which Presbyterianism was itself revealed as the root of sectarianism, it enabled them to cite the Presbyterians against themselves. In the satires on enthusiasm Swift is not much interested in making such direct and explicit polemical points; but, as the *Tale* exemplifies with dizzying intensity, he was fascinated by the satirical potential of authorial and narrative voices. One of the most memorable episodes recounted in *Gangraena*, of which L'Estrange reminds his readers in his one-line summaries, is that of Samuel Oats the Anabaptist weaver:

> There is one *Samuel Oats* a Weaver (a man whom I have spoken of in my former Book, and in this too, page 10) who being of Lams Church, is sent out as a Dipper and Emissary into the Countries ... this yeer he was sent out into *Essex* about three or four months ago, and for many weeks together went up and down from place to place, and Town to Town about *Bochin, Braintry,* and *Tarling,* and those parts, preaching his erroneous Doctrines, and dipping in many rivers; this is a young lusty fellow, and hath traded chiefly with young women and young maids, dipping many of them, though all is fish that comes to his net ... A godly Minister of *Essex* coming out of those parts related, he hath baptized a great number of women, and that they were call'd out of their beds to go a dipping in rivers, dipping many of them in the night, so that their husbands and Masters could not keep them in their houses, and 'tis commonly reported that this *Oats* had for his pains 10 shillings apeece for dipping the richer, and two shillings six pence for the poorer ... There was another woman also whom he baptized, as a godly Minister that came out of those parts, and had been at *Baintree* related to me from a good hand, whom after he [Oats] baptized, he bid her gape, and she gaped, and he did blow three times into her mouth, saying words to this purpose, *either receive the holy Ghost, or now thou hast received the holy Ghost.*[27]

---

[25] *Tale of a Tub*, 7; Harold Williams, *Dean Swift's Library* (Cambridge: Cambridge University Press, 1932), no. 514. *The Dissenters Sayings. Two Parts in One* is dated 1685 on the title page but refers to L'Estrange's recent death in 1704 and is given a 1705 date by *Eighteenth-Century Collections On-Line*.

[26] Astell, *Moderation Truly Stated*, 51–2, 80; *A Fair Way with the Dissenters*, in *Mary Astell: Political Writings*, ed. Patricia Springborg (Cambridge: Cambridge University Press, 1996), 115–16, 119, 121.

[27] L'Estrange, *The Dissenters Sayings. Two Parts in One*, 9; *Gangraena*, 2: 146–7.

This story is representative of Edwards's narrative style and illustrates his technique of recording, rather than arguing with, the heresies he claimed were spreading like a fatal infection through the English body politic. It is typical also in its concern with accuracy of detail ('two shillings six pence') and with credibility—the information comes from a 'godly minister' or is 'related at good hand'. Edwards points out that Oats has form, a claim that the reader can verify by cross-referencing *Gangraena*. There is a characteristic association of heresy with social and sexual inversion: the uneducated weaver usurps the role of the ordained minister, claiming spiritual inspiration (but with the true design, Edwards implies, of cheating the weak-minded out of their money). Oats preys in particular on wives and female servants, seducing them away from their husbands and masters to frolic naked in rivers around Essex. Edwards includes a marginal manicule to direct the reader to the account of Oats's blowing into the mouth of a female acolyte, so he obviously regarded it as a significant example of sectarian behaviour. The Oats episode in *Gangraena* is a prime example, known to Swift and repeated by L'Estrange, of the sort of anti-sectarian motifs and narratives which are worked into episodic satiric fantasy in the *Tale*. In the description of the Æolist sect the enthusiastic claim to divine inspiration is bathetically literalized as the Æolist priests, 'their mouths gaping wide against a Storm', issue 'Belches ... received for sacred, the sourer the better, and swallowed with infinite Consolation by their meager devotees'. The Æolist priest has 'a secret funnel ... conveyed from his posteriors to the bottom of the barrel, which admits new supplies of inspiration' and enables him to deliver 'oracular belches to his panting disciples', who run 'greedily gaping after the sanctified Breath'.[28] Swift picks up on the inherent but unintentional comedy of heresiographical episodes such as those of the Anabaptist weaver, which Edwards recorded to shock and horrify his readers.

Edwards's constant concern with the threat to learning of rise of the sects—he tells his readers that the ignorant heretics who populate *Gangraena* believe there to be 'no need of learning, nor for reading of Authors for Preachers, but all books and learning must go down, it comes from want of the Spirit, that men write such great volumes, and make such adoe of learning'—reminds us that the critical tendency to divide the *Tale* into satire on the abuses of learning and satire on the abuses of religion imposes a dichotomy that early moderns would not have recognized.[29] The Æolists identify learning with wind because they interpret Scripture literally, in this case Corinthians 8:1, and Swift exploits this literal-mindedness to develop his satire on the enthusiastic substitution of spiritual inspiration for book-learning:

> it is generally confirmed, or confessed, that learning *puffeth men up* ... For this reason, the philosophers among them did in their schools deliver to their pupils all their doctrines and opinions by eructation, wherein they had acquired a wonderful eloquence, and of incredible variety. But the great characteristic by which their

---

[28] *Tale of a Tub*, 100–1, 102. Higgins notes that Swift 'could have read in *Gangraena*' the story of Samuel Oats (*Swift's Politics*, 111).

[29] *Gangraena*, 1: 30–1.

chief sages were best distinguished, was a certain position of countenance, which gave undoubted intelligence to what degree or proportion the spirit agitated the inward mass.

The tale-teller adds that the Æolists believe women make particularly good preachers because of the greater room in their sexual organs for the wind to pass through, an ability they have been able to modulate from a 'carnal into a spiritual ecstasy'.[30] In his gloss on the text here Swift makes the connection with 'our *modern* Æolists', the Quakers.

The notion that sectarian religion was merely an excuse for sexual promiscuity has a long history in anti-Puritan and anti-sectarian polemic, going back in England at least to representations of the perfectionist sect the Family of Love in the late Elizabethan period—Swift does in fact compare the Quakers to the Family of Love in the 'History of Fanaticism' in the *Mechanical Operation*. The speaker in the *Mechanical Operation* claims to have discovered that 'there is one fundamental point wherein [all enthusiasts] are bound to agree, and that is the *community of women*'. He then goes on to disclose that 'a very eminent member of the faculty assured me that when the Quakers first appeared, he seldom was without some female patients among them for the *furor* [*Uterinus*]'. The inner light is diagnosed, in other words, as nymphomania. Among Swift's contemporaries, Charles Leslie accused the Quakers of holding women in common.[31] But in *Gangraena* Swift would have found not simply accusations but *narratives* of sectarian sexual excess. As we saw with the Oats episode, Edwards repeatedly makes the connection between sectarian activity and sexual disorder among wives and female servants, and he includes a series of lurid stories concerning the sexual exploits of sectarian preachers, clearly designed to titillate as well as create anxiety: 'Of adulteries and fornications … if I should set downe all the instances of this kind that I have had from good hands, and relate the stories at large, I could fill some sheets … There are divers of the dippers and mechanic preachers of the sectaries, not only shrewdly suspected for filthiness and uncleanesses, but some of them accused by women.'[32]

Women preachers are for Edwards the ultimate vindication of his representation of sectarianism as subversive of social, religious, and gender hierarchies. He claims that 'all the confusion and disorder in Church-matters both of opinions and practises' is due to 'all sorts of Mechanicks taking upon them to preach and baptize, as Smiths, Taylors, Shoomakers, Pedlars, Weavers &c. there are also some women-preachers in our times'. In fact, the monstrous appearance of women preachers tends to be the climax of Edwards's near hysterical declamations about the descent of England into blasphemy:

> How do sects and schisms increase and grow daily, Sectaries doing even what they will, committing insolencies and outrages, not only against the truth of God and the

---

[30] *Tale of a Tub*, 100, 102.
[31] *Tale of a Tub*, 185–6. See the charge of sexual licence among the Quakers in Leslie's *The Snake in the Grass* (1696), 90, 95–6, a tract that Swift could have read while writing the *Tale*.
[32] *Gangraena*, 3: 188.

peace of the Church, but the Civil state also, going up and down Countries, causing riots, yea tumults and disturbances in the publike Assemblies! How do persons cast out of other Countries for their Errours, not only live here, but gather Churches, preach publikely their Opinions! What swarmes are there of all sorts of illiterate Mechanick preachers, yea of Women and Boy preachers![33]

As always Edwards has a specific narrative to hand, telling us at length about a 'lace-woman' who 'disclaimed that she took upon her to Preach, but only to exercise her gifts; for she could not be evinced that any in the world this day living, had any Commission to preach'. This 'lace-woman', who is later named as Mrs. Attaway, is of course revealed to be an adulteress: she is said to have left her husband for a sectary called William Jenny, citing Milton's arguments for divorce.[34] In Edwards's 'straight' heresiographical narratives as well as John Taylor's comic fictions, the sexual motive behind the sectarian claim to spiritual purity is revealed.

Such exposure of the claim to inspiration as caused by or as an excuse for sexual disorder is key to Swift's satiric narratives, such as the oft-quoted discussion in the *Mechanical Operation* of why zealous people are the most '*amorous*': 'Nay, to bring this argument yet closer, I have been informed by certain sanguine brethren of the first class that in the height and *orgasmus* of their spiritual exercise, it has been frequent with them * * * * *; immediately after which they found the spirit to relax and flag of a sudden with the nerves, and they were forced to hasten to a conclusion.' The visual form of this mock self-censorship recalls how Edwards self-censors his text to accentuate the depravity of the heresies that he describes. Here Edwards recounts what he has heard with his usual precision of detail, except the blasphemy becomes so extreme that he must leave it to the imagination of the reader:

> On April 9. 1645. Being that day commonly called Easter Wednesday, Mr. Cole Book-Seller in Cornhill, in his own shop (I going to him to help me to an unlicensed book) amongst other Discourse told me, That divers persons whom about 4 years ago he thought as godly as any, were now fallen to deny all things in matter of Religion, and held nothing, but laboured to plunder men of their Faith; and that many of these were vicious in their lives, as well as Heretical in their judgements; and some of them would come into his Shop, and had spoken fearfull Blasphemies not fit to be named; as that the Virgin *Mary* was — — — (I forbear to mention what followed.)[35]

The febrile Edwards tells us just enough to make us start thinking about what sort of blasphemy, almost certainly sexual in nature and too terrible to be enunciated, this might be.

Edwards emphasizes that heresy flourishes among the 'illiterate', in the pre-nineteenth-century sense of those lacking Latin and a classical education, and among

---

[33] *Gangraena*, 1: 84, 1, sig. a1v.
[34] *Gangraena*, 1: 88, 2: 11.
[35] *Tale of a Tub*, 186; Edwards, *Gangraena*, 1: 82–3.

'mechanicks'. 'Mechanick' and 'mechanical' were familiar forms of class distinction in early modern England. Edwards, like other heresiographers of the 1640s, frequently refers to the bloody Anabaptist uprisings in Münster in the 1530s, which briefly led to a form of communism, to tar contemporary sectarianism with the same brush.[36] In his 'history of *fanaticism*' Swift's speaker refers to John of Leyden, the leader of the Münster Anabaptists, as one of the 'last *fanatics* of note', 'whose visions and revelations always terminated in *leading about half a dozen sisters apiece*'; 'Dutch Jack' is one of the offspring of Jack Calvin in the parable of the three brothers.[37] While Swift is following in an established tradition of class-based rhetoric in anti-sectarian polemic, he picks up on the term 'mechanic' that Edwards and other heresiographers of the 1640s use repeatedly to stigmatize sectarian enthusiasts—in *The Dippers Dipts* (1645), Daniel Featley, a Calvinist episcopalian, laments the rise of 'Mechanick Enthusiasts', 'sublime Coachmen', and 'Illuminated Tradesmen' who turn 'Tubs into Pulpits'—and makes it serve a dual satirical purpose. In the *Mechanical Operation*, enthusiasm is not only 'mechanical' in the sense of being 'an effect of artifice' rather than of spiritual infusion, but in the sense of being espoused by mechanicals: 'It is, therefore, upon the *Mechanical Operation of the Spirit* that I mean to treat, as it is at present performed by our *British Workmen*.'[38] At the same time, the apparently antipathetic twin targets of Swift's satire, Hobbesian materialism and Quaker enthusiasm, are reduced to, and fused in, a single word—'mechanical'.

The charges of sexual licence and stereotypes of the illiterate heretic that Swift incorporates into his satires on enthusiasm, and which he would have found in *Gangraena*, were the common currency of anti-sectarian literature and Swift would have found them in many other texts, from before and after the 1640s. But what may have particularly caught Swift's fancy in *Gangraena* is its unusual textual form and idiosyncratic authorial voice—a voice that, as we shall see, Edwards's own immediate contemporaries found a ripe subject for parody. Edwards is anxious throughout *Gangraena* to represent himself as the faithful reporter of truth, or as what Michael McKeon would call a 'naïve empiricist'.[39] Typically Edwards makes his point through the kind of straight-faced exaggeration which distinguishes the tone of the text: his book, he insists, is 'of so much truth that I beleeve no Book written this hundred years having so much variety and particularity in it will be found to have more'. We might recall here the tale-teller's pride in having written 'three large Volumes in Folio' on '*zeal*; which is perhaps the most significant word that hath ever been yet produced in any language'.[40] The three parts of *Gangraena* are largely made up of factual narratives identifying individuals holding and preaching heretical doctrine in the mid-1640s, stating when, where, and with whom they did so. As we have seen, Edwards is obsessively concerned

---

[36] See e.g., Edwards, *Gangraena*, 1, sig. B3.
[37] *Tale of a Tub*, 85.
[38] Featley, *The Dippers Dipt* (1645), sigs. B3v, B4v; *Tale of a Tub*, 173.
[39] Michael McKeon, *The Origins of the English Novel, 1600–1740* (Baltimore, Maryland: John Hopkins University Press, 1987), 45–7.
[40] *Gangraena*, 2: 44; *Tale of a Tub*, 38.

to certify the accuracy and veracity of these narratives. He prints letters and eye-witness accounts from correspondents all over the country which confirm his story, or which offer new narrative detail. The credibility of his testimony is crucial to Edwards, as he makes clear in the long discussion of his methodology in the first part of *Gangraena*. He has interrogated informants if they were 'ear and eye witnesses, yet if there was but one single witness, I have used to question, who else was present? And to enquire after circumstances and occasions, and accordingly to have gone to other persons named, from one to another, to finde out the bottome and truth both of opinions held, and practices used'. Edwards represents himself as a man who has dedicated himself absolutely to the universal cataloguing of error: 'I have a long time used to write down daily the same day, yea the same hour (when I could get the opportunity of privacie) the occurrences both of opinions and practises that concern our sectaries.' *Gangraena* is presented, in other words, as both a work of the moment and as a compendium, encompassing every error 'now in being, alive in these present times, all of them vented and broached within these four years last past, yea most of them within these last two years'. The text is supposed to be a taxonomy of heresy, working upon vaguely Ramist principles of relation and differentiation: the 'undigested Chaos' of sectarian 'errours and strange opinions' has been 'carefully declined in this following discourse, by joyning in one things scattered and divided', putting them 'under certain heads, and ... into their proper places, in a methodical way for memories sake, that the Reader may easily finde them'. He promises 'a Synopsis of sectarisme ... drawn as it were into one table' and seeks to control his ever-enlarging bulk of information through systematic lists and numbering schemes.[41]

However, as the publication of two more parts of *Gangraena* in quick succession indicates, 'Edward's present-mindedness continually sabotaged his attempts to impose structure on his material ... lists of errors, methodological principles, practices, blasphemies, and corollaries follow each other in hectic confusion.'[42] The list of errors in the first part simply keeps on going until Edwards stops at the arbitrary figure of 176, with many of the descriptions of particular heresies repeated in only slightly different phrasing, and then repeated again in subsequent parts: in a supplementary list of errors in the second part, Edwards had to revise his numbering when he suddenly realized that the eleventh error had already appeared in the first part. But in one of many Shandean moments, this realization and revision takes place *within* the published text, albeit in a marginal note: 'The 11th errour specified in the former part of this Book is in the Catalogue of Errours contained in the first part of *Gangraena*, which slipt me before I was aware: and therefore upon comparing both together, I put it out, and reckon not that, but make these Errours to begin here at number 23 which otherwise should have been number 24' (2: 140). Clearly Edwards did not have time for revision and we get a

---

[41] *Gangraena*, 1: 1, 4, 5–7.
[42] Hughes, *Gangraena and the Struggle*, 98, 100. On the form of *Gangraena*, see also Kristen Poole, *Radical Religion from Shakespeare to Milton: Figures of Nonconformity in Early Modern England* (Cambridge: Cambridge University Press, 2000), 104–23.

vivid sense of a man sending his pages to the printer as he wrote. Edwards kept adding bits on to the text even as it was going to press—another appendix, another postscript. In the final pages of the second part the size of the print is even reduced so that all the information can be fitted into the page. In one sense Edwards's failure to impose formal order on his material makes his point and is a rhetorical effect—the proliferation of blasphemous opinions in 1640s England is so out of control that he struggles to keep his records up-to-date. At the same time the chaotic form of *Gangraena* is an embodiment of what Hughes calls 'the air of obsessive paranoia' that hangs over the text as Edwards vainly strives to incorporate every single heresy circulating in England while repeatedly asserting his own credibility.[43]

The 1640s marked the beginning of the democratization and alleged vulgarization of the literary system against which Swift and his fellow Scriblerians reacted in their elaborate satirical assaults on Grub Street and its 'hack' authors. The numerous references to and citations from recent 'heretical' books in *Gangraena*, many of which (such as Milton's divorce tracts of 1643–5) Edwards demands should be publicly burned, are a testament to this phenomenon. Edwards repeatedly complains about the downwards dissemination of print among the laity and the shocking involvement of 'illiterate Mechanick persons' in the publication of theological speculation. This flood of controversial publishing during the Civil War, and the plethora of competing claims to truth, led to increasing awareness of 'the insecurity of the printed medium as a channel of communication' and consequently to a lack of faith in 'the idea of the "text" as concurrent with divine order'.[44] The battle over truth was at its fiercest in the Civil War newsbooks, with polemicists of each party asserting the veracity of their own accounts and denouncing the claims of their enemies as romance fiction—a phenomenon that McKeon regards as the 'climax of the early modern revolution in narrative epistemology, and ... of fundamental importance in the origins of the English novel'.[45] While Edwards himself poured scorn on the 'false reports ... vented in weekly news Books' (2: 208), *Gangraena* 'dealt with the same kind of material, and used them on occasion as sources'.[46] Emerging from the pamphlet wars of the 1640s, which had left the truth of the printed word as an epistemologically unstable category, Edwards is constantly anxious to convince his readers that they can have complete faith in him and his text because he catalogues all error, producing (what he presents as) impeccable testimony and proof for each claim. All challenges to his book are therefore false—but in the new climate of printed debate, when texts were 'anatomized, split up and reused in an opponent's animadversion', the challenges must be *proved* to be false.[47]

---

[43] Hughes, *Gangraena and the Struggle*, 101.
[44] *Gangraena*, 1, sig. A5v; Lucasta Miller, '"The Shattered *Violl*": Print and Textuality in the 1640s', in *Essays and Studies*, 46 (1993), 23–38 (27).
[45] McKeon, *Origins of the English Novel*, 48.
[46] *Gangraena*, 2: 208; Hughes, *Gangraena and the Struggle*, 120.
[47] Nigel Smith, *Literature and Revolution in England, 1640–1660* (New Haven and London: Yale University Press 1994), 42.

In an influential essay, Marcus Walsh has argued that one context for the self-consciousness of the *Tale* about its 'textual nature and status' is the Anglican defence of the authority of scriptural texts against Roman Catholic arguments that the Bible, as a printed text, was an insufficient rule of faith: Catholics maintained it was the tradition of interpretation and ceremony embodied by Rome which 'provides the text with a reader'.[48] But it might be remembered that Anglicans were also in debate on their other flank with Presbyterian and Baptist claims of *sola Scriptura*, the doctrine that the biblical text is the only infallible rule of faith. The Anglican tradition of rejecting Puritan biblical fundamentalism in favour of arguments from natural reason and probability, as well as ecclesiastical tradition, stretches back to the great Elizabethan bishop, Richard Hooker (1554–1600). To that extent, a degree of scepticism had long 'reinforced [the Church of England's] authority and was part of its orthodoxy'.[49] During the 1640s, when the Church of England was in ruins and the establishment of a Presbyterian national church government looked close, some Laudian intellectuals began to incorporate the very arguments about the inevitable corruption of the biblical texts in their historical transmission to which Catholic polemicists turned in their critique of Protestant Biblicism. In *The Liberty of Prophesying* (1647), Jeremy Taylor (1613–67), Bishop of Down and Connor after the Restoration and an important intellectual influence on the Latitudinarian movement, argues on historical and textual, as well as hermeneutical, grounds that the Bible can provide no decisive answers concerning speculative theology. It was probably the pressure to respond to the rise of enthusiasm in the 1640s as much as the threat of Presbyterian dominance that led Taylor to this radical position. The orthodox Reformed position that revelation had ceased, shared by Anglicans and Presbyterians as well as the more conservative Independents, was the basis of the claim that only an educated and trained ministry was qualified to make an authoritative interpretation of Scripture. This claim was now furiously denied and indeed inverted by mechanic preachers such as the cobbler Samuel How, who in the popular *The Sufficiencie of the Spirits Teaching without Humane Learning* (1640) declared that 'such as are taught by the Spirit, destitute of human learning, are the learned ones who truly understand the Scriptures'.[50] By denying the absolute authority of the Bible on textual grounds, Taylor could also deny the authority of the popular enthusiast who claimed to find sacred truth autonomously in a prophetic reading of the vernacular texts.

How's belief in the possibility of the mechanic's illiterate but inspired exegesis was anathema to Swift, as indeed it was to Thomas Edwards. But, just as for Jeremy Taylor the enthusiastic, anti-clerical claim to inspired scriptural interpretation depended on and

---

[48] Walsh, 'Text, "Text", and "A Tale of a Tub"', 294–5.

[49] J. G. A. Pocock, 'Within the Margins: The Definitions of Orthodoxy', in Roger D. Lund (ed.), *The Margins of Orthodoxy: Heterodox Writing and Cultural Response, 1660–1750* (Cambridge: Cambridge University Press, 1995), 33–53 (50).

[50] Samuel How, *The Sufficiencie of the Spirits Teaching without Humane Learning* (1640), 12–13. See further Nicholas McDowell, 'The Ghost in the Marble: Jeremy Taylor's Liberty of Prophesying (1647) and Its Readers', in Ariel Hessayon and Nicholas Keene (eds), *Scripture and Scholarship in Early Modern England* (Aldershot: Ashgate, 2006), 176–91 (182–4).

developed from the Puritan insistence on *sola Scriptura*, for Swift it was Presbyterian clerics like Edwards who had 'spawned' enthusiasts like How. Swift is finally more concerned in the *Tale* with the dissenting than the Catholic threat precisely because of the fresh and bitter memory of the Civil Wars: hence the creative energies he put into the invention of the Æolist sect and the comparatively mild and unmemorable treatment of Catholicism in the narrative of Peter, Martin, and Jack. The narrators of the *Tale* and the *Mechanical Operation* assert the absolute, transparent, and encyclopaedic truth of their texts in the manner of those dissenters and sectarians who would argue for *sola Scriptura*, while the textual anarchy of Swift's satires subverts any authorial claim for the perfect concurrence of the text with divine order. *Gangraena* is, as we have seen, a Presbyterian text which repeatedly and anxiously asserts its own infallibility, while staging in its very textual form its inadequacy as a true representation of reality. In its endlessly digressive narrative form, the *Tale* makes the object of explicit parody the sort of chaotic textual progression that we find in *Gangraena*, as Edwards quixotically, sometimes desperately, seeks to impose a godly textual order on a constantly proliferating swarm of blasphemy and heresy. And, like Edwards, the tale-teller always returns from his rambling and disordered narrative to assert its historicity: 'However, I shall by no means forget my character of an historian, to follow the truth, step by step, whatever happens, or wherever it may lead me.' Aspects of this claim to historicity in the *Tale* include the insistence on immediacy—'this minute I am writing'; 'the very garret I am now writing in'—and the accumulation of obscure information, such as the account of the 'macrocephali'.[51] In the *Mechanical Operation*, the speaker similarly represents himself as a compendious scholar of enthusiasm, describing in pseudo-physiological terms the various methods of 'ejaculating the soul': though these methods are 'branches of a very different nature', they have all 'arisen from the same original'. He then provides his brief history of fanatics, going right back to the ancient Egyptians: 'I have collected their systems from infinite reading', he tells us, as well as from observing 'the gesture, the motion, and the countenance, of some choice professors in their most familiar actions'.[52]

The massive polemical operation against the Independents in *Gangraena*, the most famous heresiography of the Civil War period, became a quarry for late Restoration Anglican controversialists, who found in Edwards's three volumes a treasure-trove of anti-sectarian material that they could use against Edwards's Presbyterian heirs. In this chapter, I have suggested that Swift would not only have found in his copy of *Gangraena* a host of unintentionally comic narratives of strange sectarian behaviour, but a credulous and shrill authorial voice which had lost control of its own text even as it made repeated assertions of unimpeachable textual authority. And it was the voice of the Presbyterian clergy, a tribe whom Swift hated as the 'Parent Sect' of all the others which had plagued England in the seventeenth century. But if the argument that *Gangraena* provided specific material for Swift's satires remains ultimately unprovable for works characterized

---

[51] *Tale of a Tub*, 87, 23, 109.
[52] *Tale of a Tub*, 172–3, 183.

by the unbounded heterogeneity of their textual and cultural origins, we might yet conclude that the authorial voices of the *Tale* and the *Mechanical Operation* parody the voice not only of the enthusiast, the Hobbesian, the Royal Society member, and the Grub Street hack but of another character who made the mad claim to be the cataloguer of universal truth—the heresiographer. And if the *Tale* left itself open to accusations of impiety and irreligion by refusing to offer a norm by which religious heterodoxy could be judged, then this may be because Swift's characteristic impulse to invade the design of other literary forms and subvert their premises leads him not only to anatomize sectarian folly but to parody some of the prose forms of anti-sectarian literature.

CHAPTER 19

HISTORIES

NIALL ALLSOPP

HISTORY AND ALLEGIANCE

HISTORY writing of the later Stuart period was, scholars agree, 'dominated by partisan warfare'.[1] In a bitterly partisan climate, the past supplied a powerful resource for defining, consolidating, and even ritualizing a sense of collective political identity, and for delegitimizing others. This process drew on a diverse range of historical sources, but the central, defining touchstone was the collective memory of the Civil Wars.[2] One eighteenth-century Tory marked every anniversary of the Restoration by having his son recite passages from Clarendon's *History of the Rebellion*.[3] For twentieth-century historians, the political intensity of seventeenth-century history writing provided the origin point for what they called a "historical revolution", in which political bias, didacticism, and superstition were eventually swept aside in favour of a newly enlightened understanding of impartiality, of critical rigour, and of causation and change—which established history, in their view, as a modern academic discipline.[4] More recent scholars have questioned that narrative, highlighting the continued role of ideology and political rhetoric in history writing throughout the eighteenth century and beyond. Others highlight the ideological currents that continue to shape the historiography of

---

[1] Ashley Marshall, *Swift and History: Politics and the English Past* (Cambridge: Cambridge University Press, 2015), 25.

[2] Matthew Neufeld, *The Civil Wars after 1660: Public Remembering in Late Stuart England* (Woodbridge: Boydell & Brewer, 2013), 18–49, 88–95; Judith Pollmann, *Memory in Early Modern Europe, 1500–1900* (Oxford: Oxford University Press, 2017), 143–53.

[3] Daniel R. Woolf, *Reading History in Early Modern England* (Cambridge: Cambridge University Press, 2000), 121, discussing Henry Prescott.

[4] F. S. Fussner, *The Historical Revolution: English Historical Writing and Thought 1580–1640* (London: Routledge, 1962), 299–305; F. J. Levy, *Tudor Historical Thought* (San Marino CA: The Huntington Library, 1967), 287–8; Arthur B. Ferguson, *Clio Unbound: Perception of the Social and Cultural Past in Renaissance England* (Durham, NC: Duke University Press, 1979).

the English Revolution in the modern era.[5] The partisanship of seventeenth-century historians did not deter them from almost unanimously invoking a language of 'impartiality'—reminding us how the language of 'impartiality' tacitly gestures to a context of interpretation which is partial, and contested.[6]

This chapter aims to clarify what it means to describe history writing as partisan by applying current historians' frameworks for understanding how mass partisanship worked in a period before the existence of organized parties or a highly centralized state. The Roundheads and Cavaliers have been re-described as 'rainbow' or 'fissiparous' coalitions, shaped contingently around discrete aims, occasions, and personalities, through which sympathies could be mobilized into active military, logistical, or financial support. Coalitions were fashioned through sermons, pamphlets, petitions, declarations, journalism—all forms in which writers worked to resolve complex events into comprehensible and galvanizing narratives.[7] All of these drew on the resources of history in their search for causes, precedents, justifications, and common rallying-points. In light of this complex and nuanced picture of political mobilization, we clearly need to reassess what it means to describe history writing as 'partisan'. That is the aim of this chapter: to ask whether this picture is mirrored in the work of seventeenth-century historians—firstly in their account of partisanship during the Civil Wars, and secondly in their understanding of how history-reading might itself mobilize readers. While the 'Warre between the Penns' has always been recognized as one of their major themes, further work is needed to assess how they understood political mobilization.[8] My survey is necessarily schematic and provisional, but it will conclude by highlighting some striking examples in which history-reading itself is shown to be a galvanizing political force.

---

[5] David Womersley, 'Against the Teleology of Technique', and Mark Knights, 'The Tory Interpretation of History in the Rage of Parties', in Paulina Kewes (ed.), *The Uses of History in Early Modern England* (San Marino, CA: Huntington Library, 2006), 91–104, 347–66; David Norbrook, *Poetry and Politics in the English Renaissance* (1984; 2nd edn, Oxford: Oxford University Press, 2002), 270–89.

[6] Joad Raymond, 'Exporting Impartiality' and Christine Gerrard, 'The Language of Impartiality and Party-Political Discourse in England, 1680–1745', in Kathryn Murphy and Anita Traninger (eds.), *The Emergence of Impartiality* (Leiden: Brill, 2014), 151–5, 212–15.

[7] Barbara Donagan, 'Varieties of Royalism', in Jason McElligott and David L. Smith (eds.), *Royalists and Royalism during the English Civil Wars* (Cambridge: Cambridge University Press, 2007), 66–88; Rachel Foxley, 'Varieties of Parliamentarianism', in Michael Braddick (ed.), *The Oxford Handbook of the English Revolution* (Oxford: Oxford University Press, 2015), 414–29; Michael Braddick, 'Mobilisation, Anxiety and Creativity in England during the 1640s', in John Morrow and Jonathan Scott (eds.), *Liberty, Authority, Formality: Political Ideas and Culture, 1600–1900* (Exeter: Imprint Academic, 2008), 207–30; David R. Como, *Radical Parliamentarians and the English Civil War* (Oxford: Oxford University Press, 2018), 6–19. See also Chapter 27 on 'Political Debate' by Mark Knights and Chapter 35 on 'Sermons' by Warren Johnston.

[8] Thomas Hobbes, *Behemoth*, ed. Paul Seaward (Oxford: Oxford University Press, 2010), 212; all further references to *Behemoth* are to this edition. A partial exception is Ingrid Creppell's consideration of Hobbes's responses to 'mass-mobilization' and 'mass politicization' in 'The Democratic Element in Hobbes's *Behemoth*', in Tomaž Mastnak (ed.), *Hobbes's Behemoth: Religion and Democracy* (Exeter: Imprint Academic, 2009), 347–9.

Reading history can be a viscerally political experience. Readers' enduring involvement in the passions of the Civil Wars can be witnessed in surviving annotated copies of Thomas Hobbes's *Behemoth*. One reader, 'W: Champernoone', recorded his violent agreement with Hobbes's anti-puritan invective. This he distilled into splenetic slogans scrawled in the margins: 'K: Charles I[t] murdered by the Presbyterians'; 'Presbiterian tubb-Preacchers destroyed the peace of the kingdome'.[9] These annotations may have served to vent Champernoone's feelings—he clearly needed no reminding that Oliver Cromwell was a 'Usurpinge Rebellious Rogue'. They were perhaps targeted at other readers of the copy, to induct peers or household members into a shared political identity.[10] Another copy of *Behemoth* annotated by the diarist John Evelyn marks Hobbes's polemic more coolly, with silent underlining and the occasional 'N.B.'. Evelyn instead recorded another kind of investment, annotating the text with his own participation in the events narrated. At the execution of Strafford he notes, 'I saw him beheaded'; in the prolonged crisis that preceded the Restoration, he inserts his own (unavailing) efforts to lobby on behalf of Charles II.[11] Both examples, in different ways, suggest how history can galvanize its readers into political action: an urge to commemorate, to amplify, and to project oneself into the events narrated. Yet they also reveal the uncertainties inherent in different readers' temperaments, and ambiguities about how reading translates into action.

This chapter will focus on three of the most significant examples from the voluminous and rancorous historiography of the Civil Wars that grew up in the decades following the conflict.[12] Clarendon's *History*, Hobbes's *Behemoth*, and Lucy Hutchinson's *Memoirs of the Life of Colonel Hutchinson* were all written to instruct and mobilize readers to partisan ends. Edward Hyde, Earl of Clarendon, had served as Charles I's secretary and Charles II's Lord Chancellor; an experienced propagandist, he sought to defend a sovereign monarchy, legitimized by its subscription to binding promises. The *History*'s posthumous publication was timed to coincide with the 1702 Tory election campaign.[13] Hobbes's *Behemoth* presents a dialogue between a pupil, 'B', and a teacher, 'A', who analyse the Civil Wars through a distinctively Hobbesian theoretical framework. While Hobbes also sought to defend sovereignty against Presbyterian preachers and 'democraticall gentlemen', his uncompromising views horrified mainstream Royalists

---

[9] The shelf-mark is British Library, 1481.bb.15: 39, 155, 177. Champernoone signed the volume in 1699; his family hailed from Hobbes's old neighbourhood, in Chesterfield, Derbyshire.

[10] British Library, 1481.bb.15: 226. Compare the copy of the 1707 edition of Clarendon's *History* in Marsh's Library, Dublin, which carries Jonathan Swift's similarly furious annotations, largely directed against Scottish Presbyterians, 'Cursed, abominable, hellish Scottish villains everlasting Traitors etc'. See extract at www.marshlibrary.ie/digi/items/show/592 (accessed 1st August 2023).

[11] The shelf-mark is British Library, Eve.a.14:94, 129, and end paper; see also 87, 136, 278.

[12] Royce MacGillivray, *Restoration Historians and the English Civil War* (The Hague: Martinus Nijhoff, 1974), 1–4.

[13] Edward Hyde, Earl of Clarendon, *The History of the Rebellion and Civil Wars in England begun in the year 1641*, ed. William Dunn Macray, 6 vols. (Oxford, 1888, repr. 1992); a new edition by Paul Seaward is forthcoming, but see currently *The History of the Rebellion: A New Selection*, ed. Paul Seaward (Oxford: Oxford University Press, 2009).

(including Clarendon). *Behemoth* was proscribed from publication, though five unauthorized editions did appear in Hobbes's lifetime, and a further posthumous edition in 1682.[14] In contrast, Hutchinson's *Memoirs* are comparable with other narratives by defeated and marginalized puritans, like that of Edmund Ludlow—written to maintain morale and solidarity by commemorating (and retrospectively defining) what they now termed the Good Old Cause. Since their rediscovery and publication in 1806, the *Memoirs* have been valued for their far-reaching analysis of the social and religious causes of the conflict, and more recently, the space Hutchinson opens up for women's political agency.[15] Though they clearly have very different political outlooks, Hobbes, Clarendon, and Hutchinson are united by a shared political aim, to transmit the terms of the conflict into contemporary political struggles.

Generic Contexts

What twentieth-century scholars perceived as partisanship can be explained as a result of the early modern understanding that history was primarily a rhetorical and morally didactic genre. This view was founded on Cicero's description of history as 'the life of memory and teacher of life' (*'vita memoriae, magistra vitae'*). As explained in the 1620s by Degory Wheare, Camden Professor of Ancient History at the University of Oxford, this meant: 'the Register and Explication of particular affairs, undertaken to the end that the memory of them may be preserved, and so universals may be the more evidently Confirm'd, by which we may be instructed how to live well and Happily'.[16] The emphasis was on moral instruction, which carried particular rhetorical demands, but also a particular risk, that rhetorical invention might carry the historian beyond the bounds of factual veracity.[17] Some historians, like the Oxford scholar Mathias Prideaux, tried to defend factual history from association with romance fictions, a 'Bastard sort of Histories' which wasted time in 'transporting and deluding the affections'.[18] Most

---

[14] See the account in Seaward, 'General Introduction', in Hobbes, *Behemoth*, 15–16.

[15] Lucy Hutchinson, *Memoirs of the Life of Colonel Hutchinson*, ed. James Sutherland (Oxford: Oxford University Press, 1973); a new edition by David Norbrook is forthcoming. See Claire Gheeraert-Graffeuille, *Lucy Hutchinson and the English Revolution: Gender, Genre, and History Writing* (Oxford: Oxford University Press, 2022).

[16] Degory Wheare, *The Method and Order of Reading both Civil and Ecclesiastical Histories*, tr. Edmund Bohun (1685), 15. See Anthony Grafton, *What was History? The Art of History in Early Modern Europe* (Cambridge: Cambridge University Press, 2007), 21–35; J. H. Salmon, 'Precept, Example, and Truth: Degory Wheare and the *ars historica*', in Donald R. Kelley and David Harris Sacks (eds.), *The Historical Imagination in Early Modern Britain: History, Rhetoric, and Fiction, 1500–1800* (Cambridge: Cambridge University Press, 1997), 12–23.

[17] Daniel Woolf, *The Idea of History in Early Stuart England* (Toronto: University of Toronto Press, 1990), 16–24; Patrick Collinson, 'Truth, Lies, and Fiction in Sixteenth-Century Protestant Historiography', in Kelley and Sacks (eds.), *Historical Imagination*, 37–68 (42–6).

[18] Mathias Prideaux, *An Easy and Compendious Introduction for Reading all sorts of Histories* (1648), 343.

readers, however, experienced this divide in more nuanced ways—a fact illustrated by the catalogue Hobbes's publisher William Crooke appended to his posthumous edition of *Behemoth* (1682). Crooke's highly porous list of 'Histories' includes chronicles like James Heath's *A Brief Chronicle of the Late Intestine War* (second edition, 1676), Hobbes's principal factual source—though one which still described itself in poetic terms as 'the English Iliads in a nut-shel'. But it also features obviously poetic romances, like Hobbes's translation of the *Odyssey* (1675, double-counted under two different titles).[19] Readers could move omnivorously between scholarly history and fiction: the puritan clergyman Ralph Josselin made detailed studies of biblical historians like James Ussher to bolster his religious teaching, but also records in his diary his 'singular affection' for reading history—when he was 'exceeding yong', he recalls, he liked to imagine 'the conquering of kingdoms' and 'write historyes of such exploits'. The Royalist Margaret Cavendish memorably described history and fiction as productively complimentary: 'Poesy is beautiful and spritely; History is brown and lovely.'[20]

If history used rhetorical invention to instruct readers, so historians could also use rhetoric to excite and galvanize political passions. No historian drew on the power of rhetoric so forcibly as Clarendon, renowned both for his memorable aphorisms (his pithy description of Cromwell as 'a brave, bad man') and for his imposing, copious sentences: 'It will be wondered at hereafter, that, in a judging and discerning state, where men had, or seemed to have, their faculties of reason and understanding at the height [they were inflamed] into the most prodigious and boldest rebellion that any age or country ever brought forth.'[21] Clarendon's rhetoric captures a sense of grand tragedy—the awareness of posterity, or 'hereafter', that constantly weighs on him. But it also projects the detached irony ('had, or seemed to have') that befitted an astute political analyst. Hutchinson, too, achieves some electrifying effects—her witnessing of providence's role in history gives her account a wider social and spiritual sweep than Clarendon's. Her story begins 'when the dawne of the Gospell began to break upon this Isle after the darke midnight of Papacy', a metaphor of spiritual light that spans across the whole work, until the Restoration is secured by the Convention Parliament of 1660, 'whose sunne of liberty then sett, and all their glorie gave place to the fowlest mists that ever overspread a miserable people'.[22] In contrast to these examples, Hobbes's *Behemoth* employs a plainer and often acidic style, seemingly designed to puncture any temptation to frame the conflict in epic terms. When 'A' offers an unflattering description of Clarendon's cherished theory of power shared between king and parliament, 'B' asks 'But how if they cannot

---

[19] Thomas Hobbes, *Behemoth, the History of the Causes of the Civil-Wars of England* (1682), sig. Z2r; James Heath, *A Brief Chronicle of all the Chief Actions So Fatally Falling Out in the Three Kingdoms* (1662), 'To the Reader' (n.p.).

[20] *The Diary of Ralph Josselin, 1616–1683*, ed. Alan MacFarlane (London: British Academy, 1976), 1–2 and 119; Margaret Cavendish, *The Worlds Olio* (1655), 7; Daniel Woolf, 'A Feminine Past? Gender, Genre, and Historical Knowledge in England, 1500–1800', *American Historical Review*, 102 (1997), 647–8, 660–2.

[21] Clarendon, *History*, 2: 81; Martine Watson-Brownley, *Clarendon and the Rhetoric of Historical Form* (Philadelphia PA: University of Pennsylvania Press, 1985), 38–49.

[22] Hutchinson, *Memoirs*, 38, 224.

agree?', to which 'A' responds sardonically, 'I think they never thought of that'.[23] The evidence of William Champernoone's annotations may suggest that Hobbes's rough-hewn cynicism could be even more exciting to readers than Clarendon's lofty rhetoric. These differences of approach notwithstanding, all three histories discussed here are didactic works, which draw on the different emotional and imaginative resources of rhetoric to bring an avowedly partisan interpretation of history to life.

The hybrid and rhetorical nature of the genre notwithstanding, several changes were underway in later seventeenth-century history writing which impacted on the historians under consideration here. Without reinstating the teleological frame of a 'historical revolution', it has been shown that contemporary developments nevertheless brought about several significant intellectual 'transitions' in thinking about historiographical issues of chronology, causation, and proof.[24] The old chronicle form was slowly declining from its sixteenth-century heyday; a new, non-narrative history of things and places—antiquarianism—was growing in popularity under the influence of writers like William Camden and John Selden.[25] Narrative history was increasingly dominated by the 'politic' history practised influentially by humanists like Niccolò Machiavelli and, in England, Francis Bacon. Politic history foregrounded the morally equivocal rules of political prudence. It replaced the eloquent didacticism of Cicero with the terse cynicism of Tacitus, a more detached style embodied contrastingly by Hobbes's plain speaking and Clarendon's ironies and aphorisms.[26] Hobbes's translation of Thucydides (1628) had established him as a major English practitioner of politic history. Though by the 1660s he had developed doubts about the value of prudence, *Behemoth* signals at least some residual allegiance to this tradition in its proclaimed focus not on events, but on the 'Causes and Councells' that shaped them.[27] Clarendon, who prominently cites both Tacitus and Machiavelli, also signals a debt to politic history. In 1647 he described his work as a 'digested relation', an alimentary metaphor borrowed from Bacon's category of 'Ruminated History', which consists in 'politic discourse and observation thereupon'.[28]

---

[23] Hobbes, *Behemoth*, 150; see also Seaward, 'General Introduction', *Behemoth*, 18–21.

[24] Daniel Woolf, 'From Hystories to the Historical: Five Transitions in Thinking about the Past, 1500–1700', in Kewes (ed.), *Uses of History*, 31–68 (34–6).

[25] See Chapter 6 on 'Antiquarian Writing' by Thomas Roebuck; Woolf, *Reading History*, 14–25, 48–65; Daniel Woolf, *The Social Circulation of the Past: English Historical Culture 1500–1730* (Oxford: Oxford University Press, 2003), 141–82.

[26] Anthony Grafton and Lisa Jardine, 'Studied for Action: How Gabriel Harvey read his Livy', *Past and Present*, 129 (1990), 30–78; Peter Burke, 'Tacitism, Scepticism, and Reason of State', in J. H. Burns (ed.), *The Cambridge History of Political Thought, 1450–1700* (Cambridge: Cambridge University Press, 1991), 477–98; Paulina Kewes, 'Henry Savile's Tacitus and the Politics of Roman History in Late Elizabethan England', *Huntington Library Quarterly*, 74 (2011), 515–51.

[27] *Behemoth*, 166. See Kinch Hoekstra, 'Hobbes's Thucydides', and Tomaž Mastnak, 'Making History: The Politics of Hobbes's *Behemoth*', in A. P. Martinich and Kinch Hoekstra (eds.), *The Oxford Handbook of Hobbes* (Oxford: Oxford University Press, 2016), 547–74 (547–9, 569–71), 575–602 (580–93).

[28] *State Papers Collected by Edward, Earl of Clarendon*, ed. Richard Scrope, 3 vols. (Oxford, 1767–86), 2: 357; Francis Bacon, *The Advancement of Learning*, ed. Michael Kiernan (Oxford: Oxford University Press, 2000), 70; Paul Seaward, 'Clarendon, Tacitism, and the Civil Wars of Europe', in Kewes (ed.), *Uses of History*, 289–311 (286–8, 302–6).

When a historian has actually lived through the events they are narrating, history also blurs symbiotically with memoir. This was especially the case for politic history, because political prudence was derived from personal experience—history offered a means of topping up one's experience artificially, by reading other people's.[29] For this reason, Francis Bacon argued that 'lives' excelled other forms of history, 'chronicles' and 'relations'. Margaret Cavendish ventured a colourful adaptation of Bacon's view in her Civil War memoir of her husband, the Marquis of Newcastle—identifying 'lives' as the most 'heroicall' kind of history, as they are governed by a single, monarch-like figure.[30] But memoir was also governed by personal experience in less lofty ways—in narrating her husband's exploits, Cavendish was also 'effectively presenting Charles II with a bill' for his services. Autobiography infiltrates all three of the histories under discussion here. Hutchinson's *Memoirs* have been interpreted as a reaction against Cavendish's Royalist appropriation of biography, working to vindicate John Hutchinson from any suspicion of complicity in the Restoration.[31] In *Behemoth*, though both interlocutors reflect Hobbes's views in different ways, 'A', the older and wiser speaker, stresses that he is speaking from his personal experience of the Civil Wars.[32] Clarendon's *History*, meanwhile, belongs to a sub-genre of memoirs written by retired statesmen. The first draft of the 'Historical Narration', written in exile in 1647–8, is highly coloured by his personal experiences; this text was later interleaved with an explicitly autobiographical 'Life', written in Clarendon's second exile after 1667.[33] The autobiographical histories of the seventeenth century were fuelled by a culture of private note-taking: Hutchinson's *Memoirs* are written up from 'private memorials', a more fragmentary notebook that survives in the British Library. Charles I sought to assist Clarendon by sending him his 'own short memorials and journal'.[34] The ultimate example of a hybrid memoir-chronicle was the *Memorials of the English Affairs* by the Cromwellian statesman Bulstrode Whitelocke—a private diary, later tidied up and

---

[29] For classic statements of these generic views, see Thomas Hobbes, 'To the Reader', in *Eight Bookes of the Peloponnesian Warre written by Thucydides* (1629), sig. A3v; and Thomas Hobbes, *Leviathan*, ed. Noel Malcolm, 3 vols. (Oxford: Oxford University Press, 2012), 3: 42–4. All further references to *Leviathan* are to Malcolm's edition.

[30] Bacon, *Advancement of Learning*, 66; Margaret Cavendish, *The Life of the Thrice Noble, High, and Puissant Prince William Cavendishe* (1667), sig. c1r. The other kinds are 'national histories' (aristocratic/politic), and 'general histories' (democratic/mechanical, and hence the lowest).

[31] David Norbrook, 'Margaret Cavendish and Lucy Hutchinson: Identity, Ideology, and Politics', *In-Between: Essays & Studies in Literary Criticism*, 9 (2000), 179–203 (195); David Norbrook, 'Memoirs and Oblivion: Lucy Hutchinson and the Restoration', *Huntington Library Quarterly*, 75 (2012), 233–82.

[32] Seaward, 'General Introduction', *Behemoth*, 18–21.

[33] Paul Seaward, 'The *Life* of Clarendon: History and Memoir in England and France', in Philip Major (ed.), *Clarendon Reconsidered: Law, Loyalty, Literature, 1640–1674* (Abingdon: Routledge, 2017), 123–43 (123–5).

[34] Hutchinson, *Memoirs*, 157; Clarendon, *History*, 4: 3–4. See Anna Wall, '"Not So Much Open Professed Enemies as Close Hypocritical False-Hearted People": Lucy Hutchinson's Manuscript Account of the Services of John Hutchinson and Mid-Seventeenth-Century Factionalism', *The Seventeenth Century*, 36/4 (2021), 623–51.

posthumously published (in 1682), in which public and private affairs become 'hopelessly confused'.[35]

Historians and Political Print

The Civil Wars transformed the work of a historian most dramatically through the explosion and politicization of printing. A wealth of primary information was now available, which either had not been printed before—newsbooks, parliamentary speeches, even the king's private correspondence—or never with such intensity—petitions, proclamations, pamphlets. This deluge could be read as a sort of accelerated chronicle: John Cleveland described weekly news as 'an Historie in Snippets' (there was authority for this in Bacon, who had categorized 'journals' together with 'annals').[36] There was also a proliferation of printed documents—declarations and petitions—which asserted their own historical significance while retailing a self-justifying interpretation of the war and its causes. For example, the Grand Remonstrance of 1641, itself designed as a milestone text, entrenched a narrative of Charles's corruption at the hands of 'malignant' counsellors which came to define parliamentarian historiography.[37] The outpour of such texts led to the unlikely politicization of another historical genre, the edited collection of documents. The first of these, Edward Husband's *An Exact Collection of all Remonstrances, Declarations, Votes, Orders, Ordinances, Proclamations, Petitions, Messages, Answeres, and other Remarkable Passages* (1643), was commissioned by parliament to recapitulate the various definitions and justifications of the cause, to bolster government officials in the face of local opposition. Collections were hybrid works of journalism and antiquarianism. The best-known example, John Rushworth's *Historical Collections* (1659–1701), clearly aspired to a monumental status, and it was scrupulously edited from Rushworth's extensive personal archive.[38] But behind this scholarly façade, the selection and editing could be as partisan as the source material itself. Rushworth's *Historical Collections*, originally dedicated to Richard Cromwell, provoked a Royalist counterblast, John Nalson's *Impartial Collection*—the term 'impartial' again tacitly acknowledging a context of partisan interpretation.[39] The collections remained an inescapable presence in the contested historiography of the Civil Wars: Whitelocke's

---

[35] Blair Worden, 'The "Diary" of Bulstrode Whitelocke, 1605–1675', *English Historical Review*, 108 (1993), 123–9.

[36] Woolf, *Reading History*, 28–31; Bacon, *Advancement of Learning*, II, 69–70.

[37] David Cressy, 'Remembrancers of the Revolution: Histories and Historiographers of the 1640s', in Kewes (ed.), *Uses of History*, 253–62 (257).

[38] Michael Braddick, *God's Fury, England's Fire: A New History of the English Civil Wars* (London: Allen Lane, 2008), 272–3; Frances Henderson, '"Posterity to Judge": John Rushworth and his "Historicall Collections"', *Bodleian Library Record*, 15 (1996), 247–59.

[39] Joad Raymond, 'Exporting Impartiality', 143–7; MacGillivray, *Restoration Historians*, 96–116.

Memorials and Clarendon's *History* are interspersed with long verbatim excerpts from printed documents.

Clarendon, Hobbes, and Hutchinson's relation to the printed landscape is complicated by their histories' initial lives in manuscript. Forbidden from printing *Behemoth*, Hobbes had to content himself with manuscript circulation—even after a pirate copy had appeared in 1677, refusing to sanction an official version until after his death.[40] Clarendon acknowledged that his *History* was 'not likely to be published', and would 'make mad work among friends and foes' if it were, though he left detailed instructions for posthumous editing and publishing in a will drawn up in 1647.[41] Hutchinson, who harboured cultural and religious ambivalences about the propriety of print publication, frames her text as a private, didactic manuscript dedicated to her sons. But here also we cannot rule out a possible hope of posthumous publication: her manuscript works display affinities with print genres, including pamphlets and didactic 'mother's legacy' texts.[42]

All three of these manuscript texts conduct a close conversation with printed sources and paratexts. Hutchinson's reference to her husband reading 'all the publick papers ... besides many other private treatises' attests to the close proximity between texts in print and manuscript, consumed alongside one another.[43] Clarendon, who (as already noted) relied partly on the king's own manuscript journals, confessed to Charles that he also refreshed his 'ill memory' with 'some few pamphlets and diurnals', drawing verbatim on a large number of printed texts. In private, he defended his use of pamphlet material from both sides as 'the foundations upon which all that was after done, was built', citing the Italian historian Davila as an authoritative model.[44] Relying on pamphlets could bring pitfalls: Hobbes made an incautious slip by summarizing the parliamentarians' position from a tendentious pamphlet that had in fact been drafted anonymously by Clarendon.[45] Nevertheless, the dialogue in *Behemoth* presents a running commentary on compendia like Husband's *Exact Collection* and Heath's *Brief Chronicle*. At one point 'A' abdicates his responsibilities as a narrator: 'for the proceeding of the Warre, I referre you to the History thereof written at large in English', whereafter he promises to resume his analysis of the roundheads' 'iniustice, impudence, and hypocrisy'.[46] Hutchinson very similarly sends her reader to consult a narrative before continuing her analysis: 'I shall desire you to informe your selves better' from 'their owne

---

[40] Seaward, 'General Introduction', *Behemoth*, 10–17.

[41] Clarendon, *History*, 1: 2–3; *Clarendon State Papers*, 2: 288, 357.

[42] See Wall, 'Lucy Hutchinson's Manuscript Account'; Jennifer Heller, *The Mother's Legacy in Early Modern England* (Farnham: Ashgate, 2011); Gheeraert-Graffuille, *Lucy Hutchinson*, 5–8.

[43] Hutchinson, *Memoirs*, 53, 65.

[44] *Clarendon State Papers*, 2: 385 and 333. Seaward, 'Clarendon, Tacitism, and the Civil Wars of Europe', 291–4; Jason Peacey, 'A Royalist Reads the News: Sir Edward Hyde and Civil War Journalism', in Major (ed.), *Clarendon Reconsidered*, 16–36 (29–30).

[45] Hobbes, *Behemoth*, 33, 244.

[46] Hobbes, *Behemoth*, 267; see Paul Seaward, '"Chief of the Ways of God": Form and Meaning in the "Behemoth" of Thomas Hobbes' in Mastnak (ed.), *Hobbes's Behemoth*, 73–92 (76–9).

printed papers and Mr. Maye's History'.[47] Presumably Thomas May's *The History of the Parliament of England* (1647) along with a collection of parliamentarian texts (perhaps compiled in Husband's *Exact Collection*) were available to consult in the Hutchinsons' library alongside the manuscript of the *Memoir*. Hutchinson situates her account within a sprawling print controversy:

> if any one have a desire of more particular information, there were so many bookes then written as will sufficiently give it them; and although those of our enemies are all fraught with abominable lies, yet if all ours were suppresst, even their owne writings impartially consider'd would be a sufficient chronicle of their injustice and oppression[.][48]

Her borrowing of the word 'chronicle' suggests how this pamphlet literature could be viewed as a historical resource in its own right. However misleading as to events, Royalist pamphlets at least record the 'injustice' of their cause. At the same time, Hutchinson positions herself *not* as a chronicler, but rather as an interpreter of this printed sphere, framing the controversy through a partisan language of 'ours' and 'theirs'. Similarly, Clarendon admits of the attainder against Strafford in 1641: 'of the argument itself I shall say little, it being in print and in many hands; I shall only remember two notable propositions, which are sufficient characters of the person and the time'.[49] These historians envisaged their task as to navigate through the published documents—applying partisan frameworks, selecting salient details, and drawing out hidden meanings, to wrest interpretive control from the voluminous printed record.

Recording Mobilization

The writers studied here could not ignore the centrality of print culture in driving Civil War partisanship. It remains to see, however, how their understanding of this process matches up to modern historians' subtle understandings of mobilization and coalition-forming. Hutchinson, Hobbes, and Clarendon all make a central distinction between passive sympathy and active mobilization. Clarendon notes how the Worcestershire gentry were 'well affected to the king', but 'came not to him' in his hour of need; Hobbes, that the king's 'passionate complaint to his people ... made them pity him, but not yet rise in his behalfe'.[50] His proximity to the Royalist war effort gave Clarendon a particularly acute insight into the different ways in which mobilization drove the conduct of war: it could involve office-holding, or more informal kinds of logistical or financial support,

---

[47] Hutchinson, *Memoirs*, 53.
[48] Hutchinson, *Memoirs*, 37.
[49] Clarendon, *History*, 1: 307.
[50] Clarendon, *History*, 5: 187 (on 'indigested affection', see also 4: 332); Hobbes, *Behemoth*, 305.

or the more nebulous social legitimation of acquiescence. Thus Clarendon recounts how parliament's Vote of No Addresses (1648) was 'so publicly detested, that many who had served the Parliament in several unwarrantable employments ... withdrew themselves from the service'. Losing crucial support from the gentry who 'had been seduced to do them service' forced parliament to lean more heavily on an expensive army, and on 'a more inferior sort of the common people', compounding problems of logistics and legitimacy.[51] Clarendon reveals here a subtle grasp of the connections between mobilization and perceptions of legitimacy. Yet his understanding of mobilization is also clouded, on the other hand, by a tendency to conceptualize it as working from the top down, and commonly in nefarious ways—using a pejorative language of 'seduction' of an 'inferior sort'.

Himself an accomplished propagandist, Clarendon plays close attention to the printed propaganda through which parliament attempted to 'publish the temper of the people'—'publish' is used here in the ordinary sense, of making public, but also apparently in a more complex, transitive sense, of trying to define or manipulate the public 'temper' through publication. He dissects the 'false and fallacious mediums' used in parliamentarian rhetoric to 'dazzle' the 'clearness of men's understandings', to cement their own coalition. Politicians and pamphleteers, he alleges, sought to escalate the crisis and whip up hysteria, trapping opponents into 'the impertinency of arguing against a supposition that was not like to be real', while trapping allies into being 'for the future captivated and pre-engaged by their own votes'.[52] This rhetorical coalition-building was also co-ordinated with networks of dissemination, as he notes seditious material 'being printed and scattered amongst the people' to draw 'multitudes of mean people' into the streets of Westminster. These aspects of Clarendon's account reveal striking affinities with recent studies of 1640s mobilization and coalition-forming. Yet modern historians have granted greater agency to grassroots, extramural politics than permitted by Clarendon—for whom social status combines with the assumptions of politic history to privilege a model of top-down manipulation. This can be seen, for instance, in the passive constructions which encourage the reader to scour the narrative for agency—'it was quickly understood abroad that the Commons liked well the visitation of their neighbours'—deftly presupposing an elite and conspiratorial explanation for events.[53] These assumptions also apply to Clarendon's descriptions of Royalist mobilization: his account of the 1648 Kent Rising highlights the propagandist Roger L'Estrange's circulation of 'declarations and engagements as he thought most likely to prevail with the people', bolstered by the Kentish gentry 'stirring up and inflaming' the local mariners.[54]

---

[51] Clarendon, *History*, 4: 285–6; See also his assessment of the precarious parliamentarian coalition at 3: 247.

[52] Clarendon, *History*, 1: 269; 2: 83; *OED*, 'publish, v.', see obsolete sense 4a: 'to brand *as*'.

[53] Clarendon, *History*, 1: 450–1 (see also at 1: 263–4); contrast Como, *Radical Parliamentarians*, 107–14, or John Walter, *Covenanting Citizens: The Protestation Oath and Popular Political Culture in the English Revolution* (Oxford: Oxford University Press, 2016), 60–5.

[54] Clarendon, *History*, 4: 334–5.

In this way, Clarendon reified his 'obsession with gentry influence', a preoccupation with the highest levels of leadership which arguably exaggerated their real agency in the face of events—as if the gentry and their hired pens could turn popular mobilization on and off like a tap.[55]

Whereas Clarendon consistently portrays parliamentarian allegiance in a nefarious light—as 'private interest ... covered under public pretences'—Hutchinson undertook the opposite task of bearing witness to genuine godly conviction.[56] Unlike Hobbes or Clarendon, she situates the Civil Wars in a more expansive historical narrative, familiar from Protestant histories like Foxe's Book of Martyrs, of a beleaguered minority of saints who have 'the name of Puritane fix'd upon them'.[57] Hutchinson's fundamentally binary model of a Papist and 'Puritane party' may look simplistic by contrast with recent historians' nuanced models of 'fissiparous coalitions'. However, her very adoption of 'the name of Puritane' can be read as itself an instrument of coalition-building: 'labelling' was 'intrinsic to the process of polarization', supplying 'discursive poles around which people were mobilized'.[58] Hutchinson also reveals striking affinities with Clarendon in her close analysis of the duplicitous verbal strategies by which the Royalists appropriated parliamentarian rhetoric to mobilize support for their own cause. The King's Commissions of Array (1642), she notes, 'mockt the Parliament, using their owne words', which had originally 'invited men to arme for the defence of the Protestant religion'. This linguistic appropriation, repeating the same phrase, 'using their owne words', perversely 'deceiv'd many people, and got contributions of plate, mony and armes'.[59] Hutchinson echoes Clarendon not only in her close scrutiny of rhetorical tactics, but also in her anti-populist contempt for cheap print. Colonel Hutchinson refuses to have his deeds reported in the newspapers because he 'never would give anything to buy the flatteries of those scriblers'.[60]

Hobbes, by contrast, is impatient of and even hostile towards political print. 'B' portrays the king's willingness to 'entertaine so many Petitions, Messages, Declarations and Remonstrances, and [to] vouchsafe his answers' as a serious strategic error. The 'common people', he explains, 'vnderstood not the reasons of either party', but rather 'by his complyance' contracted 'an opinion that the Parliament was likely to haue the victory'. For a king to demean himself as a mere interlocutor eroded the 'opinion' of omnipotence which was, in Hobbes's political theory, integral to sovereign power.[61] This argument is a not-so-covert attack on Clarendon, the Royalists' leading propagandist. Clarendon, Hobbes alleges, 'dream't of a mixt power of the King and the two Houses' and hence was 'alwaies vrging the King to Declarations and Treaties', which merely

---

[55] Ronald Hutton, 'Clarendon's *History of the Rebellion*', *English Historical Review*, 97 (1982), 70–88.
[56] Clarendon, *History*, 1: 442 (see also 3: 495).
[57] Hutchinson, *Memoirs*, 43; Collinson, 'Protestant Historiography', 49–57.
[58] Thomas Leng, 'The Meanings of "Malignancy": the Language of Enmity and the Construction of the Parliamentarian Cause in the English Revolution', *Journal of British Studies*, 53 (2014), 835–58 (854).
[59] Hutchinson, *Memoirs*, 58.
[60] Hutchinson, *Memoirs*, 68.
[61] Hobbes, *Behemoth*, 242, 275.

'increased the hope and courage of the rebels, but did the King little good'.[62] Clarendon responded with scorn to these criticisms, insisting that Hobbes's 'too peremtory adhering to some Philosophical Notions … had misled him in the investigation of Policy'. It was experienced practitioners, not theorists, who made the best historians.[63] In his *Life*, Clarendon defends both his qualifications as a statesman and his role as a propagandist. He recalls his own appointment to the king's staff by describing how 'infinitely discomposed' the parliamentarians had been by the 'new … secretary the king had found, who supplied him with so much resolution and bitterness'.[64] What elevates Clarendon's own propaganda above self-flattering bitterness is a recurring rhetorical topos of 'undeceiving'. He quotes a royal Declaration (which he had drafted) in which Charles declares that he will 'let himself fall to any office that might undeceive his people, and to take more pains that way by his own pen than ever king had done', whatever the cost. This language is echoed in the *History*'s opening declaration, 'that posterity be not deceived'.[65] Seen in this light, Clarendon's position may not look altogether different from Hobbes's view that the sovereign ruler was the sole authority on doctrinal truths. But Clarendon went further than Hobbes in ascribing to himself, as the sovereign's loyal scribe, a leading role in professing such truths.[66]

While print was undeniably central, all three writers complicate its status—and in so doing echo modern historians—by emphasizing that print was only a part of a wider circulation loop driven by oral dissemination. The other crucial ingredient was preaching. As Clarendon disapprovingly observed, the 'license of printing and preaching' often worked together in tandem, witnessed by the 'monuments' of 'seditious sermons' that survive in printed form. His use of the grandiose term 'monuments' offers a distinctly ironic acknowledgement of the survival of cheap and ephemeral print as a kind of historical resource.[67] Preaching disrupts elite domination of politics by appealing orally to assembled congregations. In Hutchinson's *Memoirs* preaching is especially powerful in revealing spaces of grassroots mobilization. Private sermons in the Hutchinsons' household prove instrumental in their conversion to Baptism; but such heterodoxy is meanwhile 'revil'd' in the 'public sermons' given in Nottingham churches, where Presbyterian ministers 'preach up their faction openly' against Colonel Hutchinson's regime.[68] Hutchinson's testimony lends weight to recent studies of mobilization networks between Westminster politicians and their extramural supporters in the provinces, mediated

---

[62] Hobbes, *Behemoth*, 275.

[63] Edward Hyde, Earl of Clarendon, *A Brief View and Survey of the Dangerous and Pernicious Errors to Church and State in Mr Hobbes's Book, Entitled Leviathan* (Oxford, 1676), 322.

[64] From the *Life*, 2.37–40, in *The History of the Rebellion*, ed. Seaward, 127–8.

[65] [Edward Hyde], *His Majesties Answer, by way of Declaration, to a Printed Paper, intituled, A Declaration of both Houses of Parliament, in Answer to his Majesties last Message concerning the Militia* (1642), 1; Clarendon, *History*, 2: 65; 1: 1.

[66] Jon Parkin, 'Clarendon Against Hobbes?', in Major (ed.), *Clarendon Reconsidered*, 84–97 (92–3); and *Leviathan*, XVIII, 2: 272.

[67] Clarendon, *History*, 1: 269; 4: 194; 2: 320; on orality in historical culture, see Woolf, *Reading History*.

[68] Hutchinson, *Memoirs*, 168–9.

by preachers.[69] Hobbes also bears witness to this function of orality, going so far as to blame the Civil Wars on Presbyterian ministers who 'by a long practised Histrionick faculty, preached vp the Rebellion powerfully', and on so-called 'democratical' MPs who spread sedition through 'their Harangues in the Parliament, and by their discourses and communication with people in the Country'.[70] Hobbes's emphasis on oratory, however, was primarily motivated by his political philosophy. *Leviathan* had identified inflammatory speeches as one of the greatest dangers to the state. Yet this fear is also coupled with a recognition, in *Leviathan* but even more pronouncedly in *Behemoth*, that oratory may also be politically necessary: 'I cannot thinke that preaching to the people the points of their duty, both to God and Man, can be too frequent.'[71] This stress on preaching signals a striking shift in Hobbes's understanding of political allegiance in *Behemoth*, which retreats markedly from previous works' emphasis on his abstract theory of social contract, and instead goes much further to root allegiance in cultural and emotional forces. The latter had always been an element in Hobbes's thought, but in *Behemoth* it becomes dominant. He concedes that the only way to guarantee the loyalty of armies is through 'Preachers and Gentlemen that inibibe good principles in their youth', and that such preachers must be 'graue, discreet, and ancient' men who are 'reuerenced by the people'.[72] This emphasis also explains Hobbes's dismissive attitude towards printed propaganda—because he saw preaching as the most powerful and therefore the most dangerous tool of mobilization.

So far, we have seen how all three writers display an ambivalent relationship with the printed records of the Civil Wars: sometimes denigrating political print, but always engaging closely with it. At times, this conveys a nuanced understanding of the role of print in driving mobilization: their close analysis of rhetorical techniques; their awareness of circulation loops between politicians, propagandists, and grassroots support; and their emphasis on preaching alongside (and in Hobbes's case, over and above) political print. At the same time Hobbes and Clarendon are particularly constrained by a tendency to read mobilization through an exaggerated sense of elite manipulation. Hutchinson does this too, although her accounts of preaching open up some sense of the social roots of parliamentarian activism. The elite emphasis is unsurprising—the effect of politic history's generic emphasis on 'Causes and Counsells', and of the texts' gestation as manuscript histories aimed at instructing a circumscribed and socially elite audience. This latter point now requires closer attention—with the aim of revealing how these authors saw histories themselves as instruments for galvanizing their readers' political commitments.

---

[69] Como, *Radical Parliamentarians*, 245–55.
[70] Hobbes, *Behemoth*, 108–9, 136–7, 323.
[71] Hobbes, *Behemoth*, 190. See *Leviathan*, XIX, 2: 290, and 'Review and Conclusion', 3: 1132–3, and Quentin Skinner, *Reason and Rhetoric in the Philosophy of Thomas Hobbes* (Cambridge: Cambridge University Press, 1996), 347–56, 382–3.
[72] Hobbes, *Behemoth*, 183 and 211. See Richard Tuck, 'The Utopianism of Leviathan', in Tom Sorell and Luc Foisneau (eds.), *Leviathan After 350 Years* (Oxford: Oxford University Press, 2004), 125–38 (132).

History-Reading as Mobilization

We can glean vital clues in the reflexive moments where history-reading itself figures in the narrative. Hobbes viewed the potentially inflammatory power of history-reading with intense distrust: he blamed the Civil Wars on those 'democratical' men who 'hauing read the bookes written by famous men of the ancient Græcian and Roman Commonwealths became thereby in loue with their formes of gouernment'.[73] This anxiety, that heroic histories of tyrannicide may encourage seditious behaviour, was a driving factor in Hobbes's earlier translation of Thucydides; the charge here is repeated almost verbatim from *Leviathan*.[74] The phrase 'in loue with their forms of gouernment' suggests how this suspicion of history-reading stemmed from Hobbes's cynical view of human psychology. Again, it echoes a related passage in *Leviathan*, which argues that people must be taught 'not to be in love with any forme of Government they see in their neighbour Nations'.[75] Studying the histories of rival forms or government, or of successful rebellions, may (Hobbes feared) stimulate our naturally errant tendencies to rash desire and vainglorious pride: 'the Folly of those fine men, which out of their reading of Tully, Seneca, or other Antimonarchiques, thinke themselues sufficient Politicks'.[76] In this way, Hobbes develops a psychology of history-reading, albeit one that imagines readers as rather simple-minded blank tablets, who naively download their 'Principles … from Enemies of Monarchy'.[77] This view stems, again, from *Leviathan*, which imagines 'the Common peoples minds' as 'clean paper', liable to be 'scribbled over', or to 'receive whatsoever by Publique Authority shall be imprinted on them'.[78] These anxieties about history-reading may suggest why Hobbes withheld from describing *Behemoth* itself as a 'history'.[79] Instead, as an imaginary conversation, *Behemoth* models the kind of oral teaching—supplementary to the preaching described above—which Hobbes saw as the only reliable method of political re-education.

Hutchinson, working from a very different standpoint to Hobbes, took a more nuanced view of the effects of history-reading. When Mr. Hutchinson sits down to 'read all the publick papers that came forth betweene the King and Parliament, besides many other private treatises' (including Thomas May's *History*), he becomes an idealized example of a diligent reader who 'became abundantly inform'd in his understanding, and convinc'd in conscience of the righteousnesse of the Parliament's cause'. Significantly, however, Mr. Hutchinson's intellectual conviction does not convert automatically into

---

[73] Hobbes, *Behemoth*, 110.
[74] Hoekstra, 'Hobbes's Thucydides', 547–8; Hobbes, *Leviathan*, XXIX, 2: 506–8.
[75] Hobbes, *Leviathan*, XXX, 2: 524.
[76] Hobbes, *Behemoth*, 318; See Julie Cooper, 'Vainglory, Modesty, and Political Agency in the Political Theory of Thomas Hobbes', *Review of Politics*, 72 (2010), 241–69.
[77] Hobbes, *Behemoth*, 322.
[78] Hobbes, *Leviathan*, XXX, 2: 524.
[79] Seaward (ed.), *Behemoth*, 50–7.

mobilization: 'although he was clearely sway'd by his owne judgement and reason to the Parliament', he felt 'he had no warrantable call to doe anything more at that time'; though he 'could gladly at that time have engag'd', he 'did not then find a cleare call from the Lord'.[80] For Hutchinson, intellectual assent drawn from reading is a crucial ingredient in mobilization, but—in contrast to Hobbes's blank-tablet model—it proves insufficient without an additional feeling of spiritual calling. When John's sense of vocation does belatedly arrive, it is determined not by his reading, but by his locality. He accepts a commission as commander of Nottingham Castle, 'believing that God hereby call'd him to the defence of his country'—'country' in the early modern sense, meaning the county.[81] This strong sense of local identity may not be informed directly by history-reading, but it nevertheless draws on an informal but deeply embedded sense of a shared past—or what Daniel Woolf has called 'the social circulation of the past'.[82] For instance, when Mr Hutchinson prevents the Royalists from seizing the Nottingham munition stores he invokes a local solidarity based on historic precedent: 'the Country would not be willing to part with their pouder', arguing that 'they all had interest in it as bought with their mony for the particular defence of the County'.[83] This sense of shared past is perhaps most obvious in Hutchinson's narrative of an embattled puritan party (discussed earlier), but it is also invested in locality. It can cut across class and confessional divides—as when the recalcitrant townsfolk are mobilized against a besieging Royalist army: 'they should be no longer slothfull in their owne defence, but take armes to preserve their famelies and houses'.[84] While history-reading offers valuable preparation, and a sense of calling is available to a select few, it is this more dispersed sense of a shared past that proves crucial for Hutchinson in driving mobilization.

Clarendon's weighty sense of duty to posterity led him to continually imagine how his words might be read by future generations. His inclusion of other printed texts within the narrative create frequent opportunities to imagine ideal readers' responses: 'I presume many who without passion do now read those depositions, (for they are in all hands to be read,) do marvel how such conclusions could result to his majesty's disadvantage.' On such occasions, Clarendon invokes a discourse of impartiality—'they might be both impartially read and examined'.[85] Again, though memorialization can be presented as a disinterested act, the language of impartiality tacitly acknowledges a context of partisan interpretation. One 'remembrance' concerns a puritan clergyman and 'incendiary of the rude people' named Whitehall, who allegedly used to carry around in his pocket 'several papers of memorials of his own obscene and scurrilous behaviour with several women'. Here, Clarendon uses the highly loaded terms 'remembrance' and

---

[80] Hutchinson, *Memoirs*, 53, 65.
[81] Hutchinson, *Memoirs*, 83, again at 106.
[82] Woolf, *Social Circulation*, 290–303; Martyn Bennett, '"Every County Had More or Lesse the Civill Warre within It Selfe": the Realities of War in Lucy Hutchinson's Midland Shires', *The Seventeenth Century*, 30 (2015), 191–206.
[83] Hutchinson, *Memoirs*, 55–6.
[84] Hutchinson, *Memoirs*, 115.
[85] Clarendon, *History*, 2: 106.

'memorials'—once again ironically, but nevertheless appealing to a sense of posterity, describing as preservation what was really an act of projection, a memorial strategically selected to suggest the 'lewd and vicious' character of parliamentarians.[86] By contrast, Clarendon's digressions on leading Royalists, pre-eminently his friend Viscount Falkland, are justified as 'one of the principal ends and duties of history', namely 'celebrating the memory of eminent and extraordinary persons, and transmitting their great virtues for the imitation of posterity'.[87] This was a conventional humanist statement of history's morally didactic purpose—looking back to Cicero's 'teacher of life', and shared with Hutchinson's memorialization of her husband. But in Clarendon's case, didacticism can shade into something more like veneration, slipping into the devotional language of the *Eikon Basilike*. A letter written by Charles I shortly before the regicide is inserted verbatim as 'so lively an expression of his own soul that no pen else could have written it, and deserves to be transmitted to posterity, as a part of the portraiture of that incomparable King'.[88] The key concept being 'transmitted to posterity' here is not a moral lesson, but rather the passion and veneration aroused by the Stuart cause.

Clarendon's insistent use of the phrase 'transmitted to posterity' reveals how historians of the Civil Wars sought to keep the intense passions of the conflict alive in the factional politics of the Restoration period. The manuscript histories considered here proceed through detailed conversation with the flood of printed sources produced in the 1640s, though it would be misleading to see in this an origin point for the modern academic practice of critical source analysis. Rather, 'impartiality' provided a rhetorical guise under which the historians wrested the voluminous printed record into a partisan interpretive framework. Printing was central but not all-important for these historians, who each reveal a complex sense of the emotional and psychological dynamics of coalition-forming. For Hutchinson, political mobilization arises from a complex interaction between the circulation of print controversy and more diffuse kinds of historical thinking embedded in local and confessional identity. For the elect this had also to be combined with a conviction of divine calling, which emanated from somewhere outside of history. For Hobbes, print was subservient to the more tangible power of public oratory and preaching—though this view sits awkwardly with his alarmist portrayal of the history-reader as a seditious bogeyman. Hobbes's psychology of allegiance is more schematic than Hutchinson's—Clarendon accused it of being simplistic. As an experienced propagandist, Clarendon valued printed materials as an emotive resource for historical interpretation, manipulating a language of memorialization to pour scorn on the parliamentarians but to preserve the passions of royalism for posterity. This rhetoric helped to cement Clarendon's central place in the canon—as a reservoir of Tory ideology, and as a definitive example of history from above, describing the Civil Wars in terms of elite calculation. By applying the modern framework of mobilization, we

---

[86] Clarendon, *History*, 2: 69.
[87] Clarendon, *History*, 3: 21; 3: 178.
[88] Clarendon, *History*, 4: 74.

have been able to recover how these elite manuscript histories responded to the mass participation in politics that gave the Civil Wars their radical and enduring impact. This highlights the emotional responses which shaped the historians' understanding of political partisanship, and through which they sought to galvanize their own readers into action.

CHAPTER 20

KEYS

NICHOLAS MCDOWELL

In *Rabelais and His World* (first published in Russian in 1965), Mikhail Bakhtin presented François Rabelais's great masterpiece of comic and satirical prose, *Gargantua and Pantagruel* (five books, 1532–64), as exemplifying the spirit of festive comedy that Bakhtin believed was characteristic of folk culture in medieval and Renaissance Europe. Sympathy with the forms of 'carnival humour' that animate Rabelais's loosely related tales of gluttonous, bibulous giants and their fantastic adventures began to be lost, according to Bakhtin, during the latter half of the seventeenth century. The process of loss is illustrated by the rise of what he calls the 'historic-allegorical interpretation' of Rabelais. This interpretative approach reveals how 'a specific character or event can be found behind each of Rabelais's images. The entire novel is [shown to be] a system of historical allusions'. Although there was interest in *le sens historique* of *Gargantua and Pantagruel* among the French *érudits* and *libertins* of the earlier seventeenth century, and a historical 'key' to Rabelais first appeared in a Brussels edition of his *Œuvres* in 1659, the 'true initiator of the historic-allegorical method', Bakhtin declared, was Pierre Antoine Le Motteux (1663–1718) in his English editions of the 1690s. The critical apparatus and commentary that Motteux added to the English translations of Rabelais that he issued in 1694 became, Bakhtin states, 'the main source' of the method of reading *Gargantua and Pantagruel* as a work that allegorically represents real historical protagonists, an interpretative method that supposedly held sway until Bakhtin himself restored to readers the true, carnivalesque nature of the work. Since the 'historic-allegorical method illustrates the disintegration of laughter that took place in the seventeenth century', the charge against Motteux is a weighty one.[1]

Modern readers are probably sympathetic to Bakhtin's disdain for the notion that Rabelaisian comedy can be treated as a *roman à clef*, with the vigorous linguistic excess that has attracted readers from Sterne to Joyce constrained to one-to-one political

---

[1] Mikhail Bakhtin, *Rabelais and His World*, trans. Helene Iswolsky (Bloomington: Indiana University Press, 1984), 112–16; Marcel de Grève, 'Les érudits du XVII siècle en quête de la clef de Rabelais', *Études Rabelaisiennes*, 5 (1964), 41–63.

allegory. But it is historically naïve to assume that such a method of reading was not attractive to earlier readers, and scholarship has recovered aspects of the ways in which early moderns read between the lines of fictive texts, in particular romances, to find contemporary political meaning.[2] Moreover, the contemporary popularity of such modes of reading is evident in the publication of numerous 'keys' to literary works, including *A Tale of a Tub* (1704), *Gulliver's Travels* (1726), and *The Dunciad* (1728–43), purporting to reveal their exact allegorical meaning and relation to actual events and individuals. The form came into fashion in the late Restoration in the immediate aftermath of John Dryden's *Absalom and Achitophel* (1681–2), with the swift appearance of printed texts which claimed to provide a key to Dryden's poem, encouraging readers to index their own copies with the supposed real-life identities of its protagonists. Interest remained strong enough for Jacob Tonson to print a 'Key to Both Parts of *Absalom and Achitophel*' in his edition of Dryden's *Miscellany Poems* in 1716.[3] Such 'keys' became a speciality of the publisher Edmund Curll (1675–1747) and got him into prolonged and bitter conflict with Pope and Swift.

Pope produced his own *A Key to the Lock, or, A Treatise Proving, Beyond all Contradiction, the Dangerous Tendency of a Late Poem, Entitled The Rape of the Lock, to Government and Religion* (1715) to mock the form and its claims to find religious and political allegory in poetry and fiction. Pope adopts the persona of a commentator, 'Esdras Barnivelt', who uncovers the 'intricate' allegories of *The Rape of the Lock* (1714) in the interests of Britain's national security:

> Now that the Author of this Poem is professedly a *Papist*, is well known; and that a Genius so capable of doing Service to that Cause, may have been corrupted in the Course of his Education by *Jesuits* or others, is justly very much to be suspected; notwithstanding that seeming *Coolness* and *Moderation*, which he has been (perhaps artfully) reproached with, by those of his own Profession. They are sensible that this Nation is secured with good and wholesome Laws to prevent all evil Practices of the Church of *Rome;* particularly the Publication of Books, that may in any sort propagate that Doctrine: Their Authors are therefore obliged to couch their Designs the deeper … In all things which are intricate, as Allegories in their own Nature are, and especially those that are industriously made so, it is not to be expected we should find the Clue at first sight; but when once we have laid hold on that, we shall trace

---

[2] The classic work in this area, although it is concerned largely with pre-Civil War England, remains Annabel Patterson, *Censorship and Interpretation: The Conditions of Writing and Reading in Early Modern England* (Madison, Wisc.: University of Wisconsin Press, 1984). See also, more recently, Thomas Keymer, *Poetics of the Pillory: Literature and Seditious Libel, 1660–1820* (Oxford: Oxford University Press, 2019); and Chapter 1 by Thomas Keymer on 'Circulation'.

[3] [Christopher Ness], *A Key (With the Whip) To Open the Mystery and Iniquity of the Poem called, Absalom and Achitophel: Shewing its Scurrilous Reflections Upon both King and Kingdom* (1682); *Absolon's IX Worthies, or, A Key to a late Book or Poem, Entituled A. B. & A. C.* (1682). For early readers' creation of their own 'keys' to the poem, see Alan Roper, 'Who's Who in *Absalom and Achitophel*?', *Huntington Library Quarterly*, 63 (2000), 98–138; Rhodri Lewis, 'An Early Reader of Dryden's *Absolom and Achitophel*', *Notes and Queries*, 57 (2010), 67–9.

this our Author through all the Labyrinths, Doublings and Turnings of this intricate Composition.

In fact, the allegories are not 'intricate' at all but absurd in their crudity—the lock of hair itself is revealed as a symbol for the 1713 Barrier Treaty between Britain and the Dutch republic—and Pope sets out 'to mingle absurdity and plausibility together, to the general effect of rendering any political reading of the poem ridiculous'.[4] Pope was surely in part inspired by the 'Apology' that prefaced the 1710 edition of *A Tale of a Tub*, in which Swift both insists the *Tale* is an allegory of contemporary religious 'abuses' and rejects those interpretations of passages 'which prejudiced or ignorant Readers have drawn by great Force to hint at ill Meanings ... [the Author] never once had it in his Thoughts that any thing he said would in the least be capable of such Interpretations'.[5] At the end of the *Key*'s absurdly strained interpretation of *The Rape of the Lock* as rabidly pro-Catholic propaganda, 'Barnivelt' cites the key to '*Rabelais's Gargantua*' as a model for such revelation of 'Secret Satyrs upon the State', insisting his own interpretation has been 'deduced as naturally, and with as little force'.[6]

Edmund Curll had Whig sympathies but his main motivation in publishing 'keys' was commercial; Motteux was also primarily a commercially motivated writer, but the sincerity of his political and religious reading of *Gargantua and Pantagruel* is not to be doubted, and it is a reading shaped by his own experience as a Huguenot refugee. The 'historic-allegorical method' of interpretation developed by Motteux in his English versions of Rabelais, mocked by Pope and excoriated as narrowly reductive by Bakhtin, needs to be understood in the context of Motteux's own personal history as one of the thousands of Huguenot refugees who arrived in England after the Revocation of the Edict of Nantes in 1685. Motteux presented the comic episodes of *Gargantua and Pantagruel* as encoding bitter attacks upon the history of intolerance and persecution in early modern France. He sought to offer this anti-Catholic Rabelais to leading English Whigs as the ideal author for an English nation that, by means of the Glorious Revolution of 1688, had avoided the Catholic intolerance that had forced Motteux out of his own country. In the format of its original publication, which included extensive prefaces and commentaries, Motteux's Rabelais articulates the sentiment that was common among Whigs and Dissenters when they evaluated the events of 1688–9 in a

---

[4] Howard Erskine-Hill, *Poetry of Opposition and Revolution: Dryden to Wordsworth* (Oxford: Oxford University Press, 1996), 87.

[5] *The Cambridge Edition of the Works of Jonathan Swift: A Tale of a Tub and Other Works*, ed. Marcus Walsh (Cambridge: Cambridge University Press, 2010), 8.

[6] 'Esdras Barnivelt' [Alexander Pope], *A Key to the Lock. Or, A Treatise Proving ... the Dangerous Tendency of a Late Poem, entitled The Rape of the Lock, to Government and Religion* (1715), 9, 11, 32–3. On Curll, see Paul Baines and Pat Rogers, *Edmund Curll, Bookseller* (Oxford: Oxford University Press, 2007); for interesting recent work on Pope's 'key' to his own poem, see Tim Morris, 'Lock and Key: Hermeneutics, Symbols, and Signifying in Pope's *The Rape of the Lock*', *English*, 64 (2015), 183–203; Freya Johnston, 'Alexander Pope: Unlocking the Key', *Review of English Studies*, 67 (2016), 897–913; Abigail Williams, *Reading It Wrong: An Alternative History of Early Eighteenth-Century Literature* (Prnceton, NJ, and Oxford: Princeton University Press, 2024), 156–8.

European context: that the Glorious Revolution 'was in many respects England's answer to the Revocation of the Edict of Nantes'.[7]

The sense of 'key' as 'something which enables the interpretation of an allegorical, cryptic, or otherwise obscure work' enters English, according to the *OED*, with Francis Bacon's *Advancement of Learning* in 1605; this sense also encompasses 'a means of translating a foreign text', exemplified by a citation from a 1715 guide to translating Ovid, *Clavis Ovidiana*.[8] The rudimentary keys to Rabelais that had circulated on the Continent, which comprised little more than an index identifying the historical or real counterparts of fictional protagonists, were transformed by Motteux's commentary on his English translation into a complex allegorical superstructure that offered a politicized model for reading a modern literary 'classic' like *Gargantua and Pantagruel*. It is a model that writers like Swift and Sterne were provoked not simply to mock, but also to incorporate into the very fabric of their comic fictions: the late Restoration genre of the 'key' was part of the complex of literary materials that went into the development of the eighteenth-century novel in English.

Satire, Translation, and Allegory

Motteux's involvement with the English Rabelais began in 1694, the year in which *The Gentleman's Journal* came to an end, when he edited the first three books of *Gargantua and Pantagruel* in the translation of the Scottish laird Sir Thomas Urquhart (1611–60), whose brilliant rendering of books one and two had incongruously appeared in 1653, on the cusp of the Cromwellian Protectorate and while Urquhart himself was prisoner of war after being captured at the Battle of Worcester.[9] Motteux claimed that the manuscript of Urquhart's translation of the third book had been found after his death 'among his papers somewhat incorrect' and that a 'Gentleman' called 'Mr Kimes' who 'is a very great linguist'—very likely Motteux himself, given there is no other trace of this 'Mr Kimes' and 'kime' is an obscure English word for 'fool'—had been asked to revise the text of all three of Urquhart's books.[10] The questions of how Urquhart's manuscript came

---

[7] G. C. Gibbs, 'Reception of the Huguenots in England and the Dutch Republic, 1680–1690', in Ole Peter Grell, Jonathan Israel, and Nicholas Tyacke (eds.), *From Persecution to Toleration: The Glorious Revolution and Religion in England*, (Oxford: Oxford University Press, 1991), 275–306 (294).

[8] *OED*, 'key', 5b.

[9] On the (surprising) circumstances surrounding the publication of the imprisoned Urquhart's Rabelais, see Nicholas McDowell, 'Urquhart's Rabelais: Translation, Patronage and Cultural Politics', *English Literary Renaissance*, 32 (2005), 273–303.

[10] Motteux, 'Preface. Wherein is given an Account of the Design and Nature of this Work, and a Key to some of its most difficult Passages', in *The Works of Mr Francis Rabelais ... done out of French by Sir Tho. Urchard, Kt., and others*, I, p. xliii. The third book of *Gargantua and Pantagruel* was first published separately, with a title page dated 1693, without any prefatory apparatus or reference to Motteux's role in the revision of Urquhart's manuscript. It is advertised as the work of 'Thomas Urwhat' and Motteux's name is absent, although the publisher (Richard Baldwin) is the same as for Motteux's 1694 publications.

to light, and to what extent the previously unpublished version of the *Tiers Livre* is the work of Motteux himself, remain a matter of conjecture, but Motteux's behaviour over matters of authorship and appropriation was soon to come into question with a rancorous public argument over whether his comedy *Love's Jest* (1696) incorporated material from a dramatic manuscript given to him by an actor.[11] In July 1694, presumably spurred on by the commercial success of the earlier volume, Motteux issued his own translations of the fourth and fifth books—the fifth book is now considered probably not to be (entirely) the work of Rabelais, but its authenticity was not questioned in the early modern period—and then in 1708 Motteux combined his translation with Urquhart's version to create the first complete English rendering of *Gargantua and Pantagruel*. This translation, as up-dated with further notes and commentary by Ozell, who incorporated aspects of the commentary by Jacob Le Duchat (1658–1735), another Huguenot, in his great French edition of 1711, was the one used by eighteenth-century novelists such as Sterne.[12]

Motteux's 1694 edition of Urquhart's version of the first three books of *Gargantua and Pantagruel* was published by Richard Baldwin (c.1653–98), who had emerged during the Exclusion Crisis as a publisher 'instrumental in the Whig propaganda machine' and was frequently in trouble with the authorities in 1681–3. Baldwin kept quiet during the reign of James II, but after 1688 he returned to publishing 'Whig tracts on a large scale'.[13] His core business was in political and satirical pamphlets and newspapers, but he also published periodicals of other kinds, including *The Gentleman's Journal*. Baldwin's interest in Huguenot affairs is evident in the fact that he continued to get into trouble after the accession of William III for his views on France and on England's failure to act against a French state represented in his publications as bent on establishing a papist tyranny in Europe. In 1691 Baldwin was summoned before the House of Commons for remarks about Louis XIV that appeared in one of the periodicals in his stock, while his newspaper *The Postman*, which appeared from 1695, is characterized by its anti-Catholic and specifically anti-French content.[14] Indeed by 1697, Baldwin's publications, such as *The Secret History of Whitehall*, increasingly represented even the Glorious Revolution itself as part of a wider French plot for Roman Catholic domination of Europe.[15] In this

---

[11] See Paulina Kewes, *Authorship and Appropriation: Writing for the Stage in England, 1660–1710* (Oxford: Oxford University Press, 1998), 73–5.

[12] See Regan, 'Translating Rabelais'; Antony Coleman, 'Sterne's Use of the Motteux-Ozell "Rabelais"', *Notes and Queries*, 223 (1978), 55–8. Le Duchat's commentary exhibits his knowledge of Motteux's key to *Gargantua and Pantagruel*, about which Le Duchat had corresponded with Pierre Bayle before undertaking his own edition of the text; see Theodore P. Fraser, *Le Duchat, First Editor of Rabelais* (Geneva: Droz, 1971), 22–3, 72–5.

[13] See Beth Lynch, 'Baldwin, Richard (c.1653–1698)', in *ODNB*. Mark Knights refers to Baldwin as a 'steadfastly Whiggish bookseller' (*The Devil in Disguise: Deception, Delusion, and Fanaticism in the Early English Enlightenment* (Oxford: Oxford University Press, 2011), 244).

[14] Leona Rostenberg, *Literary, Political, Scientific, Religious, and Legal Publishing, Printing, and Bookselling in England, 1551–1700: Twelve Studies*, 2 vols. (New York: Burt Franklin, 1965), 2: 369–415.

[15] See Rebecca Bullard, 'Signs of the Times? Reading Signatures in Two Late Seventeenth-Century Secret Histories', in Eve Patten and Jason McElligot (eds.), *The Perils of Print Culture: Book, Print and*

respect, Baldwin's activities are representative of the concerns of the more radical or 'Real' Whigs in the later 1690s, who had come to regard the formation of a Protestant alliance in Europe that would curb the ambitions of Louis XIV to be the keystone that would maintain civil and religious liberty in Britain.[16] Among other books that Baldwin published in 1694, and which was advertised at the back of his edition of Motteux's translation of Rabelais, was Milton's *Letters of State* (1694), selected correspondence from Milton's period as Secretary for Foreign Tongues under the Commonwealth and Protectorate as translated by his nephew Edward Phillips. Attached to Baldwin's edition of Urquhart's Rabelais, as edited by Motteux, is a dedicatory poem to Baldwin himself by Nahum Tate (c.1652–1715), the firmly Williamite Irish writer made Poet Laureate in 1692. Tate presents Baldwin as 'Still playing th' honest wight in thy Vocation, / And printing dang'rous Truths to serve the Nation'.[17] It seems Tate regarded an English Rabelais published with Motteux's key as a book which could convey such 'dangerous truths'.

Motteux's edition of Urquhart's translations is dedicated to Edward Russell (1652–1727). Brother of William Russell, executed in 1683 for his part in the Rye House Plot, Edward was one of the 'Immortal Seven' who issued the invitation to William of Orange to depose James II, and subsequently a member of the so-called 'Whig Junto' that sought to control parliamentary politics during the 1690s and beyond. In 1692 he had become Commander-in-Chief of the Anglo-Dutch naval force that destroyed the French fleet at Barfleur, a decisive victory in the War of the Grand Alliance; Russell went on in 1694 to become First Lord of the Admiralty and Earl of Orford.[18] Motteux offers his Rabelais to Russell as though it were further French bounty, captured to enrich English culture: Motteux, as 'a lover of Britain', 'envying to *France* such a Treasure, has made it a Prize; and now sets it out with English colours, fearless of its Enemies, under your Powerful Patronage'.[19] Immediately, in the opening pages of Motteux's edition, the English Rabelais is represented as a 'Prize' in the European conflict between Protestant and Catholic nations, paving the way for Motteux's interpretation of the whole work as a satire on the violent Catholic intolerance that justifies the actions of Russell and the

---

Publishing History in Theory and Practice (Basingstoke: Palgrave, 2014), 125–6, 128–9; see also Chapter 34 by Rebecca Bullard, 'Secret Histories'.

[16] See Rachael Hammersley, *The English Republican Tradition and Eighteenth-Century France: Between the Ancients and the Moderns* (Manchester: Manchester University Press, 2010), chap. 2.

[17] *The Fifth Book of the Works of Francis Rabelais, M.D., Containing the Heroic Deeds and Sayings of the Great Pantagruel to Which is Added the Pantagruelian Prognostication, Rabelais's Letters, and Several Other Pieces by That Author/Done out of French by P.M.*, final leaf; Tate, 'A Familiar Epistle to Mr Baldwin on his Publishing of the Translation of Rabelais', in *The Works of Mr Francis Rabelais … Done out of French by Sir Tho. Urchard, Kt., and others*, sig. *1.

[18] Grant Tapsell, 'Immortal Seven (*act.* 1688)', in *ODNB*; Stuart Handley, 'Whig Junto (*act.* c.1694–c.1716)', in *ODNB*; D. D. Alfridge, entry for 'Edward Russell (1652–1727)', in *ODNB*.

[19] Motteux, 'To the Right Honourable *Edward Russel*, Esq', in *The Works of Mr Francis Rabelais … Done out of French by Sir Tho. Urchard, Kt., and others*, sig. A2v. See also Robert Newton Cunningham, 'A Bibliography of the Writings of Peter Anthony Motteux', *Proceedings and Papers of the Oxford Bibliographical Society*, 3 vols. (1933), 3: 317–37.

other Whigs in deposing James II and preventing the same sort of religious tyranny in England.

The dedication to Russell is followed by a brief life of Rabelais and then a 'Preface. Wherein is given an Account of the Design and Nature of this Work, and a Key to some of its most difficult Passages'. Motteux seeks to illustrate how in both his life and his work, Rabelais, 'in a jesting manner, exposed the *Roman* clergy's persecuting manner'. Motteux begins by declaring that he will explain 'the Truths which are hid under the dark veil of Allegories in that incomparable work': 'most of the Adventures which are mystically represented by Rabelais', we are told, 'relate to affairs of Religion'. Motteux's explanation of how his key to *Gargantua and Pantagruel* goes beyond philological matters to develop for the first time a full-scale account of the work's allegorical meaning is worth quoting in full, in part because its language of unlocking anticipates so closely that of Pope's 'Barnivelt':

> In the late Editions, some learned Men have given us a Vocabulary, wherein they explain the Names and Terms in it which are originally, Greek, Latin, Hebrew, or of other Tongues, that the Text might thus be made more intelligible, and their work may be useful to those who do not understand those Tongues. But they have not had the same success in their pretended Explications of the Names which *Rabelais* has given to the real Actors in this Farce; and thus they have indeed fram'd a Key, but, if I may use the Allegory, 'twas without having known the Wards and Springs of the Lock. What I advance, will doubtless be owned to be true by those who may have observed that by that Key, none can discover in those *Pythagorical* Symbols (as they are call'd in the Author's Prologue to the first Book) any Event that has a Relation to the History of those to whom the Names mention'd by *Rabelais*, have been applied by those that made that pretended Key.[20]

Motteux's reference to earlier, inferior keys to Rabelais is likely to the 1663 Elzevier edition published in Amsterdam, to which was appended an alphabetized key glossing difficult words and phrases and providing a rudimentary, one-to-one identification of the historical identity of characters and places in the text.[21]

The interest among Huguenot exiles in this allegorical reading is evident in a copy of the two-volume 1666 Leiden edition of Rabelais which belonged to Élie Bouhéreau (1643–1719), who fled France for England after the 1685 Revocation before eventually ending up in Ireland as the first Keeper of Marsh's Library in Dublin, where all his papers and books remain today. Bouhéreau and his fellow Huguenot exiles were keen readers of Rabelais: in his diary, for example, Bouhéreau records on 6 June 1711 being 'dans une compagnie' where the discussion turned to the meaning of some old French words 'dont il est parlé dans Rabelais'. Notes at the back of his edition, probably

---

[20] Motteux, 'The Life of Dr *Francis Rabelais*', and 'Preface', in *Works of Mr Francis Rabelais*, pp. ix, xlv–xlvi.

[21] For some discussion of the 1663 Elzevier 'alphabet', see Samuel Kinser, *Rabelais's Carnival: Text, Context, Metatext* (Berkeley: University of California Press, 1990), 155–9.

by Bouhéreau himself, reproduce the key to the Elzevier edition, to which Bouhéreau presumably compared his Leiden edition at the date recorded in the headnote ('À la fin du Rabelais de Paris. 1669'): Gargantua is identified as Francis I and Pantagruel as his son Henry II, both kings of France during Rabelais's life and both notable persecutors of the Huguenots.[22] Bouhéreau's inscribed copy indicates the culture among Huguenot refugees of reading Rabelais historically and allegorically, a culture from which Motteux's vastly more detailed and complex commentary emerges.

Motteux's methodological justification for this reading of the text as an allegory of religious controversy in mid-sixteenth-century France relies on a completely literal reading of the 'Author's Prologue' to the first book of *Gargantua and Pantagruel*, in which Rabelais insists that his book is one of those 'that seem easie and superficial, but are not so readily fathom'd': readers must be prepared to 'break the bone and suck out the substantial marrow, that is my allegorical Sense'. If they do so, the book will disclose to them 'dreadful Mysteries, as well as in what concerneth your Religion, as Matters of the Publick State'.[23] Motteux quickly skates over the fact that Rabelais flatly contradicts this claim in the next paragraph, ridiculing those commentators who have tried to interpret Homer allegorically, and insisting that he thought nothing of the reader when writing *Gargantua and Pantagruel* because he only wrote while drunk. 'I know that he immediately after this passes off with a banter what he had assur'd very seriously,' Motteux admits, 'but this was an admirable piece of prudence.' Motteux prefers to look away from Rabelais's characteristic tricksiness about his intentions and instead compare the work to seventeenth-century romances that he regards as having encoded political meaning and replayed contemporary events in early modern France under the cover of fiction, including Honoré d'Urfé's *L'Astrée* (5 vols., 1607–28) and John Barclay's much-translated Latin work *Argenis* (1621).[24] A key to *Argenis* identifying the various historical figures supposedly signified by Barclay's fictional personae was included in the Latin version of 1627 and then in the second, 1636 edition of Kingsmill Long's English translation (first published, 1625), in which the narrative is revealed to be an allegorical representation of later sixteenth-century France under the rule of Henry III and Henry IV. In *A Key to the Lock*, Pope cites 'Barclays Argenis', as well as 'Rabelais's Gargrantua', as an example of a literary work that is revealed to be a satire 'upon the State' through application of its accompanying key.[25]

Modern scholars such as Annabel Patterson and Blair Worden have resurrected this tradition of providing a *clavis* or key to works of prose fiction, emphasizing the historical grounds for reading early modern romance, whether *Argenis* or Sidney's *Arcadia* (1590), as political allegory: as Worden puts it, 'the contemporary resonance of Sidney's

---

[22] For Bouhéreau's diary, which covers the years 1689–1719, see Marsh's Library, Dublin, MS. 302. 2. 2. 2, 120–1; *Les Œuvres de François Rabelais*, 2 vols. ([Leiden], 1666), Marsh's Library, Dublin, Class R. 2. Tab. 8, nos. 26, 27.
[23] *Works of Mr Francis Rabelais*, sig. B3v ('The Author's Prologue').
[24] Motteux, 'Preface', in *Works of Mr Francis Rabelais*, pp. xli, lxv.
[25] [Pope], *Key to the Lock*, 34.

language is a key to his art, not a debasement of it'.[26] Motteux places *Gargantua and Pantagruel* in the *clavis* tradition by insisting that Rabelais developed a fictive mode of discussing contemporary religious and political events in his comic romance to evade censorship and persecution, and it is a mode of writing that requires reading between the lines to understand its true sense.[27] Motteux continually reminds us of 'those Enemies of Truth, who would not have failed to have burned him alive, in that Persecuting Age, had he less Wit and Prudence than they shewed Ignorance and Malice'. Rabelais' continual purpose was to 'insinuate a Contempt of the Church of Rome's Fopperies' through his comic allegories and fictions, an alternative mode of attack from within while 'the Protestants publicly were indeavouring a thorough Reformation'.[28]

Motteux provides a list of characters in *Gargantua and Pantagruel* and explains exactly which historical persons they represent, in the manner of the Elzevier 'alphabet', but whereas the alphabet had identified the Rabelaisian giants with kings who were persecutors of the Huguenots, Motteux rather identifies Gargantua with Henri d'Albret, King of Navarre (1503–55), renowned for his sympathy towards the Huguenots, and Panurge is identified as Jean de Monluc, Bishop of Valence (1502–79): while Jean de Monluc was the eldest brother, as Motteux puts it, 'of the Marschal de Montluc, the most violent Enemy which the Huguenots had in those Days', Jean himself is represented as a closet Calvinist, with a secret wife and son. So when Gargantua's brain is purged by his new schoolmaster Ponocrates of the useless scholastic information that he has been taught by his previous tutors the Sophisters, the episode is decoded by Motteux as Henry of Navarre, who had shown 'little improvement' in his studies 'under Popish governors', undergoing the cleansing education of 'a Protestant prince' by means of 'Arguments drawn from Reason, and the Scripture, oppos'd to the Authority of the Popish Church'. Motteux writes of Rabelais, Henry of Navarre, and 'others in these Times, who were against the Errors of the Church of Rome in their Hearts [and] favored the Reformation perhaps even more than those who openly professed it'.[29] Rabelais's own closet confessional allegiance becomes apparent in the revelation of the true signification of his comic stories, and each of his major characters is revealed to represent a prominent figure of his time who was either sympathetic to the Huguenots, or who was actually and secretly Protestant themselves.

---

[26] Blair Worden, *The Sound of Virtue: Philip Sidney's* Arcadia *and Elizabethan Politics* (New Haven and London: Yale University Press, 1996), 8. See also Patterson, *Censorship and Interpretation*, 184: '[Argenis] was quickly recognized as an encoded and fictionalized account of European history.'

[27] For the continuation of this interpretation in modern criticism, see e.g. Kenneth Borris, *Allegory and Epic in English Renaissance Literature: Heroic Form in Sidney, Spenser and Milton* (Cambridge: Cambridge University Press, 2000), 19, who cites the example of the prologue in the first book of *Gargantua and Pantagruel* to justify the reading of early modern works as political allegories: 'The comment of Rabelais, who himself used secondary or hidden meanings to gain some latitude of political and religious expression, may itself be partly an alibi to shield his own practice from possible sanctions.'

[28] Motteux, 'Preface', in *Works of Mr Francis Rabelais*, pp. xcii, cxliv.

[29] Motteux, 'Preface', in *Works of Mr Francis Rabelais*, pp. lxv, lxx.

Motteux extends this one interpretative approach to every detail of a vast and cornucopian text. A striking reading of Rabelais through the lens of Motteux's own experience of fleeing religious persecution in France is found in his commentary on the celebrated episode of the frozen words that Pantagruel and Panurge encounter in chapters 55 and 56 of the fourth book—sounds of a naval battle that have been frozen as material substance and then, as they melt, fill the air with noise. This is an episode that was popular with eighteenth-century readers, most prominently Swift, who adapted the theme of words as material objects for the depiction of the Academy of Lagado in *Gulliver's Travels*; as with the fourth and fifth books of *Gargantua and Pantagruel*, the third book of *Gulliver's Travels* takes the form of a voyage to several islands and becomes more explicit in its contemporary allusion. Motteux, now simply referring to persecuted French Protestants as 'Pantagruelists', explains that this episode is an allegory for how in Rabelais's time Huguenots 'did not dare discover their minds, so that their words were in a manner frozen within their mouths, which Fear and Interest kept shut'. The melting of the words, he continues, signifies when they had escaped France for lands that welcomed them as Protestant refugees: 'But when they were out of danger, they could no longer thus contain their words, and then everyone distinctly heard them, murmuring words against those Bigots, very sharp words, bloody words, terrible words, angry words, occasion'd by Reflections made on the Idolatrous Persecutors.'[30] 'Pantagruelist' has been redefined, not as a term for a comic, drunken protagonist—in Edward Phillips's *The New World of English Words* (1658), a 'Pantagruelist' is listed as a word of French derivation for 'a merry drunkard, or good fellow'—but one persecuted for their religion and who must either dissemble to conceal their true allegiance, or leave behind their home country. The redefinition is of course reductive, even absurdly so, but it also derives some emotional power from its source in Motteux's own personal experience as a religious refugee.[31] Motteux also offers an alternative signification for the unfrozen words which emphasizes the Huguenot experience, and his own personal experience, of persecution: 'Those frozen words that were thaw'd, and then were heard, may also mean the Books publish'd at that time at Geneva and elsewhere against Popery and the Persecution. Those who fled from it to Places of Safety, with a great deal of freedom, fill'd their Writings with such Truths as were not to be spoken amongst the biggotted *Romanists*.' And he makes it clear that the situation is as bad now as it was in Rabelais's time: 'This has been and still is observable in France', he declares.[32] One of those persecuted French Protestants who fled to a 'place of safety' was Motteux himself, and the prefaces and commentary that he attached to his editions of the English Rabelais were conceived as one of these Huguenot books published 'against Popery and the Persecution' in France. Post-revolutionary England, on the other hand, is represented by Motteux as a nation which has evaded the

---

[30] Motteux, 'Explanatory Remarks', in *Pantagruel's Voyage to the Oracle of the Bottle*, pp. lvii-lviii.
[31] Edward Phillips, *The New World of English Words, or, A General Dictionary Containing the Interpretations of Such Hard Words as are Derived from Other Languages* (London, 1658), s.v. 'Pantagruelist'; a similar definition is given in Elisha Coles, *An English Dictionary* (London, 1677).
[32] Motteux, 'Explanatory Remarks', in *Pantagruel's Voyage to the Oracle of the Bottle*, pp. lviii, lxii.

terrible fate of popish domination that has befallen France, and which offers persecuted Protestants a haven of liberty and tolerance.

FABLE, RIDDLE, AND THE NOVEL

In the earlier 1680s Tories had denounced the use of tales of the atrocities suffered by the Huguenots in Whiggish literature as sensationalist anti-Catholic scare stories; in response, Whigs had attacked the lack of Tory sympathy for their fellow persecuted Protestants as evidence of their true attitude towards dissenters. In 1681, Henry Care (1646/7–88), the inveterate Whig polemicist, attacked Roger L'Estrange (1616–1704), who had assiduously sought to suppress dissenting literature in his role as Licenser of the Press from 1663 to 1679, for claiming in his newsbook *The Observator* that the Whigs were exaggerating the Huguenots' suffering for political reasons. As Care sarcastically put it: 'Pitty them! What sure you won't turn Fool in your Old Age? Those *Hugenots* are *Presbyterians*, man! And *errant dissenters*.' Care's real target here was obviously the persecution of English dissenters, and it was a central theme of his anti-Catholic polemic to identify the sufferings of the French Protestants under Louis XIV with those of English dissenters under Charles II.[33] The sufferings of the persecuted Huguenots became a polemical topic in the war of words between Whig and Tory, providing 'rhetorical opportunities' for non-conformist, conformist, and Catholic, regardless of whether or not the Huguenots who came to England really sought to align themselves with dissent.[34] Motteux's Rabelais illustrates how those sufferings continued to be a part of confessional and political polemic after the Glorious Revolution, and more specifically how anti-Catholic rhetoric was continued in England by Huguenot émigrés, encompassing even works of commercial literary translation that might at first look like unlikely vehicles of confessional propaganda.

As with so many Whig and pro-tolerationist works of the 1670s and 1680s, it may be the case that Motteux's Rabelais is in dialogue with L'Estrange's publications, in this case the translation of Aesop's *Fables* that L'Estrange published in 1692. In explaining how Rabelais encoded his commentary on French religious politics, Motteux advises that Rabelais chose to write in such a manner because 'Mankind is naturally addicted

---

[33] Anne Dunan-Page, 'Roger L'Estrange and the Huguenots: Continental Protestantism and the Church of England', in Anne Dunan-Page and Beth Lynch (eds.), *Roger L'Estrange and the Making of Restoration Culture* (Aldershot: Ashgate, 2008), 109–30 (129), quoting Henry Care, *Weekly Pacquet of Advice from Rome*, 3. 60 (29 July 1681); Gregory Dodds, '"Sham Liberty of Conscience": Huguenots and the Problem of Religious Toleration in Restoration England', in D. J. B. Trim (ed.), *The Huguenots: History and Memory in Transnational Context* (Leiden: Brill, 2011), 69–102 (90–2).

[34] Dodd, 'Sham Liberty of Conscience', 93. See also Bernard Cottret, *The Huguenots in England: Immigration and Settlement, c. 1550–1700*, trans. Peregrine Stevenson (Cambridge: Cambridge University Press, 1991), 267: 'Even when [the refugee communities] refused to conform to the established Church, they never entirely shared the characteristics of dissent.'

to the Love of Fables'. One of the commendatory poems to Motteux's Rabelais explicitly compares his achievement with L'Estrange's Aesop: 'Thus *Aesop* is familiar with the Town; / Inspir'd with English by a learned Pen.'[35] The poet here—one 'J. Drake', probably the London doctor and literary man about town, James Drake (*bap.* 1666, *d.* 1707)—is generous to L'Estrange, whose version of Aesop was very popular into the eighteenth century and beyond and is still in print today. But L'Estrange, who had been arrested on suspicion of Jacobite activity the previous year, leaves little doubt in his preface that his fables are a form of coded political protest against Williamite England, 'covertly addressed to readers', as Thomas Keymer has put it, 'in circumvention of censorship':

> For there's Nothing makes a Deeper Impression upon the Minds of Men, or comes more Lively to their Understanding, then Those Instructive Notices that are Convey'd to them by Glances, Insinuations, and Surprize; and under the Cover of some Allegory or Riddle... As what's more Ordinary, for Example, then for the most Arbitrary of Tyrants, to set up for the Advocates and Patrons of Common Liberty; or for the most Profligate of Scoffers and Atheists, to Value themselves upon a Zeal for the Power, and Purity of the Gospel? In two Words, What's more Familiar then to see Men Fighting the Lord's Battels (as they call it) against Blasphemy and Prophaneness, with One hand; and at the same time offering Violence to his Holy Altars, Church and Ministers with the Other: Now These People are not to be dealt withal, but by a Train of Mystery and Circumlocution.[36]

Indeed, the riddle is not hard to decipher: L'Estrange's fables replay quite transparently the events of 1688–9 from an anti-Williamite perspective (with allusions also to the execution of Charles I and Cromwellian rule) as the calamitous decision of a people who invited in a foreign tyrant, much worse than the rule whom he replaced. Fable 20, for example, describes 'how the *Pigeons* finding themselves persecuted by the *Kite*, made Choice of the *Hawk* for their Guardian. The *Hawk* sets up for their Protector; but under Countenance of That Authority makes more Havock in the *Dove-House* in Two Days, then the *Kite* could have in Twice as many months'. L'Estrange then provides a 'Moral' ('Tis a Dangerous Thing for People to call in a Powerful and an Ambitious man for their Protector') and a 'Reflexion' ('This Fable in One Word was never more Exactly Moralized than in our Broils of Famous Memory').[37] If Motteux did have L'Estrange's

---

[35] Motteux, 'Preface', and J. Drake, 'On the Works of Rabelais Translated', in *Works of Mr Francis Rabelais*, p. cxix, sig H3v. See further Chapter 16 by Jayne Lewis on 'Fables and Fairytales'.

[36] Thomas Keymer, 'Pamela's Fables: Æsopian Writing and Political Implication in Samuel Richardson and Sir Roger L'Estrange', *Bulletin de la société d'études anglo-américaines des XVIIe et XVIIIe siècles*, 41 (1995), 92; Roger L'Estrange, *Fables, of Æsop and Other Eminent Mythologists with Morals and Reflexions* (1692), preface, sigs. A2–A2v. On L'Estrange's arrest, see Harold Love, entry for 'Roger L'Estrange (1616–1704)', in *ODNB*.

[37] L'Estrange, *Fables*, 21. For the argument that the Jacobite politics of the Aesop translation is less prominent than L'Estrange's wider, more philosophical concerns, see Line Cottegnies, '"The Art of Schooling Mankind": the Uses of the Fable in Roger L'Estrange's *Aesop's Fables*', in Dunan-Page and Lynch (eds.), *Roger L'Estrange*, 131–48.

rather thinly disguised political allegories of 1692 in mind when compiling the commentary upon his English Rabelais in 1694, then there is an ironic circularity to this literary history of what Motteux calls the 'artful evasion' of censorship through fable. For just as Motteux was now free in Williamite England to explain how Rabelais was forced to resort to allegory while living under a persecutory French regime in the mid-sixteenth century, L'Estrange, the formerly feared censor of dissent, had to resort to his own form of polemical allegory to attack the post-revolutionary England to which persecuted Huguenots fled for sanctuary and tolerance.

Alexander Pope lived and wrote as a Roman Catholic in a later generation and his anxiety about the influence of Motteux's ideological interpretation of *Gargantua and Pantagruel* may be apparent in his denial of any consistent allegory in the work, and insistence that Rabelais really only wrote 'nonsense':

> Rabelais had written some sensible pieces, which the world did not regard at all. 'I will write something, (says he), that they shall take notice of': and so sat down to writing nonsense. Everybody allows that there are several things without any manner of meaning in his Pantagruel … His concealed characters are touched only in part, and by fits: as for example, though the King's Mistress be meant in such a particular, related of Gargantua's mare; the very next thing that is said of the mare, will not, perhaps, at all apply to the Mistress.[38]

As Pope well knew, the English version of *Gargantua and Pantagruel* was couched in a commentary that asserted the continual and concerted allegorical meaning of the work that Pope himself here denies. In Pope's 1728 prose satire *Peri Bathous, or, The Art of Sinking*, Motteux is memorably described (alongside Lewis Theobald, 'Tibbald' himself, the first 'hero' of *The Dunciad*) as one of those '*Eels*', 'obscene authors that wrap themselves up in *their own mud*, but are *nimble and pert*'. 'Pert' was, for Pope, a term descriptive of literary style as well as moral character: the 'pert style' is specifically associated in the *Peri Bathous* with Grub Street translations, with '*modernizing* and *adapting* to the *taste of the times* the work of the ancients. This we rightly phrase *doing* them *into English*, and *making* them *English*; two expressions of great propriety, the one denoting our *neglect* of the *manner how*, the other the *force* and *compulsion* with which it is brought about. It is by virtue of this style that Tacitus talks like a coffee-house politician, Josephus like the *British gazeteer*'.[39] Might Motteux have one inspiration for Pope's 'Esdras Barnivelt', who reveals himself to be a '*naturalized*' citizen of Great Britain, exposing the Catholic sedition encoded everywhere in *The Rape of the Lock* in the public interest of his adopted country? (Pope plays with the nationality of Barnivelt: the name sounds Dutch, and one mock-commendatory poem addressed to Barnivelt is signed 'High German Doctor'; but another refers to 'Thy Works in *Spanish*'.) As with Rabelais himself, Barnivelt has a

---

[38] Joseph Spence, *Anecdotes, Observations, and Characters, of Books and Men. Collected from the Conversation of Mr. Pope*, ed. James M. Osborn, 2 vols. (Oxford: Oxford University Press, 1966), 1: 217–18.

[39] Alexander Pope, *Major Works*, ed. Pat Rogers (Oxford: Oxford University Press, 2006), 206, 227.

medical training—one of the mock-commendatory poems calls him 'Pharmacopolitan', a rare term for a seller of drugs or remedies—and connects his profession of apothecary with his literary method, offering his revelation of the 'Labyrinths, Doublings, and Turnings of this intricate Composition' as 'an Antidote against the Poyson which has been so artfully distilled through [Pope's] Quill' into the body politic of England.[40]

The mock politico-religious allegory that Pope developed in the *Key to the Lock*, which itself develops aspects of Swift's response to the controversy provoked by *A Tale of a Tub*, is one aspect of the apparatus of mock scholarship that constitutes what might be called the Scriblerian ethos.[41] It is an ancestor of the satirical footnotes of *The Dunciad* and related to other forms of comically over-determined reading, such as the satirical index, notably employed by William King in his 'Short Account of Dr Bentley by Way of Index', appended to Charles Boyles's *Dr Bentley's Dissertations* (1698), and also used prolifically by Pope in *The Dunciad*. The Scriblerians may have sneered at 'index learning' as a symptom, like 'keys' to allegorical interpretation, of the abuse of learning in modern times—in *Discourse of the Mechanical Operation of the Spirit* (1704), Swift scorns 'a sort of Modern Authors' who 'pretend to understand a Book, by scouting thro'the *Index*, as if a traveller should go about to describe a *Palace*, when he had seen nothing but the *Privy*'—but they set about with gusto exploiting these supposedly corrupt textual forms, turning them into the organizing principles of their own satire.[42] As Howard Erskine-Hill observes in what remains one of the best introductions to *Gulliver's Travels*: 'Writing a book obviously indebted to Rabelais, Swift probably remembered Peter Motteux's interpretations of *Gargantua and Pantagruel*, Books Four and Five. Almost certainly Swift played on his readership's expectations of finding originals in his text.' *Gulliver's Travels* does not offer the sort of one-to-one political allegory that Swift encountered in the prefaces and commentary of Baldwin and Motteux's Whig Rabelais; but it would then be mistaken to assume that it thus contains no covert political references at all. Rather Swift was able to exploit the recent tradition of allegorical commentary on Rabelais to 'keep up our sense of the possibility of identification, offering, sometimes, almost enough to establish it', and thereby add another dimension to the experience of reading *Gulliver's Travels*, which spawned an array of publications claiming to offer a key to the historical and political meaning of its episodes, as *A Tale of a Tub* had before it.[43] Pope had supplied a separate mock key to *The Rape of the Lock*; in *Gulliver's Travels*,

---

[40] 'Epistle Dedicatory to Mr. Pope', in [Pope], *Key*, p. iii, 6, 8, 13. Pope's use of 'pharmacopolitan' is the second of only two recorded in the *OED*. Martinus Scriblerus himself is also revealed to be a naturalized citizen in one of Pope's notes to *Peri Bathous*.

[41] See e.g., Brean Hammond, 'Scriblerian Self-Fashioning', *The Yearbook of English Studies*, 18 (1988), 108–24, and Chapter 21 on 'Learned Wit and Mock-Scholarship' by Henry Power.

[42] *A Tale of a Tub and Other Works*, ed. Walsh, 184; Roger D. Lund, 'The Eel of Science: Index Learning, Scriblerian Satire, and the Rise of Information Culture', *Eighteenth-Century Life*, 22 (1998), 18–42. See also Dennis Duncan, 'Indexes', in Dennis Duncan and Adam Smyth (eds.), *Book Parts* (Oxford: Oxford University Press, 2019), 263–74 (272–3).

[43] Howard Erskine-Hill, *Jonathan Swift: Gulliver's Travels* (Cambridge: Cambridge University Press, 1993), 36. See e.g. *A Key, being Observations and Explanatory Notes, upon the Travels of Lemuel Gulliver* (1726).

Swift took the further step within his original book of turning such stiffly imposed allegories into 'a riddling device, furthering and protecting rather than breaching the mysterious specificity of the original'.[44] The Kingdom of Tribnia in the third book of *Gulliver's Travels*, a transparent allegory of Britain, is characterized by its 'Set of Artists very dextrous in finding out the mysterious Meanings of Words, Syllables, Letters. For instance, they can decypher a Close-Stool to signify a Privy-Council; a Flock of Geese, a Senate; a lame Dog, an Invader; the Plague, a standing Army'; and so the list goes on for a dozen more examples. Yet this mockery of the nonsense of finding continual political allegory in a text is itself, according to modern editors, in part an allegorical account of the trial of Bishop Atterbury in 1722 on the charge of a Jacobite plot, dismissed in Jacobite publications as a Whig fabrication.[45]

The modern novel began to develop in the last decades of the seventeenth century 'through intersections and interactions among texts, readers, writers, and publishing and critical institutions that linked together Britain and France', and the reception and translation history of *Gargantua and Pantagruel*, the greatest of French comic romances, is one (comparatively neglected) aspect of that development.[46] A fuller understanding of that history may also allow us to reconcile the claims of Sterne and his friends for the Rabelaisian inheritance of *Tristram Shandy* (1759–67)—Sterne was proclaimed on the novel's publication as the 'English Rabelais' and Yorick carries a copy of *Gargantua and Pantagruel* in his pocket—with what we now know of Sterne's extensive reliance on the example of various 'moderns'. Thomas Keymer has suggested that 'the noise Sterne makes about Rabelais and Cervantes could pre-empt allegations of indebtedness to his immediate contemporaries and so assist, paradoxically, his standing as an original himself'.[47] Motteux and Ozell were not exactly immediate contemporaries, but they can be counted among the 'moderns' from whom Sterne disassociates himself in favour of those Renaissance authors, pre-eminently Rabelais, who had by the later eighteenth century attained a status akin to the classics. Yet Sterne came to Rabelais through Motteux's edition and its Whig commentary, and Motteux's key to *Gargantua and Pantagruel* is an obvious source for the 'Key' appended to Sterne's *A Political Romance* (1759), in which the members of a 'political club' in York dispute the precise allegory encoded in the manuscript 'Romance' that they discover on the ground in the Minster: 'It was instantly agreed to, by a great Majority, That it was a Political Romance; but concerning what State or Potentate, could not so easily be settled amongst them.' Sterne even compares the multiple subjective interpretations imposed on the romance with the fate of *Gargantua and Pantagruel*:

---

[44] Johnston, 'Alexander Pope: Unlocking the Key', 902.

[45] Jonathan Swift, *Gulliver's Travels*, ed. Claude Rawson and Ian Higgins (Oxford: Oxford University Press, 2005), 178–9, 332.

[46] Margaret Cohen and Carolyn Dever, 'Introduction', in Cohen and Dever (eds.), *The Literary Channel: The Inter-National Invention of the Novel* (Princeton, NJ.: Princeton University Press, 2001), 1–34 (2).

[47] Thomas Keymer, *Sterne, the Moderns, and the Novel* (Oxford: Oxford University Press, 2002), 19; for Sterne's Whig associations, see 184–214.

Thus every Man turn'd the Story to what was swimming uppermost in his own Brain;—so that, before all was over, there were full as many Satyres spun out of it,—and as great a Variety of Personages, Opinions, Transactions, and Truths, found to lay hid under the dark Veil of its Allegory, as ever were discovered in the thrice-renowned History of the Acts of *Gargantua and Pantagruel*.[48]

Motteux's political key to Rabelais—blamed by Bakhtin for the 'disintegration of laughter' in eighteenth-century Europe—in fact became the stuff of comic fiction in Sterne.

---

[48] Sterne, *A Sentimental Journey and Other Writings*, ed. Tim Parnell (Oxford: Oxford University Press, 2003), 169, 172. See the brief but suggestive note by Michael Fardon, 'A Rabelaisian Source for the "Key" to Sterne's A Political Romance', *Review of English Studies*, 26 (1975), 47–50. For wider reflections on the influence of Rabelais on Sterne's early writings, although Motteux is not cited, see Marcus Walsh, 'Scriblerian Satire, A Political Romance, the "Rabelaisian Fragment", and the Origins of *Tristram Shandy*', in Thomas Keymer (ed.), *The Cambridge Companion to Laurence Sterne* (Cambridge: Cambridge University Press, 2009), 21–33.

CHAPTER 21

LEARNED WIT AND MOCK-SCHOLARSHIP

HENRY POWER

SAMUEL Johnson, in his life of Alexander Pope, tells us that Pope, Jonathan Swift, John Gay, Thomas Parnell, and John Arbuthnot 'used to meet in the time of Queen Anne, and denominated themselves the *Scriblerus Club*'—their purpose being 'to censure the abuses of learning'.[1] There are reasons to be sceptical about this account—there is, for example, no contemporary evidence that these not especially clubbable men actually regarded themselves as belonging to the 'Scriblerus Club': the denomination may have come later.[2] And they did not meet in 'the time of Queen Anne' so much as in the last year of her reign (also the final year covered by this volume): 1714. But there is little doubt that something extraordinary happened in that Scriblerus year. Over the following three decades, Pope, Swift, Gay, Parnell, and Arbuthnot were all to draw on satirical routines developed during these meetings. We find their traces in works such as *Gulliver's Travels* (1726), the *Dunciad* (1728–43)—especially its prose elements— and the *Memoirs of Martinus Scriblerus* (c.1714; publ. 1741). And, however we might apply scholarly caution to the notion of a coherent or formalized 'club', there is plenty of evidence that eighteenth-century readers recognized the concept of Scriblerianism and associated it with a particular aesthetic approach (whether or not they found this approach rewarding or enjoyable). When in 1744 Samuel Richardson expressed his dislike for 'Scriblerus-Prolegomena-Stuff', it is clear enough what aspect of Pope's work he was referring to.[3] And when Henry Fielding assumed the identity of 'H. Scriblerus

---

[1] *Lives of the Poets*, ed. Roger Lonsdale, 4 vols. (Oxford: Clarendon Press, 2006), 4: 47.

[2] For a strongly sceptical view, see Ashley Marshall, 'The Myth of Scriblerus', *Journal for Eighteenth-Century Studies*, 31 (2008), 77–99.

[3] Richardson to Aaron Hill, 19 January 1744, in *Selected Letters of Samuel Richardson*, ed. John Carroll (Oxford: Clarendon Press, 1964), 60. Claude Rawson suggests that Richardson's dislike of the Scriblerian circle can be attributed to the fact that 'Fielding had early assumed the mantle of Scriblerus Secundus' (*Satire and Sentiment, 1660–1830* (New Haven, CT: Yale University Press, 1994), 217).

Secundus' (adopted for the first time in *The Tragedy of Tragedies* (1731)), he was not only declaring a particular cultural affiliation but also signalling a particular satirical technique—the comic deployment of the language and apparatus of scholarship. The Scriblerians were not by any means the first authors to exploit the idea of the mock-book in order to land a satirical blow.[4] What set them apart from previous satirists was the way in which their mock-books were animated by a distrust of developments in scholarship in the final decade of the seventeenth century.

What were the 'abuses of learning' that the Scriblerians set out to censure? The professionalization of scholarship over the course of the seventeenth century seemed—through the mechanical application of philological tools—to threaten the proper appreciation of classical literature. The greatest works of Greek and Latin literature contained universal truths for mankind, which modern scholars tended to overlook, treating them instead as mere pieces of evidence whose meaning (far from being universal) was contingent on the time and place of their composition. This modern approach to literature was associated above all with the Cambridge classicist Richard Bentley, who came to prominence during the debate over the authenticity of the *Epistles* of Phalaris in the 1690s. There is no space here for a full discussion of the Phalaris controversy, which has been comprehensively discussed elsewhere, but its basic outline is as follows.[5] Sir William Temple published his *Essay upon Ancient and Modern Learning* in 1690. This was intended as a challenge to progressive theories of knowledge and culture which valued modern learning over ancient. Temple held up as a shining example of ancient superiority the *Epistles* of the Sicilian tyrant Phalaris, supposedly written early in the sixth century BC—and therefore, significantly, held to be among the oldest texts in existence. Temple's broad claims were rebutted by William Wotton in 1694, in an essay which asserted the great achievements of post-Renaissance Europe.

Wotton's work was republished in 1697 alongside an essay by Bentley arguing that the *Epistles* of Phalaris must be later forgeries. In his *Dissertation Upon the Epistles of Phalaris*, Bentley drew on a deep knowledge of ancient material culture, including archaeology and numismatics. He also insisted that his knowledge of linguistic shifts in Greek enabled him to offer a precise date for the *Epistles*: 'Every living Language, like the perspiring Bodies of living Creatures, is in perpetual motion and alteration ... For what *Englishman* does not think himself able, from the very turn and fashion of the Stile, to distinguish a fresh *English* composition from another a hundred years old.'[6] This appeal to the fluctuating nature of Greek inevitably enraged those who were determined to hold up works of classical literature as timeless artefacts capable of communicating

---

[4] For a good example of an earlier writer (Marvell) exploiting these satirical possibilities see Matthew Augustine, '"A Mastery in Fooling": Marvell, the Mock-Book, and the Surprising Life of "Mr. Bayes"', *Studies in Philology*, 112 (2015), 353–78.

[5] Joseph M. Levine, *Battle of the Books: History and Literature in the Augustan Age* (Ithaca, NY: Cornell University Press, 1991), 13–84; Kristine Haugen, *Richard Bentley: Poetry and Enlightenment* (Cambridge, MA: Harvard University Press, 2011), 100–23.

[6] Richard Bentley, *A Dissertation Upon the Epistles of Phalaris, Themistocles, Socrates, Euripides, and Others; and the Fables of Aesop* (1697), 51–2.

their meaning effortlessly to subsequent generations. Charles Boyle countered that Bentley was wrong to 'confound the most holding Tongue in the World' with 'the most fickle and fleeting of any'.[7] (Bentley's typically abrasive retort was that Boyle 'had better have *holden his Tongue* than to have talked so crudely and erroneously'.[8]) What is still more striking about Bentley's approach is that he hardly engages with Temple's major claim about the Epistles—that is, that they are works of spirit, wit, and genius—and instead focuses on minutiae: linguistic forms, ancient coinage, mentions of weights and measures. As Kristine Haugen puts it, the Dissertation 'dealt with tiny passages of a very long work, virtually never commenting on the impression given by the text as a whole. Specific, empirical details were at the heart of Bentley's assault'.[9]

The fine detail of the argument in the *Dissertation* on Phalaris established Bentley's popular reputation as a scholar more comfortable with tiny details and shattered pieces than with a complete work (here it is relevant that Bentley had already published editions of poets who existed only in fragmentary form, most notably Callimachus in 1693). William King anticipated later attacks on Bentley, and on modern philology more broadly, in his *Dialogues of the Dead* (1699), in which Bentley features prominently as 'Bentivolglio'. King has Democritus telling Heraclitus (in a discussion of the Phalaris controversy): 'It is not a Critick's business to read Marbles, but out of *Broken pieces* to guess at 'em, and then positively to restore 'em.'[10] This view of Bentleian scholarship was to prove remarkably durable: almost half a century later we find Pope echoing the sentiment in the final book of the *Dunciad* (published as the *New Dunciad* in 1741 and incorporated into the larger poem the following year), when he has Bentley speak the following words:

> In ancient Sense if any needs will deal,
> Be sure I give them Fragments, not a Meal;
> What Gellius or Stobaeus hash'd before,
> Or chew'd by blind old Scholiasts o'er and o'er.
> The critic Eye, that microscope of Wit,
> Sees hairs and pores, examines bit by bit.[11]

Bentley's alleged love of fragments was relentlessly parodied by Swift, and ultimately became part of the Scriblerian aesthetic, in which lacunae are deployed with devastating

---

[7] Charles Boyle, *Dr. Bentley's Dissertations on the Epistles of Phalaris and the Fables of Aesop Examin'd* (1698), 72. Boyle's response may in fact have been largely the work of Francis Atterbury: see G. V. Bennett, *The Tory Crisis in Church and State 1688-1720: The Career of Francis Atterbury* (Oxford: Clarendon Press, 1975), 40-2.

[8] Richard Bentley, *A Dissertation Upon the Epistles of Phalaris with an Answer to the Objections of the Honourable Charles Boyle, Esquire* (1699), 404.

[9] Haugen, *Richard Bentley*, 113.

[10] William King, *Dialogues of the Dead Relating to the Present Controversy Concerning the Epistle of Phalaris* (1699), 46.

[11] Alexander Pope, *The Dunciad in Four Books*, ed. Valerie Rumbold (1999; London and New York: Routledge, 2014), 305-6 (4: 229-34).

comic effect. The text of *The Battel of the Books* is peppered with gaps, which apparently become larger as the narrative progresses, signalled by Latin tags: 'Hic pauca desunt'; 'Desunt non-nulla'; 'Ingens hiatus hic in MS'; 'Alter hiatus in MS'; 'Hiatus valdè deflendus in MS.'[12]

Brean Hammond, in a rich discussion of Scriblerian literature, identifies the target of these early works:

> The Scriblerian target is *homo mechanicus*, a species both produced by and producing the new scientific learning, but at a cost to fundamental humanity, to naturalness, and to good writing. 'Scriblerian' satire inhabits many different kinds of writing, but in its early phase it employs as its 'host' sub-literary kinds such as the biography or learned essay or critical treatise, because initially it works by parodying the kinds that seem to endanger 'valuable' writing.[13]

While Hammond is right to identify *homo mechanicus* as the principal target of Scriblerian wit, I find it harder agree that the scholarly treatise is a mere early host from which this parasitic mode eventually migrates. A profound distaste for—and a paradoxical imaginative attraction towards—the forms and foibles of modern scholarship are at the heart of Scriblerian literature.[14] The presentation of the Battel as an ancient manuscript—with venerable lacunae—sits awkwardly with the title page's declaration that this is an account of a battle fought 'last FRIDAY'. It implies an excessive, Bentleian focus on textuality as opposed to meaning. The reader is told in an initial note from the Bookseller not to apply 'to persons what is here meant only of books, in the most literal sense. So, when *Virgil* is mentioned, we are not to understand the person of a famous poet called by that name; but only certain sheets of paper bound up in leather, containing in print the works of the said poet'.[15] The suggestion is in one sense absurd—that the attacks on formerly revered ancient authors are no more than attacks on the leather, paper, and ink through which their meaning is communicated. But at the same time, it perfectly skewers the nature of the Bentleian approach to ancient learning, which (Swift's argument might run, were he prepared to put it in remotely straightforward terms) focuses on the constituent parts of a literary work at the expense of recognizing its genius or spirit. Significantly, when Bentley himself appears as a character in the Battel his armour is 'patch'd up of a thousand incoherent Pieces'.[16]

---

[12] *The Cambridge Edition of the Works of Jonathan Swift: A Tale of a Tub and Other Works*, ed. Marcus Walsh (Cambridge: Cambridge University Press, 2010), 156–8, 160.

[13] Brean S. Hammond, 'Scriblerian Self-Fashioning', *The Yearbook in English Studies*, 18 (1988), 108–24 (118)118.

[14] Hammond goes on to say that there is a strain of Scriblerian satire that is autonomous from its historical moment of origin; he names Beckett and Borges—and to these we might add Sterne and Nabokov. Fundamental to each of these authors' latterday Scriblerianism is that sense of play with the form of scholarship, even if some of the sting has disappeared.

[15] *Tale of a Tub and Other Works*, ed. Walsh, 141.

[16] *Tale of a Tub and Other Works*, ed. Walsh, 160.

Swift's volume of 1704, comprising *The Battel of the Books*, *A Tale of a Tub*, and *A Mechanical Operation of the Sprit*, all of which relentlessly target scholarly pedantry and mercantile opportunism, is in many ways his most Scriblerian creation. These works were written earlier still and are firmly anchored in the scholarly debates of the 1690s. But though they predate the establishment (if we can call it that) of the 'Club', the set of prejudices, enthusiasms, and preoccupations which formed the *Tale* were also crucial in directing the activities of the Scriblerians after 1714. The *Tale* is, as Pat Rogers writes, 'a pre-Scriblerian example of Scriblerus humour'; and it must have struck the club's members as a central template for their collaborative enterprises.[17] Again, the *Tale* attacks the Bentleian preoccupation with fragments. A 'True Critick', says the tale-teller, 'in the Perusal of a Book, is like a *Dog* at a Feast, whose Thoughts and Stomach are wholly set upon what Guests *fling away*, and consequently, is apt to *Snarl* most, when there are fewest *Bones*'.[18] Quite apart from being more interested in scraps than in entire joints, Bentley was known for his tendency to growl; William King's Bentivoglio is referred to as a 'snarling critic', and the term is frequently applied in contemporary attacks. But in the *Tale*, the modern scholarly interest in the fragmentary is also reflected in the form of the work as a whole.[19]

The central narrative of *A Tale of a Tub* is simple: a father dies, leaving each of his three sons—Peter, Martin, and Jack—a coat. His will also provides his sons with firm instructions on the proper management and upkeep of these coats: its gist is that they are not to be tampered with. The sons, however, wilfully misread the will in order to accessorize their clothes, adding shoulder-knots, gold lace, flame-coloured linings, and other appendages. Martin and Jack eventually recognize the folly of this course of action and remove the extraneous items, Martin doing so with great care and Jack doing so in a fanatical rage which leaves him 'a Meddley of *Rags*, and *Lace*, and *Rents*, and *Fringes*'; Peter continues in his garish and unlicensed pomp.[20] The underlying message of this fable is clear enough. The three brothers stand for the Roman Catholic church, for the Church of England, and for the dissenting Protestants: their differing attitudes to their coats represent the different paths taken since the reformation, with Martin's moderate behaviour representing the *via media* of the Anglican church. The simplicity and integrity of the ancient church should be respected; and lest we miss the connection between religious observance and critical practice, the brothers' differing attitudes to their coats are reflected in their approach to reading their father's instructions. Peter wants to find some scriptural authority for his decision to add shoulder-knots to his

---

[17] Pat Rogers, *The Alexander Pope Encyclopedia* (Westport, CT: Greenwood, 2004), *s.v.* 'Scriblerus Club'.

[18] *Tale of a Tub and Other Works*, ed. Walsh, 67.

[19] On this aspect of the *Tale*, see (most usefully), John R. Clark, *Form and Frenzy in Swift's Tale of a Tub* (Ithaca, NY: Cornell University Press, 1970); Robert Phiddian, *Swift's Parody* (Cambridge: Cambridge University Press, 1995), esp. 140–203; Marcus Walsh, 'Swift's *Tale of a Tub* and the Mock Book', in Paddy Bullard and James McLaverty (eds.), *Jonathan Swift and the Eighteenth-Century Book* (Cambridge: Cambridge University Press, 2013), 101–18.

[20] *Tale of a Tub and Other Works*, ed. Walsh, 93.

coat: '*'Tis true, said he, there is nothing here in this Will, totidem verbis, making mention of Shoulder-knots, but I dare conjecture, we may find them* inclusivè, *or* totidem syllabis.'[21] Peter's interest in the plain and lasting meaning of the will is minimal; he eschews the opportunity to read what it says 'in so many words', and instead breaks it down into its constituent syllables. That is, he is on firmer ground when attempting (like King's Bentivoglio) to restore it out of broken pieces.

This account makes the *Tale* sound almost straightforward—and is thus grossly misleading. The narrator of the *Tale* is, he tells us, the 'most devoted Servant of all Modern Forms', and Swift sets about inhabiting a modern form with gusto.[22] Its digressions, ellipses, and sharp changes of tack are evidence of the narrator's febrile state of mind and of the perversions of modern literature, though there is no doubting Swift's adeptness at manipulating these ultra-modern formal characteristics, nor the pleasure he takes in it. The digressive nature of the *Tale* again takes its cue above all from Bentley, who in the *Dissertation* on Phalaris meanders back and forth over a vast range of topics and subdisciplines, demonstrating the inauthenticity of the Epistles not through a well-rounded argument but through attrition. These modern critics fail to recognize the universal appeal and beauty of the texts they mine for evidence, and that failure of understanding is reflected in the texts they produce themselves: baggy, digressive, ill-formed. 'I have sometimes *heard* of an *Iliad* in a *Nut-shell*', says the teller at the start of his 'Digression in Praise of Digressions', 'but it hath been my Fortune to have much oftner *seen* a *Nut-shell* in an *Iliad*'.[23] To see a nutshell (many nutshells, in fact) in an *Iliad* is to reduce a great—perhaps the greatest—work of literature to a mere repository of nugatory factoids. And when judged by such a standard, the works of the ancients will come a poor second to the dissertations of the moderns.

The teller hopes that a 'famous Modern' will soon compose a 'universal System in a small portable volume, of all things that are to be known, or Believed, or Imagined, or Practised in Life'—the famous Modern he has in mind is a certain 'Dr. B---tly'.[24] This projected work, of universal consequence, is implicitly contrasted with the work of Homer, whom Temple had described as 'without dispute, the most universal genius that has been known in the world'.[25] There is a misunderstanding here about the way in which Homer might be seen as universal. The teller tells us that 'we are assured, [Homer] design'd his Work for a compleat Body of all Knowledge Human, Divine, Political, and Mechanick', before chastising him for 'his gross Ignorance in the Common Laws of this Realm, and in the Doctrine as well as Discipline of the Church of England', not to mention his unsatisfactory treatments of topics such as political wagering, the spleen,

---

[21] *Tale of a Tub and Other Works*, ed. Walsh, 54.
[22] *Tale of a Tub and Other Works*, ed. Walsh, 28. Cf. the discussion of the targets of the satire of the *Tale* in Chapter 18 on 'Heresiography and Religious Controversy' by Nicholas McDowell.
[23] *Tale of a Tub and Other Works*, ed. Walsh, 95.
[24] *Tale of a Tub and Other Works*, ed. Walsh, 82.
[25] Sir William Temple, *Five Miscellaneous Essays*, ed. Samuel H. Monk (Ann Arbor: University of Michigan Press, 1963), 181.

and tea. But the source of this assurance is, we learn from a marginal note, Xenophon's statement that Homer has 'embraced all human affairs in his poems'.[26] The teller of the *Tale* is not interested in the kind of universality that can enable communication across the centuries—by, for example, describing unchanging aspects of human nature. For him universality is the ability to address directly a large number of singular questions. This interest in particulars at the expense of universals can be seen in the list of 'Treatises wrote by the same Author' which precedes the *Tale*. Here the author's advertisement of earlier works such as *A Panegyrical Essay upon the Number THREE* and *A general History of Ears* suggests an idiosyncrasy that is close to madness. This is the context in which we must understand his enthusiasm for Wotton's contribution to the Phalaris debate: 'A Book never to be sufficiently valued, whether we consider the happy Turns and Flowings of the Author's Wit, the great usefulness of his Discoveries upon the subjects of Flies and Spittle, or the laborious eloquence of his Stile.'[27] It is, in other words, impossible for an author to speak *to* the present age without speaking *of* it.

Weights and measures, flies and spittle, tea, coins, spleen, parts of speech. The new criticism attacked by Swift finds value in all sorts of strange things, while failing to recognize the true value that inheres in a text. The usual word applied to this failure of vision is pedantry, which Swift defined elsewhere as the 'over-rating any kind of Knowledge we pretend to. And, if that kind of Knowledge be a Trifle in itself, the Pedantry is the greater'.[28] It is not that Swift himself disregarded such things—coins and tea, in particular, were matters of some interest to him—but that there was a proper place for them. Pedantry was of course one of the 'abuses of learning' mocked by the Scriblerians; their co-creation 'Martinus Scriblerus' was a pedant above all else, the fastidious annotator of Pope's *Dunciad Variorum* and (he boasts in his memoirs) the actual author of many of Bentley's critical works: '[Martin's] Terence and Horace are in every body's hands, under the names Richard B—ley, and Francis H-re [Hare]. And we have convincing proofs that the late Edition of Milton publish'd in the name of the former of these, was in truth the Work of no other than our Scriblerus.'[29] But pedantry was a preoccupation for many other writers during the period, including those who were tentatively interested in the new mode of scholarship. In some cases, the Scriblerian mode of mock-scholarship became a means of reinforcing an author against accusations of critical myopia.

Joseph Addison was one such author, who regularly adopted what might be called a Scriblerian scepticism towards modern trends in scholarship, while remaining open to its possibilities. The *Spectator* is concerned with both great and small matters, in fairly regular alternation. Certainly, it is possible to pick up numerous details about life in early eighteenth-century London from its pages—and its first readers must have seen their own lives reflected there—but they also instruct the reader in how to read Milton,

---

[26] *Tale of a Tub and Other Works*, ed. Walsh, 83.
[27] *Tale of a Tub and Other Works*, ed. Walsh, 4, 83.
[28] *Works of the Reverend Dr Jonathan Swift*, 11 vols. (1762), 1: 309.
[29] *The Memoirs of the Extraordinary Life, Works, and Discoveries of Martinus Scriblerus*, ed. Charles Kerby-Miller (New York and Oxford: Oxford University Press), 129.

in theories of landscape and painting, and in proper modes of social and ethical conduct. Addison's stated aim was to bring 'Philosophy out of Closets and Libraries, Schools and Colleges, to dwell in Clubs and Assemblies, at Tea-Tables, and in Coffeehouses'.[30] Accordingly, both tea and classical literature have a place in the *Spectator*, as do coins, flies, and parts of speech; but Addison (in particular) is at pains to stress the importance of proper perspective or, as he terms it, 'Discretion': 'There are many more shining Qualities in the mind of Man, but there is none so useful as Discretion; it is this indeed which gives a Value to all the rest, which sets them at work in their proper Times and Places, and turns them to the Advantage of the Person who is possessed of them. Without it Learning is Pedantry, and Wit Impertinence.' Learned men who do not exercise discretion in such matters suffer from a kind of 'short-Sightedness, that discovers the minutest Objects which are near at hand, but is not able to discern things at a distance'. Discretion, on the other hand, 'has large and extended Views, and, like a well-formed Eye, commands a whole Horizon'.[31] We are perhaps intended to think of (for example) Mr Spectator's visit to the Royal Exchange (*Spectator*, no. 69, 19 May 1711), where his capacious and generous view allows him to see the relationship between the contents of his tea cup (the 'Infusion of a *China* Plant sweetened with the Pith of an *Indian* Cane') and the global networks being established by English merchants, which 'without enlarging the British Territories, has given us a kind of additional Empire'.[32] We might alternatively think of Addison's papers on *Paradise Lost* (*Spectator*, nos. 267-86), in which he attempts to persuade his readers away from a narrow focus on neoclassical rules, which might make them pay excessively close attention to Milton's 'faults' or 'beauties', and instead encourages them to develop a subjective appreciation for the poem as a whole.[33]

This exhortation to subjective judgement, and this emphasis on readerly response to an organic whole, finds an unexpected analogy in *Spectator*, no. 409, in which Addison compares literary criticism to connoisseurship in tea. He tells the reader that he knows of a person 'that after having tasted ten different Kinds of Tea ... would distinguish, without seeing the Colour of it, the particular sort that was offered him'; and is also able, when served a blended tea, to ascertain the origin of the various constituent elements:

> A Man of a fine Taste in Writing will discern, after the same manner, not only the general Beauties and Imperfections of an Author, but discover the several Ways of thinking and expressing himself, which diversify him from all other Authors, with

---

[30] *The Spectator*, no. 10 (12 March 1711), in Donald F. Bond (ed.), *The Spectator*, 5 vols. (Oxford: Oxford University Press, 1987), 1: 44. On *The Spectator*, see also Chapter 15 on 'Essays' by Kathryn Murphy and Chapter 26 on 'Periodical Literature' by Brian Cowan.
[31] *The Spectator*, no. 225 (17 November 1711), in Bond (ed.), *Spectator*, 2: 376.
[32] *The Spectator*, no. 69 (19 May 1711), in Bond (ed.), *Spectator*, 1: 295-6.
[33] For an excellent recent discussion of these papers, see Denise Gigante, 'Milton's Spots: Addison on *Paradise Lost*', in Blair Hoxby and Ann Baynes Coiro (eds.), *Milton in the Long Restoration* (Oxford: Oxford University Press, 2016), 7-21.

the several Foreign Infusions of Thought and Language, and the particular Authors from whom they were borrowed[.][34]

Addison makes the comparison seem natural enough; *Paradise Lost* certainly has its share of 'Foreign Infusions' (the phrase also evokes the drink that Mr Spectator describes at the Royal Exchange). The analogy has its limits, though. We may like or dislike tea—or prefer one sort to another—and attract no opprobrium. But if when sampling 'the celebrated Works of Antiquity, which have stood the Test of so many different Ages and Countries' a reader finds 'a Coldness and Indifference in his Thoughts, he ought to conclude, not (as is too usual among tasteless readers) that the Author wants those Perfections that have been admired in him, but that he himself wants the Faculty of discovering them'. There is a difference, then, one which Coleridge was to express playfully a century later when he disparaged the foolish reader 'who literally considers *taste* to be one and the same thing, whether it be the taste of venison or a taste for Virgil'.[35] There is a sense of playfulness in Addison's use of the analogy too. Readers are in fact expected to exercise some discernment (or discretion) as they read the paper, and to develop an awareness of how drinking tea is not (or not exactly) like reading *Paradise Lost*.

Addison combined a distaste for pedantry with an interest in the new approach to learning pioneered by Bentley and others. This results in a tension which is occasionally visible in the *Spectator* papers, but which is on far more prominent display in his early prose work, *Dialogues upon the Usefulness of Ancient Medals*, published posthumously in 1721 but in fact the product of Addison's relative youth; he seems to have written it between 1702 and 1707, shortly after developing an interest in numismatics while in Rome. The major purpose of the work is to demonstrate that the study of ancient coins and medals is indeed useful, above all for the help it can provide in the interpretation of ancient poetry. But Addison's dialogue format allows for this modern scholarly position to be challenged by a more sceptical approach; throughout the dialogues the numismatist Philander is challenged (and even mocked) by the sceptical Cynthio, with their friend Eugenius mediating between the two. Cynthio's position is presented with enough energy and wit that we have to conclude that Addison was not entirely unsympathetic to it. To give an example of the kind of arguments made by Philander, he remarks on a Claudian coin on which the emperor is depicted with his neck and arms uncovered. Before seeing this, he tells his friends: 'I have sometimes wondered to see the *Roman* Poets in their descriptions of a beautiful man, so oft mentioning the Turn of his Neck and Arms, that in our modern dresses lie out of sight, and are covered under part of the cloathing.'[36] This insight helps us to make sense of Horace's thirteenth Ode, in which

---

[34] *The Spectator*, no. 409 (19 June 1712), in Bond (ed.), *Spectator*, 3: 527–8.

[35] Bond (ed.), *Spectator*, 3: 528; *Collected Works of Samuel Taylor Coleridge*, ed. H. J. Jackson and J. R. de J. Jackson, 11 vols. (1995; Princeton, NJ: Princeton University Press, 2019), 11, pt. 1, 363.

[36] Joseph Addison, *Miscellaneous Works*, ed. A. C. Guthkelch, 2 vols. (London: G. Bell, 1914), 2: 334–5. For a recent account of the connections between ancient numismatics and the circulation of texts and ideas in Addison's *Dialogues Upon the Usefulness of Ancient Medals*, see Henry Power, 'Coins and

the poet mentions Telephus's 'rosy neck and wax-like arms' ('Cervicem roseam, et cerea Telephi … brachia'). This is typical of Philander's approach: we are taken directly from an account of a coin to some lines of Latin poetry on which it sheds light. It is both practical and enlivening. The poem is to some degree animated by this turn to material culture—especially so in this case, as Philander/Addison offers a translation of the Ode in which Telephus' *cerea brachia* are rendered as 'winding arms': it is as though the wax is animated through Philander's scholarly endeavours.

Examples like this are intended to demonstrate that the new scholarship can steer clear of pedantry, and bring ancient texts to life. But there is a counterpoint, and Addison allows it to be put forcefully. In the first dialogue, Philander indicates that one of the great advantages of studying coins is that they give a sense of a much broader range of material culture: weaponry, religious ritual, architecture, and costume. The mention of costume—anticipating his reflections on Horace's ode—provokes a contemptuous response from Cynthio, who sees this as emblematic of a type of knowledge which 'contributes rather to make a man learned than wise, and is neither capable of pleasing the understanding or imagination'. In a subsequent flight of fancy, he imagines what would happen if a similarly inclined future scholar turned his attention to the early eighteenth century:

> To set them in their natural light, let us fancy, if you please, that about a thousand years hence, some profound author shall write a learned treatise on the Habits of the present age, distinguished into the following Titles and Chapters.
>
> *Of the old* British *Trowser.*
> *Of the Ruff and Collar-band.*
> *The opinion of several learned men concerning the use of the Shoulder-knot.*
> *Such a one mistaken in his account of the Surtout,* &c.[37]

The list of idiosyncratic and wrong-headed works is markedly similar to the one we find at the start of the 1710 edition of *A Tale of a Tub* (and the mention of a learned treatise on shoulder-knots suggests that Addison may have revised this section having read the *Tale*). The dialogue format allows Addison to pre-empt and neutralize an obvious objection to his work, and he does so using strikingly proto-Scriblerian humour.

As Marcus Walsh has pointed out, the *Tale* does not merely 'contain or speak through parodies, but presents itself in many different ways as a parodic book'.[38] This was true on its first appearance in 1704, but became truer still in 1710, when Swift added a host of annotations and paratextual materials to the fifth edition. In this it is typical of, and the prototype for, Scriblerian literature, which focuses relentlessly on the material

---

Circulation in Addison's Prose', in Paul Davis (ed.), *Joseph Addison: Tercentenary Essays* (Oxford: Oxford University Press, 2021), 80–94.

[37] Addison, *Miscellaneous Works*, 2: 286–7.
[38] Walsh, 'Swift's *Tale of a Tub* and the Mock Book', 102.

form of the scholarly works it attacks. The most significant aspect of scholarly form targeted by the Scriblerians was the scholarly note; indeed, it could be argued that they inaugurated a lasting tradition of satirical annotation. Annotation in itself was neither new nor threatening. As Jenny Davidson points out, the scholarly practice is 'older not only than print but even than the form of the codex'.[39] Various forms of annotation were well-known (and widely revered) during our period: patristic commentaries on biblical texts, Servius on Virgil, Eustathius on Homer. The footnote, as it emerged towards the end of the seventeenth century, was different. As Walsh puts it, the footnote 'is modern, modernist, philological. The use of the footnote, and the associated lists, divisions and addenda of the new learning, enact a transition from an older, narrative history or philological scholarship to a new scholarly humanism'. Walsh, following Anthony Grafton (who makes a similar argument about the connection between annotation and the professionalization of scholarship), places the emergence of the footnote in the final decades of the seventeenth century.[40]

Again, it was Richard Bentley who provided the most salient and provocative example for satirists to kick against. In 1711, he published an edition of Horace's poetry in which he altered the text of the vulgate (previously thought of as a fairly stable one) in over 700 places. Here was a scholar imposing his own ideas on a well-known and widely revered work of ancient literature (and justifying his actions by stressing his own critical 'sagacity'). Especially provocative were Bentley's notes, in which he justified his depredations on the text in combative Latin. He regarded many of his predecessors as rubbish, and wasn't afraid to say so, frequently labelling rejected readings as *nugae* (trash). In one famously literal-minded emendation to Ode I. 23, he insisted that in *early* spring there are no leaves to rustle on the trees, and so corrects 'mobilibus veris inhorruit / adventus foliis' ('the arrival of spring terrifies with its rustling leaves') to 'mobilibus vepris inhorruit / ad ventum foliis' ('the branch terrifies with its leaves rustling in the wind').[41] Bentley's Horace again reinforced the perception of his techniques and proclivities that had taken hold following the Phalaris dispute. Here was a critic more interested in dissecting, or fragmenting, individual words than in understanding the work as a whole. And his use of notes as the vehicle for his attacks on the text reinforced the idea of the scholar at war with literature. Needless to say, Martinus Scriblerus was soon enlisted to the cause of Bentleian conjectural criticism. In Arbuthnot's 'Virgilius Restauratus' (only published as an appendix to the 1729 *Dunciad Variorum*, but which is likely to have originated as a response to Bentley's Horace), Scriblerus offers a series of hare-brained conjectures on the text of Virgil's *Aeneid*, and is quick to shout 'Nugae!' where he senses

[39] Jenny Davidson, 'Footnotes', in Dennis Duncan and Adam Smyth (eds.), *Book Parts* (Oxford: Oxford University Press, 2019), 237–50 (239).

[40] Marcus Walsh, 'Scholarly Documentation in the Enlightenment: Validation and Interpretation', in Paddy Bullard and Alexis Tadié (eds.), *Ancients and Moderns in Europe: Comparative Perspectives* (Oxford: Voltaire Foundation, 2016), 97–112 (101); Anthony Grafton, *The Footnote: A Curious History* (Cambridge, MA: Harvard University Press, 1997).

[41] *In Q. Horatium Flaccum Notae & Emendationes Richardi Bentleii* (Cambridge, 1711), 37–8.

possible disagreement. Arbuthnot has moments like the reworking of *Odes* 1. 23 in his sights when he has Scriblerus dismantle perfectly serviceable Virgilian lines. Thus, for example, 'Excutitur pronusque magister / Volvitur in caput' ['The helmsman is knocked off, and bending down is rolled on his head'] becomes 'Excutitur: pronusque magis ter / Volvitur in caput' ['He is shaken off and bending down three times more is rolled on his head'].[42]

Kristine Haugen has recently given us a more nuanced view of Bentley's Horace, pointing out that it was not such a radical departure from previous approaches as has been previously suggested, and that he did in fact pay due respect to the manuscript tradition—even the description of previous lections as *nugae* was an act of homage to Bentley's idol, the Dutch philologist Joseph Scaliger.[43] It is also worth adding that a very large proportion of Bentley's conjectures were vindicated by later manuscript discoveries. Still, it was the satirical version of Bentley—as portrayed by the Scriblerians and others—that prevailed. An indication of Bentley's high profile is the existence of an English version of his commentary on Horace, antagonistically translated in the hope that Bentley's arrogant disregard for literature will be evidenced through his own words—but with the helpful addition of some satirical 'notes upon notes, done in the Bentleian Stile and Manner'. So, on the emendation of Ode 23, readers are first treated to Bentley's own confident assertion of his superlative critical intelligence: 'Nothing can be more certain than this Conjecture. It has so much Light of its own to shew itself by, that the Authority of an hundred Manuscripts could not give it more.' Readers are then assured that '*Certainty* and *Conjecture* do not very well consist together, but the Meaning of the Place is this, that our Commentator's *Conjectures* are as good as other Mens *Demonstrations*'.[44] As the sample indicates, the standard of the satire is not high; yet its major satiric effect inheres not in the taunting of Bentley but in the form of the publication itself. In presenting his attack in a series of 'Notes upon Notes', the author stresses the supposed tendency of modern philology to focus attention away from the canonical work and towards spurious and pedantic scholarly debates. The most celebrated appearance of the footnote in eighteenth-century literature was to come in Pope's *Dunciad Variorum* in 1729, in which the notes of various scholars—real and invented—are put into battle with Pope's own verse, threatening at times to force it from the page. Pope, in Grafton's phrase, uses 'the footnote throughout as the hockey-masked villain in an American horror film uses a chainsaw: to dismember his victims'.[45]

The mock-scholarly (or Scriblerian) mode reached its peak in the 1720s—and even then it was a late flowering; a belated return to battles which had their origin in the 1690s. But the idea of a comic, chaotic, or antagonistic scholarly presence within

---

[42] *The Poems of Alexander Pope. Volume 3: The Dunciad (1728) and The Dunciad Variorum (1729)*, ed. Valerie Rumbold (2007; London and New York: Routledge, 2022), 'Appendix IV', 336.

[43] Haugen, *Richard Bentley*, esp. 130–54.

[44] *The Odes of Horace in Latin and English; with a Translation of Dr. Bentley's Notes. To Which Are Added, Notes Upon Notes; Done in the Bentleian Stile and Manner ... Part V* (1712), 19–21.

[45] Grafton, *The Footnote*, 114.

a text had a long afterlife. We see it most prominently in the fictions of the later eighteenth century. In *Tom Jones* (1749), Fielding's narrator turns Bentleian critic when he announces a pressing need to step in and provide some explanation 'as the great beauty of the simile may possibly sleep these hundred years, till some future commentator shall take this work in hand...'.[46] Indeed Fielding's trademark intrusive narration, complete with regular addresses to a 'sagacious Reader', can be seen as a development of the Scriblerian attacks on Bentley.[47] *Tristram Shandy* (1759–67) features occasional disruptive footnotes ('The author is here twice mistaken...'), but more fundamentally Tristram cannot resist serving as the commentator on his own narrative—subjecting the reader to endless delay but in the process providing much of the novel's interest and giving it its distinctive shape.[48] Perhaps this accounts for Johnson's famous dislike of Sterne's novel; Johnson was wary of excessive annotation, and he had in mind the debates of the earlier eighteenth century when he argued that it stood in the way of imaginative engagement with great works of literature ('The mind is refrigerated by interruption').[49] But there is clearly a category of literature which draws its energy from the interplay of authorial and pseudo-scholarly voices: *Tom Jones* and *Tristram Shandy* fall into that category, and it ultimately emerges from the various experiments with mock-scholarship within our period.

---

[46] Henry Fielding, *The History of Tom Jones, a Foundling*, ed. Martin C. Battestin and Fredson Bowers, 2 vols. (Oxford: Clarendon Press, 1974), 1: 47 (I.vi).

[47] See Henry Power, 'Henry Fielding, Richard Bentley, and the 'Sagacious Reader' of *Tom Jones*', *The Review of English Studies*, 61 (2010), 749–72.

[48] Laurence Sterne, *The Life and Opinions of Tristram Shandy, Gentleman*, ed. Melvyn New and Joan New (London: Penguin, 1997), 121 (II. xix). On Sterne's footnotes, see Helen Williams, *Laurence Sterne and the Eighteenth-Century Book* (Cambridge: Cambridge University Press, 2021), 138–68.

[49] Samuel Johnson, 'Preface' to *The Plays of Shakespeare* (1765) in *Samuel Johnson*, ed. David Womersley (Oxford: Oxford University Press, 2018), 758.

CHAPTER 22

LETTERS

DIANA G. BARNES

Over the period 1640–1714 the prose letter was a tremendously pervasive and varied print form. Examples range from serious to frivolous, witty to quotidian, pedagogical to entertaining, historical to contemporary reportage, private to political, exemplary of virtue/conduct to scandalous, and reverential classical imitation to ephemera. It is an academic commonplace to talk about *the republic of letters*, an ideal realized in manuscript and disseminated in print, and that concept usefully highlights the connection between epistolary form and a proto-democratic social, intellectual, and political ethos. The letter is the genre of community par excellence: always involving a dialogue between at least two writers, and often situating that dialogue within a broader social context. It was firmly associated with the modelling of social relationships of all kinds and with theorizing what binds individuals together in sociable enterprise. However, the inclusive spirit of the republic of letters was not upheld by all epistolary modes. Consider the familiar letter and the love letter. Both provide a portrait of the writer as a 'self in familiar form'.[1] Both concern the affective bonds between writers; both stand in for face-to-face conversation; and thereby both overcome barriers of distance and time. The classical model of the familiar letter, following Cicero and Seneca, is of a quotidian conversation between male friends where friendship is defined by equality and sameness. This mode is associated with the republic of letters. By contrast, the love letter draws much of its rhetoric and ethos from Ovid's verse epistles. This form involves uneven pairs of writers, conventionally differentiated by gender, unsated desire, and the abuse of power. This mode is associated with exclusion, violation, abuses of power, and their rhetorical redress. As the genre is so prevalent, it is impossible to provide a comprehensive overview in the space available here. The following chapter will provide a judicious selection of the epistolary subspecies that dominated the print marketplace: the epistolary manuals that laid down the theory; mock-manuals that parodied those principles; cabinets of

---

[1] Annabel Patterson, *Censorship and Interpretation: The Conditions of Writing and Reading in Early Modern England* (Madison, University of Wisconsin Press, 1984), 211–40.

secret letters; love letters; religious letters; and intellectual letters. In closing, it will spotlight three epistolary agents: a publisher (Humphrey Moseley), an author (Margaret Cavendish) and a reader (of the *Tatler*).

LETTERS: AN OVERVIEW

The letter is an everyday mode of communication, dignified by classical precedent. For this reason from medieval times it was central to the teaching of classically derived rhetorical precepts, and from Francesco Petrarch's recovery of Cicero's letters to his friends the form was admired for its familiar, practical, and vernacular scope.[2] Much letter writing and its theory circulated in manuscript, or Latin, that is, in closed circuits.[3] But from the 1560s, when the first English letter-writing manuals were published, this culture and its ideals (specifically that good letter writing could facilitate social improvement) were disseminated more widely to 'any learner'.[4] According to Frank Whigham, Elizabethan epistolary-manual 'rhetoric *maintained* and altered the *status quo*; it was at once conservative and disruptive', but Lynne Magnusson finds that while Erasmian epistolary theory 'offer[ed] both the equipment to replicate and the equipment to critique and alter existing social relations' this was not adapted to the early English manuals.[5] As literacy increased, and the number of individuals who wrote letters, and enjoyed reading them, swelled, a proliferation of miscellaneous letter collections, translations, prefatory letters, pamphlets addressed 'To a friend', and other subspecies went to press.[6]

Around 1640, however, this well-established print genre underwent a major shift. During the civil war period censorship broke down, and the print marketplace was flooded with domestic news of the mounting political tensions, much of it in epistolary form. In this context the familiar letter, defined as it was as the conversation of equals, became an important means of challenging age-old privilege-bound information circuits and of modelling minority or dissenting communities defined by shared

---

[2] Patterson, *Censorship and Interpretation*, 212–13; Lisa Jardine, *Erasmus, Man of Letters: The Construction of Charisma in Print* (Princeton: Princeton University Press, 1993); Alan Stewart, 'Letters', in Andrew Hadfield (ed.), *The Oxford Handbook of English Prose 1500–1640* (Oxford: Oxford University Press, 2013), 417–33.

[3] James Daybell, *The Material Letter in Early Modern England: Manuscript Letters and the Culture and Practices of Letter-Writing, 1512–1635* (Basingstoke: Palgrave, 2012).

[4] Jonathan Goldberg, *Writing Matter: From the Hands of the English Renaissance* (Madison: University of Wisconsin Press, 1990), 251.

[5] Frank Whigham, *Ambition and Privilege: The Social Tropes of Elizabethan Courtesy Theory* (Berkeley and Los Angeles: University of California Press, 1984), 18–20; Lynne Magnusson, *Shakespeare and Social Dialogue: Dramatic Language and Elizabethan Letters* (Cambridge: Cambridge University Press, 1999), 64.

[6] Gary Schneider, *The Culture of Epistolarity: Vernacular Letters and Letter Writing in Early Modern England, 1500–1700* (Newark: University of Delaware Press, 2005).

political, religious, and moral values and notions of citizenship. Over the 1640s a number of cabinets of private (friendship and love) letters were published, many without the permission of the authors. These publications divided traditional loyalties and established new ones. Over the 1650s the letter's association with classical stoicism (Cicero and Seneca) provided the ideal foundations for articulating covert Royalism during the interregnum. At the Restoration, print letters served to document recent history with a personal twist. During the 1670s and 1680s love letters came into vogue. These novelistic and digressive collections rework the passionate terms of the verse epistle to address contemporary political scandal. From the 1690s, letters in serialized journals drew readers into a public sphere of debate, and they modelled their responsibilities within it.

Epistolary Manuals

Epistolary manuals, derived from the medieval *ars dictaminis*, disseminated the humanist promise that rhetorical know-how translated directly into practical social and political agency. They had tremendous popular appeal, often going through multiple editions. John Hill's *The Young Secretary's Guide, or, Speedy Help to Learning* (twelve editions between 1687 and 1713) was one of the most frequently reprinted epistolary guides of the period. Like the epistolary manuals of the preceding generation, such as Angel Day's *The English Secretary* (1586), which Hill's title references, manuals published 1640–1714 teach the art of letter writing through the copious, even slavish, elaboration of rules, examples, and rhetorical exegesis. They liberally borrow, adapt, and rearrange materials and sample letters from earlier manuals to fit new fashions and contexts.[7] They offer a broad sampling of letters, from the prodigal son to his parents, to the wife to her husband, or the servant to his master.[8] According to Linda C. Mitchell, while the emphasis upon classical rhetoric diminished, the 'stress on letter writing as a practical skill for the rising classes', indeed one that might improve the skilled writer's

---

[7] Linda C. Mitchell observes that 'roughly 80 percent of the [seventeenth- and eighteenth-century] manuals [she surveyed] share roughly 75 percent of their material in common, despite the claims to originality' see 'Entertainment and Instruction: Women's Roles in the English Epistolary Tradition', *Huntington Library Quarterly*, 79 (2016), 439–54 (440).

[8] Some prosaic manuals were addressed specifically at women, such as Henry Care's *The Female Secretary* (1671), and the instructions for letter writing in Hannah Wooley's domestic manuals *The Gentlewoman's Companion* (1673, 1675, 1682) and *A Supplement to the Queen-like Closet, or, A Little of Everything. Presented to All Ingenious Ladies and Gentlewomen* (1674, 1680, 1684). See Linda C. Mitchell, 'Entertainment and Instruction'; Sanna-Kaisa Tanskanen, '"Proper to their Sex": Letter-Writing Instruction and Epistolary Model Dialogues in Henry Care's *The Female Secretary*', in Matti Paikola et al. (eds.), *Instructional Writing in English: Studies in Honour of Risto Hiltunen* (Amsterdam: John Benjamins, 2009), 125–40; Lawrence H. Green, 'Dictamen in England, 1500–1700', in Carol Poster and Linda C. Mitchell (eds.), *Letter-Writing Manuals and Instruction from Antiquity to the Present: Historical and Bibliographical Studies* (Columbia: University of South Carolina Press, 2007), 102–26 (112–13); Elaine Hobby, *Virtue of Necessity: English Women's Writing 1649-88* (London: Virago, 1988) 171–2.

position, remained constant.[9] Making a direct pitch at readers' desire for upward mobility, Hill promises to 'prove in some kind, serviceable even to the Learned' but 'dare[s] presage it will stand those in much stead who want those large Indowments' by providing 'Forms and Precedents ready drawn up' ('The Epistle to the Reader', 1687). There is very little hard evidence, however, for how closely the social world constructed by the manuals represented that of actual readers, or the degree to which they shaped the 'real' practice of letter writing.[10] Manuals were read, and used, in a variety of piecemeal ways. Eve Tavor Bannet argues that the epistolary discourse they formulated and circulated facilitated the 'administrative centralization' necessary for global trade and colonial expansion.[11]

MOCK-MANUALS AND ACADEMIES

French letters came into vogue as the French Queen consort, Henrietta Maria, gained influence in the English court over the 1630s. English translations of the letters of courtiers and salon members, Jean-Louis Guez de Balzac (1634, repr. 1638, new editions 1639, 1654, and 1658), Puget de la Serre (*The Secretary in Fashion*, seven editions between 1640 and 1685), and a little later Vincent Voiture (1657, 1696, 1700) went through numerous editions.[12] The title *The Secretary in Fashion* misleadingly suggests a continuity with the English manual tradition, but these were letters of compliment modelling *precosité* and devout humanism, a courtly code of civility involving compliment, wit, and honesty.[13] Nevertheless the pedagogical promise persisted as the complimenting mode was adapted to English mores in the popular mock civility manuals which included letters within a mix of prose, poetry, and dialogue. The word 'academy' appears in many of the

---

[9] Linda C. Mitchell, 'Letter-Writing Instruction Manuals in Seventeenth- and Eighteenth-Century England', in Poster and Mitchell (eds.), *Letter-Writing Manuals*, 178. See also Jean Robertson, *The Art of Letter Writing: An Essay on the Handbooks Published in England During the Sixteenth and Seventeenth Centuries* (Liverpool: University Press of Liverpool, 1942); Diana G. Barnes, *Epistolary Community in Print 1580–1663* (Farnham: Ashgate, 2013), 19.

[10] Alan Stewart and Heather Wolff, *Letter Writing in Renaissance England* (Washington, DC: Folger Shakespeare Library, 2004), 21.

[11] Eve Tavor Bannet, *Empire of Letters: Letter Manuals and Transatlantic Correspondence, 1680–1820* (Cambridge: Cambridge University Press, 2005), pp. ix–x.

[12] *The Letters of Monsieur de Balzac*, trans. William Tirwhyt (1634, 1638), *New Epistles of Monsieur de Balzac*, trans. Sir Richard Baker (1638, 1639), *A Collection of Modern Epistles by Monsieur de Balzac*, trans. Thomas Powell (1639), and further editions in 1654, 1658. See William Henry Irving, *The Providence of Wit in the English Letter Writers* (Durham, NC: Duke University Press, 1955), 62–9; and for French influence in Elizabethan and Jacobean letters see Stewart, 'Letters'.

[13] Katherine Gee Hornbeak, 'The Complete Letter Writer in English 1568–1800', *Smith College Studies in Modern Languages*, 15 (April–July 1934) 50; Erica Veevers, *Images of Love and Religion: Queen Henrietta Maria and Court Entertainments* (Cambridge: Cambridge University Press, 1989). Lawrence H. Green, 'Dictamen in England, 1500–1700', in Poster and Mitchell (eds.), *Letter-Writing Manuals*, 102–26 (114).

titles for example, *Wits Academy* (1640), *The Academy of Pleasure. Furnished with all Kindes of Complemental Letters, Discourses, and Dialogues* (1665), or Milophilus' *A New Academy, or, The Accomplish'd Secretary* (1698). An academy suggested a club, society, salon, or elite school with restricted membership to which diligent readers might gain access with some rhetorical training. Academy letters offer neither rules nor rhetorical exegesis, however. As Roger Chartier argues of French letters of compliment, 'they nourished a social knowhow and a social imaginary' for a print readership hungry for information about the 'remote' and 'exotic' 'universe [. . .] of aristocratic ways'.[14] This is made plain in the title of *The Academy of Complements. Wherein Ladyes, Gentlewomen, Schollers, and Strangers may Accommodate their Courtly Practice* (nine editions between 1639 and 1685).[15]

Academy letters are characterized by over-blown encomium, a 'sleazie' 'bombast of words, and smooth affected complement' as English letter writer James Howell described them disparagingly.[16] Typically exchanges of compliment between lovers, friends, and acquaintances are driven by the overwhelming desire to perform service to others, and to have that service graciously acknowledged. For example, 'The Garden-Knot of Faire and Rare Letters of Complement' in *The Academy of Complements* opens with the following brief letter:

> Sir, These strokes of my hand, shall serve to intreat you to honour me with yours, and to confirme to you anew the purpose I have always had in my soule, which is a perfect will to live faithfully, that I may die constant.
> Yours, Sir.[17]

Here the writer's exaggeratedly sensual language parodies the passionate mode of male friendship letters in Ciceronian style. This writer presents his commitment to faithful service and honourable reciprocity as moral credentials that underwrite a heartfelt request. Such letters express what one letter writer describes as 'a fervent passion perfectly zealous for [the addressee's] service' (192). Writers strive to ingratiate themselves, or improve their position. As another writer acknowledges, their success in this endeavour depends upon the reader's judgement: 'being overcome to see your passions so great, I cannot but commit my love, my honour, my selfe, and all to your affection and wise government' (201). In terms conventional to complaint poetry, men and women weep and rail. Letters to unfaithful, cruel, or unresponsive lovers are blotted with 'streames of teares' (185), and 'love and crueltie' (219), pleasure and pain are at war. As an anguished

---

[14] Roger Chartier, 'Introduction: An Ordinary Kind of Writing', in Roger Chartier, Alain Boureau, and Cecile Dauphin (eds.), *Correspondence: Models of Letter-Writing from the Middle Ages to the Nineteenth Century*, trans. Christopher Woodall (Princeton, NJ: Princeton University Press, 1997) 5.
[15] Other academies in this tradition include Charles Sackville et al., *The New Academy of Complements* (1669, 1671, 1681, 1695, 1699); and John Shirley, *The Compleat Courtier, or, Cupids Academy* (1683).
[16] Howell, *A New Volume of Letters* (1647); see Barnes, *Epistolary Community*, 148.
[17] J.[ohn] G.[ough], *The Academy of Complements* (1640 edn), 179.

writer puts it in distinctly Ovidian terms 'the despaire of Love, hath put the pen into my hand, with a purpose if it returne me no redress, to change it into a sword, which promises mee a full though a cruell healing' (197).

Academy letters parody the practical application of ideals promulgated in epistolary handbooks. By offering courtly compliment and wit under critique implied by a wry satirical tone, the academies initiate the absorption of those ideals into quotidian epistolary discourse. For example, as Bannet shows, Hill's manual redeploys the techniques by which 'social distance' is articulated in courtly letters (specifically Serre's *The Secretary in Fashion*) to redress the disadvantages of an underclass of serving women and men.[18] The courtly ethos of the academies carried a distinctly political valence in England during the interregnum when Royalism was under threat and the court absent.[19] For example, after lengthy sections covering rhetorical theory and commonplaces, Thomas Blount's *The Academy of Eloquence* (five editions between 1654 and 1683) offers a selection of readily identifiable Royalist letters by 'W. M.' or William Montagu, 'W. D.' or Sir William Davenant, and others. Here the seemingly phatic performance of civility exemplified by the exchange of epistolary compliments nourishes the memory of a political life centred on the court.

Cabinets and Packets of Letters Exposed

The most historically significant epistolary publication between 1640 and 1714 was *The King's Cabinet Open'd* (1645). Parliament capitalized upon its military victory at the Battle of Naseby (June 1645) by publishing a selection of the king's personal correspondence discovered amongst the battle spoils. Quick to recognize the propaganda value in the king's letters, Parliament established a committee to decode partially enciphered letters, and it prepared a selection for publication within months.[20] The cabinet letters draw upon the political uses to which letters had been put prior to the outbreak of civil war, specifically the role they played in dividing the Crown from the people. Both sides used letters to garner political support. For example, in 1639 letters of prominent courtiers and the queen herself were published to proclaim support for Roman Catholics (*A Copy of 1. The Letter sent by the Queene's Majestie concerning the collection of the Recusants Mony*, 1639), and in the 1640s this was countered successfully with crypto-Roman Catholic manuscript letters presented to the House of Commons as

---

[18] Bannet, *Empire of Letters*, 110–21.

[19] Barnes, *Epistolary Community*, 77–8, 139–41.

[20] R. E. Maddison, "'The King's Cabinet Opened': A Case Study in Pamphlet History", *Notes and Queries*, 13 (1966), 2–9; C. V. Wedgewood, *The King's War, 1641-1647* (Harmondsworth: Penguin, 2001), 458.

evidence of a mounting conspiracy supported by the Crown. The cabinet letters reveal hidden truths, specifically the duplicity of Charles I, his knowing division of his sovereignty, his collusion with foreigners, and his protection of English and Irish Roman Catholics. The editors present the letters as direct transcriptions or *true* copies of originals, and, thereby detract attention from how epistolary discourse, and its presentation in print, shaped readers' interpretation of the contents. Such formative strategies include: a preface encouraging readers to recognize that their antipathy or sympathy to the letters makes them either friends or enemies to Parliament; thematic, rather than chronological, grouping of letters within the collection; variation of typeface; interpolation of symbols to underscore certain passages; and lengthy concluding annotations.[21] As I have argued elsewhere, the collection draws upon the conventions of familiar and love letters to present the king as disloyal to his country or loyal followers, owing to his devotion to his Roman Catholic queen, that is, as a man weakened by love to betray the code of friendship.[22]

The King's Cabinet exemplifies the capacities of the print letter to effect political change; it also irrevocably altered the status of the letter as a print genre.[23] Once letters had discredited Royalism by opening the king's private and familiar correspondence with his wife and friends to public scrutiny and judgement, the genre became more pervasive in print. Other cabinets of intercepted letters were published; as Joad Raymond argues, the 'Pamphlet-of-letters-as exposure' came into vogue.[24] In reaction, some defences of Royalism used familiar epistolary discourse—in conventional letter-to-a-friend form—to establish sympathy between writer and reader, and extend it to the king. The anonymous author of *A Letter in which the Arguments of the Annotator and Three other Speeches Upon their Majesties Letters Published at London are Examined and Answered* (1645), for example, acknowledges his initial disillusionment on reading *The King's Cabinet*. Careful attention to the king's epistolary style, particularly its robust 'masculine' and 'reasonable' tone, he explains, renews loyalist affections: 'He that writes thus deserves to govern' (3), he asserts. Here the affective and deliberative epistolary discourse of friends musters readers' political allegiance.

---

[21] Derek Hirst, 'Reading the Royal Romance: Or, Intimacy in a King's Cabinet', *The Seventeenth Century*, 18 (2003), 211–29; Laura Knoppers, *Politicizing Domesticity from Henrietta Maria to Milton's Eve* (Cambridge: Cambridge University Press, 2011), 42–67; Michelle Anne White, *Henrietta Maria and the English Civil Wars* (Farnham: Ashgate 2006), 165–78.

[22] Barnes, *Epistolary Community*, 103–35.

[23] Michael McKeon, *The Secret History of Domesticity: Public, Private, and the Division of Knowledge* (Baltimore: Johns Hopkins University Press, 2003), 482–6; Cecile Jagodzinski, *Privacy and Print: Reading and Writing in Seventeenth-Century England* (Charlottesville: University Press of Virginia, 1999), 78–86; Frances E. Dolan, *Whores of Babylon: Catholicism, Gender and Seventeenth-Century Print Culture* (Ithaca: Cornell University Press, 1999), 126–52.

[24] Joad Raymond, *Pamphlets and Pamphleteering in Early Modern Britain* (Cambridge: Cambridge University Press, 2003) 214–18. For example, *The Lord Digby's Cabinet . . . Taken at the Battle of Sherborn* (1647); *The Kings Packet of Letters Taken by Colonel Rossiter* (1645); *The Irish Cabinet, or, His Majesties Secret Papers* (1645).

Love Letters: Secrecy, Passion, and the Public World

The publication of *The King's Cabinet* also decisively transformed the love letter. In Elizabethan and Jacobean epistolary manuals (such as Day's) and collections (Nicholas Breton's *A Packet of Mad Letters*, 1602; 11th edn, 1635), love letters provide amusing portraits of lovers rhetorically tempering the distractions of love, and regulating their passions and discourse to fit situations. Following *The King's Cabinet*'s revelation that private passions are deeply implicated in political affairs, the love letter was no longer simply a vehicle for the witty display of amatory rhetoric. At the Restoration, Royalists attempting to overturn anti-Royalist rhetoric turned to the love letter. *Coll. Henry Marten's Familiar Letters to His Lady of Delight* (1662), for example, presents the letters of regicide and parliamentary radical, Henry Marten to his *de facto* wife, alongside some 'salacious' confections of the editor 'Edmundus De Speciosâ Villa' or Royalist hack Edmund Gayton. In a *faux* address to Marten, Gayton asserts 'The Letters of Yours to Yours, had not seene the world, if you yourself had not given just occasion for the incivilitie'. He reminds readers that Marten voted for the publication of the cabinet letters, and 'tore in pieces, with [his] own hands, the Kings Commission of Array'.[25] The scurrilous tone of Gayton's epistolary retribution set a standard for subsequent publications.

The word 'Cavalier' in *Five Love-Letters From A Nun To A Cavalier* (1678), the title of Roger L'Estrange's translation of the popular French text *Lettres d'une religieuse portugaise* (1669), makes an empty allusion to the ethos of Civil War and interregnum Royalism. This is a collection of prose letters written by Mariana to the 'Inconsiderate, Improvident, and most unfortunate Love[r]' (2) who has abandoned her. Over and again she complains 'my sorrows are Inconsolable, and the very Remembrance of my past Enjoyments makes up a great part of my present pain' (20). Mariana's pain is fuelled by the endless replay of fleeting moments of ecstasy. In this sense, like the Ovidian template the volume adapts, it has what Linda Kauffman describes as an 'iterative narrative'.[26] Her letters create a moving portrait of her anguish designed to move her reader. With each word she strives to engender feeling in her lover and reader, but she fears that it will fall on deaf ears, or worse that the emotion it stirs up will serve no purpose. Mariana opines 'I do not know what 'tis I write for. Perhaps you'l pitty me; but what good will that pitty do me?' (42). Persuasive affect is the aim rather than escape. She declares 'I do not at all repent of my Passion for you; Nay, I am well enough

---

[25] *Coll. Henry Marten's familiar letters to his lady of delight* (1662), sigs. A2r–A3r.

[26] Linda S. Kauffman, *Discourses of Desire: Gender, Genre, and Epistolary Fictions* (Ithaca: Cornell University Press, 1986), 44. See also Peggy Kamuf, *Fictions of Feminine Desire: Disclosures of Heloise* (Lincoln: University of Nebraska Press, 1982), 56–66.

satisfi'd that you have seduc'd me' (27). Disoriented by the strength of her feelings, she complains that she has 'Lov'd ... to the very Loss of my Reason' (114). She relishes her pain, writing 'My Love, you see, has distracted me; and yet I make no complaint at all of the violence of it: for I am so wonted to Persecutions, that I have discover'd a kind of pleasure in them, which I would not live without, and which I enjoy' (62–3). Reluctantly she '[tries] to get the Mastery of [her] Passion' (84) and to arrest 'A thousand ... Sighs' (5) 'a thousand afflictions' (63) and 'Many, and Many a Tear; A thousand, and a thousand Agonies, and Distractions, more than you can imagine' (88). Sequels—*Seven Portuguese Letters* (1681), and *Five Love Letters Written by a Cavalier* (1683)—further iterate Mariana's anguish.

Whereas L'Estrange's gesture to cavalier politics is nominal, Aphra Behn's epistolary novel *Love-Letters of a Nobleman to his Sister* (1684–7) presents a close parallel between passionate letters of complaint and an unfolding political-sexual scandal: the elopement of Lady Henriette Berkeley and Lord Grey of Werke. Berkeley was from a Tory family, and Grey a supporter of James, Duke of Monmouth, in the Rye House Plot (1683), Monmouth's failed rebellion against James II. The novel transposes the English political situation to France and an attempted Huguenot *coup*. This is played out in a competition between Silvia's lovers: Philander the 'French Whigg' and supporter of the would-be usurper 'Cesario', and Octavio the 'Tory'. Underscoring the cabinet letters that nominally give licence to this libertine fiction of conflict within Royalism, the prefatory 'Argument' claims that the letters were 'found in [the lovers'] cabinets'. This *roman à clef* is not a neat political allegory, however; contemporary events and the public airing of private cabinet letters are starting points for a complex three-part digressive narrative which develops from pure epistolary exchange in the first part to letters integrated through subjective third-person narration. The discourse of complaint provides the terms and rhetoric to express the agonies of unsated passion; both female and male lovers weep, complain, and faint under the strains of powerful and overwhelming, but not enduring, passions. In an iterative chain of events, heartfelt letters are exchanged, lost, stolen, recovered, and faked, as Silvia and Philander experience competing and oscillating passions for others. This is not pure Ovidian adaptation, however. As Janet Todd argues, the novel draws upon other epistolary codes such as contemporary postal conditions, the use of epistolary evidence in legal trials, particularly that concerning Berkeley and Grey, and diplomatic letters of intelligence supply tropes of secrecy, spying, subterfuge, and doubleness.[27]

---

[27] Janet Todd, 'Fatal Fluency: Behn's Fiction and the Restoration Letter', *Eighteenth-Century Fiction*, 12 (2000), 417–34. The familiar letter displaced the love letter when the spy letter came into vogue with William Bradshaw's English translation of Giovanni Paolo Murana's eight-volume collection *Letters Writ by a Turkish Spy* (1687) and its sequel Daniel Defoe's *Continuation of Letters Writ by a Turkish Spy* (1718). See Rosalind Ballaster, *Fabulous Oriental Fictions of the East in England, 1662–1785* (Oxford: Oxford University Press, 2005), 145–71.

Religious Letters

Authorized by Biblical precedent—specifically St Paul's epistles—the letter was associated with the definition of religious community and terms of faith, and it was readily adapted to represent religious minorities and dissent. The publication of *A Collection of Letters* (1660) by known Roman Catholic Tobie Matthews served this purpose.[28] Letters also dominate Quaker publications. As titles such as Margaret Fell Fox's *Letter to the King on Persecution* (1660) and Dorothy White's *An Epistle of Love and of Consolation unto Israel* (1661) suggest, many Quaker tracts began as manuscript letters.[29] There was no clear distinction between printed or scribally published materials.[30] Once such letters entered the network, authors had little control over whether or not their writings went to press, or indeed the accuracy of transcription. Margaret Fell and George Fox selected, edited, and reshaped letters for publication.[31] Over time a subset of letters within the published corpus of Quaker letters, those of Fox and Fell, for example, gained 'quasi-official' authority.[32]

Quaker letters also served to circulate news and to hold dispersed Friends together.[33] The proximity between epistolary discourse and conversation gave Quaker minister William Dewsberry the terms to establish virtual religious community. He writes 'I am with you, though absent in body'; then, drawing upon the connection between the letter and oratory, as though preaching, he directs readers to 'examine your consciences' (*Several Letters Written to the Saints Most High*, 1654). According to Matthew Horn, letters supplied 'a mechanism of balance between the individual worshipper's need for personal apprehension of religious experience and the corporate movement's need to maintain body unity'. Letters also provided a means of distinguishing between 'essential beliefs or actions' and those open to individual interpretation.[34] For example, the letter by Quaker leader James Nayler appended to the multi-authored pamphlet, *A Brief Discovery of a Threefold Estate of Antichrist* (1653), closes:

---

[28] See Barnes, *Epistolary Community*, 73–102.

[29] Peter Green and Kate Peters, 'Religious Publishing in England 1640–1695', in John Barnard and D. F. MacKenzie (eds.), *The Cambridge History of the Book in Britain. Volume IV: 1557–1695* (Cambridge: Cambridge University Press, 2002), 67–94.

[30] Kate Peters, 'Quakers and the Culture of Print in the 1650s', in Laura Lunger Knoppers (ed.), *The Oxford Handbook of Literature and the English Revolution* (Oxford: Oxford University Press, 2012), 567–90.

[31] Marjon Ames, *Margaret Fell, Letters, and the Making of Quakerism* (London: Routledge, 2016).

[32] Matthew Horn, 'Texted Authority: How Letters Helped Unify the Quakers in the Long Seventeenth Century', *The Seventeenth Century*, 23 (2008), 290–314 (304).

[33] Kate Peters, *Print Culture and the Early Quakers* (Cambridge: Cambridge University Press, 2005), 40.

[34] Horn, 'Texted Authority', 290, 299.

Dear, friends meet often together and take heed of what exhalteth itself above his brother; but keep low, and serve one another in love; for the Lords sake let all friends know how it is with us, that God may have the praise of all.
My dear love to my friend
James Nayler
Written from Kellet
October 27. 1652.[35]

Nayler's impassioned injunction regarding worship is strengthened by the intimate discourse of epistolary friendship. As the letter to a friend remained a key mode within Quaker publications through the period, it was also a favoured form for criticism, for example, J. L., *A Letter of an English Reformed Quaker, to His Friend of the Same Persuasion: with the Answer and Reply Thereto* (1700) or William Mucklow, *A Bemoaning Letter of an Ingenious Quaker to a Friend of His: Wherein the Government of the Quakers Among Themselves (as It Hath Been Exercised by George Fox, and Others of Their Ring-Leaders) Brought to Light; Wherein Their Tyrannical and Persecuting Practices Are Detected and Redarged* [sic]: *Also a Preface to the Reader Giving an Account of How the Said Letter Came to the Hand of the Publisher* (1700).

The familiar letter, as the letter of friends, fit the Quaker ethos perfectly, but it was also used in other publications of religious dissent. Richard Baxter, for example, made use of a prefatory familiar letter to address his collection of sermons entitled *The Mischiefs of Self-Ignorance* (1662) directly to the Kidderminster parish at which he had preached over the years 1641–2 and 1647–60, but from which he had been removed at the Restoration owing to his dissenting views.[36] On another occasion when promoting the cause of Christian unity, he opened with an epistle addressed more generally to 'Men and Brethren' (*Catholic Unity, or, The Only Way to Bring Us All to be of One Religion*, 1660), thereby, once again, manipulating the familiar epistolary rhetoric of the prefatory letter to fit the specific religious issue motivating the publication.

NEW KNOWLEDGE IN EPISTOLARY FORM

The growing respect for experience-derived knowledge is enshrined in letters that give (or claim to give) witness to a journey or historical period. Examples include the collection *Cabala: sive scrinia sacra: Mysteries of State and Government in Letters of Illustrious Persons and Great Agents in the Reigns of Henry the Eighth, Queen Elizabeth, K: James, and the Late King Charls: In Two Parts, in Which the Secrets of Empire and Public Manage of Affairs Are Contained* (1654); James Howell's partly confected

---

[35] 'A Copy of a Letter to Some Friends Concerning *George Foxes* Tryal', in [Samuel Buttivant], *A Brief Discovery of a Threefold Estate of Antichrist* (1653), 13.

[36] N. H. Keeble, entry for 'Baxter, Richard (1615–1691)', in *ODNB*.

Epistolae Ho-Eliane: Familiar Letters Domestic and Forren Partly Historical Political and Phylosophical (1645–55); or Delarivier Manley's fictional *Letters Writen by Mrs Manley* (1696). The letter's admired capacity to convey personal testimony explains its prominence in the emergent hybrid print genres associated with empirical science and the new philosophy. The letters of English philosophers, Thomas Hobbes and Henry More, were first published in the 'Objections and Replies' appended to the works of René Descartes, modelling a practice of sociable philosophical exchange that generated new ideas. Interestingly in *A Collection of Several Philosophical Writings of Dr Henry More ... as Namely, His Antidote Against Atheism, Appendix to the Said Antidote, Enthusiasmus Triumphatus, Letters to Des-Cartes* (1662), More's letters to Descartes appear in Latin, the language in which he corresponded with Descartes, although the rest of the volume is in English. These letters do not expand the community of inquiry beyond educated readers.

Letters are integral to *Philosophical Transactions*, the journal Henry Oldenburg, secretary to the Royal Society, established in 1665.[37] In a dedicatory letter 'To the Royal Society', Oldenburg politely distinguishes the new periodical from the society, acknowledging 'It will not become me, to adde my Attributes to a Title, which has a Fulness of Lustre from his Majesties Denomination' (n.p.). Nevertheless it was published under the society's imprimateur by its official printers John Martyn and James Allestrye, and was approved for publication by a society committee, and as such, it was firmly associated with the society. Oldenburg continues 'In these Rude Collections, which are onely the Gleanings of my private diversions in broken hours, it may appear, that many Minds and Hands are in many places industriously employed under Your Countenance and by Your Example'. When Oldenburg describes his extensive personal correspondence as 'Rude Collections' he underscores the fact that, unlike philosophical tracts, letters have the unpolished *ex tempore* quality of a face-to-face conversation. And like a conversation they outline brief reports on new findings and arguments without the formality of elaborating a whole system.[38] Oldenburg appeals to the letter's established use as a conduit of news, when he promises that the 'Parcels' of published letters will provide 'Glimpses of Light' that will 'benefit' 'every man'. The opening of this cabinet will make public the otherwise closed exchanges of society members and their associates.

The familiar letter grafted credibility onto the empirical observations and hypotheses presented in *Philosophical Transactions*, by tying them to a community of male friends. It cast disagreement as reasoned and civil exchange.[39] A single-authored tract was more vulnerable to critique and censorship than the communal endeavour of 'many Minds

---

[37] On letters as vehicles for communicating scientific knowledge, see Chapter 33 on 'Scientific Transactions' by Felicity Henderson.

[38] Adrian Johns, 'Miscellaneous Methods: Authors, Societies and Journals in Early Modern England', *British Journal for the History of Science*, 33 (2000), 159–86 (164).

[39] Bryce Allen, Jian Qin, and F.W. Lancaster, 'Persuasive Communities: A Longitudinal Analysis of References in the *Philosophical Transactions* of the Royal Society, 1665–1990', *Social Studies of Science*, 24 (1994), 293–5.

and Hands', or the extended mind, of the Royal Society. Letters embed the emerging method of objective observation within the sociable assurances and guarantees of friendship, courteous exchange, and shared values.[40] For example, in the second issue (3 April 1665), the anonymous writer of the 'Extract of a Letter, written from Paris' responds to a letter concerning observations of 'the late Comet' published in the previous issue. He concludes, asserting that he writes as he would speak to his friends, 'Hence it was, that I assured my friends here, that the following daies we should no more see it so bright, because I knew, that there were none such small bright Starrs in the way, which by my former observations I conjectured it was to move' (19). Like other devices that conferred scholarly authority in print, such as footnotes and citations, the letters 'call into existence' a 'persuasive community' or 'an entourage of supporting opinion' designed to convince readers of the validity of the ideas by rehearsing the bonds of mutual respect that bind the group. As such, letters model how rational and civil dialogue between trusted friends fosters new and unsettling ideas.[41]

Letters published in the *Philosophical Transactions* provide evidence of the internationalism that defined the Royal Society's intellectual activity.[42] The classical epistolary understanding of friendship as entailing sameness and equality had to be tweaked, even compromised, to accommodate European intellectuals, however. In some letters, national rivalries are barely veiled. For example, the fourth issue (5 June 1665) includes a letter by Royal Society member, Robert Hooke, addressed to Adrien Auzout, French astronomer and philosopher whose review of Hooke's *Micrographia* (1665) had appeared in the previous issue. Much of Hooke's text is a point-by-point response to Auzout's criticisms presented through the civilities of familiar epistolary rhetoric. He stresses his gratitude and debt: 'I thought myself obliged, both for your satisfaction and my own Vindication, to return to you my present thoughts upon these Objections' (63). After justifying an omission noted by Auzout, he adds: '(though I did not tell the Reader so much, to the end that he might have the more freedom to examine and judge of the contrivance, yet)' (63). He highlights his commitment to the principle of mutual respect foundational to epistolary friendship, using parentheses to cast his addendum as a polite interpolation into a friendly conversation with Auzout.

Hooke is keen to disabuse Auzout of the belief that he speaks for the Royal Society. He attributes his critic's error either to his feeble grasp of English or his failure to read the book's 'Dedication to the Royal Society'. In it, Hooke stresses, Auzout 'would have found, how careful I was, that that Illustrious Society should not be prejudiced by my Errors, that could be so little advantaged by my Actions' (64). Either by choice or inability, Hooke implies, Auzout does not read diligently. Furthermore, Auzout's objections are

---

[40] On the civilities of the Royal Society see Johns, 'Miscellaneous Methods', 165; on objective method see Peter Harrison, 'The Natural Philosopher and the Virtues', in Conal Condren and Stephen Gaukroger (eds.), *The Philosopher in Early Modern Europe* (Cambridge: Cambridge University Press, 2006), 202–28.

[41] Allen, Qin, and Lancaster, 'Persuasive Communities', 295–301.

[42] Michael Hunter, *Establishing the New Science: The Experience of the Early Royal Society* (Woodbridge: Boydell, 1989), 245–6, 251.

based upon mere 'speculation' rather than 'experiment', that is, upon theory rather than empirical evidence. Hooke laces his counter with protestations of his own graciousness, writing, for example, 'I must take the liberty to doubt, whether ever my Animadversor saw a long Glass, that was otherwise; as he might presently satisfie himself by a way I could shew him' (64–5). Thus Hooke presents his rebuttal of Azout's review as the kind of civil disagreement permitted within friendship. He invokes the liberties of epistolary amity, however, to signal its limits particularly for a misinformed *French* critic. Such protestations distinguish classes of participants within the epistolary community of *Philosophical Transactions*. Evidently on this point Hooke did not speak for the Royal Society, as Auzout was elected a member the following year.

Other published English philosophical letters deliberately hail a broad readership. Much of the oeuvre of Oxford theologian John Norris, for example, either takes epistolary form or interpolates letters.[43] Some works address a generic 'friend', such as *An Idea of Happiness, in a Letter to a Friend Enquiring Wherein the Greatest Happiness Attainable by Man in this Life Does Consist* (1683); *The Charge of Schism Continued Being a Justification of the Author of Christian Blessedness for His Charging the Separatists with Schism, not Withstanding the Toleration: In a Letter to a City-Friend* (1691); and *A Collection of Miscellanies Consisting of Poems, Essays, Discourses, and Letters Occasionally Written* (1687), which includes a selection of friendship letters (including a reprint of *An Idea of Happiness*).[44] Others specify the addressee as Lady [Damaris] Masham, Henry More, or 'the author of a serious proposal for the ladies' (Mary Astell).[45] Norris's *An Idea of Happiness* blends epistolary discourse with the conventions of scholarly publication. In the manner of a letter, it addresses an unnamed generic 'Dear SIR', and like a tract discussion points are numbered in the margin. Epistolary form offers certain advantages: it documents the sociable motivation for the expression of his ideas, and thus enhances the persuasive force of his argument. For example, he concludes one point conversationally as follows: 'This I suppose is the utmost that can be said or conceiv'd of it, and less than this will not be enough. And thus far we are all agreed' (399). The terms of familiar epistolary discourse allow him to glide seamlessly from 'I' to a consensual 'we'. In other places Norris redirects the passion of male friendship, and the empirical method it supports, towards love of God. Like *Philosophical Transactions*, Norris uses epistolary form as a means of soliciting readers' sympathy.

---

[43] On Robert Boyle's epistolary persona see Steven Shapin, *A Social History of Truth* (Chicago: University of Chicago Press, 1994), 177.

[44] See also John Norris, *Miscelleneous [sic] Poems, with … A Letter Concerning the True Notion of Plato's Ideas, and of Platonick Love* (1696); and *Two Treatises Concerning the Divine Light* (1692). See also Edmund Elys, *A Letter from Edmund … to John Norris* (1693).

[45] John Norris, *The Theory and Regulation of Love a Moral Essay, in Two Parts: to Which Are Added Letters Philosophical and Moral between the Author and Dr. Henry More* (1688, 1694); *Reflections upon the Conduct of Human Life with Reference to the Study of Learning and Knowledge: in a Letter to the Excellent Lady, the Lady Masham* (1690); and *Letters Concerning the Love of God between the Author of the Proposal to the Ladies and Mr. John Norris* (1695).

A Publisher: Humphrey Moseley

Letters were a key element in the publications of Humphrey Moseley, the London bookseller whom David Kastan credits with 'developing a market for [English] literary works' over the period he was active from the late 1630s through until his death in 1661.[46] Moseley achieved this by harnessing the technologies of print to 'erect a stable set of relations among differing books, authors, publishers, and readers', as Randal Ingram argues.[47] Serialization and regularization of format allowed the success of one publication to flow to the next. Single-issue plays, for example, were published in octavo with an engraved frontispiece foregrounding the author's name. As Paulina Kewes explains, this was accompanied by a 'wealth of author-centred paratextual material'.[48] Much of this material was epistolary. Dedicatory epistles, authorial letters to the reader, letters by friends of the author, and, on occasion, letters of 'the Stationer' by Moseley himself set the agenda for the reception of the works.[49] For example the stationer's letter appended to John Milton's *Poems* (1645) seeks to hail discerning readers in order to create a niche for learned yet 'vendible' English poetry in a market flooded by pamphlet ephemera. This is achieved by coaxing the 'gentle reader' in familiar respectful terms. 'I know not thy palat how it relishes such dainties, nor how harmonious thy soul is; [. . .] perhaps more Trivial Airs may please thee better' but surely, he implies, the judicious reader will be swayed by 'the unparall'd attestation of that renowned Provost of Eton, Sir Henry Wotton' whose gracious 1638 letter to his new friend Milton appears midway in the volume, prior to the republished 'A Mask [. . .] presented at Ludlow Castle'.

The values Moseley promoted in epistolary paratexts have a distinctly Royalist tint. This ethos is expressed as nostalgia for court culture in letters of compliment, mock-manuals, and academies that he published; these included: *The Academy of Compliments*, Blount's *The Academy of Eloquence* (1654), 'Philomusus', *The Marrow of Complements* (1654), Serre's *The Secretary in Fashion* (repr. 1654). It is also implied by the distinctly Royalist account of history given in his editions of James Howell's *Epistolae Ho-Eliana: Familiar Letters Domestic and Forren Partly Historical Political and Phylosophical* (1645) and *Letters Between Lord George Digby and Sir Kenelm Digby*

---

[46] David Scott Kastan, 'Humphrey Moseley and the Invention of English Literature', in Sabrina Alcorn, Eric N. Linquist, and Eleanor F. Shevlin (eds.), *Agent of Change: Print Culture Studies after Elizabeth L. Eisenstein* (Amherst: University of Massachusetts Press, 2007), 105–24 (113).

[47] Randall Ingram, 'First Words and Second Thoughts: Margaret Cavendish, Humphrey Moseley, and "the Book"', *Journal of Medieval and Early Modern Studies*, 30 (2000), 101–24 (108).

[48] Paulina Kewes, '"Give me the Sociable Pocket-Bookes . . .": Humphrey Moseley's Serial Publication of Octavo Play Collections', *Publishing History*, 38 (1995), 5–21 (10–11).

[49] Maureen Bell, 'Booksellers without an Author, 1627–1685', in Gary Taylor and John Lavagnino (eds.), *Thomas Middleton and Early Modern Textual Culture: A Companion to the Collected Works* (Oxford: Oxford: University Press, 2017), 260–85 (273).

concerning Religion (1650). As Moseley acknowledges in 'The Preface' to Procopius' *The History of the Wars of the Emperor Justinian* (1653), those historians who are 'personally concerned in the actions they write of' are 'biased'. This is a valuable quality. By this definition, the historical account provided by eyewitness letters is valuable because it is 'partial'. Evidently the attraction of Howell's letters is that they provide a 'faction'ed and sided' historical account.[50] Indeed the epistolary segments of Moseley's corpus all convey a Royalist bias.

The frontispiece of Moseley's *Fragmenta Aurea: A Collection of all the Incompararable Peeces Written by Sir John Suckling* (1645) does not mention the *Letters to Divers Eminent Personages* which take up 44 of the 119 pages. It does, however, present the volume as an act of friendship, 'published by a Friend to perpetuate his memory. Printed by his owne Copies.' In a letter 'To the reader', the anonymous friend (possibly Moseley) introduces the works of the deceased poet as a passport to further friendship. He writes: 'But I keep back the Ingenuous Reader, by my unworthy Preface: The gate is open, and thy soule invited to a Garden of ravishing variety, admire his wit, that created these for thy delight, while I with draw into a shade, and contemplate who must follow' (sig. A4r). Those 'knowing Gentlemen' who 'convers'd with [Suckling] when alive' need no introduction, but those who 'liv'd so much in darkness' should read with 'Civility and Understanding' in order to correct this deficit. This is an effect elaborated in *Letters to Divers Eminent Personages* which presents a varied selection of Suckling's letters to a beloved, a friend, a patron, and so forth. A sequence addressed to 'Aglaura', the female character for whom Suckling's 1637 play is named, links the letters to his dramatic oeuvre and to Moseley's 1646 republication of that play. The tone of compliment pervades an exchange between two friends debating marriage. One writer protests that a widow is 'a kind of chew'd meat!' His friend counters that she 'is rather the chewer, then thing chewed'; it would be 'strangely fantastical' to prefer a new 'straight-boot' over a comfortable pre-stretched one (68–71). It would seem a strain to read this exchange as articulating an ideological preference for the Crown as comfortable old boot over Parliament as pinching new boot in the wars underway at the time of publication. Rather this masculine banter is the flourish of cavalier discourse 'taught' in the mock-manuals also published by Moseley. Such letters display the 'ravishing variety [of the] wit' for which Suckling was celebrated as 'an Ornament of our Age' ('To the Reader', sigs. A3v–A4r). Other letters reference the Civil Wars explicitly. In a letter thanking a 'Noble Lord' for a letter received, for example, Suckling apologizes for not having written earlier as 'the places we are come to, have afforded rather blood than Inke: and of all things, Sheets have been the hardest to come by, specially those of Paper' (66). Thus in Suckling's posthumous letters Moseley strives to keep the threatened spirit of Royalism alive.

---

[50] James Howell's *Epistolae Ho-Eliana* (1645), sig. A2r.

An Author: Margaret Cavendish, Duchess of Newcastle

Margaret Cavendish published two volumes of letters, *Sociable Letters* (1664) and *Philosophical Letters* (1664), and made a fine art of the copious epistolary paratext.[51] By 1664 when her volumes of letters were published she was already an author with a public reputation largely generated by paratextual letters to her husband, her brother-in-law, her readers, ladies, the universities or learned men, and usually supplemented by an epistle addressed to the author herself. Her first publication, *Poems and Fancies* (1653), for example, includes: 'The Epistle Dedicatory To Sir Charles Cavendish', 'To all Noble and Worthy Ladies', 'An Epistle to Mistress Toppe' with Toppe's reply, 'To Natural Philosophers' and 'To the Reader'. These prefatory letters present an image of the author situated within sociable networks that confer privilege and authority. As the frontispiece announces, 'the Right Honourable, the Lady Newcastle' did not need patronage in the conventional sense. Nonetheless she addresses Sir Charles Cavendish, her brother-in-law, as a patron who 'may gain [her] Book a Respect, and Esteem in the World, by the favour of [his] Protection' (sig. A2r). This is a defensive move, as she stresses in the letter that follows: 'But I imagine I shall be censur'd by my owne Sex, and Men will cast a smile of scorne upon my Book, because they think thereby, Women incroach too much upon their Perogatives' ('To all Noble and Worthy Ladies', sig. A3r). Although Mistress Topp presents Cavendish as 'the first English Poet of [her] Sex' (n.p.), Cavendish presents herself as continuing a tradition begun by Lady Mary Wroth, Sir Philip Sidney's niece. In the opening sentence of her letter to her brother-in-law she describes her writing as 'her Work' and then in her letter 'To all Noble, and Worthy Ladies' she quotes Edward Denny, Baron of Waltham's censuring directive to Wroth: 'Work lady, work, let writing Books alone' (sig. A3v). Thus she develops an image of herself as shunning the duties conventionally assigned to women in favour of writing; anticipating the 'scorn' men bestow when '*Women* incroach too much on their *Prerogatives*'; and yet resiliently determined to seek fame (sigs. A3r–v). She authorizes this intervention by reworking the stoic legacy associated with epistolary form via Cicero and Seneca, particularly the idea of the ethical reasoned retreat from the excesses and abuses of the public world, to present her writing as resulting from an enforced retreat from social and familial roles conventional for women of her class: first she has no children to tend; second, owing to her husband's exile (1645–60), she has

---

[51] On Cavendish's paratexts see James Fitzmaurice, 'Fancy and the Family: Self-Characterizations of Margaret Cavendish', *Huntington Library Quarterly*, 53 (1990), 198–209; Ingram, 'First Words and Second Thoughts'; Katherine R. Larson, *Early Modern Women in Conversation* (Basingstoke: Palgrave, 2011), 138–65; and T. Skouen, 'Margaret Cavendish and the Stigma of Haste', *Studies in Philology*, 111 (2014), 547–70.

no household to manage ('To the Reader' n.p.); and third she prefers not to waste her time on women's trivial and malicious gossip ('To all Noble, and Worthy Ladies', sig. A3v). It is true that elements of her life belie this claim; it should be understood within the conventions of the familiar letter. After the 1653 publication of *Poems and Fancies* and its companion volume *Philosophical Fancies*, Cavendish's subsequent publications are accompanied by a letter, or verse epistle, of endorsement by her husband, William Cavendish, Duke of Newcastle. The purpose of Newcastle's intervention is made plain in the title of his first contribution to his wife's paratexts: 'An Epistle to justifie the Lady Newcastle, and Truth against falsehood, laying those false, and malicious aspersions of her, that she was not Authour of her BOOKS.'[52]

Sociable Letters and *Philosophical Letters* are not solely concerned to present Margaret Cavendish as author as the paratextual letters are. Some of the letters in *Sociable Letters* do convey autobiographical snippets—for example, the negative reception of her *Playes* (1662) (§173), the failings of her education (§175), and the civil disorder she witnessed in Paris (§172)—but others are generic friendship letters concerning social behaviour, etiquette, marriage, and health and their terms derive from epistolary and civility handbooks. Anticipating her critics, and nodding to the academy letters of compliment, Cavendish writes: 'I fear the'l say, they are not written in a Mode-style, that is, in A Complementing, and Romantical way, with High Words, and Mystical Expressions, as most of our Modern Letter-writers use to do' ('The Preface', sig. C1r). Cavendish eschews the discourses hitherto associated with Royalist letters—that is, courtly compliment, frivolous cavalier wit, and the passionate extremes of love—in favour of the tempered civility of female friendship. This is modelled in the ladies' reasoned approach to everyday topics such as gossip, the infidelity of husbands, and friendship. Cavendish stresses 'the disturbance in this Countrey hath made no breach of Friendship betwixt us, for though there hath been a Civil War in the Kingdom, and a general War amongst the Men, yet there hath been none amongst the Women' (§16). As women's friendship is not implicated in the recent wars, Cavendish presents it as a pristine spring for the renewal of Royalist values and culture. In the partner volume, *Philosophical Letters*, women's friendship letters distil the foundational principles for such renewal. Each letter presents a fragment of philosophical argument ostensibly prompted by the questions of her friend, the same 'Dear Madam' to whom most of the sociable letters are addressed. Female friendship gives a social context and motivation for the author's reasoned response to the leading philosophers of the day. These letters make little reference to Cavendish as author, but the decorous civilities of female friendship elaborated in *Sociable Letters* signals a deliberate intervention in the conventions of masculine intellectual discourse and culture represented by Descartes, Thomas Hobbes, Henry More, and the other philosophers whose work she addresses in *Philosophical Letters*.

---

[52] Margaret Cavendish, *The Philosophical and Physical Opinions* (1655), sig. Av.

Fashionable Readers

Letters had been a feature of periodical publication from the corantos printed in England in the 1630s. These early serialized news publications incorporate epistolary reports from abroad, and eyewitness accounts.[53] Thus early newspapers used letters to build the impression that information was gathered from multiple sources, and that it was the output of a social group into which the reader gained membership. These features worked to underwrite the authenticity and trustworthiness of print news. The integration of letters established the multivocal quality that came to define periodical publications, and which critics associate with the rise of a public sphere of debate.

The Athenian Gazette or Casuistical Mercury (1691–7) was a periodical entirely devoted to responding to readers' letters. From its first issue readers were invited to send in their 'Divine, Moral and Natural' inquiries via the 'Penny-Post'. The editors explained 'The design [was] to endeavor the Answering of any Reasonable question which should be proposed', and promised that such questions would receive 'a kind reception by the Ingenious', that is, from members of the Athenian Society which included editor-publisher John Dunton and philosopher John Norris.[54] This learned college of experts and its publication mimicked the Royal Society and *Philosophical Transactions*. Although the *Philosophical Transactions* included letters and some replies, both society membership and discussion topics were tightly controlled. *The Athenian Gazette* aimed 'to remove those Difficulties and Dissatisfactions, that shame or feare of appearing ridiculous by asking Questions, may cause several Persons to labour under' (1). In the format developed for *The Athenian Gazette* (and adapted in *The Female Mercury*) citations from letters document a conversation directed by male and female readers.[55] Daniel Defoe's *A Weekly Review of the Affairs of France* (1704–13) broadened the scope to include full letters, and to consider questions of etiquette and social propriety in order to shape public opinion and political attitudes.[56]

Discussion of urban civilities dominates the letters included in the most successful periodicals of the day, Richard Steele's *The Tatler* (1709–11) and Steele and Joseph Addison's *The Spectator* (1711–14). As the letter was viewed as a written conversation whose discourse was determined by the relationship between reader and recipient, it had a long association with the theorization of conduct. This made it an ideal forum for the era's increasing obsession with manners and civility. In the *Tatler* and *Spectator* the elision between face-to-face conversation and letters was represented

---

[53] David Randall, 'Epistolary Rhetoric, the Newspaper, and the Public Sphere', *Past and Present*, 189 (2008), 3–32.
[54] 'The Preface to the First Volume', in *The Athenian Gazette* (17 March–30 May, 1691), sig. A2r.
[55] Helen Berry, 'An Early Coffee House Periodical and its Readers: The *Athenian Mercury*, 1691-1697', *The London Journal*, 25 (2000), 14–33. See also Johns, 'Miscellaneous Methods', 175, 179–82.
[56] J. A. Downie, 'Stating Facts Right about Defoe's Review', *Prose Studies*, 16 (1993), 8–22.

through readers' letters presented in full, extracted, or cited as the motivation for an essay.[57] Letters were embedded in the social world depicted around the fictional editor 'Isaac Bickerstaff' (a satirical pseudonym first used in 1708 in hoax pamphlets by Jonathan Swift, an occasional contributor, and then taken up by Richard Steele presumably to bolster sales of the *Tatler*).[58] For example, in *Tatler*, no. 83 (20 October 1709), Bickerstaff describes doing the rounds of the coffee-house and exchange 'to observe what Reception my Works meet with in the World, and what good Effects I may promise myself from my Labours' (26). Afterwards he receives delivery of a love letter signed 'Your admirer, Maria'. Bickerstaff recounts his pleasure in receiving further evidence of his positive reception, but he rationalizes that Maria has judged his discourse and not his person. Being no longer young, he observes, 'I must not pretend to write to a Lady civil Things, as *Maria* desires' (29) and in a polite reply he expresses his unsuitability.[59] A key rule of epistolary discourse is seemliness, that is, the principle that the discourse of a letter must fit the social relationship between the writer and recipient. Bickerstaff upholds these standards by bowing out of improper, ill-fitting relations. The incident does not end there, however.

In *Tatler*, no. 91 (8 November 1709) Bickerstaff receives a visit from a lady who reveals herself to be 'Maria'. Having accepted the terms of Bickerstaff's reply, Maria seeks his advice on suitors. Just as Bickerstaff ventures beyond the pages of the *Tatler* with his perambulation from his apartment into the town and back, so too does Maria via epistolary transmission. Her letter is delivered by post, read by Bickerstaff in his parlour, and published in the *Tatler*. Following this Maria appears in Bickerstaff's apartment in person, and this visit is reported in the *Tatler*. Thus the *Tatler* models how conversations begun in letters extend into other, and in this case more appropriate, sociable contexts. Once Maria leaves, the epistolary sequence continues. Bickerstaff's maid brings him another letter, whose 'Style' suggests it 'was left by Nick Doubt'; it questions the veracity of yet another letter published in *Tatler*, no. 89.[60] Letters construct a complex discursive social network around Bickerstaff in which readers participate as writers, spectators, and judges. Indeed conversations begun in *Tatler* and *Spectator* were continued in the private correspondence of readers.[61] Epistolary form provides a means of examining the discourse and civilities proper to these relationships. As the Bickerstaff–Maria example shows, this was not a static representation of a status quo, but rather a portrait of sociable dialogue under witty civil critique.

---

[57] Nicola Parsons, *Reading Gossip in Early Eighteenth-Century England* (Basingstoke: Palgrave, 2009), 94–5.

[58] Calhoun Winton, '*The Tatler*: From Half Sheet to Book', in Thomas N. Corns and J.A. Downie (eds.), *Telling People What to Think: Early Eighteenth-Century Periodicals from The Review to The Rambler* (Abingdon: Frank Cass, 1993), 26–9.

[59] Donald F. Bond (ed.), *The Tatler*, 3 vols. (Oxford: Clarendon Press, 1987), 2: 26–31.

[60] *Tatler*, 2: 68–73; *Tatler*, 2: 58–63.

[61] On the *Tatler* see Parsons, *Reading Gossip*, 97–100; on the *Spectator* see Brian Cowan, 'Mr Spectator and the Coffee House Public Sphere', *Eighteenth-Century Studies*, 37 (2004), 345–66 (346). See further Chapter 26 on 'Periodical Literature' by Brian Cowan.

Conclusion

Over the period 1640–1714, the prose letter was an extraordinarily varied print form, adapted to fit a range of different agendas. Defined by its proximity to conversation, what unifies this plethora of examples is the genre's capacity to model social relations. This was also the case for the print letters of the earlier period, 1580–1640. What changed dramatically and decisively over 1640–1714 was that the print letter became tied up with formative debates taking place in print. Such debates were not simply focused upon the exposure of startling political information as in *The King's Cabinet*; the revelation of new philosophical or scientific ideas in *The Philosophical Transactions*; or the assertion of dissenting spiritual values as in Quaker epistolary tracts. Rather what is significant about these debates is that they utilize epistolary form in order to reshape readers. In this sense they seem to follow the script laid down in the manuals to fashion the reader variously: as a supporter of Parliament in *The King's Cabinet*; as a true believer of the Quaker values that bound Friends together; as the armchair intellectual who trusts his friends and his senses in *Philosophical Transactions*; as the bemused and slightly superior critic of social codes and conventions in the academies; and as the reader, writer, judge, and social actor in the *Tatler*.

CHAPTER 23

LITERARY HISTORY

NICK HARDY

INTRODUCTION: THE EXAMPLE OF DRYDEN'S 'DISCOURSE'

NEAR the end of the 'Discourse Concerning the Original and Progress of Satire' that prefaced his 1693 translations of Juvenal and Persius, John Dryden appears to draw his long essay towards a conclusion: "Tis but necessary, that after so much has been said of Satire, some Definition of it should be given.'[1] Used to the neoclassical rigour and prescriptiveness of later seventeenth-century criticism, Dryden's readers might well expect something like the short, neat definition of tragedy that appears in Aristotle's *Poetics*.[2] But that is not what they get. Instead of proffering a definition of his own, or one drawn from an ancient authority, Dryden quotes that of Daniel Heinsius, a Dutch scholar, satirist, and poet of the earlier seventeenth century:[3]

> Satire is a kind of Poetry, without a Series of Action, invented for the purging of our Minds; in which Humane Vices, Ignorance, and Errors, and all things besides, which are produced from them, in every Man, are severely Reprehended; partly Dramatically, partly Simply, and sometimes in both kinds of speaking; but for the most part Figuratively, and Occultly; consisting in a low and familiar way, chiefly in a

---

I would like to thank Kirsten Macfarlane, Marcus Walsh, and the editors for their comments on this chapter.

[1] John Dryden, 'Discourse Concerning the Original and Progress of Satire', in *The Works of John Dryden*, ed. Edward Niles Hooker, H. T. Swedenberg, and Vinton A. Dearing, 20 vols. (Berkeley: University of California Press, 1956–2000), 4: 77. Cited hereafter as *Works*.

[2] Aristotle, *Poetics* 6 (1449b).

[3] For Heinsius's scholarship and his literary output, see J. H. Meter, *The Literary Theories of Daniel Heinsius: A Study of the Development and Background of His Views on Literary Theory and Criticism during the Period from 1602 to 1612*, trans. Ina Swart (Assen: Van Gorcum, 1984).

sharp and pungent manner of Speech; but partly, also, in a Facetious and Civil way of Jesting; by which, either Hatred, or Laughter, or Indignation is mov'd.[4]

After quoting Heinsius's definition, moreover, Dryden immediately rejects it. He accuses it of being 'obscure and perplex'd'; a 'Description' rather than a 'Definition'; and, furthermore, 'wholly accommodated to the *Horatian* way; and excluding the Works of *Juvenal* and *Persius*, as foreign from that kind of Poem'. In particular, Dryden asserts that Heinsius's insistence that satire has a 'low familiar way of speech' corresponds only with the style of Horace's satires, not those of Juvenal or Persius. Having abandoned Heinsius, readers might expect Dryden finally to offer his own definition. But he confounds his readers' expectations once more, by failing to do so. Dryden's essay tails off with some suggestions about thematic unity and versification in modern English, not ancient satire, and an outline of the policies which he has followed in rendering Juvenal and Persius. The definition which Dryden had only just identified as 'necessary' is conspicuous by its absence.

The refusal of Dryden's 'Discourse' to define its subject can tell us a lot about the nature and functions of 'literary history' in Dryden's work, and in Restoration literary culture as a whole. The present chapter argues that Dryden stopped short of defining satire because he had been confronted with its overwhelming historical specificity, to the point where totalizing, philosophical definitions of the genre no longer seemed possible or desirable. In this respect, the 'Discourse' was the culmination of a long, humanist tradition of empirical, historically minded scholarship that placed literature in its immediate social, political, and intellectual contexts, treating it as a heterogeneous, changing phenomenon that varied from one cultural setting or moment to the next. In the century leading up to Dryden's 'Discourse', this tradition vied with a countervailing tendency to divest literature of its cultural associations by dividing it into neatly defined genres and identifying principles of literary composition and appreciation that could survive the passage from one culture to another. Dryden quoted Daniel Heinsius, and took issue with his definition, because Heinsius, as we shall see, was one of several earlier seventeenth-century scholars whose work on the history of satire embodied this tension between particularism and universalism.

The presence of historicist tendencies within Dryden's criticism receives little attention from modern scholars.[5] Indeed, so does the 'Discourse' itself.[6] Instead, the central document of Dryden's career in literary criticism is his early *Essay of Dramatick Poesie*.[7] The fractured, dialogic format of the *Essay* makes it similarly inconclusive to

---

[4] The translation is Dryden's. For the original Latin, see Daniel Heinsius (ed.), 'De satyra Horatiana libri duo', in *Quintus Horatius Flaccus* (2nd edn, Leiden, 1629), 54.

[5] For an exception, covering Dryden's statements about Aristotelian dramatic theory, see Joshua Scodel, 'Dryden the Critic's Historicist and Cosmopolitan Mean', in *Au-delà de la Pöetique: Aristote et la littérature de la Renaissance*, ed. Ullrich Langer (Geneva: Droz, 2002), 79–81.

[6] The 'Discourse' receives two brief and dismissive mentions in H. B. Nisbet and Claude Rawson (eds.), *The Cambridge History of Literary Criticism. Volume 4: The Eighteenth Century* (Cambridge: Cambridge University Press, 1997).

[7] John Dryden, 'An Essay of Dramatick Poesie', in *Works*, 17: 3–81.

the 'Discourse';[8] but the *Essay* concerns itself largely with questions of unity of time and place, the intrinsic virtues and vices of drama's formal characteristics, and its effects on a hypothetical audience or readership. Unlike the 'Discourse', the *Essay* does not provide a linear narrative of drama's development over time, or explain the changes which it underwent. The *Essay* concentrates, moreover, on recent English drama as well as classical models, and engages primarily with recent French neoclassical criticism. The same could be said of a lot of other Restoration criticism. As a result, Dryden's 'Discourse' can seem like an outlier in relation both to the author's own work and to the broader literary scene. Its relative disregard for English satirists, its reliance on writers like Heinsius rather than Rapin and Boileau, and its resistance to synthetic, transhistorical accounts of poetry all place it outside the mainstream.

However, it is far from clear that the 'Discourse' would have seemed marginal to Dryden himself, or to its earliest readers. On the contrary, Dryden's increasing attention to historical particularity and change was just one of several contemporary attempts to fuse 'polite' and neoclassical literary appreciation with more erudite, academic ways of studying poetry.[9] These attempts were made by authors as diverse as Richard Bentley, Thomas Pope Blount, and the third Earl of Shaftesbury, as recent work on them has shown.[10] Until now, however, Dryden has resisted assimilation with critics such as these. Even Michael Werth Gelber, the scholar who has devoted most attention to Dryden's use of historical scholarship in his later critical writings, only accords it an attenuated and instrumental function: for all their learning and technical competence, the scholars of ancient satire on whom Dryden relied could only provide 'the basic or essential facts out of which sound opinions may be formed', because they were 'frequently incapable of forming such opinions themselves'.[11] In this view, Dryden's French and English contemporaries might be opinionated interlocutors with whom he is constantly in dialogue, but the humanists like Heinsius whose works on satire he studied were merely sources of atomized details and observations. Not only does this understate the intellectual creativity and aesthetic commitments of later humanist scholarship,[12] it also denies Dryden's 'Discourse' the place within larger literary-critical developments which is so often accorded to Dryden's *Essay*. Whereas the *Essay* can stand synecdochically for

---

[8] As noted in Paul Hammond, *Dryden and the Traces of Classical Rome* (Oxford: Oxford University Press, 1999), 145.

[9] For the scholarly dimensions and broader intellectual contexts of vernacular literary studies in this period, see Marcus Walsh, *Shakespeare, Milton and Eighteenth-Century Literary Editing: The Beginnings of Interpretative Scholarship* (Cambridge: Cambridge University Press, 1997).

[10] Kristine Louise Haugen, *Richard Bentley: Poetry and Enlightenment* (Cambridge, MA: Harvard University Press, 2011); Kelsey Jackson Williams, 'Canon before Canon, Literature before Literature: Thomas Pope Blount and the Scope of Early Modern Learning', *Huntington Library Quarterly*, 77 (2014), 177–99; Karen Collis, 'Shaftesbury and Literary Criticism: Philosophers and Critics in Early Eighteenth-Century England', *The Review of English Studies*, 67 (2016), 294–315.

[11] Michael Werth Gelber, *The Just and the Lively: The Literary Criticism of John Dryden* (Manchester: Manchester University Press, 1999), 204.

[12] For humanists' views about, and creative imitation of, ancient satire, see Ingrid A. R. de Smet, *Menippean Satire and the Republic of Letters, 1581–1655* (Geneva: Droz, 1996).

Restoration neoclassicism or an embryonic Tory aesthetic, the 'Discourse' remains no more than a perceptive study of a particular literary genre that digested and regurgitated Continental scholarship for domestic readers.[13]

There are several ways to correct this imbalance. First of all, it is necessary to treat Dryden's precursors in the study of satire as more than mere repositories of specific facts and assertions about the genre. Scholars like Heinsius had their own broad visions of how classical texts should be read, appreciated, and imitated, and they struggled to articulate and defend those visions in the face of competing alternatives just as much as Restoration critics did. Their work was animated by deep theoretical and methodological concerns about the relationship between literary criticism and literary history, and the value of erudition to students of poetry. Dryden could take much more from their work than narrow insights into particular genres, texts, and authors. We can start to see this by telling the story of late humanist scholarship in its own terms. Indeed, this is the only way to appreciate how much was at stake when Dryden dismantled Heinsius's definition and avoided replacing it with one of his own making.

BEFORE DRYDEN: CRITICISM, POETICS, AND THE HISTORY OF SATIRE IN THE LATE RENAISSANCE

Before considering Heinsius, we must start with the pivotal figure of Isaac Casaubon, the scholar on whom Dryden relied most heavily and with whom he most frequently agreed.[14] Casaubon's 1605 monograph on satire, *De satyrica Graecorum poesi, & Romanorum satira*, represented the boiling point of a conflict that had long simmered between philosophical and empirical-historical accounts of poetry.[15] The final chapter of Casaubon's book made his own allegiance clear. Its principal subject was the question of whether satire deserved to be classed as 'poetry'. According to Casaubon, the sheer diversity of poetic genres and forms, and the range of opinions that had been expressed about them from classical antiquity onwards, indicated that poetry could not be defined any more precisely than as 'speech constrained by metre'.[16] In proposing such a loose definition of poetry, Casaubon was pitting himself against several influential authorities in Renaissance poetic theory. Neither Plato's definitions of poetry nor Aristotle's satisfied

---

[13] Howard D. Weinbrot, 'The Achievement of Dryden's "Discourse on Satyr"', in *Eighteenth-Century Satire: Essays on Text and Context from Dryden to Peter Pindar* (Cambridge: Cambridge University Press, 1988), esp. 2, 6.

[14] As recognized in William Frost, 'Dryden's Theory and Practice of Satire', in Bruce King and John Heath-Stubbs (eds.), *Dryden's Mind and Art* (Edinburgh: Oliver & Boyd, 1969), 195.

[15] Isaac Casaubon, *De satyrica Graecorum poesi, & Romanorum satira libri duo* (Paris, 1605).

[16] Casaubon, *De satyrica Graecorum poesi*, 353 (2.5): 'all speech constrained by metre both can and should be called a poem'.

him, since both philosophers would have excluded verse satire from the category.[17] Casaubon added that their opinions were limited by the historical moment in which they wrote, when epic and, above all, drama had become so dominant that those genres alone provided the models for their accounts of the art.[18]

Although his conclusion pertained to poetry in general, it was not a coincidence that Casaubon articulated it in a study of verse satire, one of the most unruly ancient genres. The poetry of the three principal Roman verse satirists, Horace, Juvenal, and Persius, varied considerably in its form and subject matter, and often lowered itself in the direction of less obviously poetic forms of speech and writing. The variety of satire and its proximity to non-literary speech was an explicit theme of their work.[19] Horace described his satires as 'conversations' (*sermones*), Juvenal called his a *farrago*, and Persius described himself as a 'half-poet'.[20] The ambivalence of these authors' own self-representations was compounded by the relative dearth of ancient discussions of the genre's origins and its key components. Early modern scholars of satire could not ground their reflections in the longer, more coherent, and purportedly comprehensive accounts which Plato and Aristotle had provided for epic and drama. Instead, they had to comb a miscellany of sources that treated satirical verse only in passing, from Livy and Tacitus's historical works to grammatical and rhetorical manuals like Diomedes' *Ars grammatica* and Quintilian's *Institutio oratoria*. Their reliance on this fragmentary evidence about satire pointed scholars in a number of different, often mutually exclusive directions. Some sources required scholars to take an ethnographer's perspective, asking under what circumstances primitive society elevated rudimentary personal invective into an art form; others required them to be antiquarians, examining non-literary evidence such as inscriptions and carved gemstones. Equally, while some sources appeared to stress satire's affinities with the Greek dramatic genres of satyr-play and Old Comedy,

---

[17] For Casaubon's discussions of Plato and Aristotle, see Casaubon, *De satyrica Graecorum poesi*, 335–48 (2.5).

[18] Casaubon, *De satyrica Graecorum poesi*, 338 (2.5): 'This was the opinion of the common man and of Socrates. In that period poetry was practised most often in theatres and [dramatic] contests. This kind of poetry consisted mainly in the composition of plots, arranged into tragedy, satyr-play, and comedy. From there the error gradually insinuated itself into the minds of men that caused them to talk and think of poetry as though they acknowledged no other form than that used in theatres and contests. This was a huge error, of course, and one which learned men ought to correct when others make it, rather than consolidating it by their own authority and reputation. But custom is capable of anything.'

[19] See the introduction to Horace, *Satires. Book 1*, ed. Emily Gowers (Cambridge: Cambridge University Press, 2012), 6–14.

[20] This interpretation of the phrase *semipaganus* in the Prologue to Persius's *Satires* had been proposed in the ancient commentary attributed to Cornutus, and was followed by the majority of late Renaissance commentators, including Casaubon. See Persius, *Satyrarum liber*, ed. Élie Vinet (Poitiers, 1560–3), vol. II, 3. For the reception of this commentary in the Renaissance, see James E. G. Zetzel, *Marginal Scholarship and Textual Deviance: The Commentarium Cornuti and the Early Scholia on Persius* (London: Institute of Classical Studies, 2005), 162–79; and for the Renaissance reception of Persius in general, see F. Edward Cranz and Dorothy M. Robathan, 'A. Persius Flaccus', in *Catalogus Translationum et Commentariorum*, ed. Paul Oskar Kristeller and F. Edward Cranz, vol. III (Washington: Catholic University of America Press, 1976), 201–312.

others suggested that it had native, Roman roots. The study of satire, in other words, encouraged scholars to regard literary works as complex, overdetermined cultural products of forces which were social and political as well as artistic.

The humanists' view of ancient literature was not, however, restricted to satire. We have already seen that Casaubon regarded poetry in general as being impossible to define in precise terms, and that he objected to the hegemony of Platonic and Aristotelian accounts of the art. But his misgivings about definition were animated by a broader concern about the nature and functions of what he called the 'art of criticism'. Just as Casaubon was more reluctant to define poetry than previous critics had been, so too was he trying to set 'criticism' on different epistemic and methodological foundations from some of its earlier practitioners. This broader vision of criticism may have informed Dryden's deployment of late humanist erudition just as much as any of Casaubon's specific statements about the origins and progress of satire.

This is because Casaubon's conception of criticism was fundamentally erudite. Drawing on ancient uses of the term 'criticism' (κριτική/*critica*) and its cognates, Casaubon regarded the art of criticism as deeply empirical, grounded in the study of philological and historical particulars and of the material evidence, particularly manuscripts, of ancient literary culture. It was thus broader, more open-ended, and more inter-disciplinary than anything which modern Anglo-American studies of Renaissance 'literary criticism' naïvely and ahistorically understand by the term.[21] It was also more descriptive and less prescriptive. Casaubon and his peers were relatively uninterested in elevating a given text, author, or mode of writing to the status of an ideal, transcendent model or in drawing clear boundaries between one genre and another.[22]

This differentiated Casaubon from the most famous 'critic' of the previous generation, Julius Caesar Scaliger.[23] In his *Seven Books of Poetics* (*Poetices libri septem*), Scaliger maintained that epic poetry was the most distinguished genre; that Virgil was its unsurpassable master; and that the true 'critic' was the philosopher, not the 'grammarian' who dealt only in atomized facts and examples.[24] Scaliger's vast handbook routinely

---

[21] The best treatments are Benedetto Bravo, '*Critice* in the Sixteenth and Seventeenth Centuries and the Rise of the Notion of Historical Criticism', in *History of Scholarship*, ed. Christopher Ligota and Jean-Louis Quantin (Oxford: Oxford University Press, 2006), 135–95; and Jean Jehasse, *La renaissance de la critique: l'essor de l'humanisme érudit de 1560 à 1614* (2nd edn, Paris: Champion, 2002). See also Nicholas Hardy, *Criticism and Confession: The Bible in the Seventeenth-Century Republic of Letters* (Oxford: Oxford University Press, 2017), 21–46.

[22] Dirk van Miert, 'Joseph Scaliger, Claude Saumaise, Isaac Casaubon and the Discovery of the Palatine Anthology (1606)', *Journal of the Warburg and Courtauld Institutes* 74 (2011), 241–61.

[23] Casaubon's *De satyrica Graecorum poesi* rarely mentioned Scaliger by name, but his notes and drafts for the work show that Casaubon read his *Poetics* very carefully. See Bodleian Library, MS Casaubon 31, fols. 30r–57v.

[24] Julius Caesar Scaliger, *Poetices libri septem* = *Sieben Bücher über die Dichtkunst*, ed. Luc Deitz and Gregor Vogt-Spira (Stuttgart-Bad Cannstatt: Frommann-Holzboog, 1994), I: 6–8, 126 (1.5); For the philosophical underpinnings of Scaliger's criticism, see Luc Deitz, 'Scholastic Logic and Renaissance Poetics: A Few Observations on J.C. Scaliger's *Poetices Libri Septem* (1561)', in George Hugo Tucker (ed.), *Forms of the 'Medieval' in the 'Renaissance': A Multidisciplinary Exploration of a Cultural Continuum* (Charlottesville, VA: Rookwood Press, 2000), 49–62.

castigated 'grammarians' ancient and modern for allowing themselves to be led astray by their own erudition. In the particular case of satire, their knowledge of obscure historical customs and terms had formed the basis of an implausible conjecture about the genre's Roman origins: its name referred to the *lanx satura*, a dish composed of a varying mixture of ingredients, extended to satire because of its miscellaneous and unpredictable form and content. Scaliger, by contrast, contended that the Roman genre was a non-dramatic strain of the Greek satyr-play.[25] Scaliger was telling a streamlined story about one literary genre's beginnings in another literary genre, following a familiar, linear trajectory from Greece into Rome. It was paralleled by Scaliger's similarly neat hierarchy of Roman satirists, with Juvenal at the top and Persius a distant third, primarily on account of his unintelligibility and ostentatious learning.

On both counts, Casaubon challenged Scaliger's assertions. As far as the origin of Roman satire was concerned, it was easy to show that the grammarians were, in fact, correct, and that Scaliger was not.[26] As for the relative merits of its practitioners, it was possible to make a case for Persius's possession of virtues which were specific to his historical circumstances and his own intellectual commitments, although Casaubon stopped short of trying to invert Scaliger's hierarchy altogether. This is what erudition and criticism meant to Casaubon: not a replacement of a 'wrong' account by a 'true' one, but a fracturing of simple, monolithic histories of, and value-judgements about, literature. Modern scholarship identifies Casaubon's recognition that Roman satire did not originate in Greek satyr-play as the principal achievement of his *De satyrica*, and the main insight which he passed on to Dryden.[27] But this overlooks the broader point which Casaubon was making about the nature of literary history. Far from simply refuting the connection which Scaliger and others had made between satyr-play and satire, Casaubon replaced a monogenetic story of satire's origins with a polygenetic one. He showed that it shared common origins with native iambic verse lampoons and the rustic 'Fescennine' verses alluded to by Horace;[28] and that it had later been influenced by the Greek genres not of satyr-play but of Old Comedy and *silloi*, a form of epigrammatic verse invective of which very few examples had survived.[29] The open-ended story which Casaubon told about the genre's development was mirrored in his judgements about the three major Roman satirists. In rescuing Persius from Scaliger's condescension, Casaubon was also making a broader point that each of the

---

[25] Scaliger, *Poetices libri septem*, I: 186 (1.12). See further D. J. Shaw, 'More about the "Dramatic Satyre"', *Bibliothèque d'Humanisme et Renaissance*, 30 (1968), 318–19.

[26] J. W. Jolliffe, 'Satyre: *Satura*: Σάτυρος: A Study in Confusion', *Bibliothèque d'Humanisme et Renaissance*, 18 (1956), 84–95.

[27] William Frost, 'Dryden and "Satire"', *Studies in English Literature, 1500–1900*, 11 (1971), 401–16 (408–9); Dustin H. Griffin, *Satire: A Critical Reintroduction* (Lexington: University Press of Kentucky, 1994), 12–13, albeit with a broader awareness of the richness of Casaubon's treatment of the genre in the following pages (13–24).

[28] Casaubon, *De satyrica Graecorum poesi*, 233–7.

[29] Casaubon, *De satyrica Graecorum poesi*, 274, 282–4.

three satirists embodied a certain distinctive quality, and should be judged by different standards.[30]

The distinctive achievement of Casaubon's *De satyrica* lay not so much in its disentangling of satyr-play from satire, then, as in its openness to history. The same openness characterized other subsequent treatments of satire: not only Dryden's, but also those of Casaubon's more immediate followers such as Daniel Heinsius. This is not to say, however, that Casaubon's method had decisively triumphed against Scaliger's. Heinsius actually retained some of Scaliger's prescriptivism, although, as Dryden pointed out, he regarded Horace, not Juvenal, as the ideal model for verse satire. Heinsius made his case on the grounds that the former had best preserved the essence of the Greek dramatic genres in which satire had originated,[31] whereas the latter had pushed the genre too far in the directions of tragedy, epic, and oratory.[32] Nonetheless, Heinsius conceded that satire had a wider range of influences than Scaliger had recognized, including the *silloi* as well as Old Comedy and the satyr-play. Even Heinsius, who was still prepared to offer a general definition of satire as a genre, softened his essentialism in responding to Casaubon's treatise.

By the time Dryden wrote his 'Discourse', then, he could draw on several different models for writing the history of Roman satire and for evaluating its three most famous authors. But as well as providing different methods, arguments, and conclusions, Scaliger, Heinsius, and Casaubon were each operating within very different formal, cultural, and institutional parameters. As well as helping to explain how each critic arrived at such different conclusions, these parameters can also illuminate the meaning of the choices which Dryden was making at every stage of his 'Discourse'.

First of all, each scholar presented his work in a different format. Scaliger's remarks appeared within an exhaustive manual of poetics, which was dedicated to one of his sons, Sylvius. Scaliger's *Poetics* formed part of a larger programme of juvenile literary education: it was meant to lay down guidelines for the composition of Latin poetry, rather than establishing literary criticism as an autonomous discipline or research agenda. Scaliger's prescriptive tendencies and his limited, perfunctory treatments of literary-historical questions cannot be separated from the *Poetics*' pedagogical orientation. Heinsius, too, shared something of Scalige's pedagogical preoccupations: his dissertation on Horatian

---

[30] Peter E. Medine, 'Isaac Casaubon's *Prolegomena* to the *Satires* of Persius: An Introduction, Text and Translation', *English Literary Renaissance*, 6 (1976), 271–98 (294).

[31] Heinsius, 'De satyra Horatiana', 83: 'If the divine gentleman Caesar Scaliger had weighed these things correctly, he never would have compared Juvenal with Horace in this respect. This is because it seems unworthy, in my opinion, for anyone, even of mediocre judgement, to prefer [Juvenal]; not to mention anyone who both understands the foundations of Satire and investigates its relationship to the Old Comedy and satyr-plays. For nothing less becomes a philosopher than to praise something in a writer which was never part of the essence and form of his work. For [Horace] is playful, like a comedian; Juvenal frequently strikes your spirit, like a tragedian. The former's work produces laughter, together with the greatest pleasure; the latter's, terror and indignation in equal measure.' Heinsius summarizes his view of the close relationship between Old Comedy, satyr-play, the *silloi* and Roman verse satire at 'De satyra Horatiana', 35–6. See also Heinsius, 'De satyra Horatiana', 28–9, 33–7, 76, 140–4, 218–21.

[32] Heinsius, 'De satyra Horatiana', 7–8, 70, 171.

satire had been conceived while he held a chair of poetry at Leiden University.[33] Like many Renaissance commentaries and the prefaces affixed to them, Heinsius's work on Horace must have emerged from his teaching of that author to undergraduates, and his Horatian partisanship surely reflected the dominance of teaching centred on individual poets within a structured university curriculum. As well as sharing an interest in literary education, moreover, both Scaliger and Heinsius were creative authors in their own right. Heinsius, in particular, had already become an accomplished author of Latin satire, albeit in prose rather than verse, before he published his dissertation, and this clearly affected his handling of the genre's ancient manifestations. It is surely no coincidence, for example, that Heinsius preferred satirists who openly criticized specific contemporary figures over those, such as Juvenal and Persius, who tended not to do so: this preference reflected the policy of his own writings.[34]

In all of these respects, Casaubon was different. Most importantly, he operated outside of any specific institutional framework, and this freed him to depart further from the prescriptive format of the poetics textbook or the commentary on a single author. Casaubon's 1605 commentary on Persius had, admittedly, grown out of a series of lectures on the poet which he had first given at the Reformed Academy of Geneva in the early 1590s.[35] But by 1605, Casaubon had moved to Paris, where he was prohibited from teaching publicly on account of his Protestantism and instead supported by direct grants from the French crown.[36] Casaubon's freedom from teaching allowed him to transform a line-by-line exposition of Persius into one of the most substantial and sophisticated of all Renaissance commentaries.[37] More importantly, he also produced his *De satyrica*, a book too wide-ranging to fit neatly into a standard course of undergraduate lectures on an individual poet. Indeed, Heinsius himself warned Casaubon that his long, digressive commentary 'would not be useful to students', and this warning in turn prompted Casaubon to publish the *De satyrica* as a separate piece rather than as a preface to the edition of Persius.[38] It is worth pausing to appreciate just how unusual the standalone format of the *De satyrica* was, regardless of its methods or conclusions. It was perhaps

---

[33] Paul R. Sellin, *Daniel Heinsius and Stuart England* (Leiden: University Press; New York: Oxford University Press), 16–17.

[34] Heinsius, 'De satyra Horatiana', 66–7. For instance, his *Hercules Tuam Fidem* (Leiden, 1608), an attack on the Jesuit polemicist Kaspar Schoppe and the rest of his order. On Schoppe, see Herbert Jaumann (ed.), *Kaspar Schoppe (1576–1649), Philologe im Dienste der Gegenreformation: Beiträge zur Gelehrtenkultur des europäischen Späthumanismus* (Frankfurt: Vittorio Klostermann, 1998).

[35] Mark Pattison, *Isaac Casaubon, 1559–1614* (2nd edn, Oxford: Clarendon Press, 1892), 43–6, 99–101.

[36] Pattison, *Isaac Casaubon*, 156–67; Hardy, *Criticism and Confession*, 32–5, 55–7.

[37] On Casaubon's commentary and its significance, see Mark Morford, *Persius* (Boston: Twayne Publishers, 1984), 100–01.

[38] Casaubon to Heinsius, 11 July 1605, Isaac Casaubon, *Epistolae*, ed. Theodoor Jansson van Almeloveen (Rotterdam, 1709), 242: 'After … you persuaded me that the verbal *largesse* which I had used in [my commentary on] Persius would not be useful to students, I decided not to be sparing with my words, and not always to keep count of them in writing. The result of this was that two little books emerged out of the argument which I had initially intended to form the Prolegomena.'

the first modern 'monograph', a term which Casaubon himself adopted,[39] on a literary-historical subject. Few, if any, books had narrated the history of a single mode of writing in such a focused and exacting way.

At the same time, Casaubon's arguments were also shaped by his own place within late Renaissance literary culture. Few late humanist scholars of ancient satire were not also authors or assiduous readers of modern satirical writing.[40] Casaubon's commentary on Persius contains long digressions on topics of contemporary relevance, such as whether French poetry can be composed in blank verse and classical metres.[41] Most importantly, unlike Heinsius, Casaubon was not an author of satire, and his socio-political orientation inclined him towards the genre's less directly polemical, more oblique, and philosophical tendencies. This can be seen in his account of how Roman satire gradually cast off its primitive associations with the 'excessive and immoderate liberty of insulting anyone and everyone, whether they were a private individual or magistrate', which its first practitioner, Lucilius, had imported from the Attic Old Comedy.[42] As J. H. M. Salmon has suggested,[43] Casaubon's squeamishness may have reflected the specific religio-political situation in which he was writing, after his patron, King Henri IV, had engineered the end of the French Wars of Religion. The Wars had been an age of vicious, personal libels and lampoons, which sometimes justified their methods by alleging precedents in Roman verse satire and ultimately in the figure of the melancholic, abusive 'satyr' with whom that genre was customarily associated.[44] By downplaying satire's links to Old Comedy and to cultures of public invective, Casaubon was not simply offering a revisionist history of an ancient genre: he was also trying to signal the end of a certain vernacular tradition. But Casaubon's stance also had an immediate personal significance. Whereas Heinsius was the author of satirical invective, Casaubon was the target of it: like other prominent Protestant intellectuals, he was routinely lampooned in Latin prose satires by Jesuit and other Catholic polemicists.[45] It was in the dedication of his *De satyrica* that Casaubon first lamented this tendency in print,[46] and he spent the remaining years of his life resisting the urge to retaliate against his enemies.

---

[39] For Casaubon's use of the Latinized Greek term 'monobibla' to refer to books treating a single subject within ancient history, see his letters to Jacques-Auguste de Thou, 27 October 1593, and to Jean Vassan, 5 October 1607 (Casaubon, *Epistolae*, 6 and 302).

[40] Anthony Grafton, 'Petronius and Neo-Latin Satire: The Reception of the Cena Trimalchionis', *Journal of the Warburg and Courtauld Institutes*, 53 (1990), 237–49.

[41] Persius, *Satirarum Liber*, ed. Isaac Casaubon (Paris, 1605), 131–4.

[42] Casaubon, *De satyrica Graecorum poesi*, 274–6 (2.3), here 276.

[43] J. H. M. Salmon, 'French Satire in the Late Sixteenth Century', in *Renaissance and Revolt: Essays in the Intellectual and Social History of Early Modern France* (Cambridge: Cambridge University Press, 1987), 73–97 (94–5).

[44] See, for instance, the long and rich discussion of the role of personal insult in Roman verse satire and its Greek origins in the printer's second preface to the famous *Satyre Ménippée: de la vertu du catholicon de'Espagne et de la tenue des estats de Paris* (Paris: Champion, 2007), 160–1.

[45] Pattison, *Isaac Casaubon*, 217–18, 389–91.

[46] Casaubon, *De satyrica Graecorum poesi*, sig. a3v.

Last of all the underlying factors that separated Scaliger's work from Casaubon's was the relationship between their methods and their scholarly ethos. Scaliger was a harsh critic: besides castigating Persius for his obscurity and the ancient grammarians for their learned ignorance, he famously entered into drawn-out polemics with Erasmus,[47] and with the natural philosopher Girolamo Cardano.[48] Scaliger's self-confident, aggressive mode of argument had an epistemological as well as a psychological dimension: as a philosopher-polymath, he claimed to be able to transcend knowledge of particulars and see into the true natures of things and of disciplines. Casaubon, by contrast, preferred humility in both his intellectual practices and his rhetoric. His preface to Persius cautioned that judging poetry was difficult, for good judgement, as the author of the ancient treatise *On the Sublime* had remarked, could only be acquired through long experience.[49] Casaubon's disagreements with Scaliger were tempered by praise of his profound learning, and he preferred in general not to name scholars whose claims he was disputing.[50] 'Modesty' was a watchword of Casaubon's scholarship.

Historicism and Value-Judgement in the 'Discourse'

Having surveyed the intellectual, literary, and cultural landscape in which Dryden's late humanist precursors were working, it is now possible to see that Dryden engaged just as much with their basic sympathies and preoccupations as he did with those of their insular, vernacular contemporaries, Shakespeare and Jonson. Of course, this distinction between Continental and domestic culture can be overdrawn. Casaubon spent the last four years of his life in London, under the patronage of James I. As one contemporary of Dryden noted, he died in communion with the Church of England and he was buried in Westminster Abbey with a prominent monument.[51] His work on ancient

---

[47] Anthony Grafton, 'Scaliger, Julius Caesar', in Peter G. Bietenholz and Thomas Brian Deutscher (eds.), *Contemporaries of Erasmus: A Biographical Register of the Renaissance and Reformation*, 3 vols. (Toronto: University of Toronto Press, 1985), 3: 212–14.

[48] Guido Giglioni, 'Scaliger versus Cardano versus Scaliger', in Jill Kraye, David A. Lines, and Marc Laureys (eds.), *Forms of Conflict and Rivalries in Renaissance Europe* (Göttingen: Vandenhoeck & Ruprecht, 2015), 109–30.

[49] For the quotation, see Medine, 'Isaac Casaubon's *Prolegomena* to the *Satires* of Persius', 278 (erroneously printing χρίσις for the 1605 edition's κρίσις). Casaubon quotes from pseudo-Longinus, *On the Sublime*, 1.6. For the translation, see Aristotle, Pseudo-Longinus, and Demetrius, *Poetics; On the Sublime; On Style*, trans. Stephen Halliwell et al. (2nd edn, Cambridge, MA: Harvard University Press, 1995), 177: 'judgement in literature is the ultimate fruit of ripe experience'.

[50] Medine, 'Isaac Casaubon's *Prolegomena* to the *Satires* of Persius', 288–9.

[51] Thomas Smith to John Batteley, 22 October 1698, Bodleian Library, MS Smith 56, 23: 'our Church, whose constitution hee admired, and in whose communion hee dyed, Bishop Andrews [Lancelot Andrewes] giving him the holy Sacrament.' For Casaubon's funeral and burial, see Pattison, *Isaac Casaubon*, 418.

poets, including Persius, influenced Jonson;[52] his edition of Persius was republished in England by his son, a prominent Anglican clergyman,[53] and his writings found their way into student reading lists.[54] Casaubon thus has a reasonable claim to being Renaissance England's greatest literary critic. Heinsius's connections with England are similarly well documented.[55] Even if Casaubon and Heinsius had enjoyed much less contact with England, however, they would still have loomed large in Dryden's own view of the recent history of criticism. It is now possible to appreciate that their works were much more to Dryden than repositories of literary-historical facts and observations, as his casual reference to the 'informations' provided by earlier scholars might suggest.[56]

Dryden's debts begin with the very form of the 'Discourse'. Arranged primarily as a historical narrative of the genre, and dealing with all of the major Roman satirists rather than concentrating on one in particular, the 'Discourse' closely resembles Casaubon's 'monograph' *De satyrica*. The long, essayistic study of a genre's entire history was still not a popular format by Dryden's time, and there were few models at his disposal other than Casaubon's.[57] Even Dryden himself tended to keep his critical works shorter, more desultory, and more closely tied to the poems and translations which they prefaced.

The copiousness of the 'Discourse' reinforced the impression of a genre which was heterogeneous, historically unstable, and still up for grabs, and it underlined Dryden's commitment to a tentative, relativist, and subjective mode of criticism. Dryden used Casaubon, Heinsius, Rigault, and Dacier to paint a portrait of a porous genre which was constantly surrounded by a number of generic alternatives, with each of its manifestations being affected by those alternatives in different ways. In its early history, especially, Roman satire was close to several other cultural forms, not all of which were strictly poetic: these included extemporized, semi-prosaic lampoons delivered at religious festivals; dramatic farces and interludes; parody; burlesque; and verse invectives levelled at specific individuals.[58] Both satire and its counterparts were written in a

---

[52] Wesley Trimpi, *Ben Jonson's Poems: A Study of the Plain Style* (Stanford: Stanford University Press, 1962), 77; David McPherson, 'Ben Jonson's Library and Marginalia: An Annotated Catalogue', *Studies in Philology*, 71 (1974), 3–106 (14); Medine, 'Isaac Casaubon's *Prolegomena* to the *Satires* of Persius', 271; Eugene D. Hill, 'A Generic Prompt in Jonson's *Timber, or, Discoveries*', in A. D. Cousins and Alison V. Scott (eds.), *Ben Jonson and the Politics of Genre* (Cambridge: Cambridge University Press, 2009), 190–7 (192–5).

[53] Persius, *Satirarum Liber*, ed. Isaac Casaubon and Meric Casaubon (3rd edn, London, 1647). On Meric Casaubon, see the introduction to *Generall Learning: A Seventeenth-Century Treatise on the Formation of the General Scholar by Meric Casaubon*, ed. Richard Serjeantson (Cambridge: RTM Publications, 1999).

[54] Mordechai Feingold, 'The Humanities', in Nicholas Tyacke (ed.), *The History of the University of Oxford. Volume 4: Seventeenth Century Oxford* (Oxford: Clarendon Press, 1997), 211–357 (249, 258).

[55] Sellin, *Daniel Heinsius and Stuart England*; David McPherson, 'Ben Jonson Meets Daniel Heinsius, 1613', *English Language Notes*, 14 (1976): 105–9.

[56] Dryden, 'Discourse', 28; cited by Gelber, *The Just and the Lively*, 204.

[57] Haugen, *Richard Bentley*, 77.

[58] Dryden, 'Discourse', 30–42, esp. the concluding summary at 42: 'So that the Ancient Satire of the *Romans* was in Extemporary Reproaches: The next was Farce, which was brought from *Tuscany*: To that Succeeded the Plays of [Livius] *Andronicus*, from the old Comedy of the *Grecians*: And out of all these, sprung two several Branches of new *Roman* Satire; like different Cyens from the same Root.'

mixture of metres, including the more conversational iambic as well as the heroic hexameter.[59] Some of its influences were native, including the 'Saturnian' and 'Fescennine' verses and the improvised Atellan farces;[60] others, including the Old Comedy and iambic invectives, were Greek imports.[61]

This part of Dryden's account was, for the most part, a sort of negative history: a story of satire distancing himself from the aforementioned forms, most of which were 'rusti' and more suited to a society which was closer to a state of nature than a fully realized civilization.[62] But Dryden did not draw this distinction very sharply. The Old Comedy of the Greeks was the product of a mature, culturally sophisticated city-state, and it had no less influence on the early Roman satires than their more rudimentary indigenous dramatic and verse forms. Sometimes, satirists abandoned more obscene or invective-laden modes of writing because they faced legal sanction or pressure from their patrons, not because they were deliberately trying to refine their genre.[63] And when such modes were eschewed by later satirists, it was often because they had simply been displaced into other genres, rather than abandoned altogether: Horace, for example, kept his satires relatively genteel by channelling his most splenetic, personal diatribes into his *Odes* and *Epodes*.[64] Even while Dryden made his own preference for a poetry stripped of its primitive baggage clear, he stopped short of excluding it from the definition of satire altogether. Iambic invectives, for example, were described with a typically tentative metaphor as 'the Under-wood of Satire, rather than the Timber-Trees'.[65] Even later Roman satire, Dryden had to admit, could be so devastatingly obscene as to invite censorship.[66]

On the other side of satire, Dryden placed the more cultivated and civilized cultural forms with which satirists ought to align themselves: namely, philosophy and heroic poetry. Philosophy drew satirists' attention away from merely personal quarrels and towards general principles of ethics and civic conduct;[67] by aligning satire with epic, moreover, they distanced the genre metrically from iambic verse and drama, but also committed itself to the 'variety' in subject matter and 'Universal Learning' which were the distinctive merits of heroic poetry, as well as the inculcation of virtue. The variety which epic and satire shared was important to Dryden because it justified his departure from the Aristotelian, neoclassical language of formal perfection and unity. Dryden made this clear near the beginning of the 'Discourse', by first enumerating the Aristotelian unities of action, time, and place, of which tragedy was capable; but proceeding to assert that 'an Heroique poem is certainly the greatest Work of Human Nature' on the grounds of that it has 'more Ornament, and Variety'; that it is instructive

---

[59] Dryden, 'Discourse', 38, 42, 45.
[60] Dryden, 'Discourse', 38, 41.
[61] See, respectively, Dryden, 'Discourse', 42–4, 35.
[62] Dryden, 'Discourse', 29–30, 32, 39.
[63] Dryden, 'Discourse', 32–3, 53, 57–8, 65–7.
[64] Dryden, 'Discourse', 35–6, 58–9.
[65] Dryden, 'Discourse', 35.
[66] Dryden, 'Discourse', 54.
[67] Dryden, 'Discourse', 55–6, 62.

and character-forming; and that it demands 'Universal Genius' and 'Universal Learning' in its creator.[68] All the same things could be said of satire, as Dryden went on to describe it. Indeed, the later story of Roman satire was in part a story of its interactions with epic and its aspirations to the noble, 'masculine' sublimity of heroic verse.[69] It is surely no co-incidence that Dryden claimed that Virgil would have been the greatest satirist if he had tried his hand at the genre.[70]

Dryden's account of satire thus opposed itself to the strictures of neoclassicism, and, whether it associated satire with rustic invective or civilized epic, made a virtue of the genre's diversity. But another aspect of Dryden's opposition to neoclassical criticism manifested itself in the tonal and rhetorical strategies which he used to engage with other scholars and advance his own arguments. Like Casaubon, Dryden laid bare his own investment in more refined, dignified versions of satire and his opposition to obscenity and personal invective. This was a product of his own status as a victim of public mockery, from Buckingham's famous lampoon, *The Rehearsal*, onwards.[71] Dryden's self-consciousness in this case was just one instance of a broader propensity to acknowledge the inevitable subjectivity of literary-critical judgement, especially when it rested on imperfect knowledge of historical particulars that might always be reinterpreted or supplemented by new evidence. He thus made an example of the critic who had spectacularly failed to show any epistemic humility, the 'insolent' Julius Caesar Scaliger, who asserted the continuity of Greek satyr-play and Roman satire with very tenuous evidence.[72] A much better example had been set by Casaubon: in demolishing the 'supercilious' and 'vain-glorious' Scaliger's assumptions, Casaubon dealt with Scaliger, if anything, too leniently: 'as a Modest Scholar with a Master'.[73] Dryden himself, accordingly, signalled his readiness to defer to the common consensus and 'better Judgments' of the critics when discussing the legal status of verse invective in early Roman history,[74] and designated his discussion of the relative merits of Horace and Juvenal as no more than 'my own Opinion'.[75]

The language and style of the 'Discourse' mirrored the provisionality of the genre itself, as Dryden had depicted it. This mirroring is clearest at the point when Dryden launches into his account of satire and outlines the overarching aims of the 'Discourse': 'To Describe, if not Define, the Nature of that Poem, with its several Qualifications and Virtues, together with the several sorts of it. To compare the Excellencies of *Horace*, *Persius* and *Juvenal*, and shew the particular Manners of their Satires.'[76] The project of

---

[68] Dryden, 'Discourse', 26–7.
[69] Dryden, 'Discourse', 63, 65; cf. the recommendations concerning versification in English satire, 81–2.
[70] Dryden, 'Discourse', 64–5.
[71] Dryden, 'Discourse', 8–9, 59–60.
[72] Dryden, 'Discourse', 36–7.
[73] Dryden, 'Discourse', 52–3.
[74] Dryden, 'Discourse', 33.
[75] Dryden, 'Discourse', 58.
[76] Dryden, 'Discourse', 26.

'definition' is presented as a receding, possibly unachievable goal, to be replaced by discussion of its 'several sorts' and the 'particular Manners' of its authors. With this evasive declaration of intent, Dryden prepares his readers for his own failure to replace Heinsius's definition of satire with something more reliable.

Conclusion

Both the objective facts about satire and the subjective problems of judgement made Dryden reluctant to attempt to define the genre. In this respect, Dryden's 'Discourse' was a representative of a long tradition of literary-historical scholarship that had risen to prominence in the Latinate, humanistic world of the late Renaissance and was now starting to pervade vernacular English literary criticism as well. But the idea that Dryden was writing a form of 'literary history' does not sit comfortably with current scholarly orthodoxies, for a number of reasons.

The first reason is that the abundant precedents for Dryden's approach in earlier literary criticism have been overlooked. The history of literary criticism in the Renaissance, and especially in Renaissance England, gives very little space to anything that resembles Casaubon, Heinsius, and Dryden's 'literary history'. Its heroes are figures like Philip Sidney, and its awareness of Continental, Latinate alternatives to English vernacular poetics and rhetoric is dim.[77] This is partly because early modernists do not cope well with Latin sources that have not already been translated, and so their understanding of 'humanist' literary criticism begins and ends with canonical earlier writers like Erasmus. But it is also because of a much deeper-running bias in their understanding of classical poetics as a whole. Classical poetics was more empirical in its methods and more preoccupied by historical particulars than most scholars of its early modern reception have acknowledged.[78] Early modern critics themselves could see this scholarly tradition clearly enough, because their knowledge of ancient 'criticism' stretched beyond Aristotle's *Poetics*, Plato, Horace, Quintilian, and Longinus to encompass grammarians, anonymous scholiasts, and other commentators whose work did not simply replicate or dispute philosophical abstractions.[79] Early modern scholars' identification of 'criticism' as an art rooted in history was not without classical foundations.

---

[77] The essays gathered in Glyn P. Norton (ed.), *The Cambridge History of Literary Criticism. Volume 3: The Renaissance* (Cambridge: Cambridge University Press, 1999) are representative.

[78] The literature on the scholarly dimensions of ancient literary criticism is substantial. For some particularly important sources and recent discussions, see Sextus Empiricus, *Against the Grammarians (Adversus Mathematicos I)*, ed. and trans. David L. Blank (Oxford: Clarendon Press, 1998), secs 43–4, 76–9, 91–5, 248–54; Suetonius, *De grammaticis et rhetoribus*, ed. Robert A. Kaster (Oxford: Oxford University Press, 1995), sec. 4.1–6, 24.1–4.

[79] For Casaubon's use of ancient scholia, see Anthony Grafton and Joanna Weinberg, *'I Have Always Loved the Holy Tongue': Isaac Casaubon, the Jews, and a Forgotten Chapter in Renaissance Scholarship* (Cambridge, MA: Belknap Press, 2011), 15–17.

Indeed, they could even find support for it in Aristotle himself, when they looked beyond the relatively lean, abstract *Poetics* and considered the role of historical erudition in the rest of his works.[80]

If scholars of the later Renaissance have overlooked humanist literary history, however, scholars of Restoration criticism are no less guilty of doing so. Putting aside the challenges of working across two periods, this neglect can be put down to the fact that the historical orientation of late Renaissance criticism upsets widespread assumptions about the distinctiveness of post-Restoration literary culture. It is now common, for example, to attribute the scepticism and subjectivism of Dryden's critical prose to the forms of research and styles of writing advocated by practitioners of the new experimental natural philosophy.[81] Even Douglas Lane Patey's magisterial, broad-minded survey of pre- and post-Restoration thinking about the relationship between probability and certainty in philosophical and literary discourse gave very little attention to historical writing,[82] and preferred to trace the sceptical tendencies in Dryden's critical prose to the rise of the new philosophy or to restrict them to the genre of dialogue.[83] As a result, it has become harder for specialists in post-Restoration criticism to see any longer-term continuities, and appreciate how Dryden might have learned to write a provisional, open-ended literary history from late Renaissance scholars whose work owed nothing to experimental philosophy and whose overriding interest was in the study of culture, not nature.

A further reason for the eclipse of Dryden's literary-historical interests has to do with ingrained assumptions about the ultimate incompatibility of 'scholarly' or 'historicist' approaches to literary texts and approaches that prioritize value-judgement, appreciation, and edification. These assumptions can be found in studies of the late Renaissance, but they are especially prominent in the various, overlapping historiographies of literary criticism in the long eighteenth century, from the 'Quarrel of the Ancients and Moderns' and the 'Battle of the Books', to the many studies of the diverging paths supposedly taken by academic and 'polite', 'public', or 'gentlemanly' forms of literary criticism in the long eighteenth century. We are only just starting to push beyond the assumption that the late seventeenth and early eighteenth centuries witnessed an inevitable clash between two competing branches of the humanist legacy: on the one hand, those who devoted themselves to the study of classical literature for its enduring moral, intellectual, and

---

[80] For the role of erudition in Aristotle's writings on poetics, see Philodemus, *On Poems: Books 3-4. With the Fragments of Aristotle, On Poets*, ed. Richard Janko (Oxford: Oxford University Press, 2011), 317–18, 321–2, 390–7. For the relationship between Aristotelian philosophy and scholarship in the period more generally, see Gianna Pomata and Nancy G. Siraisi (eds.), Historia: *Empiricism and Erudition in Early Modern Europe* (Cambridge, Mass.: MIT Press, 2005).

[81] Michael Gavin, *Invention of English Criticism* (Cambridge: Cambridge University Press, 2015), 39–43; drawing on the seminal study by Steven Shapin and Simon Schaffer, *Leviathan and the Air-Pump: Hobbes, Boyle, and the Experimental Life* (Princeton: Princeton University Press, 1985).

[82] Douglas Lane Patey, *Probability and Literary Form: Philosophic Theory and Literary Practice in the Augustan Age* (Cambridge: Cambridge University Press, 1984), 47.

[83] See the discussion of Dryden's *Essay*, Patey, *Probability and Literary Form*, 173–4.

aesthetic value, and on the other, the more specialized scholars who used historical criticism to show that ancient values were in fact incommensurable with modern ones.[84] Similarly, it is often said that Augustan and later literary critics placed themselves firmly on the non-academic, non-technical side of any divide between 'polite' culture and professional scholarship.[85] But Dryden's work on satire is too steeped in erudition which it neither repudiates nor masks to be placed firmly in one or the other of these categories. For all their learning, Dryden and his scholarly precursors remained concerned with questions of value, even as they proposed softer, more qualified answers to them than critics like Julius Caesar Scaliger had.[86] As such, their work is difficult to insert into any narrative of a conflict between value-laden and value-free approaches to texts. This may indicate that historians of late Renaissance and early Enlightenment criticism need a new narrative, one based on the hypothesis that historicism and value-judgement were compatible or even complementary.

The final reason for the diminished stature of Dryden's 'Discourse' within the Augustan critical canon is perhaps the most important, because it has to do with the ways in which the history of criticism is structured and written. The history of criticism is still, for the most part, a history of significant individual texts, ideas, critics, and, occasionally, set-piece debates. It is rarely, on the other hand, approached as a history of critical practices: as a kind of work on a set of primary sources whose outcome is determined not only by the ideas, ideology, or writing style of the critic doing it, but also on that critic's technical abilities, working methods, and bibliographical resources. More than most of his critical writing, Dryden's 'Discourse' demands that its readers take the latter approach as well as the former, and pay attention to the depths of his intellectual labour as well as the surfaces of his prose. In this respect, it may seem derivative. But what appears to be dutiful borrowing from Casaubon, Heinsius, Rigault, and Dacier actually turns out to be a dynamic dialogue with multiple generations of earlier critics, which required Dryden to face the same profound, consequential decisions about the relationship between literature, criticism, and history as his humanist precursors had.

---

[84] This was the theme of Joseph M. Levine, *The Battle of the Books: History and Literature in the Augustan Age* (Ithaca: Cornell University Press, 1991). See the perceptive and forceful essay review by John Traugott in *Modern Philology* 91 (1994), 501–8. For more recent critiques from various perspectives, see the studies cited in n. 10.

[85] Gavin, *Invention of English Criticism*, 22; Robin Valenza, *Literature, Language, and the Rise of the Intellectual Disciplines in Britain, 1680–1820* (Cambridge: Cambridge University Press, 2009), 18, 50.

[86] Casaubon's conception of 'criticism' encompassed value-judgement as well as historical interpretation and reconstruction: see Hardy, *Criticism and Confession*, 40–1. The same was true of Heinsius: see esp. Meter, *The Literary Theories of Daniel Heinsius*, 16–18.

CHAPTER 24

MOCK-SCIENTIFIC LITERATURE

GREGORY LYNALL

Parody and Science in the Culture of Print

In Section V of Jonathan Swift's *A Tale of a Tub* (1704), 'A Digression in the Modern Kind', the narrator remarks upon the apparent brilliance of William Wotton's *Reflections upon Ancient and Modern Learning* (1694), which had been commissioned by the Royal Society to chronicle the achievements of recent thinkers and experimenters:

> A Book never to be sufficiently valued, whether we consider the happy Turns and Flowings of the Author's Wit, the greatest Usefulness of his Sublime Discoveries upon the Subject of *Flies* and *Spittle*, or the laborious Eloquence of his Stile. And I cannot forbear doing that Author the Justice of my publick Acknowledgements, for the great *Helps* and *Liftings* I had out of his incomparable Piece, while I was penning this Treatise.[1]

This mock-encomium captures some of the ways in which 'scientific' writing was viewed by its antagonists in the Restoration and early eighteenth century: it is not only suspicious of the utility of the kinds of learning the new experimental philosophy was producing, but also abusive towards what it perceives to be the prosaic dissemination of that knowledge. Within the ironies of the second sentence, however, is Swift's own admission that *Reflections* was a significant source of information, parodic borrowing, and satirical provocation when he wrote the *Tale* and its associated works in the late 1690s.

---

[1] Jonathan Swift, *A Tale of a Tub and Other Works*, ed. Marcus Walsh (Cambridge: Cambridge University Press, 2010), 83–4.

The complex relationship between hypotext and parody suggested by the *Tale* is also apparent in the period's many other mock-scientific works. The mode generally designated 'parody' creates a variety of reverential, comic, and satiric effects which lie across a wide tonal spectrum, from near-pastiche at one end to travesty at the other. Whilst there have been attempts to sub-divide, or even substantially re-define parody,[2] discrete distinctions will not be made here, since such classifications reduce our awareness of the multiple inflections contained within a work towards its originating hypotext (as the *Tale* passage illustrates). Similarly, the chapter uses the term 'scientific' interchangeably with 'natural philosophical' and 'natural historical' to describe the kinds of knowledge and practice we now associate with the natural sciences. As I argue elsewhere, satire and parody as cultural modes were involved in determining the disciplinary and social boundaries of the new sciences during this period.[3] This chapter considers more specifically the imitation and mockery of the *writing* of science: the formal, stylistic, and paratextual parameters of which were themselves under significant development in the mid- to late seventeenth century. Such parodies were not always, or at least not only, critiques of the sciences they alluded to but also served as vehicles of satire against other targets, particularly the religious and political.

Natural philosophers were highly attentive to the linguistic propriety of their writings and took care to persuade that written accounts had the authority to provide proof of matter of fact. Thomas Sprat claimed that Royal Society members aspired to a 'primitive purity' in verbal expression, discarding 'amplifications, digressions, and swellings of style' in favour of a 'naked, natural way of speaking'.[4] This movement to a 'plain style' is misinterpreted sometimes as a rejection of all figurative language, rather than its excesses; whereas in reality, scientists were open to the possibilities of rhetorical tropes and 'literary' modes.[5] Historians of science have also shown how, in order to enhance the plausibility of their observations and experiments, many Royal Society fellows eschewed making generalized statements in their essays and instead narrated the first-person experience of the observer within specific events, in order to create a kind of 'virtual witnessing' within the reader. This emphasis on circumstantial detail was allied with investment in the figure of the author as guarantor of truth.[6] What has been hitherto missing from scholarship, however, is a recognition of the ways in which mock-scientific writings (normally published anonymously or pseudonymously) staged their

---

[2] See esp. Gérard Genette, *Palimpsests: Literature in the Second Degree*, trans. Channa Newman and Claude Doubinsky (Lincoln: University of Nebraska Press, 1997), 24–5.

[3] See Gregory Lynall, 'Science', in *The Oxford Handbook of Eighteenth-Century Satire*, ed. Paddy Bullard (Oxford: Oxford University Press, 2019), 387–402.

[4] Thomas Sprat, *The History of the Royal-Society of London, For the Improving of Natural Knowledge* (1667), 113.

[5] See esp. Claire Preston, *The Poetics of Scientific Investigation in Seventeenth-Century England* (Oxford: Oxford University Press, 2015).

[6] See esp. Steven Shapin, 'Pump and Circumstance: Robert Boyle's Literary Technology', *Social Studies of Science*, 14 (1984), 481–520, and Peter Dear, '*Totius in verba*: Rhetoric and Authority in the Early Royal Society', *Isis*, 76 (1985), 145–61 (152–4).

own appeals to trustworthiness in order to not only ridicule the essay form's credentials in communicating the validity of natural knowledge but also gain satiric authority for their spoofing.

The importance of Wotton's popularizing *Reflections* to the *Tale*'s engagement with science draws attention to the many different (and evolving) forms of prose writing which then encompassed 'scientific literature'. Along with the essay, these included the epistle, dialogue, compendium, cosmogonical narrative, physico-theological sermon, and travel account, and these forms also found rhetorical means to corroborate the veracity of the learning they promoted. Correspondingly, mock-scientific works exploited the discursive multiplicities and stylistic pretensions of their 'genuine' counterparts. Samuel Butler's 'An Occasional Reflection on Dr. Charleton's Feeling a Dog's Pulse at Gresham College by R. B. Esq.', for instance, reports on Royal Society experiments in the form of Robert Boyle's meditative, heavily stylized, and analogizing writing. It argues hyperbolically that 'a Dog's Leg [may] contribute something to the public Good of Mankind, and Commonwealth of Learning', serving to caricature both the physico-theological moments of Boyle's *Occasional Reflections upon Several Subjects* (1665) and the utilitarian discourse of the Society's *Philosophical Transactions*. Moreover, Butler charges Boyle's prose with a pompous verbosity, far removed from plain style, which aggrandizes experimental practice in the meanest of fields, when a physician 'condescend[s] to animadvert the languishing diastole of an expiring mongrel'.[7]

Print itself had a role to play in the dissemination of science, as writers and editors took advantage of the ways in which book design (including illustration and paratextual citation) could help to validate new, often practical, knowledge.[8] Yet, as we will see, parodic works exploited these same textual elements in order to confer epistemic authority upon their own attacks. Publishing scientific knowledge within periodicals also bestowed new kinds of credibility, although this was dependent upon careful management of corporate identity and publishing practicalities. In particular, the *Philosophical Transactions*, first published in 1665, presented themselves as collaborative productions whose individual essays (reports of experiments performed at Society meetings, or extracts of correspondence) had been approved by a royal-chartered institution, despite this periodical almost always being under the stewardship of a single editor (the Society's secretary) as a private enterprise. As will be explored later in the chapter, William King both targeted satirically and utilized parodically the problems associated with the *Transactions* as an individual venture. The bookseller John Dunton's *Athenian Mercury* (originally *Athenian Gazette*) (1691–7), however, exploited the authority accorded the institutionalized periodical by presenting itself as the publication

---

[7] *The Genuine Remains in Verse and Prose of Mr. Samuel Butler*, ed. Robert Thyer, 2 vols. (1759), 1: 406, 410. Swift's *A Meditation upon a Broom-Stick* (1701) also parodies Boyle's 'meleteticks', but its engagement with science is more subtle. See Gregory Lynall, *Swift and Science: The Satire, Politics, and Theology of Natural Knowledge, 1690–1730* (Basingstoke: Palgrave Macmillan, 2012), 23–32.

[8] See Adrian Johns, *The Nature of the Book: Print and Knowledge in the Making* (Chicago: University of Chicago Press, 1998), esp. 31, 44.

of a group of virtuosi: in reality, this 'society' existed only in print, and all articles were written by Dunton with just two or three others.[9] Publishing translations of articles from continental journals such as *Acta Eruditorum* added to its overall credentials, as did the tendency to cite scientific authorities when answering any sort of query.[10] Yet this preoccupation with cultivating intellectual credibility did not stop the *Mercury* from occasionally mocking the writing of contributors to the *Transactions*. The devotional raptures of Boyle and Antoni van Leeuwenhoek, for instance, inform the excited celebrations of such topics as the abundance of animalcula in semen, which receives the appropriately ejaculatory *'Marvellous are thy works, O Lord!'*.[11] Indeed, such sly pokes assert an air of stylistic superiority, gentlemanly disinterest, and sober but witty collaboration in the *Mercury*'s query-answering, over what it caricatures as the personalized, sometimes even histrionic *Transactions* papers: a pose which King would repeat ad nauseam.

To illustrate the parodic complexity and satiric power of mock-scientific prose in further detail, the rest of the chapter will explore works by Swift, Daniel Defoe, William King, Joseph Addison, and Richard Steele. The other authors warrant little introduction, but King—the least famous, and yet most prolific writer of the mock-scientific—will be considered more thoroughly. To varying degrees, the five authors' writings testify to the sizeable imaginative potency of science within comic, parodic, and satiric prose of the period, and show how mock-scientific literature contributed to debates about the epistemological, rhetorical, and socio-political parameters of natural knowledge.

SWIFT, DEFOE, AND THE MECHANICS OF MOCK-SCIENCE

Swift's *A Tale of a Tub*, 'Written for the Universal Improvement of Mankind', is a veritable *omnium gatherum* of different forms of knowledge, often conflated to form the narrator's mock-scientific systems, cosmologies, and principles: Section I's 'Physicological Scheme' uses Epicurean notions of gravity and Boylean pneumatics to explain the power of words; the Taylor-worshippers' clothes cosmology in Section II fuses alchemical notions with corpuscular philosophy and physico-theology; Section

---

[9] See Adrian Johns, 'Miscellaneous Methods: Authors, Societies and Journals in Early Modern England', *The British Journal for the History of Science*, 33 (2000), 159–86 (179–85).

[10] See, for example, The Supplement to the first Volume of *The Athenian Gazette*, 1. 18 (23 May 1691), and *The Athenian Mercury*, 6. 27 (26 March 1692), 1.

[11] *The Athenian Oracle: Being an Entire Collection of the Valuable Questions and Answers in the Old Athenian Mercuries*, 3rd edn, 4 vols. (1728), 1: 516. See T. Christopher Bond, 'Keeping up with the Latest Transactions: The Literary Critique of Scientific Writing in the Hans Sloane Years', *Eighteenth-Century Life*, 22 (1998), 1–17 (12).

IX narrativizes madness through both humoral and iatro-mechanical discourses.[12] Structurally, however, Swift's most 'mock-scientific' early work is probably the *Discourse Concerning the Mechanical Operation of the Spirit* appended to the *Tale*. The putative author reports to be a member of Gresham College (and, by association, the Royal Society) and has written a 'Letter to a Friend' reminiscent of epistles published in the *Philosophical Transactions*.[13] The central topic, the artificiality of the '*lifting up of the Soul or its Faculties above Matter*' by dissenters, seems to be derived from Meric Casaubon's *Treatise Concerning Enthusiasme* (1655), which asserted Anglican suspicion of the possibility of inspiration and assigned such episodes of religious ecstasy to medical causes. Like Swift's narrator, the humanist Casaubon cites classical analogues and calls upon the authority of physicians and naturalists.[14] What Swift adds to this tradition of anti-enthusiasm, however, is a virtuoso-narrator whose 'scientific' credentials are borne out less in the subject matter and more in his approach, which is apparently based on 'many judicious Observations', traces the 'whole Course and Method', 'produc[es] parallel Instances, and relat[es] certain Discoveries' (172–3). The narrator also seeks to immerse readers within the reported experience through a kind of vicarious witnessing: 'a small glimmering Light begins to appear, and dance before you. Then, by frequently moving your Body up and down, you perceive the Vapors to ascend very fast, till you are perfectly dosed [then] you find your self prompted [. . .] by a meer spontaneous Impulse' (176). Guiding the audience's imaginations through second-person address acts as a textual simulation of the hypnotic action of the 'Spirit', and yet the instructional mode heightens the sense of artificiality.

The narrator also brings an array of scientific interests into play in order to explain the phenomenon of mechanical enthusiasm, as befits an eclectic virtuoso during this 'pre-disciplinary' period. He pays excessive attention to geometrical shape and subscribes to the theory of the mother's woman's imagination ('These Heads, thus formed into a perfect Sphere [. . .], were most exposed to the view of the Female Sort, which did influence their Conceptions so effectually'), reduces the brain to 'only a Crowd of little Animals' (parodying Thomas Willis's neurology), cites 'Chymists', and, like the *Tale*'s narrator, tries to evaluate the physical 'Force, or Energy' of words.[15] The closest we might come to identifying a parodic hypotext is Joseph Glanvill's *Scepsis Scientifica* (1665), which Swift read during the late 1690s when working on the *Tale*, and dismissed as a 'fustian piece of abominable curious Virtuoso Stuff'.[16] There Glanvill acknowledges how the

---

[12] *Tale*, 3, 39, 49–50, 106–8. See Gregory Lynall, 'Swift's Pneumatics, Fanatics, and Satiric Mechanics', *Swift Studies*, 29 (2014), 6–23, and Lynall, *Swift and Science*, 35–9, 42–5.

[13] *The Mechanical Operation of the Spirit*, in *Tale*, 170. On the *Philosophical Transactions*, see further Chapter 33 on 'Scientific Transactions' by Felicity Henderson.

[14] *Mechanical Operation*, 172, 182, 186, and Meric Casaubon, *A Treatise Concerning Enthusiasme* (1665), 18, 28. See esp. Phillip Harth, *Swift and Anglican Rationalism: The Religious Background of 'A Tale of A Tub'* (Chicago: University of Chicago Press, 1961), 72–5.

[15] *Mechanical Operation*, 174, 179, 186, 180. On parodying Thomas Willis, see Clive T. Probyn, 'Swift's Anatomy of the Brain: The Hexagonal Bite of Poetry', *Notes & Queries*, 219 (1974), 250–1.

[16] Swift to John Winder, 13 January 1698[–9], in *The Correspondence of Jonathan Swift, D. D.*, ed. David Woolley, 4 vols. (Frankfurt am Main: Lang, 1999–2007), 1: 137.

'*Mechanical* way of conveyance and direction of the *Spirits* in *Animal performances* is yet undiscover'd'; and yet his attempt to even speculate on the connection between soul and body was, for Swift's Christian scepticism, perhaps a step too far.[17]

For all of the narrator's ambition to clear up the 'Mystery' of the mechanical operation of the spirit, the 'whole Process of the Operation' is left as a textual lacuna, since the editor 'thought [it] neither safe nor Convenient to Print' (179). We are left with only those elements used to cultivate a (mock-) sense of authority in the absent 'science part'. Ultimately, in applying scientific methodology and theories to religious (and often sexually suggestive) ritual, the *Mechanical Operation* simultaneously ridicules the pretentiousness of the narrating virtuoso in his thinking and writing and, more importantly, uses a materializing gaze to condemn dissenting worship as an artificial, vacuous practice. Yet the precise 'Operation' of Swift's satire in this work, beginning with the identity of the hypotext, is itself often intentionally obfuscatory.

In comparison, the parodic and satiric trajectories of Daniel Defoe's *The Consolidator* (1705) are much more distinguishable. Despite the multiple meanings of 'transaction', *The Consolidator*'s subtitle—*Memoirs of Sundry Transactions From the World in the Moon*—divulges that the Royal Society's journal is one of its parodic models. Its narrative structure and perspective closely resemble the travel accounts found in the *Philosophical Transactions*, and its focus on the discoveries and technologies of Chinese and Lunar societies suggests the narrator is seeking to gratify a virtuoso readership. Although *The Consolidator* alludes to various activities of Royal Society members, it is doubtful that this institution and its periodical are themselves objects of ridicule (especially given Defoe's endorsement of natural philosophy elsewhere).[18] Instead, many of the work's ironies are structural, aimed at a narrator who unblinkingly considers all Chinese and Lunar learning to be far superior to anything the Royal Society is capable of, and whose credulous exoticism extends to believing that the Chinese can even mind-read.[19]

Through the defamiliarizing lens of the moon voyage, science and technology operate as Defoe's principal vehicles of political and religious satire. Partly inspired by Swift's conceits in the *Tale* and *Mechanical Operation*, the narrator's mock-mechanistic analysis allows the Dissenting Defoe to anatomize self-consciously and in intricate detail the 'vast mysterious dark World' of the English church and state.[20] *The Consolidator*'s targets, however, include the High Church Anglican (and Irish) Swift:

---

[17] Joseph Glanvill, *Scepsis Scientifica* (1665), 30. See Swift's sermon *On the Trinity*, in *The Prose Writings of Jonathan Swift*, eds. Herbert Davis and others, 14 vols. (Oxford: Blackwell, 1939–68), 9: 164.

[18] See Ilse Vickers, *Defoe and the New Sciences* (Cambridge: Cambridge University Press, 1996), 70, 56–7.

[19] Daniel Defoe, *The Consolidator, or, Memoirs of Sundry Transactions From the World in the Moon* (1705), 15, 10. The narrator's veneration of China is perhaps intended to satirize William Temple: see G. A. Starr, 'Defoe and China', *Eighteenth-Century Studies*, 43 (2010), 5–54 (43).

[20] See *Consolidator*, 33, 99, 109, 82.

among his Mechanick Operations of the Spirit, [. . .] he form'd his System wholly upon the mistaken Notion of *Wind*, which Learned Hypothesis being directly contrary to the Nature of things in this Climate, where the *Elasticity* of the Air is quite different, and where the *pressure of the Atmosphere* has for want of Vapour no Force, all his Notion dissolv'd [. . .] and flew upward in [. . .] a livid Flame call'd *Blasphemy*, which burnt up all the Wit and Fancy of the Author, and left a strange *Stench* behind. (61–2)

The *Tale*'s anti-Puritan satire is condemned via a conflation of the formal language of Boylean pneumatics with a scatological punchline worthy of Swift himself.[21] Defoe's deployment of natural knowledge brings a tight logic to this satirical conceit: the narrator makes pseudo-factual claims and pursues them as physical principles. This technique is also present in the *Tale* (in Section I's pneumatic account of oratory, for example) but in Swift's hands is often combined with ironic undercutting, textual hiatus, or *reductio ad absurdum* which serve to expose the limits of such tropes, suggesting greater suspicion of science as an explanatory model.

King of Parody

A similar recognition of science's epistemological limitations is evident in the works of William King (1663–1712), who came to prominence as one of Oxford's Christ Church 'Wits'. Like Swift's *Tale* and *Battel of the Books*, the Christ Church collaborations defended the classical scholarship of Charles Boyle against the philological methods of Richard Bentley during the 'Phalaris affair': an intellectual dispute concerning the 'Ancients' and 'Moderns' which also reflected religious, political, and social divisions to some extent (High versus Low Church, Tory against Whig, gentleman-amateur versus professional), and which became increasingly personal.[22] Whilst Swift's *Tale* came under attack from King (at least half-seriously) for its apparent blasphemy and vulgarity, King's works share the *Tale*'s ideological allegiances and their satiric appropriation of the mock-scientific and paratextual, hinting at mutual influence.[23]

King's Lucianic *Dialogues of the Dead* (1699) was directed predominantly at Bentley but struck blows at others in the Moderns' camp. In the ninth dialogue, King's ironies

---

[21] Cf. *Tale*, 34, 38, 99, 105. See further Chapter 18 on 'Heresiography and Religious Controversy' by Nicholas McDowell.

[22] See esp. Lynall, *Swift and Science*, 57–9. On the literary consequences of the Phalaris affair, see further Chapter 21 on 'Learned Wit and Mock-Scholarship' by Henry Power.

[23] See William King, *Some Remarks on The Tale of a Tub* (1704), and Gregory Lynall and Marcus Walsh, 'Edifying by the Margent: Echoing Voices in Swift's *Tale*', in *Reading Swift: Papers from the Sixth Münster Symposium on Jonathan Swift*, eds. Kirsten Juhas, Hermann J. Real, and Sandra Simon (München: Fink, 2013), 159–70 (160–2).

take swipe at natural history and experimental philosophy using what had become, over the seventeenth century, the conventional jokes against the virtuoso:

> *Indifferentio.* Where have you been *Moderno?* [...] you make such a hideous Figure, and are so Dirty, that no Gentleman would come near you? What has your Horse thrown you? Or what's the matter?
> *Moderno.* The matter! Why *I have been in a Ditch.*
> *Indifferentio.* By some Accident, I suppose.
> *Moderno.* Accident! [...] Gentlemen of my *Estate, Fortune, Education, Parts* and *Learning,* don't *use to go into a Ditch* by Accident, but *choice. There has been more true Experience in Natural Philosophy gather'd out of Ditches* in this latter Century, than *Pliny* and *Aristotle* were Masters of both together.[24]

This comic exchange foregrounds how the modern pursuit of natural knowledge came into conflict with the accepted image of the gentleman and the ideals of humanist learning.[25] In particular, the Baconian natural history required the collection of physical specimens to form the basis of taxonomies. The only people with the leisure time and resources to carry out such studies sufficiently were gentlemen, and whilst a degree of learning was needed for genteel accomplishment, 'too much', or of the 'wrong' sort, was the sign of an unhealthy pedant (whose social impropriety is literalized through Moderno's presence in 'Ditches', with all its sexual connotations).[26]

As well as achieving general satire upon the figure of the virtuoso, King's deadpan Moderno is a thinly veiled lampoon of William Wotton. In *Reflections*, Wotton documented the intellectual impact of the Moderns through extensive use of marginal citation, and King's dialogue not only parodied (and quoted verbatim) Wotton's words, but also caricatured his book on the physical page, with side-notes and lengthy, intrusive footnotes which dominate the text. These paratextual excesses perhaps seek to parody at a formal level Wotton's inability to distinguish between significant information and mere trivia.[27] Yet in this imaginative investment in marginalia, King revealed an affinity with the very errors he sought to expose. King is alleged to have made notes on over 22,000 books and manuscripts at Christ Church,[28] and in the *Dialogues* he embraces learned writing and paratextual structures as not only a target but also a vehicle of his satire. To quote, to cite, to index—themselves often disparaged as frivolous pedantry—each

---

[24] William King, *Dialogues of the Dead* (1699), 66–7.

[25] See Steven Shapin, *Never Pure: Historical Studies of Science as if It Was Produced by People with Bodies, Situated in Time, Space, Culture, and Society, and Struggling for Credibility and Authority* (Baltimore: Johns Hopkins University Press, 2010), 171.

[26] Mary Astell's virtuoso has similarly rejected the gentlemanly lifestyle (selling his 'Estate in Land to purchase one in *Scallop*' and abandoning the 'Society of Men for that of *Insects*'), but King's dialogue frame heightens the strangeness and comedy of 'Moderno' in comparison to Astell's characterology. See *An Essay in Defence of the Female Sex* (1696), 96–7.

[27] See Lynall and Walsh, 'Edifying by the Margent', 162.

[28] See Joseph Browne, *Memoirs of the Late Learned and Ingenious Dr. William King* (1732), 16.

served as a method of satiric collection somewhat analogous to the virtuoso's foraging for specimens, of diligently cataloguing 'fault' in every place it was found.

Wotton, echoing Sprat, concluded his *Reflections* by voicing an anxiety that a decline in the study of natural philosophy had been caused by its satiric mistreatment:

> the *ROYAL SOCIETY* has weathered the rude Attacks [...] That Studying of Natural Philosophy and Mathematicks, was a ready Method to introduce Scepticism at least, if not Atheism into the World: Yet the sly Insinuations of the *Men of Wit*, [...] That every Man whom they call a *Virtuoso*, must needs be a *Sir Nicholas Gim-crack*, have so far taken off the Edge of those who have opulent Fortunes, and a Love to Learning, that Physiological Studies begin to be contracted amongst Physicians and Mechanicks. [...] one must spend a good deal of Time and Pains, of Industry and Attention, before he will be able thoroughly to relish them.[29]

These were blossoming yet fragile times for this institution, when the discoveries, theories, and literary methods of scientific practitioners encountered intense scrutiny from 'serious' critics and 'wits' alike. Yet Wotton considers misinformed ironic 'insinuation', not religiously attuned invective, to be doing the damage. This ridicule apparently does not discriminate enough: it condemns the whole 'species' of the virtuoso, and not just those who exhibit the extreme forms of behaviour reminiscent of Gimcrack in Thomas Shadwell's play *The Virtuoso* (1678). Modelled directly on Wotton's conclusion, Moderno states that 'nothing wounds so much as Jest, and when Men once become Ridiculous, their Labours will be slighted, and they will find few Imitators. How far this may deaden the Industry of the Philosophers of the next Age, is not easie to tell'.[30] King's deployment of the word 'Industry' renders the new philosophy as a kind of commercial trade, ironically emphasizing intellectual 'Labour' at a time when the disinterested gentleman-amateur still possessed considerable power as an aspirational model. King's parody of Wotton's worrying demonstrates that taking a stand against one's critics often runs the risk of granting their laughter further exposure.

In *The Transactioneer*, published anonymously in 1700, King continued to interrogate this 'Industry of the Philosophers', and particularly the *Philosophical Transactions* under its current editor, Hans Sloane. King's mocking pamphlet, however, is not a formal parody of the journal, but instead transplants quotations from the *Transactions* into two dialogues, condemning Sloane and his contributors auto-parodically through their own words, which are unexaggerated but often placed out of context. The first dialogue is between a 'gentleman' and a 'virtuoso': the 'gentleman' knows little about the Society, and from this detached vantage point, and with the credit associated with his class, he maintains a cynical, ironic lens through which he interrogates the discourse of natural knowledge; the 'virtuoso' represents a typical, unquestioning reader of the *Transactions* who cannot detect the gentleman's ironies. The second dialogue is between this same

---

[29] William Wotton, *Reflections upon Ancient and Modern Learning* (1694), 357. Cf. Sprat, *History*, 417.
[30] King, *Dialogues*, 57.

'gentleman' and the 'Transactioneer' himself, the fictionalized editor of the *Transactions*, whose suffixed name (-eer) suggests professional and commercial pretensions. This editor is less naïve than the virtuoso, and can recognize when the gentleman is poking fun, but is surprised by the gentleman's attitude and tries to convince him of the importance of the journal and the ideas it disseminates. In effect, the dialogues socialize the *Transactions*, exposing them to scrutiny through interaction with a disinterested, polite audience.

In *The Transactioneer*, Sloane's journal comes under attack for claiming to advance natural knowledge whilst over-valuing the trivial, rare, and exotic, seeming to make no effort to corroborate far-fetched testimony and prioritizing 'Story' over matter of fact, citing such genuine *Transactions* topics as Chinese ear-pickers, a Bolton man who claimed to be 150 years old, and a rain-shower made of butter.[31] Sloane is implied to be a 'Master of only Scraps' who assembles accounts indiscriminately in the same way he augments chaotically his cabinets of physical curiosities. However, King's satirical method—of cataloguing intellectual and stylistic error, by populating the dialogues with quotations collected from the genuine *Transactions*—is in some way analogous to the accusations made of Sloane's editorial process. King also finds much satiric mileage in the journal's stylistic infelicities. For example, the 'virtuoso' cites unsuspectingly the poor syntax one might find, commending the Transactioneer's 'strange Tallent at Stile' in producing such essay titles as: 'Representation of a Limestone Marble found in *Wales*, when polished.'[32] Many of the quotations are accompanied with genuine citations to the *Transactions* (some in the form of side-notes), and this philological attention to detail confers additional satiric authority. The contents page, as a manifestation of the deluge of matters of fact, also shows King to be delighting in the satirical possibilities of the paratext.

The Preface to *The Transactioneer* claims that, in criticizing the current editorial policy, it is offering disciplinary and institutional protection: 'I am mov'd by the Respect I have for Natural Studies, and ... by the trifling and shallow Management of one who wants every Qualification that is requisite for such a Post.' This declaration has been read as wholly ironic, confirming King's 'hostility toward modern virtuosi', or as a 'relatively serious, straightforward statement of the author's attitude' toward Sloane's role as editor.[33] Neither argument is entirely convincing: the *Transactions* were perhaps just as full of unenlightened trivia when his predecessors Henry Oldenburg and Robert Plot were in charge; but this does not prove King's 'anti-scientific' agenda. One could, instead, see the Preface's claims of allegiance as deliberately mischievous, exploiting the

---

[31] William King, *The Transactioneer* (1700), 15, 46, 65.

[32] King, *The Transactioneer*, sig. A2v, 4.

[33] King, *The Transactioneer*, sig. A2v. See Roger D. Lund, '"More Strange than True": Sir Hans Sloane, King's "Transactioneer", and the Deformation of English Prose', *Studies in Eighteenth-Century Culture*, 14 (1985), 213–30 (217), and David G. Engel, '"The Ingenious Dr. King": The Life and Works of Dr William King (1663–1712), with Particular Reference to the Tradition of Menippean Satire', PhD thesis, University of Edinburgh, 1989, 270.

Society's existing fault-lines, which ran between scientific disciplines, social and political affiliations, and personalities. These differences were particularly acute between natural history and natural philosophy, although even within disciplines there was much disagreement about the purpose and value of their studies, and rivalry between competing theories. Correspondingly, the *Transactions* material King chooses *not* to include is perhaps significant in itself. There are, for instance, several mathematics papers edited by Sloane absent from *The Transactioneer*, but it is unclear if this suggests King's tacit approval of a subject with ancient pedigree or that there are limits to the comic potential of algebra compared with such reports as 'A Woman that talk'd Obscenely and offer'd her Cow for a Bag-pipe'.[34]

Whatever the intention, *The Transactioneer* seemed to touch a nerve and was read widely by the scientific community, not just within the small circle of Christ Church. Sloane wrote to the Oxford mathematician John Wallis that he was 'not the least concerned at it', but his desire to know the author's identity shows he was clearly rattled.[35] Wallis knew the author and saw it as beneath someone of King's social standing 'to trifle at that rate ... Such writers are best answered By using night chad. They hurt no body more than themselves'.[36] By the time Sloane received this reply, he had already complained to the Royal Society's Council, and they were investigating (with a view to taking legal action) his accusation that members John Woodward and John Harris had written *The Transactioneer*.[37] In his statement to the Council, Harris commented that the *Transactions* under Sloane were 'not much to the [Society's] Honour', and that he considered satire to be a valid response, but that King had not gone far enough, passing by faults 'y^t do justly deserve Animadversion & Censure'.[38] Although King was allegedly a Christ Church 'Ancient', the concerns he raised were not confined to the margins.[39]

King's comic gaze revisited the Royal Society in 1709, publishing *Useful Transactions in Philosophy and other sorts of Learning* in three issues across the year. His *Journey to London* (1698) had parodied physician and FRS Martin Lister's *A Journey to Paris* (1698) by employing a virtuoso-narrator who made '*Curious* Enquiries after Dust' and celebrated collections of rarities, but King's new mock-journal showed him taking parodic ventriloquism to a new level, writing whole essays which imitate the style and content of *Philosophical Transactions* articles.[40] King revels in the ways the genuine essays represent the acquisition of knowledge and justify its utility. In particular, he exaggerates how the essays represent rhetorically the methodologies of observation and experiment,

---

[34] King, *The Transactioneer*, sig. A4r.
[35] Hans Sloane to John Wallis, 6 February 1699/1700, Wellcome Library MS 7633/1.
[36] Wallis to Sloane, 19 February 1699/1700, Wellcome Library MS 7633/1.
[37] See Charles Richard Weld, *A History of the Royal Society, with Memoirs of the Presidents*, 2 vols. (1838), 1: 353–5.
[38] John Harris to Sir John Hoskins, 27 February 1699/1700, British Library, Sloane MS 4026, fol. 253. See also John Woodward to Hoskins, 28 February 1699/1700, British Library, Sloane MS 3334, fol. 58r.
[39] See esp. Joseph M. Levine, *Dr. Woodward's Shield: History, Science, and Satire in Augustan England* (Berkeley: University of California Press, 1977), 86.
[40] William King, *A Journey to London* (1698), 11, 14–22.

and especially how the narrators position themselves as witnesses of discovery. King seems to suggest that there are limits to empirical narration, hinting that the essay form cannot adequately convey the nature of the specimens under analysis, quoting the microscopist van Leeuwenhoek's lament: 'if I could but represent them to any other Bodies Eyes in the same manner as I saw them my self, they would cry out, WHAT WONDERS ARE THESE.'[41] Ironically, these wondrous topics include the tongue of a wine porter with a hangover, inviting the reader to explore what constitutes suitable objects (from social, moral, theological, philosophical, and utilitarian perspectives) worthy of 'learned and large Dissertation[s]'.[42] Akin to *Dialogues of the Dead*, there is also a social aspect to King's mockery, with the Preface to the first issue parodying Sprat's egalitarian ambitions in its claim that 'Pedlars, Semstresses, Poets, Gipsies, and indeed all sorts of professions, may be useful to the world, if they study Philosophy'.[43]

The second issue of *Useful Transactions* includes 'A Letter Concerning the Migration of Cuckoo's, [...] Communicated by Mr. Martin Cheapum', parodying William Derham's letter to Sloane 'concerning the Migration of Birds'.[44] King's imitation is substantially longer than its hypotext, taking from the original the initial premise of Derham the natural historian narrating his own personal observations of returning migratory birds. This ornithological narrative develops, however, into a comic skit in which the reader learns more and more about Cheapum's unhealthy mind. King parodies Derham's circumstantial and anthropomorphic narration with superfluous details which, rather than affirming to readers the truthfulness of Cheapum's testimony, make us question his sanity: 'I was then walking in my Garden in my new Silk Night-Gown, and a Velvet-Cap. At first I thought he [the Cuckoo] might be surpriz'd at seeing me in that Habit, as having left me in a Stuff one last Year. But upon farther list'ning to him (being vers'd as I shall hereafter acquaint you in the Language of Birds) the first Word he spoke distinctly was *Summer, Summer*.'[45] Cheapum's delusion serves as a structural irony which undermines the utility of knowledge about bird migration and the evidential narration used to support its credibility. But the ultimate impression one gets from this essay, and many of the others in the *Useful Transactions*, is of King's parodies revelling in the ludic comedy of their conceits, with his spoof essays indulging in the kinds of speculation and discourse given licence by Sloane's journal, rather than brutally satirizing the Society's work. Indeed, Cheapum's essay becomes a kind of satirical anatomy, pursuing the ornithological conceit as a means of cultural and social satire which encompasses Thomas

---

[41] William King, *Useful Transactions in Philosophy, and Other Sorts of Learning, For the Months of March and April, 1709* (1709), 29, quoting Antoni van Leeuwenhoek, 'Microscopical Observations upon the Tongue', *Philosophical Transactions*, 26 (1708–9), 122.

[42] See *Useful Transactions ... March and April, 1709*, 16, and *Useful Transactions in Philosophy, For the Months of January and February, 1708-9*, in *The Original Works in Verse and Prose of Dr. William King*, 3 vols. (1776), 2: 59.

[43] *Useful Transactions ... January and February, 1708-9*, 60. See Sprat, *History*, 63–7.

[44] See William Derham, 'Part of a Letter from the Reverend Mr. W. Derham, F.R.S. to Dr. Hans Sloane, R.S. Secr. concerning the Migration of Birds', *Philosophical Transactions*, 26 (1708–9), 123–34.

[45] *Useful Transactions ... March and April, 1709*, 38.

D'Urfey's play *The Wonders of the Sun, or, The Kingdom of the Birds* (1706) and prostitution in Drury Lane, migrating into non-scientific modes of discourse (including theatrical criticism) (41–5).

Other hybrid pieces in the issue create fictional narratives within which they embed scientific papers. For instance, 'The Eunuch's Child' reports on a Venetian legal case in which a scientific expert witness (Seignior Aerio) seeks to prove that a eunuch is the father of a child of disputed parentage. Aerio testifies that potent '*Effluvia*' has been transferred to the mother without contact, in a way analogous to the generation of static electricity, and he proceeds to quote verbatim from Francis Hauksbee's recent papers (3).[46] Placing Hauksbee's accounts of artificial electricity in this fictional context draws out unintended *double endentres*: of giving motion to effluvia 'by the Approach of one's Hand', and of 'GENTLY RUBBING [amber] with my Hand, in the Dark (which was the Head of my Cane)' to produce sparks of light (4, 8). Hauksbee was at this time the Royal Society's curator of experiments, the technician whose manual skills were at the fellows' command, and since 1706 had carried out many of these trials specifically at their instruction, as his essays declared.[47] His experiments—in which hands were crucial in generating and indicating the presence of electricity—are reduced by King to a kind of masturbation, where scientific discovery is dependent upon how quickly one can rub with one's hands rather than think with one's mind. Whilst King's appropriations have hilarious consequences, they also foreground contemporaneous debates about the proximity of gentlemanly and artisanal labour and knowledge, since it was questioned whether 'hands' (referring both to the limbs and employees of experimenters) could generate reliable philosophy as well as visually entertaining demonstrations.[48]

King's third issue was devoted to parodying Sloane's account of his time in Jamaica, and appeared with a frontispiece depicting the Royal College of Physicians on Warwick Lane. Sloane was admitted a fellow in 1687, and the doorway motto 'Enter in order to profit' is a common one for an educational institution but is included here perhaps in order to mock Sloane's mercenary ambitions. The quotation at the bottom of the page— 'He gains each point who has mixed the useful with the pleasing'—is from Horace's *Ars Poetica* and perhaps alludes self-consciously to King's parodic transformation of the *Transactions*.[49] Most interesting about this illustration, however, is the image of the speaking cuckoo soaring high above the college. It has been known since the time of Aristotle that most varieties of cuckoo lay their eggs in the nests of other species.[50]

---

[46] Hauksbee's papers include 'An Account of Some Experiments, Touching the Electricity and Light Producible on the Attrition of Several Bodies', *Philosophical Transactions*, 26 (1708–9), 87–92.

[47] See Hauksbee, 'An Account of Some Experiments', 87.

[48] See Simon Schaffer, 'Experimenters' Techniques, Dyers' Hands, and the Electric Planetarium', *Isis*, 88 (1997), 456–83 (456, 459).

[49] William King, *Useful Transactions in Philosophy, and other sorts of Learning, For the Months of May, June, July, August and September, 1709* (1709), frontispiece; Horace, *Epistles Book II and Epistle to the Pisones (Ars Poetica)*, ed. Niall Rudd (Cambridge: Cambridge University Press, 1989), 70 (l. 343).

[50] See Herbert Friedmann, 'The History of our Knowledge of Avian Brood Parasitism', *Centaurus*, 10 (June 1965), 282–304. The satirical currency of this behaviour is also evident in *The Fable of the Cuckoo, or, The Sentence on the Ill Bird that Defiled his own Nest* (1701).

The behaviour of the cuckoo as a brood parasite is a brilliant metaphor of what King's parody does in creatively invading and living off scientific writing, and this graphic motif shows us again how aspects of the material book could be deployed satirically.

In the *Useful Transactions* especially, King honed the parodic techniques of Butler, Swift, and others into a rich vein of mock-science. Yet the limitations of his mode were soon recognized, as John Gay explained: King had 'a World of Wit, yet as it lies in one particular way of Raillery, the Town soon grew weary'.[51] Just as King's *Useful Transactions* ran its course, the more versatile essays of Addison and Steele were going from strength to strength, and their mock-scientific moments adapted Swift and King's sceptical witness into more of a homage to scientific writing.

FROGS, FACTS, AND FABLES

Addison and Steele were significant figures in the popularization of natural philosophy in early eighteenth-century London. Steele had been educated at Charterhouse school by Thomas Burnet, whose *Sacred Theory of the Earth* (1681) he later commended in the *Spectator*.[52] Steele also invited the controversial Newtonian William Whiston to lecture at Button's coffee-house, publicly endorsed Whiston's longitude method and Derham's *Physico-Theology* (1713) in *The Guardian*, and was something of a projector himself (co-designing a mobile pool for the importation of live fish).[53] Meanwhile, Addison's *Spectator* essays on the pleasures of the imagination promoted natural philosophy, particularly Newtonianism, as a fashionable interest within polite society, associating its pursuit with particular codes of civility and sociability.[54]

However, Addison and Steele's periodicals the *Tatler* (1709–11), the *Spectator* (1711–12), and *The Guardian* (1713) also contained satirical engagements with scientific knowledge. The 'Isaac Bickerstaff' and 'Mr. Spectator' personae pursued a kind of social anthropology through their close observations of the vagaries of human behaviour and deployed stereotypes as a kind of satirical shorthand against the excessive tendencies they witnessed.[55] Some of their essays, therefore, recited the standard repertoire of

---

[51] Gay, *The Present State of Wit* (1711), in *John Gay: Poetry and Prose*, eds. V. A. Dearing and C. E. Beckwith, 2 vols. (Oxford: Clarendon Press, 1974), 2: 449.

[52] *Spectator*, no. 146 (17 August 1711), in Donald F. Bond (ed.), *The Spectator*, 5 vols. (Oxford: Clarendon Press, 1965), 2: 76–7.

[53] On Whiston's lectures, see Marjorie Hope Nicolson and G. S. Rousseau, *'This Long Disease, My Life': Alexander Pope and the Sciences* (Princeton: Princeton University Press, 1968), 142–4, 147; *Guardian*, no. 107 (14 July 1713) and no. 175 (1 October 1713), in *The Guardian*, ed. John Calhoun Stephens (Lexington: University Press of Kentucky, 1982), 371–2, 569–71; Richard Steele, 'An Account of the Fish-Pool' (1718), in *Tracts and Pamphlets*, ed. Rae Blanchard (Baltimore: The Johns Hopkins Press, 1944), 419–52.

[54] See esp. *Spectator*, no. 393 (31 May 1712) and no. 413 (24 June 1712), in Bond (ed.), *Spectator*, 3: 475, 547.

[55] See Charles A. Knight, *A Political Biography of Richard Steele* (London: Pickering & Chatto, 2009), 52–3.

complaints against virtuosi, who are 'utter Strangers to the common Occurrences of Life' and concerned with the 'most minute and trivial Parts of the Creation'.[56] These parodies, like King's, poked fun particularly at what they presented as the scientist's compulsion to publish, which bypassed any consideration of need in favour of profit and self-promotion. For instance, seeking to build on his recent 'Story of the Lion', one of the *Guardian*'s narrators boasts of how 'a considerable number of *Virtuosi* have offered, when my Collections shall swell into a reasonable Bulk, to contribute very handsomely, by way of Subscription, towards the Printing of them in *Folio*'.[57] The ambiguity regarding whether such 'Collections' are textual or anatomical underscores the narrator's misguided principles, focused on material acquisition, to the detriment of intellectual and stylistic value.

Other essays, however, utilized scientific writing more as an agent than a target of satire. For instance, Mr Spectator's dreams of 'Visionary Dissection' by an 'Assembly of Virtuoso's', upon a beau's head and coquet's heart, brilliantly appropriate the languages of anatomy, optics, and thermometry for the purpose of social satire.[58] These related pieces are clearly inspired by Swift's 'Digression on Madness', whose narrator confesses seeing a 'Woman *flay'd*' and ordering a 'Carcass of a *Beau* to be stript'. Yet Addison and Steele replace the *Tale*'s sardonic narration with an urbane speaker whose anatomical indulgences are restricted to the dream realm and operate almost entirely as satirical vehicles: discovering, for instance, how the 'Muscle which turns the [beau's] Eye towards Heaven, did not appear to have been used at all'.[59] Whilst the *Tale*'s autopsical excesses associate scientific investigation with physical and moral violation of the human, Addison and Steele show how the genteel periodical essay form can be a potent medium for the exploration of scientifically inspired conceits which will not compromise their wider endorsement of natural knowledge.

One of their most interesting examples is *Tatler*, no. 236, in which the putative editor Bickerstaff prints a letter on the 'History of the Migration of Frogs' into Ireland, a species importation which in recent years had been overseen by the Royal Society. Bickerstaff remarks that 'The Matter of Fact contained in [the letter] is literally true, tho' the diverting Manner in which it is told may give it the Colour of a Fable'. This clash of content and style, of factual dissemination undermined by appeals to the reader, problematizes the issue of genre in relation to the historiography of science. Ironically, many of the material 'facts' (names, dates, and so forth) are missing, and this 'History' thrives on its quasi-mythical or fairy-tale elements ('A Frog was never known to take Three Leaps upon *Irish* Turf, before he stretched himself out and died'). It also critiques the scientific investment in this colonialist project, since the Society's first attempt

---

[56] *Tatler*, no. 216 (26 August 1710), in Donald F. Bond (ed.), *The Tatler* (Oxford: Clarendon Press, 1987), 3: 132. See also *Tatler*, no. 119 (12 January 1710) and no. 221 (7 September 1710), in Bond (ed.), *Tatler*, 2: 205–09 and 3: 153–7, and *Spectator*, no. 242 (7 December 1711), in Bond (ed.), *Spectator*, 2: 442.

[57] *Guardian*, no. 146 (28 August 1713), in Stephens (ed.), *Guardian*, 479.

[58] *Spectator*, no. 275 (15 January 1712) and no. 281 (22 January 1712), in Bond (ed.), *Spectator*, 2: 570 and 2: 594.

[59] Swift, *Tale*, 112; Bond (ed.), *Spectator*, 3: 572–3.

involved 'a sound Able-bodied Frog ... that had given Proofs of his Vigour by several Leaps which he made before that Learned Body'.[60] The condition of this single specimen received collective verification, but this illustrious body failed to acknowledge that more than one frog is needed to put into practice the (sexual) 'Vigour' necessary for colonization.

The narrative of species introduction outlined by the anonymous correspondent has obvious fabulistic affinities, but it is also abundant with politically allegorical potential, emphasized by mention of frogs' proverbial nickname of '*Dutch* Nightingales', the Battle of the Boyne, French Protestant colonies, and other references which locate it firmly within the Irish colonial context. The introduction of the frogs is itself characterized as a religio-political (and superstitious) act, since the 'very ingenious Physician' and 'very good Protestant' (probably Dr Charles Gwythers or Guither) who successfully imported the frogs showed his 'Zeal against Popery' by placing 'some of the most promising Spawn' in 'St. *Patrick's Well*'.[61] Appropriately, Bickerstaff's concluding comments not only follow the conventional criticisms of the virtuosi, who 'contract and fix' the mind upon 'Trifles', but also hint at the Royal Society's political trespass, calling this institution a 'Confederacy against Men of polite Genius, noble Thought, and diffusive Learning'. Yet the final joke is aimed at Bickerstaff himself, as he proclaims: 'I have made Observations in this Matter so long, that when I meet with a young Fellow ... more dull than the rest of the Company, I conclude him to be a Fellow of the Royal Society'.[62] Bickerstaff's own (cod-anthropological) 'Observations' are themselves on a trifling, pedestrian topic (the social conduct of curious men) and so from his own perspective he is as guilty of dullness as those he condemns. To mock the scientific with sufficient rhetorical authority, one must observe, experiment, catalogue, and classify: an irony never far from the surface throughout this period.

---

[60] *Tatler*, no. 236 (12 October 1710), in Bond (ed.), *Tatler*, 3: 216–18).

[61] Bond (ed.), *Spectator*, 3: 219. Swift draws out similar political parallels: see Swift to John Temple, 15 June 1706, in *Correspondence*, 1: 161. On Gwythers, see J. D. H. Widdess, *A History of the Royal College of Physicians of Ireland, 1654–1963* (Edinburgh: Livingstone, 1963), 38. Editors of the *Tatler* assume erroneously that this 'ingenious Physician' is Sloane.

[62] Bond (ed.), *Spectator*, 3: 218–19, 220.

CHAPTER 25

NEW WORLD WRITING AND CAPTIVITY NARRATIVES

CATHERINE ARMSTRONG

THE three-quarters of a century following 1640 represent a crucial turning point in the exploration and settlement of the so-called 'New World'. Correspondingly a new type of prose literature was produced in this period, reflecting England's growing confidence in conceptually controlling the region, which accompanied her uncertainty about what colony and empire would mean for the mother country. This chapter will discuss two ways of understanding the New World literature written in English, during this period: firstly, the domestic versus imperial discourse and secondly, the flowering of the use of the trope of racial difference used by authors confronting the 'others' in the region. First, though, a word about the region itself. Although the 'New World' is a phrase that was current in the seventeenth century when describing the American hemisphere, its Eurocentric formulation has been increasingly problematic to historians and literature scholars in recent times. Much of the work on the development of European colonies in the Americas during the early modern period now uses the conceptual framework of the Atlantic World, a region bounding an ocean, in which national boundaries are less significant than broader regional, cross-cultural continuities and changes.[1] This chapter will discuss English authors travelling in and writing about North America, the Caribbean, and Central America. To be truly Atlantic, it must also acknowledge the emergence of Africa in the literature of the English, and this will be touched upon briefly in the discussion of black slavery.

This period is characterized by the emergence of a colonial literature within North America and its similarities and differences to the discourse about the region emanating from London. In this period, the book trades in North America were undeveloped, apart from in New England. Most authors based in the colonies still relied on connections

---

[1] David Armitage and Michael Braddick (eds.), *The British Atlantic World 1500–1800* (London: Palgrave, 2009) is a seminal work in the field.

in London for their work to be printed and distributed. The majority of books bought in North America were purchased via London agents and shipped across the Atlantic.[2] Thus, although in terms of content, distinct domestic and imperial concerns were emerging in the literature of this period, the production and distribution of knowledge in both regions was intimately linked by the trade. This chapter will explore the ways in which a distinct American identity was emerging, triggered by settlers' engagement with the realities of life in America and encounters with its people. It will examine the changes in colonial life that caused this evolution within the literature, by comparing mid-seventeenth-century literature to that of the Elizabethan era, as well as charting significant evolution in the nature and content of the literature published between 1640 and 1714.

North America was not the only area of focus in the 'New World' during this period and, for the first time, in 1648, an English author, Thomas Gage, reported on his travels and experiences in Spanish America (modern-day Mexico and Guatemala) in *The English-American* (1648). But following the partial success of the Western Design, which resulted in the British gaining a foothold in Jamaica, the potential of the Caribbean entered the English mindset for the first time. In all of these regions, despite rhetorical pleas to the contrary, the English did not have the lands to themselves, and throughout the Atlantic region the encounters with the Native Americans helped to define the English experience. Although the feelings of confusion and wonder of the first contact period had past, Native Americans still posed a considerable conceptual problem for English authors who tried to imagine their role within an English America. This period was also one in which the systematic use of slave labour in all parts of the English Atlantic was established and this development is reflected in the prose literature, both factual and fictional. Handbooks began appearing advising on the use and management of slaves in agricultural endeavours in the New World, balancing a Christian approach to slave treatment with the racialized view of work in the region.[3] The African and his enslavement penetrated the world of fiction too, with the most notable example being Aphra Behn's *Oroonoko* in 1688.[4] While Africans always remained an 'other', this is the period in which, for the English, slavery and its use in the New World became normalized.

This chapter will bring to the fore three important themes within the diverse literature of this period about the Atlantic World. These themes centre on the ways in an uncertain and insecure world that the landscape and its inhabitants were conceptualized. From the century after the settling of Jamestown in 1607, authors metaphorically brought under control the American landscape and its natural commodities through their urge to observe, record, and evaluate them. Towards the end of the seventeenth century, such attempts at cataloguing emerged differently from authors who had been born in

---

[2] See, for example, Hugh Amory and David Hall (eds.), *A History of the Book in America. Vol. I: The Colonial Book in the Atlantic World* (Cambridge: Cambridge University Press, 1999).
[3] For example, Morgan Godwyn, *The Negro's and Indians Advocate* (1685)
[4] Aphra Behn, *Oroonoko, or, The Royal Slave, A True History* (1688).

America or spent much of their life there. Such positioning of observers as English or American can also be useful when we survey the representation of Native Americans and their tensions with Euro-American settlers. Emerging in the literature, even in this early period decades before independence, there are some nascent cultural differences between English and American identities. Finally, much literature, especially that written by visitors to, rather than residents of, the Americas, emphasized the landscape of the region as a site of cruelty or excess, thus rhetorically both distancing and fascinating the English readership. Theirs was a different motive to those writers trying to encourage practical engagement by investors and emigrants, for whom the potential of the flora and fauna was a main focus.

The Second Contact Period?

After 1640 there was a shift in the prose literature about the Americas, away from the exploration narratives and early, overly optimistic, promotional literature to a more measured, even uncertain appraisal of England's role across the Atlantic. When the English first began to explore and settle North America during Elizabeth's and James's reigns, collections of travel accounts gathered by Richard Hakluyt and Samuel Purchas showed the possibilities of the region for Protestant expansion and social engineering by removing some of England's poor.[5] Flora and fauna were catalogued depending on their potential for trade or food and medicine for settlers, while the overall fecundity of the New World was universally lauded. The only dark clouds on the horizon were the inscrutable natives, who many believed were living in an uncivilized state akin to the ancient Britons.[6] Initially friendly and cooperative, according to English depictions, the natives became treacherous seemingly without reason and refused to help the newcomers, even attacking their former friends. At this stage of first contact, depictions of the natives grew darker, as accusations of cannibalism became the literary trope through which enmity was expressed. These first authors made sense of the Americas by trying to fit what they saw into their pre-existing mental world, reaching for comparisons with the landscape and people of Europe and the near East, or looking back to the Classical world for interpretive models. When the New World refused to easily fit into these intellectual straitjackets, some authors such as George Chapman, Ben Jonson, and John Marston in their play *Eastward Hoe!*, printed in 1605, turned to satire and ridiculed the idea that everywhere in the New World was paved with gold. A few others such as Thomas Hariot and John Smith, who both experienced extended periods in America, appeared to listen to the natives,

---

[5] Richard Hakluyt, *Principall Navigations* (1589); Samuel Purchas, *Hakluytus Postumus, or, Purchas, His Pilgrims* (1626).

[6] As depicted in John White's watercolours of the Algonquin natives of Roanoke.

appreciating that it was from them that they might learn as much as they could about this strange new land.[7]

The early days of fear and instability having passed, the literature of the 1620s and 1630s turned more to the potential of staple crops and also the sheer size of the landscape, potentially accommodating a vast array of settlements. The arrival of religious migrants such as the 'Pilgrim Fathers' who landed at Plymouth, and the Puritan settlers led by John Winthrop in Massachusetts, changed the tone of the literature as much of it focused on leaving one's country to establish a 'city upon a hill', in Winthrop's famous phrase, that might provide a beacon of light to illuminate the religious errors of Laudian England.[8] The religious jeremiad depicting the metaphorical and literal journey that these separatist and Puritan migrants took became a common literary form throughout the middle part of the seventeenth century. An example of this was Edward Johnson's *Wonder-working Providence of Sion's Saviour in New England*, published in London in 1654. But more practical texts such as William Wood's *New England's Prospect* of 1639 were also published, showing migrants how they might best maximize their chances of survival, both of the fearful crossing and the difficult first few years in the so-called 'wilderness'. By 1640, settlements in Virginia, Plymouth, and Massachusetts were well established and, in the later seventeenth and early eighteenth centuries, various further models of colonization were tried. For example, donation of land in the New World became a way that Charles II, newly restored to the throne, could reward his supporters. The 1660s saw the development of Carolina, a colonial venture built on the seemingly contradictory foundations of Lockean tolerance and systematic race-based chattel slavery.

Since the failed settlement of Roanoke disappeared in the late 1580s, English perceptions of the Atlantic World had been defined by rivalry with Spain, who had settled in regions with untold riches. Initial disappointment at the lack of mineral wealth in North America gave way to fear in Carolina of Spanish territorial encroachment from the south in Florida. This borderland region became a haven for runaway slaves from the Carolinas, further exacerbating the tensions between the European nations. The French also began to exert their influence from the north in Quebec and, with their exploration of the Mississippi River from the 1680s onwards, the English felt squeezed from all sides. The ever-changing alliances between European nations and native tribes along the eastern seaboard further complicated the picture. From the Restoration onwards, explorers adopted new scientific methods as observers of the natural world. Fascinated by the differences to be found in America, they examined the flora and fauna of the region armed with instructions from the nascent Royal Society, formed in 1660. When the Royal Society collected reports about North America for its journal, the *Philosophical Transactions*, it always mentioned when eyewitness testimony was the origin of the report. In 1676 a report by Thomas Glover about Virginia not only emphasized that

---

[7] Thomas Harriot, *A Brief and True Report of the New Found Land of Virginia* (1588).

[8] John Winthrop, 'A Model of Christian Charity' (1630), in *Collections of the Massachusetts Historical Society* (Boston, 1838), 3rd series, 7, 31–48.

Glover had seen Virginia personally but that he was 'an ingenious Chirugion that hath lived some years in that country'.[9] Glover's position as a settler rather than a visitor to Virginia, as well as his professional standing, rendered him a more reliable witness in the eyes of the members of the Royal Society. Networks of transatlantic communication on scientific matters developed during this period and English became a key language of information exchange.

This 'second contact' period was unique in witnessing an increase both in certainty about the survival of English settlements in the Americas and in uncertainty about what this would mean economically, politically, and socially for the mother country. Settlers in the colonies struggled from the start to conceptualize what their migration meant in terms of their own identity. First generation migrants considered themselves English, with an Englishman's rights and privileges, but later American-born generations began to question this and, despite those from the elites regularly travelling across the Atlantic, saw themselves as different. The London elite saw 'colonials' as different too, raised in a different soil, breathing different air. This environmental determinism led them to judge the human products of America as inferior to their English-born brothers, just as the flora and fauna were.

COLONIAL VERSUS METROPOLITAN LITERATURES

A case study of two early historians of the English settlement in the Americas shows the increasing differences in approach of colonial and metropolitan literatures. On the face of it, Robert Beverley and John Oldmixon, writing at the turn of the eighteenth century, were men from similar backgrounds. Robert Beverley wrote the 1705 work *The History and Present State of the Colony of Virginia*, which was reprinted many times and became a key source of information for other authors about early Virginia. Beverley's father moved from Yorkshire to Virginia and his three sons, all members of the Virginia political elite, were born in the colony. Robert Beverley was tied by marriage and by the marriage of his children to the most important planter families of the colony, including the Carters and the Byrds. John Oldmixon, only six years Robert's junior, was also raised in an elite military family and became interested in overseas trade. He was also a writer of plays and poetry, but his most famous work was published in 1708 and recounted the history of *The British Empire in America*. Later he turned his attention to British history, writing a controversial history of the civil war era, which had Whiggish leanings. Both men wrote, among other reasons, in order to make sense of a century's history of English permanent settlement in North America and what this meant for the English identity. But they had very different interpretations of the significance of the settlement

---

[9] Thomas Glover, 'An Account of Virginia', *Philosophical Transactions*, 11/116 (1676), 623.

of Virginia. Beverley's intentions were to show that as an eyewitness on the ground in Virginia, his word on its history was to be trusted, whereas Oldmixon's main aim was to encourage migration and prove that it was possible for English bodies, vulnerable to alien environments, to thrive in the different climate of North America. Beverley contradicted Oldmixon on this point, stating that the act of migrating to Virginia had changed his fellow Englishmen in some way and he expressed this by claiming a shared identity with the Native Americans: 'I am an Indian', he wrote, and in doing so also complicated the supposed racial worldview of white settlers at this period.[10]

We can see further that the differences, between colonial and metropolitan representations of the New World regarding trade, magnified once the Carolina settlement was established in the 1680s. Thomas Ashe, who, in 1680, was sent to Carolina to make a note of the 'state of that country by his majesties special command', wrote that Carolina was 'a jewel to the crown of England', a status that would later be afforded to India.[11] The early 1680s saw an upsurge of interest in Carolina, as non-conformist residents of England, and also the Irish, were encouraged to migrate. As well as persuading migrants to go, Thomas Ashe also directed his rhetoric towards those remaining in the Old World concerned about the new territorial acquisitions. However, in presenting images of useful and easily accessible commodities, authors knew that they had to do this without artifice or pretence because such lies would be found out with an increasing number of authors writing about the New World. Emphasizing his honesty, John Lawson dedicated his 1714 tract to the Lords Proprietors of Carolina, telling them that he would give a description 'of your own country for the most part in her natural dress and therefore less vitiated with fraud and luxury'.[12] Publications produced by authors based in England and targeted at an English readership often took a more strictly promotional tone, encouraging migration not only for individual benefits but also for the benefit of England as a whole. During this period, the literature on the potential of the southern colonies for silk cultivation began to emerge. It culminated later in the century in the 1730s and 1740s when Georgia had been settled. This promotional material had little to do with the realities of life in the Americas (and the expertise of those who had settled there) and everything to do with the imperial policy of the English hoping to circumvent expensive sources of silk that came via continental Europe.

Colonial authors who lived in Carolina tended to discuss in more detail the particular threats and challenges to their security that they faced. These threats were from European rivals and their native allies. The French were particularly feared because of their proximity to the English, the possibility that they might convert the natives and turn them against Carolina, and the worry that they might dominate the trade of the region because of their control of the great river. Another concern was that the

---

[10] Robert Beverley, *The History and Present State of the Colony of Virginia* (1705), p. vii.
[11] Thomas Ashe, *Carolina or a Description of the Present State of that Country* (1682), epistle dedicatory, sig A2r.
[12] John Lawson, *A History of Carolina* (1714), epistle dedicatory, sig A2.

French were making more effort to document and understand the landscape, and their accounts were being published for entertainment and to promote that understanding back in Europe. John Lawson wrote in the preface to his natural history of Carolina that it was a shame that many of the English settlers 'are persons of the meaner sort uncapable of giving any reasonable account of what they met withal in these remote parts', and that, by contrast, the French 'outstrip us' by sending out clergy and gentlemen who record their travels in journals. This problem inspired Lawson to write his seminal account.

Another important concern for colonial authors was rivalry between different settlements. In a land-rich, labour-poor environment such as North America, being able to attract new settlers was crucial. Authors contrasted the fortunes of each region in order to boost the reputation of their preferred colony. The promoters of Carolina were especially adept at doing this. In the epistle dedicatory to Carolina proprietor Lord Ashley, John Lederer's 1672 report of his explorations in North Carolina explained that Carolina was 'the beauty and envy of North America', and he criticized Virginians for being so mean as to complain about the amount of money he spent on his expedition.[13] Lederer's report was widely read in London and encouraged a great deal of interest in the new colony of Carolina. Lederer was German-born and initially wrote his report in Latin; it was translated into English by Sir William Talbot, governor of Maryland—where Lederer had settled. The map which accompanied this volume, along with its errors about the position of the Great Dismal Swamp of North Carolina, was reproduced throughout the eighteenth century in printed volumes.

Other English Atlantic Interests

It was not only North America that interested the English during this second contact period. Accounts of Spanish America written by English authors were incredibly rare because of the limitations on non-Spanish migration placed on the region. But in 1648, Thomas Gage, educated at St. Omer by his English Catholic family and a one-time Dominican friar, having spent twelve years travelling round the Spanish New World, returned home to England and published an account of his travels. He renounced Catholicism, became an informer for Cromwell's authorities, and became a 'preacher of the word', an Anglican minister with Puritan leanings, at a parish in Kent. His account *The English-American* caused a sensation and impressed Cromwell, who hired him to be a clergyman on board the Western Design ships trying to wrest control of Hispaniola from the Spanish. Gage's luck ran out though, and he died of disease in Jamaica. The shape taken by *The English-American* was determined by English readers'

---

[13] John Lederer, *The Discoveries of John Lederer* (1672), sig A1r. Lederer's account is also interesting because it records that the drinking of the King's health in brandy at a particular spot had taken over from the symbolic planting of the cross as the English ritual of claiming possession of an area (22).

desire for material on the Black Legend. Popular since the mid-sixteenth century when Gage's fellow Dominican, Bartolomé de las Casas, published his account of the horrors perpetrated against the Native Americans by the conquistadors, Black Legend material was an intrinsic part of the development of an English Protestant national identity during the reign of Elizabeth I and beyond. The first English version of Las Casas's work was published in 1583 (following the Spanish version in 1552, and the Dutch and French editions of 1578). Las Casas' work was republished in 1656 as *The Tears of the Indians* by John Phillips, the nephew of John Milton who worked for Cromwell's government. As well as justifying colonization and challenging the Spanish in the New World, this material also provided English readers with an ethnographic understanding of Native Americans and a geographical understanding of America. It also made money for printers and booksellers as the sensational, titillating stories attracted a wide readership, in the format of large collections of travel narratives for the richer book buyer and smaller pamphlet literature for the poorer buyer. Gage's work fits into this trajectory and was popular because it was written by an Englishman, who, even though he was a renegade educated abroad, was seen as more trustworthy than the Spanish authors previously relied upon, who were read in translation. Prior to Gage's book, the only Englishmen to report on life in New Spain had been illiterate sailors, such as Miles Philips whose oral account was recorded and published by Richard Hakluyt as 'The Voyage of Miles Phillips one of the company put on shore by Sir John Hawkins 1558'.[14]

Gage's *The English-American* tells as much about his self-perception as about the realities of life in Central America. The title of the book shows how conflicted Gage was about his own identity and leads the reader to doubt his assertions that he arrived in England as a Protestant Englishman. In his epistle dedicatory to Sir Thomas Fairfax, he asserted his dual reason for writing, to narrate his conversion and to convey information useful to his countrymen. He depicted England and Protestantism as his 'home', writing about 'my returning home, not onely to my country but to the true knowledge and free profession of the Gospel's purity'.[15] But the title *The English-American* complicates this certainty. He might have chosen a title reflecting his assuredness, perhaps describing his book, in the popular style of the time, as 'a true account of an English man's travels in New Spain'. But instead he chose the title *The English-American*. That this choice of title was his is reinforced in the text when Gage acknowledged that his story allowed readers 'to observe an English man become American, travailing many thousands miles there'.[16] This choice of title is rendered stranger because, in the seventeenth-century meaning of the word, calling someone 'an American' did not bring to mind a white Englishman settled in America but rather either one of two enemies: a man of Spanish descent who lived in the New World, or a Native American. Through his choice of title, Gage

---

[14] Richard Hakluyt, *The Principal Navigations Voyages Traffiques and Discoveries of the English Nation*, 12 vols. (Cambridge: Cambridge University Press, 2014), 9: 398
[15] Gage, *English-American*, sig. A2r.
[16] Gage, *English-American*, 81.

situated himself in his readers' minds as an 'other', saying 'I am not like you; I have been changed by my journey', further complicating his liminal identity as an English renegade Catholic.

Gage's death in Jamaica in 1656 occurred just at the point when this lucrative island was being violently transferred from Spanish to English control. This process was not sudden and decisive, complicated by the presence of Native Americans and maroons who changed sides as and when it suited them. The presence of outlaw sailors and pirates of many nationalities and ethnicities at the port towns further exacerbated the confusing situation. But, by 1713, the island of Jamaica was securely in English hands. Initial literature about the island followed the previous pattern of works on Virginia. Promotional tracts encouraging settlement discussed the natural world of Jamaica in glowing terms, glossing over the concerns over the susceptibility of English bodies to disease there, and over the natural disasters of hurricanes and earthquakes. These tracts were followed a few years later by complaints from local planters in print about the calibre of settler being sent to the region, specifically in Jamaica's case, the tendency to send Irish and Scottish prisoners of war for a period of forced servitude, usually seven years. One of the most significant texts about Jamaica of this era was written and published in 1672 by cartographer and stationer Richard Blome, taken from the notes of the governor of Jamaica and 'other distinguished persons of the region'. Although the title of the book gives the impression of being about Jamaica, it actually documents the whole of the English holdings in the region, and is accompanied by maps. Of Jamaica's climate, the book states that it is 'temperate and healthful', while disease was only prevalent among the immoral visitor, prone to 'ill diet, drunkenness and slothfulness'.[17]

Unsurprisingly, Blome's work justifies the English taking of Jamaica from the Spanish and frequently refers back to the Black Legend. Blome argues that the Spanish mistreated the native populations. When it suited the English to do so, they confirmed the native title to the land. As Blome puts it: 'The Indians, who are the natural proprietors of America, do abominate and hate the Spaniards for their cruelty and avarice; and upon every occasion will shew their willingness to give themselves and their Countreys, freely into the power and protection of the English.'[18] This was the same justification used by Scottish adventurers and settlers involved in the Darien expedition to modern-day Panama a generation later in the 1690s. This expedition and its failure generated a great deal of literature. In July 1698, five ships sailed from Leith carrying over a thousand migrants, many of whom were starving highlanders. The organizer of the enterprise, William Paterson, carried a package to be opened once aboard ship, revealing their destination. Paterson had raised a huge amount of money to support the voyage with many investors each putting in thousands of pounds; at £500,000 his company's coffers contained around half of Scotland's available national capital.

---

[17] Richard Blome, *A Description of the Island of Jamaica* (1672), 6, 26.
[18] Blome, *Description*, 56.

Of course, the reality of Darien was far from a fabled land of plenty. By March 1699, settlers were dying at the rate of ten per day, and the survivors abandoned New Edinburgh and Fort St. Andrews, limping home via Jamaica, still more dying on the way. The second wave of settlers had no idea of this tragic turn of events and three more ships, carrying 1300 more migrants, left in August 1699, soon to be followed by five more relief ships from Leith. Arriving in Darien to find it abandoned and battered by storms, they set out to try to rebuild the shattered colony, but once again disease led to a breakdown in law and order and many lucky colonists escaped to Jamaica and the North American mainland, rather than stay in Darien. Darien was finally surrendered to the Spanish in April 1700. The literature about Darien includes four pamphlets written by authors, several of whom, along with the printers and sellers of their texts, were put at risk of arrest and imprisonment.[19] Books were burned by the hangman and proclamations issued offering large rewards for the capture of the pamphleteers who were seen, in the words of one of William III's earliest proclamations on the subject, to be 'stirring up sedition and rebellion between English and Scots'.[20]

This period was also known as 'the golden age of piracy', as much for the literary representations of these outlaws as for the reality of their activities in the Atlantic and the East Indies. The first important tome gathering oral history accounts of piracy into written prose emerged during this period. Later, Daniel Defoe would write his own similar work, telling among others the stories of notorious female pirates such as Anne Bonny. But the first of the genre, written by A. O. Exquemelin, was written first in Dutch as *De Americaensche Zee-rovers* in 1674, before being translated into English as *The Buccaneers of America* in 1684. Exquemelin's origins are unclear, but he was a sailor in the Caribbean himself, at times as a forced labourer. He was trusted by the notorious 'pirate' Henry Morgan, and it was Morgan's escapades in Cartagena and Portobello that formed the centrepiece to Exquemelin's book. His account is part travel narrative, with detailed descriptions of the flora and fauna of Tortuga, for example, and part adventure story, with breathtaking accounts of storms, shipwrecks, and sea battles. One of the most titillating aspects for readers were detailed accounts of the torture and cruelty used by Morgan and his men on traditional enemies of the English, such as when they encountered the Spanish governor of Maracaibo, and 'they put him again upon the Rack, lifting him up on high with Cords, and tying huge weights unto his feet and neck. Besides which cruel and stretching torment, they burnt him alive, applying Palm-leaves burning unto his face. Under which miseries he died in half an hour'.[21]

---

[19] *A Short Account from and Description of Darien* (Edinburgh, 1699); *A Defence of the Scots Abdicating Darien* (1699); *Caledonia, or, The Pedlar Turn'd Merchant: A Tragi-Comedy as was Acted by His Majesties Subjects in Scotland in the King of Spain's Province at Darien* (1700); G. Ridpath, *Scotlands Grievances Relating to Darien Humbly Offered to the Consideration of the Parliament* (Edinburgh, 1700).

[20] *By the King. A Proclamation. William R.* (1699), broadsheet.

[21] A. O. Exquemelin, *The Buccaneers of America* (1684), 119

The Problem of the Native Americans

Exquemelin spent much of his narrative describing the lives of the Native Americans in Central and Southern America. Like all Europeans of the period, he wrote in a way to 'other' them by highlighting stories that deliberately distanced and alienated them from 'civilized' European society. An example of this is his description of the custom of the natives of the Yucatan peninsula who took a newborn child and left him untended in the temple for the first night, to tempt animals. Any animal which approached was then considered that child's spirit animal. But many babies were injured in this way, and Exquemelin calls the natives 'miserable and ignorant' for engaging in such superstitious practices.[22]

During the late seventeenth century, English understanding of native life and culture was greatly influenced by the captivity narrative genre. The most famous Indian captivity narrative was that by Mary Rowlandson. It was so popular that in 1682 it went through four editions and was published in both Boston and London. Rowlandson and her three children from Lancaster, Massachusetts were taken captive during King Phillip's War by natives close to Phillip himself. She spent over eleven weeks in captivity during which time she travelled over 150 miles and one of her children died. Some editors of her work, such as Wendy Martin, have claimed that Rowlandson had no interest in her 'exterior' world during her captivity but a close reading of her narrative shows this is not the case. Rowlandson immediately establishes the controversy over the possession of the landscape she moves through, saying that she was captured by the Indians in revenge for English encroachment on 'their' land and she refers to the places where she travelled as 'Narragansett country' and 'Nipmug country'.[23] Rowlandson also highlights the vulnerability of the English position in this landscape saying that this vulnerability was not entirely the fault of the natives, that Lancaster was a 'small town, remote from the aid of others and not being garrison'd as it might'.[24] She depicts a native population entirely at ease moving through the whites' built environment, showing them clambering on barn roofs in order to get better angles for shooting their victims, while she initially feels uncomfortable and fearful in their landscape. David Minter has argued that the captivity narratives, especially Rowlandson's, are 'intensely adverse' in their portrayal of the natural world.[25]

Much of Rowlandson's landscape description is symbolic and her experience travelling through it is a sign from God, as she tells of the 'waterless pit' of despair into which she was cast on her seizure.[26] Her descriptions of turning her back 'on the town

---

[22] Exquemelin, *Buccaneers*, 44.
[23] M. Rowlandson, *A True Account of the Captivity and Restoration of Mrs Mary Rowlandson* (1682), in *Colonial American Travel Narratives*, ed. Wendy Martin (London: Penguin, 1994), 5.
[24] Rowlandson, *A True Account*, 6.
[25] David Minter, 'Dens of Lions: Notes on Stylization in Early Puritan Captivity Narratives', *American Literature*, 45 (1973), 335–47 (345).
[26] Rowlandson, *A True Account*, 8.

and travel[ling] with them into the vast and desolate wilderness' are designed to establish the locus of her redemption as much as to actually describe the landscape. But as well as symbolism these descriptions reflect what Rowlandson saw and experienced. For example, on her fourth remove she refers to the landscape as a 'desolate place in the wilderness' but qualifies this by saying 'there were no wigwams or inhabitants before', and that it was 'cold, wet and snowy'.[27] This indicates that Rowlandson was acutely aware of her exterior world and not simply presenting her journey to reinforce her religious message. Water is a constant theme in Rowlandson's narrative, as it is in many of the captivity stories. She claims that several times she had to cross a stream with water up to her knees and flowing with such force that she was nearly carried away. This has a religious symbolism of new baptism and Moses leading his people across the river, but it also emphasizes the great role played by rivers, creeks, and swamps in the lives of any American traveller of this period, forced or not.

The captivity narratives occupy a complex position in American and British print culture of the late seventeenth and early eighteenth centuries. The stories they tell also appeared in newspapers published both in London and Boston. Therefore, the political situation in Europe—the Restoration, the Glorious Revolution, and the ongoing wars of succession in Europe—must also be considered.[28] There they were presented as part of the political reporting of the various wars with the French and Indians. The conflict known as King Philip's war was the most serious of this period, but even this did not threaten to dislodge the English settlements of New England as they were, by now, numerous enough to be secure, unlike during the earlier era of the Virginia Massacre of 1622 in which one-third of English settlers in the region were murdered. However, the causes of King Philip's war were still hotly debated in the anonymous pamphlet literature during the years 1675 and 1676, and in longer books written by William Hubbard and Richard Hutchinson and published in London. Many of these shorter works were based on letters from settlers in the region, such as *A Brief and True Narration of the Late Wars Risen in New England*, published in 1675, that, using the theme of the perfidious natives, claimed that 'All the Indians quite through the Countrey are in Arms, yet pretend favour to the English; however we trust them not, as knowing they wait a fit occasion against us'.[29] Following the convention of authors of travel narratives throughout the seventeenth century, the writer is at pains to emphasize the veracity of his words, stating that his prose is 'without aggravating or diminishing of our *Troubles* here'.[30]

Captivity narratives were less like travel accounts and more closely resembled the Puritan jeremiads produced by New Englanders after their arrival in America in the 1630s. These accounts told of tests of faith and redemption in which an individual or community was sent out into the wilderness and suffered hardship and strife only

---

[27] Rowlandson, *A True Account*, 18.
[28] Teresa Toulouse, *The Captive's Position: Female Narrative, Male Identity and Royal Authority in Colonial New England* (Philadelphia: University of Pennsylvania Press, 2006), 74.
[29] *A Brief and True Narration of the Late War Risen in New England* (1675), 6.
[30] *Brief and True Narration of the Late War Risen in New England*, 3.

to be redeemed through God's love. The texts worked as a plea for repentance and a commitment to turning away from previous sinful ways. But they also offered hope for survival on a dangerous frontier, encouraging people to believe they could be self-sufficient.[31] Initially the 'wilderness' described in jeremiads was America itself, seen as an exile from the mother country, and the hardships faced were through simply trying to survive. In the captivity narratives these patterns were altered, and the wilderness described was the frontier territory and the hardships were endured during captivity. The narratives also fit into the genre of the anti-Catholic literature that was emerging on both sides of the Atlantic, stirred up both by James II's controversial reign, evoking fears that he might spread Catholicism around the English empire, and also, in the early eighteenth century, by the Jacobite rebellion. The literature included tales of forced conversions and subversions of true religious practice, and of conniving Jesuits, as in the anonymous *A True Narrative of the Horrid Hellish Popish Plot* (2 pts., 1682). Anti-Catholic playwrighting reached its peak with Elkanah Settle's misogynistic *The Female Prelate* (1680). This was accompanied by a vivid anti-Catholic visual culture, for example Roger L'Estrange's *The Committee or Popery in Masquerade* of 1680 and by street performance in London such as pope-burning processions. In the captivity narratives this anti-Catholicism takes on a national, political dimension because of its anti-French slant.

Many captives, including Mary Rowlandson, argued that they had no intention of publishing their tale but that they were persuaded to do so by family, friends, or their minister, and while this is true in some cases, historians must also be wary of taking this statement at face value. It is regularly seen as part of the 'modesty trope', popular among writers since the early seventeenth century, in which they proclaimed their work's suitability for publication for the very reason that they did not seek it. Subsequent editions of earlier captivity narratives were released in 1720 at the height of Massachusetts' conflict with the Abenakis to try to promote an aggressive policy towards them, and also in 1754 when anti-French sentiments were at their peak due to the outbreak of the Seven Years War. Mary Rowlandson's account was published again in the 1770s as a commentary on the Boston Massacre, a violent altercation where British soldiers attacked a Patriot mob during the incendiary period prior to American independence, when it was intended to promote local patriotism and self-defence.[32]

RACE AND SLAVERY

Aphra Behn's *Oroonoko* is one of the most famous works of literature of this era for many reasons, among them the gender of the author and the detailed anti-colonial

---

[31] Tara Fitzpatrick, 'The Figure of Captivity', *American Literary History*, 3 (1991), 1–26 (4).
[32] Rowlandson, *A True Account*, 358.

commentary found within it. But Behn's 1688 work was not anti-slavery or abolitionist in tendency; instead it focused on the social and psychological frameworks of the cruelty of one human being to another.[33] She did not challenge the validity of slave trading or a slave labour system, nor did she use the book to examine the racial 'othering' of Africans during the period. Behn's tale is full of sympathetic black characters, especially Oroonoke and Imoinda who are shown to be cultured and civilized. Africa as a place is also praised in her book, with Coromantien having a highly developed social order, albeit one built on the profits of the slave trade. But she still exoticized the black bodies she wrote about, and their pain and suffering. Indeed, Behn was more concerned with English cruelty and barbarism at home, commenting on the Civil War and execution of Charles I. But in placing a black African at the centre of her story, Behn alerted London audiences to the increasingly important truth, which was that English expansion overseas in this period was intrinsically bound up with the slave trade.

Contemporary commentators believed that the climate of the southern colonies and the Caribbean and the staple crops grown there necessitated the development of the slave labour system. Representations of the landscape and of slavery entered the literature early in the history of Carolina and Georgia. In Carolina, rice growing was thought to be possible only with slave labour. In his dialectical pamphlet of 1712 about plantation life in Carolina, John Norris explained to an English readership what a slave was: 'those we call slaves are a sort of black people here commonly call'd Blackamoors some few kept here in England by Gentry for their pleasure but are there bought by the Inhabitants ... their masters or owners have then as good a right or title to them during their lives as a man has here to a horse or ox after he has bought them.'[34] The pamphlet explained that the benefit of having slaves is that white men have the freedom to raise themselves up to even greater wealth. To emphasize this point, the white planter in Norris's dialogue was called James *Freeman*. Norris was also aware that the heavy labour involved in rice cultivation might be undesirable for wealthier settlers, so he was one of the rare commentators who, in his text, discussed slaves' working lives in depth. He described their working day, including the custom of taking a siesta in the hottest part of the day, and suggested crops that could be grown in order to feed them such as 'pompions and West India potatoes' which would feed hogs and swine 'tho either is very serviceable and paliatable [sic] for a family of slaves'.[35] Although Norris wrote at great length about the requirements for growing rice, he also included in his tract the formulaic list of animals, plants, fruits, fish, and wildfowl that are typical in descriptions of this period.

---

[33] The difference between abolitionist and anti-slavery works is that abolitionist material called for the complete end to slavery because of its horrific treatment of slaves, and often for black men and women to be treated equally. Anti-slavery material could be any piece of writing that suggested that the slave system was problematic. Anti-slavery works did not necessarily call for the immediate end to slavery and did not always depict black people positively.

[34] John Norris, *Profitable Advice for Rich and Poor in a Dialogue or Discourse* (1712), 17.

[35] Norris, *Profitable Advice*, 37, 43.

Commentators based in North America reported very positively about the benefits of incorporating slavery into the colonies' economy: 'A planter can make more tar in any one year here with 50 slaves than they can do with double the number in those places [Virginia and the northern colonies].' Edward Randolph attributed this difference to the following factor: 'their slaves living here at very easy rates with few clothes.'[36] Contrary to the arguments made following the slave uprising in 1739 in the Stono River area of coastal Carolina, 'R. F.' argued in 1682 that Carolina's slave population enhanced the security of the colony and prevented a threat from Native Americans because, as he put it, there was 'a natural antipathy the Native and the Negro [have] one against another'.[37]

Not all commentators commended the slave system. Although there were few authors criticizing slavery during this period, Morgan Godwyn, who in the 1670s lived in Virginia and Barbados as an Anglican minister, wrote a tract in 1680 claiming that slaves and natives should be converted to Christianity, emphasizing their humanity and criticizing the white Carolinians' cruelty. He entitled his tract *The Negro's and Indian's Advocate*, making a judgement as he did so on the behaviour of other English men who had neglected and mistreated those of the other races that they had encountered in the New World. Godwyn was certainly not challenging the necessity of slavery or calling for its abolition, although he saw enslavement purely for profit as a sin unless accompanied by a desire to improve the lives of the slave. He called for the amelioration in slaves' conditions, and he saw a Christian education as the best way in which to do this. As well as practical considerations, like Behn, Godwyn condemned the nascent racism he saw in the Atlantic World, the belief that 'the *Negro's*, though in their Figure they carry some resemblances of Manhood, yet are indeed *no Men*'.[38] Also like Behn, Godwyn connected this to imperialism, but in a very different way from her. He accused Englishmen of borrowing this racist belief from the Catholic Spanish who had used it to justify their mistreatment of the natives, once again raising the spectre of the Black Legend, a century after its first invention. In fact, Godwyn asserted the 'rights' of the 'negroes' as men: 'the *Negro's* (both Slaves and others) have naturally an *equal Right* with other Men to the *Exercise and Privileges* of *Religion;* of which 'tis most unjust in any part to deprive them.'[39] Godwin also did not pull any punches when describing the hypocrisy of European settlers who denied slaves' humanity and yet used enslaved women, and occasionally men, as sexual playthings. He wrote that 'if Slavery hath such a faculty or power as to transmute Men into Beasts, or if all *Negro's* be naturally such, may we not be bold to demand what will become of those *Debauches,* that so frequently do make use of them for their *unnatural* Pleasures and Lusts?'[40] In asking such questions, Godwyn

---

[36] 'Letter of Sir Edward Randolph to the Board of Trade, 16 Mar. 1698/9', in *Narratives of Early Carolina, 1650–1708,* ed. A. S. Salley (New York: Scribner, 1911), 208.
[37] R. F., *The Present State of Carolina with Advice to the Settlers* (1682), 5.
[38] Godwyn, *The Negro's and Indians Advocate,* 3.
[39] Godwyn, *The Negro's and Indians Advocate,* 7.
[40] Godwyn, *The Negro's and Indians Advocate,* 30.

prefigured the later eighteenth-century debate over abolition, which also suggested that the slave trade was an abomination because it turned white men into sinners.

Conclusion

As well as being significant for their prose, the texts discussed in this chapter were also artefacts of material culture in themselves. The actual physical books have an important historical significance, just as do the texts contained within them. During this period, the vast majority of printed works about the Americas were published in London. The few exceptions to this were items of local political concern, such as summaries of local laws. The main reason for this was that the printing and bookselling trades were still poorly represented in British North America and the Caribbean. Boston's role was developing slowly, but the town would only acquire a flourishing book trade as the eighteenth century progressed. The other reason is the perception of contemporary authors, patrons, and publishers of books that their main readership would be in London and the rest of England. Sometimes manuscripts were sent to England to be published on behalf of the author. Other times they were carried across the Atlantic by the author on a visit to England. On still other occasions, the author's eyewitness experiences would be harnessed and recorded while he was in England, having had no intention to write about his life prior to his journey.

This chapter has attempted to address two key questions. First, what had changed in this period compared to the first contact and early settlement era of the late sixteenth and early seventeenth centuries? And second, as more Englishmen and women settled permanently in the New World, what were the differences between their literature and that of interested commentators back in London, who had never crossed the Atlantic? In this second contact period, the two most significant changes are that English settlers became confident of the survival of the settlements, despite ongoing violence and tensions with the Native Americans and with other European nations. This period also saw the solidification in the English mind of the possibilities of the slave labour system in North America and of the gains to be made by becoming involved in the slave trade itself. The founding of the Royal Africa Company in 1660 represented a new chapter, a state-led foray into that most destructive of Atlantic World trades. These two changes are reflected in much of the literature written about the New World between 1640 and 1713. But there are also continuities, showing that some of the ways of writing about the Americas from the Elizabethan and Jacobean eras still endured. Two examples come to the fore: the continuing presence of the Black Legend as a motif for describing encounters with the Spanish and Native Americans; and the persistence in the interest in listing the commodities of the New World. The ever-present lists of flora and fauna, whether of use to local settlers or the new imperial markets, or of interest to scientists, still appeared in much of the travel literature of this second contact period. What really separates this second contact period from the first is the presence of native-born authors who considered America as their home and who had little or no experience of life in Europe. Their literature naturally often had a better sense of local environmental and safety concerns, of the threats from the natural world or from natives or other European settlers or military forces. They were keen to prove to Englishmen who had never crossed the Atlantic that their colonies and their people and commodities were not weaker than those of Europe, but in many cases should be considered superior.

CHAPTER 26

PERIODICAL LITERATURE

BRIAN COWAN

Inventing the Periodical

In the first issue of the *Tatler* (1709–11), Richard Steele announced that the 'End and Purpose of this my Paper' was to offer something to 'Persons of strong Zeal and weak Intellects', whereby they 'may be instructed, after their Reading, what to think'.[1] Steele's *Tatler* is often seen, along with its even better-known successor, the *Spectator* (1711–12, 1714), as the progenitor of that quintessentially eighteenth-century genre, the periodical essay. Anthologists and critics of the romantic era agreed that the *Tatler* and the *Spectator* initiated and exemplified a new style of essay-writing: the periodical. Anthologies such as Harrison's *British Classicks* (1785) and Alexander Chalmers's *British Essayists* (1802–3) gave the *Tatler* and the *Spectator* essays pride of place amongst their many volumes, and Nathan Drake's *Essays, Biographical, Critical and Historical: Illustrative of the Tatler, Spectator, and Guardian* (1805) declared that Steele and his main collaborator, Joseph Addison, were 'the fathers and founders of periodical writing, and round them, as round two mighty orbs, must be arranged in just order, and with a subserviency due from inferior luminaries, the numerous literati who, however slightly in degree, have contributed to heighten the lustre of the system to which they were attached'.[2] Critics such as Drake sought to link the periodical essay to earlier literary forms, such as Italian courtly dialogues and conduct manuals like Baldassare Castiglione's *Cortegiano* (1528) and Giovanni Della Casa's *Galateo* (1558), French essayists such as Michel de Montaigne, or neo-Theophrastan character writing such as Jean de La Bruyère's *Caractères* (1688), but they all nevertheless emphasized that it was Addison and Steele who brought these

---

[1] *The Tatler*, no. 1 (12 April 1709), in Donald F. Bond (ed.), *The Tatler*, 3 vols. (Oxford: Clarendon Press, 1987), 1: 15.

[2] Nathan Drake, *Essays, Biographical, Critical and Historical: Illustrative of the Tatler, Spectator, and Guardian*, 3 vols. (1805), 1, pp. iv–v.

continental influences into contact with the more traditionally English practice of periodical prose writing.

The connection between periodical prose and news writing could hardly be denied, but Drake tried to avoid drawing attention to it. Earlier attempts at periodical essay writing that focused on news, politics, or trade were dismissed as 'abortive attempts'.[3] Samuel Johnson's influential 'Life of Addison' (1781) probably did the most work in promoting the *Tatler* and the *Spectator* as progenitors of the periodical essay.

> Before the Tatler and the Spectator ... England had no masters of common life. No writers had yet undertaken to reform either the savageness of neglect, or the impertinence of civility; to shew when to speak, or to be silent; how to refuse, or how to comply. We had many books to teach us our more important duties, and to settle opinions in philosophy and politicks; but an *Arbiter elegantiarum*, a judge of propriety, was yet wanting, who should survey the track of daily conversation, and free it from thorns and prickles, which tease the passer, though they do not wound him.

Johnson knew what he was doing when he set the *Tatler* and *Spectator* up as innovative paragons of politeness. He understood well that these journals were far from the first English periodicals, and he knew that 'this mode of conveying cheap and easy knowledge began among us in the Civil War, when it was much the interest of either party to raise and fix the prejudices of the people'. Johnson then invoked the names of three prominent civil war era periodicals—*Mercurius Aulicus* (1643–6), *Mercurius Rusticus* (1643), and *Mercurius Civicus* (1643)—as well as later journals of political opinion, such as Roger L'Estrange's *Observator* (1681–7) and Charles Leslie's *Rehearsal* (1704–9), before dismissing journals of this type as works that 'taught many to talk, whom they could not teach to judge'.[4] By praising Addison's and Steele's periodical essays as the first '*arbitres elegantiarum*' in English prose, Johnson aimed to contest and denigrate the tradition of partisan periodical writing that began during the civil wars of the 1640s. In its place, he constructed a new genealogy for the periodical that began with the ostensibly non-partisan essays on manners, culture, and character found in the *Tatler* and the *Spectator*.

Johnson's alternative, not-so-secret history of the English periodical resonated with readers and critics in the later eighteenth and nineteenth centuries, and it provided the basis for the canon of periodical works reprinted and anthologized by later editors such as Chalmers and Drake. Johnson's new canon of Augustan periodical essay writings has survived in some sense up to the present day.[5] This 'Spectatorial' narrative of periodical

---

[3] Drake, *Essays*, 1: 24. See Richard Squibbs, *Urban Enlightenment and the Eighteenth-Century Periodical Essay: Transatlantic Retrospects* (Houndmills: Palgrave, 2014) for this process of genre formation.

[4] Samuel Johnson, *The Lives of the Most Eminent English Poets*, ed. Roger Lonsdale, 4 vols. (Oxford: Oxford University Press, 2006), 3: 7–8. For an earlier example of this kind of genealogy of periodical writing, see *British Mercury*, no. 369 (30 July–2 August 1712).

[5] Squibbs, *Urban Enlightenment*; Denise Gigante (ed.), *The Great Age of the English Essay: An Anthology* (New Haven: Yale University Press, 2008); Iona Italia, *The Rise of Literary Journalism in the Eighteenth Century: Anxious Employment* (London: Routledge, 2005); Clifford Siskin, *The Work of*

writing emphasizes the distinctive and novel aspects of the *Tatler* and the *Spectator* essays as well as a welcome break from the partisan bickering that occupied the pages of so many later Stuart era periodicals.[6] It also recognizes the long-lasting influence of Addison's and Steele's writings on the eighteenth- and nineteenth-century essays. In his 1818 lecture 'On the Periodical Essayists', William Hazlitt skipped straight from Michel de Montaigne to Richard Steele when constructing his genealogy of the founding fathers of the periodical essay.[7] Thus was established a relatively apolitical narrative of the rise of the English 'literary periodical' that has remained persistently predominant in histories of periodical writing.[8]

Rather than looking forward from the *Tatler* to the polite essays of the eighteenth and nineteenth centuries, this chapter seeks to recover the history of periodical prose writing that Johnson sought to occlude. For the periodical journal was an invention of the partisan political divisions that erupted as a result of the civil wars, and it persisted long after the resolution of armed hostilities. Viewed from this perspective, the periodical emerged as a closer cousin to news writing than to the essayistic tradition of Montaigne and Francis Bacon that later critics such as Johnson sought to accentuate. Like newspapers, periodicals were published regularly and sequentially, thus creating an expectation that they would address topics of current interest and do so on an ongoing basis. They often announced their topicality by using their date of publication as an identifying marker, and more often than not, they were published as separate issues with sequential numbering.[9]

Unlike news writing, however, seventeenth-century periodical writing gradually evolved as a slightly different species. News sought to offer 'a perfect diurnal', 'weekly intelligence', or a 'true relation' of the events of the day; it presented a direct reportage of events, and its prose was supposed to be dry and factual.[10] News was supposed to be descriptive above all, even if it presented its facts with a perspective favouring one side or another and despite the reputation of many news writers for mendacity. As such,

---

Writing: Literature and Social Change in Britain 1700–1830 (Baltimore: Johns Hopkins University Press, 1998), 155–71.

[6] Addison and Steele likely intended their essays to be understood as a break with the tradition of partisan periodical writing that preceded them: see Brian Cowan, 'Mr. Spectator and the Coffeehouse Public Sphere', *Eighteenth-Century Studies*, 37 (2004), 345–66.

[7] William Hazlitt, 'On the Periodical Essayists' (1819), in *The Complete Works of William Hazlitt*, P. P. Howe (ed.), 22 vols. (London: J. M. Dent, 1931), 6: 91–105.

[8] Walter Graham, *The Beginnings of English Literary Periodicals: A Study of Periodical Literature, 1665–1715* (Oxford: Oxford University Press, 1926); Walter Graham, *English Literary Periodicals* (New York: Thomas Nelson, 1930).

[9] *Diurnall Occurences, or, The Heads of the Proceedings in Both Houses of Parliament*, no. 5 (31 January–7 February 1642), is the first newsbook to use sequential numbering mentioned in Joad Raymond (ed.), *Making the News: An Anthology of the Newsbooks of Revolutionary England 1641–1660* (Little Window: Windrush, 1993), 43. The practice became standard soon thereafter.

[10] These phrases recur in the titles of civil war era newsbooks, see Raymond (ed.), *Making the News*; Joad Raymond, 'News Writing', in Andrew Hadfield (ed.), *The Oxford Handbook of English Prose 1500–1640* (Oxford: Oxford University Press, 2013), 396–414.

it was closely related to other contemporary genres of topical prose writings, such as the pamphlet and the 'true relation'; the first periodical newspapers were called 'weekly News pamphlets' by contemporaries. Many, perhaps even the majority of the earliest periodical publications were considered to be 'newsbooks' by their readers; even the canonical *Tatler* began its run by publishing news stories along with its better-known essays, commentaries, and letters.[11] The generic boundaries between these forms of reportage remained fluid in the early modern era.

Periodical prose did not just report on the news of the day; it offered commentary on the news. Periodical literature emerged as a potent form of persuasive prose: it 'told people what to think', as Steele recognized when he commenced writing for the *Tatler*. A key rhetorical tactic for periodicals was to adopt a characteristic voice for the journal. While in some cases this simply reflected the party line supported by the periodical, the authorial voice often took on a sort of life of its own. Regular writers for periodicals became associated with a journal, and sometimes developed a persona tailored to the paper's particular voice. For this reason, writers like Roger L'Estrange or John Tutchin became known as the 'Observator', and Daniel Defoe could be called 'Mr. Review'. Some journals developed fictional personae that were in some sense distinct from their authors: the *Tatler*'s Isaac Bickerstaffe and Mr Spectator were exemplary in this regard, and this is yet another reason why Addison's and Steele's writings were seen as models for subsequent periodical writers. They perfected the art of periodical rhetoric and managed to construct identities for their papers that were instantly recognizable and sympathetic voices for their readers. These nominally fictional voices for periodical writing have often been identified as 'eidolons', or ghostly voices, by modern critics since at least the 1950s, although references to the term as a shorthand for the personae adopted by periodical writers can be found as early as 1830.[12] While Bickerstaffe and Mr Spectator epitomized the eidolon for imitators and admirers of Addison and Steele, the rhetorical stance had developed much earlier in the propaganda efforts of later Stuart era serials and newsbooks.

Just as news writing flourished in response to the demand amongst English readers for information about what was happening as their country was torn apart by the civil wars, periodical writing also emerged out of the exigencies created by the partisan political divisions between Royalists and Parliamentarians to mobilize support for each side, and to provide partisans with a storehouse of arguments to use against their opponents.[13] Thus was established a recognizable new genre of periodical advice

---

[11] Joad Raymond, *Pamphlets and Pamphleteering in Early Modern Britain* (Cambridge: Cambridge University Press, 2003), 101; Frances E. Dolan, *True Relations: Reading, Literature, and Evidence in Seventeenth-Century England* (Philadelphia: University of Pennsylvania Press, 2013); Charles A. Knight, *A Political Biography of Richard Steele* (London: Pickering, 2009), 46–50.

[12] Manushag N. Powell, *Performing Authorship in Eighteenth-Century English Periodicals* (Lewisburg: Bucknell University Press, 2012), 23–4.

[13] Michael Braddick, 'Mobilisation, Anxiety and Creativity in England during the 1640s', in John Morrow and Jonathan Scott (eds.), *Liberty, Authority, Formality: Political Ideas and Culture, 1600–1900: Essays in Honour of Colin Davis* (Exeter: Imprint Academic, 2008), 175–94; Jason Peacey, *Print and Politics in the English Revolution* (Cambridge: Cambridge University Press, 2013).

literature that would endure well after the restoration of the monarchy and would increasingly shape the contours of political debate for the rest of the later Stuart period. While deeply influenced by and often anchored in the sphere of political contestation, the purview of periodical writing would expand beyond strictly partisan concerns in the later seventeenth century. Matters of commercial interest, literary or scientific topics, and moral problems could all be tackled by periodical writers as the genre flourished and took on a multiplicity of different guises. By the time that Steele founded the *Tatler*, periodical writing was already a diverse and hybrid genre.

Revolution (1643–60)

By any means of reckoning, the publication of the first royalist newsbook, *Mercurius Aulicus* (January 1643–September 1645), or 'The Court Mercury' as it came to be known, was a momentous occasion in the history of periodical writing. *Aulicus* presented itself as a newsbook: the subtitle to the first issue announced its design of 'communicating the intelligence, and affairs of the Court, to the rest of the Kingdome'. But its broader purpose as a partisan voice for the royalist cause was announced in its first paragraph:

> The world hath long enough beene abused with falshoods: And there's a weekly cheat put out to nourish the abuse amongst the people, and make them pay for their seducement. And that the world may see that the Court is neither so barren of intelligence, as it is conceived; nor the affairs thereof in so unprosperous a condition, as these Pamphlets make them: it is thought fit to let them truly understand the estate of things that so they may no longer pretend ignorance, or be deceived with untruthes: which being premised once for all, we now go on unto the businesse; wherein we shall proceed with all truth and candor.[14]

The advent of *Mercurius Aulicus* has been identified as 'the beginnings of advocacy journalism' and 'the first journal of opinion'.[15] Its publication set in motion a process of partisan propaganda production that would long outlast the armed hostilities that convinced King Charles I and his supporters to abandon their traditional hostility to news culture. *Aulicus* began publication in Oxford in January 1643 and continued for an additional 118 issues until it was terminated in September 1645 as the military hopes for the royalist cause began to look bleak. The Laudian cleric Peter Heylyn was the journal's first editor, but *Aulicus* soon became closely associated with the work of Heylyn's assistant and principal writer, John Berkenhead. It developed into the voice

---

[14] *Mercurius Aulicus* (1–7 January 1643), {2.09} in Raymond, *Making the News*, 92.
[15] Andrew Pettegree, *The Invention of News: How the World Came to Know About Itself* (New Haven: Yale University Press, 2014), 222; C. John Sommerville, *The News Revolution in England: Cultural Dynamics of Daily Information* (New York: Oxford University Press, 1996), 38.

of uncompromising royalism and demand for it was strong enough to allow for what would have otherwise been a cheap one penny quarto to sell for as much as eighteen pence after being smuggled into parliamentarian London.[16]

A key characteristic of early modern periodical publishing was the tendency for one journal to be 'answered' by another, usually from an opposing partisan perspective. In the civil war context out of which *Aulicus* emerged, it could hardly be otherwise. Within months, the parliamentarian cause had produced its own journal of opinion, the *Mercurius Britannicus* (August 1643–May 1646). Like *Aulicus*, *Britannicus* was a collective effort with official sponsorship (in this case probably the House of Commons itself), but it commonly became associated with the work of perhaps the most industrious journalist of the civil war and interregnum era, Marchamont Nedham.[17] *Britannicus*'s subtitle claimed that its aim was 'communicating the affaires of great Britaine: For the better information of the People', but its main aim was to refute the claims and the spin on current events offered by royalist publications such as *Aulicus*. The 'paper war' between the two journals would be the longest and most vitriolic of the civil war era and it would set the template for later contests between other conflicting periodicals.

Nedham notoriously wrote for both the parliamentarian and the royalist cause, and in August 1647, he switched his allegiance to the king and launched a new journal, *Mercurius Pragmaticus* (September 1647–March 1649). Although his allegiance had changed, Nedham's style had not. His characteristic mode was the joco-serious, an attempt to convey grave truths through a jocular, jesting style: 'yet I would have you know, in the midst of jest I am much in earnest.'[18] This was not a novel stance—one can find John Bastwick invoking the 'mingling *ioca seriis et seria iocis*' in his own defence before the outbreak of the civil wars—but Nedham developed the joco-serious style into a characteristic mode of expression that would endure throughout the many partisan tergiversations of his lifetime. Contemporaries claimed classical and humanist precedent for the joco-serious style in the works of Lucian and Sir Thomas More, and Nedham developed the deliberate mixing of 'jest and earnest' pronouncements into something of a personal motto. He claimed (not without irony) to 'set it down for a sure Maxim of State, *To live in Jest, and never to be in Earnest, except it be in order to die*'.[19]

---

[16] Jason Peacey, *Politicians and Pamphleteers: Propaganda During the English Civil Wars and Interregnum* (Aldershot: Ashgate, 2004), 189–90; Jason McElligott, *Royalism, Print and Censorship in Revolutionary England* (Woodbridge: Boydell, 2007), 19–20, 27.

[17] Peacey, *Politicians and Pamphleteers*, 190–1; Jason Peacey, 'The Struggle for *Mercurius Britanicus*: Factional Politics and the Parliamentarian Press, 1643–1646', *Huntington Library Quarterly*, 68 (2005), 517–43; Joad Raymond, 'Marchamont Nedham', in Laura Lunger Knoppers (ed.), *The Oxford Handbook of Literature and the English Revolution* (Oxford: Oxford University Press, 2012), 375–93.

[18] *Mercurius Pragmaticus*, no. 1 (28 March–4 April 1648), 2.

[19] John Bastwick, *The Letany of John Bastwick, Doctor of Phisicke* (Leiden, 1637), sig. A2r. Andrew McRae, *Literature, Satire and the Early Stuart State* (Cambridge: Cambridge University Press, 2004), 193; *Mercurius Politicus*, no. 352 (5–12 March 1657), {8.17} in Raymond, *Making the News*, 370; Blair Worden, *Literature and Politics in Cromwellian England: John Milton, Andrew Marvell, Marchamont Nedham*

Nedham's joco-serious style established a model for future periodical writers. The dialogue between jest and earnest would be imitated by periodical writers throughout the later Stuart era.[20] Journals such as Thomas Flatman's often reprinted, and frequently imitated, *Heraclitus Ridens* (February 1681–August 1682) would later use the conceit as a framework for rehearsing political arguments between 'jest' and 'earnest'.[21]

When Nedham's political loyalties turned again after the regicide from royalism to defending the new commonwealth, he nevertheless maintained his allegiance to wit. Nedham's prospectus for the commonwealth's journal *Mercurius Politicus* (June 1650–April 1660) explained his purpose:

> The designe of this Pamphlett being to undeceive the People, it must bee written in a Jocular way, or else it will never bee cryed up: For those truths which the Multitude regard not in a serious dresse, being represented in pleasing popular Aires, make Musick to the Common sence, and charme the Phantsie; which ever swayes the Scepter in Vulgar Judgements; much more then Reason.
>
> I entitle it Politicus, because the present Gouernment is veram πολιτεία [politeia] as it is opposed to the despotick forme. It shalbee my care to sayle in a middle way, between the Scylla and Charybdis of Scurrility and prophanenes ... I desire suplyes of the best Intelligence of State; and that Tuesday may bee the weekly day, because most convenient for dispersing it through the Nation.
>
> I desire likewise that some Order may bee passed to authorize it.[22]

Mercurius Politicus largely lived up to Nedham's promises. The first issue announced its arrival by asking: 'Why Should not the Common-wealth have a Fool, as well as the King had?'[23] Nedham's desire to 'undeceive the people' would be reiterated frequently by subsequent periodical writers, as was his claim to forge a 'middle way' that would help him avoid accusations of impropriety, even if his work attracted criticism for its demotic and railing style. As early as 1643, one of Nedham's critics claimed that his writing was

---

(Oxford: Oxford University Press, 2007), 37, 75, 316. On the reception and use of Lucianic satire in the period, see Nicholas McDowell, 'The Double Personality of Lucianic Satire from Dryden to Fielding', in Paddy Bullard (ed.), *The Oxford Handbook of Eighteenth-Century Satire* (Oxford: Oxford University Press, 2019), 145–60.

[20] John Spurr, 'Style, Wit and Religion in Restoration England', in Stephen Taylor and Grant Tapsell (eds.), *The Nature of the English Revolution Revisited: Essays in Honour of John Morrill* (Woodbridge: Boydell, 2013), 240–1. See also Raymond A. Anselment, *'Betwixt Jest and Earnest': Marprelate, Milton, Marvell, Swift and the Decorum of Religious Ridicule* (Toronto: University of Toronto Press, 1979).

[21] See *Democritus Ridens, or, Comus and Momus, a New Jest and Earnest Pratling Concerning the Times*, no. 1 (17 March 1681); *The New Heraclitus Ridens, or, An Old Dialogue Between Jest and Earnest Revived*, no. 1 (24 May 1689); [William Pittis], *Heraclitus Ridens, in a Dialogue Between Jest and Earnest, Concerning the Times* (August 1703–March 1704).

[22] J. Milton French (ed.), *The Life Records of John Milton, Volume II: 1639–1651* (New Brunswick, NJ: Rutgers University Press, 1950), 310–11; compare Raymond, 'Marchamont Nedham', 385; and Peacey, *Politicians and Pamphleteers*, 319.

[23] *Mercurius Politicus*, no. 1 (6–13 June 1650), 1.

recognizable by its 'impudence' and 'we cannot say that this Fellow writes, but vomits'. It was the equivalent of 'the biting of [a] Mad-Dogge'.[24]

Equally influential was the way in which Nedham imitated the manner of news writing by publishing his journal weekly and with the advantage of having advance supply of intelligence to work from and comment upon. His periodical would be both timely and opinionated. The issues written under the commonwealth contained a series of opinion pieces that borrowed from his previously published *The Case of the Common-wealth of England Stated* (1650), and other material would appear later in *The Excellencie of a Free State* (1656). Although some have claimed that Nedham's style 'flattened' after the commonwealth gave way to Cromwell's protectorate, he could be provoked to return to satiric form when engaging with James Harrington's *Oceana* (1656).[25] *Politicus* was highly profitable, especially under the Cromwellian protectorate when Nedham was granted an effective monopoly on news publication. Nedham was granted half of the profits from the sales of *Politicus* and at times earned a state pension as well. By the later years of the protectorate, Nedham was remitting nearly a quarter of the paper's profits back to secretary of state John Thurloe in return for intelligence provided for publication in *Politicus*.[26] The symbiotic relationship between Nedham's periodical and the propaganda and information management needs of the interregnum governments proved to be highly successful. *Politicus* would be among the longest lived periodicals of the later Stuart era, remaining in print for almost an entire decade and ending only when the restoration of the monarchy made Nedham's position untenable.

Nevertheless, a model had been set. Nedham proved that a government-approved periodical of news mixed with opinion could be a valuable tool in shaping opinion and legitimizing the policies of the regime in power. Before the outbreak of the civil wars and the installation of a post-regicide regime, there had been little need for a government-sponsored propaganda journal. After the restoration of the monarchy, there was hope in some quarters that matters would return to the *status quo ante bellum* and 'all our discourse will bee of Hunting & Hawkeing, Boling, Cocking, & such things', but there was no going back. While Roger L'Estrange castigated Nedham in 1660 as 'the *Goliah* of the *Philistines*' and 'the great Champion of the late Vsurper', he would later put his pen to the service of defending the new government with a periodical of his own.[27]

---

[24] Joad Raymond, *The Invention of the Newspaper: English Newsbooks 1641–1649* (Oxford: Clarendon Press, 1996), 155, citing *Anti-Britannicus*, no. 2 [11 Aug. 1645], 11.

[25] Raymond, *Making the News*, 335–6; compare Kevin Sharpe, *Image Wars: Promoting Kings and Commonwealths in England 1603–1660* (New Haven: Yale University Press, 2010), 420.

[26] Jason Peacey, *Politicians and Pamphleteers*, 195; Jason Peacey, 'Cromwellian England: A Propaganda State?' *History*, 91 (2006), 193, 196; Joad Raymond, '"A Mercury with a Winged Conscience": Marchamont Nedham, Monopoly and Censorship', *Media History*, 4 (1998), 13, 15.

[27] Thomas Slaughter (ed.), *Ideology and Politics on the Eve of Restoration: Newcastle's Advice to Charles* (Philadelphia: American Philosophical Society, 1984), 56; Roger L'Estrange, *A Rope for a Pol* (1660), in Raymond (ed.), *Making the News*, 332.

Restoration (1660–88)

Periodical writing flourished after the restoration of the monarchy. The Licensing Act of 1662 restored pre-publication censorship and over a year later Sir Roger L'Estrange was appointed to be chief licensor of the press. L'Estrange also obtained his own licence to publish news under the guise of a new publication that appeared on Mondays as *The Intelligencer* and on Thursdays as *The Newes* (August 1663–January 1666). Here he famously and somewhat paradoxically claimed that news publication 'makes the multitude too familiar with the actions, and counsels of their superiors, too pragmaticall and censorious, and gives them, not only an itch, but a kind of colourable right, and licence, to be meddling with the government' as a way of introducing his readers to his own newspaper, which he thought would 'redeem the vulgar from their former mistakes, and delusions, and to preserve them from the like for the time to come'. Nevertheless, L'Estrange continued to publish his *Intelligencer* and *Newes* until it was decided to make the *London Gazette* the only licensed newspaper. L'Estrange was compensated with the promise of an annual pension of £200, a sum which would prove to be unreliably paid.[28] Although he was obliged to give up his news writing, L'Estrange did not abandon his periodical writing.

L'Estrange would in fact become perhaps the most influential periodical writer of the Restoration era. The furore over the rumours of a popish plot to kill the king in the late 1670s and the further polarization of the political culture between Whigs and Tories in the 1680s encouraged the rebirth of polemic prose writing in periodical form. Two authors in particular—one writing for the Whigs and the other for the Tories—shaped the development of periodical writing at the moment when party politics began to take shape for the first time. Henry Care's Whiggish *Weekly Pacquet of Advice from Rome* (December 1678–July 1683) presented church history and especially the history of the reformation in weekly essays that provided partisan context for the popish plot debates. On the other side, Roger L'Estrange's *The Observator* (April 1681–March 1687) presented a demotic Tory perspective on the politics of the last years of Charles II's reign and continued to support the Crown's positions under James II. Care's *Weekly Paquet* and L'Estrange's *Observator* would be the two longest lived periodicals of the era.

While working in a genre established by civil war era periodical writers, Care and L'Estrange also managed to innovate by imagining their publications to exist not only as occasional papers written in response to the immediate debates of the present but also as works that would be bound up together as volumes and later read as first-draft histories

---

[28] *The Intelligencer*, no. 1 (31 August 1663), 1; Geoff Kemp, 'The Works of Roger L'Estrange: An Annotated Bibliography', in Anne Duncan-Page and Beth Lynch (eds.), *Roger L'Estrange and the Making of Restoration Culture* (Aldershot: Ashgate, 2008), 211–12; George Kitchin, *Sir Roger L'Estrange: A Contribution to the History of the Press in the Seventeenth Century* (London: Kegan Paul, 1913), 129, 150–4; Peter Hinds, *'The Horrid Popish Plot': Roger L'Estrange and the Circulation of Political Discourse in Late-Seventeenth-Century London* (Oxford: British Academy, 2010), 37.

of their moment. Despite his dislike for both authors, Macaulay used their periodicals as rich source material for his picture of late seventeenth-century English society.[29] A distinctive temporal awareness of periodical writing emerged in the Restoration era: it was, on the one hand, firmly anchored in the concerns of the present whilst, on the other, also consciously looking forward to being consulted by future readers as a witness to the history of the times.

The temporal orientation of Restoration era periodicals was tripartite rather than simply dual, for these works were deeply concerned with the past as well as the present and posterity. Care's *Weekly Pacquet* presented a history of popery that was meant to explain why contemporary readers should be concerned about the nefarious plots and actions of present-day Roman Catholics. Ecclesiastical history was used to illustrate a process whereby 'step by step the mystery of Iniquity was working apace, and Superstition and Tyranny [were] growing up mainly in the Church' of Rome.[30] L'Estrange, too, used an awareness of the past to energize his political commitments in the present, but for him it was the domestic history of the civil wars and the interregnum that animated his prose. L'Estrange argued that the key to understanding the rise of Whig politics in Charles II's reign was to see it as a rehearsal of the growth of opposition to the policies of Charles I that led to the outbreak of civil wars and ultimately to regicide. This was a common Tory talking point that was hardly unique to L'Estrange, but no other writer of his age hammered the message home with greater enthusiasm or persistence than he. Sceptical readers of the day may have thought the claim that the conflicts of 1681 were a reiteration of the unfortunate events of 1641 was 'Nothing but crying 40 & 41' over and over again, but the comparison was politically effective for the Tory cause.[31]

Both Care and L'Estrange sought to distinguish their periodical writings from more downmarket publications such as pamphlets and newspapers, yet neither writer was ashamed to admit that their desired readership was not elite. Care decried against those who 'clamour that [*The Weekly Pacquet*] was but a pamphlet, [and hence] is below an intelligent mans regards; as if sense and reason were confin'd to folio's, and could not be delivered but in vast cumbersome tracts'. He also proudly declared that he would 'gladly assist the vulgar, whose souls are equally precious, and more in danger' than those of the learned and he was forthright about the propagandistic aims of his periodical. It was published in 'single sheets' like newspapers and pamphlets so that 'it might the better and more easily fall into the hands and hearts of the middle or meaner rank; who having not time nor coyn to buy or peruse chargeable, tedious, and various books, might

---

[29] Lois Schwoerer, *The Ingenious Mr. Henry Care, Restoration Publicist* (Baltimore: Johns Hopkins University Press, 2001), 227; T. A. Birrell, 'Sir Roger L'Estrange: The Journalism of Orality', in John Barnard and D. F. McKenzie (eds.), *The Cambridge History of the Book in Britain, Volume IV: 1557–1695* (Cambridge: Cambridge University Press, 2002), 657–61 (661).

[30] *Weekly Pacquet of Advice from Rome*, vol. 2, no. 1 (11 July 1679), 6.

[31] Tim Harris, *London Crowds in the Age of Charles II: Propaganda and Politics from the Restoration until the Exclusion Crisis* (Cambridge: Cambridge University Press, 1987), 134–8; Matthew Neufeld, *The Civil Wars after 1660: Public Remembering in Late Stuart England* (Woodbridge: Boydell, 2013); MS note on *Heraclitus Ridens*, no. 19 (7 June 1681) in Bodleian Library, Nichols Newspapers, vol. 3b.

readily and cheaply be furnisht here with a general scheme of Popery'.[32] Nevertheless, the papers would later be published as volumes fit to be bound, and supplemented by such paratextual apparatus as an index for the fourth volume.[33]

L'Estrange was equally forthright about his aims for the *Observator*. This was a journal aimed at telling the people what to think, and to do so in order to correct the errors promoted by Whig writers such as Care. L'Estrange affirmed in the preface to the first volume of the journal that his 'papers were written, indifferently, for the enformation of the multitude; and for the reproof of a faction ... but if I could have resolved upon a dedication, with any particular mark, or epithete of distinction; it should have been, to the IGNORANT, the SEDITIOUS, or the SCHISMATICALL Reader; for there, properly, lies my bus'ness'.[34] L'Estrange did not disparage his plebian readers for their social station. Instead, he sought to elevate and educate them. He thought that the lower sort of people would rest content in their station 'if other people would but let 'em alone, in the bed and position, where the order of nature and policy has lodg'd them' but since 'their minds are weak; their faculties of discerning things are dark, and heavy: for want of use, study, application, letters and experience. They are easily wrought upon by appearances, colours and paradox, because they cannot enter into the depth, the truth, and the reason of things'.[35] For this reason, L'Estrange decided to speak directly to these commoners through his periodical writing.

The *Observator* was carefully designed to exist both as a coffee-house paper that would provoke immediate debate and as an impressive bound folio volume that would document the moment for posterity. L'Estrange boasted in the paper itself that 'there are hundreds and hundreds of setts of [*Observators*], fairly bound up, posted and preserved in a condition to be delivered over to posterity', and 'that in time to come, these collections will be lookt upon with the same reverence that we our selves pay, at this day, to the most authentique manuscripts of former times'.[36] The bound folios also included prefaces, often a frontispiece portrait of Sir Roger L'Estrange himself, and elaborate indexes. The indexes were necessary, for the prose was prolix and the topics covered were wide-ranging but the references were often obscure, even to contemporary readers. Even L'Estrange admitted that some readers might find 'Digesting such a Medly of Thoughts' difficult, especially 'when Every Day started New Argument; and Every Paper was to be Accommodated to the Accidents and Emergences of the Season'.[37]

Given that the periodical was published two to four times a week over the course of six years, the medley of thoughts produced by L'Estrange was indeed extensive. All told, the *Observators* comprised 931 issues covering 1,866 pages and including more than

---

[32] *Weekly Pacquet of Advice from Rome*, vol. 1 (3 December 1678–4 July 1679), sig. A2v; vol. 2 (11 July–5 December 1679), sig. A2r.

[33] *History of Popery, or, Pacquet of Advice from Rome*, vol. 4 (1682 [30 December 1681–18 August 1682]).

[34] *Observator in Dialogue. The First Volume* (1684), unpaginated preface.

[35] *Observator*, third series, no. 206 (4 September 1686).

[36] *Observator*, first series, no. 259 (16 December 1682).

[37] *Observator in Dialogue. The First Volume* (1684), unpaginated postscript to the preface.

2.4 million words. Care's *Pacquet* was not nearly so prolix but remains impressive nevertheless; all 5 volumes of the periodical comprised 240 issues with a possible total print run of 542,800 copies published over the course of its four and a half years in publication. Like the *Observator*, the *Pacquet* was also sold in bound volumes with prefaces and tables of contents to guide readers who wished to navigate its copious content.[38] Paratextual efforts of this kind encouraged readers to understand these periodicals as something more than just an ephemeral newspaper: they were encouraged to collect and bind the entire print run in complete volumes.

In this way, Care and L'Estrange further developed the new genre of periodical writing. They continued writing in Nedham's joco-serious style and attempted to advance an earnest partisan political agenda couched in an informal, sometimes humorous, manner that emulated the vernacular speech often heard on the streets of London in the later seventeenth century.[39] Their prose was replete with topical and personal references that would only make sense to readers who were familiar with current events and metropolitan society. At the same time, they cultivated a sense that the corpus of their works would endure for posterity as valuable commentary on the age. The periodical writings of the Restoration would indeed remain etched in the memories of the next generation and the distinctive style (and indeed often the very titles of the works) developed by authors such as Care and L'Estrange would be imitated by the next generation of writers after the Revolution of 1688.

Post-Revolution (1689–1714)

When the Glorious Revolution upended English politics, periodical writing was well ensconced as a fixture of the publishing world. While the numbers of periodical titles and issues dropped precipitously after 1681 in the wake of the Tory reaction against Whig agitation for an exclusion bill, they began to creep up again after the Glorious Revolution. By 1691, there were as many periodical titles being published as had appeared at the height of the exclusion crisis in 1680–1, and the average number of issues published per year was nearly as high.[40] Periodical writing re-emerged as vibrant as ever after the Revolution, and the contents found in post-revolutionary periodicals became even more diversified than ever.

While the Revolution reintroduced periodicals to the reading public, it did not inaugurate a renaissance of partisan political periodical publication. Despite the persistence of significant pockets of Jacobite allegiance to the now exiled King James II, and despite the continued publication of clandestine Jacobite propaganda, no attempt

---

[38] Kemp, 'The Works of Roger L'Estrange', 213; Schwoerer, *Ingenious Mr. Henry Care*, 74.
[39] Schwoerer, *Ingenious Mr. Henry Care*, 147–50; Birrell, 'Sir Roger L'Estrange'.
[40] Carolyn Nelson and Matthew Seccomb, 'The Creation of the Periodical Press, 1620–1695', in Barnard and McKenzie (eds.), *Cambridge History of the Book. Volume IV*, 533–50 (figure 25.1, 534).

was made to produce a major Jacobite periodical in the 1690s. Charles Leslie's Jacobite-friendly opinions in *Rehearsal* (August 1704–March 1709) would ultimately appear along with the resurgence of the 'rage of party' in Anne's reign, but the 1690s witnessed a temporary break in the furious partisanship that had become a signal feature of the last years of Charles II's reign.[41] Instead, the era saw the efflorescence of periodicals devoted to miscellaneous topics of general interest, including literary entertainment, such as Peter Motteux's *Gentleman's Journal, or, The Monthly Miscellany* (January 1692–June 1697); commercial affairs, such as John Houghton's *Collection for the Improvement of Husbandry and Trade* (March 1692–September 1703); or social and ethical concerns, such as John Dunton's *Athenian Mercury* (May 1691–June 1697). While some pre-revolutionary periodicals made attempts to address similar topics, only after the 1690s did non-political periodicals become long-standing commercially successful ventures. These miscellany periodicals made the intellectual interests of seventeenth-century virtuoso culture accessible to a wider reading public. Early modern English virtuosity was defined above all by an almost insatiable curiosity about natural and social phenomena and how to explain them through careful eye-witnessing and rational inquiry.[42] The greatest testament to English virtuoso culture was the *Philosophical Transactions* (1665–present) of the Royal Society, which published the findings and reports of both English and foreign virtuosi in a periodical that is often thought to be the first academic journal of scientific investigations.[43] While the *Philosophical Transactions* was not a commercial endeavour nor was it aimed at a general reading public, its success in the Restoration era surely offered a model and an inspiration for the more profit-motivated publications of enterprising journalists such as Motteux, Houghton, and Dunton.

The circumstances of the post-revolutionary era made the 1690s a particularly propitious moment for the success of the new miscellany periodicals. The advent of war with France prompted novel experiments in public and private joint-stock investments, and the war made it imperative for merchants and tradespeople to be aware of how the war might affect their business affairs. Political arithmetic, or the use of quantitative methods to better understand (and attempt to control) the natural and social worlds, moved from closed counsels of state ministers to the public sphere. This post-revolutionary financial revolution provided an added fillip to the already extensive culture of projecting and improvement that was a distinctive feature of later Stuart England.[44] After the lapsing of the Licensing Act in 1695, it became even easier for publishing entrepreneurs to bring new ventures to market that attempted to satisfy this demand for new information.

---

[41] Paul Kléber Monod, *Jacobitism and the English People, 1688–1788* (Cambridge: Cambridge University Press, 1989), 28–44.

[42] Brian Cowan, 'An Open Elite: The Peculiarities of Connoisseurship in Early Modern England', *Modern Intellectual History*, 1 (2004), 151–83; Brian Cowan, *The Social Life of Coffee: The Emergence of the British Coffeehouse* (New Haven: Yale University Press, 2005).

[43] On the *Philosophical Transactions*, see Chapter 24 on 'Mock-Scientific Literature' by Gregory Lynall and Chapter 33 on 'Scientific Transactions' by Felicity Henderson.

[44] Paul Slack, *The Invention of Improvement: Information and Material Progress in Seventeenth-Century England* (Oxford: Oxford University Press, 2015).

Houghton's *Collection* was most obviously designed to fit the need for information regarding matters such as financial affairs, international commerce, and local trades. He stated that his journal was intended for small scale and large scale traders involved in both local and international markets. The periodical provided commodity prices as well as the prices of joint-stock shares in the East India Company, the Guinea Company, and the Hudson's Bay Company. Houghton saw his *Collection* as a sort of virtual coffee-house: 'Altho' they that live at London, may, every noon and night on working days, go to Garraway's Coffee-House, and see what prices the actions bear of most companies trading in joynt-stocks, yet for those whose occasions permit not there to see, they may be satisfied once a week how it is, and thereby the whole kingdom may reap advantage by those trades.' His was a project of national improvement. Thus he proclaimed: 'Without doubt, if those trades were better known, 'twould be a great advantage to the kingdom.'[45] Houghton's *Collection* became the journal of post-revolutionary England's financial revolution, and the data it reported has proved to be a valuable resource for historians of the early stock market. But each issue also contained a leading essay written by Houghton on various aspects of practical trades such as soap making as well as financial trading on the newly established stock market.

Houghton was a Fellow of the Royal Society and he boasted of its support for his project in the pages of his *Collection*. He had previously contributed to the *Philosophical Transactions* and it appears that Houghton imagined his periodical to be something of a companion to the Royal Society's journal of scientific discoveries as well as a 'hand maid' to the newspapers of the kingdom. Like the periodicals, and unlike newspapers, however, Houghton's *Collection* was also intended to be collected and bound in volumes with indexes, including 'an index of all the Advertisements, whereby for ages to come, they may be useful'.[46] His essays on agriculture and trade contributed to the Royal Society's Baconian project of promoting and publishing a history of trades that would present the current state of knowledge in all of the productive industries of the kingdom.[47] His collections of advertisements were also remarkable as Houghton sought to use his periodical to promote and develop new markets such as brokerage services and even matchmaking. In 1695, he published what may well be considered the first personal ad. He prefaced it by emphasizing that he has always 'undertaken to advertize all sorts of things that are honourable; and what follows, is not otherwise', adding as well that 'I am well paid for it'. The ad stated: 'A gentleman about 30 years of age, that says he has a very good estate, would willingly match himself to some good young gentlewoman, that has a fortune of 3,000 l. or thereabout, and he will make settlement to content.'[48]

---

[45] *A Collection for Improvement of Husbandry and Trade*, vol. 1, no. 1 (30 March 1692); vol. 1, no. 2 (6 April 1692).

[46] *Collection for Improvement of Husbandry and Trade*, vol. 3, no. 52 (28 July 1693).

[47] Natasha Glaisyer, 'Readers, Correspondence and Communities: John Houghton's *A Collection for Improvement of Husbandry and Trade (1692–1703)*', in Alexandra Shepard and Phil Withington (eds.), *Communities in Early Modern England: Networks, Place, Rhetoric* (Manchester: Manchester University Press, 2000), 235–51.

[48] *Collection for Improvement of Husbandry and Trade*, vol. 7, no. 156 (26 July 1695).

If Houghton produced the first periodical devoted to commerce and finance, John Dunton's *Athenian Mercury* invented the social periodical. Just as Houghton's *Collection* brought the Baconian history of trades to a wider public, so did Dunton's *Mercury* introduce casuistic reasoning to its readers. Indeed, it was later published in collected form as the *Athenian Gazette, or, Casuistical Mercury*. Dunton addressed cases of conscience that troubled his readers and he invited his readers to send their queries to the journal to be answered by its ostensible authors, the 'Athenian Society'. This interactive feature and the club motif would both prove to be key innovations that would be imitated in later periodicals such as Defoe's Scandal Club in his *Review* (February 1704–June 1713) and especially in the *Tatler* and *Spectator*. Although Dunton also addressed matters of scientific or commercial interest in his periodical, questions of a social nature predominated and they constituted its primary appeal. It offered a public forum for the discussion of matters that might otherwise be considered private concerns.

The *Mercury* addressed questions related to social relations, gender, manners, marriage, and sexuality with an unprecedented degree of detail. In one volume for the first half of 1692, just under a third of all the questions answered concerned courtship, marriage, or personal relationships, far more than the second largest category of questions related to religious matters.[49] The questions could be provocative, although the answers often bordered on the facetious, such as the response to the query if it is possible 'for one woman to love another as passionately and constantly as if the love were between the different sexes?' Dunton replied 'As constantly they soon may, but as passionately how should they, unless they're of the race of Tiresias?'[50]

Dunton's *Mercury* was one of the first periodicals that cultivated female as well as male readers. It actively courted them, as in a notice published in one of the early issues of the journal pronounced clearly: 'We have receiv'd this week a very Ingenious Letter from a Lady in the Country, who desires to know whether her Sex might not send us Questions as well as men, to which we answer Yes, they may. Our design being to answer all manner of questions sent to us by either sex, that may be either useful to the public or to particular persons.'[51] The appeal worked, and the *Mercury* both received and published a substantial number of queries from its female readers. In this way, the *Mercury* created a precedent for Richard Steele's famous resolve 'to have something which may be of Entertainment to the Fair Sex, in Honour of whom I have invented the Title of this Paper'—namely the *Tatler*—or Addison's later declaration in the *Spectator* that 'there are none to whom this Paper will be more useful than to the female World'.[52]

---

[49] Helen Berry, *Gender, Society and Print Culture in Late-Stuart England: The Cultural World of the Athenian Mercury* (Aldershot: Ashgate, 2003), 28, 244.

[50] *Athenian Mercury*, vol. 11, no. 25 (3 October 1693).

[51] *Athenian Mercury*, vol. 1, no. 13 (5 May 1691).

[52] Berry, *Gender, Society and Print Culture*, 61, 246; *Tatler*, no. 1 (12 April 1709), in Bond (ed.), *Tatler*, 1: 15; *The Spectator*, no. 10 (12 March 1711), in Donald F. Bond (ed.), *The Spectator*, 5 vols. (Oxford: Clarendon Press, 1965) 1: 46.

Dunton's cultivation of a female readership and his invitation of women to contribute to the journal itself was a radical innovation and it created a new model for conceiving of the periodical as means of addressing matters of social concern—often styled as feminine topics, even if they also appealed to men—that would prove to be powerfully influential in the eighteenth century.[53]

While the 1690s saw a brief hiatus in the fervid publication of partisan periodicals that had come to define the genre after its emergence during the civil wars, the practice returned with renewed vigour as the rage of party burned with greater ferocity in Queen Anne's reign. The periodicals adopted the techniques of their Restoration era predecessors, using dialogues and eidolons such as Mr Review and Mr Observator. In some cases, the titles of older periodicals were revived under a new guise. Thomas Flatman's Tory *Heraclitus Ridens* (February 1681–August 1682) was launched anew by William Pittis under the same title and ran from July 1703 until March 1704. Most notable perhaps was the return of the *Observator* (April 1702–July 1712), but this time as a Whig periodical authored at first by John Tutchin and later, after Tutchin's death in 1707, by George Ridpath. The Whig *Observator* was launched within a month of the accidental death of William III and announced its intention to defend the Protestant succession in the face of Jacobite challenges. It quickly took up the Whig case against the high church and Tory revival that followed upon Queen Anne's accession and it vigorously prosecuted the case for war against Louis XIV's France in the War of the Spanish Succession. Although Anne's accession as queen was largely uncontested, it raised new questions as to the basis for her royal title: was it statutory or hereditary? And the queen's lack of heirs meant that the Protestant succession would depend upon the Act of Settlement, only recently passed in 1701. To a large degree, the political vitriol of Anne's reign derived from the uncertainties regarding the nature of her reign and, even more so, the viability of a Hanoverian succession to what now appeared to be the last Stuart monarch.[54]

The return of the *Observator* as a Whig periodical surely prompted Flatman's revival of *Heraclitus Ridens* a year later, and by 1704 they were joined by two significant new journals, Leslie's fervently high church *Rehearsal* and Daniel Defoe's *Review* (February 1704–June 1713). Defoe's periodical was surely subsidized by Robert Harley and it soon became known as the public voice of the government, even if the contents of each issue remained Defoe's responsibility. Defoe's *Review* holds an important place in the transformations of the English periodical in the later Stuart era.[55] It was designed to be a journal of political propaganda much like the works of Nedham, L'Estrange, and Care,

---

[53] Jennie Batchelor and Manushag N. Powell (eds.), *Women's Periodicals and Print Culture in Britain, 1690–1820s* (Edinburgh: Edinburgh University Press, 2018).

[54] Edward Taylor, 'John Tutchin's Observator, Comment Serials and the "Rage of Party" in Britain, 1678-c.1730', *Historical Journal*, 63 (2020), 862–84; Joseph Hone, *Literature and Party Politics at the Accession of Queen Anne* (Oxford: Oxford University Press, 2017).

[55] Brian Cowan, 'Daniel Defoe's Review and the Transformations of the English Periodical', *Huntington Library Quarterly*, 77 (2014), 79–110.

but it also incorporated elements of Houghton's commercial writings and Dunton's interactive social agenda. For almost a decade, and over the course of over 5,600 pages of print and close to four million words of prose, Defoe addressed a variety of different topics including current events, political theory, international relations, trade, and commerce, as well as social and moral concerns. He switched the policy slant of the *Review* to align with the shifting priorities of the various ministries of Anne's reign, even managing to maintain the support of the Whig junto after Harley's resignation and retaining Harley's confidence after his triumphal return to office. Throughout its run, Defoe managed to use the *Review* to tack between the high church, divine right Jacobitism of Leslie's *Rehearsal*, and the extremist country Whiggery of Tutchin's and Ridpath's *Observator*.

This pose of moderation would prove to be effective, and it too would be echoed in Addison's claims in the *Spectator* that the 'paper has not in it a single word of news, a reflection in politics, nor a stroke of party' and that 'among those Advantages which the Publick may reap from this Paper, it is not the least, that it draws Mens Minds off from the Bitterness of Party'.[56] Despite these protestations, both the *Tatler* and the *Spectator* were obviously partisan Whig periodicals and they were understood as such by contemporaries. Nevertheless, their extremely polished style and the ways in which they almost seamlessly merged social commentary with a sly political posture made them stand out amongst the crowd. As much as they tried to deny it, the periodical writers of the later Stuart era were indebted to news writing and the rise of the newspaper business. From the civil wars onward, reporting on current events was a highly politicized endeavour. News invited commentary, and this created an opening for the invention of periodicals of opinion. News could not simply be reported; it also had to be 'spun' to make it palatable (or even comprehensible) to the polarized reading public. Even after the restoration of the monarchy made the divisions between Royalists and Parliamentarians a thing of the past, the tendency to view current events through one frame or the other remained; and thus few could be surprised when the succession crisis provoked by the real prospect of a Catholic successor in James, the Duke of York, reanimated the old animosities of the past in the form of Whig and Tory partisanship. Nor did the Revolution that replaced the Catholic James II with a new Protestant regime and the assurance of a Protestant succession in the future allay this divide, as the return of partisan journalism in Anne's reign proved decisively.

When Steele and Addison began to write their *Tatler* and *Spectator* essays with the aim of telling people what to think, they were participating in this tradition. The main difference from their predecessors is that they did so in the guise of impartial moralists rather than as declared or thinly disguised partisans. Speaking of Steele's Isaac Bickerstaff, John Gay wrote 'Instead of complying with the false Sentiments or Vicious tasts of the Age, either in Morality, Criticism, or Good Breeding, he has boldly assur'd them, that they were altogether in the wrong, and commanded them with an Authority,

---

[56] *Spectator*, no. 262 (31 December 1711), 2: 517, 519.

which perfectly well became him, to surrender themselves to his Arguments, for Vertue and Good Sense'.[57] By adopting the guise of impartial moral censors, Addison and Steele reinvented partisan periodical writing for a new age of politeness in the eighteenth century. The undeniable success of their venture has occluded the debt they owed to the predecessors against which they strived so hard to distinguish themselves.

---

[57] John Gay, 'The Present State of Wit' (29 May 1711), in John Gay, *Poetry and Prose*, ed. Vinton A. Dearing and Charles E. Beckwith, 2 vols. (Oxford: Oxford University Press, 1974), 2: 452.

CHAPTER 27

POLITICAL DEBATE

MARK KNIGHTS

This chapter examines both what was at stake in political debates in the period and, more importantly, how their style and conduct became a matter of interest and concern to contemporaries. Content and style were intimately connected. It often became difficult to separate the refutation of a rival position from a critique of how that position had been put forward. Political debate and prose style went hand in hand because the pressure of heated disputes disturbed both ideological and literary norms. Partisanship was thus a stance taken both on the political debates of the day and on how those debates were conducted; and this had important consequences, as we shall see, on truth-claims, on the art of polemics, on satire, and on ideals of impartiality and civil or polite ways of arguing. Partisan debate, it will be argued, was a highly disruptive but also creative force.

The chapter begins by asking what constituted political debate, and it stresses that contemporaries did not neatly divide the political from the religious or the economic or the social. In mapping out the key fault-lines of political debate, it becomes clear that the 'political' has to be considered a capacious category and that the boundaries of politics were also expanding in the seventeenth century.[1] One model, put forward by the sociologist Jürgen Habermas, highlights this development by talking in terms of the emergence of the 'public sphere', a concept that has shaped a good deal of the recent literature about political discourse. The chapter then shifts to examining the inventive polemic and invective of the period, highlighting the shift from civil war to paper war and the growing role that 'propaganda' assumed for both those in authority and those challenging it. The need to appeal to the people, it is argued, stimulated innovations in the discursive format in the print media, in the style of debate, and in the imaginative frameworks within which that debate took place. The chapter ends by considering the ramifications of these developments: an anxiety that political lying had become so endemic that politics had become a realm of fiction; that political debate had become

---

[1] For useful remarks on a similar topic for the period before 1640 see Nicholas McDowell, 'Political Prose', in Andrew Hadfield (ed.), *The Oxford Handbook of English Prose, 1500–1640* (Oxford: Oxford University Press, 2013), 360–79.

abusive, railing, and over-zealous; and that new ways of talking needed to be developed to contain and constrain partisan passions.

What Constituted 'Politics'?

The expansive nature of political debate is evident when we identify key points of controversy.[2] One strand of discourse, important before the Civil War but also after the restoration of the monarchy in 1660, concerned the proper limits of royal authority. This constitutional debate often revolved around the extent to which the king was above the laws enacted by parliament or by customary practice, but almost immediately after 1640 this became a wider debate about where political sovereignty lay. The champions of exalted claims for royal authority had suggested that the king was divinely appointed and that he was sovereign in his own right, answerable to none; but a rival construction of political power located sovereignty in the people.[3] The concept of popular sovereignty had large implications: it meant that the king was entrusted by the people to act for their benefit; that if he failed to do so the people had a right to protest against this; and that they might even have a right of resistance. But it was not just the boundaries of royal authority that were in dispute, since there was also disagreement, throughout the period, about the reach and power of parliament. Were MPs delegates mandated by the people, or representatives entitled to act on their own discretion? Was parliament a sovereign institution, with popular sovereignty expressed only in this institutional form, or was the popular voice to be heard in other ways, such as through mass-petitioning or protest? Who were the 'people': the landed elite, the county freeholders, the urban bourgeoisie, the commercial community, or the mass of the labouring poor? Politics, then, in this broader ideological debate, was also a social and cultural question.

---

[2] For overviews of the ideological divisions see David Armitage, *The Ideological Origins of the British Empire* (Cambridge: Cambridge University Press, 2000); G. R. Aylmer, *The Struggle for the Constitution, 1603–1689* (Cambridge: Cambridge University Press, 1986); Michael Braddick (ed.), *The Oxford Handbook of the English Revolution* (Oxford: Oxford University Press, 2014); Barry Coward, *A Companion to Stuart Britain* (Oxford: Blackwell, 2007); Barry Coward, *The Stuart Age* (London: Routledge, 2014); Tim Harris, *Politics Under the Later Stuarts: Party Conflict in a Divided Society 1660–1715* (New York: Longman, 1993); John Morrill, 'The Causes of the British Civil Wars', *Journal of Ecclesiastical History*, 43 (1992), 624–33; John Morrill, 'The Causes and Course of the British Civil Wars', in N. H. Keeble (ed.), *The Cambridge Companion to Writing of the English Revolution* (Cambridge: Cambridge University Press, 2001); Steve Pincus, *1688: The First Modern Revolution* (New Haven: Yale University Press, 2009); Conrad Russell, *The Causes of the English Civil War* (Oxford: Oxford University Press, 1990); Jonathan Scott, *England's Troubles: Seventeenth-Century English Political Instability in European Context* (Cambridge: Cambridge University Press, 2000); John Walter, *Understanding Popular Violence in the English Revolution: The Colchester Plunderers* (Cambridge: Cambridge University Press, 1999).

[3] Edmund S. Morgan, *Inventing the People: The Rise of Popular Sovereignty in England and America* (New York: W.W. Norton, 1988).

Contestations over the roots and boundaries of authority also had economic implications. In this period, large armies were raised—whether this was to fight civil war or, after 1689, to fight war against France in continental Europe and across the globe—and were hugely expensive, demanding unprecedented levels of taxation in the 1640s and the creation of new financial structures, such as the Bank of England, in the 1690s that some historians have termed a 'financial revolution'.[4] Heavy taxation inevitably created a vigorous public discussion about whether money was being well spent and whether the means to raise it were valid and fair. Moreover, it was disputed how far either monarch or parliament should direct commercial policy. Throughout this period there were debates over whether monopolistic rights could be granted to certain traders and, more broadly, how far the state had a right or duty to protect trade through its foreign policy and its tax regime. Disputes over sovereignty and the legitimate extent of power were thus intrinsically economic as well as political. 'Political economy', the interaction of the two, was avidly discussed.

Furthermore, issues of power and sovereignty were almost impossible to separate from religion, not just because of the concept of divine right and the strong interdependence of the church and monarchy after the Reformation had yoked the two institutions so closely together, but also because 'puritan' ideas challenged the monarch's religious policy and the way in which the church was structured and governed, attacking the hierarchical model in which the bishops exercised power. The proliferation of religious sects in the 1640s and 1650s, followed by their proscription as 'non-conformists' or 'dissenters' after the restoration of the national church in 1660, also questioned the proper boundaries between church and state, a debate that often became focused on how far it was possible to tolerate religious diversity.[5] After a period of relative religious toleration in the 1650s, Scotland, Ireland, and England all experienced far more restrictive religious frameworks in the 1660s, with laws penalizing those who could not conform to the restored national churches. The campaign to achieve religious toleration—apparent throughout the period, even after the passage of the Toleration Act in 1689, because of the antipathies still harboured by those resolutely loyal to an exclusive Church of England—was inherently political because it required legislative and dynastic change.

---

[4] John Brewer, *The Sinews of Power: War, Money, and the English State, 1688–1783* (Cambridge, MA: Harvard University Press, 1989); Mike Braddick, *The Nerves of the State: Taxation and the Financing of the English State 1558–1714* (Manchester: Manchester University Press, 1997); Steve Pincus, 'Whigs, Political Economy and the Revolution of 1688-9', in David Womersley, Paddy Bullard, and Abigail Williams (eds.), *'Cultures of Whiggism': New Essays on English Literature and Culture in the Long Eighteenth Century* (Newark: University of Delaware Press, 2005), 62–85.

[5] See Chapter 18 on 'Heresiography and Religious Controversy' by Nicholas McDowell; John Coffey and Paul Lim (eds.), *The Cambridge Companion to Puritanism* (Cambridge: Cambridge University Press, 2008); John Coffey, *Persecution and Toleration in Protestant England 1558–1689* (London: Longman, 2000); W.K. Jordan, *The Development of Religious Toleration in England*, 4 vols. (1932-4); John Spurr, *The Restoration Church of England 1646–1689* (New Haven: Yale University Press, 1991); Alex Walsham, *Charitable Hatred: Tolerance and Intolerance in England 1500–1700* (Manchester: Manchester University Press, 2006).

The establishment of the Protestant Hanoverian line that acceded to the throne in 1714 was the direct outcome of this politics of religion.

Politics thus embraced constitutional and ideological division but also diverging views about economics and religion. This multi-faceted notion of politics is embodied in the parties which in 1679 were first called Whig and Tory, labels which were to endure beyond the end of our period. Clashes between Whigs and Tories could be classed as party politics, but the issues over which they divided were numerous: foreign policy, religious policy, economic policy, and at times social policy too. These divisions and partisanship affected literary culture because, as we shall see, they provoked writers to take up their pens and coincided with growing freedom and output of the press. As this highly schematic overview suggests, issues of power, authority, and sovereignty could not be compartmentalized from social, economic, and religious ones. 'Politics', then, has to be seen as a wide field and it included the 'literary': the prose of this period was often intensely political and the ablest pens were deployed on controversy. Separate domains of 'politics' and 'literature' simply collapse.[6] Whilst 'new historicism', putting literature in historical context, might be ebbing from its initial high-tide, paying attention to the interplay between literature and politics is extremely productive for this period.

The connections across our modern disciplinary boundaries are easier to see because the chronology of this handbook brings together the two seventeenth-century revolutions of the 1640/50s and 1680/90s. Considering them separately, as has so often been the case, led earlier generations of scholars to miss the connections across them. Thinking of the two revolutions as conceptually linked is useful because, as we have seen, many of the same issues were at stake in both; because the innovations in one revolution affected the other; and because the revolutions had a cumulative impact that is best discerned across a reasonably long time-frame. Assessing the impact of the civil wars of 1642–9 or the 'Glorious Revolution' of 1688–9 can only be done by looking at the period 1640–1714 as a whole. 'Revolution' thus becomes a *process*, not an event. Examining that process also enables us to be expansive geographically: both revolutions affected, and in part were driven by divisions in, Scotland and Ireland, leading to temporary union of all three kingdoms in the 1650s and the permanent union with Scotland in 1707, but the revolutions also affected the colonies in the Americas and the trading posts in the East Indies.[7]

---

[6] For the earlier part of our period, see e.g., Nigel Smith, *Literature and Revolution, 1640–1660* (New Haven: Yale University Press, 1994).

[7] For these issues, see e.g., Brendan Bradshaw and John Morrill, *The British Problem 1504–1707: State Formation in the Atlantic Archipelago* (Basingstoke: Macmillan, 1996); Steven G. Ellis and Sarah Barber (eds.), *Conquest and Union: Fashioning a British State, 1485–1725* (London: Longman, 1995); Glenn Burgess, *The New British History: Founding a Modern State, 1603–1715* (London: I.B. Tauris, 1999); Nicholas Canny (ed.), *The Oxford History of the British Empire, Volume I: The Origins of Empire* (Oxford: Oxford University Press, 1998); Colin Kidd, *British Identities before Nationalism: Ethnicity and Nationhood in the Atlantic World, 1600–1800* (Cambridge: Cambridge University Press, 1999); Bruce Lenman, *England's Colonial Wars 1550–1688: Conflicts, Empire and National Identity* (London: Longman, 2001).

Combining the argument for the expansive nature of politics and the cumulative impact of two revolutions across nations and colonies, it should be no surprise that the category of politics itself was being reshaped during this period. In the period before 1640 'politics', considered as the study of government and the state, was well established but politics as meaning the activities of the state ('domestic politics') was only emerging in the seventeenth century, as we can see in linguistic innovation necessary to describe the new situation. Politics as denoting public life or a profession was a notion only apparent in the later Stuart period, as was politics as a set of ideas, beliefs, or commitments of a particular individual or organization: *OED* gives 1662 as the first use of this meaning. Similarly, whilst the adjective 'political', to describe the form or organization of an institution, was a sixteenth-century coinage, it was not until the mid-seventeenth century that it was used in relation to the theory or practice of politics (such as 'political wisdom', coined in 1646) and only in the later Stuart period that it was used to describe those involved or interested in politics. 'Political arithmetic'—the study of the economics and demography of a state—and 'political economy' were again later Stuart inventions (both coined by Sir William Petty in the 1680s). *OED* gives 1656 as the first use of 'political history'; 1668 for 'political philosophy'; and 1676 for 'political union'. The philosopher Thomas Hobbes also popularized the phrase 'political science' in his 1651 *Leviathan*. 'Party politics' was a mid-eighteenth-century coinage, but in Anne's reign contemporaries talked about 'party rage' to denote the furious clash between different ranks of supporters. In other words, linguistic innovation around the terms politics and political suggest that the period 1640–1714 was witnessing interesting expansions of vocabulary, reflecting novel modes of doing politics.

One of the ways in which the concept of politics was expanding was through the notion of the public. Whilst it is true that mass politics was still an object of suspicion—a political crowd or populace was termed a 'mob' in the 1680s and appeals to the people condemned throughout the seventeenth century as 'popularity'—large numbers of people were included in political debate. The people were mobilized in many ways. First, as soldiers in ideological wars: tens of thousands fought in the civil wars (with even larger civilian casualties, especially in Ireland where the population loss was about 20–40 per cent) and the forces in the wars against France that raged between 1689 and 1713, with just a short respite 1697–1702, numbered, at their high-point, about 135,000. Second, the people were mobilized as oath-takers (all adult males being required to take oaths or pledge allegiance in 1641, 1643, 1650, and 1696) and mass subscribers to petitions and addresses. David Zaret notes about 500 petitions in the period 1640–60 and there were ten times that number in the period 1660–1714, with many thousands of signatures.[8] Third, the people were mobilized as voters: elections became particularly

---

[8] Mark Knights, *Representation and Misrepresentation in Later Stuart Britian: Partisanship and Political Culture* (Oxford: Oxford University Press, 2005), 109–62; David Zaret, 'Petitions and the "Invention" of Public Opinion in the English Revolution', *American Journal of Sociology*, 101 (1996), 1497–555; David Zaret, *The Origins of Democratic Culture: Printing, Petitions and the Public Sphere* (Princeton: Princeton University Press, 2000).

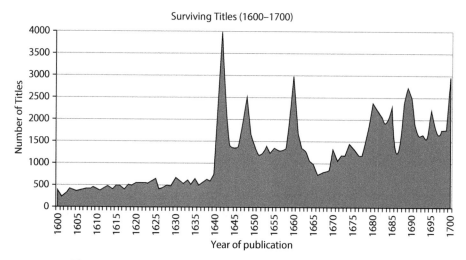

FIGURE 27.1 Fluctuations in Press Output, 1600–1700 (five-year intervals). Data drawn from Alain Veylit, 'Some Statistics on the Number of Surviving Printed Titles for Great Britain and Dependencies from the Beginnings of Print in England to the Year 1800', https://cbsr.ucr.edu/ESTC/ESTCStatistics.html

frequent after 1678 when there were 15 national polls over the next 34 years and the electorate increased to about 330,000 by the end of the period (a higher proportion of adult males than at any time before 1868). Finally, the people were mobilized as readers: after the collapse of censorship in 1641 censorship there were periodic moments of freedom 1658–60, 1679–83, 1688–90, and permanently after 1695, leading to huge waves of print (Figure 27.1).

Between 1640 and 1661 the book collector and publisher George Thomason assembled a collection of nearly 15,000 pamphlets and more than 7,000 newspapers. In 1642 John Taylor thought that print 'would goe neere (if it were laid sheet by sheet) to cover the whole Kingdom'.[9] The press was increasingly accessible: literacy rates doubled between 1600 and 1675 (to 45 per cent of adult males; female literacy rose sharply in the second half of the century, reaching 48 per cent in the 1690s) and print was greedily consumed in taverns, marketplaces, and the new coffee-houses that rapidly proliferated after the first one opened in Oxford in 1650 (there were over sixty in London by the 1670s and most provincial towns had one by the 1680s).[10] The wars, petitioning campaigns, frequent and partisan electioneering, and press freedom all widened the scope of political debate to include very large numbers of people.

---

[9] Taylor, *A Cluster of Coxcombes* (1642), un-paginated, penultimate page.
[10] See further Chapter 1 by Thomas Keymer on 'Circulation' and Chapter 26 by Brian Cowan on 'Periodical Literature'; David Cressy, *Literacy and the Social Order: Reading and Writing in Tudor and Stuart England* (Cambridge: Cambridge University Press, 1980); Adam Fox, *Oral and Literate Culture in England, 1500–1700* (Oxford: Oxford University Press, 2000); Steve Pincus, '"Coffee Politicians Does Create": Coffeehouses and Restoration Political Culture', *Journal of Modern History*, 67 (1995), 807–34.

Jürgen Habermas suggested that all this amounted to the emergence of a 'public sphere', though he located this in the 1690s rather than across the period as a whole, which might have been more useful because it would have integrated religious dispute into his model and recognized the social dimensions of popular debate.[11] Instead, Habermas saw the public sphere as bourgeois (linked to the financial revolution and the investments the public made in the stock market, bank, and other fiscal innovations), and as an interface between the private sphere and the state, capable of exerting pressure on the latter especially through public discussion which he thought marked by the rational, informed discussion evident in the newly free press. His model has come in for a good deal of criticism, and the rest of this chapter will question how far rational discussion did characterize the prose of the period; but we can use it loosely to identify something really significant in terms of the expansion of public participation in politics.

PROPAGANDA AND POLEMIC: WARS OF WORDS

Although the adjective 'invective' was a late medieval one, its evolution into a noun, to denote a violent verbal attack (first attested by *OED* in 1523) or vehement denunciatory language (first attested 1602) were later innovations that had much to do with political and religious conflict and debate.[12] Polemic (vehement verbal attacks in controversial writing) was another seventeenth-century word. OED gives 1614 as the first usage of polemic as an adjective and 1626 as a noun; but again it was in the mid-century revolution, in the 1650s in particular, that the word really took off. A 1658 dictionary defined polemical as 'Military, belonging to war' but the same dictionary, in its 1706 edition, recognized its literary meaning too: 'Polemick(s)' meant 'Disputations, Treatises, or Discourses about controversial Points.'[13] In 1656 Thomas Blount defined polemics as 'verses treating of war, or treatises of war, or strifes'. Polemic was also a central feature of the war between the parties which reached a peak in the reign of Queen Anne (1702–14).

As this chronology and etymology suggests, there was a close connection between polemic and war. Contemporaries were aware that war on the battlefield was joined, and then replaced in our period, by a war of words. In this paper war, words were dangerous and contemporaries often made the connection between verbal and military campaigns.

---

[11] Jürgen Habermas, *The Structural Transformation of the Public Sphere*, trans. Thomas Burger (Cambridge, MA: MIT Press, 1989).

[12] See Jesse M. Lander, *Inventing Polemic: Religion, Print, and Literary Culture in Early Modern England* (Cambridge: Cambridge University Press, 2006). For a set of essays arguing instead for continuity across medieval and early modern polemic see Almut Suerbaum, George Southcombe, and Benjamin Thompson (eds.), *Polemic: Language as Violence in Medieval and Early Modern Discourse* (Farnham: Ashgate, 2015).

[13] Edward Phillips, *The New World of Words* (1658; 1706).

When arguing in favour of press censorship in 1664, Richard Atkyns thus suggested 'that these paper pellets became as dangerous as bullets' and Andrew Marvell thought that 'Lead, when moulded into Bullets, is not so mortal as when founded into Letters'.[14] Lewis Griffin warned that 'Pollemciall discourses are like shooting at a mark'.[15] John Nalson, royalist historian, did not know 'any one thing that more hurt the King th[a]n the paper Bullets of the Press'.[16] The idea of a 'paper war' became a commonplace. In 1704, for example, Charles Davenenant talked of men enlisting in the national disputes between the parties with the result that 'the Paper-War has been carry'd on with Industry, Wit, and Sharpness... inflaming Oratory, Satyr, and Invectives, go off with another sort of Relish, gain more Attention, and please better, than their cold Precepts whose Aim it is to lay before the People what is Honest, Safe, and Advantagious to the Publick'.[17] A verse attack on Daniel Defoe argued that

> Satyr and Scandal Ammunition are,
> And Pen, and Ink declare a Paper War,
> Where Scribblers, like our Daniel, fear a Peace,
> Who draw their whole Subsistence from the Press:
> Print is their Standard, Publishers their Drums,
> Feud is the Word, and Pamphlets are their Guns.[18]

A 1709 print, 'Faction Display'd', shows Defoe as part of a canon of Whig authors, their heads atop an actual cannon being fired at a cleric, Henry Sacheverell, who was prosecuted in 1709–10 for a sermon that questioned the 'revolution principles' that had been established since 1688 (Figure 27.2). The year 1710 duly saw a 'Paper-war betwixt High and Low Church'.[19]

Polemic was thus belligerent and aggressive argumentation; but its verbal violence was proxy for armed combat. Occasionally argument did still provoke blows—1714–15 saw unrest, Jacobites rebelled in 1715 to try to restore the Stuarts to the throne and the following year violent groups of Whigs took part in the Mug House riots of 1716, attacking Jacobites in London—but the proliferation of the paper war may also have reduced the amount of physical violence by channelling hostility into words. Nevertheless, the function of polemical writing was also, as in a physical war, to marshal the troops of supporters, bolster their resolve, and equip them with the weapons with which to fight their opponents as well as to persuade deserters to join their camp

---

[14] Richard Atkyns, *The Original and Growth of Printing* (1664), 7; Andrew Marvell, *The Rehearsal Transpos'd* (1672), 4. See also Harold Weber, *Paper Bullets: Print and Kingship under Charles II* (Lexington: The University Press of Kentucky, 1996); Joad Raymond, *The Invention of the Newspaper: English Newsbooks, 1641–1649* (Oxford: Oxford University Press, 2005), 184–231.
[15] L[ewis] G[riffin], *Essayes and Characters* (1661), 'To the Reader'.
[16] John Nalson, *An Impartial Collection of the Great Affairs of State*, 2 vols. (1682), 2: 809.
[17] Charles Davenant, *Essays Upon Peace at home and war abroad* (1704), 6.
[18] *Poems on Affairs of State, from 1620 to this Present Year 1707* (1707), 8.
[19] Edward Ward, *The Fourth Part of Vulgus Britannicus* (1710), sub-title.

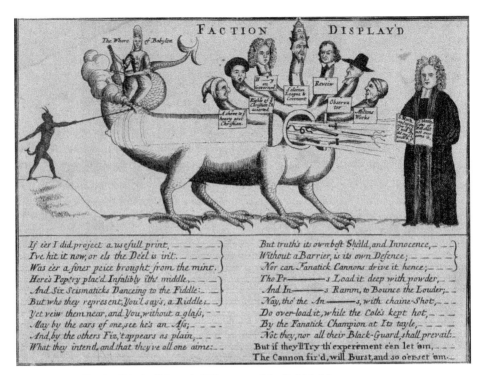

FIGURE 27.2 *Faction Display'd* (1709). © Trustees of the British Museum

or bludgeon enemies into submission with the force of argument or denunciation. Polemical prose might thus be called propagandistic. Jason Peacey uses the term 'Propaganda' to describe the pamphleteering of the mid-century revolution, much of which 'bore little visible evidence of official backing, but which can nevertheless be demonstrated to have been produced in collusion with the authorities, and with financial and organizational backing, not to say official impetus'.[20] Similarly J. A. Downie uses the word 'propaganda' to describe the literary campaign orchestrated by Robert Harley in the reign of Queen Anne.[21] Common to both revolutionary uses of propaganda was the government's (or at least canny politicians within the government's) recruitment of writers who could influence the public with their pens. Milton turned to prose in 1649 and during the 1650s to support the republican and Cromwellian regimes; Marchmont Nedham put his wit at the disposal of both parliamentary and royalist sides; the prolific Roger L'Estrange published at least 130 pro-government titles, with some 64,000 copies of his works circulating in the two crisis years before 1681 alone; and Jonathan

---

[20] Jason Peacey, *Politicians and Pamphleteers: Propaganda during the English Civil Wars ad Interregnum* (Farnham: Ashgate, 2014); Jason Peacey, 'Cromwellian England: A Propaganda State?' *History*, 91 (2006), 188.

[21] J. A. Downie, *Robert Harley and the Press: Propaganda and Public Opinion in the Age of Swift and Defoe* (Cambridge: Cambridge University Press, 1979).

Swift and Daniel Defoe both engaged in political pamphleteering for the government.[22] These writers in turn achieved notoriety and fame. The political writer as celebrity became part of the literary culture, nicknamed, satirized, and pilloried, creating a canon of authors, one that is nevertheless rather different from the literary canon today, since it was composed of those whose pens provoked and responded to controversy in a creative and eye-catching way. Indeed, such figures fascinated contemporaries and their identities and characters became part of the political debate.

Polemic was a mode not a genre; indeed, it made use of and colonized a number of different genres—dialogues, printed letters, mock trials, parodies, 'characters', as well as reflections and 'animadversions'—and these had an enduring literary impact. Before examining this, however, it is worth noting that the generic promiscuity of polemic was in part dictated by the need to appeal to as large a number of people as possible. Polemic was inherently public—it aired differences openly but also sought to involve the public in the disputes. It also relied as much on passion as it did on reason—evoking emotional responses in readers was important if a work was to carry a punch. This meant that genres that relied on affective manipulation were particularly useful to a polemicist. In order to be both affective and effective in mobilizing and manipulating the people, political prose had to be inventive. Although the prose of this period drew on earlier literary and printed battles—the debt to the Marprelate controversy of the 1580s was evident in the rebirth of its central character, Martin Marprelate, as a figure of future-Leveller Richard Overton's pamphleteering in the 1640s, and then again in the satires of the Restoration dissenter Ralph Wallis in the 1660s—some elements were either new or developed to new heights or in new ways.[23] This creativity took a number of forms that are worth charting, since they highlight some of the fruits of politically heated prose.

Keywords and Labels

One remarkable feature of prose writing in these years is the highly charged nature of particular words. This involved more than the deployment of striking phrases, though to be sure the intensity of word usage achieved a remarkable vividness of phrase in the hands of L'Estrange and his fellows who delighted in memorable 'bites' in order to

---

[22] For L'Estrange, see Violet Jordain (ed.), *Selections from the Observator (1681-7)* (Los Angeles: William Andrews Clark Memorial Library, 1970), p. i.

[23] Richard Overton, *The Araignment of Mr Persecution...by Younge Martin Mar-Priest, Son to Old Martin the Metropolitane* (1645); Richard Overton, *Martin's Eccho* (1645); *The Ordinance for Tythes Dismounted...by...his superlative Holyness, reverend young Martin Mar-Priest* (1645). On Wallis and Marprelate, see Stephen Bardle, *The Literary Underground in Restoration England: Andrew Marvell, George Wither, Ralph Wallis, and the World of Restoration Satire and Pamphleteering* (Oxford: Oxford University Press, 2012), 49–54.

capture and move their audience.[24] Beyond this verbal brilliance, certain keywords were both powerful in their effect and fought over, as each side sought to claim them for their own, giving them their own distinctive set of meanings that excluded their opponents' alternative definitions. Thus 'Liberty', 'Property', and 'Public Good' became highly contested terms with rival sets of resonances, and the struggle between partisans was thus in one sense a linguistic struggle to assert a control over meanings of terms.[25] Marchmont Nedham warned in 1677 that the critics of Charles II 'tickled' the people with 'frequent mentions of ancient laws, the good laws and the ancient customs of England, and like phrases; which make a noise and great noises usually take the weaker sort of people; yea and engage them too'.[26] Certain key words thus had an almost magical influence on readers. The 'faction', Nedham believed, misled the people 'as witches do with charms' to make them 'run headlong into civil wars'.[27] Charles Leslie also believed that the abuse of words had helped to cause the revolution of 1641 and in 1705 threatened to do so again: 'Four P's carry'd on the whole revolution of forty-one. These were people, parliament, property and popery ... the inchantment of these words is not yet over with us.'[28] The Tories were convinced that the Whigs used a set of words to mislead the public, with 'liberty' as their best rallying cry. The word, alleged one pamphleteer, 'has been the protection of all sorts and degrees of criminals and debauchees; it can swear and fight, plunder and kill through all the points of the compass: backbiting, perjury and libelling of princes, sodomy, incest and all the unnatural lusts have defended themselves with the pompous name of liberty'.[29]

But the Whigs were equally convinced that Tories redefined words for their own evil ends. One writer thus attacked High Church Tory tactics: 'They first get the reader as far from any settled meaning to the word schism as they can, and then come around him with some horrid crime they would have him think of the like nature; and awaken his apprehension and even fears of damnation at the thoughts of such guilt'.[30] The author condemned Tory writers for their 'misapplication of several hard words, with which they expect to amuse the weak and ignorant, and work them into such wicked purposes as they find it in their interest to prosecute'.[31] Another complained that whenever an 'honest, well-meaning people' was misled it always 'proceeded from some popular word, misunderstood by those who make the most use of it'.[32] 'Monarchy, Prerogative, Liberty,

---

[24] See Chapter 8 by John McTague on 'Bites and Shams'.
[25] Mark Knights, 'Politics after the Glorious Revolution', in Barry Coward (ed.), *A Companion to Stuart Britain* (Oxford: Blackwell, 2008), 455–73.
[26] Marchmont Nedham, *A Second Paquet of Advices and Animadversions Sent to the Men of Shaftesbury* (1677), 11.
[27] Nedham, *A Second Paquet*, 62.
[28] *The Rehearsal* (7–14 April 1705).
[29] T. R., *A True Protestant Bridle* (1694), 13–14.
[30] *Reflections on the Management of some Late Party-Disputes* (1715), 1–2
[31] *Reflections on the Management of some Late Party-Disputes*, 33.
[32] [Defoe], *The Mercy of Government Vindicated* (1716), 4–5.

Property, the Church, Popery and Fanaticism are words that in this kingdom enchant and enflame and almost bereave us of our senses', commented Charlwood Lawton in 1706.[33] Or, as another writer advised any would-be polemicist:

> Let but any one take a few rattling words for his materials, such as schismatic, atheist, rebels, traitors, miscreants, monsters, enthusiasts, hypocrites, Lord's anointed, sacred majesty, God's viceregent, impious, blasphemers, damnation; stir these together in a warm head and after a little shaking, bring them out, scum and all, distribute them into several periods and your work is half done.[34]

So elusive did stable meanings of words become that in 1710 rival Whig and Tory tracts published, in emulation of dictionaries, 'explanations of some hard terms now in use', with completely different definitions of key terms.[35]

The pressure on words was also evident in the multiplicity of labels that were coined and fired at opponents as weapons of abuse: Puritan, Cavalier, Roundhead, Ranter, Quaker, Fanatic, Commonwealthsman, Whig, Tory, High Churchman, Low Churchman, and Republican. These labels were useful and powerful fictions, enabling polemicists to distil what they believed to be the quintessence of their enemies' characteristics into a single term. As Jonathan Swift observed, a '*Whig* forms an Image of a *Tory* just after the Thing he most abhors, and that Image serves to represent the whole Body'.[36] Those labelled had to decide whether to try to reject, redefine, or even embrace such terms which, as the Marquis of Halifax noted, could be highly misleading and even dangerous:

> Amongst all the engines of dissention, there hath been none more powerful in all times, than the fixing names upon one another of contumely and reproach, and the reason is plain, in respect of the people, who tho[ugh] generally they are uncapable of making a syllogism or forming an argument, yet they can pronounce a word: and that serveth their turn to throw it with all their dull malice at the head of those they do not like; such things ever begin in jest and end in blood.[37]

The meaning of those labels thus became part of the paper war, keywords that could be manipulated with important consequences precisely because they were used by the public to identify politicians and their own allegiances. The names given to groups were thus part of the political game.

---

[33] *A Second Letter Concerning Civil Comprehension* (1706), 3.

[34] T. Bradbury, *The Lawfulness of Resisting Tyrants* (2nd edn, 1714), preface. A period was, in rhetorical terms, a complete sentence.

[35] *The True Genuine Tory Address and the True Genuine Whig-Address, Set One Against the Other* (1710) set these out in dictionary format.

[36] *Examiner*, no. 33 (22 March 1710), in Herbert Davis (ed.), *The Prose Works of Jonathan Swift, Volume III: The Examiner and other Pieces written in 1710-11* (Oxford: Blackwell, 1940), 111.

[37] George Savile, Marquis of Halifax, *The Character of a Trimmer Concerning Religion, Laws and Liberties* (1683), preface.

'Characters' and Stereotypes

This contest over the representative identities of rival groups becomes evident in the genre of polemical 'characters': prose portraits of groups that filled out the label with short character sketches.[38] This genre was not new—it dated back to Theophrastus's work in classical antiquity and influenced Ben Jonson in the earlier seventeenth century—but its polemical potential was realized in the period after 1640 when writers demonized their opponents in damning, simplified, and exaggerated sketches of their motivations and ideas.[39] A flavour of their extraordinary colourfulness can be obtained from an attack on Oliver Cromwell, a character sketch of a tyrant who 'eats up the people like bread, and drinks their blood like sweet wine, commanding all as if he made all, making his Creators his creatures, his Makers his meat, his Lords his Loons'.[40] The year 1642 saw a spate of characterizations of the 'Malignant partie', allegedly made up of prelatists, papists, Cavaliers, evil counsellors, and corrupt judges.[41] On occasion, such 'characters' could be more nuanced and sympathetic: *A Character of an Anti-Malignant* (1642) was a relatively complex treatment of the supporter of parliament. More generally, however, the genre set up stereotypes of enemies who lacked human characters or even, since they often equated them with insects or animals, marks of humanity. The broadsheet *Character of a Tory* (1681) thus described its subject as a 'Monster' and likened him to caterpillars who devoured the nation as well as to beasts of prey and even 'a sort of wild Boars that would root out the Constitution'. Stereotyping was not new—Reformation and post-Reformation anti-Catholicism manipulated stereotypes of the Catholics for a multiplicity of ends—but political prose in the century after the outbreak of civil war pushed stereotyping to its extreme.[42]

Public Disclosures of the Private: Dialogues and Letters

Stock characters were also a feature of the prose dialogues that proliferated in the period. Over 2,000 of these were published, in part because the shutting of the theatres

---

[38] See also Chapter 9 by Kate Bennett on 'Brief Lives and Characters'.
[39] Benjamin Boyce, *The Polemic Character 1640–1661* (Lincoln: University of Nebraska Press, 1955).
[40] J[ohn] P[rice], *Tyrants and Protectors Set forth...in Several Characters* (1654), 7.
[41] *The Lively Character of the Malignant Partie* (1642); *A Plea for the Parliament, or, XIX. Considerations for the Satisfaction of Such, Who Are Apt to be Misled by a Malignant Party Against the Parliament* (1642).
[42] Mark Knights, 'Historical Stereotypes and Histories of Stereotypes', in Cristian Tileagă and Jovan Byford (eds.), *Psychology and History: Interdisciplinary Explorations* (Cambridge: Cambridge University Press, 2015), 242–67; Peter Lake, 'Anti-Popery: the Structure of a Prejudice', in Richard Cust and Ann Hughes (eds.), *Conflict in Early Stuart England* (London: Routledge, 1989), 72–106.

in the 1640s and 1650s channelled drama into prose form, but more importantly because dialogues were such an accessible and flexible way to discuss politics, emulating the conversations taking place across the country.[43] Prose dialogues could both reflect the debate and shape it: the philosophical mode of dialogic point and counter-point could easily give way to a more didactic and controlling form of writing that sought to direct readers towards fairly unambiguous conclusions (often signalled by the coded or symbolic names of interlocutors). Prose dialogues thus became a way of instructing the people how to make sense of the news, countering along the way any possible objection from opponents. Dialogues could also expose what was conspiratorially hidden, being able to put words into the mouths of characters that they might only have said (if at all) in private. For these reasons, although dialogue was far from being a new form (indeed it was one of the oldest literary genres) there were large spikes of output in the 1640s, 1660s, 1680–90s, and again in the early eighteenth century, a sign that the genre was particularly suited to political crises.[44]

The polemical public revelation of the private sphere, apparent in many prose dialogues, was also achieved through the publication of real or, more often, invented letters. As manuscript letter writing took off in the period, so too did printed emulations of the more private form. The printed letter, with its feigned personal intimacy, was thought to be persuasive and its content sincere. Printed political letters were thus less polemical but still emotionally manipulative.[45] Letters were also the means by which political news was shared and circulated—as we shall see, information from letters formed much of the core content of newspapers—and so emulating the format for discursive purposes was a logical extension of function. To be sure, the printed letter was not a new genre; but hundreds of 'Letters to' or 'Letters from' were published after 1640 and became potent tools in discursive campaigns, especially as they were a way of connecting (both conceptually and virtually) London and provincial or even colonial opinion. Printed letters to and from the Country or the City were thus common. Like the dialogue, the printed letter was an adaptable form, capable of addressing any political topic. It was relatively short and could reflect the dialogic nature of political debate, with replies and answers provoked by the initial missive.

Prose dialogues and letters, as well as the vogue for 'secret histories', thus played with the distinctions between the private and the public, destabilizing any sharp division between them.[46] Dialogues and letters also featured in a new genre of the period, the newspaper and periodical. The lapse of governmental control over the press in 1641, and again in 1660 and 1679, led to periods in which newspapers and periodicals developed and flourished as some of the most influential forms of political prose writing. Several

---

[43] Jake Halford, '"Of Dialogue, That Great and Powerful Art": A Study of the Dialogue Genre in Seventeenth-Century England', unpublished PhD thesis, Warwick University, 2016.

[44] See Cathy Shrank, 'All Talk and No Action: Early Modern Political Dialogue', in Hadfield (ed.), *Oxford Handbook of English Prose, 1500–1640*, 27–42.

[45] See further Chapter 22 by Diana G. Barnes on 'Letters'.

[46] See further Chapter 34 by Rebecca Bullard on 'Secret Histories'.

innovations are worth highlighting in terms of political debate. One was the integration of letter writing into the format of a periodical. The innovation was made by John Dunton whose *Athenian Mercury* in the 1690s pioneered interaction with readers in this way, and other periodicals adopted the idea. In the hands of Jacobite publishers such as Henry Crossgrove, who published the *Norwich Gazette*, it became a potent political tool. Political debate could thus involve a two-way conversation between readers and publishers. Another innovation was the use of dialogue within a newspaper or periodical. Perhaps the best example of this was Roger L'Estrange's *Observator* (1681–7), which initially took the form of a dialogue between Whig and Tory and then between Trimmer and Observator. L'Estrange's paper also illustrates a third development in political debate: the emergence of comment on the news as well as 'factual' reporting. Reflecting on news items in order to shape the response of readers was apparent in the journalism of Marchmont Nedham in the 1640s and 1650s, but the era of party rivalries in the later Stuart period heightened the need to guide readers about what to think. This development in turn gave way to the political essays refined by Joseph Addison and Richard Steele in *The Spectator* (1711–12), even if these claimed to eschew partisan zeal, and many other periodicals of the early eighteenth century.

This overview of generic innovation nevertheless misses ways in which political debate stimulated certain types of writing. Nedham's and L'Estrange's contributions remind us that political debate was also a form of entertainment. Nedham recognized that a combination of 'jest and earnest' was highly effective. He felt the need in the 1650s to adopt a 'jocular' style for his *Mercurius Politicus* 'or else it will never bee cryed up: For those truths which the Multitude regard not in a serious dresse, being represented in pleasing popular Aires, make Musick to the Common sence, and charme the Phantsie; which ever swayes the Scepter in Vulgar Judgements; much more then Reason'.[47] His mixture of banter, mockery, and satire used humour to deepen the interpretative effect of his comments and his work entertained as well as informed. Royalist news-writer Sir John Berkenhead was witty in a more refined way but also aimed to entertain: an opponent admitted that his paper, *Mercurius Aulicus*, knew how to 'mix folly and knavery, and Roguery too, and do it handsomely, like an Artist'.[48] Politics had always been something of a spectacle that entertained but earlier in the century it had been Court affairs that chiefly provided the drama; after 1640 both the political stage and audience were bigger. The wit John Cleveland jested that 'since the Stages were voted downe, the onely Play-house is at *Westminster*'.[49] Thinking about political debate as entertainment is productive for exploring the interaction between historical and literary studies, though

---

[47] Joseph Frank, *Cromwell's Press Agent: A Critical Biography of Marchamont Nedham, 1620–1678* (Lantham, MD: University Press of America, 1980), 90; Joad Raymond, 'Marchamont Nedham', in Laura Lunger Knoppers (ed.), *The Oxford Handbook of Literature and the English Revolution* (Oxford: Oxford University Press, 2012), 375–93.

[48] P. W. Thomas, *Sir John Berkenhead 1617–1679: A Royalist Career in Politics and Polemics* (Oxford: Clarendon Press, 1969), 61, citing *Good Newes from All Quarters of the Kingdome* (13 September 1643).

[49] John Cleveland, *The Character of a London Diurnal* (1644), 2.

it challenges the Habermasian notion that the early public sphere was different to the 'candyfloss entertainment' he associated with the decayed public sphere of modernity. Political debate could thus take a polemical, vituperative, aggressive, snarling form, but also a lighter, more mocking tone that sought to entertain. Partisan passions were ambiguous: they provoked both anger and laughter.

THE LITERARY IMPACT OF PARTISAN DEBATE

Partisan debate also created uncertain representations of 'truth' that enemies called fictions.[50] It is no coincidence that novelists such as Daniel Defoe and Jonathan Swift cut their literary teeth on political debate: the political and fictional realms were not so different. The first female author to earn her living through her journalism, Delarivier Manley, similarly fused political debate and fiction in her novelistic treatments of contemporary politics, such as the *New Atalantis* (1709), which drew thinly veiled versions of Whig politicians in order to attack them. Partisan exchanges destabilized what was credible or true, and they fostered fictionality. Partisans told lies; they misrepresented their opponents; they destabilized words and meanings; they played around with the distinction between private and public, and political comment and controversy became a form of entertainment. Pamphleteers created enduring fictional characters through whom to talk about politics: Charles Davenant created Tom Double who represented the hypocrisy and duplicity of the 'new' Whigs who grasped after power, and John Arbuthnot created the archetypal Briton, John Bull, in 1711 in order to discuss the ways in which the nation had been tricked in matters of foreign policy.

J. Paul Hunter has argued that the newspapers and periodicals of the period fostered the rise of the novel because they created unfolding prose dramas populated by characters who attracted attention.[51] But the fictionality of political debate could both enrage and amuse, sometimes almost simultaneously. The deceptions and misrepresentations peddled to readers and voters were deeply resented as misleading the people in dangerous as well as delightful ways. The author of *Study to be Quiet* (1680) thought that pamphlets were 'filled with lies and falsehood' but that they were read 'with delight and complacency' so that 'the sharper and more satirical they are' the more the print found a 'ready and approved reception'.[52] Arbuthnot, despite (or perhaps because of) his own fictionalizing of politics, drew up a mock prospectus for a volume in 1712 which he proposed to call *The Art of Political Lying*. This satire depicted politics as 'an elaborate and endless glass-bead game of lies' and he suggested, tongue in cheek, that

---

[50] These ideas are set out at length in Knights, *Representation and Misrepresentation*.

[51] J. Paul Hunter, *Before Novels: The Cultural Contexts of Eighteenth-century English Fiction* (New York: W.W. Norton, 1990).

[52] *Study to be Quiet* (1680), 6.

the people had no right to political truth but could invent and spread lies to pull down governments of which they were weary.[53] Arbuthnot's satire was both in jest and earnest.

Reaction against the bitter railing of combative polemic and the anxieties about the prevalence of fictions, lying, and dissimulation contributed to the idealization of a more polite, impartial, moderate, and rational form of political debate. In other words, the rational conventions governing the public sphere, which Habermas saw as emerging in the later Stuart period, were in many ways a contemporary idealization of how political debate *ought* to operate, formulated because of, and in reaction to, the decayed and irrational debate that contemporaries saw all around them. The ideal of politeness, argues Lawrence Klein, was developed in the period 1700–15, and offered a 'public, secular gentility' that sought to distinguish polite debate, manners, and behaviour from 'impolite' ones. Politeness, a linguistic and cultural code which shaped dress, fashion, taste, leisure, and design, offered a way of moderating the passions of partisanship and gave the elite a cohesion that the political divisions otherwise threatened.[54] *The Spectator* thus argued that it sought 'to extinguish that pernicious Spirit of Passion and Prejudice, which rages with the same Violence in all Parties'.[55] *The Second Part of the Character of a Good Man, neither Whig nor Tory* (1682) idealized a participant 'that avoids all modern exasperating names of distinction … and makes a very charitable construction of other men's words and actions'.[56] He was inclined to be 'very cautious of running into extreams and in things of a controversial nature inclines to believe the moderators to be the wisest men'.[57] Politeness thus rejected polemical tactics, prizing instead, as one pamphleteer put it, 'TRUTH and REASON'.[58] The author went on to condemn the current state of debate and idealize an alternative:

> One side calls the other Jacobite, High-Flier, Tory, Perkinnite &c the other returns the compliment, and clamours mightily with the exprobations of Whig, Phanatick, Republican, Forty One Man and the like. Thus they endeavour to stigmatize each other's arguments with names instead of confuting them by reasons … whereas in right reason the argument ought to be look'd on, not the person or his principle who urges it, or what side he is of. A just friend to truth wou'd take this method, and all who do not are truly high-fliers on one side or the other and therefore equally criminated.[59]

---

[53] Conal Condren, *Satire, Lies and Politics: The Case of Dr Arbuthnot* (Basingstoke: Palgrave, 1997), 123.

[54] Lawrence Klein, *Shaftesbury and the Culture of Politeness: Moral Discourse and Cultural Politics in Early Eighteenth-Century England* (Cambridge: Cambridge University Press, 1994), 21. See also now Ross Carroll, *Uncivil Mirth: Ridicule in Enlightenment England* (Princton, NJ: Princeton University Press, 2021).

[55] *Spectator*, no. 126 (25 July 1711), in Donald Bond (ed.), *The Spectator*, 5 vols. (Oxford: Oxford University Press, 1967), 2: 3.

[56] *The Second Part of the Character of a Good Man* (1682), side 1.

[57] *The Second Part of the Character of a Good Man*, side 2.

[58] *The Balance, or, A New Test of the High-Fliers of Both Sides* (1705), 37.

[59] *The Balance*, 37.

Political passion, the tract concluded, was 'irrational'.[60] Reason required moderation: 'Moderation in general will amount to the due observation of a mean betwixt all unjustifiable excesses in matters of difference and contest among men, proceding from a just amplitude and ingenuity of spirit, and aiming alwaies at the advancement of the most publick and extensive good.'[61] Reason, it was said, demanded fact and demonstration in a quasi-scientific or quasi-legal way. Rather than regulation of political debate by formal governmental censorship, politeness urged a set of informal self-imposed restraints that were policed by the public.

This aspiration to impartiality and moderation was, of course, itself a rhetorical pose that masked partisan loyalties—the champions of politeness, Addison and Steele, were both Whig MPs—so politeness became part of the political game. Reason, moderation, and impartiality could all be used to help argue a partisan position, delegitimizing an opponent for the way they argued as much as for what was said. Thus *The Moderator* (1702) ostensibly sought to 'allay this publick phrensy' by reconciling the parties, both of which the author criticized for the violent 'heat and scandal' which they published; but the author was a Whig supporter who castigated the Tories for aiming at 'private malice'.[62] Similarly the ideal of moderation was invoked by the High Church pamphlet *The Introduction to the Reconcilers* (1713), which attacked partisan wranglers for whom 'the heat of the dispute has rais'd a smoke and a mist before their understandings, which has made them miss the truth'; but the 'truth' consisted in support for the High Church Tory partisan, Henry Sacheverell.[63] Political debate still aimed at beating the opponent; and politeness could be a way to achieve the defeat. Moreover, the new rhetorical ploy often excluded those lower down the social scale and women, both groups being depicted as irrational and passionate. Politeness restrained but also constrained political debate.

Yet those exclusions are not quite the whole story, for the inventive, exuberant, and biting polemical prose of the period did have a longer life in which it became accessible to the poor and marginalized. In 1817 a radical publisher of cheap print, William Hone, was put on trial by the government for his searing parodies of government corruption and his defence involved bringing into court a pile of tracts published in the 1640–1714 era. Hone began collecting many printed parodies from this period as well as the works of the mid-century Leveller John Lilburne, with whom he identified as a martyr for a free press and the right to criticize the government.[64] The political debate of the two revolutions of the seventeenth century thus reverberated into the nineteenth and were still available a century and a half after publication as a template and inspiration for radical, and often impolite, satire.

---

[60] *The Balance*, 44.
[61] George Tullie, *Moderation Recommended in a Sermon* (1689), 4.
[62] *The Moderator* (1702), 4–5, 19, 33.
[63] *The Introduction to the Reconcilers* (1713), 5, 25.
[64] Mark Knights, '"Was a Laugh Treason?" Corruption, Satire, Parody and the Press in Early Modern Britain', in Mark Knights and Adam Morton (eds.), *The Power of Laughter and Satire in Early Modern Britain, 1500–1800* (London: Boydell & Brewer, 2017), 190–210.

CHAPTER 28

POLITICAL SPECULATIONS

NIGEL SMITH

[A] civil war has miscarried in our days; which was founded (at least pretendedly) upon defence of the people's own rights: in which, although they had as clear a victory in the end, as ever any contest upon earth had, yet could they never reap the least advantage in the world by it; but went from one tyranny to another, from Barebone's Parliament, to Cromwell's reign; and from that, to a committee of safety.[1]

At the beginning of the crisis between King and Parliament that would lead rapidly to a Civil War in three kingdoms, readers of books in English were not able to have access in writing to a set of political concepts that would enable them to think beyond the idea that England was ruled by a mixed constitution, whereby the monarch ruled through Parliament. The assumptions of loyalty and deference were heavily and primarily monarchical, then aristocratic, and in a social order that was heavily patriarchal. Most political thought was transmitted in Latin, and, in the European vernaculars, the most advanced political ideas in the previous century had been expressed in Italian. English common law, in which the constitution of the mixed monarchy was expressed, was a mixture of French, Latin, and English. Yet by the beginning of the next century there was a new and extensive discourse of popular sovereignty, consent, (limited) toleration, and the natural rights of individuals. All of this was available in a rich body of writings in English that are notable for their originality, sometimes for their striking literary qualities, and in a few cases for works that quickly gained highly influential status. They would subsequently become enduring classics of political thought and taught across large parts of the globe. Even after the intensely prolific period of the Civil War

---

[1] Henry Neville, *Plato Redivivus* (2nd edn, 1681), in *Two English Republican Tracts*, ed. Caroline Robbins (Cambridge: Cambridge University Press, 1969), 177.

and Interregnum, when print publication of political material during the years of the restored monarchy was much more difficult, the new perceptions stuck. My concern in this chapter is not with a history of the evolution of the political ideas articulated, a subject thoroughly addressed in many other works, but with the way in which these ideas were articulated and made accessible to readers in English prose.

We should also be clear that the subject is *political prose*. Although it is impossible to separate religion from politics in early modern England, and although much political expression remained religious in nature, or aligned with particular religious views, the focus here is on prose that articulated political concepts (and neither poetry nor drama that used both verse and prose, even though these literary forms were important for the exploration of political ideas). Furthermore, who were the readers? While most political prose before 1640 remained the preserve of the political elite, with the local gentry and highest 'middling sort' being the lowest rung of that elite, the upheavals of mid-century produced a much broader readership, thoroughly embracing many more 'middling sort' readers and, with the reading aloud of political writing in various kinds of community, the extension of the 'political nation' at least for a period even among the urban and rural poor. We see the rise to literacy and entry to the category of authorship of people of the humblest backgrounds: sons and daughters of shoemakers and ploughmen. There is a further distinction to be made here between political discourse concerned with contingent controversial issues (such as the 'Engagement Controversy', the printed debate about the Oath of Allegiance required by the new commonwealth government in 1650; or the extended exchange from the late 1660s into the 1670s concerning toleration or 'liberty of conscience') and less locally engaged discourse in which political concepts were articulated in a more general or even speculative way. Specific context makes it sometimes hard to extract the political ideas or their expression themselves for a modern evaluative purpose.[2] This chapter is less concerned with controversial writing, moving instead through other genres such as utopias, some romances, and romance-oriented fiction to works of pure political theory and correspondence where political concepts were debated and instantiated.

Seventeenth-century England should be of interest greatly here because it was the time during which the threat from the monarchy to become absolute and rule without Parliament was avoided, and a more limited, constitutional, and mixed monarchical government finally emerged. However, before we commit to a narrative of English or British exceptionality, let us acknowledge that there were arenas outside of the British Isles in which non-monarchal politics and political understanding were beginning to assert themselves that were also crucially important for English authors. The Netherlands, France, and Switzerland were places of exile for many English and Scottish people during the period, and it is through residence in and connections with Dutch intellectuals that the perceptions of one of the giants of English political thought at this

---

[2] A point made by Clive Holmes, 'The Remonstrance of the Army and the Execution of Charles I', *History*, 104 (2019), 585–605.

time, John Locke, were refined.[3] Italian political life and thought continued to exercise a considerable impact on English thinking.[4] At the same time, the settlement of English and Scottish colonial North America, the Caribbean, and small parts of South America produced not only novel predicaments (the interaction, usually violent, of Europeans with indigenous populations, with other Europeans, and with the forcibly transported African slave populations) but also new modes of political writing concerned with these vexing transformative matters.

What was political theory and political thought and how does its textual construction matter? Political wisdom is the description of how societies emerge in time and how they are best governed. The most enduring statements here were made by Aristotle in the *Politics* and the *Nicomachean Ethics*, widely adopted in the medieval and early modern worlds, especially in the universities. Before that was Plato, and along with this tradition in the early modern period came, for Europeans, a growing sense of how the Bible represented the political order.[5] Medieval scholastic philosophy provided commentary on these fundamental texts and such commentaries were studied in the universities. At the same time 'advice to princes' literature began to distil this wisdom into a shorter and more intelligible form.[6] Thomas Hobbes would stand out among seventeenth-century English writers because he tried to meet both goals: the production of a complete science of politics, separate from, against, and exceeding Aristotle, integrated with a full account of nature and human nature, as well as works that were designed to educate princes.

There are some further paradigm features that govern the sixteenth and seventeenth centuries. Printing changed much, making it possible for far greater extents of literacy to develop and to be used either to accept restraint or to fuel critical dissent in a regime. In the long-term history of print, early printed Bible translations fostered lay political knowledge distinctly in a vernacular language, which then became a foundation for asserting the possibilities and limitations of liberty in the future, effectively a paradigm of the semantics of liberty down into the eighteenth century and beyond.[7] The force of religious dissent in the sixteenth century, most notably Protestantism, led eventually to a shared sense that a ruler might be righteously resisted, and even removed by force, where that ruler has not listened to their subjects, so that an accusation of tyranny

---

[3] Gaby Mahlberg, *The English Republican Exiles in Europe during the Restoration* (Cambridge: Cambridge University Press, 2020).

[4] See, for example, Blair Worden, 'The Machiavellian Tradition', pt. iii of 'English Republicanism', in J. H. Burns (ed.), *The Cambridge History of Political Thought, 1450–1700* (Cambridge: Cambridge University Press, 1991), 464–75.

[5] See Alan Ryan, *On Politics: A History of Political Thought from Herodotus to the Present* (New York: Liveright, 2012).

[6] See, for example, Judith Ferster, *Fictions Of Advice: The Literature and Politics of Counsel in Late Medieval England* (Philadelphia: University of Pennsylvania Press, 2016); Ivan Lupić, *Subjects of Advice: Drama and Counsel from More to Shakespeare* (Philadelphia: University of Pennsylvania Press, 2019).

[7] See the essays in John Coffey (ed.), *The Oxford History of Protestant Dissenting Traditions, Volume I: The Post-Reformation Era, 1559–1689* (Oxford: Oxford University Press, 2020).

was made.[8] In the later sixteenth century this was the special province of the French Huguenots (Calvinist Protestants) who dispersed across Europe in several directions, not least in the hugely influential *Vindiciae contra tyrannos* (c.1574–9).[9] Religious affiliation and expression of support for controversial religious positions is not in an abstract sense political, but once inside the arena of the Civil War, where the fate of King Charles I became an overriding concern, it plays its role, as much as did the Stuart monarchs' claim to rule by divine right directly from God. This claim was also powerfully extended through the printing press, using a combination of words and images, as in the King's posthumously published explanation of his actions, *Eikon Basilike* (1649), probably written by one or more of his advisers.[10] It is out of the religious-political struggle between Civil War factions, mostly elite, but some decidedly not so, that we find discourses proposing new constitutions and guaranteeing a greater degree of personal freedom than had ever been the case before. Such statements are recorded in debates that were transcribed in the first instance and then printed up in truncated form. They would be joined by various kinds of discursive text and newsbook commentary.[11] With a press functioning in a relatively unhindered way, a public sphere emerged in which various proposals could be heard and debated.[12]

HOBBES AND HARRINGTON

The astonishing, bold, original project of Thomas Hobbes (1588–1679) was to produce not a history or a commentary on history (although he did that too, along with translations of both Homer and Thucydides) but a *scientia* of human life, a complete knowledge system, beginning with his materialist account of human psychology and ending with the consequent description of society and political behaviour: the book of how everything is. Atoms bombard your eyeballs, and that is sight; sheer fear of violence, the threat to self-preservation, drives the need to appoint a sovereign who will govern in order to stop the otherwise endless war of everyone against everyone else. By the time this *scientia* had evolved to its third iteration in *Leviathan*, the humanist-trained

---

[8] As most influentially discussed by Quentin Skinner, *The Foundations of Modern Political Thought*, 2 vols. (Cambridge: Cambridge University Press, 1978).

[9] See [Hubert Languet], *Vindiciae Contra Tyrannos*, ed. George Garnett (Cambridge: Cambridge University Press, 2003).

[10] See Robert Wilcher, '*Eikon Basilike*: The Printing, Composition, Strategy, and Impact of "The King's Book"', in Laura Lunger Knoppers (ed.), *The Oxford Handbook of the Literature and the English Revolution* (Oxford: Oxford University Press, 2012), 289–308.

[11] Nigel Smith, *Literature and Revolution in England 1640–1660* (New Haven: Yale University Press, 1994); Joad Raymond, *The Invention of the Newspaper: English Newsbooks, 1641–1649* (Oxford: Oxford University Press, 1996); Joad Raymond, *Pamphlets and Pamphleteering in Early Modern Britain* (Cambridge: Cambridge University Press, 2003).

[12] See Chapter 27 on 'Political Debate' by Mark Knights.

secretary, deeply immersed in the natural philosophy of his day, offered a mechanistic account of society that was also rhetorically amazing; after three hundred and seventy years it is still capable of captivating the reader and dominating their perceptions:

> Nature (the Art whereby God hath made and governes the World) is by the *Art* of man, as in many other things, so in this also imitated, that it can make an Artificial Animal. For seeing life is but a motion of Limbs, the beginning whereof is in some principall part within; why may we not say, that all *Automata* (Engines that move themselves by springs and wheeles as doth a watch) have an artificiall life? For what is the *Heart*, but a *Spring*, and the *Nerves*, but so many *Strings*; and the *Joynts*, but so many *Wheeles*, giving motion to the whole Body, such as was intended by the Artificer? *Art* goes yet further, imitating that Rationall and most excellent worke of Nature, *Man*. For by Art is created that great leviathan called a common-wealth, or STATE, (in latine civitas) which is but an Artificiall Man; though of greater stature and strength than the Naturall, for whose protection and defence it was intended; and in which, the *Soveraignty* is an Artificiall *Soul*, as giving life and motion to the whole body.[13]

Hobbes sought to attack Aristotelian epistemology and physics (he had once been Francis Bacon's secretary), and what he saw as a huge investment in English humanist education in ancient oratory: the eloquent Ciceronian elevation of 'liberty' as a positive quality that one sought to acquire and protect. By contrast, Hobbes argued that liberty could only be defined negatively, the set of political arrangements that protected people from the encumbrances of Necessity, such as defending themselves from the encroachments of their neighbours. Making a social contract with a sovereign (which could be *any* kind of body, but he thought monarchs were best) gave you that protection, but you had to obey them. To most English people then and now, this looked like an argument for absolute monarchy and a violation of the ancient constitution, to say nothing of an atheistic argument grounded in a materialist Epicureanism that scornfully mocked traditionally conceived religious truth (which Hobbes himself vigorously denied, always claiming he was true to the Bible).

Quentin Skinner has made a powerful case for the mature Hobbes's return to the ancient *ars rhetorica* in order to make the argument for the social contract stick in *Leviathan*, a significant change from his position in the earlier works. This has been contested on the grounds that Hobbes's works were much more consistent with each other: the humanist (never too optimistic in the positive power of rhetoric) and the materialist modernist much more coherently intertwined throughout the body of writing.[14] Much has also been said against authoritarian Hobbes for the degree to which he defended the liberty due to a person (the right to self-defence and liberty of

---

[13] See Thomas Hobbes, *Leviathan*, ed. Noel Malcolm, 3 vols. (Oxford: Oxford University Press, 2012), 1: 16.

[14] Quentin Skinner, *Reason and Rhetoric in the Philosophy of Hobbes* (Cambridge: Cambridge University Press, 1996); cf. Timothy Raylor, *Philosophy, Rhetoric, and Thomas Hobbes* (Oxford: Oxford University Press, 2018).

thought), but there is no doubting the huge influence of Hobbes that has been detected in the later seventeenth century, even down to the publishing of Locke's major works. Hobbes is for some the greatest and most influential English political philosopher, and his entirely memorable way of expressing his concepts has much to do with it, turning key expressions of those with whom he disagrees or those he claims have been misinterpreted to his own distinctive ends. Thus, the ancient and Renaissance image of eloquence, with the orator's persuasive words represented as a chain extending from his mouth to the ears of his entranced audience, is refashioned to represent sovereign power exerting itself through civil laws:

> as men, for the atteyning of peace, and conservation of themselves thereby, have made an Artificiall Man, which we call a Common-wealth; so also have they made Artificiall Chains, called *Civill Lawes*, which they themselves, by mutuall covenants, have fastned at one end, to the lips of that Man, or Assembly, to whom they have given the Soveraigne Power; and at the other end to their own Ears. These Bonds in their own nature but weak, may neverthelesse be made to hold, by the danger, though not by the difficulty of breaking them.[15]

James Harrington, who had been a personal attendant of Charles I, as Hobbes had been the tutor of his son, the future Charles II, saw the force of Hobbes' analysis and the strength of its debt to the new natural philosophy. But he took issue with Hobbes's iconoclastic treatment of intellectual tradition and thought that in doing so Hobbes had missed its central teaching: that political influence in a state depends fundamentally upon who owns the property in it. In a powerful invocation of Plato, he offered a view of the republic of England as in the first instance a crystallizing in the mind of the author of the entire scope of political learning. Political theory sits in your head as you try to figure out what is accurate. Property ownership relations produce a balance of power, and if that balance is not reflected in constitutional arrangements, then there will be civil strife. Thus Harrington understood that the property redistribution of the English Reformation had greatly advanced the standing of the gentry who needed to be acknowledged in the politics of the nation, alongside the traditional aristocracy. He thought that Queen Elizabeth had understood this well, and that her deftly managed relations with her subjects had played to her advantage and the nation's. Indeed, it was as if Elizabeth managed with her counsellors a republic, largely agricultural in nature (unlike say Venice) but not without commerce, and having rid itself in 1649 of a monarchy that misunderstood its place, the best move for the Commonwealth that replaced it was to become as quickly as possible the republic of greater and smaller property owners that it was, productively enabled by the founding laws of an initiating intelligence such as—in 1656, when Harrington published his first major statement, the utopian *Oceana*—Lord Protector Oliver Cromwell. It is the matter of ownership that

---

[15] Hobbes, *Leviathan*, ed. Malcolm, 1: 328. Malcolm notes a source of the image in Lucian, *Heracles*, 1–3, and its association of the image with the ruler in French political iconography.

determines political stability—not the virtue of individual citizens nor the social contract. Harrington sees this in terms of natural philosophy: it is so by nature, and hence it is not a theory that asserts as a foundation the value of acts of political virtue, even as it points up the importance of liberty and the benefits of political choice through voting:

> Equal rotation is equal vicissitude in government, or succession unto magistracy conferred for such convenient terms, enjoying equal vacations, as take in the whole body by parts, succeeding others through the free election or suffrage of the people.
>
> The contrary whereunto is prolongation of magistracy which, trashing the wheel of rotation, destroys the life or natural motion of a commonwealth.
>
> The election or suffrage of the people is freest where it is made or given in such a manner that it can neither oblige (*qui beneficium accepit libertatem vendidit*) nor disoblige another, or through fear of an enemy, or bashfulness towards a friend, impair a man's liberty.[16]

This involves a comparative approach to different political practices, and one that never excludes history, as we can see in this explanation of Venice:

> An equal commonwealth (by that which hath been said) is a government established upon an equal agrarian, arising into the superstructures or three orders, the senate debating and proposing, the people resolving, and the magistracy executing by an equal rotation through the suffrage of the people given by the ballot. For though rotation may be without the ballot, and the ballot without rotation, yet the ballot not only as to the ensuing model includeth both, but is by far the most equal way; for which cause under the name of the ballot I shall hereafter understand both that and rotation too.[17]

Oceana's terminology is complicated, and enshrined in the coded fictions of political romance, and perhaps detrimentally so. (Did Cromwell actually understand it?) Until recently, historians of political thought have been less interested in the way in which *Oceana* was constructed and have even dismissed the intellectual tradition marshalled by the author as the work of an amateur. But, in an important new study, the signalling by literary scholars of Harrington's peculiar language is developed by Rachel Hammersley.[18] The stacking up of genres, authorities, and concepts and the thinking through of their viewpoints may be seen in the 'Introduction or Order of the Work'. Harrington seeks to explain what he sees as an English situation in which freedom inheres not in grovelling royal courts but in a country life that is inherently and simply democratic:

> in the way of parliaments, which was the government of this realm, men of country lives have been still entrusted with the greatest affairs and the people have constantly

---

[16] James Harrington, *The Commonwealth of Oceana; and, A System of Politics*, ed. J. G. A. Pocock (Cambridge: Cambridge University Press, 1992), 33.

[17] Harrington, *The Commonwealth of Oceana*, 34.

[18] Rachel Hammersley, *James Harrington: An Intellectual Biography* (Oxford: Oxford University Press, 2019).

had an aversion from the ways of the court. Ambition, loving to be gay and to fawn, hath been a gallantry looked upon as having something of the livery, and husbandry or the country way of life, though of a grosser spinning, as the best stuff of a commonwealth, according unto Aristotle, *agricolarum democratica respublica optima*; such an one being the most obstinate assertress of her liberty and the least subject unto innovation or turbulency. Wherefore, till the foundations (as will be hereafter shown) were removed, this people was observed to be the least subject unto shakings and turbulency of any; whereas commonwealths upon which the city life hath had the stronger influence, as Athens, have seldom or never been quiet, but at the best are found to have injured their own business by overdoing it.[19]

It may not be immediately apparent what he is driving at but it does have a cumulative force, one that reveals to the patient reader Harrington's conceptual progression: a building of political wisdom through history, starting with Aristotle's *Politics* and landing in early modern agricultural England—that sense of rustic manners no doubt informed by English pastoral poetry and drama.

Much of Harrington's energy would be directed to long subsequent works in which he tried to clarify his proposals to a perplexed readership, and through his role as leader of the Rota, a political debating society. During the Restoration he became an increasingly distracted and pitifully reduced figure. Nonetheless, he had provided a nascent republican movement with its most serious intellectual matter, the essence of which was the subject of intense debate among Commonwealth supporters across the ranks, and up and down the social scale. Former Levellers and Fifth Monarchists would embrace his ideas, ensuring that they circulated in shorter, more affordable pamphlets. *Oceana* and its associated texts would provide the bedrock on which later eighteenth-century republicanism would be built, in Britain, in North America, and in France and Germany.[20] We see here how far older political forms could be reinvested in the age of print with new force. The most significant of these was the utopia: no longer the ludic juxtaposition of unsatisfactory reality with ideal vision of what could never quite realistically be, but a plain blueprint for a better future.

UTOPIA AND TRAVEL WRITING

In 1668 appeared a short text detailing the discovery of a remote ocean island.[21] This island was found to be populated with more than a thousand English-speaking people,

---

[19] Harrington, *The Commonwealth of Oceana*, 5.

[20] See further J. G. A. Pocock, *The Machiavellian Moment: Florentine Political Thought and the Atlantic Republican Tradition* (Princeton, NJ: Princeton University Press, 1975); Gaby Mahlberg and Dirk Wiemann (eds.), *European Contexts for English Republicanism* (Aldershot: Ashgate, 2013).

[21] [Henry Neville], *The Isle of Pines* (1668); included in Derek Hughes (ed.), *Versions of Blackness: Key Texts on Slavery from the Seventeenth Century* (Cambridge: Cambridge University Press, 2007), 3–116; see also Henry Neville, *The Isle of Pines and Plato Redivivus*, ed. David Womersley (Carmel, IN: Liberty Fund, 2020).

the discovery having been made by a Dutch East Indiaman. A second edition would reveal the captain to be Henry Cornelius van Sloetten and in that edition we learn that the text was forwarded to its London publisher by Abraham Keek (or Keck), in fact a real life Amsterdam merchant with connections to English radicals.[22] The text is a kind of dystopia, telling the story of the shipwreck in 1567 of an English merchantman bound for India, the only survivors being an apprentice called George Pine, his master's daughter, two servant women ('maids'), and a further African serving woman. They soon realized they had found a paradise, and as their European clothes rotted, and they resorted to the state of nature, formal relations of hierarchy and servitude (and perhaps also slavery) ended, and they managed to generate many children between them, so that by the time they are discovered by Van Sloetten, three generations later, in 1589 there are well over one thousand English-speaking naked islanders, all living without modern European technology. A little more than ten pages has gone by. Nonetheless there are a lot of disagreements between the settlers, some violent dissent, despite the adoption of harsh laws imposed by Pine. The date of 1668 suggested not a true story, as some took it, but an obvious satire of the lax English court, widely blamed for the humiliation at the hands of the Dutch Navy in the River Medway the previous year. The author would turn out to be none other than Henry Neville (1620–94), who came from a wealthy landed Berkshire family with good court connections. However, by the late 1640s he was a pioneer republican, deeply versed in Machiavelli, the master of a mode of what has been called 'porno-political' satire, and someone who would have much time for Harrington's republican thought.[23] He fled to Italy in 1660 and enjoyed the reputation of a dangerous republican who might return and stir dissent and subversion.

That as many as twenty editions appeared in six different languages within the first year of the work's publication is a testimony to its marketability, and that market delivered Neville a European-wide publishing coup, putting his satire at the heart of literary attention, from Sweden in the north to France in the south and Germany in the east. The text was enormously popular, but what was its language of politics? The island proves a paradise, free from dangers and with much provided by nature. The thing that happens initially between humans is sex, and while George Pine does not disguise his pleasure at first in having four different partners, his interest as a narrator looking back on events is reproduction and the population of the island; the making of a people. What we have described is the fruitful operation of polygamy, since he tends to talk of his partners as 'consorts': they are natural law wives. Polygamy is mentioned in some of the

---

[22] See Gaby M. Mahlberg, 'Authors Losing Control: The European Transformations of Henry Neville's "The Isle of Pines" (1668)', *Book History*, 15 (2012), 3; William Poole, ed., *Five Restoration Travel Hoaxes* (Oxford: Editiones Rariores No. 3, 2024), 5, 8–14, 32–4.

[23] Susan Wiseman, '"Adam, the Father of all Flesh": Porno-Political Rhetoric and Political Theory In and After the English Civil War', in James Holstun (ed.), *Pamphlet Wars: Prose in the English Revolution* (London: Frank Cass, 1992), 134–57; Madison R. Wolfert, "The Racial Biopolitics of Sex in the Work of Henry Neville." *English Literary Renaissance*, 54, no. 3 (2024): 346–73. .

religious utopias attempted by English people at this time.[24] This is the central concern of the initial, shorter narrative, and to which all other concerns are subordinate. Food supply is readily explained by the plentiful environment on the island, but Van Sloetten's crew will eventually build William Pines a governor's 'palace' with their tools in 1667, so in fact the arts of civilization are limited.

The augmented second version, in which we meet Van Sloetten, includes a history of the island after the death of George, the father of his people. It is a harsh and unpleasant parody of the Book of Genesis: failure to read the Bible by one faction leads to open and wanton fornication. This may have been acceptable through necessity in the beginning but it leads quickly to sexual tyranny: violent rape and the forcing of wills. There is a disciplining of the wanton faction by the sacrificial punishment of John Phill, second son of the African slave Philippa. He is thrown to his death in the sea from some high cliffs. The imposed discipline of some incredibly strict commandments that impose sexual order follows: a crude Ten Commandments. Acts of starvation, whipping, burning, and maiming look like the history of persecution since antiquity, and perhaps especially after the Reformation, but Neville saves up for adultery these punishments: 'for the first crime the Male shall lose his Privities, and the Woman have her right eye bored out, if after that she was again taken in the act, she should die without mercy.'[25] Some paradise.

A primitive Christianity with regulated marriage at its core has evolved. The Dutch go on an expedition and in the course of hunting goats with guns scare the hut-dwelling locals. These primitive English now begin to resemble the indigenous Americans, like the Aztecs, in Spanish narratives of New World contact and conquest.[26] The people might be English-speaking savages to the civilized Dutch, but the animals seem less wild than in Europe since less a prey to mankind's ravages: 'whether it were as having enough to satiate themselves without ravening upon others, or that they never before saw the sight of man, nor heard the report of murdering Guns, I leave it to others to determine.'[27] The Pines think a set of bagpipes is a living creature, and if, as Van Sloetten says, they are ingenious and so like their European forebears, they prosper by lacking the means to express themselves, the source of corruption in the old world. The satire of the Stuart court becomes complete, and as they leave the Dutch sailors are forced to intervene in a rape case, since another Phill has ravished a Trevor (the tribal names are derived from the family names of the original inhabitants) and the island is in civil uproar. Only armed intervention enables William Pine to restore his authority and exercise judgement over the offender. Van Sloetten's stay was less than a month, so the implication is that the Isle of Pines is repeatedly vitiated by these disputes.

---

[24] Such as the society of 'Jewish Christians' led by the Seventh Day Baptist Thomas Tillam at Wied near Bonn and then at Lobenfeld in the Palatinate during the 1660s and 1670s. For the longer tradition, see Leo Miller, *Milton Among the Polygamists* (New York: Loewenthal Press, 1974).

[25] Neville, *The Isle of Pines*, in Hughes (ed.), *Versions of Blackness*, 18.

[26] See, for example, Bernal Díaz del Castillo, *The True History of the Conquest of New Spain*, ed. and trans. Janet Burke and Ted Humphrey (Indianapolis, Indiana: Hackett, 2012).

[27] Neville, *The Isle of Pines*, 20.

Prose fiction narrative, even a travel narrative-come-utopia/dystopia like *The Isle of Pines* was a perfectly proper way to investigate the political, following the famous and much discussed elements of the political in Sidney's *Arcadia* (1590), the allegorical *roman à clef* of John Barclay's *Argenis* (Paris, 1621), and the long Royalist prose romances of the 1650s, most of them translations from French originals, which were a way of representing defeated, elite selves in the 1650s, and sometimes an industry of occupation for those confined to their estates. Behind them lay the ideal society tradition embodied in Plato's *Republic* and Sir Thomas More's *Utopia*. This third category of political fiction, often of huge length, became the source for the more distilled but no less political, and no less Royalist, romances of Aphra Behn, and others.[28] Romance informed both Hobbes's *Leviathan*, where it was spurned, and Harrington's *Oceana*, where its conventions were incorporated in the narrative structure. These two texts are represented as the barrels towed by a ship in Jonathan Swift's first major work, *The Tale of a Tub* (1704), put there in order to distract the whale, perhaps representing the people, the masses, from disturbing, or even capsizing, the ship of state.

Neville's resort to fiction reflected the fact that it was far harder to publish speculative political ideas during the Restoration. The publisher's preface to the reader of Neville's *Plato Redivivus* (1681) acknowledged that it was 'lawful' to publish something like *Oceana* in the 1650s: 'talking of state-affairs in a monarchy must needs be more offensive, than it was in the democracy where Plato lived', but, being assured that it was the work of a 'gentleman', and showing it to a 'gentleman friend', the publisher was sure it should be published and that it was part of a long line of texts stretching back before *Oceana* alleging 'that empire was founded in property, and discoursed rationally upon it'.[29] This was something of a ruse, no less than the publishers' assurances that the attentive reader of the canon of history and political theory books will always lead to Harrington's conclusions. Inevitability or determinism is more evident than in Harrington when we read in Neville that 'England was not capable of any other government than a democracy', and that this is as compatible with a monarchy as with a republic. More precisely this is said to be 'redressing and supporting one of the best monarchies in the world', which almost implies the conversion of it to a true free state. Before the dialogue begins comes a book-list of reason-of-state and historical writing, from Machiavelli to Boccalini, the very books usually taken to be the context in which Harrington's *Oceana* was framed.[30] Harrington and some of Neville's works would become part of this canon

---

[28] See further Chapter 5 on 'Amatory Fiction' by Melissa E. Sanchez and Chapter 14 on 'Encounters with the East' by Matthew Dimmock.

[29] Neville, *Plato Redivivus*, 68–9.

[30] See Mark Goldie, 'The Civil Religion of James Harrington', in Anthony Pagden (ed.), *The Languages of Political Theory in Early-Modern Europe* (Cambridge: Cambridge University Press, 1987), 197–222; David Womersley, 'Henry Neville's Booklist', in Alex W. Barber and Katherine A. East (eds.), *Radical Ideas and the Crisis of Christianity in England, 1640-1740: The Politics of Religion* (Woodbridge: The Boydell Press, 2024), 58–77..

by the 1690s when, under the Whig Junto, John Toland was able to publish substantial folio editions of Milton and Harrington. The problem in 1681 was not, as Neville saw it, popery, the focus of Whig alarm when Charles II was to be succeeded by his Roman Catholic brother, but the matter of giving due representation to those with landed property.

Radicalism

The use of actual Machiavellian texts to analyse popular political action from popular as opposed to elite, substantially propertied perspectives begins in England in the Levelling campaigns of the mid- and later 1640s, if in untypical style. The Levellers were a loose alliance of city radical Puritans and New Model Army soldiers who emerged in the later stages of the First Civil War demanding greater religious toleration, economic redress, and political representation than the Parliamentarian consensus was prepared to grant. They ran effective pamphlet campaigns (featuring accounts of the unjust persecution of the Leveller figurehead John Lilburne as he sought to defend his rights as a free born Englishman), live protests, and eventually mutinies. The candidate in question here is the pamphlet *Vox Plebis*, which has been ascribed to Richard Overton and John Wildman, both Levellers, but is now attributed with some confidence to the republican journalist Marchamont Nedham, famous for changing sides.[31] Much of the tract translates the Latin of medieval English common law into the vernacular:

> as *Bracton l. 3. fol.* 136. witnesseth in these words, *Qui pro crimine, vel felonia magna, sicut pro morte hominis captus fuerit, & imprisonatus, vel sub custodia detentus; non debet spoliari bonis suis, nec de terris suis disseisiri: sed debet inde sustentari donec de crimine sibi imposito se defenderit, vel convictus fuerit, quia ante convictionem nihil forisfacit. Et si quis contra hoc secerit, fiat Vic. tale brev. Rex Vic. salute, Scias quod provisum est in Curia nostra coram nobis, quod nullus homo captus pro morte hominis, vel alia felonia pro qua debeat imprisonari, disseiseatur de terris, tenementis, vel catallis suis, quousque convictus fuerit de felonia de qua indictus est, &c.* In English thus, Where any man for a crime, or great felony, as, for murder; shall be taken and imprisoned, or detained under custody, he ought not to be spoyled of his goods, nor disseised of his lands; but ought to be maintained of the same, untill he shall acquit himselfe of the crime charged upon him, or shall be convicted thereof, because, *Before conviction he shall forfeit nothing.*[32]

---

[31] For the attribution see the discussion in Jonathan Scott, *Commonwealth Principles: Republican Writing of the English Revolution* (Cambridge: Cambridge University Press, 2004), 83; Rachel Foxley, *The Levellers: Radical Political Thought in the English Revolution* (Manchester: Manchester University Press, 2013), 201, 213, 222–5.

[32] *Vox Plebis, or, The Peoples Out-Cry Against Oppression, Injustice, and Tyranny* (1646), 14–15.

Until the last section, there are only a couple of small giveaways that might suggest knowledge of ancient history and modern commentary on it. The more interesting is an animal fable from the Venetian Giovanni Battista Ramusio's innovative compilation of travel narratives (the first volume appearing in 1550), and then stories of the abuse of prisoners from English sources that morphs into comparison with Lucian, the second century Greek satirist:

> [Lucian] saith, that *Homer upon a time had drunk too much of the sweet wine of Chios, his native Countrey, and fell a spewing; and there came* Pindarus, *and* Virgil, *and* Homer, *and a great many more, and lickt up his spewings, and thereby became inspired with Poetry, every one according to the quantity of the spewings that he lickt up.* So these *Goalers,* upon the dissolution of *Regall Authority,* each of them hath lickt up a part of the spewings of it, & are become exercisers of this illegal arbitrary power, so far as their Wits will give them way, to the extream vexation and oppression of their prisoners.[33]

Then comes another story from Reynard the Fox, the popular medieval allegorical tale, known throughout north-west Europe.

This allusive style would indeed not be beyond the Levellers Richard Overton and William Walwyn, the follower of Montaigne, but more Nedhamesque are the Greek and Roman examples of the republics' guardians who were themselves subjected to cruel treatment by the state. The comparisons come straight into recent history with Fernando Cortes and Jan van Oldenbarnevelt, both victims of princely displeasure despite their patriotic accomplishments.[34] Two sentences then become more telling still, since Nedham is now renowned for his grasp of Machiavelli: 'For *Seneca* saith, *Mitius imperanti melius paretur,* they are best obeyed, that govern most mildly. And *Machiavel ubi supra,* p. 542. observes, that one act of humanity was of more force with the conquered *Falisci,* then many violent acts of hostility.'[35] Raleigh's *History of the World* and Guicciardini provide many examples of how harsh treatments of populations by native or foreign governments will result in such resistance that their power will end, but it is Machiavelli who is deemed more insightful with his claim that the Roman republic failed because of 'contention' between parties under the agrarian law that divided conquered property among citizens, and when elite groups were able to hold on to power and make themselves tyrannous.[36] Dominion is thought of here in a liberal way:

> We know that Common-wealths have never been much amplified, neither in dominion nor riches, *unlesse only during their Liberties;* for it is no mans particular good that amplifies the Kingdome. We know that those that have in their hands the

---

[33] *Vox Plebis,* 52–3.
[34] *Vox Plebis,* 61. For Overton and for Walwyn's use of Montaigne, see Chapter 30 on 'Radical and Deist Writing' by Nicholas McDowell and Giovanni Tarantino.
[35] *Vox Plebis,* 62.
[36] *Vox Plebis,* 66.

Government of a State, ought to increase the number of their free Subjects, *and make them as their Associates, and not Vassals.* We know that it is more honourable and profitable unto a State, moderately to use their Subjects meanes, thereby to keep their State in perpetuity, then through covetousnesse to devour them in one day, and in their losse to undoe themselves for ever.[37]

Moreover, 'the pretence of necessity in a Prince or State, *is but the Bawde to Tyrannie*'. It is Raleigh again who provides the evidence from ancient Rome of a hero, Caius Flaminius, who stood up against state tyranny and saved the republic: '*understanding the Majesty of Rome to be wholly in the people, and no otherwise in the Senate, then by way of delegacy, or grand Commission.*'[38] He was, it is implied, and as the publisher's note suggests in two pamphlets recording his persecution, the Roman John Lilburne, a decidedly populist version of a Roman republican.

If Nedham was a keen ventriloquizer of the Levellers, as well as a brilliant and authentic follower of Machiavelli, and someone interested in the role of the mere people in a nation's political life, he did not quite imitate all of the voices within the Leveller spectrum. He might have respected Lilburne and enjoyed his company in prison, and he might have shared satirical-political common ground with Overton, but Walwyn's post-Montaignian scepticism was of a different order, as was the juridical thinking of John Wildman and John Warr. The republican and Independent Lucy Hutchinson recorded that she and her New Model Army commander husband John had much sympathy for the Levellers but drew the line among popular movements at the New Levellers, or Diggers.[39] We have had to wait a very long time for a properly prepared and annotated edition of the main Digger author Gerrard Winstanley, who built a remarkable vision of a property-less mystical communion of God and man through the cultivation of the land, and where all land would be treated as held in common. That union, with a God called Reason and defined in a pantheistic way, stood out as notably different, Winstanley's pellucid prose briefly drawing much popular interest in London in 1651–2.[40]

The commune failed quickly because it could not overcome local resistance, and despite the Diggers proclaiming themselves loyal servants of the Commonwealth and drawing the approval of Lord Fairfax, until June 1650 still the Commander in Chief of the New Model. How did Winstanley's writings circulate and live on, if at all? They were not entirely forgotten, but were understood to plead for universal salvation, certainly one of Winstanley's heterodox positions. The utopia of *The Law of Freedom* (1652) is generally thought to have been more pessimistic than the earlier pamphlets, with heavy

---

[37] *Vox Plebis*, 67.
[38] *Vox Plebis*, 67–8.
[39] Lucy Hutchinson, *Memoirs of the Life of Colonel Hutchinson* (1806; Cambridge: Cambridge University Press, 2010), 285.
[40] Gerrard Winstanley, *Complete Works*, ed. Thomas N. Corns, Ann Hughes, and David Loewenstein, 2 vols. (Oxford: Oxford University Press, 2009). On Winstanley and 'Reason', see Chapter 30 on 'Radical and Deist Writing' by Nicholas McDowell and Giovanni Tarantino.

punishments stipulated for those who committed crimes or refused to live 'in common'. This may or may not have been an issue for later seventeenth-century readers who made contact with Winstanley's writings. But the universalism, the promise of redemption for all and for all of nature, aligns Winstanley with the mystical enthusiasts of the 1680s and 1690s, especially the Philadelphian Society, followers of both the early seventeenth-century mystic Jakob Böhme and the blind prophet Jane Lead, who would become internationally revered among the Pietists in the Netherlands and the north German principalities. Winstanley venerated a redefined 'Reason' who was God, whereas Lead recommended an irrational or extra-rational rapture, figuratively represented as the decollation of the head of the body politic, reason itself. The proof that Winstanley was being read in these circles is the evidence recently discovered of his translation into Dutch by the millenarian and Behmenist Amsterdam merchant Petrus Serrarius (1600–69), although the text itself does not survive.[41]

In these international, ecumenical circles, utopian communities, at once spiritualist and utilitarian, were entertained (such as the 1663 Delaware settlement planned and led by Pieter Plockhoy, who had previously tried to win the support of Oliver Cromwell in 1650s England), so we should not be surprised.[42] Yet in the universe of discourse, Winstanley fused mystical communism with the semantics of extreme poverty and marginal, vagabond living:

> The man of the flesh, judges it a righteous thing, That some men that are cloathed with the objects of the earth, and so called rich men, whether it be got by right or wrong, should be Magistrates to rule over the poor; and that the poor should be servants nay rather slaves to the rich.
>
> But the spiritual man, which is Christ, doth judge according to the light of equity and reason, That al man-kinde ought to have a quiet substance and freedome, to live upon earth; and that there shal be no bond-man nor begger in all his holy mountain.
>
> Gen. 1.28 Man-kinde was made to live in the freedome of the spirit, not under the bondage of the flesh, though the lordly flesh hath got a power for a time, as I said before; for every one was made to be a Lord over the Creation of the Earth, Cattle, Fish, Fowl, Grasse, Trees, not any one to be a bond-slave and a beggar under the Creation of his own kinde.[43]

Working at this level, where freeborn Englishmen, minimally propertied masters, are replaced by the humbler poor, the narrative begins to look like that more shocking discourse of the early American English settlements where settlers of all kinds, from various European places, come together with indigenous people and enslaved Africans to find new heaven (or its opposite) in the earth that they must clear to make workable, to

---

[41] Ariel Hessayon, 'Gerrard Winstanley in Translation', *Notes and Queries*, 66 (2019), 544–6.

[42] Pieter Plockhoy, *A Way Propounded to Make the Poor in these and other Nations Happy* (1659); Henk Looisteijn, 'Between Sin and Salvation: The Seventeenth-Century Dutch Artisan Pieter Plockhoy and His Ethics of Work', *International Review of Social History*, 56 (2011), 69–88.

[43] Winstanley, *The New Law of Righteousness* (1649), 34, in *Complete Works*, 1: 502.

ensure survival, and perhaps even to provide a profit.[44] A factual link might be provided by the evidence of those who agreed to be indentured servants in London only to find themselves transported to the Caribbean to be subjected to such harsh conditions of servitude they may as well have been called slaves.[45]

Mary Rowlandson's captivity narrative makes this point of deprivation in the New World in another way:

> *After a restless and hungry night there, we had a wearisome time of it the next day.* The Swamp by which we lay, was, as it were, a deep Dungeon, and an exceeding high and steep hill before it. Before I got to the top of the hill, I thought my heart and legs, and all would have broken, and failed me. What through faintness, and soreness of body, it was a grievous day of travel to me. *As we went along, I saw a place where* English *Cattle had been: that was comfort to me, such as it was: quickly after that we came to an* English *Path, which so took with me, that I thought I could have freely lyan down and dyed.* That day, a little after noon, we came to *Squaukheag*, where the *Indians* quickly spread themselves over the deserted *English* Fields, gleaning what they could find; some pickt up ears of Wheat that were crickled down, some found ears of *Indian* Corn, some found Ground-nuts, and others sheaves of Wheat that were frozen together in the shock, & went to threshing of them out[.] My self got two ears of *Indian* Corn, and whilst I did but turn my back, one of them was stolen from me, which much troubled me[.] There came an *Indian* to them at that time, with a basket of Horse-liver; I asked him to give me a piece: *What*, says he, *can you eat Horse-liver?* I told him, I would try.[46]

Such a perspective was frankly terrifying, and its vicarious attractiveness to readers would result in the popularity of major works of fiction in the period and the years ahead, many of which made some kind of claim to be a depiction of reality. It is no surprise to find these works of fiction interacting with the major works of political thought at that time, Hobbes or Locke. Winstanley described a political vision to redeem the destitute; it is not far at all from transatlantic expression.

Conclusion: Toleration

As the century drew to a close, and as the victory of the Whigs in the Glorious Revolution became more assured in the 1690s, many works were finally printed that had been circulated in clandestine limited groups during the Restoration, or not circulated at all.

---

[44] See Chapter 25 on 'New World Writing and Captivity Narratives' by Catherine Armstrong.

[45] John Donoghue, *Fire Under the Ashes: An Atlantic History of the English Revolution* (Chicago: University of Chicago Press, 2013).

[46] Mary White Rowlandson, *The Soveraignty & Goodness of God, Together, with the Faithfulness of His Promises Displayed; Being a Narrative of the Captivity and Restauration of Mrs. Mary Rowlandson* (Cambridge, MA, 1682), 21.

John Locke's several writings would become hugely influential, in some ways the 'official ideology' of the English in the eighteenth century. What is striking in Locke, howsoever he inherited elements from such predecessors as Hobbes, is the simple clarity of his sentences, sweeping away eons of convention, and the previous generation's obsession with constitutions, for a newly defined set of ground rules. This was writing not free of controversy, but it was so widely read that we can say it escaped these conjunctions. The *Letter Concerning Toleration* was originally composed in Latin, and then translated by Locke's secretary and Andrew Marvell's nephew, William Popple, so most readers will encounter it through the lens of the translation. Nonetheless, Popple captures Locke's definitional force:

> For whatsoever some People boast of the Antiquity of Places and Names, or of the Pomp of their Outward Worship; Others, of the Reformation of their Discipline; All, of the Orthodoxy of their Faith; (for every one is Orthodox to himself): these things, and all others of this nature, are much rather Marks of Men striving for Power and Empire over one another, than of the Church of Christ. Let any one have never so true a Claim to all these things, yet if he be destitute of Charity, Meekness, and Goodwill in general towards all Mankind; even to those that are not Christians, he is certainly yet short of being a true Christian himself.[47]

The *Letter* was written in exile in the Netherlands and addressed to Philippus van Limborch, a leading Remonstrant divine whom Locke had met in Amsterdam at a public dissection. The relatively open society of the Dutch Republic is apparent and where Locke himself encountered the nearly complete separation of church and state. Passion is expelled and all is clear. The prose enacts banishment of the persecuting spirit that Locke saw among some Puritans as well as among Anglicans.

How much Locke could be read in print before 1689 was strictly limited. The major works, with all of their remarkable force and clarity, come late, in the fundamentally reorienting decade of the 1690s. In the generation before that happened much English political writing was a tortured thing, outside of ordinary calls for obedience in church and state. Commonwealth loyalists knew political life had changed, and that they must adapt, but they experienced the silencing hand of persecution. They also had a far greater control of insight and vocabulary than they would have done if written by their equivalents in 1595. This picture might suggest a satisfaction with the terms of the 1689 settlement, and indeed even as the fall of the House of Stuart, which would prove after the death of Queen Anne in 1714 to be permanent, ensured the emergence of Jacobitism in substance and style, so old republicans still alive returned home, sometimes to publish within the safe parameters of the new regime. This was the case with the remarkable fishing manual-cum-allegory that confessed Cromwellian and New Model allegiance, Richard Franck's *Northern Memoirs* (1694).[48] The reset that came with 1689, which we

---

[47] John Locke, *A Letter Concerning Toleration and Other Writings*, ed. Mark Goldie (Indianapolis: Liberty Fund, 2010), 7–8.
[48] See Nigel Smith, 'Oliver Cromwell's Angler', *The Seventeenth Century*, 8 (1993), 51–65.

now know was not nearly so 'bloodless' as once assumed, resulted in the quick establishment of commercial society, much more extensive if still limited toleration, and a public sphere where the two poles of political identity established during the Civil War could survive as marketable styles in the periodical journals. In this way the literary 'styles' of Royalism and Parliamentarianism, Tory versus Whig, could become more extensively invested in aesthetic debates and questions of taste.

CHAPTER 29

PORNOGRAPHY

HAL GLADFELDER

The word *pornography* is a faux-classical coinage of the nineteenth century. Its derivation from the ancient Greek words *pornē* (prostitute) and *graphē* (writing or visual mark) gives the word a spurious air of antiquity, but apart from a single usage of *pornographoi* (to mean painters of prostitutes) in the second century AD the word is unknown before its reinvention by the French author Rétif de la Bretonne for the title of his 1769 treatise on prostitution, *Le Pornographe*. In its present-day meaning of any sexually explicit writing or image, *pornographique* was first used in French in 1806, and *pornography* as a noun in English in 1842.[1] Given this history, it is often argued that to apply the word to texts from the eighteenth century and earlier is anachronistic.[2] But while it is certainly true that no one in the period would have used the words *pornographic* or *pornography*, it does not follow that to use these as terms of historical analysis is to impose a post-Enlightenment or post-modern model of sexuality, the body, or erotic desire on early modern texts, nor does it presume that seventeenth-century readers thought about sex, gender, desire, or pleasure in the same ways that 'we' do. Rather, the very strangeness of the word *pornography* in a seventeenth-century context might help to illuminate the disruptive force of a new species of erotic writing which began to appear in England in the 1680s, and which was almost immediately regarded as constituting a new 'canon of depravity'.[3]

---

[1] On the use of *pornographoi* by Athenaeus in the second century, see Ian Moulton, *Before Pornography: Erotic Writing in Early Modern England* (Oxford: Oxford University Press, 2000), 8, and Walter Kendrick, *The Secret Museum: Pornography in Modern Culture* (Berkeley: University of California Press, 1996), 11–12. On Rétif and *Le Pornographe*, see James A. Steintrager, 'What Happened to the Porn in Pornography? Rétif, Regulating Prostitution, and the History of Dirty Books', *Symposium*, 60 (2006), 189–204. On the 1806 *pornographique*, see Lynn Hunt, 'Introduction', in Hunt (ed.), *The Invention of Pornography: Obscenity and the Origins of Modernity, 1500–1800* (New York: Zone, 1993), 9–45 (14). The 1842 use of 'pornography' in its modern sense is cited in the *OED*.

[2] See Moulton, *Before Pornography*, 8–15; Bradford K. Mudge, *The Whore's Story: Women, Pornography, and the British Novel, 1684–1830* (Oxford: Oxford University Press, 2000), 27–30.

[3] James Grantham Turner, 'Libertine Literature Forty Years On', *The Book Collector*, 54 (2005), 29–51 and 231–56 (29).

If the Restoration, and particularly the years 1679–85 during which the Licensing Act was allowed to lapse, saw the emergence of an obscene or pornographic canon, this canon was in vital ways *anti*-canonical. Its key texts—*The School of Venus* (1680), *The Whores Rhetorick* (1683), *Venus in the Cloister, or, The Nun in Her Smock* (1683), and *A Dialogue between a Married Lady and a Maid* (1684)—were translated, usually unfaithfully, from French and Italian originals, and mixed libertine with moralistic strains, high with low linguistic registers, dialogic with narrative modes, and female with male subject positions. Generically, thematically, and linguistically these were hybrid, heterodox works, whose hybridity grew out of their engagement with difference: the interaction of innocence and experience, native and foreign, female and male, visible and hidden. Animated by opposition and struggle, these foundational texts set the terms of the proliferation over the following two centuries of pornography not as a stable category but as a site of contestation—in Walter Kendrick's phrase, 'an argument, not a thing'.[4] It is the unstable, unrespectable, defiantly impure character of pornography that makes it a useful term of analysis even for writing produced in periods before the word existed.[5]

As critics from David Foxon and Lynn Hunt to Sarah Toulalan have shown, the realm of the pornographic is defined by a dialectic between the authorial or readerly aim of arousal and the censorial aim of regulation: pornography is as much a legal as a literary term.[6] Indeed, vexingly for censors, legal prohibition makes pornography all the more arousing. In this chapter, I read the four key early pornographic texts in relation to the histories of their translation, publication, and prosecution to explain their contradictory status as prohibited classics, canonical outlaws. Emulating the form and content of Pietro Aretino's *Ragionamenti* (Dialogues) of 1534–6, in which an older woman tutors a younger in the language and practice of *eros*, the French-, Latin-, and Italian-derived English texts of the 1680s also drew on native English traditions of bawdy tales and sexual burlesque, as had such predecessors as *The Crafty Whore* (1658) and the periodical miscellany *The Wandering Whore* (1660–3). While many authors of the period, from ballad-mongers to courtier rakehells, continued to treat erotic and obscene subjects in verse, the modern prose dialogue form offered new ways of thinking about the relationship between subjectivity and sex, in large part due to the 'promiscuity' and flexibility of prose itself. As with the contemporaneous emergence of the novel in France (for example, Mme de Lafayette's 1678 *Princesse de Clèves*), the pornographic prose dialogue focuses less on visible bodies and acts than on interiority—on sensation, memory, and desire. But in their hybrid English versions, these dialogues also incorporated the

---

[4] Kendrick, *Secret Museum*, 31.

[5] The most comprehensive overviews of the range of eroto-pornographic writing in the period are Roger Thompson, *Unfit for Modest Ears* (Totowa, NJ: Rowman and Littlefield, 1979); Peter Wagner, *Eros Revived: Erotica of the Enlightenment in England and America* (London: Paladin, 1990); and Julie Peakman, *Mighty Lewd Books: The Development of Pornography in Eighteenth-Century England* (Basingstoke: Palgrave Macmillan, 2012).

[6] David Foxon, *Libertine Literature in England, 1660–1745* (New Hyde Park, NY: University Books, 1965); Hunt, 'Introduction'; Sarah Toulalan, *Imagining Sex: Pornography and Bodies in Seventeenth-Century England* (Oxford: Oxford University Press, 2007).

scabrous, coarse language of the native English obscene—in James Grantham Turner's phrase, the 'touches of blustering rudeness typical of Restoration England'—so that their subtle analysis of sensation and affect is roughened by raucous laughter.[7]

ANCESTORS: ARETINO AND *THE CRAFTY WHORE*

The first volume of the *Ragionamenti* or Dialogues of Pietro Aretino (1492–1556), published in 1534, provided the formal and thematic model for all of the foundational pornographic texts examined here and was the wellspring of all later erotic literature. Over the course of three days, two courtesans, Nanna and Antonia, discuss the three modes of life available to women—nun, wife, whore—in order to determine which will be best for Nanna's daughter Pippa to follow. Not too surprisingly, they conclude that it is the profession of whore that offers women the greatest degree of control over themselves and others; and even though it is less sexually explicit than the first day's dialogue on the orgiastic excesses of life in a convent, the third dialogue, on the life and stratagems of whores, had a wider circulation and the greatest influence on later pornographic writing.[8] Nanna, the older and more experienced of the two, is the principal speaker throughout, and over the course of the dialogues she recounts the history of her sexual initiation as a narrative of education. As in many later pornographic narratives, spying on the sexual activities of others is a crucial early step in the narrator's progress, and Nanna's first-person narrative serves the same purpose as sexual spying: as a source of both instruction and erotic excitement.

Aretino's works were placed on the Catholic *Index Librorum Prohibitorum* as early as 1559; but in 1584 the London printer John Wolfe published an unexpurgated edition of the *Ragionamenti* which was reprinted in London c.1597 and at least four times on the Continent between 1600 and 1650.[9] Wolfe's edition was intended mainly for the Continental market, but its production in London not only made the text available to such English readers as Ben Jonson and Queen Elizabeth's chief adviser, William Cecil, but also attests to the closeness of the English and Continental book trades from the late sixteenth century. Pornographic writing was only one component of the international

---

[7] Turner, 'Libertine Literature', 49. See also Thompson, who in *Unfit for Modest Ears* writes of the 'Restoration obsessions with the indecent and the scabrous, with brutality and obscenity' (11)—a theme developed in his 'Conclusion', 212–15.

[8] On the publishing history of the *Ragionamenti*, see Foxon, *Libertine*, 25–7. As he explains, the third dialogue was frequently published on its own, particularly in translation. On the *Ragionamenti* as social critique, see Moulton, *Before Pornography*, 127–36. A second volume, in whose three dialogues Nanna imparts to her daughter the knowledge needed for a successful career in prostitution, was published in 1536.

[9] Foxon, *Libertine*, 26; Moulton, *Before Pornography*, 146.

trade in prohibited books, which also included works banned for their subversive, immoral, or anti-religious contents—and Aretino's presence on the *Index* was due at least as much to his scathing attacks on Catholic churchmen and politicians as to his erotic works: the great Italian poet Ariosto tagged Aretino *il flagello de' principi* (the scourge of princes).[10] But the overlapping of *eros* and political critique in Aretino's writing was to prove one of the defining traits of pornography's long later history, from the anti-monastic satire of *Venus in the Cloister* to French anti-royalist screeds of the 1780s and 1790s.[11]

Another instance of the international circulation of forbidden texts was the publication, in 1658, of a loose (in every sense) translation of the third dialogue of the *Ragionamenti* called *The Crafty Whore*. It follows the basic pattern of Aretino's work—one prostitute tells another the story of the various tricks by which she gained money and independence from men—but places it into a moralistic frame, so that the dialogue is preceded by a preface in which the author states his intention 'to trie what good I could do, by shewing you the wildnesse and perniciousnesse of those, who make it their sole lively-hood to commit whoredome ... [so that] you may be admonisht to avoid and beware of the like'.[12] The dialogue departs from Aretino's original by ending with Nanna (here named Thais) resolving to pack herself off to 'some remote Cell or Hermitage' where 'my lustfull & deceitfull crimes will I number by my sighs and groanes' (95); and this in turn is followed by a sixteen-page 'Dehortation from Lust', which consists mainly of a set of lurid stories of sex and death, of the kind often recorded in ballads or chapbooks. One might wonder whether all this apparatus of moral condemnation is meant to be taken seriously, or if it plays facetiously with the convention that sensational or lascivious tales always had to be enclosed within trite moral lessons or warnings as a tax the reader had to pay to enjoy the narrative contents. Of course seventeenth-century readers believed in sin and providential retribution: 'see God's revenging hand', the author of the 'Dehortation' writes, before showing us the spectacle of a 'lustfull' lady and her 'comely' servant, discovered dead on her bed after a night of 'venereall skirmishes ... lying in a most shamefull and beastly manner' (110–11). How would readers have responded to such a tableau—with prim distaste, fear and trembling, shameful excitement, rude laughter, or some combination of these? In its prurient language, the scene allows for and even encourages multiple, conflicting reactions, just as it incites readers to conjure a mental image of the lustful, comely couple lying in a 'shamefull and beastly manner'.

Certainly the moral cladding of *The Crafty Whore* sits uneasily with the snarky, bawdy tone of Thais's storytelling and Antonia's cynical comments. Early in her career, Thais takes a Spaniard, a Frenchman, and an Englishman as lovers—the joke-like structure of

---

[10] Ludovico Ariosto, *Orlando furioso*, 46. 14, lines 3–4.

[11] On eighteenth-century France, see Lynn Hunt, 'Pornography and the French Revolution', in Hunt, *Invention*, 301–39; and Robert Darnton, *The Forbidden Bestsellers of Pre-Revolutionary France* (London: HarperCollins, 1996).

[12] *The Crafty Whore* (1658), sigs. A1v–A2r.

three lovers embodying three national stereotypes is typical of the work as a whole—and of the Englishman, she says, 'This my noble lover spent very freely upon me, and in me' (32), punning on 'spent' as a synonym for 'ejaculated'. Her English lover contracts 'a terrible clap' from a prostitute and passes it on to Thais, prompting Antonia to comment, 'What can he expect lesse, who partakes of the nature of a Dog, in this, that he takes his pleasure with every Bitch he meets'. Continuing with the animal imagery, Antonia says of the infected whore, 'Truly (Sister) I believe she is paid home in the same coyne that makes her ------ a stable for every Asse to litter in, sometimes she may meet withall a *Running Nag*' (32). This passage is typical of *The Crafty Whore* in its puns, its use of cant or slang ('running nag' was cant for a venereal running sore), its 'low' use of barnyard metaphors, its use of dashes as a device for avoiding an obscene word but 'in such a way as to emphasize even more the term replaced' (here, presumably, 'cunt').[13] It is also typical in its utter absence of sympathy or good nature: every person the speakers encounter is a fool or dupe who deserves whatever they get. So it comes as a surprise when Antonia follows her '*Running Nag*' pun with a little sermon on the wickedness of bawdy-houses: 'Modesty that should be a Woman's glory is hence banisht; nothing but what is lascivious and wanton must be entertained there' (32–3). But Thais sees through her friend's posturing: 'For all thy preaching, I really think it was not thou that left first this bittersweet sin, but it did thee, and I think thou doest wish well to it still' (33). Morality in this roguish world is just another con, and repentance just a tactic for duping another fool.

In that light one might also question whether Thais's plan to retire to a hermit's cell can possibly be taken seriously, especially as it is outlined so perfunctorily on the text's last page. Some scepticism is warranted if we recall an earlier episode, when Thais 'pretended … that I would now bid adieu to the world, by sequestring my self in a Nunnery from its rumours & manifold trouble' (48)—a stratagem for entrapping a rich husband in the persona of a virtuous wife, 'counterfeiting the lives of the Saints'. This husband is no sooner snared than she cuckolds him with multiple lovers, spends all his money, and kills him, laughing all the while. By any ethical standard, Thais's actions are appalling; but if we read *The Crafty Whore* as a rogue narrative—heartless, amoral, crudely and cheerfully obscene—the text's moral cladding becomes just one more object of burlesque.

In *The Crafty Whore*, the Aretine dialogue of sexual instruction and female initiation is contaminated with contradictory strains of moral sermonizing and ribald cruelty, the 'brutality and obscenity' that Roger Thompson argued is characteristic of Restoration eroticism. English authors, Thompson contended, 'excelled at making sex shocking as they failed to make it either exciting or funny. They could disgust; they could not arouse or amuse. Their response to sexuality was smut, or burlesque, or rage, or outrage'.[14]

---

[13] Armando Marchi, 'Obscene Literature in Eighteenth-Century Italy: An Historical and Bibliographical Note', trans. James Coke and David Marsh, in Robert Purks Maccubbin (ed.), *'Tis Nature's Fault: Unauthorized Sexuality during the Enlightenment* (Cambridge: Cambridge University Press, 1987), 244–60 (246)

[14] Thompson, *Unfit*, 215.

Rage and disgust also run through the *Wandring Whore* pamphlets of 1660–1, whose title exploits the notoriety of the Italian prose dialogue *La puttana errante* (the errant or wandering whore) often misattributed in the period to Aretino.[15] *The Wandring Whore* (which despite the title has nothing to do with *La puttana errante*) mixes Aretine dialogue with rogue narrative, joke-book jests, classified adverts offering rewards for the return of goods stolen by 'thieving whores', and lists of 'all the Crafty Bawds, Maidenhead-sellers, Common Whores, Night-walkers ... Pimps and Trappanners' practicing in London. This makes for an obscene hodgepodge, whose catalogue of sexual practice can be startling, as in one sketch of clients at a brothel: a young merchant 'who will not be contented with doing the business, but will have half a dozen Girles stand stark naked round about a Table whilst he lyes snarling underneath as if he would bite off their whibb-bobs, and eat them for his pains; another will needs shite in one of our wenches mouth's (which is odd lechery) ...' and so on.[16] Such 'monstrous scenes', as Turner calls them, combine carnivalesque 'rough music' with a debasement of female bodies that anticipates Sade's *120 Days of Sodom* of 1782–5 but also reflects a longer history of misogynistic bawdry. Although similarly founded on the model of the *Ragionamenti*, the four 'canonical' works of the 1680s depart notably from *The Crafty* or *Wandring Whore* in their greater emphasis on sensation and subjectivity: that is, on the feelings of fear, pain, desire, and pleasure experienced by their female protagonists both during the sexual scene itself and in the acts of remembering and retelling it to another woman.

'UNA VEZ TO DECHARGER': TRANSLATION AND THE ENGLISH PORNOGRAPHIC CANON

The only seventeenth-century reader to leave a precise account of his purchase, reading, and reaction to a pornographic text is the diarist Samuel Pepys, whose 1668 encounter with the French *L'École des filles* has been much pored over.[17] Coming across it one day

---

[15] There are two completely unrelated Italian texts titled *La puttana errante*: a mock-epic verse satire from c. 1538 by Lorenzo Venier (or Veniero) and a prose dialogue modelled on the *Ragionamenti* from c. 1660. Both works were wrongly attributed to Aretino, whose name had become a kind of brand associated with all things lascivious. See Foxon, *Libertine*, 27–30; Moulton, *Before Pornography*, 148–52.

[16] [John Garfield], *The Wandring Whore Continued* [issue number 3 of 5] (1660), 9. On Garfield, see Foxon, *Libertine*, 9, 28. A 'sixth part' of *The Wandring Whore* appeared in 1663, but according to Turner this 'is clearly a different enterprise from a different publisher': James Grantham Turner, *Libertines and Radicals in Early Modern London: Sexuality, Politics, and Literary Culture, 1630–1685* (Cambridge: Cambridge University Press, 2002), 127 and 302 n. 15. On the passage quoted here, see Turner, *Libertines*, 144–50. (Parts 2, 3, and 5 of *The Wandring Whore* are available on *EEBO*.)

[17] The fullest reading is in James Grantham Turner, *Schooling Sex: Libertine Literature and Erotic Education in Italy, France, and England, 1534–1685* (Oxford: Oxford University Press, 2003), 1–6 and 226–40. See also Moulton, *Before Pornography*, 36–7, and Hal Gladfelder, 'Literature and Pornography, 1660–1800', *Oxford Handbooks Online* (New York: Oxford University Press, 2013).

in a bookshop, Pepys read a few pages and was startled to find that 'it is the most bawdy, lewd book that ever I saw, rather worse than *putana errante* — so that I was ashamed of reading in it'.[18] Why ashamed? Pepys's shame is in direct proportion to his desire to keep reading even after he has discovered what sort of book he has picked up. There is no shame in looking into a book entitled *The School for Girls*, only in continuing to read it after discovering it to be 'lewd'. But as his reference to the *Puttana errante* reveals, *L'École* wasn't the first such book Pepys had read; and the fact that he knew enough to make the comparison—to recognize the two books as belonging to the same species—may have been another source of shame.

Pepys was unusual in being able to make such a comparison: not only did he have to be literate, in a period when literacy was linked to social rank; he had to be able to read in French and Italian as well as English. Indeed, the presence of *L'École des filles* in a London bookshop at a time when it was outlawed in France—the French authorities had burned all the copies they could track down of its first print run—not only confirms the close ties between Continental and English literary cultures but suggests that as far as English censors were concerned, a foreign book, whose readership was limited to a linguistic elite, posed no threat to public morals. In his survey of legal actions against obscene books from 1660 to 1745, Foxon found only one case, from 1677, in which a bookseller's shop was closed down for 'several hours' for stocking some foreign-language pornography—including the French *École des filles*. As the bookseller's brother-in-law wrote to the high-ranking civil servant Sir Joseph Williamson, 'he did not conceive in any way' that such books were 'prohibited in England'.[19] It was only when foreign texts were translated into English, putting them in reach of less privileged readers, that they became targets of prosecution—as happened with the English translation of *L'École* as *The School of Venus* in 1680.[20]

Pepys's shame did not stop him from returning to Martin's bookshop three weeks later to purchase a copy of *L'École*. Indeed his desire for the text is inextricable from the shame his desire aroused, and he notes that he took it home 'in plain binding... because I resolve, as soon as I have read it, to burn it, that it may not stand in the list of books, nor among them, to disgrace them if it should be found'. The next day, he had friends over: 'We sang till almost night, and drank my good store of wine; and then they parted and I to my chamber, where I did read through *L'escholle des Filles*; a lewd book, but what doth me no wrong to read for information sake (but it did hazer my prick para stand all the while, and una vez to decharger); and after I had done it, I burned it, that it might not be among my books to my shame'.[21] Even shame, however, does not prevent Pepys

---

[18] *The Diary of Samuel Pepys*, ed. Robert Latham and William Matthews, volume IX (London: HarperCollins, 1971), 21–2.

[19] Foxon, *Libertine*, 9.

[20] In 1680, John Coxe was indicted for publishing *The School of Venus*, as was Joseph Streater in 1688, for a reprint of the same translation: see Roger Thompson, 'Two Early Editions of Restoration Erotica', *The Library*, 5th ser., 32 (1977), 45–8; Turner, 'Libertine Literature', 45, and *Schooling Sex*, pp. xxv–xxvi; Foxon, *Libertine*, 10–11.

[21] Pepys, *Diary* IX, 57–9.

from recording the whole episode in explicit detail: as Turner notes, while the entry was written in Pepys's cryptic shorthand, the book's title is fully written out in longhand, as is the French word *decharger* (ejaculate), which suggests that Pepys was highlighting as much as concealing his orgasmic response to the shaming text. Pepys's shift into a babel of English, Spanish, and French at the moment of climax signals the infiltration of English domestic space by a foreign invader or seducer but also suggests a continuity between foreign and domestic, just as his secret reading in the solitude of his chamber is continuous with his sociable carousing with friends, woven into a single sentence. Pepys's response to the text is pornographic precisely because it undoes the boundaries between private (chamber) and public (bookshop), foreign (*decharger*) and domestic (*prick*), instruction ('for information sake') and arousal, female (the text's speakers, reciting their own orgasmic pleasures) and male (the reader who identifies with the speakers and takes vicarious part in the same pleasures).

The text's translation into *The School of Venus* twelve years later served as the first step in the making of an English pornographic canon in which foreignness itself often stands for sexual excitement, excess, sophistication, perversity, and danger. Only one copy of this work has been located, at the Bayerische Staatsbibliothek in Munich; this has recently been transcribed and reprinted in an edition supervised by Bradford K. Mudge.[22] The bookseller John Coxe was indicted in 1680 for publishing *School*, and legal documents from 1688 and 1745 include indictments of the printers and publishers of later editions, of which there are no surviving copies. Those indictments, however, include passages transcribed from the 1688 and 1744 editions which establish that these were 'verbally identical' with the 1680 text.[23] The fact that the same text was printed multiple times over more than sixty years in the face of censorial opposition shows not only that publishers thought there was enough readerly interest in the work to make the risk of prosecution worth braving, but also that the English pornographic canon was both stable and small: the same few titles turn up again and again from the later seventeenth through most of the eighteenth century.

In its translation from French to English, *The School of Venus* lost the original subtitle, *La Philosophie des dames*, indicating a paring back of the more 'philosophical' passages of the 1655 French text. The change from *École des filles* to *School of Venus* also suggests a shift to a blunter, bawdier tone, as 'School of Venus' was slang in the period for bawdy-house or brothel. Even without those passages in which the French speakers articulated the work's 'ostensible philosophy of enlightened hedonism', however, a rough-and-ready form of philosophical materialism does run through the English text, as when Katy, the younger of the dialogue's two speakers, reports back to Frances after her first sexual experience: 'I tell you what, since Mr. *Roger* has fucked me, and I know what is what, I find all my Mothers stories to be but Bug-bears, and good for nothing but to fright Children,

---

[22] *The School of Venus* (1680) in Bradford K. Mudge (ed.), *When Flesh Becomes Word: An Anthology of Early Eighteenth-Century Libertine Literature* (New York: Oxford University Press, 2004).

[23] Turner, 'Libertine Literature', 46. On the prosecutions of those who printed and sold *The School of Venus*, see Foxon, *Libertine*, 10–11, 15–18, 30–7; Turner, *Schooling Sex*, xxv–xxvi.

for my part I believe we were created for fucking, and when we begin to fuck, we begin to live.'[24] This statement is typical of the text as a whole in two respects: in its articulation of the claim that sex is a universal drive which trumps morality; and in its plain, even coarse language. The universalizing claim appears in various formulations, as when Frances tells Katy that 'all People of all ranks and degrees participate therein, even from the King to the Cobler, from the Queen to the Scullion Wench, in short, one half of the World Fuckes the other' (10–11; 9). The 'levelling' message, that sex erases social distinctions, is based in a materialist view of nature: as Frances sums up, 'To be short, Fucking is so natural, that one way or another Leachery will have it's vent in all sorts and conditions of People' (113–14; 47). Moreover, this levelling model of sexual desire pertains as much to gender distinctions as to class: females and males can equally be active subjects of the verb 'fuck', as Katy implies when she wonders 'why is the pleasure greater when the Woman gets upon the Man and Fucks him, then when she is passive and lyes under' (124; 50). Frances's answer to this undermines, in fact, any faith in fixed gender identities or roles: 'it is a kind of Metamorphosis', she asserts, 'for when the Woman is a top, the Man is possessed with feminine thoughts, and the Woman with Masculine passions, each having assumed the contrary Sex by the postures they are in' (125; 50). Biological sex is not a stable concept, but an endlessly mutable one.[25]

The *School of Venus*'s plain language is itself a topic of discussion within the text. Katy balks when Frances first says the word 'prick', but Frances tells her, 'if you are minded to hear such Discourse, you must not be so Scrupulous', going on to insist, 'I must use the very words without Mincing, Cunt, Arse, Prick, Bollocks, &c.' (13; 10). In arguing for the merits of 'plain *English*', Frances privileges clarity and directness over 'affected modesty' (16; 11), and in so doing she gestures towards a theory of pornographic prose, which rejects euphemism, or the 'tedious demonstrations' of metaphorical invention, in favour of 'call[ing] every thing by it's right name' (107–8; 44). Such plain English is valued not just for its clarity, however, but also for its erotic force. Early in the first of their two dialogues, when Frances is tutoring the as yet inexperienced Katy in the elements of love, she tells her, 'When a man thrusts his prick into a Womans Cunt, it is called Fucking, But pray do'nt talk of such kind of things before Company, for they will call you an immodest baudy Wench, and chide you for it' (16; 11). Modest speech is the currency of public sociability, as plain speech is of sexual passion. In the second dialogue, which follows her sexual initiation, Katy notes that 'when Mr. *Roger* and I am alone together, he makes me often name these words, which amongst Lovers is very pleasing' (80; 34), as if the immodesty of the words carried an erotic charge. As Frances puts it, 'heat of love will neither give us leave or time to run divisions, so that all we can pronounce is, come my dear Soul, take me by the Prick, and put it into thy Cunt, which sure is much better than

---

[24] *The School of Venus* (1680), 59. Subsequent references will be given in the text, with the original page number followed by the page number of the transcription in Mudge (ed.), *When Flesh Becomes Word* (here 26); 'ostensible philosophy of enlightened hedonism' is from Turner, 'Libertine Literature', 49.

[25] In the 1680 edition, Frances's name is printed as *Frank* before her speeches, as if to allow us to read her as either male or female, or both, or neither exclusively.

to say, take me by the Gristle, which grows at the bottom of my Belly, and put it into thy Loves Paradice' (108; 44). It is only in plain or obscene words that lovers can express the urgency of desire.

Both the plain language and the view of sex as a universal, natural force that cancels out social distinctions could suggest that desire in *The School of Venus* begins and ends with the body, and that the pornographic text is solely concerned with the flesh: that is, with the outward appearance and actions of visible, tangible, material bodies in motion. Frances declares that 'the greatest and chiefest cause of love, is the pleasure our Bodies receive' (103; 43) and argues that 'all love is Brutal' (103; 43), by which she means reducible to copulation. In keeping with such a theory of desire, the dialogue is replete with minutely detailed descriptions of male and female bodies and sexual postures; so it can seem there is no place for anything other than bodies in Venus's *School*. But if desire, like love, originates in the body, the very form of the dialogue shifts the locus of erotic passion from the bedrooms where Frances and Katy meet their lovers to the secluded room where they retell each other their sexual encounters. The scene of sexual arousal is the room where the dialogue takes place. Again and again, Katy and Frances tell one another how listening to such lascivious scenes affects them. In the first dialogue, after Frances has given a detailed account of one night with her husband, Katy says that 'the very Relation you have given me makes me mad for Horseing, in plain English my Cunt Itcheth like Wild-Fire ... I am for downright Fucking without any more ado' (44; 22). Similarly, in the second dialogue Katy interrupts Frances's discourse on 'Tongue-kissing' with the outburst, 'Enough, Enough of this Cousin, or else you'le make me spend' (124; 50). Throughout *The School of Venus*, the remembrance and narration of sexual scenes elicits desire, even orgasm, in speaker and listener alike—offering readers a model for how they might respond, vicariously and bodily, to the text.

This imaginative response of listener and reader to the pornographic text suggests that if *eros* originates in the body, it is nurtured and embellished in the imagination, in memory and language. The 'plain English' words that Mr. Roger makes Katy speak intensify erotic sensation; while the 'greater pleasure' produced 'when the woman is a top' stems, Frances argues, from an imagined 'Metamorphosis' whereby 'the Man is possessed with feminine thoughts, and the Woman with Masculine passions' (125; 50). Near the end of the second dialogue Katy says that 'when I am absent from my friend I always think of the pleasant pastime I have in his company, and not considering his other perfections, I am so strangely besotted with his Stones and Prick, that ... I think it tumbleth the very coggles of my heart, these imaginations make me so damnable Prick proud, that I spend with the very conceit of them' (130–1; 52). Conceit or thought stands in for the absent body, arousing the imagination just as the shameful words of *L'École des filles* induced Pepys 'una vez to decharger'.

Despite the 1680 indictment of John Coxe for publishing this English *School of Venus*, it must have been a money-spinner, for not only was the same text republished in 1688 (leading to a second round of prosecutions) but it evidently inspired the translation and publication of the three other key texts in the making of an English pornographic canon: *The Whores Rhetorick* and *Venus in the Cloister* (both 1683) and the 1684

Dialogue between a Married Lady and a Maid.[26] Although none of these later works is as raw in language or as explicit in sexual detail as the *School*, they share its self-conscious concern with the effects of erotic representations on their audiences, and its amoral, materialist theory of sex as a natural force. For all their attention to the body, they follow the *School of Venus*'s lead in emphasizing the subjective and imaginative dimensions of *eros*, which becomes a constitutive feature of the pornographic form in this period. Each adapts the Aretine model of an educative dialogue between women 'to the Meridian of London'—that is, to the tastes and expectations of English readers—while preserving some flavour of their sources' foreign, and thus 'exotic' and potentially wicked, origins.[27]

The Whores Rhetorick presents itself as a 'straight' translation of Ferrante Pallavicino's 1642 *Retorica delle puttane*, but as Turner has shown, it is an unfaithful, mongrel text that recasts Pallavicino's sophisticated, satirical 'eroto-didactic treatise' as a dialogue in the mould of *The School of Venus*, interlarding pieces of Pallavicino with passages cribbed from Aretino's *Ragionamenti*, and mixing in topical references to celebrities and scandals from contemporary London.[28] Pallavicino's nameless female professor of rhetoric is translated into Mother Creswel or Cresswell, a notorious London bawd, who in the *Rhetorick*'s introductory narrative offers to teach the 'young and most beautiful Virgin' Dorothea how to thrive as a 'Woman of the Town' by mastering 'the *Whores Rhetorick*'.[29] This 'rhetoric', she explains, 'is nothing else, but the art to multiply insinuating words, and feigned pretences to perswade, and move the minds of those men, who falling into their nets, do become the trophies of their victories' (36). The bulk of the ensuing text is a catalogue of 'Cheats, Slights and Juggles' (114), by which a well-schooled whore can secure her fortune. Mother Creswel's method is based on the principle that 'your whole life must be one continued act of dissimulation' (40) and entails rigorous self-discipline, to the point that the whore must repudiate her 'natural' gender identity: as she tells Dorothea (lifting a line from the *Ragionamenti*), 'a Whore is a Whore, but a Whore is not a Woman' (144). In a crisp departure from the timeworn misogynist *doxa* that all women are whores, this epigram suggests instead that all identities, including gender identities, are roles or masks—a 'continued act of dissimulation'. The role of whore simply makes this 'act' explicit.

This emphasis on rigorous self-policing in order to dissimulate more effectively means that Creswel pays scant attention to sexual pleasure (except *as* performance) or love (except as a weakness to be shunned), which differentiates *The Whore's Rhetorick* from the other key texts addressed here. But in one passage the erotic imagination does come to the fore, in the context of a self-reflexive discussion of pornography itself.

---

[26] On the 1688 prosecutions, see Foxon, *Libertine*, 11.

[27] The quoted phrase is from the full title of *The Whores Rhetorick, Calculated to the Meridian of London, and Conformed to the Rules of Art* (1683).

[28] Turner, *Schooling Sex*, 74–87 (on Pallavicino's *Retorica*) and 315–18 (on *The Whores Rhetorick*). The quoted phrase is from p. 78. See also Foxon, *Libertine*, 9–10.

[29] *The Whores Rhetorick*, 1, 15, 19. Subsequent references will be given in the text.

Mother Creswel tells Dorothea that she needs to stock up on 'lascivious Pictures, obscene Images and Representations to raise her own and her Lovers joys' (166). Such pictures answer a practical need: 'When you are detained in ugly, sordid, or ungrateful embraces; it would be difficult without the artificial aid of a picture to counterfeit those ecstasies which every comer may expect for his money.' To form a mental image of a 'comely Youth ... whose shadow will create a greater gust than could be raised by a nauseous though real enjoyment', the whore requires a visual prompt: 'The Picture of this charming Boy may very fitly be placed near your Bed, to imprint the fancy deeper in your imagination, and enable you to fall into ... sweet transports' (166). In Creswel's scenario, it is not the ugly client's body, but a 'fancy' imprinted in the whore's imagination by a lascivious picture, that brings her to orgasm or 'sweet transports'. And from this imagined scene Creswel derives a universal theory of desire, telling Dorothea, 'the whole series of carnal satisfaction *does purely consist in fancy*, and he effectually enjoys most, whose imagination is strongest' (167–8; emphasis added). Pictures, or the speaking pictures of pornographic texts, arouse the viewer's or listener's fancy and so produce 'carnal satisfaction', which is a function not of the body (even if it is felt *on* the body) but of the desiring imagination.

Published the same year as *The Whore's Rhetorick*, *Venus in the Cloister* was unusual in having been translated almost immediately, and pretty faithfully, from the original French of *Vénus dans le cloître* (also 1683; usually attributed to Jean Barrin). A later translation by Robert Samber was the focus of the publisher Edmund Curll's 1725–8 trials for obscene libel, in which the prosecution, led by the attorney general Sir Philip Yorke, successfully argued that if a publication 'is destructive of morality in general; if it does, or may, affect all the king's subjects, it then is an offence of a public nature'.[30] That argument provided the legal basis for all subsequent regulation of obscene publications in Britain; but no legal case was made against the 1683 version, perhaps because it could be taken as a satirical exposé of the evils of Catholicism, with its scenes of sexual licence and 'perversity'—from masturbation to voyeurism to whipping—in an outwardly respectable convent. Taking its inspiration from the first of Aretino's *Ragionamenti*, on the sex lives of nuns, *Venus* comprises three dialogues between the nineteen-year-old libertine Angelica and the less worldly, sixteen-year-old Agnes, starting from a moment when Angelica spies through a keyhole on Agnes secretly masturbating in her cell.[31] This originary scene is important, for it not only establishes a pattern of voyeuristic eroticism

---

[30] Quoted in Foxon, *Libertine*, 15. On the Curll trials, see Paul Baines and Pat Rogers, *Edmund Curll, Bookseller* (Oxford: Oxford University Press, 2007), 155–69, and 'The Prosecutions of Edmund Curll, 1725-28', *The Library*, 5 (2004), 176–94; Alexander Pettit, '*Rex v. Curll*: Pornography and Punishment in Court and on the Page', *Studies in the Literary Imagination*, 34 (2001), 63–78; Donald Thomas, *A Long Time Burning: A History of Literary Censorship in England* (London: Routledge and Kegan Paul, 1969), 78–85; Foxon, *Libertine*, 14–15.

[31] Although the 1683 French and English texts consisted of just three dialogues, further dialogues were added in later decades, very different in tone and sexual content, reaching a total of six in early eighteenth-century French editions. The Samber translation published by Curll in 1724 contained five dialogues, but not the sixth.

running through the text, but infuses Angelica and Agnes's dialogues with a homoerotic intensity at odds with their ostensibly 'heterosexual' content. That is, while most of Angelica's educational stories concern sex between men and women, their intention is more seductive than instructive. Even before the dialogue proper begins, Angelica asks Agnes's permission to embrace her, 'that our hearts may speak to one another in the midst of our kisses'; and so warm is her embrace that it takes Agnes to the threshold of combustion: 'Ah God! how thou graspest me in thy Arms, thou little thinkest I am naked in my Smock! Ah! thou hast set me all on a Fire.'[32] In this hot setting it is not surprising that when Angelica tells Agnes what she spied through the keyhole, she takes action as well: 'I saw thee in such a Posture and Action as if thou pleas'st I will serve thee in myself; wherein my hand shall at present do thee the Office which thy own a while ago did so charitably render to another part of thy Body' (8). Homoerotic currents flit through such earlier pornographic texts as *The School of Venus*, too—when Katy invites Frances to look at her 'White, Smooth and Plump' thighs, for instance, Frances reminds her that 'I have often seen and handled them before now, when we lay together' (63; 28)—but sexual desire between women is the driving force in *Venus in the Cloister*, and the dialogue closes with a declaration of same-sex love: 'Adieu *Agnes*, Adieu my *Heart*, my *Souls-Delight*, my *Love*' (161).

Since its story originates in a scene of voyeurism—it is what she sees through the keyhole that draws Angelica into Agnes's room and precipitates their conversation—*Venus* foregrounds the tension between private and public, visible and hidden, which animates much early modern pornographic writing. As Sarah Toulalan writes, 'in a world in which there was in actuality very little privacy ... pornography offers the *illusion* of a private sexual world that we are not meant to see — but that is held up for us to see'.[33] The publication, or making-public, of that private world, she argues, 'produces an erotic charge'.[34] In *Venus*, the reader gains imaginative access to the claustral female space of a Catholic nun's cell—which for English readers especially would have carried the charge of the illicit—but more generally, the pornographic text gives access to realms that would otherwise be off-limits. This idea of a hidden realm of the sexual is bound up with the educative premise of the Aretine pornographic dialogue, as is also evident in the title of the last of the key texts in the seventeenth-century English pornographic canon, the 1684 *Dialogue between a Married Lady and a Maid*, in which the married lady Tullia's task is to prepare the virgin or maid Octavia for her wedding night by teaching her the physical details of sexual love. As Octavia puts it, over the course of their dialogues 'I am

---

[32] *Venus in the Cloister, or, The Nun in her Smock ... Done out of French* (1683), 5.
[33] Toulalan, *Imagining Sex*, 162; see 161–93 for a full discussion of notions of privacy in early modern pornography.
[34] Toulalan, *Imagining Sex*, 162. See also James Grantham Turner, '*The Whore's Rhetorick*: Narrative, Pornography, and the Origins of the Novel', *Studies in Eighteenth-Century Culture*, 24 (1995), 297–306, in which he notes that 'even the ostensible exposé communicates a furtive erotic pleasure, the pleasure of revealing secrets' (302).

to learn Secrets I cannot yet comprehend': to gain access to the hidden realm of adult sexuality.[35]

No copies of the 1684 *Dialogue between a Married Lady and a Maid* are known to have survived; but a single line quoted in the indictment of that edition is so close to the same line in an edition from 1740 which *does* survive (in a single copy), that it seems probable the 1740 text reproduces, or nearly so, the lost 1684 version.[36] That lost text, which was republished at least twice, in 1688 (when it was again the object of legal action) and 1740, was a heavily edited translation, or alteration, of Nicolas Chorier's Latin work in seven dialogues, *Satyra Sotadica* [Sotadic—that is, pornographic—Satire], probably the most influential and surely the most extreme or 'advanced' pornographic text of the seventeenth and eighteenth centuries.[37] The *Dialogue* is a considerably expurgated version of portions of Chorier's first, fourth, and fifth dialogues, and while sexually explicit—even, perhaps, blunter in language than the original—it replaces Chorier's transgressive, violent, 'anarchistic' libertinism with a paean to the sexual pleasures of faithful married love.[38] It consists of three dialogues: the first introduces the speakers; the second features Tullia's descriptions of male and female genitals, and an account of her wedding night; in the third, Octavia reciprocates with a report of her own erotic initiation with Philander. Its plot is the same as that of the *School of Venus*, but made respectable by confining sex to marriage (Katy's Mr. Roger in the *School* is a 'fucking Friend' [25; 14], not a husband.)

For a twenty-first-century reader, the most surprising point in the *Dialogue*'s portrayal of sexual initiation may be the presence of third parties in the bedroom, especially mothers, whose salacious pleasure in their daughters' defloration contrasts starkly with the moralistic role of Katy's mother in the *School*. Early in their dialogue, Tullia tells Octavia that 'Thy mother is overjoyed with the Reputation [your fiancé] has of being the best provided young Man in all the City, but it will cost thee some Tears' (368; 240–1)—his 'provision' being the size of his 'P—ck'. (In the 1740 text of the *Dialogue*, the 'plain English' words are printed as 'P—ck' and 'C—t'; it is not known if this was also true in the 1684 text.) As she goes on to tell the story of her own first sexual experience, Tullia says that at the moment she and her husband, Horatio, 'died' in each other's arms, both

---

[35] *A Dialogue between a Married Lady and a Maid* (1740), facsimile edition in *Eighteenth-Century British Erotica I*, general eds. Alexander Pettit and Patrick Spedding, volume 2, ed. Kevin L. Cope, 355–401, on 365. Subsequent references to this edition will be given in the text, followed by the page number of the transcription in Mudge (ed.), *When Flesh Becomes Word* (here 239).

[36] See Turner, *Schooling Sex*, 337. The 1684 indictment was first noted in Thompson, 'Two Early Editions', 47.

[37] *Satyra Sotadica* is the short title of *Aloisiae Sigeae Toletanae Satyra Sotadica de Arcanis Amoris et Veneris* (c.1660) [Aloisia Sigea of Toledo's Sotadic Satire on the Secrets of Love and Venus]. It is also often referred to as *Aloisia Sigea*, after the name of its supposed Spanish female author, or as *Johannis Meursii elegantiae Latini sermonis* [Johannes Meursius's elegant Latin sermons] or simply *Meursius*, after the name of its supposed Dutch translator into Latin. Its complex textual history is most fully told in Turner, *Schooling Sex*, 165–220, 335–43. See also Foxon, *Libertine*, 38–43. The text also circulated widely in a French version, *L'Académie des dames* (1680).

[38] Foxon describes the *Satyra Sotadica* as 'brilliantly anarchistic' (and also 'repugnant') in *Libertine*, 38.

her mother and her friend Pomponia (who had been hiding in the bedroom) ran up to the naked couple, hugging and congratulating them and even having a snack together. Although Tullia recalls feeling 'ashamed to hear my Mother's Voice so near' and unable 'to look my Mother in the Face' (379; 246), her mother laughs at her shame, and has Pomponia pull the couple from under the sheets. Tullia's mother laughs again when Horatio 'roguishly' gets on top of Tullia and starts having intercourse with her, even after Tullia cries 'Ah! My dear *Pomponia*, come and deliver me from the murdering Man' (380; 246). The mother's laughter is both sadistic and celebratory, reading Tullia's pain as a pledge of eventual pleasure and rite of passage into maturity; but it also evokes the rude, raucous laughter of native English bawdry.

Octavia's mother, too, has a starring role in the third and last dialogue, in which Octavia recounts her wedding-day adventures. Having left the couple alone as the wedding guests arrive for dinner, Octavia's mother returns to their room only to see Philander 'with his Breeches and Drawers down, and his Thing stiff and red'. As Octavia reports, 'My Mother taking Notice of the Bigness of it[,] *Gemini!* said she, what a Monster is this! But be not daunted, Daughter, it will be so much the more pleasant to you in Time' (384; 248). Leaving the room a second time, she returns at the moment of Octavia's orgasm, and when she asks Octavia for a full account, 'I obey'd', Octavia tells Tullia; 'and, as I made the Description, her Eyes sparkled; her Veins swelled; and, embra[c]ing me, she almost fell away in my Arms, with the Sense of my Pleasures' (387; 249). Octavia's story elicits her own mother's orgasm, and she falls away in Octavia's arms like a lover: testament to the power of erotic narrative over the listener's or reader's imagination and to the fluidity of subject positions. Octavia's mother, so eagerly present at the scene while it unfolds, shares in Octavia's recollected sensations, as Tullia does when Octavia tells the story again: 'Thou makes me mad with thy Descriptions', Tullia says, 'and the Image of thy Pleasures create such in me, as comes very near thy own' (399; 254–5). Through the medium of erotic narrative, the arousal of desire, and its bodily gratification, pass from one subject to another.

Conclusion

The four canonical texts on which I have focused present fictions of female desire and pleasure to appeal, primarily, to a male audience. Although the question of who read erotic writing in the early modern period can never be settled—and even if it seems likely that women would have had access, as listeners or readers, to eroto-pornographic texts consumed at home—the limited evidence suggests that men were the principal authors, publishers, and readers of the works considered here.[39] Yet the scene of secret

---

[39] On the vexed question of readership, see Toulalan, *Imagining Sex*, 52–61; Peakman, *Mighty Lewd Books*, 25–8, 33–9, 44; Karen Harvey, *Reading Sex in the Eighteenth Century: Bodies and Gender in English Erotic Culture* (Cambridge: Cambridge University Press, 2004), 35–77.

conversations between women, like the fantasy-image of the solitary female reader corrupted by illicit texts, dominates the canon of pornographic literature. That this canon was already recognized as such by 1683 is evident from an exchange between Agnes and Angelica near the end of *Venus in the Cloister*: 'What canst thou say', asks Angelica, 'of the *School of Venus*, and of that *Infamous Phylosophy*, that has nothing but what's flat and insipid, and all whose poor and silly Reasonings can only perswade low and vulgar spirits' (155). Although Agnes, too, is unimpressed by the *School*'s explicit crudeness, she is captivated by 'the Wit and Ingenuity' (155) of *Satyra Sotadica*: 'Lord, Lord, how ingenious it is in inventing new Pleasures for a satiated and disgusted mind! With what Points and with what Spurs does it revive that Lust that is the most lulled asleep, the most languishing, nay and that which is no longer able! What extravagant Appetites! What strange Objects! What unknown Meats does it offer!' (156–7).[40] As Turner suggests, by commenting in detail on these precursors, *Venus*'s author situates it as third and best in a sequence, avowing its generic affiliations.[41] While there were many literary forms treating sexual subjects in the period—from smutty verse to marriage manuals to adultery trial reports—the Aretine erotic dialogue between women conveyed feelings as well as physiologies. In its English versions, juxtaposing supple depictions of desire with the raucous laughter of 'crafty whores', it displays the deeply conflicted attitudes towards sexuality in Britain in the closing years of the seventeenth century.

---

[40] In this text, the *Satyra*'s title is given as *The Academy of Ladyes, or, The Seven Satyrical Dialogues of Aloisia* (156).

[41] Turner, *Schooling Sex*, 344.

CHAPTER 30

RADICAL AND DEIST WRITING

NICHOLAS McDOWELL AND
GIOVANNI TARANTINO

In the beginning of time, the great Creator Reason, made the Earth to be a common Treasury, to preserve Beasts, Birds, Fishes, and Man, the Lord that was to govern this Creation; for Man had Domination given to him, over the Beasts, Birds, and Fishes; but not one word was spoken in the beginning, that one branch of mankind should rule over another. And the reason is this, Every single Man, Male and Female, is a perfect Creature of himself; and the same Spirit that made the Globe, dwells in man to govern the Globe; so that the flesh of man being subject to Reason, his Maker, hath him to be his Teacher and Ruler within himself, therefore needs not run abroad after any Teacher and Ruler without him, for he needs not that any man should teach him, for the same Anoynting that ruled in the Son of man, teacheth him all things.[1]

THE opening lines of Gerrard Winstanley's *A Declaration to the Powers of England* (1649), also known as the *True Levellers' Standard Advanced*, have a good claim to be among the most radical pieces of English prose to appear in print in the entire period covered by this volume. Winstanley (1609–76) rewrites the opening of Genesis ('In the beginning was the Word') and, with breathtaking daring, the identity of the 'Creator' is redefined as 'Reason'—a 'Spirit' that not only 'made the Globe' but dwells within 'Every single Man' (and, as Winstanley immediately makes clear, by this he also means every single woman). This is not quite the materialistic pantheism or animism often ascribed to Winstanley, for 'Reason' is a property given to humanity but not to the rest of nature and the animal world, over which human beings have explicitly been given 'Domination'.[2] Yet the redefinition of

---

[1] *A Declaration to the Powers of England* (1649), in *The Complete Works of Gerrard Winstanley*, ed. Thomas N. Corns, Ann Hughes, and David Loewenstein, 2 vols. (Oxford: Oxford University Press, 2009), 2: 4.

[2] The Diggers were rather unthinkingly associated with a proto-Romantic pantheism when they were rediscovered in mid-twentieth-century history and criticism; for a more sophisticated, contextualized

God as 'Reason', turning the person of the divine into an abstract, yet nonetheless universal, property of every human being, accomplishes at one fell swoop the delegitimizing of slavery and any concept of a natural social hierarchy, as well as the subversion of social institutions, such as the clergy, based on hierarchies of education and learning. These sentences also reveal why Winstanley's thought is virtually *sui generis* in the seventeenth century: the notion that the spirit of God resides within each person, rendering external forms of authority and education—including the Bible that Winstanley does not hesitate to rewrite—subordinate to inner promptings, sounds like a clear case of what was polemically known in the period as 'enthusiasm'.[3] At the same time, Winstanley's identification of the divine with human reason is at odds with the enthusiastic tradition embodied by other Civil War religious radicals, such as the 'Ranters' and the early Quakers, in which the very categories of reason and human learning are rejected as stumbling blocks to the supra-rational wisdom released by experience of the Spirit within. It aligns Winstanley rather with a more politically directed radical tradition which encourages the common people to break free from intellectual and political subjection by exercising their reason.

In this latter tradition, exemplified in the 1640s by the leading Levellers William Walwyn (1600–81) and Richard Overton (fl. 1640–63), issues of language and literacy are seen in relation to wider questions of political representation and social organization. To generalize, enthusiastic or prophetic radicalism is an extension of Calvinist doctrine in that human nature and reason are seen as inherently depraved, even though the enthusiast, and usually some of his or her fellow members of their sect, have been redeemed by the infusion of the Holy Spirit and have undergone an 'internalized apocalypse'.[4] Antinomianism, or 'free grace' as its proponents preferred to call it, in effect pushed Calvinist theology to its logical conclusions by denying the earthly application of moral and religious law, but only to the elect. Rational radicalism, on the other hand, is driven by an optimistic conception of humanity and its natural capacities, often expressed theologically as a belief in universal grace, or at least a universal capacity to obtain grace. In Leveller thought this confidence in individual natural reason was a corollary of demands for an extension of the franchise and greater popular participation in the political process. Winstanley, the most innovative thinker of all the Civil War radicals, bridges these positions by fusing an enthusiastic theology of the Spirit within, which speaks to each person apart from the Word in Scripture, with a theology of universal grace and a practical plan for political, social, and economic reform, which he

---

discussion of Winstanley in relation to discourses of 'animist materialism' in the mid-seventeenth century, see John Rogers, *The Matter of Revolution: Science, Poetry and Politics in the Age of Milton* (Ithaca, NY: Cornell University Press, 1996), 40–50. See also Chapter 28 on 'Political Speculations' by Nigel Smith.

[3] For a cogent account of the rise to prominence of the term 'enthusiasm', particularly in the Restoration, see Michael Heyd, *Be Sober and Reasonable: The Critique of Enthusiasm in the Seventeenth and Early Eighteenth Centuries* (Leiden: Brill, 1995).

[4] The term 'internalized apocalypse' is taken from M. H. Abrams, 'Apocalypse: Themes and Variations', in C. A. Patrides and Joseph Wittreich (eds.), *The Apocalypse in English Renaissance Literature and Thought* (Ithaca, NY: Cornell University Press, 1984), 342–68.

later outlined in detail in *The Law of Freedom* (1652), after the failed attempt to establish Digger communities on St. George's Hill in Surrey and elsewhere.[5]

It is certainly the case that the 'period in English history between 1640 and 1832 was marked by some common conditions and characteristics, bestowing a consistency upon those who pursued a political or religious vision different from that required by the state'.[6] Yet the fundamental epistemological distinction between enthusiastic and rational radicalism, which issues in important distinctions of expression and style, as well as thought, in radical prose, tends to become blurred in attempts to map a continuous tradition of 'freethinking and libertinism' in Britain and Ireland, stretching from the English Revolution to the aftermath of the French Revolution.[7] Those who were called deists and who liked to call themselves 'freethinkers', in the later seventeenth and early eighteenth centuries, were as hostile to enthusiasm and prophecy as they were to 'priestcraft' and clerical privilege.[8] A telling example is the editorial work of John Toland (1670–1722), the Donegal-born free-thinker who was key to ensuring the survival of the mid-seventeenth-century political tradition in the early eighteenth century through his involvement in the republication of a series of republican writings by John Milton and James Harrington, among others. In his edition of the regicide Edmund Ludlow's *Memoirs* (3 vols., 1698–9), Toland systematically excised the apocalyptic and prophetic elements in Ludlow's thought to turn him into a more respectably rational and secular republican—a radical Whig as opposed to a radical Puritan.[9]

---

[5] For a detailed account of these events, see John Gurney, *Brave Community: The Digger Movement in the English Revolution* (Manchester: Manchester University Press, 2007).

[6] Timothy Morton and Nigel Smith, 'Introduction', in Morton and Smith (eds.), *Radicalism in British Literary Culture, 1650–1830* (Cambridge: Cambridge University Press, 2002), 1.

[7] For an example of this blurring of enthusiasm and rationalism, see e.g., Christopher Hill, 'Freethinking and Libertinism: The Legacy of the English Revolution', in Roger D. Lund (ed.), *The Margins of Orthodoxy: Heterodox Writing and Cultural Response, 1660–1750* (Cambridge: Cambridge University Press, 1995), 54–72. The utility of the anachronistic terms 'radical' and 'radicalism' was much contested in politicized, occasionally bitter, historiographical debates of the 1980s and 1990s, but now seems to be generally accepted in light of the more flexible definitions proposed by, among others, Glenn Burgess, who has argued for the need to move away from what he calls a 'substantive' concept of radicalism, which posits 'a continuous radical tradition of definable identity', towards a 'situational' one, in which radicalism is identified in a particular context through study of the interaction between the 'history of events' and the 'history of languages and/or ideas'. See Glenn Burgess, 'A Matter of Context: "Radicalism" and the English Revolution', and, for the contribution of literary criticism to advancing the debate, Nicholas McDowell, 'Writing the Literary and Cultural History of Radicalism in the English Revolution', both in Mario Caricchio and Giovanni Tarantino (eds.), *Cromohs Virtual Seminars: Recent Historiographical Trends of the British Studies (17th-18th Centuries)* (2006–7): https://oajournals.fupress.net/index.php/cromohs/article/view/11246; https://oajournals.fupress.net/index.php/cromohs/article/view/11244. .

[8] This point has been well made in response to Christopher Hill's argument for a continuous tradition stretching from Civil War prophets to Restoration free-thinkers and libertines by Sarah Ellenzweig, *The Fringes of Belief: English Literature, Ancient Heresy, and the Politics of Freethinking, 1660–1700* (Stanford: Stanford University Press, 2008), 35–7.

[9] See Blair Worden, 'Whig History and Puritan Politics: The *Memoirs* of Edmund Ludlow Revisited', *Historical Research*, 75 (2002), 209–37. See further Chapter 7 on 'Biography and Autobiography' by Julie A. Eckerle.

Prophetic radicals of the mid-century tended to regard the vernacular Bible as an allegory both of external historical events and their internal spiritual experiences: so Winstanley regarded the Fall and redemption as an allegory of every individual's inner life. Deists and free-thinkers, however, incorporated developments in biblical and textual criticism—as often derived from orthodox scholarly sources in the vernacular, such as the Anglican bishop Edmund Stillingfleet, or heterodox foreign authors such as Spinoza—to question the reliability and authority of the biblical texts.[10] And whereas the self-proclaimed prophets proclaimed the irrelevance of humanist intellectual tradition to the experience of the internal Spirit or 'inner light', the deists and free-thinkers made their bookishness and access to the classical tradition a key element of their appeal to a superior rationality. Where there is some ideological overlap between the traditions is in a shared and vigorous anticlericalism; but there is also a stylistic continuity in the use of irony, satire, and parody by university-educated radicals of the mid-century, who drew on their knowledge of learned culture and their experience of institutional education to launch rhetorically elaborate attacks on those systems and structures of knowledge and the uses to which they were put in establishing clerical elites.[11] Ironic and satirical forms of polemic were habitually adopted in deist writing, and the ethics and consequences of this mode of attack became the subject of important theoretical treatises on rhetoric, such as the third Earl of Shaftesbury's *Essay on the Freedom of Wit and Humour* (1709).

The Rhetoric of Enthusiasm

The enthusiastic or prophetic tradition is characterized by the development of a rhetoric of irrationality and madness to articulate the strangeness of the internal experience of the Spirit and its distance from orthodox modes of speech, writing, and education. Civil War prophets repeatedly claimed Pauline authority to speak publicly, representing themselves as new Apostles raised from the ranks of the lowly and uneducated. As the Welsh prophet Arise Evans announced in *The Bloudy Vision* (1653): 'I am as the Paul of this time … he was a mechanic, a tent-maker, Acts 18.3. I am a tailor.' In the posthumously published *Sufficiencie of the Spirits Teaching without Humane Learning*, much cited in polemics against the rise of the 'Mechanick Enthusiast', the cobbler Samuel How, pastor of a separatist church in pre-war London, condemned the notion that 'knowledge of arts and sciences, diverse tongues, much reading' in any way increased

---

[10] On the Bible as internal allegory in radical religious writing, see Nigel Smith, *Perfection Proclaimed: Language and Literature in English Radical Religion, 1640–1660* (Oxford: Clarendon Press, 1989); on deist use of Anglican biblical scholarship, see e.g., Joseph M. Levine, 'Deists and Anglicans: The Ancient Wisdom and the Idea of Progress', in Lund (ed.), *Margins of Orthodoxy*, 219–39.

[11] The importance of anticlericalism in connecting a British radical tradition between the English and French revolutions was emphasized by Justin Champion in a series of powerful essays; see e.g., Champion, ' "May the Last King be Strangled in the Bowels of the Last Priest": Irreligion and the English Enlightenment, 1649–1789', in Morton and Smith (eds.), *Radicalism in British Literary Culture*, 29–44.

a person's ability to 'understand the mind of God in his word'. How declared that 'such as are taught by the Spirit, destitute of human learning, are the learned ones who truly understand the Scriptures', for 'the wisdom of the world is foolishness with God (1 Cor. 3:19)'.[12] One of the most influential statements of the sufficiency of the Spirit's teaching comes from George Fox, foremost of the early Quakers and one-time apprentice to a sheep grazier, in his journal entry for 1646:

> At another time, as I was walking in a field on a First-day morning, the Lord opened unto me, 'that being bred at Oxford and Cambridge was not enough to fit and qualify men to be ministers of Christ': and I stranged at it, because it was the common belief of people. But I saw clearly, as the Lord opened it to me, and I was satisfied ... But my relations were much troubled at me, that I would not go with them to hear the priest: for I would get into the orchard, or the fields, with my Bible, by myself ... And I saw that being bred at Oxford or Cambridge, did not qualify of fit a man to be a minister of Christ; and what then should I follow such for?[13]

Winstanley proclaimed in 1649 that 'the declaration of the Son of man was first declared by Fisher-men, & men that the learned, covetous Scholars despised: the declaration of righteous law shall spring up from the poor, the base and despised ones, and fools of the world'.[14] The Pauline language of inversion and paradox provided radicals of the English Revolution with scriptural sanction for the reversal of hierarchies of social status, education, and gender that had been regarded as God-given, authorizing the remarkable female prophetic speech and writing of the period. As Anna Trapnel exclaimed in *A Legacy for Saints* (1654): 'oh what a manner of love is this! That makes no difference between fools and learned ones, preferring idiots before the wisdom of the world, making the ignorant and erring Spirit to have the greatest understanding?'[15]

The Pauline model of self-fashioning also offered radicals of various strands the rhetorical persona of the prophet whose articulation of divine truths looks like folly and madness to the corrupt and godless. In Christopher Hill's *The World Turned Upside Down* (1972)—flawed and much criticized as a piece of historiography but unquestionably the work that has done most to establish radical writing as a category of historical and cultural study—the chapter entitled 'The Island of Great Bedlam' lists a succession of self-proclaimed prophets who invoked as their authority to speak and write publicly such biblical touchstones as 1 Corinthians 1:25 ('For the foolishness of God is wiser than

---

[12] The phrase 'Mechanick Enthusiast' is from Daniel Featley's popular heresiography *The Dippers Dipt* (1645; 5th edn, 1647), sig. B3v; Samuel How, *The Sufficiency of the Spirts Teaching without Humane Learning* (1640), 12–13, 25–6.

[13] George Fox, *The Journal* (1694), ed. Nigel Smith (Harmondsworth: Penguin, 1998), 10.

[14] Winstanley, *The New Law of Righteousness Budding Forth, in Restoring the Whole Creation from the Bondage of the Curse* (1649), in Corns, Hughes, and Loewenstein (eds.), *Complete Works of Gerrard Winstanley*, 1: 528.

[15] Anna Trapnel, *A Legacy for Saints* (1654), 16. See further Nicholas McDowell, *The English Radicall Imagination: Culture, Religion, and Revolution, 1630–1660* (Oxford: Clarendon Press, 2003), 1–21.

man's wisdom').[16] Thus the 'Ranter' Joseph Salmon wrote in 1649 to the New Model Army leaders informing them that 'I was once as wise as well as you, but now I am a fool, I care not who knows it ... and it is for your sakes that I am so'. The so-called 'Seeker' and future Quaker Isaac Pennington began in 1650 to 'prefer folly at my very heart above wisdom ... In this state of folly I find a new state of things springing up in me'.[17] 'What a Stage of Vanity is this world, where every Art and Science is made up of madnesse and folly?', asked the New Model Army chaplain and leading 'antinomian' Henry Pinnell in his account of a prophetic vision—'this earthquake within me'—that he had related to Oliver Cromwell in December 1647. In the 'Seeker' William Erbery's *The Mad Mans Plea* (1653), the persona of the holy fool provided licence for the satirical style adopted by Erbery: 'If God had not made me a fool, surely I should never have made the Ministers mad ... Babylon's last fall shall be in the fall of these last Churches, who shall be thrown down ... by the mighty approach of God in his people, Rev. 18. Neither is it by controversy (as before) nor by disputes (as now) but by derision and scorn.'[18]

The most stylistically inventive instance of this rhetoric of folly is the 'Ranter' Abiezer Coppe (1619–72), who repeatedly parodies academic language, as in his address to 'my Cronies, the scholars of *Oxford*':

> Well, hie you, learne apace, when you have learned all that your *Pedagogues* can teach you, you shall go to Schole no longer, you shall be [*Sub ferula*] no longer, under the lash no longer, but be set to the *University* [of the universall Assembly], and entered into Christs Church, [the Church of the first born, which are written in heaven,] and when you once come to know that you are *there*, you will hear no Mechanick Preach; (no, not a *Peter*, if he be a Fisher-man) but the learned Apostle, who speaks with tongues more then *they—all*,—and then you will fall upon your books (as if ye were *besides* your *selves*) and bring your books together; and burne them before all men; so mightily will [ὁ λόγος—] *the word* grow in you, and prevaile upon you, that men shall say you are not only in a Lunatick-------------Moode.[19]

While the persecutory authorities seek to burn books they deem blasphemous—Coppe's own *A Fiery Flying Roll* (1649) would suffer this fate under Parliament's 1650 Blasphemy Act—those who have undergone 'internalized apocalypse' will engage in a

---

[16] Christopher Hill, *The World Turned Upside Down: Radical Ideas During the English Revolution* (1972; Harmondsworth: Penguin, 1991), 277–84. For a variety of opinions about the validity and influence of *The World Turned Upside Down*, see the special issue of *Prose Studies*, 36/3: 'Christopher Hill's *The World Turned Upside Down*, Revisited', ed. Michael J. Braddick (2014).

[17] Joseph Salmon, *A Rout, A Rout* (1649), 13; Isaac Pennington, *Light or Darknesse* (1650), sig. A2v.

[18] Henry Pinnell, *A Word of Prophesy, Concerning the Parliament, Generall, and the Army* (1648), sig. A8r; William Erbery, *The Mad Mans Plea* (1653), 3.

[19] Coppe, *Some Sweet Sips, of some Spiritual Wine* (1649), in *A Collection of Ranter Writings: Spiritual Liberty and Sexual Freedom in the English Revolution*, ed. Nigel Smith (London: Pluto Press, 2014), 54; for an interesting attempt to place the 'manic style' of Coppe in an English literary tradition, see Clement Hawes, *Mania and Literary Style: The Rhetoric of Enthusiasm from the Ranters to Christopher Smart* (Cambridge: Cambridge University Press, 1996).

spiritual *auto-da-fé*: the corrupt forms of knowledge in which they have been educated will be burned away by the Word rising within them. The syntactical and typographical disruption is a stylistic embodiment of what looks to the unregenerate like a 'Lunatick' fit. But Coppe's prose is also continually sprinkled with Latin and Greek (and elsewhere Hebrew) phrases and the address to his former 'Cronies' at Oxford emphasizes that he had himself been an Oxford student—he was at All Souls College and then Merton College in the late 1630s, leaving before finishing his degree, and his use of 'cronies' as a term of university slang predates its first entry in the *OED* by fourteen years. Effective parody depends, after all, upon familiarity with the languages and conventions being mocked. Coppe possesses, and carefully shows himself to possess, that very facility with Latin and the biblical languages upon which the clergy's false claim to superior religious knowledge is founded.[20]

In an influential 1982 lecture on 'Radical Prose in Seventeenth-Century England', Christopher Hill contended that radical texts brought 'the speech of ordinary people' into the previously elite sphere of printed opinion and were addressed to a popular rather than a 'Latin-educated or court audience'. They were designed to be read by 'craftsmen and yeoman' and 'read aloud to illiterate audiences'. Eloquent in its rough, natural simplicity, radical writing was seen to have its roots in 'utilitarian artisans' prose' rather than the grammatical and rhetorical training of the early modern schoolroom.[21] Subsequently radical writing tended to be valued by critics as a record of early modern popular belief that was not mediated through sources produced by the elite, the learned, and educated few at the top of society. But even a glance at a page from Coppe's printed works is proof that the social and educational background of radical prose writers was more diverse than Hill's characterization would have us believe. Indeed, of the four writers whom I quoted above for their adoption of the persona of the holy fool, three had been to university (Erbery, Pennington, and Pinnell) and only Joseph Salmon, a soldier, fits the type of the artisan radical. This has implications for how we understand radical style, for university-educated radicals such as Coppe often drew on their knowledge of learned culture and their experience of institutional education to launch rhetorically elaborate attacks on those systems and structures of knowledge in a manner that can seem to owe as much to the culture that produced Erasmus's great humanist satire, the *Moriae Encomium*, or *Praise of Folly* (1509; first publ., 1511), as to untutored personal encounter with the King James Bible. After all, towards the end of the *Praise of Folly*, Erasmus himself increasingly dwells on the theme of Christian folly, concluding, as one editor puts it, 'with a remarkable feat of double irony as [the work] transforms itself from a mock encomium into a real one'.[22]

---

[20] See further McDowell, *English Radical Imagination*, 89–136.

[21] 'Radical Prose in Seventeenth-Century England: From Marprelate to the Levellers', *Essays in Criticism*, 32 (1982), 95–118. Similar arguments are made in another classic work by Christopher Hill, *The English Bible and the Seventeenth-Century Revolution* (Harmondsworth: Penguin, 1993).

[22] Erasmus, *Praise of Folly*, ed. A. H. T. Levi, trans. Betty Radice (Harmondsworth: Penguin, 1971), 186 n. 22.

The example of Henry Pinnell is instructive about the bookish resources of radical style in the mid-seventeenth century. Pinnell left the Army in 1648, disappointed by Cromwell's lack of social radicalism, and turned to editing the sermons of Tobias Crisp, the foremost pre-Civil-War proponent of 'free grace', assuming in the same year the position of rector of Brinkworth in Wiltshire that Crisp had held until his death in 1642. If we extract single-line statements from Pinnell's writings of the late 1640s and early 1650s, he appears to be an obvious representative of the plain-speaking, vernacular, anti-intellectual tradition of radical prose identified by Hill. In *A Word of Prophecy* (1648), he claims that he 'got more from simple country people, husbandmen, weavers, &c. about Brinkworth, Sandwich, and those parts in Wiltshire than ever I did, or yet have by books and preachers'. Yet Pinnell had been at Oxford, matriculating at Hart Hall in 1632, and his prose is marked by a satirical liveliness that depends upon his reading. His display of his learning in the moment of ridiculing its value is illustrated in his use of Latin tags and stylistic juxtaposition of the colloquial and the Latinate. Nor were the rhetorical resources of Pinnell's anti-intellectualism restricted to Corinthians:

> If any think me too sharp and Satyrical in what I have written I excuse myself as *Democritus* Junior did,
> > *Hor. Dixero si quid forte jocosius, hoc mihi juris*
> > > *Cum venia dabis—*
> > Take in good part
> > The milde and tart.
> [...]
> —*Ridentem dicere verum*
> —*Quid vetat?*
> If it be true that men are evill,
> A jerking jest is not uncivil.[23]

Pinnell invokes Robert Burton's disingenuous and elusive response in 'Democritus Junior to the Reader', the 'Satyrical Preface' to *The Anatomy of Melancholy* (1621–38), to those who might consider his book 'too light and Comicall for a divine, too Satyrical for one of my profession'. In the passage to which Pinnell refers, and from which he faithfully quotes the lines from Horace's *Satires*, Burton summons the example of Erasmus's impersonation of the voice of Folly to justify his satirical style: 'I will presume to answer with *Erasmus*, in this case, 'tis not I, but *Democritus, Democritus dixit* ... and what liberty those old Satyrists have had, it is a *Cento* collected from others, not but they that say it.' Burton's footnote cites the *Moriae Encomium*; he then quotes from Erasmus's defence of the *Moriae Encomium* in his *Letter to Martin Dorp* (1515) to assure those that might take offence at his satire that 'I hate their vices, not their persons'. The persona of Democritus, the laughing philosopher who analysed madness to distract from his own

---

[23] Pinnell, *A Word of Prophecy*, [59]; Pinnell, *Nil Novi. This Years Fruit, from The Last Years Root* (1654), 40.

melancholy disposition, gives Pinnell an ironic distance from the inverted values of the world in a similar fashion to that of the Pauline holy fool adopted by Erbery and other radicals.[24] The prophetic radicalism of the English Revolution was a more stylistically, as well as socially and intellectually, diverse phenomenon than its either seventeenth-century opponents or twentieth-century historiographers would have us believe, even if its deployment of reading to scorn the uses of 'humane' reason was a very different polemical strategy from that of the ostentatiously bookish free-thinkers of the later seventeenth century.

The Rhetoric of Rationalism

Enthusiasts tended to distrust the powers of reason and education because they derived from the Calvinist tradition a view of the unredeemed human creature as inherently corrupt and sinful. However, the Levellers Walwyn and Overton—as well as the self-proclaimed 'True Leveller' Winstanley—viewed all men as endowed with grace and the capacity to improve themselves and their society through the exercise of reason. These rational radicals were as much the heirs of the humanist as the Puritan tradition—of the Erasmian emphasis on man's capacity for self-sufficient rational virtue. Consequently, they regarded education as essential to the spiritual and moral formation of all men, not merely of a clerical caste which would then instruct the laity in spiritual matters. What they objected to was the appropriation of the humanist curriculum to define ruling elites of church and state, bolstered by the equation of Latin literacy with social and religious hierarchy.[25] Moreover, if education is the key to moral improvement, then reading must be unprejudiced and the circulation of knowledge must be free. Walwyn provocatively directed his clerical opponents to one of the most celebrated parts of Montaigne's *Essays* (1580–95), 'On Cannibals', to ridicule their lack of Christian charity:

> And in his twentieth Chapter, pag: 102. he saies, speaking of the Cannibals, the very words that import lying, falsehood, treason, dissimulation, covetousnesse, envy, detraction, and pardon, were never heard of amongst them. These and like flowers, I think it lawfull to gather out of his Wildernesse, and to give them room in my Garden; yet this worthy Montaign was but a Roman Catholique; yet to observe with what contentment and swoln joy he recites these cogitations, is wonderful to consider: and now what shall I say? Go to this honest Papist, or to these innocent

---

[24] Robert Burton, *The Anatomy of Melancholy*, ed. Thomas C. Faulkner, Nicolas K. Keissling, and Rhonda L. Blair, 3 vols. (Oxford: Clarendon Press, 1989), 1: 110–11.

[25] On the ambivalence in mainstream Puritanism concerning the role of reason and education in religion, see John Morgan, *Godly Learning: Puritan Attitudes towards Reason, Learning, and Education, 1560–1640* (Cambridge: Cambridge University Press, 1986). For further discussion of these strands in English radical thought, see Nicholas McDowell, 'Levelling Language: The Politics of Literacy in the English Radical Tradition', *Critical Quarterly*, 46 (2004), 39–62.

Cannibals, ye Independent Churches, to learn civility, humanity, simplicity of heart; yea, charity and Christianity.[26]

Walwyn puts into practice Milton's argument in *Areopagitica* (1644) that 'truth lies in the choices made available to the individual in the course of acquiring knowledge, that is reading'; though he goes beyond Milton in his explicit recommendation of the moral teaching to be obtained from Roman Catholic books. Indeed Walwyn's attitude towards books brings out the radical implications of Milton's own assertion—one that sits uneasily with Milton's exclusion from toleration of 'Popery and open superstition'—that '[t]o the pure all things are pure [Titus 1:15], not only meats and drinks, but all kinde of knowledge whether of good or evill; the knowledge cannot defile, nor consequently the books, if the will and conscience be not defiled.'[27]

This radical allegiance to natural reason over institutional dictate is exemplified in Richard Overton's *Mans Mortalitie*, published in 1644 before he became a leading figure in the Leveller movement, in which Overton made the most explicit argument yet printed in English for the mortality of the soul, setting out to show, as the (anonymous) title page puts it, 'both Theologically and Philosophically, that whole Man (as a *rationall Creature*) is a Compound wholly mortal, contrary to that common distinction of *Soule* and *Body*'. In doing so, Overton was resurrecting a controversy that had been key to the theological debates about the existence of Purgatory that marked the Reformation in England and, before that, provoked the Fifth Lateran Council (1512–17) to assert the truth of the Christian doctrine of the immortal soul over the materialist philosophies being recovered from classical thought by Italian humanists such as Pomponazzi. In the course of his argument, Overton makes over two dozen references to classical sources and supplies a sophisticated account of how Platonic dualism was grafted onto Judaeo-Christian belief to produce the pernicious fiction of the immortal soul, which he argues has no basis in either Scripture or natural reason. Rather than argue in solemnly doctrinal language, Overton developed a witty, satirical style to expose the bizarre logic of orthodox dualistic metaphysics:

> Now seeing all this while we have had to do with an immortall Soul, we cannot find, or the *Soularies* tell us what it is, such likewise is its residence; for if we ask, where it is? They *flap us i'th mouthwith a Ridle, tota in toto, & tota in qualibet parte*, the whole in the whole, and the whole in every part: that is, the whole immortall Soul in the whole body, and the whole Soul wholy in every part of the body … and so, were a man minced into Atomes, cut into innumerable bits, then we would be so many innumerable Souls, else could it not be wholy in every part.

---

[26] *Walwyns Just Defence* (1649), in *The Writings of William Walwyn*, ed. J. R. McMichael and B. Taft (Athens, GA: University of Georgia Press, 1989), 399–400.

[27] Nigel Smith, '*Areopagitica*: Voicing Contexts, 1643–5', in David Loewenstein and James Grantham Turner (eds.), *Politics, Poetics and Hermeneutics in Milton's Prose* (Cambridge: Cambridge University Press, 1990), 106; *Complete Prose Works of John Milton*, ed. D. M. Wolfe et al., 10 vols. in 8 (New Haven: Yale University Press, 1953–82), 2: 512, 565.

Monstrum horrendum, ingens; cui quot sunt
Corpore crines,
Tot vigiles Animæ *supter, mirabile dictu*!
And thus the *Ridle* is unfolded.[28]

Overton modulates between Latin phrases and tags and a colloquial vernacular, displaying his own education—he had been at Cambridge in the 1630s—to ridicule more effectively the pointlessness of theological speculation about the nature of the soul. Here he comically rewrites the famous description of Fame in the *Aeneid*, 4. 181 (to make it mean 'Ominous, awful, vast; for every hair on the body is a waking soul beneath, wonderful to tell'), suggesting that the real motive of the 'Soularies' in their obsession with scrutinizing the soul is not truth but reputation. While it appeared a couple of years before the rise of the Leveller movement, the monistic materialism developed in *Mans Mortalitie* established a metaphysical framework for his Leveller political philosophy of individual liberty and agency: 'To every Individuall in nature is given an individuall property by nature, not to be invaded or usupred by any ... For by naturall birth all men are equally and alike borne to like propriety, liberty and freedome.'[29]

Overton made clear his belief in an ultimate resurrection at which heaven and hell will come into being and all human beings will be raised bodily to face God's final judgement: his mortalism should thus not be confused with atheism or secularism. And yet what has often been described as the process of secularization in England in the later seventeenth century is less 'a refutation of religion but an attempt to rescue it from clericalism, from "priestcraft", from dogmatism, from superstition and fanaticism'.[30] Compared to the brazenly satiric rationalism of *Mans Mortalite*, published in the aftermath of the temporary breakdown of mechanisms of censorship in the early 1640s, deist writing in the Restoration tended to approach the same material indirectly, developing an ironic tone of high scholarly pursuit.[31] In *Anima Mundi* (1679), Charles Blount (1654–93) repeatedly and excessively asserted his orthodoxy while outlining in detail the pagan origins of the idea of the immortal soul in the claims of figures such as Pythagoras, who 'feign'd himself to be risen from the dead, preaching up Rewards and Punishments in another life, to the great terrour of the People', and,

---

[28] [Richard Overton], *Mans Mortalitie*, ed. Harold Fisch (Liverpool: Liverpool University Press, 1968), 72.

[29] [Richard Overton], *An Arrow Against All Tyrants and Tyranny* (1646), 3. For the relationship between Overton's monism and his Leveller politics, see Nicholas McDowell, 'Ideas of Creation in the Writings of Richard Overton the Leveller and *Paradise Lost*', *Journal of the History of Ideas*, 66 (2005), 59–78.

[30] Blair Worden, 'The Question of Secularization', in Alan Houston and Steven Pincus (eds.), *A Nation Transformed: England after the Restoration* (Cambridge: Cambridge University Press, 2001), 20–40 (28).

[31] It should be emphasized that the terms 'deism' and 'deist' emerged from attacks on those called deists and do not denote a single religious identity, but they are used to group various writers and thinkers who had broadly similar intellectual (and stylistic) approaches to institutional Christianity; see for example the sensible comments in Wayne Hudson, *The English Deists* (London: Pickering & Chatto, 2009), 1–28.

at the same time, 'the most plausible Arguments [the pagans] had to justifie their wicked Opinion of the Soul's mortality, or unrewarded condition', by quoting chunks of Epicurean philosophy from Lucretius. The 'news of separate Souls in coelestial Joys, or infernal Agonies, *Enumerus* the Atheist says most impiously, were as hard to prove as the *Elysian* fields, *Acheron* or *Styx*, or *Pluto* with his infernal guard': impious or not, the implication, of course, is that Christian ideas of reward and punishment in the afterlife are as about as plausible and authentic as these pagan notions.[32] Blount's materialist reflections later went way beyond the thematic boundaries of the classical tradition in *Miracles, no Violations of the Laws of Nature* (1683), in which Blount included his own translation of the sixth chapter of Spinoza's *Tractatus theologico-politicus* (Amsterdam, 1670).

In his *Letters to Serena*, John Toland similarly combined the translation and discussion of Spinoza's materialist metaphysics with a 'history of the soul's immortality among the Heathens'. As with Blount, Toland offered his history as a disinterested, scholarly account, but his true design in showing 'the gradual Progress of [the doctrine of the immortal soul] thro all the Parts of the Earth then known, together with the true Original of the Poetical Fables concerning the Elysian Fields, the Rivers, Judges, Gates, and Ferrymen of Hell, of Souls being disquieted for want of orderly Burial', was evidently to foster scepticism about the legitimacy of Christian ideas of heaven, hell, and the afterlife by placing them in a comparative religious history. In ostensibly excavating the origins merely of pagan idolatry, Toland carefully employed the language of Christian doctrine as he listed the 'reasons how People came to imagine that Heaven (or the Palace of the good) was over their Heads, and that Hell (or the Prison of the Wicked) was under their Feet'. Toland invoked such recent works of polemical comparative religion as *Second Thoughts concerning Human Soul* (1702), a 500-page work published under the pseudonym of 'Estibius Psychaletes' by William Coward, an Oxford doctor. For Coward, the immortality of the soul was in origin an ancient Egyptian myth that contradicted not only Aristotelian naturalism but Christianity itself; or as the title-page succinctly put it: 'A plain Heathenish invention, and not consonant to the principles of philosophy, reason, or religion; but the ground only of many absurd, and superstitious opinions, abominable to the Reformed Churches, and derogatory in general to the True Christianity'. Toland's accounts of Spinoza's materialism (though couched in the form of a refutation, as so often in deist writing) and the pagan origins of the soul's immortality are combined with a bravura opening chapter on the 'Origin and Force of Prejudices', in which he condemns the pernicious indoctrination of superstition by educational structures that have been designed by a self-interested clergy intent on instilling obedience through fear: 'whereby it comes to pass that we swallow the Poison of their Errors with inexpressible Pleasure, and lay a large Foundation for future Credulity, insensibly acquiring a Disposition for hearing things rare and wonderful, to imagin[e] we believe

---

[32] Charles Blount, *Anima Mundi, or, An Historical Narration of the Opinions of the Ancients Concerning Mans Soul After this Life* (1679), 4, 15, 24.

what we only dread or desire, to think when we are but puzzl'd that we are convinc'd, and to swallow what we cannot comprehend.'[33]

In fusing philosophies of political and religious liberty with a materialist metaphysics, Blount and Toland were able to incorporate figures who would seem to be intellectually incompatible into their thought, such as Thomas Hobbes and Milton (though the nineteenth-century discovery of the manuscript of Milton's Latin work of systematic divinity, *De Doctrina Christiana*, shows Milton also came to believe in the mortality of the soul).[34] Blount essentially repackaged Milton's *Areopagitica* for his own generation in his protest against licensing laws in *A Just Vindication of Learning* (1678), but he also published two years later an anthology of quotations from Hobbes (*The Last Sayings, or, Dying Legacy of Mr Thomas Hobbs* (1680)). In truth, the deist style, if generalizations can be made given the diversity of the writers involved, owes much more to Hobbesian than Miltonic example. Hobbes's extended satirical attack in *Leviathan* (1651) on post-biblical claims to prophetic inspiration shapes the deists' attacks on enthusiasm, for all their political debt to the republican thinking of the 1650s. In probably his most influential work, *Christianity not Mysterious, or, A Treatise Shewing There is Nothing in the Gospel Contrary to Reason, Nor Above It* (1696), Toland made the rejection of inspiration central to his elevation of reason as the rule of faith: '*Divine Faith* is either when God speaks to us immediately himself, or when we acquiesce in the Words or Writings of those to whom we believe he has spoken. All *Faith* now in the World is of this last sort, and by consequence entirely built upon *Ratiocination*.' Consequently, there is no 'different Rule to be follow'd in the Interpretation of *Scripture* from what is common to all other Books'; to think Scripture can be interpreted differently is to become 'Enthusiasts or Impostors [rather] than the taught of God, who has no Interest to delude his Creatures, nor wants Ability to inform them rightly.'[35]

Thus, 'rather than trash the claims of Scripture, the Church Fathers and ecclesiastical tradition', as the Civil War prophets had done, 'Toland became expert in the knowledge of these discourses'.[36] Whereas prophets such as Coppe and Pinnell used their learning satirically to mock the authority of learning, free-thinkers such as Toland used their erudition to expose the intellectual poverty of their clerical opponents. Writers like Toland and Blount in effect collapsed the orthodox critique of enthusiasm into their own critique of the pernicious ideology of 'priestcraft', ironically representing the very clerics who so fulminated against the dangers of enthusiasm into types of enthusiasts themselves in their adherence to irrational superstitions such as the immortal soul. If Lucretius's account of Epicurean philosophy in the *De Rerum Natura* offered the deists a classical philosophical model, it was the Greek satirical prose of Lucian that offered them

---

[33] John Toland, *Letters to Serena* (1702), sigs. b6v, b8, 6.

[34] On Milton's mortalism in context, see Nicholas McDowell, 'Dead Souls and Modern Minds? Mortalism and the Early Modern Imagination from Marlowe to Milton', *Journal of Medieval and Early Modern Studies*, 40 (2010), 559–92.

[35] John Toland, *Christianity not Mysterious* (2nd edn, 1696), 127.

[36] Justin Champion, *Republican Learning: John Toland and the Crisis of Christian Culture, 1696–1722* (Manchester: Manchester University Press, 2003), 14.

a model of attack against both clerical hypocrisy and false claims to prophecy. The first complete English translation of Lucian eventually appeared in print in three volumes in 1710–11 but had been completed in the mid-1690s: it includes several translations of key Lucianic satires done by Blount, who had killed himself in 1693 (as well as an introduction and life of Lucian by John Dryden (1631–1700), who was the first, according to the *OED*, to use the term 'deism' in the preface to his poem *Religio Laici* (1682)).[37]

The Lucianic style of Hobbes—who was specifically paired with Lucian by early opponents—particularly appealed to the free-thinkers in their ridicule of claims to exclusive spiritual authority, clerical or enthusiastic. Anthony Collins (1676–1729), along with Blount and Toland the most significant of the deist writers, wrote in his *Discourse of Ridicule and Irony in Writing* (1729) of how Hobbes was a '*Philosophical Drole*', who displayed a 'great deal of *Wit* of the *drolling* kind'. Whereas for earlier commentators such as Joseph Glanvil, in his *Reflections on Drollery and Atheism* (1668), this Hobbesian method of ridicule threatened to bring all religion into disrepute, for Collins, 'the Opinions and Pratices of Men in all Matters, and especially in Matters of Religion, are generally so absurd and ridiculous that it is impossible for them not to be the Subjects of Ridicule'.[38] Yet freethinkers such as Toland and Collins, writing in the period of the 1695 Licensing Act and then the 1698 Blasphemy Act, tended to indulge less in open ridicule than to dissimulate their unconventional tenets ironically, through reticence, insinuation, and deliberately shaky argumentation. In one of his last works, Toland gave an oblique justification for this 'veiled' mode of attack in an extended dicussion of 'exoteric' and 'esoteric' meanings:

> While the priests industriously conceal'd their mysteries, lest, being clearly understood, they might by the philosophers be expos'd to the laughter of the people, as fabulous, false and useless: the philosophers, on the other hand, conceal'd their sentiments of the nature of things, under the veil of divine allegories; lest being accused of impiety by the priests (which often happen'd) they might be expos'd in their turn to the hatred, if not to the fury of the vulgar.

Toland offered readers in search of the author's implicit or even just insinuated meaning, of the esoteric doctrine intended for the alert few, an interpretative clue: 'When a man maintains what's commonly believ'd, or professes what's publicly injoin'd, it is not always a sure rule that he speaks what he thinks: but when he seriously maintains the contrary of what's by law established, and openly declares for what most others oppose, then there's a strong presumption that he utters his mind.'[39]

---

[37] On the deist involvement in translating Lucian, see further Nicholas McDowell, 'The Double Personality of Lucianic Satire from Dryden to Fielding', in Paddy Bullard (ed.), *The Oxford Handbook of Eighteenth-Century Satire* (Oxford: Oxford University Press, 2019), 155–7.

[38] [Anthony Collins], *A Discourse Concerning Ridicule and Irony in Writing* (1729), 43, 19; on this work, see Jacopo Agnesina, 'Sur l'attribution à Anthony Collins du *Discourse Concerning Ridicule and Irony in Writing*', *La Lettre Clandestine: Revue d'Information sur la Littérature Clandestine de l'Âge Classique*, 17 (2009), 277–89. On Hobbes and the model of 'heterodox wit', see Roger D. Lund, 'The Bite of *Leviathan*: Hobbes and Philosophic Drollery', *English Literary History*, 65 (1998), 825–55.

[39] Toland, 'Clidophorus', in *Tetradymus* (1720), 94, 96.

Anthony Ashley-Cooper (1671–1713), third Earl of Shaftesbury, the powerful Whig politician who collaborated with Toland on a number of projects in the late 1690s, recognized that open ridicule could only be possible under a political and religious system which guarantees liberty of expression: 'wit can never have its liberty, where the freedom of raillery is taken away: for against serious extravagancies, and splenetic humors, there is no other remedy than this.' For Toland, freedom of speech was similarly a key foundation for toleration.[40] It was in their consistent argument for liberty of expression that the Miltonic influence was strongest on the free-thinkers. In his *Discourse of Free-Thinking* (1713), Collins meditated on whether necessity, utility, and the *salus populi* were ever, as Hobbes had argued, a justification for the restraint of free thought and the social imposition of 'speculations', and concluded otherwise:

> It is objected, *That certain speculations (tho false) are necessary to be impos'd on men, in order to assist the magistrate in preserving the peace of society: And that it is therefore as reasonable to deceive men into opinions for their own good, as it is in certain cases to deceive children; and consequently it must be absurd to engage men in thinking on subjects where error is useful and truth injurious to them* ... I will grant the reasoning contain'd in the objection to be found on a just principle, *viz*. That the good of society is the Rule of whatever is to be allow'd or restrain'd; and I will likewise grant, that if errors are useful to human society, they ought to be impos'd: and consequently I must allow the inference, That thinking ought be restrain'd. But then I affirm, That the Rule is as falsly as it is irreligiously apply'd, and that both experience and reason demonstrate the imposition of speculations, whether true or false, to be so far from being a benefit, that it has been and must be the greatest mischief that has ever befel[l] or can befal[l] mankind.

Collins invokes Cicero's *De natura deorum* as his authority to reject the notion that 'they who would not be govern'd by Reason, might be influenc'd by Religion to do their Duty'.[41] Collins's *Discourse* attracted enough attention for Jonathan Swift to respond almost immediately with a characteristic satirical impersonation of Collins's voice, but Swift struggles somewhat to make the free-thinker sound like the enthusiast who would seek to impose their world-view on all others—'It is the indispensable Duty of a *Free Thinker*, to endeavour *forcing* all the World to think as he does, and by that means make them *Free Thinkers* too'—when such imposition is precisely what Collins argues against.[42] Collins is not explicitly indebted to *Areopagitica* in the way that Blount was in his protest against licensing laws in 1678—though the continuity of radical thought is suggested by Collins's impressive library, which included copies of Milton's prose alongside Leveller tracts, Winstanley's *Law of Freedom*, and Samuel How's *Sufficiencie of the*

---

[40] [Shaftesbury], *A Letter Concerning Enthusiasm* (1708), 31; Toland, *Tetradymus*, 223.

[41] Anthony Collins, *A Discourse of Free-Thinking* (1713), 94–5. On Collins's use of Cicero, see Giovanni Tarantino, 'Collins's Cicero, Freethinker', in Wayne Hudson, Diego Lucci, and Jeffrey R. Wigelsworth (eds.), *Atheism and Deism Revalued: Heterodox Religious Identities in Britain, 1650–1800* (Farnham: Ashgate, 2014), 81–99.

[42] [Jonathan Swift], *Mr C—ns's Discourse of Free-Thinking* (1713), 15. On Swift's difficulties with his satirical mimicry of Collins, see Judith C. Mueller, 'The Ethics of Reading in Swift's *Abstract* on Freethinking', *Studies in English Literature, 1500–1990*, 31 (1991), 483–98.

Spirits Teaching, among others. Collins's defence of the social value of error points to how Miltonic thinking about liberty was not only imbibed directly into late Restoration freethought through Toland's 1690s editions of Milton's prose and his brilliant and enduring 1698 *Life* of Milton, the motors of which are, in the words of Justin Champion, 'the defence of liberty and the critique of priestcraft'.[43]

There were English influences on Toland and Collins beyond the Miltonic, such as Martin Clifford's defence of toleration in *Treatise of Human Reason* (1674). Clifford (1624–77), secretary to the second Duke of Buckingham and subsequently master of the London Charterhouse, is explicit about the confusion likely to be suffered by any human being looking for the certainty of religious truth:

> The Samaritan says, I have an infallible rule, which is the *Books of Moses*, and only them. The Jew says, I cannot erre for I follow the *Old Testament*, which is infallible, and only that. The Christian assures himself of the Truth as long as he is guided by the *Evangelists* and *Apostles*, whose Writings are the infallible dictates of the *Holy Ghost*. The Turk assumes the same from the *Alcoran*; and the Heathen from *Oracles*, *Sybill's Books*, and the like. What shall I do? None of all these Books can be believed by their own light, for there are things equally strange in them all.

In response to this potentially disabling scepticism, Clifford affirms that everyone should reflect upon the grounds of their beliefs and declare them honestly, without allowing their moral independence to be compromised by any authority, '[w]hereas on the contrary side, the submitting our judgments to Authority, or any thing else whatsoever, gives universality and perpetuity to every error'. As has been well observed of Clifford's work, the reception of which seems to have in part prompted Dryden's application of the term 'deist' in *Religio Laici*: 'Perhaps the most revealing feature of the treatise is the notion that dissent and divergence are in themselves ultimate values, regardless of what they stand for or what they diverge from.' Human beings, Clifford argues, should be guided by the inner conviction that they are in the right, following their 'peculiar Reason ... with constancy, diligence and sobriety', without looking back over their shoulders all the time or recklessly taking other paths, unless induced to do so by some just cause.[44] The corollary of sexual equality implicit in Clifford's pamphlet did not escape the attention of his many critics:

> [If] lapsed reason in its more accurate state (as it is possessed by the wits) may be made a slave to the wills, interests, or the prejudices of men ... what confusion shall

---

[43] Champion, *Republican Learning*, 101. On Collins's library, see Giovanni Tarantino, 'The Books and Times of Anthony Collins, Free-Thinker, Radical Reader and Independent Whig', in Ariel Hessayon and David Finnegan (eds.), *Varieties of Seventeenth- and Early Eighteenth-Century English Radicalism in Context* (Farnham: Ashgate, 2011), 221–40.

[44] Martin Clifford, *A Treatise of Humane Reason* (1674), 4–5, 28–9, 87–8; E. N. Hooker, 'Dryden and the Atoms of Epicurus', *English Literary History*, 24 (1957), 181. On Clifford's importance in the development of deism, see Giovanni Tarantino, *Martin Clifford, 1624–1677. Deismo e tolleranza nell'Inghilterra della Restaurazione* (Florence: Leo S. Olschki, 2000).

we have when all sorts of people whether men, *women, &c.* (for you except none) shall be allowed the priviledge to govern themselves from within, without the least regard had either to example or authority?[45]

Clifford encourages the reader to embrace a philosophical religion that nurtures doubt and tolerance, and in calm, non-polemical prose presents the pursuit of happiness as a question of individual responsibility. In doing so, Clifford's *Treatise* paved the way for Enlightenment thought in England and beyond.[46]

---

[45] George Blundell, *Remarks upon a Tract, Intituled, A Treatise of Humane Reason, and upon Mr. Warren's Late Defence of It* (1683), 10–11.

[46] On the European reception of Clifford's work, see Giovanni Tarantino, 'Martin Clifford and his *Treatise of Humane Reason* (1674): A Europe-Wide Debate', in Ruth Savage (ed.), *Philosophy and Religion in Enlightenment Britain: New Case Studies* (Oxford: Oxford University Press, 2012), 9–28.

CHAPTER 31

RECIPE BOOKS

HENRY POWER

A recipe describes the ingredients and procedure required to make a dish, or a medicinal preparation. It is tempting to imagine that these sets of instructions offer an accurate portrait of domestic life in the seventeenth and eighteenth centuries. They do not. As Wendy Wall points out in her study of what she calls 'recipe culture', 'most of what people cooked or made was so familiar that it could be produced without consulting a book'.[1] The recipes that have been recorded, whether in manuscript or in print, serve a literary as well as (perhaps more than) a didactic purpose. That is not to say that they were not used—as we will see, there is material evidence that they were—but it is worth bearing in mind that they often had a function beyond the mere transmission of domestic instructions. Recipes could be nostalgic, aspirational, or political. They could be prized for their origins (always emphasized by the word *receipt*) as much as for their content. And their easily identifiable generic conventions also made them ripe for parody; the period abounds in satirical recipes (a few of which I discuss in the final section of this chapter).[2]

The first English recipe book to be printed, *The Boke of Cokery*, appeared in 1500, and by 1600, according to Gilly Lehmann's calculation, there were 14,500 copies of recipe books in circulation, in twenty-nine editions.[3] However, it was in our period that the recipe book flourished as a genre in England, and took on the characteristics that are still recognizable today. A major shift in the nature of recipe books started to take place during the 1650s. Elizabethan recipe books tended to be compendiums of domestic

---

[1] Wendy Wall, *Recipes for Thought: Knowledge and Taste in the Early Modern Kitchen* (Philadelphia: University of Pennsylvania Press, 2016), 5.

[2] For an analysis of the formulaic conventions of early modern recipes, see Francisco Alonso-Almeida, 'Genre Conventions in English Recipes, 1600–1800', in Michelle DiMeo and Sara Pennell (eds.), *Reading and Writing Recipe Books, 1550–1800* (Manchester: Manchester University Press, 2013), 68–90.

[3] See Gilly Lehmann, *The British Housewife: Cookery Books, Cooking and Society in Eighteenth-Century Britain* (Totnes, Devon: Prospect Books, 2003), 30.

knowledge, paying as much attention to medicine and household maintenance as to gastronomy. Books of this sort continued to be published in large numbers throughout our period and well into the eighteenth century. *The Ladies Cabinet Enlarged and Opened* (1654) is fairly typical in its recipes being 'comprized under three general Heads' of 'preserving, Conserving, Candying, &c.', 'Physick and Chirugery', and 'Cookery and Housewifery'. However, the period also saw the publication of the first exclusively culinary recipe books, including Joseph Cooper's *The Art of Cookery* (1654), Theodore de Mayerne's *Archimagirus Anglo-Gallicus* (1658), Robert May's *The Accomplisht Cook* (1660), and William Rabisha's *The Whole Body of Cookery Dissected* (1675). These works, generally written by male authors, competed for attention with books written according to a more traditional model.

The rise of the male cookery expert is at least partly associated with the rise of French cuisine, which exerted a strong influence on English cookery (especially at court and the tables of various aristocrats) from the middle of the seventeenth century.[4] The seminal French text was La Varenne's *Le Cuisinier francois* (1651), translated into English as *The French Cook* in 1653, which initiated (or at least registered in print for the first time) a radical shift away from a medieval tradition focused on roast meats and dishes flavoured with sugar and spices, and towards a modern approach to cookery which involved the systematic creation of stocks and essences, thus enabling the creation of a whole battery of sauces. A systematized form of cookery went hand in hand with a more methodically arranged style of recipe book: French cookery writers (and their English imitators) usually offer a basic recipe followed by a series of variations, as opposed to the more haphazard arrangement of recipes found in traditional English books. French books are also more likely to be equipped with an index. This generic difference is linked to a fundamentally different set of assumptions: La Varrene instructs readers how to cook from scratch, whereas books emerging from English households published in the same period assume a much more thorough knowledge of cooking times and preparation techniques.

So, over the course of this period, two distinct strains of recipe book emerge. Books by male authors overwhelmingly emphasize professional expertise, while female authors tended to stress the efficient management of the household; one strain speaks *from* and the other *to* the domestic sphere. The preface to Joseph Cooper's *The Art of Cookery* (1654) highlights the distinction:

> Ladies, forgive my confidence if I tell you, that I know this piece will prove your favourite; and if any thing displeases you, it will be to see so many uncommon, and undeflour'd Receipts prostituted to the publique view, which perchance you will think might have been plac'd better in a few of your Cabinets; but 'tis easie to pardon that offence, which is only committed in favour of the Common good.[5]

---

[4] For details of this significant development, I am indebted to Lehmann, *The British Housewife*, esp. 40–54.

[5] Joseph Cooper, *The Art of Cookery* (1654), sigs. A2–A2v.

Cooper had been chief cook to Charles I, and trades on his position. The highly sexualized language suggests (deliberately or not) masculine intrusion into a largely feminine world—and here the familiar metaphor of the closet or cabinet opened (to be discussed further below) takes on a sinister edge.

The difference between these two traditions is not simply a matter of prose style or organization. Although there were inevitably (and increasingly) overlaps between the styles of cookery described, one might easily taste the difference between the dishes described in a book that emerged from an English household and those described in a book written by a French chef (or by an English writer working in the Continental tradition). Indeed the presence or absence of sugar in dishes (or, rather, the separation of dishes into the sweet and savoury categories we would recognize today) became a crucial generic marker. Broadly speaking, male authors drew a clearer distinction between the two—with female authors more likely to offer recipes which are distinctly English, and where meat and sugar appear in the same recipes. The distinction is not absolute, and over the course of the period (and well into the eighteenth century) the French courtly style gradually influences English domestic cookery. But the tension between the two written traditions persists and we still find Hannah Glasse inveighing against the wastefulness and trickery of French cookery, in contrast to the uprightness and solidity of English food, in 1747: 'So much is the blind Folly of this Age, that they would rather be impos'd on by a *French* Booby, than give Encouragement to a good *English* Cook!'[6]

Though most of the examples mentioned in this chapter are printed recipe books, it is important to stress that a far greater number of recipe books existed and circulated in manuscript. A *receipt*, the word more commonly used for recipe in our period, reveals the way in which these short pieces of prose found their way into books or manuscript collections: they were received—gathered from a variety of sources—and always retained the potential to be redistributed and set within new collections, perhaps in modified form. Thus a recipe in the period was never a stable or static document, and a manuscript recipe book still less so. A printed recipe book is essentially an ossified version of an evolving document; one might draw a comparison with the transcription of ancient oral epic, which preserves a snapshot of a fluid text for future readers. But the boundary between print and manuscript was even more porous than this analogy implies, and there is plenty of evidence that readers modified and annotated printed collections.[7]

One result of the fact that recipes are gathered over time, and then often bequeathed after death, is that a collection of recipes might be drawn from across several generations.

---

[6] *The Art of Cookery, Made Plain and Easy. By a Lady* (1747), sig. a1v. Glasse was identified as the author on the title page of the fourth edition (1751).

[7] Elaine Leong, *Recipes and Everyday Knowledge: Medicine, Science, and the Household in Early Modern England* (Chicago: University of Chicago Press, 2018), esp. 147–72; on readers' annotations to *The Queen's Closet Open'd* (1655), see also Laura Lunger Knoppers, *Politicizing Domesticity from Henrietta Maria to Milton's Eve* (Cambridge: Cambridge University Press, 2011), 99–100, 113.

To give one example, when Rebecca Brandreth died in 1740 she left her daughter two recipe books, which she described as follows in her will: 'two receipt books in folio written by myself... both of the said books being bound with leather and on the inside Lidds of each of them is mentioned that they were written in the year 1683 by Rebecca Price (that being my maiden name)'.[8] Conversely, the fact that a manuscript collection had generated a printed book did not necessarily mark the end of its useful life. Both *A Choice Manual, or, Rare and Select Secrets in Physick and Chirurgery* (1651) and *A True Gentlewoman's Delight* (1653) originated from a receipt book in the household of Elizabeth Talbot, Countess of Kent (1582–1651)—but the manuscript itself continued to grow until the early nineteenth century.[9]

In the seventeenth century many printed recipe books advertised themselves as revealing the secrets of previously private collections. This was naturally true of the recipe books of the famous, such as *The Queen's Closet Open'd* (1655), the Countess of Lennox's *Choice and Profitable Secrets* (1656), and *The Closet of... Sir Kenelm Digby Kt, Opened* (1669), but it was also true in the case of works such as *The Ladies Cabinet Enlarged and Opened* (1656), William Lovell's *The Dukes Desk Newly Broken Up* (1656), Hannah Woolley's *The Queen-Like Closet, or, Rich Cabinet* (1675), and John Shirley's *The Accomplished Ladies Rich Closet of Rarities* (1690). The metaphor of the 'closet opened' is a telling one. In the seventeenth century the word *closet* signified a private space used for all sorts of purposes—including writing, prayer, sleep, and socializing. It was an intimate and lockable space 'in which privacy was habitually sought, and privacy was uniquely found'.[10] Elizabeth Spiller makes the important point that there is nothing intrinsically 'secret' about a recipe (which is by definition usually received from elsewhere), and that they are never described as such in manuscript collections from which printed books are usually derived. Through a strange paradox, it is only at the moment of their being issued in print and made widely available that they take on claims of secrecy.[11] Nonetheless, the idea that the consumer was being given access to a previously private world was clearly part of the appeal of these books. Even where title pages and prefaces are evasive about a collection's origins, they still often evoke the image of the cabinet opened; the Countess of Kent is not named in the early editions of *A True*

---

[8] *The Compleat Cook, or, Secrets of a Seventeenth-Century Housewife, by Rebecca Price*, ed. Madeline Musso and Anthony Vaughan (London: Routledge and Kegan Paul, 1974), 345.

[9] It is now in the possession of the University of Pennsylvania (UPenn MS. Codex 1601).

[10] Lena Cowen Orlin, 'Gertrude's Closet', *Shakespeare Jahrbuch*, 134 (1998), 44–67 (46); Lean Cowan Orlin, *Locating Privacy in Tudor London* (Oxford: Oxford University Press, 2008), 296–326. Orlin stresses that a closet was often a space shared by several members of a household. See also Lynette Hunter, 'Cookery Books: A Cabinet of Rare Devices and Conceits', *Petits Propos Culinaires*, 5 (1980), 19–34; Lynette Hunter, 'Books for Daily Life: Household, Husbandry, Behaviour', in John Barnard and D.F. McKenzie (eds.), with Maureen Bell, *The Cambridge History of the Book in Britain, Vol. IV: 1557–1695* (Cambridge: Cambridge University Press, 2002), 514–32.

[11] *Seventeenth-Century English Recipe Books: Cooking, Physic, and Chirurgery in the Works of Elizabeth Talbot Grey and Aletheia Talbot Howard*, ed. Elizabeth Spiller (London and New York: Routledge, 2008), p. xv.

Gentlewoman's Delight, but readers are assured that the work is both a 'rich magazine of experience' and 'that it was once esteemed a rich Cabinet of knowledge, by a person truly Honourable'.[12]

Naturally, significant labour was involved in transforming a manuscript miscellany into a printed text. One interesting example is *The Closet of ... Sir Kenelm Digby Kt, Opened*, assembled from Digby's posthumous papers and published in 1669, four years after his death. As described above, the published collection (to say nothing of the collection of papers on which it is based) contains recipes gathered from a wide social circle and over several decades; the earliest recipe is perhaps the one for 'Sir Walter Raleigh's great Cordial' (Raleigh died in 1616). This popular book (which went through several editions in the last decades of the seventeenth century) had been preceded in 1668 by Digby's *Choice and Experimented Receipts in Physick*. Both books were put together from Digby's private papers by his steward and factotum, George Hartman. Hartman's name did not appear on either of these initial publications, but he later published *The True Preserver and Restorer of Health ... Together with Excellent Directions for Cookery* under his own name. It is clear, as Peter Davidson and Jane Stevenson have shown, that the recipes in *The True Preserver* draw on the same manuscript sources as *The Closet ... Opened*. Variants between the two texts (which have 122 recipes in common) often seem to be the result of divergent attempts to read Digby's handwriting.[13]

The case of Digby's recipes shows that a process of selection tended to be applied when manuscript collections came to be printed; in reality, there was a great deal more to do than simply opening a closet. When authors organized their own collections of recipes, they often did so in such a way as to make an emphatic statement about the function and purpose of the recipe book. Wendy Wall's discussion of Hannah Woolley's work makes it clear that Woolley was at pains to move away from the growing emphasis on professional (and usually male) expertise, and to re-emphasize the significance of good domestic management. As Wall puts it, Woolley aimed

> to reset the scene and meaning of recipe work. As she returned food preparation to its earlier placement alongside medical care, distilling, carving, dairying, and confectionery, Woolley also expanded recipe topics to include manners, deportment, letter writing, handwriting, decorating, arithmetic, money handling, wax working, and moral behaviour.[14]

The heterogeneity of Woolley's recipes is, in other words, far from accidental. In gesturing back to earlier cookery books (as well as anticipating the compendious later works produced by writers like Isabella Beeton and Martha Stewart), she makes a clear

---

[12] [Elizabeth Talbot Grey], *A True Gentlewoman's Delight* (1653), sig. A2. See also Spiller (ed.), *Seventeenth-Century English Recipe Books*, p. xxxii.

[13] *The Closet of Sir Kenelm Digby, Opened* (1669), ed. Peter Davidson and Jane Stevenson (Totnes, Devon: Prospect Books, 1997), 257–68.

[14] Wall, *Recipes for Thought*, 42.

political statement—about the Englishness of her work and about the centrality of women in the business of domestic management.

The Politics of Recipe Books

The first recipe given in Robert May's *The Accomplisht Cook* (1660) is for a Twelfth Night entertainment. The recipe starts straightforwardly enough (assuming the reader is a skilled pastry maker): 'Make the likeness of a Ship in pasteboard, with flags and streamers, the guns belonging to it of Kickses [the hollow stems of plants].' But straightforward as this may seem, we soon learn that this is just the beginning: the cannon should be fully functioning and charged with live gunpowder. The ship is to be placed on a large charger, and then—on a separate charger—the cook should place a pastry model of a stag, filled with claret so that it can bleed at an appropriate moment.

> At each side of the Charger wherein is the Stag, place a Pie made of course Paste, in one of which let there be some live Frogs, in the other live Birds; make these Pies of course Paste filled with bran, and yellowed over with Saffron or Yolks of Eggs, gild them over in spots, as also the Stag, the Ship, and Castle; bake them, and place them with gilt bay-leaves on the turrets and tunnels of the Castle and Pies; being baked, make a hole in the bottom of your pies, take out the bran, put in your Frogs and Birds, and close up the holes with the same course paste; then cut the lids neatly up, to be taken off by the Tunnels: being all placed in order upon the Table, before you fire the trains of powder, order it so that some of the Ladies may be perswaded to pluck the Arrow out of the Stag, then will the Claret wine follow as blood running out of a wound.

At this point, the ladies are encouraged to remove the piecrusts so that the live frogs and birds can jump out. Music starts playing, and the good times roll. But the recipe comes with a sting in the tail: this is not so much a set of instructions to enable future jollity as a record of English hospitality before the country was divided by civil war: 'These were formerly the delights of the Nobility, before good House-Keeping had left England, and the Sword really acted that which was onely counterfeited in such honest and laudable Exercises as these.'[15]

For twenty-first-century readers, recipe books are often both aspirational and nostalgic, interlarded with photographs which hint at a lost commensality: large families sitting around trestle tables in the Tuscan hills, large groups of friends (none of them holding phones) relaxing together in improbably spacious houses in East London. May's nostalgia is sharper than this, though. The book is dedicated to five members of the aristocracy and gentry widely-known (May tells us) for their 'generous House-keepings',

---

[15] Robert May, *The Accomplish't Cook, or, The Art and Mystery of Cookery* (1660), sigs. A7v–A8.

and in the dedication he mourns the fact that 'Hospitality, which was once a relique of Gentry, and a known Cognizance to all ancient Houses, hath lost her Title through the unhappy and cruel Disturbance of these Times, she is now reposing of her lately so alarum'd Head on your Beds of Honour'. May's book is a product of the long 'Cavalier winter' of 1646 to 1660, during which Royalists retreated to their estates.[16] Although the title page bears the date 1660, the dedication is dated 24 January 1659. It is a prose counterpart to estate poems like Thomas Carew's 'To Saxham', in which the land is gripped by winter and life retreats to the estates of the Royalist gentry:

> The season hardly did afford
> Course cates unto thy neighbours board,
> Yet thou hadst daintyes, as the skie
> Had only been thy Volarie;
> Or else the birds, fearing the snow
> Might to another deluge grow:
> The Pheasant, Partridge, and the Larke,
> Flew to thy house, as to the Arke.[17]

The frontispiece of *The Accomplisht Cook* draws on the same imagery; the poem below May's portrait on the title page describes the author as the leading figure among that 'race of those that for the *Gusto* stand, / whose Tables a whole Ark command / Of Natures plentie'.[18]

A similar strain of nostalgic conservatism can be found in other recipe books of the period. Madeline Bassnett points out the 'consistent identification of receipt book authors with royalist figures and the deposed monarchy'.[19] At least three of the cookery books published during the interregnum were produced by members of the royal household, and several others were issued in the name of Royalist noblemen and women. *The Queens Closet Open'd*, published in 1656, strongly emphasizes the sources of the *receipts* it contains. In the preface, 'W. M.' (that is, the Queen's secretary William Montagu) explains that he has taken the extraordinary step of publishing these papers in order to 'continue my Soveraine Ladies remembrance in the breasts and loves of those persons of

---

[16] May, *Accomplish't Cook*, sig. A3v. On the iconography of the Cavalier winter, see Earl Miner, *The Cavalier Mode from Jonson to Cotton* (Princeton, NJ: Princeton University Press, 1971); Robert Wilcher, *The Writing of Royalism* (Cambridge: Cambridge University Press, 2001), 309–11.

[17] Carew, 'To Saxham' (1640), in *Poetry and Revolution: An Anthology of British and Irish Verse 1625–1660*, ed. Peter Davidson (Oxford: Oxford University Press, 1998), 207–9, lines 15–21.

[18] For a more obviously political application of the story of Noah's Ark to the Interregnum and Restoration, see Thomas Ross's poem to Charles II, part of the prefatory material to his translation of Silius Italicus: 'And (like the Great Restorer, when the Flood / O'reran the Universe) an Ark prepare, / To which all such, as Good, and Loyal are, / For Safety flie' ('To the King', in *The Second Punick War between Hannibal, and the Romanes, Englished from the Latine of Silius Italicus by Thomas Ross* (1661), sigs. B3–B3v).

[19] Madeline Bassnett, 'Restoring the Royal Household: Royalist Politics and the Commonwealth Recipe Book', *Early English Studies*, 2 (2009), 1–32 (8).

honor and quality, who presented most of these rare Receipts to her'—that is to say, the Royalist networks that have been dispersed, or driven underground or overseas, survive here in printed form.[20] During the Civil War, the name-dropping tendencies inherent in the genre take on a political flavour; the first culinary recipe in the volume is '*To make a Posset, the Earle of* Arundels *Way*' (the courtier Thomas Howard, Earl of Arundel, had died in exile in Padua in 1652). Elizabeth Spiller suggests that even the ingredients recommended may have struck some readers as old-fashioned. Whereas French recipe books of the 1650s no longer mention saffron, its use in English recipes intensifies. During the long Cavalier winter, readers could reflect on tastes associated with the Stuart court: 'these texts are not old-fashioned because they were printed belatedly (and usually posthumously); rather they were printed precisely because they were old-fashioned.'[21]

There is another respect in which *The Queen's Closet Open'd* is a political text. Its title and presentation strongly suggest that it was issued in response to the unlicensed publication, in 1645, of a series of letters between Charles I and Henrietta Maria on both domestic and political matters: *The Kings Cabinet Opened*. Laura Lunger Knoppers has shown how these letters were edited and sequenced in order to give the impression of 'a royal household in disorder, with a domineering wife and a dangerously uxorious husband'.[22] *Eikon Basilike* (1649), the work of spiritual autobiography and reflection published in Charles' name immediately after his execution, is partly concerned with refuting the imputations of the unlicensed publication; it shows that there is more than one way to delve into a King's cabinet. The Queen's cookery book is a kind of culinary *Eikon Basilike*, which shows a consort operating in her proper sphere, presiding over a well-organized household. There was, as Bassnett points out, a tendency for recipe books to 'link good household management to the monarchy, thereby claiming that royalists could and should heal, order, and feed the nation'.[23] Another recipe book with obviously Royalist sympathies was *The Court and Kitchin of Elizabeth, Commonly Known as Joan Cromwel[l]* (1664), a satirical work published only after the Restoration—with Cromwell dead, and when Elizabeth had retreated into obscurity. This volume again played on the relationship between domestic and political competence. The preface details the sordidness, parsimony, and chaos that apparently characterized the Cromwells' running of the palace at Whitehall, typified by their employment of a drunken cook, who was summoned to Cromwell's presence to be disciplined and then 'delivered himself by Vomit, in the very Face of his Master, and was thereupon dismissed the House'.[24] The preface is a polemical *tour de force*, brimming with scurrilous political anecdotes and

---

[20] W.[illiam] M.[ontagu], *The Queens Closet Opened* (4th edn, 1658), sig. A4.

[21] Elizabeth Spiller, 'Printed Recipe Books', in Laura Lunger Knoppers (ed.), *The Oxford Handbook of Literature and the English Revolution* (Oxford: Oxford University Press, 2012), 516–33 (519).

[22] Knoppers, *Politicizing Domesticity*, 55.

[23] Bassnett, 'Restoring the Royal Household', 2.

[24] *The Court and Kitchin of Elizabeth, Commonly Known as Joan Cromwel* (1664), 25. See further Laura Lunger Knoppers, 'Opening the Queen's Closet: Henrietta Maria, Elizabeth Cromwell and the Politics of Cookery', *Renaissance Quarterly*, 60 (2007), 464–99.

quoting (in the original) from Persius and Epictetus. The recipes that follow are unremarkable and seem to have been chosen more or less at random—although there may be a dig at the Cromwells' homeliness and East Anglian origins in the several recipes for eels.

Food is always political. Besides the co-option of recipe books by the Royalist faction during (and in the aftermath of) the Civil War, the rise of the recipe book played a crucial role in the broader cultural politics of the period. We have already seen that there were two distinct types of recipe books published in the period, which might loosely be described as domestic and Continental. This subtle distinction was often simplified into a dichotomy between the plain roast meats favoured by the English and the miscellaneous and mysterious concoctions eaten in Continental Europe (and also adopted at court and at various aristocratic tables). Even writers who are very obviously indebted to the Continental tradition are often at pains to stress their resistance to excessively modish or Frenchified cuisine. Robert May for example, though he learned his trade in France and includes many French recipes in *The Accomplisht Cook*, writes in his preface that 'the French by their Insinuations, not without enough of Ignorance, have bewitcht some of the Gallants of our Nation with Epigram Dishes, smoakt rather than drest, so strangely to captivate the Gusto, their Mushroom'd Experiences for Sauce rather than Diet, for the generality howsoever called A-la-mode, not worthy of being taken notice on'.[25] Recipe books both introduced consumers to a range of dishes from Continental Europe and encouraged a kind of gastronomic chauvinism. This tension goes back to the earliest English cookery books; Gervase Markham included a recipe for Olla Podrida in the *English Huswife* (1615), but also encourages the virtuous housewife to content herself with 'the provision of her own yard' and to let her cooking be 'esteemed rather for the familiar acquaintance she hath with it, than for the strangenesse and rarity it bringeth from other Countries'.[26] There is no doubt that such Continental dishes were eaten and enjoyed during the period; Pepys writes in 1669 of being treated to 'a Spanish *Oleo*' at friend's house, and describes it as 'a noble dish, such as I never saw better, or any more of'.[27] But at the same time olios, ragouts, and fricasees became emblematic of a foreign style of cookery which was characterized by miscegenation and which served as a metaphor for moral, aesthetic, or political confusion. The author of the broadsheet, *An Excellent Receipt to Make a Compleat Common-Wealth-Oleo* (1659), finds an easy parallel between the chaos that followed Cromwell's death and the stomach-churning of Continental cuisine. The 'oleo' contains ingredients such as 'a drachme of the scrapings of the Divell's cloven foot; five spoon-fulls of the marrow of old Oliver's nose ... together

---

[25] May, *Accomplish't Cook*, sigs. A4–A4v.
[26] G.[ervaise] M.[arkham], *The English House-Wife. Containing the Inward and Outward Vertues Which Ought to be in a Complete Woman* (4th edn, 1631), 4. The 1615 edition appeared under the title *Country Contentments, in Two Bookes...The Second Intituled, The English Huswife*.
[27] *The Diaries of Samuel Pepys: A Selection*, ed. Robert Latham (Harmondsworth: Penguin, 2003), 1005 (5 April 1669). On the olio and character writing, see also Chapter 9 by Kate Bennett on 'Brief Lives and Characters'.

with a Kilderkinfull of Hugh Peter's sighs and tears ... you may throw in (if you see cause) a barrell or two of Gunpowder'.

Continental recipe books also provide the impetus for Pope's 'Receipt to Make an Epick Poem', published in the *Guardian* in 1713, in which the suggestion is that an epic poem might be produced according to the same kind of culinary system advocated by La Varenne and his followers. The joke here is the over-elevation of domestic science, now applied to the highest form of literature, and Pope starts with a suitably portentous statement: 'An Epic Poem, Critics agree, is the greatest work human nature is capable of', which closely echoes Dryden's famous pronouncement in the *Dedication* of his translation of the *Aeneid*: 'an heroick Poem, truly such, is undoubtedly the greatest Work which the Soul of Man is capable to perform.' But Pope (or his comic creation—later revealed to be none other than Martin Scriblerus when the piece was repurposed as the final section of *Peri Bathous, or, Martinus Scriblerus his Treatise of the Art of Sinking in Poetry*, in 1728) contends that an epic poem may 'be made *without a genius*' if only his instructions are followed. 'To make an EPISODE', for example, 'take any remaining adventure of your former collection, in which you could no way involve your Hero: or any unfortunate accident that was too good to be thrown away; and it will be of use, applied to any other person, who may be lost and *evaporate* in the course of the work, without the least damage to the composition'.[28]

The 'Receipt' pokes fun at those with an over-mechanical approach to literary composition; it has been argued that those who blindly follow the rules for composing an epic poem of the French critic René le Bossu (1631–80) are a particular target.[29] It is thus an imaginative fleshing out of Pope's early observation, in *An Essay on Criticism* (1711), that 'Some dryly plain, without Invention's Aid, / Write dull *Receits* how Poems may be made'.[30] But beyond this, it is striking how many of the quasi-culinary instructions are concerned with the reuse of existing literature. The passage quoted above, which recommends recycling adventures, is a good example—but there are several others. Battle scenes should be purloined from Homer and Virgil, but 'if there remain any overplus, you may lay them by for a *Skirmish*'; 'For the *Under-Characters*, gather them from Homer and Virgil, and change the names as occasion serves'; the fable can be taken 'out of any old Poem, History-book, Romance, or Legend'.[31] An approach which may count as good practice in the kitchen (and which is especially associated with the new French cookery) also evokes a particular kind of lazy and incompetent poet; one who allowed

---

[28] *The Prose Works of Alexander Pope, Vol. II. The Major Works, 1725–1744*, ed. by Rosemary Cowler (Oxford: Blackwell, 1986), 228; *The Works of John Dryden: Volumes V–VI: The Works of Virgil in English, 1697*, ed. by William Frost and Vinton A. Dearing (Berkeley, CA: University of California Press, 1987), 5: 267. See further Henry Power, *Epic into Novel: Henry Fielding, Scriblerian Satire, and the Consumption of Classical Literature* (Oxford: Oxford University Press, 2015), 93–119.

[29] Loyd Douglas, 'A Severe Animadversion on Bossu', *Proceedings of the Modern language Association*, 62 (1947), 690–706.

[30] *The Twickenham Edition of the Poems of Alexander Pope*, gen. ed. John Butt, 11 vols. (London, 1939–68), 1: 252, lines 114–15.

[31] 'Receipt to Make an Epic Poem', in Cowler (ed.), *Prose Works of Alexander Pope, Vol. II*, 228–30.

no piece of writing—however poor—to travel unremunerated to the wastepaper basket. Behaviour of this sort is plainly at odds with Dryden's pronouncement that an epic poem is the great work, not merely of the mind, but of the soul. It also violates a central tenet of epic theory, as stressed by le Bossu himself: 'An *Episode*, according to *Aristotle*, should not be taken from something else and added to the Action.'[32]

Swift also ridiculed Continental cuisine: both its miscellaneity and the self-regard of those who promoted it. The ultra-modern narrator of Swift's *A Tale of a Tub* professes his admiration for the 'late Refinements in Knowledge, running parallel to those of Dyet in our Nation, which among Men of a judicious Taste, are drest up in various Compounds, consisting in *Soups* and *Ollio's*, *Fricassées* and *Ragousts*'. The teller sets himself squarely against those who 'pretend utterly to disrelish these polite Innovations'.[33] The nay-sayers he dismisses include, we might infer, Swift himself, who had a particular distaste for adulterated food. We find Pulteney writing to him in 1726, to promise that 'you shall not have one Dish of Meat at my Table so disguised, but you shall know easily what it is'.[34] For both Pope and Swift, unappealing modern developments in cuisine are emblematic of a parallel set of equally unappealing intellectual developments. It is tempting to regard the 'receipt' element of the parody as purely incidental, given Pope's quite serious aesthetic agenda (which also lies behind more substantial later works such as *Peri Bathous* and the *Dunciad*). But one should not underestimate the popular animus against French cookery around the turn of the eighteenth century.

Isaac Bickerstaff, in *Tatler*, no. 148, opens his account of 'the Diet of this great City' with 'a very earnest and serious Exhortation to all my well-disposed Readers, that they would return to the Food of their Forefathers, and reconcile themselves to Beef and Mutton'. This diet, he says, was responsible for England's greatest victories, at Crecy and Agincourt. But now, at least among the upper classes, such honest fare is rejected by 'false Delicates', who allow a set of perverse rules to dictate their diet. The home-grown alternative to these maligned olios and ragouts is roast beef. This is a point on which Bickerstaff is clear:

> I was now in great Hunger and Confusion, when methoughts I smelled the agreeable Savour of Roast Beef, but could not tell from which Dish it arose, but I did not question but it lay disguised in one of them. Upon turning my Head, I saw a noble Sirloin upon the Side of the Table smoking in the most delicious Manner. I had

---

[32] René Le Bossu, *Monsieur Bossu's Treastise of the Epick Poem. Done into English from the French, with a New Original Preface upon the Same Subject, by W.J.* (1719), 64.

[33] *The Cambridge Edition of the Works of Jonathan Swift: A Tale of a Tub and Other Works*, ed. Marcus Walsh (Cambridge: Cambridge University Press, 2010), 95.

[34] *The Correspondence of Jonathan Swift*, ed. Harold Williams, 5 vols. (Oxford, 1963–5), 3: 162 (3 September 1726). Cf. *A Modest Proposal* (1729), where the projector suggests that 'a young healthy Child, well Nursed is at a year Old, a most delicious, nourishing, and wholesome Food; whether *Stewed, Roasted, Baked*, or *Boyled*, and I make no doubt, that it will equally serve in a *Fricasie*, or *Ragoust*' (*The Cambridge Edition of the Works of Jonathan Swift: Irish Political Writings after 1725*, ed. David Hayton and Adam Rounce (Cambridge: Cambridge University Press, 2018), 149–50).

recourse to it more than once, and could not see without some Indignation that substantial *English* Dish banished in so ignominious a Manner to make Way for *French* Kickshaws.[35]

Ben Rogers has charted the journey by which, over the course of the eighteenth century, roast beef became associated with a nostalgic, rural Tory viewpoint, while elaborate Continental recipes were increasingly identified with urban Whiggish cultural and political innovation.[36] These (supposed) proclivities are clearest when they are being parodied: Swift's olio-loving teller is a comic construct, as is the beef-eating, arch-Tory Bickerstaff—*Tatler*, no. 148 was in fact written by the cosmopolitan Whig, Joseph Addison, who would presumably have felt rather less affronted by French 'kickshaws'. The Englishness of roast beef found its apotheosis in the solid figure of John Bull, who made his first appearance in John Arbuthnot's *Law is a Bottomless Pit* (1712); Bull's meat-eating, which was amplified in later appearances, is a marker of his plain-speaking, rustic Toryism. This particular culinary–political faultline has proved remarkably durable. In 2008, the Tory columnist Boris Johnson (who as prime minister would later withdraw Britain from the European Union) drew a connection between Tony Blair's Continental tastes and his (allegedly) slippery politics, writing of 'The Tuscan Palazzo of Count Girolamo Strozzi where he [Blair] forged one of New Labour's few hard-edged ideological positions: he was pro-sciutto and anti-pasto'.[37]

One of the strangest engagements with the recipes of the period is William King's *The Art of Cookery*. The core of the work is a version of Horace's *Ars Poetica* in which aesthetic precepts are replaced by culinary ones at every possible moment. To emphasize the joke, Horace's Latin was printed opposite King's, in a move which anticipates the presentation of Pope's Horatian imitations of the 1730s. But the work as a whole is a kind of Menippean satire; King's poem is accompanied by a series of 'Letters to Dr. Lister, and Others' in which he mocks the physician and polymath Martin Lister for his recent scholarly edition of the Roman cookery book attributed to Apicius.[38] King plainly found such an expenditure of scholarly labour ridiculous—the application of considerable intellectual resources to a book about mushrooms, lentils, and anchovy paste. The Moderns who disregard Homer are apparently interested enough in gravy. The prefatory letters play—like the poem—on an imagined equivalence between food and literature. King ironically bemoans the fact that gastronomy is not adequately taught in schools:

---

[35] *The Tatler*, no. 148 (18 March 1710), in Donald F. Bond (ed.), *The Tatler*, 3 vols. (Oxford, 1987), 2: 337–8. 'Kickshaw', a word common in eighteenth-century English descriptions of French food, is a contemptuous corruption of *quelque chose*.

[36] Ben Rogers, *Beef and Liberty: Roast Beef, John Bull and the English Nation* (London: Chatto & Windus, 2003), esp. 31–109.

[37] *The Oxford Book of Humorous Quotations*, ed. Gyles Brandreth, 5th edn (Oxford: Oxford University Press, 2013), 323.

[38] *Apicii Cœlii de Opsoniis et Condimentis, sive de Arte Coquinaria Libri Decem, cum Annotationibus M. Lister* (1705).

For what hopes can there be of any Progress in Learning, whilst our Gentlemen suffer their Sons at *Westminster*, *Eaton*, and *Winchester*, to eat nothing but *Salt* with their *Mutton*, and *Vinegar* with their *Roast Beef* upon Holidays? What Extensiveness can there be in their Souls? Especially when upon their going thence to the University, their Knowledge in *Culinary Matters* is seldom enlarg'd, and their Diet continues very much the same; and as to *Sauces*, they are in profound ignorance.[39]

Eighteenth-century schoolboys subsisted largely on a diet of ancient epic, the literary equivalent of plain roast meat. The suggestion is that this education does not equip them adequately for engaging with the range of dishes, or literary forms, currently available. But the suggestion is ironically made. The *Art of Cookery* has a strong anti-gallic flavour: King flaunts a John Bull-ish distaste for the murky ragouts and fricassees favoured by both the Moderns and the French. For John Fuller, 'this contrast between beef, the food of heroes, and the particularly nasty forms of food attributed to the taste of England's enemy is central to an understanding of what King is up to'.[40] Gastronomic politics stand for a broader cultural stance; King is not just in favour of plain meat, but on the side of canonical literature and Tory politics (both of these enthusiasms were—and presumably are—expected of members of the Beefsteak Club, of which King was a founding member in 1705).

Recipe books predate this period, and the genre continued to evolve after 1714; indeed, the later eighteenth century is widely regarded as the golden age of the form, with Hannah Glasse's *The Art of Cookery, Made Plain and Easy* (1747) often cited as the first best-selling recipe book. But it was during the period from 1640 to 1714 that the conventions of the genre began to emerge—and in particular the tension between those written in *haut-en-bas* style by male professionals and those written by women with direct experience of household management. The boundaries between these categories became increasingly porous, and some of the tensions explored in this chapter are visible in Glasse's work, which manages to be both cosmopolitan and insular, both forward-looking and nostalgic.[41]

---

[39] [William King], *The Art of Cookery, in Imitation of Horace's Art of Poetry. With Some Letters to Dr. Lister, and Others* (1708), 3–4.

[40] John Fuller, 'Carving Trifles: William King's Imitation of Horace', *Proceedings of the British Academy*, 62 (1976), 269–91 (279). See also Joan Hildreth Owen, 'Philosophy in the Kitchen, or, Problems in Eighteenth-Century Culinary Aesthetics', *Eighteenth-Century Life*, 3 (1977), 77–9; Power, *Epic into Novel*, 31–4.

[41] On Glasse, see Lehmann, *The British Housewife*, 226–32.

CHAPTER 32

RELIGIOUS AUTOBIOGRAPHY

BROOKE CONTI

If any single work can be said to have invented the early modern spiritual autobiography, it is John Bunyan's *Grace Abounding to the Chief of Sinners*. This is not because Bunyan wrote the era's first religious autobiography—he missed that distinction by decades, if not a full century—or because of his influence on later autobiographers, though that was considerable.[1] Rather, the category of 'spiritual autobiography' was devised in the twentieth century to explain and contextualize Bunyan's narrative. Never theorized or precisely defined, the term itself dates to the late nineteenth century and early usage applied it promiscuously to both fiction and nonfiction in a variety of genres.[2] Starting in 1948, however, Roger Sharrock took up the term and promoted it energetically across a number of articles and books as he sought to place *Grace Abounding* within the literary

---

[1] Depending on how one defines 'early modern' and 'autobiography' there are many earlier English-language contenders for the title, dating back at least to John Bale's *Vocacyon* (1553). For the influence of *Grace Abounding* on later autobiographers, see for example D. Bruce Hindmarsh, *The Evangelical Conversion Narrative: Spiritual Autobiography in Early Modern England* (Oxford: Oxford University Press, 2005), 51–2, 57–8; John N. Morris, *Versions of the Self* (New York: Basic Books, 1966), 89–90; Linda H. Peterson, *Victorian Autobiography: The Tradition of Self-Interpretation* (New Haven: Yale University Press, 1986), esp. 1–28.

[2] 'Spiritual autobiography' was frequently used to describe the life stories of contemporary churchmen and women (usually of an evangelical strain), but it was also applied, just as early, to works of fiction, including Goethe's *Faust*. Examples of the former include Adoniram Judson Gordon, *How Christ Came to Church: The Pastor's Dream: A Spiritual Autobiography* (American Baptist Publication Society, 1895); Hannah Whittal Smith, *The Unselfishness of God and How I Discovered It: A Spiritual Autobiography* (New York: Fleming H. Revell, 1903). Contemporary fiction was sometimes described as providing either the author or main character's spiritual autobiography. See *The New York Times*'s review of Orestes Brownson's *Charles Elwood* (9 September 1883, p. 10) or *Literary Digest*'s review of Mrs. Humphrey Ward's *Robert Ellsmere* (*Literary Digest* 26: 18 April 1903, p. 576). Older works were also sometimes retrospectively labelled spiritual autobiographies. One *New York Times* book review, of a biography of Goethe, calls *Faust* the German's spiritual autobiography, and another, of a new edition of George Herbert, notes that the editor arranges to the poems in such a way that they become a spiritual autobiography (February 13, 1881; November 11, 1905).

culture of Bunyan's contemporaries.[3] Neither Sharrock nor his immediate successors paused to comment on the term's origins or implications, but their examination of nonconformist and Quaker conversion narratives, and the theology that provided their discursive template, brought them to the attention of a wide scholarly audience.[4]

According to these early studies, the spiritual autobiography was an essentially Puritan genre, one that fused the Pauline or Augustinian experience of conversion with Calvinist anxieties about salvation, leading to a continual search for signs of election. A typical story of the soul's growth in grace might begin with an account of the author's youthful sinfulness, interspersed with evidence of God's providential interventions; proceed to the author's acceptance that he or she could do nothing to merit salvation; and culminate in a profound experience of God's grace and the assurance of election. By the 1960s and 1970s this understanding of the genre was so widespread that scholars working in both autobiography studies and the study of the novel were claiming the spiritual autobiography as an important ancestor.[5] In these narratives of origin, what distinguished the spiritual autobiography was its focus on the interior drama of an ordinary life. The term itself may have encouraged this reading ('spiritual autobiography' suggests more intimacy than 'conversion narrative'), but so too did *Grace Abounding*. For though numerous scholars have noted how unusual Bunyan's work is in its intensive focus on its author's emotional and psychological state, *Grace Abounding* is undoubtedly the most frequently read religious autobiography of the seventeenth century.[6] Thus a link was forged between spiritual autobiography and the nonconformist conversion narrative, and with it a belief in the latter's unprecedented degree of interiority.

In recent decades this narrative has been seriously challenged. Although there is no disputing that many works fit the conventions outlined above, even among so-called Puritans not all works of religious autobiography feature moments of conversion—those of John Milton, John Lilburne, and Agnes Beaumont do not—nor do they necessarily linger over their authors' inner experience.[7] There has also been tremendous interest in

---

[3] See Roger Sharrock, 'Spiritual Autobiography in *The Pilgrim's Progress*', *Review of English Studies*, 24/94 (1948), 102–20; *John Bunyan* (New York: St. Martin's, 1968 [reprint; Hutchinson, 1954]), 53–68; 'Spiritual Autobiography: Bunyan's *Grace Abounding*', in Anne Laurence, W. R. Owens, and Stuart Sims (eds.), *John Bunyan and His England* (London: Bloomsbury, 1990), 97–104; and Sharrock's editions of *Grace Abounding* (Oxford: Clarendon Press, 1962), pp. xxvii–xxx, and *Pilgrim's Progress* (Oxford: Clarendon Press, 1960). Sharrock was not the first scholar to argue that *Grace Abounding* be read alongside autobiographies by his contemporaries and co-religionists; that appears to have been William York Tindall, in *John Bunyan, Mechanick Preacher* (New York: Columbia University Press, 1934). However, Tindall does not use the term 'spiritual autobiography'.

[4] In addition to Sharrock and Tindall, important early treatments of the genre include Daniel B. Shea, *Spiritual Autobiography in Early America* (Princeton, NJ: Princeton University Press, 1968); Owen C. Watkins, *The Puritan Experience: Studies in Spiritual Autobiography* (New York: Schocken, 1972).

[5] See G. A. Starr, *Spiritual Autobiography and the Rise of the Novel* (Princeton: Princeton University Press, 1965); Morris, *Versions of the Self*, 1–9; Peterson, *Victorian Autobiography*, 1–28; Michael McKeon, *Origins of the English Novel: 1600–1740* (Baltimore: Johns Hopkins University Press, 1987), 90–6.

[6] See Sharrock (ed.), *Grace Abounding*, pp. xxxi–xxxii.

[7] For a discussion of how poorly Milton fits the paradigm, see Stephen M. Fallon, *Milton's Peculiar Grace: Self-Representation and Authority* (Ithaca: Cornell University Press, 2007), 21–44.

the autobiographies of writers elsewhere on the religious spectrum, which show even more narrative and formal variety. In the face of this diversity, 'spiritual autobiography' no longer seems the appropriate term; it is limited on the one hand by a scholarly history that has long considered it synonymous with the Calvinist conversion narrative, and on the other by the word 'spiritual', with its implicit restriction to works that deal with the author's interior life or affective relationship to the divine.[8] A more capacious understanding of what constitutes early modern religious autobiography would include works written in institutional contexts that follow relatively set forms (such as those written upon joining a nonconformist congregation or a Catholic seminary); essentially private works, such as diaries, letters, and biblical paraphrases written for devotional use; self-vindications and accounts of juridical proceedings; and autobiographical fragments in sermons, speeches, and works of religious controversy.[9]

But if early modern religious autobiography turns out not to be defined by a set of common narrative or formal characteristics, that does not mean that these texts have nothing in common. Whatever else they may be doing, religious autobiographies strive to locate their authors within a larger Christian framework—one that reaches beyond the denominational or sectarian. As a result, the autobiographies of early modern recusants, conformists, and nonconformists often display similar strategies of self-presentation (and show similar anxieties about that presentation).[10] Twentieth-century Bunyan scholars were right in seeing *Grace Abounding* as a window onto the religious culture of seventeenth-century nonconformity. But if we place Bunyan alongside writers from elsewhere on the denominational spectrum, we will see that his autobiography does not just reflect the concerns of his co-religionists; in the wake of the Reformation, some desires and fears were common to all Christians.

The religious upheavals of the sixteenth and seventeenth centuries jeopardized any easy narrative of Christian continuity, making it harder for individuals to see themselves as part of an unbroken chain of the faithful. Protestants had to account for the centuries of corruption that separated them from the disciples (a period that included their own immediate ancestors), while English Catholics had to account for the extirpation of their religion on their native soil. The era's battles over ecclesiology and worship, with their sometimes obsessive interest in the practices of the early church, were one

---

[8] A looser definition is arguably truer to the term's original usage, and when it comes to contemporary autobiographies it may have much to recommend it. However, in the case of early modern life-writing I believe its limitations render it too confusing to be useful.

[9] See further Chapter 7 by Julie A. Eckerle on 'Biography and Autobiography'; Chapter 9 on 'Brief Lives and Characters' by Kate Bennett, and Chapter 12 on 'Diaries' by Adam Smyth.

[10] This is not to say that sectarian identity is irrelevant; just as *Grace Abounding* is indebted to Calvinist theology and comes into sharper focus when it is read among works by Bunyan's co-religionists, autobiographers from other confessional positions must be understood as emerging from their respective theological and devotional communities. However, I see no evidence that differences in doctrine or worship translate into consistent or readily identifiable stylistic or formal differences, as was frequently asserted in early studies of these texts. See for example Joan Webber, *The Eloquent 'I': Style and Self in Seventeenth-Century Literature* (Madison: University of Wisconsin Press, 1968); Dean Ebner, *Autobiography in Seventeenth-Century England* (The Hague: Mouton, 1971).

way of claiming direct descent from the apostles. At the same time, the intractable nature of those debates was a reminder of just how distant those ancestors were and how fractured the Christian community had become. Autobiography provided a different means to the same end, allowing writers to claim membership in a timeless Christian Church without entangling themselves in an endless cycle of controversy. What these works reveal is how Christians of all stripes navigated the identity crisis at the heart of the Reformation.

One common thread in many religious autobiographies is the expression of dismay at religious controversy. Autobiographers rarely attempt to disguise their authors' denominational or sectarian identity, but they consistently lament the fragmentation of the church and emphasize the futility of religious disputes. At the conformist end of the spectrum, Thomas Browne asserts, in *Religio Medici* (1643), that 'there remains not many controversies worth a passion, yet never any disputed without [it],' and notes that he, personally, 'could never divide [him] selfe from any man upon a difference of an opinion'.[11] Similarly, John Donne, in *Devotions Upon Emergent Occasions* (1623), laments 'uncharitable *disputations*' over such things as religious images and bell-ringing, beseeching that Christians 'not breake the *Communion of Saints*, in that which was intended for the *advancement* of it'.[12] Such sentiments are equally common among nonconformists. Late in *Grace Abounding* Bunyan notes that in his preaching he 'never cared to meddle with things that were controverted and in dispute amongst the Saints',[13] and in *Reliquiae Baxterianae* (1696) Richard Baxter expresses regret that in his younger years he was 'apt to stir up Controversies'.[14] As a way of illustrating how peripheral controversial disputes are to sound Christian belief, Baxter proposes an extended metaphor of a tree, in which the roots are the fundamentals of Christianity and the most important parts of religion are those nearest them. As he says, 'the Stock [i.e., trunk] of the Tree affordeth Timber to build Houses and Cities, when the small though higher multifarious Branches are but to make a Crow's Nest, or a Blaze'.[15] Like Baxter, the Fifth Monarchist Anna Trapnel also renounces her prior interest in disputed matters, and in the process gestures toward the kind of solution that I am arguing autobiography affords. In *A Legacy for Saints* (1654),

---

[11] Thomas Browne, *Religio Medici 1643* (Menston: Scolar Press, 1970), 2.3, 1.6. All quotations refer to this facsimile edition, with part and section numbers hereafter cited in the text (or page numbers, in the case of front matter).

[12] John Donne, *Devotions Upon Emergent Occasions*, ed. Anthony Raspa (Montreal: McGill-Queens University Press, 1975), 84. For a discussion of the somewhat self-serving nature of these pleas, see Richard Strier, 'Donne and the Politics of Devotion', in Donna B. Hamilton and Richard Strier (eds.), *Religion, Literature, and Politics in Post-Reformation England* (Cambridge: Cambridge University Press 1996), 93–114.

[13] Bunyan, *Grace Abounding*, §284. All quotations from *Grace Abounding* refer to Roger Sharrock's 1962 edition, and are cited by section numbers (or page numbers, in the case of front matter).

[14] Richard Baxter, *Reliquiae Baxterianae* (1696), 125. Page numbers are hereafter cited in the text. Baxter's autobiography was published posthumously, but was mainly written in 1664–5 and 1670–85. There is now a state-of-the-art, fully annotated modern edition: *Reliquiae Baxterianae*, ed. N. H. Keeble et al., 5 vols. (Oxford: Oxford University Press, 2020).

[15] Baxter, *Reliquiae Baxterianae*, 127.

Trapnel notes that in her earlier days she had 'an eager pressing after the way of worship', so that 'night and day' she spent 'study[ing] Ordinances, and the right administrations, according to that practice in the time of the Apostles'.[16] Unfortunately, in the churches of her own day, she 'could not find any come up unto [them]'. Eventually, Trapnel says, she concluded that this obsession with the practices of the apostles was a kind of idolatry, and so urges that 'all the Saints' should 'have a care' not to exalt any ordinance above Christ himself.[17] But although Trapnel's response to the diversity of forms of worship is to declare that it is impossible to perfectly reproduce the conditions of the early church, she still has faith in the fundamental continuity of Christian experience. This leads her to focus her attentions elsewhere—in her case, on her unmediated encounters with God, who sends her the visions and prophecies that occupy much of her three autobiographical works.[18]

Most early modern religious autobiographies are not accounts of their authors' visions, but a longing for an authentic and unmediated Christian identity can be seen in virtually all of them; writers seek to locate the source of their authority not in external forms but in the witness of their individual experience. In addition to lamenting the existence of religious controversy, then, most autobiographers de-emphasize their own disputatious beliefs. Compared to Bunyan's other nonfiction, *Grace Abounding* virtually ignores sacramental and devotional issues, instead focusing on doubts and anxieties with a more universal resonance.[19] The work's effectiveness depends on the reader's willingness to believe not only that Bunyan has experienced what he says he has but also that those experiences reflect something fundamentally Christian. All religious autobiographies do something similar, at least implicitly; the works of the Leveller John Lilburne, the young recusant Nicholas Hart, and the ejected bishop Joseph Hall are all quite unlike Bunyan's, not least in their disinclination to dwell on their authors' inner experiences.[20] But when Lilburne asserts God's presence when he was whipped through

---

[16] Anna Trapnel, *Legacy for Saints* (1654), 18.

[17] Trapnel, *Legacy for Saints*, 18–19.

[18] In addition to *Legacy for Saints*, Trapnel's autobiographical works (somewhat different in form but both published in 1654) are *Cry of a Stone* and *Report and Plea*.

[19] The closest Bunyan comes to critiquing the practices of the state church is in §16, where he mentions, in passing, that as a newly married man he took some small steps toward religion, and 'fell in very eagerly with the religion of the times'. He adds that, although 'retaining my wicked life ... I was so overrun with the spirit of superstition, that I adored ... the high place, priest, clerk, vestments, [and] service'. Even this, however, is not quite a critique of the state church, since the focus is on *Bunyan's* failings: he retains his wicked life and approaches religion with a spirit of superstition.

[20] Lilburne's *A Worke of the Beast* (1638) and *Christian Man's Triall* (1641) both recount his punishment for refusing to take the Oath of Star Chamber. Hart's autobiography was written upon joining the Jesuit seminary at Rome, and responds to the standard questions developed by Robert Persons for young recusant seminarians. See *Responsa Scholarum of the English College, Rome: Part 1 1598–1621*, ed. Anthony Kenny (Catholic Record Society, 1962), 25–9. Hall's two autobiographies, *Observations of Some Specialties in the Life of Joseph Hall*, and *Bishop Hall's Hard Measure*, were both written in 1647 after Hall's ejection from the bishopric of Norwich during the civil wars, but published posthumously in *The Shaking of the Olive-Tree: The Remaining Works of that Incomparable Prelate Joseph Hall* (1660).

the streets and the divine inspiration that allowed him to speak eloquently from the scaffold, as when Hart and Hall itemize God's providential interventions in their lives, these events stand as testimonials not just to their authors' sincerity but to the authenticity of their beliefs.[21] Whether a writer *itemizes* those beliefs or explains their superiority to others is beside the point (some do, but they are never their works' focus); the life of each is his witness and implicit proof of his membership in a universal Christian identity.

Foregrounding one's engagement with Christian fundamentals may sometimes be a deliberate authorial strategy, whether in an effort to reach a wider audience or simply to make the writer look or feel better. But no autobiographer is ever in complete control of what his or her text reveals, and it is best to see a writer's self-presentation as an unstable mix of the intentional and the inadvertent.[22] Ultimately, whether the attempt to articulate a universal Christian identity is 'calculated' or 'sincere' does not much matter. What these autobiographies demonstrate is that in an age of increasing sectarian fragmentation, a coherent religious identity—and the authority that goes with it—are tied to how well an autobiographer can connect his life and experiences to a timeless church, one that rises above temporal and national divisions.

This longing to connect with one's ancestors in the faith can result, however, not only in downplaying doctrinal specifics but sometimes in actually seeming to cast aspersions on the religion of the present day, including that of the authors' supposed co-religionists. We saw some of this in the passage from Anna Trapnel quoted above, but dissatisfaction with contemporary religious practice is not limited to matters of worship. It includes the ways believers narrate their own lives, which is to say, the very form of religious autobiography itself. Even *Grace Abounding* betrays misgivings about the enterprise. In the work's preface, addressing the congregation he has been separated from by his imprisonment, Bunyan explains that he is publishing the book so that 'others may be put in remembrance of what [God] hath done for their Souls, by reading his work upon me.'[23] He urges them to reflect on their own lives in order to see themselves as part of the universal Christian narrative. 'Call to mind,' he says, 'the former days, the years of ancient times; remember also your songs in the night.... your tears and prayers to God; yea, how you sighed under every hedge for mercy.... Have you forgot the Close, the Milk-house, the Stable, the Barn, and the like, where *God* did visit your Soul?'[24] Just as the operations of grace in Bunyan's life should match up with his readers' own, so should the events of 'ancient times'—which is to say, of past ages and the lives of past Christians—map onto whatever his contemporaries experience in the more homely circumstances of the milk-house and the stable. But despite this initial assertion of the similarity of all Christian

---

[21] Lilburne, *A Worke of the Beast* (1638), 8–9, 19; Kenny, *Responsa Scholarum*, 26–7; Hall, *Observations*, 4–14.
[22] Brooke Conti, *Confessions of Faith in Early Modern England* (Philadelphia: Pennsylvania University Press, 2014), esp. 1–13.
[23] Bunyan, *Grace Abounding*, 2.
[24] Bunyan, *Grace Abounding*, 3.

lives, in the body of *Grace Abounding*, Bunyan confesses that not all autobiographies are created equal and that he himself is much more interested in those of 'former days... [and] ancient times'. In fact, his longing for a larger Christian community results in impatience with the narratives of his contemporaries.

Approximately a third of the way through the work, as Bunyan emerged from his first series of temptations to commit the sin against the Holy Ghost, he says that he found himself searching for writers who might have experienced something similar and left an account. He writes:

> Before I had got thus far out of these my temptations, I did greatly long to see some ancient Godly man's Experience, who had writ some hundred of years before I was born; for, those who had writ in our days, I thought (but I desire them now to pardon me) that they had Writ only that which others felt, or else had, thorow the strength of their Wits and Parts, studied to answer such Objections as they perceived others were perplexed with, without going down themselves into the deep.

What Bunyan does *not* want to read is an autobiography from the present day. He does not dispute that such works reflect events or emotions that are widely shared—or even that those might parallel his own experiences—but he seems not to trust them, suspicious that their authors are just following a template. Either they import 'what others felt' into their own life stories or they cunningly manipulate those stories so that they appear to address 'what others were perplexed with', or a common set of theological or salvational anxieties.

This passage has implications for autobiographers beyond Bunyan. First, it suggests that seventeenth-century nonconformists were not only conscious but perhaps sometimes weary of their own narrative tropes. It may even be that Bunyan's autobiography, so prized by later readers, is a conscious attempt to improve upon the genre by conveying what he found lacking in other autobiographies: the emotional experience of 'going down ... into the deep'. Second, the passage suggests that what Bunyan and other nonconformists may have been looking for in conversion narratives was not so different from what they were looking for in their ecclesiology, worship, and devotion: a connection less to the horizontal community of their contemporary co-religionists than to the vertical community of their ancestors in the faith.

In Bunyan's case, he finds that connection in 'a book of *Martin Luther*, his comment on the *Galathians*'. Bunyan emphasizes his sense of the work's antiquity, and hence authority. It was, he says, 'so old that it was ready to fall piece from piece, if I did but turn it over'. He adds 'I was pleased much that such an old book had fallen into my hand', and its consonance with his experience makes him marvel: 'for thus thought I, this man could not know anything of the state of Christians now, but must needs write and speak of the Experience of former days.'[25] Vera Camden has written persuasively about the importance of Luther's *Commentary* for Bunyan's autobiography, arguing that Luther's more

---

[25] Bunyan, *Grace Abounding*, §129.

affective account of the operations of grace spoke to Bunyan in ways unlike the conversion narratives of his contemporaries (which Camden characterizes as more focused on doctrine than 'authentic inward experience').[26] She is surely right, and I would not wish to dismiss the importance of Luther to Bunyan's religious development. But the passage does not emphasize the content of Luther's text so much as its distance from Bunyan in time; its value lies in the fact that Luther, despite 'not know[ing] anything of the state of Christians now', nevertheless describes experiences that are consonant with theirs. Just as in the work's epistle, where Bunyan urges his readers to think of 'the former days' of Christianity, here he longs for 'some ancient Godly man's Experience', one who 'writ some hundred of years' ago. Indeed, it is possible that Bunyan sees Luther as a gateway to a yet earlier era, connecting him not just to the dawn of Protestantism in the 1530s but also to the dawn of Christianity itself. After all, the work is not Luther's autobiography, though he writes in the first person and addresses his readers with great intimacy and urgency. Rather, it is an explication of Paul, and at times there is significant slippage between Luther's voice and the apostle he purports to be channelling. When Luther paraphrases Paul's exhortations to the church at Galatia to rely upon faith and reject the works of the law, Bunyan might well believe that his state is the same as that of the Galatians.

Bunyan is not the only autobiographer to express dissatisfaction with the contemporary conversion narrative or to seek a warrant for his experiences outside of that genre. Both Trapnel and Baxter do something similar. In *A Legacy for Saints*, Trapnel starts conventionally enough with an account of her childhood, her gradual coming to Christ, and her temptations along the way—but acknowledges that in some particulars her life may seem to diverge from the conventional pattern. She writes, 'if I vary concerning some experiences in this, in respect of doubting, and questioning union after sealing [i.e., after receiving confirmation that she was among the elect], it is my own experience, I must not record anothers experience'.[27] Baxter does much the same, beginning with a list of the chief sins of his youth and various providential escapes, but then veering off course. In recounting his coming to Christ in his early adolescence, Baxter notes that, although there was one particular moment when he felt that God 'awaken[ed] my soul, and shew[ed] me the folly of Sinning', he is not quite sure that this amounts to the kind of transformative moment of conversion that others so confidently identify in their own lives: 'Yet whether sincere Conversion began *now*, or *before*, or *after*, I was never able to this day to know.'[28] Several paragraphs later, he returns to this perplexity and his longstanding fear that he might not be saved because his sense

---

[26] See Vera J. Camden, '"Most Fit for a Wounded Conscience": The Place of Luther's "Commentary on Galatians" in *Grace Abounding*', *Renaissance Quarterly*, 50 (1997), 822.

[27] Trapnel, *A Legacy for Saints*, 12. For Trapnel's influence on the English conversion narrative—including, perhaps, Bunyan's own—see Maria Magro, 'Spiritual Autobiography and Radical Sectarian Women's Discourse: Anna Trapnel and the Bad Girls of the English Revolution', *Journal of Medieval and Early Modern Studies*, 34 (2004), 405–37.

[28] Baxter, *Reliquiae Baxterianae*, 3.

of the motions of the spirit upon his heart did not conform to the experiences of others. Eventually, he says, he came to understand 'that the Soul is in too dark and passionate a plight at first, to be able to keep an exact account of the order of its own Operations.... it is not possible that one of very many should be able to give any true account of the *just Time* when Special Grace began'.[29] Baxter bolsters this claim by noting that he has 'heard many [others] make the very same Complaints' about their inability to fit their life experiences into the standard template; these include 'People of whom I had the best esteem, for the uprightness and holiness of their Lives'.[30] Based on these witnesses, Baxter ultimately concludes that 'God breaketh not all Mens hearts alike'.[31] Like Bunyan and Trapnel, Baxter takes for granted that many aspects of a Christian's experiences are common to all—elsewhere in his autobiography he will say that he finds it 'somewhat unsavory to recite' the events of his faith life, 'seeing God's Dealings are much what the same with all his Servants'—but when a Christian's life does not conform to the expected narrative, he asserts the necessary validity of that unique experience.[32]

These three writers demonstrate the difficulty autobiographers have in presenting themselves as authentically Christian in ways that are recognizable not only to others but also to themselves. When present-day precedents such as those of the conversion narrative fail, they grope for parallels in the experiences of others or fall back on their own sense of assurance. Inner conviction may well be the only kind that a believer ever gets, but by its nature it is invisible to others. It is still less communicable textually. From a literary standpoint, the only proof of an author's membership in the elect is how persuasively she communicates it. What counts as 'sincere' or 'authentic' may differ from writer to writer, but one of the paradoxes of a narrative convention is that conformity to that convention can simultaneously authorize and delegitimate an individual's experience. Bunyan's suspicion that the normative conversion narrative might allow anyone to take the usual tropes and shoehorn in her own autobiographical details implies that a certain degree of idiosyncrasy might be understood, even in an age less attracted to novelty than our own, as evidence of emotional truth.

Although concerns about authenticity and generic self-presentation might seem most common among nonconformists conscious of writing within a prescriptive genre, writers from other confessional positions wrestle with them too. Browne's *Religio Medici* initially seems as unlike *Grace Abounding* as it is possible for an autobiographical work by a Protestant near-contemporary to get. Written by a generally conforming member of the Church of England, the *Religio* is not a conversion narrative; in fact, it is not a narrative at all, and it provides few details about the specifics of Browne's life. Instead, it is a series of essayistic first-person meditations on religious topics, focused particularly

---

[29] Baxter, *Reliquiae Baxterianae*, 6.
[30] Baxter, *Reliquiae Baxterianae*, 9.
[31] Baxter, *Reliquiae Baxterianae*, 7.
[32] Baxter, *Reliquiae Baxterianae*, 124. For more on Baxter's struggles with the conventions of nonconformist life-writing, see Kathleen Lynch, *Protestant Autobiography in the Seventeenth-Century Anglophone World* (Oxford: Oxford University Press, 2012), 231–70.

on the relationship between faith and reason. Like *Grace Abounding*, however, it was spectacularly popular: Bunyan's work went through six editions in its author's lifetime, while Browne's went through seven (and was immediately translated into Latin, Dutch, and French).[33] Moreover, its popularity seems to have been due in part to its originality, in this case Browne's seemingly tolerant and ecumenical persona; he, too, attempts to stand outside of controversy, presenting himself as simply Christian.[34] To my knowledge, the two works have never been directly compared, but putting these texts that sit at opposite stylistic and doctrinal poles into conversation suggests just how widespread were the phenomena that I have been discussing.[35] Many believers, it seems, used autobiography to imagine themselves into a larger and transhistorical Christian identity.

Like Bunyan, Browne seems dissatisfied with the religion of the present day. The *Religio*'s opening lines contain a defiant assertion of Browne's Christian identity behind which seems to lurk displeasure at *having* to assert it—that is, at the idea that anyone might assume otherwise:

> For my Religion, though there be severall circumstances that might perswade the world I have none at all, as the generall scandall of my profession, the naturall course of my studies, the indifferency of my behaviour and discourse in matters of Religion, neither violently defending one, nor with that common ardour and contention opposing another; yet in despight hereof I dare, without usurpation, assume the honorable stile of a Christian.[36]

Browne expresses exasperation at the perception that all doctors are atheists—and also, and at greater length, at the idea that avoiding religious controversy makes for a lukewarm faith. In defiance of this assumption Browne labels himself a Christian, *tout court*, and initially refuses to be more specific. It will take several more sentences before Browne grudgingly circles around to admitting that he is a Protestant, acknowledging that, in his day, 'the name of a Christian is become too generall to express our faith, there being a Geography of Religions as well as Lands ... To be particular, I am of that reformed new-cast Religion, wherein I dislike nothing but the name'.[37] Even in extending himself thus far, Browne makes it clear that he is unhappy about the fragmentation of the church; he will go on to say of Catholics 'we have reformed from them, not against them' and 'there is between us one common name and appellation, one faith and

---

[33] See Thomas Browne, *Religio Medici: Edited from the Manuscript Copies and the Early Editions*, ed. Jean-Jacques Denonain (Cambridge: Cambridge University Press, 1953).

[34] Reid Barbour, *Sir Thomas Browne: A Life* (Oxford: Oxford University Press, 2013), 279–83.

[35] A number of books focusing on autobiography or authorial voice do contain chapters on both works, but the two are not compared in any sustained way. Examples include Margaret Bottrall, *Every Man A Phoenix: Studies in Seventeenth-Century Autobiography* (London: John Murray, 1958); Webber, *Eloquent 'I'*; Stanley Fish, *Self-Consuming Artifacts: The Experience of Seventeenth-Century Literature* (Berkeley: University of California Press, 1972); Conti, *Confessions of Faith*.

[36] Browne, *Religio Medici*, 1.1.

[37] Browne, *Religio Medici*, 1.2.

necessary body of principles'.[38] Still, Browne regretfully concludes that, 'though peaceable Spirits doe desire' it, Christian reunification seems unlikely.[39] However, his reluctance to abandon a more universal Christian identity persists. Even after he manages to call himself a Protestant, it is not until the work's fifth section (on page eight of the original quarto volume) that he announces himself as a member of the Church of England. Again, he almost immediately qualifies that statement by asserting his independence of thought, claiming that he belongs to that church not only because it is the national church, but because none other 'so squares unto my conscience'. He adds, 'I condemne not all things in the Councell of *Trent*, nor approve all in the Synod of *Dort* ... I borrow not the rules of my Religion from *Rome* or *Geneva*, but the dictates of my owne reason'.[40] In all these ways, Browne strives to establish himself, from the very first page, as one free from sectarianism and whose Christianity requires no mediation; he can engage directly with scripture, with the teachings of different sects, and with the documents from Trent or Dort, and yet come to his own conclusions.

Still, like the nonconformists whose ambivalence about the normative conversion narrative I have discussed, Browne's insistence on the reliability of his own judgement in matters of faith sometimes gives way to anxiety about seeming too far outside the larger community of Christian believers. Despite his reluctance to be classified as something more specific than a Christian and his belief that a strong faith may 'exercise [itself] in the difficultest point[s]' of religion,[41] at certain moments he repudiates this freedom. At the end of the work's first part he declares that his beliefs may contain 'many things singular ... yet, if they square not with maturer Judgements, I disclaim them, and doe no further father them, than the learned and best Judgements shall authorize them'.[42] He says something similar in the epistle to the reader, where he claims that the work was composed seven years earlier and reflects only 'the sense of [his] conceptions at that time' and was not intended as 'an example or rule unto any other'.[43] Autobiographers may be impatient with the religion of the present day and yet remain sensitive to charges of being too far outside the main line of Christian belief.

Religious doubt, which preoccupies both Browne and Bunyan, sits precariously between these two extremes: it can be reassuringly normative or dangerously singular. On the one hand, doubt is an experience common to all believers, and an autobiographer's descriptions of his struggles with doubt can contribute to an impression of authenticity. On the other hand, doubt can destroy the very grounds of belief and place him among the dangerous and unredeemable. Both Bunyan and Browne make nervous references to those whose doubts led them to despair, even as both men frame their own experiences as triumphs over such dangers. Bunyan twice references Francis Spira, an

---

[38] Browne, *Religio Medici*, 1.3.
[39] Browne, *Religio Medici*, 1.4.
[40] Browne, *Religio Medici*, 1.5.
[41] Browne, *Religio Medici*, 1.9.
[42] Browne, *Religio Medici*, 1.58.
[43] Browne, *Religio Medici*, sigs. Av–A2r.

Italian apostate who believed himself to have committed the sin against the Holy Ghost and died in despair, allegedly by suicide.[44] And Browne, though insisting that his own doubts have never led him into danger, acknowledges that some are not so lucky. He mentions 'a Doctor in Physick of Italy' and a French 'Divine and man of singular parts' who could not accept the immortality of the soul; despite the efforts of their friends, nothing anyone could say could 'expell the poyson of [their] errour'.[45]

Given these dangers, early modern autobiographers circumscribe their own experiences of doubt in a variety of ways in order to contain and defuse their seriousness. Bunyan's doubts during the long central portion of *Grace Abounding* are lurid and compulsive, practically leaping from the page. But these are placed in the past, and the conclusion of each one comes triumphantly. Bunyan does admit to having had doubts since then, including depressive periods in prison, but those he deals with briskly. As he says in what are virtually the last lines of his autobiography proper, all his trials have left his 'heart full of comfort' because of the 'teaching' he has had by them.[46] Browne does something similar. Though he declares that 'no man hath knowne' more doubts than he, Browne claims that he conquered them—past tense—'not in a martiall posture, but on my knees'.[47] He will go on to itemize a few of these doubts, noting that scholars are particularly susceptible because the devil prompts them to consider natural explanations for seeming miracles in scripture, such as the fire that consumed Sodom and Gomorrah. However, he never gives the sense that he was ever in great danger, nor do the kinds of doubts he describes as troubling himself or other scholars—such as where Lazarus's soul went in the interim between his death and resurrection, or how Noah could have fit all the animals into the ark along with enough food to maintain them—seem very serious. Browne himself dismisses them as 'nicities' and 'paradoxes' that cannot be proven or disproven.[48]

But despite their authors' attempts to downplay the seriousness of their doubts, early modern religious autobiographies often reveal their uncertainties about fundamental Christian beliefs. Not only are Bunyan's doubts not completely past—he mentions them even in the very last lines of *Grace Abounding*, albeit in passages that are less vivid than those in the central portion of the work—but they are also not merely *personal* doubts about whether he himself has merited (or thrown away) salvation. Early in the work Bunyan describes his younger self wondering whether Christians 'were of the Israelites, or no', and thus truly God's chosen people, and becoming disconsolate when his father tells him otherwise.[49] Even as he grows in faith, he wonders whether it might be possible

---

[44] Bunyan, *Grace Abounding*, §163, §179. Spira, a Lutheran who renounced his faith under pressure from the Inquisition, was a figure of terrified fascination for many seventeenth-century Protestants, and multiple books told his story. Bunyan's immediate source appears to be Nathaniel Bacon's *A Relation of the Fearful Estate of Francis Spira, in the Year 1548* (1649). For more on Spira's lasting influence on Bunyan, see Sharrock's edition of *Grace Abounding*, 146 n. 163.

[45] Browne, *Religio Medici*, 1.21.

[46] Bunyan, *Grace Abounding*, §339.

[47] Browne, *Religio Medici*, 1.14.

[48] Browne, *Religio Medici*, 1.22.

[49] Bunyan, *Grace Abounding*, §18.

that Mohammed was the saviour rather than Christ, for, as he reasons, 'everyone doth think his own religion rightest, both Jews, and Moors, and Pagans; and how if all our faith, and Christ, and Scriptures, should be but a think-so too?'[50] After receiving his initial assurance of election, Bunyan still periodically doubts 'whether ... there were no such thing' as God and 'no such thing as a Day of Judgement [and] that we should not rise again'.[51] In fact, the work ends with Bunyan's announcing that he still regularly doubts these things. In a separate, seven-paragraph section entitled 'The Conclusion', Bunyan writes 'Of all the temptations that ever I met with in my life, to question the being of God, and the truth of the Gospel, is the worst, and worst to be born. When this temptation comes, it ... removeth the very foundations from under me'.[52] A few paragraphs later he reiterates that he continues to struggle with 'inclinings to unbelief'.[53] These doubts about whether Jesus is the messiah or whether God even exists have received relatively little attention compared to Bunyan's doubts about his salvation, and *Grace Abounding* does work to downplay them, implying by their brief references that they are only fleeting or shallow fears. But this is not what the work *says*. Ultimately, we might see all of Bunyan's doubts as of a piece: doubts about Christianity's truth claims, like doubts about his own salvation, are all fears about not belonging to a community of saints that stretches across time and space.

Similar doubts appear in a range of early modern religious autobiographies. Although it would be absurd to claim that religious doubt is itself a product of the Reformation (on the evidence of the New Testament, believers have had trouble with many doctrines since the beginning), it may well be that the fragmentation of the church and the era's endless disputes over everything from the relative importance of faith and works to the proper form of church government left individuals more vulnerable to doubt; questions about seemingly minor matters of worship could open the door to larger questions about Christian history and even its very truth claims. The Quaker John Crook's autobiography, *A Short History of the Life of John Crook* (1706), hints at just such a progression. Like Trapnel and others, Crook was in his younger days troubled by 'many Questionings about the way of worship', and the Independent congregation he belonged to was so concerned about 'whether [they] were in the right Order of the Gospel' that they began to dispute among themselves. This led to 'Questionings about divers [other] things not at all questioned before', until eventually, as he reports, 'we began not only to be remiss in our Meetings, but also confused in our Preachings ... so that at last we did not meet at all'.[54] Crook claims that he overcame these doubts when he met the Quakers, who seemed to him 'like as if the old Apostles were again risen from the Dead', but not all autobiographers place their doubts as firmly in the past. Like Bunyan, Baxter admits

---

[50] Bunyan, *Grace Abounding*, §97.
[51] Bunyan, *Grace Abounding*, §101, 161; see also §240.
[52] Bunyan, *Grace Abounding*, Conclusion §1.
[53] Bunyan, *Grace Abounding*, Conclusion §6.
[54] John Crook, *A Short History*, in *Grace Abounding with Other Spiritual Autobiographies*, ed. John Stachniewski and Anita Pacheco (Oxford: Oxford University Press, 1998), 165–6.

that his are ongoing; in fact, he says that with age have come doubts about the very existence of God, which he never had in his youth.[55]

However, it is Browne whose doubts occupy a portion of his work that is most closely equivalent to the space taken up by Bunyan's. I have already noted the way Browne tries to distance himself from religious doubt, especially by implying that many doubts are essentially trivial and not fundamental to religious belief. But there are hints throughout the work that Browne is troubled by the nature of the Trinity (in particular, the problem of 'priority' among the three persons) and the question of whether the soul is mortal or immortal.[56] Unlike Bunyan he does not seem to question Christianity's superiority to Judaism or Islam, but the persistence and strength of those religions do trouble him, as does his belief that Christians are more prone to become Jews and Muslims than the other way around.[57] But Browne's most tenacious doubts seem to concern death, salvation, judgement, and resurrection; these occupy a large portion of the *Religio,* including a contiguous sequence of sections that amounts to approximately one-quarter of the entire work. And at moments the discussion feels as personal as it does in Bunyan.

Early in the *Religio* Browne identifies as one of his youthful 'heresies' the belief 'that God would not persist in his vengeance for ever, but after a definite time of his wrath he would release the damned soules from torture' (Browne 1.9), and toward the end of the work's first section he returns to this problem, fretting over how God can be both all just and all merciful and asserting that he 'desire[s] with God, that all, but yet affirme[s] with men, that few shall know salvation'.[58] The first part of this sentence is perfectly orthodox: God *desires* that all men should be saved, but because humans are depraved and turn away from him, not all can be saved. The second part is stranger: it is *men,* Browne says, not God, who affirm that few shall know salvation. Browne seems to get to have it both ways here, asserting both God's justice and his mercy, while leaving open the possibility that men are wrong and that it might, after all, be possible that 'after a definite time of his wrath' God will admit all to salvation. Indeed, in the next sentence Browne reproves 'those who doe confine the Church of God, either to particular Nations, Churches, or Families' for making God's kingdom 'farre narrower than our Saviour ever meant it'. Meditating upon how arrogantly Christians of various stripes assign others to salvation or damnation provokes a moment of seeming anxiety on Browne's part: 'That name and compellation of *little Flocke,* doth not comfort but deject my devotion, especially when I reflect upon mine owne unworthinesse, wherein, according to my humble apprehensions, I am below them all.'[59] In the next section, he returns to this issue, seemingly feeling that it is unresolved: 'Againe,' he says, as the first sentence in this section, 'I am confident, and fully persuaded, yet dare not take my oath of my salvation; I am as it were sure, and do beleeve, without all doubt, that there is such a City as *Constantinople,*

---

[55] Baxter, *Reliquiae Baxterianae,* 127.
[56] Browne, *Religio Medici,* 1.7, 12, 36, 37.
[57] Browne, *Religio Medici,* 1.25.
[58] Browne, *Religio Medici,* 1.9, 1.53.
[59] Browne, *Religio Medici,* 1.56.

yet for me to take my oath thereon, were a kinde of perjury, because I hold no infallible warrant from my owne sense to confirme me in the certainty thereof."[60] This is different in tone from Bunyan's obsessive and almost hallucinatory fears about his salvation, but not necessarily different in substance. Nonconformists, after all, were not the only Christians to doubt their salvation, nor the only ones to use autobiography to work through those anxieties and assert, if only by implication, their membership in a universal and transhistorical church.

What early modern religious autobiography demonstrates is how many Christians, in the wake of the Reformation, sought an identity that linked them to a community larger than any available in the present day. It is not that seventeenth-century Christians were the first to look backward and seek connections with their forebears in the faith; but in an age of division and when one's own immediate ancestors were compromised by their participation in an un- or imperfectly reformed church (or an apostate one), reconnecting with more distant ancestors may have felt all the more urgent. Religious autobiography is thus both a response to religious upheaval and an attempt to transcend it through the assertion of a common Christian identity. However, as we have seen, both the form in which an autobiographer expresses that identity and the nature and authenticity of that shared experience may themselves be as disputable as any of the practices and institutions debated in the wake of the Reformation.

---

[60] Browne, *Religio Medici*, 1.56.

CHAPTER 33

SCIENTIFIC TRANSACTIONS

FELICITY HENDERSON

> ... each Page in the great Volume of Nature is full of real Hieroglyphicks, where (by an inverted way of Expression) Things stand for Words, and their Qualities for Letters.[1]

THE relationship between words and things occupied writers of scientific texts perhaps more than any other writers in the early modern period.[2] Their investigations into the 'great Volume of Nature', as Robert Boyle suggested, opened up to them a world in which things had meanings beyond those traditionally assigned to them in biblical or classical sources. For those who could learn to read the 'real Hieroglyphicks' of the natural world, untold secrets awaited.[3] Yet bringing those secrets to light would require translating them into words—spoken, written, and printed. Just as there was not yet an established method of doing science, nor was there an agreed format for communicating science. The written 'scientific transactions' of the period took place in a heterodox array of forms—notebooks, letters, reports and eye-witness accounts, dialogues, collections of aphorisms, mathematical proofs, museum catalogues, natural history taxonomies, books of recipes or secrets, pharmacopoeias, journal articles and book reviews, printed books, lists and tables of data, diaries or day-books—and other forms not easily classified. Scientific writing was protean, easily morphing into (or out of) theological

---

[1] Robert Boyle, 'The Usefulness of Natural Philosophy', in Michael Hunter and Edward B. Davis (eds.), *The Works of Robert Boyle, Volume 3: The Usefulness of Natural Philosophy and sequels to Spring of the Air, 1662–3* (London: Pickering and Chatto, 1999), 232.

[2] A note on terminology: the words 'science', and 'scientific' were not used in their modern sense in this period (terms such as 'natural knowledge', 'new philosophy', or 'experimental philosophy' were used to describe knowledge gained by methods we would now broadly understand as scientific). I have used them here, though, because they are more immediately comprehensible for a wide audience.

[3] On the 'characters' to be found in natural forms, see also Robert Hooke, *Micrographia* (1665), 154.

discourse, fiction, utopian writing, travel accounts, or philosophical tracts depending on the aims of the author and, in part, the intended audience. The scientific revolution had been gathering pace since the sixteenth century, but for many of those not directly involved, science still seemed a useless endeavour, or worse, one that was distinctly irreligious. Scientific writers needed to tackle these underlying concerns if they wanted to communicate their ideas to a more general audience.

This was also the period when Europe's scientific societies began to be founded and to produce texts of their own. In England, a small group of scientific gentlemen began meeting in London in 1660 to discuss the 'new philosophy'. With the assent of Charles II, newly restored to the throne, these Fellows took the name of the Royal Society of London for Improving Natural Knowledge. The Royal Society began its own regime of record-keeping and information-gathering, and lent its name to the first scientific journal, the *Philosophical Transactions of the Royal Society*, founded in 1665.[4] The Society quickly became an information hub for those who wanted to make and share their own experiments and observations, or to keep up with new developments. Although of course there were scientific writers in the period who were not Fellows, many of the writers whose works I discuss below were connected to the Society in some way. The Fellows were completely aware of the indifference or outright ridicule their endeavours met with amongst their peers, but at the same time they were far too excited about their discoveries not to want to share them as widely as possible. For some, this meant reforming the English language at the same time as reforming natural knowledge.[5]

New Philosophy, New Prose?

Perhaps the most frequently cited statement about scientific prose in the early modern period is Thomas Sprat's assertion that the Royal Society Fellows had resolved to

> reject all the Amplification, Digressions, and Swellings of Style; to return back to the primitive Purity and Shortness, when Men deliver'd so many *Things*, almost in an equal Number of *Words*. They have exacted from all their Members, a close, naked, natural way of Speaking; positive Expressions, clear Senses; a native Easiness; bringing all Things as near the mathematical Plainness as they can; and preferring

---

[4] The French *Journal des Sçavans* appeared slightly earlier in 1665 but had a much wider subject range; for the *Philosophical Transactions* see Noah Moxham, 'Fit for Print: Developing an Institutional Model of Scientific Periodical Publishing in England, 1665-ca. 1714', *Notes and Records of the Royal Society*, 69 (2015), 241–60.

[5] For the attempts of Royal Society Fellows and others to reform language in the period, see Rhodri Lewis, *Language, Mind and Nature: Artificial Languages in England from Bacon to Locke* (Cambridge: Cambridge University Press, 2007); Francis Lodwick, *On Language, Theology, and Utopia*, ed. Felicity Henderson and William Poole (Oxford: Oxford University Press, 2011).

the Language of Artizans, Countrymen, and Merchants, before that of Wits, or Scholars.[6]

This was the only remedy, Sprat assured his readers, for 'the Luxury and Redundance of *Speech*' which had infected 'most other parts of Learning'.[7] This and similar statements elsewhere led some modern critics to argue that early modern scientific writers generally advocated a plain style and rejected rhetoric.[8] However, the evidence of their actual writing suggests otherwise, as other critics have pointed out in the course of various arguments against a straightforward equation of science with a plain style.[9] The quest to understand this apparent contradiction between scientific writers' ostensible rejection, and continued use, of rhetoric in their work continues.[10] Sprat's comments highlight some of the concerns felt by scientific writers at the time. It was agreed that the tricks and flourishes of rhetoric could be used to persuade listeners (or readers) by appealing to the emotions rather than to reason. Skill in rhetoric was strongly associated with a style of scholastic argument whose protagonists were more interested in chopping logic and scoring points than arriving at an essential truth. And when used as mere decoration, rhetorical devices were empty and thus counter to the somewhat utilitarian ideals espoused by the early Royal Society (particularly evident in Sprat's work, as the previous quote shows). However, even a very cursory inspection of the early Fellows' prose demonstrates their continued use of rhetoric both as an explanatory tool (by using, for example, metaphors and 'similitudes' to underpin scientific arguments) and for more ornamental purposes. For the most part trained at the English universities, it should come as no surprise that scientific writers used the literary techniques with which they were familiar from their extensive classical reading.[11]

---

[6] Thomas Sprat, *The History of the Royal Society of London* (1667), 113.

[7] Sprat, *History*, 111, 112.

[8] The most influential exponent was Richard F. Jones: see in particular his 'Science and English Prose Style in the Third Quarter of the Seventeenth Century', *Publications of the Modern Language Association*, 45 (1930), 977–1009.

[9] Brian Vickers, 'The Royal Society and English Prose Style: A Reassessment', in Brian Vickers and Nancy S. Struever (eds.), *Rhetoric and the Pursuit of Truth: Language Change in the Seventeenth and Eighteenth Centuries* (Los Angeles, CA: William Andrews Clark Memorial Library, 1985), 1–76; Claire Preston, 'English Scientific Prose: Bacon, Browne, Boyle', in Andrew Hadfield (ed.), *The Oxford Handbook of English Prose 1500–1640* (Oxford: Oxford University Press, 2013), 268–91; Richard Nate, 'Rhetoric in the Early Royal Society', in Tina Skouen and Ryan J. Stark (eds.), *Rhetoric and the Early Royal Society: A Sourcebook* (Leiden: Brill, 2014), 77–93; John T. Harwood, 'Rhetoric and Graphics in *Micrographia*', in Michael Hunter and Simon Schaffer (eds.), *Robert Hooke: New Studies* (Woodbridge: The Boydell Press, 1989), 119–47.

[10] Recent contributions include Ryan J. Stark, 'Language Reform in the Late Seventeenth Century', in Skouen and Stark (eds.), *Rhetoric and the Early Royal Society*, 94–127; David Burchell, '"A Plain Blunt Man": Hobbes, Science, and Rhetoric Revisited', in Juliet Cummins and David Burchell (eds.), *Science, Literature and Rhetoric in Early Modern England* (Aldershot: Ashgate, 2007), 52–72.

[11] See in particular Claire Preston, *The Poetics of Scientific Investigation in Seventeenth-Century England* (Oxford: Oxford University Press, 2015).

A preference for 'mathematical Plainness' as a prose style did not necessarily mean similarly pared-back content in scientific writing. Nehemiah Grew, introducing his catalogue of the Royal Society's museum collection, noted that some readers might think his descriptions of the museum artefacts unnecessarily long. Not so, claimed Grew. In Pliny's *Natural History*, though commendable, the entries are so brief as to be 'rather a *Nomenclature*, than a History'. If Pliny, and other writers of natural histories had

> been more particular in the Matters they treat of: their Commentators had engaged their own and their Readers Time much better, than in so many fruitless and endless Disquisitions and Contests. It were certainly a Thing both in it self Desirable, and of much Consequence; To have such an Inventory of Nature, wherein, as on the one hand, nothing should be Wanting; so nothing Repeated or Confounded, on the other. For which, there is no way without a cleer and full Description of Things.
>
> Besides, that in such Descriptions, many Particulars relating to the Nature and Use of Things, will occur to the Authors mind, which otherwise he would never have thought of. And may give occasion to his Readers, for the consideration of many more.[12]

Grew's advocacy for plenitude over brevity was founded on a conviction that a more detailed description would not only be more useful for both authors and readers but would also be clearer and would thus avoid the kinds of quibbling over meanings that had taken the place of proper scientific research in the previous centuries. Modern critics have also seen this kind of 'full Description', particularly when used to recount experimental procedures, as a way for scientific writers to develop a new form of authority. Historians of science have argued that experimental results (or 'matters of fact', in contemporary language) had to be agreed upon by multiple witnesses in order for them to attain the status of evidence. In an influential account of Robert Boyle's writing practices, Steven Shapin argued that Boyle's densely circumstantial accounts of his experiments were attempts to enlist his readers as 'virtual' witnesses of these experiments, by creating a very vivid image of them in the reader's mind.[13]

Boyle himself, in the preface 'To the Reader' of his *New Experiments Physico-Mechanical, Touching the Spring of the Air and its Effects* (Oxford, 1660), gave four reasons for being 'somewhat prolix'. The experiments being quite new, he felt they needed to be 'circumstantially related, to keep the Reader from distrusting them'; he recorded the details 'for fear of forgetting them'; and in some cases his intention was to enable readers to repeat the experiments. Most commonly, though, he intended his rich, detailed descriptions to do away with the necessity of replication: knowing the difficulty and expense of preparing the experiments, he hoped that by 'punctually relating' what

---

[12] Nehemiah Grew, *Musaeum Regalis Societatis* (1681), sig. [A4]r–v (italics reversed).

[13] Steven Shapin, 'Pump and Circumstance: Robert Boyle's Literary Technology', *Social Studies of Science*, 14 (1984), 481–520. See also Steven Shapin and Simon Schaffer, *Leviathan and the Air-Pump: Hobbes, Boyle, and the Experimental Life* (Princeton, NJ: Princeton University Press, 1985; rev. edn 2011), esp. 60–4.

he had carefully observed, his readers might 'look upon these Narratives as standing Records in our new Pneumaticks, and need not reiterate themselves an Experiment to have as distinct an Idea of it, as may suffice them to ground their Reflections and Speculations upon'.[14] As Shapin argued, Boyle needed to present himself as a reliable narrator if he wanted his readers to take his 'Narratives' as 'standing Records'. Thus his authorial persona, and choices about tone and form, were also influenced by the intention that his narratives stand as evidence.

Robert Boyle's self-proclaimed 'prolix' prose style should not be taken as representative of the entire field of scientific writers, but, as the quotation from Nehemiah Grew suggests, he was not alone in his belief that seemingly small details were important. We should look beyond the notion of virtual witnessing at a range of factors that may have influenced this belief. Francis Bacon's insistence that common, everyday things were just as significant as the exotic or unusual was widely repeated by early modern scientific authors, who reminded their readers not to lose sight of such things just because they were very familiar.[15] Writers were probably also drawing on older models of proof, such as the classical notion of 'circumstances' as the foundation for persuasive arguments, including those presented in legal cases.[16] As Boyle has demonstrated, scientific writers acknowledged that no one really knew which details of an observation were going to be significant and so it made sense to retain as much information as possible, for themselves as much as for anyone else. Finally, as Shapin and other critics have stressed in their discussions, the social context of early modern science was important. There was a sense in which English authors wanted readers to be 'virtual actors' rather than virtual witnesses.[17] By asking readers to enter the experimental scene, writers hoped to engender a sense of involvement in the scientific enterprise in order to swell the ranks of their supporters and encourage others to experiment for themselves.

The social world of early modern science has been seen to influence scientific prose in other ways. Again largely drawing on Boyle as an exemplar, Steven Shapin has argued that one method of establishing authority for early modern science was by ensuring the English scientific community conformed to the standards of conduct expected from English gentlemen: specifically with regard to disinterested behaviour, truth-telling, and politeness.[18] Politeness was particularly important when it came to entering into scientific disputes, especially those played out through the medium of print. Shapin

---

[14] Robert Boyle, *New Experiments Physico-Mechanical* (1660), in Michael Hunter and Edward B. Davis (eds.), *The Works of Robert Boyle, Volume 1: General Introduction, Textual Note, Publications to 1660* (London: Pickering and Chatto, 1999), 143–4.

[15] See Robert Hooke, 'A General Scheme, or, Idea of the Present State of Natural Philosophy', in Richard Waller (ed.), *The Posthumous Works of Dr Robert Hooke* (1705), 27.

[16] For this see Lorna Hutson, *Circumstantial Shakespeare* (Oxford: Oxford University Press, 2015), esp. 2, 57–8.

[17] Shapin uses this phrase in 'Pump and Circumstance', 511.

[18] As argued by Steven Shapin, *A Social History of Truth: Civility and Science in Seventeenth-Century England* (Chicago: University of Chicago Press, 1994). For a refutation, see Mordechai Feingold, 'When Facts Matter', *Isis*, 87 (1996), 131–9.

pointed out Boyle's instructions for the management of disputes, which included urging philosophers to avoid *ad hominem* attacks and instead to concentrate on calmly refuting incorrect assertions. Indeed Shapin argued that the structure of Boyle's *The Skeptical Chymist* (1661), written in the form of a conversation between several proponents of opposing scientific theories, was intended to guide philosophers in their real-life conduct.[19] Though not uniformly practised, there were certainly good reasons for the English scientific community to avoid controversy in print. They were small in number and their endeavours were routinely ridiculed by onlookers: internal tensions, especially those played out publicly, weakened the enterprise even further.[20] In post-Civil War England, there was a strong sense that divisions needed to be healed rather than exacerbated, and at least some of the founding Royal Society Fellows saw science as a calm and rational escape from political or theological bickering.[21] Rejecting argument may also have been linked with the rejection of scholastic debate, which was seen as empty point-scoring that did nothing to advance real knowledge. So, while most early modern scientists would have thought of themselves as gentlemen, and in general scientific writers avoided fierce dissent, it is not really necessary to attribute such avoidance to social status.

SCIENTIFIC STYLE IN PRACTICE

When discussing the 'scientific' style in early modern English texts, critics have tended to focus on a few key figures: Robert Boyle, in particular, but also Francis Bacon, Thomas Browne, and Isaac Newton.[22] Boyle's status as a major figure in English science, and its most prolific publisher in this period, means that he is hard to ignore. However, he may have exercised more of an influence over his twentieth-century commentators than he did over the prose style of his contemporaries: no one else had quite the same gift for involved phrasing. His approach to writing has been described as 'additive' or

---

[19] Shapin, 'Pump and Circumstance', 503–4.
[20] See Adrian Johns, *The Nature of the Book: Print and Knowledge in the Making* (Chicago: University of Chicago Press, 1998), 543–621. See also Chapter 24 on 'Mock-Scientific Literature' by Gregory Lynall.
[21] See, for example, Sprat, *History*, 53–6.
[22] On Boyle, see Shapin, 'Pump and Circumstance'; Jan V. Golinski, 'Robert Boyle: Scepticism and Authority in Seventeenth-Century Chemical Discourse', in Andrew E. Benjamin, Geoffrey N. Cantor, and John R. R. Christie (eds.), *The Figural and the Literal: Problems of Language in the History of Science and Philosophy, 1630–1800* (Manchester: Manchester University Press, 1987), 58–82, John T. Harwood, 'Science Writing and Writing Science: Boyle and Rhetorical Theory', in Michael Hunter (ed.), *Robert Boyle Reconsidered* (Cambridge: Cambridge University Press, 1994), 37–56; on Browne, see Claire Preston, *Thomas Browne and the Writing of Early Modern Science* (Cambridge: Cambridge University Press, 2005) and Preston, *The Poetics of Scientific Investigation*, 34–67; Lara Dodds, '"Art and Fallacy" or "The Naked Offer"? Style and Science in Sir Thomas Browne's *Pseudodoxia Epidemica*', *Prose Studies*, 28 (2006), 222–33; on Newton see Alan G. Gross, 'On the Shoulders of Giants: Seventeenth-Century Optics as an Argument Field', *Quarterly Journal of Speech*, 74 (1988), 1–17.

'incremental', meaning that he preferred 'loosely structured discourses' that enabled him to add or rearrange material if necessary.[23] He was more willing to discuss his style than many of his colleagues. He remarked at the outset of *Certain Physiological Essays* (1661): 'as for the style of our Experimental Essaies, I suppose you will readily find that I have endeavour'd to write rather in a Philosophical than a Rhetorical strain, as desiring that my Expressions should be rather clear and significant, than curiously adorn'd.' He explained this with the comment that since here he aimed simply to 'inform Readers, not to delight or perswade them', 'Perspicuity' should be seen as one of the best features of his style. Boyle's justification for his style here is linked with his intention to inform, rather than to entertain or persuade; he did not rule out rhetorical flourishes altogether, but reserved them for a different purpose.[24]

Other writers approached their task differently. Thomas Browne, whose writings continued to be popular throughout this period, used a rich allusive language peppered with neologisms. His style is witty and meditative, and despite his famous project to eradicate error, he was fascinated by stories, Biblical, mythical, and local. Often these stories were his point of entry into a discussion of scientific content. Newton, in contrast, writing in English later in the period (following earlier publications in Latin), expressed himself as economically as possible. His *Opticks* (1704) begins with a series of definitions, followed by axioms: 'the summ of what hath hitherto been treated of in Opticks'; before moving on to the more advanced section of his text, divided into 'Propositions' that were each backed up with 'The Proof by Experiments'. Newton's style here is straightforward and matter-of-fact: he was not required to invent new words, and he described a pared-back, idealized version of the experiment rather than Boyle's very circumstantial account of a specific occasion: 'In a very dark Chamber at a round hole about one third part of an Inch broad made in the Shut of a Window I placed a Glass Prism, whereby the beam of the Sun's Light which came in at that hole might be refracted upwards toward the opposite Wall of the Chamber, and there form a coloured Image of the Sun.'[25] Newton routinely used the indefinite article for his experimental apparatus, suggesting that any dark chamber, prism, and window might be used to confirm his findings.[26] The experiment was universal, but the experience recounted here was still firmly Newton's, stamped with the authority of 'I'. In the *Opticks*, Newton linked his prose style with his pedagogic aim: '... in the Description of these Experiments, I have set down such Circumstances by which either the Phænomenon might be rendred more conspicuous, or a Novice might more easily try them, or by which I did try them only.'[27]

---

[23] Harwood, 'Science Writing and Writing Science', 46–7.

[24] On this see Nate, 'Rhetoric in the early Royal Society'.

[25] Isaac Newton, *Opticks, or, A Treatise of the Reflexions, Refractions, Inflexions and Colours of Light* (1704), I.18. Newton does occasionally use 'my... Chamber' in the *Opticks* (see, for example, II.114), but these instances are rare.

[26] Peter Dear has cited the text of Newton's lectures at Cambridge to make the same point. See Dear, 'Totius in verba', 155; Isaac Newton, *Optical Lectures Read in the Publick Schools of the University of Cambridge* (1728), 7.

[27] Newton, *Opticks*, I.17.

Yet this was not the first time that Newton had described an experiment with a prism in a darkened room, and an earlier iteration reads very differently. In a letter dated 6 February 1672, Newton wrote:

> I procured me a Triangular glass-Prisme, to try therewith the celebrated *Phænomena of Colours*. And in order thereto having darkened my chamber, and made a small hole in my window-shuts, to let in a convenient quantity of the Suns light, I placed my Prisme at his entrance, that it might be thereby refracted to the opposite wall. It was at first a very pleasing divertisement, to view the vivid and intense colours produced thereby; but after a while applying my self to consider them more circumspectly, I became surprised to see them in an *oblong* form; which, according to the received laws of Refraction, I expected should have been *circular*.[28]

In this account Newton is much more present, and his initial emotions of pleasure and surprise are as significant a part of the experiment's outcome as the further investigation prompted by his rational self. Yet, as Peter Dear has pointed out, historians agree that Newton's experiments with light were conducted over a number of years and therefore both of these narratives describing a single experience were in some sense false. Dear argued that the Royal Society required Newton, and other writers, to describe their experiments or observations as discrete events, because '[t]he specificity and consequent verisimilitude of the presentation lent the described experience an authority functionally equivalent to, but different from, that deriving from the use of an authoritative ancient text'.[29] Thus Dear links form and function in a way that emphasizes the need for early modern scientific writers to establish their authority.

By concentrating on the printed works of just two high-profile authors associated with the Royal Society, we risk being unrepresentative.[30] If we include the works of other active Royal Society Fellows and authors such as John Evelyn, John Ray, Martin Lister, Robert Hooke, John Wilkins, Joseph Glanvill, John Aubrey, and Nehemiah Grew, we find a wide variety of styles, but we also find points of comparison. One common thread, clearly, is the requirement to establish a new form of authority for the new philosophy. Shapin and Dear have suggested some ways in which the form and content of scientific prose works were shaped by this necessity; other aspects worth considering here include the narrative voice or authorial persona, strategies for presenting evidence, and references to other texts.[31] A preference for clarity over ornamentation is another common theme, although as we have seen this could be interpreted in various ways by different authors. As with more literary writing, the intended audience for scientific works influenced authorial choices about tone and

---

[28] Isaac Newton, 'A Letter of Mr. Isaac Newton ... containing his New Theory about Light and Colors', *Philosophical Transactions*, 6 (1671), 3075–6.

[29] Dear, 'Totius in verba', 154.

[30] Sir Thomas Browne was never officially a Fellow of the Royal Society, although his son Edward was, and Sir Thomas was well-connected with the London philosophers.

[31] On techniques for establishing authority in printed texts see also Johns, *Nature of the Book*.

style. Some texts were written primarily for consumption in the context of the Royal Society meetings—Newton's letter to Oldenburg, quoted above, is an example, and this perhaps explains its slightly more conversational style compared with Newton's later printed account of the same experiment. Boyle's printed works were intended for a somewhat wider audience of virtuosi and gentlemen interested in the latest discoveries of the new philosophy.[32] Robert Hooke's lavishly illustrated *Micrographia* (1665) was written in response to a request from Charles II, and here Hooke's prose seems designed to appeal to an even wider proportion of the book-buying public, with its many metaphors, its lyrical descriptions of the microscopic world, and its occasional jokes. Other texts, such as John Beale's aphorisms on cider, discussed below, suggest their authors may have intended them for a more practical instruction to yeomen, artisans, or merchants, although it is difficult to ascertain whether they were indeed read more widely.

Prose Forms

While scientific writers were broadly in agreement that their prose should make its point clearly and with a minimum of ornamentation, there was no real drive towards standardisation of form in this period. The book-length, printed treatise dealing with a single scientific topic was actually something of a rarity, its numbers dwarfed by communications in other formats, including letters, short reports, collections of aphorisms, dialogues, answers to queries, catalogues, tables, and lists, in both manuscript and print. For the moment I am deliberately excluding 'journal article' as a form, because even after the establishment of Henry Oldenburg's journal *Philosophical Transactions* in 1665, the idea of writing a piece of text specifically and solely for printing in the journal was slow to gain ground in the philosophical community. Most of the texts that were printed in the *Philosophical Transactions* in this period were either read and discussed at a meeting of the Royal Society or had been sent to the Society's secretary or another Fellow with the intention that they would be presented at a meeting in this way. The relationship between oral and written prose will be discussed below, but here I would like to concentrate on three formats: the scientific report, which recorded experiments or observations; the aphorism; and the descriptive catalogue. Each of these attempted to do something different, indicating some of the ways in which scientific prose could adapt to individual notions of scientific method.

When the Herefordshire-born divine and agriculturalist John Beale sent his recommendations about growing cider-apples to the Royal Society in 1662, they arrived in the form of fifty-seven aphorisms. Printed as an appendix to John Evelyn's *Sylva*

---

[32] On the publication of Boyle's works see Hunter and Davis, 'General Introduction', in *Works of Robert Boyle, Volume 1*, pp. xxi–lxxxviii.

(1664), the aphorisms are a series of numbered paragraphs, beginning: 'He that would treat exactly of *Cider* and *Perry* must lay his foundation so deep as to begin with the *Soyl*: For as no Culture or Graffs [i.e. Grafts] will exalt the *French Wines* to compare with the *Wines* of *Greece, Canaries*, and *Montefiasco*; so neither will the *Cider* of *Bromyard* and *Ledbury* equal that of *Allensmore, Ham-lacy*, and *Kings-Capell* in the same small County of *Hereford*.'[33] While we might not consider this to be short and pithy enough to warrant the name aphorism, Beale does in general present one key point in each. His intentions, however, were not quite as overbearing as the form might suggest. Evelyn felt it necessary to add a note to the beginning of the aphorisms, explaining that they were not intended to be '*dogmatical*, or arrogant'; rather, they were 'but occasional *Papers*... they do not pretend to fine, and elaborate *Methods*, but to the *Things* as they may be of use, and are in their kind considerable'.[34] Beale was not alone in his choice of the aphorism: presumably influenced by him, Richard Haines published in 1684 *Aphorisms upon the New Way of Improving Cyder, or making Cyder-royal*; the astrologer and meteorologist John Goad distilled decades of weather observations into *Astro-Meteorologica, or, Aphorisms and Discourses of the Bodies Cœlestial, their Natures and Influences* (1686), and Flemish physician and alchemist Franciscus Mercurius van Helmont's *CLIII Aphorismi Chemici* (Amsterdam, 1688) was quickly translated into English as *One Hundred Fifty Three Chymical Aphorisms, Briefly Containing Whatsoever Belongs to the Chymical Science* (1688).[35]

While van Helmont's work points to parallel traditions of aphorism-writing elsewhere, contemporary English readers of Beale, Haines, and Goad would have recognized a conscious nod to Francis Bacon, who promoted the form in several of his works. He famously referred to the aphorism as 'a knowledge broken', to be preferred to the polished treatise because the former (by its unfinished nature) invited or provoked the reader to further research whereas the latter discouraged it.[36] The aphorism was a form that allowed, even encouraged, recombination and reconfiguration of the material presented to the reader, potentially opening up fruitful new avenues of research. It was also seen as a productive form for writers on political, theological, and legal matters—a connection with the world of affairs that perhaps appealed to Beale in particular, whose treatise was intended to advance the agricultural economy of England.[37] Thus while not taken up extensively by scientific writers, aphorism as a form points to the continuing

---

[33] John Beale, 'Aphorisms Concerning Cider', in John Evelyn, *Sylva, or, A Discourse of Forest-Trees* (1664), 21 (second pagination). Montefiascone is a wine-producing town in central Italy.

[34] John Evelyn, 'Animadversion', *Sylva, or, A Discourse of Forest-Trees* (1664), sig. [π]1r (italics reversed).

[35] On Goad, see Patrick Curry, entry for 'Goad, John (1616–89)', *ODNB*.

[36] *The Oxford Francis Bacon, Volume 4: The Advancement of Learning*, ed. Michael Kiernan (Oxford: Oxford University Press, 2000), 124; see also Alvin Snider, 'Francis Bacon and the Authority of Aphorism', *Prose Studies*, 11 (1988), 60–71; Brian Vickers, *Francis Bacon and Renaissance Prose* (Cambridge: Cambridge University Press, 1968), esp. 60–95.

[37] Snider, 'Bacon and Aphorism', 66; Reid Barbour, 'The Power of the Broken: Sir Thomas Browne's *Religio Medici* and Aphoristic Writing', *Huntington Library Quarterly*, 79 (2016), 591–610, esp. 596.

Baconianism of early modern science, and the attempt to communicate in a way that reflected this.[38]

If the aphorism was a form which communicated knowledge largely based on the personal observation and long experience of its author, we might see the descriptive natural history or museum catalogue as its polar opposite. This popular Renaissance genre traditionally gathered together the opinions of as many authorities as possible, combing through classical, patristic, and modern works in order to compare names, descriptions, and attributes of plants and animals. The resulting compendia were encyclopaedic volumes which very often added little new material to the information they gathered from their sources. The new emphasis on direct observation, however, had an effect here too, and writers of natural history catalogues from later in the period were keen to distance themselves from their unscientific predecessors. In the preface to *The Ornithology of Francis Willughby* (1678), Willughby's posthumous editor John Ray explained that the book's aim was to describe and classify each species of birds accurately, but that

> we have wholly omitted what we find in other Authors concerning *Homonymous* and *Synonymous* words, or the divers names of Birds, *Hieroglyphics, Emblems, Morals, Fables, Presages*, or ought else appertaining to *Divinity, Ethics, Grammar*, or any sort of Humane Learning: And present [the Reader] only with what properly relates to their Natural History. Neither have we scraped together whatever of this nature is any where extant, but have used choice, and inserted only such particulars as our selves can warrant upon our own knowledge and experience, or whereof we have assurance by the testimony of good Authors, or sufficient Witnesses.[39]

They also deliberately ignored any previous errors, thinking it enough to present the correct descriptions in their own volume. As for style, Ray says they had taken 'greater care to render the Sense perspicuous than the Language ornate'. Thus they were working in what we can see becoming the stated norm for scientific writing: stripping out off-topic material pertaining to 'Humane Learning'; stating only what they know, or are assured is correct; and focusing more on clarity than ornamentation. Even in the deliberately narrow bounds of the catalogue entry, however, we still see scope for imagination. Among the first entries in Nehemiah Grew's catalogue of the Royal Society's 'repository' of natural and man-made artefacts were descriptions of a male and female skeleton. Having pointed out that the male's jaw was larger, as suited a body capable of harder work than the female's, he also mentioned that the male skeleton's skull was much larger than the female's, 'and so capable of more Brains'. Rather than finishing on this prosaic note, however, he added a final thought: 'Although a little House may be well

---

[38] Scholars have debated the extent to which the early modern experimental philosophers actually followed Bacon's methods, but the Royal Society as an institution, and many of its Fellows, certainly endorsed Baconian science. See William T. Lynch, 'A Society of Baconians? The Collective Development of Bacon's Method in the Royal Society of London', in Julie Robin Solomon and Catherine Gimelli Martin (eds.), *Francis Bacon and the Refiguring of Early Modern Thought* (London: Routledge, 2016), 173–202.

[39] Francis Willughby, *The Ornithology of Francis Willughby* (London, 1678), sig. [AA2]r.

furnished, and look better than a great one that stands empty.'[40] Even with a focus firmly on observable features and their logical interpretation, the opportunity to make a moral point remained.

Given the range of activities that constituted the scientific endeavour in the period, it is not surprising that a range of prose forms were employed to describe them. However, the majority of communications within the scientific community fall into the (very loose) category of what we might call the scientific report. This was a factual account of anything from observations of microscopic objects to calculations of astronomical distances, and along with the subject matter the style of these communications varied enormously. Many such reports were sent in the form of letters to scientific colleagues, and were thus influenced to a certain extent by the norms that governed epistolary prose in the period.[41] Some were discrete texts, others conceived as part of a series; some brief, others long; some intended as a personal memorandum, others for wider dissemination. With such a vast array of texts in circulation, it is perhaps unwise to place too much emphasis on any common features that might be discerned: the key point should be that this was not yet a stable form, and it was one that could slip in any number of directions, as shall be discussed below. If there was a process of standardisation beginning to take place, it can most clearly be seen in the journal begun by Henry Oldenburg and carried on by successive Royal Society secretaries, the *Philosophical Transactions*.

As the Royal Society's secretary, one of Oldenburg's main tasks was to manage the institution's ever-expanding correspondence with philosophers in Britain and beyond. This correspondence formed the basis for his journal, the first issue of which appeared in March 1665. Despite the close connection between the Society and the *Philosophical Transactions*, it was initially Oldenburg's journal, not a corporate endeavour of the Society's. Oldenburg was at pains to point this out in a dedicatory epistle accompanying his first volume, where he called the *Transactions* 'Rude Collections ... the Gleanings of my *private* diversions', which should in no way be taken as the whole output of the Society.[42] Oldenburg's short introduction to the first issue stressed the importance of communication for the scientific endeavour, and expressed the hope that reading about 'progress' and 'attempts', as well as new discoveries, would encourage those 'addicted to and conversant in such matters' to continue their work.[43] The narrative voice is often Oldenburg's, relating the contents of letters or reports read to the Society, but he also printed extracts and thus retained the original narrator's voice. Oldenburg's editorial hand, though, still shaped the journal. He chose the material for inclusion, selecting extracts from longer texts as necessary. He introduced the articles, very often introducing their authors and explaining the circumstances of composition or reception at the same time: for example, a typical article begins 'This Relation was ... made to

---

[40] Nehemiah Grew, *Musaeum Regalis Societatis, or, A Catalogue and Description of the Natural and Artificial Rarities belonging to the Royal Society and Preserved at Gresham Colledge* (1681), 6.
[41] See Chapter 22 on 'Letters' by Diana G. Barnes.
[42] 'To the Royal Society', *Philosophical Transactions*, 1 (1665–6), sig. [π]r (italics reversed).
[43] 'Introduction', *Philosophical Transactions*, 1 (1665–6), 2.

the *Royal Society*, by that Eminent *Virtuoso* Sir R[obert] Moray'.[44] If reading individual articles provided information about recent scientific progress, reading the journal as a whole provided an introduction to the social world of early modern science.

The Society's link with, and influence over, the *Transactions* became stronger as the journal continued. It was regularly suggested that papers presented at meetings should be published in the journal, and following a period of abeyance after Oldenburg's death in 1677 the Society began to take a more active role in publication.[45] Articles ranged over all the subject matter considered by the Royal Society Fellows in an institutional context, which included information about crafts and trades, languages, archaeology, and antiquarian pursuits as well as subjects we would more commonly identify as scientific.[46] However there were some broad points of similarity. Most articles appeared in English, and most were relatively brief. Oldenburg's format generally consisted of a brief introduction followed by a longer narrative of an experiment or observation, but in later periods articles often took the form of letters to the editor, or extracts from longer texts. The narration normally included some indication of the relationship between the narrator and the events discussed (that is, as an eye-witness, informed by witnesses, or the recipient of a letter via an intermediary). Sometimes the author provided an interpretation of the observations or experiments described, but this was certainly not a requirement; sometimes the subject matter was linked with previous work on the same topic. The language and content were usually straightforward and relatively concise, but this depended on the author. Annotations on original manuscripts in the Royal Society archives show that some editorial intervention took place, but this was not particularly standardised. For example, the manuscript account of some 'parhelia' (mock-suns) observed in Suffolk by a 'Grave Divine' in 1698 originally began 'The works of God are Wonderfull', but this has been struck through in the manuscript and was omitted from the printed article, presumably because it was not felt to be relevant to the ensuing account.[47] On the other hand, Zachary Mayne's letter describing a waterspout at Topsham on the river Exe in 1694 concluded with the comment that it was 'no small Mercy' no one had been injured, and his final thought, 'God shews us what he can do, happy we, if we understood his meaning, and comply with it; but alas, Mercies and Judgments are soon forgotten', was included in the printed version.[48]

---

[44] 'A Relation of Persons Killed with Subterraneous Damps', *Philosophical Transactions*, 1 (1665–6), 44.

[45] For an early example of the Society suggesting a paper be published in the *Philosophical Transactions*, see the minutes of the meeting on 13 January 1670, printed in Thomas Birch, *The History of the Royal Society of London*, 4 vols. (1756–7), 2: 415. On the journal's editors see Moxham, 'Fit for Print', n4.

[46] The Society had a broad remit, but tended not to discuss supernatural matters in an institutional setting, despite some Fellows' individual interests; on this see Michael Hunter, 'The Royal Society and the Decline of Magic', *Notes and Records of the Royal Society*, 65 (2011), 103–19.

[47] Royal Society Archives EL/B2/49; 'The Extract of a Letter from Mr Petto, a Grave Divine, Concerning some Parelii seen at Sudbury in Suffolk, Decemb. 28th, 1698. Communicated by Dr. Beverley', *Philosophical Transactions*, 21 (1699), 107–8.

[48] 'Mr Zachary Mayne's Letter, 1694. Concerning a Spout of Water that Happened at Topsham on the River between the Sea and Exeter', *Philosophical Transactions*, 19 (1695), 28–31.

Up to this point I have concentrated on texts in which we would consider the whole content to be fairly straightforwardly 'scientific', and as the example of Ray's preface to Willughby's *Ornithology* suggests, there was a sense among some scientific writers that certain types of content should be excluded from their writing. It is important to point out, though, that, like other prose forms in the period, scientific writing was nothing if not protean. In terms of the questions it asked, and its methods, the 'new philosophy' was not yet clearly distinguished from other ways of gaining knowledge about the natural world. Equally, 'scientific' knowledge was often mixed with other kinds of knowledge in the prose works of the period. Two examples will serve to illustrate this. In 1676 the horticulturalist Ralph Austen published *A Dialogue (Or Familiar Discourse) and Conference Betweene the Husbandman and Fruit-trees* (Oxford, 1676). The content was drawn from Austen's long experience as a nurseryman, although he had published a fuller technical manual on the topic twenty years earlier in *A Treatise of Fruit-trees* (Oxford, 1653). Austen's aim in his *Dialogue* was to use the wisdom drawn from growing fruit-trees to reinforce spiritual or moral points. Thus, for example, the husbandman observed that trees grown in '*a very rich soyle, deepe, and fatt*' were large and stately but bore less fruit. His fruit-trees responded: 'consider thou whether our unfruitfulnesse be not occasioned by our *too fatt, and Plentifull feeding*; for thou knowest that *Repletion is an enemy to Generation*, in all Creatures, according to their kinds.' This served not only to introduce the maxim '*Moderation is best*', but also gave occasion for '*A just Reproofe of the Carnall Careless Gentry*', who even though they were 'Trees planted (by Gods providence) in a rich, and fertile soyle' produced little in the way of spiritual fruits.[49] Austen was by no means the only writer to harness scientific content to a theological agenda: for those who saw the book of nature as complementary with the book of God's word, the two sat naturally together and could be used to expound on similar questions.

Other writers wove scientific material into narratives we would now describe as science fiction, although the term is a much later development. One of the earliest of these texts in English was Francis Godwin's *The Man in the Moone* (1638). Godwin's account of a journey from the Earth to the moon in a flying-machine powered by geese is generically hard to pin down, part travelogue, part romance; but it does make some serious points in favour of Copernicanism. Equally difficult to categorize is Margaret Cavendish's *The Blazing World* (1666), a prose fiction published in the same volume as her non-fictional scientific work, *Observations upon Experimental Philosophy*. Again, *The Blazing World* mixes romance with travelogue, as well as philosophical dialogue and (auto)biography. Here Cavendish repeated in narrative form scientific arguments that she had also made in her *Observations*, inserting them into the mouth of her semi-autobiographical protagonist, the Empress of the Blazing World. By doing so, she enabled an imaginary exchange of philosophical opinions to take place between herself and the experimentalists of the Royal Society (imperfectly disguised as bear-, bird-, and

---

[49] Austen, *A Dialogue ... Betweene the Husbandman and Fruit-trees*, 29–30.

other animal-men)—a conversation that Cavendish's gender seems to have precluded in the real world.[50]

Speech, Image, Manuscript, Print

Inevitably, the history of science in this period has largely been written from textual evidence because texts are what survive. Particularly after 1660 the story is incredibly rich, illuminated by an uninterrupted run of archives in the Royal Society. The early Fellows knew from the outset that their enterprise of improving natural knowledge would be doomed without an efficient record-keeping system, and they quickly set up a process for keeping minutes of meetings and transcribing scientific papers and correspondence into large ledgers. We need to remember, however, that a large number of these records were either composed to be communicated orally at meetings of the Royal Society, or are a more or less perfect register of speech made by someone other than the speaker: minutes taken by the secretary recording the rambling discussions that took place at Royal Society meetings, or reports of evidence delivered by eye-witnesses from every social sphere. This raises the question of whether the spoken origins of these texts might affect their prose style. For example, the note-taking methods and stylistic habits of successive secretaries must have influenced reports of Royal Society meetings. The scientific community's emphasis on gentlemanly modes of conduct and the avoidance of dispute, discussed above, may have led to conversational records being framed in a way that played down dissent. The opportunity to deliver scientific reports orally to the assembled Royal Society Fellows before providing a final text for publication in the *Philosophical Transactions* or elsewhere gave authors the opportunity to test out ideas and modify them if necessary; in this case, it is likely that some papers ended up as an amalgam of the original writer's words and the voices of his colleagues. And the reported speech of informants must have been incorporated into scientific texts more or less faithfully, depending on a number of factors, such as the status of the speaker, and the requirements of the author involved. Though it is difficult to disentangle all these strands, it seems possible that the orality of the early Royal Society may have had a homogenizing effect on prose produced in this institutional context, with the assembled Fellows tolerating fewer flights of fancy than those found in works produced independently.

The traditional emphasis on prose texts has also obscured the significance of images in the history of science. During the whole of the period under consideration, images were understood to be a powerful tool for communicating new knowledge; they were also a tool for thinking. Recent research has begun to focus on the role of images in

---

[50] Cavendish did visit the Royal Society, the only woman to do so during this period, but she does not seem to have been taken very seriously by the Fellows; see Birch, *History*, 2: 177–8; Robert Latham and William Matthews (eds.), *The Diary of Samuel Pepys*, 11 vols. (London, 1970–83), 8: 243.

constructing scientific knowledge in the period, and so it is worthwhile thinking about how this role affected the production and consumption of scientific prose.[51] Sometimes the presence of an image could stand in for a complex description, and thus in a sense took the place of prose. Most images, though, only depicted an object in one state or at a single moment in time.[52] In this case, the accompanying prose could concentrate on describing movements rather than structures. The detailed (and arresting) engravings accompanying Robert Hooke's *Micrographia* enabled him to explain aspects of the microscopic world that must otherwise have remained mystifying for his readers. In many places his prose relies so heavily on the images that it makes little sense without them:

> the joints of [a flea's legs] are so adapted, that he can, as 'twere, fold them short one within another, and suddenly stretch, or spring them out to their whole length, that is, of the fore-leggs, the part A, of the 34th *Scheme*, lies within B, and B within C, parallel to, or side by side each other; but the parts of the two next, lie quite contrary, that is, D without E, and E without F, but parallel also; but the parts of the hinder leggs, G, H and I, bend one within another, like the parts of a double jointed Ruler, or like the foot, legg and thigh of a man; these six leggs he clitches up altogether, and when he leaps, springs them all out, and thereby exerts his whole strength at once.[53]

The similes that Hooke employed here, comparing the flea's legs to 'a double jointed Ruler' or a man's legs and feet, enabled him to transform the static image (Figure 33.1) into a three-dimensional moving object in the minds of his readers. The inclusion of images in a scientific text immediately gives readers a sense of confidence in the material, perhaps enabling the writer to adopt a more playful tone without any danger of relinquishing his authority, or allowing him to appeal to the reader's own judgement in confirmation of hypotheses. There were limited opportunities for texts to be linked in this way with material objects, such as scientific instruments, simply because they were available to very few potential readers. However, Hooke, Robert Boyle, and others did include detailed descriptions of their apparatus, partly to enable others to repeat experiments or observations using similarly constructed equipment, and partly to bolster their claims to credibility by showing readers exactly how experiments were conducted.[54]

---

[51] See, for example, the essays in Felicity Henderson, Sachiko Kusukawa, and Alexander Marr (eds.), *Curiously Drawn: Early Modern Science as a Visual Pursuit*, special issue of *Huntington Library Quarterly*, 78 (2015).

[52] Makers of scientific images worked hard to remedy this, using techniques such as dotted lines to indicate a different state (of, for example, an instrument with moving parts), or putting several images together on a single plate (for example showing a plant's roots, leaves, flower, and fruit simultaneously).

[53] Hooke, *Micrographia*, 210.

[54] See, for example, Hooke's description of his microscopes in *Micrographia*, sig. fv-[f2]r), and Boyle's description of the air-pump in *New Experiments Physico-Mechanical*. Illustrations of both these instruments are included in the respective texts.

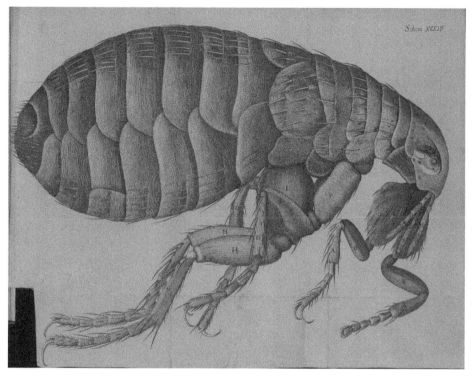

FIGURE 33.1 Engraving of a flea in Robert Hooke, *Micrographia* (1665). Wellcome Collection. Attribution 4.0 International (CC BY 4.0).

Source: Wellcome Collection.

Scientific Prose in Translation

Despite the continued dominance of Latin as a learned language at the English universities, English was the preferred language for scientific writing in England. Several factors seem to have influenced this: nationalistic pride, along with early scientists' commitment to intelligibility and a wide audience, and their desire to distance themselves from the kinds of university learning that they and others deemed overly argumentative and lacking in substance. Latin was still the main language of international communication, and so writers who wanted a Continental audience either published in Latin at the outset, or, like Robert Boyle, oversaw Latin translations of their works that appeared soon after the English edition.[55] However, by choice or necessity, many important new scientific works appeared in European vernaculars. Given that the subject matter was often of universal interest, there was a demand for English translations

---

[55] See Hunter and Davis (eds.), 'General Introduction', in *Works of Robert Boyle, Volume 1*, pp. lx–lxxiv.

of both printed scientific material and personal correspondence arriving from the Continent. It is certainly not the case that because these accounts were factual, their translation was somehow straightforward or mechanical. Investigating the translations, and noting aspects such as the language used, the ways in which translations deviate from the source text, identities of translators, and how they approach their task, can provide useful clues about scientific prose in England. One example is the translation of Dutch microscopist Jan Swammerdam's *Ephemeri Vita* (Amsterdam, 1675), a long work describing the natural history of the mayfly, interspersed with poetry and prayers, printed in Dutch. The English merchant and linguist Francis Lodwick (later F. R. S.) translated the volume, probably at the instigation and with the assistance of Robert Hooke and the physician Edward Tyson. The latter contributed a preface to the translation, where he noted that the 'frequent, Pious Meditations, and Poetry' of the original work had been left out.[56] No doubt there were various reasons for this: the resulting translation was much shorter (and therefore quicker and cheaper to produce), and Swammerdam was not such an important figure in England as in his native country. However it also seems likely that the omissions were influenced by the sense that such things were inappropriate distractions in a work of natural history.[57] Other translators felt equally at liberty to cut sections of their source texts or to add material of their own (or both).[58] The general aim seems to have been to present the subject matter as clearly as possible to the English audience, but like other scientific writers in the period, translators saw their efforts (and the work of the authors they were translating) as part of an ongoing conversation. No printed text represented the final word on any given topic; all texts were open to revision and expansion.[59]

Conclusion

Scientific writers in the early modern period were keenly aware of the need to communicate their ideas in a way that was both straightforwardly informative and rhetorically persuasive. Writers of works intended for print publication, in particular, would have been aware that not all their readers would understand or sympathise with the aims of the new philosophy. In order to communicate effectively with such readers, some writers chose to use the forms and language familiar from more literary prose works.

---

[56] Jan Swammerdam, *Ephemeri Vita, or, The Natural History and Anatomy of the Ephemeron* (1681), sig. A2r.

[57] Other writers, however, saw poetry as perfectly compatible with natural history: Evelyn's *Sylva* is interlarded with extracts from the classical poets, particularly Virgil.

[58] Felicity Henderson, 'Faithful Interpreters? Translation Theory and Practice at the Early Royal Society', *Notes and Records of the Royal Society*, 67 (2013), 101–22.

[59] Elizabeth Yale demonstrates this very clearly in contemporary natural history writing in her *Sociable Knowledge: Natural History and the Nation in Early Modern Britain* (Philadelphia: University of Pennsylvania Press, 2016), esp. 116–67.

We should not be surprised that the largely university-educated members of the scientific community sometimes enjoyed putting their rhetorical training to use in their scientific writings. Much of the concern expressed by scientific writers in the period about rhetoric actually stems from their concern about whether, and how, their readers would understand new scientific ideas. Rhetoric, as John Donne demonstrates with his description of the '*metaphors ... Curtaines* of *Allegories ... third Heauens* of *Hyperboles*' found in Scripture, can be confusing: science needs to be clear.[60] Rhetoric exerts all its power to persuade listeners to agree with the speaker; science needs its audience to make up their own minds on the basis of experimental or observational evidence. In Thomas Sprat's summary, rhetoric is the province of 'wits and scholars' who delight in empty arguments and point-scoring; science conveys solid learning about matters of fact. It should not be surprising, then, that ostentatious displays of rhetoric were seen to have no part in communicating science. The sticking-point, though, is the fact that rhetoric can also make texts and ideas come alive for people, and science does need this. Hence the ambivalence.

The prose 'Transactions' of science in this period were much more than the procedural, business-like, matters of fact that the title might suggest. As I have argued, communication of scientific ideas took place in such a diverse array of forms, written by and for such a disparate range of people, that it is difficult to find common ground. Perhaps the aspect that is most engaging for modern readers, though, is the sense of excitement and wonder in all of these texts. While they were aware, on some level, of the need for clarity and sobriety, and the need to construct an authoritative narrative voice, most scientific writers allow their enthusiasm for their subject to show. They want their readers to do more than simply understand and assent to their propositions: they want them to join in and begin their own course of experiments and observations. They were aware that the process of scientific discovery was just beginning. But they were contributing to a larger discourse: it was both allowable and newly fashionable to communicate unfinished thoughts, 'essays', and 'attempts', and to leave interpretation in the hands of readers.[61]

---

[60] John Donne, '19. Expostulation', in *Devotions upon Emergent Occasions* (1624), 480–1.
[61] See further Chapter 15 by Kathryn Murphy on 'Essays'.

CHAPTER 34

SECRET HISTORIES

REBECCA BULLARD

In the four decades between 1674 and 1714, more than sixty separate published titles claimed to be 'the secret history of' something. A large proportion of these were overtly polemical exposés of topical, political targets—'of popery', 'of the four last monarchs of Great-Britain', 'of the French King', 'of White-hall', 'of the Geertruydenbergh negociation', 'of the Chevalier de St. George' (otherwise known as the Pretender), of 'the Calves-Head Club'—a republican drinking club.[1] Their revelations combined sexual and political scandal, as the titles of many—including secret histories of 'the royal mistresses of France', 'the amours of Madam de Maintenon, with the French King', and 'the amours and marriage of an English nobleman with a famous Italian Lady'—attest.[2] A significant subset focused on historically distant figures and settings, such as 'the court of the Emperor Justinian', 'the most renowned Q. Elizabeth and the E. of Essex', 'the Duke of Alançon and Q. Elizabeth', 'the house of Medicis', 'Lewis XI, King of France', and 'Mack-Beth, King of Scotland'—sometimes, but not always, with a view to comparing courts and rulers past and present.[3] A few, including secret histories of 'a silver chamber-pot' and 'gaming [and] sharping Tricks and Cheats', offered an irreverent glimpse into

---

[1] Edmund Hickeringhill, *The Devil's Dream, or, A Secret History of Popery* (1709); *The Secret History of the Four Last Monarchs of Great Britain* (1691); David Jones, *The Secret History of White-hall* (1697); *The Secret History of the Geertruydenbergh Negociation* (1712); *The Safety of France to Monsieur the Dauphin, or, The Secret History of the French King* (1690); *The Secret History of the Chevalier de St. George* (1714); Edward Ward, *The Secret History of the Calves-Head Club* (1702).

[2] Claude Vanel, *The Royal Mistresses of France, or, The Secret History of the Amours of all the French Kings* (1695); [Eustache le Noble], *The Cabinet Open'd, or, The Secret History of the Amours of Madam de Maintenon, with the French King* (1690); *A Secret History of the Amours and Marriage of an English Nobleman with a Famous Italian Lady* ([1712]).

[3] Procopius of Caesarea, *The Secret History of the Court of the Emperor Justinian* (1674); *The Secret History of the Most Renowned Q. Elizabeth and the E. of Essex* (Cologne [i.e. London], 1680); *The Secret History of the Duke of Alançon and Q. Elizabeth* (1691); Antoine Varillas, *Anekdota heterouriaka [sic], or, The Secret History of the House of Medicis* (1686); Jean de Roye, *The Secret History of Lewis XI, King of France* (1712); Marie-Catherine Le Jumel de Barneville, baronne d'Aulnoy, *The Earl of Douglas ... with the Secret History of Mack-Beth King of Scotland* (1708).

hidden underworlds and private lives, rather than the courts and cabinets of monarchs, ministers, and their mistresses.[4] All of these secret histories, however, share some significant characteristics: they disclose, in the highly public medium of print, privileged information about private worlds from which their readers 'ought' to be excluded. They are voyeuristic and iconoclastic, trading in the display of bodies, minds, and feelings. They were consumed with relish—many achieving multiple editions and translations into and out of languages including French and Dutch—but they were also regarded with suspicion, outrage, and contempt by opponents who objected to them on both political and literary grounds.

In this chapter, I want to explore the ways in which secret history evolved over the course of later Stuart Britain—stretching the end date of this volume just a little to 1715 so as to explore the impact of the Hanoverian accession on writers in this tradition. My analysis falls into three sections, each one reflecting a stage in secret history's development. The first covers the longest stretch of time: from the 1640s to 1688. This period witnesses the first use in English of the title tag 'secret history', as well as early attempts to define this genre as a form of neoclassical historiography. Secret history, however, refused to submit to singular definition. Like many other prose genres covered in this volume of chapters, it cross-fertilizes with other literary forms. The first section of this chapter, then, explores secret history's relationship with genres including pamphlet polemic and romance, as well as neoclassical 'perfect' or explanatory history. The second section of the chapter turns to secret history during the reign of William and Mary (and, after Mary's death, of William III alone). Following the revolution of 1688–9, secret history became a genre of choice for Whig polemicists seeking to distance the new Protestant regime from the perceived machinations of the Catholic and crypto-Catholic Stuart courts that had preceded it. But even as propagandists deploy secret history as a weapon in a paper war, they begin to expose some of its rhetorical complexities—complexities that sometimes pose a challenge to its polemical purpose. Secret history's ongoing experimentation is the focus of the third section, which explores this genre during the reign of Queen Anne (1702–14) and the first year of the reign of George I (1714–15). While some Whig partisans continue to exploit secret history for immediate, political purposes—using it to depict the Hanoverian succession as a 'revolution' akin to that of 1688, for instance—other writers took the genre in new directions, apparently enjoying the range of tonal and expressive possibilities afforded by secret history's by-now-distinctive conventions.

The self-consciousness of secret historians during the second part of the long seventeenth century is one reason why studying this genre offers us insight into more than just the particular contours of a single literary tradition. Although, as we will see shortly, secret history has classical antecedents, it is a genre discovered anew in and forged through the political ferment and literary experimentalism of the later Stuart period, bearing

---

[4] *The Lady's Journey to Oxford, or, The Secret History of a Silver Chamber-Pot* (1709); *Memoirs of the Lives, Intrigues, and Comical Adventures of the Most Famous Gamesters and Celebrated Sharpers* (1714).

the distinctive marks of this period in its formal conventions and rhetorical strategies. Practitioners and opponents of this genre developed, between them, a complex literary form that interrogates the relationship between history and fiction, gender and genre, literature and politics. These concerns are also, of course, central to the development of secret history's close cousin, the novel. But unlike the novel, secret history does not flourish long beyond the period of its first formation. It offers us, then, an opportunity to investigate the development of an early modern genre without becoming caught in a teleological current. In the conclusion to this chapter, I want to consider the ways in which secret history challenges some familiar ideas about genre in later Stuart Britain.

Secret History, 1640–89

The first work in English to bear the generic title 'secret history' appeared in 1674. *The Secret History of the Court of the Emperor Justinian* was an anonymous translation of *Anekdota*, a scurrilous account of the Emperor Justinian's reign written by a Byzantine official, Procopius of Caesarea, in the mid-sixth century. Procopius's work was not widely distributed during his lifetime because, as he put it, 'it was not possible to elude the vigilance of multitudes of spies, nor, if detected, to escape a most cruel death'.[5] After his death it lay, apparently forgotten, for over a thousand years until it was rediscovered in the Vatican library and published in a Latin translation in 1623 by Niccolò Alemanni. It was this Latin translation that turned *Anekdota*, or 'unpublished things', into *Arcana historia*, or 'secret history', for the first time.[6] The first reference to this text in English, in the preface to a 1653 translation of another of Procopius's works, calls it 'Ἀνέκδοτα, or, Secret History'.[7] The 1674 English translation was, however, based on a French translation by Leonor de Mauger: *Histoire secrète de Procope de Césarée*, published in 1669.

The phrase 'secret history' quickly became associated with the kind of history written by Procopius in *Anekdota*—to the extent that the latinized term, *anecdota*, and the anglicized 'anecdotes' became synonymous with secret history. In *Anekdota*, Procopius reveals that the laudatory, official version of Justinian's reign that he had composed in his *History of the Wars* concealed the truth about Justinian's court, character, and actions. *Anekdota*, he claims, will set the record straight, disclosing the real reasons behind the events that he had depicted in *History of the Wars*. Almost all of these reasons involve the machinations of women—especially Antonina, wife of Justinian's General Belisarius, and the Empress Theodora, Justinian's wife. Low-born, bloodthirsty, greedy,

---

[5] Procopius, *Secret History*, trans. H. B. Dewing (Cambridge, MA: Harvard University Press, 1954; repr. 2004), 3.

[6] The title *Anekdota* comes from the Suda and may not be Procopius's own; see Averil Cameron, *Procopius and the Sixth Century* (London: Routledge, 1996), 50.

[7] Procopius, *History of the Warres of the Emperour Justinian in Eight Books*, trans. Henry Holcroft (1653), sig. A3v.

and sexually depraved, Theodora and Antonina control their uxorious husbands using a combination of sexual and supernatural power, and wreak havoc in the commonwealth. Secret history on Procopius's model, then, revises received accounts of the past by offering scandalous revelations that focus on women, private lives, and secret spaces, rather than on public events.

Many seventeenth-century commentators—some in England, and more in France—were intrigued but also embarrassed and even horrified by this 'new', ancient exemplar. After the publication of the Latin translation of *Anekdota*, Thomas Ryves attacks Procopius's pretensions to the title 'historian', claiming that *Arcana historia* is nothing more than a 'satire of vices'.[8] François la Mothe le Vayer suggests that Procopius himself was ashamed of this work: both the title, *Anekdota*, and the long concealment of this text 'shows that this is a secret work and that its author did not want [his name] to be revealed'.[9] Writing after the publication of vernacular translations of *Anekdota*, René Rapin notes that a key requirement of ancient and modern history writing is 'the decyphering of what is secret and of importance, in the designs and intentions of those whose Actions it divulges'.[10] In case this precept threatens to erase the distinction between proper neoclassical history and secret history, however, Rapin asserts that Procopius 'forget[s] to circumstance what is important, and is very careful in circumstancing what is not so'—perhaps an allusion to his detailed description of the Empress Theodora's erotic performances in the public theatre.[11]

In fact, Rapin's attempt to distinguish between secret history and other kinds of neoclassical history ultimately serves to draw attention to their proximity.[12] Certainly other contemporary commentators on secret history were keen to emphasize Procopius's credentials as an ancient. Antoine Varillas includes a lengthy critical preface on the genre in his *Anecdotes de Florence, ou, L'Histoire secréte de la maison de Medicis* (1685), in which he asserts that Procopius performs 'the Duty of a perfect Historian'—that is, a historian who details not only events but also the causes behind them.[13] The secret historian, indeed, provides a considerably more 'perfect' account than most classical and neoclassical historians, who are content to 'draw [their subjects] such as they were in the Army, or in the tumult of Cities', whereas the secret historian 'endeavours by all means to get open their Closet-doors' and 'makes his main of what occurs in Secret and Solitude'.[14] The secret historian's interest in private life, and especially in sexual intrigue,

---

[8] 'conuitiorum satyra'; Thomas Ryves, *Imperatoris Iustiniani defensio aduersus Alemannum* (1626), 9.

[9] 'Le nom d'Anecdotes monstre que c'est un travail secret, & que son Auteur ne vouloit pas estre divulgué' (François de la Mothe le Vayer, *Oeuvres*, 2 vols. (3rd edn, Paris, 1662), 1: 356.

[10] René Rapin, *Instructions for History* (1680), 59.

[11] Rapin, *Instructions for History*, 54–5.

[12] On the relationship between secret history and other kinds of history writing, see Noelle Gallagher, *Historical Literatures: Writing About the Past in England, 1660–1740* (Manchester: Manchester University Press, 2012) and Robert Mayer, *History and the Early English Novel: Matters of Fact from Bacon to Defoe* (Cambridge: Cambridge University Press, 1997).

[13] Varillas, *Anekdota heterouriaka*, sig. a2v.

[14] Varillas, *Anekdota heterouriaka*, sigs. a4v–a5r.

may mean that his or her subject matter is different from that found in orthodox historical accounts, but Varillas is insistent that the 'Anecdoto-grapher' 'cannot dispence himself from any of the Rules that *Aristotle, Cicero, Plutarch* and the other Masters of th'Art have so judiciously prescrib'd for Publick History'.[15] Varillas' English translator, Ferrand Spence, agreed, insisting that Varillas himself 'has the Gravity of *Livy*, the Politeness of *Salust*, the Policy of *Tacitus*', just as Varillas had affirmed his ancient predecessor's literary status.[16]

In emphasizing more erotic aspects of secret history, French commentators like la Mothe le Vayer, Rapin, and Varillas play down its political resonances. English writers, on the other hand, were keen to exploit the polemical potential of a text that was aimed, as the first English translation puts it, 'at such persons who are desirous to govern in an Arbitrary way', that they 'might discover, by the misfortune of those whom I mention, the destiny that attends them, and the just recompence they are to expect of their crimes'.[17] While the French translation of *Anekdota* was published *avec privilège* as part of a prestigious complete works of Procopius, the material form of the English translation sends out very different rhetorical signals. In 1682 the prominent Whig stationer Richard Baldwin issued a new edition of the text with a revised title: *The Debaucht Court, or, The Lives of the Emperor Justinian, and His Empress Theodora the Comedian*. Published towards the end of the Exclusion Crisis, this version of the *Anekdota* implicitly encourages readers to identify parallels between the 'Debaucht Court' of Charles II and that of Justinian.

In this respect, secret history is a tributary of the river of iconoclastic, polemical writing that runs through the late seventeenth century. The English translation of Procopius may have been the first text to use the title tag 'secret history' but the idea of printing the secrets of those in power as a political strategy was current long before 1674. *The Kings Cabinet Open'd* (1645), for instance, offers readers a series of putative letters from Charles I to Queen Henrietta Maria supposedly taken from the King's private quarters after the battle of Naseby, under a title that pre-empts Antoine Varillas' assertion that the secret historian 'endeavours by all means to get open ... Closet-doors'.[18] The letters that make up this text share many characteristics with later secret histories, including the motif of a corrupt woman who controls an uxorious and treacherous leader. Against the secrecy and silence of arbitrary or absolute power and the mysteries of popery, texts like *The Kings Cabinet Open'd* exploit the populism and publicity of print. In particular, the text's epistolary format gives readers an impression of something akin to direct access to the monarch's body, his 'Hand' and 'Heart'.[19] During the Commonwealth

---

[15] Varillas, *Anekdota heterouriaka*, sigs. a1v–a2r.
[16] Varillas, *Anekdota heterouriaka*, sig. A6v.
[17] Procopius, *Secret History*, 2.
[18] On the recurrent image within the period of the closet or cabinet opened, see Chapter 31 on 'Recipe Books' by Henry Power.
[19] The title page's insistence that these letters were 'Written with the Kings own Hand', and Charles's chosen salutation, 'Dear Heart', add to the impression of physical and affective proximity created by the epistolary format.

period *Cabala; sive Scrinia Sacra [or, Sacred Cabinet]* (1654) also offers royal letters up to public scrutiny—this time between James I, Charles I, and their ministers of state. The preface again emphasizes the physical exposure that these letters facilitate: here, 'the great *Ministers* of *State* are presented naked, their *Consultations, Designs, Policies,* the things done by them, are exposed to every mans eye'.[20] These texts remind us that, in the seventeenth century, a 'secret' need not be an object (a piece of concealed information) but might also be a method or process known only to the initiate—something like a craft or trade. *Cabala* offers its readers 'the mysteries of *Government,* the wisdom, and manage of Publick businesses in the late Reigns'—not so much particular pieces of intelligence (though it does offer those) as strategies by which the Stuart kings had ruled.[21] Texts like these attack would-be arbitrary monarchs not only by inviting ridicule at their 'naked[ness]', but also by rendering explicit the tacit dimensions of absolutist government.[22]

Iconoclastic texts that reveal and thereby attack the secret aims and ambitions of monarchs and their ministers continued to be published after the Restoration—among them the Earl of Shaftesbury's *Letter from a Person of Quality to his Friend in the Country* (1675) and Andrew Marvell's *Account of the Growth of Popery and Arbitrary Government* (1677).[23] Not all Restoration secret histories attack the royal prerogative, however—and not all of them adopt the kind of direct, revelatory strategies that we find in those texts that label and publish state secrets. Aphra Behn's *Love-Letters Between a Nobleman and His Sister* (1684, 1685, 1687) is a Tory secret history which capitalizes on topical literary and political developments to attack Whig supporters of the Duke of Monmouth: Charles II's illegitimate son who mounted a challenge to the succession of the Roman Catholic heir to the throne, James Duke of York. *Love-Letters* is a literary experiment, which blends aspects of polemical secret history with a well-established European tradition of allegorical romance and its more recent, French sub-genres, *histoire galante* or *histoire amoureuse*.[24] It does so not by focusing directly on Monmouth, to whom Behn gives the ironic, allegorical name Cesario, but rather by giving a behind-the-scenes (or inside-the-cabinet) glimpse at two other contemporary figures: Monmouth's close associate Ford, Lord Grey, whom Behn depicts as Philander, and Grey's sister-in-law, Henrietta Berkeley, given the moniker Silvia. Philander's seduction and abandonment of Silvia, and Silvia's subsequent development into a female rake,

---

[20] *Cabala: sive Scrinia sacra* (1654), sig. A3r.
[21] *Cabala: sive Scrinia sacra,* A3r.
[22] On secret history as a form that renders the 'tacit' aspects of government 'explicit', see Michael McKeon, *The Secret History of Domesticity: Public, Private, and the Division of Knowledge* (Baltimore: The Johns Hopkins University Press, 2005), 5–6.
[23] On this tradition during the Restoration, see Annabel Patterson, *Early Modern Liberalism* (Cambridge: Cambridge University Press, 1997), 153–231.
[24] On the particular debt that seventeenth-century English fiction owes to French romance, see Ros Ballaster, *Seductive Forms: Women's Amatory Fiction, 1684–1740* (Oxford: Clarendon Press, 1992), 42–9. On Behn's *Love-Letters Between a Nobleman and His Sister* see also Chapter 5 on 'Amatory Fiction' by Melissa E. Sanchez and Chapter 22 on 'Letters' by Diana G. Barnes.

reflects the political treachery that Behn wants her readers to associate with the Whig cause. But the way in which Behn adapts a 'real-life' story of seduction and betrayal—Grey's trial for the rape and abduction of Henrietta Berkeley was taking place even as Behn was publishing this multi-part text—also reveals the sophistication with which she adapts and reflects on the conventions of secret history.

In *Love-Letters*, the act of revelation often leads not to secure and confident knowledge of previously concealed information, but rather to the discovery or suspicion that there might be further secrets to uncover, and an attendant sense of uncertainty, scepticism, even fear. In one of his early letters to Silvia, Philander asserts: 'I move about this unregarded world, appear every day in the great Senate House at Clubs, Caballs, and private consultations (for *Silvia* knows all the business of my Soul, even its politicks of State as well as Love) I say I appear indeed, and give my Voice in publick business, but oh my Heart more kindly is imploy'd, that and my thoughts are *Silvia*'s!'[25] Philander's account of the way he spends his time suggests that he occupies not just one secret ('unregarded') world but several. Within the Senate House, or Parliament, are a set of inner circles of decreasing size and increasing secrecy—'Clubs, Caballs, and private consultations'. Indeed, Philander's phrasing suggests that 'appear[ing]' in the Senate House is, for him, the same thing as participating in clubs and cabals, to the extent that it is difficult to know quite what he means by 'publick business': it might signify anything from participation in the business of the House of Lords to attendance at a 'private consultation'. Even in relatively private spaces, however, Philander still harbours a secret: his absent 'Heart' and 'thoughts' remain with Silvia. Philander delights in the fact that not even his co-conspirators reach the bottom of his affairs. Philander and Cesario's cabals are not just unstable because they consist of (inherently treacherous) Whigs, but because any group held together by apparently shared, secret knowledge is vulnerable to the impact of future revelations from within the group itself.

As readers, we feel the destabilizing force of secrecy through *Love-Letters*'s formal characteristics. A *roman à clef*, *Love-Letters* veils the identities of historical referents even as it apparently reveals secrets about them. The dangers of such 'Hieroglyfick'd' narratives are highlighted in the third part of *Love-Letters*, when the 'fawning Wizard' Fergusano equivocates with and deceives his dupe, Cesario, by showing him an apparition 'so very like ... to himself, as if he had seen his proper Figure in a Glass'—a description that might be applied to Behn's own narrative as much as to Fergusano's conjured vision.[26] The three-part structure of Behn's narrative also serves to challenge the idea that revelation leads to political enlightenment. The epistolary format of the first part, published in 1684, mimics texts like *The Kings Cabinet Open'd* in giving readers voyeuristic access to private correspondence. The publication of two subsequent parts, however, and a gradual move away from epistolary form towards diegetic narration suggest the risks involved in taking a series of published letters as the whole story. Published

---

[25] Aphra Behn, *Love-Letters between a Nobleman and his Sister*, ed. Janet Todd, in *The Works of Aphra Behn*, 7 vols. (London: William Pickering, 1993), 2: 20.

[26] Behn, *Love-Letters*, 2: 404, 2: 403, 2: 405.

in a decade that witnessed repeated 'discoveries' of plots by both Catholic conspirators (including the Popish Plot of 1678–9 and Meal-tub Plot of 1679) and Whig opponents of a Catholic succession (including the Rye-House Plot of 1683), *Love-Letters* stages in print the dangers and difficulties involved in trusting secrets.

By the end of the 1680s, modern writers of secret history had forged a recognizable new literary genre. It was one that brought together literary traditions of neoclassical history writing, albeit of a rather dubious kind, radical polemic, and romance. It focused on the illegitimate political power of women and the inextricability of sex, passions, and appetite from politics. It highlighted the centrality of secrecy to political discourse, but it also registered the dangers of trusting in secrets and, by implication, the proximity of secret revelations both to history and to fiction.

Secret History, 1689–1702

Although the first text to call itself a 'secret history' was published in 1674, it was not until the 1690s that this title formula really became in vogue. The sudden upsurge in self-styled secret histories published during this decade is a literary by-product of the political revolution that in 1688 brought the Protestant monarchs William and Mary to the throne in place of their Roman Catholic predecessor, James II. Secret historians who, from the 1640s to the 1680s, had mostly focused on revealing the secrets of those currently in positions of power and influence now began to publish secrets about the ousted King James, his brother and predecessor, Charles II, and their much more powerful ally, the French king, Louis XIV. The kind of revelations that we find in texts like *The Secret History of the Reigns of K. Charles II and K. James II* (1690), *The Secret History of the Duchess of Portsmouth* (1690), and *The Secret History of the French King* (1690) show evidence of continuity with earlier participants in this tradition: they depict male would-be tyrants who are nonetheless controlled by the sexual power of women and who, while in power, posed a direct threat to the religious and political liberties of their subjects. But the fact that secret histories of the 1690s are published in the wake of a revolution that seemed, at least to most commentators, to have resulted in the overthrow of a pro-French, Catholic, or crypto-Catholic regime means that these texts offer their readers a significantly different experience from the kind created by many of their literary forbears.

Secret history offers Whig polemicists of the 1690s the opportunity to celebrate the revolution by contrasting the new regime with the corrupt machinations of the former Stuart kings, Charles and James. A number of secret historians make this contrast explicit. One declares his intent to 'let all the World judg of the Furberies and Tyranny of those Times, and the Integrity, Sincerity, and Sweetness of Their Present Majesties Reign'.[27] Writing towards the end of William III's reign, the Whig peer, John, Baron Somers likewise asserts: 'Some People tell us, that *Truth is not always to be spoken*;

---

[27] *The Secret History of the Reigns of K. Charles II. and K. James II* (1690), sig. A2v.

which perhaps might be so, while we were under the Arbitrary Government of the late King; but we now live in a Reign, *where Truth does not pass for Treason.*'[28] These writers align themselves with their political forbears (Somers's assertion contains an allusion to the scaffold speech of Whig martyr, Algernon Sidney)[29] but they also emphasize the differences in their circumstances, as they celebrate the triumph of liberty and enlightenment over tyranny and monarchical oppression.[30]

The relationship between secret history in England and France affirms the growing association of this form with a Whig perspective on national and international politics. From the 1660s to the 1680s, ideas about secret history had often been imported into England from France, whether in the form of vernacular translations of Procopius, neoclassical commentaries on secret history as an 'ancient' form of historiography, or politically inflected romance narratives. In the 1690s, however, a marked increase in the publication of *histoire secrète* in France is closely connected to events across the channel. Many *histoires secrètes* from this decade focus on English affairs—for instance, *La Cour de St. Germain* (1695), translated into English as *The Secret History of James II*, and *Histoire secrète du voyage de Jacques II à Calais* (1696) recount the amatory and political intrigues of the Jacobite court in exile. Both English Whig publishers and opposition writers in France exploit the connection between secret history and the revolution of 1688–9, 'importing' this genre's strong association with political and religious liberty into Louis XIV's absolutist state.[31]

Not all Whig secret histories, however, appear unequivocally to be products of a new era of political liberty under William and Mary. One published attack on *The Secret History of the Reigns of K. Charles II and K. James II* accuses its author of writing a narrative '*calculated* merely for the *Common-wealthish Meridian*, and directly levell'd at the bespattering all Kings alike … out of his Hatred to Royalty and Monarchical Government'.[32] This secret history explicitly praises William and Mary in its preface but, as its opponent observes, it has 'No Author's, Printer's, or Licenser's Name to it; no, not so much as the Name of the Place where it was Printed', and consequently resembles quite closely contemporary French *histoires secrètes*, which routinely used false imprints to dodge state censors.[33] It is difficult to tell whether this secret history really is an

---

[28] John Somers, *The True Secret History of the Lives and Reigns of all the Kings and Queens of England* (1702), sig. A2v.

[29] On the scaffold before his execution, Sidney declared that he 'live[s] in an age that makes *Truth* pass for *Treason*'; Algernon Sidney, *Col. Sidney's Speech, Delivered to the Sheriff on the Scaffold* (1683), 1.

[30] These early, Whig secret historians arguably initiated the historiographical tradition, continued by more august writers including Thomas Babington Macaulay and G. M. Trevelyan, to which Herbert Butterfield objected in his influential volume, *The Whig Interpretation of History* (London: G. Bell and Sons, 1931).

[31] On the relationship between secret history in England and France during this decade, see Rebecca Bullard, *The Politics of Disclosure, 1674–1725: Secret History Narratives* (London: Pickering & Chatto, 2009), 51–2 and Allison Stedman, 'Secret History in Pre-Revolutionary France', in Rebecca Bullard and Rachel Carnell (eds.), *The Secret History in Literature, 1660–1820* (Cambridge: Cambridge University Press, 2017), 205–15.

[32] N. N., *The Blatant Beast Muzzl'd* (1691), sig. A6v.

[33] N. N., *The Blatant Beast Muzzl'd*, 1.

attempt to undermine monarchical government altogether, or whether it just aims to capitalize on the *frisson* associated with illicit publication. Other secret histories, however, reflect more self-consciously on the act of disclosing secret intelligence in such a way as to challenge the apparent political function of their own revelations.

The Secret History of White-hall (1697), a series of letters written by a spy at the French court and edited by the historian David Jones, presents itself as a text written in the well-established tradition of Whig opposition to arbitrary government. Rather than celebrating 1688 as a watershed moment, however, which led to a new era of political liberty marked, in part, by the growth of secret history, *The Secret History of White-hall* insists that England remains under threat from the forces of popery and arbitrary government. One of the letters in this secret history informs readers that 'the *French* keep their Correspondence among, and make Tools of Men and Parties most averse to them in their Neighbour-Nations, and who, no manner of Motives would ever be prevalent enough to make instrumental to promote an Interest so hateful to them, did they but know who they wrought for'.[34] Although this letter was ostensibly written before 1688, Jones's preface makes it clear that little has changed since the revolution, asserting that 'no one *Party*, or sect of Men in *England*, much less the Court exempted' is free from French influence, since 'they have all of them, in their respective turns, though many quite against their Knowledge, been imposed upon by *French Emissaries* and made *Tools* of to serve the Interest of *France*, to the prejudice of themselves, and of their own Country'.[35] The idea that even the most loyal courtier might be an unwitting 'tool' of France speaks to the same sceptical view of secret revelations that we find in Behn's *Love-Letters*. Instead of providing secure intelligence that leads to increased political knowledge, this secret history highlights the fact that any secret revelation has the capacity to lead to the discovery of yet more, still more carefully concealed, secrets. The secret springs behind the visible events of history are here arranged as a 'Wheel within a Wheel'—a series of ever more minute interlocking cogs that lead those who discover them towards an increasingly sceptical view of the possibility of political agency.[36]

Over the course of the 1690s, then, secret history develops in a number of new ways. The long-standing association between this form and the Whig opposition to an extended royal prerogative (or arbitrary government, as they called it) means that, after the Williamite revolution of 1688 secret history becomes a symbol of political liberty. These texts are no longer straightforwardly oppositional, but rather represent a celebration of a new era of political history. Not all Whig secret history, however, expresses confidence in 1688 as a definitive triumph over the secretive forces of arbitrary government. Conscious that revelations have the potential to lead to further discoveries, ad infinitum, some secret historians of this period use their chosen form to highlight the instability of any kind of political knowledge, and the ongoing threat of absolutist rule.

---

[34] Jones, *Secret History of White-hall*, 57.
[35] Jones, *Secret History of White-hall*, sig. A8r.
[36] Jones, *Secret History of White-hall*, sigs. Ffffff1v-Ffffff2r (Letter XLV).

Secret History, 1702–15

Towards the end of Queen Anne's reign, Whig polemicists returned to secret history as a weapon in a new skirmish with the forces of French-style absolutism and arbitrary government. John Oldmixon in *The Secret History of Europe* (1712–15) and *Arcana Gallica, or, The Secret History of France* (1714) and John Dunton in *Neck or Nothing* (1713–14) were determined to reveal 'the *True* Character or *Secret History* of the PRESENT MINISTRY'.[37] They claimed that the Tory administration of Robert Harley, Earl of Oxford, which had been in power since 1710, was engaged in secret negotiations with France with the ultimate aim of installing James Edward Francis Stuart, the son of James II otherwise known as the Pretender, on the English throne. Oxford was a notoriously secretive politician whose humour, as one of his political opponents described it, was 'never to deal clearly or openly, but always with Reserve, if not Dissimulation, or rather Simulation; & to love Tricks even where not necessary, but from an inward Satisfaction he took in applauding his own Cunning'.[38] Even without taking the personal qualities of its primary target into account, however, Whig secret histories of Anne's reign are notable for the fact that they pay much more attention to ministers than to monarchs: an index of the power shift in British politics that had taken place after 1688.

If Whig writers used secret history to attack Oxford's ministry while it was in power, they deployed it with even greater enthusiasm to celebrate his fall from grace just days before the death of Queen Anne in the summer of 1714. Anne was succeeded not by her Jacobite half-brother, as the Whigs had feared, but rather by the Protestant Hanoverian, George I. Secret historians compared the events of 1714–15 with 1688–9, asserting that they 'are founded on such a visible Analogy of Causes and Effects, that they may well bear the same name, viz. THE REVOLUTION'.[39] In both cases, the revolution brought to an end a four-year 'reign' that aimed to 'bring in Popery and Slavery'.[40] And although secret history flourished in the wake of this second revolution, as it had after the first, some secret historians observed that the form was now redundant in an age free from secret political machinations. 'I might have continu'd down to the Present Times', writes John Oldmixon in the preface to the fourth and final volume of his *Secret History of Europe*, 'had not an end been put to my Design, by his Majesty's happy Accession to the Throne'.[41]

But although political circumstances towards the end of Queen Anne's reign led to a resurgence in Whig secret history, the first fifteen years of the eighteenth century also

---

[37] John Dunton, *Neck or Nothing* (1713), title page.
[38] William Cowper, *The Private Diary of William, First Earl Cowper*, ed. E. C. Hawtrey (Eton: Roxburghe Club, 1833), 33.
[39] *A Secret History of One Year* (1714), 3.
[40] John Dunton, *Queen Robin, or, The Second Part of Neck or Nothing, Detecting the Secret Reign of the Four Last Years* (1714); William Stoughton, *The Secret History of the Late Ministry* (1715), sig. a*7v.
[41] John Oldmixon, *The Secret History of Europe. Part 4* (1715), sig. A4r.

witnessed the diversification of this tradition. In particular, Tory polemicists began to use this form—previously so closely associated with Whig polemic—to claim that Whig ministers, including Lord Godolphin, intended to 'Dethrone' the Queen and become 'Rulers of Unlimited Sway'.[42] *The Secret History of Queen Zarah and the Zarazians* (1705) is especially close to the Procopian model of secret history, identifying the Queen's Whig favourite, Sarah Churchill, as the corrupt power behind the throne. The fact that Tory secret histories under Queen Anne resemble their Whig counterparts so closely reflects the development of political parties as a permanent feature of the British political landscape in the early eighteenth century, and the attendant attempts of partisans on each side to appropriate cultural and linguistic forms associated with the other.[43] Some Tory writers are, however, more overtly experimental in the ways they adapt this genre to new political circumstances. Among these writers are two perhaps best known for their contribution to the development of the early novel: Delarivier Manley and Daniel Defoe.

Delarivier Manley's *Secret Memoirs and Manners of Several Persons of Quality, of both Sexes, from the New Atalantis* (1709) is better known just by the last three words of that long title. *The New Atalantis* is a peculiarly self-reflexive secret history because of the structural device that frames its revelations: a conversation between the allegorical figures Astrea, goddess of Justice; Virtue; and Intelligence, 'First lady of the bedchamber to the Princess Fame'.[44] Intelligence—her name signifying secret information, rather than cognitive ability—is a figure for secret history itself. She 'bustles up and down, and has a World of Business on her Hands', discovering and reporting on the secrets of the residents of Atalantis, a thinly veiled version of contemporary Britain. 'Her garments are all hieroglyphics', we are told—a description that not only recalls Aphra Behn's reference to 'Hieroglyfick'd' histories in *Love-Letters* but also alludes to the fact that both Manley's and Behn's texts are *romans à clef*.[45] *The New Atalantis* was published with a key that was, itself, 'disemvowelled'—that is, the names of many of the figures named in the key were obscured by removing some of their letters. Manley may have used the 'hieroglyphic' strategies of *roman à clef* to evade prosecution (though, in fact, she was arrested for seditious libel shortly after the publication of *The New Atalantis*) but they serve a rhetorical, as well as a practical, function.[46] They mean that every revelation also involves an act of concealment—that the text adds a layer of secrecy even as it discloses previously concealed information. They encourage speculation and

---

[42] Colley Cibber, *The Secret History of Arlus and Odolphus* (1710), 9.

[43] See, for instance, Mark Knights, 'The Tory Interpretation of History in the Rage of Party', *Huntington Library Quarterly*, 68 (2005), 353–73. See further Chapter 27 on 'Political Debate' by Mark Knights.

[44] Delarivier Manley, *The New Atalantis*, ed. Rosalind Ballaster (Harmondsworth: Penguin, 1991), 13.

[45] Manley, *New Atalantis*, 13.

[46] For two different interpretations of the rhetorical significance of Manley's keys, see Catherine Gallagher, *Nobody's Story: The Vanishing Acts of Women Writers in the Marketplace, 1670–1820* (Berkeley and Los Angeles: University of California Press, 1994), 88–144; Nicola Parsons, *Reading Gossip in Early Eighteenth-Century England* (Basingstoke: Palgrave Macmillan, 2009), 48–55. For the pre-1700 history of the 'key' to prose fictions, see Chapter 20 on 'Keys' by Nicholas McDowell.

conversation, harnessing the energy of extra-textual gossip to amplify the conversation of the three central characters.

Manley's *New Atalantis* is, then, not just a secret history but also a narrative about the production and consumption of secret history. It draws attention to the fact that secret history rarely stands alone, but usually exists in relation to other forms of discourse, whether 'orthodox' neoclassical history, printed keys, or common gossip. It highlights the ambiguous position that secret history occupies on the borders of fact and fiction: 'I take Truth with me when I can get her', observes Intelligence, but 'sometimes indeed she's so hard to recover, that Fame grows impatient, and will not suffer me to wait for her slow approach.'[47] Most significantly, however, it foregrounds gender as a primary concern of secret history. Earlier texts in this tradition had, of course, depicted women as corrupt influences behind the throne, and to some extent *The New Atalantis* also exploits this convention. For instance, in a section of the narrative that gives the history of an island called 'Utopia'—a fictionalized version of recent British history—Manley depicts Sarah Churchill, Duchess of Marlborough, under the guise of 'Madam de Caria' as a pernicious influence on Olympia/Queen Anne in ways that recall *The Secret History of Queen Zarah and the Zarazians*. In Manley's narrative, however, there is not a simple or straightforward distinction between the subjects of secret history and its producers and consumers. Intelligence—who, like the Duchess of Marlborough, holds the office of first lady of the bedchamber—is part of the murky world of backstairs intrigue that she also exposes. As it empowers its readers through a form of printed gossip, secret history also positions them as part of a female-gendered sphere of indirect power. The association between secret history and 'feminine' forms of literary and political expression may have been particularly evident at a time when a female monarch held power in Britain, and in the hands of a female secret historian. The idea that this genre embodies in literary form political structures in which gossip, innuendo, and sexual intrigue hold sway is nonetheless evident from Procopius onwards.

Delarivier Manley was not the only anti-Whig polemicist during the early years of the eighteenth century to write a self-reflexive secret history. Daniel Defoe's *Secret History of the White-Staff* was published in three parts in 1714 and 1715, ostensibly as a rebuttal to the Whig secret histories of the Earl of Oxford that (as we have already seen) became popular after the Hanoverian accession. Defoe's relationship with Oxford had begun a decade previously when the latter—then known just as Robert Harley—employed Defoe as part of a nationwide intelligence network.[48] Defoe's enthusiasm for his new employer's secretive methods of working is evident in their correspondence, in which Defoe asserts, for instance, that 'Intelligence is the Soul of all Publick bussiness', and that 'As Intelligence Abroad is So Considerable, it follows in Proportion That The

---

[47] Manley, *New Atalantis*, 162.

[48] On the beginnings of this relationship, see Max Novak, *Daniel Defoe: Master of Fictions* (Oxford: Oxford University Press, 2003), 195–9.

Most usefull Thing at home is Secrecy.'[49] In *The Secret History of the White-Staff*, written after Oxford's fall from power, Defoe defends his former employer on the very grounds that, for Oxford's political opponents, proved his treachery: his secrecy. While writers like John Oldmixon and John Dunton accused Oxford of conspiring with Jacobites, Defoe suggests that any negotiations with supporters of the Pretender were, in fact, part of a secret strategy designed to neutralize the Jacobite threat. In *The Secret History of the White-Staff* a fictionalized Jacobite peer fulminates against Oxford as he reveals to one of his co-conspirators Oxford's apparent betrayal of the Jacobite cause: 'we are all trick'd and bubbl'd from the Beginning ... wheedled in to be the Instrument of our own Disappointment, by a Management [of] which none of us had Penetration enough to take notice.'[50] In his defence of Oxford, Defoe exploits the same metaphor David Jones used in *The Secret History of White-hall*: that secrets are like 'Wheels' in a 'Machine' and that behind every secret lies another, still more carefully hidden.

Oxford's secrecy underpins not only the content of Defoe's defence of his former employer, but also its formal structure. *The Secret History of the White-Staff* is published in three parts, none of which claims to give a full account of the final years of Queen Anne's reign. The second part supplements the first, 'introduc[ing] the Matters which are behind', and the third part concludes inconclusively, with the assertion that 'there are yet several large Fields that are not mentioned, or entred into, and which have some *Arcana* of publick Matters to bring to light, before the History of the *White-Staff* can be said to be compleat'.[51] In part, Defoe seems to aim at highlighting the effectiveness of Oxford's secrecy: not even a secret historian, he suggests, can provide a complete account of this ministry. Another result of this strategy, however, is to raise extreme scepticism towards secret history itself. Indeed, between the publication of the second and third part of *The Secret History of the White-Staff*, Defoe published (anonymously) another text, *The Secret History of the Secret History of the White-Staff* (1715) which claims, as its title suggests, to reveal the 'truth' behind Defoe's pamphlets. This tract declares that the pamphlet war between the secret historians who had recently condemned the Earl of Oxford, and those who had attempted to defend him, was in fact a publisher's ruse with just one, mercenary aim: 'that the said Books *may Sell*.'[52] It is difficult to know exactly why Defoe attempted to undermine his own, previous attempts to defend Oxford in this way. In a sense, however, he was following the logic of secret history to an extreme conclusion. Many secret historians over the course of the later Stuart period had acknowledged that the scepticism that they asked their readers to exercise towards received narratives of the past might also be directed towards their own iconoclastic narratives. Defoe stretches this sceptical impulse to its fullest extent, representing the power of the secret historian as

---

[49] 'Daniel Defoe to Robert Harley' [July–August c.1704] in *The Letters of Daniel Defoe*, ed. G. H. Healey (Oxford: Clarendon Press, 1955), 36, 38.
[50] Daniel Defoe, *The Secret History of the White-Staff*, 3 parts (1714), 2: 20–1.
[51] Defoe, *The Secret History of the White-Staff*, 2: 21, 3: 80.
[52] Daniel Defoe, *The Secret History of the Secret History of the White-Staff, Purse and Mitre* (1715), 19.

just another form of tyranny that 'caus[es] the deceiv'd People to Dance in the Circles of their drawing'.[53]

Secret history in the early eighteenth century repeatedly reminds its readers that it is part of a decades-old literary tradition. In some cases, this generic self-consciousness is designed to affirm the political continuity between opponents of the Stuart kings—in the 1640s, the 1670s, the 1690s, and, finally, in the 1710s. But one effect of these self-reflexive tendencies is that eighteenth-century secret histories begin to challenge both the political ideology and the rhetorical strategies that had underpinned earlier texts in this tradition. As secret history is used in the service of a wider range of political causes, so its attitudes towards questions of gender and genre become more intensely self-referential, complex, and experimental.

Conclusion

Secret history as a genre was fostered and shaped by the political upheaval and literary innovations of the late seventeenth and early eighteenth centuries. The polemical aggression that characterized this form at its inception became less pronounced in the politically quieter years that followed 1715. In the mid- to late eighteenth century, aspects of secret history's gossipy, anecdotal style, its interest in private life, sex, and women's experience, and even its scepticism towards the act of disclosure become evident in other emerging genres including it-narratives periodicals, oriental tales, and early Gothic literature, as well as—of course—the novel.[54] Secret history's heyday remains, however, defined by political events—from its emergence during the civil wars, through the revolution of 1688–9 that accelerated its popularity, to the Hanoverian accession that substantially ended its widespread use as a political instrument.

As a consequence of its relatively circumscribed period of popularity, secret history illuminates aspects of seventeenth- and eighteenth-century attitudes towards genre that are less visible in longer-lived literary forms. Chief among secret history's characteristics is its generic self-consciousness. From the 1680s through to the early years of the eighteenth century, numerous secret histories begin with prefaces that define their own formal characteristics.[55] They allude to and quote from one another, affirming their

---

[53] Defoe, *The Secret History of the Secret History*, 8.

[54] On the relationship between secret history and other genres, including it-narratives, periodicals, and oriental tales, see essays in Bullard and Carnell (eds.), *Secret History in Literature*. On secret history's vexed relationship with the novel, see McKeon, *Secret History*, 621–718, Rachel Carnell, 'Slipping from Secret History to Novel', *Eighteenth-Century Fiction*, 28/1 (2015), 1–24, and Srinivas Aravamudan, *Enlightenment Orientalism: Resisting the Rise of the Novel* (Chicago: The University of Chicago Press, 2011), chap. 5.

[55] Varillas, *Anekdota Heterouiaka*, sigs. A3r–A8v, a1r–d4r; *Secret History of … K. Charles II and K. James II*, sigs. A2r–v; Jones, *Secret History of White-hall*, A3r–A8r; Somers, *True Secret History*, sigs. A2r–A3v; [Joseph Browne?], *The Secret History of Queen Zarah and the Zarazians* (Albigion [i.e. London], 1705), sigs. A2r–A8v, a1r–a6v.

coherence as a tradition. The care that so many secret historians take to delineate and comment on their chosen genre presents a challenge to those late twentieth-century scholarly analyses of later Stuart prose which place more emphasis on the continuities between different kinds of text—news, novels, periodicals, and pamphlets—than on their generic particularities.[56] Secret historians take pains to define their form as a distinctive historiographical tradition—not as an evolutionary stage on the way to the novel.[57] And yet, as we have also seen, secret history often interacts with other generic traditions, especially neoclassical history, romance, partisan polemic, and satire.

Secret history seems, then, to require an approach towards generic categorization that is more *both/and* than *either/or*. It is *both* a distinct tradition *and* one that hybridizes readily. Indeed, its capacity to mix with other genres is due in no small part to its practitioners' awareness of the distinctive characteristics of their chosen form. Approaching secret history in this manner illuminates other ways in which the genre challenges singular definition. It is both an ancient form and a self-consciously modern one; it is playful, even frivolous, but also serious, sincere, and politically potent; it is aware of its proximity to oral forms like gossip, and also emphatic about the ideological implications of the publicity of print. Secret history, then, has the capacity to open up ways of looking at seventeenth- and eighteenth-century prose fiction that foreground apparent contradictions and, rather than seeking to reconcile them or explain them away, instead acknowledges their literary energy and political force.

---

[56] See, for instance, Lennard Davis, *Factual Fictions: The Origins of the English Novel* (New York: Columbia University Press, 1983), which advocates a 'news/novels matrix'.

[57] As suggested, for instance, by William Warner, *Licensing Entertainment: The Elevation of Novel Reading in Britain, 1684–1750* (Berkeley: University of California Press, 1998), 1–127.

CHAPTER 35

SERMONS

WARREN JOHNSTON

THE significant cultural footprint of sermons in early modern British society is widely recognized. Recent studies have demonstrated not only the breadth of ideas that early modern sermons conveyed but also the variety of occasions and purposes for which they were preached, including services at the royal court, at assize court sessions, at funerals and farewells, for significant anniversaries, national thanksgivings, and fast days, and at other local and national commemorations.[1] These were in addition to the hundreds that were normally preached weekly in parish churches throughout England. This range of events marked by and incorporating preaching shows just how expansive and diverse sermons were in the sixteenth, seventeenth, and eighteenth centuries.

The essential role of preaching was entrenched and emphasized by Protestant reformers, who prescribed sermons as an integral component of church services. Protestant churchgoers came to appreciate and expect them as a vital part of their worship experience by the early seventeenth century. The popularity of sermons continued throughout the seventeenth and into the eighteenth century. The appeal and prominent societal impact of sermons is also revealed by their conspicuousness in print in the seventeenth and eighteenth centuries: scholars have calculated that sermons made

---

[1] See in particular Peter McCullough, *Sermons at Court: Politics and Religion in Elizabethan and Jacobean Preaching* (Cambridge: Cambridge University Press, 1998); Lori Anne Ferrell, *Government By Polemic: James I, the King's Preachers' and the Rhetorics of Conformity, 1603–1625* (Stanford: Stanford University Press, 1998); Lori Anne Ferrell and Peter McCullough (eds.), *The English Sermon Revised: Religion, Literature, and History 1600–1750* (Manchester: Manchester University Press, 2000); Susan Wabuda, *Preaching During the English Reformation* (Cambridge: Cambridge University Press, 2002); Arnold Hunt, *The Art of Hearing: English Preachers and Their Audiences* (Cambridge: Cambridge University Press, 2010); Mary Morrissey, *Politics and the Paul's Cross Sermons, 1558–1642* (Oxford: Oxford University Press, 2011); Jennifer Farooq, *Preaching in Eighteenth-Century London* (Woodbridge: The Boydell Press, 2013); Keith Francis and William Gibson (eds.), *The Oxford Handbook of the British Sermon, 1689–1901* (Oxford: Oxford University Press, 2012); Peter McCullough, Hugh Adlington, and Emma Rhatigan (eds.), *The Oxford Handbook of the Early Modern Sermon* (Oxford: Oxford University Press, 2011).

up 15 per cent of publications in England from the late fifteenth century to 1640, and that, from 1660 to 1783, somewhere between 12,000 and 15,000 sermons were printed.[2]

This chapter considers sermons in printed form from 1640 to 1714. However, the large number of sermons published during these years presents a difficulty: any attempt to consider this wealth of sources in its entirety in a short essay would achieve little meaningful detail. Therefore, to narrow the focus, it will use fast-day sermons as a representative case study of sermon literature during this period. Though only one subcategory, an examination of fast sermons allows a greater depth of analysis, while also revealing the forms and kinds of ideas found in sermons of all types.

Structures and Characteristics of Early Modern Sermons

To place fast sermons within the wider genre, it is necessary to discuss some general aspects of sermons in the period from the mid-seventeenth to the early eighteenth century. Structurally, sermons were introduced with and centred around a short scriptural text, after which the preacher would examine the biblical and historical context of the passage and explain its meaning, often through extensive glosses on key words and phrases in the text. The main points of argument (often called 'doctrines') for the sermon were listed and then extrapolated around a particular set of spiritual issues and concerns. The preacher would then apply these themes (often referred to as 'uses') to theological lessons, as well as to contemporary circumstances facing the auditors and the nation. Some combination, and frequently all, of these elements were present in sermons from this period, though the order in which they appeared and the space committed to each varied, depending on the preacher's preferences in composition.

In regard to homiletical method, the seventeenth century was a period of transition connected with the growing preference towards 'plain' style preaching. Already evident in the period before 1640, plain style became the predominant form in the later seventeenth century in England, moving away from elaborate rhetorical and linguistic flourishes to a more direct and clear exposition of scriptural meaning.[3] For example,

---

[2] Mary Morrissey, 'Interdisciplinarity and the Study of Early Modern Sermons', *The Historical Journal*, 42 (1999), 1111–1123 (1112); Ian Green, 'Orality, Script and Print: The Case of the English Sermon c. 1530–1700', in Heinz Schilling and István György Tóth (eds.), *Cultural Exchange in Early Modern Europe, Volume I: Religion and Cultural Exchange in Europe, 1400–1700* (Cambridge: Cambridge University Press, 2006), 236–55 (250–1).

[3] See further Millar MacLure, *The Paul's Cross Sermons 1534–1642* (Toronto: University of Toronto Press, 1958), 147, 152–3; Morrissey, 'Interdisciplinarity', 1119–20; Mary Morrissey, 'Scripture, Style and Persuasion in Seventeenth-Century English Theories of Preaching', *Journal of Ecclesiastical History*, 53 (2002), 686–706 (694); Tom Kilton, 'Post-Restoration English Commemorative Sermons—Observations on Their Form and Content', *Journal of Library History*, 14 (1979), 297–318 (311); Andrew Lacey, *The Cult of King Charles the Martyr* (Woodbridge: The Boydell Press, 2003), 146–50.

Richard Kentish described his sermon as 'plain and shalow' and himself as one 'who savours nothing of delicacy nor depth', indicating his intent to not 'tickle the ears' but, instead, 'to move the affection, and touch the heart'.[4] Twelve years later Richard Baxter noted the changing styles, declaring his sermon contained 'nothing but plain English ... less affecting such ornaments in sacred discourses, then formerly I have done'.[5]

The movement towards plain style should not be interpreted as underestimating early modern audiences' ability to understand the foundations of the sermons they heard.[6] Congregations were expected to sit in church and listen to sermons that were thirty minutes to an hour in length; many took notes to reflect on at home, and there was the expectation that the sermon would be discussed and repeated later for the benefit of individuals within the household and the community.[7] Preachers clearly expected their audience would absorb a wide variety of substantial theological ideas and the scriptural examples used to reinforce them.

Another item of consideration was the time devoted to the sermon. In the mid-seventeenth century sermons were generally about an hour in length, and pulpits often had hourglasses attached to them, which were used by preachers to time their discourses.[8] Remarks within published versions of sermons occasionally give a sense of time restrictions. In his sermon to the House of Commons, Richard Byfield introduced the final point of his sermon by acknowledging 'the time is over, and I fear to detaine you beyond what is meet'.[9] Similarly, Matthew Barker explained that he had not preached the end of his sermon 'because I was prevented by time, chusing rather to be abrupt then tedious'.[10] There is also evidence that some did not abide by standardized temporal restraints: in 1642 Edmund Calamy proudly informed the House of Commons 'you have heard a Sermon of two houres'.[11] However, the length of preached sermons was

---

[4] Richard Kentish, *Sure Stay ... Sermon ... at Margarets Westminster before the. . . House of Commons... Nov. 24. 1647* (1648), 'Epistle Dedicatory' (n.p.).

[5] Richard Baxter, *Sermon of Repentance. ... before the... Commons ... April 30. 1660* (1660), sig. A4r.

[6] Tom Webster, 'Preaching and Parliament, 1640–1659', in McCullough, Adlington, and Rhatigan (eds.), *Early Modern Sermon*, 404–22 (417); Hunt, *Art of Hearing*, 10.

[7] David Appleby, 'Issues of Audience and Reception in Restoration Preaching', in Geoff Baker and Ann McGruer (eds.), *Readers, Audiences and Coteries in Early Modern England* (Newcastle: Cambridge Scholars Press, 2006), 10–27 (17); Jeremy Gregory, '"For All Sorts and Conditions of Men": The Social Life of the Book of Common Prayer during the Long Eighteenth Century, or, Bringing the History of Religion and Social History Together', *Social History*, 34 (2009), 29–54 (39–40); John Spurr, *The Laity and Preaching in Post-Reformation England* (London: Dr Williams's Trust, 2013), 9–12; Morrissey, *Politics*, 39–41; Kevin Killeen, 'Veiled Speech: Preaching, Politics and Scriptural Typology', in McCullough, Adlington, and Rhatigan (eds.), *Early Modern Sermon*, 387–403 (396); Wabuda, *Preaching*, 97; Caroline Francis Richardson, *English Preachers and Preaching, 1640–1670: A Secular Study* (London: S.P.C.K., 1928), 49, 70.

[8] Appleby, 'Issues', 18; Emma Rhatigan, 'Preaching Venues: Architecture and Auditories', in McCullough, Adlington, and Rhatigan (eds.), *Early Modern Sermon*, 88–119 (93–4).

[9] Richard Byfield, *Zion's Answer ... Sermon... before the ... Commons ... Junii 25. 1645* (1645), 36.

[10] Matthew Barker, *Faithful and Wise Servant ... Sermon ... in the Parliament House, Jan. 9, 1656* (1657), sig. A3r.

[11] Edmund Calamy, *Gods Free Mercy ... Sermon ...before the ... Commons ... Feb. 23. 1641* (1642), 51.

changing: by the end of the seventeenth century sermons were expected to be only half an hour long, a timeframe that also made a convenient length for publication.[12]

SERMONS IN PRINT

The transition from their original oral delivery into print is another topic that applies to all types of sermons. Prior to the Reformation, sermons were considered texts intended to be received aurally by their audiences. This began to change in the late sixteenth and early seventeenth century due to the growth of the print trade. Though sermons were almost always still first delivered orally to congregations at the local level, they were also becoming important as printed works whose distribution and audiences extended further. This conversion of sermons into texts that were written and read was not a seamless one, and was connected to ideas of proper method and mind-set in the pulpit.[13] In the first half of the seventeenth century *ex tempore* delivery was viewed as the soundest form, but by the later seventeenth century sermons were frequently delivered based on thorough written notes, and by the mid-eighteenth century increasingly preachers were reading sermons as full and refined written texts.[14]

Published sermons give some sense of concerns over the sometimes problematic journey from pulpit to print. After a delay in printing his sermon, Robert Harris explained it was constructed from 'onely broken notes' but attempted to 'come as neere my selfe, as my notes will help mee'.[15] Daniel Burgess introduced his thirty-one page octavo version as 'little more than a Skeleton of our Fast Day's Discourse'.[16] Assessing

---

[12] Tony Claydon, 'The Sermon, the "Public Sphere" and the Political Culture of Late Seventeenth-Century England', in Ferrell and McCullough (eds.), *English Sermon*, 208–34 (213); Jennifer Farooq, 'The Politicising Influence of Print: The Responses of Hearers and Readers to the Sermons of Gilbert Burnet and Henry Sacheverell', in Baker and McGruer (eds.), *Readers, Audiences and Coteries*, 28–46 (31).

[13] There is a growing scholarly discussion about differences and similarities between oral and printed sermons, as well as audience reception of both forms. See for example: Hunt, *Art of Hearing*, 11–12, 94, 148, 393; Morrissey, *Politics*, 35, 49, 63, 66–7; Appleby, 'Issues', 11; Jacqueline Eales, 'Provincial Preaching and Allegiance in the First English Civil War, 1640-6', in Thomas Cogswell, Richard Cust, and Peter Lake (eds.), *Politics, Religion and Popularity in Early Stuart Britain: Essays in Honour of Conrad Russell* (Cambridge: Cambridge University Press, 2002), 185–210 (187); Rosemary Dixon, 'Sermons in Print, 1660–1700', and John Craig, 'Sermon Reception', in McCullough, Adlington, and Rhatigan (eds.), *Early Modern Sermon*, 460–79 (461); 179–93 (179, 190); Webster, 'Preaching', 417; Richardson, *English Preachers*, 120; Farooq, *Preaching*, 114–17.

[14] Green, 'Orality', 237–40, 248, 254–5; Hunt, *Art of Hearing*, 12–13, 54, 59, 119, 124, 126, 131–5, 184, 394; Eric Josef Carlson, 'The Boring of the Ear: Shaping the Pastoral Vision of Preaching in England, 1540-1640', in Larissa Taylor (ed.), *Preachers and People in the Reformations and Early Modern Period* (Leiden: Brill, 2001), 249–96 (282); Farooq, *Preaching*, 9–11; Françoise Deconinck-Brossard, 'Eighteenth-Century Sermons and the Age', in W.M. Jacob and Nigel Yates (eds.), *Crown and Mitre: Religion and Society in Northern Europe Since the Reformation* (Woodbridge: The Boydell Press, 1993), 105–23 (111–13); William Gibson, *The Church of England 1688-1832: Unity and Accord* (London: Routledge, 2001), 224–5.

[15] Robert Harris, *Sermon...to the...Commons...May, 25. 1642* (1642), sig. A2r.

[16] Daniel Burgess, *Seasonable Words...Sermon...January the 14th, 1707/8* (1708), sig A2r.

the differences between oral and printed delivery, John Ward confirmed he 'knew well that the same Sermon, as to the life of it, is scarcely the same in the hearing, and in the reading', and Thomas Bradbury opened his prefatory remarks by pronouncing his sermon as 'designed for no other Sense than the Ear', adding he took no 'New Pains to prepare it for the Publick Tast[e]'.[17]

Some clergymen were cautious about publishing their sermons. This was based on perceptions in the late sixteenth and early seventeenth century that the ear was more effective than the eye for receiving spiritual messages and that publishing took ministers away from their principal pastoral roles.[18] Remarking on the Commons' order to print his 1644 sermon, George Gipps characterized printing as something he had 'not hitherto been *guilty of*.[19] Similarly hesitant, Edward Reyner protested that 'Those small abilities God hath given me ... lye ... rather through the Pulpit then the Presse'.[20]

Uneasiness about publishing was also apparent in the ritualized humility repeated by preachers-cum-authors from the 1640s through to the 1710s. This conceit was ubiquitous, and it took the forms of protestations of unwillingness to publish, yielding to requests from auditors, or expressions of unworthiness of the sermon. A few examples include Henry Hall declaring his work 'weake and course-spun', and Peter Sterry attributing his sermon's ideas to 'my Scanty Store, in the midst of that Thick Ignorance'.[21] Without the request of his parishioners, John Harris said he would 'have judg'd this Discourse by no means worthy of coming abroad'.[22] Using violent imagery, Samuel Fisher described the requests from auditors to publish his 1673 sermon as 'an honest rape' due to avowals that they would combine notes and print it 'without my leave' if he did not do so himself.[23]

Despite such apprehension, wide availability of printed sermons by the mid-seventeenth century indicated preachers' willingness to publish their work. It was becoming recognized that printed sermons had benefits that overcame earlier concerns. These advantages included the chance to reach a much wider audience than the original spoken delivery, the permanence and extended life of the printed sermon, the ability to expose more people to more sermons, and the growing appreciation among clerical

---

[17] John Ward, *God Judging ... Sermon ... before the ... Commons ... March 26. 1645* (1645), sig. A2r; Thomas Bradbury, *God's Empire ... Sermon ... January 19, 1703/4* (1704), sig. A2r.

[18] Carlson, 'Boring of the Ear', 280–2; James Rigney, 'Sermons in Print', in McCullough, Adlington, and Rhatigan (eds.), *Early Modern Sermon*, 198–212 (200); James Rigney, '"To Lye Upon a Stationers Stall, Like a Piece of Coarse Flesh in a Shambles": The Sermon, Print and the English Civil War', in Ferrell and McCullough (eds.), *English Sermon*, 188–207 (189); Hunt, *Art of Hearing*, 119.

[19] George Gipps, *Sermon ... to the ... Commons ... Novemb. 27* [1644] ... (1644), sig. A2r. (emphasis mine).

[20] Edward Reyner, *Orders from the Lord ... Sermon ... at ... Newark ... 27th of March, 1646 ...* (1646), sig. A2r.

[21] Henry Hall, *Heaven Ravished ... Sermon to the ... Commons ... May 29. 1644* (1644), sig. A2r; Peter Sterry, *Clouds ... Sermon before the ... Commons ... Octob. 27, 1647* (1648), sig. A2v.

[22] John Harris, *Sermon ... in ... St. Mary Magdalen, Old Fish-Street ... Twenty Sixth of May, 1703* (1703), sig. A2r.

[23] Samuel Fisher, *Honour the King ... Sermon ... January 30, 1672/3 ... At Birmingham* (1673), sig. A2r.

and lay contemporaries (including booksellers) of sermons as useful, interesting, and popular publications.[24]

Some structures also benefited printed sermons over their spoken counterparts. Even in sermons where the written text mirrored what had been spoken, publication allowed the use of devices to augment the preacher's objectives. Title pages often included the place the sermon had been preached, the audience, and the occasion, in order to pique the potential readers' interest. Prefaces and dedicatory epistles could introduce, explain, and elaborate on the discourse that followed, as well as thank or attract the attention of important auditors and potential patrons. Marginal notes expanded and consolidated ideas contained in the text. In addition, many printed sermons included marginal Latin, Greek, and sometimes Hebrew passages from contemporary and ancient authors, not only providing further information for learned readers but also displaying the author's erudite abilities. All of these elements enhanced the sermon as a piece of printed prose.

A final physical feature of the printed sermon to consider is size. In the fast sermons used for this study,[25] quarto was the most common page format for sermons from 1640 to 1700, with only two examples of the smaller octavo format, and none in larger, folio editions. By the early eighteenth century a mixture of quarto and octavo versions appeared. A consideration of average page counts in this fast sermon sample also reveals trends in sermon length. From 1640 to 1648 (182 sermons), the average length of a printed quarto fast sermon was 40.2 pages; though no other decade of the period reached that concentration of fast sermon publication, if the quarto sermons (121) from 1660 to 1714 are used as a comparison, the average length was 30.46 pages. A final comparator can be found in the octavo fast sermons from 1704 to 1714: the average length in this group (26) is 24.42 pages. Taken together, this data suggests that the length of printed sermons was decreasing by the later seventeenth and early eighteenth century.

Features of Fast Sermons

So far this chapter has considered attributes shared by all types of sermons from 1640 to 1714. As a subgenre, fast sermons had certain elements specific to their purpose and meaning. They were a part of fast-day services, a type of national public worship (others included thanksgiving days and days of prayer) that had been observed in England since the medieval period, and were intended to focus people spiritually in the interest of the

---

[24] Green, 'Orality', 241–2, 243, 251; Rigney, 'Sermons', 200–05; Rigney, 'To Lye Upon a Stationers Stall ...', 190–3; Morrissey, *Politics*, 42; Morrissey, 'Interdisciplinarity', 1112; Dixon, 'Sermons', 463; Alexandra Walsham, *Providence in Early Modern England* (Oxford: Oxford University Press, 1999), 55–6; Pasi Ihalainen, *Protestant Nations Redefined: Changing Perceptions of National Identity in the Rhetoric of the English, Dutch and Swedish Public Churches, 1685–1772* (Leiden: Brill, 2005), 27; Claydon, 'Sermon', 213–14; Farooq, 'Politicising Influence', 36–8, 45.

[25] First editions have been used whenever available; however, editions and variations in other formats may also have been printed.

kingdom.[26] The objective of a fast was to turn people's attention to issues of concern to the community by considering themes of sinfulness and repentance, confronting audiences with considerations of the nation's and their own failings. Though it is not certain how widely the fasts were kept outside of London in the 1640s, by the late seventeenth and early eighteenth century fasts and thanksgivings enjoyed a widespread participation throughout the country.[27]

Discussion of the nation's sins was ubiquitous in fast sermons, often illustrated with lists of the improprieties perpetrated. In 1642 John Pigott, curate of St Sepulchre in London,[28] bewailed 'all the abominations that are committed … in our Hierusalem … how hath pride jetted in one street? drunkennesse reeled in another … oppression marched … in another … adultery with all her wanton positures minced in another street? wee have justified Sodome in all her abominations'.[29] In the same year, for the London preacher Simeon Ashe it was 'our sinnes, personall sins, Family sinnes, City sinnes, Country sinnes, Kingdom sinnes, Pride, Passion, Prodigality, Hypocrisy, Oaths, Blasphemy, polluting Gods Ordinances, Sacrilegious lavishing our holy time'.[30] In 1691 the Bristol vicar, Thomas Cary, was still decrying 'contempt for God's Word and Worship, for prophaning his Holy Day, dishonouring his sacred Name, by Customary Swearing and Cursing, for Drunkenness, Adultery, Pride, and Dissolute living'.[31]

Fast sermons were full of directions to repent. In the early 1640s, the royal chaplain Richard Love declared repentance was 'the summe of every Sermon' and, similarly, Obadiah Sedgwick, Presbyterian minister of Coggeshall in Essex, found the essential answer to the needs of 'our sinfull and distracted Kingdome' in the word '*Repent*, and in that … all our safeties and hopes are contained'.[32] Accompanying the need to repent were warnings about current and impending punishments for the people's and the nation's refusal to do so. Perhaps the epitome of this type of message came in the mid-1660s, with the occurrence of two disasters in quick succession. In 1666 the twin calamities of fire and plague over the previous year and a half caused Edward

---

[26] Natalie Mears, 'Public Worship and Political Participation in Elizabethan England', *Journal of British Studies*, 51 (2012), 4–25 (6, 7, 12, 21–2); Tony Claydon, *William III and the Godly Revolution* (Cambridge: Cambridge University Press, 1996), 101.

[27] Claydon, *William III*, 109–10; Farooq, *Preaching*, 222.

[28] Unless otherwise noted, biographical details of preachers were obtained from information in the published sermons themselves and, where necessary, more detail has been obtained from the *Clergy of the Church of England 1540–1835* database (http://theclergydatabase.org.uk/) or A. G. Matthews, *Calamy Revised: Being a Revision of Edmund Calamy's Account of the Ministers and Others Ejected and Silenced, 1660–2* (Oxford: Oxford University Press, 1988).

[29] John Pigott, *Hierusalem Bedewed … Sermon … at St. Mary Woolnoth London … Martii, 30. 1642* (1642), 22.

[30] Simeon Ashe, *Best Refuge … Sermon.. to the … Commons … March 30, 1642* (1642), 10.

[31] Thomas Cary, *Sermon … in … St. Philip and Jacob, in … Bristol … 15th of July, 1691* (1691), 6.

[32] Richard Love, *Watchmans Watchword … Sermon … at White-Hall … 30 of March* [1642] . . . ([Cambridge], 1642), 7; Obadiah Sedgwick, *England's Preservation … Sermon … to the … Commons … May, 25. 1642* (1642), sig. A3v (emphasis in the original).

Stillingfleet, rector of St Andrew's Holborn in London and a royal chaplain, to reflect on God's anger with England. Recounting the iniquities of its citizens, he concluded with London advising 'her inhabitants not weep for her miseries, but for their own sins'.[33] On the same occasion, William Sancroft, dean of St Paul's Cathedral, envisaged a 'slow-moving Cloud ... o're our Heads, ... and without our serious Amendment we have no Rainbow to assure us, that we shall not again be drencht in that horrible Tempest'.[34]

The wars of the early eighteenth century provided further evidence of divine dissatisfaction. Queen Anne's royal chaplain Ofspring Blackall asserted 'that all temporal Judgments are Expressions of God's Displeasure against Sin', and that national punishments struck both the 'good' and the 'wicked' at 'random' as a sign of God's displeasure.[35] Fellow royal chaplain Andrew Snape interpreted the long conflict with France as a product of the nation's wickedness, aptly warning that 'the Artillery of Heaven is never to be exhausted' and God continued 'to regard our Actions ... [and] chastise us for 'em'.[36] The London Presbyterian minister John Shower agreed that war continued because of the many 'bare-faced Impieties and Provocations of our Age and Nation'.[37]

In order to prevent God's wrath, preachers encouraged people to change the way they lived their lives. This alteration was often expressed in terms of a personal 'reformation', which would prepare the godly for their work. Stephen Marshall, a Presbyterian minister and prominent parliamentary preacher in the 1640s, saw humiliation and reformation encompassing 'the very life of unfained repentance, and the spirituall part of a Religious Fast'.[38] In 1642 fellow Presbyterian Thomas Hill asked the House of Commons 'How can you be good Reformers both of State and Church, unless you be first Reformers of your selves, and your owne Families?'[39] In the early Restoration Nathaniel Hardy, vicar of St Martin in the Fields in London and a royal chaplain, continued the call for 'a thorough Reformation, not of our Religion ... but of manner and lives of people which are excessively bad'.[40] Such appeals for individual reform were found in English sermons of all kinds throughout the early modern period,[41] and in the 1690s a movement was

---

[33] Edward Stillingfleet, *Sermon ... before the ... Commons, at St. Margarets Westminster Octob. 10. 1666* (1666), 3, 15–16.

[34] William Sancroft, *Lex Ignea ... Sermon ... before the King, Octob. 10, 1666* (1666), 34.

[35] Ofspring Blackall, *Sermon ... before ... the Lord Mayor, Aldermen ... of London, at the Cathedral-Church of St. Paul, January the 19th. 1703/4* (1704), 6, 25.

[36] Andrew Snape, *Sermon ... before the ... Commons ... 28th of March, 1711* (1711), 6–7, 19.

[37] John Shower, *Fast-Sermon, on the Account of the Present War* (1705), 23.

[38] Stephen Marshall, *Reformation and Desolation ... Sermon ... to the ... Commons ... Decemb. 22, 1641* (1642), 17.

[39] Thomas Hill, *Trade of Truth ... Sermon ... to the ... Commons, ... Iuly 27. 1642* (1642), 22.

[40] Nathaniel Hardy, *Loud Call ... Sermon ... 30th of January 1661 ... before the ... Commons ... in ... Saint Margarets Westminster* (1662), sig. A4r.

[41] Martin Ingrim, 'Reformation of Manners in Early Modern England', in Paul Griffiths, Adam Fox, and Steve Hindle (eds.), *The Experience of Authority in Early Modern England* (New York: St. Martin's, 1996), 47–88.

established, which the Congregational minister Thomas Bradbury expressly identified to his audience in 1704 as 'a Zeal for the REFORMATION of MANNERS'.[42]

Fast Sermons during the Civil War

All types of sermons held the possibility of a preacher weighing-in on current issues and affairs, making them much more than just texts for theological and spiritual instruction. As days of national worship focused on prominent events, fast sermons were even more likely to inspire such comment. Despite being part of a particular type of service, with repeated themes and shared purpose, they incorporated a broad range of subjects into their messages, and opinions on contemporary political and religious circumstances informed many of them. The nature and focus of such remarks depended upon the preacher and the context. In the 1640s, political division and religious divergence had different meanings depending on the denomination and political leanings of the preacher. In the Restoration, contention often centred around Protestant nonconformity, as well as around differing ideas on constitutional structures and principles, distinctions that continued into the early eighteenth century.

The 1640s ushered in an intense period of fast sermon publication. This group of sermons is best known because of their association with the Civil Wars, and due to several focused scholarly studies.[43] From 1630 to 1641 there had only been three occasions of national fasting in England.[44] However, concerns over domestic political circumstances and rebellion in Ireland spurred parliament to petition Charles I to implement more regular fasts and preaching, and in early January 1642 he instituted monthly public fasts for the kingdom, with specific provision for parliamentary sermons; this resulted in eighty-five monthly fast days being observed from February 1642 to February 1649.[45] A vast majority of the fast sermons published in the 1640s were preached before one or both houses of parliament. Here the concerns of preachers intersected with crucial political and religious affairs of the nation.

The exceptional nature of the events of the decade makes it unsurprising that clergymen weighed in on these matters. In the early 1640s fast sermons commented on

---

[42] Bradbury, *God's Empire*, 31 (emphasis in the original). The foundation of societies for the Reformation of Manners after 1690 saw endowed sermons preached specifically on this theme. See Dudley Bahlman, *The Moral Revolution of 1688* (New Haven: Yale University Press, 1957).

[43] John F. Wilson, *Pulpit in Parliament: Puritanism During the English Civil Wars, 1640–1648* (Princeton, NJ: Princeton University Press, 1969), 60–97; Christopher Durston, '"For the Better Humiliation of the People": Public Days of Fasting and Thanksgiving during the English Revolution', *The Seventeenth Century*, 7/2 (1992), 129–49; Webster, 'Preaching', 404–20.

[44] Natalie Mears et al. (with Lucy Bates), *National Prayers: Special Worship Since the Reformation, Volume I: Special Prayers, Fasts and Thanksgivings in the British Isles, 1533–1688*, Church of England Record Society 20 (Woodbridge: The Boydell Press, 2013), pp. cxviii–cxix.

[45] Wilson, *Pulpit*, 57, 60; Durston, ' "For the Better Humiliation…" ', 132–3.

the legislative successes of parliament and on the unique dangers that faced the nation. Suggestively, Edward Reynolds, rector of Braunston in Northamptonshire and later a member of the Westminster Assembly of Divines, pronounced 'Liberty, Property, Priviledges are sacred and pretious things, not to be in the least manner betrayed'.[46] The Presbyterian minister, and fellow member of the Westminster Assembly, Thomas Case blamed 'the cursed policy of desperate Malignant Courtiers, and Counsellors' for inciting 'Princes and Potentates against the poor people of God'.[47] Some preachers also legitimized parliament's resistance to the king, a theme that became especially important after civil war broke out. In his June 1642 sermon William Gouge, preacher at St Ann Blackfriars in London, justified parliament's 'Subsidies, Pole-money, Land-rate, Loanes, and other meanes' as necessary measures, and seven months later fellow London preacher Walter Bridges similarly laid out a series of arguments defending parliament's position and the policies implemented to support the war.[48] Though a few sermons sincerely appealed for the political breach between the king and parliament to be quickly healed, the fact that the ministers were invited by parliament to preach clearly suggested their perspective on the conflict.

A vast majority of the parliamentary fast preachers were Presbyterian or Congregational ministers, and criticisms of existing ecclesiastical policies formed a significant undercurrent of justification in their sermons. These combined with an intent to promote change in church government and worship. Preachers emphasized religious reform as parliament's first and most important responsibility. Stephen Marshall told the Commons 'God hath raised you up to attempt glorious things for his name, for purging of his house, and the establishment of this great people in the peace of the Gospel', while the Scottish minister Robert Baillie prioritized parliament's responsibilities by asserting 'The ordering of the State and Kingdom ... ought not to precede the setling of the Church'.[49] Fellow Presbyterian Matthew Newcomen described the 'great work God hath called you to ... to rescue truth from the jaws of those monstrous errours, that had almost devoured it; to disburthen the worship of God of those corruptions, that have long clogged and defiled it'.[50]

In the second half of 1643, the convening of the Westminster Assembly of Divines and the signing of the Solemn League and Covenant with the Scots provided further impetus for religious reform. Only days after parliament accepted the agreement in September, Humphrey Chambers, a Presbyterian member of the Westminster Assembly, voiced his

---

[46] Edward Reynolds, *Israels Petition ... Sermon ... in St. Margarets Church at Westminster ... before the ... Commons ... July, 27. 1642* (1642), 25. In the Restoration, Reynolds would become the bishop of Norwich.

[47] Thomas Case, *Gods Rising... Sermon before the ... Commons ... 26. Octob. 1642* (1644), 11.

[48] William Gouge, *Saints Support ... Sermon ... before the ... Commons ... 29. Iune, 1642* (1642), 21; Walter Bridges, *Ioabs Counsell... Sermon before the ... Commons ... Feb. 22* (1643), sigs. A3r–A4r, 11.

[49] Marshall, *Reformation*, 7; Robert Baillie, *Satan the Leader ... Sermon to the ... Commons ... Febr. 28. 1643* (1643), sig. A2v.

[50] Matthew Newcomen, *Jerusalems Watch-Men ... Sermon ... at the Abbie at Westminster, before Both Houses of Parliament, and the Assembly of Divines ... Iuly 7. 1643* (1643), sig. A2r.

hope 'that that solemne Covenant ... shall ... bring forth a blessed Church'.[51] In turn, the Edinburgh minister Alexander Henderson proclaimed 'Amongst all the great things which the honourable Houses of Parliament have done, there is none more acceptable to God ... then that a Church-assembly is called'.[52] However, initial optimism gave way to concern that parliament was not as zealous as it should be in moving to implement the terms of the Covenant and push forward real reform. Already in December 1644 Edmund Calamy, the Presbyterian pastor of St Mary Aldermanbury in London, felt compelled to tell the Lords to 'Consider the late Nationall Covenant you have taken ... remember it is not the taking but the keeping of Covenant that prevailes with God'.[53] By early 1646 Gaspar Hickes, another Presbyterian member of the Westminster Assembly, would cynically pronounce that 'the Covenant is like mariners vows in a storm, as sick-bed promises, quite forgotten now we are safe and sound'.[54]

A slowing pace of reform was not the only apprehension. By the mid-1640s fast sermons revealed mounting concern over the emergence of heterodox beliefs. Preachers recited lists of sects and false doctrines as a catalogue of errors for their audiences to be wary of. Robert Baillie complained that heresies ate 'like a Gangreen, and Canker [through] ... the whole land', and Obadiah Sedgwick portrayed heretical ideas 'like circles in a pond, one circle begets another, ... monstrous opinions have been built upon errours which seemed but little at first'.[55] John Whincop, a minster from Clothall in Hertfordshire, warned the Commons that the sects not only endangered 'all Order, Discipline, and Charity, but threaten many Godly and Orthodox Divines, threaten the Assembly, threaten the Parliament, nay threaten you, and the Government you shall establish'.[56]

After Charles I surrendered in 1646, unease over the condition of the nation grew, with particular apprehension over the unresolved relationship between the king and parliament. Parliament's own shortcomings did not escape preachers' notice. Having returned from Massachusetts the previous year, Nathaniel Ward was invited to preach for the 30 June 1647 fast, and expressed dissatisfaction at the lack of a political settlement. Ward told the Commons to 'Lament if you have not sufficiently attended the re-establishing of the Royall Scepter', and he maintained that 'If a Common-wealth bee headlesse the people will be brainlesse'.[57] In a sermon from the previous month, William Hussey, a

---

[51] Humphrey Chambers, *Divine Ballance ... Sermon ... before the ... Commons, in S. Margarets Westminster ... Sept. 27. 1643* (1643), 15.

[52] Alexander Henderson, *Sermon ... to the ... Commons ... December 27, 1643* (Edinburgh, 1644), 5.

[53] Edmund Calamy, *Indictment against England ... Sermon ... before the ... Lords ... Abby Church at Westminster ... December 25. 1644* (1645), 22.

[54] Gaspar Hickes, *Advantage of Afflictions: ... Sermon ... before the ... Peers, January 28. 1645. in the Abbey Church, Westminster* ([1646]), 12.

[55] Baillie, *Satan*, sig. A3r; Obadiah Sedgwick, *Nature and Danger of Heresies ... Sermon before the ... Commons, January 27. 1646. At Margarets Westminster* (1647), 25.

[56] John Whincop, *Gods Call ... Sermon before the ... Commons ... January 29, 1644* (1645), 27.

[57] Nathaniel Ward, *Sermon ... before the ... Commons ... June 30. 1647* (1647), sig. A3v, 19, 20. On Ward, see Wilson, *Pulpit*, 92, 132.

minister from Chislehurst in Kent, told the Lords that the war had been fought to have their old rights re-established, and complained that parliament was now initiating 'a new quarrell upon a new cause, upon grounds not knowne'.[58]

There was also concern over parliament's failure to push forward the agenda of religious reform. Calling it 'lamentable for a Kingdome to have perfidious and Covenant-breaking guides', George Hughes, a Presbyterian minister from Plymouth, accused the Commons of being 'remisse and carelesse of Gods affaires in reforming his House, and setling his Ordinances', and London Presbyterian Samuel Annesley chastised parliament for having 'let slip seasons of Reformation', allowing 'monstrous births of Prophaneness and Blasphemy'.[59] Charging parliament with being 'harvest sleepers, [and] summer sluggards' for their failure to reform the church, fellow Presbyterian William Jenkyn described the religious settlement as 'so imperfect, and discountenanced ... that it is rather a scorne then a curb to men disaffected to holinesse'.[60]

Though the number of printed fast sermons slowed markedly by the end of 1648, several were published that give insight into the unprecedented events occurring at that time. Taken in the context of the coming trial and execution of the king, these sermons had clear messages for the audiences that heard and read them. In late November, the Congregational preacher George Cokayn told the Commons 'God is no respecter of persons' and advised his audience to 'Delay not to act for the peoples good who have intrusted you'. Encouraging the radical political turn parliament was about to take, Cokayn warned them 'not to save your selves by an unrighteous saving of them, who are the Lords and the Peoples known Enemies', and told his audience 'God hath spoken aloud to you in these last years; I beseech you be not dull of hearing'.[61] In the fast at the end of December, and with parliament's path now determined, Thomas Brooks, minister of St Thomas Apostle in London, reminded the Commons of the damaging effects of the Civil War, and declared that any neglect of justice would transfer to them 'the treachery, and murther, and bloud, and crueltie, and tyranny of others'.[62]

The Restoration

Nothing would come close to matching the output of printed fast sermons from the 1640s. During the 1650s there were fewer national fasting occasions and few sermons

---

[58] William Hussey, *Magistrates Charge ... Sermon ... before the ... Peeres ... in the Abbey Church at Westminster ... May 26. 1647* (1647), 16.

[59] George Hughes, *Wo-Joy-Trumpet ... Sermon before the ... Commons ... May 26. 1647* (1647), 32; Samuel Annesley, *Sermon ... to the ... Commons, July 26. 1648. At Margarets Westminster* (1648), 11–12, 25.

[60] William Jenkyn, *Sleeping Sicknes ... Sermon ... before the ... Peeres ... in the Abby-Church at Westminster ... 27th of January* (1647), 28, sig. A3r.

[61] George Cokayn, *Flesh Expiring ... Sermon before the ... Commons. Nov. 29. 1648* (1648), 5, 24, 26, 28.

[62] Thomas Brooks, *Gods Delight ... Sermon before the ... Commons ... December 26. 1648* (1649), 16–17.

from them printed.[63] The number of fast days observed in England from 1660 to 1688 was far less (twelve, plus monthly fasts in the summer of 1665[64]) than during the 1640s. Other characteristics also changed for all types of printed sermons. Many more published sermons began to appear that were originally preached from a wider variety of locations and to other audiences beyond London and parliament, and sermons preached by Anglicans represented a majority of those published after 1660.[65] Of course, the political and religious contexts also changed, both from those of the 1640s and also within the over fifty years from 1660 to 1714. Still, it is apparent that there was some continuity in the way sermons were used.

In early April 1660 a fast was called by the Convention Parliament, a body convened after the dissolution of the Long Parliament, which facilitated the return of monarchy in the person of Charles II. Two ministers from differing denominational perspectives preached sermons to the House of Commons on that occasion, and their sermons demonstrated how fasts continued to provide a forum where preachers displayed their particular political and religious sympathies. The Presbyterian Richard Baxter's sermon was moderate, criticizing intemperate name-calling from all sides of the religious divisions, and advising people to look at their own faults first. Baxter reminded his audience that he, along with 'the generality of the Orthodox sober Ministers, and godly people of this Nation, did never consent to King-killing, nor to the change of the ancient Government of this Land'. Still, near the end of his sermon, Baxter echoed some refrains of the 1640s, appealing to the Commons to support godliness and good preaching, as well as calling for policy that would not 'ensnare our consciences with any unscripturall inventions of men'.[66]

The other April 1660 preacher was John Gauden, who had remained a proponent of the Church of England during the Interregnum and would become bishop of Exeter by the end of the year. Gauden was also the likely author of *Eikon Basilike*, the very popular and apologetic memoir of Charles I which became a best-seller immediately after the king's execution in 1649.[67] Showing that wounds from the 1640s and 1650s were still fresh, Gauden condemned 'partial and fanatick interests' and those 'damners of their own souls, who pretend to build Religion and Reformation on the ruines of Iustice and Civil Laws, by sacriledge, and violence'. He demanded compensation for 'the Church and Clergy of England' and relief from those 'Harpyes ... who are pretenders to Reformation'.[68]

A key element of the Restoration response to the Civil Wars and Interregnum was the establishment of a fast day in memory of Charles I. Legislation passed by parliament in

---

[63] Wilson, *Pulpit*, 96; Webster, 'Preaching', 409.

[64] Mears et al., *National Prayers*, I, pp. cxxviii–cxxx.

[65] Deconinck-Brossard, 'Eighteenth-Century Sermons', 106–09.

[66] Baxter, *Sermon of Repentance*, 18–19, 43–4, 45.

[67] Jim Daems and Holly Faith Nelson, 'Introduction', in *Eikon Basilike with Selections from Eikonoklastes* (Peterborough, Ontario: Broadview Press, 2006), 16–21.

[68] John Gauden, *Gods Great Demonstrations ... Sermon before the ... Commons ... April 30. 1660* (1660), 3, 21, 54, 62.

1661 set 30 January, the anniversary of Charles's death, to be commemorated annually.[69] Each year sermons from 30 January fasts reminded audiences of the lasting impact of the upheavals of the mid-seventeenth century, but they also showed how even very specific occasions and traditions could still be used by preachers to remark on other matters. Unsurprisingly, criticism of those who rebelled against Charles I was a prominent theme of the 30 January sermons. Anglican preachers used terms like 'usurping Tyrants' and 'bloodthirsty' subjects to describe the regicides.[70] The 30 January sermons also reinforced the image of Charles I as a suffering martyr. His treatment and execution were frequently compared to the trial and death of Christ: though preachers realized that this association was not quite appropriate, they made it anyway. Emanuel Langford, rector of Whitnash in Warwickshire, recognized that he could not say Charles was without sin but went on to assert 'certainly He had as few to answer for as any prince ever had'.[71] More directly, William Delaune, president of St John's College, Oxford, said 'tho' the Divinity of Christ forbids any comparison between him and the person of our Martyr ... yet their Sufferings were attended with too many of the same circumstances, to be either hid or deny'd'.[72] Many of the sermons also dramatically re-enacted the scaffold scene and praised Charles's saintly demeanour to evoke sympathetic emotions from their audiences. One example here should suffice: 'with rapturous Eyes looking unto Jesus, ... see him so resolutely and meekly go as a Lamb to the Slaughter, and lay down his Neck with such Humility, and Devotion, and his innocent Blood spilt upon the Ground, like Water.'[73]

During the Restoration period, 30 January sermons were overwhelmingly sympathetic towards the royal martyr. However, by the early eighteenth century it is clear that the unconditional condemnation of Charles I's opponents was waning, with some preachers now including accounts of the king's shortcomings. Though calling the Civil War 'unnatural' and the king's execution 'deplorable', White Kennett, rector of St Botolph without Aldgate in London, blamed the influence of a 'French Interest' at court, as well as Charles's extra-parliamentary taxation, for instigating the conflict.[74] Fellow London rector, of St Paul's Covent Garden, Robert Lloyd suggested that Charles should have forgiven his friends as well as his enemies on the scaffold because 'His ill-chose Popish Queen, with her accurs'd French Adherents, did more towards his fatal Tragedy,

---

[69] Lacey, *Cult of King Charles*, 130, 132–3.
[70] Francis Turner, *Sermon ... before the King ... 30/1 of January 1680/1* (1681), 25; Thomas Husbands, *Great Sin ... Sermon ... at the Cathedral-Church in Hereford ... XXXth of January, 1713* (1713), 8.
[71] Emanuel Langford, *Sermon ... before the Commons ... for the Martyrdom of King Charles I* (1698), 17.
[72] William Delaune, *Sermon ... before the ... Commons, at St. Margaret's Westminster, January 30. 1702/3* (1703), 2.
[73] Thomas Cooke, *Way to Peace ... Two Sermons ... January 16 ... And January 30 ... at Kingston in Surry* (1712), 34.
[74] White Kennett, *Compassionate Enquiry ... Sermon ... in ... St. Botolph Aldgate ... January XXXI, 1703/4* ([1704]), 2, 4, 11.

than all his open Enemys'.[75] Royal chaplain Francis Browne acknowledged some royal 'Miscarriages' and commended those who had been 'Zealous to preserve the Right of Parliaments, and the Liberty of the Subject'.[76]

Despite an express purpose of remembering the past, 30 January sermons also commented on current circumstances. The ejected Presbyterian minister Samuel Fisher used his 1673 sermon to demonstrate he was as willing to obey lawful authority as other subjects. Though noting he would not violate his conscience, Fisher only justified methods of passive disobedience such as sending petitions to and seeking mediation with the king.[77] In a sermon preached to Charles II only a week before the king died early in 1685, Francis Turner, bishop of Ely and later a nonjuror, took an opposing perspective, attacking dissenters for setting up 'Fanatic Schools, and their Country Academies ... to breed up their Children ... to make them Rebels ... such Parents go far towards the making Regicides both of themselves and their Children'.[78] In 1713, near the end of Anne's reign, the Herefordshire vicar Thomas Husbands found the memorial fast a perfect occasion to endorse the Tory ideology of unqualified passive obedience and non-resistance, while, conversely, Robert Lloyd used his sermon to demonstrate 'Unshaken Zeal for the Revolution, and Protestant Succession'.[79]

Beyond the 30 January commemorations, other occasional fasts occurred during the Restoration. Concerns around parliament and threats to the kingdom inspired several national fasts in the late 1670s and in 1680. Revelations of the Popish Plot caused William Sancroft, now the Archbishop of Canterbury, to claim that enemies intended to destroy the English church and its people, and he used the apocalyptic image of the dragon (Revelation 12: 4) to implicate the machinations of the Church of Rome in this effort.[80] Referring to the recent anniversary of the Gunpowder Plot, Benjamin Camfield, rector of Aylestone in Leicestershire, told his congregation in November 1678 that 'the same kind of Agents are at work again ... to Destroy both His Sacred Majesty, and ... our Liberties and Religion'; Camfield listed 'Romish Agents, Priests and Jesuites, and others of that Communion, abetted with Foreign Powers,' as enemies of the nation.[81]

Though the Church of Rome was the obvious target at this time, preachers also identified domestic concerns. In a sermon to the House of Commons in 1679, William Jane, chaplain to the bishop of London, blamed 'Fanaticks' and dissenters for having 'so far weakned the Protestant Interest, as to give incouragement to the Papists in their

---

[75] Robert Lloyd, *Sermon ... at St. Paul's Covent-Garden ... Thirtieth of January, 1709* (1710), 6–7; Robert Lloyd, *Sermon ... at St. Paul's Covent-Garden ... 30th of January, 1713–14* (1714), 13.
[76] Francis Browne, *Sermon before the ... Lord Mayor, Aldermen ... of London; at the Cathedral-Church of St. Paul's ... January 30. 1712–13* (1713), 10, 11.
[77] Fisher, *Honour*, sig. A4r, 6.
[78] Francis Turner, *Sermon ... before the King ... 30th of January, 1684/5* (1685), 22.
[79] Husbands, *Great Sin*, sigs. A2v–A3r; Robert Lloyd, *Sermon ... at St. Paul's Covent-Garden ... 30th of January, 1711 ...* (1712), Epistle Dedicatory (n.p.).
[80] William Sancroft, *Sermon ... to the ... Peers, Novemb. 13th, 1678* (1678), 9, 13.
[81] Benjamin Camfield, *Sermon ... November the XIIIth, 1678* (1678), 1–2, 45–6.

present attempts against us, and our Religion'.[82] According to John Sharp, rector of St Giles in the Fields in London and future archbishop of York, the problem was 'the Unnatural, Un-Christian Feuds and Divisions that are amongst us, our Nations being rent and torn into so many Parties and Factions, and the cruel and bitter Animosities with which each party does prosecute each the other'.[83] Despite calling for the reconciliation of 'all Parties', Robert Dixon, vice-dean of Rochester Cathedral, spent a long passage of his sermon complaining that the Presbyterians had not yet 'come into us'.[84]

The Late Seventeenth and Early Eighteenth Century

There were no national fast days in England from 1681 to 1688.[85] However, when William III and Mary II came to the throne in 1689, they instituted a regular series of fasts, and this revival extended into the early eighteenth century.[86] These supported the nation's war efforts in Europe, which called for the kingdom to look outward in a substantial way to identify international concerns. Preachers like William Wake, chaplain to the new monarchs and later Archbishop of Canterbury in George I's reign, told their audiences 'Behold this day the Eyes not of your own Nation only, but of all the Nations round us, fix'd upon you ... the Fortunes of all the Reformed Churches, and distressed Countries of Europe, depending on the success of our present Enterprizes'.[87] Calling William 'our Joshua' in 1696, the Northumberland schoolmaster William Bewick described him as having 'gone over Jordan, to assist the Weak, and set the Afflicted free'.[88]

The war abroad captured attention, but fast sermons continued pointing out problems at home. Especially worrying was religious and political disunity in the kingdom. The royal chaplain Thomas Comber named 'a Schism which some Angry Men are forming in her own Bowels' among the church's concerns.[89] In 1690 John Tillotson, who would become Archbishop of Canterbury the next year, hoped 'that these Names and Distinctions of Parties should be laid down and abolish'd for ever'.[90] Worry over political divisions in

---

[82] William Jane, *Sermon ... April the 11th, 1679, at St. Margarets Westminster before the ... Commons* (1679), 40–1.

[83] John Sharp, *Sermon ... April the 11th, 1679, at St. Margarets Westminster, before the ... Commons* (1679), 18.

[84] Robert Dixon, *Sermon ... December 22. 1680 ... in the Cathedral ... of Rochester* (1681), 29, 41–2.

[85] Mears et al., *National Prayers*, I, pp. cxxx–cxxxi.

[86] Claydon, *William III*, 96, 105.

[87] William Wake, *Sermon ... before the ... Commons, at St. Margaret's Westminster June 5th. 1689* (1689), 31.

[88] William Bewick, *A Sermon ... at Hexham in Northumberland ... 26th of June, 1696* (1696), 16.

[89] Thomas Comber, *Reasons of Prayer ... Sermon ... before the Queen at Whitehall ... August 29th, 1694* (1694), 16.

[90] John Tillotson, *Sermon ... at St Mary Le Bow before the Lord Mayor, ... Aldermen ... of London ... 18th of June* (1690), 31.

England grew in subsequent years. Over a decade later the bishop of Oxford, William Talbot, continued to lament 'Are we not still miserably torn into Parties and Factions? Are not too many among us more zealous to promote the Designes of their Party, than the Interest of the Nation?'[91] Charles Palmer, vicar of Towcester in Northamptonshire, also observed 'Divisions and Animosities amongst our selves ... tho' we both argue and pray for Union, we are indispos'd to embrace it, unless it be attain'd by our own Devices and Parties'.[92] Frustrated by political disunity, in 1711 the Cambridgeshire vicar John Thory advised 'while Exalted Tories talk of Male-Administration in the last, and Whiggs deride the present Measures, Let us ... lay aside all odious Party-Distinctions, and ... act with the true Spirit of Moderation'.[93]

Though the particular points of contention were different, the sermons at the end of Anne's reign showed national fasts being used for political polemical purposes, just as the ones in the 1640s had. In the 1710s, the political divisions of the country and the issue of war came to a head over the new Tory ministry's push for a peace treaty with France. Preaching in St Martin in the Fields in London, Joseph Trapp criticized those whose loud 'Clamours' strongly opposed the peace, asking 'is not Peace between Nation and Nation a very great Blessing[?]'[94] In a sermon to his congregation in Sandford in Somerset, Robert Ham expounded how the war had 'cost the Lives of many Thousands; exhausted our Wealth and Riches; and brought the Nation into Straits and Difficulties', and he concluded that most of the nation was crying for peace.[95] While acknowledging the war was just and honourable, Roger Altham, rector of St Botolph without Bishopsgate in London, argued it was a 'Calamity' to the nation because 'the necessary Expence both of Blood and Treasure requir'd in one Year for the Support ... is more than can be repair'd in the compass of Many'.[96]

For the very same January 1712 fast, other preachers argued strongly against peace. Though recognizing war as 'a sore Judgment', William Butler, chaplain to the lord mayor of London, cautioned that peace could be 'a more grievous' one.[97] The Presbyterian minister to Kingston upon Thames, Daniel Mayo, criticized 'those Male-contents in our Nation, who are grumbling at the necessary Taxes', and he argued that further military successes would be what secured a 'good and lasting Peace'. Mayo also pressed another hot political button of his day, directing his congregation to pray that the laws enacting

---

[91] William Talbot, *Sermon ... before the Lords ... in the Abbey-Church of Westminster ... Jan. 19. 1703/4* (1704), 23.

[92] Charles Palmer, *Sermon ... at Towcester ... June 10th 1702* (Oxford, 1702), 1.

[93] John Thory, *Piety and Loyalty ... Sermon ... at Hattly St. George, and Caxton, in Cambridgeshire ... March the 28th, 1711 ...* (n.d.), 5.

[94] Joseph Trapp, *Sermon ... at ... St. Martin in the Fields; January the 16th 1711* (1712), 7–8.

[95] Robert Ham, *Right Way ... Sermon ... in Sandford Church ... January the 16th. 1711/12* (Exeter, 1712), 3, 4.

[96] Roger Altham, *Sermon ... before the ... Commons ... at ... St. Margaret Westminster ... Jan. 16. 1711/12* (1712), 19–20.

[97] William Butler, *Sermon ... before the ... Lord-Mayor, the Aldermen ... of London, at the Cathedral Church of St. Paul ... January 16th. 1711/12* (1712), 14.

the Protestant Hanoverian succession be upheld.[98] Defending those justifiably 'afraid of an insecure Peace', the bishop of St Asaph, William Fleetwood, suggested that those who now alleged the war was 'entred wrong into ... are those ... who would have us go wrong out of it'.[99] Prevented from preaching his January 1712 fast sermon to the House of Lords, Fleetwood published it anyway.[100] Despite Fleetwood's defiance, the permission to publish a sermon was fairly typical of sermons in the period: of the sermons read for this study, 64 per cent (217) had some kind of imprimatur—included in the first few pages, on the title page, or on the back pages—in the form of some official or body authorizing their publication.

Fast sermons are only one subset of early modern sermons but they can be used to display a number of aspects of the genre as a whole in the period from 1640 to 1714. They demonstrate how preachers dealt with the process of turning a vehicle for the spoken word into a published, written form. They also show how printed devices and structures could be used to augment sermons, making them something more than they had been in their original delivery. The sample of fast sermons used here also indicates some of the changes in length and form occurring in sermons from the mid-seventeenth to the early eighteenth century. In addition, even as a specific type of work, fast sermons show that, while being called to fit into a particular form of worship, the way preachers chose their subjects, constructed their arguments, and supported their ideas made sermons extremely varied and not restricted by set forms or prescribed topics. Sermons, as a whole, went far beyond theological and spiritual edification in their messages, and preachers used them to convey thoughts about politics, ecclesiastical policy, and the significant issues facing the nation.

---

[98] Daniel Mayo, *Pray for the Peace ... Sermon ... at Kingston Upon Thames ... January 16. 1711/2* (1712), 6, 11.

[99] [William Fleetwood], *Sermon ... January the Sixteenth, 1711/12* (1712), 19, 21.

[100] James Caudle, 'Preaching in Parliament: Patronage, Publicity and Politics in Britain, 1701–60', in Ferrell and McCullough (eds.), *English Sermon*, 235–63 (245).

CHAPTER 36

TRUE ACCOUNTS

SOPHIE GEE

'TRUE Accounts' are a subgenre of English prose that proliferated during the later seventeenth and early eighteenth centuries. They were usually brief (fewer than ten pages), plainly written, and cheaply produced, occasionally with a crude woodblock illustration accompanying the text. In *EEBO* there are around thirty-five examples of True Accounts with woodblock illustrations printed between 1680 and 1750. Of these, only three belong to the eighteenth century proper. Their subjects involved odd or sensational matters of fact, as these sample titles suggest: *A Full and True Account of the Behaviors, Confessions; and last Dying Speeches of the Condemn'd Criminals, that were Executed at Tyburn on Friday the 24th of May*; *Salt-Water Sweetened, or, A True Account of the Great Advantages of this New Invention both by Sea and by Land* (1683).[1] But they rarely confined themselves to fact, since in reality they aimed to bring readers around to their point of view on a subject that was difficult or impossible to verify (ghost sightings, colonial activity, the moral status of executed criminals). True Accounts are self-consciously not non-fictions (as histories or learned treatises were, for example), and neither are they fictional. They assign themselves a generic identity distinct from journalism, opinion-writing, or political propaganda, since (unlike these other forms) they don't acknowledge the author's bias or point of view. And yet they call our attention to ways in which all these genres

---

[1] Some other examples, to give a sense both of the topical variety and tonal uniformity of the genre: *The Whipster of Woodstreet, or, A True Account of the Barbarous and Horrid Murther Commited on the Body of Mary Cox, Late Servant in Woodstreet*; *A New Wonder, or, A Strange and True Account from Shrewsbury of a Dreadful Storm Which Happened on the 4th of May Last*, (1681); Richard Baxter, *Church-History of the Government of Bishops and Their Councils Abbreviated Including the Chief Part of the Government of Christian Princes and Popes, and a True Account of the Most Troubling Controversies and Heresies Till the Reformation* (1681); *A True Account of the Dreadful Fire Which Happened on Sunday the 19th of November, Between Ten and Eleven at Night in Wapping as Also, of What Persons Were Hurt and Burnt, and of One That Was Taken Suspected to Have Fire-Balls* (1682); *The Tryals of the Persons Who Committed the Barbarous and Inhumane Murther Upon the Body of Thomas Thynn, Esq. on the 12th of this Instant February* (1682); *A Full and True Account of the Landing and Reception of the Late King James at Kinsale with the Particulars of the Ships, Arms, Ammunition, Men, and Money That He Brought with Him: in a Letter from Bristol April 1st* (1689).

became simultaneously distinct and paradoxically interdependent in the early eighteenth century. True Accounts remind us that the issue of 'truth' was at once unprecedentedly important and unstable in English intellectual culture after the Restoration.

The most common topics for True Accounts were descriptions of 'horrid murders' or 'brutal deaths' of children, women, or criminals. The phrase was sometimes used in the titles of religious polemic arguing for a particular doctrinal or disciplinary position, and it was also used in documents reporting on the 'true' conditions of far-off colonial disputes.[2] Interestingly, nearly twice as many True Accounts were printed in the decade of the 1680s as in the century before or in the half-century afterward, and they were especially concentrated around 1688.[3] This detail is noteworthy because of the political shifts that were taking place in England at that time, when Stuart succession was interrupted and replaced by King William of Orange, the Protestant Dutch *stadtholder*, married to James II's daughter Mary. The crisis represented the symbolic and literal defiance of the divine right of monarchial succession, and the assertion of human autonomy over absolute or unalterable authority.[4] The 1688 Revolution, then, demonstrated the theoretical and actual ability of English subjects to adjudicate what was 'true'. That assertion of the role of human reason in political affairs coincided with another landmark event in intellectual history: the rise of the novel.[5] Novelistic narrative, which was committed both to a standard of plausibility and a capacity for imaginative speculation, negotiated complex relationships between empirical truths and speculative, or counterfactual, truth-claims.[6] Just one example of this are the attempts to distinguish between 'fiction' and mere 'untruth' in reaction to early novels, in which novels were assigned a place on the continuum between natural histories, whose narrative ideology, in Michael McKeon's words, was that 'the truths of nature will obtain an unimpeded mediation', and what McKeon calls the 'credulous mystifications of "romance," especially when associated

---

[2] On 'true accounts' of happenings in the New World, see Chapter 25 on 'New Word Writing and Captivity Narratives' by Catherine Armstrong.

[3] *EEBO* records 136 True Accounts between 1580 and 1680; 543 True Accounts between 1650 and 1750; 125 between 1650 and 1680; 311 in the decade of the 1680s, of which 107 were printed between 1687 and 1689; 155 during the 1690s; 39 between 1700 and 1750.

[4] Of the events leading from the regicide to the Civil War and thence the Glorious Revolution, Jonathan Lamb writes: 'These ... decisive interruptions of legal and dynastic continuity inclined many people to believe that history had evolved not from an immemorial ancient constitution or the dateless prerogatives of sovereignty, but from their own consent'; '"Lay Aside My Character": The Personate Novel and Beyond', *The Eighteenth Century: Theory and Interpretation*, 52 (2011), 271–87 (275).

[5] On the relationship between political and social authority and narrative autonomy, see Victoria Kahn, *Wayward Contracts: The Crisis of Political Obligation in England, 1640–1674* (Princeton, NJ: Princeton University Press, 2004), esp. 81–111.

[6] On the counterfactual aspects of fiction, see Catherine Gallagher, 'Telling It Like It Wasn't', *Pacific Coast Philology*, 45 (2010), 12–25 (19): 'counterfactual histories and alternate histories limit their personae to historically existent individuals who draw their significance extra-diegetically, whereas the novels are not only invented narratives but also narratives of invented personae, or fictional characters. The novelistic genre has the resources that fictional characters provide by their very lack of historical reference, which allows for the illusion of a more complete alternative reality.'

with the discredited authority of the ancients'.[7] Non-fictions asserted the human capacity to establish and define the parameters of knowledge, seen for example in Robert Hooke's *Micrographia* (1665) or Thomas Sprat's *History of the Royal Society* (1667). The idea that humans could have authority over their own narratives reveals a new clarity and optimism regarding the separation of fiction from non-fiction; truth from untruth. At the same time, with the rise of the novel came the accompanying realization that fiction need not compete with new standards of truth, but could, like factual narratives, promote them.

Fiction and non-fiction become increasingly interfused even as they pulled in different directions and became generically distinct.[8] We know from histories of the early novel that the emergence of fictionality and factuality as distinct categories is related to the rise of the new science, rational religion, and natural philosophy—with a pervasive commitment to marking the possibilities and limits of human authority. J. Paul Hunter describes a 'literary revolution' beginning in the early eighteenth century featuring 'new readers, new modes of literary production, changing tastes, and a growing belief that traditional forms and conventions were too constricted and rigid to represent modern reality or to reach modern readers'.[9] The emphasis of this 'revolution' was, in Hunter's view, on novelty across genres for a considerable stretch of time before it was on the novel per se. The idea that narrative could and should be doing new and distinct intellectual work had, in other words, to do with large cultural and political shifts in categorizing knowledge and the production of knowledge; what Hunter calls 'a wholly new mode of interpreting fact and event', grounded in the perception that 'a merely factual response to the itch for knowledge was not enough'.[10]

Another explanation, offered by scholars in cognitive literary theory, is that a complex set of mental responses are triggered by texts in which non-factual information is presented in a 'true' way and, conversely, texts in which factual information is presented in narrative form: 'the most "fantastic" story contains a number of contingently useful "truths" about the world, whereas the most "factual" narrative manipulates facts by virtue of being a *narrative*.'[11] The condition that enabled such conflations of perception

---

[7] For accounts of the novel as mediating between fact and fiction see Michael McKeon, *The Origins of the English Novel: 1600–1740* (1987; Baltimore: Johns Hopkins University Press, 2002); J. Paul Hunter, *Before Novels: The Cultural Contexts of Eighteenth-Century English Fiction* (New York: W.W. Norton, 1990); Leonard Davis, *Factual Fictions: The Origins of the English Novel* (Philadelphia: University of Pennsylvania Press, 1983). An alternative critical strain has developed around the concept of 'fictionality', which argues that fiction occupies a distinct epistemological ground in which its power derives from its separation from the literature of fact. For a synopsis of the state of the field, see Simona Zetterburg Gjerlevsen, 'A Novel History of Fictionality', *Narrative*, 24 (2016), 174–89.

[8] For another recent account of this phenomenon, see Jesse Molesworth, *Chance and the Eighteenth-Century Novel: Realism, Probability, Magic* (Cambridge: Cambridge University Press, 2010).

[9] Hunter, *Before Novels*, 10.

[10] Hunter, *Before Novels*, 197.

[11] Lisa Zunshine, 'Eighteenth-Century Print Culture and the "Truth" of Fictional Narrative', *Philosophy and Literature*, 25/2 (2001), 215–32 (215).

was a disposition and newfound confidence in 'reading' the empirical world, with the individual reader granted unprecedented authority:

> Mere facts ... were only the most direct route to secrets of nature, for in the wake of scientific advancement and the growing emphasis on observation and experience, the world seemed there to be read, and the discovery, accumulation, and recording of miscellaneous facts could point to larger patterns of understanding. The recording of everyday observations and events came to seem essential as a means to knowing the nature of things; the record became, in fact, a kind of rival to life itself.[12]

Lisa Zunshine argues that when early eighteenth-century readers encountered fictional or factual narratives, they oscillated or toggled cognitively between processing the information as true and processing it as either false or speculative. The experience of being in contact with narrative, in other words, was to experience hermeneutic ambivalence, even paralysis. Zunshine's focus is on 'what happens *before* certain texts get explicitly marked as fiction and stored as perpetual scope-representations, and in how writers may attempt to capitalize on the cognitive uncertainty (predicated arguably upon the representational complexity of the text in question) accompanying this labeling/categorization process'.[13]

Work in cognitive anthropology suggests that in early eighteenth-century texts the reader is often intentionally caught between two competing, incompatible truth-values that he or she is ultimately unable to reconcile: 'at certain historical junctures, when a new medium is entering a culture and the cues needed to evaluate ... the "truth" of narratives transmitted through this medium appear to be in flux, the proliferation of those hard-to-classify narratives leaves people deeply anxious, grasping for "labels" and uncertain about the new rules of "labeling"'.[14] Assessing the same phenomenon through the lens of eighteenth-century aesthetic theory, Sarah Tindal Kareem labels the experience of cognitive suspense, of being caught between interpretative and generic certainties, as wonder, 'a powerful psychological response to novelty that momentarily suspends the cognitive process'.[15] In Kareem's account, the state of interpretative or intellectual inaction is a moral and philosophical problem for thinkers from Thomas Hobbes to Samuel Johnson, a form of mental paralysis that removes the hard-won agency which characterizes individual cognitive autonomy after 1688, and which places the individual in a condition of aesthetic destabilization or impotence. At the same time, Kareem finds that wonder instils the individual with an enhanced capacity for attention, for the formation of a 'deep impression' on the mind, opening the way to more rigorous understanding.[16]

---

[12] Zunshine, 'Truth of Fictional Narrative', 199.
[13] Zunshine, 'Truth of Fictional Narrative', 220.
[14] Zunshine, 'Truth of Fictional Narrative', 217.
[15] Sarah Tindal Kareem, *Eighteenth-Century Fiction and the Reinvention of Wonder* (Oxford: Oxford University Press, 2014), 39.
[16] Kareem, *Reinvention of Wonder*, 40.

True Accounts have, then, a perverse relation to the period's most important literary genre. They posed a challenge to novels in that they promoted non-empirical 'truths' that did not rely for their authentication on the conventions of fictionality. But they also shed light on a seeming contradiction in the novel form. Despite its nominal commitment to the real, realist fiction often compromised or undermined its own relationship with empirical truth. While appearing to enable and be enabled by empirical knowledge, realism, like its rogue sibling the True Account, could more correctly be seen as threatening and destabilizing to readers' understanding of empirical data. The significance of the interstitial, occasional prose works known as True Accounts lies in their pointing to more pervasive ambivalences across eighteenth-century intellectual culture. Instability and epistemological uncertainty are, in other words, among the important intellectual legacies of eighteenth-century English prose. The capacity—theoretical and actual—for humans to assert their agency, control, and freedom, and the evolving commitment to distinguishing between reality and illusion (the project of empiricism) leads, paradoxically, to deeper recognition of the impossibility of full human reason, autonomy, and cessation of credulity. 'An optimistic faith in the power of empirical method to discover natural essences points in one direction; a wary scepticism of the evidence of the senses and its mediating capacity points in quite another,' writes McKeon.[17] This is among the most fascinating paradoxes of eighteenth-century intellectual life. Perhaps more interesting still is the discovery that when limits on human reason and autonomy are perceived, they too are simultaneously denied and obscured by the same narrative conventions that enabled their exposure. We see this shift taking place across all the prose genres of the period. In True Accounts we see it in crude form, with workaday writers cobbling together 'truth' from semi-realities and would-be histories, recruiting scraps of fictional and factual narrative to assert their superiority to both.

While True Accounts varied a good deal in style and subject matter, they have one thing in common: they are almost never true. In the single-sheet pamphlet, *Full and True Account of the Behaviors, Confessions; and last Dying Speeches of the Condemn'd Criminals* (1700), for example, the author tells the story of arson and robbery committed by a man named John Shirl[e]y, alias Davis, '22 years old, condemn'd for firing the house of Dr. Sloan' in a well-heeled neighbourhood of London. Shirley was hanged with other felons at Tyburn on 24 May 1700. The report given of Shirley's life and situation is neither 'full' nor self-evidently 'true', relying as it does on biographical cliché and an absence of distinguishing or verifiable narrative details. It is literally generic: reminiscent of the beginning of an early eighteenth-century prose-fiction (like *Robinson Crusoe* (1719) or *Gulliver's Travels* (1726)) in which the author offers a plausible, morally instructive backstory for the hero in order to give readers a point of sympathetic entry into the narrative. Shirley, a.k.a. Davis, is a classic black sheep: 'descended of a good Family, that his Parents, who tenderly loved him, Educated him at School a considerable time, but growing Headstrong, he ran away from them.' It's perfectly possible that this is true

---

[17] McKeon, *Origins of the English Novel*, 68.

(it's a common story, after all), but it sounds more like fiction than fact; it captures the reader's interest because of its general applicability, not its particularity. Even the faintly quirky detail of John Shirley's feminine last name is smoothed into the generic Davis, itself a criminal fiction intended to assure his anonymity. The account makes an appeal to particularity only when it comes to describing the robbery of Dr. Sloan's house:

> At length they resolv'd to break open this House in *Bloomsbury Square*, which they attempted in several Places, but could not effect; then they resolv'd to burn it; and accordingly one of them struck a Light, and cut a little Door into Splinters, then breaking the Glass and part of the Wood in the Window, set a Candle to it, which caus'd the Window to blaze: Their Design as he said, was to throw Stones at the upper Windows, to awaken the Family when the Fire had got a Head, and so under Pretence of helping them to carry away their best Goods, and Rob them of all that was valuable.

These details embed the passage in history; the crime feels singular in the sense of belonging to a historical moment in which such circumstances would be intuitively recognizable to readers. The author might be referring to any well-appointed house in the Bloomsbury area, made vulnerable by the omnipresence of fire and darkness in the early eighteenth-century world. The detail of the plan to throws stones at windows and so wake the family to warn them of danger evokes a strange hybrid of sophistication and crudity characteristic of early modern urban crime-stories. The physical details of the splintered door and broken glass are what make Davis's testimony against himself ring true. This is not the same as truth, of course: the description is on the same porous representational boundary as realism—between hard, singular fact and plausible fiction. True Accounts and realist fictions, then, are densely interrelated while ostensibly being opposed.

The interrelation is illuminated by Francis Ferguson's reflections on what she calls literary 'hailing' in novels, a process that involves 'our recognizing texts and feeling recognized by them'.[18] We, the readers of novels, 'spend time in the company of imaginary characters and think that they're talking to us', despite our knowledge that they are not. Ferguson asks: 'why doesn't the consciousness of all our differences from one another ... block a sense of affinity, and affinity even with characters who seem very unlike us?' This sense of extreme proximity or identification that novels can produce, in Ferguson's account, both results in and makes necessary the evolution of free indirect style. This singular resource of the novel draws readers into a sense of recognition or identification with fictional characters albeit unwittingly, or involuntarily, since free indirect style is 'almost silent', a 'verbal version of peripheral vision'.[19] This identification is fuller, more transparent, than relationships in reality and it encompasses, too, the

---

[18] Francis Ferguson, 'Now It's Personal: D.A. Miller and Too-Close Reading', *Critical Inquiry*, 41 (2015), 521–40 (524).

[19] Ferguson, 'Now It's Personal', 523, 528.

reader's uncanny sense of being recognized by a character whom they know does not exist. The identificatory economy in which True Accounts participate is closely related to the one Ferguson lays out, while being seemingly opposed. True Accounts lead readers away from as well as towards their narrative—they must insist on an unbridgeable gap between the reader's experience and the one being described. I would argue that this is an alternative (and less imaginative) solution to the same realization with which eighteenth-century fictions contend: that truth in reality can be only partially and provisionally apprehended. In True Accounts, then, the fictional strategy of hailing is reversed and the text refuses to hail or acknowledge its readers in anything other than purely general or generic terms. Whenever the True Account is particular, whenever it reports details eccentric enough to sound 'real', it discourages the reader's direct identification and assumes that they are in want of more information. Where fiction closes the gap between reality and representation by way of fantasies about identification, the True Account closes the gap by supplying the reader with 'truth' so real, so eccentric, as to render identification impossible.

True Accounts claim authority by implying that their value exceeds that of a fiction, because they don't need recourse to invention. Their reason for existing, and the appeal they make to a broad, non-elite readership, is based on the implication that they are more authentic than other prose genres. They critique the unspoken counter-claim being made by fiction, that greater (and more nuanced) authenticity is located in narratives that aren't true. In classic accounts of the novel, fiction is said to arise out of non-fiction. To draw on Jonathan Lamb's elegant framing, the 'experimental procedures and rhetorical austerities that define the production of facts among scientists, navigators, virtuosos and historians of the seventeenth century' provide the ontological and epistemological underwriting for 'the credibility of fiction and the currency of its characters'.[20] But a close look at True Accounts yields the discovery that the new conventions of realist fiction were reclaimed and co-opted to produce counter-fictions: the pseudo-factual narratives of True Accounts. This is hardly surprising. Bruno Latour has argued that the Enlightenment scepticism of hard facts, the insistence on the relative nature of truth, is 'one critique too late' in the twenty-first century to address the crisis around factuality. No longer, writes Latour, is the primary threat 'an excessive confidence in ideological arguments posturing as matters of fact'—the posture adopted by True Accounts—but from 'an excessive *distrust* of good matters of fact disguised as bad ideological biases!'[21] Latour's appeal affirms what is most important about the True Account genre: that the important work of establishing truth both in fiction and non-fiction depended, in part, on dismissing the True Account's claim to be factual.

An account from 1701, a single-sheet pamphlet entitled *A Full and True Account of a Strange and Wonderful Discovery, of an Unknown Person That Was Found on Saturday*

---

[20] Lamb, 'Personate Novel', 274.
[21] Bruno Latour, 'Why Has Critique Run out of Steam? From Matters of Fact to Matters of Concern', *Critical Inquiry*, 30 (2004), 225–48 (227).

Last, within the Top of a Chimney, in the House of 'Squire Pimm in Aurendel-Street, Pickadelia, tells of a human body found cured and preserved in a London chimney, 'supposed to have lain there for several years, his skin, and flesh being dry'd hard as shoeleather; with several strange circumstances relating thereto, the like having not been heard of in the memory of any man living'. The feature that gives this True Account an appearance of veracity is its singularity: 'the like having not been heard of.' In the face of such singularity, the writer is compelled to defend his credibility by endorsing the explanation he deems most reasonable:

> Various are the discourses, concerning the original cause of this strange and unknown Person's lying Dead in that place: some supposing that he had been conceal'd in the House with an intent to Robb it, and being apprehensive of Danger went out at the Garret Window, and so down that chimney for his supposed safety ... others (with more reason) imagine that he was one of those Thieves, who attempted to Rob the Lord Lovelace's house about 7 or 8 years ago.

This emphasis on a plausible explanation bolsters the believability of the tale. But reasonableness, or believability, widens the range of genres that this account might belong to, thus reducing the extent to which it exclusively fits the bill of the True Account. The form runs up against its central challenge of making its claims credible without losing the eccentricity or singularity that holds it apart from the more respectable or orthodox contemporary prose forms: the newspaper report, the novel, the essay, the inquiry. The need for plausibility, in other words, vies with the simultaneous pressure to remain implausible. Exceptionality—the readers' sense that this could *not* have happened to them—must trump the unexceptionable or believable. True Accounts exist in a generic by-way where they seem real because they do not feel realistic. The intellectual and emotional appeals they make to readers cannot stray into overfamiliarity.

The interdependence of fictional and factual narrative emerges with the ostensible separation of fact from fiction; of hard truth from mere possibility or speculative opinion. A 1698 pamphlet, *A True Account of the Forts and Castles Belonging to the Royal African Company Upon the Gold Coast in Africa, with the Number of Men, and Guns, the Nature of the Said Forts and Castles, and the Guns Planted on Them, as Taken from Sundry Persons Very Lately Come from Thence* (1698), presents its findings on the state of fortified slave-ports in Africa. It is presented as a table, a literal accounting. To the right of the ledger are notes. This table presents a set of seemingly unambiguous facts—fort names, numbers of guns and people, the condition of the fortifications. But in reality the author is expressing a strongly partisan (Tory) viewpoint, namely that the Royal African Company, a monopoly trading company supplying slaves to North America and the Caribbean, is essential for the continued prosperity of the transatlantic slave trade.[22]

---

[22] During the 1690s and into the eighteenth century, extensive parliamentary debates took place on the question of whether the slave trade should be conducted by a monopoly, state-endorsed company (the Royal African Company) or by free traders. For details on the political and ideological expediency

The document assumes the reader's conviction that the Royal African Company's fortified ports are the only effective trading model; if the table raises a question at all, that question is whether there are *enough* guns and white people on site. The account suppresses its political bias by effacing the alternative point of view (that deregulated free trade would make slavery more efficient). It's important to note that the opposition view to the one expressed here is the abolition not of slavery but of monopoly slave-trading; it was, in reality, a successfully deregulated slave trade that enabled the vast expansion of the trade and increase in profits.[23] Facts and fragments of fact support the document's central fiction about the Royal African Company, although the facts are non-verifiable and likely to have changed even in the time it took for the information to travel to London. More interestingly still, the pseudo-facts about guns and men feel real because of the prevailing fiction that fortification and militarization are necessary for the inter-colonial trade in humans. Even as fictional narratives were being engineered out of the language of facts, factuality reciprocally depended upon and was constructed out of prevailing fictions.

Perhaps the oddest of the early eighteenth-century True Accounts is a short pamphlet titled *A Most Strange, but True Account of a Very Large Sea-Monster, That Was Found Last Saturday in a Common-Shore in New Fleet-Street in Spittle-Fields* (1704). The story is of a porpoise found in the Fleet Ditch, London's underground waterway, which served as a city sewer. Unlike other True Accounts, this pamphlet's writer eschews rational explanation, remarking, rather, that since porpoises 'appear in multitudes against an approaching Storm, tumbling after a strange manner with their Bellies upwards about Ships that are on their several Voyages' it is amazing 'that it should leave the Deep to rove up into fresh Water Rivers, and more especially to crawl so far up a Common-Shore'. The author adds the digression that the porpoise 'fish' is 'vulgarly called a Sea-Hog, from its being like a Swine both in Shape and Flesh', perhaps by way of explaining the animal's attraction to the sewer. The dead porpoise, we learn, is now a marvel which 'is to be seen at the Sign of the Black-Swan an Alehouse, in New Fleet Street in Spittle Fields'. This final claim would presumably have been possible to verify, opening the likelihood that the account is, after all, 'true'. But the pamphlet takes a bizarre turn in which the writer remarks that almanacs are being consulted to interpret the porpoise's arrival. 'There is a now great turning over of Partridge', the speaker notes—Partridge being the notorious

---

of monopoly in the post-1688 economy, see William Pettigrew and George van Cleve, 'Parting Companies: The Glorious Revolution, Company Power and Imperial Mercantilism', *The Historical Journal*, 57 (2014), 617–38; Steve Pincus, 'Addison's Empire: Whig Conceptions of Empire in the Early 18th Century', *Parliamentary History*, 31/1 (2012), 99–117; Philip J. Stern, 'Companies: Monopoly, Sovereignty and the East Indies', in Philip J. Stern and Carl Wennerlind (eds.), *Mercantilism Reimagined: Political Economy In Early Modern Britain and Its Empire* (New York: Oxford University Press, 2014), 177–95.

[23] See further William Pettigrew, 'Free to Enslave: Politics and the Escalation of Britain's Transatlantic Slave Trade, 1688–1714', *The William and Mary Quarterly*, 64 (2007), 3–38; Abigail Swingen, *Competing Visions of Empire: Labor, Slavery and the Origins of the British Atlantic Empire* (New Haven, Yale University Press, 2015).

Whig astrologer and almanac-maker of the early century, an object of Jonathan Swift's satirical scorn.[24] But, we are informed, no reference can be found to the porpoise, which leads the anonymous author to reprise popular interpretations of the event, circulating through London:

> The general Conjecture of this Creature's rambling so far up a sh[itte]n Concavity under Ground is, that it either came from the *French* coasts, and signifies *Lewis* [sic] is ready to beshit himself, for fear the Affairs will not go as they should do in Spain; or else it came from the *Spanish* Coasts, and intimates by his Obscurity that the Duke of Anjou had rather hide his head than fight.

This extraordinary and baffling conclusion reveals that the pamphlet is not recording a marvel, but mounting a satirical attack against Whig propagandists and popular opinion-makers (like Partridge). The 'general conjecture' about the allegorical meaning of the drowned porpoise alludes to the major players in the War of Spanish Succession (Louis XIV of France and his nephew the Duke d'Anjou, crowned Louis XV in 1715). This protracted struggle over the balance of power in Europe had reached a stalemate in the opening years of the century and become a source of considerable political discontent in England. Reactions to the war fell mostly along party lines, with the Tories favouring the protection of Anglo-French relations and the Whigs favouring a pan-European balance of power that built more dispersed Protestant diplomatic alliances.[25] The pamphlet, in other words, is rather complicated mock-propaganda, probably written by a Tory as a satirical attack on Whig anti-French, reformed Protestant sentiment. The complexities of the narrative are only increased when we recall that the heir apparent to the French throne was known as the 'Dauphin'—that is, the Dolphin (alluding to his coat-of-arms and seat in the Dauphine region of south-eastern France). 'Dauphin' would become the formal title of the Duke d'Anjou when the three other Dauphins died, which in 1704 seemed likely. The Dauphine region was, additionally, a Huguenot (French Protestant) stronghold, which during the late seventeenth and early eighteenth centuries suffered persecution: yet another sign of the threat French Catholicism posed to European Protestantism. The pamphlet likely also alludes to the notorious English 'dolphin' of the period, the Tory Earl of Godolphin (Go-dolphin), and Lord High Treasurer during the War. Godolphin's daughter in law became the first Duchess of Marlborough, cementing

---

[24] True Accounts are generically related to another popular form of eighteenth-century alternative factuality, the mock-treatise or pseudo-learned tract. These were Swift's preferred forms for prose that purported to be factual while being entirely speculative or satirical. The proliferation of mock-texts alongside True Accounts again confirms the instability or negotiability of factuality in the period. See, for example, Valerie Rumbold's introduction to her edition of Swift's *Parodies, Hoaxes, Mock Treatises* (Cambridge: Cambridge University Press, 2013); Paddy Bullard, 'The Scriblerian Mock-Arts: Pseudo-Technical Satire in Swift and His Contemporaries', *Studies in Philology*, 110/3 (2013), 611–36. See further Chapter 21 on 'Learned Wit and Mock-Scholarship' by Henry Power.

[25] For an overview of the politics of the war see Renger E. de Bruin et al. (eds.), *Performances of Peace: Utrecht 1713* (Leiden: Brill, 2013).

a strong association between the Godolphin family and the Tory Stuart monarchs, since Lord Marlborough was rewarded the Dukedom for his service in the War of Spanish Succession. The satire attacks pan-European Protestant consensus and endorses nationalism, conservative church orthodoxy, and Tory-Jacobite factionalism in early eighteenth-century England.

True Accounts make ridiculous claims intended to appeal to credulous readers, in implied opposition to the new prose forms of the post-revolutionary era. Amid the hundreds of pamphlets by anonymous or obscure hacks are *A True Relation of the Apparition of One Mrs. Veal, the Next Day After Her Death: To One Mrs. Bargrave at Canterbury* (1706); *A True Account of the Design, and Advantages of the South-Sea Trade* (1711); and *The True and Genuine Account of the Life and Actions of the Late Jonathan Wild: Not Made Up of Fiction and Fable, but Taken from His Own Mouth, and Collected from Papers of His Own Writing* (1725). These three True Accounts have been attributed to Daniel Defoe, though in each case the attribution has been questioned. *The Apparition of Mrs. Veal* was queried on the grounds that Defoe's puritanism would have disqualified his belief in ghosts, which the pamphlet nominally endorses.[26] *The True Account of the South Sea Trade* has been questioned on the grounds that it splices together excerpts from an earlier tract by another Tory propagandist, Abel Boyer.[27] *Jonathan Wild* has been questioned on the grounds that Defoe's style in *Applebee's Original Weekly Journal*, whose publisher, John Applebee, also printed the original edition of the *Life*, is not consistent enough to warrant assigning authorship to the longer work.[28] The disputed authorship is as interesting as the attributions themselves. While it is customary to connect Defoe's fictions with his political propaganda on a biographical level, they are generally assumed to be stylistically and imaginatively distinct. But the attribution confusion over the True Accounts suggests not only that Defoe's prose, fiction and non-fiction alike, evades voice and style but also that his imaginative originality consists precisely in the process of borrowing from and grafting onto existing narratives that True Accounts typically involve.

It is relatively easy to see why Defoe, seemingly alone among the major authors of the early century, might have been drawn to the True Account, which furnished him with a ready-made form that positioned itself against more reputable prose genres. It

---

[26] See George Starr, 'Why Defoe Probably Did Not Write the Apparition of Mrs. Veal', *Eighteenth-Century Fiction*, 15 (2003), 421–50. See also Ashley Marshall, 'Beyond Furbank and Owens: A New Consideration of the Evidence for the 'Defoe' Canon', *Studies in Bibliography*, 59 (2015), 131–90.

[27] See Arne Bialuschewski, 'A True Account of the Design, and Advantages of the South-Sea Trade: Profits, Propaganda, and the Peace Preliminaries of 1711', *Huntington Library Quarterly*, 73/2 (2010), 273–85.

[28] For the original query see P. N. Furbank, and W. R. Owens, 'The Myth of Defoe as "Applebee's Man"', *Review of English Studies*, 190 (1997), 198–204. For the cultural context of the Defoe/Mist relationship, see Pat Rogers, 'Nathaniel Mist, Daniel Defoe, and the Perils of Publishing', *The Library*, 10 (2009), 298–313. For defences of Defoe's authorship see Maximillian Novak, 'Daniel Defoe and Applebee's Original Weekly Journal: An Attempt at Re-Attribution', *Eighteenth-Century Studies*, 45/4 (2012), 585–608; Maximillian Novak, 'Defoe's Role in the Weekly Journal: Gesture and Rhetoric, Archive and Canon, and the Uses of Literary History in Attribution', *Studies in Philology*, 113 (2016), 694–711.

refuses the liberating status of fiction as simultaneously authoritative yet *not* true and it evades the broadly accepted standards for empirical verification in the mainstream non-fiction forms. In the essay that placed him in his greatest professional peril, *The Shortest Way with Dissenters* (1702), Defoe relinquished his identity and ventriloquized the voice of a genocidal High Anglican, calling for the extirpation of dissenters. If he did write these True Accounts, and even if he merely had a hand in their composition, it suggests that the relinquishing of autonomy and literary authority is a central part of Defoe's self-fashioning as a writer. Difficulty of attribution, in other words, should not be taken as a sign that Defoe's writing has misfired.

In any case, it doesn't really matter whether *The Apparition of Mrs. Veal* and *Jonathan Wild* are Defoe's work or the work of another skilled writer in Defoe's milieu. Defoe would undoubtedly have known the writer, if it wasn't himself, given his close connection to *Applebee's Journal* and the fact that *Mrs Veal's* publisher Benjamin Bragg printed both legitimate and pirated copies of Defoe's *Jure Divino* in the same year that *Mrs. Veal* came out.[29] *The Apparition of Mrs Veal* and *Jonathan Wild* are sophisticated documents. The Preface to *The Apparition of Mrs. Veal* begins:

> This relation is Matter of Fact, and attended with such Circumstances, as may induce any Reasonable Man to believe it. It was sent by a Gentleman, a Justice of Peace at Maidstone in Kent, and a very Intelligent Person, to his Friend in London, as it is here Worded; which Discourse is attested by a very sober and understanding Gentlewoman, a Kinswoman of the said Gentlemans, who lives in Canterbury, within a few Doors of the House in which the within named *Mrs. Bargrave* lives; who believes his Kinswoman to be of so discerning a Spirit, as not to be put upon by any Fallacy, and who positively assured him, that the whole Matter, as it is here Related and laid down, is what is really True; and what She her self had in the same Words (as near as may be) from *Mrs. Bargrave's* own Mouth. (n.p.)

The language here reworks cliches familiar from other true accounts to achieve more complex effects. The opening phrase, 'this relation is matter of fact', captures the central paradox of the True Account genre, that the 'fact' it presents relies ontologically on the narrative that contains it, the 'relation'. In other words, the True Account justifies its existence on the grounds that it reports fact transparently, but it merely reveals that pseudo-fact can be manufactured out of rumour, speculation, and opinion, given the right narrative conditions. 'This relation is matter of fact' is a piece of understated misdirection that throws into relief the amplified claims to authority and control over secular narratives that characterize both fiction and non-fiction in the early eighteenth century, and, at the same time, the recognition that the new knowledge, while overtly more assured than in the past, could only ever be partial and provisional. Like other True Accounts, however, *Mrs. Veal* proclaims its truth unequivocally, petitioning the rational

---

[29] See Maximillian Novak, *Daniel Defoe: Master of Fictions* (Oxford: Oxford University Press, 2003), 278.

reader to accept it. The speaker protests too much, as if anticipating the reader's incredulity while failing to address its causes. The account immediately lays out a confusing and convoluted series of communications between Mrs. Bargrave (the woman who sees Mrs. Veal's apparition) and the unnamed friend in London who presumably tells the tale to Defoe's own speaker (though this chain of relationships is left blank). While the sequence of retellings is ostensibly included to add precision to the account, it has the opposite effect; there are just too many people involved to keep facts straight. Even at the close of the second sentence, the parenthetical 'as near as may be' acknowledges the probability that Mrs. Bargrave's words have been distorted, a likelihood that the reader readily assents to after hearing the laundry-list of persons involved in reporting the story.

As with other True Accounts, this one makes use of devices that would become conventions in realist fiction. The many voices involved in conveying the story from its origin in Dover to Benjamin Bragg's publishing house in Paternoster Row in London are reminiscent of a gossips' circle, a prototype for the unreliable tattlers in eighteenth-century domestic fictions, who subsequently morph into the unreliable narrators of Victorian novels. At the end of the tale Defoe's speaker declares that 'Mrs Bargrave is the Person to whom Mrs. Veal appeared after death; she is my intimate Friend, and I can avouch for her Reputation'. Since few readers will recall the identity of 'I' by this point in the story, this assurance of veracity by a speaker whose identity has been long-since forgotten merely serves as a reminder that the account is unlikely to be true. The narrating 'I' retreats further into obscurity as he or she continues to ponder the credibility of Mrs. Bargrave's story:

> this Thing has very much affected me; and I am as well satisfi'd, as I am of the best grounded Matter of Fact. And why we should dispute the Matter of Fact, because we cannot solve Things of which we can have no certain of demonstrative Notions, seems strange to me. *Mrs. Bargraves* Authority and Sincerity alone, would have been undoubted in any other Case. (9)

When it is confirmed toward the end of the story that Mrs. Bargrave has, indeed, seen Mrs. Veal's apparition, the crucial piece of evidence is a reference to her dress fabric, which Mrs Bargrave has already noted as being of 'scower'd silk' (silk treated to improve the fastness of dye). She touches the fabric earlier in the account when she 'commends' Mrs. Veal's gown in an attempt to distract her from morbid ramblings about the life to come. Mrs. Veal has veered off course in their conversation, moving away from predictable chat about their former times as neighbours and starting to describe her experiences beyond the grave: 'Says Mrs. Veal, Dear Mrs. Bargrave, If the Eyes of our Faith were as open as the Eyes of our Body, we should see numbers of Angels about us for our Guard: The notions we have of Heaven now, are nothing like what it is, as Drelincourt says. Therefore be comforted under your Afflictions' (3). Mrs. Bargrave's reaching out to make material contact with Mrs. Veal comes at a timely moment in the narrative, pulling the story back to the realm of the empirical and forensic as it begins to sound too speculative and spectral.

Mrs. Veal has become a canonical instance of the 'apparition narrative', a paradigm for reading other supernatural and gothic fictions.[30] Unlike the many cruder examples of the sub-genre that proliferated across the century, *Mrs. Veal* fashions itself as demonstrably literary. In addition to the elaborate architecture of the narrative itself and the use of narrative strategies drawn from contemporary fiction, the volume is printed with a Preface and the tale makes reference to several specific titles drawn from a large body of writing on the status of the soul after death.[31] The text deploys the techniques of fiction, including the juxtaposition between natural and supernatural evidence that Defoe would use to such effect in the episode of the footprint in *Robinson Crusoe*. *Mrs. Veal* is formed out of ordinary details: Mrs. Bargrave's trip upstairs to fetch *Drelincourt's Book of Death*; the almost-kiss that the women give each other on meeting (though Mrs. Veal turns away, so they never make contact); the sewing Mrs. Bargrave is at work on when the apparition arrives. These details create a brilliantly uneasy effect, particularly when coupled with the figure of Mrs. Veal herself, who behaves like a regular character in a domestic novel, apparently unaware that her new knowledge about the invisible world has come about because she is dead. The reader's knowledge that she is an apparition (flagged in the title but not in the story itself) creates a remarkable instance of the uncanny. But the aspects of the tale that are most interesting to readers—the virtuosic literary effects Defoe creates—go unremarked and unacknowledged by the narrator, who remains fixed on his mission to persuade readers that this really is a True Account of 'matter of fact'.

Defoe wrote *The True and Genuine Account of the Life and Actions of the Late Jonathan Wild* in 1725 and so it takes us beyond the historical boundary of this volume; but it is a text which is instructive about how the emergence of the True Account in the final decades of the seventeenth century relates to later, eighteenth-century developments in realist fiction. This version of the Jonathan Wild story was succeeded by two much better known, John Gay's *The Beggar's Opera* (1728) and Henry Fielding's *Jonathan Wild* (1743). By the time Gay and Fielding wrote, Wild's story was well accepted as an allegory for contemporary political corruption and the tale had already hardened into a kind of national myth. But Defoe's *Jonathan Wild*, like virtually all his writing, claims hybrid territory at the intersection of fiction, history, and allegory. This hybridity announces itself in the title page, which is arranged to look like a work of history, philosophy, or religious reflection, and which sits opposite an illustrated frontispiece of Wild in prison. It also includes an elaborate Preface and Introduction. The most prominently printed words on the title page are 'Account' and 'Jonathan Wild'. *Account* encourages us to assume that we are reading non-fiction, since the term implies the rigour of a ledger,

---

[30] See Jayne Lewis's account of the *Mrs. Veal* phenomenon in *Air's Appearance: Literary Atmosphere in British Fiction, 1660–1794* (Chicago: University of Chicago Press, 2012), 120–3. For an earlier and important analysis of the rise of the apparition narrative see McKeon, *Origins of the English Novel*, 83–9.

[31] The volume Mrs. Bargrave fetches from upstairs at Mrs. Veal's request is Charles Drelincourt's *The Christian's Defence Against the Fears of Death* (1651), the sales of which increased greatly after Defoe's *True Relation* was published. Drelincourt was a Huguenot clergyman in France.

but the prominence of Wild's name hints that the text is more likely to be allegorical in its nature. The name Wild solicits allegorical interpretation, since it's neither singular enough to feel factual nor generic enough to sound like the hero of a realist novel. In the Preface to the work, however, Defoe rejects all attempts to allegorize or fictionalize Wild's life, lamenting the 'absurd and ridiculous accounts' of Wild's conduct, which turn it into a 'kind of Romance' imposed on the 'Credulous World'. Yet Defoe's language attests to the multiplicity of genres in which Wild's life might simultaneously be cast. He purports to present Wild's 'history, which is indeed a Tragedy of itself ... in a Method agreeable to the Fact', acknowledging in a single sentence no less than three genres that would accommodate the narrative (history, tragedy, and non-fiction). The note on the title page, 'not made up of *Fiction* or *Fable*, but taken from his own mouth', alerts readers to two other prose genres that might be (and perhaps already have been) attached to Wild's story.

What is interesting about Defoe's *True and Genuine Account* is not so much that it seeks to preserve truth from the distortions of fiction and fable, but that it implicitly recognizes truth as a species of narrative, appealing to a different set of desires and cognitive priorities than other narrative forms. Defoe's preoccupation with the status of the text as true extends beyond generic convention. In the Preface he explains that by printing early advertisements of the work, he avoids the reader being 'impos'd' on by false or pirated versions of his text. The notion that a material text could be a true or false object had been disseminated along with the rise of literary piracy in the eighteenth century and, like most matters pertaining to truth in the period, turns out to be less clear cut than it initially appears. While writers theoretically feared their texts becoming the object of piracy (illegal printing prior to legitimate publication), the pirating of manuscripts also conferred reputation and prestige on the authorized version.[32] The true text thus depended on the false one; its real value was in some ways produced by its theoretically unwanted rival.

Defoe makes it clear that Wild's life, as he tells it, is entirely singular: 'the Life of Jonathan Wild is a perfectly new scene; as his conduct has been inimitable, so his Imployment has been singular to him.' Defoe's version of the story cannot, in other words, be confused for the plausible or believable details of realist fiction, or the open-ended generality of allegory or religious typology. Wild's career is unrepeatable. Indeed, since his associates are unlikely to use Wild's now-notorious tricks, his employment is likely to 'die with him'. The condition of singularity that Defoe insists on at the opening of *Jonathan Wild* sheds unexpected light on his novels. *Robinson Crusoe, Moll Flanders* (1722), and *Roxana* (1724) are, of course, seminal texts that defined and determined the development of the genre. But at the same time, the peculiar mark of Defoe's fictions

---

[32] See Pat Rogers, 'The Uses of the Miscellany: Swift, Curll and Piracy', in Paddy Bullard and James McLaverty (eds.), *Jonathan Swift and the Eighteenth-Century Book* (Cambridge: Cambridge University Press, 2013), 87–100; Adrian Johns, *Piracy: The Intellectual Property Wars from Gutenberg to Gates* (Chicago: University of Chicago Press, 2009), 41–56.

is that their details are so deliberately singular that readers might well (and often did) mistake them for truth. The lingering possibility, improbable as it is, that novelistic narrative might, indeed, be true creates a destabilizing effect in the fiction. Since singularity, or circumstantial eccentricity, is the narrative mechanism True Accounts use to keep themselves separate from fiction, Defoe's use of the technique in his novels is, perversely, disruptive to his form. Actual reality doesn't make realist narrative seem more true.

But as the story develops, *Jonathan Wild* adopts the realistic or plausible ring of fiction, not the eccentricity of a True Account. Several times the narrative veers toward religious allegory, too, forging a link between the literary conventions of criminal biography and spiritual conversion narrative. When Defoe gives Wild's family background he emphasizes that he's one of three brothers, following in their father's buckle-making trade but dissenting from it into criminality. 'All three Brothers have had some Acquaintance with the inside of a Goal, though on different Accounts.'[33] The trio of brothers, their rebellious fraternal rivalry, their dissent from a father's advice are all standard tropes of Protestant allegory, including the allegorical narrative invoked at the beginning of *Robinson Crusoe* when Crusoe breaks with his father. They also recall the fighting brothers at the opening of Swift's *A Tale of a Tub* (1704), which parodies the schematic familial relations of spiritual allegory. When Jonathan Wild comes to London after his apprenticeship, he proves unwilling to be content with his legitimate 'day labor'. In describing his lapsed professional identity, Defoe again hints at religious allegory by framing Wild's criminal conduct in moral and temperamental terms: 'What he could get at his day Labour, but ill serv'd to maintain him, whose Temper even then was not much given to Frugality.'[34]

Early in his criminal career, Wild meets the prostitute Mary Milliner, with whom he enters into a bigamous second 'marriage'. The narrative here sounds exactly like realist fiction (indeed like *Moll Flanders*), making specific references to modern London and its criminal underworld. A long sentence, rich in believable local colour, meanders through a description of Wild's complicated relationship with Mrs. Milliner:

> Whether it was that she was frequently brought in there in her Night Rambles, and might receive some Favours from him on that Occasion, it being much in his way to favour such as she was, he being as a kind of Keeper set over them; or whether they Contracted a Friendship at first sight, or what other Incident brought it about I know not; but Mr. Wild not only became acquainted with her, but a more than common Intimacy soon grew between them; insomuch, that she began to teach him a great many New, and to him unknown Ways of getting Money, and brought him into her own Gang, whether of Thieves or Whores, or of both, is not much Material.[35]

---

[33] *Jonathan Wild*, 2.
[34] *Jonathan Wild*, 3.
[35] *Jonathan Wild*, 4.

Defoe's sprawling prose matches and conveys the sense of a distended, chaotic urban landscape. He doesn't gloss the underclass terminology, allowing contemporary readers a sense of being urban insiders when they understand what it means to say 'it being much in his way to favour such as she was' or to guess that when Milliner carried Wild 'upon the twang' it means that she taught him the tricks of her trade. Milliner's name, like Wild's, feels more suited to allegory or proto-fiction than a True Account. It casts her squarely within the aspirational working class, a girl with a taste for finery, eager to attract men's attention, with a dependable manual skill. That Mary Milliner is *not* a milliner but a whore anticipates Gay's move in *The Beggar's Opera* (1728) to make the criminal Peachum family upwardly mobile bourgeoisie. (Her respectable name gives her the opposite air to Moll Flanders, whose sensibilities she otherwise shares.) Mary Milliner's name sounds as if it ought to offer meaningful information about her character, though logically it should do nothing of the sort, given that she was a real person. The ironic antithesis between her name and the character Defoe gives her sustains the fiction of fiction, as does Defoe's critical attention to the power of names in the story. Defoe repeatedly implies the fictional and allegorical commonplace that names are meaningful; that they communicate information about a person's identity. 'Mr. Wild has left several Widows behind him at his *Exit*, whether they go by Name or not, that he himself could not inform us.' The speaker describes Wild's third wife as 'a true Penitent for all her former Life, [who] made him an excellent Wife'.[36] The woman's penitence here substitutes for a name, implying a connection between names and characters, but of course the text's claim to be true also refutes the kind of interpretative readings its literary devices encourage.

Defoe figures both Wild's and Milliner's criminality as entrepreneurial, again imposing the conventions of fictional narrative on a True Account. He tells us how Wild parts ways with Milliner once he becomes 'A Proficient in his Business' positioning Wild as a criminal apprentice, and Milliner master to the more ambitious pupil. When Wild becomes successful, Defoe announces Wild's 'taking a new house' in the Old Bailey with his sixth wife. Wild runs his thief-taking business on a strictly professional footing: 'he openly kept his Compting House, or Office, like a Man of Business, and had his Books to enter every thing in with the utmost Exactness and Regularity.'[37] Defoe encourages us to remember that the story he tells is literally, demonstrably true, even as he adheres to the language used in texts claiming fictional or spiritual truth. Describing the paucity of information around Wild's criminal system he writes: 'If it was asked, how they come to know who the Goods were taken from? It was always answer'd, That it was merely Providential; being, by meer Accident, at a Tavern, or at a Friend's House in the Neighbourhood, they heard that such a Gentleman had his House broken open, and such and such Goods Stolen, and the like.' Wild relies on Providence (or Accident) for his information. The use of providence and accident as synonyms here are reminders

---

[36] *Jonathan Wild*, 18.
[37] *Jonathan Wild*, 21.

that, in the period Defoe was writing, 'accident' denoted the spiritual or non-essential attributes of divine substance. The rumours that prove so helpful to Wild's business themselves sound as much like biblical parables as criminal narratives: 'a Gentleman had his House broken open, and such Goods Stolen.' Wild himself is figured as a kind of anti-Messiah, delivering the English people by sacrificing a few sinners along the way: he was 'oblig'd' from time to time 'to give up every now and then one or two of his Clients to the Gallows, to support his rising Reputation: In which cases, he never fail'd to proclaim his own Credit in bringing Offenders to Justice, and in delivering his Country from such dangerous People.' His double-dealing as a liaison between the criminal underworld and the magistrates is figured sacerdotally, with Wild as Priest: 'some have gone so far as to tell us the very Particulars which recommended any of the Gangs to him for a Sacrifice.'[38]

At one point Defoe goes so far as to suggest that Wild usurps divine prerogative by dispensing fate before God has the opportunity:

> He acted in a more difficult Station, as placing himself in the middle, between the Law and the Offender, in a manner, commuting the Felony, and making a kind of Composition where the Fact was Punishable; which Punishment no Man had Power to anticipate, but the Hand above, which had Power also to remit the Penalty; namely, the supreame Magistrate.[39]

These passages about Wild's providential authority establish two paradoxical or contradictory claims within the text of *Jonathan Wild*. On the one hand, Defoe's speaker uses the example of Wild to insist on the reality of divine providence: Wild's infamy lies in his having attempted to usurp God's authority. But on the other hand, Wild's conduct implies the contingency, or indeterminacy of authority, since Wild did usurp providence successfully, on earth; he did in fact determine others' fates. This contradiction offers important information about the problematic epistemology of True Accounts, but, perhaps more importantly, of fictions like the ones Defoe had written. These competing yet coexistent claims about the simultaneously fixed and negotiable status of truth hold it to be simultaneously possible that divine providence can be demonstrated and at the same time that providential traces on earth can be interrupted or altered by human agents. One broad social and intellectual consequence of this paradox would be the rise of natural religion, with its declaration that the divine kingdom exists beyond the jurisdiction of humans, and that human action should be rewarded and punished only as a matter of civil government, without consequences for salvation. The complete separation of religion and civic power was indeed the solution that Defoe supported, and this aspect of his work—the many essays in which he advocates for the complete removal of religious worship from civil life and independence of matters of conscience from political and

---

[38] *Jonathan Wild*, 11–12.
[39] *Jonathan Wild*, 16.

legal authority—has thus a logical connection to these seemingly unrelated instances in which he makes use of the True Account format.

Jonathan Wild offers a template for suggesting that in eighteenth-century writing, fixed and contingent truths can, and indeed must, coexist in narrative. True Accounts raise the possibility that narrative resists—perhaps even occludes—the separations that were happening ontologically and epistemologically outside narrative: in law, in religion, in marriage, in natural sciences. These were separations between the value of assured and speculative knowledge; between real and false facts; between truth and partial or un-truth that could be treated as authentic by readers who rejected the established conventions used to differentiate fact from fiction. This distinguishes the True Account from realist fiction and at the same time connects the modes to one another more interestingly. If we have seen that the factual content of True Accounts is constantly threatened or undermined by its use of fictions, we can also see that the opposite is true: that fiction is always compromised by the lingering and undermining presence of residual fact.

Index

For the benefit of digital users, indexed terms that span two pages (e.g., 52–53) may, on occasion, appear on only one of those pages.

Figures are indicated by an italic *f* following the page number.

Addison, Joseph *see also Spectator, The*
   Button's Coffee House 162–63
   Dialogues upon the Usefulness of Ancient Medals 374–75
   on the English language 48–49
   and the essay form 84, 272–73
   on fairy tales 296–97
   Johnson's 'Life of Addison' 451
   literary style 57–58, 60, 61
   on modern scholarship 372–75
   and Pope's *Guardian* 40 sham 167
   popularization of natural philosophy 430
   role of philosophy 275, 372–73
   works in Latin 9–10
amatory fiction *see also* romance
   affect and sexuality in 103–5
   autoeroticism 105–6
   commodification and sexual violation of women 108, 112–13, 115–18
   Daphnis and Chloe 103–4, 109–12
   devotion vs. self-preservation 112–17
   Lettres portugaises 103–4, 109–12, 113–14, 386–87
   Love-Letters between a Nobleman and His Sister 103–4, 112–18, 387
   pastoral codes 108–9
   reading practices for 104–5, 107
   unrequited love 109–10, 111–12
   virtuous passion vs. cynical manipulation 109–11
   women readers' innocence 106–7
Anabaptists 320–21, 325–26
Anderton, William 33–34, 38–39
Andrewes, Lancelot 305–6, 311, 314–15

Anglican Church
   Defoe's *The Shortest-Way* sham 37–38, 157–62, 232–33, 628–29
   occasional conformity 158–59
Anne, Queen 238, 465
annotation
   diary as-annotation practices 219–20
   in modern scholarship 375–77
antiquarianism
   scholarship on 119–21
   seventeenth-century practices 123–24, 130–31
antiquarian writing
   Anglo-Saxon prose in translation 127–30, 133
   archaic prose style 126–27, 129–30
   Aubrey's rhapsodic style for 124–25, 134–35
   Brady's *Complete History of England* 133–35
   Camden's *Britannia* 120–21, 122–26, 131, 134–35
   canonical scholarship 125–26
   county histories 120–21
   edited collections of documents 339–40
   genre 120–22, 337
   letters 121
   manuscripts 121
   materiality of texts 125–26
   on medieval documents 121–22, 126, 129–30
   move to stylistic heterogeneity 122–26, 130–31, 134–35
   plain prose style 131–33, 134–35, 337
   on Roman Britain 123–24, 126
   systematic/miscellaneous tensions in the organisation of 121–23, 124, 130–31

antiquarian writing (*cont.*)
   translation debates 122–24, 127–29, 133
   use of classical authorities 129–30, 131–32
   women writers 128–29
anti-sectarian polemic
   see also heresiographies; polemical prose
   anti-Catholic rhetoric 360
   anti-Williamite writings 360–62
   Gangraena as source material 320–22, 324, 325, 326–27, 329–31
   in New World literature 444
   pamphlets 317–19
   Presbyterian anti-sectarianism 320–22
   sexual promiscuity in 323, 324, 325
   in Swift's library 319
   Swift's *Tale of a Tub* as 316–17, 318–19, 325–26, 329–30
   tub imagery 317–18
Applebee, John 215, 628
Apuleius 188, 189–90
Arbuthnot, John 366–67, 376–77, 483–84
Aretino, Pietro 505–7, 515–17
Aristotle 62–63, 66–67, 131, 403–5, 414–15, 488, 490
Arnold, Matthew 1–2, 3–4, 9, 10, 60
Ashe, Thomas 438
Astell, Mary 321–22
astrology
   propagandistic use of 153–56
   Swift's anti-Partridge sham 153–57, 626–27
Atherton, John 203–4
Atkyns, Richard 22
Atlantic World *see* New World literature
Aubrey, John
   constructed diary of 222–23
   'An Idea of Education of Young Gentlemen' 182
   on instructional literature 300–1
   Minutes of Lives (*Brief Lives*) 79, 168–70, 172–73, 175–76, 178, 180, 181–83
   Monumenta Britannica 124
   prose style 572–73
   research information for Wood's *Athenae Oxonienses* 172–73
Austen, Ralph 578
authorship
   party writing 20

   satirised in *A Tale of a Tub* 17–20, 25–26
   separation of author and persona in shams 158–59, 160–62
auto/biographical writing *see also* brief lives; historical writing; spiritual autobiographies
   authorial self-interests 144–45, 147–48, 180–81
   bio-bibliography 223–25
   biographical romances 146
   brief lives as distinct from 169–70
   Calthorpe's *Short History* 146–47, 150–51
   Cavendish's *Life of William Cavendish* 143, 144–46, 338–39
   Clarendon's *Life* 147–50
   classical influences 78–79
   concerns over 136, 137, 140, 145
   consolatory motivations 137–38, 139–40, 143–44
   cultural contexts 141
   by dissenters 230
   on the East 251
   Eikon Basilike 320, 347–48, 488–89, 544–45, 612
   ethical and moral challenges 137–38, 139–41
   exemplarity tradition 136–37, 139, 140
   family histories 150–51
   female-authored 143–47, 150
   as a form of stewardship 146–47
   generic hybridity 141–42, 148, 150–51
   Hamilton's *The Exemplary Life and Character of James Bonnell* 136, 137–38, 140
   Hutchinson's *Life of John Hutchinson* 143–44
   hybrid memoir-chronicles 338–39
   Ludlow's *Memoirs* 147–48, 334–35
   male-authored biographies of women 147
   manuscript forms 150
   memorialization function 137–39, 143–44
   political motivations 143–45, 147–51
   as a practice 136–37, 141, 142–43
   pre-modern forms 141–43
   range of subjects 136–37
   reputational defence 143–44, 145–46, 147–48
   source material 140–41
Auzout, Adrien 391–92

Bacon, Francis
   The Advancement of Learning 83–84, 353
   on the English language 47–48, 49–51
   the essay form 84, 279, 306–7, 452
   Rabelais quotations 88
   scientific writings 569, 570–71
   tripartite distinction of history 78–79, 337
   use of aphorism 574–75
Bakhtin, Mikhail 350–51, 365
Baldwin, Richard 354–55, 588
ballads 204
Ballaster, Ros 112–13, 186–87, 260–62
Bank of England 193, 206–7, 470
Barclay, John 84–85, 357, 496
Barrow, Dr Isaac 169–70
Bastian, Frank 160–62
Baxter, Richard
   dangers of romances 44
   dissenting writing 230, 231
   on exemplary lives 244
   on sermon styles 601–2
   spiritual autobiography 553–54, 557–58, 562–63
Bayle, Pierre 155–56
Beadle, John 226–27
Beale, John 572–75
Beattie, J. M., 202–3, 205
Beaumont, Agnes 230, 551–52
Behn, Aphra
   engagement with print culture 28
   Love-Letters between a Nobleman and His Sister 7–8, 87–88, 103–4, 112–18, 387, 589–91, 593, 595–96
   Oroonoko 91, 434, 445–46, 447–48
   translations of French philosophical texts 81, 90
belles lettres, term 81–82
Bell, Maureen 16
   Bentley, Richard (1645–97) 22, 82–83
Bentley, Richard (1662–1742)
   annotation and Horace's poetry 376–77
   King's parody of 423–24
   Latin prose 9–10
   mock scholarship 363–64, 368–69, 370, 371, 372, 374–75, 376–78
   the Phalaris dispute 9–10, 98–99, 367–68, 371–72, 376–77, 402–3, 423

Beverley, Robert 437–38
Bible, the
   literacy rates and reading practices 41–42, 43–44
   print culture and 488–89
   and prophetic radical thought 523
   Protestant Biblicism 329–30
   scriptural interpretation debates 329–30
Bigold, Melanie 28
biography *see* auto/biographical writing
bites *see also* shams
   definition 152–53
   in prose writing 152
Blair, Hugh 57–58, 60
Blome, Richard 441
Blount, Charles 530–31, 532–33
Blount, Edward 174–75
Blount, Thomas 384, 393–94, 402–3, 474
Boate, Arnold 147
Boate, Margaret 147
Bohun, Edmund 67–68, 69–70
Bolingbroke, Henry St John, 1st Viscount 36, 58
Bonnell, James 136, 137–41
Bonnell, Jane 137–41
book trade *see also* print culture
   annual book production 22–26, 24f, 473f
   book ownership 20–21, 42–43, 71, 74, 76–77
   in foreign books 86–87, 506–7, 509–10
   pricing 20–21
   production centres 23
   publications in foreign languages 86–87
   punishment of printers 32–35, 36–37
   regulation of 21–23, 29–30
   works in Latin 71
Bouhéreau, Élie 356–57
Boyer, Abel 89–90, 95, 97, 291–92, 628
Boyle, Charles 367–68, 423
Boyle, Robert
   authorial persona 419, 565–66, 568–69
   the essay form 272, 273
   experiments 568–69
   Latin translations of 581–82
   in mock science writings 419–20
   prose style 419–20, 570–71, 580
   on scientific disputes 569–70
Brady, Robert 133–34

brief lives
- archival fidelity 172–73
- Aubrey's *Lives* 79, 168–70, 172–73, 175–76, 178, 180, 181–83
- character types 173–76
- the Civil War in 170–72
- as distinct from auto/biographical writings 169–70
- exemplary lives 168, 180
- libelous content 172
- memorialization function 171–72
- personal anecdotes 169–70

Brightland, John 52–53
Brinsley, John 44
Brome, Alexander 3–4
Brown, David 43–44
Browne, Thomas
- prose style 570–71
- *Religio Medici* as spiritual autobiography 553–54, 558–61, 563–64
- *Religio Medici*'s confessional tone 269, 270–71

Brugis, Thomas 307–8
Bruns, Gerald R., 292
Buckingham, George Villiers, 2nd Duke 28, 178, 413, 535
Bulteel, John 75–76
Bunyan, John
- dissenting writing 230, 235–36, 240–41
- *Grace Abounding* 230, 240–41, 550–51, 552, 553–57, 558–59, 560–62
- imprisonment 247
- Martin Luther's influence on 556–57
- *The Pilgrim's Progress* 40, 42–43, 49–51, 174–75, 230, 241, 247–48
- reading aloud 42–43
- simplicity in written style 49–51

Bunyan, Thomas 7–8
Burgess, Anthony 54
Burles, Edward 65
Burnet, Thomas 278–79, 430
Burton, William 126
Butler, Charles 46–47, 48
Butler, Samuel
- *Hudibras* 316–17, 318–19
- mock scientific works 419
- use of characters 173, 175–76, 178, 179–80

Butler, William 169–70
Button's Coffee House 162–63

Calthorpe, Dorothy 146–47, 150–51
Camden, Vera 556–57
Camden, William 120–21, 122–26, 131, 134–35
captivity narratives 443–45, 501
Care, Henry 32–33, 360, 458–61
Carew, Thomas 542–43
Caribbean 434, 441–42
Casaubon, Isaac
- on the art of criticism 405–7
- in England 410–11
- study of verse satire 403–5, 406–7, 408–10

Casaubon, Meric 420–21
Cavaliers *see* Royalists
Cavendish, Margaret
- auto/biographical writing 143, 144–46, 338–39, 396
- *The Blazing World* 578–79
- on character types 175–76, 177
- engagement with print culture 28
- on the genre of history 335–36
- letters 395–96

censorship *see* press control
Chambers, Ephraim 51–52, 56–57
Chambers, Robert 54
Chantry, John 75
chapbooks 89–90, 203, 204, 207–8
characters
- amplification in 175–76
- in Aubrey's *Lives* 181–82
- cultural role 174, 183
- definition 173
- Hooke's louse 178–80
- of John Earle 173, 175, 176, 181–82
- in the letters of Dorothy Osborne 48–51, 182–83
- for life lessons 182–83
- microscopic analysis 180–81
- 'Overbury' characters 174–75, 176
- in polemical prose 480
- as polite satire 176–78
- in prose dialogues 480–81
- of Samuel Butler 173, 175–76, 178, 179–80
- Theophrastus' ethical characters 173, 174–75, 177, 480

Charles I
  Eikon Basilike 320, 347–48, 488–89, 544–45, 612
  fast days 608, 612–13
  The King's Cabinet Open'd 384–86, 399, 544–45, 588–89, 590–91
  sermons on 612–14
Charles II
  Declaration of Breda 233–34
  Declaration of Indulgence 236–37
  in oriental scandal fiction 261–62
  Rye-House Plot 153–54, 355–56, 387, 590–91
Charlett, Arthur 122–23
Chorier, Nicolas 517
Cicero 64, 70, 129–30, 131–32, 335–36, 337, 534–35
  L'Estrange's translation of *de Officiis* 68–70
circulation
  book ownership 20–21
  of foreign books 86–87
  growth in published titles 22–26, 24f
  legislation 29–39
  manuscript transmission 26–27
  metaphors for 15–19
  numbers 19–26
  press control 29–30
  and the print trade 16
  proliferation of print culture 16–19
  of translated texts 91–92
circulation narratives *see also* spy narratives
  animation 185, 189–90, 191–93, 196–98
  continuity of memory 184–85, 187–88, 189
  currency and national identity 184, 193–95
  genre 184, 185–86
  The Golden Spy 185–86, 191–95
  gold's influence on human morality 191–93
  metamorphosis in 184–85, 187–93
  The New Metamorphosis 185–86, 188–91
  observation and representation in 184–85, 197–98, 199
  personification 195–96, 197–99
  term 185–86
  transformative nature of money 192–93
  vice witnessed in 188–91
Civil War
  in brief lives 170–72
  in historical writing 332–33
  preaching and mobilization 344–45
  and the 'prosification' of England 1–2, 3–4, 6–7
Clarendon, Edward Hyde, Earl of
  allegations of bribe-taking 172
  authorial bias 180–81
  Civil War mobilization and propaganda 341–44, 348–49
  historical writing 77–78
  on history-reading 347–48
  on John Seldon 172–73
  The Life of Edward Earl of Clarendon 147–50
  politic history 342–43, 345
  rhetoric 336–37
  True Historical Narration of the Rebellion and Civil Wars in England 168, 170–71, 180–81, 332–33, 334–35, 338–44
classical texts
  accessible translations 71, 74–77
  the Ancients and the Moderns' literary quarrel 98–99, 296, 367–69, 371–72
  applicability to contemporary society 66–70
  biographical writing 78–79
  Camden's Greek Grammar 64, 65
  classical allusions in modern prose 69–70
  classical authorities in antiquarian writings 129–30, 131–32
  dialogues 77–78
  English historical writing 77–78
  epistolary genre 79–80
  the essay form 77–78, 84
  in grammar school education 63–67
  humanist scholarship on 401–3
  influence on English prose 62–63, 72–74, 77, 79–80
  Lily's Latin Grammar 64, 65–66
  manuals 303–5
  rhetoric 64
  the romance 79–80, 84–85
  Theophrastus' ethical characters 173, 174–75, 177, 480
  in translation 70–77
  in university education 66–67
  verse satire 404–5
Clegg, Cyndia Susan 30–31, 36

Cleveland, John 48, 51, 339–40, 482–83
Clifford, Isaac 246
Clifford, Lady Anne 42–44
Clifford, Martin 535–36
Cockin, William 52–53
coffee-houses 35–36, 221–22, 228, 275–76, 397–98, 430, 463, 473
coinage
    counterfeiting 206–7
    currency and national identity 184–85, 193–95
    Dialogues upon the Usefulness of Ancient Medals 374–75
    gold's influence on human morality 191–93
    recoinage debate 192–93
Coleridge, Samuel Taylor 54, 60
College, Stephen 32–33
Collier, Jeremy 278–80
Collins, Anthony 533, 534–35
colonial literature of the New World 433–34, 437–39, 448–49
Congreve, William 91, 176
Cooper, Christopher 52–53
Cooper, Joseph 537–38
Coppe, Abiezer 525–26, 532–33
corantos 217–18
Cordingly, David 214–15
Cornwallis, Sir William 84
Cotton, Charles 84, 266–68, 269
Cotton, Robert 121
Cowley, Abraham
    essays 56–57, 84, 267–68, 270–71, 273, 275–76
    ode to the Royal Society 179–80
    Works 27
crime
    the criminal classes 203–4
    financial crimes 206–7
    highwaymen 203–4, 211–14
    in the press 215
    rural/urban divides 201–2, 211–12
    in true accounts 619–20, 622–24
    witchcraft 206
    by women 205–6, 207–9, 223
criminal literature
    compendia of criminal lives 208, 212–13

    and developments in the legal system 201–7
    everyday lives in/social commentary 200–1
    genre 200, 215
    highwaymen 211–14
    moralizing fables 204
    picaresque 209–11
    pirate tales 211, 213–15
    Richard Head's *The English Rogue* 209–10
    rogue's tales 207–9, 211
    satire in 201
    transcripts of judicial hearings 205
    witchcraft 206
criminology 201
Croll, Morris 6–7
Cromwell, Oliver
    characterization of 480
    disinterment of 204–5
    satirized in recipe books 544–46
Crook, John 561–62
Culliford, John 32–33
Curll, Edmund 203–4, 206, 350–51, 352–53, 515–16
Curtis, Jane 32–33

Daines, Simon 52–53
d'Aulnoy, Marie-Catherine
    fairy tales 288–90, 296–99
    translations of 89–90, 91–92
Davenant, Charles 483
Dawks, Ichabod 28–29
Defoe, Daniel
    ambiguity of the post-licensing regime 38–39
    censorship of 37–39
    The Compleat English Tradesman 15
    The Consolidator 422
    discussions of national improvement 274
    the essay form 274
    in *Faction Display'd* 475, 476f
    impartiality in the authorial voice 281
    Jonathan Wild 628, 629, 631–36
    A Journal of the Plague Year 229
    Letters Writ by a Turkish Spy 186–87, 262
    mock science writings 422
    Moll Flanders 205–6, 207–8, 210–11, 229
    pillorying 37–38, 157–60, 161–62, 205

piracy in the works of 214, 442
polemic against 474–75
political writings 475–77, 483
Robinson Crusoe 53–56, 61, 248–49, 258, 259–60
Roxana 207–8, 210–11
Secret History of the White-Staff 596–98
The Shortest-Way with the Dissenters 37–38, 157–62, 232–33, 628–29
on the taking of Anglican communion 158–59, 238
A Tour thro' the Whole Island of Great Britain 15
True Accounts 628–36
A Weekly Review of the Affairs of France 397, 453, 465–66
deism *see also* Blount, Charles; Toland, John
freedom of expression 534–35
toleration debates 534–36
deist writing
biblical and textual criticism 523, 531–33, 534–35
Hobbes' influence on 532
ironic tone 530–31
polemical prose 523
term 532–33
DeJean, Joan 91–93
Demaus, Robert 58–59
Dennis, John 48–49, 176
Dent, Arthur 42–43
Derham, William 428–29, 430
Descartes, René 389–90, 396
diaries
almanac diaries 218–20
bio-bibliographical works 223–25
diary-as-annotation practice 219–20
financial accounting and 217–18, 219, 220–21, 225, 227–28, 242
genre 216–17, 228
materiality of texts 220, 222–23
practices of diary-writing 218–19, 221–23
self-representation in 217–18, 220–23, 227
spiritual diary-keeping 225–28, 242
within wider life-writings 225
Diggers 499–500, 521–22
'Discourse Concerning the Original and Progress of Satire' (Dryden)

critical antecedents for 403–11
definition of satire 400–1, 413–14
epic poetry and satire 412–13
on the genre of satire 411–13
as literary history 401–3, 414–16
particularism and universalism tensions 401, 402–3
tonal and rhetorical strategies 413–14
dissenters *see also* toleration debates
arguments against religious uniformity 234–35
Defoe's sham piece on 37–38, 157–62, 232–33, 628–29
epitaphs 245–46
imprisonment 246
individualism and freedom of expression 234–36, 534
legislation against 233–34, 236–37
persecution of 235–37
in political debate 470–71
sects 234, 237
taking of Anglican communion 158–59, 237–38
Toleration Act 237–38, 316–17, 470–71
dissenting writing
auto/biographical writing 230
censorship 232–33, 238–40
for comfort and support 244–45, 388–89
commemoration in 245–46
conformist criticism of 238–40
emotional and bodily suffering in 243–44
language and style 238–42
prison writing 246–48
religious letters 388–89
Robinson Crusoe as 248–49
role of print culture 230, 231–32, 233, 248–49
and the spiritual condition 241–42
spiritual diary-keeping 225–28, 242
Dodsworth, Roger 121
Dodwell, Henry 67
Donaworth, Jane 42, 43–44
Donne, John 88, 553–54, 582–83
Doody, Margaret Anne 105–6, 108–9
Downie, J. A., 36
Drake, Nathan 450–52

Dryden, John *see also* 'Discourse Concerning the Original and Progress of Satire' (Dryden)
  classical translations 20–21, 72–75
  Of Dramatic Poesy 56–57
  on the English language 46–47, 48–51, 73–74
  Essay of Dramatick Poesie 401–3
  essays 267–68
  keys to 350–51
  life of Hobbes 180–81
  'Life of Plutarch' 77–78, 79, 169–70
  Mac Flecknoe 16–17
  prefaces 57
  public mockery of 413
  use of historical scholarship 401–3
Dugard, William 93
Dugdale, William
  Antiquities of Warwickshire 120–21, 131–33, 218–19
  anti-sectarian polemic 321–22
  life-writing 218–19
  Monasticon Anglicanum 121, 218–19
  plain prose style 131–33
  use of classical authorities 129–30
Dunton, John 25–26, 227, 419–20, 461–62, 464, 481–82, 594, 596–97
Dyche, Thomas 52–53
Dyer, John 28–29, 36

Earle, John 170, 173, 175, 181–82
East, the
  Arabian Nights 82–83, 89–90, 263–65, 291–92
  in early travel writings 251–52
  fictional engagement with 260–61
  imaginative engagement with 259–60, 264, 265
  literary influences in *Robinson Crusoe* 258, 259–60
  oriental scandal fiction 261–62
  Ottoman Empire 257–58, 261–62
  in prose writing 250–51
  scholarship on Islam 255–58
  translation of *Ḥayy ibn Yaqẓan* 258–59, 263–64
  translations 291–92

translations of the Qur'an 252–56
as a vehicle for national self-examination 263
Edmonds, J. M., 108–9
education
  applicability of classical learning to contemporary society 66–70
  ars historica tradition 66–70
  classical literature's influence on 63–70
  discussions of national improvement 273–74
  grammar schools 63–64, 407–8, 548–49
  'An Idea of Education of Young Gentlemen' (Aubrey) 182
  in Latin and Greek 64–66
  memorisation of classical references 69–70
  role of philosophy 275
  university education 66–67
  women 65
Edwards, Thomas 319–23, 324–28, 329–31
Ellwood, Thomas 231–32
Elstob, Elizabeth 128–29
enslavement
  Behn's *Oroonoko* 91, 434, 445–46, 447–48
  English trade in 194–95
  handbooks on slave management 434
  in New World literature 433, 434, 445–49
  Royal African Company 625–26
Epictetus 303–5
epistolary genre 79–80
Erasmus, Desiderius 304–5, 526, 528
essay form
  apolitical, polite essays in periodicals 450–52, 466–67
  classical influences 77–78, 84
  cultural and literary criticism 267–68
  definitions 267
  dialogic forms 277, 278–80
  discussions of national improvement 273–74
  the essayistic voice 280–82
  language and style of 267–68, 274, 276
  miscellaneity of the genre 266–70
  in mock science 427–28
  Montaignean confessional style 84, 266–71, 278–79, 280–81, 282
  and a national literature 84, 85–86

the practical arts 276
and scientific pursuits 271–73
and the transmission of knowledge 275–77
Evelyn, John 43–44, 309–11, 572–74
Exclusion Crisis 22–25, 31–33
Exquemelin, Alexandre Olivier 213–15, 442–43
Ezell, Margaret 26–27, 45–46

fables
autodidactic potential 287–88
didactic function of *Telemachus* 288, 289–91
ironization of 296, 298–99
L'Estrange's *Fables of Aesop* 283–84, 286, 287, 293–95, 360–62
for moral instruction 283–85, 290–94
moralizing fables in criminal literature 204
pedagogical function 294–95
in political prose 498
prose style of 290–91, 292, 293–94
prose versions of Aesop 286–88, 290–91
in *The Spectator* 286–88
and Swift's *A Tale of a Tub* 296
translations of *Arabian Nights* 291–92
fairy tales
d'Aulnoy's tales 288–90, 296–99
female readership 297–98
ironization of 296–97
and literacy rates 296–97
literary fairy tales 288
for moral instruction 284–85, 297–98
prose style of 289, 291–92
realism and reason in 297–99
translations from French 89–90, 288–89, 296–97
Fancourt, Samuel 16
Featley, John 226–27
Fell, Margaret 42, 43–44
Fénelon, François, *Telemachus* 89–90, 97–98, 288, 289–91
Ferguson, Francis 623–24
Fielding, Henry 366–67, 377–78, 631–32
Filmer, Robert 28
Flatman, Thomas 465–66
Fontanelle, Bernard Le Bovier de 81, 83, 90
Fox, George 49–51, 230, 246, 523–24

France *see also* Huguenots
Anglo-French linguistic networks 81–83, 86–87, 91–96, 99–100
Anglo-French periodical press 93–94
cuisine 537–39
English satires on Continental cuisine 545–49
fairy tales 89–90, 288–89, 296–97
French plays 82–83
letters 382–83
philosophical texts 81, 90
pornography 509–14, 515–16, 517–19
romances 87–88, 496
secret histories 592, 593
translations of French texts 82–83, 87–90
women writers 91–92
Franck, Richard 502–3
freedom
dissenters' individualism and freedom of expression 234–36
of expression 534–35
press freedoms 35–36
in reading practices 254
of thought 275–76, 285–86
freethinkers *see* deism
Fuller, Thomas 79
Fulman, William 121

Gadbury, John 155–56
Gage, Thomas 434, 439–41
Gale, Thomas 121
Galland, Antoine 82–83, 89–90, 263–65, 291–92
Gardiner, Judith Kegan 112–13, 117–18
Gauden, John 612
Gay, John 168, 213, 366–67, 631–32, 634
Gayton, Edmund 172
Gibson, Edmund 122–26, 134–35
Gifford, George 41
Gildon, Charles
The Golden Spy 185–86, 191–95
The New Metamorphosis 185–86, 188–91
The Post-Boy Robb'd of His Mail 186–87
Glanvill, Joseph 270–71, 421–22, 533, 572–73
Glasse, Hannah 539, 549
Godolphin, Lord 28–29, 594–95
Godwin, Francis 89–90, 578–79

Godwyn, Morgan 447–48
Goldhill, Simon 107, 108–9
Goodwin, Thomas 65–66
grammars *see also* punctuation
    Camden's Greek Grammar 64, 65
    definition 56–57
    expansion in 56–57
    Lily's Latin Grammar 64, 65–66
    prescriptivist grammars 56–58
Green, Jody 34–35
Grew, Nehemiah 568, 569, 572–73, 575–76
Guardian
    mock science 430–31
    Pope's writing for 162, 164–66, 546
Guillory, John 2

Habermas, Jürgen 35–36, 468–69, 473, 484
Hale, George 312
Halifax, Marquis 479
Hallam, Henry 56–57, 59–60
Hamilton, Elizabeth 52–53
Hamilton, William 136, 137–38, 140
Hammond, Brean 369
handbooks *see* instructional literature
Harley, Robert (Earl of Oxford) 36–37, 38–39, 465–66, 475–77, 594, 596–98
Harrington, James 126–27, 491–93, 496–97, 522
Harvey, William 15
Hauksbee, Francis 429
Hazlitt, William 84
Head, Richard 209–10
Healey, John 303–5
Hearne, Thomas 125–26, 224–25
Heinsius, Daniel 400–1, 402–3, 407–8, 409, 410–11
Heliodorus 84–85
Herbert, George 41, 43–44
heresiographies *see also* anti-sectarian polemic
    authorial voice 320, 323, 326–28
    Gangraena 319–23, 324–28, 329–31
    Gangraena as source material for anti-sectarian polemic 320–22, 324, 325, 326–27, 329–31
    illiteracy and 323–24, 325–27, 328
    by Irenaeus 316–17, 319, 320

    sexual promiscuity in 323, 324, 325, 326–27
    textual veracity 328
    used against the Presbyterians 320–23
    women preachers 324–25
Heywood, Oliver 244, 245
Hickes, George 127–29
Hill, Abraham 169, 171–72
Hill, Christopher 524–25, 526, 527
Hill, John 381–82
Hind, James 208–9, 211, 212–13
historical writing *see also* antiquarian writing; secret histories
    Clarendon's *History of the Rebellion* 168, 170–71, 180–81, 332–33, 334–35, 336–37, 338–43
    classical influences on 77–78
    edited collections of documents 339–41
    generic conceptions of history 335–36
    history-reading as mobilization 334, 346–49
    Hobbes' *Behemoth* 335–37, 338–39, 340–42, 343–45, 346
    Hutchinson's *Life of John Hutchinson* 336–37, 338–39, 340–41, 343, 344–45, 346–47
    hybrid memoir-chronicles 338–39
    ideology and political rhetoric 332–33, 335–37
    language of 'impartiality' 332–33, 348–49
    mobilization and coalition-forming 341–45, 348–49
    partisanship in 332–33, 335–36, 341–42
    periodicals as 458–59
    plain prose style 337
    political history 337–39
    print culture and 339–40, 344–45, 348–49
    seventeenth-century changes in 337
Hobbes, Thomas
    Behemoth 334–37, 338–39, 340–42, 343–45, 346
    on Bible reading practices 42
    on classical learning 66–67
    classical translations 72–73, 76–77, 489–90
    on the English language 48
    historical writing 77–78
    on history-reading 346
    Latin prose 9–10
    letters 389–90, 396

Leviathan 346, 472, 489–91, 532
Lucianic style 533
on oratory 344–45
in Overbury's *Characters* 175
political prose 5–6, 488
on preaching and mobilization 344–45, 348–49
rhetoric 490–91
Holdsworth, Richard 65–67, 70
Holland, Philemon 73, 74, 76–77, 122–24
Homer 97–99, 289–90, 371–72, 498, 546–47
Hone, William 485
Hooke, Robert
  on history writing 250–52
  interest in the East 250–51, 264, 265
  the louse/flea from *Micrographia* 178–80, 579–80, 581f
  Micrographia 391–92, 579–80, 619–20
  preface to Knox's *Historical Relation of the Island Ceylon* 250, 259, 264, 265
  prose style 572–73
  Royal Society 178
  translation work 581–82
Horace 376–77, 404–5, 407–8, 548
Houghton, John 461–62, 463–64, 465–66
Howe, John 233–34, 235–36
How, Samuel 329–30, 523–24, 534–35
Huet, Pierre-Daniel 92–93
Huguenots
  careers of French women writers 91–92
  in England 93, 96–97, 99–100
  French book market for in London 81, 86–87
  Motteux's key to *Gargantua and Pantagruel* 356–57, 359–60
  periodical literature 9–10, 93–94
  political prose 488–89
  refugees and French translations 81, 93
  Revocation of the Edict of Nantes 352–53
  translations by 89–90, 97–98
Hume, David 35–36, 275, 276, 277
Hunter, J. Paul 42–43, 44–46, 483, 620
Hurt, William 36
Husband, Edward 339–41
Hutchinson, Lucy
  accounts of preaching 344–45
  on Civil War coalition-building 343
  on history-reading 343, 344–45, 346–47
  on the Levellers 499
  Life of John Hutchinson as auto/biographical writing 143–44
  Life of John Hutchinson as historical writing 336–37, 338–39, 340–41, 343, 344–45, 346–47
  rhetoric 336–37, 338–39

imperialism 1–2, 194–95
Independents *see also* Hutchinson, Lucy
  dissenting writing 230, 231, 243–44
  individualism and freedom of expression 235
  polemic of *Gangraena* 330–31
  Presbyterian-Independents division 234, 320–21
instructional literature *see also* manuals
  classical literature 64–65
  didactic obliqueness 301–2
  genre 302–3
  growth in published titles 25–26
  as pastoral 301–2
  on punctuation 52–53
  socio-economic context 300–2, 308–10
invective, term 474
Ireland 23, 87
Irenaeus 316–17, 319, 320
Isham, Elizabeth 42, 43–44
Islam
  and Protestant religious doubt 561–62
  scholarship on 255–58
  translations of the Qur'an 252–56
it-narratives 184–86, 187–88, 198–99

Jacobitism 34–35, 38–39, 316–17, 361, 444, 461–62, 475–77
Jamaica 208, 429–30, 434, 439–40, 441
James I 588–89
James II
  absolutist ambitions 133–34
  Declaration of Indulgence 237
Jameson, Fredric 104–5
Janeway, James 242
Jeffreys, George 203, 210
Jenkins, Leoline 170–71
jestbooks 208–9

Johnson, Samuel
 on the changing nature of English 47–48, 59
 and the essay form 84
 on grammar 56–57
 history of the periodical 451–52
 life of Alexander Pope 366–67
 life of Joseph Addison 451
 on prose style 57, 61
Jones, R. F., 6–7, 49–51
Jonson, Ben 84, 88, 176, 182–83
Josephus 71–72
journalism 215, *see also* newspapers
Junius, Franciscus 128
Juvenal 400, 401, 404–5, 407–8

Kadar, Marlene 142–43
Kareem, Sarah Tindal 621
Keith, George 241, 258
Kentish, Richard 601–2
Keymer, Thomas 205, 361, 364
keys, literary
 the *clavis* tradition 87–88
 commercial markets 352–53
 to Dryden 350–51
 and *Gulliver's Travels* 350–51, 359–60, 363–64
 historical-allegorical method 350, 352–53
 to L'Estrange's *Fables of Aesop* 360–62
 Motteaux's key to Rabelais' *Gargantua* 350–53, 356–60, 364–65
 Pope's *A Key to the Lock* 87, 162, 163–65, 166–67, 351–52, 362–64
 popularity of 350–51
King, Gregory 20
King, William
 The Art of Cookery 548–49
 and the biography of James Bonnell 137–38, 139–41
 as a Christ Church Wit 423, 427
 Dialogues of the Dead 423–25
 parodies of the essay format 427–28
 parody of Swift 423
 The Transactioneer 419–20, 425–27
 Useful Transactions in Philosophy 427–30
Kirkman, Francis 208, 209
Knox, Robert 250–51, 259, 264

Lambarde, William 127–28, 133
language *see also* Latin
 Anglo-French linguistic networks 81–83, 86–87, 91–96, 99–100
 borrowings from European languages 81–82
 the changing nature of English 47–48, 59
 criticism of the English language 46–42, 49
 English and prose 40, 46
 English in scientific writing 581–82
 European languages 46–47, 48–49
 keywords and labels in political debate 477–79
 Latin's influence on English 81–82
 of the legal system 202
 praise for the English language 46–47, 48–49
Lanham, Richard 53, 55–56
La Rochefoucauld, François de 83, 90
La Roche-Guilhem, Anne de 91–92
Las Casas, Bartolomé de 439–40
Latin
 in antiquarian writings 122–24
 in the domestic print trade 71
 and the evolution of the English language 81–82
 in grammar school education 64–66, 407–8
 neo-Latin writing 9–10, 83–84
 pornographic works 517
 in scientific writing 581–82
Latour, Bruno 624
Laud, William 305–6, 314–15
Lawson, John 438–39
Leake, William 74
legal system *see also* crime; criminal literature; press control
 court procedures 202–3
 developments in 200, 206–7
 jury system 202–3
 law enforcement 201–2
 legislation against dissent 233–34
 manuals 308–9
 Old Bailey Sessional Papers 202, 215
 pillorying 32–33, 36–38, 157–60, 161–62, 205
 punishments 203, 204–5, 206–7
 Toleration Act 237–38, 316–17, 470–71

Lejeune, Philippe 216–17, 218, 229
Leslie, Charles 233, 316–17, 324, 451, 461–62, 465–66, 477–78
L'Estrange, Roger
    alleged Jacobitism 361
    anti-sectarian writings 321–22, 323
    Civil War mobilization and propaganda 342–43
    The Committee or Popery in Masquerade 444
    The Dissenters Sayings 321–22
    on dissenting writing 232, 239–40
    Fables of Aesop 283–84, 286, 287, 293–95, 360–62
    Five Love-Letters From A Nun To A Cavalier 22–23, 28–29, 87–88, 109–12, 386–87
    as Licenser of the Press 21–22, 28–29, 30–34, 321–22, 360, 458
    The Observator 360, 451, 458, 460–61
    periodical writing 458–61
    political writings 475–77, 482–83
    prose style 477–78
    translation of Cicero's *de Officiis* 68–70
    translation of Josephus 71–72
    translation of *Lettres portugaises* 87–88, 103–4, 109–12, 113–14, 386–87
    translations from French 87–88
letters
    antiquarian writings 121
    Behn's *Love-Letters between a Nobleman and His Sister* 7–8, 87–88, 103–4, 112–18, 387, 589–91, 593, 595–96
    cabinets of secret letters 379–81, 384–85, 588–89
    during the Civil War era 380–81, 384–86
    empirical science and the new philosophy 389–92
    epistolary manuals 379–80, 381–82
    genre 379–81, 399
    informality and intimacy 27, 176–77, 379–80
    The King's Cabinet Open'd 384–86, 399, 588–89
    L'Estrange's *Five Love-Letters From A Nun To A Cavalier* 22–23, 28–29, 87–88, 109–12, 386–87

as a literary form 27
love letters 176–78, 182–83, 380–81, 386–87
of Margaret Cavendish 395–96
mock-manuals and academies of letters 379–80, 382–84
in periodicals 397–98, 481–82
in *Philosophical Transactions* 390–92, 397, 576–77
political debate in 481–82
in print culture 380–81, 385
published by Humphrey Moseley 393–94
religious letters 388–89
rhetoric 380, 381–82
in the Royal Society's *Philosophical Transactions* 28, 42–43, 390–92, 397, 399
translations of French letters 382–83
Levellers 31, 485, 497–99, 520–22, 528, 534–35
libraries 16, 43–44
life-writing *see also* auto/biographical writing; diaries; spiritual autobiographies
    practices of 142–43, 218–19
    Puritanism's influence on 217–18, 225–26
Lilburne, John 31, 485, 497, 551–52, 554–55
Lister, Martin 427–28, 548, 572–73
literacy rates 20–21, 40, 41–42, 217–18, 296–97, 473, 487
literary history
    the Ancients and the Moderns' literary quarrel 401, 415–16
    Casaubon's study of verse satire 403–5, 406–7, 408–10
    Dryden's 'Discourse' as 401–3, 414–16
Littlebury, Isaac 290–91
Livy 71–72, 74, 404–5
Lloyd, David 75, 168, 180
Locke, John
    Aesop's Fables 287–88
    the concept of the 'mind' 284–85
    essay form 83–84, 266–67, 273, 277
    influence of eastern writings 257–58
    journals 225
    the knowledge of things 285–86
    language and style of 501–3
    Letter Concerning Toleration 501–3
    pedagogy 296
    political writings 487–88
    translations of 83–84

Lodge, Thomas 71–72
London
  crime rates 201–2
  criminal literature 201–2
  great show trials 202–3
  law enforcement 201–2
  literacy rates 20, 42–43
  Old Bailey Sessional Papers 202, 215
  population 19–20, 201–2
Longus, *Daphnis and Chloe* 103–4, 105–9
Lovelace, Richard 3–4
Loveman, Kate 152, 153, 157–58
Lucian 74–75, 455–56, 498, 532–33
Ludlow, Edmund 147–48, 334–35, 522
Luther, Martin 255, 556–57
Lynch, Kathleen 27
Lytton, Sir Edward Bulwer 60

Macaulay, Thomas 35–36, 222–23
Machiavelli, Niccolò 337, 493–94, 498, 499
Mackenzie, George 85
Mack, Maynard 166
Madox, Thomas 121–22
Maizeaux, Pierre Des 94–95
Makin, Bathsua 65–66
Mandeville, Sir John 251–52, 263
Manley, Delarivier 49–51, 91, 389–90, 483, 595–97
Mansell, Francis 170–71
manuals
  classical influences 303–5
  for devotional practice 304–7, 314–15
  epistolary manuals 379–80, 381–82
  female readership 308–9
  Franck's *Northern Memoirs* 502–3
  genre 302–3
  handbooks on slave management 434
  instruction in processes 301–2, 312, 313–14
  legal 308–9
  mechanical processes 309–11, 314–15
  mock-manuals for letters 379–80, 382–84
  for professionals 307–8
  recreational vs. business pursuits 313
  size 310–11
  statesman's *vade mecum* 306–7
  Walton's *The Compleat Angler* 301–2, 311–15

manuscripts
  antiquarian writings 121
  auto/biographical writing 150
  censorship 28–29
  clandestine satire 28–29
  of the classical golden age 18–19
  commercial markets 28–29
  life-writing 27
  materiality 27
  political treatises 28
  print-manuscript hybridisation 28–29
  print-manuscript hybrid recipe books 539–41
  prose categories 26–27
  transgressive wit in 28
  transmission 26–27
  women writers and 28
Marana, Giovanni Paolo 186–87, 262–63
Marprelate, Martin 477
Marshall, Ashley 159–60
Marvell, Andrew 7–8, 28–29, 178, 589–90
Mascuch, Michael 142–43
May, Robert 537–38, 542–43, 545–46
McIntosh, Carey 57–58
McKenzie, D. F., 16, 21–22, 23–25, 29–30, 31, 33–34, 51–52
McKenzie, Sir George 270–71, 275–76, 282
McKeon, Michael 7, 104–6, 113–14, 118, 328, 619–20, 622
McMurran, Mary Helen 87–88
medicine 15, 307–8
metaphors
  of circulation 15
  of opened closets/cabinets in recipe books 537–38, 540–41
  in pornography 507–8
  of war in polemical prose 474
Milton, John
  Areopagitica 254, 529, 532, 534–35
  on classical schooling 64–65
  condemnation of heresiography 319
  divorce tracts 328
  historical writing 77–78
  as a Latin prose stylist 9–10
  Letters of State 354–55
  Poems 393
  political writings 475–77, 522

prose/poetry opposition 1, 3–4, 11
   in *The Spectator* 372–73, 374
   spiritual autobiography 551–52
Minto, William 52–53, 54
mock science *see also* Scriblerianism
   appeals to trustworthiness 418–19, 428–29
   of Defoe 422
   epistemic validity 419–20
   the essay form 427–28
   genre 418
   parodies of Bentley 423–24
   parodies of Swift's *Tale of a Tub* 422–23
   parodies of the Royal Society 425–30, 432
   parodies of William Wotton 417, 424–25
   in periodicals 430–32
   stylistic imitation 419, 426
   Swift's satires on enthusiasm 420–22
   Swift's *Tale of a Tub* as 363–64, 417–18, 420–22, 431
   textual elements 419–20, 424–25
modern scholarship *see also* 'Discourse Concerning the Original and Progress of Satire'
   Addison's writings on 372–75
   the Ancients and the Moderns' literary quarrel 98–99, 296, 367–69, 371–72, 401, 415–16, 423, 548
   annotation and footnotes 375–77
   Bentley and the Phalaris dispute 9–10, 98–99, 367–68, 371–72, 376–77, 423
   parodied as recipes 546–47, 548–49
   Scriblerian attacks on 366–69, 371–72, 375–78, 546–47
Momigliano, Arnaldo 130–31
Montaigne, Michel de
   essay form 84, 266–67, 269, 277, 280–81, 282, 450–52, 528
   translations 84, 266–68
Montesquieu 186–87, 262
morality
   ethical and moral challenges of auto/biographical writing 137–38, 139–41
   fables and fairy tales and moral instruction 283–85, 290–94, 297–98
   gold's influence on human morality 191–92, 193
   moralizing fables in criminal literature 204

Mordaunt, Elizabeth, Viscount 227–28
More, Henry 303–4, 389–90, 396
More, Sir Thomas 455–56, 496
Morgan, Matthew 73
Moseley, Humphrey 393–94
Motteux, Pierre Antoine Le
   the Ancients and the Moderns' literary quarrel 99
   anti-Catholic reading of Rabelais 352–53, 355–57, 358–61
   the *Gentleman's Journal* 93–94, 353–55, 461–62
   historical-allegorical method 350, 352–53
   Huguenot exile 9–10, 93, 96–97, 352–53
   key to *Gargantua and Pantagruel* 350–53, 356–60, 364–65
   and L'Estrange's *Fables of Aesop* 360–62
   Pope on 362–63
   translation of Cervantes 89
   translations of Rabelais 9–10, 88, 353–56, 364
Moxon, Joseph 309–11, 314–15
Murray, Lindley 56–57

national identity
   and coinage 184, 185, 193–94
   discussions of national improvement 273–74
national literature
   canonical classics 125–26
   the English romance 84–86
   genres and the formation of 83–84, 85–86, 91
natural philosophy *see also* Hooke, Robert; mock science; modern scholarship; Royal Society
   Hobbes' *Leviathan* 490–92
   mirrored in brief lives writing 180
   in periodicals 93–94
   prose style 272, 415
Nayler, James 388–89
Nedham, Marchamont 455–57, 461, 475–78, 497–98
Ness, Christopher 230
Neville, Henry 493–97
New Historicism 5
newsbooks 3–4

newspapers
  in French 93, 94
  political debate in 481–82
  proliferation 28–29, 42–43
Newton, Isaac 570–73
New World literature
  American identity-formation 433–35, 437–38, 448–49
  Black Legend motif 439–40, 441, 448–49
  captivity narrative genre 443–45, 501
  Caribbean 434, 441–42
  cataloguing of the American landscape 434–37, 446, 448–49
  colonial literature 433–34, 437–39, 448–49
  the Darien expedition 441
  deprivation in 500–1
  handbooks on slave management 434
  King Philip's war 443, 444
  metropolitan literature on 437–38, 448–49
  Native Americans 434, 443–45
  on piracy 442
  political prose 487–88
  the print trade 433–34, 448
  promotion of migration to 436, 437–38, 439
  Puritan writings 436, 444–45
  on race and slavery 433, 434, 445–49
  representation of Native Americans 434–36, 437–38, 439–40
  Spanish America 434, 436–37, 439–41
  term 433
Nichol Smith, David 168
Nicolson, William 127–28
Norris, John 392, 397
North, Thomas 71–72, 73–74, 76–77
novel
  Bentley's collections of 22, 82–83
  criticism texts 92–93
  early novel 619–20, 622
  European influences on English prose 364
  identification and 623–24
  influence of French writers in translation 91–92
  pre-history of 7
  transnational origins 92–93
  True Accounts and 619–20, 622

Oldenburg, Henry 390, 573, 576–77
Oldmixon, John 437–38, 594, 596–97
Osborne, Dorothy 27, 176–78, 182–83
Ottoman Empire 257–58, 261–62
Overton, Richard 477, 497, 498, 521–22, 528, 529–31
Oxford, Robert Harley, 1st Earl 36–37, 38–39, 465–66, 475–77, 594, 596–98
Ozell, John 89–90, 97–99, 353–54, 364

Palmer, Thomas 28–29
pamphlets
  'Bickerstaff Papers' 153–54, 155–57
  criminal literature 208
  Defoe's *The Shortest-Way with the Dissenters* 37–38, 157–62, 232–33, 628–29
  metaphors for 16
  Partridge's *Mene Tekel* 154–56
  polemical 317–19
  proliferation 3–4, 42–43
  Wandring Whore pamphlets 508–9
Parker, Samuel 239–40, 278–79
Parliamentarians
  auto/biographical writing 143–44
  periodical press 455
Partridge, John 153–57, 626–27
patronage 20
Payne, Joseph 59
Penn, William 49–51
Pepys, Samuel
  on continental food 545–46
  on pornography 27, 509–11
  reading of scientific writing 42–43
  use of a cipher 27
  writing-experience gap 220
periodicals *see also Philosophical Transactions; Spectator, The; Tatler*
  the Ancients and the Moderns' literary quarrel 99
  Anglo-French production and readership 93–94
  apolitical, polite essays 451–52, 466–67
  The Athenian Gazette or Casuistical Mercury 397
  Care's *Weekly Pacquet* 458–61
  on commerce and finance 462–64
  Defoe's *Review* 397, 453, 465–66

Dunton's *Athenian Mercury* 419–20, 464–66, 481–82
  female readership 464–65
  general interest publications 461–62
  government-approved news 457
  as historiography 458–59, 460
  Houghton's *Collection* and 463–64, 465–66
  Jacobitism in 461–62
  joco-serious style 455–57, 461, 482–83
  L'Estrange's *The Observator* 458–61
  letters in 397–98, 481–82
  literary quarrels 97
  Mercurius Aulicus 217–18, 451, 454
  Mercurius Britannicus 217–18, 455
  Mercurius Politicus 456–57, 482–83
  Mercurius Pragmaticus 455–56
  news writing 451, 452–53
  Nouvelles de la Republique des Lettres 93–95
  partisanship in 461–62, 465
  philosophy in 276–77
  political debate in 451, 453–54, 481–82
  post-Revolution 461–67
  readership 459–60
  of the Restoration 458–61
  of the Revolution 454–57
  rhetorical tactics 453
  of the Royalists 454–55
  scientific writings in 419–20
  social periodicals 464–66
  Whig-Tory political culture 458–61, 465–66
Perrault, Charles 89–90, 98–99, 284–85, 297
Persius 400, 401, 404–5, 407–9, 410–11
Phalaris dispute 9–10, 98–99, 367– , 68– , 423
Philips, Ambrose 162–63, 164–65, 166–67
Philosophical Transactions
  articles 577
  English virtuoso culture 461–62
  as an epistolary community 390–92, 397, 576–77
  eyewitness testimony 436–37
  foundation of 390, 566, 576–77
  Houghton's *Collection* and 463
  internationalism 391–92
  new sciences in 28, 42–43
  Oldenburg's editorship 576–77
  parodies of 419–20, 422, 425–27
  reports about North America 436–37
philosophy
  empirical pivot 285–86
  Epictetus' *Enchiridion* 303–5
  epistolary philosophical exchange 389–92
  the essay form for 275–77
  in the periodical press 276–77
picaresque 89, 91, 209–11
Pinnell, Henry 525, 526, 527–28, 532–33
piracy
  in criminal literature 211, 213–15
  in New World literature 442
Plato 62–63, 70–71, 77–78, 278, 403–5
Pliny 568
Plot, Robert 120–21, 131–32
Plutarch 62–63, 71–72, 73–75, 76–77, 79, 169–70
Pococke, Edward 255–56, 257–58, 263
poetry
  and Cavalier self-fashioning 3–4
  epic poetry and satire 412–13, 546–47
  pastorals 162–63
  prose/poetry opposition 3–4, 11, 60, 403–4
  prose's influence on 1–2
  satire 403–5
polemical prose *see also* anti-sectarian polemic; political debate; secret histories
  characters and stereotypes 480
  in deist writing 523
  genre 477
  keywords in political debate 477–79
  labels 479
  paper war concept 475
  as propaganda 475–77
  rise of politeness 484–85
  war metaphors 474
polemic, term 474
policing 201–2
politeness
  and political debate 450–52, 466–67, 484–85
  in scientific disputes 391–92, 569–70, 579
political arithmetic 20, 201, 462, 472
political debate *see also* anti-sectarian polemic; periodical press; polemical prose
  concepts of politics 468–74
  as entertainment 482–83

political debate (*cont.*)
   and the era's revolutions 471–72
   issues of power and sovereignty 469–70
   keywords and partisanship 477–78
   literary impact of 483–85
   in newspapers and periodicals 481–82
   and politeness 450–52, 466–67, 484–85
   political critiques in pornography 506–7
   political economy 472
   in printed letters 481–82
   in prose dialogues 480–81
   prose style 468, 487
   the public sphere 472–74
   on religious diversity 470–71
   representations of 'truth' 483–84
political prose
   Continental influences 487–88, 499–500
   the Diggers 499–500
   emergence of 486–87, 488
   Harrington's *Oceana* 491–93, 496–97, 522
   Hobbes' *Leviathan* 489–91
   issues of power and sovereignty 487–89
   language and style of 490–91, 492–93
   the Levellers 497–99
   of Locke 501–3
   manuscript exchange 28
   Neville's *The Isle of Pines* 493–97
   in New World literature 487–88
   print culture and 488–89
   publication of 496–97, 501–3
   radicalism 497–501
   readership 487
   and the romance genre 496
   socio-economic context 488–89
   use of Machiavellian texts 497, 498–99
   utopias/dystopias 493–97
   Vox Plebis 497–98
politics, as term 472
Pope, Alexander
   classical translations 72–73, 548
   The Dunciad 18–19, 363–64, 366–67, 368, 372
   essays 267–68
   on 'index' learning 363–64
   A Key to the Lock 87, 162, 163–65, 166–67, 351–52, 362–64
   literary quarrels 97–99

   and Motteux's key to *Gargantua and Pantagruel* 362–63
   pastorals 162–63
   Peri Bathous 362–63
   'Receipt to Make an Epick Poem' 546
   the *Scriblerus Club* 366–67, 546
   shams 162–67
   writes as 'Esdras Barnivelt' 356, 362–63
Pope, Walter 169–70
pornography
   Aretino's *Ragionamenti* 505–7, 515–17
   censorship 505–7, 515–16
   The Crafty Whore 507–9
   dialogic forms 505–7, 508–9, 513, 514, 515–17
   Dialogue between a Married Lady and a Maid 516–18
   and the English bawdry tradition 505–6, 508–9, 511–12, 517–18
   the erotic imagination 513, 514–15
   generic hybridity 505
   homoeroticism in 515–16
   international book trade 506–7, 509–10
   language and style of 505–6, 507–8, 512–13
   L'Ecole des filles/The School of Venus 509–14, 515–16, 517–19
   levelling model of sexual desire 511–13
   owned by Pepys 27, 509–11
   political critique in 506–7
   readership 518–19
   sexual spying 506, 515–18
   term 504
   translations from French, Italian and Latin 505, 509–10, 514, 517
   Venus in the Cloister 515–17, 518–19
   Wandring Whore pamphlets 508–9
   The Whores Rhetorick 513–15
Presbyterians
   in anti-sectarian polemic 320–22
   interpretation of Scripture 329
   Presbyterian-Independents division 320–21
press control *see also* L'Estrange, Roger
   ambiguity of the post-licensing regime 32–33, 34–39
   calls for in heresiographical writing 319
   common law of seditious libel 36–38
   compliance with 29–30, 31

Copyright Act of 1710 34–35
Court of the Star Chamber 29–30, 31–32
dissenting writing 232–33, 238–40
enforcement of 28, 31–35, 36, 232–33
impact on book circulation 29–30
Licensing Act of 1662 30–31, 34–35, 36, 37–38, 205, 232, 283–84, 287, 458, 462
Licensing Order of 1643 30–31
pillorying 32–33, 36–38, 157–60, 161–62, 205
of pornography 505–7, 515–16
and public opinion 31–32, 35–36
in the Restoration era 16, 21–23, 28–29, 30–33
and the rule of law 36
of scribal materials 28–29
sedition trials 205
Stamp Act 34–35, 36
print culture *see also* book trade
books as luxury items 20
circulation metaphors 16
and historical writing 339–40, 344–45, 348–49
materiality 27
proliferation 16–19, 42–43, 473
satirised in *A Tale of a Tub* 17–20
scribal publications 26–27
self-representation and 217–18
of the 1630–60 period 3–5
subscription publishing 20
textual veracity 328
Pritchard, Allan 136–37, 150–51
Procopius of Caesarea 77–78, 586–88
propaganda
astrology as 153–56
Civil War mobilization 341–45, 348–49
government-approved periodicals 457
Jacobite 461–62
polemical prose as 475–77
Royalist periodical press 454–55
true accounts as mock-propaganda 626–28
prose dialogues 480–81
Protestants *see also* Huguenots
Biblicism 329–30
dissenters 157–59
radical 'Real' Whigs 354–55
self-reflection 141, 217–18, 225–26
Prynne, William 31–32, 36–38

punctuation
evolution of 51–52
for reading aloud 52–53
in *Robinson Crusoe* 53–56
Puritans
in the Americas 436
anti-sectarian polemics against 320–21
focus on individual grace 230
focus on the particular 225–26
plain prose style 238–39
reading practices 41–43
sola Scriptura belief 329–30
spiritual autobiography 551

Quakers 51, 324, 388–89, 550–51, 561–62
Quarles, Francis 307, 311

Rabelais, François
anti-Catholic reading of 352–53, 355–57, 358–60
Gargantua and Pantagruel 88, 350–60
historical-allegorical interpretations of 350
influence on the English novel 364
translations of 88, 353–54
radicalism *see also* deism; dissenters; dissenting writing
biblical and textual criticism 523, 528–32
the divine and human reason 520–21
the enthusiastic/prophetic tradition 520–28, 532–33
female prophetic speech 524
language and style of 523, 526, 529–30
in political prose 497–501
rational radicalism 521–22, 528–36
rhetoric 523
role of individual natural reason 520–22, 528–29
Swift's satires on enthusiasm 317–18, 322, 326–27, 420–22, 534–35
Winstanley's *Declaration* 520–21
Raven, James 20–21, 22, 25–26
Ray, John 131, 572–73, 575–76
reading practices
for amatory fiction 104–5, 107
the Bible 41–42, 43–44
close reading 104–5
concerns over 44, 45–46

reading practices (*cont.*)
　expansion in　40
　freedom in　254
　and intellectual empowerment　42–44
　new ways　45–46
　paranoid reading　104–5
　parodic modes　164–66
　reading aloud　52–53
　of women　44, 106–7, 308–9, 464–65
recipe books
　cultural politics of　545–49
　English domestic cookery　537–39, 541–42, 545–46, 549
　French cuisine　537–39, 545–49
　genre　537–39, 549
　influence of French cuisine　538
　male authorship　537–38
　May's *The Accomplisht Cook*　537–38, 542–43, 545–46
　metaphors of opened closets/cabinets　537–38, 540–41
　nostalgia for Royalist hospitality　542–46
　olios　175–76, 545–46
　print-manuscript hybrids　539–41
　The Queens Closet Open'd　543–45
　satires on Continental cuisine　545–49
　satires on domestic politics　537, 544–46
religious writings *see also* sermons; spiritual autobiographies
　captivity narrative genre　443–45
　conversion narratives　27
　devotional manuals　304–7, 314–15
　growth in published titles　25–26
　letters　388–89
　literacy rates　41–42
　literary style　47–48, 49–51
　by Puritans in the Americas　436, 444–45
　spiritual diary-keeping　225–28, 242
Restoration
　press control　16, 21–23, 28–29, 30–33
　taxation levels　20
rhetoric
　of the enthusiastic tradition　523–28
　in historical writing　332–33, 335–37
　of Hobbes' *Leviathan*　490–91
　in letters　380, 381–82
　in radical writing　523

　of rational radicalism　528–36
　in scientific writing　566–67, 582–83
　in university education　66–67
Robertson, Joseph　51, 52–53
romance *see also* amatory fiction
　biographical romances　146
　classical influences　79–80, 84–85
　English genre　84–85
　political prose and　496
　translations from French　87–88, 496
Rose, Mark　34–35
Ross, Alexander　252–56
Rousseau, Jean-Jacques　141
Rowe, Elizabeth　76–77
Rowlandson, Mary　443–44, 445, 501
Royalists
　auto/biographical writing　144–45
　the Cavalier Winter　542–43
　hospitality　542–43
　life writings　170–71
　nostalgia for Royalist hospitality　542–46
　periodical press　454–55
　re-descriptions　333
Royal Society *see also Philosophical Transactions*
　archives　579
　character types for　178–79
　codification of mechanical processes　309–11
　Cowley's ode to　179–80
　foundation of　566
　orality and prose style　579
　parodies of　425–30, 432, 569–70
　reports about North America　436–37
　simplicity in written discourse　49–51, 418–19, 566–67
Russell, Edward　355–56
Rycaut, Paul　257–58, 261–62, 263
Rye-House Plot　154, 355–56, 387, 590–91
Rymer, Thomas　48–49

Saint-Evremond, Charles de　94–95
satire *see also* 'Discourse Concerning the Original and Progress of Satire' (Dryden); Scriblerianism
　anti-sectarian satire　316–17, 318–19
　Casaubon's study of verse satire　403–5, 406–7, 408–10

in criminal literature 201
Dryden's definition of 400–1, 413–14
epic poetry and satire 412–13, 546–47
late Renaissance scholarship on 400–1
in manuscript 28–29
mock-manuals and academies of letters 382–84
poetry as 403–4
recipe books 537, 544–46
Restoration verse satire 316–17
satires on Continental cuisine 545–49
Scriblerian satire 363–64
true accounts as 626–28
verse satire 404–5
Scaliger, Julius Caesar 405–8, 410, 413, 415–16
scientific writings *see also* mock science; *Philosophical Transactions*
aphorism 572–75
authorial voice and truth 418–19, 568, 569–70, 572–73
cataloguing and describing the American landscape 434–37
detailed descriptions in 568–69, 579–80
and the essay form 271–73
generic hybridity 565–66, 578–79
genre 419
Hooke's louse from *Micrographia* 178–80
images 579–80
language and style of 49–51, 418–19, 565–66, 570–73, 582–83
natural history catalogues 568, 575
parodies 417–18
in periodicals 419–20
politeness and scientific disputes 391–92, 569–70, 579
and print culture 42–43, 419–20
prose forms 573–79
scientific reports 576, 579
translations 419–20, 581–82
use of metaphor 51
use of rhetoric 566–67, 582–83
scribal publications 26–27
Scriblerus Club
aesthetic 366–67, 368–69
attacks on modern scholarship 363–64, 366–69, 371–72, 375–78
ethos 10–11

fragments and the Phalaris debate 368–69
homo mechanicus as the target of 369
Memoirs of Martinus Scriblerus 366–67, 372
mock scholarship 276, 363–64
satire of Grub Street 328
Swift's *Tale of a Tub* and 370–72, 375–76
Scudéry, Madeleine de 87–88, 178
secret histories
Behn's *Love-Letters* as 589–91, 593, 595–96
classical antecedents 77–78, 585–88
Defoe's *Secret History* 596–98
at the end of Queen Anne's reign 594–95
genre 585–86, 591, 598–99
iconoclastic texts 588–90
and international politics 592, 593
James I's letters 588–89
The King's Cabinet Open'd 588–89, 590–91
Manley's *New Atalantis* 595–97
polemical genre of 77–78, 584–85, 588–89, 591–92
scandalous revelations 584–85, 586–88
as a symbol of political liberty 593
term 586–87, 591
by the Tories 594–98
by the Whigs 591–95
Sedgwick, Eve 104–5
Selden, John 172–73
sermons
of the 1640s 605–11
of the 1650–60s 611–12
during Anne's reign 616
audiences 602, 604
on Charles I 612–14
dismay over religious controversy 614–15
duration 602–3
fast-day sermons 601, 605–6, 616–17
genre 600, 601, 616–17
national sin in 605–7
orality of 603–4
plain style 601–2
political content 608–9, 611
in print culture 600–1, 603–5, 611–12
on religious reform 609–11
on repentance and reformation 606–8
during the Restoration 613–15
ritualized humility 604
role in Protestantism 600–1

sermons (*cont.*)
    textual elements 605
    during the Williamite era 615–16
sexuality *see also* pornography
    and affect in amatory fiction 103–5
    gold's influence on human morality 191–92, 193
    scenes of witness in circulation narratives 188–91
    sexual intrigue in secret histories 584–85, 586–88
    sexual promiscuity in anti-sectarian polemic 323, 324, 325, 326–27
Shadwell, Thomas 17, 425
Shaftesbury, Anthony Ashley Cooper, 3rd Earl
    criticism of the essay form 267–69, 271, 280–81, 282
    on the English language 48–49
    Essay on the Freedom of Wit and Humour 523
    freedom of expression 534
    literary style 58
    on modern scholarship 44–45, 402–3
    on Platonic dialogue 278–79
    role of philosophy 275
    secret histories 589–90
    Stoicism and 303–5
shams
    by Alexander Pope 162–67
    definition 152–53
    Defoe's *The Shortest-Way with the Dissenters* 37–38, 157–62, 232–33, 628–29
    ironic failure 159–60, 161–62
    parodic modes of reading 164–66
    Pope's *A Key to the Lock* 87, 162, 163–65, 166–67, 351–52, 362–64
    Pope's *Guardian* 40, 162, 164–66
    and print technology 153–54, 158–59
    in prose writing 152
    separation of author and persona 158–62
    Swift's Bickerstaff papers 153–57, 167
Shapin, Steven 568–70
Sharpe, Jim 206
Shaw, David 86–87
Sidney, Algernon 28, 32–33, 591–92
Sidney, Philip 42–43, 84–85, 496
slavery *see* enslavement

Sloane, Hans 94, 425–27, 428–29
Smith, Thomas 121, 125–26, 133–34
Smollett, Tobias 209, 210–11, 262, 290–91
Smyth, Thomas 136, 137, 140, 145
Socrates 278
Somner, William 127–28, 133
Spectator, The
    Addison as model of English prose 9–10
    allegory and economic health 195–96
    apolitical, polite essays 451–52, 466–67, 484, 485
    circulation narratives 185, 186–87
    the essay form 267–68, 272–73, 450–52
    fables in 286–88
    female readership 464–65
    generic hybridity 7–8, 276–77, 372–73
    impact of the Stamp Act 34–35
    letters in 397–98
    mock science 430–31
    on modern scholarship 372–75
    Mr Spectator persona 281, 430, 453
    private reading practices 45–46
    representations of national character 196–98
Spence, Ferrand 74–75
spiritual autobiographies
    authorial self-presentation 552, 554–55, 558–59
    Browne's *Religio Medici* 553–54, 558–61, 563–64
    Bunyan's *Grace Abounding* 550–51, 552, 553–57, 558–59, 560–62
    conversion narratives 27, 551–52, 557–58
    dismay over religious controversy 552–55, 559–60, 561–62
    genre 551–66
    historical experiences of faith 555–57, 564
    the inner experience witnessed 551–52, 554–55, 557–58
    religious doubt 560–63
    religious materials 27
    Robinson Crusoe as 53–54
    spiritual diary-keeping 225–28, 242
    term 550–52
    Trapnel's *A Legacy for Saints* 553–54, 555–56, 557–58

universal Christian identities 554–56, 558, 559, 560, 564
Sprat, Thomas
  on the English language 46–49
  History of the Royal Society 47–48, 619–20
  life-writing 27
  prioritisation of knowledge 285–86
  simplicity in written discourse 49–51, 53, 59, 418–19, 566–67, 582–83
  use of metaphor 51
spy narratives *see also* circulation narratives
  dream vision 187–88, 195–96
  genre 184, 185–87
  Letters Writ by a Turkish Spy 186–87, 196, 262–63
  metamorphosis in 184–85, 187–88
  mindedness 184–85
  observation and representation in 184–85, 197–98, 199
  The Secret History of White-hall 593
  sexual spying in pornography 506, 515–18
Stamp Act 20–21, 34–35, 36
Stationers' Company 21–22, 30–31, 34–35, 86–87, 309–10
Steele, Richard *see also* Tatler
  and the essay form 84
  and Pope's *Guardian* 40 sham 162–63, 166–67
  popularization of natural philosophy 430
Stephens, Robert 'Hog' 31–32, 33–34
Sterne, Laurence 364–65
Strype, John 138, 139–40
Stubbe, Henry 256–58, 263
style, literary
  conformist and nonconformist traits 238–40
  of dissenting writing 238–42
  essay form 267–68, 274, 276
  ideal Latin style 64
  increased attention to prose style 56–58
  joco-serious style of periodicals 455–57, 461, 482–83
  loose vs. periodic sentences 52–53, 61
  plain prose style 131–33, 134–35, 238–39, 285–86, 418–19
  in religious works 49–51
  rhetorical prose style 62–63

  in *Robinson Crusoe* 53–56, 61
  in scientific writing 49–51, 418–19
  simplicity in 49–51, 62–63
  stylistic imitation in parody 419
  in translations of classical works 71–73
  Victorian periodisation 58–60
Swammerdam, Jan 581–82
Swift, Jonathan *see also Tale of a Tub, A* (Swift)
  anti-Partridge sham 153–57, 626–27
  The Battel of the Books 18–19, 98–99, 368–69, 370
  belles lettres, term 81–82
  'Bickerstaff Papers' 153–54, 155–57, 167, 228
  on Defoe's pillorying 37–38
  Discourse Concerning the Mechanical Operation of the Spirit 420–22
  on the English language 46–47, 49
  Gangraena in the library of 319, 321–22
  Gulliver's Travels 45–46, 88, 89–90, 359–60, 363–64, 366–67
  literary style 58, 61
  Mechanical Operation of the Spirit 316–17, 324, 325, 329–30
  political writings 475–77, 479, 483
  print-manuscript hybrids 28–29
  satires on enthusiasm 317–18, 322, 326–27, 420–22, 534–35
  Scriblerian writings 366–67, 370
  on style 49–51

Tacitus 62–63, 77–78, 404–5
Tale of a Tub, A (Swift)
  'Ancients' and 'Moderns' in 18–19, 98–99, 371
  as anti-sectarian satire 316–17, 318–19, 320, 325–26, 329–30
  'Apology' 317, 321–22, 351–52
  and the fabular tradition 296, 370
  fiction/non-fiction boundaries 10–11
  genealogy of heresy 320–21
  generic categories for 7–8
  Gangraena as source material 320, 323–24, 326–27, 329–30
  parodies of 422–23
  parody of scientific writing 417–18, 419, 420–22, 431
  price 20–21

Tale of a Tub, A (Swift) (*cont.*)
   as a religious allegory 17, 370
   satire on Continental cuisine 547
   satire on modern authorship 17–20, 25–26
   as a Scriblerian work 370–72, 375–76
   title 317–18
   and the Toleration Act 316–17
Tanner, Thomas 122–23, 225–26
Tate, Nahum 354–55
Tatler
   allegory and economic health 195–96
   apolitical, polite essays 451–52, 466–67, 485
   on classical texts 278
   diary-writing tradition and 228–29
   the essay form 450–52
   female readership 464–65
   generic hybridity 276–77
   Isaac Bickerstaff persona 228–29, 380–98, 430, 431–32, 453, 547–48
   letters in 397–98
   mock science 430–32
   news writing 452–53
   periodical essays 267–68
   spy narratives 185, 186–87, 195–96
Taylor, Jeremy 305–6, 314–15, 329–30, 473
Taylor, John 317–19
Temple, Sir William
   the Ancients and the Moderns' literary quarrel 18–19, 98–99, 367–68, 371–72
   Dorothy Osborne's love letters 27, 176–78
   and the essay form 57, 84, 267–68, 269–70, 306–7
   Miscellanea 266–67
Theocritus 162–63
Theophrastus 173, 174, 175, 177, 480
Thomason, George 23–26, 473
Thornley, George 103–4, 109–12
Tickell, Thomas 162–63, 167
Toland, John 147–48, 496–97, 522, 531–32, 533–34
Toleration Act (1689) 237–38, 316–17, 470–71
toleration debates
   Behn's translation of Fontanelle 90
   Defoe's *The Shortest-Way with the Dissenters* 37–38, 157–62, 232–33, 628–29
   dissenters' arguments on 234–36, 534–36
   freedom of speech 534–35
   the monarchy's stance on 236–38
   political debate 470–71

Tonson, Jacob 20–21, 22, 74–75, 162–63, 164–65, 350–51
Tories
   keywords in political debate 477–79
   party politics 470–71
   in the periodical press 458–61, 465–66
   secret histories 594–98
Torshell, Samuel 43–44
trade
   allegory and economic health 195–96
   circulation metaphors 15
   colonial literature and 433–34
   commerce in the periodical press 463–64
   financial instruments 206–7, 217–18
   and human agency 195–96
   representations of national character 196–98
translation
   abridged and excerpt translations 75–76
   of *Anekdota* 586–88
   in antiquarian writings 122–24, 127–29, 133
   Arabian Nights 82–83, 89–90, 263–65, 291–92
   of classical texts 70–77, 303–5
   of eastern literature 258–59, 263–64
   Elizabethan classical translations 71–72, 73–74, 76–77
   of European genres 83
   European influences on English prose 86–90, 91
   fairy tales 89–90, 288–89, 296–97
   of foreign books 87–88
   freer literary style 71–73
   of French letters 382–83
   of French romances 87–88, 496
   of French texts 82–83, 87–90
   of *Ḥayy ibn Yaqẓan* 258–59, 263–64
   L'Estrange's translation of Cicero's *de Officiis* 68–70
   and literary exchanges 91, 97–98
   of Montaigne 266–68, 269
   neo-Latin writing 9–10
   of pornography 505, 509–10, 514, 517
   process of 90, 97–98
   as a public service 71, 74–75
   of the Qur'an 252–56
   of Rabelais 88
   of scientific writing 419–20, 581–82
   of the Spanish picaresque 82–83, 89, 91

statesman's *vade mecum* 307
textual fidelity 72–73
vernacular literary translations 75–77
Trapnel, Anna 524, 553–54, 555–56, 557–58
Traugott, Elizabeth Closs 56–57
True Accounts
　captivity narratives 443–44, 445, 501
　of criminal activity 619–20, 622–24
　by Defoe 628–31
　Defoe's *Jonathan Wild* 628, 629, 631–36
　fiction/non-fiction hybridity 619–22, 625–26, 629–30
　genre 618–19
　historical contexts 619–20
　illustrations 618–19
　narrative devices 630–31
　and the novel form 619–20, 622
　reader experiences 623–24
　and realist fiction 622, 623, 624, 630, 631–33
　as satire 626–28
　veracity claims 618–19, 622, 623–25, 629–30
　witchcraft 206
Turner, James Grantham 85, 105–6, 505–6, 508–11, 514
Tutchin, John 36, 157–58, 160, 161–62, 465
Twyn, John 33–34
Tyrrell, James 133–34

Urquhart, Sir Thomas 88, 353–54

Valerius Maximus 70–71
Varillas, Antoine 587–89
Vine, Angus 121–22, 130–31
Virgil 163–65, 546–47
Voltaire 33–34, 86–87

Wall, Wendy 537, 541–42
Walton, Izaak 79, 301–2, 311–15
Walwyn, William 521–22, 528–29
Warburton, William 166–67
Ward, Ned 155–56, 186–87, 191
Wentworth, Anne 150, 230, 231–32, 240, 243
Wheare, Degory 67–68, 69–70
Whigs
　anti-Catholic satires 352–53, 354–56, 360
　and the John Partridge sham 153–57, 626–27

keywords in political debate 477–79
party politics 470–71
in the periodical press 458–61
in secret histories 589–91
use of secret histories 591–95
Whitelocke, Bulstrode 338–40
Wild, Jonathan 200–1, 210, 213, 631–36
Winstanley, Gerrard 499–500, 520–22, 524, 528, 534–35
women
　access to classical translations 76–77
　criminal activity 205–6, 207–9, 223
　education 65
　female prophetic speech 524
　literacy rates 40, 41–43, 473
　manuals for 308–9
　misogynistic bawdry 508–9
　preachers 324–25
　reading practices 44, 106–7, 308–9, 464–65
　sexual promiscuity in anti-sectarian polemic 323, 324, 326–27
　witchcraft 206
women writers *see also* Behn, Aphra; Cavendish, Margaret; Hutchinson, Lucy
　antiquarians 128–29
　auto/biographical writing 143–47, 150
　aversion to print 28
　careers of French women 91–92
　manuscripts 28
　recovery of writing by 5–6, 8–9
Wood, Anthony
　Athenae Oxonienses 126–27, 171–73, 218, 223
　bio-bibliography 223–24
　biography of William Dugdale 218–19
　diary-as-annotation practice 219–20
　on dissenting writing 239–40
　practice of diary-writing 218, 219, 221–23, 225–26
　revision of self 220–23
Woolf, Virginia 61
Woolley, Hannah 541–42
Worden, Blair 147–48
Wotton, William 367–68, 371–72, 417, 419, 424, 425

Zunshine, Lisa 621
Zurcher, Amelia 84–85